THE
Oliver Wendell Holmes
DEVISE

HISTORY OF
THE SUPREME COURT
OF THE UNITED STATES

VOLUME X.II

THE OLIVER WENDELL HOLMES DEVISE

History of the SUPREME COURT of the United States

VOLUME X.II
The Taft Court
Making Law for a Divided Nation, 1921–1930

Robert C. Post
Yale Law School

Shaftesbury Road, Cambridge CB2 8EA, United Kingdom

One Liberty Plaza, 20th Floor, New York, NY 10006, USA

477 Williamstown Road, Port Melbourne, VIC 3207, Australia

314–321, 3rd Floor, Plot 3, Splendor Forum, Jasola District Centre, New Delhi – 110025, India

103 Penang Road, #05–06/07, Visioncrest Commercial, Singapore 238467

Cambridge University Press is part of Cambridge University Press & Assessment, a department of the University of Cambridge.

We share the University's mission to contribute to society through the pursuit of education, learning and research at the highest international levels of excellence.

www.cambridge.org
Information on this title: www.cambridge.org/9781009336215
DOI: 10.1017/9781009336246

© The Oliver Wendell Holmes Devise 2024

This publication is in copyright. Subject to statutory exceptionand to the provisions of relevant collective licensing agreements,no reproduction of any part may take place without the writtenpermission of Cambridge University Press & Assessment.

First published 2024

Printed in the United Kingdom by TJ Books Limited, Padstow, Cornwall

A catalogue record for this publication is available from the British Library.

A Cataloging-in-Publication data record for this book is available from the Library of Congress

ISBN – 2 Volume Set 978-1-009-33621-5 Hardback
ISBN – Volume X.I 978-1-009-34621-4 Hardback
ISBN – Volume X.II 978-1-009-34617-7 Hardback

Cambridge University Press & Assessment has no responsibility for the persistence or accuracy ofURLs for external or third-party internet websites referred to in this publicationand does not guarantee that any content on such websites is, or will remain,accurate or appropriate.

PART V
SOCIAL AND ECONOMIC LEGISLATION

On the day of his inauguration, Warren G. Harding paraded down Pennsylvania Avenue. Among the spectators was Justice Brandeis's law clerk, Dean Acheson. The "most striking feature of the parade," Acheson later recalled, "was 'the biggest broom ever made,' gilded of handle, topped by an American flag, given to the President by an Oklahoma delegation to typify the 'possibilities of change of administration from Democratic to Republican.'"[1] Harding himself succinctly summarized the sweeping transformation in his Inaugural Address: "[O]ur supreme task," he said, must be "the resumption of our onward, normal way."[2]

The nation had just passed through the furnace of World War I, the country's first encounter with global warfare. It had learned that modern war required not only battlefield tactics, but also the efficient mobilization of economic resources.[3] The Wilson administration set in motion "remarkable" and "unprecedented" exercises of federal power that endowed the national government with "control over corporate and individual existence which infinitely transcends the wildest dreams of those who advocate centralized authority."[4] In 1918 Harding bitterly complained that "the radicals at home are making the republic the realm of state socialism." As a newly elected president in 1921, he intended to wield his gilded broom to cleanse the country of all such "abnormal conditions of war." If "we shackled, regulated, restrained, reproved and revised during the war," Harding proclaimed, if all this "was accepted as a war necessity," it was now time to "[b]reak the shackles of war-time legislation for both business and citizens, because the war is actually ended. ... [G]ive us the normal ways of government and of men."[5]

Nowhere did Harding's gilded broom produce more lasting change than on the Supreme Court. Harding's four appointments produced a deliberate and abrupt shift in the Court's orientation toward social and economic

The Taft Court

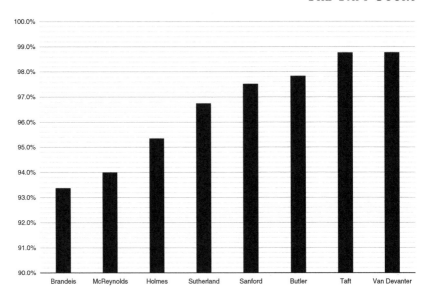

Figure V-1 Percentage of decisions in which a participating justice on the Taft Court joins or authors an opinion for the Court, 1921–1928 terms

legislation.[a] There is no doubt but that Harding selected Taft as "the judicial representative of 'normalcy.'"[6] Montana District Judge George Bourquin, who had himself been placed on the bench by Taft in 1912, observed in a published opinion: "It is said that Chief Justice White admitted that 'in my time we relaxed constitutional guarantees from fear of revolution,' and that Chief Justice Taft declared that 'at a conference I announced "I have been appointed to reverse a few decisions," and,' with his famous chuckle, 'I looked right at old man Holmes when I said it.'"[7]

By the end of Taft's tenure, the verdict of the eminent political scientist Edward S. Corwin was that Taft had succeeded in his mission. Corwin noted that if the tendency of the White Court had been to express "expansive views of governmental power, although not always, Chief Justice Taft's period, on the other hand, was one, frequently, of reaction toward earlier concepts, sometimes indeed of their exaggeration."[8] Harding's appointments created a "significant divide in the history of the Supreme Court."[9]

Writing in 1934, Felix Frankfurter observed that "after the World War, during the decade when William H. Taft was Chief Justice, the Court ... veered toward a narrow conception of the Constitution. ... Between 1920 and 1930 the Supreme Court invalidated more state legislation than during the fifty years preceding."[10] The very institution whose jurisdiction had been expanded in 1914

---

[a] The relative coherence of the voting of the Harding justices can be seen in Figure V-1.

Social and Economic Legislation

in part to create a check against conservative state court interpretations of the federal Constitution[11] was so transformed by the time of Taft's resignation that it could be fiercely attacked as "the zenith of reaction."[12] Contemporaries believed that the Court had become "particularly active since the World War in striking down legislation, both State and federal."[13] Fearing that the rush "Back to Normalcy" had warped the Court's jurisprudence,[14] many in the 1930s castigated "the Taft Court" as "an anachronism in its attempt to restore the conditions of an earlier generation."[15]

The actual story, however, is more complex. The nation's extraordinary response to World War I forever altered the landscape of the country's social and economic legislation. Although World War I made the necessity of planning all but inescapable, it simultaneously provoked a fierce backlash in favor of older ideals of *laissez-faire* individualism. The result was a "new era"[16] in which "planning reflected *both* the antistatism of American political culture *and* the modern search for national managerial capabilities."[17] On the one hand, the "values of continuity and regularity, functionality and rationality, administration and management set the form of problems and outlined their alternative solutions."[18] Yet, on the other hand, the nation demanded a president like Calvin Coolidge, who seemed dead set against all forms of managerial control.

Harding himself perfectly inhabited this ambivalence, appointing to his Cabinet both the arch-conservative Andrew Mellon, who insisted on a minimal role for government,[19] and the progressive engineer Herbert Hoover, who believed that after the convulsion of the war "there could be no complete return to the past."[20] The pairing was not inadvertent.[21] The powerful Senator Henry Cabot Lodge desperately wanted Mellon but recoiled at Hoover. Harding coldly forced his hand, telling him "Mellon and Hoover or no Mellon."[22]

Taft's personal ambivalence toward social and economic regulation[23] mirrored the muddle of Republican-dominated Washington in the new era of the 1920s. Taft would lead his Court into an erratic, jumbled jurisprudence that both restricted social and economic regulation in ways that would grow increasingly rigid and conservative, and yet that also affirmed regulation in ways that would have been all but inconceivable before the war. To unpack this complex story, we must step back and grasp the vast and subtle impact of World War I on American social and political thought.

THE TAFT COURT

Notes

1. DEAN ACHESON, MORNING AND NOON 45–46 (Boston: Houghton Mifflin Co. 1965). *See Natural Democracy Inaugural Keynote*, WASHINGTON POST (March 5, 1921), at 1.
2. *Inaugural Address*, 61 CONG. REC. 4–6 (March 4, 1921).
3. JOHN MAURICE CLARK, THE COSTS OF THE WORLD WAR TO THE AMERICAN PEOPLE 29 (New Haven: Yale University Press 1931). *See* Ernest L. Bogart, *Economic Organization for War*, 14 AMERICAN POLITICAL SCIENCE REVIEW 587, 587–88 (1920).
4. HENRY LITCHFIELD WEST, FEDERAL POWER: ITS GROWTH AND NECESSITY vii (New York: George H. Doran Co. 1918).
5. Warren G. Harding, *America in the War: Address at the Ohio Republican State Convention, Columbus, Ohio, August 27, 1918*, in RE-DEDICATING AMERICA: THE LIFE AND RECENT SPEECHES OF WARREN G. HARDING 178 (Frederick E. Schortemeier, ed., Indianapolis: Bobbs Merrill 1920); Warren G. Harding, *The Republican Party and America: Address before the Republican Rally at Memorial Hall, Columbus, Ohio, February 23, 1920, id.* at 191; Warren G. Harding, *The Problems of Business: Address before the Providence Chamber of Commerce at Providence, Rhode Island, February 25, 1920, id.* at 203; Warren G. Harding, *Auto-Intoxication: Address before the Baltimore Press Club at Baltimore, Maryland, February 5, 1920, id.* at 219.
6. Stanley I. Kutler, *Labor, the Clayton Act, and the Supreme Court*, 3 LABOR HISTORY 19, 28 (1962).
7. Investors' Syndicate v. Porter, 52 F.2d 189, 196 (D. Mont. 1931) (Bourquin, J., dissenting), *reversed*, Porter v. Investors' Syndicate, 287 U.S. 346 (1932). A month after becoming chief justice, Taft wrote Pennsylvania lawyer and legal scholar Hampton Carson: "There is no function more important in our government than that which the Supreme Court performs, no institution more sacred than that of the Constitution. Its preservation is of the essence of the life of our popular government, and I think it is because you and I think alike in respect to its proper interpretation that we both rejoice that I am to have an opportunity in that interpretation for I hope some years to come." WHT to Hampton L. Carson (July 30, 1921) (Taft papers).

Soon after Taft became chief justice, Van Devanter sent him an article by Georgetown law school professor Joseph Sullivan. *See* Joseph D. Sullivan, *Supreme Court and Social Legislation*, 10 GEORGETOWN LAW JOURNAL 1 (1921). The Supreme Court "is having difficulty in finding a sound and logical basis upon which to found its policy towards the many statutes involving social and economic problems," Sullivan wrote. He explained that the Court was divided between conservatives, like Van Devanter and McReynolds, who believed in "maintaining vested rights and the security of property," *id.* at 3, and radicals like Brandeis, Holmes, and Clarke, who sought to interpret the Constitution to "give effect to advanced legislation along social and economic lines." *Id.* at 2. Noting that "Ideas of property rights and contractual obligations inherited from the common law, and sought to be perpetuated by the Federal Constitution are in danger of radical revision if the new conceptions are adopted by" the Court, Sullivan fretted that "Much interest attaches to the attitude of Chief Justice Taft.... With which group will he align himself?" *Id.*

at 12. "Whether the conservative or liberal interpretation of our constitution" will prevail, Sullivan concluded, "will be largely a matter determined by his attitude." *Id.*

Taft thanked Van Devanter for the article and replied, "One good turn deserves another." WHT to WVD (January 8, 1922) (Taft papers). Taft sent Van Devanter a long address by Alabama attorney Forney Johnston attacking the jurisprudence of Holmes and Brandeis. Forney Johnston, *Address of Forney Johnston*, PROCEEDINGS OF THE TWENTY-SIXTH ANNUAL MEETING OF THE MARYLAND STATE BAR ASSOCIATION 149 (Baltimore: Maryland State Bar Association 1921). Johnston expressed the "growing concern on a part of the Bar over what appears to be the illusory character of the constitutional guarantees." *Id.* at 150. He worried over a "perceptible limitation upon the judicial review of all legislation, state and federal, involving the regulation of property rights in the interest of some ideal deemed for the moment by legislatures a public necessity. This tendency has become of controlling importance because of the death of the late Chief Justice, whose attitude ... was conservative in that it was based firmly upon the traditional view of the Constitution as a fixed landmark constituting a vital limitation upon arbitrary action by government rather than as a mere floating symbol to rise and fall with the preponderating opinion of the times." *Id.* at 152.

8. Edward S. Corwin, *Social Planning under the Constitution – A Study in Perspectives*, 26 AMERICAN POLITICAL SCIENCE REVIEW 1, 19 (1932).

9. ALEXANDER M. BICKEL & BENNO C. SCHMIDT, JR., THE JUDICIARY AND RESPONSIBLE GOVERNMENT 1910–1921, at 4 (New York: MacMillan Publishing Co. 1984). "Symbolizing the decade's pro-business orientation, the Taft Court invalidated state and federal regulatory laws in greater numbers and more frequently than any previous Court. Consistently, it favored the interests of private business, appeared sharply hostile to the cause of organized labor, and reasserted the doctrine of liberty of contract to void regulatory statutes." EDWARD A. PURCELL, JR., BRANDEIS AND THE PROGRESSIVE CONSTITUTION: ERIE, THE JUDICIAL POWER, AND THE POLITICS OF THE FEDERAL COURTS IN TWENTIETH-CENTURY AMERICA 21–22 (New Haven: Yale University Press 2000).

10. FELIX FRANKFURTER, LAW AND POLITICS: OCCASIONAL PAPERS OF FELIX FRANKFURTER 1913–1938, at 27 (Archibald MacLeish & E.F. Prichard, Jr., eds., New York: Harcourt, Brace & Co. 1939). *See* KEITH E. WHITTINGTON, REPUGNANT LAWS: JUDICIAL REVIEW OF ACTS OF CONGRESS FROM THE FOUNDING TO THE PRESENT 167 (Lawrence: University Press of Kansas 2019) (showing that the rate at which the Taft Court invalidated federal legislation was more than double that of the White Court). As the entry on *Judicial Review* put it in the 1937 *Encyclopaedia of the Social Sciences*, the Court's "interpretation of the due process of law clause of the Fourteenth Amendment today confers upon the court a practically discretionary veto power upon every state legislature. Sometimes this veto is mildly exercised, as between 1910 and 1920; at other times it is applied with considerable rigor, as from 1920 to 1930. Whether it is applied laxly or strictly depends upon no stable rule but upon the social philosophy of the majority of the justices." Edward S. Corwin, *Judicial Review*, in 8 ENCYCLOPAEDIA OF THE SOCIAL SCIENCES 461 (Edwin R.A. Seligman & Alvin Johnson, eds., New York: MacMillan Co. 1937).

11. *See* Act of December 23, 1914, Pub. L. 63-224, 38 Stat. 790 (1914) (authorizing the United States Supreme Court to use writs of *certiorari* to review judgments of the highest court of a state upholding a federal right). At the time it was said that the "reason for" expanding the Court's jurisdiction lay "in the increasing tendency of certain State courts to hold State laws unconstitutional, and the broader trend of the National Supreme Court decisions towards upholding the constitutionality of statutes." Charles Warren, *Legislative and Judicial Attacks on the Supreme Court of the United States*, 47 AMERICAN LAW REVIEW 1, 2 (1913). *See, e.g.*, FELIX FRANKFURTER & JAMES M. LANDIS, THE BUSINESS OF THE SUPREME COURT: A STUDY IN THE FEDERAL JUDICIAL SYSTEM 188–98 (New York: MacMillan Co. 1928); Charles Warren, *The Progressives of the United States Supreme Court*, 13 COLUMBIA LAW REVIEW 294, 296 (1913). *But see* Edward Hartnett, *Why Is the Supreme Court of the United States Protecting State Judges from Popular Democracy?*, 75 TEXAS LAW REVIEW 907, 954 (1997) (the 1914 Act was supported by conservatives to give the Supreme Court control over popularly elected state courts).

On a possible cause of what contemporaries called the Court's "Progressive Phase," LOUIS B. BOUDIN, 2 GOVERNMENT BY JUDICIARY 474 (New York: W. Godwin 1932), see Thomas Reed Powell, *The Police Power in American Constitutional Law*, 1 JOURNAL OF SOCIETY OF COMPARATIVE LEGISLATION AND INTERNATIONAL LAW 160, 171 (3d ser. 1919):

> The Bake Shop Case and the annulment of a workmen's compensation law by the New York Court of Appeals furnished munition for Mr. Roosevelt's demand in 1912 for the "recall of judicial decisions" – a device for taking direct appeals from the judiciary to the electorate on decisions annulling police measures.... As a campaign slogan it aroused wide popular interest.... The proposal shocked the conservative traditions of the American bar, but it is thought by many to have induced Courts to relax somewhat their censorship over novel police measures.

Felix Frankfurter was even more emphatic than Powell: "No student of American constitutional law can have the slightest doubt that Mr. Roosevelt's vigorous challenge of judicial abuses was mainly responsible for a temporary period of liberalism which followed in the interpretation of the due process clauses, however abhorrent the remedy of judicial recall appeared to both bar and bench. The public opinion which the Progressive campaign aroused subtly penetrated the judicial atmosphere. In cases involving social-industrial issues, public opinion, if adequately informed and sufficiently sustained, seeps into Supreme Court decisions. Roosevelt shrewdly observed: 'I may not know much about law, but I do know one can put the fear of God into judges.'" FRANKFURTER, *supra* note 10, at 15. *See The Red Terror of Judicial Reform*, 40 NEW REPUBLIC 110, 113 (1924); Victoria F. Nourse, *A Tale of Two Lochners: The Untold History of Substantive Due Process and the Idea of Fundamental Rights*, 97 CALIFORNIA LAW REVIEW 751, 778–85 (2009).

12. *Supreme Court and Interstate Commerce Commission*, 69 NEW REPUBLIC 256 (1932). *See also* Ray A. Brown, *Due Process of Law, Police Power, and the Supreme Court*, 40 HARVARD LAW REVIEW 943, 944 (1927) ("[I]n the six years since 1920 the Supreme Court has declared social and economic legislation

Social and Economic Legislation

unconstitutional under the due process clauses of either the Fifth or Fourteenth Amendment in more cases than in the entire fifty-two previous years during which the Fourteenth Amendment had been in effect."). "Scholars have long noted that until the 1920s the Supreme Court took a fairly permissive stance on industrial regulation laws." Stephen A. Siegel, *Lochner Era Jurisprudence and the American Constitutional Tradition*, 70 NORTH CAROLINA LAW REVIEW 1, 13 (1991).

13. Felix Frankfurter, *The Supreme Court and the Public*, 83 THE FORUM 329, 333 (June 1930). "The World War and its aftermath ushered in once again a period dominated by fears – the fear of change, the fear of new ideas – and these fears were written into the Constitution." Felix Frankfurter, *The United States Supreme Court Molding the Constitution*, 32 CURRENT HISTORY 235, 239 (1930). *See, e.g.*, Zechariah Chafee, Jr., *Liberal Trends in the Supreme Court*, 35 CURRENT HISTORY 338, 338 (1931). Modern historians sensitive to this periodization include David E. Bernstein, *Lochner Era Revisionism, Revised: Lochner and the Origins of Fundamental Rights Constitutionalism*, 92 GEORGETOWN LAW JOURNAL 1, 10 (2003) ("There was not one *Lochner* era, but three. The first period began in approximately 1897 and ended in about 1911, with moderate Lochnerians dominating the Court. The second era lasted from approximately 1911 to 1923, with the Court, while not explicitly repudiating *Lochner*, generally refusing to expand the liberty of contract doctrine to new scenarios, and at times seeming to drastically limit the doctrine. From 1923 to the mid-1930s, the Court was dominated by Justices who expanded *Lochner* by voting to limit the power of government in both economic and noneconomic contexts."); RUSSELL GALLOWAY, THE RICH AND THE POOR IN SUPREME COURT HISTORY 1790–1982, at 101–31 (Greenbrae: Paradigm Press 1982); Russell W. Galloway, Jr., *The Taft Court (1921–29)*, 25 SANTA CLARA LAW REVIEW 1, 1 (1985).

14. BOUDIN, *supra* note 11, at 474. *See* Joseph P. Pollard, *Justice Sutherland Dissents*, 158 OUTLOOK AND INDEPENDENT 496, 497 (August 19, 1931) ("The liberal wave that swept political thought before the war resulted in the Supreme Court sustaining a Kansas act limiting the rates to be charged by insurance companies. That was before the Harding appointees brought the court back to the 'normalcy' of Mark Hanna.").

15. ERNST SUTHERLAND BATES, THE STORY OF THE SUPREME COURT 264 (Indianapolis: Bobbs Merrill 1936). *See* Aviam Soifer, *The Paradox of Paternalism and Laissez-Faire Constitutionalism: United States Supreme Court, 1888–1921*, 5 LAW & HISTORY REVIEW 249, 254 (1987).

16. *See* AMERICA AND THE NEW ERA (Elisha M. Friedman, ed., New York: E.P. Dutton & Co. 1920).

17. GUY ALCHON, THE INVISIBLE HAND OF PLANNING: CAPITALISM, SOCIAL SCIENCE, AND THE STATE IN THE 1920S at 4 (Princeton University Press 1985) (emphasis added).

18. ROBERT H. WIEBE, THE SEARCH FOR ORDER 1877–1920, at 295 (New York: Hill & Wang 1967).

19. KENNETH WHYTE, HOOVER: AN EXTRAORDINARY LIFE IN EXTRAORDINARY TIMES 259 (New York: Alfred A. Knopf 2017). Mellon "was as orthodox as they came, insisting on a minimal role for government generally: it was responsible for national defense, the currency, customs and excise, and little else. Washington spent roughly 3 percent of gross national product before the war, and Mellon aimed to

return to that level from wartime highs of 23 percent by keeping spending tight and taxes low." *Id.*
20. HERBERT HOOVER, THE MEMOIRS OF HERBERT HOOVER: THE CABINET AND THE PRESIDENCY 1920–1933, at 41 (New York: MacMillan Co. 1952) ("The people were demanding a return to ways of prewar living – Harding's 'normalcy.' But in reality, after such a convulsion, there could be no complete return to the past. Moreover, the social sense of our people, livened by the war, was demanding change in many directions.").
21. The pairing represented Harding's effort to straddle the "ideological split" between the "conservatism of the Old Guard centered on a faith in the old, entrepreneurial, laissez-faire doctrine," and "a new conception of industrial development" that fostered "cooperation between the business sector and government." Peri Ethan Arnold, *Herbert Hoover and the Continuity of American Public Policy*, 20 PUBLIC POLICY 525, 530 (1972).
22. HOOVER, *supra* note 20, at 36.
23. *See supra* Chapter 10, at 393–94.

CHAPTER 21

"Everything Is on Edge": *World War I and the American State*

WITH MUCH POMP and ceremony, the Unknown Soldier was laid to rest in Arlington Cemetery on November 11, 1921. His burial commemorated the nation's sacrifices during the Great War. The Supreme Court attended the burial.[1] Chief Justice Taft was described as looking "strong, rosy, and cheerful."[2]

Although American participation in the war had lasted only eighteen months, from April 6, 1917, to November 11, 1918, more than 4.5 million Americans had been mobilized; 116,516 had been killed and 204,002 wounded.[3] The European slaughter left Henry James, of all people, at a loss for words. "One finds it in the midst of all this as hard to apply one's words as to endure one's thoughts. The war has used up words; they have weakened, they have deteriorated like motor car tires."[4] James's childhood friend, Oliver Wendell Holmes, was at first "disgusted by the vulgarities of the bogus sentiment" at the burial of the Unknown Soldier, but then "when I saw the coffin borne into the great rotunda of the Capitol, which became beautiful and impressive in the dim twilight, and afterwards saw the miles of people marching through, three abreast, from early morning into the next day, I realized that a feeling may be great notwithstanding its inability to get itself expressed."[5]

World War I has today all but faded from memory. It has become "the forgotten conflict of America's war-torn twentieth century."[6] Over time, the dead of other wars have been buried in the tomb of the Unknown Soldier, and Armistice Day has evolved into Veterans Day.[7] A visitor to Washington D.C. now "looks in vain for a national memorial to the soldiers of World War I."[8] This is startling, because what Brandeis called the "epochal changes"[9] of the war left the nation altogether transformed.[10] Although the war "was a pervasive presence in the lives of Americans,"[11] it presently "occupies a rather obscure corner of the collective memory."[12] A strenuous effort of historical imagination is required to recapture the paths of its immense influence.

A recurring story is that World War I killed progressivism in America.[13] But that is a serious oversimplification. Prewar progressivism was a potpourri of multiple different tendencies – ranging from the populism of Robert La Follette to the technocratic efficiency of Gifford Pinchot. Its core, however, lay in the aspiration so brilliantly described by Walter Lippmann as the effort "to substitute purpose for tradition," to seek "the infusion of scientific method" and the "careful application of administrative technique."[14] Progressivism conceived society "not as something given but as something to be shaped." At root, Lippmann asserted, the assumption of "mastery" was necessary if the country was to make popular will effective now that "self-government has become a really effective desire."[15]

From this perspective, World War I produced a transformation that "reflected the triumph of an extreme version of the progressive impulse."[16] The domestic changes wrought by the war expressed the "ultimate application of the Progressive belief in forceful, active government."[17] During America's long years of neutrality, the nation had acquired a healthy respect for German industry and organization;[18] it had come to understand the relationship between modern warfare and national planning.[19] Americans watched European belligerents deliberately organize their economies to maximize the manufacture of wartime materials.[20] Noting "that the necessities of war are driving the nations of Europe to adopt large helpings of what used to be regarded as crazy idealism," American progressives stressed "that successful war is impossible to-day for a nation that clings to a *laissez-faire* policy about property, business, labor, and social organization. Preparedness is the Trojan horse most in fashion at the moment. Reformers are not ashamed to confess that they regard the fear of war as an excellent way of improving the establishment of peace."[21]

At the very moment that Wilson came before Congress to request a declaration of war, he explicitly warned that belligerency would "involve the organization and mobilization of all the material resources of the country."[22] It was immediately obvious to all that "we can fight Germany only by reconstructing the United States."[23] "The choice is between efficiency and defeat."[24] Progressives recognized and celebrated the war's potential to inculcate precisely the "mastery" celebrated by Lippmann three years earlier:

> We shall count or fail as we succeed in remedying those defects of our national organization against which reformers have fought long before this was conceived. The enemy is bad work, corruption, special interest, administrative slack, planlessness – the typical evils of a sprawling, half-educated competitive capitalism. . . .
>
> The leadership in the work must fall naturally to the inventive civilians, to those very reformers and pioneers who all along have preached the very gospel which is now transformed from an amiable hobby into a world necessity.[25]

The Wilson administration proposed, and the nation accepted, "the most sweeping extension of national power experienced by the country up to that time."[26] Contemporaries recognized it as "a kind of governmental effort absolutely new in American history."[27] The federal government took control of the nation's railroads, its telegraphs and telephones, and its shipping industries. It assumed authority to regulate the production and prices of food and fuel. Through closely coordinated administrative interventions, it directed the country's manufacturing capacities away from civilian goods and towards the production of essential military resources.[28] It altered the fiscal structure of the government through the enactment of progressive income taxes. It imposed "massive" nationwide conscription that registered all men between 18 and 45, and that called up to service more than 4 million persons.[29] It established national labor policies and agencies. It decreed national prohibition. It almost instantaneously created institutions that would serve as prototypes fifteen years later for the New Deal.[30] To staff these institutions, "social progressives were brought en masse into government and quasi-government service."[31]

Within a month of the declaration of war, Illinois Representative James Mann could proclaim on the floor of Congress that "We are undergoing the greatest revolution in government which this country has ever seen."[32] Nothing like this explosion of federal regulatory power had ever been exercised before.[33] Surveying the scene in 1918, the *New Republic* could report with unmistakable satisfaction that the war had "forever exploded the myth that all we have to do is to leave things alone. . . . [T]he war has forced men to turn over to the state the chief means of production and to regulate monopolies, prices, wages and labor conditions. *Laissez-faire* has been adjourned . . . . We have entered upon the stage of state-capitalism in which all our main economic activities are subordinated to the public interest."[34] The domestic "story" of World War I was, in the words of Grosvenor Clarkson, director of the National Council of Defense, that "of the conversion of a-hundred million combatively individualistic people into a vast cooperative effort in which the good of the unit was sacrificed to the good of the whole."[35]

The remarkable transformation produced the distinct "sense of a political culture cracking and reforming under the war's strain."[36] For a nation long accustomed to limited government, the sudden imposition of planning and coordination seemed inimical to fundamental values. Mark Sullivan would later recall:

> Of the effects of the war on America, by far the most fundamental was our submission to autocracy in government. . . . Every businessman was shorn of dominion over his factory or store, every house-wife surrendered control of her table, every farmer was forbidden to sell his wheat except at the price the government fixed. Our institutions, the railroads, the telephones and telegraphs, the coal mines, were taken under government control . . . . The prohibition of individual liberty in the interest of the state could hardly be more complete.[37]

Almost immediately, the "near-socialism" prompted by the war's relentless dedication to "achieve one supreme end" evolved into a strenuous debate whether this kind of active state intervention should be temporary or permanent.[38] Conservatives warned "against beginning after-war reconstruction 'under the auspices of semi-Socialistic and bureaucratic paternalism.'"[39] They feared "the short-sighted provincial attitude of certain elements who are seizing the opportunity to force changes in our fundamental laws to meet theories of social life not supported by experience, and upon which there is wide divergence of opinion."[40]

Progressives, by contrast, celebrated the fact that "[w]e are more of a unified, self-conscious nation than ever before."[41] They were acutely aware that "[o]ur society today is as fluid as molten iron; it can be run into any mold," and they were determined to ensure that the "social control" that "was a necessity during the war" not be abandoned to "unrestrained private initiative"[42] after the Armistice. "What we have learned in war we shall hardly forget in peace," proclaimed Walter Weyl in 1918. "We shall no longer be content with an industrial machine which is so ill-regulated that it loses its force in waste heat and develops little drive. We shall be obliged to retain conceptions and practices acquired during the war. The new economic solidarity, once gained, can never again be surrendered."[43] The innocent confidence of progressives can be seen in a letter that William Allen White wrote his friend Mark Sullivan in January 1918:

> The war swallowed the progressive issues.... I think the big thing to do now is quietly organize a hundred or so fellows who are dependable and who may take such steps as are necessary after the war to serve all the economic and social campaigns that the war brings to us. I think price fixing should be permanent, but not done by Wall Street. I think the government should tighten its control either into ownership or operation of the railroads. I think that labor arbitration should be a permanent thing, and that we should federalize education through universal training, making it a part of the system of education.[44]

The hopes of progressives were soon dashed. Throughout the war Wilson had been "ambiguous and hesitant about expanding state control over the economy."[45] He had been elected in 1912 on the platform of the New Freedom, which Lippmann at the time mercilessly caricatured as a "deliberate attempt to create an undeliberate society," a Utopian dream of a "Golden Age" in which Americans "could drift with impunity."[46] In the face of the unprecedented managerial demands of the war, Wilson sought to remain as faithful as he could "to the country's voluntarist traditions."[47] At the close of the war, therefore, "every trace of the war organization was destroyed as rapidly as possible."[48] Wilson "allowed his administration to close in a riot of reaction."[49]

Wilson lost both Houses of Congress in the 1918 election. Diagnosing the defeat to his friend James Bryce, Henry Cabot Lodge wrote that "Mr. Wilson's defeat at the elections and the magnitude of the defeat are almost unbelievable.... The underlying cause was the dread deep down in the people's hearts of the establishment of a dictatorship, and in view of the great bureaucratic machine which has been built up the alarm was anything but ill founded."[50] Harding's crushing victory in 1920 capped a sweeping popular repudiation of wartime mastery. "After the great storm," Harding announced in his inaugural address, "we must strive for normalcy to reach stability."[51]

The advantages of government control, however, could not be so easily cast aside. For all the ambivalence associated with the massive economic regulation prompted by the war, it marked a "watershed" in the orientation of the federal government.[52] It "changed the trajectory of American political development."[53] It produced deep and irreversible transformations. The fiscal foundations of the federal government, for example, were permanently and essentially transformed.[54] The war centralized authority in the administrative agencies of the executive branch,[55] so that the administrator became "the man of the hour."[56]

No one was more opposed to the war's allocation of "excess power to the executive"[57] than Harding.[58] Yet in his first State of the Union address, despite acknowledging that the war had involved "excessive grants of authority and ... extraordinary concentration of powers in the Chief Executive,"[59] Harding nevertheless felt compelled to ask for yet more executive discretion.[60] He requested that the Tariff Commission be given amplified discretion so that it might enjoy "flexibility and elasticity ... to meet unusual and changing conditions which can not be accurately anticipated." Without a trace of irony, Harding conceded that "I must disavow any desire to enlarge the Executive's powers or add to the responsibilities of the office. They are already too large. If there were any other plan I would prefer it."[61]

Seven years later the Taft Court unanimously ratified the resulting expansion of executive power in *J.W. Hampton, Jr. & Co. v. United States*, which upheld the innovative "flexible tariff provision" on grounds that would become fundamental for the modern administrative state: "If Congress shall lay down by legislative act an intelligible principle to which the person or body authorized to fix such rates is directed to conform, such legislative action is not a forbidden delegation of legislative power."[62]

A lasting effect of World War I was the emergence of a professional bureaucracy to meet the enormous planning capacities demanded by wartime regulation.[63] Contemporaries marveled at the sheer statistical expertise suddenly required to oversee "the drafting of men, the commandeering of ships and workshops and supplies, the control of prices and output, the restriction of exports and imports, the supervision of the processes of market distribution, the regulation of consumption, the coordination and administration of transportation agencies, the solution of labor difficulties, the raising of vast sums of money through taxes and loans, and the creation of priority rights."[64] It was apparent that the acquisition of this kind of expertise profoundly altered "the possibilities ... of rationally adapting the mechanism of national life to fit national ends."[65]

The newly discovered bureaucratic capacity to manage large systems generated a concomitant responsibility to oversee essential national services. The inability of the railroads to meet national needs had forced the federal government to seize control of the rail system in 1917.[66] Although Congress refused to nationalize the railroads after the war, it nevertheless enacted the Transportation Act of 1920,[67] which revolutionized the role of the Interstate Commerce Commission ("ICC"). The Transportation Act "was a clear departure from the regulatory system established under the Interstate Commerce Act and subsequent railroad legislation. Unlike earlier policy, which was driven by the fear of railroad abuses and a concern for the rights of shippers to reasonable and just rates, the 1920 act was dominated by a recognition of the financial needs of the railroads and the desire for stability."[68] The Act imagined the railway system of the nation as a single unit, relieving railroads from the strictures of anti-trust law[69] and effectively placing both interstate and intrastate rail travel under the supervision of the ICC.

The extraordinarily far-reaching authority of the ICC to oversee the operational health of the country's railroad system was unanimously affirmed by the Taft Court in

Dayton-Goose Creek Railway Co. v. United States, which acknowledged and sustained the legislative purpose of putting "the railroad systems of the country more completely than ever under the fostering guardianship and control of the Commission, which is to supervise their issue of securities, their car supply and distribution, their joint use of terminals, their construction of new lines, their abandonment of old lines, and by a proper division of joint rates, and by fixing adequate rates for interstate commerce, and in case of discrimination, for intrastate commerce, to secure a fair return upon the properties of the carriers engaged."[70] It is difficult to imagine a more direct extension of the planning capacities created by the war.

The war also marked the beginning of "economic inquiry for purposes of managing the economic system as a whole."[71] "The business economist ... came into his own during the Great War."[72] The war "brought dozens of trained economists into government service and put them to work producing the data, tools, and understanding needed for effective performance of the new managerial tasks."[73] Suddenly economic expertise became indispensable for planning and management. In the 1920s this attitude would become "the dominant mode of thought in agencies like the Forest Service, the Geological Survey, the Bureau of Mines, and the Bureau of Public Roads," as well as the Department of Agriculture.[74]

Particularly influential was the approach adopted by the War Industries Board ("WIB"). During the war, the WIB had organized fifty-seven commodity sections, each consisting of "a chief and assistants, who usually came from the industry to be regulated, and representatives from the army, navy, and other claimant agencies."[75] The United States Chamber of Commerce, in turn, certified about 300 war service committees, which consisted of elected members of industries with trade associations or representatives selected by the Chamber itself for unorganized industries. The function of the war service committees was to advise the commodity sections.[76] The object was to set prices and priorities in ways that would maximize the production of war-related goods.

Wartime planning proceeded in close coordination with the corporate interests of the affected industries, which in the process discovered the immense advantages of cooperation with each other and with the government. The president of the United States Chamber of Commerce wrote:

> Preparation for and participation in the military struggle is accomplishing now an organization of business that will outlive the war.... Creation of the War Service Committees promises to furnish the basis for a truly national organization of industry whose proportions and opportunities are unlimited.... Industries torn apart for years by factional differences have been brought together in committees and are working with one another in closest harmony.... Competition has been put on a clean and enduring basis. The integration of business, the expressed aim of the National Chamber, is in sight. War is the stern teacher that is driving home the lesson of cooperative effort.[77]

Just as the war convinced the nation of the need for an integrated railroad system, so the "World War profoundly changed general conceptions with reference to the desirability of industrial combinations; it was found that to win the war, concentration of control was inevitable."[78] If progressivism had burst on to the national scene in a frenzy of trust-busting, the war taught the nation to appreciate consolidation and economies of scale.[79] In its final Report, the WIB urged that "practices of cooperation and coordination in industry as have been found to be clearly of public benefit should be stimulated and encouraged by a Government agency." The WIB especially praised trade associations, which it deemed "capable of carrying out purposes of greatest public benefit."[80] Even so sober an observer as Charles Evans Hughes could remark:

> The War has compelled co-operation and the Government, under this compulsion, has fostered what is previously denounced as criminal. The conduct which had been condemned by the law as a public offense was found to be necessary for the salvation of the Republic. But the public need so dramatically disclosed by the War is not ... removed by the termination of the War. Co-operation is just as necessary to secure the full benefits of peace as it was to meet the exigencies of War. And without it we shall miss the great prosperity and advance in trade to which with our skill and energy we are entitled.[81]

In the years after the war, trade associations multiplied in the United States.[82] Herbert Hoover entered the Commerce Department "with his mind made up to reestablish the essence of the plan inaugurated by the War Industries Board" and to maximize production by working with "business organizations, chambers of commerce, boards of trade, and trade associations."[83] Hoover believed:

> We have reached a stage of national development of such complexity and interdependence of economic life that we must have a national planning of industry and commerce. We have gained a larger perspective than individual business because without the prosperity of the whole, individual prosperity is impossible.... Government has a definite relationship to it, not as an agency for production and distribution of commodities, not as an economic dictator, but as the greatest contributor in the determination of fact and of cooperation with industry and commerce in the solution of its problems.[84]

Under Hoover, the Commerce Department offered "guidance for corporate planners" by publishing "the monthly *Survey of Current Business* as a sourcebook of primary and secondary statistics."[85] Using a structure derived from the WIB, Hoover divided the Commerce Department into commodity divisions that distributed relevant trade information to specific industries and sought to increase efficiency by promoting standardization and simplification.[86] Hoover was passionately committed to eliminating "national waste" that decreased "the efficiency of the entire industrial machine and ... the available commodities for distribution."[87] He believed "better distribution of information bearing upon future supply and demand"[88] would reduce information costs and increase productivity. But he also insisted on government programs that would preserve "individual initiative,"[89] and he "opposed government price fixing," commenting that "I would not propose price fixing in any form short of again reentering the trenches of a World War."[90]

The upshot was a new vision of "an 'associative state,' tied to, cooperating with, and helping to develop and guide" voluntary organizations, "particularly trade associations."[91] Hoover "saw himself both as an anti-statist and as an ardent champion of one form of positive government and national planning."[92] During the Taft Court era, Hoover's vision of state-facilitated cooperation would be tested by prewar conceptions of individualistic competition. An important question that hung over the 1920s was how the associative cooperation practiced during the war and perpetuated by Hoover's Commerce Department would fare under traditional anti-trust policy.

At first the Taft Court attempted to use prewar anti-trust doctrine to discipline innovative postwar forms of economic coordination. In *American Column & Lumber Co. v. United States*,[93] the Court held that the Sherman Act invalidated the "Open Competition Plan"[94] of a trade association of hardwood manufacturers. The announced purpose of the plan was "to disseminate among members accurate knowledge of production and market conditions so that each member may gauge the market intelligently instead of guessing at it; to make competition open and above board instead of secret and concealed." The Plan was run by a "Manager of Statistics," who circulated to the membership detailed reports that included his "suggestions as to both future prices and production." The Court held that the Plan was in effect an agreement "to bring about a concerted effort to raise prices regardless of cost or merit, and so was unlawful."[95] McKenna, Holmes, and Brandeis dissented.[96]

American Column & Lumber caused an uproar in the business community.[97] Hoover was so concerned that he immediately wrote Attorney General Daugherty to defend the "propriety" of trade associations for the "promotion and advancement of the public welfare and for progressive economic organization." Hoover boldly proposed to legitimate the informational functions of trade associations by having them transmit economic data directly to the Department of Commerce, which in turn would publish the data to the general public. "If information regarding production, capacity, and distribution by districts, with average prices for grades, brands, sizes, styles, or qualities sold in the respective districts for specified periods of time could be given to the public at the same time that such information is available to the members of an association, in my judgment, great public good would result."[98] Daugherty grudgingly conceded the legitimacy of the plan, "*provided always* that whatever is done is not used as a scheme or device to curtail production or enhance prices, and does not have the effect of suppressing competition."[99]

In 1923, however, the Taft Court struck down yet another (especially rigorous and coercive) information-sharing scheme in *United States v. American Linseed Oil*.[100] Speaking for a unanimous Court,[101] McReynolds opined that it was "not normal" for competitors to limit "their freedom of action by requiring each to reveal to all the intimate details of its affairs. ... Obviously they were not *bone fide* competitors; their claim in that regard is at war with common experience and hardly compatible with fair dealing. ... Their manifest purpose was to defeat the Sherman Act."[102] Underlying McReynolds's decision was the premise that the very essence of competition was, as Francis Walker had defined it in 1892, "the operation of individual self-interest, among the buyers and sellers of any article in any market."[103] The individual self-interest celebrated by McReynolds was quite distinct from Hoover's conception of the market as an encompassing structure of incentives designed to efficiently produce and distribute goods.

American Linseed Oil threatened to disrupt Hoover's plan to have the Department of Commerce distribute trade association information.[104] But in 1925 the Taft Court executed an abrupt and unexpected *volte face* after Stone, who had been close to Hoover in Coolidge's Cabinet,[105] joined the bench. In *Maple Flooring Manufacturers Ass'n v. United States*,[106] the Court once again considered the relationship between the Sherman Act and the exchange of price and production information within trade associations. Writing for a majority of six,[107] Stone was careful to note at the outset that "it is neither alleged nor proved that there was any agreement among the members of the Association either affecting production, fixing prices or for price maintenance."[108] The precise question, therefore, was not whether the organized exchange of information could be used to unreasonably restrain trade, which Stone conceded would be illegal, but whether such an exchange was intrinsically and necessarily incompatible with the Sherman Act.[109] In language referencing Hoover,[110] Stone held that it was not.

"It is the consensus of opinion of economists and of many of the most important agencies of government," he wrote, "that the public interest is served by the gathering and dissemination, in the widest possible manner, of information with respect to the production and distribution, cost and prices in actual sales, of market commodities because the making available of such information tends to stabilize trade and industry, to produce fairer price levels and to avoid the waste which inevitably attends the unintelligent conduct of economic enterprise."[111] "We do not conceive that the members of trade associations become ... conspirators merely because they gather and disseminate information, such as is here complained of, bearing on the business in which they are engaged and make use of it in the management and control of their individual businesses."[112] In dissent, McReynolds objected that "ordinary knowledge of human nature and of the impelling force of greed ought to permit no serious doubt" that the sharing of pertinent trade information was inimical to "that kind of competition long relied upon by the public for the establishment of fair prices."[113]

By mid-decade, in other words, the Taft Court had pivoted from the assumption that competition consisted of the atomistic "individual self-interest" of particular actors, to the quite different assumption that competition was a system of incentives designed to produce efficient outcomes. The shift in perspective was profound.[114] The very idea that "unintelligent" competition could produce "waste" presupposed that competition was itself a purposive structure whose aim was to maximize output given available resources, an insight that built on aggressive state interventions during World War I which were designed to incentivize the greatest possible production of war-related goods.

This was the insight that inspired Hoover's transformation of the Department of Commerce during the 1920s. Hoover insisted that the Sherman Act no longer be interpreted to require the maintenance of "a great host of highly competitive units in every trade," even when the resulting competition was "highly destructive." He instead believed that the statute be construed to permit "forms of collective action to eliminate definite wastes" whenever such action was "obviously in the public interest and productive of a fundamental strengthening of competition itself."[115]

In Hoover's view, efficient economic production and distribution were unquestionably "in the public interest," and this interest could be facilitated by appropriate forms of government planning and coordination. The function of government was to create "a better synchronizing of the parts of the economic machine," by, for example "eliminating waste through standardizing of dimensions, qualities of goods and business practice."[116] A lasting legacy of World War I was the belief that government policy could be used to shape economic practices to serve intelligible social purposes.[117] Hoover exemplified this progressive impulse to mastery.

What makes the 1920s so difficult to characterize is that this impulse could coexist with its opposite, with the instinctive assumption that active government intervention disrupted the "normal" and effective operation of the market. Coolidge might be said to epitomize this latter perspective.[118] He was, as Hoover said, "a real conservative, probably the equal of Benjamin Harrison."[119] By contrast, Harding had been far more ambivalent.[120]

Consider Harding's Conference on Unemployment, convened in September 1921. The country was facing a sharp recession with a consequent serious uptick in unemployment.[121] Hoover pushed Harding into sponsoring a conference with representatives of employers, labor, and the public, "to inquire into the volume and distribution of unemployment, to advise upon emergency measures that can be properly taken by employers and local authorities and civic bodies, and to consider such measures as would tend to give impulse to the recovery of business and commerce to normal."[122] This was classic Hoover activism,[123] and in fact the conference eventually recommended a rudimentary macroeconomic strategy of countercyclical spending.[124]

Harding himself inaugurated the conference, however, by frankly avowing his uncertainty about the entire enterprise: "It is fair to say," he remarked to those gathered to confer, "that you are not asked to solve the long-controverted problems of our social system. We have builded the America of to-day on the fundamentals of economic, industrial, and political life which made us what we are, and the temple requires no remaking now. We are incontestably sound. We are constitutionally strong. We are merely depressed after the fever, and we want to know the way to speediest and dependable convalescence."[125]

Harding's ambivalence is exemplary. Throughout the 1920s there was a running battle in America between those who believed that the "temple requires no remaking," and those who sought to remedy "long-controverted problems" of the "social system." The Taft Court is now chiefly remembered for its efforts to use the Constitution to referee this battle. The experience of World War I overhung its efforts. As Charles Evans Hughes had insightfully predicted in 1918, military conscription would have deep but subtle consequences for constitutional adjudication, including "a new appreciation of the power of our government":

> What will be the reaction to this new impression of power? Will it be in favor of individual liberty, or in favor of a larger measure of governmental control over

individual conduct and property in the days of peace? I am disposed to think that in some degree there will be both reactions. But I cannot escape the belief that in the main the present exercise of authority over the lives of men will hereafter find its counterpart in a more liberal exercise of power over the conduct, opportunities and possessions of men. Among the ten million young men who have been registered under the draft act, there will probably be a host who are not likely to shrink at the application of power to others if they conceive it to be in the general interest, the supremacy of which they have been bound to acknowledge. If former conceptions of property right and individual liberty are to be maintained in the years to come, it will not be through the same instinctive regard for them which has hitherto distinguished our people, but because it is the conviction that the common interest will be better served by freedom of individual opportunity than by fettering it. . . . [I]ndividual privilege when challenged will have to show cause before a public to which old traditions are no longer controlling – a public trained to sacrifice – which will have and enforce its own estimate of the extent of the common right.[126]

The Taft Court would struggle throughout the decade to discern constitutional boundaries in a world where "the common right" had grown to mammoth proportions, and yet in which "old traditions" were no longer sustained by "instinctive regard." It was a difficult, if not impossible task. Stripped of their implicit moorings in customary understandings, constitutional limitations came increasingly to seem like merely arbitrary restraints on desirable political reform.[127] The astonishing precedents of World War I stood as a continual reminder of what American society could accomplish if only the "general interest" were deemed sufficiently important. They were precedents upon which the New Deal would later freely build. But during the 1920s, as the forces of regulation unleashed by World War I washed against the uncertain dykes of constitutional restraint, an unsettling jurisprudential crisis began to loom.

To defenders of the old order, like Sanford, "the aftermath of war" produced "troubled and bewildered days, when . . . many evil passions have been turned loose that . . . seek to undermine the foundations of Liberty itself."[128] Butler remarked that the "war was followed by many new and difficult business and industrial problems; and a feeling of unrest is quite widespread."[129] Taft was apt to refer to "the depths in which we have been since the War,"[130] which he regarded as a "cataclysmic eruption" causing "tremendous upheaval."[131] The lingering efforts of the Wilson administration to exert wartime powers gave Van Devanter the queasy sensation that "everything is on edge" and that "existing conditions are not well balanced. Some day they may take a slide just as the snow does on the mountain and carry everything before them."[132]

Governments, Van Devanter observed to a friend in 1920, "cannot be maintained . . . on the principle of the sailor who thinks any port looks good in a storm."[133] Van Devanter sought to mute his elation at Harding's gilded broom by reminding himself that "so many things have to be done and done wisely to put us on a good footing again that it will be almost impossible to do what the people generally want done. Sickness, when it has become pronounced, cannot be thrown off quickly no matter who the doctor is."[134]

Notes

1. The only missing justice was Oliver Wendell Holmes, who had "allowed representations of danger to the aged to persuade me not to go to Arlington." OWH to Harold Laski (November 13, 1921), in 1 HOLMES-LASKI CORRESPONDENCE, at 381.
2. Philip Kinsley, *Throngs Watch Cortege*, CHICAGO DAILY TRIBUNE (November 12, 1921), at 1. *See* Arthur Sears Henning, *Capital Bows as Hero Is Laid in Final Couch*, CHICAGO DAILY TRIBUNE (November 12, 1921), at 1.
3. ANNE LELAND & MARI-JANA "M-J" OBOROCEANU, AMERICAN WAR AND MILITARY OPERATIONS CASUALTIES: LISTS AND STATISTICS 2 (Washington D. C.: Congressional Research Service February 26, 2010).
4. Quoted in Preston Lockwood, *Henry James's First Interview*, NEW YORK TIMES (March 21, 1915), Magazine at 3. It was left to Ernest Hemingway to create a literature of deflated words.
5. OWH to Harold Laski (November 13, 1921), in 1 HOLMES-LASKI CORRESPONDENCE, at 381.
6. David Reynolds, *America's "Forgotten War" and the Long Twentieth Century*, in WORLD WAR I AND AMERICAN ART 20 (Robert Cozzolino, Anne Classen Knutson & David M. Lubin, eds., Pennsylvania Academy of the Fine Arts, in association with Princeton University Press 2016).
7. Jennifer D. Keene, *Remembering the "Forgotten War": American Historiography on World War I*, 78 THE HISTORIAN 439, 443 (2016).
8. Reynolds, *supra* note 6, at 19.
9. LDB to Frederick Wehle (October 28, 1924), in BRANDEIS FAMILY LETTERS, at 395.
10. HAZEL HUTCHISON, THE WAR THAT USED UP WORDS: AMERICAN WRITERS AND THE FIRST WORLD WAR 14 (New Haven: Yale University Press 2015).
11. Robert Cozzolino, Anne Classen Knutson, & David M. Lubin, *Introduction*, in WORLD WAR I AND AMERICAN ART, *supra* note 6, at 11.
12. HUTCHISON, *supra* note 10, at 14.
13. *See, e.g.*, Herbert Croly, *The Eclipse of Progressivism*, 24 NEW REPUBLIC 210 (1920); William Hard et al.,*Where Are the Pre-War Radicals?*, 55 THE SURVEY 556 (1926); Frederick C. Howe, *Where Are the Pre-War Radicals?*, 56 THE SURVEY 33 (1926).
14. WALTER LIPPMANN, DRIFT AND MASTERY: AN ATTEMPT TO DIAGNOSE THE CURRENT UNREST 145, 266 (New York: Henry Holt & Co. 1917). "We can no longer treat life as something that has trickled down to us. We have to deal with it deliberately, devise its social organization, alter its tools, formulate its method, educate and control it. In endless ways we put intention where custom has reigned. We break up routines, make decisions, choose our ends, select means." *Id.* at 267. DRIFT AND MASTERY was first published in 1914. Understood as an aspiration to mastery, the progressive impulse was essentially incompatible with forms of conservative constitutional jurisprudence that located fundamental rights in custom and tradition. *See supra* Chapter 5, at 169.
15. LIPPMANN, *supra* note 14, at 171, 275. "That is what mastery means: the substitution of conscious intention for unconscious striving. Civilization, it seems to me, is just this constant effort to introduce plan where there has been clash, and purpose into the jungles of disordered growth." *Id.* at 269.

16. Steven F. Lawson, *Progressives and the Supreme Court: A Case for Judicial Reform in the 1920s*, 42 THE HISTORIAN 419, 420 (1980). *See* OTIS L. GRAHAM, JR., THE GREAT CAMPAIGNS: REFORM AND WAR IN AMERICA 1900–1928, at 97–111 (Englewood Cliffs: Prentice-Hall 1971); William E. Leuchtenburg, *The New Deal and the Analogue of War*, in CHANGE AND CONTINUITY IN TWENTIETH-CENTURY AMERICA (John Braeman, Robert H. Bremner, & Everett Walters, eds., Columbus: Ohio State University Press 1964); Stanley Shapiro, *The Great War and Reform: Liberals and Labor, 1917–1919*, 12 LABOR HISTORY 323 (1971); Charles Hirschfeld, *Nationalist Progressivism and World War I*, 45 MID-AMERICA: AN HISTORICAL REVIEW 139 (1963); Robert Cuff, *Organizing for War: Canada and the United States during World War I*, in CANADIAN HISTORICAL ASSOCIATION, HISTORICAL PAPERS 141–56 (1969).
17. MORTON KELLER, AMERICA'S THREE REGIMES: A NEW POLITICAL HISTORY 190 (Oxford University Press 2007).
18. JOHN MAURICE CLARK, THE COSTS OF THE WORLD WAR TO THE AMERICAN PEOPLE 29 (New Haven: Yale University Press 1931). *See* Elihu Root, *Address of the President*, in REPORT OF THE THIRTY-NINTH ANNUAL MEETING OF THE AMERICAN BAR ASSOCIATION 355, 356 (Baltimore: Lord Baltimore Press 1916).
19. GEORGE SOULE, PROSPERITY DECADE: FROM WAR TO DEPRESSION: 1917–1929, at 9 (New York: Rinehart & Co. 1947). *See* DANIEL T. RODGERS, ATLANTIC CROSSINGS: SOCIAL POLITICS IN A PROGRESSIVE AGE 285–86 (Cambridge: Harvard University Press 1998); Walter Lippmann, *Correspondence*, 6 NEW REPUBLIC 157–58 (1916); *Republican Resurrection*, 9 NEW REPUBLIC 172, 173 (1916).
20. Pierre Purseigle, *The First World War and the Transformations of the State*, 90 INTERNATIONAL AFFAIRS 249, 253 (2014).
21. *Preparedness – A Trojan Horse*, 5 NEW REPUBLIC 6 (1915). "What do they mean when they shout for preparedness," Walter Lippmann presciently asked in 1916. "Are they willing to unify and socialize the railroads and the means of communication, to regulate rigorously basic industries like steel and coal mining, are they willing to control the food supply and shipping and credit, are they willing to recognize labor as a national institution? Are they willing to go behind all this and create a workable, modern, scientific federalized system of education? Are they ready to end the destruction of national vitality through unemployment, child labor, overwork, and poverty? Are they willing to do all of this which is the price of coöperation for a free people? If they are not, what are they talking about so earnestly?" Walter Lippmann, *The Issues of 1916*, 7 NEW REPUBLIC 107, 108 (1916).
22. *Address by the President of the United States*, 55 CONG. REC. 101, 103 (April 2, 1917).
23. *Morale*, 10 NEW REPUBLIC 337, 337 (1917).
24. *The American Tradition and the War*, 104 THE NATION 484, 485 (1917). "War necessitates organization, system, routine, and discipline.... The executive side of the Administration will have to be strengthened by the appointment of trained specialists. Socialism will take tremendous strides forward.... We shall have to give up much of our economic freedom.... The only way to fight Prussianism is with Prussian tools. The danger is lest we forget the lesson of Prussia: that the bad brother of discipline is tyranny – which our fathers fought to put down and our

immigrants came to our shores to escape. It would be an evil day for America if we threw overbroad liberty to make room for efficiency." *Id.*
25. *Morale, supra* note 23, at 338.
26. RICHARD L. WATSON, Jr., THE DEVELOPMENT OF NATIONAL POWER: THE UNITED STATES, 1900–1919, at 219 (Boston: Houghton Mifflin 1976).
27. Charles M. Hough, *Law in War Time – 1917*, 31 HARVARD LAW REVIEW 692, 699 (1918).
28. "Non-war-related production would decrease during the war: $24.3 billion worth of war materials were produced, of which only $1.9 billion came from increased output while $22.4 billion came from diverting civilian production to war needs." MEIRION HARRIES & SUSIE HARRIES, THE LAST DAYS OF INNOCENCE: AMERICA AT WAR 1917–1918, at 279 (New York: Random House 1997). "Maintenance of a maximum production of war material is second in importance only to raising and training of an adequate army," observed Taft. "We need both to win the war." William Howard Taft, *Toward Industrial Peace* (April 4, 1918), in VIVIAN, at 46.
29. JILL LEPORE, THESE TRUTHS: A HISTORY OF THE UNITED STATES 395 (New York: W.W. Norton & Co. 2018).
30. Leuchtenburg, *supra* note 16.
31. RODGERS, *supra* note 19, at 283.
32. 55 CONG. REC. 2832 (May 24, 1917). For discussions of wartime regulation, see generally ELLIS W. HAWLEY, THE GREAT WAR AND THE SEARCH FOR A MODERN ORDER: A HISTORY OF THE AMERICAN PEOPLE AND THEIR INSTITUTIONS 1917–1933 (New York: St. Martin's Press 1979); DAVID M. KENNEDY, OVER HERE: THE FIRST WORLD WAR AND AMERICAN SOCIETY 45–190 (Oxford University Press 1980); NEIL A. WYNN, FROM PROGRESSIVISM TO PROSPERITY: WORLD WAR I AND AMERICAN SOCIETY 65–85 (New York: Holmes & Meier 1986); ROBERT HIGGS, CRISIS AND LEVIATHAN: CRITICAL EPISODES IN THE GROWTH OF AMERICAN GOVERNMENT 123–59 (Oakland: The Independent Institute 1987); RONALD SCHAFFER, AMERICA IN THE GREAT WAR: THE RISE OF THE WAR WELFARE STATE 31–61 (New York: Oxford University Press 1991); PAUL A. C. KOISTINEN, MOBILIZING FOR MODERN WAR: THE POLITICAL ECONOMY OF AMERICAN WARFARE, 1865–1919 (Lawrence: University Press of Kansas 1997). On constitutional developments during the war, see WILLIAM G. ROSS, WORLD WAR I AND THE AMERICAN CONSTITUTION (Cambridge University Press 2017).
33. *See* Melvin I. Urofsky, *The Great War, the Constitution, and the Court*, 44 JOURNAL OF SUPREME COURT HISTORY 251 (2019).
34. *Stabilizing Demand for Labor*, 16 NEW REPUBLIC 2125–26 (1918). *See* Charles Merz, *War as Pretext*, 11 NEW REPUBLIC 129, 130–31 (1917) ("Why should war not serve as a pretext to foist innovations upon the country? ... It is a certain extenuation of war that by creating enormous pressure, it makes obvious the defects in political and economic organization. We shall not in this war be accomplishing much that we are setting out to accomplish if we foreclose to ourselves the full chances of profiting from a dear experience."). *See* Neva R. Deardorff, *The Demise of a Highly Respected Doctrine*, 39 THE SURVEY 416 (1918) ("Laissez faire is dead! Long live social control! Social control not only to enable us to meet the rigorous demands of war, but also as a foundation for the peace and brotherhood that is to come. This was the theme that ran strongly through all the annual meetings of the learned societies of the social sciences which were held holiday week in Philadelphia." The learned

societies included the American Sociological Society, the American Political Science Association, the American Economic Association, the American Association for Labor Legislation, the American Statistical Association, the American Historical Association, the American Farm Management Association, and the Association of Accounting Instructors.).
35. GROSVENOR B. CLARKSON, INDUSTRIAL AMERICA IN THE WORLD WAR: THE STRATEGY BEHIND THE LINE 1917–1918, at 3–4 (Boston: Houghton Mifflin 1923).
36. RODGERS, *supra* note 19, at 289.
37. MARK SULLIVAN, OUR TIMES: AMERICA AT THE BIRTH OF THE TWENTIETH CENTURY 567 (New York: Scribner 1996).
38. J.M. Clark, *The Basis of War-Time Collectivism*, 7 AMERICAN ECONOMIC REVIEW 772, 772 (1917). "These stupendous increases in the functions of the national government are threatening to the interests and even to the survival of many powerful classes in the community. They involve a radical change in the balance of economic power, an increase of administrative as compared to legislative power which Congress will fear, and an increase of central as compared with local power which the states will dislike. All these opposing interests will regard this vast extension of national authority which is associated with the autocratic but necessary war power of the executive as ephemeral as the war power itself. Indeed what many of the most convinced opponents of government intrusion into private business mean by a reconsideration of these questions at the end of the war is in substance an automatic and inevitable return to the status quo ante. They regard the former industrial conditions as essentially normal and permanent, and the recent intrusion of the government as a catastrophe precipitated by the violent irrelevance of war." *After the War – Reaction or Reconstruction*, 13 NEW REPUBLIC 331, 331 (1918).
39. *Kahn Warns against After-War Socialism*, BOSTON DAILY GLOBE (October 11, 1918), at 3.
40. Walter George Smith, *Civil Liberty in America: Address of the President*, in REPORT OF THE FORTY-FIRST ANNUAL MEETING OF THE AMERICAN BAR ASSOCIATION 209, 216 (Baltimore: Lord Baltimore Press 1918). Taft himself cautioned that "Human nature is not going to be changed after the war." William Howard Taft, *The Socialist Impulse* (January 25, 1918), in VIVIAN, at 31. *See War Measures for War Times*, 208 NORTH AMERICAN REVIEW 180 (1918); *Constitutional Government in War and Peace*, 3 CONSTITUTIONAL REVIEW 222 (1919); Cordenio A. Severance, *Constitution and Individualism*, 8 AMERICAN BAR ASSOCIATION JOURNAL 535 (1922).
41. *Nationalism and Internationalism*, 17 NEW REPUBLIC 5 (1918). "Sectionalism, which not more than two years ago appeared to be a growing force in this country, has all but disappeared. We are hearing practically nothing of the peculiar needs and demands of South or Far West, New England or the central industrial district. Officially and unofficially, we are emphasizing the points in which the interests of labor and capital coincide and slurring the points in which they conflict. And in so far as we are thinking at all about reconstruction policies, we are instinctively adopting the premise that the interest of each group in our nation is the interest of all." *Id. See Mob Violence and War Psychology*, 16 NEW REPUBLIC 5, 7 (1918) ("The essential unity of this country has been magnificently vindicated. America is more of a nation today than she has ever been in the past and her nationality is more firmly attached than ever to democratic domestic and foreign policy.").

42. *The Uses of an Armistice*, 17 NEW REPUBLIC 59, 60–61 (1918). *See Carrying Forward of War-Time Industrial Standards*, 41 THE SURVEY 308 (1918) ("All those who had come from intimate contact during the war with the government agencies in the industrial field believe that a real and permanent gain has been made in many directions, and especially that of greater democracy in industry. But with regard to the latter set of standards, relating to the activity of the government itself, it was clearly shown that only a strong and immediate expression of public opinion can rescue from an untimely end the new agencies and methods established during the war which would be valuable in peace time.").
43. WALTER E. WEYL, THE END OF THE WAR 303–4 (New York: MacMillan Co. 1918). "It would be blind obscurantism to treat the nationalization of the railroads and the coal and food supplies of the country as the ephemeral and episodic consequence of a military emergency, and to ignore the question as to how far the breakdown of private management during the war emergency was not the natural fruits of defects which had been sufficiently conspicuous under more normal conditions. It would be no less obscurantist to surrender helplessly at the end of the war the public benefits which may have accrued from the incorporation of these essential sources into the national organization. ... Radicals have consequently a sufficient excuse for considering the compulsory nationalizing of the economic organization under the emergency of war as an illuminating experiment. It indicates the road which the American people will have to travel, in case they wish their economic and social system to serve public rather than private interests." *After the War – Reaction or Reconstruction*, *supra* note 38, at 331–32.
44. William Allen White to Mark Sullivan (January 28, 1918), in SELECTED LETTERS OF WILLIAM ALLEN WHITE 1899–1943, at 185 (Walter Johnson, ed., New York: Henry Holt & Co. 1947).
45. KENNEDY, *supra* note 32, at 137. "Throughout the mobilization president Wilson sought to separate war-related functions from the regular Executive Departments wherever possible." Robert D. Cuff, *The Politics of Labor Administration during World War I*, 21 LABOR HISTORY 546, 553 (1980). *See* KOISTINEN, *supra* note 32, at 204.
46. LIPPMANN, *supra* note 14, at 178–79. *See id.* at 132–44.
47. HARRIES & HARRIES, *supra* note 28, at 278.
48. George Soule, *Hard-Boiled Radicalism*, 65 NEW REPUBLIC 261, 262 (1931).
49. RICHARD HOFSTADTER, THE AMERICAN POLITICAL TRADITION AND THE MEN WHO MADE IT 274 (New York: A.A. Knopf 1948). *See generally* BURT NOGGLE, INTO THE TWENTIES: THE UNITED STATES FROM ARMISTICE TO NORMALCY (Urbana: University of Illinois Press 1974). "The return to 'normalcy' was to be an effective Republican slogan after the war, but in fact throughout the conflict it had been Wilson's main intention to depart from the normal as little as possible, especially in economic matters." KENNEDY, *supra* note 32, at 250.
50. Henry Cabot Lodge to James Bryce (December 14, 1918), quoted in KENNEDY, *supra* note 32, at 244–45.
51. 61 CONG. REC. 5 (March 4, 1921).
52. Paul A.C. Koistinen, *The "Industrial-Military Complex" in Historical Perspective: World War I*, 41 BUSINESS HISTORY REVIEW 378, 379–80 (1967).

53. Marc Allen Eisner, From Warfare State to Welfare State: World War I, Compensatory State Building, and the Limits of the Modern Order 2 (University Park: Pennsylvania State University Press 2000).
54. *See, e.g.*, Ajay K. Mehrotra, *Lawyers, Guns and Public Moneys: The U.S. Treasury, World War I, and the Administration of the Modern Fiscal State*, 28 Law and History Review 173, 173, 175, 179–82, 187 (2010):

> World War I was a pivotal event for U.S. political and economic development, particularly in the realm of public finance. For it was during the war that the federal government ended its traditional reliance on regressive import duties and excise taxes as principal sources of revenue and began a modern era of fiscal governance, one based primarily on the direct and progressive taxation of personal and corporate income. . . .
>
> World War I triggered a sea change in the historical development of a powerful U.S. nation-state. Unparalleled interconnections among economy, society, and polity were undergirded by fundamental transformations in public finance and federal bureaucratic capacity. After the war, the steeply progressive tax rates were scaled back, just as tariff revenues increased in response to the revival of international trade. But the national tax system did not return to either its prewar levels or even its prewar trajectory – the war was thus the pivot upon which the early twentieth-century fiscal revolution turned.

55. Eisner, *supra* note 53, at 35.
56. Elisha Friedman, *The New Era and Social Progress*, in America and the New Era 6 (Elisha M. Friedman, ed., New York: E.P. Dutton & Co. 1920). *See, e.g.*, F. Herbert Snow, *The Engineer and the State*, 45 Proceedings of the American Society of Civil Engineers 11 (January 1919) ("'Winning the War' . . . brought to the fore the Engineer as the man of the hour."); Rexford G. Tugwell, *America's War-Time Socialism*, 124 The Nation 364 (1927) ("[T]he war was an industrial engineer's Utopia.").
57. Warren G. Harding, *America in the War: Address at the Ohio Republican State Convention, Columbus, Ohio, August 27, 1918*, in Re-Dedicating America: The Life and Recent Speeches of Warren G. Harding 176 (Frederick E. Schortemeier, ed., Indianapolis: Bobbs Merrill 1920).
58. In accepting the Republican nomination for president, Harding decried "the surrender of Congress to the growing assumption of the executive." Warren G. Harding, *Speech of Acceptance, Address at Formal Notification of His Nomination for the Presidency, at Marion, Ohio, July 22, 1920*, in Re-Dedicating America, *supra* note 57, at 36. "In Woodrow Wilson was concentrated infinitely more power than had ever been given to an American President. In absolute terms it far exceeded Lincoln's, for it extended to a control of the nation's economic life that would have caused a revolution in 1863." Clinton L. Rossiter, Constitutional Dictatorship: Crisis Government in the Modern Democracies 241–42 (Princeton University Press 1948).
59. *Address by the President of the United States*, 62 Cong. Rec. 36 (December 6, 1921). "During the anxieties of war, when necessity seemed compelling, there were excessive grants of authority and an extraordinary concentration of powers in the Chief Executive. The repeal of war-time legislation and the automatic expirations which attended the peace proclamations have put an end to these emergency excesses, but I have the wish to go further than that. I want to join

you in restoring ... the spirit of coordination and cooperation, and that mutuality of confidence and respect which is necessary in representative popular government. Encroachment upon the functions of Congress or attempted dictation of its policy are not to be thought of, much less attempted." *Id.*

60. Harding frankly conceded that "the contribution of this Republic to restored normalcy in the world must come through the initiative of the executive branch of the Government." *Id.* at 36.
61. *Id.* at 37.
62. J.W. Hampton, Jr. & Co. v. United States, 276 U.S. 394, 400, 409 (1928). Taft's articulation has remained controlling, see Whitman v. American Trucking Ass'ns, Inc., 531 U.S. 457, 472 (2001), although it has recently come under some pressure. *See, e.g.*, Gundy v. United States, 139 S.Ct. 2116, 2137–42 (2019) (Gorsuch, J., dissenting); Department of Transportation v. Ass'n of American Railroads, 575 U.S. 43, 70–86 (2015) (Thomas, J., concurring in judgment). During the 1920s, many contemporaries regarded the flexible tariff as a profoundly unsettling expansion of executive power. *See supra* Chapter 11, at note 1.
63. EISNER, *supra* note 53, at 36–37.
64. Allyn A. Young, *National Statistics in War and Peace*, 59 AMERICAN STATISTICIAN 58, 58 (2005) (originally delivered as the Presidential Address of the American Statistical Association on December 27, 1917, and published in 16 JOURNAL OF THE AMERICAN STATISTICAL ASSOCIATION (1918)). "[T]he formulation and administration of wise national policies must depend upon the national self-knowledge that only statistical information, gathered on a much larger scale than we have been accustomed to think possible, can give." *Id.* at 58, 61.
65. *Id.* at 61. *See e.g.*, Wesley C. Mitchell, *Statistics and Government*, 16 PUBLICATIONS OF THE AMERICAN STATISTICAL ASSOCIATION 226 (1919): "The war forced a rapid expansion in the scope of federal statistics and the creation of new statistical agencies. What is more significant, the war led to the use of statistics ... as a vital factor in planning what should be done. ... We cherish the hope that what they helped to accomplish during the war toward the guidance of public policy by quantitative knowledge of social fact may not be lost in the period of reconstruction through which we are passing, and in the indefinite period of peace upon which we are about to enter. ... [T]he development of social science offers more hope for solving our social problems than any other line of endeavor." *Id.* at 226, 230.
66. EISNER, *supra* note 53, at 72; ROSS, *supra* note 32, at 73–82. Government take-over of the railroads was "the most drastic mobilization measure of the war." KENNEDY, *supra* note 32, at 253.
67. Pub. L. 66-152, 41 Stat. 456 (February 28, 1920).
68. EISNER, *supra* note 53, at 135. Thus the ICC after the Transportation Act, instead of setting maximum rates, set "*minimum* rates" in the interest of "preventing ruinous rate wars and promoting the stability and profitability of the industry." *Id.* In order "to bring stability and certainty of return, to restore railway credit, to place rigid restraints upon a supposedly hostile regulating body," the ICC was charged with fixing rates that would bring at least a 5.5 percent return on the "fair value" of the aggregate railway property within a given district. Gerard C. Henderson, *Railway Valuation and the Courts*, 33 HARVARD LAW REVIEW 902, 902 (1920). *See* 41 Stat. 488; Samuel W. Moore, *Railroad Rates and Revenues*, 16 VIRGINIA LAW REVIEW 243, 244 (1930).

"Everything Is on Edge": WWI & the American State

69. 41 Stat. 481–82.
70. 263 U.S. 456, 478 (1924). Butler's docket book indicates that McKenna was the only dissenting vote in conference in the case.
71. Ellis W. Hawley, *Economic Inquiry and the State in New Era America: Antistatist Corporatism and Positive Statism in Uneasy Coexistence*, in THE STATE AND ECONOMIC KNOWLEDGE: THE AMERICAN AND BRITISH EXPERIENCES 288 (Mary O. Furner & Barry Supple, eds., Cambridge University Press 1990). *See* SOULE, *supra* note 19, at 62: "[T]he eyes of many who had participated in the war planning or who had observed it with understanding, were opened to the possibilities of managing the economy for chosen ends. Whereas in previous years the behavior of the economic order had seemed like a series of unpredictable and uncontrollable natural phenomena, it now was analyzed with the aid of masses of new statistics and more detailed examination of cause and effect. It began to be possible to speak in terms of relative magnitudes and large aggregates, and to apply deliberate social controls by policies of priority and other devices. Toward the end of the war, a relatively few people began to ask why, if production and distribution could be governed even by a hastily improvised organization for war purposes, even better results might not be achieved over a longer period for purposes regarded as desirable in peace."
72. Hugh P. Baker, *Practical Problems of Trade Associations*, 11 PROCEEDINGS OF THE ACADEMY OF POLITICAL SCIENCE IN THE CITY OF NEW YORK 629, 632 (1926).
73. Hawley, *supra* note 71, at 289.
74. Ellis W. Hawley, *"Industrial Policy" in the 1920s and 1930s*, in THE POLITICS OF INDUSTRIAL POLICY 65 (Claude E. Barfield & William A. Schambra, eds., Washington D.C.: American Enterprise Institute for Public Policy Research 1986). *See, e.g.*, Ernest L. Bogart, *Economic Organization for War*, 14 AMERICAN POLITICAL SCIENCE REVIEW 587, 606 (1920).
75. KOISTINEN, *supra* note 32, at 211.
76. *Id.* at 209–11. "The war service committees secured business far more immunity from the antitrust laws than even the most sanguine advocates of industrial cooperation had espoused during the Progressive years. A private commercial body, not the federal government, certified that the committees represented the collective interests of business." *Id.* at 209.
77. Harry W. Wheeler, *Putting Our Resources on Tap*, 6 NATION'S BUSINESS 9 (August 1918). "So well has the system operated thus far that it is only a step to the time when the system of competitive bidding on war orders will be obsolete. Bidding is made unnecessary when manufacturers are ready to lay their cost sheets on the table before their competitors and let the government fix its own price on their products. And the government is coming to see that orders must be placed with a view to conserving industry as a whole, that the industrial structure must not be torn down." *Id.* Left-wing journalist George P. West remarked in wonder at the newly created wartime bureaucracy: "American business is in the saddle at Washington. In no other field could the Government find expert knowledge and executive efficiency. Our radicals are nowhere. ... For the most part our radicals stand by speechless, helpless, while the conduct of affairs passes to men who are ... efficient, men who know their jobs .... Business is being nationalized; but the process is in its own hands, – in the hands of its high priests." George P. West, *Business Takes Charge*, THE PUBLIC (May 11, 1917), at 456–57.

78. E.F. Albertsworth, *The Federal Supreme Court and Industrial Development*, 16 AMERICAN BAR ASSOCIATION JOURNAL 317, 319 (1930).
79. Thus Mark Sullivan wrote in 1925:

> With the war, solidarity of industry, coöperation among the units composing each industry, was seen to be, for purpose of the war, not reprehensible but desirable.... Out of this... came a greater popular tolerance of combination. The economic benefits of production on a large scale, and the reduced costs that accompany it, came to outweigh, to some extent, the popular hostility toward combinations because of the suspicion against the power put into the hands of the individuals who control these combinations. Along with this went a greater tolerance on the part of government.
>
> For nearly two decades, it was a major issue in American politics to prevent consolidation of the railroads.... Twenty years later, the Government is actually demanding consolidation of the railroads into larger units; and the machinery is at this moment under way bringing practically all the railroads of the country into a smaller number of units.

Mark Sullivan, *Looking Back on La Follette*, 49 WORLD'S WORK 324, 330 (January 1925).
80. BERNARD M. BARUCH, AMERICAN INDUSTRY IN THE WAR: A REPORT OF THE WAR INDUSTRIES BOARD 105, 107 (Washington D.C.: Government Printing Office 1921).

> They can increase the amount of wealth available for the comfort of the people by inaugurating rules designed to eliminate wasteful practices attendant upon multiplicity of styles and types of articles in the various trades; they can assist, in cultivating the public taste for rational types of commodities; by exchange of trade information, extravagant methods of production and distribution can be avoided through them, and production will tend to be localized in places best suited economically for it. By acting as centers of information, furnishing lists of sourses to purchasers and lists of purchasers to producers, supply and demand can be more economically balanced. From the point of vantage which competent men have at the central bureau of an association, not only can new demands be cultivated, but new sources of unexploited wealth can be indicated.

Id. at 105–6.
81. Charles Evans Hughes, *Our After-War Dangers*, 61 THE FORUM 237 (February 1919).
82. EISNER, *supra* note 53, at 89–91.
83. George T. Odell, *Herbert Hoover – Super-Business Man*, 121 THE NATION 325, 325–26 (September 23, 1925). *See* Peri Ethan Arnold, *Herbert Hoover and the Continuity of American Public Policy*, 20 PUBLIC POLICY 525, 530–35 (1972); Tugwell, *supra* note 56, at 367 ("The sole representative of the War Industries idea in Washington today is Mr. Hoover, and the contrast between the activities of his Department and the attitude of President Coolidge and his Department of Justice is amusing and instructive."). On Hoover's intellectual debt to Brandeis and his views of competition, see LAURA PHILLIPS SAWYER, AMERICAN FAIR TRADE: PROPRIETARY CAPITALISM, CORPORATISM, AND THE "NEW COMPETITION," 1890–1940, at 107–95 (Cambridge University Press 2018).
84. Quoted in *Hoover Says Boom Should Not Bring Inflation Perils*, NEW YORK TIMES (May 9, 1923), at 7. Both Brandeis and Franklin Delano Roosevelt pushed the Democratic Party to nominate Hoover for president in 1920. Marc Winerman &

"Everything Is on Edge": WWI & the American State

William E. Kovacic, *Outpost Years for a Start-Up Agency: The FTC from 1921–1925*, 77 ANTITRUST LAW JOURNAL 145, 160 (2010).

85. Evan Metcalf, *Secretary Hoover and the Emergence of Macroeconomic Management*, 49 BUSINESS HISTORY REVIEW 60, 61, 68 (1975).
86. Arnold, *supra* note 83, at 535–36; Metcalf, *supra* note 85, at 69; HERBERT HOOVER, THE MEMOIRS OF HERBERT HOOVER: THE CABINET AND THE PRESIDENCY 1920–1933, at 66 (New York: MacMillan Co. 1952). *See Address by Hon. Herbert Hoover*, in DEPARTMENT OF COMMERCE, BUREAU OF STANDARDS, FOURTEENTH ANNUAL CONFERENCE ON WEIGHTS AND MEASURES 79 (Washington D.C.: Government Printing Office 1922) ("The whole conception of standardization has changed in recent years and has come to the first rank of importance. ... [T]he question of standards has become a question embracing the very fundamentals of efficiency in our whole commercial and industrial fabric."). Of essential importance was the standardization of cost-accounting principles. SAWYER, *supra* note 83, at 157.
87. Herbert Hoover, *The World Economic Situation: Address of Herbert Hoover before the San Francisco Commercial Club* (October 9, 1919), at 15 (available at http://hdl.handle.net/2027/uc2.ark:/13960/t9v11xx20).
88. Quoted in Arnold, *supra* note 83, at 535.
89. Quoted in *Hoover Says Boom Should Not Bring Inflation Perils, supra* note 84, at 7. Thus, insisted Hoover, "To curb the forces in business which would destroy equality of opportunity and yet to maintain the initiative and creative faculties of our people are the twin objects we must attain. To preserve the former we must regulate that type of activity that would dominate. To preserve the latter, the Government must keep out of production and distribution of commodities and services. This is the deadline between our system and socialism. Regulation to prevent domination and unfair practices, yet preserving rightful initiative, are in keeping with our social foundations. Nationalization of industry or business is their negation." HERBERT HOOVER, AMERICAN INDIVIDUALISM 54–55 (New York: Doubleday, Page & Co. 1923).
90. Quoted in Joan Hoff Wilson, *Herbert Hoover's Agricultural Policies, 1921–1928*, in ELLIS W. HAWLEY, HERBERT HOOVER AS SECRETARY OF COMMERCE: STUDIES IN NEW ERA THOUGHT AND PRACTICE 121 (Iowa City: University of Iowa Press 1981). Price fixing was necessary during the war, Hoover said, because government was "forced into ... becoming the dominant purchaser and thereby, willingly or unwillingly, the price determiner in particular commodities." Herbert Hoover to Woodrow Wilson (March 26, 1918), in *Board to Determine War Policy with Respect to Meat Industry*, 2 OFFICIAL BULLETIN 1, 6 (No. 272) (April 1, 1918).
91. Ellis W. Hawley, *Herbert Hoover, the Commerce Secretariat, and the Vision of an "Associative State," 1921–1928*, 61 JOURNAL OF AMERICAN HISTORY 117–18 (1974). Hoover regarded trade associations as groups within which "the individual finds an opportunity for self-expression and participation in the moulding of ideas, a field for training and the stepping stones for leadership." HOOVER, *supra* note 89, at 42.
92. Hawley, *supra* note 91, at 118.
93. 257 U.S. 377 (1921). The case had originally been argued on October 20–21, 1920; it was reargued a year later on October 12–13, 1921, after Taft joined the Court. The

opinion was authored by Clarke, who considered the case "one of the most important anti-trust cases ever decided by [the] Court for it involved for the first time 'the Open Competition Plan' which was devised with all the cunning astute lawyers & conscienceless business men could command to defeat or circumvent the law. It seemed to me and to six others that it was a most flagrant case of law breaking." JHC to Woodrow Wilson (September 9, 1922) (Wilson papers).

94. The plan was sometimes called "The New Competition." *American Column & Lumber*, 257 U.S. at 392. This was likely a reference to ARTHUR JEROME EDDY, THE NEW COMPETITION (New York: D. Appleton & Co. 1912), which strongly endorsed the creation of "open-price" associations.

95. *American Column & Lumber*, 257 U.S. at 392, 397, 399, 409. The Court explained: "In the presence of this record it is futile to argue that the purpose of the Plan was simply to furnish those engaged in this industry, with widely scattered units, the equivalent of such information as is contained in the newspaper and government publications with respect to the market for commodities sold on Boards of Trade or Stock Exchanges. One distinguishing and sufficient difference is that the published reports go to both seller and buyer, but these reports go to the seller only; and another is that there is no skilled interpreter of the published reports, such as we have in this case, to insistently recommend harmony of action likely to prove profitable in proportion as it is unitedly pursued." *Id.* at 411.

96. There is an undated note in Taft's papers entitled "Votes" (reproduced in Reel 617 of the Taft papers), in which Taft counts among the dissenters in *American Column & Lumber Co.* "Brandeis, Vandevanter [sic], Holmes, McKenna." Apparently, Van Devanter subsequently acquiesced to the Court's published opinion, although his sympathy to trade associations would emerge later in the decade. In his powerful dissent, Brandeis argued that "it was neither the aim of the Plan, nor the practice under it, to regulate competition in any way. Its purpose was to make rational competition possible, by supplying data not otherwise available, and without which most of those engaged in the trade would be unable to trade intelligently." 257 U.S. at 415 (Brandeis, J., dissenting). Brandeis stressed that "No information gathered under the Plan was kept secret from any producer, any buyer, or the public. Ever since its inception in 1917, a copy of every report made and of every market letter published has been filed with the Department of Justice, and with the Federal Trade Commission." *Id.*

> Concerning grain, cotton, coal, and oil, the government collects and publishes regularly, at frequent intervals, current information on production, consumption, and stocks on hand; and Boards of Trade furnish freely to the public details of current market prices of those commodities, the volume of sales, and even individual sales, as recorded in daily transactions. Persons interested in such commodities are enabled through this information to deal with one another on an equal footing. The absence of such information in the hardwood lumber trade enables dealers in the large centers more readily to secure advantage over the isolated producer. And the large concerns, which are able to establish their own bureaus of statistics, secure an advantage over smaller concerns. Surely it is not against the public interest to distribute knowledge of trade facts, however detailed.

Id. at 415–16 (Brandeis, J., dissenting). Brandeis was quite pleased with his dissent. "I was waiting for a chance to say some of those things." LDB to Felix Frankfurter (December 31, 1921), in 5 LETTERS OF LOUIS D. BRANDEIS, at 41.

"Everything Is on Edge": WWI & the American State

97. M. Browning Carrott, *The Supreme Court and American Trade Associations, 1921–1925*, 44 BUSINESS HISTORY REVIEW 320, 329–30 (1970). *See* Homer Hoyt, *Trade Associations and the Sherman Act*, 1 NORTH CAROLINA LAW REVIEW 21, 21 (1922) (The case "has aroused more discussion among business men than any decision of the Supreme Court of the United States within the last two or three years, for the interpretation of the Sherman Law adopted in the case apparently throws into question the legality of the trade association – a type of co-operative business activity that has grown rapidly since the war. ... Thousands of business men are wondering today whether activities that seem indispensable to the efficient conduct of their business have been outlawed by this case."). One commentator observed that the decision "manifestly goes counter to the trend of our national commercial life," because "co-operation is the tocsin of the new age. Almost every interest in the community has its local organization" whose "prime purpose" is "to collect data and to co-operate for mutual benefit. Furthermore, government bureaus and boards of trade have been organized with the same general purpose. They furnish details of sales and current prices in daily transactions." *Restraint of Trade: "Open Competition Plan" Violates Sherman Anti-Trust Act*, 10 CALIFORNIA LAW REVIEW 350, 352 (1922).
98. Herbert Hoover to Harry Daugherty (February 3, 1922), in FRANKLIN D. JONES, TRADE ASSOCIATION ACTIVITIES AND THE LAW 327–28 (New York: McGraw-Hill 1922). *See* Franklin D. Jones, *Business Statistics as a Means of Stabilizing Business*, 11 PROCEEDINGS OF THE ACADEMY OF POLITICAL SCIENCE IN THE CITY OF NEW YORK 598 (1926). For a discussion of Hoover's response to *American Column*, see Arnold, *supra* note 83, at 538–39.
99. Harry Daugherty to Herbert Hoover (February 8, 1922), in JONES, *supra* note 98, at 332. Prominent corporate attorney Gilbert H. Montague supported Hoover's plan. *See* Gilbert H. Montague, *Trade Associations and the Government*, 215 NORTH AMERICAN REVIEW 751 (1922). Montague noted with some irony that "Less than four years ago, the Government was fervently urging businessmen everywhere to combine with their competitors into trade committees or trade associations in order to stabilize supply and demand, restrict competition, and even agree upon prices, in coöperation with the United States Fuel Administration, the United States Food Administration, and the War Industries Board. ... Many business men have experienced during the war, for the first time in their careers, the tremendous advantages, both to themselves and to the general public, of combination, of cooperation and common action, with their natural competitors." *Id.* at 751. Yet in *American Column & Lumber Co.* the Court has "declared that it is criminal for a trade association to collect and disseminate information among its members regarding supply and demand and prices, if in the association's meetings and bulletins the members are told how they may best act upon this information." *Id.* at 752. Montague asserted that "No development in business life is more significant than the increase of financial and industrial services that furnish information to enable business executives to take their bearings and determine their course." Id. at 758–59. Interpreting *American Column & Lumber Co.* as turning on the distribution of advice about how to act on pricing information, Montague endorsed Hoover's offer for the government "to disseminate promptly and periodically all information collected by trade associations and filed with him for distribution." *Id.* at 760. Montague suggested that trade associations could gather statistics with a level of "detail and freshness" that could not be duplicated by any government agency. *Id.* at 758.

In the Hardwood case, the mischief began when the Association in its meetings and bulletins tried to instruct its members how best to act upon trade information. May it not, therefore, be possible for trade associations merely to collect such trade information from their members, and to distribute it not only among their members but also among the Government bureaus, the trade press, the daily newspapers so far as they are interested, and the fast growing number of statistical service organizations that in recent years have sprung up for the purpose of interpreting to business men the tendencies and developments in business throughout the country?

Id. at 758.

Montague pioneered the development of a legal practice focused on federal regulations of business. *See* Wyatt Wells, *Counterpoint to Reform: Gilbert H. Montague and the Business of Regulation*, 78 BUSINESS HISTORY REVIEW 423 (2004).

100. 262 U.S. 371 (1923). William J. Donovan later commented about *American Linseed Oil Co.* that the case was inaccurately "designated as a trade association case." "The defendants . . . were not members of a trade association group, but they had bound themselves by contract to a so-called 'business bureau' which had certain of the attributes of a pool. The defendants entered into an agreement, with provisions for financial forfeiture in the event of violation, for the organization and maintenance of a bureau, the function of which was to gather and disseminate information among members as to all price lists. Adherence to these prices was required of members and all information was treated as confidential and concealed from the buyers." William J. Donovan, *The Legality of Trade Associations*, in PROCEEDINGS OF THE ACADEMY OF POLITICAL SCIENCE, *supra* note 98, at 573.

101. Butler's surviving docket book for the 1922 term indicates that the surface show of unanimity may perhaps have been misleading. At conference, Butler's notation strongly suggests that Holmes, Brandeis, and Sutherland, and perhaps even Butler himself, were uncertain about how to vote, and that McKenna had affirmatively voted against McReynolds' judgment.

102. *American Linseed Oil*, 262 U.S. at 389–90. In the press, it was reported that "The Court's decision is regarded here as sufficiently sweeping to cause all trade associations which have continued to disseminate price information among their members to cease doing so. The co-called 'open price' associations were a development of war-time conditions. . . . Government officials, however, have recognized a need for more complete statistics relative to production, consumption and prices of major commodities and the Department of Commerce has endeavored to expand its statistical service as far as it could do so along this line without running counter to the law." Grafton Wilcox, *Linseed Trade Plans Are Hit*, LOS ANGELES TIMES (June 5, 1923), at 15.

103. FRANCIS A. WALKER, POLITICAL ECONOMY 91–92 (London: MacMillan & Co. 1892). *See* Herbert Hovenkamp, *Labor Conspiracies in American Law, 1880–1930*, 66 TEXAS LAW REVIEW 919, 936 (1988).

104. Ellis W. Hawley, *Herbert Hoover and the Sherman Act, 1921–1933*, 74 IOWA LAW REVIEW 1067, 1079–83 (1989); ROBERT F. HIMMELBERG, THE ORIGINS OF THE NATIONAL RECOVERY ADMINISTRATION: BUSINESS, GOVERNMENT, AND THE TRADE ASSOCIATION ISSUE, 1921–1933, at 26–42 (New York: Fordham University Press 1993). Following *American Linseed Oil Co.*, "the opinion gained currency among lawyers as well as among laymen that the mere collection and

dissemination of statistical information was unlawful." Donovan, *supra* note 100, at 574.

105. As attorney general, Stone had strongly supported Hoover's view of trade associations. He may even have been involved in the selection of Maple Flooring Manufacturers Ass'n v. United States, 268 U.S. 563 (1925), as a test case. HIMMELBERG, *supra* note 104, at 45–47; RUDOLPH J.R. PERITZ, COMPETITION POLICY IN AMERICA: HISTORY, RHETORIC, LAW 87 (Oxford University Press 1996); SAWYER, *supra* note 83, at 187.

106. 268 U.S. 563 (1925). The case had been originally argued on December 1–2, 1924, but after McKenna's retirement it was reset for argument on March 3, 1925. The case was paired with Cement Manufacturers Protective Ass'n v. United States, 268 U.S. 588 (1925). On March 5, Holmes wrote Laski that "We have been having some cases under the Sherman Act, which I loathe and despise – and I am pleased to know that Brandeis who used to uphold it, doesn't think it does any good. I am wondering whether I shall be in a minority. I don't mean to let my disbelief in the act affect my application of it – but I think it has been enlarged by construction in ways that I regret." OWH to Harold Laski (March 5, 1925), in 1 HOLMES-LASKI CORRESPONDENCE, at 719.

107. Taft, McReynolds, and Sanford dissented. Van Devanter's defection from the position seemingly implied by his public vote in *American Column & Lumber Co.* was foreshadowed by his initial vote in conference in that case. *See supra* note 96. Sutherland's and Butler's seeming shift from their public votes in *American Linseed Oil Co.* might also have been foreshadowed by their uncertainty in conference in that case. *See supra* note 101. In 1927, Van Devanter, Sutherland, and Butler would silently dissent from Stone's opinion for the Court in United States v. Trenton Potteries Co., 273 U.S. 392 (1927), which held that an agreement to fix prices was illegal even if the price agreed upon was reasonable. By contrast, Taft wrote Stone about his opinion in *Trenton Potteries* that "This is one of the best opinions written by you or anyone this term. I felicitate you." (Stone papers). Holmes wrote Stone, "I defer, but unwillingly." (Stone papers).

In his notes of the conference of December 6, 1924, after the first argument of *Maple Floor Manufacturers Ass'n*, Butler briefly summarized the position of each voting justice. He wrote that Taft argued that the district court decree enjoining the plan should be affirmed "under the language of McR in Linseed Oil Case – Change of method not a change of purpose." McKenna voted with Taft to affirm the decree. Holmes, by contrast, blasted the decree as a "Disgrace to the U.S." Butler recorded Van Devanter as commenting, "Wrong – reverse." McReynolds and Sanford voted to affirm; Brandeis, Sutherland, and Butler to reverse. Taft was ill during the conference of March 27, 1925, that followed the reargument of the case, see *supra* note 106, and it was Holmes, as the presiding senior justice, who assigned the opinion to Stone. W. Barton Leach, Jr. to Felix Frankfurter (May 31, 1938) (Holmes papers).

Taft subsequently urged William J. Donovan, who headed the Department of Justice's anti-trust division, that "it may be properly argued in future cases that the Cement and Maple Flooring cases are not a departure from the wholesome rule laid down by Justice McReynolds in the Lindseed [sic] Oil case." WHT to William J. Donovan (September 4, 1925) (Taft papers). Taft teased Van Devanter that if their mutual friend Solicitor General William D. Mitchell had briefed the case,

"some of you people in the majority might have seen the proper light." WHT to WVD (September 11, 1925) (Van Devanter papers). *See infra* note 113.
108. *Maple Flooring Manufacturers*, 268 U.S. at 567. Nor was there any evidence that the exchange of information had influenced prices, either by producing a "practical uniformity of net delivered prices" or by affecting "prices adversely to consumers." *Id.*
109. *Id.* at 572. Stone emphasized that "all reports of sales and prices dealt exclusively with past and closed transactions," and that the statistics were "published in trade journals which are read by from 90 to 95% of the persons who purchase the products of Association members. They are sent to the Department of Commerce which publishes a monthly survey of current business." *Id.* at 573–74. He noted that the statistics did not "differ in any essential respect from trade or business statistics which are freely gathered and publicly disseminated in numerous branches of industry producing a standardized product such as grain, cotton, oil." *Id.* at 574. In contrast to *American Column & Lumber Co.*, "there was no discussion of prices in meetings. . . . [T]he Association was advised by counsel that future prices were not a proper subject of discussion." *Id.* at 575.
110. SAWYER, *supra* note 83, at 186–87.
111. *Maple Flooring Manufacturers*, 268 U.S. at 582–83. Stone was in direct correspondence with Hoover while drafting the opinion. *See* Herbert Hoover to HFS (April 3, 1925) (Stone papers); HFS to Herbert Hoover (April 4, 1925) (Stone papers); Herbert Hoover to HFS (April 18, 1925) (Stone papers); HFS to Herbert Hoover (April 20, 1925) (Stone papers) ("What I was especially interested in when I telephoned to you the other day was in getting information as to how far there was any general distribution of information as to the cost of standardized products of industry."); HFS to Herbert Hoover (June 1, 1925) (Stone papers). Hoover found Stone's opinion "of the most powerful interest and extraordinarily helpful. It is a great economic document!" Herbert Hoover to HFS (June 3, 1925) (Stone papers).

In his opinion, Stone stressed that "Exchange of price quotations of market commodities tends to produce uniformity of prices in the markets of the world. Knowledge of the supplies of available merchandise tends to prevent overproduction and to avoid the economic disturbances produced by business crises resulting from overproduction. But the natural effect of the acquisition of wider and more scientific knowledge of business conditions, on the minds of the individuals engaged in commerce and its consequent effect in stabilizing production and price, can hardly be deemed a restraint of commerce, or, if so, it cannot, we think be said to be an unreasonable restraint, or in any respect unlawful." 268 U.S. at 582.

> It was not the purpose or the intent of the Sherman Anti-Trust Law to inhibit the intelligent conduct of business operations, nor do we conceive that its purpose was to suppress such influences as might affect the operations of interstate commerce through the application to them of the individual intelligence of those engaged in commerce, enlightened by accurate information as to the essential elements of the economics of a trade or business, however gathered or disseminated. Persons who unite in gathering and disseminating information in trade journals and statistical reports on industry, who gather and publish statistics as to the amount of production of commodities in interstate commerce, and who report market prices, are not engaged in unlawful conspiracies in restraint of trade merely because the ultimate result of their efforts may be to stabilize prices or limit production through a better understanding of economic laws and a more general ability to conform to them, for

the simple reason that the Sherman Law neither repeals economic laws nor prohibits the gathering and dissemination of information.

268 U.S. at 583–84.

112. *Id.* at 584. Holmes called Stone's opinion "Good sense and good law." (Stone papers). Brandeis commented about *Maple Flooring Manufacturers Ass'n* and *Cement Manufacturers Protective Ass'n* that "These are two uncommonly good opinions." (Stone papers). He thought them Stone's "best work." LDB to Felix Frankfurter (June 2, 1925), in 5 LETTERS OF LOUIS D. BRANDEIS, at 175. Van Devanter noted on Stone's draft that it was "a model opinion in every respect." (Stone papers). Sutherland remarked that "I think you have done a good and useful job." (Stone papers).

113. *Maple Flooring Manufacturers*, 268 U.S. at 587 (McReynolds, J., dissenting). Taft and Sanford separately dissented in both *Maple Flooring Manufacturers Ass'n* and *Cement Manufacturers Protective Ass'n* on the ground that "the evidence established in each case brings it substantially within the rules stated in the *American Column Co.* and *American Linseed Oil Co. Cases*, the authority of which ... is not questioned in the opinions of the majority of the Court." *Id.* at 586 (Taft, C. J. and Sanford, J., dissenting). In contrast to McReynolds, Taft and Sanford did not contend that the exchange of information constituted a *per se* violation of the Sherman Act. They instead believed that there were sufficient facts in the record to demonstrate the existence of an independent agreement to fix prices. (The government later filed an unsuccessful petition for rehearing in both cases on precisely these grounds. Donovan, *supra* note 100, at 576–77.) After publication of the Court's opinion, Taft received a letter from his good friend Charles D. Hilles, the vice chair of the Republican National Committee, expressing surprise "at the majority opinion in the Trades Associations case. It is difficult to see how practically the Government can permit the intimate interchanges between competitors which the decision legalizes and still prevent, or even detect, the meeting of minds on prices." Charles D. Hilles to WHT (June 8, 1925) (Taft papers). Taft replied that "I was disappointed in the Trade Association cases, and I think this decision may return to plague the majority, but we shall see." WHT to Charles D. Hilles (June 9, 1925) (Taft papers).

114. *See* Emerson P. Schmidt, *The Changing Economics of the Supreme Court*, 147 ANNALS OF THE AMERICAN ACADEMY OF POLITICAL AND SOCIAL SCIENCE 66 (1930). As the labor economist W. Jett Lauck explained to a Senate committee in the context of labor regulation:

> Prior to the war industry was considered as being primarily conducted for profit, the theory being that by competition and by free play of selfish, economic forces, the greatest advantages to the greatest number – labor, capital, and the public – would be accomplished. On the other hand, in recent years the idea has been gaining ground and growing in force and acceptance that in reality industry is a social institution. In its most conservative form it finds expression in the claim that industry should not be conducted in a spirit of relentless economic self-interest for profit, but that while the stimulus of profit should be retained and the fundamental rights of capital and labor should be protected and conserved, industrial promotion, expansion, and operation should also be a social service ....
>
> Out of the war has come the idea, which is widely accepted, that industry must serve the common good.

Statement of Mr. W.J. Lauck on the Report of the Industrial Conference, in Hearing before the Senate Committee on Education and Labor, 66th CONG. 2nd SESS. (April 8, 1920), at 9–10. *See* W. Jett Lauck, *Labor and Production*, 90 ANNALS OF THE AMERICAN ACADEMY OF POLITICAL AND SOCIAL SCIENCE 94, 99 (1920). Herbert Hoover praised Lauck's articulation of the altered understanding of industry in postwar America as "a very able and a very strong statement." Statement of Hon. Herbert Hoover, Vice President of the Industrial Conference, on the Report of the Industrial Conference, in Hearing before the Senate Committee on Education and Labor, *supra*, at 36.

115. Herbert Hoover, *We Can Cooperate and Yet Compete*, 14 NATION'S BUSINESS 11 (June 5, 1926). Hoover illustrated his point with the example of agricultural cooperatives. In 1928 the Taft Court would accept this insight. *See* Liberty Warehouse Co. v. Burley Tobacco Growers' Co-Operative Marketing Ass'n, 276 U.S. 71 (1928); *infra* Chapter 42, at 1405–6.

116. Hoover, *supra* note 115, at 11. "These accomplishments," Hoover wrote, "involve not only the units of a given trade but also cooperation between the many producing and consuming trades of a given commodity. . . . I might cite the widely successful organized cooperation between several score different shippers' and transportation organizations for the more regular and efficient transport of goods. These undertakings result not only in greater economy in production and consumption, but also eventuate in less costs to consumers." In this extraordinary essay, Hoover also discussed the increasing separation of ownership from control within American business, and hence the growth of "a new profession, business administration." "The expert has passed from the land of derision to the land of esteem. We have realized from this . . . great advances in quality of leadership, in technology, organization and adaptability to new ideas and to shifting demand."

117. A decade later, in the weeks immediately following the Wall Street stock market crash of October 1929, when Hoover called conference after conference at the White House, it was said in the press that Hoover was seen "to be playing a new role, 'asserting a mastery over conditions which once had to be left largely to Providence and accidents.'" *A Great National Fight on for Prosperity*, 103 LITERARY DIGEST 7–8 (December 7, 1929). It was remarked that Hoover "treated business very much as it was treated at the beginning of the Great War, when it was invited to Washington and enlisted in the service of the country in what was a national emergency." *Id.* at 7.

118. In the immortal words of Walter Lippmann: "Mr. Coolidge's genius for inactivity is developed to a very high point. It is far from being an indolent inactivity. It is a grim, determined, alert inactivity which keeps Mr. Coolidge occupied constantly. Nobody has ever worked harder at inactivity, with such force of character, with such unremitting attention to detail, with such conscientious devotion to the task. Inactivity is a political philosophy and a party program with Mr. Coolidge." WALTER LIPPMANN, MEN OF DESTINY 12–13 (New York: MacMillan Co. 1927).

119. HOOVER, *supra* note 86, at 56. Coolidge disliked Hoover. Marc Winerman & William E. Kovacic, *The William Humphrey and Abram Myers Years: The FTC from 1925 to 1929*, 77 ANTITRUST LAW JOURNAL 701, 709 (2011). "Harding openly admired Hoover's intelligence and efficiency, often calling him 'the smartest gink I know.' Coolidge, however, resented Hoover and snidely referred

to him as 'the wonder boy'. . . . [Hoover's] activism jarred with the President's personal belief in the virtues of restrained government." NIALL PALMER, THE TWENTIES IN AMERICA: POLITICS AND HISTORY 133 (Edinburgh University Press 2006).

120. "Harding's conservatism had been forged in the hard-headed and corrupt arena of Ohio state politics, an arena in which pragmatism and deal-making were prerequisites of political success. Consequently, Harding's political philosophy mixed an emotional attachment to conservative principles with a practical willingness to consider policies which smacked to some of progressivism and to pursue an interventionist path when necessary. Coolidge's beliefs, on the other hand, were rooted in the values of rural New England and its small towns and hamlets, where thrift, honesty, temperance and hard work were regarded as cardinal virtues and government activism was deeply distrusted. Coolidgean conservatism, rooted in this solid, Puritan environment, was far more resilient than Harding's. It also appealed to many Americans who, in the restless decade of the 1920s, wallowed in nostalgia for a vanishing and over-romanticised past, even as they excitedly welcomed accelerating socioeconomic and cultural change." PALMER, *supra* note 119, at 102–3.

121. In Taft's words, "We had been through the greatest war of history and were attempting to return to peace conditions, and had reached a time in 1920 when business was bad and financial disaster threatened. . . . [W]e were in the grip of a nation-wide industrial and business depression." United States v. Stone & Downer Co., 274 U.S. 225, 240 (1927).

122. REPORT OF THE PRESIDENT'S CONFERENCE ON UNEMPLOYMENT 16 (Washington D.C.: Government Printing Office 1921).

123. "Intervention of such a scale by a federal 'quasi-voluntary body,' as Hoover described it, 'to handle the whole problem of unemployment . . . on a nation-wide basis,' would have been inconceivable before the war. Hoover and aides like Arthur Woods brought to this peacetime problem the experience of numerous war agencies in similar drives to mobilize local and private groups to act with a national purpose. More than one observer compared the conference's method of issuing an 'official appeal . . . for unofficial action' to the wartime appeals of Hoover's Food Administration for meatless and wheatless days, 'without the passage of any law.'" Metcalf, *supra* note 85, at 72. Seven years later, in his first major speech as a presidential candidate, Hoover would proudly endorse the conference as exemplifying his belief that "Full employment depends not only upon a strong and progressive economic system but upon the sound policies of and the vigorous cooperation by the government to promote economic welfare." *Text of Herbert Hoover's Opening Campaign Speech Last Night at Newark*, BALTIMORE SUN (September 18, 1928), at 13.

124. On "Hoover's introduction of macroeconomic policy into official thinking the 1920s," see Metcalf, *supra* note 85, at 79. The Conference on Unemployment recommended, *inter alia*:

> 7. Public construction is better than relief. The municipalities should expand their school, street, sewage, repair work, and public buildings to the fullest possible volume compatible with the existing circumstances. That existing circumstances are favorable is indicated by the fact that over $700,000,000 of municipal bonds, the largest amount in history, have been sold in 1921. Of these,

$106,000,000 were sold by 333 municipalities in August. Municipalities should give short-time employment the same as other employers. ...

9. The Federal authorities, including the Federal Reserve Banks, should expedite the construction of public buildings and public works covered by existing appropriations.

REPORT OF THE PRESIDENT'S CONFERENCE ON UNEMPLOYMENT, *supra* note 122, at 20.

Hoover was frustrated that the conference did not produce legislative results. "Specifically, he wanted something permitting the countercyclical phasing of public works, an idea too advanced even for so progressive a senator as Nebraska's George Norris, who said, 'We had better let God run [the economy] as in the past.' Hoover's partisans nonetheless declared victory: bond issues for local public works hit record highs within months of the gathering, and several federal departments advanced spending projects that had been lingering on drawing boards." KENNETH WHYTE, HOOVER: AN EXTRAORDINARY LIFE IN EXTRAORDINARY TIMES 263 (New York: Alfred A. Knopf 2017). In the press it was said that the "response" to the Conference's recommendations "was not unlike that which we all made to Mr. Hoover's wartime appeals for the conservation of food." *Cycles of Unemployment*, NEW YORK TIMES (April 3, 1922), at 12. On the left, however, it was said that "The most acute criticism made of the United States Food Administration was that Herbert Hoover conceived the American food problem to be a temporary emergency, and that when the war was over nothing of permanent service to the nation was left. That is also true of the unemployment conference. ... What the recent Washington conference did was to consider the industrial depression and to offer business suggestions." William L. Chenery, *Mr. Hoover's Hand*, 47 THE SURVEY 107, 107, 110 (1921).

125. REPORT OF THE PRESIDENT'S CONFERENCE ON UNEMPLOYMENT, *supra* note 122, at 27.
126. Charles E. Hughes, *New Phases of National Development*, 4 AMERICAN BAR ASSOCIATION Journal 92, 107–8 (1918). It was common during the 1920s for contemporaries to experience a tension between peacetime constitutional precedents and the need to exercise powers during wartime. *See* Edward S. Corwin, *War, the Constitution Moulder*, 11 NEW REPUBLIC 153, 153–54 (1917) ("The war has overtaken us at a peculiarly favorable moment for effecting lasting constitutional changes. For several years forces have been accumulating behind the barriers of the old Constitution, straining and weakening them at many points, yet without finding adequate enlargement. Where the stress of war falls coincident with such forces we may expect it to thrust aside accepted principles, not for the time only, but permanently.").
127. Consider John W. Davis's assessment of the impact of the war in 1923:

The Great War and its aftermath have profoundly disturbed the foundations of society and government. ... Men and women were taken from their normal and accustomed occupations and set to new and strange tasks. They were required to reverse the orderly habit and custom of their lives. Power was given to those who before had been impotent. ... It is not to be wondered at that in the name of reform one remedy after another is offered to a world whose discontent makes it eager to embrace any gospel, even when condemned by all past experience. ... Some Senators of the United States and other would-be

> leaders are willing, or would have themselves believed to be willing, to strike down our whole theory of constitutional government by transferring from the Courts to Congress the ultimate power to determine when the limit of constitutional authority has been overstepped.

John W. Davis, *Some Current Activities of the American Bar Association*, 29 WEST VIRGINIA LAW QUARTERLY 109, 117–18 (1923).

128. Edward T. Sanford, Address to the Harvard Alumni Association, June 19, 1924 (Sanford papers at the University of Tennessee at Knoxville).
129. Pierce Butler, *Some Opportunities and Duties of Lawyers*, in REPORT OF THE FORTY-SIXTH ANNUAL MEETING OF THE AMERICAN BAR ASSOCIATION 221 (Baltimore: Lord Baltimore Press 1923).
130. WHT to Mrs. Bellamy Storer (September 4, 1924) (Taft papers).
131. Quoted in Basil Manly, *Chief Justice Taft Replies to Three Vital Questions*, BOSTON GLOBE (January 9, 1929), at 32.
132. WVD to J.H. Farley (February 12, 1920) (Van Devanter papers).
133. *Id.*
134. WVD to John C. Pollock (November 4, 1920) (Van Devanter papers). Consider Stone's remarks to the New Jersey Bar on February 26, 1921:

> In recent years we have been trying some dangerous experiments in autocracy in this country, in passing numerous laws under which administrative officers are given extraordinary powers over the liberty and property of individuals without those safeguards afforded by judicial review and by our traditional legal procedure. Even if these laws do not infringe upon the constitutional rights of citizens and of "persons within the United States," which in many instances is doubtful, they mark an abandonment of the protection which substantive law and established modes of procedure have heretofore customarily thrown about the rights and liberties of the individual, and they afford large scope and opportunity for violation of law and abuse of power by administrative officials. Many of these laws, such as the Espionage Law, the Deportation Law, laws for the regulation of food and fuel, the War Tax Law, the law for the enforcement of the Eighteenth Amendment, are an outgrowth of the war and we have acquiesced in their official interpretations and methods of enforcement because of our loyalty to the government and our desire to give the greatest possible effectiveness to our war effort. But the war is now ended. These laws are still in our statute books and we are passively enduring the encroachment on individual liberty and rights of property of a regime of law created and administered by bureaucratic officials. Unless there is a change in public sentiment we shall soon harvest a crop of similar laws in the several States. ... Yet collectively in our Bar organizations and individually we are silent, acquiescing by mere force of inertia without critical examination, in fundamental changes in our laws which are more far reaching in their consequences than any change that has taken place in a hundred years.

Harlan Fiske Stone, *Address of Mr. Harlan F. Stone*, in NEW JERSEY STATE BAR ASSOCIATION YEAR BOOK 1921–1922, at 60–61 (1922).

CHAPTER 22

Cabining the Constitutional Implications of the War

THE FIRST STEP in curing the illness of the war was to reimpose a proper sense of constitutional limitations. "Congress is passing extraordinary legislation and the Administration is doing many extraordinary things," George Sutherland wrote his friend Arthur Thomas, the ex-governor of Utah, in September 1917.[1] "On the whole, while mistakes are being made, I think war matters are being pretty well handled, though I have no doubt both legislative and executive powers are being exceeded in many particulars, the reckoning for which will come after the war. As soon as peace is declared, the flood of litigation will begin and Washington ought to be a place where a lawyer can earn bread and butter."[2]

One of Taft's first duties as chief justice was to preside over a memorial to his predecessor, Edward Douglass White. In that ceremony Taft praised White's "genius ... as a statesman and a jurist," singling out White's opinions "in the World War ... supporting statutes enacted to enable the Government to carry on the struggle, to mass all its resources of men and money in the country's defense."[3] During his own time as chief justice, Taft would preside over many decisions examining the scope of the government's powers during war. Although his Court would largely validate the exercise of government authority during times of war,[4] it would simultaneously strive to prevent that enlarged authority from leaching into times of peace. As the Court unanimously put it in 1926, war "is abnormal and exceptional; and, while the supreme necessities which it imposes require that, in many respects, the rules which govern the relations of the respective citizens of the belligerent powers in time of peace must be modified or entirely put aside, there is no tendency in our day at least to extend them to results clearly beyond the need and the duration of the need."[5]

A good example of the strain of simultaneously validating and containing the exercise of powers during war may be found in *Highland v. Russell Car & Snowplow Co.*, in which the Taft Court, speaking unanimously through an opinion by Butler,[6] upheld the power of Congress in the Lever Act[7] to authorize the president during the war "to fix the price of coal, to regulate distribution among dealers and consumers, ... and to require producers to sell only to the United States through a designated agency empowered to regulate resale prices."[8] The pressure of upholding price fixing in war, and yet simultaneously withholding constitutional authorization for price fixing in peace (except with respect to property affected with a public interest),[9] contorts the reasoning of the opinion into virtual incoherence.

In *Highland*, the owner of a coal mine had contracted with a buyer to sell coal at $4.05 per ton, but the buyer eventually paid only $2.45 per ton, which was the price set by the federal government. The seller's suit for the difference turned on the constitutionality of the president's executive order fixing the price. The most obvious way to justify the Wilson administration's price controls would have been to emphasize the strength of the government's interest in controlling costs during the war. But to take this route would have required the Taft Court affirmatively to articulate state interests that might justify price controls, which the Court was unwilling to do. No matter what standard the Court might articulate, it was certain to be advanced in one circumstance or another to justify price controls in peace, and the Court was intent on altogether shutting down such price fixing.[10] As a consequence, the Court in *Highland* was forced to elaborate an all but incomprehensible rationale for the Wilson administration's executive order.

"It is everywhere recognized," Butler began, "that the freedom of the people to enter into and carry out contracts in respect of their property and private affairs is a matter of great public concern and that such liberty may not lightly be impaired." Citing *Adkins v. Children's Hospital of the District of Columbia*,[11] Butler underscored the central point that he sought to convey, which was that the right to contract was "protected by the due process clauses of the Fifth and Fourteenth Amendments." Yet Butler also conceded that the right was "not absolute or universal," and "Congress may regulate the making and performance of such contracts whenever reasonably necessary to effect any of the great purposes for which the national government was created." Butler then explained that:

> The principal purpose of the Lever Act was to enable the President to provide food, fuel, and other things necessary to prosecute the war without exposing the government to unreasonable exactions. The authorization of the President to prescribe prices and also to requisition mines and their output made it manifest that, if adequate supplies of coal at just prices could not be obtained by negotiation and price regulation, expropriation would follow. Plaintiff was free to keep his coal, but it would have been liable to seizure by the government. The fixing of just prices was calculated to serve the convenience of producers and dealers, as well as of consumers of coal needed to carry on the war. As it does not appear that plaintiff would have been entitled to more if his coal had been requisitioned, the act and orders will be deemed to have deprived him only of the right or opportunity by negotiation to obtain more than his coal was worth.... As applied to the coal in question, the statute and executive orders were not so clearly unreasonable and arbitrary as to require them to be held repugnant to the due process clause of the Fifth Amendment.[12]

Butler's reasoning is difficult to follow. He seems to argue that because the seller would not have been entitled to a higher price than that set by the government "if his coal had been requisitioned," the loss of the contract price deprived him "only of the right or opportunity by negotiation to obtain more than his coal was worth."[13] But this logic is inconsistent with Butler's own opinion for a unanimous Court in *United States v. New River Collieries Co.*,[14] which holds that the value of coal requisitioned under the Lever Act must be determined by the "market price prevailing at the time and place of the taking."[15] *New River Collieries* explicitly rejects the argument that a coal producer is entitled only to "the 'real' value of coal as distinguished from its market value," even though the "real" value of coal is determined by "the owner's cost of production and a reasonable profit,"[16] the very criteria used by Wilson's executive order to fix the price of coal in *Highland*.[17] If the coal in *Highland* had been requisitioned, therefore, its price would have been set by the market, not by the terms of the executive order.

Butler might have argued in *Highland* that there was no market for coal during the war because of government price regulations. But any such an argument would validate the very price fixing scheme that the seller was constitutionally attacking, and Butler was not tempted to go that far.[18] In roughly analogous cases, moreover, the Taft Court had not hesitated to use a market-value test of damages for wartime takings, despite massive government interference in the market and the manifest "uncertainties of the war."[19]

Highland is puzzling for two reasons. First, the government had not requisitioned the seller's coal under the Court's own precedents.[20] Second, even if the government had requisitioned the seller's coal, the measure of damages should have been the very contract price the seller was seeking to enforce. It follows that the seller did not seek to obtain "more than his coal was worth." He sought only to obtain its market value, which the Taft Court had repeatedly held was the precise measure of its worth.

Butler ordinarily wrote straightforward opinions that were easy to follow. The unusual analytic slippage in *Highland* evidences the strain of defending wartime price fixing from attacks based on freedom of contract. Given the constitutional premise of the right "to enter into and carry out contracts" that Butler initially proposed, the most obvious path open to Butler would have been to explain why the circumstances of the war had rendered it "reasonably necessary" to regulate the price of coal.[21]

To pursue this line of analysis, however, would have required Butler to articulate criteria justifying government price fixing, and such criteria would be most unwelcome to a Court that was increasingly moving toward a *per se* rule prohibiting price fixing in the absence of a showing that regulated property was "affected with a public interest."[22] Coal was definitely not such property. In a case dealing with the Wilson administration's efforts to revive the authority of the Lever Act to control the price of coal in response to the grave national emergency provoked by the coal miner's strike of 1919, for example, the Taft Court was brusquely unsympathetic.[23] The upshot of *Highland's* strangely contorted reasoning was to validate *post hoc* the government's aggressive efforts to fix prices during

Cabining the Constitutional Implications of the War

World War I, but to leave utterly obscure the constitutional implications of that validation for government efforts to regulate prices during peacetime.

A distinct and somewhat more plausible framework for distinguishing the broad powers exercised by the government during the war – which need not themselves have been literal "war" powers – from the government's more circumscribed authority during peace, lay in the thought that the war had created a unique crisis justifying abnormal forms of regulation. According to this justification, the constitutional validity of otherwise abnormal regulations cease "upon the passing of the emergency."[24] As Taft himself wrote in 1918, "The Central Government now has very wide war powers. When peace comes, these must end, if the Republic is to be preserved."[25] The best illustration of this framework is *Chastleton Corp. v. Sinclair*,[26] which concerned the constitutionality of rent control in the District of Columbia.[27]

In 1921, the White Court had in *Block v. Hirsh* upheld a 1919 congressional statute temporarily imposing rent control in the District of Columbia in response to "emergencies growing out of the war, resulting in rental conditions in the District dangerous to the public health and burdensome to public officers, employees and accessories, and thereby embarrassing the Federal Government in the transaction of the public business."[28] Holmes, in an opinion for a five-person majority that included Brandeis, Day, Pitney, and Clarke, concluded that these emergencies converted housing in the District into property affected with a public interest, so that its price could constitutionally be regulated.

"Congress has stated the unquestionable embarrassment of Government and danger to the public health in the existing condition of things," Holmes observed. "The space in Washington is necessarily monopolized in comparatively few hands, and letting portions of it is as much a business as any other. Housing is a necessary of life. All the elements of a public interest justifying some degree of public control are present." Although legislative declarations of emergency "may not be held conclusive by the Courts," they were nevertheless entitled "to great respect," and in this case the facts establishing the emergency were "publicly notorious" and sufficient to clothe "the letting of buildings in the District of Columbia with a public interest so great as to justify regulation by law."[29]

Citing the need to respond to the same wartime emergency that convinced the Court in *Hirsh*, Congress renewed rent control in the District in 1921,[30] and again in 1922.[31] To conservative contemporaries it seemed as if Congress were under "the spell of war," which spawned the "doctrine that in emergencies the constitution must yield to the police power."[32] Although *Hirsh* did not technically involve legislation that depended upon Congress's war powers, it nevertheless demonstrated how deeply the war had altered Congress's authority to regulate property during an "emergency." *Chastleton* arose when a landlord, whose rents were controlled in 1922, alleged that the emergency justifying the 1919 statute no longer existed. He claimed that Congress's two subsequent extensions of rent control were unconstitutional. Lower courts dismissed the landlord's case on the authority of *Hirsh*.

By the time *Chastleton* was argued at the Supreme Court in April 1924, the only remaining members of the *Hirsh* majority were Holmes and Brandeis. Butler's docket book indicates that the Court voted unanimously to reverse the judgment of the lower courts. Van Devanter is recorded as taking the position that the extensions were "bad" and that this did not depend upon any "objective question of fact." Sutherland, Butler, and Sanford were noted as agreeing with Van Devanter. Holmes alone contended that the constitutionality of the rent control extensions depended upon "a question of fact"; namely, whether the "emergency" continued to exist.[33]

With characteristic shrewdness, Taft assigned the opinion to Holmes, who framed the question as whether "the emergency that justified interference with the ordinarily existing private rights in 1919 had come to an end in 1922." Holmes noted that "We repeat what was stated in *Block v. Hirsh* as to the respect due to a declaration of this kind by the Legislature so far as it relates to present facts. But even as to them a Court is not at liberty to shut its eyes to an obvious mistake, when the validity of the law depends upon the truth of what is declared. ... A law depending upon the existence of an emergency or other certain state of facts to uphold it may cease to operate if the emergency ceases or the facts change even though valid when passed."[34]

Holmes regarded it as a "matter of public knowledge that the Government has considerably diminished its demand for employees that was one of the great causes of the sudden afflux of people to Washington." And then, with deft strokes, Holmes quietly undercut the continuing influence of World War I: "If about all that remains of war conditions is the increased cost of living, that is not in itself a justification of the act. ... In that case the operation of the statute would be at an end."[35]

Holmes concluded the original draft of his opinion with a quick and efficient remand to the trial court to determine the relevant facts.[36] But at the very time *Chastleton* was under consideration, Congress was debating whether to extend rent control in the District to 1925. The conservative members of the Court were determined to draw a sharper constitutional line between the extraordinary emergency of the war and the normal conditions then obtaining under Calvin Coolidge.[37] Holmes was forced to recirculate his opinion with the notation "Corrected by C.J. in accord with majority view." He altered the conclusion of the second draft to read: "[I]f the question were only whether the statute is in force today, upon the facts that we judicially know we should be compelled to say that the law has ceased to operate. Here however it is material to know the conditions of Washington at different dates in the past. Obviously, the facts should be accurately ascertained and carefully weighed, and this can be done more conveniently in the Supreme Court of the District than here."[38] The day after Holmes read his decision, Taft wrote his wife: "We have just announced an opinion by Holmes which intimates strongly that rent acts are emergency measures and that it is time to get back to 'normalcy' as poor Harding would say. I suppose this will mean another attack on the Court."[39]

Chastleton's message was that the extraordinary emergency caused by World War I could be confined within boundaries cognizable through judicial notice.[40] The limits of the abnormal could be established as a mere "matter of public knowledge." This was not a happy message to those progressives who had hoped to use wartime legislation as a "Trojan horse" to undermine antebellum

Cabining the Constitutional Implications of the War

constitutional restrictions. Fiorello LaGuardia, in the course of congressional debates about whether to extend rent control to 1925,[41] argued that rent control should be constitutional whether or not there was a wartime emergency. He complained that "the only blessing that came from the war is that it brought a condition which gave the legislatures of the various States sufficient courage to pass, for the first time in history, regulatory powers over dwellings in cities."[42] But progressive pleas that such powers receive peacetime constitutional sanction were insufficient to halt the Taft Court's determined march toward normalcy.

THE TAFT COURT
Notes

1. GS to Arthur L. Thomas (September 21, 1917) (Sutherland papers). Thomas had written Sutherland: "I fear, very much fear, that the day of reckoning is not far off. The old fashioned idea of a government of balanced powers is rapidly being displaced by the most absolute centralization of power the world has ever known, and this is happening in the Great American Republic." Arthur L. Thomas to GS (September 10, 1917) (Sutherland papers).
2. GS to Arthur L. Thomas (September 21, 1917) (Sutherland papers).
3. *Remarks of Chief Justice Taft*, 257 U.S. xxiv, xxvii (1921). Taft admired White's "intense patriotic appreciation of the necessity of vesting full powers in the nation when its integrity is threatened and of the existence of ample authority to this end in the Constitution." *Id.*
4. The Taft Court did extend to civil actions the holding of the White Court that the provision of the Lever Act prohibiting "unjust or unreasonable" or "excessive" charges for "necessaries" was unconstitutionally vague. See A.B. Small Co. v. American Sugar Refining Co., 267 U.S. 233 (1925); United States v. Cohen Grocery Co., 255 U.S. 81 (1921).
5. Sutherland v. Mayer, 271 U.S. 272, 287 (1926).
6. Stone's docket book shows that McReynolds had initially "passed" at conference.
7. Pub. L. 65-41, 40 Stat. 276 (August 10, 1917).
8. 279 U.S. 253, 259 (1929).
9. On the Taft Court's hostility to price fixing, see *infra* Chapter 25.
10. *See infra* Chapter 25, at 801–3.
11. 261 U.S. 525 (1923).
12. *Highland*, 279 U.S. at 261–62.
13. *Id.* at 262. Butler was correct to equate the requisition of property with the constitutional taking of that property through eminent domain. *See* Liggett & Myers Tobacco Co. v. United States, 274 U.S. 215 (1927) (opinion by Butler). But there was no reason to think that in *Highland* the seller's coal had been requisitioned. Controlling Taft Court decisions held that war time fixing of coal prices did not constitute the taking of contracts to sell coal. *See, e.g.,* Morrisdale Coal Co. v. United States, 259 U.S. 188, 190 (1922) ("The claimant in consequence of the regulation ... sold some of its coal to other parties at a less price than what it would otherwise have got. That is all. ... Making the rule was not a taking and no lawmaking power promises by implication to make good losses that may be incurred by obedience to its commands.").

There were powerfully pragmatic reasons for the Taft Court, in reviewing wartime regulation, carefully to distinguish between the frustration of contracts and the taking of contracts. In Omnia Commercial Co. v. United States, 261 U.S. 502 (1923), for example, Omnia Commercial Co. had a contract with Allegheny Steel Co. for steel plate. "The contract was of great value, and if carried out would have produced large profits." But the contract was foiled when "the United States government requisitioned the steel company's entire production of steel plate for the year 1918," directing the company "not to comply with the terms" of Omnia's contract. Omnia brought an action alleging that the government had "taken" its contract with Allegheny and seeking lost profits as damages. Speaking for a unanimous Court, Sutherland conceded that the contract "was property within the meaning of the Fifth Amendment" and that if it had been "taken for public use

Cabining the Constitutional Implications of the War

the government would be liable." *Id.* at 508, 510. But the Court ruled that the government had merely rendered performance of the contract "impossible"; it had not "appropriated" the contract itself. *Id.* at 511. "The government took over during the war railroads, steel mills, shipyards, telephone and telegraph lines, the capacity output of factories and other producing activities. If appellant's contention is sound, the government thereby took and became liable to pay for an appalling number of existing contracts for future service or delivery, the performance of which its action made impossible. This is inadmissible. Frustration and appropriation are essentially different things." *Id.* at 513.

14. 262 U.S. 341 (1923). As published, *New River Collieries* is unanimous, but Butler's docket book indicates that McReynolds and Sanford had dissented in conference.

15. *New River Collieries*, 262 U.S. at 344. *See* Standard Oil Co. of New Jersey v. Southern Pacific Co., 268 U.S. 146, 155–56 (1925). The alleged taking in *New River Collieries* occurred after the war. In expropriation cases arising from the war, Butler was meticulous to enforce the "government's obligation" under eminent domain "to put the owners in as good a position pecuniarily as if the use of their property had not been taken." Phelps v. United States, 274 U.S. 341, 344 (1927). *See* Seaboard Air Line Railway Co. v. United States, 261 U.S. 299 (1923).

16. *New River Collieries*, 262 U.S. at 343–44. Butler was insistent, as he wrote Stone, that the "'value' of private property is that sum which would constitute just compensation if it were taken by exertion of the sovereign power of eminent domain for public use." PB to HFS (May 9, 1929) (Stone papers, in the case file of Lucas v. Alexander, 279 U.S. 573 (1929)).

17. "The basis prescribed for the determination of prices to be charged by producers of coal was the cost of production, including the expense of operation, maintenance, depreciation, and depletion, plus a just and reasonable profit. And prices to be charged by dealers were to be made by adding to their cost a just and reasonable sum for profit." *Highland*, 279 U.S. at 259–60. In *New River Collieries*, Butler explicitly held that "[t]he owner's cost, profit, or loss did not tend to prove market price or value at the time of taking." 262 U.S. at 344. *See* Davis v. George B. Newton Coal Co., 267 U.S. 292 (1925).

18. Indeed, Butler finds that government wartime price fixing was justified only "as applied to the coal in question." This is an extremely narrow conclusion, especially because, as Butler repeatedly emphasizes, the purchaser in *Highland* was the manufacturer of railroad equipment needed by the government and hence any increase in the price of coal "would have been directly opposed to the interest of the government." 279 U.S. at 262. The "as applied" holding of *Highland* is consistent with the Taft Court's decision in Matthew Addy Co. v. United States, 264 U.S. 239 (1924), in which the Taft Court held unanimously that government regulations of the price of coal did not apply retroactively to jobbers who had already purchased coal at unregulated prices. The Court was explicit that any other construction of the executive order fixing the price of coal would require consideration of the "grave constitutional question" of congressional "power to fix prices at which persons then owning coal must sell thereafter, if they sold at all, without providing compensation for losses . . . . If this difficulty can be eliminated by some reasonable construction of the order, it should be accepted." *Id.* at 245. Butler's docket book shows that at conference Holmes was "*dubitante*" about the Court's conclusion.

19. Brooks-Scanlon Corp. v. United States, 265 U.S. 106, 123–26 (1924) (opinion by Butler). *See* Russell Motor Car Co. v. United States, 261 U.S. 514 (1923).
20. *See supra* note 13.
21. The closest Butler came to any such argument was the proposition that wartime price fixing was necessary "to prevent manipulations to enhance prices by those having coal for sale and to lessen apprehension on the part of consumers in respect of their supply and the prices liable to be exacted." 279 U.S. at 261. It would perhaps be too easy to make such a showing to justify peacetime price fixing when necessary to effect legitimate national interests during coal emergencies.
22. *See infra* Chapter 25.
23. Davis v. George B. Newton Coal Co., 267 U.S. 292 (1925). For a contemporary discussion, see Sidney Post Simpson, *Due Process and Coal Price Regulation*, 9 IOWA LAW BULLETIN 145 (1924). In Hamilton v. Kentucky Distilleries Co., 251 U.S. 146 (1919) and Jacob Ruppert v. Caffey, 251 U.S. 264 (1920), the White Court had extended the authority of Congress's war powers long after the Armistice. The question of when wartime authority ought constitutionally to terminate provoked a lively debate. *See* Matthew C. Waxman, *Constitutional War Powers in World War I: Charles Evans Hughes and the Power to Wage War Successfully*, 44 JOURNAL OF SUPREME COURT HISTORY 267, 272–75 (2019).
24. Russell Motor Car Co. v. United States, 261 U.S. 514, 521–22 (1923).
25. WHT to Allen B. Lincoln (September 2, 1918) (Taft papers).
26. 264 U.S. 543 (1924).
27. The story of *Chastleton* is well told in CHRISTOPHER N. MAY, IN THE NAME OF WAR: JUDICIAL REVIEW AND THE WAR POWERS SINCE 1918, at 223–53 (Cambridge: Harvard University Press 1989).
28. 256 U.S. 135, 154 (1921). The Court simultaneously upheld rent control within New York City. *See* Marcus Brown Holding Co., Inc. v. Feldman, 256 U.S. 170, 199 (1921). On the controversial nature of the congressional statute, see *Constitutional Government in War and Peace*, 3 CONSTITUTIONAL REVIEW 222, 230–32 (1919) ("It is the disposition of people to demand, and of legislators to adopt, such measures as seem to them good without regard to what the constitutions may have to say. That is symptomatic, and it is disquieting.").
29. *Hirsh*, 256 U.S. at 154–56. There was a strong dissent by McKenna. Joined by White, Van Devanter, and McReynolds, McKenna complained that the decision relegated the Constitution to "an anachronism," an "'archeological relic' no longer to be an efficient factor in affairs but something only to engage and entertain the studies of antiquarians." *Id.* at 163. McKenna asked:

> Have conditions come, not only to the District of Columbia, embarrassing the Federal Government, but to the world as well, that are not amenable to passing palliatives, so that socialism, or some form of socialism, is the only permanent corrective or accommodation? It is indeed strange that this court, in effect, is called upon to make way for it and, through the instrument of a constitution based on personal rights and the purposeful encouragement of individual incentive and energy, to declare legal a power exerted for their destruction. The inquiry occurs, Have we come to the realization of the observation that "War unless it be fought for liberty is the most deadly enemy of liberty?"

Id. at 162–63 (McKenna, J., dissenting). "There can be no conception of property aside from its control and use," McKenna argued. "Protection to it has been

Cabining the Constitutional Implications of the War

regarded as a vital principle of republican institutions. . . . Our social system rests largely upon its sanctity, 'and that State or community which seeks to invade it will soon discover the error in the disaster which follows.' . . . As we understand, the assertion is, that legislation can regard a private transaction as a matter of public interest. It is not possible to express the possession or exercise of more unbounded or irresponsible power." *Id.* at 165, 167 (McKenna J., dissenting).

Two days after the announcement of the opinion Holmes wrote Frankfurter: "The best defence [sic] [of constitutional rights] I ever heard came from Brandeis many years ago – that constitutional restrictions enable a man to sleep at night and know that he won't be robbed before morning – which, in days of legislative activity and general scheming, otherwise he scarcely would feel secure about. I am afraid McKenna thinks that security at an end." OWH to Felix Frankfurter (April 20, 1921), in HOLMES-FRANKFURTER CORRESPONDENCE, at 110.

It is clear, however, that even Holmes felt some discomfort with the extent of rent control authorized by congressional statute. Eighteen months later, for example, he would write that "The late decisions upon laws dealing with the congestion of Washington and New York, caused by the war, dealt with laws intended to meet a temporary emergency and providing for compensation determined to be reasonable by an impartial board. They went to the verge of the law." Pennsylvania Coal Co. v. Mahon, 260 U.S. 393, 416 (1922).

In *Block v. Hirsh*, Holmes specifically stressed that "A limit in time, to tide over a passing trouble, well may justify a law that could not be upheld as a permanent change." 256 U.S. at 157. The next year, however, in a 6–3 opinion authored by Clarke (with McKenna, Van Devanter, and McReynolds dissenting), the Court reaffirmed the constitutionality of rent control in New York in a way that distinctly deemphasized the relevance of emergency conditions. *See* Edgar A. Levy Leasing Co. v. Siegel, 258 U.S. 242, 245 (1922). Clarke's statement of the justification for rent control glossed the concept of emergency in a manner that far transcended the specific and presumably temporary conditions caused by the war:

> The warrant for this legislative resort to the police power was the conviction on the part of the state legislators that there existed in the larger cities of the State a social emergency, caused by an insufficient supply of dwelling houses and apartments, so grave that it constituted a serious menace to the health, morality, comfort, and even to the peace of a large part of the people of the State.

Id. at 245. Clarke's only concession to the temporary quality of the "emergency" justifying rent control was to note in passing the "notorious fact that a grave social problem has arisen from the insufficient supply of dwellings in all the large cities of this and other countries, resulting from the cessation of building activities incident to the war." *Id.* at 246.

30. Act of Aug. 24, 1921, Pub. L. 67-71, 42 Stat. 200 (1921) (extending rent control until May 22, 1922).
31. Act of May 22, 1922, Pub. L. 67-222, 42 Stat. 543 (1922) (extending rent control until May 22, 1924). *Chastleton* was decided on April 21, 1924.
32. John W. Davis, quoted in *J.W. Davis Assails Reformers Who Would Alter Constitution to Regulate Individual Morals*, ST. LOUIS STAR AND TIMES (January 19, 1923), at 13. *See* John W. Davis, *Present Day Problems*, 9 AMERICAN BAR ASSOCIATION JOURNAL 553, 554 (1923).

33. Butler records that McReynolds "thinks the bill good and [should be] reversed." Brandeis is recorded as having advocated a "short cut. Validity need not be answered" because of inadequate service to the parties. *Id.* Brandeis eventually adopted this position in his separate published opinion "concurring in part." *See* 264 U.S. at 549 (Brandeis, J., concurring in part).
34. *Chastleton*, 264 U.S. at 547–48.
35. *Id.* at 548.
36. Holmes papers.
37. McReynolds, for example, replied to Holmes's circulated draft: "I will not say no. But I should much prefer to have you say that facts within the knowledge of the court make it entirely clear that no emergency exists and the act is no longer in force. This will put an end to mischievous agitation now going on in Congress and clear the air." (Holmes papers). Similarly, Sutherland wrote: "I voted to go further and reckon the Emergency to have passed on what we know. Perhaps it is better to dispose of the case as you have done, but I should like to hear what the brethren who voted as I did think about it." *Id.* Van Devanter wrote Holmes that "I have read and reread your opinion in the rent case and am still inclined to take the view that we ought to end it now, but I have not had an opportunity to take it up with others who also had that view." *Id.*
38. *Chastleton*, 264 U.S. at 548–49. Even this change, however, was not enough completely to satisfy McReynolds, who wrote Holmes: "I will acquiesce in this if it is accepted all round. But I do think that if we held conditions [existing in] 1922 were such as to show no emergency the result would be better." (Holmes papers). Justice Butler responded, "Yes, I go along with the others. Would prefer to hold law invalid and have an end of it now." *Id. Chastleton* was decided on April 21, 1924, and, on the basis of the paragraph quoted in text, the Court of Appeals of the District of Columbia declared rent control unconstitutional as of May 2, 1924. *See* Peck v. Fink, 2 F.2d 912, 913 (D.C. Cir. 1924). The appellate court could not resist making the lesson of *Chastleton* explicit: "It of course is unnecessary for us to attempt to add to the reasoning of the Supreme Court, but we may say with propriety that, if the emergency in question is not at an end, then this legislation may be extended indefinitely, and that which was 'intended to meet a temporary emergency' may become permanent law." *Id.* at 913.
39. WHT to Helen Herron Taft (April 22, 1924) (Taft papers). Taft added: "Brandeis did not dissent but thought we did not need to decide it."
40. As Brandeis wrote Frankfurter: "To fully appreciate the rent decision, recent Congressional record & files of Washington papers on proposed extension of law to 1926 must be considered." LDB to Felix Frankfurter (April 23, 1924), in 5 LETTERS OF LOUIS D. BRANDEIS, at 126. The Court's determination in *Chastleton* to use judicial notice to conclude that the wartime conditions had passed should be compared to Brandeis's opinion in Hamilton v. Kentucky Distilleries Co., 251 U.S. 146 (1919), which held that the Wartime Prohibition Act could constitutionally be applied even after the signing of the Armistice:

> Conceding, then, for the purposes of the present case, that the question of the continued validity of the war prohibition act under the changed circumstances depends upon whether it appears that there is no longer any necessity for the prohibition of the sale of distilled spirits for beverage purposes, it remains to be said that on obvious grounds every reasonable intendment must be made in favor

of its continuing validity, the prescribed period of limitation not having arrived; that to Congress in the exercise of its powers, not least the war power upon which the very life of the nation depends, a wide latitude of discretion must be accorded; and that it would require a clear case to justify a court in declaring that such an act, passed for such a purpose, had ceased to have force because the power of Congress no longer continued.

Id. at 163.

41. Remarkably, Congress did vote to extend rent control until May 22, 1925. *See* Act of May 17, 1924, Pub. L. 68-119, 43 Stat. 120 (1924). The law was judicially overturned. *See* MAY, *supra* note 27, at 244–53.
42. 65 CONG. REC. 7391–92 (April 28, 1924).

CHAPTER 23

Diminishing Judicial Deference

THE TAFT COURT'S return to normalcy was marked by a revival of turn-of-the-century principles of economic freedom. This new orientation would lead directly to the tectonic confrontations of the New Deal era, when the nation sought to revive the institutional innovations created during "the experience of economic mobilization of World War I."[1] At the heart of the Taft Court's strategy lay its determination to qualify, if not reverse, the deference with which the White Court had reviewed legislation addressing social and economic issues. The Taft Court's revision of doctrine was subtle and fundamental. To understand it, we should consider *Jay Burns Baking Co. v. Bryan*,[2] a case decided the week before *Chastleton*. Although the stakes in *Jay Burns* itself were quite small, the Court's opinion contains the seeds of much more consequential developments.

Jay Burns involved a challenge to a Nebraska statute fixing minimum and maximum weights for standard-sized loaves of bread.[3] It had been common to regulate the price and quality of bread during the first half of the nineteenth century. Bread was a necessity of life, yet urban populations lacked ovens in which they could bake their own loaves. As the Court observed in its seminal 1876 opinion in *Munn v. Illinois*,

> it has been customary in England from time immemorial, and in this country from its first colonization, to regulate ferries, common carriers, hackmen, *bakers*, millers, wharfingers, innkeepers, &c., and in so doing to fix a maximum of charge to be made for services rendered, accommodations furnished, and articles sold. To this day, statutes are to be found in many of the States upon some or all these subjects; and we think it has never yet been successfully contended that such legislation came within any of the constitutional prohibitions against interference with private property. With the Fifth Amendment in force, Congress, in 1820,

Diminishing Judicial Deference

conferred power upon the city of Washington "to regulate ... the weight and quality of bread."[4]

As home ovens came into ordinary use, bread regulation fell into desuetude. But it was revived during the progressive era as part of a general movement, exemplified by the 1901 creation of the National Bureau of Standards,[5] to promote standardized weights and measures.[6] In 1912, Taft's Secretary of Commerce and Labor (and Brandeis's brother-in-law) Charles Nagel endorsed a new organization created by the Bureau, the Annual Conference on Weights and Measures, which brought together local, state, and national weights and measures officials to create best practices for imposing uniform standards.[7] The Conference swiftly became a clearinghouse for national and local initiatives to standardize the size of bread loaves. Standardization was believed necessary because consumers had no idea of the actual weight of the loaves they were buying, which undermined the possibility of fair competition in the market for bread.[8]

The White Court was generous in its review of government efforts to standardize bread loaves. In 1913, in *Schmidinger v. Chicago*, the Court unanimously upheld a Chicago ordinance fixing minimum standard weights for bread against the charge that it was "an unreasonable and arbitrary exercise of police power and ... an unlawful interference with the freedom of contract secured" by the Due Process Clause of the Fourteenth Amendment.[9] Speaking through Day, the Court adopted a highly deferential standard of review. "This Court has frequently affirmed that the local authorities intrusted with the regulation of such matters, and not the courts, are primarily the judges of the necessities of local situations calling for such legislation, and the courts may only interfere with laws or ordinances passed in pursuance of the police power where they are so arbitrary as to be palpably and unmistakably in excess of any reasonable exercise of the authority conferred."[10]

The standardization of bread loaves reached its apogee during World War I,[11] when the United States Food Administration under Herbert Hoover decreed that bread could be served only in standard loaves of 1, 1.5, or 2 pounds, or other pound multiples.[12] The Food Administration prohibited bread loaves that weighed too much as well as loaves that weighed too little. It permitted "variations at the rate of 1 ounce per pound over and 1 ounce per pound under" the prescribed weights for loaves.[13] The success of this wartime regulation provoked a revived appreciation of "the imperative need of uniform standardization of loaf weight of bread in order to protect the purchasing public."[14]

State legislation requiring standardized bread weights was first enacted in 1919 in Indiana.[15] By 1924 similar laws had been enacted in some eighteen states,[16] as well as in the District of Columbia.[17] Of these, ten states and the District of Columbia allowed variances in weight that roughly mirrored those used by the Food Administration during the war.[18] By the middle of the decade, therefore, it was evident that "The modern trend of State legislation, in relation to the sale of bread is ... undoubtedly in favor of the principle of standard weights."[19]

Nebraska was one of the states that participated in this new trend. In 1921, it enacted a statute requiring that bread be sold in specified weights, decreeing that "a tolerance at the rate of two ounces per pound in excess of the standard weights herein fixed shall be allowed, and no more, provided that the standard weights herein prescribed shall be determined by averaging the weight of not less than twenty-five loaves of any one unit."[20] Although not a literal extension of wartime emergency legislation, as was the case in *Chastleton*, the Nebraska statute nevertheless reflected a peacetime version of popular and effective wartime regulation. The tolerances permitted by the Nebraska statute were twice as generous as those that had been permitted by the Food Administration during the war. The baking industry nevertheless challenged the statute on the ground "that the provision fixing the maximum weights ... is unnecessary, unreasonable and arbitrary" and hence an infringement of freedom of contract under the Due Process Clause.[21]

Butler's docket book indicates that the Court split 5–4 in conference, with McKenna, Holmes, Brandeis, and Sutherland voting to sustain the statute. Taft assigned the opinion to Butler, who eventually authored a decision for seven justices, with only Brandeis and Holmes dissenting.[22] Butler concluded that setting maximum weight tolerances "is not necessary for the protection of purchasers against imposition and fraud by short weights and is not calculated to effectuate that purpose, and ... it subjects bakers and sellers of bread to restrictions which are essentially unreasonable and arbitrary, and is therefore repugnant to the Fourteenth Amendment."[23] At the core of Butler's opinion lay a resolutely common-sense judgment, verging on outrage, that a law seeking to prevent fraudulently short-weighted loaves should perversely set maximum weights.[24]

The plaintiffs in *Jay Burns* sought to establish that in many conditions of humidity and temperature it was "impossible to comply with the law without wrapping the loaves or employing other artificial means to prevent or retard evaporation." Butler credited the bakers' evidence, concluding:

> The uncontradicted evidence shows that there is a strong demand by consumers for unwrapped bread. It is a wholesome article of food, and plaintiffs in error and other bakers have a right to furnish it to their customers.... It would be unreasonable to prevent unwrapped bread being furnished to those who want it in order technically to comply with a weight regulation and to keep within limits of tolerance so narrow as to require that ordinary evaporation be retarded by wrapping or other artificial means. It having been shown that during some periods in Nebraska bread made in a proper and usual way will vary in weight more than at the rate of two ounces to the pound during 24 hours after baking, the enforcement of the provision necessarily will have the effect of prohibiting the sale of unwrapped loaves when evaporation exceeds the tolerance.[25]

Examined closely, Butler's reasoning was quite odd. Progressive agitation to require that commercially baked bread be wrapped to protect it from contamination was common in the second decade of the twentieth century;[26] statutes requiring that bread be wrapped before sale had heretofore easily passed constitutional muster.[27] Indeed, at the very time *Jay Burns* was under advisement, Congress was considering a proposed "Federal Bread Act" which would require that bread be wrapped before shipment in interstate commerce.[28] Even if compliance with the maximum

Diminishing Judicial Deference

tolerances of the Nebraska statute did require that bread be wrapped, therefore, it is unclear why this result would intolerably interfere with constitutional rights.[29]

At the heart of *Jay Burns*, therefore, was not the question of wrapped or unwrapped bread, but instead the issue of whether Nebraska had sufficient reason constitutionally to impose maximum sizes on standardized loaves. In part this turned on whether it was "possible for bakers to comply with the law."[30] On this question, the plaintiffs in *Jay Burns* created an extensive record of expert testimony designed to establish the extreme difficulty of baking bread within a tolerance of plus or minus 2 ounces.[31] Nebraska produced what in retrospect seems like a largely perfunctory defense.[32] No doubt Nebraska imagined that it could afford to create a somewhat casual record because of the generously deferential standard of *Schmidinger*, and because the nation had by the middle of the decade already accumulated extensive experience with maximum bread tolerances twice as strict as those imposed by Nebraska.[33] Epitomized by the Food Administration's successful wartime regulations, it was commonly acknowledged that stricter tolerances than Nebraska's "worked like a charm."[34]

The Court was perfectly aware of this history, because it was detailed in Brandeis's extensive dissent.[35] But the Court nevertheless concluded that the Nebraska statute subjected "bakers and sellers of bread to restrictions which are essentially unreasonable and arbitrary."[36] It might perhaps be said that the Court in *Jay Burns* was scrupulous to decide the constitutionality of the Nebraska statute based only on facts placed into evidence by the parties, as though ascertaining the constitutionality of legislation were exactly analogous to rendering a verdict in a dispute between two private parties.[37] But we know from the Court's anxiety to exercise judicial notice in *Chastleton* that it was subject to no such scruples. In the words of an early draft of *Chastleton*, members of the Taft Court were prepared to acknowledge "all that a man with eyes open can see."[38] The Court knew full well that judgments of constitutionality often turn on legislative facts that have no ready analogue in merely private litigation,[39] and the Court also knew full well that since the war bakers had easily complied with tolerances far stricter than those imposed by Nebraska.

Ironically, the key holding of *Jay Burns* rested on an aggressive exercise of judicial notice. Butler struck down the statute because Nebraska could not provide an adequate justification for imposing upon bakers the burden of complying with maximum bread weights. Nebraska argued that requiring maximum weights was necessary to avoid consumer confusion, to prevent "a loaf of one standard size from being increased so much that it can readily be sold for a loaf of a larger standard size."[40] But Butler, reasoning *ex cathedra*, declared that "it is contrary to common experience and unreasonable to assume that there could be any danger of such deception."[41] Deprived of this justification, Nebraska's maximum tolerances were left exposed as "not necessary for the protection of purchasers against imposition and fraud by short weights."[42]

In effect, therefore, Butler took judicial notice of "common experience" to discredit Nebraska's justification for its statute.[43] This was a fundamental repudiation of the deferential standard of *Schmidinger*. In a brilliant and memorable dissent, Brandeis sought to rehabilitate Nebraska's justification for its statute by explaining the history of bread regulation. He defended the "administrative necessity" of prohibiting "excessive weights" if "short weights were to be prevented"[44] by recounting the limitations on excessive bread weight imposed during and after the war. Frankly admitting that he was relying on evidence "not in the record," Brandeis insisted that in deciding questions of constitutionality courts were obliged to take "judicial notice" of "the history of the experience gained under similar legislation," as well as of "the results of scientific experiments," "whether occurring before or after the enactment of the statute or of the entry of the judgment."[45]

In effect, Brandeis sought to flip the majority's use of judicial notice. He argued that if a court was to decide a case based upon evidence outside the record, it ought to consider a comprehensive history of relevant administrative experience. Brandeis had defended this approach since his pathbreaking brief in *Muller v. Oregon*.[46] In words that would reverberate for the next century, Brandeis concluded:

> Put at its highest, our function is to determine, in the light of all facts which may enrich our knowledge and enlarge our understanding, whether the measure, enacted in the exercise of an unquestioned police power and of a character inherently unobjectionable, transcends the bounds of reason; that is, whether the provision as applied is so clearly arbitrary or capricious that legislators acting reasonably could not have believed it to be necessary or appropriate for the public welfare.
>
> To decide, as a fact, that the prohibition of excess weights "is not necessary for the protection of the purchasers against imposition and fraud by short weights," that it "is not calculated to effectuate that purpose," and that it "subjects bakers and sellers of bread" to heavy burdens, is, in my opinion, an exercise of the powers of a super-Legislature – not the performance of the constitutional function of judicial review.[47]

Today we are most likely to interpret Brandeis's argument through the lens of deference. If the Court is to avoid second-guessing the outcome of the legislative process, it must *defer* to empirical legislative judgments unless those judgments are patently arbitrary and capricious. But in 1924 Brandeis's words would also sound in the register of evidentiary relevance. Brandeis was saying that no court should presume to find a legislative judgment irrational unless it had first considered all the various forms of evidence, "all facts which may enrich our knowledge and enlarge our understanding," which a legislature may have considered when enacting a statute. Brandeis believed that the rationality of the Nebraska statute should have been assessed in light of all the accumulated administrative expertise of the nation.[48] And to this form of evidence Butler was resolutely oblivious.

In *Jay Burns*, the majority of the Taft Court turned its back on government administrative expertise that had accumulated during the war, trusting instead to its own version of "common experience." *Jay Burns* was for this reason condemned as "an unexpected reversion to the past,"[49] and, more pointedly, as "reminiscent of the majority opinion in Lochner v. New York,"[50] which had struck down a New York law limiting the employment of bakers to sixty hours per week. Brandeis himself believed that *Jay Burns* was "worse even than Lochner."[51] Butler's appeal to "common experience" eerily evoked *Lochner's* appeal to "common understanding" to establish that "the trade of a baker has never been regarded as an unhealthy one."[52] Progressives repudiated *Lochner* precisely because "[t]he majority opinion was based upon 'a common understanding' as to the effect of work in bakeshops upon ... those engaged in it. 'Common understanding' has ceased to be the reliance in matters calling for essentially scientific determination."[53]

In influential and stinging words, Brandeis attacked Butler for exactly this same mistake: "Knowledge is essential to understanding; and understanding should precede judging. Sometimes, if we would guide by the light of reason, we must let our minds be bold. But, in this case, we have merely to acquaint ourselves with the art of breadmaking and the usages of the trade."[54] Popular and academic commentary on *Jay Burns* echoed Brandeis's attack. "One of the judicial reforms for which Mr. Justice Brandeis has long been contending is the abandonment of speculative, doctrinaire, a priori effusions in judicial opinions and the substitution of a realistic and concrete examination of the relevant facts. Those who wish to see both methods in their respective perfections should read Jay Burns Baking Co. v. Bryan."[55] The *New Republic* argued that no "disinterested student of constitutional law" could read *Jay Burns* "and deny that we have never had a more irresponsible period in the history" of the Court.[56]

Read in the context of *Chastleton*, *Jay Burns* is best interpreted as an effort to check what American Bar Association president and soon-to-be Democratic presidential nominee John W. Davis called the "flood of laws" that has "come to crowd our statute books and clog our courts," a flood prompted by "the fatuous belief that a ready solution can be found for every social or economic evil by invoking the agencies of government."[57] The experience of conservative elites in the 1920s was that the war had sparked a "tendency towards paternalistic legislation," which reduced "all men ... to a level of uniformity" they associated with "August 1914." In their view, a "state consisting of a powerful and paternalistic government and subservient citizens is good for nothing except war."[58] In 1923, the year before *Jay Burns*, Butler had himself cautioned against "legislative experiments to relieve people from their own just responsibilities."[59] He had long opposed the "tendency toward a kind of State socialism, which is destructive of individual initiative and development."[60]

In *Jay Burns*, the conservative majority of the Taft Court took it upon itself to restore an appropriate constitutional balance. The key move was the repudiation of the deferential standard of *Schmidinger*.[61] In its determination to return the country to antebellum normalcy, the Court was prepared to put the state to its proofs when it undertook to engage in social and economic regulation.[62] Within a month of its decision, the Court cited *Jay Burns* for the proposition that the "validity of regulatory measures may be challenged on the ground that they transgress the Constitution, and thereupon it becomes the duty of the court, in the light of the facts in the case, to determine whether the regulation is reasonable and valid or essentially unreasonable, arbitrary and void."[63] Two years later, in the important decision of *Weaver v. Palmer Brothers Co.*, the Court again cited *Jay Burns* to support the conclusion that a 1923 Pennsylvania statute prohibiting the use of "shoddy" in bedding was "purely arbitrary and violates the due process clause of the Fourteenth Amendment."[64] The opinion was again written by Butler. Holmes, Brandeis, and Stone dissented.

Shoddy is material made by grinding up old rags and waste fabric materials. The resulting fibers are then used to stuff comforters, mattresses, and other forms of bedding. Because it was believed that shoddy could spread infection, it was commonly regulated. In the years after 1915 at least nine states prohibited its use in bedding materials.[65] Whether such a ban was arbitrary, Butler wrote in *Weaver*, "depends upon the facts of the case. Legislative determinations express or implied are entitled to great weight; but it is always open to interested parties to show that the legislature has transgressed the limits of its power. Invalidity may be shown by things which will be judicially noticed or by facts established by evidence. The burden is on the attacking party to establish the invalidating facts."[66]

Because the Pennsylvania statute permitted the use of sterilized secondhand materials other than shoddy in bedding, and because it was conceded that sterilization could eliminate whatever health risk shoddy might pose, Butler concluded that the statute could not "be sustained as a measure to protect health" and that it was therefore "purely arbitrary" to prohibit shoddy. As he had noted in the context of unwrapped bread, Butler emphasized that "shoddy-filled" products "are useful articles for which there is much demand. And it is a matter of public concern that the production and sale of things necessary or convenient for use should not be forbidden."[67] By explicitly seeking to vindicate the "public concern" in protecting the normal (meaning unregulated) functioning of the market, the Taft Court decisively shifted doctrine away from the judicial deference of *Schmidinger*.

Although Butler struck down Pennsylvania's statute as "purely arbitrary," he virtually ignored Pennsylvania's key justification for the legislation. The state had argued to the Court that it was "known and recognized in the industry" that shoddy was a material whose "very nature facilitates the practice of fraud and deceit." Pennsylvania contended that although it was relatively easy for inspectors to determine whether other secondhand material had been sterilized, this was not true of shoddy. Particularly for bedding manufactured out of state, as was the case in *Weaver* itself, "the testimony clearly establishes that it is impracticable and impossible to determine by such inspection as can be made ... whether or not shoddy has been actually sterilized."[68]

Pennsylvania defended its statute based on its need for effective administrative enforcement. Butler met this defense by asserting that the statute could not "be sustained as a measure to prevent deception" because the state provided for the inspection of manufacturers, and because the state required the display of tags stating the particulars of the sterilization process. Although the Court was without evidence to support its assumption that Pennsylvania could enforce its requirement that shoddy be sterilized, particularly with respect to out-of-state manufacturers, it

Diminishing Judicial Deference

was nevertheless unwilling to accord the state any leeway on this question. It was enough to establish that sterilized shoddy would present no danger to the health of the public. Butler insisted that "constitutional guarantees may not be made to yield to mere convenience."[69]

In dissent Holmes underlined what he regarded as the key fallacy of the Court's opinion. "It is admitted to be impossible to distinguish the innocent from the infected product in any practicable way, when it is made up into the comfortables. On these premises, if the Legislature regarded the danger as very great and inspection and tagging as inadequate remedies, it seems to me that in order to prevent the spread of disease it constitutionally could forbid any use of shoddy for bedding and upholstery."[70] Holmes worried that the Court was impeaching the important White Court precedent of *Purity Extract & Tonic Co. v. Lynch*, in which, speaking through Hughes, the Court had explicitly extended deference to a state's choice of such administrative measures "as it may deem necessary in order to make" its laws "effective."[71] In unusually strong language, Holmes cautioned, "I think we are pressing the Fourteenth Amendment too far."[72]

Commentators noted that *Weaver* explicitly altered previous canons of deference,[73] emphasizing that the decision was "irreconcilable with prior police power cases."[74] Together with *Jay Burns*, *Weaver* was said to "demonstrate, if demonstration still were needed, that the due process clauses are being utilized by the Supreme Court for general revision of legislation."[75] It was apparent that the Taft Court was no longer willing to defer to government expertise on questions of administrative convenience and enforceability. This point was driven home by *Schlesinger v. Wisconsin*, which had been decided the week before *Weaver*. Speaking through McReynolds, the Court in *Schlesinger* struck down a Wisconsin statute providing that gifts made within six years of death "shall be construed to have been made in contemplation of death" and hence subject to inheritance taxes.[76] McReynolds deemed the conclusive presumption "wholly arbitrary" and hence "in plain conflict with the Fourteenth Amendment."[77]

McReynolds made absolutely clear that administrative convenience and necessity would no longer count for much in justifying the constitutionality of a statute:[78]

> The presumption and consequent taxation are defended upon the theory that, exercising judgment and discretion, the legislature found them necessary in order to prevent evasion of inheritance taxes. That is to say, "A" may be required to submit to an exactment forbidden by the Constitution if this seems necessary in order to enable the State readily to collect lawful charges against "B." Rights guaranteed by the federal Constitution are not to be so lightly treated; they are superior to this supposed necessity. The State is forbidden to deny due process of law or the equal protection of the laws for any purpose whatsoever.[79]

In dissent, Holmes penned an elegant and classic opinion:

> [I]t seems to me not too late to urge that in dealing with state legislation upon matters of substantive law we should avoid with great caution

attempts to substitute our judgment for that of the body whose business it is in the first place, with regard to questions of domestic policy that fairly are open to debate.

The present seems to me one of those questions. I leave aside the broader issues that might be considered and take the statute as it is written, putting the tax on the ground of an absolute presumption that gifts of a material part of the donor's estate made within six years of his death were made in contemplation of death. If the time were six months instead of six years I hardly think that the power of the State to pass the law would be denied, as the difficulty of proof would warrant making the presumption absolute; and while I should not dream of asking where the line can be drawn, since the great body of the law consists in drawing such lines, yet when you realize that you are dealing with a matter of degree you must realize that reasonable men may differ widely as to the place where the line should fall. I think that our discussion should end if we admit what I certainly believe, that reasonable men might regard six years as not too remote. Of course many gifts will be hit by the tax that were made with no contemplation of death. But the law allows a penumbra to be embraced that goes beyond the outline of its object in order that the object may be secured. ...

I think that with the States as with Congress when the means are not prohibited and are calculated to effect the object we ought not to inquire into the degree of the necessity for resorting to them.[80]

Brandeis and Stone joined in Holmes's dissent, which marked the exact moment at which the classic triumvirate emerged as a recognizable phenomenon.[81] Taken together, *Schlesinger* and *Weaver* cemented the Taft Court's reputation as determined to expand "the meaningless meaning of the 'due process' clause of the Fourteenth Amendment" to put "constitutional compulsion behind the private judgment of its members upon disputed and difficult questions of social policy."[82] All recognized that the Taft Court had adopted "a more rigid attitude ... toward the constitutionality of state legislation."[83]

It was left to Sutherland to endow this new attitude with crisp doctrinal articulation. *Louis K. Liggett Co. v. Baldridge*[84] involved a 1927 Pennsylvania statute providing that only licensed pharmacists could own pharmacies or drug stores. A Massachusetts corporation challenged the statute as invalid under the Fourteenth Amendment. A three-judge district court upheld the statute: "It may be the Legislature thought that a corporate owner, in purchasing drugs, might give a greater regard to the price than to the quality; and, if such was the thought of the Legislature, can this court say it was without a valid connection with the public interests, and so unreasonable as to be unlawful?"[85] On appeal, however, the Taft Court, in an opinion by Sutherland for seven justices, held that the lower court was mistaken.[86] Holmes and Brandeis dissented.

Sutherland had dedicated his 1917 American Bar Association presidential address to deploring the national "passion for making laws," which he lampooned as a "prevailing obsession ... that statutes, like crops, enrich the country in proportion to their volume."[87] The good intentions of legislation, he argued, should

Diminishing Judicial Deference

"be of small consequence, or of no consequence at all, in the domain of law," because in the name of "a diffused desire to do good" the community was nevertheless made to suffer "from the affliction of mischievous and meddlesome statutes."[88] "I have a very firm conviction," Sutherland announced to the New York State Bar Association in 1921, "that the tendency to control our activities by statutory rule is being over-emphasized. Too many laws are being passed in haste. Too many that simply reflect a temporary prejudice, a passing fad, a fleeting whim, a superficial view or an exaggerated estimate of the extent, or a mistaken impression of the quality of an evil."[89] Taking a page from his close friend Harding, Sutherland urged that the state "must not be allowed to wander too far from the sphere of its normal and traditional functions, nor interfere over-much with the liberty of the individual to work out his destiny here and his salvation hereafter in his own way."[90]

Baldridge offered Sutherland the perfect occasion to embody these concerns in the language of clear and forceful constitutional doctrine. The Pennsylvania statute, under the "masquerade"[91] of a health measure, was "obviously intended to prevent the further extension of chain drug stores."[92] Sutherland used this discrepancy to drive to the surface the implicit premise of decisions like *Jay Burns* and *Weaver*.

Sutherland began his opinion with the axiom that "appellant's business is a property right and as such entitled to protection against state legislation in contravention of the federal Constitution." It followed that "unless justified as a valid exercise of the police power, the act assailed must be declared unconstitutional because the enforcement thereof will deprive appellant of its property without due process of law." The purported goal of the act was to protect public health. Thus, Sutherland reasoned, "the determination we are called upon to make is whether the act has a real and substantial relation to that end or is a clear and arbitrary invasion of appellant's property rights guaranteed by the Constitution." In effect, therefore, courts were to strike down as "arbitrary" statutes regulating businesses if the government could not demonstrate that the statutes bore "a real and substantial relation" to an appropriate end.[93]

In *Baldridge,* the Court held the Pennsylvania statute unconstitutional because "[n]o facts are presented by the record, and, so far as appears, none were presented to the legislature which enacted the statute," that restricting ownership would contribute to public health.[94] The lesson was clear: State interference with normal market operations would be held unconstitutional absent evidence establishing a substantial relationship to an appropriate end.[95] The burden of proof was effectively shifted to the state. In this way Sutherland made elegantly explicit the dismantling of deference that had been implicit in *Jay Burns* and *Weaver*.[96] In dissent, Holmes could say only that "[b]ut for decisions to which I bow I should not think any conciliatory phrase necessary to justify what seems to me one of the incidents of legislative power. I think however that the police power as that term has been defined and explained clearly extends to a law like this, whatever I may think of its wisdom, and that the decree should be affirmed."[97]

Notes

1. William E. Leuchtenburg, *The New Deal and the Analogue of War*, in CHANGE AND CONTINUITY IN TWENTIETH-CENTURY AMERICA 83 (John Braeman, Robert H. Bremner, & Everett Walters, eds., Columbus: Ohio State University Press 1964).
2. 264 U.S. 504 (1924).
3. *Id.* at 511.
4. 94 U.S. 113, 125 (1876) (emphasis added). *See* Munn v. People, 69 Ill. 80, 91 (1873) ("Ever since the organization of our State government, the legislature has exercised ... unquestioned" power "to regulate ... the weight and price of bread."); German Alliance Insurance Co. v. Kansas, 233 U.S. 389, 417 (1914).
5. 31 Stat. 1449 (March 3, 1901).
6. DEPARTMENT OF COMMERCE AND LABOR, BUREAU OF STANDARDS, CONFERENCE ON THE WEIGHTS AND MEASURES OF THE UNITED STATES 44 (Washington D.C.: Government Printing Office 1905).
7. *Remarks of Honorable Charles Nagel, Secretary of Commerce and Labor* (February 15, 1912), in DEPARTMENT OF COMMERCE AND LABOR, BUREAU OF STANDARDS, SEVENTH ANNUAL CONFERENCE ON WEIGHTS AND MEASURES 11 (Washington D.C.: Government Printing Office 1912).
8. *See* DEPARTMENT OF COMMERCE AND LABOR, BUREAU OF STANDARDS, FIFTH ANNUAL CONFERENCE ON WEIGHTS AND MEASURES 19–22, 26–29, 58, 86, 88–89 (Washington D.C.: Government Printing Office 1911); DEPARTMENT OF COMMERCE AND LABOR, BUREAU OF STANDARDS, SIXTH ANNUAL CONFERENCE ON WEIGHTS AND MEASURES 22–23, 132–33, 157 (Washington D.C.: Government Printing Office 1912); SEVENTH ANNUAL CONFERENCE ON WEIGHTS AND MEASURES, *supra* note 7, at 24, 32, 64, 69, 75, 82; DEPARTMENT OF COMMERCE, BUREAU OF STANDARDS, EIGHTH ANNUAL CONFERENCE ON WEIGHTS AND MEASURES 23, 29, 33, 259, 278, 284, 289 (Washington D.C.: Government Printing Office 1914).
9. Schmidinger v. Chicago, 226 U.S. 578, 585 (1913). The Court stated: "To the argument that to make exactly one pound loaves is extremely difficult, if not impracticable, the supreme court of Illinois has answered, and this construction is binding upon us, that the ordinance is not intended to limit the weight of a loaf to a pound or the fractional part or multiple of a pound, but that the ordinance was passed with a view only to prevent the sale of loaves of bread which are short in weight." *Id.* at 589. In his brief to the Court, however, Schmidinger had asserted that he had been "charged with and found guilty of making and selling bread in loaves *in excess* of the prescribed weights, although correctly labeled as to the actual weight thereof." Brief of Plaintiff in Error, at 17.
10. *Schmidinger*, 226 U.S. at 587–88.
11. As a general matter, the national Bureau of Standards "received a very great impulse due to the war work." *Address of S.W. Stratton, Director of the Bureau of Standards*, in DEPARTMENT OF COMMERCE, BUREAU OF STANDARDS, TWELFTH ANNUAL CONFERENCE ON WEIGHTS AND MEASURES 24 (Washington D.C.: Government Printing Office 1920).
12. WILLIAM CLINTON MULLENDORE, HISTORY OF THE UNITED STATES FOOD ADMINISTRATION 1917–1919, at 164 (Stanford University Press 1941). The Food Administration imposed standardization in part to conserve domestic food

consumption; in part to make the production of bread more efficient; in part to promote the capacity of consumers to know what they were buying; and in part because these goals could be administratively enforced only if loaves were standardized. The Food Administration standardized not only the size of loaves, but also the recipe for bread, as well as the grades of flour that could be used in the production of bread.

13. *Id. See Hoover Fixes Standard Loaf*, NEW YORK TIMES (November 12, 1917), at 1.
14. Resolution passed at the Thirteenth Annual Conference on Weights and Measures, sponsored by the Bureau of Standards, May 27, 1920, DEPARTMENT OF COMMERCE, BUREAU OF STANDARDS, THIRTEENTH ANNUAL CONFERENCE ON WEIGHTS AND MEASURES 174–75 (Washington D.C.: Government Printing Office 1921). *See id.* at 117, 142. The resolution urged "the passage by the several states of legislation tending to bring about the adoption of such a uniform standard." The next year, after much debate, the Conference adopted a model ordinance specifying bread weights. DEPARTMENT OF COMMERCE, BUREAU OF STANDARDS, FOURTEENTH ANNUAL CONFERENCE ON WEIGHTS AND MEASURES 131 (Washington D.C.: Government Printing Office 1922). *See id.* at 24–44, 80–87. Hoover himself addressed the Conference, suggesting that "the question of bread weights" was a matter "of simplifying the process of manufacture, and in simplifying the process of manufacture you are contributing to a lower production cost and protecting both producer and consumer." *Address by Hon. Herbert Hoover* (May 25, 1921), *id.* at 79.
15. Hearings before the House Committee on Agriculture on H.R. 4533 (1924), 68th CONG. 1st SESS., at 18; DEPARTMENT OF COMMERCE, BUREAU OF STANDARDS, SEVENTEENTH ANNUAL CONFERENCE ON WEIGHTS AND MEASURES 40–41 (Washington D.C.: Government Printing Office 1924). "The demand for bakery legislation including standard bread weights followed closely the ending of the war and undoubtedly came as the result of the experiences both of the baker and of the consumer under the regulations of the United States Food Administration." I.L. Miller, *Enforcement of the Indiana Bread Law*, *id.* at 40–41. The Indiana statute permitted a tolerance of "one ounce per pound over and one ounce per pound under the standard unit weight." *Id.* at 41. The law, including its tolerances, was fully supported by Indiana bakers. *Id.* at 44–45. The movement for standardized weights for bread loaves after the war was intended both to promote educated consumption and to protect bakers against unethical competition.
16. Hearings before the House Committee on Agriculture on H.R. 4533, *supra* note 15, at 13–14, 16. To the list of states set forth in the Hearings should be added New York, North Dakota, and South Dakota. *See* DEPARTMENT OF COMMERCE, BUREAU OF STANDARDS, FEDERAL AND STATE LAWS RELATING TO WEIGHTS AND MEASURES 570, 596, 762 (3rd ed.,Washington D.C.: Government Printing Office 1926).
17. Act of March 3, 1921, Pub. L. 46-358, 41 Stat. 1217, 1220, amended by Pub. L. 67-72, 42 Stat. 201 (August 24, 1921).
18. Hearings before the House Committee on Agriculture on H.R. 4533, *supra* note 15, at 12–13. Massachusetts should be added to the list provided in the hearings. *See* FEDERAL AND STATE LAWS RELATING TO WEIGHTS AND MEASURES, *supra* note 16, at 361.

19. Statement of Mr. F.S. Holbrook, Chief of the Weights and Measures Division, Bureau of Standards, Washington D.C., in Hearings before the House Committee on Agriculture on H.R. 4533, *supra* note 15, at 16.
20. Jay Burns Baking Co. v. Bryan, 264 U.S. 504, 510–11 n.1 (1924).
21. *Id.* at 511.
22. Brandeis later reported to Frankfurter that the case "was really 5 to 4, but Van Devanter 'got busy,' in his personal way, talking & laboring with members of Court, finally led Sutherland & Sanford to suppress their dissents." *Brandeis-Frankfurter Conversations*, at 328 (July 2, 1924). Most likely Brandeis confused Sanford with McKenna, substituting in his recollection one weak justice for another. In the Brandeis papers there is a note from McKenna to Brandeis, stating: "Disturbing doubts have come to me. I am struggling with them and frankly I don't know whether they go to the conclusions or to details and reasoning." JM to LDB (Brandeis papers).
23. *Jay Burns*, 264 U.S. at 517.
24. Butler wrote: "Undoubtedly, the police power of the State may be exerted to protect purchasers from imposition by sale of short weight loaves. . . . But a state may not, under the guise of protecting the public, arbitrarily interfere with private business or prohibit lawful occupations or impose unreasonable and unnecessary restrictions upon them. . . . Constitutional protection having been invoked, it is the duty of the court to determine whether the challenged provision has reasonable relation to the protection of purchasers of bread against fraud by short weights and really tends to accomplish the purpose for which it was enacted." *Id.* at 513.
25. *Id.* at 515–16.
26. *Bakers Wrap Bread in Paper: Efforts Making to Have Practice Extended*, CHRISTIAN SCIENCE MONITOR (March 15, 1912), at 6; *Bacterial Contamination of Bread*, ATLANTA CONSTITUTION (July 21, 1912), at B7; *Wrap Bread? Sure Say Club Women*, CHICAGO DAILY TRIBUNE (March 6, 1913), at 3; *Aldermen Urge Clean Bread Law*, CHICAGO DAILY TRIBUNE (July 24, 1913), at 17; *State Board of Health Pushes Campaign for Wrapped Bread*, LOUISVILLE COURIER-JOURNAL (February 6, 1913), at 7; *Wrapped Bread Scores a Point*, LOUISVILLE COURIER-JOURNAL (October 14, 1914), at 6; *Women Oppose Bakers in Hearing on Wrapped Bread*, ST. LOUIS POST-DISPATCH (October 13, 1915), at 10; *Health Departments and Dirty Bread*, ST. LOUIS POST-DISPATCH (December 8, 1915), at 14; *Wrapped Bread to Go on Market*, LOUISVILLE COURIER-JOURNAL (March 6, 1923), at 8; DEPARTMENT OF COMMERCE, BUREAU OF STANDARDS, SIXTEENTH ANNUAL CONFERENCE ON WEIGHTS AND MEASURES 104 (Washington D.C.: Government Printing Office 1924) (noting that Louisiana required that bread be wrapped and labelled).
27. State v. Normand, 76 N.H. 541 (1913). *See* FEDERAL AND STATE LAWS RELATING TO WEIGHTS AND MEASURES, *supra* note 16, at 516.
28. Hearings before the House Committee on Agriculture on H.R. 4533, *supra* note 15, at 1–2, 5. The Federal Bread bill had originally set standard sizes for loaves that allowed "a tolerance of two ounces per pound in excess of the declared weights." *Id.* at 1–2. Herbert Hoover's Department of Commerce cooperated with the Department of Agriculture to draft the bill. H. Rep. No. 990, 68th CONG. 1st SESS. (June 5, 1924), at 1. The bill was redrafted after *Jay Burns* to increase tolerance to "three and one-half ounces per pound in excess of the standard

weights." H.R. 8981, 68th CONG. 1st SESS. (June 5, 1924). The bill was favorably reported out of a House committee but died on the floor.
29. Butler did emphasize that "The act is not a sanitary measure," 264 U.S. at 516, as though measures that would be constitutional if enacted to uphold sanitation would be unconstitutional if enacted to prevent consumer confusion.
30. *Jay Burns*, 264 U.S. at 514.
31. The evidence purporting to establish the impossibility of complying with the statute's tolerances mostly involved unwrapped bread.
32. Transcript of Record, Jay Burns Baking Co. v. Bryan, No. 94, October Term 1923. The historian Barry Cushman heavily emphasizes this point in his discussion of *Jay Burns*. See Barry Cushman, *Some Varieties and Vicissitudes of Lochnerism*, 85 BOSTON UNIVERSITY LAW REVIEW 881, 945–952 (2005). Cushman rightly observes that the Court, speaking unanimously through Justice Butler, would in 1934 uphold a subsequent Nebraska statute fixing the standard size of loaves and imposing a maximum tolerance of 3 ounces per pound. See P.F. Petersen Baking Co. v. Bryan, 290 U.S. 570. Having learned its lesson, Nebraska would offer extensive expert testimony in *Petersen* to sustain the more generous tolerances of its new law.

It is plain, however, that in *Jay Burns* Nebraska produced more than enough evidence to demonstrate to a court that wished to be deferential that bread could be baked within the tolerances of the statute, even if unwrapped. See Brief and Argument for Defendants in Error, Jay Burns Baking Co. v. Bryan, No. 94, October Term 1923, at 17–28, 49–51. Many of the plaintiffs' experts testified that in their tests they had made no effort to bake loaves whose weight would be within the tolerances of the Nebraska statute. Nebraska also offered probative evidence that the plaintiffs' experts had conducted their baking experiments under "unfair" and "artificial conditions." *Id*. at 53.
33. In 1921, for example, Charles M. Fuller, the County Sealer of Weights and Measures of the Los Angeles County, reported to the Fourteenth Annual Conference on Weights and Measures on "the result of five years' successful enforcement of a standard-weight bread law" that allowed "a tolerance of 1 ounce above the standard weight" for each pound. No tolerance for short weight was allowed. Fuller noted "that the act has worked out so successfully in eliminating the unfair competition of bakers who would cut the price by selling an underweight loaf that even those firms which were first opposed to the idea of a standard-weight bread law are now in favor of it." Charles M. Fuller, *Enforcement of Bread Legislation, Including Proper Tolerances* (May 24, 1921), FOURTEENTH ANNUAL CONFERENCE ON WEIGHTS AND MEASURES, *supra* note 14, at 37. In 1921, the Conference resolved to appoint a committee to study proper tolerances for legislation setting standardized bread weights. *Id*. at 84–87.

The next year the Committee recommended "A tolerance of 2 ounces per pound in excess and 1 ounce per pound in deficiency" on the weight of individual loaves, but a tolerance only "of 1.5 ounces per pound in excess and 1 ounce per pound in deficiency shall be allowed on the average weight of 10 or more loaves of bread of the same nominal weight." *Report of Committee on Specifications and Tolerances, On Tolerances for Bread Loaves, Presented by F.S. Holbrook, Chairman* (May 25, 1922), DEPARTMENT OF COMMERCE, BUREAU OF STANDARDS, FIFTEENTH ANNUAL CONFERENCE ON WEIGHTS AND MEASURES 79 (Washington D.C.:

Government Printing Office 1922). The committee's recommendation was based upon "a very large amount of work" weighing "several thousand loaves" of bread "in a number of small cities in the State of New York and in the city of Chicago." *On Tolerances for Bread Loaves, id.* at 80. The committee weighed 1,564 1-pound loaves baked in large Chicago bakeries, and it determined that 99.4 percent fell "within a tolerance of ±¾ ounce." "[T]he lightest loaf was 0.85 ounce underweight and the heaviest loaf was 1.05 ounces overweight." *Id.* at 82. The committee weighed 993 loaves of white bread produced in ninety-nine "small" bakeries. Ninety-seven percent "were within ±1 ounce." *Id.* The committee's report was attacked on the floor of the Conference for allowing tolerances that were "too large." *Id.* at 88, 92; SIXTEENTH ANNUAL CONFERENCE ON WEIGHTS AND MEASURES, *supra* note 26, at 114. It was agreed that the question of tolerances should be taken up with "a committee of the baking industry to endeavor to agree . . . upon tolerances which will be satisfactory to both sides." *Id.* at 93. The next year it was reported that representatives of the baking industry, who included Jay Burns himself, had rejected the concept of maximum sizes for standardized loaves and proposed a tolerance of "1 ounce per pound under the standard unit." *Synopsis of Provisions of Bill Submitted by Bakers' Committee* (May 23, 1923), SIXTEENTH ANNUAL CONFERENCE ON WEIGHTS AND MEASURES, *supra* note 26, at 112–14.

The Conference's consideration of tolerances in 1924 was derailed by the Court's decision in *Jay Burns.* SEVENTEENTH ANNUAL CONFERENCE ON WEIGHTS AND MEASURES, *supra* note 15, at 126. At the 1924 Conference, the evidence of the plaintiffs' experts in *Jay Burns* was treated with bemused skepticism. F.S. Holbrook of the National Bureau of Standards noted with incredulity that "It is a most remarkable fact that figures indicating shrinkages of as much as 3¾ to 4¼ ounces in 24 hours, on individual loaves weighing about a pound, were exhibited. The temperature and humidity of the air in these cases of excessive shrinkage were not shown, but the notation is made that it was 'dry.' Doubtless it was – very dry. In this relation I might say that the Bureau of Standards has conducted shrinkage experiments on loaves of bread commercially baked and kept in the ordinary way and has never found shrinkages at all comparable to shrinkages such as these. Our experiments are all to the effect that the range in the Nebraska law is an ample one. Figures published by other investigators are to the same effect." *Id.* at 53–54. The Conference went on to endorse the Federal Bread Act, amended to permit a tolerance of "three and one-half ounces per pound in excess of the standard weights." Even after *Jay Burns,* Arizona enacted legislation fixing the standard size of bread loaves with an excess tolerance of only 1 ounce per pound. *See* FEDERAL AND STATE LAWS RELATING TO WEIGHTS AND MEASURES, *supra* note 16, at 74.

34. "What the bakers had thought impossible before the creation of the Food Administration worked like a charm, and the trade, being relieved of the destructive competition in weight and the necessity of constantly watching the juggling of weight by their competitors, could settle down to the more important problem of furnishing the people, even under adverse conditions, with quality bread, at a price which, despite the extraordinary and oftentimes exasperating circumstances, made bread still the cheapest and best food on the American table. . . . This standard weight insisted upon by the Food Administration is one of the regulations referred to as having been found so advantageous by the majority of bakers that in a great many

cities the rule has been either voluntarily adopted as a sound business practice by the bakers or, at the instance of the trade, has been incorporated into new afterwar bakery laws and regulations." H.E. Barnard, Director, American Institute of Baking, *Bread Legislation from the Standpoint of the Baker*, FOURTEENTH ANNUAL CONFERENCE ON WEIGHTS AND MEASURES, *supra* note 14, at 27 (quoting from a paper read before the convention of the Southeastern Bakers' Association). "During the period of war control of the bakers by the United States Food Administration, it was clearly demonstrated that it was entirely feasible for bakers to bake loaves to a uniform size, and this is also admitted by the bakers themselves. This indicates that the proposal to standardize the weight of loaves of bread presents no difficulties of manufacture which may not readily be adjusted." John M. Mote, *Reasons for Standard-Weight Loaves of Bread and Enforcement of Ohio Standard-Weight Bread Law*, FIFTEENTH ANNUAL CONFERENCE ON WEIGHTS AND MEASURES, *supra* note 33, at 89.

35. Brandeis's dissent was joined by Justice Holmes, who commented that it was "A-1. A sockdologer. I agree of course." (Brandeis papers).
36. *Jay Burns*, 264 U.S. at 517.
37. On the essential and pervasive role of judicial notice and nonadjudicative facts in determining constitutionality, see Note, *The Consideration of Facts in "Due Process" Cases*, 30 COLUMBIA LAW REVIEW 360 (1930), which regarded *Jay Burns* as an example of a case in which "facts brought into the record are clearly responsible for some decisions holding legislation invalid." *Id.* at 366.
38. Holmes papers.
39. Henry Wolf Biklé, *Judicial Determination of Questions of Fact Affecting the Constitutional Validity of Legislative Action*, 38 HARVARD LAW REVIEW 6, 15–18 (1924).
40. *Jay Burns*, 264 U.S. at 519 (Brandeis, J., dissenting). *See* Brief and Argument for Defendants in Error, Jay Burns Baking Co. v. Bryan, No. 94, October Term 1923, at 49.
41. *Jay Burns*, 264 U.S. at 516–17:

> Concretely, the sole purpose of fixing the maximum weights, as held by the Supreme Court, is to prevent the sale of a loaf weighing anything over nine ounces for a one pound loaf, and the sale of anything over eighteen ounces for a pound and a half loaf, and so on. The permitted tolerance, as to the half pound loaf, gives the baker the benefit of only one ounce out of the spread of eight ounces, and as to the pound loaf the benefit of only two ounces out of a like spread. There is no evidence in support of the thought that purchasers have been or are likely to be induced to take a nine and a half or a ten ounce loaf (16 ounce) loaf, or an eighteen and a half or a 19 ounce loaf for a pound and a half (24 ounce) loaf, and it is contrary to common experience and unreasonable to assume that there could be any danger of such deception. Imposition through short weights readily could have been dealt with in a direct and effective way.

Jay Burns was thus read by some courts as flatly prohibiting maximum limits on bread weights. *See, e.g.*, Holsum Baking Co. v. Green, 45 F.2d 238, 240 (N. D. Ohio 1930):

> Manifestly, considered as a proper exercise of the state's police powers, there is a distinction between a provision for a surplus tolerance and one for

a deficiency. The latter is manifestly in the public interest as a safeguard against imposition, and, moreover, observance of it entails no substantial embarrassment to the baker, whereas the former, as observed in the *Burns* decision, serves the consuming public in no substantial manner, and it is readily seen to be a definitely hampering restriction in baking operations.

Cf. State v. Curran, 220 Ala. 4 (1929). For a contrary interpretation of *Jay Burns*, see F.S. Holbrook, *The Recent Decision of the United States Supreme Court on Nebraska Bread Law*, SEVENTEENTH ANNUAL CONFERENCE ON WEIGHTS AND MEASURES, *supra* note 15, at 51–59.

42. *Jay Burns*, 264 U.S. at 517.
43. Butler's appreciation of common experience apparently changed after the Depression. In 1934, Butler, in a case upholding a subsequent Nebraska bread regulation law, held that "The fixing of maximum weight for each size or class of loaves is not unreasonable." Peterson Baking Co. v. Bryan, 290 U.S. 570, 573 (1934). Butler then conceded that the "mere prescribing of a minimum weight for each class reasonably may be deemed not effective for there might be made such intermediate sizes as would permit deception and fraud." *Id.* at 574. Butler retroactively explained *Burns Baking* as turning primarily on the difficulty of complying with tolerances of plus or minus 2 ounces per pound. *Id.* at 573.
44. *Jay Burns*, 264 U.S. at 520 (Brandeis, J., dissenting).
45. *Id.* at 533 (Brandeis, J., dissenting). Brandeis fully acknowledged the existence of "evidence contained in the record in this case" that conflicted with the judgment that the Nebraska statute was reasonable. *Id.* But he argued that "with this conflicting evidence we have no concern. It is not our province to weigh evidence." *Id.* at 533–34.
46. 208 U.S. 412 (1908). *See supra* Chapter 8, at 300–1.
47. *Jay Burns*, 264 U.S. at 534 (Brandeis, J., dissenting). For examples of the rich subsequent history of the idea of a "super-legislature," see Obergefell v. Hodges, 576 U.S. 644, 697 (2015) (Roberts, C.J., dissenting); Ewig v. California, 538 U.S. 11, 28 (2003); Board of Trustees of University of Alabama v. Garrett, 531 U.S. 356, 384 (2001) (Breyer, J., dissenting); Heller v. Doe, 509 U.S. 312, 319 (1993); Nollan v. California Coastal Comm'n, 483 U.S. 825, 846 (1987) (Brennan, J., dissenting); Shea v. Louisiana, 470 U.S. 51, 62 (1985) (White J., dissenting); Plyler v. Doe, 457 U.S. 202, 231 (1982) (Blackmun, J., concurring); Hodel v. Indiana, 452 U.S. 314, 333 (1981); City of Mobile v. Bolden, 446 U.S. 55, 76 (1980); Exxon Corp. v. Governor of Maryland, 437 U.S. 117, 124 (1978); New Orleans v. Dukes, 427 U.S. 297, 303 (1976); Paris Adult Theatre I v. Slaton, 413 U.S. 49, 64 (1973); San Antonio Indep. Sch. Dist. v. Rodriquez, 411 U.S. 1, 31 (1973); Shapiro v. Thompson, 394 U.S. 618, 661 (1969) (Harlan, J., dissenting); Desist v. United States, 394 U.S. 244, 259 (1969) (Harlan, J., dissenting); Griswold v. Connecticut, 381 U.S. 479, 482 (1965); Ferguson v. Skrupa, 372 U.S. 726, 731 (1963); Day-Brite Lighting, Inc. v. Missouri, 342 U.S. 421, 423 (1952); Southern Pac. Co. v. Arizona *ex rel.* Sullivan, 325 U.S. 761, 788 n.4 (1945) (Black, J., dissenting); and West Virginia v. State Bd. of Educ. v. Barnette, 319 U.S. 624, 648 (1943) (Frankfurter, J., dissenting).

At the time Brandeis was writing, the phrase "super-legislature" was often used as a term of opprobrium to describe the powerful Anti-Saloon League, the promoter of prohibition, "which has long seemed to regard itself as a super-Legislature." *A Sorry Spectacle*, NEW YORK TIMES (July 31, 1923), at 16. *See Warning from the Super-Government*, NEW YORK TIMES (February 25, 1919), at 10 ("Mr. William H. Anderson, Super-intendent of the New York Anti-Saloon League, the Super-Legislature and Super-Government of the State, has issued another message."); *Drier Dryness*, NEW YORK TIMES (April 27, 1921), at 13 ("From the point of view of a few purists it may be regrettable that the league doesn't possess formally and constitutionally the powers it exercises severely in fact of a Supreme Super-Legislature and Super-Government."). Sometimes the term was also used to disparage the League of Nations. *See Mr. Root's Amendments*, NEW YORK TIMES (March 31, 1919), at 12; *Labor Indorses League after Bitter Debate*, NEW YORK TRIBUNE (June 21, 1919), at 7.

48. Or, even more capaciously, as Brandeis asserted in 1921, "What, at any particular time, is the paramount public need is, necessarily, largely a matter of judgment. Hence, in passing upon the validity of a law challenged as being unreasonable, aid may be derived from the experience of other countries and of the several States of our Union in which the common law and its conceptions of liberty and of property prevail." Truax v. Corrigan, 257 U.S. 312, 356 (1921) (Brandeis, J., dissenting).

49. Oscar E. Monnig, *Constitutional Law – Due Process – Statutes Establishing Standard Weights for Loaves of Bread*, 3 TEXAS LAW REVIEW 447, 450 (1925).

50. Robert Cushman, *Constitutional Law in 1923–1924*, 19 AMERICAN POLITICAL SCIENCE REVIEW 51, 63 (1925). *See* Lochner v. New York, 198 U.S. 45, 64 (1905).

51. LDB to Felix Frankfurter (April 23, 1924), in 5 LETTERS OF LOUIS D. BRANDEIS, at 126. The opinion prompted Holmes to comment to his friend Frederick Pollock that "The Fourteenth Amendment is a roguish thing." OWH to Frederick Pollock (May 11, 1924), in 2 HOLMES-POLLOCK CORRESPONDENCE, at 136.

52. 198 U.S. 45, 59 (1905).

53. Felix Frankfurter, *Hours of Labor and Realism in Constitutional Law*, 29 HARVARD LAW REVIEW 353, 370 (1916). *See* Ernst Freund, *Limitation of Hours of Labor and the Federal Supreme Court*, 17 GREEN BAG 411, 416 (1905) ("Has not the progress of sanitary science shown that common understanding is often equivalent to popular ignorance and fallacy? And if common understanding is to be turned into judicial notice, is there any other case of judicial notice with regard to which respectable judicial opinion is evenly divided?"). *See* HOWARD GILLMAN, THE CONSTITUTION BESIEGED 136 (Durham: Duke University Press 1993).

54. *Jay Burns*, 264 U.S. at 520 (Brandeis, J., dissenting). Brandeis famously repeated his admonition that "if we would guide by the light of reason, we must let our minds be bold" in his magnificent dissent in New Ice Co. v. Liebmann, 285 U.S. 262, 311 (1932) (Brandeis, J., dissenting). From that setting, the aphorism has frequently inspired later judges. *See, e.g.*, Boy Scouts of America v. Dale, 530 U.S. 640, 664 (2000) (Stevens, J., dissenting); Chandler v. Florida, 449 U.S. 560, 579 (1981); Whalen v. Roe, 429 U.S. 589, 597 n.20 (1977); McGautha v. California, 402 U.S. 183, 312 (1971) (Brennan, J., dissenting); Lucas v. Forty-Fourth General Assembly of the State of Colorado, 377 U.S. 713, 752 (1964) (Clark, J., dissenting). By contrast, Brandeis's warning that "Knowledge is essential to understanding, and understanding should precede judging" seems mostly to have influenced scholars. *See, e.g.*, Barry Sullivan, *Just Listening: The Equal Hearing Principle and the Moral Life of Judges*, 48 LOYOLA UNIVERSITY CHICAGO LAW JOURNAL 351, 356

n.12 (2016); Leslie W. Abramson, *What Every Judge Should Know about the Appearance of Impartiality*, 79 ALBANY LAW REVIEW 1579, 1615 (2015–2016); Joel K. Goldstein, *Edmund S. Muskie: The Environmental Leader and Champion*, 67 MAINE LAW REVIEW 225, 230 (2015); Laura Rothstein, *Disability Discrimination Law: The Impact on Legal Education and the Profession*, 51 UNIVERSITY OF LOUISVILLE LAW REVIEW 429, 433 (2013); Paul R. Baier, *Chief Justice Dixon: Twenty Years in Retrospect*, 65 TULANE LAW REVIEW 1, 10 n.42 (1990); Isabel Marcus, *Reflection on the Significance of the Sex/Gender System: Divorce Law Reform in New York*, 42 UNIVERSITY OF MIAMI LAW REVIEW 55, 63 (1987); Serbei S. Zlinkoff, *The American Investor and the Constitutionality of Section 61-B of the New York General Corporation Law*, 54 YALE LAW JOURNAL 352, 358 (1945); Walton H. Hamilton & George D Braden, *The Special Competence of the Supreme Court*, 50 YALE LAW JOURNAL 1319, 1341 n.83 (1941).

55. Thomas Reed Powell, *The Work of the Supreme Court*, 40 POLITICAL SCIENCE QUARTERLY 71, 75 (Supp. 1925). Robert Cushman cited *Jay Burns* as an example of the "willingness of the court to form its own opinion with respect to the existence or nonexistence of the facts upon which the validity of the act must in the last analysis depend, and to adhere to that opinion in the face of the conflicting testimony of experts and the contrary opinion of the legislature." Cushman, *supra* note 50, at 63. A note in the *Yale Law Journal* observed that "the distinguishing characteristic between the majority opinion of the Court ... and the minority ... lies in the absence, in the majority opinion, of any extended discussion of the facts of scientific experience in the making and distribution of bread, and in the almost exclusive devotion of the minority opinion of Justice Brandeis to an exhaustive discussion of the scientific investigations of the federal and state governments and of experts.... It is not necessary even to agree with the preponderant conclusion of the experts in order to believe that the Supreme Court made an error in substituting its own judgment as to policy or reasonableness or appropriateness of means to end for that of the legislature, sustained by the state court." Comment, *State Police Legislation and the Supreme Court*, 33 YALE LAW JOURNAL 847, 848–49 (1924).
56. *The Red Terror of Judicial Reform*, 40 NEW REPUBLIC 110, 113 (1924).
57. John W. Davis, *Drawing Up Profession's Balance Sheet*, 9 AMERICAN BAR ASSOCIATION JOURNAL 93, 94 (1923). Davis lectured American lawyers that "a crucial test of the American system" was "approaching," in which the nation would have to choose "between the doctrines of individual liberty under which we have grown to greatness, and the philosophy of collectivism which can bring in its train nothing but stagnation and decline. On one side is the conviction that the unit of society is the individual and his freedom the State's greatest care; on the other the theory that human society is a concrete whole, and the individual its mere servant." *Id.*
58. *A Phrase Deserving Immortality*, 26 LAW NOTES 221, 221–22 (1923).
59. Pierce Butler, *Some Opportunities and Duties of Lawyers*, in REPORT OF THE FORTY-SIXTH ANNUAL MEETING OF THE AMERICAN BAR ASSOCIATION 220 (Baltimore: Lord Baltimore Press 1923).
60. Pierce Butler, *Educating for Citizenship: Duties the Citizen Owes to the State*, 12 CATHOLIC EDUCATIONAL ASSOCIATION BULLETIN 123, 130 (1915).
61. The sources of this shift can plainly be heard in R.E.L. Saner's presidential address to the American Bar Association later that year: "[T]hrough paternalistic

Diminishing Judicial Deference

legislation, we hear the faint cry of maternalistic bureaus and other bureaus which are insidiously destroying our resourcefulness, our self-sufficiency and our very independence itself." R.E.L. Saner, *Governmental Review*, in REPORT OF THE FORTY-SEVENTH ANNUAL MEETING OF THE AMERICAN BAR ASSOCIATION 137–38 (Baltimore: Lord Baltimore Press 1924). "[I]f unrestrained by the Supreme Court," Saner warned, "our government would degenerate into a paternal, sumptuary bureaucracy, governing, directing and controlling every activity of its citizens, even to the method and manner of their living." *Id.* at 139.

62. This interpretation is consistent with *Jay Burns*'s odd insinuation that Nebraska would apply its statute in bad faith. The tolerances set by the statute were to "be determined by averaging the weight of not less than twenty-five loaves of any one unit." In a startling passage, Butler wrote that because individual loaves will always vary in weight, and because "any loaves of the same unit at any time on hand during 24 hours after baking may be selected to make up the 25 or more to be weighed in order to test compliance with the act," "if only a small percentage of the daily output of the loaves in large bakeries shall exceed the maximum when taken from the oven or fall below the minimum weight within 24 hours, it will always be possible to make up lots of 25 or more loaves whose average weight will be above or below the prescribed limits." 264 U.S. at 514. Butler's interpretation would seem contrary to the rather obvious purpose of taking an average weight of twenty-five loaves. It is certainly contrary to Nebraska's presentation of the statute in its brief. *See* Brief and Argument for Defendants in Error, Jay Burns Baking Co. v. Bryan, No. 94, October Term 1923, at 52. Butler's unwarranted speculations led an employee of the Bureau of Standards later to advise state officials to craft legislation explicitly requiring that "the loaves used in arriving at an average weight ... be taken at random." SEVENTEENTH ANNUAL CONFERENCE ON WEIGHTS AND MEASURES, *supra* note 15, at 58. The employee expressed shock at the Court's imputation of bad faith: "It is inconceivable that an inspector would weigh a large number of loaves and pick out all the lightest or all the heaviest ones to establish a prosecution; nor should he be allowed to do so." *Id.*

63. Norfolk & W. Ry. Co. v. Public Service Commission of West Virginia, 265 U.S. 70, 74 (1924). In *Norfolk & W. Ry Co.* the Court upheld an order of the West Virginia Public Service Commission requiring a railroad to construct and maintain a crossing for the use of vehicles to haul freight across its tracks in a small West Virginia town.

64. *Weaver*, 270 U.S. 402, 415 (1926). Oddly, the Court framed the question as whether the statutory prohibition "violates the due process clause of the equal protection clause." *Id.* at 410.

65. Brief of Appellant, Exhibit B, Weaver v. Palmer Bros., Co. No. 510, October Term 1925.

66. *Weaver*, 270 U.S. at 410.

67. *Id.* at 412, 414–15. Such articles, Butler observed, "are to be distinguished from things that the State is deemed to have power to suppress as inherently dangerous." *Id.* at 412–13.

68. Brief of Appellant 28, 33–34, 18, Weaver v. Palmer Bros., Co. No. 510, October Term 1925.

69. *Weaver*, 270 U.S. at 414–15.

70. *Id.* at 415 (Holmes, J., dissenting).

71. 226 U.S. 192, 201 (1912). "It does not follow that because a transaction, separately considered, is innocuous, it may not be included in a prohibition the scope of which is regarded as essential in the legislative judgment to accomplish a purpose within the admitted power of the government. With the wisdom of the exercise of that judgment the court has no concern." *Id. See* Sturges & Burn Manufacturing Co. v. Beauchamp, 231 U.S. 320, 325 (1913) (holding the government can "select means appropriate to make its prohibition effective."). On the Taft Court's hostility to *Purity Extract*, see *infra* Chapter 26, at 825; *infra* Chapter 30, at notes 59 and 68. *But see infra* Chapter 26, at 838–39. On the Taft Court's ambivalence toward *Purity Extract* in the context of prohibition, compare *infra* Chapter 28, at note 56 and *infra* Chapter 30, at 973 with *infra* Chapter 30, at note 51.
72. *Weaver*, 270 U.S. at 416 (Holmes, J., dissenting).
73. Cuthbert W. Pound, *Defective Law – Its Cause and Remedy*, 1 New York State Bar Association Bulletin 279, 283 (1929). *See* Alfred McCormack, *Book Review*, 26 Columbia Law Review 645, 646 (1926); Note, *Constitutionality of Co-Operative Marketing Acts*, 11 Iowa Law Review 375, 378 (1926).
74. Note, *The Constitutionality of Statutes Creating a Conclusive Presumption that Gifts within a Fixed Period of Death Were Made in Contemplation of Death*, 26 Columbia Law Review 737, 741 (1926).
75. T.F.T. Plucknett, *Book Review*, 27 Columbia Law Review 628, 630 (1927). *See* Robert Cushman, *Constitutional Law in 1925–1926*, 21 American Political Science Review 71, 84–86 (1927); Note, *Act Preventing Use of Shoddy in Manufacture of Comfortables Held Unconstitutional*, 12 Virginia Law Review 662, 663 (1926).
76. 270 U.S. 230, 236 (1926). "Twelve states besides Wisconsin, and Congress in the Federal Estate Law of 1926," had revenue codes with similar conclusive presumptions "for various periods prior to death." Note, *supra* note 74, at 738. The presumptions were "clearly based on the judgment that most gifts made within such period are in contemplation of death, and that nothing short of a conclusive presumption will prevent widespread tax evasion." *Id.*
77. *Schlesinger*, 270 U.S. at 240. The Court did not deny the power of Wisconsin "to tax gifts inter vivos," *id.* at 239, but in the Court's view the conclusive presumption arbitrarily swept certain *inter vivos* gifts into the "graduated" schedule that characterized inheritance taxes, a schedule that "could not properly be laid on all gifts, or, indeed, upon any gift without testamentary character." *Id.* at 240. Three years later, in Bromley v. McCaughn, 280 U.S. 124 (1929), the Court held in an opinion by Stone that an *inter vivos* gift tax could be graduated because it was not a "direct" tax and hence need not be uniform. Sutherland authored a dissent, joined by Van Devanter and Butler. Stone's docket book suggests that in conference McReynolds was uncertain about how to vote.
78. Sanford took the unusual step of concurring in the Court's result alone, not in its opinion.
79. *Schlesinger*, 270 U.S. at 240. The challenge in *Schlesinger* had been under both the Due Process Clause and the Equal Protection Clause. *See supra* note 64. The Court would in 1932 strike down a conclusive presumption in the federal tax code that gifts made within two years of death were made in contemplation of death. Heiner v. Donnan, 285 U.S. 312 (1932). *Heiner* interpreted *Schlesinger* to hold that the

Diminishing Judicial Deference

presumption was invalid because it was "conclusive without regard to actualities, while like gifts at other times were not thus treated." *Id.* at 325.
80. *Schlesinger*, 270 U.S. at 241 (Holmes, J., dissenting).
81. By the end of the Taft Court era, it would be common in the press to observe "the existence of two well defined groups in the nation's highest tribunal – a consistently conservative majority and an equally consistent liberal or even radical minority. In virtually every case of major importance involving constitutional or economic issues in the last three years, Justices Oliver Wendell Holmes, Louis Brandeis, and Harlan F. Stone have stood together in the minority." *3 "Liberals" in Supreme Court Again Dissent to Rail Ruling*, CHICAGO DAILY TRIBUNE (May 22, 1929), at 4. *See* Richard L. Strout, *President Hoover and the Supreme Court*, CHRISTIAN SCIENCE MONITOR (March 11, 1930), at 16.
82. *The Supreme Court as Legislator*, 46 NEW REPUBLIC 158 (1926).
83. Note, *supra* note 74, at 744.
84. 278 U.S. 105 (1928).
85. Louis K. Liggett Co. v. Baldridge, 22 F.2d 993, 996 (E.D. Pa. 1927).
86. Stone's docket book indicates that McReynolds passed in conference. Stone's failure to dissent is noteworthy. Future Justice Owen Roberts represented the appellant.
87. George Sutherland, *Address of the President: Private Rights and Government Control*, in REPORT OF THE FORTIETH ANNUAL MEETING OF THE AMERICAN BAR ASSOCIATION 198 (Baltimore: Lord Baltimore Press 1917). Sutherland decried the "widespread demand for innovating legislation – a craze for change." *Id.* at 200.
88. *Id.* at 199–200. "Unfortunately ... governmental incursions ... are being extended beyond the limits of necessity and even beyond the bounds of expediency into the domain of doubtful experiment." *Id.* at 201.
89. George Sutherland, *Principle or Expedient?*, 5 CONSTITUTIONAL REVIEW 195, 208 (1921). *See* GEORGE SUTHERLAND, SUPERFLUOUS GOVERNMENT: AN ADDRESS BY SENATOR SUTHERLAND OF UTAH 2–4 (Cleveland: Cleveland Chamber of Commerce 1914). *Compare* WILLIAM HOWARD TAFT, THE PRESIDENCY: ITS DUTIES, ITS POWERS, ITS OPPORTUNITIES AND ITS LIMITATIONS 9 (New York: Charles Scribner's Sons 1916) ("In this age and generation ... the danger to the best interests of the country, is in the overwhelming mass of ill-digested legislation."). As late as 1922 Taft could be heard publicly complaining about the "disease of excessive legislation" that has "produced tons of statutory laws under which public money is wasted." WILLIAM HOWARD TAFT, LIBERTY UNDER LAW: AN INTERPRETATION OF THE PRINCIPLES OF OUR CONSTITUTIONAL GOVERNMENT 41 (New Haven: Yale University Press 1922). *See also* WILLIAM HOWARD TAFT, REPRESENTATIVE GOVERNMENT IN THE UNITED STATES 10–13 (New York: New York University Press 1921).
90. Sutherland, *Principle or Expedient*, *supra* note 89, at 209. At about this time, Sutherland wrote a friend that "The tendency everywhere is to over-legislate and to penalize a lot of things that ought to be left to the individual to determine for himself, or at any rate, left to be dealt with by public opinion." GS to Horace H. Smith (March 2, 1921) (Sutherland papers).
91. T.R. Powell, *Supreme Court and State Police Power*, 18 VIRGINIA LAW REVIEW 1, 9 (1931).

92. Comment, *Taxation Directed against the Chain Store*, 40 YALE LAW JOURNAL 431, 435 (1931). *See* Note, 15 VIRGINIA LAW REVIEW 376, 376 (1929) ("The statute was obviously aimed at the chain store corporations operating in Pennsylvania, although the legislature gave as the purpose of the act an attempt to protect the public health and safety.").
93. *Baldridge*, 278 U.S. at 111.
94. *Id.* at 113.
95. "It is a matter of public notoriety that chain drug stores in great numbers, owned and operated by corporations, are to be found throughout the United States. They have been in operation for many years. We take judicial notice of the fact that the stock in these corporations is bought and sold upon the various stock exchanges of the country and, in the nature of things, must be held and owned to a large extent by persons who are not registered pharmacists. If detriment to the public health thereby has resulted or is threatened, some evidence of it ought to be forthcoming. None has been produced, and, so far as we are informed, either by the record or outside of it, none exists. The claim, that mere ownership of a drug store by one not a pharmacist bears a reasonable relation to the public health, finally rests upon conjecture, unsupported by anything of substance. This is not enough; and it becomes our duty to declare the act assailed to be unconstitutional as in contravention of the due process clause of the Fourteenth Amendment." *Id.* at 113–14.
96. Contemporaries observed that although an "attitude of non-interference with state policies once found expression in the majority opinions of the Court, it is now stated in dissents." Comment, *supra* note 92, at 435.
97. *Baldridge*, 278 U.S. at 115 (Holmes, J., dissenting). "Argument has not been supposed to be necessary in order to show that the divorce between the power of control and knowledge is an evil." *Id.* at 114. *Baldridge* should be compared to Roschen v. Ward, 279 U.S. 337 (1929), in which, speaking through Holmes, the Taft Court upheld a New York statute requiring a licensed physician or optometrist to "be in charge of and personal attendance" whenever prescription eyeglasses were sold. "We cannot say, as complainants would have us say, that the supposed benefits are a cloak for establishing a monopoly and a pretense." *Id.* at 340.

CHAPTER 24

Adkins v. Children's Hospital

THE DECISIONS CITED by Sutherland in *Baldridge* to which Holmes bowed were all Taft Court precedents.[1] One decision that Sutherland did not cite in *Baldridge*, but which was undoubtedly the foundation for many subsequent Taft Court cases, was his own 1923 opinion in *Adkins v. Children's Hospital of the District of Columbia*.[2] In the eyes of contemporaries, *Adkins* was the "*chef d'oeuvre* of the Taft Court."[3] It was the decision that decisively set the Taft Court on the path toward normalcy. *Adkins* held that minimum wage legislation enacted by Congress for the District of Columbia was unconstitutional under the Due Process Clause of the Fifth Amendment.

Speaking for a majority of five, Sutherland in *Adkins* laid the theoretical groundwork for the Taft Court's increasingly aggressive attitude toward exercises of the police power. "There is, of course, no such thing as absolute freedom of contract," Sutherland wrote. "But freedom of contract is, nevertheless, the general rule and restraint the exception, and the exercise of legislative authority to abridge it can be justified only by the existence of exceptional circumstances."[4] This is the precise proposition that five years later Sutherland would lucidly set in doctrine in *Baldridge*. *Adkins* would also generate a distinctively dogmatic and unbending line of Taft Court precedents that categorically prohibited price fixing unless property was "affected with a public interest." This was the line of cases that eventually drove Stone into the jurisprudential arms of Brandeis and Holmes.[5]

Adkins concerned a 1918 federal statute requiring minimum wages for women and minors in the District of Columbia.[6] The purpose of the Act was "to protect the women and minors of the District from conditions detrimental to their health and morals, resulting from wages which are inadequate to maintain decent standards of living."[7] Enacted "while the country was still inspired by war conditions to subordinate individual rights of liberty and property to the accomplishment of the common good,"[8] the Act was relatively uncontroversial, passing with only sixteen negative votes in the House[9] and only twelve negative votes in the Senate.[10] Although legislation fixing minimum wages for women was a recent innovation in the United States – the first such statute was enacted in 1912 – Congress could by 1918 draw on existing legislation in eleven states.[11] The constitutionality of gender-based minimum wage legislation had been upheld in decisions by four state supreme courts.[12]

Back in December 1914, Brandeis had himself argued before the Supreme Court when it reviewed the first of these decisions, the Oregon case of *Stettler v. O'Hara*.[13] The case mysteriously lay dormant for years, but was restored to the docket for reargument after Brandeis's appointment to the Court in 1916. By then Frankfurter had succeeded Brandeis as counsel *extraordinaire* for the National Consumers' League, and it was Frankfurter who reargued the case in January 1917.[14]

Eventually the Oregon Supreme Court decision upholding the legislation was affirmed by an equally divided Court on April 9, 1917, with Brandeis recusing himself. Most believed, therefore, that between 1916 and 1922 a majority of five justices were prepared to affirm the constitutionality of legislation establishing minimum wages for women.[15] *Adkins* was eagerly anticipated as the case that "will be the first to show the alignment of the new court,"[16] which had been augmented by Harding's appointments. When finally released, Sutherland's opinion for McKenna, Van Devanter, McReynolds, and Butler was "surprising and shocking"[17] in its prohibition of what until then had virtually been taken for granted.[18]

Stripped to its essentials, the theory of minimum wage legislation for women was that large numbers of women were receiving wages less than those required to sustain "the barest necessaries" of life.[19] The statute was justified on the ground that "the health of a considerable section of the present generation was impaired by undernourishment, demoralizing shelter and insufficient medical care. Inevitably, the coming generation was thereby threatened.... [F]inancial burdens were imposed upon the District involving excessive and unproductive taxation, for the support of charitable and quasi-charitable institutions engaged in impotent amelioration rather than prevention."[20]

The D.C. statute established a Minimum Wage Board to set a "living wage" for women. The wage was calculated to make up "for the deficit between the cost of women's labor – i.e., the means necessary to keep labor going – and any rate of women's pay below the minimum level for living, and thereby to eliminate all the evils attendant upon such a deficit on a large scale."[21] Frankfurter represented the District. He filed a sprawling 1,138-page Brandeis brief, filled with what Sutherland called a "mass of reports, opinions of special observers and students of the subject,"[22] which sought to demonstrate that the harms identified by Congress were real and that Congress's choice of a remedy was not arbitrary.[23]

The question presented by *Adkins* was whether the minimum wage statute was inconsistent with "the right to contract about one's affairs" that inhered in "the liberty of the individual protected" by the Due Process Clause.[24] The statute was challenged by the Children's Hospital of the District of Columbia, which alleged that the statute interfered with its right to employ "a number of women – scrubwomen, washerwomen, attendants, etc. – at less than the minimum wage." It was also challenged by Willie A. Lyons, a 21-year-old woman employed by the Congress Hall Hotel, who was fired after the Hotel claimed that it could not afford to employ her at the minimum wage.[25]

Adkins v. Children's Hospital

Alleging that the statute was "a 'price fixing' law, pure and simple," these plaintiffs argued that *"the amount of the charge* received ... for ... labor in private business can not *itself* be called a matter affecting the public health, morals or safety, and thus brought within the scope of the police power." "The reason for this ... is that the Constitution itself has laid down certain fundamental principles of economics in establishing private ownership of property and individual liberty; that these principles can not *themselves* be declared to be inimical to the public health, safety, morals or welfare, and changed under the guise of an exercise of the 'police power.'"[26]

Plaintiffs argued that legislation establishing minimum wages was different from legislation "limiting work in underground mines or restricting hours of labor." The latter "directly" promotes health and safety, and even if they "affect indirectly contractual relations between individuals or cause loss to one or gain to another," this redistribution is a "secondary" result, "not the 'evil' aimed at." "[T]o take the property of A and give it to B, C and D is fundamentally different, even though by enriching B, C and D, their health or morals might be promoted indirectly. Laws which would transfer the money of one individual to another or fix the amount of money to be given in exchange for property, cannot have any real or direct relation to health."[27]

To modern eyes, it might appear as if the argument framed for the Court was about Congress's actual subjective purpose in enacting minimum wage legislation. Was it to protect the health and morals of women, or was it instead to redistribute wealth from employers to women employees? It is fair to say, however, that nothing in *Adkins* turned on the subjective intent of Congress. Instead, the Court was concerned with whether government was constitutionally empowered to manipulate the price of labor to protect the health of workers.

In the years after the Civil War, the Court interpreted the Constitution to prohibit "'class', 'special', 'partial', or 'unequal' legislation, 'legislation that could not be regarded as public-regarding because it benefited certain interests groups or took from A to give to B.'"[28] It is accurate to say that "one of the central distinctions in nineteenth-century constitutional law" was that "between valid economic regulation," which served the public interest, and "invalid 'class legislation,'" which served merely factional or partial interests.[29] The Court's hostility to "class legislation" – to legislation that benefited only particular persons rather than the public as a whole – had deep roots in the antifactionalism of the Founding period, as well as in the antiprivilege stance of Jacksonian Democracy.[30] Although Holmes from the outset conceived legislation as little more than the outcome of class struggle,[31] this intellectual framework was deeply impressed on other members of the Taft Court like Taft and Sutherland.[32]

The basic idea behind prohibiting class legislation was "to distinguish between legislation for the common benefit and legislation that benefitted or burdened the few."[33] This distinction lost analytic traction, however, when states at the turn of the century began to pass laws to provide for the safety of particular occupations or groups – for example legislation limiting hours of work for underground miners[34] or for women[35] – and when this legislation was nevertheless upheld because "the whole is no greater than the sum of all the parts, and when the individual health, safety, and welfare are sacrificed or neglected, the state must suffer."[36]

757

Once the good of the entire public became indistinguishable from the good of its component parts, the very idea of class legislation became hopelessly ambiguous.[37] It was no longer clear what it meant to say that "the power of government could not be legitimately exercised to benefit one person or group at the expense of others."[38] Constitutional inquiry accordingly evolved from the question of whether legislation aided particular groups and began to focus instead on whether legislation actually created the benefits that were said to justify its enactment. The point can be illustrated by *Lochner v. New York*.[39]

In *Lochner*, the Court considered a New York statute limiting the hours of bakers to ten hours per day or sixty hours per week.[40] New York sought to justify its law as necessary to preserve the health of bakers. The question posed by the Court was whether the legislation was "a fair, reasonable, and appropriate exercise of the police power of the state, or is it an unreasonable, unnecessary, and arbitrary interference with the right of the individual to his personal liberty, or to enter into those contracts in relation to labor which may seem to him appropriate or necessary for the support of himself and his family?" Appealing to "common understanding," the Court ruled "that there can be no fair doubt that the trade of a baker, in and of itself, is not an unhealthy one to that degree which would authorize the legislature to interfere with the right to labor."[41]

The Court did not ask whether the New York statute served the interests of bakers or of the public. It instead asked whether the legislation was necessary to preserve the health of bakers. If the legislation did materially improve the health of its beneficiaries, the Court was prepared to accept it as both contributing to the public good and as justifiably interfering with the bakers' freedom of contract. *Lochner* held, however, that the "mere assertion that the subject relates, though but in a remote degree, to the public health, does not necessarily render the enactment valid. The act must have a more direct relation, as a means to an end, and the end itself must be appropriate and legitimate, before an act can be held to be valid which interferes with the general right of an individual to be free in his person and in his power to contract in relation to his own labor."[42]

The Court, in other words, began to ask whether legislation actually produced the benefits that were claimed to justify its enactment. If the causal connection between the legislation and its benefits was not close enough, the Court would hold that the legislation's impairment of contractual freedom was not constitutionally justifiable. This framework of analysis set the pattern for Taft Court decisions like *Jay Burns*, *Weaver*, or *Baldridge*, each of which focused entirely on the instrumental adequacy of a statute's justification.

In an important passage that presaged the specific argument of the plaintiffs in *Adkins*, *Lochner* also held that New York could not limit the hours of bakers merely "as a labor law, pure and simple."

> There is no reasonable ground for interfering with the liberty of person or the right of free contract, by determining the hours of labor, in the occupation of a baker. There is no contention that bakers as a class are not equal in intelligence and capacity to men in other trades or manual occupations, or that they are not able to assert their rights and care for themselves without the protecting arm of the

Adkins v. Children's Hospital

state, interfering with their independence of judgment and of action. They are in no sense wards of the state. Viewed in the light of a purely labor law, with no reference whatever to the question of health, we think that a law like the one before us involves neither the safety, the morals, nor the welfare, of the public, and that the interest of the public is not in the slightest degree affected by such an act. The law must be upheld, if at all, as a law pertaining to the health of the individual engaged in the occupation of a baker.[43]

The Court did not explain exactly why the New York legislation would be unconstitutional *per se* as a labor law.[44] Perhaps it was because, viewed as a "purely labor law," the legislation would improperly presuppose that bakers were incompetent to contract as mature adults. Or perhaps it was because a purely labor law would constitute prohibited class legislation, for its only purpose would be the forbidden objective of redistributing income from employers to bakers.[45] Or perhaps it was because the only justification of a purely labor law was the constitutionally prohibited purpose of negating the valuable constitutional "right of free contract."[46] Or perhaps it was because a purely labor law would unconstitutionally "take" property without compensation.[47] Whatever the explanation, some statutory regulations were simply off-limits for the state, and in effect that is what the plaintiffs in *Adkins* alleged.

Defending the minimum wage law, Frankfurter established in *Adkins* that Congress's stated purpose in enacting the legislation was to protect the health and morals of women. These were manifestly proper government objectives. Frankfurter then offered a mass of evidence designed to show that Congress's legislation was rationally related to these objectives.[48] Drawing on the tradition of *Lochner*, plaintiffs in *Adkins* rejected Frankfurter's arguments on the ground that fixing the wages of women could not, *as a matter of law*, be held to promote the health of women, for explicit price fixing must constitutionally be deemed "only remotely or indirectly" connected to the purpose of promoting health.[49]

Although Sutherland found for the plaintiffs, he did not accept their reasoning. He knew that government commonly regulated prices for "property affected with a public interest," as for example when it engaged in ratemaking for utilities. Sutherland therefore did not want to accept an argument that would categorically sever ratemaking and price controls from all forms of instrumental justification.

Instead, Sutherland chose to stress those aspects of *Lochner* that emphasized the need for a tight instrumental fit between the objective of legislation and its actual benefits. Restrictions on freedom of contract could be justified only if there were good evidence of "direct relation, as a means to an end" for the restrictions. In effect this put the burden of justification on the government, which was the essence of *Lochner*'s legacy. Although Sutherland asserted that this placement of the burden had "never been disapproved,"[50] the Court had in fact abandoned it in 1917 in *Bunting v. Oregon*, which, over the dissenting votes of White, Van Devanter, and McReynolds, had upheld an Oregon statute limiting work to ten hours per day for men and women "in any mill, factory or manufacturing establishment in this State."[51] Sutherland mentioned *Bunting*, but confined it to its facts.[52]

Determining whether a statute's requirements were adequately connected to its ends would seem to involve the Court in an empirical inquiry. But Sutherland explicitly ignored the massive evidentiary record presented by Frankfurter's brief, claiming that it was only "mildly persuasive" and was relevant only to "the desirability or undesirability of the legislation" and shed "no legitimate light upon the question of its validity." In a remarkable arrogation of authority, Sutherland relied on neither evidence nor precedents to conclude that the minimum wage statute was "a naked, arbitrary exercise of power."[53] Sutherland reached this conclusion based purely upon deductive reasoning.[54] With a single sweep of his hand, Sutherland ruled out as constitutionally irrelevant the evidence of administrative practice and history that Brandeis had struggled for a lifetime to introduce into the Court's constitutional repertoire.[55]

Unleashing a barrage of objections, Sutherland found much to criticize in Congress's minimum wage statute.[56] He complained that the "standard furnished by the statute for the guidance of the board is so vague as to be impossible of practical application with any reasonable degree of accuracy."[57] He argued that it was impossible to set a standard minimum wage because each worker, depending on their particular financial circumstances, required a different weekly income to meet the necessities of life.[58] He asserted that "the relation between earnings and morals is not capable of standardization."[59] He protested that the law "ignores the necessities of the employer" by imposing obligations on him "irrespective of the ability of his business to sustain the burden." He worried that the authority to fix a minimum wage implied the authority to fix a maximum wage, which would widen "the field for the operation of the police power ... to a great and dangerous degree." He objected that the law compels an employer to pay a minimum wage "because the employee needs it, but requires no service of equivalent value from the employee.... To the extent that the sum fixed exceeds the fair value of the services rendered, it amounts to a compulsory exaction from the employer for the support of a partially indigent person, for whose condition there rests upon him no peculiar responsibility."[60]

The "feature of this statute, which perhaps more than any other, puts upon it the stamp of invalidity," Sutherland wrote, "is that it exacts from the employer an arbitrary payment for a purpose and upon a basis having no causal connection with his business, or the contract or the work the employee engages to do.... The moral requirement implicit in every contract of employment, viz. that the amount to be paid and the service to be rendered shall bear to each other some relation of just equivalence, is completely ignored."[61]

The farrago of objections in Sutherland's *Adkins* opinion makes the decision confusing to parse, because it is impossible to determine what force to attribute to any given point. Taken individually, Sutherland's complaints do not amount to much. It would be bold indeed to strike down the statute because it delegated too much discretion to the Minimum Wage Board, for the Court had approved delegations that were far less specific.[62] That different individual workers might require different levels of support to meet life's requirements is a mere cavil; the same might be said of maximum hours legislation because individual workers possess different levels of physical stamina. The causal connection between low earnings and prostitution is an

Adkins v. Children's Hospital

empirical question, but Sutherland categorically repudiated the relevance of empirical data.[63] Minimum wage legislation no more ignores the "necessities" of employers than does maximum hours legislation; each limits an employer's freedom of contract in light of a categorical judgment about the needs of employees. It is, as Taft politely observed in his dissent, a simple "*non sequitur*" to claim that the power to fix a minimum wage implies the power to fix a maximum wage.[64] If it is constitutionally objectionable to exact obligations from employers without demanding corresponding obligations from employees, it is an objection that equally applies against laws limiting hours of employment.

Cutting through the thicket of complaints, the crux of Sutherland's critique lay in his claim that the statute arbitrarily required employers to pay for the needs of employees, thus violating the core "moral requirement implicit in every contract of employment" that wages and service "shall bear to each other some relation of just equivalence." Sutherland's indictment of the statute combines two distinct assertions: (1) That it is *arbitrary* to fasten on employers obligations to subsidize employee necessities for which employers bear "no peculiar responsibility"; and (2) that in so doing minimum wage legislation *ruptures* the "just" or "fair" exchange of value that is the essence of an employment contract. Sutherland asserted that regulating price, in contrast to regulating hours, goes to "the heart of the contract, that is, the amount of wages to be paid and received."[65]

With regard to the first of these assertions, minimum wage legislation rests on the premise that wages represent the primary income of most employees and that, therefore, if wages cannot cover the living costs of employees, workers will become wards of the state. Minimum wage legislation thus requires employers to internalize the cost of maintaining the lives of laborers and to pass that cost on to consumers in the form of higher prices. This is precisely the rationale that Sutherland himself had articulated in his powerful 1913 defense of workmen's compensation laws: "The great industries of to-day are engaged in producing commodities or in rendering services for the general public. The consumers of these commodities or the recipients of these services are justly obligated to pay what they cost plus a fair return upon investment.... The injury of a workman resulting in loss of earning ability or death as truly enters into the cost of production as the breaking of a piece of machinery. ... There is no reason why the industry should not bear the expense ... collecting it in the last analysis from the consumer just as it collects every other item of expense entering into the production."[66]

Workmen's compensation legislation forces employers to assume the costs of accidents that they do not individually cause, in the sense of acting negligently to injure employees. Sutherland accepted this attribution of responsibility because:

> It must be frankly recognized that the compensation law substitutes the communistic idea of benefit for the whole class in place of the individualistic theory which permits a minority of the class to recover much and the majority little or nothing. The justification for a compulsory and exclusive workmen's compensation law rests in the conception that the workmen employed in any enterprise are industrial soldiers, who being injured in its service are entitled to be cared for to a fair and equitable extent, having in view the ability of the industry to pay.[67]

Minimum wage legislation assumes the very same relationship between employers and employees as does workmen's compensation legislation.[68] In Sutherland's words, "Workmen's Compensation legislation rests upon the idea of status, not upon that of implied contract; that is, upon the conception that the injured workman is entitled to compensation for an injury sustained in the service of an industry to whose operations he contributes his work as the owner contributes his capital – the one for the sake of the wages and the other for the sake of the profits."[69]

The distinctive status of employees recognized by Sutherland in the context of workmen's compensation legislation contradicts Sutherland's claim in *Adkins* that "[i]n principle, there can be no difference between the case of selling labor and the case of selling goods."[70] When Sutherland argued in *Adkins* that the principle of minimum wage legislation would equally justify requiring a grocer to sell discounted food to a starving and penurious customer,[71] he was overlooking the obvious fact that no status relationship exists between a grocer and her customers. But Sutherland himself defended workmen's compensation legislation in terms of the special status relationship between employers and employees, and this same relationship was equally pertinent in the context of minimum wage legislation.[72] The existence of this status relationship meant that it was not *arbitrary* to allocate the costs of both industrial accidents and employee subsistence to the employer/employee nexus.

In advocating for workmen's compensation laws, Sutherland had been careful to caution that "our righteous anxiety to minimize human suffering" may be taken too far insofar as it eliminates "the stimulating necessity of personal effort which compels us to rise." "The unfortunate must be cared for; the soldiers of industry who fall must be lifted up, but no deadlier check could be put upon the upward march of civilization than to embark upon such a scheme of emotional socialism as would put upon the backs of the strong not only the care of those who can not but of those who can but will not bear their own burdens. In framing our laws we must never lose sight of the vital distinction between helplessness, which is a misfortune, and laziness, which is a vice."[73]

It was essential to Sutherland that law not impair incentives that encourage individual initiative and effort. Sutherland believed that the Constitution protected property in order to maintain "the upward march of civilization." It is possible that Sutherland's opposition to minimum wage legislation was driven by his belief that it misaligned incentives and required the strong to carry the lazy on their backs.[74] But in drafting his opinion in *Adkins*, Sutherland did not choose to offer an argument of this kind. Instead, he crafted objections sounding in morals and traditional contract law.

Sutherland argued that the federal minimum wage statute was "simply and exclusively a price fixing law"[75] that deprived employers of the "just" or "fair" exchange of value that is "the *moral* requirement implicit in every contract of employment."[76] Sutherland asserted that the mark of an employment contract is that, "generally speaking, the parties have an equal right to obtain from each other the best terms they can as the result of private bargaining."[77] By requiring that employees receive more than the "fair" or "just" value of their work, as defined by

Adkins v. Children's Hospital

voluntary exchange in the market, minimum wage legislation corrupts the "heart" of the employment contract and improperly deprives the employer of valuable property.

The difficulty with this line of argument is that it rests upon a simple and obvious fallacy. There is nothing intrinsically "fair" or "just" or "moral" about wage contracts. A wage contract represents merely what Sutherland (referencing Adam Smith) called the "higgling of the market."[78] The market does not necessarily produce fair, just, or moral bargains.[79] Indeed, the contrast between "real" and "market" value was, as we have seen, the basis of the Court's decision one month after *Adkins* in *United States v. New River Collieries Co.*,[80] in which the Court held that market price, rather than "real" value, should measure compensation for property confiscated by the state.[81] In a properly functioning market, employment wages represent a voluntary meeting of the minds that may or may not be "fair," "just" or "moral."[82]

The essential question, then, was whether there was good reason to distrust the voluntary character of women's wages determined by the "higgling" of the labor market. Sutherland himself had acknowledged the relevance of this inquiry when, in defending workmen's compensation legislation, he explained that traditional common law assumption-of-risk doctrine should be abandoned because "the laborer in modern industry in this day of sharp competition is not quite free to accept or refuse work at his pleasure."[83] Sutherland believed that workmen's compensation legislation should be based on the "status" of the employment relationship, rather than on "contract," precisely because he understood that the labor market did not permit truly voluntary bargaining in the context of workplace safety.

It is an empirical question whether in any given labor market there is a voluntary meeting of the minds between employers and employees. Much evidence suggests that there was no such voluntary meeting of the minds in the market for women wage workers. Women were paid less than men for equivalent work, and they were less well organized than men.[84] Ultimately the case for the District of Columbia minimum wage statute "depended upon the belief that women might be forced by necessity to accept" inadequate wages,[85] just as the case for workmen's compensation legislation depended upon the belief that employees might be forced by necessity to accept work that was inherently unsafe.

Sutherland's answer to the empirical question of voluntariness was characteristically formal and abstract. He asserted that the District's minimum wage statute forbade "two parties having lawful capacity ... to freely contract with one another in respect of the price for which one shall render service to the other in a purely private employment where both are willing, perhaps anxious, to agree." As for the specific status of women's labor, Sutherland remarked that the "revolutionary changes which have taken place ... in the contractual, political and civil status of women, culminating in the Nineteenth Amendment," have diminished nonphysical differences between the sexes almost "to the vanishing point."[86] "We cannot accept the doctrine that women of mature age, *sui juris*, require or may be subjected to restrictions upon their liberty of contract which could not lawfully be imposed in the case of men under similar circumstances. To do so would be to ignore all the implications to be drawn from the present day trend of legislation, as well as that of common thought and usage, by which woman is accorded emancipation from the old doctrine that she must be given special protection or be subjected to special restraint in her contractual and civil relationships."[87]

It is not clear, however, why the Nineteenth Amendment was relevant to the facts of *Adkins*.[88] Unlike the maximum hours legislation in *Muller*, the constitutional case for the District of Columbia minimum wage statute did not invoke physical differences between men and women.[89] Nor did the case for the statute rest on the claim that women, like minors, were inherently unable competently to engage in contractual bargaining, an argument that the Nineteenth Amendment might indeed have ruled out of order. Instead, the constitutionality of the statute rested on a diagnosis of the structure of the market for women's wages. The justification for the statute was that this market did not reflect the voluntary choices of women.[90] State intervention was thus justified for the same reason that Sutherland himself had acknowledged as compelling in the context of workmen's compensation laws[91] or in the context of statutes setting maximum hours for the work of underground miners.[92]

Ultimately, the argument for congressional minimum wage legislation was that "[l]ack of organization, the brevity of [women's] industrial life, the large numbers of them ready to compete for unskilled jobs, the tradition of lower wages, the presence of many women working only for pin money and underbidding those who must earn a living ... have convinced most people that women in industry" were unable to contract for the full value of their labor.[93] By refusing in *Adkins* to attend to empirical evidence that might either support or undermine the reasonableness of that claim, Sutherland undercut the ground from his own condemnation of the statute.[94]

Brandeis did not participate in the Court's deliberations because his daughter Elizabeth was secretary to the Minimum Wage Board.[95] Taft authored a dissenting opinion that Sanford joined; Holmes dissented separately.[96] *Adkins* was commonly and appropriately received as the equivalent of a close five-to-four decision.[97] Two weeks after its release, Van Devanter confided to his friend District Judge John Pollock that "[i]n many ways I have been fairly pleased with the court's work, more so than with that of two or three years. However, the narrow vote by which a sane doctrine prevailed in the Women's Minimum Wage admonishes one that he should not be too optimistic."[98]

Holmes's dissent was basically what one would expect.[99] Adopting Frankfurter's framing of the case, he affirmed that "the power of Congress seems absolutely free from doubt."

> The end, to remove conditions leading to ill health, immorality and the deterioration of the race, no one would deny to be within the scope of constitutional legislation. The means are means that have the approval of Congress, of many States, and of those governments from which we have learned our greatest lessons. When so many intelligent persons, who have studied the matter more than any of us can, have thought that the means are effective and are worth the price it seems to me impossible to deny that the belief reasonably may be held by reasonable men.[100]

Adkins v. Children's Hospital

Holmes was especially perturbed because the statute was so plainly valid when measured against any of the "specific provisions of the Constitution." No one contended, for example, that the law took "private property without just compensation."[101] Instead the Court condemned the statute using only "the vague contours of the Fifth Amendment." But this was to constrain legislative discretion based purely on a judicially created "dogma" of "Liberty of Contract." "Contract," said Holmes, "is not specially mentioned in the text that we have to construe. It is merely an example of doing what you want to do, embodied in the word liberty. But pretty much all law consists in forbidding men to do some things that they want to do, and contract is no more exempt from law than other acts."[102] Usury laws exemplified constitutional price regulations that constricted freedom of contract.

Sutherland was also wrong to think there was some untouchable "heart" to a contract; "the bargain is equally affected" by legislation restricting hours of employment. Holmes was particularly distressed that Sutherland spent more than two pages quoting at length from *Lochner*. Holmes believed that *Lochner* should instead "be allowed a deserved repose."[103] "The criterion of constitutionality," Holmes stressed, "is not whether we believe the law to be for the public good," but whether "a reasonable man reasonably" might believe it to be so. This criterion was satisfied "by a very remarkable collection of documents submitted on behalf of the appellants."[104]

If Holmes's opinion was unsurprising,[105] Taft's dissent was distinctly unexpected. But Taft had co-chaired the War Labor Board, and under his leadership the Board had declared that "all workers, including common laborers," were entitled "to a living wage."[106] Taft was therefore unlikely to accept Sutherland's glib attacks on the indeterminacy and incoherence of the very concept of a minimum wage.[107] Taft in fact chided Sutherland for relying on distinctions "formal rather than real."[108]

Taft's dissent was powerful and cogent. He precisely identified the premise of minimum wage legislation. It proceeded, Taft said, "on the assumption that employees, in the class receiving least pay, are not upon a full level of equality of choice with their employer and in their necessitous circumstances are prone to accept pretty much anything that is offered. They are peculiarly subject to the overreaching of the harsh and greedy employer. The evils of the sweating system and of the long hours and low wages which are characteristic of it are well known." That the minimum wage for any given employee may be over or under inclusive was irrelevant, so long as the specified value of the minimum wage inures "to the benefit of the general class of employees in whose interest the law is passed and so to that of the community at large."[109]

Taft also condemned Sutherland's decision to rehabilitate *Lochner*. He considered it "extreme."[110] Taft wrote that "[i]t is impossible for me to reconcile the *Bunting Case* and the *Lochner Case* and I have always supposed that the *Lochner Case* was thus overruled *sub silentio*."[111] Insofar as the Court did not mean to overrule *Bunting*, Taft argued that there was no constitutional distinction "between a minimum of wages and a maximum of hours in the limiting of liberty to a contract. . . . In absolute freedom of contract the one term is as important as the other, for both enter equally into the consideration given and received, a restriction as to one is not any greater in essence than the other, and is of the same kind. One is the multiplier and the other the multiplicand." Certainly, the Court should have respected the evidence presented "in the record and in the literature" that low wages and long hours "are equally harmful" to the "health" of employees. Taft was careful not to express an opinion about minimum wages for adult men, but he cited *Muller* for the proposition that it was peculiarly within the province of government to protect the health of women.[112]

It was a heartfelt, compact, trenchant performance,[113] but Taft would never again exercise such public independence from the gravitational pull of his conservative brethren.[114] In the course of the decade, *Adkins* would flower into a line of cases prohibiting price fixing that would set the Court on a collision course with the New Deal, and Taft would be solidly with the majority.

Adkins provoked an immediate public furor.[115] It was said that no Supreme Court decision "in many years has aroused the public interest created" by *Adkins*.[116] The shock of Sutherland's deliberate resurrection of *Lochner* can hardly be overstated.[117] Only two years before, in his Storrs Lectures at Yale, published to general acclaim as *The Nature of the Judicial Process*, the well-tempered Benjamin Cardozo had confidently referred to Holmes's *Lochner* dissent as "the voice of a new dispensation, which has written itself into law" and whose "dominance is . . . assured."[118] Within the world of scholarship, *Adkins* was received with "practically unanimous disapproval"[119] as "a step backward, to be retraced at the first opportunity."[120] T.R. Powell encapsulated the general judgment: "As a flagrant instance of insufficient reasons and of a judgment widely regarded as an indefensible judgment, the minimum-wage decision has few, if any, rivals."[121] *Adkins* was condemned as "the most deplorable pronouncement of the court since the Dred Scott decision."[122]

Adkins provoked the governors of Washington,[123] Oregon,[124] and Wisconsin[125] to call for a meeting of governors to discuss a constitutional amendment to authorize Congress to prohibit child labor and to set minimum wages.[126] Coolidge himself in his first State of the Union called for a constitutional amendment that would enable Congress to pass minimum wage legislation for women "in all cases under the exclusive jurisdiction of the Federal Government."[127] *Adkins* prompted others, like the governor of Arizona and Senator Robert La Follette, to go further and demand a constitutional amendment that would authorize Congress to override judicial decisions finding federal statutes unconstitutional.[128] *Adkins* spurred the efforts of still others, like Idaho Senator William Borah, to seek congressional legislation preventing the Supreme Court from constitutionally invalidating federal legislation with less than a seven-person majority.[129]

In the end almost nothing came from any of these movements. A few states, particularly on the West Coast, persisted in open defiance of *Adkins*, even after the Court reaffirmed the unconstitutionality of minimum wage statutes in cases involving Arizona (1925) and Arkansas (1927).[130] But with the crushing defeat of La Follette's third-party presidential bid in 1924, open agitation against the Court's power of judicial review effectively subsided for the remainder of the decade. As Taft wrote Van Devanter in June 1925, "I don't think I am mistaken in thinking that Borah and that ilk are losing interest in efforts to change the Court."[131]

Adkins v. Children's Hospital

Notes

1. To support the key assertions in his *Baldridge* opinion, Sutherland cited: "Burns Baking Co. v. Bryan, 264 U.S. 504, 513. *See also* Meyer v. Nebraska, 262 U.S. 390, 399–400; Norfolk Ry. v. Public Service Comm'n, 265 U.S. 70, 74; Pierce v. Society of Sisters, 268 U.S. 510, 534–535; Weaver v. Palmer Bros. Co., 270 U.S. 402, 412–15; Fairmont Co. v. Minnesota, 274 U.S. 1, 9–11." Louis K. Liggett Co. v. Baldridge, 278 U.S. 105, 113 (1928).
2. 261 U.S. 525 (1923).
3. Edward S. Corwin, *Social Planning under the Constitution – A Study in Perspectives*, 26 AMERICAN POLITICAL SCIENCE REVIEW 1, 19 (1932). In 1931, contemporaries believed that *Adkins* was "the case which, next to the New York Bakers case, is considered by intelligent modern thinkers to be the one most unjust and hurtful to the needs of humble men in an oppressive industrial age." Joseph P. Pollard, *Justice Sutherland Dissents*, 158 OUTLOOK AND INDEPENDENT 496 (August 19, 1931).
4. *Adkins*, 261 U.S. at 546. In 1914, Sutherland declared to the Cleveland Chamber of Commerce that "the perfect freedom of the individual, within certain broad limits, to do as he pleases is so vital to the lasting progress of humanity that whoever seeks to interfere with it must assume the burden of demonstrating the necessity. . . . [I]t must be determined in advance whether the harm resulting from the objectionable conduct is of so grave a nature as to justify its suppression by a resort to the opposing evil of interference with the freedom of the individual. . . . Generally speaking, I think individual conduct should be left to be regulated and governed by moral restraint rather than by statutory enactment, unless it can be clearly shown that interference by legislative enactment is necessary for the preservation of the rights of others or for the protection of society as a whole." GEORGE SUTHERLAND, SUPERFLUOUS GOVERNMENT: AN ADDRESS BY SENATOR SUTHERLAND OF UTAH 4–6 (Cleveland: Cleveland Chamber of Commerce 1914).
5. *See supra* Chapter 4, at 129–32.
6. Pub. L. 65-215, 40 Stat. 960 (September 19, 1918).
7. 40 Stat. 964.
8. Thomas I. Parkinson, *Minimum Wage and the Constitution*, 13 AMERICAN LABOR LEGISLATION REVIEW 131, 131 (1923).
9. 56 CONG. REC. 10732–33 (September 24, 1918).
10. 56 CONG. REC. 10285 (September 13, 1918).
11. Massachusetts (1912); California (1913); Colorado (1913); Minnesota (1913); Oregon (1913); Utah (1913); Washington (1913); Wisconsin (1913); Arkansas (1915); Kansas (1915); and Arizona (1917). The relevant statutes are in the Brief for Appellants, Adkins v. Children's Hospital of the District of Columbia, No. 795 October Term 1922, at 584–686 ("*Adkins* Brief for Appellants").
12. Stettler v. O'Hara, 69 Or. 519 (1914); State v. Crowe, 130 Ark. 272 (1917); Williams v. Evans, 139 Minn. 32 (1917); Larsen v. Rice, 100 Wash. 642 (1918).
13. 69 Or. 519 (1914), *aff'd by an equally divided court*, 243 U.S. 629 (1917). *See* LDB to Felix Frankfurter (March 29, 1937), in BRANDEIS-FRANKFURTER CORRESPONDENCE, at 594. Brandeis wrote Frankfurter on the occasion of West Coast Hotel v. Parrish, 300 U.S. 379 (1937), which overruled *Adkins*: "Overruling Adkins' Case must give you some satisfaction." Frankfurter replied: "It is

characteristically kind of you to think of the aspects of the Washington minimum wage case that would give me some satisfaction, but, unhappily, it is one of life's bitter-sweets and the bitter far outweighs the sweet." Quoted in BRANDEIS-FRANKFURTER CORRESPONDENCE, at 594 n.1.

14. On Frankfurter's substitution for Brandeis in the League's cases, see FELIX FRANKFURTER, FELIX FRANKFURTER REMINISCES: RECORDED IN TALKS WITH DR. HARLAN B. PHILLIPS 96–103 (New York: Reynal & Co. 1960).

15. In 1917 most commentators speculated that the four justices who voted to sustain the Oregon statute were McKenna, Holmes, Day, and Clarke. See Thomas Reed Powell, *The Constitutional Issue in Minimum-Wage Legislation*, 2 MINNESOTA LAW REVIEW 1, 1 (1917). But after McKenna joined Sutherland's majority opinion in *Adkins*, Powell instead postulated that the fourth Justice in 1917 might instead have been Pitney. Thomas Reed Powell, *The Judiciality of Minimum-Wage Legislation*, 37 HARVARD LAW REVIEW 545, 549–50 (1924). Given what we now know about McKenna's extreme reaction to *Block v. Hirsh*, see *supra* Chapter 22, at note 29, it is of course possible that McKenna had changed his mind about the constitutionality of price fixing in the intervening six years. In 1924, Powell postulated that "the Supreme Court from October, 1921, to June, 1922, contained six Justices who thought minimum-wage legislation constitutional." *Id.* at 550. Powell waggishly noted that if the votes of judges "outside of the United States Supreme Court" were counted, there were by the time *Adkins* was argued "twenty-nine judges thinking compulsory minimum wage legislation not wanting in due process as against four judges thinking the contrary." *Id.* at 548.

16. "*The Chief of These Is Property*," 33 NEW REPUBLIC 59, 60 (1922). The Court of Appeals of the District of Columbia had engaged in unsavory maneuvering to decide the case against the constitutionality of the statute. *Id.* at 59.

17. Frances Perkins, *Conserve – but Check – the Court*, 50 THE SURVEY 257 (1923). "No one was prepared . . . for the kind of argument presented in Justice Sutherland's opinion." *Id.* The outcome in *Adkins*, noted Charles E. Clark, showed "the effect of the change in personnel of the court made by Mr. Harding." Charles E. Clark, *The Courts and the People*, 57 LOCOMOTIVE ENGINEERS JOURNAL 626, 627 (August 1923).

18. In his 1918 presidential address to the New York State Bar, no less a figure than Charles Evans Hughes had summarized the vast changes that had transformed the constitutional capacity of government to regulate labor. "As we look to the America that is to be – the United States after the war," Hughes said, "we must know the equipment of recognized constitutional authority with which it will face its problems":

> [A]s illustrating the power of the state with respect to conditions of employment, it is to be observed that the Oregon law limiting the hours of employees in mills, factories and manufacturing establishments, to 10 hours, with provision for allowing extra time at increased pay, was upheld as a valid health regulation. It is true that the Supreme Court of the United States was equally divided with respect to the validity of the Minimum Wage Law of Oregon and hence the decision of the State Supreme Court sustaining that law was affirmed by a divided court. While this leaves the constitutional question still open to debate, it is apparent that opportunity is afforded for experimentation which cannot fail to throw light at least upon the wisdom of the legislative policy.

Adkins v. Children's Hospital

> As we contemplate future problems, in the light of these and earlier decisions, especially as we consider the importance of intelligent action with respect to conditions of labor, to labor organizations, to the relation of employers and employees in activities affected with a public interest, and the broad field for the exercise of legislative discretion, either by Congress or the states according to the nature of the subject, without invading constitutional rights of private persons, we cannot fail to realize that the failure to deal with these problems with the adequacy demanded by good sense and the spirit of fairness will not be due to lack of power so far as the Federal Constitution is concerned, but to the mis-use or non-use of the power which the nation and the states respectively possess.

Charles E. Hughes, *New Phases of National Development*, 4 AMERICAN BAR ASSOCIATION JOURNAL 92, 93, 103–4 (1918).

19. *Adkins* Brief for Appellants at xxvii. The Minimum Wage Board had determined that one could not live in the District of Columbia for less than $16 per week, but that 72.2% of women employed in hotels, 42.6% of women employed in restaurants, and 82.3% of women employed in hospitals were receiving a wage that was less than this minimum. *Id.* at xxvii–xxviii.

20. *Id.* at xxix. "If an industry can maintain itself only by paying workers less than a living wage, it is a socially unprofitable enterprise." Emilie J. Hutchinson, *Women's Wages*, 89 STUDIES IN HISTORY ECONOMICS AND PUBLIC LAW 1, 83 (1919).

21. *Adkins* Brief for Appellants, *supra* note 11, at xxx.

22. *Adkins*, 261 U.S. at 560.

23. Frankfurter detailed the operation of the minimum wage law in 11 States, in Great Britain, Australia and Canada. He argued that "No industry which fails to supply even the bare minimum living requirements of its own workers can possibly be sound." *Adkins* Brief for Appellants, *supra* note 11, at xlix.

24. *Adkins*, 261 U.S. at 545.

25. Brief for Appellees, Adkins v. Children's Hospital of the District of Columbia, No. 795 October Term 1922, 4–7 ("*Adkins* Brief for Appellees"). Lyons claimed "that the work was light and healthful, the hours short, with surroundings clean and moral, and that she was anxious to continue it for the compensation she was receiving, and that she did not earn more. Her services were satisfactory to the Hotel Company, and it would have been glad to retain her, but was obliged to dispense with her services by reason of the order of the board and on account of the penalties prescribed by the act. The wages received by this appellee were the best she was able to obtain for any work she was capable of performing, and the enforcement of the order, she alleges, deprived her of such employment and wages. She further averred that she could not secure any other position at which she could make a living, with as good physical and moral surroundings, and earn as good wages, and that she was desirous of continuing and would continue the employment, but for the order of the board." 261 U.S. at 542–43.

26. *Adkins* Brief for Appellees, *supra* note 25, at 9, 13, 14. Plaintiffs also alleged that the law was unconstitutionally vague. *Id.* at 11.

27. *Id.* at 30–31. "Laws fixing prices in the bargains between individuals are intended to change the rules for the distribution of wealth. They are attempts to correct the inequalities of fortune which follow inevitably from the very form of government which we have – a form which recognizes private ownership of property and personal liberty; they are attempts to alter the economic principles embodied in

the Constitution itself, on the ground that the operation of those very principles is itself inimical to the public health, morals and safety. This cannot be done without an amendment of the Constitution." *Id.* at 35. This argument in Appellee's brief drew heavily on the reasoning of Coppage v. Kansas, 236 U.S. 1, 17–18 (1915). *See infra* Chapter 39, at 1231–32.

28. Barry Cushman, *Some Varieties and Vicissitudes of Lochnerism*, 85 BOSTON UNIVERSITY LAW REVIEW 881, 882 (2005). The *locus classicus* for this view is HOWARD GILLMAN, THE CONSTITUTION BESIEGED (Durham: Duke University Press 1993). Other historians, however, have stressed the independent importance of liberty of contract. *See, e.g.*, David E. Bernstein, *Lochner Era Revisionism, Revised: Lochner and the Origins of Fundamental Rights Constitutionalism*, 92 GEORGETOWN LAW JOURNAL 1 (2003) (arguing *Lochner* was not decided on the basis of a hostility to class legislation but in order to protect fundamental liberties); David E. Bernstein, *Class Legislation, Fundamental Rights, and the Origins of Lochner and Liberty of Contract*, 26 GEORGE MASON LAW REVIEW 1023, 1029–33 (2019); David N. Mayer, *Substantive Due Process Rediscovered: The Rise and Fall of Liberty of Contract*, 60 MERCER LAW REVIEW 563, 625 (2008). For other views, see Gary D. Rowe, *Lochner Revisionism Revisited*, 24 LAW & SOCIAL INQUIRY 221 (1999).

29. GILLMAN, *supra* note 28, at 10. *See also* John V. Orth, *Taking From A and Giving to B: Substantive Due Process and the Case of the Shifting Paradigm*, 14 CONSTITUTIONAL COMMENTARY 337, 337–45 (1997); G. Edward White, *Revisiting Substantive Due Process and Holmes's Lochner Dissent*, 63 BROOKLYN LAW REVIEW 87, 88–89 (1997) (arguing substantive due process claims tested "the boundary between the police powers of the states and the principle that no legislature could enact 'partial' legislation, legislation that imposed burdens or conferred benefits on one class of citizens rather than the citizenry as a whole.").

30. GILLMAN, *supra* note 28, at 22–60.

31. *See supra* Chapter 5, at 169–71.

32. For a discussion, see *infra* Chapter 42, at 1404–5.

33. V.F. Nourse & Sarah A. Maguire, *The Lost History of Governance and Equal Protection*, 58 DUKE LAW JOURNAL 955, 967 (2009).

34. Holden v. Hardy, 169 U.S. 366 (1898). *Holden* upheld a Utah statute that limited work in underground mines to eight hours a day. Sutherland had been one of the architects of the statute when he was in the Utah legislature. *See supra* Chapter 1, at 40. The Utah statute was challenged under the Due Process Clause of the Fourteenth Amendment. The Court noted that it violated due process for the state unjustly to discriminate "in favor of or against a particular individual or class of individuals." *Id.* at 383. But such discrimination was nevertheless permissible "where the legislature had adjudged that a limitation is necessary for the preservation of the health of employés, and there are reasonable grounds for believing that such determination is supported by the facts. The question in each case is whether the legislature has adopted the statute in exercise of a reasonable discretion, or whether its action be a mere excuse for an unjust discrimination, or the oppression or spoliation of a particular class." *Id.* at 398.

35. Muller v. Oregon, 208 U.S. 412 (1908). *Muller* upheld against attack under the Due Process Clause an Oregon statute limiting the hours of work of women in factories

and laundries to ten hours a day. The Court reasoned: "That woman's physical structure and the performance of maternal functions place her at a disadvantage in the struggle for subsistence is obvious. This is especially true when the burdens of motherhood are upon her. Even when they are not, by abundant testimony of the medical fraternity continuance for a long time on her feet at work, repeating this from day to day, tends to injurious effects upon the body, and, as healthy mothers are essential to vigorous offspring, the physical well-being of woman becomes an object of public interest and care in order to preserve the strength and vigor of the race. . . . Differentiated by these matters from the other sex, she is properly placed in a class by herself, and legislation designed for her protection may be sustained, even when like legislation is not necessary for men, and could not be sustained. . . . The limitations which this statute places upon her contractual powers, upon her right to agree with her employer as to the time she shall labor, are not imposed solely for her benefit, but also largely for the benefit of all." *Id.* at 421–22.

36. *Holden*, 169 U.S. at 397. Conversely, in Atchison, T. & S.F. Rd. Co. v. Matthews, 174 U.S. 96, 103 (1899), the Court upheld a statute imposing unique obligations on railroads on the ground that "Special burdens are often necessary for general benefits."
37. Which did not, of course, prevent the Court from using it. *See, e.g.*, Connolly v. Union Sewer Pipe Co., 184 U.S. 540 (1902).
38. Michael Les Benedict, *Laissez-Faire and Liberty: A Re-Evaluation of the Meaning and Origins of Laissez-Faire Constitutionalism*, 3 LAW & HISTORY Review 293, 298 (1985).
39. 198 U.S. 45 (1905).
40. For a concise and excellent overview of the police power jurisprudence of the *Lochner* era, see OWEN M. FISS, TROUBLED BEGINNINGS OF THE MODERN STATE, 1888–1910, at 160–62 (New York: MacMillan 1993).
41. *Lochner*, 198 U.S. at 56, 59.
42. *Id.* at 57–58. "Statutes of the nature of that under review, limiting the hours in which grown and intelligent men may labor to earn their living, are mere meddlesome interferences with the rights of the individual, and they are not saved from condemnation by the claim that they are passed in the exercise of the police power and upon the subject of the health of the individual whose rights are interfered with, unless there be some fair ground, reasonable in and of itself, to say that there is material danger to the public health, or to the health of the employees, if the hours of labor are not curtailed." *Id.* at 61.
43. *Id.* at 57.
44. The Court said merely that "If this statute be valid, and if, therefore, a proper case is made out in which to deny the right of an individual, *sui juris*, as employer or employee, to make contracts for the labor of the latter under the protection of the provisions of the Federal Constitution, there would seem to be no length to which legislation of this nature might not go." *Id.* at 58. On the ambiguity of *Lochner*, see Matthew J. Lindsay, *The Presumptions of Classical Liberal Constitutionalism*, 102 IOWA LAW REVIEW 259, 283–85 (2017).
45. Victoria F. Nourse, *A Tale of Two Lochners: The Untold History of Substantive Due Process and the Idea of Fundamental Rights*, 97 CALIFORNIA LAW REVIEW 751, 768 (2009); FISS, *supra* note 40, at 295. Aspects of *Lochner* did indeed push toward a doctrinal framework of impermissible motives. Thus the Court

noted that "This interference on the part of the legislatures of the several states with the ordinary trades and occupations of the people seems to be on the increase.... It is impossible for us to shut our eyes to the fact that many of the laws of this character, while passed under what is claimed to be the police power for the purpose of protecting the public health or welfare, are, in reality, passed from other motives. We are justified in saying so when, from the character of the law and the subject upon which it legislates, it is apparent that the public health or welfare bears but the most remote relation to the law. The purpose of a statute must be determined from the natural and legal effect of the language employed; and whether it is or is not repugnant to the Constitution of the United States must be determined from the natural effect of such statutes when put into operation, and not from their proclaimed purpose." *Lochner*, 198 U.S. at 63–64.

46. "If this be a valid argument and a justification for this kind of legislation, it follows that the protection of the Federal Constitution from undue interference with liberty of person and freedom of contract is visionary, wherever the law is sought to be justified as a valid exercise of the police power. Scarcely any law but might find shelter under such assumptions, and conduct, properly so called, as well as contract, would come under the restrictive sway of the legislature. Not only the hours of employees, but the hours of employers, could be regulated, and doctors, lawyers, scientists, all professional men, as well as athletes and artisans, could be forbidden to fatigue their brains and bodies by prolonged hours of exercise, lest the fighting strength of the state be impaired. We mention these extreme cases because the contention is extreme. We do not believe in the soundness of the views which uphold this law. On the contrary, we think that such a law as this, although passed in the assumed exercise of the police power, and as relating to the public health, or the health of the employees named, is not within that power, and is invalid. The act is not, within any fair meaning of the term, a health law, but is an illegal interference with the rights of individuals, both employers and employees, to make contracts regarding labor upon such terms as they may think best, or which they may agree upon with the other parties to such contracts." *Id.* at 60–61.

47. Any such conclusion would stretch "takings" jurisprudence very far, for it would condemn as an expropriation of property what to any ordinary understanding was merely a restriction of liberty.

48. On the day of the oral argument, Holmes wrote his friend Nina Gray that "I have little to do except to go to Court and hear an argument on the Minimum wages for women on which I expect my friend Frankfurter will hold forth again. He always makes good arguments." OWH to Mrs. John Chipman Gray (March 14, 1923) (Holmes papers).

49. *Adkins* Brief for Appellees, *supra* note 25, at 41.

50. *Adkins*, 261 U.S. at 546–47, 549–51.

51. 243 U.S. 426, 433–34 (1917). Against the contention that the Oregon statute was "not a health regulation" and so inconsistent with the requirements of Due Process, the Court had explicitly held that it could not "assent" to "the charge of pretense against the legislation." *Id.* at 436. Against the contention "that the law ... is not either necessary or useful 'for preservation of the health of employés in mills, factories and manufacturing establishments,'" the Court stated that "The record contains no facts to support the contention, and against it is the

Adkins v. Children's Hospital

judgment of the legislature and the Supreme Court." *Id.* at 438. The Court thus held in 1917 that absent specific contradictory evidence it would credit a legislative statement of purpose and defer to a legislative judgment about the instrumental connection between legislation and the promotion of health. Sutherland gave lip service to this deference at the outset of his opinion in *Adkins*. Legislative determinations "must be given great weight," he said, and "every possible presumption" must be extended "in favor of the validity of an act of Congress until overcome beyond rational doubt." 261 U.S. at 544. But Sutherland's actual and explicit refusal to extend such deference was a crucial moment in the Taft Court's changing posture of constitutional adjudication.

Bunting had been argued by Felix Frankfurter. He recalled that "During the course of the argument McReynolds said to me, 'Ten hours! Ten hours! Ten! Why not four?' He was then the youngest member of the Court and was sitting to my extreme right. 'If ten, why not four?' in his snarling, sneering way. I paused, synthetically, self-consciously, dramatically, just said nothing. Then I moved down towards him and said, 'Your honor, if by chance I may make such a hypothesis, if your physician should find that you're eating too much meat, it isn't necessary for him to urge you to become a vegetarian.' Holmes said, 'Good for you!' very embarrassingly right from the bench. He loathed these arguments that if you go this far you must go further. 'Good for you!' Loud. Embarrassingly." FRANKFURTER, *supra* note 14, at 102.

The jurisprudential development from *Lochner* to *Bunting* paralleled the path followed by the Court in its workmen's compensation jurisprudence. The Court had initially approved workmen's compensation schemes only for dangerous occupations. But by 1922 it effectively held that any occupation in which a worker was injured was a dangerous occupation. Ward & Gow v. Krinsky, 259 U.S. 503 (1922). *See* JOHN FABIAN WITT, THE ACCIDENTAL REPUBLIC: CRIPPLED WORKINGMEN, DESTITUTE WIDOWS, AND THE REMAKING OF AMERICAN LAW 187–207 (Cambridge: Harvard University Press 2004).

52. *Adkins*, 261 U.S. at 550–51. Sutherland characterized *Bunting* as a case in which "in the absence of facts to support the contrary conclusion," the Court chose to "accept" the "judgment" of the state legislature and state supreme court that legislation was "necessary for the preservation of the health of employees." In *Adkins*, Sutherland did not even purport to find facts in the record establishing that the minimum wage statute was unnecessary for the health of women workers.

53. *Id.* at 559–60. The statute was deemed unconstitutional "by clear and indubitable demonstration." *Id.* at 544.

54. "Anyone who reads the decision written by Justice Sutherland will realize that by far the greater part of his arguments have nothing at all to do with law or precedent. He thinks that the minimum wage law is unfair to the employer, is contrary to economic and business interests, and is bad public policy. As stated again and again by the court in times past, these considerations are entirely irrelevant to the judicial function. The business of the judge is to interpret law, not to determine legislative policy." John A. Ryan, *What "Unconstitutional" Means*, 50 THE SURVEY 258 (1923).

55. "*Adkins* led Frankfurter ... to lose all hope in the Court. '[T]he possible gain isn't worth the cost of having five men without any reasonable probability that they are qualified for the task, determine the course of social policy of the state and the

nation,' he wrote Learned Hand." Brad Snyder, *The House that Built Holmes*, 30 LAW AND HISTORY REVIEW 661, 676 (2012). Frankfurter would never again argue a case in the Supreme Court.

56. Judge Charles Robb, who had joined Judge Van Orsdel's opinion holding the statute unconstitutional in the Court of Appeals for District of Columbia, see *infra* note 74, wrote Sutherland to emphasize how much Sutherland's opinion had "impressed me. It is one of the best opinions I have ever read and its logic is *irresistible*." Charles H. Robb to GS (April 12, 1923) (Sutherland papers). Sutherland also received a letter from Andrew Furuseth, the president of the International Seamen's Union of America, with whom Sutherland had worked closely in 1915 to enact the Seamen's Act of 1915, Pub. L. 63-302, 38 Stat. 1164 (March 4, 1915). Furuseth wrote: "To me the decision seems alright. In fact I should have been very much surprised if you had written any other decision on that question.... If the legislative body has the power to determine a minimum wage it seems to me to follow that it may determine a maximum wage. The equality of the sexes will thus make it possible to return to wages set by law as it was for centuries in Britain.... Those who have enjoyed freedom a long time cannot understand the real meaning of bondage, and are likely to hold out their hands for shackles." Andrew Furuseth to GS (May 5, 1923) (Sutherland papers). Sutherland replied, "You have exactly the right view of it." GS to Andrew Furuseth (May 11, 1923) (Sutherland papers).

After publication of his opinion, Sutherland received a letter from the recent Republican candidate for governor of Virginia expressing delight "that the Court has the 'guts' to stand up in defense of personal liberty against the constant encroachments of government. If the Court had done the same thing in its decision on the Adamson Law [Wilson v. New, 243 U.S. 332 (1917)], many of the troubles which we have had since and will have in the future, would have been avoided.... I think the circumstances and conditions surrounding the country at the time largely influenced that judgment.... Incidentally it is rather interesting to observe our old friend Gompers, who defends the Herrin Murders and the Dynamiting Cases on the ground of personal liberty, complaining of your decision in defense of the essential personal liberty of contract." Henry W. Anderson to GS (April 10, 1923) (Sutherland papers).

57. *Adkins*, 261 U.S. at 555. *See* Connolly v. General Construction Co., 269 U.S. 385 (1926) (striking down as unconstitutionally vague an Oklahoma statute providing that "the current rate of per diem wages in the locality where the work is performed shall be paid to ... laborers, workmen, mechanics, or other persons employed by contractors or subcontractors in the execution of any contract or contracts with the state.") (opinion by Sutherland). Vague administrative statutes were roundly condemned by Sutherland before he joined the Court. *See* George Sutherland, *Principle or Expedient?*, 5 CONSTITUTIONAL REVIEW 195, 203–5 (1921).

58. *Adkins*, 261 U.S. at 555–56. "The inquiry in respect of the necessary cost of living and of the income necessary to preserve health and morals, presents an individual and not a composite question, and must be answered for each individual considered by herself and not by a general formula prescribed by a statutory bureau." *Id.* at 556.

59. *Id.* "It cannot be shown that well paid women safeguard their morals more carefully than those who are poorly paid.... As a means of safeguarding morals the attempted classification, in our opinion, is without reasonable basis." For a discussion of the fraught concept of "standardization" during the 1920s, see *infra* Chapter 26, at 832.

Adkins v. Children's Hospital

60. *Adkins*, 261 U.S. at 557–58, 560–61. Sutherland speculated that something other than the cost of living must have motivated the Board's decisions. Although the Board set the minimum wage in restaurants and mercantile establishments at $16.50 per week, in printing shops at $15.50 per week, and in laundries at $15 per week, the cost of living of the workers in these different settings did not vary. "The board probably found it impossible to follow the indefinite standard of the statute, and brought other and different factors into the problem; and this goes far in the direction of demonstrating the fatal uncertainty of the act, an infirmity which, in our opinion, plainly exists." *Id.* at 556–57.

    It seems fair to conclude that in setting minimum wage standards the Board considered the economics of the regulated industry as well as the minimum income necessary for workers to live. After the decision in *Adkins*, therefore, Frankfurter decided to exploit Sutherland's stress on the need for "fair value" and to substitute the idea of a "fair wage" for that of a "living wage," thus leading to the eventual enactment of the Fair Labor Standards Act. The story is well told in VIVIEN HART, BOUND BY OUR CONSTITUTION: WOMEN, WORKERS, AND THE MINIMUM WAGE 122–67 (Princeton University Press 1994).

61. *Adkins*, 261 U.S. at 558.

62. As Holmes observed in his dissent: "I see no greater objection to using a Board to apply the standard fixed by the Act than there is to the other commissions with which we have become familiar." *Adkins*, 261 U.S. at 570 (Holmes, J., dissenting).

63. *See* Hutchinson, *supra* note 20, at 49 ("From the mass of material collected by vice commissions and industrial investigators, the economic connection between inadequate earnings and occasional or regular prostitution is clearly established."); Robert L. Hale, *Judicial Power and Judicial Social Theories*, 9 AMERICAN BAR ASSOCIATION JOURNAL 810, 811 (1923) ("Despite Justice Sutherland's denial, the evidence of those who know seems to prove that there is a relation between pay and morals.").

64. *Adkins*, 261 U.S. at 565 (Taft, C.J., dissenting) ("A line of distinction like the one under discussion in this case is, as the opinion elsewhere admits, a matter of degree and practical experience and not of pure logic. Certainly the wide difference between prescribing a minimum wage and a maximum wage could as a matter of degree and experience be easily affirmed."). "Surely a little calm reflection," T.R. Powell commented in a devastating critique of Sutherland's opinion, "would instill in Mr. Justice Sutherland a confidence that an approval of the minimum-wage law would not incapacitate him from distinguishing between it and a maximum-wage law." Powell, *The Judiciality of Minimum-Wage Legislation*, *supra* note 15, at 566. Brandeis commented that this article by Powell "should open eyes & cannot fail to help. Such shots continued a few years may revolutionize attitudes. He talks English. ... Some might say, 'He talks turkey.'" LDB to Felix Frankfurter (April 6, 1924), in 5 LETTERS OF LOUIS D. BRANDEIS, at 124.

65. *Adkins*, 261 U.S. at 554, 557–58.

66. *Address of Hon. George Sutherland to the Third Annual Convention of International Association of Casualty and Surety Underwriters* (June 14. 1913), Sen. Doc. No. 131, 63rd CONG. 1st SESS., at 7. *See Report of the Employers' Liability and Workmen's Compensation Commission*, Sen. Doc. No. 338, 62nd CONG. 2nd SESS. (February 12, 1912). In his defense of workmen's compensation legislation, Sutherland stressed Holmes's broad definition of the scope of the police

power in Noble State Bank v. Haskell, 219 U.S. 110 (1911), concluding that legislation may be enacted "in order to promote the public health, safety, morality, or welfare ... although it involve the taking of private property to some extent for what in its immediate purpose is a private use." *Report of the Employers' Liability and Workmen's Compensation Commission, supra*, at 31. In *Noble*, Holmes had written: "It may be said in a general way that the police power extends to all the great public needs. It may be put forth in aid of what is sanctioned by usage, or held by the prevailing morality or strong and preponderant opinion to be greatly and immediately necessary to the public welfare." 219 U.S. at 111. From this Sutherland reasoned that legislation "can not be held invalid under the fifth amendment because there is involved to a comparatively inconsiderable degree a taking of or the placing of a burden upon ... property ... not in accordance with some rule of the common law." *Report of the Employers' Liability and Workmen's Compensation Commission, supra*, at 34.

67. *Address of Hon. George Sutherland, supra* note 66, at 9. "The thought behind this movement [for workmen compensation laws] is that if society en masse for the general welfare may command the self-effacing loyalty of each of its constituent units society in turn must shape and preserve conditions which will protect each unit in the unequal struggle for individual well-being. There is a growing feeling that the individualist theory has been pushed with too much stress upon the dry logic of its doctrines and too little regard for their practical operation from the humanitarian point of view. We are discovering that we can not always regulate our economic and social relations by scientific formulae, because a good many people perversely insist upon being fed and clothed and comforted by the practical rule of thumb rather than by the exact rules of logic." *Id.* at 11.

68. Workmen's compensation laws reflected the "demand that the products of a particular industry should themselves bear the whole burden of their production, and that no industry should be permitted either to transfer to the public charge its human losses or leave those human losses to be vicariously borne. This is the justification of the Workmen's Compensation Acts, and in part of minimum wage laws." Newton D. Baker, *Labor Relations and the Law*, 8 AMERICAN BAR ASSOCIATION JOURNAL 731, 732 (1922).

69. Cudahy Packing Co. v. Parramore, 263 U.S. 418, 423 (1923) (opinion by Sutherland). See Felix Frankfurter, *The President's Industrial Conference*, 22 NEW REPUBLIC 179, 180 (1920) (with respect to the regulation of employment, it is "more accurate to say" that the development of the law has been "from contract to status: that rights and duties flow from the relationship of the parties and not from their volition. In working out the legal rights and liabilities not from contract but from the relation of the parties in the field of labor, the law is following familiar English history."). *See* Walter B. Kennedy, *Law and the Railroad Labor Problem*, 32 YALE LAW JOURNAL 553, 553 (1923) ("Out of the death of Maine's formula 'from status to contract' there is beginning to appear a new generalization 'from contract to status.'"). *Compare* W.G. Sumner, *Industrial War*, 2 THE FORUM 1, 7–8 (1886) ("The doctrines that are preached about the relations of employer and employé would go to make that relationship one of status and not of contract. ... It is very remarkable that just when all feudal relations between landlord and tenant are treated with disdain and eagerly assailed, there should be an attempt to establish feudal relations between employer

Adkins v. Children's Hospital

and employé. An employer has no obligation whatever to an employé outside of the contract, any more than an editor has to his subscribers, or a merchant to his customers, or a house-owner to his tenants, or a banker to his depositors. In a free democratic state employés are not wards of the State. They are not like Indians, or freedmen, or women, or children."). Sutherland's characterization of workmen's compensation laws was later challenged by Brandeis in dissent in Washington v. W.C. Dawson & Co., 264 U.S. 219, 233–34 (1924). Brandeis argued that a workmen's compensation law does not "create a status between employer and employee. It provides an incident to the employment which is often likened to a contractual obligation, even where the Workmen's Compensation Law is not of the class called optional." *Id.*

70. *Adkins*, 261 U.S. at 558.

> In principle, there can be no difference between the case of selling labor and the case of selling goods. If one goes to the butcher, the baker, or grocer to buy food, he is morally entitled to obtain the worth of his money; but he is not entitled to more. If what he gets is worth what he pays, he is not justified in demanding more, simply because he needs more; and the shopkeeper, having dealt fairly and honestly in that transaction, is not concerned in any peculiar sense with the question of his customer's necessities. Should a statute undertake to vest in a commission power to determine the quantity of food necessary for individual support, and require the shopkeeper, if he sell to the individual at all, to furnish that quantity at not more than a fixed maximum, it would undoubtedly fall before the constitutional test.

Id. at 558–59. This language infuriated labor leaders. Samuel Gompers wrote that "The brutality of the majority decision can beget nothing but wrath. It went so far as to unblushingly liken the purchase of the labor power of women and girls to the purchase of provisions in a grocery store, or meat in a butcher shop." Samuel Gompers, *Usurped Power*, 50 THE SURVEY 221–22 (1923).

71. *See supra* note 70.

72. Taft himself had earlier appealed to workmen's compensation statutes to illustrate "The broad distinction between one's right to protection against a direct injury to one's fundamental property right by another who has no special relation to him, and one's liability to another with whom he establishes a voluntary relation under a statute." Truax v. Corrigan, 257 U.S. 312, 329 (1921). The status of employee, said Taft, was sufficient to justify a legislative determination "that the employer shall become the insurer of the employee against injuries from the employment without regard to the negligence, if any, through which it occurred, leaving to the employer to protect himself by insurance and to compensate himself for the additional cost of production by adding to the prices he charges for his products." *Id.* at 338–39.

73. *Address of Hon. George Sutherland*, *supra* note 66, at 11–12.

74. The opinion in *Adkins* of the District of Columbia Court of Appeals explicitly invoked policy arguments of this kind:

> Legislation tending to fix the prices at which private property shall be sold, whether it be a commodity or labor, places a limitation upon the distribution of wealth, and is aimed at the correction of the inequalities of fortune which are inevitable under our form of government, due to personal liberty and the private ownership of property. . . .

> The police power cannot be employed to level inequalities of fortune. Private property cannot by mere legislative or judicial fiat be taken from one person and delivered to another, which is the logical result of price fixing....
>
> A wage based upon competitive ability is just, and leads to frugality and honest industry, and inspires an ambition to attain the highest possible efficiency, while the equal wage paralyzes ambition and promotes prodigality and indolence. It takes away the strongest incentive to human labor, thrift, and efficiency, and works injustice to employee and employer alike, thus affecting injuriously the whole social and industrial fabric....
>
> The tendency of the times to socialize property rights under the subterfuge of police regulation is dangerous, and if continued will prove destructive of our free institutions. It should be remembered that of the three fundamental principles which underlie government, and for which government exists, the protection of life, liberty, and property, the chief of these is property; not that any amount of property is more valuable than the life or liberty of the citizen, but the history of civilization proves that, when the citizen is deprived of the free use and enjoyment of his property, anarchy and revolution follow, and life and liberty are without protection....
>
> Take from the citizen the right to freely contract and sell his labor for the highest wage which his individual skill and efficiency will command, and the laborer would be reduced to an automaton – a mere creature of the state. It is paternalism in the highest degree, and the struggle of the centuries to establish the principle that the state exists for the citizen, and not the citizen for the state, would be lost.

Children's Hospital of the District of Columbia v. Adkins, 284 F. 613, 617, 621–23 (D.C. Ct. App. 1922). As Coolidge would later famously opine: "Government price fixing, once started, has alike no justice and no end. It is an economic folly from which this country has every right to be spared." *Message to the Senate Returning without Approval S. 4808 – The McNary-Haugen Farm Relief Bill*, 68 CONG. REC. 4771 (February 25, 1927).

75. *Adkins*, 261 U.S. at 554.
76. *Id.* at 558 (emphasis added).
77. *Id.* at 545.
78. Sutherland, *supra* note 57, at 206 ("[T]he owner has an inherent, constitutional right to the market price, fixed by what is called the 'higgling of the market,' irrespective of the extent of his profits. Such a right is, indeed, itself essentially property which stands upon an equality with life and liberty, under the guaranties of the Fifth and Fourteenth Amendments.").
79. Sutherland's assumption of an objective "fair value" presupposes a "fallacy ... which could have been pointed out by any competent conventional economist." Hale, *supra* note 63, at 811. *See* Thomas Reed Powell, *Protecting Property and Liberty, 1922–1924*, 40 POLITICAL SCIENCE QUARTERLY 404, 414 (1925) ("Mr. Justice Sutherland assumes that there is some determinable 'fair value of the services rendered' by employees, and he declares the statute void for basing the minimum wage on the amount needed for the support of the worker rather than on this fair value of her services. Nowhere does he show how such fair value can be ascertained. He insists, however, that in so far as the sum fixed by the minimum-wage board exceeds this fair value, 'it amounts to a compulsory exaction from the employer.'").
80. 262 U.S. 341 (1923).
81. *See supra* Chapter 22, at 722.

Adkins v. Children's Hospital

82. As John W. Davis, the Democratic candidate for president in 1924, proclaimed in his Labor Day speech during the campaign:

> Toward grown men and women, responsible citizens of the Republic, we cannot and we should not take a paternalistic and protective attitude.... [The Government] should leave adult citizens to make their own contracts, in their own way as to the terms and conditions on which their labor is to be performed. If Government can fix the limit of a day's work in ordinary industrial and commercial pursuits it can, at its own discretion, make those limits long or short. It should attempt to do neither, but leave the parties to all such contracts to bargain with each other as their mutual benefit requires. The wage contract of the adult, no less than any other contract, should be a voluntary agreement. Anything other than this I believe to be impossible, undesirable, corrupting and tyrannical.

Text of Mr. Davis's Speech, NEW YORK TIMES (September 2, 1924), at 2.

83. *See* Cudahy Packing Co. v. Parramore, 263 U.S. 418, 423 (1923); *Address of Hon. George Sutherland, supra* note 66, at 4; Lester P. Schoene & Frank Watson, *Workmen's Compensation on Interstate Railways*, 47 HARVARD LAW REVIEW 389, 390–91 (1934) (noting that common law defenses "had been grounded on the assumptions that the employee was cognizant of all risks to be encountered and that, being cognizant, his bargaining power would enable him to decline the employment if the risks were too great. These assumptions the whole history of modern industrialism denied. Legislatures intervened to eliminate the disparity between legal fictions and economic facts."). Sutherland justified imposing an eight-hour workday on the same grounds. *See* 48 CONG. REC. 6797 (May 20, 1912) (remarks of Sutherland) ("[I]n the mechanical pursuits I believe thoroughly that the 8-hour day in the end will be better for both the employer and the employee .... We cannot make such a law that will be effective unless it is compulsory; we can not very well leave to an arrangement between the employer and the employee, because in a contest of that kind I think the employee would usually be at a disadvantage as compared with the employer."). The recognition that labor contracts did not always represent a voluntary meeting of the minds was one basis for the Court's holding in *Holden* upholding the requirement of an eight-hour day for miners. *See infra* note 92.

84. Sybil Lipschultz, Workers, Wives and Mothers: The Problem of Minimum Wage Laws for Women in Early Twentieth Century America 139–40 (Ph.D. Dissertation, University of Pennsylvania 1986).

85. *The Legal Right to Starve*, 34 NEW REPUBLIC 254 (1923).

86. *Adkins*, 261 U.S. at 553–55. Sutherland had championed the Nineteenth Amendment and advocated for "equality of legal status – including the right of contract and to hold property." 53 CONG. REC. 11318 (July 20, 1916). In 1921, Ethel Smith, a member of the District of Columbia's Minimum Wage Board, had written Sutherland to ask his opinion "as to the effect of the so-called 'equal rights' amendment to the Constitution which has been proposed for introduction in the senate on behalf of the National Woman's Party." Smith was concerned that the Amendment might jeopardize "existing laws in many States and the District of Columbia, providing an 8-hour day and a minimum wage for women in industry." Ethel M. Smith to GS (December 19, 1921) (Sutherland papers). Sutherland replied:

> I have a good deal of doubt as to the advisability or wisdom of any federal constitutional amendment of the kind suggested. The women of every state in the

Union now having been accorded the privilege of equal suffrage, I am inclined to think better results will be obtained by seeking, at the hands of the various state legislatures, such remedial legislation as may be needed in each state. I was very earnestly in favor of the 19th amendment because it dealt with a question which was, to my mind, fundamentally national. But there is danger in undertaking to reach all sorts of evils by additional amendments.

> Of course, no one can predict what construction the courts will put upon the proposed amendment. I think they would struggle to give it a reasonable interpretation, and to save the state laws relating to the eight hour a day for women, and so on. But, of course, the Supreme Court might take the view that the amendment meant precisely what it said, and that a law which gave unequal advantage to women was as obnoxious to the amendment as one which was equally to their disadvantage.

GS to Ethel M. Smith (December 24, 1921) (Sutherland papers).

87. 261 U.S. at 553. In their oral argument to the Court, plaintiffs in *Adkins* stressed the opposition to single-sex minimum wage legislation of the National Woman's Party, the National Woman's Suffrage Association, and the Equal Rights Association. Oral Argument of Wade H. Ellis, at 6–7. *See Women at Odds on Laws for Them*, NEW YORK TIMES (March 25, 1923), XX at 3. Alice Paul of the National Woman's Party in fact actively cooperated with the plaintiffs' lawyer in *Adkins* to undermine what Paul regarded as old-fashioned and harmful women-protective legislation. Joan G. Zimmerman, *The Jurisprudence of Equality: The Women's Minimum Wage, the First Equal Rights Amendment, and* Adkins v. Children's Hospital, *1905–1923*, 78 JOURNAL OF AMERICAN HISTORY 188, 220–23 (1991). On the extreme tension between those like Alice Paul, who sought an Equal Rights Amendment for women, and those like Florence Kelley, who sought instead women's protective legislation like the District of Columbia minimum wage legislation, see, for example, HART, *supra* note 60, at 108–29; AMY E. BUTLER, TWO PATHS TO EQUALITY: ALICE PAUL AND ETHEL M. SMITH IN THE ERA DEBATE, 1921–1929, at 90–107 (Albany: State University of New York Press 2002); Nancy F. Cott, *Feminist Politics in the 1920s: The National Woman's Party*, 71 JOURNAL OF AMERICAN HISTORY 43 (1984); and Lipschultz, *supra* note 84, at 55–87. Citing specifically the passages quoted in text, Alice Paul praised Sutherland's opinion in *Adkins* as "vividly" expressing "the increasing tendency to regard women as adult human beings standing on an equal plane with men." Alice Paul, *Adult Human Beings*, 50 THE SURVEY 222, 256 (1923). *See National Woman's Party Acclaims as Big Victory Minimum Wage Decision*, CHRISTIAN SCIENCE MONITOR (April 12, 1923), at 1.

88. Taft would refer to Sutherland's "somewhat garish reference to the effect of the nineteenth amendment in changing the nature of women." WHT to OWH (April 4, 1923) (Holmes papers).

89. Holmes's famous aperçu that "It will need more than the Nineteenth Amendment to convince me that there are no differences between men and women, or that legislation cannot take those differences into account," 261 U.S. at 570 (Holmes, J., dissenting), may inadvertently have contributed to a misapprehension of the stakes in *Adkins*. Holmes's actual point was that physical differences between the sexes were irrelevant to the constitutional question posed in *Adkins*: "I should not hesitate to take [these differences] into account *if I thought it necessary to sustain this act*. But after *Bunting v. Oregon* I had supposed that it was not necessary." *Id.* (Emphasis added).

Adkins v. Children's Hospital

Holmes was correct to predict that the Nineteenth Amendment would not disturb the Court's jurisprudence of physical differences between the sexes. In 1924, speaking unanimously through Sutherland, the Court upheld a New York statute prohibiting women from being employed in restaurants in large cities between the hours of ten at night and six in the morning. Radice v. New York, 264 U.S. 292 (1924). The Court explicitly held that "The legislature had before it a mass of information from which it concluded that night work is substantially and especially detrimental to the health of women. We cannot say that the conclusion is without warrant. The loss of a restful night's sleep can not be fully made up by sleep in the day time, especially in busy cities, subject to the disturbances incident to modern life. The injurious consequences were thought by the legislature to bear more heavily against women than men, and, considering their more delicate organism, there would seem to be good reason for so thinking." *Id.* at 294. Sutherland distinguished *Adkins* on the ground that the latter involved a "wage-fixing law, pure and simple. It had nothing to do with the hours or conditions of labor." *Id.* at 295. Sutherland's deference to legislative facts in *Radice* contrasts starkly with his refusal to consider such facts in *Adkins*. It is hard to resist the conclusion that Sutherland was simply not interested in facts that might establish a market failure with regard to the price of labor.

Frankfurter recorded a conversation with Brandeis in which Frankfurter announced that he "was certain that Ct would decide NY statute prohibiting night work by women favorably as it did. L.D.B. took me aside and said 'You might have been certain but it was not all certain. That was one of those 5 to 4 that was teetering back & forth for some time. The man who finally wrote – Sutherland was the fifth man & after a good deal of study (for whatever you may say of him he has character & conscience) came out for the act & then wrote his opinion. That swung the others around to silence. It was deemed inadvisable to express dissent and add another 5 to 4.'" *Brandeis-Frankfurter Conversations*, at 330 (July 6, 1924). According to Butler's docket book, the dissenting votes in conference in *Radice* were McKenna, Van Devanter, McReynolds, and Butler.

The controversy in *Radice* did not so much concern the Due Process Clause as the Equal Protection Clause. Brandeis remarked to Frankfurter that "The doubt as to the statute turned on unequal protection, which now looms up even more menacingly than due process, because the statute omitted some night work & only included some." *Brandeis-Frankfurter Conversations*, at 330 (July 6, 1924). A great part of Sutherland's opinion accordingly sought to demonstrate that the statute's distinction between large cities and other cities, and that its exclusion from coverage of women "employed in restaurants as singers and performers, attendants in ladies' cloak rooms and parlors, as well as those employed in dining rooms and kitchens of hotels and in lunch rooms or restaurants conducted by employers solely for the benefit of their employees," did not violate equal protection because the classifications of the statute were not "actually and palpably unreasonable and arbitrary." 264 U.S. at 296. "If the law presumably hits the evil where it is most felt, it is not to be overthrown because there are other instances to which it might have been applied." *Id.* at 298. Butler in his docket book inscribed next to Sutherland's name: "Classification can be sustained." He inscribed next to McReynolds's name: "Doubtfully." For a discussion of equal protection doctrine during the Taft Court, see *infra* Chapter 43.

90. Hutchinson, *supra* note 20, at 83 ("What can be said of the bargaining power of the individual in such a group of young, inexperienced, untrained, shifting workers whose wage work is regarded by themselves and every one else as something to be done in the years between leaving school and getting married?... Obviously under such circumstances the employer may practically dictate the wage rate. To the degree that competition for work is active among the employees, wages will tend to the level of the most necessitous or the most ignorant.").
91. *See supra* text at note 83.
92. In *Holden*, the Court upheld legislation setting maximum hours for underground miners on the ground of an analogous failure in the labor market: "[P]roprietors of these establishments and their operatives do not stand upon an equality, and ... their interests are, to a certain extent, conflicting.... In other words, the proprietors lay down the rules, and the laborers are practically constrained to obey them. In such cases self-interest is often an unsafe guide, and the legislature may properly interpose its authority.... [T]he fact that both parties are of full age, and competent to contract, does not necessarily deprive the state of the power to interfere, where the parties do not stand upon an equality, or where the public health demands that one party to the contract shall be protected against himself." Holden v. Hardy, 169 U.S. 383, 397 (1898). Sutherland had himself advocated for the statute at issue in *Holden* when he was in the Utah legislature.
93. Edward Berman, *The Supreme Court and the Minimum Wage*, 31 JOURNAL OF POLITICAL ECONOMY 852, 855 (1923). *See* Barbara N. Grimes, *Constitutional Law: Police Power: Minimum Wage for Women*, 11 CALIFORNIA LAW REVIEW 352, 357 (1923) ("Will the learned justices of the majority be pardoned for overlooking the cardinal fact that minimum wage legislation is not and never was predicated upon political, contractual or civil inequalities of women? It is predicated rather upon evils to society, resulting from the exploitation of women in industry, who *as a class labor under a tremendous economic handicap*. The problem is one of economic fact, not of political, contractual or civil status.") (emphasis in the original); Mary Anderson, *Get Back to the Facts*, 50 THE SURVEY 256 (1923).
94. "We cannot escape the conclusion that the opinion of the court reveals an ignorance of the nature of the modern employment contract and of the facts which surround it which, in view of the court's pivotal position is determining the economic policy of the country, is nothing short of shocking. It assumes that there exists between employee and employer an equality of position which enables each to bargain with the other upon an equally advantageous footing. To suppose that such a situation exists in modern industrial society is indeed naïve." *The Supreme Court Supplants Congress*, 116 THE NATION 484 (April 25, 1923). "The trend of legislation, of public opinion, and even of Supreme Court decisions for many years has been in the direction of a recognition of the fact that between an employer with a job to give and an employee with very little choice but to accept, there is and can be no equality of contracting power. It is a bit surprising to come upon evidence of a lack of recognition of such a fact after a quarter century of legislation based on its recognition." Berman, *supra* note 93, at 854.
95. Prior to *Adkins*, Taft had in fact been in correspondence with Brandeis's daughter about the operation of the District's minimum wage legislation. *See, e.g.*, Elizabeth Brandeis to WHT (October 30, 1922) (Taft papers) ("I am concerned with the operation of the District police court because persons charged with violating the

Adkins v. Children's Hospital

minimum wage law are prosecuted in that court. My experience seems to show that anyone under prosecution in the Police Court who demands a jury trial can delay the trial of his case practically indefinitely. ... I realize that this must seem a very unimportant matter about which to ask for your help, but nevertheless I am hopeful that you may feel able to do something."); WHT to Elizabeth Brandeis (October 31, 1922) (Taft papers) ("I deeply sympathize with you in your patience [sic] at this delay in the Police Court. The demanding of a jury trial in a police court is a boon to criminals, and I can readily understand how employers, who are violating the law, and their attorneys, chuckle at the thought of the delays that protect them against punishment for violation of a plain provision of the statute. I don't think I am given any authority under the present law, but it is possible such a provision might be put through, and then you could count on my doing everything I could to help you. I shall talk it over with the Judiciary Committee.").

96. In his dissent, Taft graciously said "But for my inability to agree with some general observations in the forcible opinion of MR. JUSTICE HOLMES, who follows me, I should be silent and merely record my concurrence in what he says. It is perhaps wiser for me, however, in a case of this importance separately to give my reasons for dissenting." 261 U.S. at 567 (Taft, C.J., dissenting). Holmes wrote Taft on March 28 that Holmes had "sketched" "a few feeble words" in dissent in *Adkins*, "so as not long to delay the opinions when they are sent around." OWH to WHT (March 28, 1923) (Holmes papers). Taft replied: "I felicitate you on your dissenting opinion in the minimum wage case. It is very strong. I thank you, too, for the array of authorities. I feel as if I ought to say something on the subject. It will not be long. You have relieved me of much, but there are two or three things I would like to say. I have been wondering if we were not going to receive a recirculated opinion from Sutherland after the more careful Vandevanter [sic] has gotten in his handiwork to modify some of the extreme statements of the opinion, notably the resuscitation of the Lochner case and the somewhat garish reference to the effect of the nineteenth amendment in changing the nature of women." WHT to OWH (April 4, 1923) (Holmes papers). I was "on my lone," Holmes wrote his friend Nina Gray, because "a few general remarks that I think obvious commanded no assent." OWH to Mrs. Chapman Gray (April 23, 1923) (Holmes papers). Holmes wrote Laski that "The C.J. and Sanford seemed to think I said something dangerous or too broad so they dissented separately. ... I think that what I said was plain common sense. It was intended *inter alia* to dethrone Liberty of Contract from its ascendancy in the Liberty business. I am curious to see what the enthusiasts for liberty of contract will say with regard to liberty of speech under a State law punishing advocating the overthrow of government – by violence." OWH to Harold Laski (April 14, 1923), in 1 HOLMES-LASKI CORRESPONDENCE, at 495. Laski replied that he thought Sutherland's opinion "was windy and poor; and half of his opinion never comes near the point at all." Harold Laski to OWH (April 26, 1923), *id.* at 496.

97. *See, e.g., A One-Man Constitution*, NEW YORK WORLD (April 12, 1923), at 10 ("The decision of the Supreme Court in the minimum-wage case again makes the Constitution of the United States a matter of one man's opinion. Against his opinion, the opinion of the House of Representatives which passed the bill, the opinion of the Senate which concurred in the bill and the opinion of the President who signed the bill are swept aside as irrelevant and immaterial."); *Report of A.F. of L. Executive Council*, in REPORT OF PROCEEDINGS OF THE FORTY-THIRD ANNUAL

THE TAFT COURT

CONVENTION OF THE AMERICAN FEDERATION OF LABOR 36 (Washington D.C.: The Law Reporter Printing Co. 1923) ("One of the justices did not act, as before his appointment he had fought for minimum wage laws. Therefore the decisions [sic] was really five to four."). *See Borah Wants Minimum Wage Left to States*, NEW YORK TRIBUNE (April 11, 1923), at 2 ("Senator Borah said: 'This is practically another 5 to 4 decision.'"). The fact that Harding's four appointments had split evenly, two joining the Court and two dissenting, was also remarked upon.

98. WVD to John C. Pollock (April 25, 1923) (Van Devanter papers).
99. Brandeis commented on the draft of Holmes's dissent, "It ought to make converts." (Holmes papers).
100. *Adkins*, 261 U.S. at 567–68 (Holmes, J., dissenting).
101. As Holmes pointed out, "This statute does not compel anybody to pay anything. It simply forbids employment at rates below those fixed as the minimum requirement of health and right living." *Adkins*, 261 U.S. at 570 (Holmes, J., dissenting).
102. *Id.* at 568. Holmes cited many examples of legislative restrictions on freedom of contract, including *Schmidinger. Id.* at 569.
103. *Id.* at 569–70 (Holmes, J., dissenting).
104. *Adkins*, 261 U.S. at 570 (Holmes, J., dissenting). "If I were Frankfurter," Laski wrote Holmes, "I should rest content that I had secured the dissent from you." Harold Laski to OWH (April 26, 1923), in 1 HOLMES-LASKI CORRESPONDENCE, at 496.
105. Holmes received a letter from the acting editor of the *Brotherhood of Locomotive Engineers Journal*, commending Holmes on a dissent that "goes to the heart of the whole matter in three brief pages, and presents the social as well as legal fallacies underlying the majority decision in an unanswerable manner."

> I wonder if the majority of the Court realize just what is the effect of this and similar decisions which ignore the needs of the people and block social progress. Last night I heard an address by a well known "radical", Wm. Z. Foster of Chicago. Mr. Foster brought ringing applause from a building packed with more than 1200 people when he compared "the dictatorship of a few black-robed men of the Supreme Court" with "the dictatorship of the black-shirted Fascisti in Italy". He pointed out the injustice of permitting one man, appointed for life by a reactionary president, to nullify repeatedly legislation protecting the welfare of the people. Certain of your colleagues would be shocked to learn that their decisions are promoting radicalism faster than all the soapbox orators of the country combined.

Albert F. Coyle to OWH (May 2, 1923) (Holmes papers).

106. UNITED STATES DEPARTMENT OF LABOR, NATIONAL WAR LABOR BOARD: A HISTORY OF ITS FORMATION AND ACTIVITIES, TOGETHER WITH ITS AWARDS AND THE DOCUMENTS OF IMPORTANCE IN THE RECORD OF ITS DEVELOPMENT 33 (Bulletin of the United States Bureau of Labor Statistics No. 287) (Washington D.C.: Government Printing Office 1922). The Board fixed "minimum rates of pay ... which will insure the subsistence of the worker and his family in health and reasonable comfort." *Id. See id.* at 23–24; William Howard Taft, *Toward Industrial Peace* (April 4, 1918), in VIVIAN, at 48. Taft believed that his duty on the Board was to set wages above the "minimum limitation as to the cost of living." William Howard Taft, *Higher Street-Car Fares* (June 12, 1919), in VIVIAN, at 227. The new statistical techniques developed during the war enabled the War

Adkins v. Children's Hospital

Labor Board to use "standard of living" as a metric in determining wages. William F. Ogburn, *Standard of Living as a Basis for Wage Adjustments*, 8 PROCEEDINGS OF THE ACADEMY OF POLITICAL SCIENCE IN THE CITY OF NEW YORK 101, 107 (1919). It was said immediately after the war that the Board's "principles and investigations and decisions in regard to the minimum wage went far toward establishing that principle as an actuality in this country." Richard B. Gregg, *National War Labor Board*, 33 HARVARD LAW REVIEW 39, 59 (1919).

The War Labor Board also declared that "If it shall become necessary to employ women on work ordinarily performed by men, they must be allowed equal pay for equal work and must not be allotted tasks disproportionate to their strength." NATIONAL WAR LABOR BOARD, *supra*, at 32. In the popular mind the war was responsible for bringing women flooding into the workforce. "The war gave us new practices in regard to government control and intensified many of the problems connected with unionism, but in no place did it so completely upset preconceived notions as in the field of women's work. The war gave the finishing blow to the old tradition that woman's only place was in the home." Malcom Keir, *Post-War Causes of Labor Unrest*, 81 THE ANNALS 101, 106 (January 1919). There is evidence, however, that as many as 95 percent of women "who went into war industry came from other industries in which they had previously gained a livelihood and industrial experience. The war-time employment of women has been characterized by a shifting from the lower paid to the higher paid occupations, and from nonessential industries, rather than by any large accession of women who would not normally have come into industry in any event." A.B. Wolfe & Helen Olson, *War-Time Industrial Employment of Women in the United States*, 27 JOURNAL OF POLITICAL ECONOMY 639, 640 (1919).

107. A bare two years previously, in 1921, New York lawyer Philip Wager Lowry had rashly predicted that the "principle" of the living wage, "as announced by the National War Labor Board ... will probably stand, in peace times as it did in war, as an absolute rule of law in American courts of whatsoever jurisdiction, as long as the wage system survives." Philip Wager Lowry, *Strikes and the Law*, 21 COLUMBIA LAW REVIEW 783, 793 (1921).

108. *Adkins*, 261 U.S. at 562 (Taft, C.J., dissenting).

109. *Id.* at 562–63 (Taft, C.J., dissenting).

110. While the case was under submission, Taft expressed to Holmes his hope that Van Devanter would be able to "modify some of the extreme statements of the opinion, notably the resuscitation of the Lochner case." WHT to OWH (April 4, 1923) (Holmes papers). Evidently Van Devanter approved of *Lochner*'s revival.

111. *Adkins*, 261 U.S. at 564 (Taft, C.J., dissenting). Taft had predicted the demise of *Lochner* as early as 1914 when he affirmed that rights of liberty and property "have to be exercised with reference to the exercise of similar rights by other individuals in the same community, and with due regard to community welfare, and that the permissible limitations upon their enjoyment must be affected by the changing conditions prevailing in society." WILLIAM HOWARD TAFT, THE ANTI-TRUST ACT AND THE SUPREME COURT 43 (New York: Harper & Brothers 1914). "The urban population has greatly increased in proportion to the rural population," Taft noted, "while the feeding of the people and their clothing, their education, their health, and their domestic comfort have necessarily cut down somewhat the free exercise of individual rights, which was wider half a century ago; and the courts

have recognized the change." *Id.* at 44. For this reason, Taft observed, "With the changed personnel of the court and the present trend of their decisions, I am inclined to think that a similar case" as *Lochner* would now "meet a different fate. The truth is that the court as at present constituted has shown itself as appreciative of the change and the necessity for a liberal construction of the restrictions of the Constitution ... as any court could be." *Id.* at 45. *See* Nourse, *supra* note 45, at 784.

112. *Adkins*, 261 U.S. at 564–65 (Taft, C.J., dissenting). Taft's brother Horace wrote him that "The women folk are singing your praises" because of your dissent, but "I daresay that is praise that you have no stomach for." Horace D. Taft to WHT (April 17, 1923) (Taft papers).

113. Clarke sent Taft a letter affirming that "I should have been with you in the Minimum Wage case, you may be sure." JHC to WHT (April 29, 1923) (Taft papers). Taft replied, "In the minimum wage case, I think some of my brethren went too far, even if they had to take that view on the merits of the case. I think there are expressions in Sutherland's opinion that will merely return to plague us. However, we are getting along very well, and I have no reason to complain of the brethren, except that one has passed his usefulness, and as to another of them, whom you know, there is some question as to how much of usefulness ever existed." WHT to JHC (May 3, 1923) (Taft papers). Clarke promptly replied, "I agree with you that there are passages in the opinion likely to return to plague the Court. The spirit of the contention in the Conference Room is apparent in every paragraph – it even mars the English of it! But the outstanding feature seems to me to be the strongest statement I remember of the rule that statutes shall be overthrown only in clear cases. He says the invalidity must appear 'beyond a rational doubt' & then goes forward & declares the statute invalid with the C.J. & 2 (3!) other judges in clearly reasoned opinions differing with him. One would think three of his brethren one the Chief Justice differing [illegible] thus sharply would be sufficient to start 'a rational doubt' as to the validity of his own thinking. I remember saying when on the Court that I would never be one of five to overthrow an act of Congress or of a state legislature because I would respect the opinions of my four dissenting brethren to the extent of saying that their views raised the doubt in my mind which prevented such a holding. So good a lawyer [illegible] as Judge Day urged me not to anticipate such a case & particularly not to take that position as I might wish to modify it. But I had worked it out more carefully than he thought I had. Observance of the rule, voluntarily by the Court, may save its jurisdiction from being mutilated by Congress in an amendment." JHC to WHT (May 5, 1923) (Taft papers). Clarke later reiterated these criticisms of *Adkins* in print in the "New Federalist Series": *John C. Clarke Writes of "Judicial Power to Declare Legislation Unconstitutional,"* 9 AMERICAN BAR ASSOCIATION JOURNAL 689 (1923). Clarke emphasized that the rule that legislation be upheld unless it could be shown to be unconstitutional "'beyond a rational doubt' ... by 'clear and indubitable demonstration'" was "of the utmost importance to our country. It is no new suggestion that if the Court would give real and sympathetic effect to this rule by declining to hold a statute unconstitutional whenever several of the Justices conclude that it is valid – by conceding that two or more being of such opinion in any case must necessarily raise a 'rational

Adkins v. Children's Hospital

doubt' – an end would be made of five to four constitutional decisions and great benefit would result to our country and to the Court." *Id.* at 692.

114. *Adkins* was twice reaffirmed during the 1920s: in Murphy v. Sardell, 269 U.S. 530 (1925) (Arizona), and then again in Donham v. West-Nelson Co., 273 U.S. 657 (1927) (Arkansas). Barry Cushman describes the votes in *Sardell* recorded in Stone's docket book:

> Next to the votes to affirm of Taft, Holmes, and Sanford – the three dissenters in *Adkins* (Brandeis had not participated) – Stone wrote "on authority [illegible] [illegible]." Stone also wrote this next to his own vote to affirm. The illegibility of the latter two words in Stone's notation makes it difficult to be certain, but it seems very likely that these four Justices indicated at the conference that they were voting to invalidate the statute only because they regarded themselves as bound by the recent authority of *Adkins*. If that is the case, then after McKenna's replacement by Stone in 1925, there was a majority of the Court that believed that *Adkins* had been wrongly decided. Four of those five Justices continued to strike down state minimum wage laws solely on the basis of a precedent that they believed was demonstrably erroneous. This no doubt frustrated Brandeis, whose solo dissents from [the *Sardell* and *Donham*] decisions might be read as opposing not only their results, but also the fealty to stare decisis that he soon would criticize in his celebrated dissent in *Burnet v Coronado Oil & Gas Co.*, 285 U.S. 393, 406–10 (1932) (Brandeis, J., dissenting).

Barry Cushman, *Inside the Taft Court: Lessons from the Docket Books*, 2015 SUPREME COURT REVIEW 345, 382–83.

I have also found the words in Stone's docket book to be unintelligible, but Cushman's interpretation is almost certainly correct. After *Sardell*, Stone wrote Thomas Reed Powell to thank him for a copy of a volume of commentary on *Adkins* that Florence Kelley had compiled in frustration after *Sardell* – THE SUPREME COURT AND MINIMUM WAGE LEGISLATION: COMMENT BY THE LEGAL PROFESSION ON THE DISTRICT OF COLUMBIA CASE (New York: New Republic, Inc. 1925). Stone remarked, "I had some views on this subject when the Adkins case was decided. Such limited experience as I have had, has strengthened them, but I suppose it is the part of prudence not to express them until the proper opportunity is presented." HFS to Thomas Reed Powell (January 16, 1926) (Stone papers). In a similar vein, Stone wrote Walter Wheeler Cook the next year in the context of Bedford Cut Stone Co. v. Journeyman Stone Cutters' Ass'n of North America, 274 U.S. 37 (1927): "I think there is a difference between being one of five and one of six to uphold an earlier opinion with which the Judge does not agree. That, at any rate, was my view both in the Bedford case and in the second minimum wage case." HFS to Walter Wheeler Cook (May 4, 1927) (Stone papers). For Stone's ultimate views on the minimum wage, see Morehead v. New York *ex rel.* Tipaldo, 298 U.S. 587, 631 (1936) (Stone, J., dissenting).

At the time of *Sardell*, Holmes wrote Laski, "Don't make a mistake about Stone. He is a mighty sound and liberal-minded thinker. In the case to which I suppose you to refer he thought as I did but also thought that no countenance should be given to the notion that the decisions of the Court were subject to a change of personnel and therefore refrained from joining in my declaration." OWH to Harold Laski (November 29, 1925) in 1 HOLMES-LASKI CORRESPONDENCE, at 800. In

THE TAFT COURT

Sardell, the official memorandum opinion of the Court notes: "Mr. Justice Holmes requests that it be stated that his concurrence is solely upon the ground that he regards himself bound by the decision in *Adkins v. Children's Hospital*." 269 U.S. 530 (1925). Brandeis dissented in both *Sardell* and *Donham*.

On popular reaction to *Sardell*, see *Tightening the Bonds*, 44 NEW REPUBLIC 271 (1925) (*Adkins* "gave a jolt to the administration of minimum wage laws all over this country. But the states with changing degrees of energy persisted in their policy in the hope that the Adkins case was after all not the pronouncement of a generalized principle of law but the disposition of a specific statute related to a rather narrow set of circumstances in the District of Columbia. That hope is now dashed by the recent decision of the Supreme Court in the Arizona Minimum Wage case.").

115. Two days after the decision was announced, Taft's brother Horace wrote him, "Well, you folks *are* raising hell. We are now going to revise the Constitution from the ground up." Horace D. Taft to WHT (April 11, 1923) (Taft papers). Sutherland appeared blithely unconcerned about public criticism of his opinion, attributing it to the question of whose "toes are trod on." George Sutherland, *Address of Justice Sutherland*, 20 PROCEEDINGS OF THE TWENTIETH ANNUAL SESSION OF THE STATE BAR OF UTAH 55, 66 (1924).

116. *The Minimum Wage Law Decision*, NEW YORK LAW JOURNAL (April 16, 1923), at 192. For a blistering symposium on the case, see *The Minimum Wage – What Next?*, 50 THE SURVEY 215 (1923).

117. It was said that "the Court had gone prancing back to dear old Justice Peckham." *Changeable Silk*, 8 THE FREEMAN 609, 612 (March 5, 1924). The emphasis on *Lochner* "suggests that the majority of the court is disposed to return to the attitude of the court in the Lochner case and to emphasize the individual's right to freedom from restraint, rather than the public welfare which justifies legislative restriction of that freedom." Parkinson, *supra* note 8, at 134. The "revival of the *Lochner* case is among the most significant points of the opinion, for we are thrown back upon a decision arrived at without adequate investigation of the facts upon which the Statute was based." Harry Cohen, *Minimum Wage Legislation and the Adkins Case*, 2 NEW YORK UNIVERSITY LAW REVIEW 48, 53 (1925). The "vice" of *Lochner* was said to be its reliance "upon 'common understanding' which Prof. Freund suggests, 'is often equivalent to popular ignorance and fallacy.'" *Id.* at 53–54. See E.M. Borchard, *The Supreme Court and the Minimum Wage*, 32 YALE LAW JOURNAL 829, 830 (1923) ("Now after all these years comes the Supreme Court with a somewhat altered membership and in a majority opinion using arguments similar to those believed to be discredited since the *Lochner* case, the majority holds invalid in a five to three (practically five to four) decision, the minimum wage law for women of the District of Columbia, a law similar to that under which thirteen states had for years been acting and which several state courts had held constitutional.").

118. BENJAMIN N. CARDOZO, THE NATURE OF THE JUDICIAL PROCESS 79–80 (New Haven: Yale University Press 1921). Cardozo quoted Holmes's dissent to the effect that "A constitution is not intended to embody a particular economic theory, whether of paternalism and the organic relation of the citizen to the state, or of *laissez faire*. . . . The word liberty in the Fourteenth Amendment is perverted when it is held to prevent the natural outcome of a dominant opinion, unless it can be said

that a rational and fair man necessarily would admit that the statute proposed would infringe fundamental principles as they have been understood by the traditions of our people and our law." *Id.* at 79–80 (quoting Lochner v. New York, 198 U.S. 45, 75 (1905) (Holmes, J., dissenting)). "That," said Cardozo in 1921, referring to Holmes's famous 1905 dissent, "is the conception of liberty which is dominant today." *Id.* at 80.

119. Clark, *supra* note 17, at 627. *See* Ray A. Brown, *Book Review*, 39 HARVARD LAW REVIEW 909, 909 (1926) (referring to "the unpopularity of the decision with teachers and students of law and the social sciences").
120. Frank M. Parrish, *Minimum Wage Law for Women as a Violation of the Fifth Amendment*, 21 MICHIGAN LAW REVIEW 906, 910 (1923).
121. Powell, *The Judiciality of Minimum-Wage Legislation*, *supra* note 15, at 572.
122. JOHN A. RYAN, THE SUPREME COURT AND THE MINIMUM WAGE 56 (New York: The Paulist Press 1923). Governor Louis Hart of Washington suggested that *Adkins* "may be in its effect upon our economic and industrial life second only to the famous Dred Scott decision." Louis F. Hart, *A New Dred Scott Case?*, 50 THE SURVEY 218, 219 (1923). Florence Kelley, the general secretary of the National Consumers' League, decried the decision because it "obliterated a workable and necessary law for freeing wage-earning women in the District of Columbia from the 'lash of starvation.... This is a new "Dred Scott" decision.'" Florence Kelley, *Progress of Labor Legislation for Women*, in PROCEEDINGS OF THE NATIONAL CONFERENCE OF SOCIAL WORK 114 (University of Chicago Press 1923). "Sooner or later women must be added to the court," Kelley argued. "The monopoly of the interpretation and administration of the law by men alone can never again be accepted without criticism or protest. It is a survival of the age before women were full citizens." *Id.* at 115. *See Women on the Bench!*, 50 THE SURVEY 222 (1923).
123. Hart, *supra* note 122, at 219.
124. Walter M. Pierce, *Protect the Untrained Worker*, 50 THE SURVEY 218 (1923).
125. Frank W. Kuehl, *For an Amendment*, 50 THE SURVEY 219 (1923).
126. *See Does the Constitution Prevent Justice?*, 133 THE OUTLOOK 694, 696 (1923); *Mr. Untermeyer on the Minimum Wage Decision*, 30 AMERICAN FEDERATIONIST 408 (1923); Ryan, *supra* note 54, at 258; Minor Bronaugh, *Minimum-Wage Laws*, in THE SUPREME COURT AND MINIMUM WAGE LEGISLATION, *supra* note 114, at 219; Stephen F. Lawson, *Progressives and the Supreme Court: A Case for Judicial Reform in the 1920s*, 42 THE HISTORIAN 419, 426 (1980).
127. *Address of the President*, 65 CONG. REC. 99 (December 6, 1923). Coolidge had supported minimum wage legislation as Massachusetts governor. Sean Beienburg, *Progressivism and States' Rights: Constitutional Dialogue between the States and Federal Courts on Minimum Wages and Liberty of Contract*, 8 AMERICAN POLITICAL THOUGHT 25, 31 n.21 (2019).
128. George W.P. Hunt, *Ridiculous Reasoning*, 50 THE SURVEY 217 (1923); *Full Text of La Follette's Speech*, NEW YORK TIMES (September 19, 1924), at 2. *See also* Gompers, *supra* note 70; *The Supreme Court Supplants Congress*, *supra* note 94, at 485.
129. *See Wage Act Voiding Stirs Demand for Majority Decision*, NEW YORK WORLD (April 11, 1923), at 2 ("The Court's action has added to the complaints of Congressmen, labor leaders and others who feel that steps should be taken to

prevent the setting aside of laws by close decisions. Senator Borah (R. Ida.) issued a statement saying it 'was time for the practice to stop in the interest of good Government.'"); *A One-Man Constitution, supra* note 97, at 10 ("Senator Borah is right when he insists that 'a law which has the approval of both the other departments of the Government as being constitutional ought not to be held void upon a mere 5 to 4 decision, or ought not to turn upon a single view or the opinion of one Judge.' On this point public sentiment is rapidly becoming unanimous. The Constitution of the United States cannot remain indefinitely a one-man Constitution."); Perkins, *supra* note 17, at 258; W. Jett Lauck, *Require a Two-Thirds Vote*, 50 THE SURVEY 260 (1923); Ryan, *supra* note 54, at 258; *Cf. Progressives to Curb Power of High Court*, SPRINGFIELD DAILY REPUBLICAN (April 11, 1923), at 8 ("Progressive circles in Congress seethed today with renewed demands of a constitutional amendment designed to curb the present unlimited power of the United States supreme court to declare legislation unconstitutional by the barest of majorities. . . . [L]egislation to limit the court's power is virtually certain of introduction in the next Congress. . . . Senator Borah . . . said today that as soon as the next Congress convenes he will introduce a bill compelling a 7-to-2 vote by the court before it can declare an act of Congress unconstitutional. Another plan, sponsored by Senator La Follette, Republican, of Wisconsin, would give Congress the power to re-enact laws by a two-thirds vote over an adverse decision by the supreme court. . . . A third, proposed by Senator Fess, Republican, of Ohio, would require a two-thirds vote of the nine supreme court's justices to make effective any decision holding an act of Congress unconstitutional. All three plans drew ardent supporters today as a result of the minimum wage decree."); John R. Commons, *Restore the Balance of Power*, 50 THE SURVEY 261 (1923) ("[T]he time has come for a constitutional amendment requiring at least a two-thirds vote or a three-fourths vote to declare an act of Congress unconstitutional. The same rule should apply when state legislation is before the United States court."); *Borah Wants Minimum Wage Left to States*, *supra* note 97, at 2 ("A proposal to amend the Constitution of the United States to make it possible for the states to enact minimum wage legislation probably will grow out of the decision of the Supreme Court of the United States yesterday invalidating the District of Columbia minimum wage law for women."); *Curb on Supreme Court Projected*, NEW YORK WORLD (April 13, 1923), at 8 ("Plans have been laid by La Follette progressives for passage next Congress of some measures restricting the power of the Supreme Court to nullify laws by so-called 'one man' decisions. An arrangement has been made with Democratic leaders by which the progressives will be given the balance of power on the House Judiciary committee before which this legislation will come. . . . Some leading Democrats are in favor of requiring the Supreme Court to come to a two-thirds vote before it can declare an act unconstitutional. La Follette progressives would go further, although they are divided, with La Follette himself wanting Congress to override the Supreme Court by a two-thirds vote and Frear (R. Wis.) seeking a unanimous decision of the Court.").

Despite worry that Harding's appointments would determine the "complexion" of the Court "for a decade," the *New Republic* regarded Borah's proposed bill as "so clearly unconstitutional that we suspect he introduced it more with the thought of keeping the issue alive than the hope of relieving the pain caused by

Adkins v. Children's Hospital

five to four decisions." *The Supreme Court Again*, 34 NEW REPUBLIC 59, 59 (1923). The *New Republic* cautioned that if the public was coming to believe "that a great number constitutional decisions turn upon the court's view of what is best for the country," the Court was running the risk of "provoking some such sweeping impairment of judicial independence as that proposed by Mr. Frear. We can see little harm and much virtue in a constitutional requirement that the court act with some degree of unanimity on questions where it, itself, has said that it will not act unless the case is clear." But "Mr. Frear's sweeping proposals for the recall of the judges and the decisions of the court go far beyond the justification of experience." *Id.* at 60.

Proposals like Borah's particularly irked Taft. He wrote his son that "The vote of five to three . . . on the minimum wage, has accentuated the attack on the power of five in the Court to set aside a law. It is said to be a 'one-man' decision. Of course this is unjust. It is just as unjust as it would be to require that every measure that passed the House and the Senate should be passed by a two-thirds vote. They speak glibly of putting through a law of that sort. I think they will have very great difficulty in sustaining such a law if they ever get it through." WHT to Robert A. Taft (April 16, 1923) (Taft papers).

130. *See supra* note 114. The story is nicely told in Beienburg, *supra* note 127. The continuous open defiance of the State of Washington, together with the strong support of the local Washington business community, explains why in West Coast Hotel Co. v. Parrish, 300 U.S. 379 (1937), the Court could marvel that the minimum wage statute of Washington had been "in force" through the "entire period" since *Adkins*. *Id.* at 391.

131. WHT to WVD (June 19, 1925) (Van Devanter papers).

CHAPTER 25

Price Fixing and Property Affected with a Public Interest

As mobilized opposition to judicial review subsided, the Taft Court seized the opportunity to develop a line of cases stringently tightening constitutional restrictions on government price controls. Building on *Adkins*, the Court explicitly distinguished price fixing from all other forms of police power regulation. The Court held that price fixing was permissible only with respect to property constitutionally classified as "affected with a public interest." By sharply and arbitrarily limiting the category of property affected with a public interest, the Court effectively prohibited price fixing from expanding beyond its prewar scope.

Famously first propounded in the 1876 case of *Munn v. Illinois*,[1] the doctrine of property affected with a public interest identified the kinds of property or businesses that could constitutionally be subject to comprehensive administrative control, including rate regulation.[2] Citing Lord Chief Justice Hale, Chief Justice Waite broadly proclaimed in *Munn* that "[p]roperty does become clothed with a public interest when used in a manner to make it of public consequence, and affect the community at large."[3] By the end of the nineteenth century, railroads and utilities had come to exemplify property affected with a public interest. The category of such property expanded steadily but erratically until the 1920s.

The apex of that expansion was perhaps the Court's 1914 decision in *German Alliance Insurance Co. v. Kansas*, which held that the business of fire insurance was "so far affected with a public interest as to justify legislative regulation of its rates." Citing precedents like *Schmidinger* and *Muller*, McKenna, writing for six justices, declared in *German Alliance* that the "underlying principle is that business of certain kinds holds such a peculiar relation to the public interests that there is superinduced upon it the right of public regulation." "Contracts of insurance," McKenna explained, belong to the category of property affected with a public interest because they "have greater public consequences than contracts between individuals to do or not to do a particular thing whose effect stops with the individuals."[4]

Price Fixing & Property Affected with a Public Interest

McKenna pointedly refused to draw any distinction between government regulation of a business's conduct and government regulation of its prices. "It is idle," he said, "to debate whether the liberty of contract guaranteed by the Constitution of the United States is more intimately involved in price regulation than in the other forms of regulation as to the validity of which there is no dispute. ... [H]ow can it be said that fixing the price of insurance is beyond [the power of government] and other instances of regulation are not?"[5]

In a forceful dissent, Joseph Lamar, joined by Van Devanter and White, argued that "The fixing of the price for the use of private property is as much a taking as though the fee itself had been condemned for a lump sum. ... But the court in this case holds that there is no distinction between the power to take for public use and the power to regulate the exercise of private rights for the public good. ... [I]f, as seems to be implied, the fact that a business may be regulated is to be the test of the power to fix rates, it would follow, since all can be regulated, the price charged by all can be regulated."[6]

World War I realized Lamar's and Van Devanter's worst nightmare. "The extraordinary circumstances of the war" brought a wide swath of businesses "clearly into the category of those which are affected with a public interest and which demand immediate and thorough-going public regulation."[7] The government engaged in aggressive and comprehensive price fixing,[8] which the White Court permitted to bleed over into peacetime rent control in cases like *Block v. Hirsh*.[9] By 1922, Rexford Tugwell could observe that "The definition of police power in all of the recent cases brings it into the broad field of public interest, so that the regulation of business in its economic aspects, its prices and its standards of service, flows from the general interest of the public just as does the right of regulation of business to secure the health, morals and safety of the community."[10]

In their quest for normalcy, however, Harding's judicial appointments almost immediately initiated what contemporaries correctly perceived as "a flat reversal of direction."[11] *Adkins*, with its sharp distinction between regulating hours of employment and regulating wages, was the opening salvo. Only two months later, speaking through Taft, the Court unanimously decided the pivotal case of *Charles Wolff Packing Company v. Kansas Court of Industrial Relations*,[12] which in *dicta* sought deliberately to contract the definition of property affected with a public interest.

At issue in *Wolff Packing* was the constitutionality of an ambitious Kansas statute declaring that industries involved in the production or manufacture of clothing, food, and fuel were "affected with a public interest." The statute established a Court of Industrial Relations with authority to fix wages and other conditions of operation within these industries whenever their "continuity or efficiency" were endangered.[13] Because the statute prohibited strikes, it was widely regarded as imposing compulsory arbitration.[14]

The case for the Kansas statute essentially rested on *Wilson v. New*,[15] in which the White Court had considered congressional legislation setting an eight-hour day and temporarily setting a wage-scale for employees of interstate railroads.[16] The legislation had been enacted during an "emergency";[17] it was intended to avert an imminent nationwide strike that "would leave the public helpless, the whole people ruined and all the homes of the land submitted to a danger of the most serious character."[18]

Over the dissents of Day, Van Devanter, Pitney, and McReynolds, the Court upheld the legislation. It held that "the business of common carriers by rail is in a sense a public business because of the interest of society in the continued operation and rightful conduct of such business," and that this "public interest begets a public right of regulation to the full extent necessary to secure and protect it." It was irrelevant that wages were ordinarily "primarily private" and "not subject" to the control of "public authority." The "dispute between the employers and employees as to a standard of wages" and "their failure to agree" imminently threatened "the entire interruption of interstate commerce ... and the infinite injury to the public interest."[19]

Wilson v. New was decided only one month before the nation entered World War I. The urgent need for national integration and unification permeates the opinion. The Kansas statute at issue in *Wolff Packing* was an effort to project that same sense of public necessity into the postwar years. The statute had been proposed by Kansas Governor Henry Justin Allen upon his return from Europe after the war. A progressive, Bull Moose Republican,[20] Allen possessed a robust conception of the public interest that drew deeply on progressive assumptions about the priority of public to private interests.[21] Upon confronting a bitter coal strike during the freezing winter of 1919–20,[22] he recruited a volunteer army of mostly ex-servicemen to replace the striking miners.[23] Resolving that the public would never again suffer because of private labor disputes,[24] Allen proposed a statute that imposed full-fledged "legal compulsion"[25] onto the workplace.[26]

The statute created a Kansas Court of Industrial Relations ("KCIR"), which was intended to speak for a public interest that transcended the "private war"[27] of capital and labor. Its authority was succinctly summarized by a question put by Allen to Samuel Gompers during a well-publicized debate between the two men in Carnegie Hall. Gompers vigorously attacked the Kansas statute's prohibition of strikes as a denial of "liberty," an infringement of "the right to own oneself ... that he may do with his powers what best conserves his interests and his welfare."[28] Allen responded with a question: "When a dispute between capital and labor brings on a strike affecting the production or distribution of the necessaries of life, thus threatening the public peace and impairing the public health, has the public any rights in such a controversy, or is it a private war between capital and labor? If you answer this question in the affirmative, Mr. Gompers, how would you protect the rights of the public?"[29]

The KCIR was designed to enforce "the rights of the public." The Kansas statute was thus the polar opposite of "invalid 'class' legislation."[30] The KCIR was established to assert public "mastery" of public problems, exactly as the country had done during the war.[31] Postwar labor strife in the United States was so intense

Price Fixing & Property Affected with a Public Interest

that the entire nation seemed transformed into a battlefield. Wartime solutions suddenly appeared reasonable and necessary. In upholding the KCIR in 1921, the Kansas Supreme Court detailed the carnage:

> The strike record of the year 1919, however, proved to be the most disheartening one in our industrial history. The statistics are amazing, even to minds accustomed to war figures. Millions of men and women were involved. The following is a partial list of the more important strikes and lockouts shown by the government report for 1919:
>
> > "A general strike in Tacoma and Seattle in February in sympathy with the metal–trades strikers, in which 60,000 persons were involved; 65,000 employees in the Chicago stockyards struck in August; 100,000 longshoremen along the Atlantic Coast struck in October; 100,000 employees in the shipyards of New York City and vicinity struck in October; 115,000 members of the building trades were locked out in Chicago in July; 125,000 in the building trades in New York City struck in February; 250,000 railroad shop workers struck in August; 367,000 iron and steel workers struck in September; and 435,000 bituminous coal miners struck in November. The number of persons concerned in these nine strikes and lockouts was upward of 1,600,000, while the total number of persons involved in strikes and lockouts during 1919 was 4,112,507." ...
>
> The direct losses in money amounted to stupendous sums. William Z. Foster, who conducted the steel strike, says that struggle alone cost a billion dollars. The indirect losses were beyond computation. The moral effect was such that school children learned to strike; and the unspeakable crime was committed in Boston when the policemen struck.[32]

It is no wonder that the Kansas legislation captured widespread "public attention."[33] Harding was so moved that in his first annual message to Congress he ignored his own Republican Party Platform and essentially proposed "to nationalize the Kansas labor court plan"[34] by creating "judicial or quasi-judicial tribunals for the consideration and determination of all disputes which menace the public welfare."[35]

The doctrinal category that proponents of the KCIR hoped would justify its extraordinary power was that of "property affected with a public interest." The railroads in *Wilson v. New* had historically been classified as such property; it was argued, not without reason, that "the price of food and raiment" were "more important to the community than the cost of its carriage."[36] The Kansas Supreme Court adopted this theory in upholding the KCIR:

> Organized government has never been without power to make regulations whenever the conduct of business threatened public harm, and the power has been exercised as occasion required. ... In 1876, the decision in Munn v. Illinois was rendered. That decision was followed by determined reactionary efforts to limit its application to definite classes of business. ... These and other efforts to limit, and even to overthrow, the doctrine of the Munn Case, failed, and all the

795

arguments by which they were sustained were refuted in the opinion in the case of German Alliance Insurance Co. v. Kansas ... a landmark in the progress of the law almost as noteworthy as the case of Munn v. Illinois.[37]

Property affected with a public interest could constitutionally be subject to comprehensive regulation, exemplified by "the minutely detailed government supervision"[38] established by the Transportation Act of 1920.[39] The argument of the Kansas Supreme Court implied that government could apply such comprehensive regulation virtually throughout the entire economy. Essentially this would extend wartime price fixing authority into the 1920s.[40] That possibility deeply worried those who had been alarmed by the wartime expansion of government authority: "The control of business activities exercised by the Federal Government during the war ... more or less accustomed people to government supervision, restraint and direction. The assertion by the State legislatures of similar control, since the close of hostilities, therefore, has met with less opposition than naturally would have been the case without such preparation. The most striking example of this type of legislation is that furnished by the Kansas 'Industrial Court Law.'"[41]

In *Wolff Packing*, Taft, speaking for a unanimous Court,[42] used the Fourteenth Amendment to cut short any doctrinal expansion of the category of property affected with a public interest.[43] Taft's concern was not that Kansas had enacted impermissible class legislation; he was not worried that Kansas had intervened to aid either labor or management. To the contrary, both Taft and Sutherland believed that the public possessed a strong and legitimate interest in diminishing industrial strife.[44] Only four months previously Taft had authored an important unanimous opinion upholding the Railroad Labor Board, which had been created by the Transportation Act of 1920 "to act as a board of arbitration" empowered to articulate "the force of public opinion" with regard to "the economic interest of every member of the public in the undisturbed flow of interstate commerce."[45] No one disagreed that the KCIR spoke for this same public interest. In *Wolff Packing*, therefore, Taft focused not on whether the KCIR favored one class over another, but instead on whether the statute intruded too unreasonably on "the freedom of contract and of labor secured by the Fourteenth Amendment."[46]

At issue in *Wolff Packing* was a KCIR order raising wages and altering other conditions of employment within a small and unprofitable meat packing company.[47] In the original draft of his opinion, Taft had apparently based his decision on the theory that preparing human food was not "affected with the public interest."[48] In his final, published version, however, Taft merely cast strong doubt on this question and decided that, even if the Wolff Packing Company were clothed with the public interest, its owners and workers could not be ordered to continue in business "on terms fixed by an agency of the State."[49]

Taft's discussion of the "affected with the public interest" doctrine was nevertheless extensive, and it was plainly meant to be instructive.[50] It began by quoting *Adkins* to the effect that "[f]reedom is the general rule, and restraint the exception." Pointedly emphasizing that the classification of property as affected

Price Fixing & Property Affected with a Public Interest

with a public interest is "always a subject of judicial inquiry" and could never be determined by "the mere declaration by a legislature," Taft proceeded to explore the "circumstances" that might justify a "change from the status of a private business and its freedom from regulation into one in which the public have come to have an interest." Taft knew full well that "[a]ll business is subject to some kinds of public regulation," so that, in his most careful formulation, he fashioned the doctrine to determine "when the public becomes so peculiarly dependent upon a particular business that one engaging therein subjects himself to a more intimate public regulation."[51]

Taft had enormous difficulty giving analytic content to this boundary. His opinion sometimes evokes the "indispensable nature of the service and the exorbitant charges and arbitrary control to which the public might be subjected without regulation."[52] Sometimes it refers to the "fear of monopoly."[53] Sometimes it employs the image of an "owner ... devoting his business to the public use."[54] Sometimes it speaks of "great temporary public exigencies," like those that had been determinative in *New* or *Hirsh*.[55] In the end, however, Taft was forced to confess that "it is very difficult under the cases to lay down a working rule by which readily to determine when a business has become 'clothed with a public interest.'"[56]

Taft's difficulty arose because he had no functional account of the purpose of the doctrine of "affected with a public interest." While he could distinguish national emergencies, like those that had existed during the World War, he did not possess an analytic framework that could convincingly discriminate among the myriad lesser public purposes that government regulation might serve. Nor did he have an explanation of the constitutional values at stake in the classification of particular forms of property as either private or public.[57]

The most that can be said is that the rhetoric of Taft's opinion points vaguely but unmistakably to the importance of safeguarding from state intrusion a realm of freedom, whose boundaries are normative rather than functional, and whose center is located in the rounds of everyday life. "If ... the common callings are clothed with a public interest by a mere legislative declaration, which necessarily authorizes full and comprehensive regulation within legislative discretion," then there must be, Taft warned, "a revolution in the relation of government to general business."[58] "It has never been supposed," Taft wrote, "that the business of the butcher, or the baker, the tailor, the wood chopper, the mining operator, or the miner was clothed with such a public interest that the price of his product or his wages could be fixed by state regulation. ... [N]owadays one does not devote one's property or business to the public use or clothe it with a public interest merely because one makes commodities for, and sells to, the public in the common callings."[59]

Although Taft's opinion in *Wolff Packing* does not explicate why the Constitution might protect the common callings from "intimate public regulation," the debate surrounding the KCIR offers intriguing suggestions. Opposition to the KCIR centered on the claim that it brought ordinary economic life "under the managerial control of the State,"[60] that it sought to establish "managerial supervision, regulation, and control of a very extensive field of private industries."[61] This kind of supervision required the same organizational expertise, the same "science of administration and management, which rests on research, planning and cooperative control,"[62] that had flourished during World War I. Taft in *Wolff Packing* was determined to restrict the managerial prerogatives of that expertise by sharply confining the category of property affected with a public interest.[63]

Taft did not explain in *Wolff Packing* why the managerial prerogatives of the state should be constitutionally limited, nor did he offer any helpful account of how those constitutional limitations might be ascertained. Taft could only reaffirm *Adkins*'s general presumption in favor of "freedom." That presumption, however, resonated with widespread popular objections to the KCIR. The "experiment of Kansas to regulate the intimate details of the daily life of its citizens met with the disapproval and resentment of both employer and employee."[64] Opposition to the KCIR circled around the claim that it subordinated economic life to the dictates of an "administrative tribunal ... miscalled a court,"[65] empowered to manage the "common machine"[66] of industrial life.

Advocates of labor opposed the KCIR because it denied the "right of all workers to control their own lives."[67] The KCIR sought to erect "a vast machinery of state for the regulation of human activities."[68] Business interests opposed the KCIR because it violated "the American principle of economic freedom."[69] Centrist liberals opposed the KCIR because it transformed independent democratic citizens into objects of managerial supervision. "What we want is a self-reliant, independent, free people, capable of working out their own destinies. The more opportunities people can have for self-control and the less they are dominated and directed ... the more likely they are to develop in that direction."[70]

No doubt this same spectrum of views was present on the Court itself. What is striking about *Wolff Packing* is its unanimity. On the left, we know that Brandeis had "absolutely" opposed compulsory arbitration since at least 1913 because he believed that it impaired the "moral vigor" necessary to maintain "the fighting quality, the stamina, and the courage to battle for what we want when we are convinced that we are entitled to it."[71] In a note signifying his assent to Taft's opinion in *Wolff Packing*, Brandeis wrote that "In Wilson v. New there was 'clear and present danger' and the 'curse was in its bigness.'"[72] Only a month later Brandeis expounded to Frankfurter his belief that "fundamental rights" of "speech," "education," "choice of profession," and "locomotion" should "not be impaired or withdrawn except as judged by 'clear and present danger' test."[73] It is plausible to infer that Brandeis regarded the KCIR as an assault on the fundamental liberties necessary for democratic citizenship that was not justified by any clear and present danger, as had been the case in *New*.

On the right, McReynolds gave full-throated expression to the stakes at issue in *Wolff Packing* in his dissent a decade later in *Nebbia v. New York*, in which the Hughes Court overruled Taft Court precedents and upheld price fixing in the dairy industry.[74] In *Nebbia*, the Court rejected the idea that there existed any distinct category of property "affected with a public interest," noting that the phrase was the simple "equivalent of 'subject to the exercise of the police power'; and it is plain

Price Fixing & Property Affected with a Public Interest

that nothing more was intended by the expression."[75] In a dissent joined by Van Devanter, Sutherland, and Butler, McReynolds bitterly complained that fixing

> the price at which "A," engaged in an ordinary business, may sell, in order to enable "B," a producer, to improve his condition, has not been regarded as within legislative power. This is not regulation, but management, control, dictation – it amounts to the deprivation of the fundamental right which one has to conduct his own affairs honestly and along customary lines. ... [I]f it be now ruled that one dedicates his property to public use whenever he embarks on an enterprise which the Legislature may think it desirable to bring under control, this is but to declare that rights guaranteed by the Constitution exist only so long as supposed public interest does not require their extinction. To adopt such a view, of course, would put an end to liberty under the Constitution.[76]

All sides of the Court, then, acknowledged the existence of "fundamental rights" that protected a sphere of individual liberty beyond the administrative management of the state. They differed in defining the exact nature and justification of that sphere. Those on the right emphasized economic freedoms associated with "customary" common law property rights, which they regarded as necessary both for production of economic wealth and for the expression of individual agency. Those on the left focused on freedoms necessary for developing the competence of democratic citizens.[77] In *Wolff Packing* both sides could concur in striking down the KCIR.

The misfortune of Taft Court jurisprudence was that it failed to develop a normative account of the "property affected with a public interest" doctrine that might capitalize on this overlap and explain the contours and purposes of the doctrine. Instead, the Court developed the doctrine with the sole purpose of checking government authority to fix prices. In the second half of the decade, Sutherland would author three opinions for the Court, each arbitrarily constricting the scope of "property affected with a public interest," each dogmatically declaring that price fixing was impermissible except with respect to such property.

We have already discussed the first two of these decisions[78] – *Tyson & Brother v. Banton*[79] and *Ribnik v. McBride*.[80] In *Tyson*, New York had declared "that the price of or charge for admission to theatres ... is a matter affected with a public interest," and that theater tickets could not be resold "at a price in excess of fifty cents in advance of the price printed on the face" of a ticket.[81] Sutherland, writing for a bare majority of five,[82] began his analysis with the premise that "the power to regulate property, services or business can be invoked only under special circumstances."[83] Sutherland took deliberate aim at the essential holding of *German Alliance Insurance* that there was no qualitative difference between the power to regulate and the power to fix prices.[84] Sutherland wrote that "the authority to regulate the conduct of a business or to require a license, comes from a branch of the police power which may be quite distinct from the power to fix prices. The latter, ordinarily, does not exist in respect of merely private property or business, but exists only where the business of the property involved has become 'affected with a public interest.'"[85]

799

Conceding that "the full meaning" of the doctrinal category of "property affected with a public interest" "cannot be exactly defined," Sutherland nevertheless insisted that government had no constitutional authority to fix prices except with respect to property that "bore such a substantial and definite relation to the public interest as to justify an indulgence of the legal fiction of a grant by the owner to the public of an interest in the use."[86] Although in *Weller v. New York* the Taft Court had unanimously upheld New York legislation requiring ticket brokers to be licensed,[87] Sutherland explicitly held that the power to require a license falls "far short of the one here invoked to fix prices."[88]

Building on *Wolff Packing*, Sutherland, with Taft supplying the fifth vote,[89] held that the "importance" of "theatres and other places of entertainment" to the public "falls below" that of "food and shelter ... provisions or clothing." "If it be within the legitimate authority of government to fix maximum charges for admission to theatres, ... it is hard to see where the limit of power in respect of price fixing is to be drawn." "Subversions" of constitutional property protections "are fraught with the danger that, having begun on the ground of necessity, they will continue on the score of expediency, and, finally, as a mere matter of course. Constitutional principles, applied as they are written, it must be assumed, operate justly and wisely as a general thing, and they may not be remolded by lawmakers or judges to save exceptional cases of inconvenience, hardship or injustice."[90]

Sutherland's opinion in *Tyson*, like Taft's in *Wolff Packing*, is directed at checking the undue expansion of state regulatory power. Sutherland's odd claim that the Court was simply applying the Constitution as "written" was too much for Holmes, who was provoked to assert in dissent that, "as I intimated in *Adkins*, ... the notion that a business is clothed with a public interest and has been devoted to the public use is little more than a fiction intended to beautify what is disagreeable to the sufferers. The truth seems to me to be that, subject to compensation when compensation is due, the legislature may forbid or restrict any business when it has a sufficient force of public opinion behind it."

> [P]olice power often is used in a wide sense to cover and ... to apologize for the general power of the legislature to make a part of the community uncomfortable by a change. I do not believe in such apologies. I think the proper course is to recognize that a state legislature can do whatever it sees fit to do unless it is restrained by some express prohibition in the Constitution of the United States or of the State, and that Courts should be careful not to extend such prohibitions beyond their obvious meaning by reading into them conceptions of public policy that the particular Court may happen to entertain.[91]

This was remarkably strong and pointed language for Holmes, whose opinion was joined by Brandeis.[92]

Stone and Sanford each dissented on the narrower ground that the New York legislation was not aimed at theaters, but at ticket brokers, who, "by virtue of arrangements which they make with the theater owners, ordinarily acquire an absolute control of the most desirable seats in the theaters, by which they ... are enabled to exact an extortionate advance in prices for the sale of such tickets to the

Price Fixing & Property Affected with a Public Interest

public."[93] Stone and Sanford each sought to give rational economic meaning to the doctrine of "affected with the public interest." They believed that the doctrine should be interpreted to authorize price fixing whenever the normal "'free' competition among buyers and sellers" had, for one reason or another, broken down.[94]

"No comment on Mr. Justice Sutherland's elaboration of the words 'affected with a public interest' could be more cruel," wrote Thomas Reed Powell, "than to place his discourse in juxtaposition with Mr. Justice Stone's elucidation of its question-begging meaninglessness."[95] But Powell missed the larger point. Although Sutherland purported to value the higgling of the market, he was in fact uninterested in the empirics of actual market failure. Sutherland did not intend to fashion doctrine that would offer helpful guidelines about when price fixing was constitutional and when it was not. His aim was instead to stop the postwar expansion of price fixing regulations altogether.[96] And in this *Tyson* succeeded. Commentators immediately recognized that it was an "epochal case" that marked the "road to the supremacy of the Supreme Court over legislative action."[97]

The Court advanced a step further down that road the following year in *Ribnik v. McBride*,[98] when Sutherland authored an opinion for five justices striking down a New Jersey statute requiring that employment agencies charge only reasonable fees.[99] *Ribnik* hardened the holding of *Tyson* into a flat, mechanical, arbitrary rule.[100] Even though employment agents were extensively regulated and licensed, "the power to require a license for and to regulate the conduct of a business is distinct from the power to fix prices."[101] Even though the public was properly and "deeply interested" in the behavior of employment agencies, its interest "is not different in quality or character from its interest" in the behavior of druggists, butchers, bakers, grocers, real estate rentals, and real estate brokers, and "in none of them is the interest that 'public interest' which the law contemplates as the basis for legislative price control." "Under the decisions of this Court it is no longer fairly open to question that, at least in the absence of a grave emergency, the fixing of prices for food or clothing, of house rental or of wages to be paid, whether minimum or maximum, is beyond the legislative power. And we perceive no reason for applying a different rule in the case of legislation controlling prices to be paid for services rendered in securing a place for an employee or an employee for a place."[102] The employment brokers in *Ribnik* were no different from the ticket brokers in *Tyson*; both were essentially "private" businesses.[103]

This was a constitutional law of labels. The labels were fashioned to authorize ongoing price fixing in areas that had been traditional before the war,[104] like railroads and utilities, while preventing the expansion of the practice to other "common callings," like employment agencies or the manufacturers of food.[105] It was a deliberately nonpurposive form of constitutional law, indifferent as to why price fixing might be permissible for railroads but not for employment agencies. It refused to ask what function the doctrinal category of "property affected with a public interest" might meaningfully be designed to serve.

801

Stone authored a brutal dissent. He argued that there was no "controlling difference between reasonable regulation of price, if appropriate to the evil to be remedied, and other forms of appropriate regulation which curtail liberty of contract or the use and enjoyment of property."[106] Taking a leaf from Brandeis's dissent in *Jay Burns*, Stone marshaled the data of "repeated investigations, official and unofficial," to mount a devastating case of widespread abuses in the employment agency business and demonstrating that price control was the only effective remedy for those abuses. It was one thing, Stone acerbically noted, "[t]o overcharge a man for the privilege of hearing the opera, ... to control the possibility of his earning a livelihood would appear to be quite another." Matters of such importance should not be decided with eyes closed "to available data throwing light on the problem with which the Legislature had to deal."[107]

Ribnik was roundly and justifiably criticized.[108] Rexford Tugwell, for example, celebrated the "pragmatic view of human necessity" informing Stone's dissent and condemned the "blind adherence to some outmoded faith" animating Sutherland's majority opinion. He was appalled by the "pure and unreasoned dogma" of Sutherland's decision, its "obvious ... prejudice and dislike for bureaucratic meddling."[109] It is precisely this quality that drove Stone to reorient his understanding of the judicial role to accept the necessity of deference in the context of social and economic legislation. Courts ought to avoid even the appearance of imposing "personal economic predilections."[110]

A year after *Ribnik*, the Taft Court in *Williams v. Standard Oil Co.* struck down a Tennessee statute regulating the price of gasoline. Sutherland's opinion for the Court was essentially a victory lap. "It is settled by recent decisions of this court," he said, "that a state Legislature is without constitutional power to fix prices at which commodities may be sold, services rendered, or property used, unless the business or property involved is 'affected with a public interest.'" Although Sutherland acknowledged that "Nothing is gained by reiterating the statement that the phrase is indefinite," he nevertheless insisted that the "phrase ... has become the established test by which the legislative power to fix prices of commodities, use of property, or services, must be measured."[111]

Property was not to be classified as affected with a public interest "merely because it is large or because the public are warranted in having a feeling of concern in respect of its maintenance." It did not matter that gasoline "has become necessary and indispensable in carrying on commercial and other activities within the state. ... [W]e are here concerned with the character of the business, not with its size or the extent to which the commodity is used. Gasoline is one of the ordinary commodities of trade, differing, so far as the question here is affected, in no essential respect from a great variety of other articles commonly bought and sold by merchants and private dealers in the country."[112]

Sutherland could not have been clearer that the Court would arrogate to itself the authority to determine when price fixing was warranted, and that it would exercise its authority in a manner that was indifferent to purposive considerations of public policy. He could not have been clearer that the Court was determined to protect freedom to conduct "ordinary" economic transactions. As Robert Jackson

Price Fixing & Property Affected with a Public Interest

subsequently put it, "'Due Process,' meant uncontrolled prices except where the Court saw fit to hold otherwise. ... The Court pulled the teeth of regulation."[113] The Taft Court was prepared to allow price fixing where it had been imposed before the war, but it would not permit an expansion of that authority. Stone was correct when he observed that in Sutherland's elegant hands the "phrase 'business affected with a public interest' ... tends in use to become only a convenient expression for describing those businesses, regulation of which has been permitted in the past."[114] Sutherland and the Taft Court resolutely refused to justify this bright line.

One can readily understand why this kind of decision-making might be perceived as arbitrary. At the beginning of the twentieth century, Roscoe Pound had famously condemned the *Lochner* Court as exemplifying a mere "mechanical jurisprudence,"[115] blundering through a "cloud of rules ... at the expense of practical results" and appealing "to artificial criteria of general application" that prevented "effective judicial investigation or consideration of the situations of fact behind or bearing upon the statutes."[116] But the Taft Court was not blundering. It was engaged in a deadly serious effort to use the Constitution to contain the regulatory explosion unleashed by the war. The Court was in effect asking the American people to trust the Court's intuitions that wartime economic planning needed to be kept on a very short leash.

The adamant resolution of the conservative bloc wore down the opposition. Brandeis and Stone concurred in the result in *Williams*. Holmes was disgusted. He dissented, but without opinion. He wrote Stone that "in spite of Brandeis's exhortations I do not intend to write. I have said my say. I thought I should say this: 'Of course I yield to the authority of decided cases, and although I thought this case might be distinguished from its predecessor it is for the propriety that established the precedents to say how far the violet rays of the Fourteenth Amendment reach.'" "I am rather pleased with the innuendo of 'violet rays,'" Holmes added, with a sardonic twinkle.[117]

Stone was not amused. "I like your phrase about the violet rays of the Fourteenth Amendment and would like to join you in it," he wrote. "I hesitate merely because there are so many solemn-minded people, unembarrassed by any sense of humor, who might feel that we were treating lightly and irreverently a very serious matter. I shall, of necessity, touch the susceptibilities of such people often enough, so that I hesitate to do it unnecessarily. Of course there is a good deal in the majority opinion which seems utter rubbish to me."[118]

Notes

1. 94 U.S. 113, 126 (1876). For a good discussion of the background and implications of *Munn*, see Harry N. Scheiber, *The Road to Munn: Eminent Domain and the Concept of Public Purpose in the State Courts*, 5 PERSPECTIVES IN AMERICAN HISTORY 329, 402 (1971); and William J. Novak, *The Public Utility Idea and the Origins of Modern Business Regulation*, in CORPORATIONS AND AMERICAN DEMOCRACY (Naomi R. Lamoreaux & William J. Novak, eds., Cambridge: Harvard University Press 2017).
2. For accounts of the doctrine in the 1920s, see Walton H. Hamilton, *Affectation with Public Interest*, 39 YALE LAW JOURNAL 1089, 1089–112 (1930); Breck P. McAllister, *Lord Hale and Business Affected with a Public Interest*, 43 HARVARD LAW REVIEW 759, 759–91 (1930); Dexter Merriam Keezer, *Some Questions Involved in the Application of the "Public Interest" Doctrine*, 25 MICHIGAN LAW REVIEW 596, 596–621 (1927); Gustavus H. Robinson, *The Public Utility: A Problem in Social Engineering*, 14 CORNELL LAW QUARTERLY 1, 1–27 (1928); and Gustavus H. Robinson, *The Public Utility Concept in American Law*, 41 HARVARD LAW REVIEW 277, 277–308 (1928).
3. *Munn*, 94 U.S. at 126.
4. 233 U.S. 389, 406, 411, 413 (1914). McKenna added:

> To the contention that the business is private we have opposed the conception of the public interest. We have shown that the business of insurance has very definite characteristics, with a reach of influence and consequence beyond and different from that of the ordinary businesses of the commercial world, to pursue which a greater liberty may be asserted. The transactions of the latter are independent and individual, terminating in their effect with the instances. The contracts of insurance may be said to be interdependent. They cannot be regarded singly, or isolatedly, and the effect of their relation is to create a fund of assurance and credit.

Id. at 414.

5. *Id.* at 415–16. McKenna continued:

> We may venture to observe that the price of insurance is not fixed over the counters of the companies by what Adam Smith calls the higgling of the market, but formed in the councils of the underwriters, promulgated in schedules of practically controlling constancy which the applicant for insurance is powerless to oppose and which, therefore, has led to the assertion that the business of insurance is of monopolistic character and that "it is illusory to speak of liberty of contract." It is in the alternative presented of accepting the rates of the companies or refraining from insurance, business necessity impelling if not compelling it, that we may discover the inducement of the Kansas statute; and the problem presented is whether the legislature could regard it of as much moment to the public that they who seek insurance should no more be constrained by arbitrary terms than they who seek transportation by railroads, steam, or street, or by coaches whose itinerary may be only a few city blocks, or who seek the use of grain elevators, or to be secured in a night's accommodation at a wayside inn, or in the weight of a 5 cent loaf of bread. We do not say this to belittle such rights or to exaggerate the effect of insurance, but to exhibit the principle which exists in all and brings all under the same governmental power.

Id. at 417.

6. *Id.* at 419, 423–24 (Lamar, J., dissenting). Lamar continued, "[G]reat and pervasive as is the power to regulate, it cannot override the constitutional principle that private property cannot be taken for private purposes. That limitation on the power of government over the individual and his property cannot be avoided by calling an

Price Fixing & Property Affected with a Public Interest

unlawful taking a reasonable regulation. Indeed, the protection of property is an incident of the more fundamental and important right of liberty guaranteed by the Constitution, and which entitled the citizen freely to engage in any honest calling, and to make contracts as buyer or seller, as employer or employee, in order to support himself and family." *Id.* at 424.

7. Charles Evans Hughes, *War Powers under the Constitution*, in REPORT OF THE FORTIETH ANNUAL MEETING OF THE AMERICAN BAR ASSOCIATION 232, 247 (Baltimore: Lord Baltimore Press 1917).
8. On the vast extent of wartime price fixing, see Lewis H. Haney, *Price Fixing in the United States during the War*, 34 POLITICAL SCIENCE QUARTERLY 104 (1919). *See* WILLIAM G. ROSS, WORLD WAR I AND THE AMERICAN CONSTITUTION 56–65 (Cambridge University Press 2017). In an effort to avoid postwar inflation, government price fixing extended well into 1919, and in some instances into 1920. *Id.* The Court struck down on grounds of vagueness the price fixing provisions of the Lever Act in United States v. Cohen Grocery Co., 255 U.S. 81 (1921), and in Weeds v. United States, 255 U.S. 89 (1921), thus avoiding any determination about exactly how long Congress's price fixing powers remained in effect after the Armistice.
9. 256 U.S. 135 (1921). *See supra* Chapter 22, at 723.
10. REXFORD G. TUGWELL, THE ECONOMIC BASIS OF PUBLIC INTEREST 124 (New York: George Banta Publishing Co. 1922).
11. Arthur L Haugan, *Vicissitudes of the Price Fixing Doctrine*, 2 DAKOTA LAW REVIEW 430, 431 (1929); *see also* R. G. Tugwell, *That Living Constitution*, 55 NEW REPUBLIC 120 (1928).
12. 262 U.S. 522 (1923). For good discussions of the remarkable facts surrounding *Wolff Packing*, see David A. Schwarz, *Compelled Consent: Wolff Packing and the Constitutionality of Compulsory Arbitration*, 12 NEW YORK UNIVERSITY JOURNAL OF LAW & LIBERTY 14 (2018); and James Gray Pope, *Labor's Constitution of Freedom*, 106 YALE LAW JOURNAL 941, 1023–24 (1997). For a good collection of articles discussing the case, see Thomas Reed Powell, *The Supreme Court's Control over the Issue of Injunctions in Labor Disputes*, 13 PROCEEDINGS OF THE AMERICAN ACADEMY OF POLITICAL SCIENCE 37, 66 n.48 (1928).
13. The complete statute is reproduced in State v. Howat, 198 P. 686, 705–10 (Kan. 1921). For good discussions of the historical background of the unusual Kansas court, see DOMENICO GAGLIARDO, THE KANSAS INDUSTRIAL COURT: AN EXPERIMENT IN COMPULSORY ARBITRATION (Lawrence: University of Kansas Press 1941); NATIONAL INDUSTRIAL CONFERENCE BOARD, THE KANSAS COURT OF INDUSTRIAL RELATIONS (Research Report No. 67) (New York: National Industrial Conference Board 1924); BUREAU OF LABOR STATISTICS, UNITED STATES DEPARTMENT OF LABOR, KANSAS COURT OF INDUSTRIAL RELATIONS (Bulletin of the United States Bureau of Labor Statistics No. 322) (Washington D.C.: Government Printing Office 1923). The Kansas Court produced several decisions in the United States Supreme Court. *See* Dorchy v. Kansas, 272 U.S. 306 (1926); Charles Wolff Packing Co. v. Court of Indus. Relations, 267 U.S. 552 (1925); Dorchy v. Kansas, 264 U.S. 286 (1924); Howat v. Kansas, 258 U.S. 181 (1922).
14. *See, e.g.*, Charles Wolff Packing Co. v. Court of Indus. Relations, 267 U.S. 552, 564–65 (1925); Howat v. Kansas, 258 U.S. 181, 184 (1922). In 1921, before becoming chief justice, Taft referred to the Kansas scheme as creating "drastic

procedure" to support "industrial machinery for compulsory arbitration." William Howard Taft, *Labor and the Farmers* (June 29, 1921), in VIVIAN, at 592.
15. 243 U.S. 332 (1917). For discussions of *Wilson*, see Powell, *supra* note 12, at 67 n.51.
16. In Taft's view, the Adamson law upheld by *Wilson* was "a humiliating page in the history of congressional legislation, when a comparatively small body of men performing a function indispensable to the life of the country 'held Congress up,' rejected arbitration and demanded and received its own price. This was pure sovietism." William Howard Taft, *The Inauguration* (March 4, 1921), in VIVIAN, at 551.
17. *New*, 243 U.S. at 348 ("[E]mergency may afford a reason for the exertion of a living power already enjoyed.").
18. *Id*. at 351. The court explained:

> The President of the United States invited a conference between the parties. He proposed arbitration. The employers agreed to it and the employees rejected it. The President then suggested the eight-hour standard of work and wages. The employers rejected this and the employees accepted it. Before the disagreement was resolved the representatives of the employees abruptly called a general strike throughout the whole country, fixed for an early day. The President, stating his efforts to relieve the situation, and pointing out that no resources at law were at his disposal for compulsory arbitration, to save the commercial disaster, the property injury and the personal suffering of all, not to say starvation, which would be brought to many among the vast body of the people if the strike was not prevented, asked Congress, first, that the eight-hour standard of work and wages be fixed by law, and second, that an official body be created to observe during a reasonable time the operation of the legislation, and that an explicit assurance be given that if the result of such observation established such an increased cost to the employers as justified an increased rate, the power would be given to the Interstate Commerce Commission to authorize it. Congress responded by enacting the statute whose validity, as we have said, we are called upon to consider.

Id. at 342.
19. *Id*. at 347–48.
20. *See* HOMER E. SOCOLOFSKY, KANSAS GOVERNORS 152–55 (Lawrence: University Press of Kansas 1990); *May Day in Kansas*, 125 THE OUTLOOK 58 (May 12, 1920).
21. According to Allen, the Court of Industrial Relations was not "for the general regulation of business, of capital, or of labor, but for the protection of the public in an emergency when the processes of production are threatened and all efforts at conciliation have been exhausted. The law adds to the provisions of the second industrial conference: when that fails then the law takes hold." Quoted in P.F. Walker, *A Year of the Kansas Industrial Court*, 1 MANAGEMENT EFFICIENCY 171, 174 (1921).
22. *See* Henry J. Allen, *A Substitute for Strikes*, 192 SATURDAY EVENING POST 6–7 (March 6, 1920).
23. *See The Annual Banquet of the League*, 2 LAW AND LABOR 82, 85 (1920) (Speech by Henry J. Allen); Henry J. Allen, *Liberty and Law in Kansas*, 61 AMERICAN REVIEW OF REVIEWS 597, 597 (1920).
24. *See* Edna Osborne Whitcomb, *Governor Allen's Solution: How Kansas Undertakes to Abolish Industrial Strife*, 61 AMERICAN REVIEW OF REVIEWS 292, 292 (1920) ("Governor Allen determined to deal with the problem of strikes and other labor troubles by legislation"); Ray Yarnell, *Speaking of Anti-Strike Laws*, 8 NATION'S BUSINESS 16, 17 (1920).
25. *Arbitration – Compulsory or Voluntary?*, 22 NEW REPUBLIC 396, 397 (1920).

26. *See, e.g.*, Willard Atkins, *The Kansas Court of Industrial Relations*, 28 JOURNAL OF POLITICAL ECONOMY 339, 339 (1920); John A. Fitch, *Government Coercion in Labor Disputes*, 90 ANNALS OF AMERICAN ACADEMY OF POLITICAL & SOCIAL SCIENCE 74–77 (July 1920). Even as early as 1918, writers like Thorstein Veblen were advocating that "the derangement of conditions caused by the war, as well as the degree in which the public attention now centres on public questions, mark the present as the appointed time to take stock and adopt any necessary change in the domestic policy." Thorstein Veblen, *A Policy of Reconstruction*, 14 NEW REPUBLIC 318 (1918). Veblen advocated public control over industrial disputes, because, "seen from the point of view of the interest of the community," private rights in property and in the right to strike "figure up to something that may be called a right to exercise an unlimited sabotage, in order to gain a private end, regardless of the community's urgent need of having the work go on without interruption and at full capacity." *Id.* at 319. For a similar view, see Walter Lippmann, *Unrest*, 20 NEW REPUBLIC 315–22 (1919).

27. *The Court of Industrial Relations*, 61 AMERICAN REVIEW OF REVIEWS 294, 294 (1920). The metaphor of "industrial war," *see* William Allen White, *Industrial Justice – Not Peace*, 10 NATION'S BUSINESS 14, 15 (May 1922), was prevalent in contemporary discussions of the Kansas Court, so much so that the Kansas statute was sometimes characterized as a "war against war." William Leavitt Stoddard, *Industrial Courts, Collectives Agreements, or What?*, 4 ADMINISTRATION 261, 268 (September 1922). The *New York Times* could refer to the statute as "legislation born in the stress of war." *Industrial Relations Courts*, NEW YORK TIMES (June 12, 1921), at 14. *See* WALTER GORDON MERRITT, SOCIAL CONTROL OF INDUSTRIAL WARFARE (New York: League for Industrial Rights 1921); William Reynolds Vance, *The Kansas Court of Industrial Relations with Its Background*, 30 YALE LAW JOURNAL 456, 465 (1921); William L. Higgins, *Just What Has the Supreme Court Done to the Kansas Industrial Act? Why Did It Do It?*, 11 AMERICAN BAR ASSOCIATION JOURNAL 363, 364 (1925). Allen himself argued:

> The Kansas court of industrial relations is founded upon the principle that government should have the same power to protect society against the ruthless offenses of an industrial strife that it has always had to protect against recognized crime.... It was time... when a tribunal should be established having the power to take under its jurisdiction the offenses committed against society in the name of industrial warfare.

Henry J. Allen, *How Kansas Broke a Strike and Would Solve the Labor Problem*, 68 CURRENT OPINION 472, 474–77 (April 1920); Allen, *supra* note 23, at 600–1. Sometimes the industrial strife justifying public intervention was described not as "war" but as "a free-for-all exemplification of the Darwinian doctrine of the survival of the fittest." Ben Hooper, *Peaceful Settlement of Differences between Carriers and Employees*, 2 STATION AGENT 19, 21 (February 1922).

28. DEBATE BETWEEN SAMUEL GOMPERS AND HENRY J. ALLEN AT CARNEGIE HALL MAY 28, 1920, at 9 (New York: E.P. Dutton & Co. 1920).

29. *Id.* at 37–38. The question sparked a huge literature. *See, e.g.*, Ralph M. Easley, *Is the Labor Problem Unsolvable?*, 5 NATIONAL CIVIC FEDERATION REVIEW 1 (1920); J.B. Gardiner, *Labor – the New Tyrant*, 67 THE FORUM 396, 400 (May 1922); *The Industrial Court*, NEW YORK TIMES (February 18, 1921), at 10. Gompers eventually responded to Allen's question by arguing that there was no

public wholly separate and apart from employers and employees. *See* HENRY J. ALLEN, THE PARTY OF THE THIRD PART: THE STORY OF THE KANSAS INDUSTRIAL RELATIONS COURT 114–16 (New York: Harper & Bros. 1921). For an example of the discomfort of progressives who both opposed the antistrike provisions of the Kansas statute and who believed in the transcendent prerogatives of the public, see *The Kansas Challenge to Unionism*, 27 NEW REPUBLIC 3, 4 (1921) ("Are we to accept the thesis of the extreme defenders of trade unionism methods that the interest of the public is in the long run identical with the interest of labor, and that therefore the public ought to bear with good grace the inconveniences and sufferings incident to the labor struggle?"). For an articulate explanation of this discomfort, see Walter Lippmann, *Can the Strike Be Abandoned?*, 21 NEW REPUBLIC 224 (1920).

30. HOWARD GILLMAN, THE CONSTITUTION BESIEGED 10 (Durham: Duke University Press 1993). The Kansas Industrial Court had "the distinction of being opposed by both capital and labor." White, *supra* note 27, at 14. *See* John A. Fitch, *Industrial Peace by Law – The Kansas Wage*, 44 THE SURVEY 7 (1920).

31. *See, e.g.*, WALTER LIPPMANN, DRIFT AND MASTERY: AN ATTEMPT TO DIAGNOSE THE CURRENT UNREST (New York: Henry Holt & Co. 1917); John Spargo, *The Public in Industrial Warfare*, 103 THE INDEPENDENT 173 (August 14, 1920). Henry Allen put it this way: "We stand at this hour to give evidence that no class under government shall live above the law." Henry J. Allen, *How Kansas Settles Its Labor Disputes*, 6 WORLD OUTLOOK 39 (August 1920). As the Kansas Supreme Court announced in upholding the KCIR: "Heretofore, the industrial relationship has been tacitly regarded as existing between two members, industrial manager and industrial worker. They have joined wholeheartedly in excluding others. The Legislature proceeded on the theory there is a third member of those industrial relationships which have to do with production, preparation, and distribution of the necessaries of life, the public. The Legislature also proceeded on the theory the public is not a silent partner. Whenever the dissensions of the other two become flagrant, the third member may see to it the business does not stop.... The rights of society as a whole... are dominant over industry." State *ex rel.* Hopkins v. Howat, 198 P. 686, 705 (Kan. 1921).

32. State *ex rel.* Hopkins v. Howat, 198 P. 686, 697 (Kan. 1921).

33. George Wickersham, *Recent Extensions of the State Police Power*, 54 AMERICAN LAW REVIEW 801, 801 (1920) ("Few measures of recent legislative enactment have attracted so much public attention, as that by which the State of Kansas attempted to grapple with the strike of coal miners during the winter of 1919–1920."). As the *St. Louis Daily Globe-Democrat* observed, "Probably no industrial legislation in recent years has attracted as much public attention as the Kansas act creating an industrial court." *The Industrial Court Decision*, ST. LOUIS DAILY GLOBE-DEMOCRAT (June 13, 1923), at 14. Analogous legislation was "introduced in State after State." *Courts of Industrial Injustice*, 110 THE NATION 416 (1920); *see also* K.H. Condit, *The Kansas Industrial Court*, 53 AMERICAN MACHINIST 749, 752 (October 21, 1920); John A. Fitch, *Shall Strikes Become Crimes: The "Industrial Court" Movement and What It Means*, 11 LABOR AGE 2 (March 1922); *Gompers Sees Labor Defying Court Law: Warns that an Industrial Relations Act Here Will Not Be Obeyed*, NEW YORK TIMES (January 6, 1922), at 19; *Industrial Relations Courts*, NEW YORK TIMES (June 14, 1921), at 14; *Labor*

Price Fixing & Property Affected with a Public Interest

Opposing Anti-Strike Bill: Illinois Measure to Prohibit "Unwarranted Industrial Warfare" Would, It Is Alleged, Do Away with Trade Unions, CHRISTIAN SCIENCE MONITOR (March 23, 1921), at 5; *Manufacturers in 21 States Seek Industrial Court Law*, NEW YORK CALL (February 20, 1921), at 2; Glenn E. Plumb, *Plumb Dissects Oklahoma Industrial Court Bill; It Is Similar to Labor Laws Proposed for Several States*, LABOR (February 5, 1921), at 21; *The Public and the Strike*, NEW YORK TIMES (February 9, 1922), at 16; REPORT OF THE PROCEEDINGS OF THE FORTIETH ANNUAL CONVENTION OF THE AMERICAN FEDERATION OF LABOR 90, 262, 264–65, 378–83 (Washington D.C.: Law Reporter Printing Co. 1920); *State Control of Strikes*, 108 INDEPENDENT & WEEKLY REVIEW 192 (February 25, 1922); Harry Tipner, *Labor Courts Do Not Solve Problem*, 46 AUTOMOTIVE INDUSTRIES 629 (March 16, 1922) ("There are pending in ten states bills modeled along the lines of the Kansas law for the establishment of industrial courts with the expectation of eliminating strikes."). *See A National Court for Labor*, 64 LITERARY DIGEST 14 (January 10, 1920). For a discussion of these various proposals, see *Legislative Attacks on Trade Unions*, in REPORT OF THE PROCEEDINGS OF THE FORTY-SECOND ANNUAL CONVENTION OF THE AMERICAN FEDERATION OF LABOR 51–57 (Washington D.C.: Law Reporter Printing Co. 1922).

    Allen energetically promoted the KCIR, and at one time Allen was even considered a presidential possibility because of it. *See* Fitch, *supra* note 30; Frank P. Walsh, *Henry Allen's Industrial Court*, 110 THE NATION 755 (1920) ("The one big campaign card of Governor Allen as a candidate for the Presidency is the passage of his Kansas Industrial Court Bill last January."). Brandeis wrote on his return to Taft's draft opinion in *Wolff Packing* that "this will clarify thought and bury the ashes of a sometime presidential boom." (Taft papers).

34. Arthur Sears Henning, *Harding Hits U.S. Traditions in His Message*, CHICAGO DAILY TRIBUNE (December 7, 1921), at 1. *See President Urges Industrial Court*, CHRISTIAN SCIENCE MONITOR (December 7, 1921), at 8 (Harding was "apparently following the general idea embodied in the Kansas Industrial Court."). Harding declared that "In an industrial society such as ours the strike, the lockout, and the boycott are as much out of place and as disastrous in their results as is war or armed revolution in the domain of politics. The same disposition to reasonableness, ... the same provision of fair and recognized tribunals and processes, ought to make it possible to solve the one set of questions as easily as the other." *Address by the President of the United States*, 62 CONG. REC. 39 (December 6, 1921).

35. *Address by the President of the United States*, *supra* note 34, at 39. "The President's suggestion for the solution of labor problems ... aroused more comment perhaps than any other portion of his speech." Henning, *supra* note 34, at 1. *See* J.F. Essary, *Harding Opens War on "Blocs" in Congress*, BALTIMORE SUN (December 7, 1921), at 1 ("The President created particular interest in some quarters by advocating the enactment of a 'code' applicable to labor disputes, a measure which it was widely assumed would provide for the creation of judicial tribunals fashioned somewhat on the lines of the Kansas Industrial Court to decide labor disputes."). Samuel Gompers protested "the presidential proposal for judicial tribunals to arbitrarily force labor and all industry under the tyrannical rule of courts." Samuel Gompers, *Forward, Onward and Upward in 1922*, 29 AMERICAN FEDERATIONIST 43, 44 (1922). *See* Samuel Gompers, *President Harding's Labor Proposal*, 29 AMERICAN FEDERATIONIST 49, 50 (1922) ("It is quite evident that the

President has in mind the establishment of a court or courts to determine the conditions and wages of the working people, and evidently with the aim that these courts can and will prevent strikes and lockouts. To secure the best terms under which ... labor and service may be given is worthy of encouragement rather than antagonism and particular the antagonism and reactionary spirit that would undertake to tie men to their jobs by law and introduce what was not only abolished by our Civil War but guaranteed against by the Thirteenth Amendment to the Constitution, the enforcement of compulsory labor or involuntary servitude.").

Harding's proposal was inconsistent with the 1920 Republican Party Platform, which had affirmed that "In private industries we do not advocate the principle of compulsory arbitration, but we favor impartial commissions and better facilities for voluntary mediation, conciliation and arbitration supplemented by the full publicity which will enlist the influence of an aroused public opinion. The government should take the initiative in inviting the establishment of tribunals or commissions for the purpose of voluntary arbitration and of investigation of disputed issues." Republican Party Platform 1920, available at www.presidency.ucsb.edu/documents/republican-party-platform-1920. By 1924, Coolidge would bluntly oppose compulsory arbitration. *Text of the President's Speech*, NEW YORK TIMES (September 2, 1924), at 2.

36. George B. Rose, *The War and the Constitution*, 24 CASE AND COMMENT 374, 377 (October 1917).
37. State *ex rel.* Hopkins v. Howat, 198 P. 686, 701 (Kan. 1921).
38. *Wolff Packing*, 262 U.S. at 543.
39. *See supra* Chapter 21, at 693–94.
40. During the war, the Food Administration had set prices on the theory "that in times of war all businesses were 'affected with a public interest.'" Novak, *supra* note 1, at 141.
41. Wickersham, *supra* note 33, at 817. Cordenio Severance, the president of the American Bar Association, directly attacked this peacetime expansion of the category of property affected with a public interest: "If a legislature can by a simple resolution declare that a business or occupation never before deemed to be affected with a public interest and thus subject to regulation, is in fact so affected, what limits are there to what it may do? The enlargement of the scope of the police power in recent years has gone far in the direction of a communistic state." Cordenio A. Severance, *Constitution and Individualism*, 8 AMERICAN BAR ASSOCIATION JOURNAL 535, 539 (1922).
42. Butler's docket books indicates that the case was unanimous in conference.
43. The political point of the decision did not go unnoticed. The *Providence Journal*, for example, stressed the "exceptional importance" of *Wolff Packing*, noting that "it comes at a time when the general tendency has been too strongly in the direction of interferences by State and national authority with private industry, and its effect may be to modify that tendency very materially." *The Kansas Industrial Court*, PROVIDENCE JOURNAL (June 14, 1923), at 16. *See In the Kansas Case*, PHILADELPHIA PUBLIC LEDGER (June 13, 1923), at 10 ("The opinion calls a sharp halt on the efforts of legislators, State and national, who for a generation have been steadily encroaching upon the rights of the individual in attempts to regulate business and industry in 'the public interest.' The Nation had come to a place where a line had to be drawn as nearly as possible between what is undoubtedly the 'public interest' and what is not.").
44. *See e.g.*, William Howard Taft, *Industrial Peace* (May 26, 1919), in VIVIAN, at 216–17; *see also Red Control of Labor* (October 18, 1919), *id.* at 287–89; *Gary*

Price Fixing & Property Affected with a Public Interest

and Unionism (April 27, 1921), *id.* at 571–72; *Labor and the Farmers* (June 29, 1921), *id.* at 591–93; GS to Warren G. Harding (June 26, 1920) (Sutherland papers).

45. Pennsylvania R. Co. v. United States Railroad Labor Board, 261 U.S. 72, 79, 84 (1923).
46. *Wolff Packing*, 262 U.S. at 540. Progressives like Felix Frankfurter were simultaneously relieved and concerned by the *Wolff Packing* decision. "The Kansas Court of Industrial Relations is dead. That great achievement of the Middle Western 'law and order' movement is killed by the Supreme Court of the land. . . . Thus fails another social experiment, not because it has been tried and found wanting, but because it has been tried and found unconstitutional. . . . The New Republic is opposed to the idea which underlay the Kansas Industrial Court. . . . We . . . disbelieve in compulsory arbitration as a social policy; but we do not disbelieve in Kansas or any other state venturing a trial of the experiment. . . . We too rejoice with Messrs. Gompers and Emery over the death of the Kansas Industrial Court; but it was for the legislature of Kansas, and not for the Supreme Court, to kill it." *Exit the Kansas Court*, 35 NEW REPUBLIC 112–13 (1923). Compare Hoover's carefully ambivalent characterization of the Kansas legislation in 1920:

   > [L]abor legislation of Kansas . . . provides for the repression of the right to strike or lockout, for the compulsory settlement of labor disputes, for the determination of a fair wage and a fair profit, and as a final resort the conduct of the industry by the state. The experiment may succeed. It is, however, an experiment with many dangers, for it sacrifices a right of labor for the sake of problematical gains. The sacrifice of liberty is an insecure road to progress. If it does succeed it will again vindicate a broad tolerance of political experimentation by a pioneering state for the benefit of the others in the Union. Furthermore, it will justify the comparative study of political procedure among our states and abroad. . . . The experiment may be worth while for the determination to the American people of its futility and any such determination is of value in social progress.

   Herbert Hoover, *Foreword*, in AMERICA AND THE NEW ERA xxix (Elisha M. Friedman, ed., New York: E.P. Dutton & Co. 1920).
47. For a report of the decision of the KCIR, see *The Kansas Court of Industrial Relations Regulates Labor Relations in the Packing Industry*, 3 LAW AND LABOR 144 (June 1921). The KCIR ordered, *inter alia*, that "women workers should receive the same wages as men engaged in the same class and kind of work." *Id.* at 146. See *Decision of the Court of Industrial Relations of Kansas in Meat Packing Company Case*, 13 MONTHLY LABOR REVIEW 206–7 (July 1921). Many rulings of the KCIR were highly favorable to labor. For example, the KCIR held that workers were entitled to a "living wage," meaning "a wage which enables the worker to supply himself and those absolutely dependent upon him with sufficient food to maintain life and health; with a shelter from the inclemencies of the weather; with sufficient clothing to preserve the body from the cold and to enable persons to mingle among their fellows in such ways as may be necessary in the preservation of life." State v. Topeka Edison Co., No. 3254 (March 29, 1920), reproduced in WILLIAM L. HUGGINS, LABOR AND DEMOCRACY 165 (New York: MacMillan Co. 1922). The KCIR also held that workers were entitled to a "fair wage," by which it meant, among many other things, that "'first-class workers' as well as 'skilled workers' . . . are entitled to a wage which will enable them by industry and economy not only to supply themselves with opportunities for intellectual advancement and reasonable

recreation, but also to enable the parents working together to furnish the children ample opportunities for intellectual and moral advancement, for education, and for an equal opportunity in the race of life. A fair wage will also allow the frugal man to provide reasonably for sickness and old age." *Id.* at 166–67. The KCIR was nevertheless bitterly opposed by Kansas coal miners. *See* Dorchy v. Kansas, 264 U.S. 286 (1924); Dorchy v. Kansas, 272 U.S. 306 (1926); EDWIN E. WITTE, THE GOVERNMENT IN LABOR DISPUTES 255–58 (New York: McGraw-Hill Book Co. 1932).

48. We do not have the original draft of Taft's opinion, but on May 29, 1923, he wrote Van Devanter asking him to review the manuscript and make "suggestions." WHT to WVD (May 29, 1923) (Taft papers). Van Devanter responded with a long (undated) analysis:

> As a whole, I fear the opinion will leave the impression that if only the Wolf [sic] Company's business were affected with a public interest, the provisions of the statute as applied to it would be valid. To my mind this would not be so. Take for instance an elevator business and concede that it is so far affected with a public interest that the legislature may prescribe the rates to be charged to the public. Does this carry with it a power to make the owner continue the business, or a power to fix the wages which he must pay and his employees must accept, etc.? This hardly can be so. I cannot believe that all business affected with a public interest may be put on the same ground, nor that the power of regulation concededly extending to some features of such a business extends to every feature. The phrase "affected with a public interest" to me does not convey a definite conception of uniform application. . . .
>
> Even if Kansas could regulate the price at which the Wolf [sic] Company may sell its meat products, I do not think this carries with it what really is in question in the present case. I fear that the opinion lays too much stress upon the question of when a business is affected with a public interest and not enough on the other questions.

WVD to WHT (undated) (Taft papers). Taft thanked Van Devanter for his "frank note," and said that he could alter his opinion to put it "on the ground that regulation of businesses that develop by change of conditions . . . into those affected with a public interest can not be regulated to secure their continuity and compel use of property and services by labor. I agree with you that the character of permissible regulation must vary with the kind of business but the cases are not such that it is easy to draw useful distinctions." WHT to WVD (undated) (Van Devanter papers).

49. *Wolff Packing*, 262 U.S. at 534. For examples of the Taft Court's willingness to require continuity of service with respect to property affected with a public interest, see Western & Atl. R.R. v. Georgia Pub. Serv. Comm'n, 267 U.S. 493, 496–98 (1925) (holding that an order requiring a railroad company to continue service on an industrial side track did not deprive the company of its property without due process of law); Southern Ry. Co. v. Clift, 260 U.S. 316, 321 (1922) ("The service of a railroad is in the public interest; it is compulsory."); United Fuel Gas Co. v. Railroad Commission of Kentucky, 278 U.S. 300, 309 (1929) (approving the order of a state commission compelling a public utility gas company "to continue their service in the cities named."). In *Wolff*, however, Taft held that such "continuity of a business" could only be required "where the obligation to the public of continuous service is direct, clear and mandatory and arises as a contractual condition express or implied of entering the business either as owner or worker. It can

only arise when investment by the owner and entering the employment by the worker create a conventional relation to the public somewhat equivalent to the appointment of officers and the enlistment of soldiers and sailors in military service." 262 U.S. at 541.

Supporters of the KCIR had advanced precisely the metaphor that employers and employees were conscripted into public service. Thus prominent Kansas lawyer F. Dumont Smith argued that employees in necessary industries were like a "locomotive engineer" who is not free to quit while the train is running, but must "remain with his engine until he reaches the next division point."

> When once we get that principle, we will understand ... that this law is constitutional; when we establish that these industries are essential to human life and to human health, whoever enters those industries in effect enlists exactly as does the soldier or the policeman in the preservation of the public peace. He is bound, not to continue to work individually – he may retire from that employment at any moment. But he can't conspire, he can't stir up a mutiny that shall destroy the army of the public weal.

F. Dumont Smith, *The Kansas Industrial Court*, in REPORT OF THE FORTY-FIFTH ANNUAL MEETING OF THE AMERICAN BAR ASSOCIATION 208, 214 (Baltimore: Lord Baltimore Press 1922); *see also The Right to Strike*, 110 THE NATION 389 (1920) (quoting remarks of Judge Wendell Phillips Stafford of the Supreme Court of the District of Columbia to the effect that public employees "have no more right to strike than any other soldier has."). Taft himself invoked the image of employees as soldiers in his condemnation of the Boston police strike of 1919. *See* William Howard Taft, Address of William Howard Taft at Malden, Massachusetts 20 (October 30, 1919) (Taft papers) (Police "are not compelled to serve. Their duty is as high as that of soldiers and sailors in the army of the United States, but they are not as strictly bound. A soldier or sailor can not resign – a policeman may. He is not compelled to serve, but he may not combine with his fellows to embarrass the state he serves by a strike which shall leave that state helpless. That is a combination that ought never to be permitted and ought to be denounced by law. With soldiers and sailors it would be punishable as mutiny, and morally it is the same offense with policemen.").

50. When two years later the Taft Court unanimously revisited the constitutionality of the KCIR, Van Devanter was explicit about these aspects of Taft's opinion:

> Various matters which were relied on as justifying the attempted restraint or abridgment were considered and pronounced inadequate. Among them was the assumption in the act that a business like that in question – preparing food for sale and human consumption – is so far affected with a public interest that the state may compel its continuance, and, if the owner and employees cannot agree, may fix the terms through a public agency to the end that there shall be continuity of operation and production. This assumption was held to be without any sound basis and its indulgence by the state Legislature was declared not controlling. The court recognized that, in a sense, all business is of some concern to the public, and subject to some measure of regulation, but made it plain that the extent to which regulation reasonably may go varies greatly with different classes of business and is not a matter of legislative discretion solely, but is a judicial question to be determined with due regard to the rights of the owner and employees.

Charles Wolff Packing Co. v. Court of Industrial Relations of Kansas, 267 U.S. 552, 566–67 (1925).

51. *Wolff Packing*, 262 U.S. at 534, 536, 538–39.
52. *Id.* at 538.
53. *Id.* "There is no monopoly in the preparation of foods. The prices charged by plaintiff in error are, it is conceded, fixed by competition throughout the country at large. Food is now produced in greater volume and variety than ever before. Given uninterrupted interstate commerce, the sources of the food supply in Kansas are country-wide, a short supply is not likely, and the danger from local monopolistic control less than ever." *Id.*
54. *Id.* at 535. "In a sense, the public is concerned about all lawful business because it contributes to the prosperity and well being of the people. The public may suffer from high prices or strikes in many trades, but the expression 'clothed with a public interest,' as applied to a business, means more than that the public welfare is affected by continuity or by the price at which a commodity is sold or a service rendered. The circumstances which clothe a particular kind of business with a public interest, in the sense of *Munn v. Illinois* and the other cases, must be such as to create a peculiarly close relation between the public and those engaged in it, and raise implications of an affirmative obligation on their part to be reasonable in dealing with the public." *Id.* at 536.
55. *Id.* at 541–42. "It is urged that under this act the exercise of the power of compulsory arbitration rests upon the existence of a temporary emergency as in *Wilson v. New*. If that is a real factor here, as in *Wilson v. New*, and in *Block v. Hirsh*, . . . it is enough to say that the great temporary public exigencies, recognized by all and declared by Congress, were very different from that upon which the control under this act is asserted. Here it is said to be the danger that a strike in one establishment may spread to all the other similar establishments of the state and country, and thence to all the national sources of food supply so as to produce a shortage. . . . The small extent of the injury to the food supply of Kansas to be inflicted by a strike and suspension of this packing company's plant is shown in the language of the Kansas Supreme Court in this case." *Id.* at 542–43.
56. *Id.* at 538.
57. Taft proposed a tripartite schema of "businesses said to be clothed with a public interest justifying some public regulation" that was endlessly repeated and that was wholly unhelpful:

    (1) Those which are carried on under the authority of a public grant of privileges which either expressly or impliedly imposes the affirmative duty of rendering a public service demanded by any member of the public. Such are the railroads, other common carriers and public utilities.
    (2) Certain occupations, regarded as exceptional, the public interest attaching to which, recognized from earliest times, . . . Such are those of the keepers of inns, cabs and grist mills.
    (3) Business which though not public at their inception may be fairly said to have risen to be such and have become subject in consequence to some government regulation. They have come to hold such a peculiar relation to the public that this is superimposed upon them. In the language of the cases, the owner by devoting his business to the public use, in effect grants the public an interest in that use and subjects himself to public regulation to the extent of that interest although the property continues to belong to its private owner and to be entitled to protection accordingly.

    Id. at 535.

Price Fixing & Property Affected with a Public Interest

58. *Id.* at 539. After the publication of his opinion in *Wolff Packing*, Taft received a letter of praise from labor attorney Frank P. Walsh, with whom Taft had co-chaired the War Labor Board. "[I]t is my sincere thought that your opinion in this case will go down in the history of your high court as one of its greatest decisions." Frank P. Walsh to WHT (June 18, 1923) (Taft papers). Any other conclusion, Walsh wrote, "would have been a great stride towards state socialism, the bridge over which it is urged the march must be made to a communistic state."

59. *Wolff Packing*, 262 U.S. at 537. Resonating in Taft's language is a well-known nursery-rhyme that evokes the quotidian: "The butcher, the baker, the candlestick maker...." So far as I can tell, the phrase "common callings" was judicially introduced into American court opinions in Bradley's concurring opinion in Butchers' Union Slaughter-House & Live-Stocking Land Co. v. Crescent City Live-Stock Landing & Slaughter-House Co., 111 U.S. 747, 763 (1884) (Bradley, J., concurring) ("[T]he ordinary pursuits of life, forming the large mass of industrial avocations, are and ought to be free and open to all, subject only to such general regulations, applying equally to all, as the general good may demand; and the grant to a favored few of a monopoly in any of these common callings is necessarily an outrage upon the liberty of the citizen as exhibited in one of its most important aspects, the liberty of pursuit."). The phrase was used an additional six times in federal and state opinions in the thirty-three years before World War I, including once in an opinion by Holmes that distinguished "common callings" from public utilities. Terminal Taxicab Co. v. Kutz, 241 U.S. 252, 256 (1916). Between the outbreak of the war and the end of 1929, however, the phrase was used at approximately four times the rate of the previous three decades.

60. *Kansas Labor Court between Two Fires*, NEW YORK TIMES (February 25, 1922), at 19 (Remarks of Harry Sharp, Secretary of Associated Industries of Kansas).

61. Matthew Woll, *How the Kansas Plan Defies Fundamental American Freedom*, 29 AMERICAN FEDERATIONIST 317, 321 (1922); *see also Kansas Labor Court between Two Fires*, *supra* note 60 (remarks of John S. Dean, counsel for Associated Industries of Kansas).

62. George Soule, *Hard-Boiled Radicalism*, 65 NEW REPUBLIC 261, 265 (1931). *See* Felix Frankfurter, *The Zeitgeist and the Judiciary*, 29 SURVEY 542 (1913): "The tremendous economic and social changes of the last fifty years have inevitably reacted upon the functions of the state. More and more government is conceived as the biggest organized social effort for dealing with social problems.... Growing democratic sympathies, justified by the social message of modern scientists, demand to be translated into legislation for economic betterment, based upon the conviction that laws can make men better by affecting the conditions of living."

63. It is fair to say that supporters of the KCIR believed that the domains of economic life regulated by the KCIR had already been colonized by forms of managerial organization. Thus Elmer T. Peterson, associate editor of the *Wichita Beacon* (of which Henry J. Allen was the editor), wrote:

> Organization, advanced by specialization, invention and other modern developments, has set up an invisible government. The only way the people have of retrieving their political power and staving off economic pressure is to erect governmental tribunals with power to prevent economic strangulation.

Elmer T. Peterson, *Is the Labor Problem Unsolvable?*, 5 NATIONAL CIVIL FEDERATION REVIEW 14 (September 25, 1920). The logic of the KCIR, in other words, was to use state organizational force to counteract private organizational power.

64. Minor Bronaugh, *Business Clothed with a Public Interest Justifying State Regulation*, 27 LAW NOTES 87, 89 (1923). The experiment "may be said to have ... served a useful purpose," Bronaugh continued, because "it furnished the occasion for the restatement, or should we say re-establishment, of the doctrine of individual liberty embodied in the Constitution but apparently lost sight of by many of our legislators and members of the judiciary in recent years." *Id.*

65. Howat v. Kansas, 258 U.S. 181, 183 (1922); *see also* State *ex rel.* Hopkins v. Howat, 198 P. 686, 694 (Kan. 1921).

66. Henry J. Allen, *The Settlement of Labor Disputes*, ELECTRIC RAILWAY JOURNAL (October 16, 1920), at 753 ("All reasonable men, whether they belong in the ranks of capital or labor, realize that we are working under modern conditions and that all the elements of manufacturing, production, transportation, and distribution are mixed together in a common machine; that a break in one part of the far-flung machinery breaks down the whole public relations.").

67. Walsh, *supra* note 33, at 757. In his justly famous address at Cooper Union on January 10, 1908, Taft, then secretary of war and soon-to-be presidential candidate, observed that "It is a very serious question whether under our Constitution a decree of a tribunal under a compulsory arbitration law could be enforced against the side of the laborers. It would come very close to the violation of the thirteenth amendment, which forbids involuntary servitude." William Howard Taft, *Address at Cooper Union*, in ROBERT LEE DUNN, WILLIAM HOWARD TAFT: AMERICAN 236 (Boston: Chapple Publishing Co. 1908). The *American Federationist* argued that the KCIR would "legislate men into serfdom," because "the very essence of democracy is found" in "the trade union practice of collective bargaining and ... trade agreement." Samuel Gompers, *What's the Matter with Kansas?*, 27 AMERICAN FEDERATIONIST 155, 156 (1920). On labor opposition to the KCIR, see W.B. Rubin, *The Kansas Industrial Act and the United States Supreme Court*, 30 AMERICAN FEDERATIONIST 832, 833 (1923) ("The right to free contract, the right to work or not to work, the right to advise or not to advise someone to join with another in such things marks the boundary line between slavery and freedom."); Matthew Woll, *Industry's Eternal Triangle*, 8 NATION'S BUSINESS 17–18 (June 1920); Alexander Howat, *Kansas Stands for Freedom*, 10 LABOR AGE 12, 13 (December 1921); *Report of A.F. of L. Executive Council*, in REPORT OF PROCEEDINGS OF THE FORTY-FIRST ANNUAL CONVENTION OF THE AMERICAN FEDERATION OF LABOR 52–54 (Washington D.C.: Law Reporter Printing Co. 1921); *Kansas Industrial Law Dismembered*, in REPORT OF PROCEEDINGS OF THE FORTY-THIRD ANNUAL CONVENTION OF THE AMERICAN FEDERATION OF LABOR 56–57 (Washington D.C.: Law Reporter Printing Co. 1923).

68. Samuel Gompers, *The Courts and Mr. Taft on Labor*, 28 AMERICAN FEDERATIONIST 220, 223 (1921).

69. *The Kansas Decision*, NEW YORK TRIBUNE (June 13, 1923), at 12; *see also Kansas Industrial Court Dead*, BROOKLYN DAILY EAGLE (June 12, 1923), at 6; *The Kansas Industrial Court*, NEW YORK TIMES (June 13, 1923), at 18. The *Philadelphia Public Ledger* interpreted *Wolff Packing* as a direct warning to "progressives" in

Price Fixing & Property Affected with a Public Interest

the Senate who sought to regulate business: "Not alone for its effect on the nationally known Kansas Court, ... but as a warning to the 'Progressive bloc' in the next Congress, bent on governmental regulation of all manner of industries – chiefly coal, sugar, gasoline – was the Supreme Court's decision held to be of the highest importance." Robert Barry, *High Court Halts State Wage Fixing*, PHILADELPHIA PUBLIC LEDGER (June 12, 1923), at 1. In a subsequent editorial, the *Public Ledger* observed that "If progressives of both parties ... have been seeking a sign from the Supreme Court, they now have that sign. They know now what that tribunal's attitude will be toward more government in industry at the expense of the individual's rights." *In the Kansas Case*, PHILADELPHIA PUBLIC LEDGER (June 13, 1923), at 10.

70. John A. Fitch, *The Case against the Law*, 44 THE SURVEY 303 (1920).
71. Quoted in *Brandeis on the Labor Problem: How Far Have We Come on the Road to Industrial Democracy?*, 5 LA FOLLETTE'S WEEKLY MAGAZINE 5–15 (May 24, 1913). Brandeis declared that "the old common law, which assures the employer the right to discharge and the employee the right to quit work, for any reason or for no reason in either case, is a necessary guaranty of industrial liberty."
72. LDB to WHT (n.d.) (Taft papers).
73. *Brandeis-Frankfurter Conversations*, at 320 (July 19, 1923). *See supra* Chapter 8, at 320. Four years later Brandeis would cite *Meyer* (and *Pierce*) in his concurring opinion in Whitney v. California, 274 U.S. 357 (1927), for the proposition that "The right of free speech, the right to teach and the right of assembly are, of course, fundamental rights. . . . These may not be denied or abridged." *Id*. at 373 (Brandeis, J., concurring).
74. 291 U.S. 502 (1934).
75. *Nebbia*, 291 U.S. at 533. "It is clear that there is no closed class or category of businesses affected with a public interest, and the function of courts in the application of the Fifth and Fourteenth Amendments is to determine in each case whether circumstances vindicate the challenged regulation as a reasonable exertion of governmental authority or condemn it as arbitrary or discriminatory. The phrase 'affected with a public interest' can, in the nature of things, mean no more than that an industry, for adequate reason, is subject to control for the public good." *Id*. at 536.
76. *Id*. at 554–55 (McReynolds, J., dissenting).
77. Brandeis believed that it was "absurd, as Holmes says," to deem property "fundamental in the sense that you can't curtail its use or its accumulation or power. There may be some aspects of property that are fundamental – but not regard as fundamental specific limitations upon it. Whereas right to your education & to utter speech is fundamental *except* clear and present danger." *Brandeis-Frankfurter Conversations*, at 320 (July 19, 1923).
78. *See supra* Chapter 4, at 129–31.
79. 273 U.S. 418 (1927).
80. 277 U.S. 350 (1928).
81. *Tyson*, 273 U.S. at 427.
82. Holmes, Brandeis, Sanford, and Stone dissented.
83. *Tyson*, 273 U.S. at 429.
84. *German Alliance*, Sutherland wrote, "marks the extreme limit to which this court thus far has gone in sustaining price fixing legislation." *Id*. at 434.

85. *Id.* at 430. The power to regulate prices, Sutherland asserted, "is not only a more definite and serious invasion of the rights of property and contract, but its exercise cannot always be justified by circumstances which have been held to justify legislative regulation of the manner in which a business shall be carried on." *Id.* at 431. Sutherland had vigorously defended this position before joining the Court. *See supra* Chapter 1, at note 58. Sutherland opposed price fixing as a matter of "great political principle." George Sutherland, *Principle or Expedient?*, 5 CONSTITUTIONAL REVIEW 195, 206 (1921). For a previous attack on the theory of *Munn* and government price regulation, see Budd v. New York, 143 U.S. 517, 551 (1892) (Brewer, J., dissenting) ("The paternal theory of government is to me odious. The utmost possible liberty to the individual, and the fullest possible protection to him and his property, is both the limitation and duty of government. If it may regulate the price of one service which is not a public service, or the compensation for the use of one kind of property, which is not devoted to a public use, why may it not with equal reason regulate the price of all service, and the compensation to be paid for the use of all property? And, if so, 'Looking Backward' is nearer than a dream.").
86. *Tyson*, 273 U.S. at 430, 438.
87. 268 U.S. 319 (1925). In conference in *Weller* Taft opined that "Within power to license brokers. Doubt as to price." Barry Cushman, *Inside the Taft Court: Lessons from the Docket Books*, 2015 SUPREME COURT REVIEW 345, 362 (2015). Sutherland sent Taft a memorandum in *Weller* stating that although it was a "rather close question, ... I am disposed to think that a theatre is not a business impressed with a public interest, but a private enterprise as much under the control of the owner as a shop for the sale of goods. I do not see upon what theory the legislature could fix the price at which the owner should sell tickets of admission; and I think the middleman stands in the same situation." GS to WHT (April 23, 1925) (Taft papers).
88. *Tyson*, 273 U.S. at 441.
89. Taft believed that *Tyson* was "a fine opinion." WHT to GS (January 31, 1927) (Taft papers).
90. *Tyson*, 273 U.S. at 440, 442, 445.
91. *Id.* at 446 (Holmes, J., dissenting). Holmes described his dissent as "a few sardonic remarks" that took "a whack at 'police power' and 'dedicated to a public use' – as apologetic phrases springing from the unwillingness to recognize the fact of power." OWH to Harold Laski (February 25, 1927), in 2 HOLMES-LASKI CORRESPONDENCE, at 921; OWH to Harold Laski (March 17, 1927), *id.* at 927. Learned Hand wrote Holmes about his dissent, "It said much that I had always wanted to have said, and said it in a way that especially reached my vitals, the ganglia where the pleasure centers are." Learned Hand to OWH (March 7, 1927) (Holmes papers). Holmes replied, "I am more than pleased that you approve of my dissent in the theatre ticket case. I had some doubt whether it was worth printing but Brandeis and my secretary said fire it off." OWH to Learned Hand (March 10, 1927) (Holmes papers). Frankfurter wrote Holmes rejoicing "over your new declaration of independence of all those sterile 'apologies' which 'police power' and 'affected with public interest' cover. You have never written a more illuminating opinion on Due Process and I throw my hat into the air for it." Felix Frankfurter to OWH (March 19, 1927), in HOLMES-FRANKFURTER CORRESPONDENCE, at 212.

Price Fixing & Property Affected with a Public Interest

92. Brandeis's view, as he was later to express it in New State Ice Co. v. Liebmann, 285 U.S. 262 (1932), was that the "notion of a distinct category of business 'affected with a public interest,' employing property 'devoted to a public use,' rests upon historical error," and that "the true principle is that the state's power extends to every regulation of any business reasonably required and appropriate for public protection. I find in the due process clause no other limitation upon the character or the scope of regulation permissible." *Id.* at 302–3 (Brandeis, J., dissenting).
93. *Tyson*, 273 U.S. at 455 (Sanford, J., dissenting). "The question as stated is not one of reasonable prices, but of the constitutional right in the circumstances of this case to exact exorbitant profits beyond reasonable prices. ... Laws against monopoly which aim at the same evil and accomplish their end by interference with private rights quite as much as the present law are not regarded as arbitrary or unreasonable or unconstitutional because they are not limited in their application to dealings in the bare necessities of life." *Id.* at 452–53 (Stone, J., dissenting). Holmes and Brandeis joined Stone's dissent.
94. *Id.* at 451 (Stone, J., dissenting).
95. Thomas Reed Powell, *State Utilities and the Supreme Court, 1922–1930*, 29 MICHIGAN LAW REVIEW 811, 836 (1931). Taft snorted apropos of Powell's attack on *Tyson* that "If his views were followed, it would mean that we would have no Constitution at all." WHT to Moses Strauss (March 31, 1927) (Taft papers). Sutherland's opinion was blasted in the law reviews as "legal phlogiston." Maurice Finkelstein, *From* Munn v. Illinois *to* Tyson v. Banton: *A Study in the Judicial Process*, 27 COLUMBIA LAW REVIEW 769, 778 (1927). For a summary of the academic literature disapproving the decision, see Maurice H. Merrill, *The New Judicial Approach to Due Process and Price Fixing*, 18 KENTUCKY LAW JOURNAL 3, 16 n.56 (1929). Taft wrote his brother that *Tyson* "has awakened the condemnation of a good many, but it is right, and that is the way the academicians and those who are not in favor of any Constitution get even with us." WHT to Horace D. Taft (January 7, 1929) (Taft papers). *See* Horace D. Taft to WHT (January 4, 1929) (Taft papers).
96. As Rexford Tugwell put it, "Under war-pressure industry had experimented with a kind of voluntary socialism – and liked it. It liked the substitution of solidarity for suspicion, of unity for compelled disunion, of cooperation for competition, of a common purpose for haphazard growth. But when the war was over, old ideas which had been in suspension again stirred in the politicians' minds. ... The Supreme Court drew a long breath and eyed the war powers arrogated by the Administration with the chilly disfavor which recently found expression in the Tyson case, decisively turning back legislative efforts to regulate prices." Rexford G. Tugwell, *America's War-Time Socialism*, 124 THE NATION 364, 366 (1927). The *New Republic* correctly viewed *Tyson* as consolidating a sharp rightward swing in the Court's jurisprudence. "Until recent years the Court could generally be counted on to take a liberal attitude toward statutes outside the labor field. ... The last three years have witnessed a marked change. The Nebraska bread law, the Pennsylvania shoddy law, and now the New York scalping law, have been successively invalidated. ... [I]f the trend of the past three years continues, the due process clause will furnish an increasingly effective obstruction to every effort of legislature or city council." *The Constitution Shelters the Ticket Speculator*, 50 NEW REPUBLIC 84, 86 (1927).
97. Finkelstein, *supra* note 95, at 769, 782. It was said in the press that "Few decisions of the Supreme Court of the United States have attracted as much attention among

legislators as the ruling this week that state legislators have no authority to specify what prices shall be charged for so-called necessities or luxuries of life." David Lawrence, *Theater Ticket Case Decision Is Significant*, ITHACA JOURNAL (March 3, 1927), at 1. Noting that "the line" between businesses affected with a public interest and those that are constitutionally deemed private "tends to narrow rather than widen in normal times," the syndicated columnist David Lawrence read *Tyson* as "warning" that a "state cannot interfere in the arrangement between buyer and seller of any commodity except those like rail and motor transportation, power rates and other quasi-monopolistic businesses." *Id.* at 2. Louis Marshall, who had argued the case for the ticket brokers, explained that "Had the decision gone the other way it would have opened the way to price fixing legislation against butchers, grocers, or any other class of trade or industry which happened at the moment to be unpopular.... The Supreme Court acted in this case according to the same logic followed by President Coolidge in his veto of the McNary-Haugen farm bill. That bill was designed to fix prices at an advance, while the New York provision governing the sale of theatre tickets was intended to fix prices at a low level. The principle was the same, however." Quoted in *Big Agencies Keep Ticket Price Level*, NEW YORK TIMES (March 1, 1927), at 12. For Coolidge's condemnation of price fixing, see *President's Annual Message*, 69 CONG. REC. 103, 105 (December 6, 1927) ("Government price fixing is known to be unsound and bound to result in disaster."). For a survey of press reaction to *Tyson*, see *The Ticket Scalper Now Free to Scalp*, 92 LITERARY DIGEST 14 (March 19, 1927).

98. 277 U.S. 350 (1928).
99. Stone, joined by Holmes and Brandeis, dissented. Sanford concurred "upon the controlling authority of *Tyson*, which, as applied to the question in this case, I am unable to distinguish." 277 U.S. at 359 (Sanford, J., concurring).
100. "A few years ago, when the business of insuring against fire was brought within the category of those businesses which are so 'affected with a public interest' as to make them regulable, it seemed that the Court might easily go on extending this classification to other employments hitherto regarded as private. The Tyson case reversed the trend. Ribnik vs. McBride confirms the reversal." Tugwell, *supra* note 11, at 120.
101. *Ribnik*, 277 U.S. at 358. In response to the Court's judgment in *Ribnik*, New Jersey enacted a strict licensing law that required, among other things, employment agencies to post a public schedule of fees. *See* Chapter 283, 1928 N.J. Laws 775–84.
102. *Ribnik*, 277 U.S. at 357. Sutherland made this announcement at a time when, as the Executive Committee of the AFL reported to its national convention, "No question caused greater concern than that of acute unemployment in the United States." REPORT OF THE PROCEEDINGS OF THE FORTY-EIGHTH ANNUAL CONVENTION OF THE AMERICAN FEDERATION OF LABOR 81 (Washington D.C.: Law Reporter Printing Co. 1928). *See Unemployment in the Midst of Prosperity*, 96 LITERARY DIGEST 8 (February 25, 1928); *Our Jobless Millions*, 97 LITERARY DIGEST 5 (April 7, 1928).
103. *Ribnik*, 277 U.S. at 357.
104. The Taft Court was quite willing to affirm price controls in contexts in which prices had been regulated before the war. *See, e.g.*, Washington *ex rel.* Stimson

Price Fixing & Property Affected with a Public Interest

Lumber Co. v. Kuykendall, 275 U.S. 207 (1927) (upholding state rates imposed upon towboats who were properly deemed common carriers).

105. *Ribnik* was particularly significant because at the time more than twenty-eight states imposed some form of price regulation on employment agencies. *See* Note, *The Regulation of Employment Agencies*, 38 YALE LAW JOURNAL 225, 229–30 (1928). The Note characterizes *Tyson* and *Ribnik* as "radical innovations." *Id.* at 234. "It is surprising," the author of the Note writes, "to find Justice Sutherland disposing of an issue in public policy by a purely conceptual argument; it is disturbing to find the selection of concepts resting upon nothing more basic than an arbitrary choice." *Id.* at 233.

106. *Ribnik*, 277 U.S. at 373 (Stone, J., dissenting). Stone continued: "[I] can see no difference between a reasonable regulation of price and a reasonable regulation of the use of property, which affects its price or economic return. The privilege of contract and the free use of property are as seriously cut down in the one case as in the other." *Id.* at 374. *See supra* Chapter 4, at note 162.

107. *Ribnik*, 277 U.S. at 362–63, 373 (Stone, J., dissenting). At about the time of *Ribnik*, Stone began to complain that argumentation before the Court did not provide the data necessary for decision. "Verbal logic chopping, with no apparent consciousness of the social and economic forces which are really involved, are about all we get. If anything more appears in the opinion it is because some member of the court takes the time and energy to go on an exploring expedition of its [sic] own." HFS to John Bassett Moore (June 5, 1928) (Stone papers); *see also* HFS to Hessel E. Yntema (October 24, 1928) (Stone papers) ("[T]here is still much to be done in the education of lawyers and judges. Take, for example, the recent case of Ribnik and McBride, in which I wrote a dissenting opinion. You will search in vain in briefs and prevailing opinions for any reference to the considerable amount of material to which I referred in my dissenting opinion. It seems not to have occurred to any of them that such data had very much to do with the case.").

108. For a review of highly unfavorable academic reactions to *Ribnik*, see Merrill, *supra* note 95, at 16 n.56. Merrill regarded the "sinister aspect" of *Ribnik* to lie in its "apparent abandonment of the fruitful practicality of the method of approach to which expression was given in the *Wolff* case in favor of a rigidly unyielding judicial prohibition against further extension of the public utility concept." *Id.* at 15. He also characterized *Tyson* and *Ribnik* as a "radical departure" from the "realistic method" of past decisions. *Id.* at 8.

109. Tugwell, *supra* note 11, at 121.

110. Morehead v. New York *ex rel.* Tipaldo, 298 U.S. 587, 633 (1936) (Stone, J., dissenting). *See supra* Chapter 4, at 131–32.

111. 278 U.S. 235, 239 (1929).

112. *Id.* at 240.

113. ROBERT JACKSON, THE STRUGGLE FOR JUDICIAL SUPREMACY 56–57 (New York: Alfred A. Knopf 1941).

114. *Tyson*, 273 U.S. at 451 (Stone, J., dissenting).

115. Roscoe Pound, *Mechanical Jurisprudence*, 8 COLUMBIA LAW REVIEW 605, 616 (1908).

116. Roscoe Pound, *Liberty of Contract*, 18 YALE LAW JOURNAL 454, 457–58 (1909).

117. OWH to HFS (December 20, 1928) (Stone papers).

118. HFS to OWH (December 21, 1928) (Stone papers).

CHAPTER 26

The Protected Realm of Freedom

It is worth taking a moment to think carefully about the protected realm of economic freedom that the Taft Court struggled so hard to shield from bureaucratic overreach. Consider the Court's decision in *Fairmont Creamery Co. v. Minnesota*, decided only two months after *Tyson*, when the Court's rightward turn began to gather unstoppable momentum. Written by McReynolds, with Holmes, Brandeis, and Stone dissenting, *Fairmont Creamery* addressed a 1923 Minnesota statute requiring those buying milk products to pay the same price in all areas of the state "after making due allowance for the difference ... in the actual cost of transportation." The statute was aimed at large centralized creameries who overbid on milk products to acquire monopoly positions.[1]

McReynolds objected that the statute did not contain a scienter requirement to distinguish between price differentials innocently caused by the natural operation of the market and price differentials deliberately used for the purpose "of destroying competition."[2] "As the inhibition of the statute applies irrespective of motive," McReynolds reasoned,

> we have an obvious attempt to destroy plaintiff in error's liberty to enter into normal contracts, long regarded, not only as essential to the freedom of trade and commerce, but also as beneficial to the public. Buyers in competitive markets must accommodate their bids to prices offered by others, and the payment of different prices at different places is the ordinary consequent. Enforcement of the statute would amount to fixing the price at which plaintiff in error may buy, since one purchase would establish this for all points, without regard to ordinary trade conditions.
>
> The real question comes to this – May the state, in order to prevent some strong buyers of cream from doing things which may tend to monopoly, inhibit plaintiff in error from carrying on its business in the usual way heretofore

The Protected Realm of Freedom

regarded as both moral and beneficial to the public and not shown now to be accompanied by evil results as ordinary incidents?[3]

McReynolds defines economic transactions that merit constitutional protection by appealing to tropes of the "normal," the "usual," and the "ordinary." These metaphors pervade the oeuvre of the Taft Court. *Fairmont Creamery* does not invoke the Due Process Clause to prohibit class legislation. It instead invokes the Due Process Clause to protect the freedom to participate in customary market practices. The Minnesota legislation was unconstitutional because "the inhibition of the statute has no *reasonable relation* to the anticipated evil – high bidding by some with purpose to monopolize or destroy competition."[4]

When legislation forbids conduct to prevent harm, the causal connection between the proscription and the harm is usually understood as an empirical question. Without actual evidence, one cannot know whether or to what degree the proscription will avert the harm. What is striking about *Fairmont Creamery* is that McReynolds makes no effort to pursue any such empirical inquiry. He is not curious about the nature or extent of the problem of monopolization in the Minnesota dairy industry; he does not ask whether or how much the statute before him might reduce that monopolization. It is puzzling, therefore, what McReynolds means when he flatly condemns the Minnesota legislation as unreasonable. "Looking through form to substance," McReynolds writes, the statute "clearly and unmistakably infringes private rights, whose exercise does not ordinarily produce evil consequences, but the reverse."[5]

What seems plain is that, just as in *Jay Burns* or *Adkins*, the Court's judgment in *Fairmont Creamery* is not driven by empirical inquiry, but instead by common sense intuition. Judicial intuition both defines the conduct worthy of constitutional protection (*normal* participation in the market) and establishes the scope of constitutional protection (government restraints on freedom of contracts must be *reasonable*). With regard to the object of constitutional protection, the Taft Court sought constitutionally to safeguard "normal contracts, long regarded, not only as essential to the freedom of trade and commerce, but also as beneficial to the public." The object of the Court's protection was thus determined by common law rules distinguishing normal from deviant contracts.

During the Taft Court era, common law rules were routinely contrasted to positive legislation. The common law was thought to reflect "public sentiment.... crystallized in general custom." It expressed the "settled conviction of the people as to what the rule of right and conduct should be on the subject to which it relates, and for that reason. ... likely to receive spontaneously the obedience that statutes exact by compulsion."[6] Charles Evans Hughes, for example, argued in 1924 that "the spirit of the common law," which is "the law of a free people, springing from custom, responsive to their sense of justice," should be "opposed to those insidious encroachments upon liberty which take the form of an uncontrolled administrative authority – the modern guise of an ancient tyranny, not the more welcome to intelligent free men because it may bear the label of democracy."[7]

Grounded in the history and intuitions of the common law, the Taft Court interpreted the Due Process Clause to protect customary business practices from the tyranny of statutory regulation. The Court accorded these practices a form of protection that was also rooted in the common law. The Court prohibited government from regulating ordinary business practices unless legislative restraints bore a "reasonable relation" to an "anticipated evil." In determining whether a regulation was "reasonable," the Court adopted a standard of "reasonableness after the essential method of the common law."[8] Although the Court did not read the Due Process Clause to withhold from "legislatures the authority to enact reasonable measures to promote the safety, health, morals and welfare of the people," it distinguished constitutional from unconstitutional regulation on the basis of intuitions that were themselves rooted in the experience of traditional practices.[9]

When Taft sought to describe this analytic framework to the general public, he explained that what constitutes a constitutionally reasonable restraint on "personal liberty of action ... is really a matter of degree. It is to be settled by the general and dominant opinion of all the people in a community of common purpose, common ideals and the common enjoyment of the blessings of liberty and justice. This crystallizes into a kind of moral code based on the vicious effect of practices sufficiently serious to affect the welfare of the community. Our courts recognize this crystallization of public sentiment."[10]

Underlying this approach was the implicit premise that courts were better able to discern public sentiment than were legislatures. In interpreting the Constitution, federal courts assumed the same broad authority as traditional common law courts. Their obligation was to articulate and defend society's "general and dominant opinion," its "common purpose" and "common ideals."

The Taft Court jealously guarded its authority to make such judgments. It insisted on making itself the ultimate arbiter of reasonableness. The Court came down hard when the Federal Trade Commission ("FTC") sought to exercise its statutory prerogatives to regulate ordinary market practices. Quoting from an earlier decision, the Court declared:

> The words "unfair method of competition" are not defined by the statute and their exact meaning is in dispute. It is for the courts, not the Commission, ultimately to determine as matter of law what they include. They are clearly inapplicable to practices never heretofore regarded as opposed to good morals because characterized by deception, bad faith, fraud or oppression, or as against public policy because of their dangerous tendency unduly to hinder competition or create monopoly. The act was certainly not intended to fetter free and fair competition as commonly understood and practiced by honorable opponents in trade.[11]

The Taft Court held that the FTC "has no general authority to compel competitors to a common level, to interfere with ordinary business methods or to prescribe arbitrary standards for those engaged in the conflict for advantage called competition. The great purpose of [the Federal Trade Commission Act[12] and the Clayton

The Protected Realm of Freedom

Act[13]] was to advance the public interest by securing fair opportunity for the play of the contending forces ordinarily engendered by an honest desire for gain."[14]

The Court's hostility to the FTC stands in sharp contrast to the deference that it typically accorded to Interstate Commerce Commission ("ICC") regulation of railroads.[15] Brandeis wrote Taft that "I think the Court's treatment of the Federal Trade Commn – is much like that given the I.C.C. in its early years – and I fear that the fruit of our action may be again bitter. It is not good statesmanship to clamp down safety valves."[16] To modern eyes, the Court's review of the ICC and the FTC should have been controlled by the same general principles of administrative law. But from the perspective of the Taft Court the two agencies were quite distinct. The mission of the ICC was to regulate property affected with a public interest, which, as *Wolff Packing* acknowledged, could be subject to "intimate public regulation."[17] The task of the FTC was, by contrast, to regulate "ordinary business methods" that were protected by the same due process standards as those enforced by *Fairmont Creamery*.

To protect the realm of normal market practices, the Taft Court fashioned doctrine that eerily anticipates the contemporary First Amendment concept of "overbreadth." In 1912 in *Purity Extract & Tonic Co. v. Lynch*, the White Court had explicitly sanctioned overinclusive state economic regulations. "It does not follow," the Court had said, "that because a transaction, separately considered, is innocuous, it may not be included in a prohibition the scope of which is regarded as essential in the legislative judgment to accomplish a purpose within the admitted power of the government."[18] But the Taft Court effectively overruled *Purity Extract*, requiring that regulations of ordinary market transactions not restrict more innocuous conduct than was necessary.[19]

This was the essence of Sutherland's reasoning in *Tyson*. After concluding that theatres were private businesses, Sutherland argued that price fixing was an unconstitutional method of regulating "fraud, extortion, collusive arrangements between the management and those engaged in reselling tickets," because it "ignores the righteous distinction between guilt and innocence, since it applies wholly irrespective of the existence of fraud, collusion or extortion. ... It is not permissible to enact a law which, in effect, spreads an all-inclusive net for the feet of everybody upon the chance that, while the innocent will surely be entangled in its meshes, some wrongdoers also may be caught."[20] McReynolds cited this passage from *Tyson* in *Fairmont Creamery* to support his conclusion that Minnesota could not suppress the price competition of all to prevent the improper overbidding of some.[21] In both *Tyson* and *Fairmont Creamery*, the Court strongly intimated that a proper scienter requirement would solve the problem of overbreadth.[22]

At no time did the Taft Court explain why the realm of ordinary economic transactions required special judicial solicitude of this kind. But it is easy to infer that these transactions embodied, at least for some Taft Court justices, the prerogatives of property itself. As the Court had explained in 1915, "Included in the right of personal liberty and the right of private property – partaking of the nature of each – is the right to make contracts for the acquisition of property."[23] By the end of the nineteenth century, American jurists had redefined property to mean not merely tangible things, like land, but also "the pursuit of one's trade, or the conduct of one's business."[24] Protecting this property was seen as necessary to sustain both the entrepreneurial energy required for civilization and the independent agency essential to full personhood. In the words of William Graham Sumner, one of Taft's favorite professors at Yale,[25] because "[t]here is no time when a man is more supremely sovereign and independent than when he is making a contract," "if one man can force another, by virtue of law and social force, to enter into a contract which is not satisfactory to him . . . . then the latter is a slave, and the relationship might serve as a definition of slavery."[26]

Because economic liberty was deemed essential for moral agency, respect for the prerogatives of market participation was indistinguishable from respect for persons.[27] Undue abridgement of "the independent action of the individual," Sutherland affirmed in 1914, threatens to undermine "the quality and extent of his powers of self-help, self-restraint, and self-reliance."[28] To deny a person the "property which is the fruit and badge of his liberty," said Sutherland, is to "leave him a slave."[29] Sutherland's rhetoric reaffirms the "'Free Labor' ideology" of the nineteenth century,[30] in which "[f]reedom meant economic independence, ownership of productive property – not as an end in itself primarily, but because such independence was essential to participating freely in the public realm."[31]

The legacy of this ideology permeated everyday political culture during the 1920s. In *Shaw v. Gibson-Zahniser Oil Corp.*, for example, the Court addressed the issue of whether Oklahoma could tax land purchased for "a full blood Creek Indian" by the secretary of the interior. The federal government decreed that the land could not "be alienated or leased during the lifetime of the grantee prior to April 26, 1931." The constitutional question, Stone wrote for a unanimous Court, turned upon "the purpose and character of the legislation" creating the Indian land allotment.[32]

Whereas "early legislation affecting" Indians had "as its immediate object the closest control by the government of their lives and property," so as to shield them "alike from their own improvidence and the spoliation of others," later legislation sought to lead them to "the more independent and responsible status of citizens and property owners" by "the gradual relinquishment of restrictions upon the lands originally allotted to the Indians," and "by encouraging their acquisition of other property and gradually enlarging their control over it until independence should be achieved." Thus, said Stone, to hold such lands immune from state taxation "would be inconsistent with one of the very purposes of their creation, to educate the Indians in responsibility."[33]

Stone's equation of the prerogatives of property with adult self-mastery and "the independent and responsible status of citizens"[34] well expresses premises behind the Taft Court's constitutional protection of ordinary economic transactions. This equation almost certainly underlay a unanimous opinion like *Wolff Packing*. It was in fact a commonplace during the 1920s. Protections for property rested "on the supposition that ... self-determination could not exist without scrupulous respect for titles to property and a free hand for individuals in acquiring it and using it."[35] The owner of private property, affirmed one popular text, enjoys "a greater amount of independence; he develops personality."[36] Property "acts as a character-builder."[37]

The Protected Realm of Freedom

"Our primary conception of a free man," said Taft, "is one who can enjoy what he earns, who can spend it for his comfort or pleasure if he would, who can save it and keep it for his future use and benefit if he has the foresight and self-restraint to do so. This is the right of property."[38]

I stress the normative dimensions of property ownership, rather than its instrumental connection to economic development, because the normative aspect of property is almost invisible to modern readers. It is hard for us now to appreciate just how thoroughly members of the Taft Court conceptualized property as constitutive of personality, as prerequisite for the formation of adult independence and agency. Broadly understood, property was "the essence of personal right and freedom."[39] And this was true not merely of property, but also of many other customary prerogatives recognized by the common law. The point can plainly be seen in two Taft Court precedents that remain vital today, *Meyer v. Nebraska*[40] and *Pierce v. Society of Sisters*,[41] each authored by McReynolds.

Decided a week before *Wolff Packing*, *Meyer* struck down a Nebraska statute prohibiting the teaching of foreign languages before eighth grade and the offering of private school instruction "in any language other than . . . English."[42] Legislation of this kind had been enacted by twenty-one states "in the patriotic stress of war,"[43] creating restrictions that by the 1920s were commonly regarded as springing "out of a war hysteria."[44] As Barbara Woodhouse has observed, these restrictions were "supported by many who described themselves as progressive," in part because of their commitment to Americanization as a vehicle for creating "one common people, united for the common good in a just society, free from divisions of class and race."[45] Indeed, when the Nebraska Supreme Court upheld the statute, it stressed that it was not "class legislation, discriminating against some and favoring others," but was instead "necessary for the public good." Hence "individual rights must yield to the general public benefit."[46]

The issue for the Taft Court in reviewing the statute was not whether it was "'class,' 'special,' 'partial,' or 'unequal' legislation,"[47] but rather "whether the statute as construed and applied unreasonably infringes the liberty guaranteed to the plaintiff . . . by the Fourteenth Amendment."[48] McReynolds, speaking for seven justices,[49] crafted an eloquent opinion defining constitutional liberty in terms that far transcend the narrow realm of ordinary market transactions:

> While this Court has not attempted to define with exactness the liberty thus guaranteed, the term has received much consideration. . . . Without doubt it denotes not merely freedom from bodily restraint, but also the right of the individual to contract, to engage in any of the common occupations of life, to acquire useful knowledge, to marry, establish a home and bring up children, to worship God according to the dictates of his own conscience, and, generally, to enjoy those privileges long recognized at common law as essential to the orderly pursuit of happiness by free men. . . . The established doctrine is that this liberty may not be interfered with, under the guise of protecting the public interest, by legislative action which is arbitrary or without reasonable relation to some purpose within the competency of the State to effect. Determination

by the legislature of what constitutes proper exercise of police power is not final or conclusive, but is subject to supervision by the courts.[50]

The passage is extraordinarily rich and allusive. It expands from "the common occupations of life" explicitly affirmed in opinions like *Jay Burns, Wolff Packing,* and *Tyson,* to embrace a wide range of freedoms "long recognized at common law as essential to the orderly pursuit of happiness by free men." These freedoms include acquiring useful knowledge, marrying, establishing a home, and bringing up children. Emphasizing the interdependence of these freedoms with what we would now call economic prerogatives, McReynolds cites for support a long string of due process decisions that range from *Lochner* to *Adkins.*[51] *Meyer* would itself be cited by subsequent Taft Court cases dealing specifically with economic freedoms.[52]

We now inhabit a post-New Deal jurisprudential world, in which economic rights are sharply distinguished from other rights. But in the 1920s, this distinction had not yet evolved into an unbridgeable chasm. *Meyer* illustrates that the pre-New Deal Court did not categorically separate economic liberties from other liberties; it did not sharply distinguish "property" from "liberty" when describing the practices protected by the Due Process Clause.[53] The blended prerogatives of property and liberty protected the many different entitlements required for the maintenance of personal independence and adult moral agency.[54]

It is for this reason mistaken to read *Meyer* as a pinched and narrow opinion. It did not turn merely on the right to property, understood in the restricted sense of a market-oriented right.[55] It is true that *Meyer* emphasized the right of teachers of modern languages to pursue their "calling," which McReynolds pointedly noted had always "been regarded as useful and honorable, essential, indeed, to the public welfare."[56] But the opinion also embraced "the natural duty of the parent to give his children education suitable to their station in life,"[57] and it stressed that "the American people have always regarded education and acquisition of knowledge as matters of supreme importance which should be diligently promoted."[58] The opinion emphasized a wide range of "fundamental rights" traditionally protected at common law because deemed prerequisite for a fully realized life.[59] The decision was contemporaneously characterized as protecting "liberty."[60] "The decision is rightly based on the ground," said *The Nation,* "that to forbid the learning of any tongue is an infringement upon personal liberty."[61] Taft himself glossed *Meyer* as preventing states from banning the study of "foreign language, because such study was not the study of anything vicious," and because such bans "curtailed, in violation of the 14th Amendment, the liberty which the States were not permitted to deny to persons within its jurisdiction."[62]

Holmes dissented from *Meyer* on the classic progressive ground that "I am not prepared to say that it is unreasonable to provide" that youth, raised in conditions of extreme linguistic pluralism, "shall hear and speak only English at school." If "men reasonably might differ" about the importance of the policy, "it is not an undue restriction of the liberty either of teacher or scholar."[63] Brandeis, by contrast, abandoned his usual pattern of progressive deference and joined McReynolds's opinion. Brandeis observed to Frankfurter one month after *Meyer*'s publication

The Protected Realm of Freedom

that "fundamental rights" concerning "education" and "choice of profession" should "not be impaired or withdrawn except as judged by 'clear and present danger' test."[64]

The jurisprudential difference between Holmes and Brandeis is significant. For Holmes, deference signified judicial respect for "the will of the dominant forces of the community,"[65] which he deemed equivalent to sovereign commands that courts were bound to honor.[66] For Brandeis, by contrast, deference signified judicial respect for democratic self-government.[67] Because the right to education at issue in *Meyer* was itself a prerequisite for democracy, deference was inappropriate. Thus, in an editorial likely written by Walter Lippmann, the *New York World* praised *Meyer* for preventing states from dictating "what shall be and shall not be taught. This is a power which a free people can never surrender to any majority."

> [W]ithout liberty of opinion, which includes reasonable liberty of teaching, the majority which is often wrong is deprived of the means by which it can set itself right. For that reason, of all liberties the liberty to think and teach is the most fundamental. It is the one liberty above all others which a people cannot destroy and still remain free.
>
> Therefore the judgment of the Supreme Court is to be welcomed as a very important landmark in the recovery of American liberty from the vandalism of the non-combatants who went mad during the war....
>
> The dissenting opinion of Mr. Justice Holmes is actuated, as we understand it, by no affection for these particular laws but by a strong conviction that the Federal power should not be used to interfere with the sovereignty of the States.... With this conviction of Mr. Justice Holmes The World would on almost any other issue agree.
>
> Nothing is more important constitutionally than to preserve against Federal aggrandizement the authority of the States. There is, it seems to us, however, one thing which is still more important, democratically, and that is to preserve liberty of thought against all governmental authority.[68]

"*Meyer* was a watershed," writes Gerald Gunther, because it split the progressive community.[69] Unlike Lippmann, "Hand and Frankfurter quickly embraced Holmes's position."[70] By the late 1920s, Hand's loss of confidence "in the practicability of truly popular government"[71] had induced him to adopt a purely Holmesian positivism in which the function of a court was simply to implement the dominant opinion of society. But Brandeis never lost faith in the ideal of self-government, and throughout the decade he would seek to explore how courts might sustain the democratic project.[72] Brandeis believed in the rights of democratic citizens because he believed in the responsibilities of democratic citizenship. Rights necessary for that citizenship were to be protected by the "clear and present danger" test. It was Brandeis's perspective, not Holmes's, that lay the groundwork for contemporary liberalism.

McReynolds's opinion in *Meyer*, like Stone's opinion in *Shaw*, reflects a republican logic that is analogous to Brandeis. Because citizens are obligated to govern, they are entitled to the rights necessary to underwrite personal independence. This political theme pervades McReynolds's opinion in *Meyer*. Nebraska had defended its statute on the ground that it was necessary "to promote civic development by inhibiting training and education of the immature in foreign tongues and ideals before they could learn English and acquire American ideals." But McReynolds proposed a very different image of the relationship between the state and its citizens:

> In order to submerge the individual and develop ideal citizens, Sparta assembled the males at seven into barracks and intrusted their subsequent education and training to official guardians. Although such measures have been deliberately approved by men of great genius, their ideas touching the relation between individual and State were wholly different from those upon which our institutions rest; and it hardly will be affirmed that any legislature could impose such restrictions upon the people of a State without doing violence to both letter and spirit of the Constitution.
>
> The desire of the legislature to foster a homogeneous people with American ideals prepared readily to understand current discussions of civic matters is easy to appreciate. Unfortunate experiences during the late war and aversion toward every characteristic of truculent adversaries were certainly enough to quicken that aspiration. But the means adopted, we think, exceed the limitations upon the power of the State and conflict with rights assured to plaintiff in error. The interference is plain enough and no adequate reason therefor in time of peace and domestic tranquility has been shown.[73]

Unlike ancient Sparta, the American state is founded on the principle of republican accountability. The people do not serve the state; the state serves the people. It follows that government in America cannot mold the American people into whatever shape the state desires, for the state would then control the people rather than answer to their wishes. The Due Process Clause protects the independence of persons, in part so that they may direct the state. The contemporary Court still uses the Due Process Clause in this way, to safeguard "from unjustified interference by the State" those aspects of "the culture and traditions of the Nation" deemed necessary for "the ability independently to define one's identity that is central to any concept of liberty."[74]

Two years after *Meyer*, in *Pierce v. Society of Sisters*,[75] McReynolds again interpreted the Due Process Clause in light of the independent agency required for republican citizenship. In *Pierce*, McReynolds spoke for a unanimous Court[76] to strike down an Oregon statute that had been adopted by referendum and that effectively prohibited private schooling for children between 8 and 16 years of age.[77] Unlike *Meyer*, which involved a constitutional defense to a state criminal prosecution, *Pierce* arose in a federal suit for injunctive relief against the operation of the statute. The plaintiffs were two corporations; one was a private Catholic religious school and the other a private military academy. As a matter of technical

The Protected Realm of Freedom

constitutional law, neither corporation could plead a violation of their liberty under the Fourteenth Amendment.[78] But they could and did claim that the statute irreparably damaged their business and thus impaired their property rights. The substantive constitutional question in the case was whether the Oregon statute was a legitimate exercise of state power.

The key holding of *Pierce* is that:

> Under the doctrine of *Meyer v. Nebraska*, we think it entirely plain that the Act of 1922 unreasonably interferes with the liberty of parents and guardians to direct the upbringing and education of children under their control. As often heretofore pointed out, rights guaranteed by the Constitution may not be abridged by legislation which has no reasonable relation to some purpose within the competency of the State. The fundamental theory of liberty upon which all governments in this Union repose excludes any general power of the State to standardize its children by forcing them to accept instruction from public teachers only. The child is not the mere creature of the State; those who nurture him and direct his destiny have the right, coupled with the high duty, to recognize and prepare him for additional obligations.[79]

Pierce explicitly reiterates the logic of *Meyer*. The state lacks competence "to standardize its children by forcing them to accept instruction from public teachers only," because the "child is not the mere creature of the state." Although McReynolds was prepared to cede the state a good deal of discretion over compulsory education,[80] he was also determined to set limits to that discretion. The precise holding of *Pierce* is that the state cannot require all children to receive an identical publicly supervised education. It cannot "standardize" children. The full import of this holding can be appreciated only in the context of developments in compulsory public-school education in the United States.

During the oral argument of *Meyer*, the defendant's attorney had rhetorically asked: "When was the first compulsory school law passed? Within the lifetime of people in this court room. . . . The compulsory system, requiring children to attend some school, public or private, was first enacted in 1852."[81] Until the end of the nineteenth century, however, compulsory school laws were largely "symbolic" because they "were unenforced and probably unenforceable."[82] After 1890, the compulsory schooling movement entered what historians call its "bureaucratic stage," in which mandatory school attendance was extended to high school and enforced by increasingly complex administrative mechanisms, "including requirements for censuses to determine how many children there were, attendance hours, elaborate 'pupil accounting,' and often state financing of schools in proportion to average daily attendance."[83] "Each year," Stanford Professor of Education Elwood P. Cubberley wrote exultingly in 1909, "the child is coming to belong more and more to the state, and less and less to the parent."[84]

The creation of professional school administration was a major achievement of the progressive era. But it meant that the domain of childhood was increasingly colonized by administrative techniques analogous to those used by government agencies to regulate the market. The expansion of state control in

831

education aroused the same worries of objectification, independence, and agency, as those provoked by managerial supervision in the economic sphere. As in *Meyer*, a "central concern of *Pierce* is the substantial threat to liberty posed by state-compelled identity."[85] Taft considered *Pierce* "the *Meyer* case over again."[86]

Pierce turns explicitly on the proposition that the state cannot "standardize its children."[87] The word "standardize" strongly suggests an underlying hostility to the mass administrative techniques so triumphantly featured during World War I and carried forward by Hoover's Commerce Department,[88] which celebrated "the man who has a standard automobile, a standard telephone, a standard bathtub, a standard electric light, [and] a standard radio."[89] In their ballot argument against the proposed Oregon statute, the Seventh Day Adventists of Oregon argued that the "government that turns its citizens into subjects and makes them mere cogs in a wheel, without any rights of their own, is a government that is transforming itself into a tyranny."[90]

Standardization was equated with the potential for government tyranny. In postwar America, fear of standardization was associated with hostility both to Prussian autocracy and communist Russia. A ballot argument against the proposed Oregon statute argued that "This measure initiates the method of public education which brought Prussia to her deserved destruction – giving the state dictatorial powers over the training of children and destroying independence of character and freedom of thought. In the present day Russia the Bolshevist government treats the child as the ward of the state. This measure proposes to adopt this method and to substitute state control for the authority and guidance of the parents and is destructive of American independence."[91] The proposed statute was "destructive of true Americanism."[92]

The ideal of "true Americanism" was extremely complex in the 1920s. On the one hand, it meant republican independence. It meant a sphere of private liberty that was immune from standardization. The preservation of that sphere was necessary to ensure that the state remained accountable to the people. Yet, on the other hand, Americanization also referred to a complex of principles and ideals to which persons were expected to give their unreserved and total allegiance. Just as the necessities of the war had promoted economic integration and planning, so they had inspired impulses toward national unity that demanded "100 per cent Americanism."[93]

Progressive, professional, well-intentioned educators had long viewed the public school as an essential pathway for "Americanizing" the huge influx of foreign immigrants who came to this country without comprehending American civic institutions, a project that accelerated during the 1920s.[94] In the absence of a countervailing commitment to a private sphere immune from compulsory inculcation, however, the project of Americanization could easily slide into a process of total standardization. In the "tribal twenties,"[95] when the nation suffered sharp increases in nativism, xenophobia, and intolerance of all kinds,[96] the project could become an instrument of oppression and prejudice.

The Protected Realm of Freedom

This is the story of the Oregon statute. The ballot argument for the statute offered sober reasons that might have been articulated by elite educators anywhere in the country. Public schools, it asserted,

> are the creators of true citizens by common education, which teaches those ideals and standards upon which our government rests. . . .
>
> The assimilation and education of our foreign born citizens in the principles of our government, the hopes and inspiration of our people, are best secured by and through attendance of all children in our public schools.
>
> We must now halt those coming to our country from forming groups, establishing schools, and thereby bringing up their children in an environment often antagonistic to the principles of our government.
>
> Mix the children of the foreign born with the native born, and the rich with the poor. Mix those with prejudices in the public school melting pot for a few years while their minds are plastic, and finally bring out the finished product – a true American.[97]

Yet the Oregon statute was in fact the direct product of the Ku Klux Klan's "'One Flag, One School' campaign," which was a "centerpiece of the Klan's platform of 100 percent Americanism."[98] The Court was well aware of the initiative's connection to the Klan,[99] which had become a notorious powerhouse in Oregon.[100] The Klan's primary target was the Catholic Church and its system of parochial schools.[101] The Klan believed that Catholic and Jewish children should be compelled to undergo indoctrination by the Protestant majorities they assumed would control public schools. Americanism, in the hands of the Klan, sought an ideological uniformity that was inconsistent with republican independence.

In the twenty-first century, independent moral agency is protected by specific constitutional rights that police the boundary between public and private spheres. *Pierce*, which "has proved the single, solid survivor of the era of substantive due process,"[102] would now probably be categorized as a case involving religious liberty. A statute that deliberately suppressed private religious education would likely fall afoul of the Free Exercise Clause. The plaintiffs' lawyers in *Pierce* did in fact repeatedly raise questions of religious liberty.[103] When *Pierce* was decided, however, the Free Exercise Clause had not yet been incorporated into the Due Process Clause for application against the states. The Court would take its first tentative steps in that direction one week later in *Gitlow v. New York*,[104] when it incorporated the right of free speech. But the Court would refrain from incorporating the Free Exercise Clause for another fifteen years.[105]

Pierce instead deployed the Due Process Clause to negotiate the boundary between a public sphere of state control and a private sphere of independent moral agency.[106] Because the Clause says nothing specific about this boundary, the Court's appeal to the Clause was necessarily informed by implicit philosophical understandings that must be reconstructed.[107] We can learn from *Meyer* and *Pierce* that, in contrast to Holmes, the Court's two most moralistic justices, Brandeis and McReynolds, were each fiercely committed constitutionally to immunizing private

833

individuals from totalizing state regulation. A plausible reconstruction is that each defined the constitutionally protected private sphere in terms of what he believed necessary to ensure that persons would become and remain independent moral agents.

McReynolds and Brandeis differed, however, in how they defined the substance of constitutionally protected moral agency. McReynolds was far more likely than Brandeis to stress the importance of entrepreneurialism. This is because McReynolds tacitly connected the concept of personhood to active participation in the market. From *Meyer*, we can infer that McReynolds also regarded other traditional common law rights as essential to the definition of personhood. Common law rights were for McReynolds "a source of liberty,"[108] which is why McReynolds invoked the Fourteenth Amendment to prevent states from suppressing common law rights.[109] Implicit in McReynolds's approach was the assumption that the common law reliably adjudicated when the agency of one individual became unacceptably oppressive to that of another.[110]

Like McReynolds, Brandeis valued small entrepreneurs, but unlike McReynolds he was deeply concerned about the many ways in which the private power of some inhibited the personal development of others. Brandeis was keenly aware that the "vast mass of property no longer consists of the instruments of individual activity and the objects of individual desire," but was owned by large corporations and institutions and used in ways that exercised "immense influence on the lives of other people, both consumers and employés."[111] For that reason Brandeis was far more likely than McReynolds to embrace innovative government interventions designed to offset the potentially crushing effects of private power authorized by traditional common law rules. Brandeis was concerned less with the economic entrepreneurialism than with the preconditions of meaningful political participation.

A case like *Meyer* reveals the overlap between the vision of McReynolds and that of Brandeis. The unanimity of decisions like *Wolff Packing* and *Pierce* suggests that some such line between public and private existed in one way or another for all members of the Taft Court. In theory, each justice revealed something of his understanding of the construction of independent moral agency by how he was prepared to draw the line between public and private spheres of life. McReynolds and Brandeis are particularly clear cases because of their intense moralism.

For justices like Taft and Sutherland, by contrast, it is often difficult to disentangle their commitment to the construction of individual agency from their commitment to the systemic incentive effects of property rights, which they believed were necessary to propel the economic growth required for civilization.[112] In *Adkins*, for example, Sutherland stressed that the fairness and justice of the wage bargain should be immunized from the interference of minimum wage legislation. This would seem to suggest that Sutherland's primary objective was to use the Due Process Clause to protect voluntary agreements that expressed the independent moral agency of workers and employers.[113] Yet it is equally plausible to interpret *Adkins* as expressing Sutherland's view that minimum wage

The Protected Realm of Freedom

legislation was unconstitutional because it was bad economic policy that obscured "the vital distinction between helplessness, which is a misfortune, and laziness, which is a vice."[114] On this account, minimum wage legislation was unconstitutional because it undermined necessary economic incentives. After a century, it is almost impossible to know which interpretation of Sutherland's motivation is correct. All that we can say with assurance is that Sutherland's categorical refusal to attend to empirical evidence demonstrating the involuntary compulsions of sweat labor raises a reasonable doubt about how seriously he took the question of independent moral agency.

Adkins illustrates the difficulty of constructing any simple, single account of the Taft Court's resurrection of *Lochnerian* due process doctrine. What makes decisions like *Meyer* and *Pierce* so historically important is that they clearly establish that the Taft Court did in fact use the doctrine to preserve the moral independence of citizens. It is this underlying clarity that accounts for the ongoing vitality of these decisions. The cataclysm of the Great Depression has made it difficult for us to appreciate the extent to which members of the Taft Court regarded property as connected to the necessary moral independence of citizens. In our own time, in the wake of the constitutional revisions of the New Deal, property has largely been drained of this moral significance.

During the Taft Court era, property disconnected from the construction of independent moral agency was typically classified as property affected with a public interest. Such property could be regulated with relatively few constitutional restraints. When constitutional restraints were imposed, they were not justified in terms of protecting the moral independence of persons, but instead in terms of protecting the incentives necessary to facilitate economic growth. The Taft Court's efforts to enforce such restraints on utility ratemaking would eventually expose it to fierce backlash.[115]

One of the Taft Court's most important and fascinating decisions about the reach of the Due Process Clause did not involve property affected with a public interest, but instead ordinary property that, most unusually, was not readily experienced as a vehicle for the construction of autonomous moral agency. In *Village of Euclid v. Ambler Realty Co.*,[116] the Court, speaking through Sutherland, unexpectedly upheld the constitutional authority of cities to pursue comprehensive municipal zoning. Van Devanter, McReynolds, and Butler each dissented without opinion.

It is hard to overstate the importance of *Euclid*. The decision "has had a profound effect on American life and jurisprudence," providing "the constitutional foundation for an explosive growth in modern zoning, subdivision controls, and other governmental land use regulation that has transformed the organization and development of land and communities."[117] The case arose when the tiny village of Euclid, located just outside the municipal boundaries of Cleveland, invoked the authority of Ohio's new zoning-enabling legislation to adopt a comprehensive zoning ordinance in 1922.[118] The ordinance restricted to residential uses development on much of the land owned by the Ambler Realty Company, thus (allegedly) reducing the land's value from $10,000 per acre to $2,500 per acre.[119] Ambler hired Newton D. Baker, Wilson's secretary of war and the former reform mayor of

Cleveland, to represent its interests. Baker promptly sought an injunction in federal court declaring the Euclid ordinance unconstitutional on its face.

It was the first federal lawsuit challenging the constitutionality of comprehensive zoning.[120] "There was ample ground" for suspicion, wrote Alfred Bettman, a national expert on zoning whose amicus brief would prove influential in *Euclid*'s resolution, "that the Ambler Realty Company ... represented a larger group seeking to destroy the zoning movement."[121] *Euclid* might have been selected as a test case because many zoning experts considered the town's ordinance "a piece of arbitrary zoning and on the facts not justifiable."[122]

At the time of *Euclid*, comprehensive zoning was a relatively recent phenomenon in American land use law. The first comprehensive zoning ordinance had been enacted by New York City in 1916.[123] It was motivated chiefly by the desire of upscale Fifth Avenue merchants to keep the rabble of the garment industry south of midtown.[124] The value of New York real estate was so interconnected that rapid changes in the character of a neighborhood could destroy millions of dollars of real estate investment. New York therefore stressed the need for zoning to secure stable property values, which were necessary to attract investment.[125] New York also emphasized the importance of "city planning" to "the health, comfort and welfare of the city and its inhabitants. New York City has reached a point beyond which continued unplanned growth cannot take place without inviting social and economic disaster. It is too big a city .... to permit the continuance of the *laissez faire* methods of earlier days."[126] Without planning, the city could not adequately provide necessary services like fire suppression, traffic control, rapid transit, sewage removal, street cleaning, public improvements, or water distribution.[127] Nor could it adequately secure the "public health" of its residents.[128]

The New York ordinance set off a national stampede. Fueled by rapid urbanization,[129] the "growth of zoning in the United States was phenomenal. It swept the nation in the 1920s."[130] Immediately appreciating the importance of zoning, Hoover in September 1921 convened an advisory committee to consider the subject.[131] The committee published a Model Zoning Enabling Act[132] and *A Zoning Primer*.[133] Both were enormously influential,[134] providing a "great national impetus to the practice of zoning."[135] By the end of 1923, "zoning was in effect in 218 municipalities, with more than 22,000,000 inhabitants"; by 1925, nineteen states had adopted the Model Act.[136]

Baker filed his Bill of Complaint in May 1923. He sought to stem the legislative tide toward zoning by alleging that the Euclid ordinance, which was mostly an unexceptional instance of the genre,

> was enacted for the purpose of preserving the ideas of beauty officially entertained by the members of the council of said village and excluding uses of private property in said village offensive to the eccentric and supersensitive taste of said members of council and arresting and diverting the normal and lawful development of the lands of the plaintiff ... in said village from those industrial, commercial and residence uses for which it is best suited and most available, all of which this plaintiff avers is done by ... restrictions which invade alike the

The Protected Realm of Freedom

rights of private property and personal liberty guaranteed by the Constitution of the United States.[137]

The district judge, D.C. Westenhaver, was Baker's former law partner. He had replaced Clarke on the Ohio bench after the latter's promotion to the Supreme Court.[138] Westenhaver handed Baker a complete victory. Citing *Adkins* and *Wolff Packing*, as well as Holmes's opinion in *Pennsylvania Coal Co. v. Mahon*,[139] Westenhaver concluded that Euclid had effectively confiscated Ambler's property and so owed it compensation.[140] "There can be no conception of property aside from its control and use," Westenhaver reasoned. The Euclid zoning ordinance drastically limited Ambler's use of its property in a manner that had no "real and substantial relation to the maintenance and preservation of the public peace, public order, public morals, or public safety."[141] Westenhaver in effect ruled "that zoning ordinances are necessarily unconstitutional."[142]

The opinion threw the entire future of the burgeoning zoning movement into disarray. With the case headed to the Supreme Court, leaders of the National Conference on City Planning, which had been founded in 1910 to promote city planning, reluctantly yielded to the entreaties of Bettman and decided to submit an amicus brief to the Court.[143] Euclid was represented by James Metzenbaum, a determined bulldog of a lawyer who produced a sprawling hodge-podge of a brief.[144] Bettman's submission, by contrast, was a disciplined professional effort that effectively summarized existing case law,[145] distinguished zoning regulations from the confiscation of property,[146] explained that the purpose of zoning was not merely aesthetics,[147] and cast zoning law as analogous to but not coterminous with traditional nuisance regulation.[148]

Unfortunately, in a delicious irony bearing on the foresight of city planners, Bettman missed the deadline for filing his brief because of an "oversight."[149] His brief had been due on the date of oral argument, which was January 27, 1926. On that day *Euclid* was argued before a bench from which Sutherland was absent.[150] Worried about what he believed to be misrepresentations in the final minutes of Baker's oral argument, Metzenbaum on January 29 sought permission to file a reply brief. On February 2, Metzenbaum was given one week to file a brief, and Baker was given one subsequent week to respond.[151] Baker filed his brief on February 16, the last day of the deadline. Yet, according to Stone's docket book,[152] the Court had already met on February 13 and voted 5–3 to sustain Westenhaver's opinion. Sutherland and Taft were in the majority;[153] dissenting were Brandeis, Sanford, and Stone.[154] There is no vote recorded one way or another for Holmes. Most unusually, there is no marking in Stone's docket book indicating the justice to whom the opinion was assigned for authorship.

On the same day as the Court's conference, February 13, Bettman discovered his mistake and wrote Taft, who was a friend from Cincinnati,[155] seeking leave to file his amicus brief. Taft brought the request to conference, which approved Bettman's request on February 26.[156] In Stone's docket book there is an undated note, written in a hand that Barry Cushman plausibly speculates is that of Alfred

McCormack, Stone's law clerk during that term,[157] which states: "Rehearing suggested by Sutherland, J., and case set down for rehearing in October Term 1926."[158] Taft announced the rehearing on March 1.[159] *Euclid* was reargued on October 12, 1926, and six weeks later Sutherland produced his opinion.[160] Sutherland and Taft had switched their votes.[161]

Zoning was a quintessential form of progressive "social planning."[162] As Bettman forthrightly acknowledged in his brief, zoning "represents the application of foresight and intelligence to the development of the community."[163] In *Adkins*, Sutherland had expressed hostility to the subordination of ordinary property to such planning. Contemporaries found it "difficult to believe that it is the same Mr. Justice Sutherland who wrote the majority opinions in" *Tyson* and *Euclid*.[164] *Euclid's* endorsement of zoning "must surely be acknowledged as . . . . the most important redefinition of the nature of private property ever made in United States courts."[165] It was exceedingly odd that it was at the hands of a justice like Sutherland, who was generally perceived as "a property man."[166]

In his brief, Baker stressed that zoning interrupts "the operation of natural economic laws" by channeling development in ways that are "arbitrary and unnatural" insofar as they do not reflect "the operation of economic laws," but instead "arbitrary considerations of taste enacted into hard and fast legislation."[167] "The theory of our liberty," Baker wrote, "has always been to maintain the right of the individual to his liberty and to his property and to allow free play to economic laws, private contract and personal choice."[168] The idea that freedom was to be measured by the rhythm of "natural" market transactions, with which it was unconstitutional folly to interfere, should have been attractive to Sutherland, because he had himself expressed similar sentiments in 1921.[169] "[T]here are certain fundamental social and economic laws which are beyond the power ... of official control," Sutherland had written, "and any attempt to interfere with their operations inevitably ends in confusion, if not disaster. These laws and principles may be compared with the forces of nature whose movements are entirely outside the scope of human power."[170]

The discrepancy between Sutherland in 1926 and Sutherland in 1921, however, is less stark than might appear at first glance. Sutherland adroitly fashioned *Euclid* to turn on a very modern distinction between "facial" and "as applied" challenges to legislation. "[I]t may happen," Sutherland wrote, "that not only offensive or dangerous industries will be excluded, but those which are neither offensive nor dangerous will share the same fate."

> But this is no more than happens in respect of many practice-forbidding laws which this court has upheld, although drawn in general terms so as to include individual cases that may turn out to be innocuous in themselves. ... The inclusion of a reasonable margin, to insure effective enforcement, will not put upon a law, otherwise valid, the stamp of invalidity. Such laws may also find their justification in the fact that, in some fields, the bad fades into the good by such insensible degrees that the two are not capable of being readily distinguished and separated in terms of legislation. In the light of these considerations, we are not

The Protected Realm of Freedom

prepared to say that the end in view was not sufficient to justify the general rule of the ordinance, although some industries of an innocent character might fall within the proscribed class. It cannot be said that the ordinance in this respect "passes the bounds of reason and assumes the character of a merely arbitrary fiat."[171]

Whereas in *Tyson* Sutherland facially invalidated overbroad legislation that failed to respect "the righteous distinction between guilt and innocence,"[172] in *Euclid* he recognized that zoning laws could and would be overinclusive. Sutherland found the Euclid ordinance *facially* constitutional because he chose to endow it with "a reasonable margin to insure effective enforcement."[173] The very existence of that margin, however, also created the possibility of challenges to the *application* of zoning ordinances to the particular circumstances of individual plaintiffs.[174] Sutherland embraced the vehicle of "as applied" challenges eighteen months later in *Nectow v. City of Cambridge*,[175] when, speaking for a unanimous Court, he struck down the application of a zoning law.[176] *Euclid* did not insulate zoning ordinances from constitutional supervision; it merely validated the generic municipal project of imposing an overall plan on urban growth.[177]

That having been said, it is nevertheless important to note the striking contrast between an opinion like *Euclid* and an opinion like *Adkins*. In *Adkins*, Sutherland had airily dismissed the "mass of reports, opinions of special observers and students of the subject, and the like," which Frankfurter had put before the Court. Sutherland had found them "interesting, but only mildly persuasive." He rejected the "large number of printed opinions approving the policy of the minimum wage" on the explicit ground that such expertise was "proper enough for the consideration of the lawmaking bodies" but shed "no legitimate light upon the question of its validity, and that is what we are called upon to decide."[178]

In *Euclid*, by contrast, Sutherland expressed great deference to the many "commissions and experts" who had discussed the necessity of zoning to serve the public health, safety, morals and welfare.[179] "The results of their investigations," Sutherland explained, "have been set forth in comprehensive reports" which "bear every evidence of painstaking consideration." If Sutherland was not quite ready to concede that the judgments of city planners "demonstrate the wisdom or sound policy in all respects" of zoning restrictions, he was nevertheless prepared to affirm that these judgments "at least" offered "reasons" that were "sufficiently cogent to preclude us from saying, as it must be said before the ordinance can be declared unconstitutional, that such provisions are clearly arbitrary and unreasonable, having no substantial relation to the public health, safety, morals, or general welfare."[180] Nothing could be further from the judicial sensibility of *Adkins*.

The experts in *Euclid* conveyed in a single voice the massive and systematic interconnectedness of urban life.[181] Justices like McReynolds, Van Devanter, and Butler valued private property because it facilitated the exercise of autonomous, individual moral agency. But "the increasing 'interdependence of modern city dwellers'"[182] made urban property particularly vulnerable to blight, meaning that the best and most intelligent efforts of any single individual could be frustrated by how neighbors chose to use their property. In the context of urban land, the significance of an agent's independent choices could be rapidly, radically, and unforeseeably undercut by the unrestricted economic agency of third parties.

The dense reports supporting New York City's pioneering zoning law, which Metzenbaum had painstakingly caused to be delivered to each justice, and especially to Sutherland,[183] demonstrated the pressing need for zoning to stabilize the prices of urban property.[184] In his amicus brief Bettman cleverly extracted long passages from 1916 testimony to the New York City Zoning Commission by Taft's intimate, lifelong friend – his college classmate and fellow member of Skull and Bones – the New York mortgage banker Clarence H. Kelsey. Kelsey declared that if New York refuses to enact "a well considered plan," it "is failing to protect itself and property values as well. Its present policy of allowing every owner of real estate to do as he pleases with his own, is a policy of self-destruction. . . . I have no doubt of the favorable effect of this proposed control of the improvement and use of real estate. . . . These restrictions will tend to steady values and enable all real estate owners to make reasonable use of their property. This is certainly better for the city as a whole than to continue to allow a few out of many to make unfair use of their property and depress still further the value of the remaining property and ultimately their own as well."[185]

Insofar as urban congestion and interdependence made obvious and inescapable the need for systematic planning to stabilize prices and to provide essential city services like traffic control, fire suppression, sewerage removal, and the like,[186] it also undermined the moral experience of autonomy on the part of individual property owners. "There is little resentment at the traffic policeman who halts us at a busy corner," observed a Chamber of Commerce pamphlet excerpted in Bettman's brief, "for it is obvious that the regulation of traffic benefits us all."[187] Although extensive traffic regulation strictly constrained individual freedom of action, it did not restrict socially meaningful freedom. No sane driver would experience freedom from traffic regulation as a site for the construction of independent moral agency.

The interdependence of city real estate analogously drained moral significance from the freedom to use urban property. Sutherland gently referenced this point when he observed in *Euclid* that "restrictions in respect of the use and occupation of private lands in urban communities" that would have seemed "arbitrary and oppressive" a half century before, are now "sustained, under the complex conditions of our day, for reasons analogous to those which justify traffic regulations, which, before the advent of automobiles and rapid transit street railways, would have been condemned as fatally arbitrary and unreasonable."[188]

It is striking that in *Euclid* Sutherland does not conceptualize urban property from the point of view of the owner, but from the perspective of the complex social system in which such property is embedded. So, for example, he writes that "the question whether the power exists to forbid the erection of a building of a particular kind or for a particular use, like the question whether a particular thing is a nuisance, is to be determined, not by an abstract consideration of the building or of the thing considered apart, but by considering it in connection with the circumstances and the locality."[189] By stressing such systemic constraints on the use of urban property,

The Protected Realm of Freedom

Sutherland deemphasized the importance of the property to the construction of independent moral agency.[190] An urban property owner does not become a slave if prevented from using his land in ways that disrupt the choices of neighboring property owners. He is no more transformed into a creature of the state than is a driver who obeys traffic regulations.

What is especially unusual about *Euclid* is that Sutherland, like Taft, usually understood property through the lens of individual incentives. "Any attempt to fix a limit to personal acquisition is filled with danger," Sutherland had written in 1921, "since, being arbitrary, it is sure to be fluctuating, tending always toward narrower and narrower limits and, in the end, destructive of that great incentive to individual effort which is furnished by the feeling of certainty that one will be allowed to enjoy the fruits of his own industry and genius."[191] This view of property had come to dominate American legal thinking in the nineteenth century, when American common law diverged from its English roots. For justices like Taft, Sutherland, and Butler, private property was almost always understood as an institution designed to facilitate economic growth and development.[192] Whereas English property law stressed the protection of existing entitlements, American law instead emphasized unrestrained market participation as a means of promoting economic expansion.[193] That is why American constitutional law regarded property law from the perspective of the owner.

Zoning was based upon a very different understanding of urban real property. Zoning "privileged security over freedom."[194] When the *Minneapolis Star Tribune* editorialized in favor of a proposed zoning statute, it emphasized the need for "realty values" to be "made more stable" and for "residential communities" to be "given better insurance against undesirable invasion."[195] If Sutherland usually immunized property from regulation to facilitate individual initiative and economic development, zoning aspired instead to make urban land a safe investment by preventing uncontrolled speculation.[196] It converted urban property into a haven insulated from transformation, rather like the nostalgic restored villages that sprung up during the unsettled 1920s.[197] In the words of Robert Wiebe's influential interpretation of the period, the nation had come to prioritize "the regulative, hierarchical needs of urban-industrial life," which "sought continuity and predictability in a world of endless change."[198]

The upshot was that *Euclid* endorsed a framework of urban land regulation that had more in common with traditional, static, English conceptions of real property than with American nineteenth-century precedents.[199] Zoning favored the maintenance of the *status quo* over the allure of a boundless future. But this meant that zoning also froze into place existing class stratification. This was obvious to contemporaries.[200] Westenhaver had struck down Euclid's ordinance in part because it constituted prohibited class legislation. "In the last analysis," said Westenhaver, "the result to be accomplished is to classify the population and segregate them according to their income or situation in life. The true reason why some persons live in a mansion and others in a shack, why some live in a single-family dwelling and others in a double-family dwelling, why some live in a two-family dwelling and others in an apartment, or why some live in a well-kept apartment and others in a tenement, is primarily economic. It is a matter of income and wealth."[201] In 1904 the great Ernst Freund, in his magisterial treatise on the police power, had definitively opined that "It is certain . . . . that in defining nuisances no standards may be established which discriminate against the poor."[202]

Postwar America, however, was hungry for normalcy. It wanted to preserve existing values rather than sacrifice stability on the altar of future development. Robert H. Whitten, an important figure in the development of American zoning legislation who had testified as an expert on the village's behalf in the trial of *Euclid*,[203] frankly admitted "that zoning tends inevitably toward the segregation of the different economic classes." Whitten considered this effect "merely incidental" and "neither undemocratic nor anti-social."[204] A policy that promoted the stability of urban property necessarily meant a policy that reinforced existing forms of social stratification.

In contrast to Westenhaver, Sutherland did not display a trace of anticlass ideology. Sutherland authored an opinion that considered only the liberty to use and control urban land. This narrow focus ignored darker social developments that were associated with the zoning movement. Questions of preservation and stability were in the 1920s characteristically associated with anti-immigrant or overtly racist sentiments. "The immigrant," writes Seymour Toll, "is the fiber of zoning. . . . In early twentieth-century New York he is seen as a southeastern European, the lower East Side garment worker whose presence in midtown Manhattan created one of the most decisive moments in the history of zoning."[205]

Ernst Freund, while acknowledging that zoning violated the principle that police regulations "operate irrespective of class distinctions," was by the 1920s prepared to concede that the principle "not be made a fetish."[206] He sought to explain "the crux of the zoning problem" – "the residential district" – by reference to "the concept of amenity," by which he meant "residential preference." Residential preference was simply a nice way of referring to social discrimination; it could be illustrated by "the coming of colored people into a district." Although "any attempt to give official recognition to social differences would be utterly futile, partly because it would be repudiated by public sentiment, partly because it would be impossible to find an appropriate legal formula," zoning nevertheless effectively enforced residential preferences.[207] In modern times, the exclusionary zoning made possible by *Euclid* has been bluntly condemned as "racism with a progressive, technocratic veneer"; its "basic purpose is to keep Them where They belonged – Out."[208]

In *Euclid*, Sutherland found "no difficulty" in sustaining zoning regulations that separated industrial from residential uses.[209] "The serious question in the case," he wrote, "arises over the provisions of the ordinance excluding from residential districts apartment houses, business houses, retail stores and shops, and other like establishments. This question involves the validity of what is really the crux of the more recent zoning legislation, namely, the creation and maintenance of residential districts, from which business and trade of every sort, including hotels and apartment houses, are excluded."[210]

The Protected Realm of Freedom

It is on this precise question that Sutherland chose to rely on "commissions and experts." "With particular reference to apartment houses," he wrote:

> it is pointed out that the development of detached house sections is greatly retarded by the coming of apartment houses, which has sometimes resulted in destroying the entire section for private house purposes; that in such sections very often the apartment house is a mere parasite, constructed in order to take advantage of the open spaces and attractive surroundings created by the residential character of the district. Moreover, the coming of one apartment house is followed by others, interfering by their height and bulk with the free circulation of air and monopolizing the rays of the sun which otherwise would fall upon the smaller homes, and bringing, as their necessary accompaniments, the disturbing noises incident to increased traffic and business, and the occupation, by means of moving and parked automobiles, of larger portions of the streets, thus detracting from their safety and depriving children of the privilege of quiet and open spaces for play, enjoyed by those in more favored localities – until, finally, the residential character of the neighborhood and its desirability as a place of detached residences are utterly destroyed. Under these circumstances, apartment houses, which in a different environment would be not only entirely unobjectionable but highly desirable, come very near to being nuisances.[211]

Much has been written about this unfortunate passage. "Apartment houses 'retard,' 'destroy,' 'monopolize,' 'interfere,' and 'deprive'; they are 'mere parasites,' which 'take advantage' of a desirable environment created by others while carrying 'disturbing noises,' and bringing an 'occupation' of the streets."[212] "Without ever mentioning race, immigration, or tenement houses," Sutherland nevertheless managed "to call upon other code words that had the same impact."[213] Although the Court had in 1917 struck down a Louisville city ordinance that required explicit racial residential segregation,[214] *Euclid* sanctioned zoning regulations that were effective, facially neutral mechanisms "to prevent the alien or the Negro from coming into a district."[215] If in *Pierce* the Court had set its face against a nativism that paradoxically expressed itself in a demand for universal public education, in *Euclid* Sutherland supported expert planning that would lay the groundwork for future suburban segregation.[216]

We cannot attribute definitive motives to the decision of Sutherland and Taft to switch their votes in *Euclid*. We cannot ascertain whether they were influenced by the etiolation of moral agency in the context of urban property, or by the need to preserve stable urban property values, or by the need to insulate middle-class whites from the contamination of "undesirable neighbors."[217] Suffice it to say that *Euclid*, the Taft Court's most profound and lasting contribution to American property law, exists in each of these dimensions.

Notes

1. Fairmont Creamery Co. v. Minnesota, 274 U.S. 1, 3–4, 7 (1927).
2. *Id.* at 8. The Minnesota statute had originally contained such a scienter requirement, but in 1923 Minnesota "eliminated purpose as an element of the offense." *Id.* at 4.
3. *Id.* at 8–9.
4. *Id.* at 9 (emphasis added).
5. *Id.*
6. T.M. Cooley, *Labor and Capital Before the Law*, 139 NORTH AMERICAN REVIEW 504, 504 (1884).
7. Quoted in *President Hughes Responds for the Association*, 10 AMERICAN BAR ASSOCIATION JOURNAL 567, 569 (1924).
8. *Id.*
9. *Id.* Although the Taft Court did not proscribe every abrogation of traditional common law rights, it held that statutory restrictions on "normal" business practices should be scrutinized and held to a standard of "reasonableness." Depending upon how legislative restrictions struck the justices of the Court, this standard could at times be quite permissive. *See, e.g.*, Louis Pizitz Dry Goods Co. v. Yeldell, 274 U.S. 112, 115–16 (1927) ("Lord Campbell's Act and its successors, establishing liability for wrongful death where none existed before, the various Workmen's Compensation Acts imposing new types of liability, are familiar examples of the legislative creation of new rights and duties for the prevention of wrong or for satisfying social and economic needs. Their constitutionality may not be successfully challenged merely because a change in the common law is effected."); Missouri Pac. R.R. Co. v. Porter, 273 U.S. 341, 346 (1927); International Stevedoring Co. v. Haverty, 272 U.S. 50, 52 (1926).
10. William Howard Taft, *Is Prohibition a Blow at Personal Liberty?*, 36 LADIES HOME JOURNAL 31, 78 (May 1919).
11. FTC v. Beech-Nut Packing Co., 257 U.S. 441, 453–54 (1922) (quoting FTC v. Gratz, 253 U.S. 421, 427 (1920)). Sutherland had opposed the creation of the FTC, which he feared would "set the business of the country upon a sea of uncertainty for many years to come." GEORGE SUTHERLAND, SUPERFLUOUS GOVERNMENT: AN ADDRESS BY SENATOR SUTHERLAND OF UTAH 7, 10–11 (Cleveland: Cleveland Chamber of Commerce 1914).
12. Pub. L. 63-203, 38 Stat. 717 (September 26, 1914).
13. Pub. L. 63-212, 38 Stat. 730 (October 15, 1914).
14. FTC v. Sinclair Refining Co., 261 U.S. 463, 475–76 (1923).
15. *See, e.g.*, United States v. Illinois Central Railroad Co., 263 U.S. 515 (1924).
16. LDB to WHT (December 23, 1922) (Taft papers). Brandeis's note was a propos of FTC v. Curtis Pub. Co., 260 U.S. 568 (1923), in which the Court set aside an FTC finding that the appellee had engaged in unfair methods of competition. Taft wrote Brandeis that "I am disturbed by McReynolds' opinion in the Curtis Publishing Co's case – as he has put it, it seems to me that he is weighing evidence in making his conclusions as if we were a jury or a chancellor. What do you think of it?" WHT to LDB (December 23, 1922) (Brandeis papers). Brandeis replied that "I agree your criticism of the Curtis Pub. Co. opinion. You will recall that I voted the other way, and the opinion has not removed my difficulties. Indeed I differ widely from McReynolds concerning the functions and practices of the Trade Commn. – as

The Protected Realm of Freedom

you know from the Gratz Case. [FTC v. Gratz, 253 U.S. 421 (1920)]. But I have differed from the Court recently in three expressed dissents & concluded that, in this case, I had better 'shut up,' as in Junior days." LDB to WHT (December 23, 1922) (Taft papers). Brandeis eventually joined Taft's separate opinion, which was denominated as "doubting," because McReynolds's opinion for the Court "may bear the construction that the court has discretion to sum up the evidence pro and con on issues undecided by the commission, and make itself the fact-finding body." 260 U.S. at 583 (Taft, C.J., doubting). "I think it of high importance," Taft added, "that we should scrupulously comply with the evident intention of Congress that the Federal Commission be made the fact-finding body and that the court should in its rulings preserve the board's character as such, and not interject its views of the facts where there is any conflict in the evidence." *Id.*

17. Charles Wolff Packing Co. v. Court of Industrial relations, 562 U.S. 522, 539 (1923).
18. 226 U.S. 192, 201 (1912).
19. In his comprehensive summary of the Court's doctrine, Thomas Reed Powell notes the many cases in which the Court refused to allow state regulations to "extend beyond the area of actual evil in order to make more certain that no evil will escape":

> A flat prohibition of price discrimination in purchases of milk cannot be sustained as a means of preventing monopoly and restraint of trade, since such practices do not necessarily tend to monopoly and it is feasible to confine the prohibition to discrimination in aid of such ultimate vice. Maximum weights cannot be set for loaves of bread as a means of preventing fraud against customers who mistake a large small loaf for a small large one. The state cannot exclude all shoddy from a puff or comfortable in order to ensure that no unsterilized shoddy finds its way in.

Thomas Reed Powell, *The Supreme Court and State Police Power, 1922–1930 – IX*, 18 VIRGINIA LAW REVIEW 597, 615–16 (1932). *See supra* Chapter 23.

20. Tyson & Brother v. Banton, 273 U.S. 418, 442–43 (1927).
21. *Fairmont Creamery*, 274 U.S. at 11. In 1926, Butler insisted that Stone remove from a draft opinion the sentence: "Conduct itself innocuous may be so related to prohibited acts as to bring the former within the proscription of the latter in order that the permitted legislative purpose may be attained." (Stone papers, file of Van Oster v. Kansas, 272 U.S. 465 (1926)).
22. As in modern First Amendment doctrine, the Taft Court safeguarded the protected realm of freedom by developing strong doctrines of vagueness. *See, e.g.*, Small Co. v. American Sugar Refining Co., 267 U.S. 233, 235 (1925) (holding that a statute violates due process by creating a duty "so vague and indefinite as to be no rule or standard at all"); Connolly v. General Constr. Co., 269 U.S. 385, 391 (1926) (holding that "a statute which either forbids or requires the doing of an act in terms so vague that men of common intelligence must necessarily guess as to its meaning and differ as to its application, violates the first essential of due process of law"); Cline v. Frink Dairy Co., 274 U.S. 445, 458 (1927). The Taft Court also developed the equivalent of the modern doctrine of unconstitutional conditions. *See* Frost Trucking Co. v. Railroad Comm'n, 271 U.S. 583, 592–94 (1926) (holding that a state may not affix to a private carrier's privilege of using its highways the unconstitutional condition that the carrier must "assume against [its] will the

burdens and duties of a common carrier"). The Taft Court also created a doctrine of "great temporary public exigencies," see Charles Wolff Packing Co. v. Court of Indus. Relations, 267 U.S. 552, 542 (1925), which both acknowledged and cabined wartime regulations, and which functioned in a manner that seems analogous to the clear and present danger test.
23. Coppage v. Kansas, 436 U.S. 1, 14 (1915).
24. William E. Forbath, *The Ambiguities of Free Labor: Labor and the Law in the Gilded Age*, 1985 WISCONSIN LAW REVIEW 767, 798.
25. "I remember that Billy Sumner was one of our best Professors in Yale." WHT to Moses Strauss (April 1, 1929) (Taft papers).
26. W.G. Sumner, *Do We Want Industrial Peace*, 8 THE FORUM 406 (1889). "[I]t is the first prerogative of a free man," said Sumner, "to make or unmake contracts." W.G. Sumner, *Industrial War*, 2 THE FORUM 1, 6 (1886).
27. For a good discussion of the history of the moral values that Americans have attached to economic liberty, see Harry N. Scheiber, *Economic Liberty and the Constitution*, in ESSAYS IN THE HISTORY OF LIBERTY: SEAVER INSTITUTE LECTURES AT THE HUNTINGTON LIBRARY 75–99 (John Phillip Reid, ed., San Marino: Huntington Library 1988). For relatively modern statements of this position, see Charles A. Reich, *The New Property*, 73 YALE LAW JOURNAL 733, 771–74 (1964) ("[P]roperty performs the function of maintaining independence, dignity, and pluralism in society by creating zones within which the majority has to yield to the owner."); C. Edwin Baker, *Property and Its Relation to Constitutionally Protected Liberty*, 134 UNIVERSITY OF PENNSYLVANIA LAW REVIEW 741, 761–64 (1986).
28. SUTHERLAND, *supra* note 11, at 13. "[T]oo much government," Sutherland said, "carries us in the direction of tyranny and oppression and, in the language of Wendell Philips, 'kills the self-help and energy of the governed.'" *Id.* at 2.
29. George Sutherland, *Principle or Expedient?*, 5 CONSTITUTIONAL REVIEW 195, 206 (1921). Sutherland believed that "The more democratic a people is, the more it is necessary that the individual be strong and his property sacred." George Sutherland, *Address of the President: Private Rights and Government Control*, in REPORT OF THE FORTIETH ANNUAL MEETING OF THE AMERICAN BAR ASSOCIATION 213 (Baltimore: Lord Baltimore Press 1917). Even Holmes was willing to acknowledge the connection between property and identity:

> A man who has lived with a belief, however uncritically accepted, for thirty years, instinctively rejects a new truth no matter how deeply founded in reason and fact if it threatens the existing structure. He fights for his life – and that is why reason has so little of the power that we expect it to have. One of my old chestnuts is that property, friendship and truth have a common root in time. Title by prescription is the most philosophically grounded of any.

OWH to Viscount Kentaro Kaneko (August 19, 1925) (Holmes papers). Holmes believed that "We end with an arbitrary can't help." OWH to Harold Laski (February 6, 1925), in 1 HOLMES-LASKI CORRESPONDENCE, at 706.
30. *See, e.g.*, ERIC FONER, FREE SOIL, FREE LABOR, FREE MEN: THE IDEOLOGY OF THE REPUBLICAN PARTY BEFORE THE CIVIL WAR 11–39 (New York: Oxford University Press, 1970).
31. Forbath, *supra* note 24, at 774–75. Thus, the District of Columbia Court of Appeals in *Adkins* had proclaimed: "Take from the citizen the right to freely contract and sell

The Protected Realm of Freedom

his labor for the highest wage which his individual skill and efficiency will command, and the laborer would be reduced to an automaton – a mere creature of the state." Children's Hosp. v. Adkins, 284 F. 613, 623 (App. D.C. 1921), *aff'd*, 261 U.S. 525 (1923).

32. 276 U.S. 575, 577–78 (1928). Indian land allotment began in 1887 with the Dawes Act, Pub. L. 49-105, 24 Stat. 388 (February 8, 1887), which broke Indian lands into discrete allotments, to be held in trust for a term of years, to the end that "Indians should be forced to leave their collective landholdings and homogeneous communal life" and be "groomed to become fee simple agriculturalists – yeoman farmers and ranchers of Jeffersonian lore, small-time capitalists with individual stakes in the American system. . . . . Theodore Roosevelt called allotment 'a mighty pulverizing machine to break up the tribal mass. It acts directly upon the family and the individual.'" Philip P. Frickey, *Doctrine, Context, Institutional Relationships, and Commentary: The Malaise of Federal Indian Law Through the Lens of Lone Wolf*, 38 TULSA LAW REVIEW 5, 6 (2002). The allotment system proved catastrophic for Native Americans, who lost 70 percent of their land. *Id.* at 7. In 1934, the United States government abandoned the allotment policy, with its individualistic premises, and enacted the Indian Reorganization Act, Pub. L. 73-383, 48 Stat. 984 (June 18, 1934), which shifted the focus of federal policy to tribal governments. The shift was roughly analogous to that which occurred in the government's approach to the labor market in the 1930s, when federal labor policy abandoned individualistic premises and began dealing instead directly with unions. *See infra* Chapter 39, at 1260–61.

33. *Shaw*, 276 U.S. at 579–81.

34. This theme in Stone's rhetoric stretches back to the beginning of what we now call substantive due process. Thus, in one of the nation's first such opinions, an 1886 decision by the Pennsylvania Supreme Court striking down a statute requiring laborers to be paid wages in cash, the court held that the law was "an insulting attempt to put the laborer under a legislative tutelage, which is not only degrading to his manhood, but subversive of his rights as a citizen of the United States. He may sell his labor for what he thinks best." Godcharles v. Wigeman, 113 Pa. 431, 437 (1886). For a modern version of this point, see Cass R. Sunstein, *On Property and Constitutionalism*, in CONSTITUTIONALISM, IDENTITY, DIFFERENCE AND LEGITIMACY: THEORETICAL PERSPECTIVES 389–93 (Michael Rosenfeld, ed., Durham: Duke University Press 1994) ("A constitutional system that respects private property should be regarded not as an effort to oppose liberal rights to collective self-government, but instead as a way of fortifying democratic processes.").

35. *The Revival of Anti-Federalism*, 41 NEW REPUBLIC 211, 213 (1925). As Taft affirmed when he was secretary of war under Roosevelt, "We can hardly conceive the right of personal liberty without private property, because involved in personal liberty is the principle that one shall enjoy what his labor produces." William Howard Taft, *Address at Cooper Union*, in ROBERT LEE DUNN, WILLIAM HOWARD TAFT: AMERICAN 219 (Boston: Chapple Publishing Co. 1908).

36. MARGARET K. BERRY & SAMUEL B. HOWE, ACTUAL DEMOCRACY: THE PROBLEMS OF AMERICA 57 (New York: Prentice-Hall, Inc. 1923).

37. *Id. See* Walter George Smith, *Property Rights under the Constitution*, 10 AMERICAN BAR ASSOCIATION JOURNAL 242, 243 (1924) ("A man without

property is to a great extent a man without independence of action, and while far removed from the condition of a slave, until he can by his earning accumulate some wage he is helpless indeed, and, of course, dependent upon those who are more fortunate or more thrifty than himself.").

38. WILLIAM HOWARD TAFT, LIBERTY UNDER LAW: AN INTERPRETATION OF THE PRINCIPLES OF OUR CONSTITUTIONAL GOVERNMENT 25 (New Haven: Yale University Press 1922).
39. Forbath, *supra* note 24, at 800.
40. *Meyer*, 262 U.S. 390 (1923).
41. 268 U.S. 510 (1925).
42. 262 U.S. at 397. *Meyer* was decided simultaneously with Bartels v. Iowa, 262 U.S. 404 (1923), in which the Court struck down an Iowa statute similar to Nebraska's, as well as an Ohio statute specifically prohibiting the teaching of German before the eighth grade. In a letter to a friend, Taft described what he regarded as the exact parameters of the decision in *Meyer*, which he believed held

> that the liberty, secured by the 14th Amendment to the Federal Constitution against State legislation, makes invalid a State law, which forbids a private school and a private school teacher from teaching German. It does not prevent the Legislature from excluding German or any other subject from the curriculum of a public school, and it does not prevent the Legislature from requiring the study of English and the study of the fundamental branches in English in every private school, but it does prevent the Legislature from forbidding a parent to employ a private school or private school teacher to teach his child any subject matter which is not itself vicious.

WHT to George L. Fox (July 31, 1923) (Taft papers). For historical discussions of *Meyer*, see WILLIAM G. ROSS, FORGING NEW FREEDOMS: NATIVISM, EDUCATION, AND THE CONSTITUTION: 1917–1927 (Lincoln: University of Nebraska Press 1994); ORVILLE H. ZABEL, GOD AND CAESAR IN NEBRASKA: A STUDY OF THE LEGAL RELATIONSHIP OF CHURCH AND STATE, 1854–1954 (Lincoln: University of Nebraska 1955); Barbara Bennett Woodhouse, *Who Owns the Child? Meyer and Pierce and the Child as Property*, 33 WILLIAM. & MARY LAW REVIEW 995 (1992).
43. *The Right to Learn Foreign Tongues*, NEW YORK TIMES (June 6, 1923), at 20. See William G. Ross, *A Judicial Janus: Meyer v. Nebraska in Historical Perspective*, 57 UNIVERSITY OF CINCINNATI LAW REVIEW 125, 133 (1988).
44. *The Week*, 35 NEW REPUBLIC 54, 57 (1923). On the close relationship between these statutes and World War I, see Ross, *supra* note 43, at 127–34; Niel M. Johnson, *The Missouri Synod Lutherans and the War against the German Language, 1917–1923*, 56 NEBRASKA HISTORY 137–56 (1975); Carroll Engelhardt, *Compulsory Education in Iowa, 1872–1919*, 49 ANNALS OF IOWA 58, 75 (Summer/Fall 1987); Carl Zollmann, *Parental Rights and the Fourteenth Amendment*, 7 MARQUETTE LAW REVIEW 53, 53 (1923); and Note, *Foreign Languages in Private Schools – Unconstitutionality of Statutes*, 9 IOWA LAW BULLETIN 123, 124 (1924). The decision of the Iowa Supreme Court upholding the statute struck down in *Bartels* makes this connection explicit:

> The advent of the great World War revealed a situation which must have appealed very strongly to the Legislature as justifying the enactment of this statute. Men called to the colors were found to be in some instances not sufficiently familiar

The Protected Realm of Freedom

> with the English language to understand military .... orders. It was to meet this situation, to encourage the more complete assimilation of all foreigners into our American life, to expedite the full Americanization of all our citizens that the Legislature deemed this statute for the best interests of the state.

State v. Bartels, 181 N.W. 508, 513 (Iowa 1921). Although Nebraska attempted to justify its statute on the ground that "an emergency exists," *Meyer*, 262 U.S. at 397, McReynolds specifically repudiated the language of "emergency." "No emergency has arisen," McReynolds said, "which renders knowledge by a child of some language other than English so clearly harmful as to justify its inhibition with the consequent infringement of rights long freely enjoyed." *Id.* at 403.

45. Woodhouse, *supra* note 42, at 1003, 1017.
46. Nebraska Dist. of Evangelical Lutheran Synod of Missouri v. McKelvie, 187 N.W. 927, 928–29 (Neb. 1922).
47. Barry Cushman, *Some Varieties and Vicissitudes of Lochnerism*, 85 BOSTON UNIVERSITY LAW REVIEW 881, 882 (2005).
48. *Meyer*, 262 U.S. at 399. *See id.* at 403. At oral argument, Taft put the problem this way:

> Here are two conflicting principles – I hope they are not conflicting; but at any rate, they seem to be currents flowing in different directions – here is the regulatory power of the State, to require proper education among its people, to protect itself, and to protect all the people in the education of all. ... And then, on the other hand, is this freedom, this liberty.

21 LANDMARK BRIEFS AND ARGUMENTS OF THE SUPREME COURT OF THE UNITED STATES: CONSTITUTIONAL LAW 779–80 (Philip B. Kurland & Gerhard Casper, eds., Arlington: University Publications of America 1975).

49. Holmes's dissent, which was joined by Sutherland, is published in the accompanying case of Bartels v. Iowa, 262 U.S. 404, 412 (1923) (Holmes, J., dissenting). Holmes and Sutherland joined the Court in striking down Ohio's statute, which prohibited *only* the teaching of German. *Id.* at 413.
50. *Meyer*, 262 U.S. at 399–400.
51. The string of citations is:

> Slaughter-House Cases, 16 Wall. 36; Butchers' Union Co. v. Crescent City Co., 111 U.S. 746; Yick Wo v. Hopkins, 118 U.S. 356; Minnesota v. Barber, 136 U.S. 313; Allegeyer v. Louisiana, 165 U.S. 578; Lochner v. New York, 198 U.S. 45; Twining v. New Jersey 211 U.S. 78; Chicago, B.&Q.R.R. v. McGuire, 219 U.S. 549; Truax v. Raich, 239 U.S. 33; Adams v. Tanner, 244 U.S. 590; New York Life Ins. Co. v. Dodge, 246 U.S. 357; Truax v. Corrigan, 257 U.S. 312; Adkins v. Children's Hospital, 261 U.S. 525; Wyeth v. Cambridge Board of Health, 200 Mass. 474.

Id. at 399.

52. *See, e.g.*, Louis K. Liggett Co. v. Baldridge, 278 U.S. 105, 113–14 (1928); Seattle Trust Co. v. Roberge, 278 U.S. 116, 120–23 (1928); Weaver v. Palmer Bros. Co., 270 U.S. 402, 415 (1926); Charles Wolff Packing Co. v. Court of Indus. Relations, 267 U.S. 552, 562–69 (1925); Jay Burns Baking Co. v. Bryan, 264 U.S. 504, 513 (1924). Conversely, pre-New Deal decisions would cite economic due process decisions in support of extending protections to freedoms that we would now regard as civil liberties. *See, e.g.*, Near v. Minnesota, 283 U.S. 697, 707–8 (1931); Yu Cong Eng v. Trinidad, 271 U.S. 500, 527 (1926).

53. *See, e.g.,* Adair v. United States, 208 U.S. 161, 173–75 (1908); Coppage v. Kansas, 236 U.S. 1, 14 (1914).
54. Taft summarized this point in 1914: "We believe that government is, of course, for the benefit of society as a whole, but that society is composed of individuals and that the benefit of society as a whole is only consistent with the full opportunity of its members to pursue happiness and their individual liberty. This, in its broadest and proper sense, includes freedom from personal restraint, right of free labor, right of property, right of religious worship, right of contract." WILLIAM HOWARD TAFT, THE ANTI-TRUST ACT AND THE SUPREME COURT 37 (New York: Harper & Brothers 1914).
55. *See, e.g.,* William G. Ross, *The Contemporary Significance of Meyer and Pierce for Parental Rights Issues Involving Education,* 34 AKRON LAW REVIEW 177, 178 (2000).
56. *Meyer,* 262 U.S. at 400. "Mere knowledge of the German language," McReynolds continued, "cannot reasonably be regarded as harmful. Heretofore it has been commonly looked upon as helpful and desirable. [The defendant in this case] taught this language in school as part of his occupation. His right thus to teach and the right of parents to engage him so to instruct their children, we think, are within the liberty of the amendment." *Id.*
57. *Id.* At the time of *Meyer* there was considerable common law precedent establishing "virtually absolute parental authority over a child's course of study," even in public schools. Stephen Provasnik, *Judicial Activism and the Origins of Parental Choice: The Court's Role in the Institutionalization of Compulsory Education in the United States, 1891–1925,* 46 HISTORY OF EDUCATION QUARTERLY 311, 324 (2006). In 1891, for example, the Nebraska Supreme Court had affirmed the right of a father to prevent a public school from teaching his child grammar:

> The testimony tends to show that Anna Sheibley is about 15 years of age; that she is pursuing studies outside of those taught in the school, which occupy a portion of her time. Now, who is to determine what studies she shall pursue in school, – a teacher who has a mere temporary interest in her welfare, or her father, who may reasonably be supposed to be desirous of pursuing such course as will best promote the happiness of his child? The father certainly possesses superior opportunities of knowing the physical and mental capabilities of his child. It may be apparent that all the prescribed course of studies is more than the strength of the child can undergo, or he may be desirous, as is frequently the case, that his child while attending school should also take lessons in music, painting, etc., from private teachers. This he has a right to do. The right of the parent, therefore, to determine what studies his child shall pursue is paramount to that of the trustees or teacher. Schools are provided by the public, in which prescribed branches are taught, which are free to all within the district between certain ages; but no pupil attending the school can be compelled to study any prescribed branch against the protest of the parent that the child shall not study such branch, and any rule or regulation that requires the pupil to continue such studies is arbitrary and unreasonable.

Nebraska *ex rel.* Sheibley v. School Dist. No. 1 of Dixon County, 49 N.W. 393, 394–95 (Neb. 1891). *See* Nebraska *ex rel.* Kelley v. Ferguson, 144 N.W. 1039, 1040 (Neb. 1914) ("The right of a parent to make a reasonable selection from the prescribed course of studies which shall be carried by his child in the free public schools of the state is not limited to any particular school nor to any particular grade in any of such public schools. ... [W]hen a parent makes a reasonable selection from the course of studies which has been prescribed by the school authorities and requests that his child may be excused from taking the same, the request should be granted."). Common law parental rights to control the content of their children's education, however, were understood to be circumscribed by the state's authority to require parents to send their children "to public or private schools for longer or shorter periods during certain years of the life of such children." Indiana v. Bailey, 61 N.E. 730, 732 (Ind. 1901). *See* Jeffrey Shulman, *Meyer, Pierce, and the History of the Entire Human Race: Barbarism, Social Progress, and (the Fall and Rise of) Parental Rights*, 43 HASTINGS CONSTITUTIONAL LAW QUARTERLY 337, 381 n.218 (2016). The state's authority was explained on the ground that "one of the most important natural duties of the parent is his obligation to educate his child, and this duty he owes not to the child only, but to the commonwealth. If he neglects to perform it or willfully refuses to do so, he may be coerced by law to execute such civil obligation." *Bailey*, 61 N.E. at 732. In *Meyer*, McReynolds was explicit that "The power of the state to compel attendance at some school and to make reasonable regulations for all schools, including a requirement that they shall give instructions in English, is not questioned. Nor has challenge been made of the state's power to prescribe a curriculum for institutions which it supports. Those matters are not within the present controversy." 262 U.S. at 402.

58. *Meyer*, 262 U.S. at 400. The conclusion of *Meyer* is that Nebraska had materially interfered "with the calling of modern language teachers, with the opportunities of pupils to acquire knowledge, and with the power of parents to control the education of their own." *Id.* at 401. McReynolds offered an analogous definition of the relevant liberties in his subsequent opinion for the Court applying *Meyer* to the Hawaiian Islands. *See* Farrington v. Tokushige, 273 U.S. 284, 298–99 (1927) ("The general doctrine touching rights guaranteed by the Fourteenth Amendment to *owners, parents and children* in respect of attendance upon schools has been announced in recent opinions." (emphasis added)).

59. *Meyer*, 262 U.S. at 401.

60. *U.S. Court Kills Laws of 3 States Forbidding Teaching of German*, NEW YORK WORLD (June 5, 1923), at 2; *A Decision for Liberty*, 17 SCHOOL AND SOCIETY 668 (June 16, 1923).

61. 116 THE NATION 682 (1923). *See Languages in School*, CHICAGO DAILY TRIBUNE (June 6, 1923), at 8 ("If legislative majorities can enter the field of education, whether lay or sectarian, and forbid the teaching of subjects acceptedly a part of the educational equipment, they can make rather drastic inroads upon individual liberty of thought and freedom of judgment.").

62. WHT to Mrs. Bellamy Storer (June 27, 1923) (Taft papers). *See* WHT to Mrs. Frederick J. Manning (June 11, 1923) (Taft papers) ("We shall deliver opinions to-day, and some important ones, too. I deliver a unanimous opinion holding the Kansas Industrial Court Act invalid, and last week we held invalid a great many laws which forbade the teaching, in any school, public or private, of German to children before they reach the High School, or of any language but English. We are engaged in correcting the constitutional errors of some of the State legislatures.").

In 1924, Taft personally wrote the editor of the *St. Louis Globe Democrat* to urge that he oppose La Follette's presidential campaign against the Court, suggesting that "I think it might be well to point out . . . . the cases of Meyer vs. Nebraska and

Bartels v. Iowa, in which we held that the forbidding of the teaching of German in private schools under the eighth grade, or requiring of school branches to be taught in such schools in the English language, was a violation of the right of liberty under the 14th Amendment.... I should think that this illustration would convince people, especially among your readers, that they have some rights that they would rather not entrust to the Legislature or to Congress to violate. Of course I think this the most important issue in the campaign." WHT to Casper S. Yost (September 11, 1924) (Taft papers). *See supra* Chapter 19, at 614–17. Yost responded with a strong editorial. *See* Casper S. Yost to WHT (September 19, 1924) (Taft papers); *La Follette and the German Vote*, ST. LOUIS GLOBE-DEMOCRAT (September 17, 1924) ("The Supreme Court in two recent decisions has held that it was a violation of the right of liberty under the fourteenth amendment to forbid the teaching of German in private schools under the eighth grade. ... Suppose the Supreme Court ... [was] deprived of the power of declaring unconstitutional laws invalid, as La Follette proposed. Any American Congress or Legislature that chooses to pass such laws as this could then do so without hindrance. ... [T]he people, their rights and their liberties, will be constantly at the mercy of legislators, state and national, moved by passions, prejudices or unwisdom, with no constitutional restraints upon them. ... The citizens of German blood, and all others, should give serious thought to these things.").

63. Bartels v. Iowa, 262 U.S. 404, 412 (1923) (Holmes, J., dissenting). Sutherland joined Holmes's dissent. McKenna returned the draft of Holmes's opinion with a notation that "There is strength in this dissent and you have developed it but I am inclined the other way." JM to OWH (Holmes papers). To Laski, Holmes wrote that "I didn't think the dissent on teaching languages worth sending. I agreed with the Court that an Ohio law excluding German only (I believe an ebullition of Cox when he wanted to be President) was bad – but said that it was legitimate to try to make the young citizens speak English and that if a legislature thought that the best way to do that for children who could hear only Polish or German or French at home, was to make them talk only English during school hours I was not prepared to say that it was an unconstitutional limitation of the liberty of the school master." OWH to Harold Laski (June 24, 1923), in 1 HOLMES-LASKI CORRESPONDENCE, at 508. To Frankfurter, Holmes wrote that "As to teaching the young, you will find that I said little and that cautiously and was willing to agree with the Court as to the fool law against German alone." OWH to Felix Frankfurter (June 6, 1923), in HOLMES-FRANKFURTER CORRESPONDENCE, at 153.

Progressive educational experts found the decision in *Meyer* "almost incomprehensible," because it gave such short shrift to the imperative of Americanization. Ellwood P. Cubberley, *The American School Program from the Standpoint of the Nation*, in 61 ADDRESSES AND PROCEEDINGS OF THE SIXTY-FIRST ANNUAL MEETING OF PROCEEDINGS OF THE NATIONAL EDUCATION ASSOCIATION 180, 181 (Washington D.C.: National Education Association 1923). *See* Kenneth B. O'Brien, Jr., *Education, Americanization and the Supreme Court: The 1920s*, 13 AMERICAN QUARTERLY 161, 165–66 (1961); Woodhouse, *supra* note 42, at 1098–99.

64. *Brandeis-Frankfurter Conversations*, at 320 (July 19, 1923). *See supra* Chapter 8, at 320.

The Protected Realm of Freedom

65. OWH to Felix Frankfurter (March 24, 1914), in HOLMES-FRANKFURTER CORRESPONDENCE, at 19. *See supra* Chapter 5, at 170.
66. The only major exception to the deference that consistently informed Holmes's constitutional jurisprudence concerns freedom of speech, as to which Holmes was prepared to assume a stance of aggressive judicial review. Holmes believed that freedom of speech was necessary to allow the dominant opinion of society to emerge. *See* Gitlow v. New York, 268 U.S. 652, 673 (1925) (Holmes, J., dissenting).
67. *See supra* Chapter 8, at 312–15.
68. *A Decision for Liberty*, NEW YORK WORLD (June 6, 1923), at 12. "Freedom of teaching, like freedom of thought, must among a free people be put beyond the interference of majorities. For without freedom of thought and freedom of teaching there is no way by which the tyrannies and follies of temporary majorities can be peacefully resisted. A people which is to be governed by majorities must keep wide open the right of minorities to think for themselves and to attempt to persuade the majority. A majority protected against the criticism of minorities outside itself and within itself is, as de Tocqueville pointed out long ago, the most intolerable of all tyrants." *Id.* The *World* opined that "it is to be expected that people in States which are afflicted with the Bryan nonsense about 'evolution' will take advantage of this decision to vindicate the freedom of scientific inquiry."
69. GERALD GUNTHER, LEARNED HAND: THE MAN AND THE JUDGE 377 (New York: Alfred A. Knopf, 1994).
70. *Id.* The day after *Meyer*, Frankfurter wrote Hand:

> For myself, I should have voted with the minority. Of course, I regard such know-nothing legislation as uncivilized, but for the life of me I can't see how it meets the condemnation of want of "due process" unless we frankly recognize that the Supreme Court of the United States is the revisory legislative body.... That kind of confinement of the activity of our legislatures shrinks their responsibility and the sense of responsibility of our votes much beyond what is healthy for ultimate securities. The more I think about this whole "due process" business, the less I think of lodging that power in those nine gents at Washington.

Felix Frankfurter to Learned Hand (June 5, 1923), quoted *id.* at 377–78. Hand endorsed Frankfurter's position: "I can see no reason why, if a state legislature wishes to make a jackass of itself by that form of Americanization, it should not have the responsibility for doing so rather than the Supreme Court. But then, like you, I am ultra-latitudinarian in such matters." Learned Hand to Felix Frankfurter (June 6, 1923), quoted *id.* at 378. *See* Edward Corwin, *Constitutional Law in 1922–1923*, 18 AMERICAN POLITICAL SCIENCE REVIEW 49, 69–70 (1924):

> The successive decisions in the Minimum Wage cases, the Industrial Court case, and the Foreign Language cases, put the Supreme Court's doctrine of liberty on a stronger foundation than ever before. Hitherto, the term has had little significance beyond that afforded by the almost equally vague phrase "freedom of contract." Now it is apparent that the court intends to subject all legislative novelties, which are seriously restrictive of previously enjoyed freedom of action, to the test of the doctrine that "freedom is the general rule, and restraint the exception," that "the legislative authority to abridge can be justified only by exceptional circumstance" – so exceptional, indeed, that the court can take cognizance of them without proof. The result will be disliked by reformers.

The Taft Court

Appalled by Tennessee's efforts to suppress the teaching of evolution, Lippmann, in contrast to Frankfurter and Hand, believed in the need "to develop some new doctrine to protect education from majorities. My own mind has been getting steadily antidemocratic: the size of the electorate, the impossibility of educating it sufficiently, the fierce ignorance of these millions of semiliterate priest-ridden and parson-ridden people have got me to the point where I want to confine the actions of majorities." Walter Lippmann to Learned Hand (June 8 or 9, 1925), quoted in GUNTHER, *supra* note 69, at 382. Lippmann was frank to admit that Thomas Reed Powell and Morris Cohen had taken the position that "the constitutionality of the law ought not to be attacked. Such foolishness should be within the province of the legislature." *Id.*

71. Edward A. Purcell, Jr., *Learned Hand: The Jurisprudential Trajectory of an Old Progressive*, 43 BUFFALO LAW REVIEW 873, 910–11 (1995).

72. The split between old-style progressive judicial deference and a newer liberal turn toward the active protection of civil rights was accelerated by the excesses of national prohibition, as we shall see *infra* in Chapter 33.

73. *Meyer*, 262 U.S. at 402. McReynolds knew something about anti-German prejudice during the war. In Berger v. United States, 255 U.S. 22 (1921), the Court affirmed the disqualification of a federal district judge for expressing prejudice against German defendants during a criminal trial. Among other remarks, the judge said of German-born Americans: "Your hearts are reeking with disloyalty." 255 U.S. at 29. McReynolds dissented from the Court's holding on the piquant grounds that "Intense dislike of a class does not render the judge incapable of administering complete justice to one of its members. A public officer who entertained no aversion towards disloyal German immigrants during the late war was simply unfit for his place. And while 'an overspeaking judge is no well-tuned cymbal,' neither is an amorphous dummy unspotted by human emotions a becoming receptacle for judicial power." 255 U.S. at 42 (McReynolds, J., dissenting).

74. Roberts v. United States Jaycees, 468 U.S. 609, 618–19 (1984).

75. 268 U.S. 510 (1925). On the history of the *Pierce* case, see PAULA ABRAMS, CROSS PURPOSES: PIERCE V. SOCIETY OF SISTERS AND THE STRUGGLE OVER COMPULSORY EDUCATION (Ann Arbor: University of Michigan Press 2009).

76. Sutherland, who had dissented in *Meyer*, wrote that the Court's decision in *Pierce* "was the only possible one. There was never any division of sentiment in the Court from the beginning." GS to William H. Church (June 8, 1925) (Sutherland papers). Interestingly, a day later Taft wrote a close friend, "We had no difficulty after we had decided the Nebraska language case. I can tell you sometime about how we made the Court unanimous." WHT to Charles D. Hilles (June 9, 1925) (Taft papers). Whatever story Taft may have had in mind has never been revealed.

77. The circumstances of *Pierce* were manifestly on the Court's mind when deciding *Meyer* two years before. The Oregon statute had been adopted on November 7, 1922, approximately three months before the argument in *Meyer*. In December, the National Catholic Welfare Conference brought into the *Meyer* case the eminent New York Catholic lawyer William D. Guthrie, who at the age of 36 had won a decision striking down the federal income tax as unconstitutional. *See* Pollock v. Farmers' Loan & Trust Co., 158 U.S. 601 (1895). Guthrie was tasked with finding some way constitutionally to invalidate the Oregon statute. Guthrie believed that the constitutional questions were "close" and "very delicate." ABRAMS, *supra* note 75, at 90–94. Representing "various

The Protected Realm of Freedom

religious and educational institutions in the United States," Guthrie filed an amicus brief in *Meyer* that did not advocate for "either party," but that instead called the Court's attention to "the statute of Oregon" and argued that the Court ought not decide *Meyer* in any way that would affirm the "virtually unlimited" police power "of a state over the education of minors." Brief of Amici Curiae, Meyer v. Nebraska, 262 U.S. 390 (1923), No. 325, October Term 1922, at 1–2. McReynolds's reference to Plato's Commonwealth likely derived from Guthrie's brief. *See id.* at 3 ("The notion of Plato that in a Utopia the state would be the sole repository of parental authority and duty and the children be surrendered to it for upbringing and education . . . . was long ago repudiated."). Guthrie made the contemporary political implications of Plato's ideal explicit. "It adopts the favorite device of communistic Russia – the destruction of parental authority, the standardization of education despite the diversity of character, aptitude, inclination and physical capacity of children, and the monopolization by the state of the training and teaching of the young." *Id.* at 3. The oral argument in *Meyer* suggests that Guthrie's brief made a deep impression on McReynolds's thinking. *See* ABRAMS, *supra* note 75, at 120–22.

78. *Pierce*, 268 U.S. at 535.
79. *Id.* at 534–35. Unlike *Meyer*, which spoke eloquently about the promotion of education, *Pierce* seemed to turn more narrowly on the "liberty of parents and guardians to direct the upbringing and education of children under their control." This has led to interpretations of *Pierce* as a decision about parental control within the family unit. *See, e.g.*, Barbara Bennett Woodhouse, *Child Abuse, The Constitution, and the Legacy of* Pierce v. Society of Sisters, 78 UNIVERSITY OF DETROIT MERCY LAW REVIEW 479 (2001). But *Pierce* did not hold that decision-making authority within the family should be accorded to parents as distinct from children. It instead held that unreasonable state control of family decisions is constitutionally prohibited. Thus the quite precise T.R. Powell contemporaneously summarized *Pierce* as turning upon the "constitutional rights of *parents and children* to select other than public schools." T. R. Powell, *Supreme Court and State Police Power*, 17 VIRGINIA LAW REVIEW 765, 796 (1931) (emphasis added). *But see* Arthur Dean, *A Far Reaching Decision*, 27 INDUSTRIAL EDUCATION MAGAZINE 37, 38 (August 1925) (stating that by the Court's decision "we have discovered something we were forgetting, namely: Children do belong primarily to parents and only to a limited extent to the state."); *Oregon's Public School Law Not Constitutional*, CHICAGO DAILY TRIBUNE (June 2, 1925), at 16 (*Pierce* upheld "the inherent right of a parent to send his boy or girl to any school he deems best.").
80. McReynolds was careful to note that "No question is raised concerning the power of the state reasonably to regulate all schools, to inspect, supervise and examine them, their teachers and pupils; to require that all children of proper age attend some school, that teachers shall be of good moral character and patriotic disposition, that certain studies plainly essential to good citizenship must be taught, and that nothing be taught which is manifestly inimical to the public welfare." *Pierce*, 268 U.S. at 534.
81. Oral Argument of Arthur F. Mullen on Behalf of Plaintiffs-in-Error, Meyer v. Nebraska, No. 325, October Term 1922, at 8.
82. David B. Tyack, *Ways of Seeing: An Essay on the History of Compulsory Schooling*, 46 HARVARD EDUCATIONAL REVIEW 355, 359 (1976).

83. *Id.* at 361–62. *See* Michael S. Katz, A History of Compulsory Education Laws 21 (Bloomington: The Phi Delta Kappa Educational Foundation 1976) ("Between 1900 and 1930, compulsory schooling laws were transformed in many states from symbolic dead letters into reasonably effective statutes. The emergence of effective enforcement mechanisms translated an isolated phenomenon – school attendance – into an integral part of the state's systematic regulation of the conduct of school-aged youth."); George D. Strayer, *The Financing of the American Schools*, in Addresses and Proceedings of the Sixty-First Annual Meeting of Proceedings of the National Education Association, *supra* note 63, at 158 ("It is only during the last generation that we have begun to enforce compulsory education. The increase in days of attendance in our public schools was 139 per cent from 1890 to 1920.").
84. Ellwood P. Cubberley, Changing Conceptions of Education 63 (Boston: Houghton Mifflin Co. 1909). "The state oversight of private and parochial education is likely to increase slowly, especially along the lines of uniformity in statistics and records, sanitary inspection, common standards of work, and the enforcement of the attendance laws. In particular, the attitude toward the control of the child is likely to change." *Id. See* Mrs. A. H. Reeve, *Parent Power – A School Auxiliary*, in Addresses and Proceedings of the Sixty-First Annual Meeting of Proceedings of the National Education Association, *supra* note 63, at 177 ("The child of today – even the average child – is being considered less and less as the personal property of its parents, and more and more as belonging to the State."). By the end of the decade the question of whether "the child belong[s] to the parents or to the State" would be debated in the context of European fascism. *Fascism's Monopoly of the Child*, 97 Literary Digest 28 (April 21, 1928).
85. Abrams, *supra* note 75, at 215. *See id.* at 222.
86. When Taft bumped into William Guthrie, who was representing the plaintiffs in *Pierce*, and when Guthrie asked Taft for more time for argument, Taft replied, "I don't see why you want any more time. In principle, this case is simply the *Meyer* case over again." Abrams, *supra* note 75, at 180.
87. *Pierce*, 268 U.S. at 535.
88. *See supra* Chapter 21, at 695. *Cf. supra* note 77. In *Adkins*, by contrast, Sutherland had confidently pronounced that "The relation between earnings and morals is not capable of standardization." 261 U.S. at 556.
89. Herbert Hoover, *We Can Cooperate and Yet Compete*, 14 Nation's Business 11, 14 (June 5, 1926). It was common during the 1920s to complain of "the tendency to standardize everything in the United States, including our laws. . . . Our newspapers print standardized news and advertisements. The picture theaters show standardized plays. We have standardized meat and drink, and the customs of our times very nearly makes us live standardized lives." Oscar W. Underwood, Drifting Sands of Party Politics 56 (New York: The Century Co. 1928). Such complaints, however, frequently referred to the growing standardization of the national market, and not to standardization imposed by state regulation. The standardization created during World War I, and its infiltration into subsequent Commerce Department practices, fused together these two distinct kinds of standardization.
90. The Oregon School Fight: A True History 17 (Portland: A.B. Cain n.d.).
91. *Id.* at 11. When a federal district court struck down the Oregon statute, the *New York Times* celebrated: "The nearest analogy to this policy . . . is to be

The Protected Realm of Freedom

found in Russia under the present regime, and in Turkey under a bill which proposed specifically to prohibit attendance upon other than schools conducted by the Government. The law partook also of the spirit and method of the Prussian educational system. . . . Despite all that may be said of the desirability of bringing children of varying tradition, creed and social status into the common training schools, a policy of compulsion violates the very first principle of individual freedom. The State may and does require of the private and parochial schools the teaching of the same subjects, the observance of like standards, the same preparation of teachers and the same period of attendance as in the public schools. But to go further and to force all children into the public school is practically to take from the parent all discretion as to the education of the child." *The Oregon School Law*, NEW YORK TIMES (April 2, 1924), at 18.

92. THE OREGON SCHOOL FIGHT: A TRUE HISTORY, *supra* note 90, at 11.

93. *See, e.g.*, *An America Message*, CHICAGO DAILY TRIBUNE (April 24, 1918), at 8 ("The meeting of the Irish Fellowship club . . . . expressed 100 per cent Americanism and was a rebuke to hyphenism which ought to carry far."); *Elect Loyal Men to Congress, Plea of Elihu Root; 100 Per Cent Americanism Urged at National Security League Meeting*, NEW YORK TRIBUNE (May 9, 1918), at 10; *Roosevelt Joins Move to Rout Out All "Yell Dogs"; Colonel Declares Nothing Less Than 100 Per Cent Americanism Will Do*, NEW YORK TRIBUNE (July 26, 1918), at 9; *Loyalty Issue in Missouri Primary*, CHRISTIAN SCIENCE MONITOR (July 29, 1918), at 13 ("The primary campaign . . . . is, for the most part, being waged on the lines of loyalty and 100 per cent Americanism."); *A Hundred Per Cent Man*, CHICAGO DAILY TRIBUNE (September 2, 1918), at 6 ("The man who is 100 per cent American, 100 per cent patriotic, 100 per cent efficient, 100 per cent intelligent, and 100 per cent honest has no weak spots in his equipment."); *Unloyalty*, ARIZONA REPUBLICAN (September 21, 1918), at 4 ("We hear much of 100 per cent Americanism. That is a catch phrase and nothing more. 'The 100 per cent' is quite superfluous. Americanism is pure or it is nothing."); GEORGE WHARTON PEPPER, MEN AND ISSUES: A SELECTION OF SPEECHES AND ARTICLES 3 (New York: Duffield 1924) ("We often compliment a man by saying of him 'He is 100% American.'").

94. *See, e.g.*, Cubberley, *supra* note 63, at 180–81 ("[W]hen the World War began we realized . . . . how vast was the number of foreign-born peoples who had settled in our midst but had not become one with us in language or thought or spirit. . . . The problem which still faces the United States is that of assimilating into our national life and citizenship these millions of foreign-born and foreign-thinking peoples. . . . [T]his process of assimilation . . . is after all largely a problem of education and one that our schools must take the lead in solving. New peoples coming among us must be initiated into the language, traditions, hopes, and aspirations of our people if we are to preserve our National character."). In 1921, the National Education Association ("NEA") adopted in its platform a commitment to "the Americanization of the foreign-born." *A Platform of Progress*, 10 JOURNAL OF THE NATIONAL EDUCATION ASSOCIATION 120, 121 (1921). The NEA proclaimed that it was "glad to co-operate with the American Legion in the establishment of a universal requirement of English as the only basic language of instruction in all schools – public, private, and parochial – and we commend heartily their demand that thorough-going instruction in American History and Civics be required of all

students for graduation from elementary and from secondary schools." *Id. See* Woodhouse, *supra* note 42, at 1009–12. The NEA also republished and distributed H.R. Rep. No. 1201, 66th CONG. 3rd SESS. (January 7, 1921), which sought to establish a federal department of education. The Report earnestly advocated for "the Americanization of our foreign born."

> We have now more than 15,000,000 foreign-born population in the United States. More than 5,000,000 can not read or write the English language. ... This mass of ignorance ... has become and is now an active source of danger to the Republic. Alien communities where our language is not spoken, where our magazine and newspapers are not read, and where no American ideals or any understanding of our institutions are made known constitute a rich soil in which are sown the seeds of unrest and revolt. ... There is but one cure for these conditions, and that is to educate the immigrant to understand our language, our Government, and our institutions.

Id. at 8–9. *See Committee Reports Education Bill*, 10 JOURNAL OF THE NATIONAL EDUCATION ASSOCIATION 41 (1921).

95. JOHN HIGHAM, STRANGERS IN THE LAND: PATTERNS OF AMERICAN NATIVISM 1860–1925, at 264 (New York: Atheneum 1970).
96. In 1924, for example, the country reversed centuries of open immigration to sharply restrict the intake of new citizens. *See e.g.*, Immigration Act of 1924, Pub. L. 68-139, 43 Stat. 153 (May 26, 1924). Known as the Johnson-Reed Act, the legislation limited entry to the United States by adopting restrictive national origins quotas based upon the 1890 census.
97. THE OREGON SCHOOL FIGHT: A TRUE HISTORY, *supra* note 90, at 7.
98. ABRAMS, *supra* note 75, at 8. "The measure professed to be one of equality," said the *New York Times*, "but it was plainly directed most intolerantly at a single class. It was one of the most hateful by-products of the Ku Klux movement." *A Bad Law Voided*, NEW YORK TIMES (June 2, 1925), at 22. "It was a bigoted measure inspired by the Ku Klux Klan against Roman Catholics and all other non-Protestant elements – and is well out of the way." 120 THE NATION 641 (1925). "The initiation of this drastic movement was under influences connected with the Ku Klux Klan, which has a considerable membership and a larger sympathetic affiliation in Oregon. One purpose, perhaps the main purpose, was to destroy schools maintained by or under the auspices of the Catholic Church." *The Oregon School Law*, NEW YORK TIMES (August 5, 1923), at E4. On the complex relationship between the Klan and the remnants of progressivism during the 1920s, see Thomas R. Pegram, *The Anti-Saloon League and the Ku Klux Klan in 1920s Prohibition Enforcement*, 7 JOURNAL OF THE GILDED AGE AND PROGRESSIVE ERA 89 (2008).
99. In June, Taft wrote Van Devanter that "it has happened that the Ku Klux Klan and other extremists have forced upon the Court the necessity of making clear to [the] country the protection which the Constitution and the Court in interpreting and enforcing it offer to large bodies of people against a deprivation of their cherished liberty." WHT to WVD (June 19, 1925) (Van Devanter papers). In 1928, the Taft Court upheld a New York Klan registration statute. *See* New York *ex rel.* Bryant v. Zimmerman, 278 U.S. 63 (1928).
100. "Oregon vies with Texas and Oklahoma as the state in which the Ku Klux nuisance comes nearest being an actual menace." *Intolerance in Oregon*, 49 THE SURVEY

76 (1922). *See* Waldo Roberts, *The Ku-Kluxing of Oregon*, 133 THE OUTLOOK 490, 491 (1923) ("Had the war never happened, the Ku Klux Klan in Oregon never would have happened. The armistice came suddenly – too suddenly, many people believe. The fighting spirit of the American people was aroused to a high pitch. But suddenly there was no one to fight. The flood of destructive passion was arrested. It had to find an outlet somewhere. In Oregon it found an outlet through the Ku Klux Klan and against the Catholic Church.").

101. Oddly, the Klan supported a measure whose ballot argument proclaimed that "[W]e recognize and proclaim our belief in the free and compulsory education of the children of our nation in public primary schools supported by public taxation, upon which all children shall attend and be instructed in the English language only without regard to race or creed as the only sure foundation for the perpetuation and preservation of our free institutions." THE OREGON SCHOOL FIGHT: A TRUE HISTORY, *supra* note 90, at 7. It should be noted, however, that during the 1920s the Klan "did not focus on protecting white supremacy in the South. At the height of the Klan's power in 1924, Southerners formed only 16 percent of its total membership. Over 40 percent of early twentieth-century Klan members lived in the three Midwestern states of Indiana, Ohio, and Illinois. The Klan enrolled more members in New Jersey than in Alabama. Klan membership in Indianapolis was almost twice that in South Carolina and Mississippi combined." STANLEY COBEN, REBELLION AGAINST VICTORIANISM: THE IMPETUS FOR CULTURAL CHANGE IN 1920S AMERICA 136 (New York: Oxford University Press 1991).

102. Robert M. Cover, *Foreword: Nomos and Narrative*, 97 HARVARD LAW REVIEW 4, 61 (1983).

103. Themes of religious liberty pervaded Guthrie's argument. Oral Argument on Behalf of Appellee, Pierce v. Society of Sisters, No. 583, October Term 1924, at 21–22, 24–27, 29. Guthrie bitterly commented "upon this cant of Americanization on the part of the promoters of this un-American measure. Imagine destroying the most valuable right that we Americans have inherited from the inspired generation that established this Government – imagine destroying the right to religious liberty and freedom of education in the name, in the cant, on the pretense, of Americanization." *Id.* at 28. Guthrie's words must have rung true to Brandeis, who in 1915 had addressed that same cant in his famous address on "True Americanism." *See* Louis D. Brandeis, *True Americanism*, in BUSINESS – A PROFESSION 364–74 (Boston: Hale, Cushman & Flint 1933). "America," Brandeis had declared in language directly applicable to *Pierce* (and to *Meyer*), "has believed that we must not only give to the immigrant the best that we have, but must preserve for America the good that is in the immigrant and develop in him the best of which he is capable. America has believed that in differentiation, not in uniformity, lies the path of progress.... The new nationalism adopted by America proclaims that each race or people, like each individual, has the right and duty to develop, and that only through such differentiated development will high civilization be attained. Not until these principles of nationalism ... are generally accepted will liberty be fully attained and minorities be secure in their rights." *Id.* at 372–74.

104. 268 U.S. 652 (1925). *Pierce* was decided on June 1, 1925; *Gitlow* was decided the next week on June 8.

105. Cantwell v. Connecticut, 310 U.S. 296 (1940). The Court did not incorporate the Establishment Clause for another seven years. *See* Everson v. Bd. of Educ., 330 U.S. 1 (1947).
106. In cases like Planned Parenthood of Southeastern Pennsylvania v. Casey, 505 U.S. 833 (1992) (upholding a right to an abortion) and Obergefell v. Hodges, 576 U.S. 644 (2015) (upholding the right to same-sex marriage), the contemporary Court has also used the Due Process Clause to negotiate this same boundary.
107. For this reason, *Pierce* provoked in Frankfurter the same skepticism that he had experienced in the context of *Meyer*. *See supra* note 70. Frankfurter published an unsigned editorial in the *New Republic* conceding that "The Oregon decision, like its Nebraska forerunner, in and of itself, gives just cause for rejoicing. The Supreme Court did immediate service on behalf of the essential spirit of liberalism. It put the quietus on two striking manifestations of post-war obscurantism." *Can the Supreme Court Guarantee Toleration?*, 43 NEW REPUBLIC 85, 86 (1925). (Strikingly, Frankfurter omitted this passage when he later republished this editorial in FELIX FRANKFURTER, LAW AND POLITICS: OCCASIONAL PAPERS OF FELIX FRANKFURTER 1913–1938, at 196 (Archibald MacLeish & E.F. Prichard, Jr., eds., New York: Harcourt, Brace & Co. 1939), no doubt because of his subsequent hostility to *Pierce* as a justice.) But Frankfurter then went on to say that, in assessing *Pierce*, the "heavy price" of other due process decisions like "The New York bakeshop case, the invalidation of anti-trade union laws, the sanctification of the injunction in labor cases, the veto of minimum wage legislation," must also be considered. *Can the Supreme Court Guarantee Toleration, supra*, at 86. The essential problem was that "the fateful words of the Fourteenth Amendment" mean "what the shifting personnel of the United States Supreme Court from time to time makes them mean. The inclination of a single Justice, the tip of his mind – or his fears – determines the opportunity of a much-needed social experiment to survive, or frustrates, at least for a long time, intelligent attempt to deal with a social evil." *Id.* "For ourselves," Frankfurter concluded, "we regard the cost of this power of the Supreme Court on the whole as greater than its gains." *Id. See Social Policy and the Supreme Court*, 43 NEW REPUBLIC 195 (1925).

Brandeis's friend, the journalist Robert W. Bruère, had a slightly different interpretation of *Pierce*. Writing in *The Survey*, Bruère noted that precisely because the conclusions of the Court transcended "legal technicalities" and depended upon "what is broadly termed common sense," their ultimate "force" would turn on "the support of prevailing public opinion." Robert W. Bruère, *The Supreme Court on Educational Freedom*, 54 THE SURVEY 379, 380 (1925). Using this criterion, the "reaction of public opinion to the Supreme Court's verdict, insofar as it can be gauged by press comment, would seem to indicate that the majority of Americans follow the reasoning of the Court with approval." *Id.* Bruère's analysis anticipated later developments in the shifting authority of the Court. *See supra* Chapter 20, at 651–52.

Pierce was a strikingly popular opinion. "Few decisions in years.... attracted as much attention" as the "momentous" case of *Pierce*. *Oregon School Law Declared Invalid by Supreme Court*, NEW YORK TIMES (June 2, 1925), at 1; *The Oregon School Law in Court*, 85 LITERARY DIGEST 32 (April 18, 1925). The

The Protected Realm of Freedom

Literary Digest reported that "the press comment that has reached this office seem to be all in approval of the Supreme Court's decision." *Death of the Oregon School Law*, 85 LITERARY DIGEST 7, 8 (June 13, 1925). "'A new *Magna Charta* for the integrity of family life,' 'a decision against tyranny,' 'a triumph for the rights of minorities,' 'a victory for freedom of education,' 'a crushing defeat for bigotry,' 'a bulwark against the tyranny of the majority' – these are some of the characterizations of this decision by such representative dailies as the Newark *News*, Brooklyn *Eagle*, Portland *Oregonian*, New York *Herald Tribune* and *World*, and Boston *Herald*." *Id.* at 7. "The decision elicited comment in 490 newspapers in 44 States, all practically unanimous in favor of the Court's decision." Robert F. Drinan, *Parental Rights and American Law*, 172 CATHOLIC WORLD 21, 22 (October 1956).

108. Edward Rubin, *Lochner and Property*, in ADMINISTRATIVE LAW FROM THE INSIDE OUT: ESSAYS ON THEMES IN THE WORK OF JERRY L. MASHAW 406 (Nicholas R. Parrillo, ed., Cambridge University Press 2017).

109. Butler v. Perry, 240 U.S. 328 (1916), is a striking case in the McReynolds *oeuvre*. Speaking for a unanimous Court, McReynolds upheld a Florida statute requiring males between 21 and 45 years of age "to work on the roads and bridges of the several counties for six days" a year. *Id.* at 329. McReynolds noted that conscription for road work was a traditional form of tax and that the statute "introduced no novel doctrine." *Id.* at 333. "[T]o require work on public roads has never been regarded as a deprivation of either liberty or property." *Id.* Because the Fourteenth Amendment "was intended to preserve and protect fundamental rights long recognized under the common law," there was no violation of due process of law. *Id.* The case reveals the extent to which McReynolds regarded essential human freedoms as constructed by traditional and historical expectations enshrined in the common law.

110. The common law was in this regard understood to reflect the teachings of "experience." 1 THE WORKS OF JAMES WILSON 348 (Robert Green McCloskey, ed., Cambridge: Harvard University Press 1967). *See also* CHARLES B. GOODRICH, THE SCIENCE OF GOVERNMENT AS EXHIBITED IN THE INSTITUTIONS OF THE UNITED STATES OF AMERICA 239 (Boston: Little, Brown & Co. 1853); ZEPHANIAH SWIFT, 1 SYSTEM OF THE LAWS OF THE STATE OF CONNECTICUT 40 (Windham: John Bryne 1795).

111. *The Revival of Anti-Federalism, supra* note 35, at 213.

112. *See supra* Chapter 10, at 387–88. Even as Taft praised the right of property because it sustained "our primary conception of a free man," he simultaneously observed that upon the right of property "rests the motive of the individual which makes the world materially to progress. Destroy it and material progress ceases.... [T]he motive of gain is the only one which will be constant to induce industry, saving, invention and organization, which will effect an increase in production greater than the increase in population." TAFT, *supra* note 38, at 25–26.

113. *See* West Coast Hotel Co. v. Parrish, 300 U.S. 379, 408 (1937) (Sutherland, J., dissenting).

114. *Address of Hon. George Sutherland to the Third Annual Convention of International Association of Casualty and Surety Underwriters* (June 14. 1913), Sen. Doc. No. 131, 63rd CONG. 1st SESS., at 11–12.

115. *See infra* Chapter 27 at 890–94.
116. 272 U.S. 365 (1926). The dramatic and fascinating history of *Euclid* has often been told. *See, e.g.*, MICHAEL ALLAN WOLF, THE ZONING OF AMERICA: EUCLID V. AMBLER (Lawrence: University of Kansas Press 2008); SEYMOUR I. TOLL, ZONED AMERICAN 213–268 (New York: Grossman Publishers 1969); Arthur V.N. Brooks, *The Office File Box – Emanations from the Battlefield*, in ZONING AND THE AMERICAN DREAM: PROMISES STILL TO KEEP 3–30 (Charles M. Haar & Jerold S. Kayden, eds., Chicago: Planners Press, 1969); William M. Randle, *Professors, Reformers, Bureaucrats, and Cronies: The Players in* Euclid v. Ambler, *id.* at 31–70; Timothy Alan Fluck, Euclid v. Ambler: *A Retrospective*, 52 JOURNAL OF THE AMERICAN PLANNING ASSOCIATION 326 (Summer 1986); Garrett Power, *The Advent of Zoning*, 4 PLANNING PERSPECTIVES 1 (1989); Michael Allan Wolf, *"Compelled by Conscientious Duty":* Village of Euclid v. Ambler Realty Co. *as Romance*, 2 JOURNAL OF SUPREME COURT HISTORY 88 (1997); Garrett Power, *Advocates at Cross-Purposes: The Briefs on Behalf of Zoning in the Supreme Court*, 2 JOURNAL OF SUPREME COURT HISTORY 79 (1997).
117. Gerald Korngold, *The Emergence of Private Land Use Controls in Large-Scale Subdivisions: The Companion Story to* Village of Euclid v. Ambler Realty Co., 51 CASE WESTERN RESERVE LAW REVIEW 617, 617 (2001). *See* Michael Allen Wolf, *The Prescience and Centrality of* Euclid v. Ambler, in ZONING AND THE AMERICAN DREAM, *supra* note 116, at 252 ("The importance" of *Euclid* "is indisputable.").
118. TOLL, *supra* note 116, at 214–16. The preface to the zoning ordinance announced:

> Whereas, it is the desire of the citizens of said Village, and the Council thereof, to preserve the present character of said Village and the public improvements therein, to prevent congestion, and to promote and provide for the health, safety, convenience, comfort, prosperity, and general welfare of the citizens thereof, for which reason the subject matter hereof constitutes an emergency as hereinafter specifically provided.

Transcript of Record, Village of Euclid v. Ambler Realty Co, No. 31, October Term 1926, at 13.
119. Village of Euclid v. Ambler Realty Co., 272 U.S. 365, 384 (1926).
120. James Metzenbaum, *Zoning on Trial Before the U.S. Supreme Court*, 35 AMERICAN CITY MAGAZINE 74 (July 1926).
121. Alfred Bettman, *The Decision of the Supreme Court in the Euclid Village Zoning Case*, 1 UNIVERSITY OF CINCINNATI LAW REVIEW 184, 184 (1927).
122. Keith D. Revell, *The Road to* Euclid v. Ambler: *City Planning, State-Building, and the Changing Scope of the Police Power*, 13 STUDIES IN AMERICAN POLITICAL DEVELOPMENT 50, 108 (1999). Alfred Bettman believed "that the Euclid ordinance was chosen for this purpose because of certain weaknesses which were felt to inhere in its provisions." *Id.* Among those weaknesses was the fact that Euclid's ordinance was adopted without a prior comprehensive city plan and was essentially, as Euclid proudly told the Court in its Brief, "an exact duplicate of the New York City Zoning Ordinance, except as to local names and locations." Brief on Behalf of the Appellants, Village of Euclid v. Ambler Realty Co, No. 31, October Term 1926, at 96. Keith Revell regards the Euclid ordinance as "the most

The Protected Realm of Freedom

egregious use of the zoning rationale by municipal officials." Revell, *supra*, at 108. *See also* A. Dan Tarlock, *Euclid Revisited*, 34 LAND USE LAW & ZONING DIGEST 4, 5 (1982) ("*Euclid* was not the best case with which to test the constitutionality of zoning because the facts did not favor the village. When the zoning ordinance was adopted, the village's grand residential boulevard, Euclid Avenue, had deteriorated into a mixed-use area."). Euclid's zoning ordinance was adopted in part to check the planned expansion of industrial uses along Euclid Avenue, see www.hmdb.org/m.asp?m=134117, and yet "several years after the Supreme Court's decision all of Ambler Realty's land was rezoned for industry." Garrett Power, *The Advent of Zoning*, 4 PLANNING PERSPECTIVES 1, 10 (1989).

123. TOLL, *supra* note 116, at 143–87. Los Angeles had enacted proto-zoning ordinances before New York, see, e.g., Gordon Whitmall, *History of Zoning*, 155 ANNALS OF THE AMERICAN ACADEMY OF POLITICAL AND SOCIAL SCIENCE 1, 10–11 (1931), but the 1916 New York ordinance is generally taken as the moment "when comprehensive zoning was implemented in the United States." EMILY TALEN, CITY RULES: HOW REGULATIONS AFFECT URBAN FORM 23 (Washington: Island Press 2012). Zoning is "fundamentally different from a building code, which applies rules uniformly to all parts of a city." *Id.* at 21. Zoning applied different building codes to different parts of the city, so that "one area of the city was allowed to be denser, taller, and more diverse, while another area was required to be sparsely populated and more homogeneous." *Id.*

124. Yale Rabin, *Expulsive Zoning: The Inequitable Legacy of* Euclid, in ZONING AND THE AMERICAN DREAM, *supra* note 116, at 105.

125. The New York ordinance was preceded by a massive report justifying the ordinance. *See* COMMISSION ON BUILDING DISTRICTS AND RESTRICTIONS, FINAL REPORT (New York: 1916). That Report stated:

> With some eight billions already invested in New York City real estate and the certainty of added billions in the coming years, a plan of city building that will tend to conserve and protect property values becomes of vital importance not only to individual owners but to the community as a whole. Why not protect the areas as yet unspoiled and insure that the hundreds of millions that shall be spent in the improvement of real estate in the coming years shall contribute to the solid and permanent upbuilding of this great city. Permanence and stability can be secured only by a far-sighted building plan that will harmonize the private interests of owners and the health, safety and convenience of the public.

Id. at 14. *See id.* at 13: "Through haphazard construction and invasion by inappropriate uses the capital value of large areas have been greatly impaired. The destruction of capital value, not only in the central commercial and industrial section of Manhattan, but also throughout the residential sections of the five boroughs, has reached huge proportions. It does not stop with the owners in the areas immediately affected, but is reflected in depressed values throughout the city." *Id.* at 13–14.

James Metzenbaum, Euclid's lawyer, took pains to acquire bound copies of this Report (as well as of its 1913 prequel) and to distribute them to the justices of the Supreme Court. Metzenbaum sent the Reports to the clerk and noted that "I am particularly anxious that Justice Sutherland should have a copy of either the 1913 or the 1916 Report." TOLL, *supra* note 116, at 239. The clerk confirmed to Metzenbaum that he had complied with his request. *Id.* at 240.

126. FINAL REPORT, *supra* note 125, at 6.
127. *Id.* at 6–11, 20. When President Taft submitted his monumental study of federal budgeting and restructuring to Congress in 1912, see *supra* Chapter 11, at 403–4, he explained that he had "instructed the commission to indicate in its report the changes which should be made in the existing organization and to proceed in the same way as would far-seeing architects or engineers in planning for the improvement and development of a great city." William Howard Taft, *Economy and Efficiency in the Government Service*, 48 CONG. REC. 1027 (January 17, 1912).
128. FINAL Report, *supra* note 125, at 9. The Report stressed the "provision of light and air," the minimization of "nervous disorders and troubles," and the prevention of "street accidents." *Id.* at 9–12. The Report claimed that "The decline in property value . . . . is merely an economic index of the disregard of essential standards of public health, safety, and convenience in building development." *Id.* at 14. The Report emphasized that "The protection of the home environment is vital to the welfare of the state. It needs no argument to demonstrate that a business or industrial street does not furnish the most favorable environment for a home. Quiet is a prime requisite." *Id.* at 20. It decried "congested tenement" districts, noting that while "the population of the city is largely recruited from the country, the city's criminal population is largely bred right within its own congested centers." *Id.* at 21–22. The Report also discussed the relationship between zoning and moral uplift:

> The moral influences surrounding the homes are of the greatest importance. The sordid atmosphere of the ordinary business street is not a favorable environment in which to rear children. Immediate and continual proximity to the moving picture show, dance hall, pool room, cigar store, saloon, candy store and other institutions for the creation and satisfaction of appetites and habits is not good for the moral development of child. Influences and temptations resulting from the proximity of such business to the homes may affect seriously the morals of the youth of the community. Under such conditions it is difficult to cultivate the ideals of life that are essential to the preservation of our civilization.

Id. at 22.
129. Newman F. Baker, *Zoning Legislation*, 11 CORNELL LAW REVIEW 164, 164 (1926).
130. TOLL, *supra* note 116, at 188. See, e.g., *The Remarkable Spread of Zoning in American Cities*, 25 AMERICAN CITY MAGAZINE 456 (December 1921). By 1929 there were "754 cities, towns and villages, with a total population of 37,000,000" that had "the protection afforded by zoning regulations." *Zoning Laws Grow in Popularity*, 15 AMERICAN BAR ASSOCIATION JOURNAL 328 (1929). *See Zoning Legislation during 1928–1929*, 16 AMERICAN BAR ASSOCIATION JOURNAL 411 (1930).
131. The only lawyer on the committee was Edward M. Bassett, who was known as the "father of zoning" and who had been chair of the New York Commission that produced the 1916 Report. Revell, *supra* note 122, at 50, 57.
132. Advisory Committee on Zoning, A STANDARD STATE ZONING ENABLING ACT (Washington D.C.: Government Printing Office 1924). The Act was issued first in mimeographed form in August 1922. It was first printed in 1924. The text of the 1924 Act may be found at https://archive.org/stream/standardstatezono5bass/standardstatezono5bass_djvu.txt.

The Protected Realm of Freedom

133. The Advisory Committee on Zoning, A ZONING PRIMER (Washington D.C.: Government Printing Office 1922). The pamphlet stressed that zoning prevents blight and helps ensure that "property values become more stable, mortgage companies . . . more ready to lend money." *Id.* at 2. Zoning "prevents an apartment house from becoming a giant airless hive, housing human beings like crowded bees." *Id.* The *Primer* emphasized the need for systematic order:

    > We know what to think of a household in which an undisciplined daughter makes fudge in the parlor, in which her sister leaves soiled clothes soaking in the bathtub, while father throws his muddy shoes on the stairs, and little Johnny makes beautiful mud pies on the front steps.
    >
    > Yet many American cities do the same sort of thing when they allow stores to crowd in at random among private dwellings, and factories and public garages to come elbowing in among neat retail stores or well-kept apartment houses. Cities do no better when they allow office buildings so tall and bulky and so closely crowded that the lower floors not only become too dark and unsatisfactory for human use but for that very reason fail to earn a fair cash return to the individual investors. . . .
    >
    > It is this stupid, wasteful jumble which zoning will prevent and gradually correct.

    Id. at 1.

134. "In less than a month and a half . . . the Commerce Department had distributed over 25,000 copies" of the *Primer*. Ruth Knack, Stuart Meck, & Israel Stollman, *The Real Story Behind the Standard Planning and Zoning Acts of the 1920s*, 48 LAND USE LAW 3, 6 (February 1996). *See* Theodora Kimball, *Survey of City and Regional Planning in the United States, 1922*, 13 LANDSCAPE ARCHITECTURE MAGAZINE 122, 123–24 (January 1923) ("The *Zoning Primer*, issued by Secretary Hoover's Advisory Committee on Zoning . . . . has probably been circulated more widely than any previous city planning publicity leaflet."); Thomas H. Reed, *City Planning*, 17 AMERICAN POLITICAL SCIENCE REVIEW 430, 431 (1923). Bettman referred to Hoover's work and included extracts from the *Primer* in his amicus brief in *Euclid*. Brief on Behalf of the National Conference on City Planning et al., Village of Euclid v. Ambler Realty Co, No. 31, October Term 1926, at 42, 133. ("Amicus Brief on Behalf of the National Conference of City Planning et al."). *See id.* at 120.

135. Gordon Whitnall, *History of Zoning*, 155 ANNALS OF THE AMERICAN ACADEMY OF POLITICAL AND SOCIAL SCIENCE 1, 12 (1931) (Part II).

136. Herbert Hoover, *Foreword*, in ADVISORY COMMITTEE ON ZONING, A STANDARD STATE ZONING ENABLING ACT iii & n.1 (Washington D.C.: Government Printing Office 1926). As of September 1921, "only 48 cities and towns, with less than 11,000,000 inhabitants, had adopted zoning ordinances." *Id. Compare supra* note 130. *See* Joseph P. Chamberlain, *Zoning Progress*, 15 AMERICAN BAR ASSOCIATION JOURNAL 535 (1929). On Hoover's involvement with the zoning question, see Richard H. Chused, Euclid's *Historical Imagery*, 51 CASE WESTERN RESERVE LAW REVIEW 597, 598–600 (2001).

137. Transcript of Record, Village of Euclid v. Ambler Realty Co, No. 31, October Term 1926, at 11.

138. Randle, *supra* note 116, at 31, 34–35, 40–42. Westenhaver had also been law partners with Frederic C. Howe, as well as with Harry and James. R. Garfield.

Westenhaver had presided over the trial of Eugene Debs for violating the Espionage Act of 1917. *Id.* at 31.
139. 260 U.S. 393 (1922).
140. Ambler Realty Co. v. Village of Euclid, 297 F. 307, 312 (N.D. Ohio 1924). Since Westenhaver characterized Euclid's zoning ordinance as a taking, Euclid might have owed Ambler market damages for the reduced value of its land, although this was not definitively settled until First English Evangelical Lutheran Church v. County of Los Angeles, 482 U.S. 304 (1987). In *Mahon*, the Court, speaking through Holmes, had held:

> Government hardly could go on if to some extent values incident to property could not be diminished without paying for every such change in the general law. As long recognized some values are enjoyed under an implied limitation and must yield to the police power. But obviously the implied limitation must have its limits or the contract and due process clauses are gone. One fact for consideration in determining such limits is the extent of the diminution. When it reaches a certain magnitude, in most if not in all cases there must be an exercise of eminent domain and compensation to sustain the act. So the question depends upon the particular facts. The greatest weight is given to the judgment of the legislature but it always is open to interested parties to contend that the legislature has gone beyond its constitutional power.

260 U.S. at 413.
141. 297 F. at 313–14.
142. Metzenbaum, *supra* note 120, at 75. Prior to Westenhaver's opinion, the supreme courts of New York, Minnesota, Louisiana, and Kansas had ruled in favor of zoning, but the supreme courts of Texas, New Jersey, and Missouri had held them unconstitutional, either under federal or state constitutional law. By the time *Euclid* was argued at the Court, the supreme courts of California, Wisconsin, Massachusetts, Ohio, and Illinois had also affirmed the constitutionality of zoning, but the Maryland Court of Appeals, the highest court in the state, had come out against it. The Maryland court held that even though "[w]ithin the last few years a veritable flood of so-called 'zoning' legislation has swept over the country," "the power to hold, use, and enjoy property" could not be "restricted or taken away by the state under the guise of the police power for purely aesthetic reasons or for any such elastic and indeterminate object as the general prosperity without compensation." Goldman v. Crowther, 128 A. 50, 55, 57 (Md. 1925). For a discussion of the Maryland decision, see Joshua Gordon, A Euclid-*Turn*: R.B. Construction Co. v. Jackson *and the Zoning of Baltimore*, 22 MARYLAND HISTORIAN 26 (Spring/Summer 1991).
143. ROBERT AVERILL WALKER, THE PLANNING FUNCTION IN URBAN GOVERNMENT 11–12, 77 (2nd ed., University of Chicago Press 1950). The Conference was formed from an alliance among the American Institute of Architects, the American Society of Landscape Architects, the American Civic Association, and the National Conference of Charities and Corrections. The Conference was initially associated more with the impulse for city planning, and in particular with the City-Beautiful Movement, than with the zoning movement. (Sometimes zoning ordinances were connected to comprehensive city plans, and sometimes they were not. In Euclid's case, the zoning ordinance was not the product of a comprehensive city plan.)

The Protected Realm of Freedom

144. For the story of Metzenbaum's tireless involvement in the case, see JAMES METZENBAUM, THE LAW OF ZONING 108–22 (New York: Baker, Voorhis and Co. 1930).
145. Amicus Brief on Behalf of the National Conference of City Planning et al., *supra* note 134, at 13–23. The irony, of course, was that Bettman disapproved of the Euclid ordinance. *See supra* note 122.
146. Taking his cue from Westenhaver, Baker spent two pages of his brief invoking *Pennsylvania Coal Co. v. Mahon*. Brief on Behalf of the Appellee, Village of Euclid v. Ambler Realty Co, No. 31, October Term 1926, at 53–54 ("*Euclid*, Brief on Behalf of the Appellee"). Bettman sought to distinguish *Mahon* on the ground that

    > the statute involved in that case is utterly different from and remote in kind, character and degree from a zoning law or ordinance. In that case the statute destroyed, not regulated, but destroyed a property title or interest expressly created by and reserved in a deed. The right of the mining company to mine coal was created by specific and express deeds and the statute expressly abolished that right.... No property or contract right created by deed or other instrument is here in any respect abolished, suppressed, destroyed or even regulated. The property rights asserted are simply those which inhere generally in all owners of land; and it is axiomatic that all property is held subject to the general right of the public to regulate its use for the promotion of public health, safety, convenience, welfare. Zoning regulations are quite free from and outside of the scope of the Pennsylvania Coal Company case, in which specified property interests created by contract were destroyed by the statute.

    Amicus Brief on Behalf of the National Conference of City Planning et al., *supra* note 134, at 12.
147. "Appellee's attorneys constantly refer to aesthetic considerations and the promotion of beauty; seeking, apparently, to give the impression that the promotion of aesthetic values is the chief purpose of the creation of residential districts. ... Zoning does aim to improve the good order of the cities, that is the general orderliness, which is perhaps, what appellee's attorneys have in mind. That is, however, something quite different from the artistic or the beautiful. ... The essential object of promoting what might be called orderliness in the lay-out of cities is not the satisfaction of taste or aesthetic desires, but rather the promotion of those beneficial effects upon health and morals which come from living in orderly and decent surroundings. When we put the furnace in the cellar rather than in the living room, we are not actuated so much by dictates of good taste or aesthetic standards, as by the conviction that the living room will be a healthier place in which to live and the house a more generally healthful place if the furnace and the gas range and the shop, if there be one, and the other industrial, so to speak, features of the house are kept out of the living room and the sleeping rooms and the dining room." *Id.* at 28–29.
148. *Id.* at 23–24. In Bettman's words, although zoning is not "restricted to or identical with nuisance regulation," it nevertheless "represents no radically new type of property regulation, but merely a new application of sanctioned traditional methods for sanctioned traditional purposes." *Id.* at 26. Remarkably, Metzenbaum said of this argument: "We wish here to advert to the brief filed by the National Conference on City Planning, as *Amici Curiae*. With no intention of criticism and with a fitting respect for this brief, the Village nevertheless feels that

in defense of its own position it does not wish this brief, like its predecessor in the Trial Court below, to prejudice any of the rights of the Village, for (a) the Village earnestly finds itself unable to subscribe to several of the doctrines urged in this brief just as they were urged in the Trial Court, and (b) in addition thereto the Village – having studiously refrained, from resting upon citations of so-called 'nuisance' and 'semi-nuisance' cases as supporting zoning ordinances – the Village can not conscientiously subscribe to the citation of such cases in the brief of the *Amici Curiae*." Brief on Behalf of the Appellants on Rehearing, Village of Euclid v. Ambler Realty Co, No. 31, October Term 1926, at 42–43. *See* Power, *Advocates at Cross-Purposes*, *supra* note 116, at 80.

149. WALKER, *supra* note 143, at 78.
150. JOURNAL OF THE SUPREME COURT OF THE UNITED STATES (October Term 1925), at 171. On January 10, Taft wrote his daughter that "Sutherland has concluded to give up three weeks of this present session to seeking health in the South because of his blood pressure. He is our colleague from Utah and one of the strongest and ablest men we have. We are very anxious to get him away in order that he may not break himself down, as he most certainly would if he remained. We hope to have him back in March." WHT to Mrs. Frederick J. Manning (January 10, 1926) (Taft papers). On January 15, Sutherland wrote Taft from Charleston, South Carolina, to say that "I think I am feeling better and that my blood pressure has abated. The air is good and it is not too cold, though far from being tropical. Shall stick out the three weeks, though I'd rather be in Court. I miss the daily contact with you all more than I can say." GS to WHT (January 15, 1926) (Taft papers). Taft replied the next day, "I read your word to the Brethren. They all send love to you. We miss you but agree you are where you ought to be." Taft added a postscript in large handwriting, "Don't Bother. It is worry that hurts." WHT to GS (January 16, 1926) (Sutherland papers). *See* LDB to GS (January 20, 1926) (Sutherland papers) ("We miss you very much."). On January 20, Sutherland wrote Taft that "I see no reason why I should not be in good form after I get back, for the remainder of the term. I feel impatient and disgusted with myself, but am trying to accept it philosophically." GS to WHT (January 20, 1926) (Taft papers). Sutherland wrote Taft on January 25 that "We expect to be back in Washington on Tuesday, February 2nd." GS to WHT (January 25, 1926) (Taft papers). Three days later he added "I am feeling 100% better and am anxious to get back." GS to WHT (January 28, 1926) (Taft papers). On February 1, Taft wrote his wife saying that "I had a note from Mrs. S saying that they had had a pleasant stay and she thought that the vacation had done him good. But she said he was very impatient to get back and get to work. Well I have given him one important case and that is all he has. He can't overload himself with work therefore." WHT to Helen Herron Taft (February 1, 1926) (Taft papers).
151. METZENBAUM, *supra* note 144, at 117–18.
152. For an excellent analysis of the docket book entries on *Euclid*, see Barry Cushman, *Inside the Taft Court: Lessons from the Docket Books*, 2015 SUPREME COURT REVIEW 345, 392–94.
153. Sutherland's position must be reconciled with a memorandum he had sent Taft in April 1925 about the upcoming argument of New York *ex rel*. Rosevale Realty Co. v. Kleinhert, 268 U.S. 646 (1925), which involved the constitutionality of a zoning ordinance. Although the Court ultimately chose to dismiss the case on procedural

grounds, Sutherland had written Taft that "[i]n the modern development of cities and towns, zoning laws are universally recognized as necessary and proper. The question presented by the law under review is a matter of degree, and I am not prepared to say that the judgment of the local law-makers was arbitrarily exercised." GS to WHT (April 1925) (Taft papers).

154. Brandeis had been intimately involved in an earnest but largely unsuccessful effort to create a city plan for Boston in 1909. MELL SCOTT, AMERICAN CITY PLANNING SINCE 1890, at 110–17 (Berkeley: University of California Press 1969). Stone was closely associated with the planning perspectives of Hoover. Sanford would dissent the next year in *Tyson*. *See supra* Chapter 25, at 800–1.

155. Lawrence C. Gerckens, *Bettman of Cincinnati*, in THE AMERICAN PLANNER: BIOGRAPHIES AND RECOLLECTIONS 134 (New York: Methuen 1983).

156. WALKER, *supra* note 143, at 78. Bettman had conservative credentials; he had worked in the Justice Department during the war and "had gained a reputation as 'the man who put socialist Eugene Debs behind bars.'" Power, *supra* note 122, at 6.

157. Cushman, *supra* note 152, at 392.

158. Many years later McCormack would write that "Justice Sutherland . . . was writing an opinion for the majority in Village of Euclid v. Ambler Realty Co., holding the zoning ordinance unconstitutional, when talks with his dissenting brethren (principally Stone, I believe) shook his convictions and led him to request a reargument, after which he changed his mind and the ordinance was upheld." Alfred McCormack, *A Law Clerk's Recollections*, 46 COLUMBIA LAW REVIEW 710, 712 (1946). *But see* note 153 *supra*. We know that Stone thought *Euclid* to be exceedingly significant. Four days after the opinion's announcement, he wrote his son that "We had some opinions of great importance in the economic and political life of the nation. The Court, by divided vote, upheld the Ohio zoning ordinance. When one considers how important the regulation of the distribution of population in urban communities is going to be in the next twenty years, it is, I think, difficult to over estimate the importance of this decision." HFS to Lauson Stone (November 26, 1926) (Stone papers).

159. WOLF, *supra* note 116, at 76; Metzenbaum, *supra* note 120, at 75. According to WALKER, *supra* note 143, at 78, "It is understood that a divided court had decided against the validity of comprehensive zoning by one vote following the first hearing." Walker does not reveal his sources. On May 22, George T. Simpson, who had filed an amicus brief in the case in support of Ambler, wrote Baker to say:

> [T]his morning I had a talk with a man that had been the private secretary to Mr. Justice Brandeis, [and] who had just come from Washington. He is now practicing law here in Minneapolis and told me that he had had a conversation with Brandeis's secretary, who told him that the order for the reargument in the Village of Euclid case came about by reason of the fact that the court was so closely divided that neither side dared to risk a vote.
>
> Brandeis and Holmes certainly are in favor of this zoning business, McReynolds, Van Devanter and Butler opposed to it, with Taft an uncertain quantity, Stone a new member who was not fully conversant with the situation, and who desired more time that he may acquaint himself.
>
> I got the impression from what he said that the reargument was made at Stone's suggestion.

Quoted in Brooks, *supra* note 116, at 17.

160. "Had the Supreme Court's decision been adverse to zoning," acidly remarked the *Literary Digest*, "its effect might have been very upsetting, for in the past ten years 500 municipalities in the United State have followed the lead of New York and adopted zoning ordinances." *Now We Can Zone Our Cities*, 91 LITERARY DIGEST 14 (December 11, 1926).
161. On the influence of Bettman's brief on Sutherland's opinion, see Tarlock, *supra* note 122, at 8.
162. Edward S. Corwin, *Social Planning under the Constitution – A Study in Perspectives*, 26 AMERICAN POLITICAL SCIENCE REVIEW 1, 21 (1932). See Wolf, *supra* note 117, at 255 ("[I]n many ways, Euclidean zoning is a quintessential Progressive concept," in part because of "the reliance on experts to craft and enforce a regulatory scheme").
163. Amicus Brief on Behalf of the National Conference of City Planning et al., *supra* note 134, at 37.
164. Note, *Constitutional Regulation of Fees of Employment Agencies*, 14 CORNELL LAW QUARTERLY 75, 80 n.36 (1928); *see also* Robert E. Cushman, *Constitutional Law in 1926–1927*, 22 AMERICAN POLITICAL SCIENCE REVIEW 70, 94 (1928) ("The opinion of Mr. Justice Sutherland embodies a most liberal attitude toward the states' police power. In fact, it is hard to realize that he is the same justice who wrote the majority opinions in Tyson and Bro. v. Banton and the Minimum Wage Case.").
165. Charles M. Haar, *Reflections on* Euclid: *Social Contract and Private Purpose*, in ZONING AND THE AMERICAN DREAM, *supra* note 116, at 334.
166. George T. Simpson, who had filed an amicus brief supporting Ambler on behalf of the American Wood Products Company, the Northwestern Feed Company, and the Lyle Culvert & Road Equipment Company, wrote Baker that "Frankly few of us here can understand the attitude of the court, for I am convinced that if this opinion stands in its present nakedness, the property interests of this nation, on which, I think, perhaps, the whole court would agree the future welfare of the nation depends, are in danger. George Sutherland is generally understood to be a property man. I know all about his appointment, and, to have George Sutherland write an opinion of this kind makes a fellow stop and think." Quoted in Brooks, *supra* note 116, at 21. Baker himself wrote:

> Of all the people I know, Mr. Justice Sutherland seemed to me the unlikeliest to write such an opinion as the one he handed down. When he was president of the American Bar Association in 1917, he made a presidential address at the annual meeting in Saratoga Springs in which he said, "It is not enough, however, that we should continue free from the despotism of a supreme autocrat. We must keep ourselves free from the petty despotism which may come from the vesting of final discretion to regulate individual conduct in the hands of lesser officials." If he has not subjected us to the petty despotism of lesser officials in this opinion, I confess I do not see how it could be done.

Quoted in Brooks, *supra* note 116, at 20. Later in the 1926 term Sutherland explicitly upheld the system of variances that has made zoning, in form so abstract and general, so particular in practice. *See* Gorieb v. Fox, 274 U.S. 603, 607 (1927).
167. *Euclid*, Brief on Behalf of the Appellee, *supra* note 146, at 15. Baker argued that the police power "must be reasonably exercised, and that a municipality may not,

The Protected Realm of Freedom

under the guise of the police power, arbitrarily divert property from its appropriate and most economical uses or diminish its value by imposing restrictions which have no other basis than the momentary taste of the public authorities." *Id.* at 42.

168. *Id.* at 82–83.
169. Taft was also given to analogous metaphors. So, for example, in 1918 Taft had announced that "The law of supply and demand will not be entirely ignored in wages any more than the law of gravitation in the physical world." William Howard Taft, *National War Labor Board* (November 26, 1918), in VIVIAN, at 124–25.
170. Sutherland, *Principle or Expedient, supra* note 29, at 197. "We may temporarily divert the small tributaries of the Mississippi from their natural channels in the uplands," Sutherland continued, "but who is so vain as to attempt to control the forces of gravity which will finally bring their waters down to the accustomed level or change the course of the great river itself in its majestic journey to the sea?" *Id.* *See* William Howard Taft, *The Socialist Impulse* (January 25, 1918), in VIVIAN, at 31 ("Human nature is not going to be changed by the war. The love of comfort, the unwillingness to make sacrifices which have characterized our great prosperity, will be moderated, but economic laws dependent on the motive for gain will be in force, unaffected by the strain of war. There will then be neither the opportunity nor the disposition to reverse those laws and make water run uphill by legislation."). These assertions sharply contrast with *Euclid's* remarkably strong affirmation of the priority of political decision-making over natural market forces:

> It is said that the Village of Euclid is a mere suburb of the City of Cleveland; that the industrial development of that city has now reached and in some degree extended into the village, and in the obvious course of things will soon absorb the entire area for industrial enterprises; that the effect of the ordinance is to divert this natural development elsewhere, with the consequent loss of increased values to the owners of the lands within the village borders. But the village, though physically a suburb of Cleveland, is politically a separate municipality, with powers of its own and authority to govern itself as it sees fit, within the limits of the organic law of its creation and the State and Federal Constitutions. Its governing authorities, presumably representing a majority of its inhabitants and voicing their will, have determined, not that industrial development shall cease at its boundaries, but that the course of such development shall proceed within definitely fixed lines. If it be a proper exercise of the police power to relegate industrial establishments to localities separated from residential sections, it is not easy to find a sufficient reason for denying the power because the effect of its exercise is to divert an industrial flow from the course which it would follow, to the injury of the residential public, if left alone, to another course where such injury will be obviated.

272 U.S. at 389–90.
171. *Euclid*, 272 U.S. at 388–89.
172. *See supra* text at notes 19–20.
173. *Compare* Weaver v. Palmer Bros. Co., 270 U.S. 402 (1926), and Schlesinger v. Wisconsin, 270 U.S. 230 (1926), and *supra* Chapter 23, at 739.
174. *See Euclid*, 272 U.S. at 395–97:

> It is true that when, if ever, the provisions set forth in the ordinance in tedious and minute detail, come to be concretely applied to particular premises, including those of the appellee, or to particular conditions, or to be considered in connection with specific complaints, some of them, or even many of them, may be

found to be clearly arbitrary and unreasonable. But where the equitable remedy of injunction is sought, as it is here, not upon the ground of a present infringement or denial of a specific right, or of a particular injury in process of actual execution, but upon the broad ground that the mere existence and threatened enforcement of the ordinance, by materially and adversely affecting values and curtailing the opportunities of the market, constitute a present and irreparable injury, the court will not scrutinize its provisions, sentence by sentence, to ascertain by a process of piecemeal dissection whether there may be, here and there, provisions of a minor character, or relating to matters of administration, or not shown to contribute to the injury complained of, which, if attacked separately, might not withstand the test of constitutionality.... Under these circumstances, therefore, it is enough for us to determine, as we do, that the ordinance in its general scope and dominant features, so far as its provisions are here involved, is a valid exercise of authority, leaving other provisions to be dealt with as cases arise directly involving them.

175. 277 U.S. 183 (1928).
176. *See id.* at 188:

> An inspection of a plat of the city upon which the zoning districts are outlined, taken in connection with the master's findings, shows with reasonable certainty that the inclusion of the locus in question is not indispensable to the general plan.... The governmental power to interfere by zoning regulations with the general rights of the land owner by restricting the character of his use, is not unlimited, and, other questions aside, such restriction cannot be imposed if it does not bear a substantial relation to the public health, safety, morals, or general welfare.... Here, the express finding of the master, already quoted, confirmed by the court below, is that the health, safety, convenience, and general welfare of the inhabitants of the part of the city affected will not be promoted by the disposition made by the ordinance of the locus in question.

See also Remarks of Alfred Bettman, in PLANNING PROBLEMS OF TOWN, CITY AND REGION: PAPERS AND DISCUSSIONS AT THE TWENTY-FIRST NATIONAL CONFERENCE ON CITY PLANNING 98 (Philadelphia: William F. Fell Co. 1929) ("If the doctrine in the Cambridge case [is] that each part of a zoning ordinance must demonstrate its relation to the health and so forth of the immediate neighborhood, I think we are in for trouble.").

177. *See* Zahn v. Board of Public Works of City of Los Angeles, 274 U.S. 325, 327 (1927); Gorieb v. Fox, 274 U.S. 603, 609–10 (1927). Sutherland, despite Westenhaver's opinion, never so much as mentioned the possibility that Euclid's zoning regulations might constitute an unconstitutional confiscation of property requiring compensation. Sutherland neither cited nor discussed *Pennsylvania Coal Co. v. Mahon.*
178. *Adkins*, 261 U.S. at 559–60.
179. *Euclid*, 272 U.S. at 394. In a superb example of a Brandeis brief, Bettman had attached to his amicus brief an appendix with seventy-four pages of expert testimony and opinion.
180. *Euclid*, 272 U.S. at 394–95.
181. One regional planning conference in Pasadena "opened with a paper called 'The Declaration of *Interdependence.*'" Kimball, *supra* note 134, at 127. The conference was "chiefly significant for the recognition accorded the principle of community interdependence." Thomas H. Reed, *City Planning*, 17 AMERICAN POLITICAL SCIENCE REVIEW 430, 431 (1923).
182. Baker, *supra* note 129, at 166. *See* Samuel Price Wetherill, Jr., *Public Guidance in Urban Land Utilization*, 148 ANNALS OF THE AMERICAN ACADEMY OF

The Protected Realm of Freedom

POLITICAL AND SOCIAL SCIENCE 199, 202 (1930); CHESTER C. MAXEY, AN OUTLINE OF MUNICIPAL GOVERNMENT 9 (Garden City: Doubleday, Page & Co. 1924) ("[I]n the city economic independence does not exist, except as a fiction in the minds of people whom it does not please to admit that the interdependence of modern city dwellers has forever vitiated the old individualistic conception of governmental functions.").

183. *See supra* note 125.
184. "Paradoxically," writes Charles Haar, "the driving political and economic force that catapulted zoning forward was the real estate industry." Haar, *supra* note 165, at 341.
185. Amicus Brief on Behalf of the National Conference of City Planning et al., *supra* note 134, at 126–27.
186. In 1916, the distinguished Frederick Law Olmsted, son of the designer of New York's Central Park, had proclaimed:

> City planning is the attempt to exert a well-considered control on behalf of the people of a city over the development of their physical environment as a whole....
>
> The new and significant fact for which this new term, "city planning," stands is a growing appreciation of a city's organic unity, of the interdependence of its diverse elements, and of the profound and inexorable manner in which the future of this great organic unit is controlled by the actions and omissions of today.
>
> We are learning how, in the complex organism of a city, anything we decide to do or leave undone may have important and inevitable consequences wholly foreign to the motives immediately controlling the decision, but seriously affecting the welfare of the future city; and with our recognition of this is growing a sense of social responsibility for estimating these remoter consequences and giving them due weight in reaching every decision.

Frederick Law Olmsted, *Introduction*, in CITY PLANNING: A SERIES OF PAPERS PRESENTING THE ESSENTIAL ELEMENTS OF A CITY PLAN (John Nolen, ed., New York: D. Appleton & Co. 1916). In his amicus brief, Bettman quoted a letter sent by Hoover to the president of the National Conference on City Planning: "The fact is constantly brought before me as Secretary of Commerce that lack of city planning and zoning constantly hampers commerce and industry in their basic function of serving mankind. This is particularly true in connection with housing and general living conditions, while the waste and inefficiency in transportation, and losses through bad location of structures are a constant drag on our resources, and tend to retard increases in living standards." Amicus Brief on Behalf of the National Conference of City Planning et al., *supra* note 134, at 34.

187. Amicus Brief on Behalf of the National Conference of City Planning et al., *supra* note 134, at 117 (quoting *City Zoning Is Sound Business*, by John Ihlder, Manager, Civic Development Department, Chamber of Commerce of the United States). In Ihlder's words, "Zoning has a sane, common-sense purpose – so to guide the development of a city's area that each part will be put to the most effective use and the whole community benefited by the substitution of system and order for chaos and disorder." "What the regulations do is to prevent one owner from injuring his neighbor by erecting a store or a factory or a public garage in a residence district years before there is any prospect that other stores or factories or garages would come into the neighborhood. In this way the probable life of any building erected today will be greatly lengthened, and the builder will be justified in investing

a larger amount in constructing a finer building." "The zoning regulations .... protect residence districts from ...., intrusion in order that men may feel greater assurance in investing their savings in things that build up family and social life." *Id.* at 113–14, 116–17.
188. *Euclid*, 272 U.S. at 386–87.
189. *Id.* at 388.
190. The profound constitutional revolution of the New Deal can be understood as a generalization of this insight to the institution of property generally. For an early statement of this position, see Walton H. Hamilton, *Property – According to Locke*, 41 YALE LAW JOURNAL 864, 878–79 (1932):

> The individual is no longer thought of as a miniature god who has a title to his own creation. It is now impossible to place a mark of personal workmanship upon any chattel; a multitude of men have mixed their labor – and many another personal contribution beside – into such earthly possessions as a motor-car, a skyscraper, a railroad, a going concern, and a handful of intangibles. In an economic order which comprehends all men the technical contribution of the individual to usable wealth cannot be isolated and measured. ... Instead his relationship to a gigantic industrial order, into whose keeping he gives his services or his productive possessions and from whose store-house he fetches away his living, depends upon a tangled scheme of social arrangements.

191. Sutherland, *Principle or Expedient*, *supra* note 29, at 207.
192. I leave Van Devanter and Sanford out of this list because their extrajudicial writings are so scant that it is impossible to identify textual support for this proposition.
193. *See generally* MORTON J. HORWITZ, THE TRANSFORMATION OF AMERICAN LAW, 1780–1860, at 31–53, 70–80, 99, 101–8 (Cambridge: Harvard University Press 1977); Robert A. Williams, Jr., *Euclid's Lochnerian Legacy*, in ZONING AND THE AMERICAN DREAM, *supra* note 116, at 278.
194. Nadav Shoked, *The Reinvention of Ownership: The Embrace of Residential Zoning and the Modern Populist Reading of Property*, 28 YALE JOURNAL ON REGULATION 91, 143 (2011).
195. *The Proposed Zoning Ordinance*, MINNEAPOLIS STAR TRIBUNE (March 31, 1924), at 6.
196. "[T]he primary objects of zoning are ... not so much the protection of public health and safety, as the protection of the value and usefulness of urban land. ... It is predicated upon a basic principle of urban land economics, that a certain conformity in use stabilizes and insures the value of land. ... Zoning ordinances are evidence of a legislative recognition of what is fast ripening into a new property right, which might be termed, a restrictive easement against what someone has called 'illegitimate and unfair non-conformity' in use of the adjoining or neighboring parcels. They recognize that a property owner has a right to expect the municipality in some degree to protect his property from the blighting effect of non-conforming uses." Edward D. Landels, *Zoning: An Analysis of Its Purposes and Legal Sanctions*, 17 AMERICAN BAR ASSOCIATION JOURNAL 163, 165 (1931). *See* Bertram H. Saunders, *Zoning: What Can Be Done for It Where the Courts Are Unfavorable?*, 34 AMERICAN CITY MAGAZINE 237 (March 1926) ("[T]o-day in our cities population rises like a flood. Gambling in real estate grows to enormous proportions and overshadows the operations of the conservative broker. More and more the land is owned by men who will not own it to-morrow; by men whose only interest in land is to crowd

The Protected Realm of Freedom

every available foot of it with whatever structures will yield the highest and quickest profit; by men who make commerce of neighborhood amenities, and who care nothing for the detrimental community effects of their activities."); *Protection Rather Than Restriction Is the Strong Argument for Zoning*, 37 AMERICAN CITY MAGAZINE 651 (November 1927).

197. David Glassberg, *History and The Public: Legacies of the Progressive Era*, 73 JOURNAL OF AMERICAN HISTORY 957, 975 (1987). Michael Kammen usefully stresses the "contrapuntal impulses" characteristic of the 1920s, when Americans were "increasingly preoccupied with retrospection and recovering the past," "usually by fabricating a history of consensus," and at the same time increasingly committed to science, accurate history, and "debunking." MICHAEL KAMMEN, MYSTIC CHORDS OF MEMORY: THE TRANSFORMATION OF TRADITION IN AMERICAN CULTURE 481–83 (New York: Vintage 1993).

198. ROBERT H. WIEBE, THE SEARCH FOR ORDER 1877–1920, at xiv (New York: Hill & Wang 1967).

199. Shoked, *supra* note 194, at 142–43 ("Euclid reconnected the New World to the Old. . . . Euclid placed the right to security in landholding, to quiet enjoyment of the homestead, at the forefront – at the expense of free exploitation of property and commercial expansion.").

200. Martha A. Lees, *Preserving Property Values? Preserving Proper Homes? Preserving Privilege?: The Pre-Euclid Debate over Zoning for Exclusively Private Residential Areas, 1916–1926*, 56 UNIVERSITY OF PITTSBURGH LAW REVIEW 367 (1994).

201. 297 F. at 316. Westenhaver cited Buchanan v. Warley, 245 U.S. 60 (1918), in which the White Court had invalidated an ordinance "districting and restricting residential blocks so that the white and colored races should be segregated." 297 F. at 312. He reasoned that the effect of Euclid's zoning ordinance would be similar. "The blighting of property values and the congesting of population, whenever the colored or certain foreign races invade a residential section, are so well known as to be within the judicial cognizance." *Id.* at 313.

202. ERNST FREUND, THE POLICE POWER: PUBLIC POLICY AND CONSTITUTIONAL RIGHTS § 178 (Chicago: Callaghan & Co. 1904). *See* Quintini v. City of Bay St. Louis, 64 Miss. 483, 490 (1887) ("The law can know no distinction between citizens because of the superior cultivation of the one over the other. It is with common humanity that courts and legislatures must deal; and that use of property which in all common sense and reason is not a nuisance to the average man cannot be prohibited because repugnant to some sentiment of a particular class.").

203. Transcript of Record, Village of Euclid v. Ambler Realty Co., No. 31, October Term 1926, at 109–22; Randle, *supra* note 116, at 38–40.

204. Robert F. Whitten, *Social Aspects of Zoning*, 48 THE SURVEY 418–19 (1922). "My own observation," Whitten continued, "is that wherever you have a neighborhood made up of people largely in the same economic status, you have a neighborhood where there is the most independence of thought and action and the most intelligent interest in the neighborhood, city, state and national affairs. . . . The so-called industrial classes will constitute a more intelligent and self-respecting citizenship when housed in homogenous neighborhoods than when housed in areas used by all the economic classes." *Id.* at 418–19.

In 1922, Whitten proposed a zoning plan for Atlanta that created three residential districts: white, colored, and undetermined. Bruno Lasker, *The Atlanta Zoning Plan*, 48 THE SURVEY 114 (1922). Bruno Lasker observed that Whitten's "Atlanta plan is the first which makes a distinction concerning type of residents as well as type of residence. To judge from the support it has received from the local newspapers and organizations of citizens, it seems to answer the prevailing desire of the white Atlantans – the more so since the emphasis in the commission's report and in the publicity supporting it has been laid entirely to the protection of property values as the main purpose of zoning. But as a precedent it opens up the possibility of new zoning ordinances embodying restrictions against immigrants or immigrants of certain races, against persons of certain occupations, political or religious affiliations, or modes of life." *Id.* at 115. Even though Whitten's plan for Atlanta was eventually struck down by the Georgia Supreme Court, see Bowen v. City of Atlanta, 159 Ga. 145 (1924), "Atlanta officials continued to use the racial zoning map to guide its planning for decades to come." RICHARD ROTHSTEIN, THE COLOR OF LAW: A FORGOTTEN HISTORY OF HOW OUR GOVERNMENT SEGREGATED AMERICA 46 (New York: Liveright Publishing Corp. 2017).

205. TOLL, *supra* note 116, at 29. In New York, the Fifth Avenue Merchants' Association demanded zoning because "hordes of immigrant labourers violated the ambiance in which luxury retailing prospered." Power, *supra* note 122, at 3.
206. Ernst Freund, *Some Inadequately Discussed Problems of the Law of City Planning and Zoning*, 24 ILLINOIS LAW REVIEW 135, 137 (1929).
207. *Id.* at 146–47. *See* Christopher Silver, *The Racial Origins of Zoning: Southern Cities from 1910–40*, 6 PLANNING PERSPECTIVES 189 (1991).
208. FRANK J. POPPER, THE POLITICS OF LAND-USE REFORM 54–55 (Madison: University of Wisconsin Press 1981). *See* JESSICA TROUNSTINE, SEGREGATION BY DESIGN: LOCAL POLITICS AND INEQUALITY IN AMERICAN CITIES (Cambridge University Press 2018).
209. *Euclid*, 272 U.S. at 390.
210. *Id. See* Alfred Bettman, *The Present State of Court Decisions on Zoning*, 2 CITY PLANNING 24, 25 (January 1926) ("The single-family district from which the apartment house or multiple-family structure is excluded is the feature about whose validity the most anxiety is felt.").
211. *Euclid*, 272 U.S. at 394–95.
212. Shoked, *supra* note 194, at 116. As of 1926, no court in the United States had ruled that an apartment building was a nuisance.
213. Chused, *supra* note 136, at 614.
214. Buchanan v. Warley, 245 U.S. 60 (1917). On the background to *Buchanan*, see RICHARD R.W. BROOKS & CAROL M. ROSE, SAVING THE NEIGHBORHOOD: RACIALLY RESTRICTIVE COVENANTS, LAW, AND SOCIAL NORMS 38–44 (Cambridge: Harvard University Press 2013). "Many border and southern cities ignored the *Buchanan* decision." ROTHSTEIN, *supra* note 204, at 46. The Taft Court, however, invoked the authority of *Buchanan* to strike down a New Orleans ordinance that attempted to zone on the basis of race. *See* Harmon v. Tyler, 273 U.S. 668 (1927); *No Laws May Part White and Black*, 92 LITERARY DIGEST 12 (March 26, 1927). On *Buchanan*, and its relationship to

The Protected Realm of Freedom

facially neutral methods of zoning exclusion, see David E. Bernstein, *Philip Sober Controlling Philip Drunk*: Buchanan v. Warley *in Historical Perspective*, 51 VANDERBILT LAW REVIEW 797, 862–64 (1998). Holmes had dissented in conference in *Buchanan. Id.* at 855.

215. Bruno Lasker, *The Issue Restated*, 44 THE SURVEY 278, 279 (1920). Zoning "provided suburbs and other local government entities with a powerful tool to limit and define their areas on economic, social welfare, and (in practice and covertly) class and racial bases." Randle, *supra* note 116, at 41. For the view that the maintenance of racial segregation was a conscious aim of Hoover's zoning advisory committee, as well as of "city planners across the nation," see ROTHSTEIN, *supra* note 204, at 51–54.

216. Six months before *Euclid*, in Corrigan v. Buckley, 271 U.S. 323 (1926), the Taft Court refused constitutionally to prohibit the enforcement of private, racially restrictive covenants, which subsequently became a major legal vehicle for propagating residential racial segregation. See BROOKS & ROSE, *supra* note 214; Bernstein, *supra* note 214, at 864–66. In the same year as *Euclid*, the Taft Court in Gong Lum v. Rice, 275 U.S. 78 (1927), upheld explicit southern racial segregation in education. *See infra* Chapter 43, at 1437–51.

217. Lasker, *supra* note 215, at 279. There was available to Sutherland yet another explanation for the importance of preserving neighborhoods devoted to single-family residences, which was the civic and social value of the American home. This perspective was most forcefully articulated by the California Supreme Court in 1925:

> In addition to all that has been said in support of the constitutionality of residential zoning as part of a comprehensive plan, we think it may be safely and sensibly said that justification for residential zoning may, in the last analysis, be rested upon the protection of the civic and social values of the American home. The establishment of such districts is for the general welfare because it tends to promote and perpetuate the American home. It is axiomatic that the welfare, and indeed the very existence of a nation depends upon the character and caliber of its citizenry. The character and quality of manhood and womanhood are in a large measure the result of home environment. The home and its intrinsic influences are the very foundation of good citizenship, and any factor contributing to the establishment of homes and the fostering of home life doubtless tends to the enhancement not only of community life but of the life of the nation as a whole.
>
> The establishment of single family residence districts offers inducements not only to the wealthy but to those of moderate means to own their own homes. With ownership comes stability, the welding together of family ties and better attention to the rearing of children. With ownership comes increased interest in the promotion of public agencies, such as church and school, which have for their purpose a desired development of the moral and mental make-up of the citizenry of the country. With ownership of one's home comes recognition of the individual's responsibility for his share in the safeguarding of the welfare of the community and increased pride in personal achievement which must come from personal participation in projects looking toward community betterment.
>
> It is needless to further analyze and enumerate all of the factors which make a single family home more desirable for the promotion and perpetuation of family life than an apartment, hotel, or flat. It will suffice to say that there is a sentiment practically universal, that this is so. But few persons, if given their choice, would, we think, deliberately prefer to establish their homes and rear

their children in an apartment house neighborhood rather than in a single home neighborhood.

Miller v. Board of Public Works of the City of Los Angeles, 195 Cal. 477, 492–94 (1925). The court's rhetoric in *Miller* trades almost entirely on the morally beneficial influences of property. *Euclid* does not adopt the rhetoric of *Miller*. Instead, Sutherland chose to justify residential zoning exclusively in terms of values like safety, health, and financial stability.

CHAPTER 27

Ratemaking and Judicial Legitimacy

THE OVERRIDING NECESSITY of winning World War I effectively impressed with a public interest the entire American economy. The Taft Court sought to roll back this wartime presumption and constitutionally reentrench the unregulated play of the market. The line of cases initiated by *Adkins* and *Tyson* guaranteed that property owners would be immune from price controls unless they granted "to the public an interest in the use which may be controlled by the public for the common good."[1] Government remained free, however, as it had been before the war, to regulate the price of railroads and utilities, which had long been classified as property affected with a public interest.

Like the urban land at issue in *Euclid*, property affected with a public interest did not lend itself to narratives about the construction of independent moral agency. Property affected with a public interest was subject to such intimate public regulation that it could not convincingly be characterized as a meaningful site for the enactment of private, personal freedom. From a macroeconomic point of view, however, such property was plainly essential to the growth of the national economy.

Throughout the 1920s, members of the Taft Court who believed that constitutional protections for property were essential for the promotion of economic development fretted that government agencies would set prices too low to sustain adequate investment in railroads and utilities. During the course of the decade, they sought to impose increasingly stringent constitutional restrictions on government ratemaking. But because these restrictions could not be explained in the language of independent moral agency, the Court was left vulnerable to charges of imposing the personal economic philosophy of its members. These charges would explode in an intense and unexpected backlash to Hoover's nomination of Charles Evans Hughes to replace Taft in 1930.

Property affected with a public interest had since the days of the Waite Court been "subject to legislative control as to ... rates of fare and freight."[2] At first the Court ceded to legislatures effective authority over rates,[3] but within a decade the Court decided that the "power to regulate is not a power to destroy, and ... is not the equivalent of confiscation. Under pretense of regulating fares and freights, the state cannot ... do that which in law amounts to a taking of private property for public use without just compensation, or without due process of law."[4] The Court undertook to determine when rates were set so low as to constitute an unconstitutional taking of property.

As the decade of the 1920s began, the governing precedent on this question was the venerable 1898 precedent of *Smyth v. Ames*,[5] which held, in Harlan's vague and inflated prose:

> The corporation may not be required to use its property for the benefit of the public without receiving just compensation for the services rendered by it. How such compensation may be ascertained, and what are the necessary elements in such an inquiry, will always be an embarrassing question....
>
> We hold, however, that the basis of all calculations as to the reasonableness of rates to be charged by a corporation maintaining a highway under legislative sanction must be the fair value of the property being used by it for the convenience of the public. And, in order to ascertain that value, the original cost of construction, the amount expended in permanent improvements, the amount and market value of its bonds and stock, the present as compared with the original cost of construction, the probable earning capacity of the property under particular rates prescribed by statute, and the sum required to meet operating expenses, are all matters for consideration, and are to be given such weight as may be just and right in each case. We do not say that there may not be other matters to be regarded in estimating the value of the property. What the company is entitled to ask is a fair return upon the value of that which it employs for the public convenience. On the other hand, what the public is entitled to demand is that no more be exacted from it for the use of a public highway than the services rendered by it are reasonably worth.[6]

Smyth created what would become known as the "fair value" test, which held that rates were not confiscatory if they produced an adequate rate of return on the "fair value" of property conscripted to serve "for the benefit of the public."[7] The incoherence of the test was manifest in the eclectic and inconsistent factors listed by *Smyth* as relevant for assessing the fair value of property.[8]

By the 1920s, the root cause of *Smyth*'s confusion had become apparent. Because the value of regulated property depends upon rates set by the government,[9] the "fair value" test was essentially caught "in a hopeless vicious circle. We cannot tell what rates the company is to charge until we know what its value is, and we cannot tell what its value is till we know what rates it may charge."[10] Once property was immunized from the higgling of the market, in other words, its "fair value" was essentially contestable and uncertain.[11]

It was a daunting jurisprudential challenge to determine when rates were so low as to be confiscatory.[12] Taft confessed that "I am afraid we shall have in increasing numbers these so-called confiscation cases, that is the cases that involve the question of rates in public utilities. I dislike them extremely, and don't feel myself competent in them. ... I would like to get rid of all such cases. I prefer even patent cases."[13] Holmes was also explicit that "rate cases" were "of the kind I hate."[14] They raised constitutional issues Holmes regarded as essentially political and arbitrary:

> [W]e had some rate cases. ... We solemnly weigh the valuation of the property and all the tests and decide pro or con – but really it is determining a line between grabber and grabbee that turns on the feeling of the community. You say the public is entitled to this and the owners to that. I see no *a priori* reason for the propositions except that that is the way the crowd feels. I tell them that if the rate-making power will only say I have considered A.B. & C., all the elements enumerated, we accept the judgment unless it makes us puke. It is like the ideal of woman – on one end you have the dames of the *Decameron* who care only for God and man, at the other a peaked, elbowed school marm who talks on high themes and thinks man a superfluity of nature. A given community fixes its conception somewhere midway according to the dominance of companionship or dimples.[15]

Others on the Court were attracted to rate cases. As Taft wrote his son, "we have some experts on our Court. One is Pierce Butler, the other is Brandeis. And I think McReynolds aspires to figure in that field of our jurisdiction."[16] In fact, Butler, McReynolds, and Brandeis cared passionately about ratemaking cases, and they each believed that these cases involved important constitutional principles.[17] Throughout the 1920s, these three justices maintained a running battle about whether the "fair value" of property affected with a public interest should be determined by the contemporary "cost of reproduction less depreciation,"[18] or instead by the amount of capital prudently invested in the property.[19] Taft initially handled this debate with exemplary fairness.[20]

The issue arose early in the 1922 term when the Court was considering two ratemaking cases: *Georgia Ry. & Power Co. v. Railroad Commission of Georgia*,[21] argued on November 29, and *Missouri* ex rel. *Southwestern Bell Telephone Co. v. Public Service Comm'n of Missouri*,[22] argued on December 8. Butler was not confirmed until December 21, and he did not hear argument in either case.[23] Brandeis seized the occasion to launch a full-scale attack on *Smyth v. Ames* and to advance an entirely new theory. Brandeis argued that utilities were constitutionally entitled only to a fair return on funds that had been prudently invested in utility property.[24]

Apparently intrigued, Taft set aside an entire day for members of the Court to debate how confiscation claims in utility ratemaking ought to be approached. As Brandeis later recounted to Frankfurter:

> [W]e have a better atmosphere for discussion – in valuation cases. ... [I]n S.W. Telephone case there was much division & I suggested "I'll report on that if you want me to." So Taft asked me to report. I took months to prepare a memo, printed it & had it circulated, about 62 pp as a basis for discussion.

I had a job holding in McReynolds who wrote his opinion in S.W. (My memo was evoked by [Georgia Ry.] case.) But through Chief and Van the thing was held up until my report was in. We then had a whole day set aside for discussion. And it was a thorough discussion. Some didn't grasp the facts & hadn't thoroughly mastered the memo but it was a new method in consideration of issues.[25]

Taft's response to Brandeis's innovative theory bespeaks a remarkable open-mindedness, especially considering that Brandeis's approach substantially modified established precedent. Butler recorded in his docket book that the unique day-long conference to consider Brandeis's memorandum "in support of *Prudent* investment" occurred on May 12, 1923, and that the "discussion resulted in disapproval of theory."[26]

The question debated by the Court was essentially whether railroads and utilities were to be valued at their "present, current, or reproduction cost," or instead at their "original cost, including expenditures on permanent improvements."[27] There were opportunistic reasons to adopt one test or the other. In times of depressed prices, state regulatory commissions were inclined to advance the cost of reproduction theory of value because it meant lower rates. In *Smyth*, for example, William Jennings Bryan had argued for a reproduction theory of value to *decrease* railroad rates.[28] But in the 1920s conditions were different; rising prices meant that reproduction cost was "higher than original cost."[29] Utilities and railroads therefore pushed hard for a reproduction theory of value that would yield higher rates.[30]

Apart from these opportunistic incentives, the two approaches to valuation also differed on a fundamental question of policy: Should railroads and utilities be compensated based on their present marginal value, which, if accurately assessed, would efficiently allocate national economic resources, or should they instead receive only a steady and predictable rate of return because they were entities "controlled by the public for the common good,"[31] in compensation for which they were entitled to special advantages unavailable to other purely private investments (like rights of eminent domain or insulation from competition)?[32]

A disadvantage of the cost of reproduction theory was that it lacked cogent connection to the constitutional issue of confiscation, which was the primary ground for judicial intervention. The theory simply assumed that owners of public utilities were entitled to a fair return on the entire present market value of their property. This assumption was in tension with the very premise of the legal category of property affected with a public interest, which was exempt from market pricing because it was uniquely dedicated to public service.[33] The essential point of the prudential investment theory, by contrast, was to identify a rate of return on invested capital to which investors were constitutionally entitled.

An important meta-issue underlay these theoretical differences. The question was whether a hypothetical inquiry like "present reproduction cost" could ever be rigorously pursued, or whether it was so inherently speculative that it would inevitably produce arbitrary and unreliable valuations.[34] Because society values the *service* provided by public utilities,[35] not their existing physical plants,[36] the reproduction value of any given utility will necessarily depend upon the cost of available substitutes.[37] Determining the price of potential substitutes is an intrinsically uncertain task. Even ascertaining the simple reproduction cost of a single physical plant could be a contentious and indeterminate process. The enormous practical difficulties associated with assessing reproduction costs have proved so daunting that in the years since the Taft Court most regulatory bodies have come to use the prudent investment model, at least as a first cut.[38]

During the Taft Court era, debate between these two views tended to center on the question of which approach would provide sufficient compensation to incentivize adequate capital investment. As Taft wrote Van Devanter, he considered "Brandeis as the borer from within the Court on 'prudential investment' attacks on the capital of the country."[39] Taft, Sutherland, Butler, and likely Van Devanter were all especially sensitive to incentive effects because they regarded the constitutional function of property to be the promotion of economic growth. For the most part, those in favor of assessing value by the present cost of reproduction were successful during the 1920s, although Brandeis was not without some influence.

The immediate result of the May 12 conference was that McReynolds authored an opinion for five justices in *Southwestern Bell Telephone* emphasizing a cost of reproduction theory of valuation. The decision set aside a state commission's order for reduced telephone rates as confiscatory. "It is impossible to ascertain what will amount to a fair return upon properties devoted to public service without giving consideration to the cost of labor, supplies, etc., at the time the investigation is made," said McReynolds. "An honest and intelligent forecast of probable future values made upon a view of all the relevant circumstances, is essential. If the highly important element of present costs is wholly disregarded such a forecast becomes impossible. Estimates for to-morrow cannot ignore prices of to-day."[40]

Brandeis converted the memorandum that he had prepared for the May 12 conference into a memorable and influential opinion that announced his opposition to the "so-called rule of *Smyth v. Ames*" on the ground that "the thing devoted by the investor to the public use is not specific property, tangible and intangible, but capital embarked in the enterprise."[41] In authoritative and trenchant prose, Brandeis explained his newly minted prudential investment theory of ratemaking.[42] He argued that constitutional confiscation was possible only if investors were denied "the opportunity to earn a fair return" on their prudently invested capital.[43]

Three weeks after *Southwestern Bell Telephone*, Brandeis announced an opinion for the Court in *Georgia Ry. & Power*. Brandeis specifically approved gas rates set by a state commission that had given "careful consideration to the cost of reproduction" but that had "refused to adopt reproduction cost as the measure of value" on the ground that "'present fair value' is not synonymous with 'present replacement cost', particularly under abnormal conditions."[44] Butler and Sanford did not participate in the case, but McKenna dissented on the reasonable ground that the decision could not "be reconciled" with the holding of *Southwestern Bell Telephone* that the value of utility property must be determined by its "reproduction cost."[45] Brandeis later observed to

883

Frankfurter that "we got by in the Georgia case holding that reconstruction is not the measure but merely a factor. ... I think gradually Court will work out pretty satisfactorily on these cases. Trouble is they don't, most of them, understand the problem."[46]

The Court indeed displayed evidence of confusion. On the very same day that it issued *Georgia Ry. & Power*, it also released *Bluefield Water Works & Improvement Co. v. Public Service Comm'n of West Virginia*, which had been argued on January 22. In *Bluefield Water Works*, Butler, citing *Southwestern Bell Telephone*, constitutionally struck down rates set by a state commission on the ground that a state agency had "failed to give weight to cost of reproduction less depreciation on the basis of" contemporary prices.[47] Brandeis mysteriously concurred "in the judgment ... for the reasons stated by him in *Missouri* ex rel. *Southwestern Bell Telephone Co.*"[48] By releasing three inconsistent opinions in three weeks, the Court produced "not a little bewilderment"[49] and "disconcerting uncertainty."[50] It was said that "the result of the debate" in the Court about valuation "seems to have been a draw. ... [T]he original uncertainties of Smyth v. Ames still remain."[51]

In 1926, however, the Taft Court revisited these issues in *McCardle v. Indianapolis Water Co.*, in which Butler authored a forceful opinion for six justices striking down rates set for a water utility on the straightforward ground that the fair value of the utility must constitutionally be determined by "the present value" of its land "and the present cost of construction" of its plant.[52] The case was especially striking because, as a private attorney, Butler had chiefly been known for his vigorous advocacy on behalf of railroads for a cost of reproduction test for determining the value of property affected with a public interest.[53] Brandeis, joined by Stone, dissented on the ground that "reproduction cost" was "not conclusive evidence of value."[54]

Butler's "practically decisive"[55] opinion was taken by many as a "wholehearted adoption of the cost of reproduction theory"[56] and hence as a significant clarification of the ambiguities that had shrouded the Court's 1923 opinions.[57] "A majority of the United States Supreme Court seems to have gone entirely over to the theory of reproduction cost as the correct rate base, and to have defined this as reproduction cost new on the day of valuation."[58] It was thus feared that "every public utility in the country will seek to establish new schedules of rates in keeping with the decision of the supreme court," and that "millions of dollars will be taken from the American people when the principle just laid down by the supreme court has been carried through the public utility and railroad structure of the country."[59]

What lent edge to this fear was that the Interstate Commerce Commission ("ICC") was about to begin publishing the results of its massive effort to value the nation's railroads. The ICC had originally been tasked with this burden in 1913 under the Valuation Act, which required the Commission to "investigate, ascertain, and report the value of all the property" of the American railway system.[60] The task was amplified by the Transportation Act of 1920, which required the ICC to establish "uniform" group or geographical rates[61] adequate to "foster, protect and control" the nation's transportation system "with appropriate regard to the welfare

Ratemaking & Judicial Legitimacy

of those who are immediately concerned, as well as the public at large, and to promote its growth and insure its safety."[62] Because railway rates were to be set on a group basis, individual railroads would be variably profitable.[63] The Act authorized the ICC to recapture half of the excess income from successful roads, defined as those with incomes higher than 6 percent of the fair value of their property, and to redistribute that income to financially less remunerative roads, so that the fiscal health of the entire transportation system could be maintained.[64] These recapture provisions required the ICC to determine the fair value of each of the nation's railroads.

Remarkably, no case reviewing the ICC's method of determining the fair value of railroad property had been decided by the Supreme Court before Taft became chief justice. But a test of the ICC's approach was anticipated throughout the 1920s. The importance of the issue had led to insistence during Butler's confirmation hearings in 1922 that his prominent role as a private attorney pressing for cost of reproduction valuation for railroads disqualify him from participating in forthcoming railroad valuation cases, an insistence to which Butler apparently acquiesced.[65] This history was revived when *McCardle* was decided. There were complaints that Butler should have "disqualified" himself in *McCardle* because the decision "establishes the precedent, that will probably be followed in the valuation decision when it finally reaches the court."[66]

There was apprehension that the aggressive approach of *McCardle* would entitle railroads "to raise their rates so as to require the people of the United States to pay to them a billion dollars a year more than at present."[67] Within weeks of *McCardle*, Illinois Congressman Henry T. Rainey proclaimed on the floor of the House:

> The greatest lawsuit in the history of the world will soon be on its way to the Supreme Court of the United States. We are now engaged in appraising the railroad properties of the United States. ... Under the "prudent investment" theory it is estimated that the railroads are worth from fifteen to twenty billion dollars, and, of course, rates should be fixed to yield a fair return on that evaluation. According to the Wall Street Journal, if the "reproduction cost" theory is adopted the railroads will be valued at more than $35,000,000,000, and the rates must be fixed to yield a "fair return" on that amount.[68]

It is no wonder that immediately after *McCardle* Stone wrote his friend John Bassett Moore that "with the present ... reproduction cost of railroads of thirty three billions, which probably exceeds actual cost by eleven or twelve billions, we are likely to have some interesting rate problems in the next few years, the solution of which may have very far reaching consequences."[69]

As it happens, the ICC threw down the gauntlet to *McCardle* a bare three months after the decision was issued. *Excess Income of St. Louis & O'Fallon Railway Co.*[70] concerned the valuation of a minuscule but nevertheless profitable 9-mile-long coal-carrying road, for the purpose of determining its excess income. The ICC chose as its test case a proceeding that had begun in 1924 and that presented a relatively simple problem. "We are dealing here with one small railroad," it said, but "what we do in this case we must in principle do for all the railroads in the United States.... [H]aving in mind ... the whole railroad situation, the decision is of the greatest consequence from both private and public viewpoints."[71] The precise question before the ICC was what excess income it would recapture from the O'Fallon line for the years 1920–1923. But this question turned on how the ICC chose to establish the value of the line.

The Transportation Act directed that in determining value the ICC "shall give due consideration to all the elements of value recognized by the law of the land for rate-making purposes."[72] The Taft Court's entire approach to ratemaking had been oriented to the constitutional question of confiscation; its decisions focused on whether rates were set so low as to constitute a prohibited taking of property. But the ICC chose to begin its analysis of the "law of the land" from an entirely different premise.

The legislative mission of the ICC was to maintain "an adequate national system of railway transportation, capable of providing the best possible service to the public at the lowest cost consistent with full justice to the private owners." So long as the ICC valued railroad property in a manner designed to serve this mission, and so long as its valuations allowed railroads to charge rates and earn income sufficient to attract and encourage "further capital ventures," the ICC believed that it would be "idle" to discard its valuations as confiscatory.[73] The agency's approach would fit comfortably within the concept of "fair value" created by "the kaleidoscopic rule of Smyth v. Ames."[74]

The ICC directly addressed the Taft Court's recent precedents. It argued that to use "the cost of reproduction new" as "the basic measure of 'fair value,' to the exclusion of all other factors," would essentially frustrate the agency's legislative mandate. Depending on annual price variations, a cost of reproduction method of valuation would produce "violent fluctuations" in railroad rates and income that would be "utterly inconsistent with the necessary attraction of private capital." If the valuation of aggregate railroad property was taken to be $18 billion in 1919 (in 1914 prices), a cost of reproduction new methodology would have produced "a gain of 23.4 billions in 1922, a loss of 6.3 billions in 1921, a further loss of 6.8 billions in 1922, and a gain again of 3 billions in 1923. These huge 'profits' and 'losses' would have occurred without change in the railroad property used in the public service other than the theoretical and speculative change derived from a shifting of general price levels."[75] In times of rising prices, the "grotesque" speculative gains would chiefly accrue to holders of common stock, as distinct from those who provided two-thirds of actual railroad capital by investing in "bonds, notes, or preferred stock, the holders of which are limited to a fixed or maximum return."[76] In times of falling prices, the effect on railroad revenues would be catastrophic.[77]

Approaching valuation by assessing "actual, legitimate investment," by contrast, would produce a stable, predictable income that would "lend confidence to industry and investment." It would be transparent, reproducible, and reliable. It would also smooth out price fluctuations because the continuous rejuvenation of railroad property would gradually introduce price changes into the rate base. In an apparent concession to the "current cost of reproduction" methodology, however,

Ratemaking & Judicial Legitimacy

the ICC decided to "value lands at their prevailing market values."[78] Commissioner Joseph Eastman, a former "progressive protégé" of Brandeis from his days in New England battling public utilities,[79] objected to this concession.[80] But the concession proved insufficient to prevent four dissents from commissioners who, citing Taft Court precedents, argued that the "law of the land" required the agency to give "an effectual weight" to "the present as compared with the original cost of construction."[81] In the words of Commissioner Aitchison, "This is not the place to discuss the economic and political results of the enforcement of a rule laid down by the Supreme Court. Our present duty is to ascertain the rule of law and to enforce it."[82]

The ICC's judgment was immediately attacked before a three-judge district court on the ground that the agency had valued O'Fallon's property using an "assumed prudent investment basis and failed to give 'effective and dominant consideration ... to the cost of reproduction.'" On December 10, 1927, the court found that the O'Fallon line had not been prejudiced because, even accepting its own claimed self-valuation, the income which it had been allowed to retain by the ICC produced returns "for the last ten months of 1920, 6.97 per cent; for 1921, 8.71 per cent; for 1922, 8.29 per cent; for 1923, 8.43 percent." Returns of this magnitude could not constitutionally be condemned as confiscatory, and hence the ICC's order was "not open to attack upon the ground of wrongful valuation."[83]

As the case headed for resolution in the Taft Court, anticipation and tension ran high. Headlines proclaimed "The Greatest Lawsuit in History," and news stories marveled that the case would affect "the astounding sum of $52,000,000,000, and the economic interests of every man, woman and child in the United States of America."[84] The issue was framed as a "clear cut ... dispute between the Interstate Commerce Commission, which defends the principle of actual cost, or 'prudent investment,' as the proper rate base, and the carriers which assert not only the constitutional right but also the economic wisdom of the rival principle of cost of reproduction."[85] Noting that *O'Fallon* "involved issues of wide and exceptional public interest and of immense consequence to all the people of the United States," the Senate passed an unusual resolution, urged by Senator George Norris, requesting that the Court permit "Donald R. Richberg, as counsel for the ... National Conference on Valuation, to intervene in [the] O'Fallon case for the purpose of making oral argument and filing a brief therein."[86] The Court granted the Senate's request in November.[87]

Arguments were held on January 3 and 4, 1929. Butler, true to his word, did not participate.[88] The Court's opinion was authored by McReynolds, who turned his argument on the fact that the Transportation Act required the ICC in its valuation of the O'Fallon line to "give due consideration to all elements of value recognized by the law of the land for rate-making purposes." "This is an express command," McReynolds wrote, "and the carrier has a clear right to demand compliance therewith." The district court was therefore mistaken to sidestep the question of proper agency valuation. "Whether the Commission acted as directed by Congress was the fundamental question presented. If it did not, the action taken, being beyond the authority granted, was invalid."[89] Even though the excess income recaptured by the ICC may not have been confiscatory, it might nevertheless be illegal if not determined according to appropriate statutory standards.

Stressing his own opinion in *Southwestern Bell Telephone*, McReynolds observed that "the present cost of construction or reproduction" had been an element "of value recognized by the law of the land for rate-making purposes" at least since *Smyth v. Ames*.[90] The ICC, however, had carefully refrained "from stating that any consideration whatever was given to present or reproduction costs in estimating the value of the carrier's property."[91] It followed that the ICC had "disregarded the approved rule and thereby failed to discharge the definite duty imposed by Congress."[92]

As originally drafted, McReynolds's opinion seemed to accept the railroads' contention that the cost of reproduction must be the primary "rule" to be applied in valuation proceedings. But Brandeis circulated a detailed, powerful dissent demonstrating with embarrassing specificity that any such mechanical application of a cost of reproduction rule to railroad valuation would be nonsensical. Many railroad lines had "been scrapped since 1920," for example, because they had "become valueless for transportation, either because traffic ceased to be available or because competitive means of transportation precluded the establishment of remunerative rail rates. Obviously, no one would contend that their actual value just before abandonment was what it originally cost to construct them or what it would then have cost to reconstruct them."[93] The valuation of railroads thus differed from the valuation of monopolies like the water companies at issue in *Bluefield Water Works* or *McCardle*, where there was no elasticity of demand and no readily available substitutes. Any sensible evaluation of railroads must account for their ability to attract business, whereas the value of monopolies of nonsubstitutable essential goods like water and electricity need not be theoretically limited in this way.[94]

The circulation of Brandeis's dissent produced an instantaneous impact. Immediately after its distribution[95] McReynolds announced at the Court's conference of May 12 "that the CJ wanted this [paragraph] inserted & that he (McR) was willing:"[96]

> The question on which the Commission divided is this: When seeking to ascertain the value of railroad property for recapture purposes, must it give consideration to current, or reproduction costs? The weight to be accorded thereto is not the matter before us. No doubt there are some, perhaps many, railroads the ultimate value of which should be placed far below the sum necessary for reproduction. But Congress has directed that values shall be fixed upon a consideration of present costs along with all other pertinent facts, and this mandate must be obeyed.

Even in his last year on the Court, and despite his failing health, Taft was able adroitly to intervene to prevent his more ideologically inclined colleagues from imposing abstractly unworkable views.

It would have been conceptually catastrophic for the Court to have required the ICC to follow a crude cost of reproduction measure of value as a dominant consideration in valuation.[97] But Taft's paragraph specifically negated this implication.[98] It instead asserted that the ICC had committed the legal error of categorically ruling out *any* consideration of the cost of reproduction.[99] Taft's paragraph ensured that the Court said nothing whatever about how the cost of reproduction should affect any ultimate conclusion. It effectively transformed the Court's opinion into a mere slap on the ICC's wrist for having had the audacity overtly to criticize the Court's cases.[100]

Thus what began the week of May 20 as the "greatest lawsuit in history," ended the week as a bust.[101] Newspaper headlines initially reported the decision as a significant railroad victory that portended a "Possible Doubling of Present Book Value" and a "Rise in Rates."[102] Railroad stocks kited up.[103] But as the *O'Fallon* opinion was more closely scrutinized, and as the implications of Taft's crucial paragraph were digested, the decision came to appear "less clear-cut.... Rail stocks sagged again, and editors and correspondents began to wonder whether the decision would have any effect except to throw the whole valuation situation into confusion and make more work for the Interstate Commerce Commission and the railroad lawyers."[104] The realization sunk in that the "most remarkable feature of the decision by the Supreme Court of the O'Fallon case is the uncertainty in which it leaves the law concerning the valuation of public utilities, despite the tremendous effort of all the participants to obtain a clear statement of just what the law is."[105] "The Supreme Court has told the Interstate Commerce Commission how not to make a valuation. It has not told it how to make one."[106]

The upshot of *O'Fallon*'s ambiguous resolution was widespread realization that ICC determinations of value were ultimately a side issue, because "the determinant of rates is generally what the traffic will bear, and with increasing competition from water routes, trucks and buses it would be hazardous to attempt any general revision upward of rates."[107] *The World* editorialized that availability of motor vehicles to carry freight cheaply meant that railroads would not be able to take advantage of an ICC reevaluation of their capital value to raise rates.[108] No doubt that is why President Hoover almost immediately pronounced that "I am confident that there will be no increase in railway rates as the result of the O'Fallon decision."[109]

Almost inadvertently, therefore, *O'Fallon* triggered public acknowledgment of the essential premise of Brandeis's brilliant dissent. The value of railroad property ultimately depends upon public demand for railroad services, which in turn depends upon competitive substitutes. To imagine that the value of railroad property could be ascertained by reproduction costs alone, apart from the entire national system of transportation within which it was embedded, was to miss the forest for the trees.[110]

Brandeis's commitment to a purposive public law allowed him to see that the ICC's essential task in evaluating the value of railroad property was to justify rates necessary to achieve the objective of the Transportation Act, which was "the maintenance of an adequate national system of railway transportation, capable of providing the best possible service to the public at the lowest cost consistent with full justice to the private owners."[111] The value of railroad properties was thus

889

a function of the rates necessary to serve this purpose.[112] McReynolds's original opinion, by implying that railroad rates hinged instead on rights of private property that were somehow independent not merely of the purposes of the Transportation Act but also of the competitive market itself, had pushed the Court to the brink of conceptual and practical disaster.

The conservative press praised *O'Fallon* because "The Supreme Court has again stood as a bulwark against disregard of the rights of property."[113] That was indeed the ideological message conveyed by the decision.[114] But, in reality, it was only Taft's timely intervention, an intervention that rendered the *O'Fallon* decision virtually meaningless, that allowed the Court to maintain the false impression that ratemaking was somehow determined by the "independent" value of property.[115]

By the following term, however, Taft was too ill and distracted to hold back his colleagues, who were anxious to press for ever greater returns to private capital. *United Railways and Electric Co. v. West*,[116] a case involving the constitutionality of rates imposed on a Baltimore street car company, was argued on October 29, 1929, and it was not decided until January 6, 1930, the very day on which Taft decided to withdraw from the Court to recuperate from disabling illness.[117] Sutherland, writing for six justices,[118] flatly asserted that "It is the settled rule of this Court that the rate base is present value."[119] Gone was the subtlety that Taft had inserted into the *O'Fallon* opinion.

The primary controversy in *West* concerned less the valuation of the utility's property than the rate of return the company was constitutionally entitled to receive on the value of its property.[120] The operative test for this question had been explained by Butler in 1923 in *Bluefield Water Works & Improvement Co.*:

> A public utility is entitled to such rates as will permit it to earn a return on the value of the property which it employs for the convenience of the public equal to that generally being made at the same time and in the same general part of the country on investments in other business undertakings which are attended by corresponding risks and uncertainties; but it has no constitutional right to profits such as are realized or anticipated in highly profitable enterprises or speculative ventures. The return should be reasonably sufficient to assure confidence in the financial soundness of the utility and should be adequate, under efficient and economical management, to maintain and support its credit and enable it to raise the money necessary for the proper discharge of its public duties. A rate of return may be reasonable at one time and become too high or too low by changes affecting opportunities for investment, the money market and business conditions generally.[121]

Sutherland invoked this passage, adding that "the fundamental principle to be observed is that the property of a public utility, although devoted to the public service and impressed with a public interest, is still private property; and neither the corpus of that property nor the use thereof constitutionally can be taken for a compulsory price which falls below the measure of just compensation." The measure of just compensation was to be determined "by

Ratemaking & Judicial Legitimacy

present day conditions." The question is "not capable of exact mathematical demonstration. It is a matter more or less of approximation about which conclusions may differ." Sutherland suggested that "There is much evidence in the record to the effect that in order to induce the investment of capital in the enterprise or to enable the company to compete successfully in the market for money to finance its operations, a net return upon the valuation fixed by the commission should be not far from 8 per cent." But because the company itself had sought from the state commission a rate that would produce a return of only 7.44 percent, Sutherland ruled only that the enforcement of any rates "producing less than this would be confiscatory and in violation of the due process clause of the Fourteenth Amendment."[122]

This was a stunning holding, given that the Transportation Act itself had authorized rates of return of only 5.5–6 percent on the fair value of railroad property, and that the Act had authorized the recapture of income above 6 percent.[123] By requiring that utilities receive rates of return that in the Court's view would make them competitive in unregulated markets, the Court effectively endowed utilities with entitlements that would render them financially equivalent to ordinary property.

Sutherland's opinion in *West* ignored the possibility that public utilities might attract capital with a somewhat lower rate of return than ordinary businesses because they were in some respects effectively monopolies, whose stability and earning power were assured by detailed state regulation. His opinion also seemed hostile to the premise that utilities were a special form of property that could be subordinated to overriding public purposes, a premise that had informed the Transportation Act of 1920.[124] Sutherland appeared to conceptualize property affected with a public interest as entitled to profits equal to those of ordinary property in private markets. The overriding importance of the public interest, which the nation had accepted from the progressive era through the end of the war, was apparently undermined.

Sutherland made no effort to justify the Court's holding in the moralizing discourse that suffused opinions like *Adkins* or *Meyer*. That discourse would scarcely have been convincing in the highly regulated context of property affected with a public interest. Sutherland thus emphasized instead prerogatives that he understood to be inherent in the institution of property itself. These prerogatives followed directly from Sutherland's foundational belief that the constitutional function of property was to facilitate economic development. From this perspective, it may well have made sense to compare railroad rates to the earning capacity of ordinary property in unregulated markets. But to the general public, this form of reasoning seemed indistinguishable from policy judgments routinely made by legislators about the rates necessary to secure adequate capital for railroads and utilities.

Less than a month after *West* was announced, Taft officially resigned, and Hoover nominated Charles Evans Hughes to replace him. Hughes's nomination was expected to sail through the Senate, but, suddenly and unexpectedly, an "intense," "amazing fight" erupted. A "formidable" coalition of progressive Republicans and Democrats attacked Hughes because his presumed views "on economic questions" associated him with the conservative wing of the Taft Court.[125] All conceded

Hughes's distinguished professional qualifications and legal competence, but senators feared that his extensive corporate practice would lead him to view ratemaking cases through the lens of corporate interests.[126]

West became a lightning rod for opposition to Hughes.[127] The case was, in Brandeis's words, "the last straw."[128] Senator Norris read the entire opinion into the congressional record.[129] Senator after senator attacked the decision.[130] Senator La Follette noted that, "carried to its logical conclusion," *West* implied "the destruction of all regulatory power. ... [A]s you increase the rate of return which these corporations may enjoy you finally reach a point where they are entitled by judicial sanction to charge rates which are all that the traffic will bear. We are, through the action of the court, driven back to the position which we occupied when this fight for regulation of these public-service corporations first began in this country."[131]

Senators chose to discuss *West* "not because Justice Hughes was a member of the court" when it was decided,

> but for the reason that ... Justice Hughes is associated in his views with the contention which is sustained by the majority, and which, in the end, if carried to its logical conclusion, must result in great economic oppression to the people of the United States. ... As Justice Sutherland says in his majority opinion, what constitutes confiscation is not a thing that one can mathematically ascertain. ... [I]t is according to the view of whether one is thinking most about property and the rights of property or about human rights or the rights of individuals. ... [W]hen we are passing upon this matter we are entitled to take into consideration the views upon constitutional and economic questions which the nominee entertains.[132]

West was attacked on the ground that it did not declare law, but instead imposed the policy views of the conservative wing of the Taft Court. Senators accordingly asserted that they were entitled to evaluate Hughes according to his political convictions rather than his legal competence. They argued that "The views of Mr Hughes on economic questions are just as important as his legal ability."[133] The confirmation of Pierce Butler was cited as a negative precedent. Butler "on the bench ... has supported the same theories of valuation that he so ably championed as the spokesman of the carriers."[134] A bipartisan coalition of progressive senators did not wish to repeat that mistake. They openly espoused the view that the court needed justices who represented more liberal views of property, like those expressed by Brandeis.[135] They explicitly challenged the relevance of party affiliation[136] and sought instead to determine whether Hughes held "progressive" or "reactionary" views on property.[137]

Ultimately, the debate over Hughes's nomination drew into question the Court's prerogative to declare "law" that the public was obliged to "respect and obey."[138] Senators who disagreed with *West*'s interpretation of the Fourteenth Amendment defiantly objected that *West* did not properly interpret the Constitution. They argued that *West* instead reflected the personal views of six members of the Court, who were "writing economic theories into their decisions."[139] Insofar as *West* was experienced as muddying the boundary between legal and political judgment, the Court's authority as a peremptory oracle of the law was diminished.

West provoked a public debate that helped fix the popular image of the Taft Court as a bastion of ideological reaction insistent on maintaining the constitutional prerogatives of property in the face of pressing contrary public needs.[140] Only a dozen years before, the federal government had taken over the railroads, and, in the Transportation Act of 1920, Congress had insisted that public control was necessary to preserve the health of the national rail system. The Taft Court, in its ratemaking cases, seemed intent on recreating a prewar world where even property affected with a public interest could claim the same rewards as ordinary property. The Court did not purport to justify these rewards by reference to a realm of individual moral freedom. To large sectors of the country, the Court was attempting to protect property affected with a public interest based upon mere judgments of policy about the proper role of property in contributing to the material growth of civilization. The pushback was bipartisan and intense.

The Hughes hearings were in fact shocking. "There has never been such a spectacle as has just been witnessed, an open, mass attack upon the Supreme Court, a tearing away, as one senator after another said in the three days of debate, of its sanctity, of the cloak of immunity from criticism which it has heretofore generally enjoyed."[141] The day after Hughes's confirmation, progressive Washington Senator Clarence Dill rose to respond to charges "that the Senate has dragged the Supreme Court into politics as has not been done in our time."[142] Unrepentant, Dill proclaimed that "the Supreme Court of this country will be in politics or will not be in politics, depending entirely upon whether or not this system of writing into the valuations of the great public utilities that provide the necessities of life continues or not. It is for the judges to say."[143]

By February 1930, fully a third of the senators voting on the confirmation of Hughes had come to believe that the compensation owed to property affected with a public interest was a question of public policy best left in the political arena. Judges were neither qualified nor empowered to determine the incentives necessary to insure adequate capital investment in public utilities. "The Senate fight over the appointment of Charles Evans Hughes," editorialized the *Washington Daily News*, "is one of the most significant developments in the political life of the nation in many years. That is true altogether apart from the virtues or the defects of Hughes' appointment as such." This was because "the Court in major cases has ... become a policy-forming body."

> The curious and dangerous aspect of this long development of Supreme Court supremacy as a virtual law-making body is that it has occurred without public awareness.
>
> Instead of watching the Court's growing power, the unsuspecting public has come to render the Court a degree of reverence which approaches perilously close to idolatry. Of all our American institutions, including the presidency, it is the one which few dare criticize.

> We have lost the early American independence which held no political institution above the critical judgment of sovereign citizens. By what servile-mindedness, by what medieval superstition or mummery of mace and gown have we vested with perfection nine fellow citizens who are political appointees?
>
> The Senate debate on the Hughes nomination is significant because it breaks thru this hush-hush and ah-ah atmosphere surrounding the Court, daring to examine that political and very human institution for what it is worth.[144]

No doubt the justices of the Taft Court who decided *West* assumed that the Court would be accorded what we have called the authority of finality.[145] Because *West* was rendered by the Court in the course of its proper jurisdiction, and because the Court's decision was unappealable, the justices expected that its opinion would be deferentially received as a definitive declaration of existing law. But the fierce pushback to Hughes's nomination illustrates the vulnerability of the authority of finality once it is suspected that a court is pursuing a political rather than a legal agenda. In such situations the decisions of a court are authoritative only if the court itself is perceived as legitimate.

Although no one questioned the dispositive, binding authority of *West* on the parties to the case, the question debated in the Senate was whether, going forward, *West*'s doctrine was a valid interpretation of the Fourteenth Amendment, or whether the Senate should push back against the Court's interpretation by confirming only candidates who might read the Constitution differently. In reaching out in *West* to declare that a 7.44 percent return on the value of capital invested in railroads was constitutionally required, the Taft Court overreached. It reaped the whirlwind, tasting the shock and bitterness of battles yet to come. It is surely no accident that the explosion was triggered by a decision that expressed, purely and simply, the constitutional narrative that property was to be protected to ensure the material growth of the economy, rather than to safeguard the independent moral agency of persons.

Ratemaking & Judicial Legitimacy
Notes

1. *Adkins v. Children's Hospital of the District of Columbia*, 261 U.S. 525, 546 (1923).
2. Chicago, Burlington, and Quincy Railroad Co. v. Iowa, 94 U.S. 155, 161 (1876). In 1887, the economist Henry C. Adams published his pathbreaking work on businesses that "are by nature monopolies" because they followed "the principle of increasing returns." Henry C. Adams, *Relation of the State to Industrial Action*, 1 PUBLICATIONS OF THE AMERICAN ECONOMIC ASSOCIATION 1, 64 (1887). Adams considered "the railroad business" as a good illustration of a natural monopoly, and for this reason Adams believed that it required "the superior control of state power." *Id.* at 55, 61. On the influence of Adams's work, see DANIEL T. RODGERS, ATLANTIC CROSSINGS: SOCIAL POLITICS IN A PROGRESSIVE AGE 107–8 (Cambridge: Harvard University Press 1998).
3. Munn v. Illinois, 94 U.S. 113, 134 (1876).
4. Stone v. Farmers' Loan & Trust Co., 116 U.S. 307, 331 (1886).
5. 169 U.S. 466 (1898). *See* Edwin C. Goddard, *The Evolution of Cost of Reproduction as the Rate Base*, 41 HARVARD LAW REVIEW 564, 564 (1928).
6. *Smyth*, 169 U.S. at 546–47.
7. CHARLES F. PHILLIPS, JR., THE REGULATION OF PUBLIC UTILITIES: THEORY AND PRACTICE 305–7 (Arlington: Public Utilities Reports 1988).
8. "Fair value has been fixed with reference to some compound of contradictory considerations concocted by the alchemy of uncontrolled and changeful compromise." T.R. Powell, *Protecting Property and Liberty, 1922–1924*, 40 POLITICAL SCIENCE QUARTERLY 404, 407 (1925).
9. "It has long since become a commonplace of rate regulation that to judge the reasonableness of rates by the return they yield on the value of the property is to reason in a circle, for the value is the result of the rates charged." Robert L. Hale, *Political and Economic Review: Public Utility Valuation*, 9 AMERICAN BAR ASSOCIATION JOURNAL 392, 392 (1923). No one contended that the mere salvage value of railroads or utilities represented an accurate measure of their worth.
10. Gerard C. Henderson, *Railway Valuation and the Courts*, 33 HARVARD LAW REVIEW 902, 1032 (1920). *See* James C. Bonbright, *The Breakdown of "Present Value" as a Basis of Rate Control*, 14 PROCEEDINGS OF THE ACADEMY OF POLITICAL SCIENCE 75, 75 (1930).
11. "The whole doctrine of *Smyth v. Ames* rests upon a gigantic illusion. The fact which for twenty years the court has been vainly trying to find does not exist. 'Fair value' must be shelved among the great juristic myths of history, with the Law of Nature and the Social Contract. As a practical concept, from which practical conclusions can be drawn, it is valueless." Henderson, *supra* note 10, at 1051. *See* Robert L. Hale, *Rate Making and the Revision of the Property Concept*, 22 COLUMBIA LAW REVIEW 209 (1922). Stone's sympathy with this critique is evident in a letter that he wrote Herbert Hoover in 1926: "You will find the articles by Henderson and Hale quite illuminating ... and both point out what they regard as economic fallacies of the courts and [sic] determining what rates are confiscatory." HFS to Herbert Hoover (December 14, 1926) (Stone papers). *See* West v. Chesapeake & Potomac Telephone Co. of Baltimore City, 295 U.S. 662, 689–90 (1935) (Stone, J., dissenting).
12. For an illuminating discussion of the jurisprudential and intellectual controversies over ratemaking, see Stephen A. Siegel, *Understanding the Lochner Era: Lessons*

from the Controversy over Railroad and Utility Rate Regulation, 70 VIRGINIA LAW REVIEW 187 (1984).

13. WHT to Robert A. Taft (October 21, 1928) (Taft papers). When Robert L. Hale wrote Taft to point out the "vicious circle" that lay at the heart of the Court's ratemaking cases, Robert L. Hale to WHT (March 28, 1927) (Taft papers), Taft replied, "I am sorry that I can not discuss with you what you think is a vicious circle in the reasoning of the majority of the court on this question. I am afraid that if I were to enter upon the question, I should have to give up my work on other cases in the Court. The question of rates is most difficult." WHT to Robert L. Hale (April 1, 1927) (Taft papers).

14. OWH to Harold Laski (April 18, 1924), in 1 HOLMES-LASKI CORRESPONDENCE, at 610.

15. OWH to Harold Laski (October 23, 1926), in 2 HOLMES-LASKI CORRESPONDENCE, at 887–88. In Cedar Rapids Gas Light Co. v. City of Cedar Rapids, 223 U.S. 655, 669–70 (1912), Holmes conceptualized the problem of fair value not as a question of property, but instead as a question of the political bargain struck between government and its utilities:

> An adjustment of this sort under a power to regulate rates has to steer between Scylla and Charybdis. On the one side, if the franchise is taken to mean that the most profitable return that could be got, free from competition, is protected by the 14th Amendment, then the power to regulate is null. On the other hand, if the power to regulate withdraws the protection of the Amendment altogether, then the property is nought. This is not a matter of economic theory, but of fair interpretation of a bargain. Neither extreme can have been meant. A midway between them must be hit.

When Robert L. Hale sent Holmes his article arguing "that the Supreme Court should definitely repudiate Smyth v. Ames and all its brood," Robert L. Hale to OWH (April 3, 1922) (Holmes papers), Holmes responded that "I share your skepticism in large part, although I do not feel driven to some of the conclusions that I suppose to be yours." *See* OWH to Robert L. Hale (April 6, 1922) (Holmes papers). "I think I showed that I understood the difficulty years ago but the problem that my father used to put to me as a little boy – What would happen if an irresistible encountered an immovable body – or its analogue sometimes meets us in the law without reducing us to despair. And if you should say so much the worse for the judges I should not agree." *Id.*

Hale answered with a call for repudiating "*Smyth* v. *Ames* with all its progeny and starting afresh ... charting the course between Scylla and Charybdis ... by deciding consciously how close you want to sail to each, instead of pretending to steer straight for Scylla while escaping it only by tampering with the compass." Robert L. Hale to OWH (April 8, 1922) (Holmes papers). Holmes replied with a twinkle: "Possibly your letter thinks me in need of more explanation of the seeming impasse than I am. If I ever have the pleasure of seeing you I will tell you the profound formula that I once whispered in Brandeis' ear but I dare not write it. I hope that the time may come." OWH to Robert L. Hale (April 10, 1922) (Holmes papers).

16. WHT to Robert A. Taft (October 21, 1928) (Taft papers). For examples of Brandeis's opinions in this area, see Galveston Electric Co. v. City of Galveston, 258 U.S. 388 (1922); Georgia Ry. & Power Co. v. Railroad Commission of Georgia, 262 U.S. 625 (1923); and Northern Pac. Ry. Co. v. Department of Public Works of

Washington, 268 U.S. 39 (1925). For examples of Butler's opinions in this area, see City of Paducah v. Paducah Ry. Co., 261 U.S. 267 (1923); Bluefield Waterworks & Improvement Co. v. Public Service Comm'n of West Virginia, 262 U.S. 679 (1923); Banton v. Belt Line Ry. Corp., 268 U.S. 413 (1925); Board of Public Utility Comm'rs v. New York Telephone Co., 271 U.S. 23 (1926); McCardle v. Indianapolis Water Co., 272 U.S. 400 (1926); Aetna Ins. Co. v. Hyde, 275 U.S. 440 (1928); and Railroad Comm'n of California v. Los Angeles Ry. Corp., 280 U.S. 145 (1929). For examples of McReynolds's opinions in this area, see Missouri *ex rel.* Southwestern Bell Telephone Co. v. Public Service Comm'n of Missouri, 262 U.S. 276 (1923); Ottinger v. Consolidated Gas Co. of New York, 272 U.S. 576 (1926); Pacific Gas & Electric Co. v. City and County of San Francisco, 265 U.S. 403 (1924); Brimstone R. & Canal Co. v. United States, 276 U.S. 104 (1928); Gilchrist v. Interborough Rapid Transit Co., 279 U.S. 159 (1929); and St. Louis & O'Fallon Ry. Co. v. United States, 279 U.S. 461 (1929). It is odd that Taft did not mention Sutherland in this context, for Sutherland also authored many important ratemaking decisions. *See, e.g.*, Brush Electric Co. v. City of Galveston, 262 U.S. 443 (1923); Ohio Utilities Co. v. Public Utilities Comm'n of Ohio, 267 U.S. 359 (1925); Smith v. Illinois Bell Telephone Co., 270 U.S. 587 (1926); United Railways & Electric Co. of Baltimore v. West, 280 U.S. 234 (1930).

17. For Butler's strong views before coming to the Court, see Pierce Butler, *Valuation of Railway Property for Purposes of Rate Regulation*, 23 JOURNAL OF POLITICAL ECONOMY 17 (1915). Butler denied that the valuation of railroad property was caught in a vicious circle. He instead believed that "the ascertainment of the value of a thing, whether it be a vacant lot or a railroad property, is the determination of a fact, and that the same property cannot be of two or more different values at one time." *Id.* at 17. Yet Butler was notably vague about how the "fact" of the value of railroad properties was to be ascertained. He was clear that *"the same principles govern valuation of railroad property for the purpose of rate regulation as apply in the case of condemnation of private property for public use."* *Id.* at 23 (emphasis in the original). But, as Butler was the first to argue, value in ordinary takings cases was to be determined by the competitive market. *See supra* Chapter 22, at 722. The absence of an analogous competitive market for railroads, precisely because of the presence of ratemaking, rendered it unclear how Butler imagined that he had escaped from the vicious circle. Butler also held that it was "a mistake to suppose that railroad rates are, or as a practical matter can be, *made* or *based upon* the value of the property used to render the service." *Id.* at 19. Yet he was also clear that rates could by regulation be set unconstitutionally low and therefore confiscatory if they did not "yield a fair return upon the full value of the property." *Id.* at 25.

18. Bluefield Waterworks & Improvement Co. v. Public Service Commission of West Virginia, 262 U.S. 679, 692 (1923). *See* McCardle v. Indianapolis Water Co., 272 U.S. 400, 408–11 (1926).

19. Missouri *ex rel.* Southwestern Bell Telephone Co. v. Public Service Comm'n of Missouri, 262 U.S. 276, 290–91, 306–7 (1923) (Brandeis, J., dissenting from opinion). *See* McCardle v. Indianapolis Water Co., 272 U.S. 400, 421–24 (1926) (Brandeis, J., dissenting).

20. It is likely that Taft was personally committed to a cost of reproduction theory. At the time of Taft's nomination to be chief justice, he was serving as one of three arbitrators tasked with determining the value of the Grand Trunk Railway in

Canada in the context of its nationalization. *See* John A. Eagle, *Monopoly or Competition: The Nationalization of the Grands Trunk Railway*, 62 CANADIAN HISTORICAL REVIEW 3, 29 (1981). In his opinion in that proceeding, Taft urged:

> The question to be settled is of a class of questions the most difficult ever presented to a tribunal, to wit, to determine the fair value of a great railway System. . . .
>
> [I]t seemed to me a proper course to allow the company and the shareholders to offer in evidence proof of the reproduction value of the whole Grand Trunk Railway System. . . . Such evidence is held in the United States to be competent and relevant in adjudging what a railway company should earn and therefore to fix its rates. . . .
>
> Evidence of this kind here produced might have materially affected the opinion which the Board would form of the earning capacity of the road and its future possibilities, especially in view of the fact that the tendency of railway legislation in the United States, as shown by the last United States Transportation Act, is toward making the reproduction value of railroad property used economically for transportation a proper basis for fixing rates.

Reasons for Dissent by the Honourable William Howard Taft, in ANNUAL REPORT OF THE DEPARTMENT OF RAILWAYS AND CANALS FOR THE FISCAL YEAR FROM APRIL 1, 1920, TO MARCH 31, 1921, at 179, 187 (Ottawa: F.A. Acland 1921). The two non-American arbitrators, however, ruled that evidence of cost of reproduction was irrelevant to the question of value. *Reasons for Award by the Rt. Hon. Sir Thomas White*, *id.* at 169. Their ruling was upheld in England by the Privy Council. A.W. CURRIE, THE GRAND TRUNK RAILWAY OF CANADA 468 (Toronto: University of Toronto Press 1957). *See* LESLIE T. FOURNIER, RAILWAY NATIONALIZATION IN CANADA: THE PROBLEM OF THE CANADIAN NATIONAL RAILWAYS 100–116 (Toronto: MacMillan Co. of Canada 1935).
21. 262 U.S. 625 (1923).
22. 262 U.S. 276 (1923).
23. Butler's lack of participation in these cases is scrupulously noted in his docket book.
24. Brandeis apparently learned the new theory from Robert Lee Hale. The story is nicely told in DANIEL R. ERNST, TOCQUEVILLE'S NIGHTMARE: THE ADMINISTRATIVE STATE EMERGES IN AMERICA, 1900–1940, at 46–48 (Oxford University Press 2014).
25. *Brandeis-Frankfurter Conversations*, at 316 (July 1, 1923). *See* LDB to Alice Goldmark Brandeis (May 8, 1923), in 5 LETTERS OF LOUIS D. BRANDEIS, at 93 ("Next Saturday has been specifically assigned for the exclusive consideration of my elaborate memo; – so you see we are very friendly."). "Taft," observed Brandeis, "hasn't the slightest grasp of fiscal or utility aspects of these cases. P. Butler is about what people said he was. He is gunning after valuation of land grants in land grant roads." *Brandeis-Frankfurter Conversations*, at 311 (June 12, 1923).
26. The entry is under the *Georgia Ry. & Power Co.* case. Butler added: "PB takes no part in this." Butler had emphatically written in 1915 that "The substitution of *cost* for *value* and the making of rates on that basis would unjustly deny reward and profit to the owners of the best railroads of the country and amount to seizure of the use of private property without just compensation." Butler, *supra* note 17, at 24.

27. PHILLIPS, *supra* note 7, at 307–13.
28. Charles G. Ross, *An Exposition of the Vital Problem of Valuation: Prudent Investment Principle Regards All Public Utilities in Light of Servants of the State*, ST. LOUIS POST DISPATCH (May 15, 1927), at 1; Alfred Evens, *Valuation in the Supreme Court*, 16 AMERICAN BAR ASSOCIATION JOURNAL 485, 485–86 (1930).
29. Ross, *supra* note 28.
30. PHILLIPS, *supra* note 7, at 307. *See* D. PHILIP LOCKLIN, ECONOMICS OF TRANSPORTATION 380 (7th ed., Homewood: Richard D. Irwin, Inc. 1972); Hugh Evander Willis, *The Rate Base for Rate Regulation*, 3 INDIANA LAW JOURNAL 225, 230–31 (1927); Evens, *supra* note 28, at 487; *The O'Fallon Decision*, 59 NEW REPUBLIC 30 (1929).
31. *Adkins*, 261 U.S. at 546.
32. *See, e.g.*, Smyth v. Ames, 169 U.S. 466, 544 (1898) ("A railroad is a public highway, and none the less so because constructed and maintained through the agency of a corporation deriving its existence and powers from the State. Such a corporation was created for public purposes. It performs a function of the State. Its authority to exercise the right of eminent domain and to charge tolls was given primarily for the benefit of the public. It is under governmental control, though such control must be exercised with due regard to the guaranties for the protection of its property. It cannot, therefore, be admitted that a railroad corporation maintaining a highway under the authority of the State may fix its rates with a view solely to its own interests, and ignore the rights of the public."); Milheim v. Moffat Tunnel Improvement District, 262 U.S. 710, 719 (1923) ("As a railroad is a highway for public use, although owned by a private corporation, a State may impose or authorize a tax in aid of its construction and in furtherance of such public use.").
33. *See* James C. Bonbright, *The Problem of Judicial Valuation*, 27 COLUMBIA LAW REVIEW 493, 505 (1927) ("The distinction ... between rate-making value and market value ... is far from adequately recognized. Yet it is a distinction which underlies the whole theory of public utility regulation, a theory which is based on the principle that ... public utilities ... should not be allowed to charge whatever prices they might be able to charge if their power to coerce customers by means of the bargaining process were not limited.").

The difference between market value and ratemaking value in fact prompted Taft's magisterial opinion in Dayton-Goose Creek Railway Co. v. United States, 263 U.S. 456 (1924), which upheld the recapture provisions of the Transportation Act of 1920: "[T]he carrier owning and operating a railroad, however strong financially, however economical in its facilities, or favorably situated as to traffic, is not entitled as of constitutional right to more than a fair net operating income upon the value of its properties which are being devoted to transportation." *Id.* at 481. On the radical quality of Taft's reasoning, see Leslie Craven, *Railroad Valuation: A Statement of the Problem*, 9 AMERICAN BAR ASSOCIATION JOURNAL 681, 686 (1923), which argues that a failure to recognize the economic value arising from "superior location" is "an appropriation of the property rights in the physical property. ... The fact that a railroad is 'affected with a public interest' has up to this time justified its regulation in order to insure the performance of its public duties, but it has not yet been held that railroad property is so out of the category of private property as to justify the appropriation without compensation of those increments of value due to these differentials, which increments could probably not be taken from the owner of the business lots of a city or the ranch owner on the plains, without an overturning of the very government itself."

The unanswered question at the heart of the cost of reproduction theory of value is why, if the owner of a business affected with a public interest is not constitutionally entitled to the return that he might obtain in the market, including the market value of the location of the physical property of the business, he is nevertheless *constitutionally* entitled to the market value of reproducing the physical property of the business.

34. In the early days of ratemaking regulation, it was difficult to ascertain the amount of capital prudently invested in railroads and utilities, so that Brandeis's proposed test could not easily be applied. But the rationalization of capital markets had by the 1920s made it relatively simple to assess capital investments. By contrast, it was a commonplace observation that the cost of reproduction test produced erratic and unpredictable results. As Brandeis observed:

> The adoption of the amount prudently invested as the rate base and the amount of the capital charge as the measure of the rate of return would give definiteness to these two factors involved in rate controversies which are now shifting and treacherous, and which render the proceedings peculiarly burdensome and largely futile. Such measures offer a basis for decision which is certain and stable. The rate base would be ascertained as a fact, not determined as matter of opinion. It would not fluctuate with the market price of labor, or materials, or money. It would not change with hard times or shifting populations. It would not be distorted by the fickle and varying judgments of appraisers, commissions, or courts. It would, when once made in respect to any utility, be fixed, for all time, subject only to increases to represent additions to plant, after allowance for the depreciation included in the annual operating charges. The wild uncertainties of the present method of fixing the rate base under the so-called rule of Smyth v. Ames would be avoided, and likewise the fluctuations which introduce into the enterprise unnecessary elements of speculation, create useless expense, and impose upon the public a heavy, unnecessary burden.

Missouri *ex rel.* Southwestern Bell Telephone Co. v. Public Service Comm'n of Missouri, 262 U.S. 276, 306–7 (1923) (Brandeis, J., dissenting from opinion). See Willis, *supra* note 30, at 231 ("[T]he chief objection to reproduction cost is its uncertainty. It is nothing but a guess. The engineering estimates required are airy calculations on impossible assumptions."); Donald R. Richberg, *Value – By Judicial Fiat*, 40 HARVARD LAW REVIEW 567, 570 (1927) (arguing that the cost of reproduction theory "makes the entire process of valuation one of imaginative guess work. The evidence to be considered must consist wholly of opinions of partisan experts, estimating the cost of an imaginary but impossible construction, at imaginary and impossible prices, under imaginary and impossible conditions."). A particularly useful explication of the relative merits of the cost of reproduction and prudent investment theories of valuation is James C. Bonbright, *Railroad Valuation with Special Reference to the O'Fallon Decision*, 18 AMERICAN ECONOMIC REVIEW 181 (1927).

35. St. Louis & O'Fallon Railway Co. v. United States, 279 U.S. 461, 517–18, 532 (1929) (Brandeis, J., dissenting).

36. *See infra* text at note 93.

Ratemaking & Judicial Legitimacy

37. Those advocating for a cost of reproduction theory of value typically focused on the more ascertainable cost of reproducing the physical plant. *See, e.g.*, McCardle v. Indianapolis Water Co., 272 U.S. 400, 417–18 (1926) ("There is to be ascertained the value of the plant used to give the service and not the estimated cost of a different plant. Save under exceptional circumstances, the court is not required to enter upon a comparison of the merits of different systems. Such an inquiry would lead to collateral issues and investigations having only remote bearing on the fact to be found, viz. the value of the property devoted to the service of the public."). The Court's approach can be economically justified only on the assumption that the cost of reproducing a physical plant is an efficient proxy for the cost of providing the service, and this assumption is highly questionable.
38. Stephen Breyer, *Economics for Lawyers and Judges*, 33 JOURNAL OF LEGAL EDUCATION 294, 297–99 (1983). In 1924, the Progressive Party advocated in its platform for "the fixing of railroads rates upon the basis of actual, prudent investment and cost of service." Platform of the Progressive Party, 1924, available at www.presidency.ucsb.edu/documents/progressive-party-platform-1924.
39. WHT to WVD (June 22, 1927) (Van Devanter papers). In his letter, Taft was most likely referring to the discussion in Ross, *supra* note 28, which considered how votes on the Court might line up to support a prudential investment theory of valuation.
40. 262 U.S. 276, 287–88 (1923). Butler and Sanford did not participate in the decision.
41. *Southwestern Bell*, 262 U.S. at 290 (Brandeis, J., dissenting from opinion). Although Brandeis concurred with the Court's judgment of reversal, he styled his intervention as "dissenting from opinion." Holmes joined Brandeis's opinion. He wrote Brandeis: "I am inclined to follow you in this but am embarrassed by not having heard the discussion." (Brandeis papers).
42. The impact of Brandeis's opinion was immediate and powerful. *See Certainty and Confusion in Public Utility Rates*, 35 NEW REPUBLIC 33 (1923) ("The majority opinion unfortunately stands for the present as the law. In the future ... public service commissions will have to struggle with competing technical estimates as to cost of reproduction before they can determine fair rates. They will still have to reckon as part of the cost of service an arbitrary percentage on an arbitrary physical valuation, instead of the actual capital charges embodied in the contracts on which security issues are based. But the absurdity of such a proceeding condemns it to disappearance in the end. No one who reads Judge Brandeis's opinion can doubt that it outlines the law of the future."); Donald R. Richberg, *The Supreme Court Discusses Value*, 37 HARVARD LAW REVIEW 291, 296 (1924) ("During an argument upon valuation theory before the Interstate Commerce Commission in July, 1923, while the writer was quoting from the *Southwestern Bell* opinions, a railroad lawyer of considerable standing and of well-known antagonism to the 'prudent investment' theory was overheard remarking to a colleague: 'I do not know what the law is today, but in my judgment that Brandeis opinion is a statement of what the law is going to be.'"); Willis, *supra* note 30, at 226 ("The prudent investment theory ... has had the almost unanimous support of legal writers."). In 1924, La Follette reiterated his commitment to have the Interstate Commerce Commission ("ICC") "fix rates on the basis of the actual prudent investment of capital." Robert La Follette, *The La Follette Speech*, NEW YORK TIMES (September 2, 1924), at 2. *See supra* note 38.

The Taft Court

43. *Southwestern Bell*, 262 U.S. at 290 (Brandeis, J., dissenting from opinion). Taft himself, in Dayton-Goose Creek Ry. Co. v. United States, 263 U.S. 456 (1924), would later observe that "[b]y investment in a business dedicated to the public service the owner must recognize that, as compared with investment in private business, he can not expect either high or speculative dividends but that his obligation limits him to only fair or reasonable profit." *Id.* at 481.
44. 262 U.S. 625, 629–30 (1923). Taft returned the draft of Brandeis's opinion with the comment: "I confess I can't find in this opinion the dynomatic assault on that model of exact definition [unintelligible] that ever helpful guide of Harlan, J. in Smyth v. Ames. The horns of the alter are still unimpaired." McReynolds agreed to Brandeis's draft, but objected to this sentence in the proposed opinion: "The question on which this Court divided in the *Southwestern Bell Telephone* case is not involved here." McReynolds commented: "I rather think reference to a division by the court is not the best form." Brandeis retained the sentence in his published opinion. 262 U.S. at 631.
45. *Georgia Ry*, 262 U.S. at 636 (McKenna, J., dissenting).
46. *Brandeis-Frankfurter Conversations*, at 312 (June 12, 1923). Brandeis added two weeks later that he had "hoped to get Ga. Case out with Southwestern. But it was laid over for reconsideration & so was decided with full consideration, on June 11, & gained reinforcement through McKenna's dissent. Upshot is that reconstruction value is not measure but merely a factor and so needs to be considered, but in fact need not pay attention, as in Ga. Case." *Id.* at 314 (June 28, 1923).
47. *Bluefield*, 262 U.S. 679, 692 (1923). Sanford did not participate in the case.
48. *Id.* at 695 (Brandeis, J., concurring).
49. Edgar Bronson Tolman, *Review of Recent Supreme Court Decisions*, 9 American Bar Association Journal 627, 627 (1923).
50. *Public Utility Valuations for Rate Making Purposes*, 26 Michigan Law Review 89, 89 (1927). *See* William M. Wherry, *The O'Fallon Case*, 34 Commercial Law League Journal 696, 698 (1929).
51. Edward S. Corwin, *Constitutional Law in 1922–1923*, 18 American Political Science Review 49, 71 (1924). *See* Philip Barton Warren, *Value* as a *Rate Base for Public Utilities*, 6 Illinois Law Quarterly 98, 101 (1924) ("The last two apparently conflicting decisions of the United States Supreme Court, coming as they do upon the heels of the very definite and forceful pronouncement and application of the principle, in a decision handed down only a few days earlier, that any finding of value will not be sustained if it fails to give effect to reproduction costs at prevailing prices, has created the impression among advocates of original cost that the Supreme Court is not so certain that the position its previous decisions were leading to, *viz.*, that every finding of value must give substantial effect to reproduction costs, was correct. This impression is not justified."). Warren presciently noted that "Up to the date of these two apparently conflicting decisions rendered by the same court on the same day, it had been held that a commission could not immunize itself from reversal by the mere assertion in its findings that it had given consideration to reproduction costs, if as a matter of fact its value was based on original cost." *Id.* at 100.
52. 272 U.S. 400, 410–11 (1926). Holmes concurred in the result. *See* OWH to Felix Frankfurter (December 8, 1926), in Holmes-Frankfurter Correspondence, at 209. Brandeis, joined by Stone, dissented. Stone's 1925 docket book shows that the

vote at conference had been 5–4, with Sutherland and Sanford joining Brandeis and Stone. In the Brandeis papers there is a return from Sutherland on Brandeis's proposed dissent in which Sutherland remarks, "I had some doubt; but after reading Butler's opinion, I think it best to close the matter up as he has done." (Brandeis papers).

53. Butler had been rebuffed by Hughes's masterful opinion in The Minnesota Rate Cases, 230 U.S. 352 (1913). *See* ERNST, *supra* note 24, at 39–41.
54. *McCardle*, 272 U.S. at 422 (Brandeis, J., dissenting).
55. Richberg, *supra* note 34, at 567. "The majority opinion now puts a seal of approval on the practice of ascribing *decisive* weight to a method of determining value which is generally repudiated by practical men as impractical." *Id.* at 571.
56. *Public Utility Valuations for Rate Making Purposes*, *supra* note 50, at 90.
57. Gustavus H. Robinson, *The O'Fallon Case: Latest Battle in the Public Utility Valuation War*, 8 NORTH CAROLINA LAW REVIEW 3, 5 (1929) (*McCardle* "put the Supreme Court more definitely in opposition to Mr. Justice Brandeis' view.").
58. Willis, *supra* note 30, at 228–29. *See U.S. Supreme Court Deals with Important Utility Questions*, 40 AMERICAN CITY MAGAZINE 90 (June 1929) (stating *McCardle* came out "flatly for reproduction cost"). For the contrary view, that *McCardle* merely "reaffirmed Smyth v. Ames," *see* Evens, *supra* note 28, at 490. Evens cites Butler's observation that "The weight to be given to ... cost figures and other items or classes of evidence is to be determined in the light of the facts of the case at hand." 272 U.S. at 410.
59. *Again the American People Will Pay*, CAPITAL TIMES (December 7, 1926), at 20.
60. Pub. L. 62-400, 37 Stat. 701 (March 1, 1913). The Act provided that the ICC "shall ascertain and report in detail as to each piece of property owned or used by said common carrier for its purposes as a common carrier, the original cost to date, the cost of reproduction new, the cost of reproduction less depreciation, and an analysis of the methods by which these several costs are obtained." *Id.* The Act had been pushed by Robert La Follette to expose what he believed to be watered railroad stock. *Working on the Railroads*, 151 OUTLOOK AND INDEPENDENT 100 (January 16, 1929).
61. 41 Stat. 481, 489 (February 28, 1920).
62. Dayton-Goose Creek Railway Co. v. United States, 263 U.S. 456, 478 (1924).
63. The Taft Court endorsed the idea of aggregate rates in Aetna Insurance Co. v. Hyde, 275 U.S. 440 (1928). "The Fourteenth Amendment does not protect against competition.... It has never been and cannot reasonably be held that state-made rates violate the Fourteenth Amendment merely because the aggregate collections are not sufficient to yield a reasonable profit or just compensation to all companies that happen to be engaged in the affected business." *Id.* at 447.
64. 41 Stat. 489. The constitutionality of the redistribution scheme was upheld in Dayton-Goose Creek Railway Co. v. United States, 263 U.S. 456 (1924).
65. *See* DAVID J. DANELSKI, A SUPREME COURT JUSTICE IS APPOINTED 128, 137 (New York: Random House 1964); DREW PEARSON & ROBERT S. ALLEN, THE NINE OLD MEN 119 (Garden City: Doubleday, Doran & Co. 1937). Speaking on the floor of the Senate in 1933, Henrik Shipstead of Minnesota recalled visiting Washington in 1922 to protest Butler's confirmation. "The three distinguished Senators on the subcommittee of the Committee on the Judiciary were Senator Knute Nelson, Senator Cummins, and Senator Walsh of Montana.... As a result of

my objection, they all agreed that Justice Butler would be disqualified from sitting in a case affecting the valuation of railroads when the Supreme Court should finally decide that question. ... But the first case involving valuation for rate-making purposes was the *Indianapolis Water Rate case*, and the decision was written by Justice Butler, and the rule was fixed in that case." 77 CONG. REC. 4411–12 (May 27, 1933). Joining the discussion, George Norris recalled the Butler confirmation controversy "so distinctly that I can pick out the seat of practically every Senator who participated in that debate." *Id.* at 4412. Norris affirmed that because Butler had been "at the head of the list of attorneys who were making the fight on behalf of the railroads," it was accepted that he would "stand aside and would not participate" when ICC evaluations of railroad property were brought before the Court for constitutional review. *Id.*

> Then what happened? The *O'Fallon case* was soon coming on to be argued in the Supreme Court, but ahead of that case came the *Indianapolis Water Works case*, where identically the same question was involved.... The rate the company could charge for water depended upon the valuation ... and the same controversy was under consideration in the *O'Fallon case*....
>
> That question was argued in the Supreme Court before the *Railroad case* was argued. Everyone knew the identical question was involved in both; and the man who had been confirmed sat with the Court in determining that question. Not only that but when the Court reached a conclusion ... he wrote the opinion of the Court, and it became the law of the land that governed railroad-valuation cases just as completely as though the decision had been made in those cases. So when the question of the valuation of railroads came into the Court then with that question already determined, true to what Senators said here, behind closed doors when that nomination was under consideration, the man who had been confirmed at that time stepped aside and did not participate in the railroad case. ... [I]t was not necessary for him to step aside; the question had been previously determined.

Id. See Samuel Gompers, *Why Pierce Butler?*, 30 AMERICAN FEDERATIONIST 76, 77 (1923) ("Within a short time the United States Interstate Commerce Commission must complete its valuation of the physical property of the railroads. It is assured as a fact in advance that this valuation will be promptly contested in the courts by the railroads, no matter what the figures may be. In due course of time the court contests will reach the Supreme Court of the United States. And there will be Pierce Butler, the valuation expert!").

66. George Norris to Donald R. Richberg (December 1, 1926) (Norris papers). It was said in the press that "a pretty good summary of" *McCardle* "can be obtained by reading Justice Butler's argument as a railroad attorney before the Interstate Commerce Commission." *Supreme Court Ethics*, NEW YORK TELEGRAM (October 2, 1927), at 4.
67. Willis, *supra* note 30, at 229. *See* Herbert Little, *The Omnipotent Nine*, 15 AMERICAN MERCURY 48, 53 (September 1928) (*McCardle* "tickled Wall Street, for under it public utility rates in most of the cities of the nation can now be increased materially by the mere process of applying to a Federal court.").
68. 68 CONG. REC. 167 (December 9, 1926). Rainey pointed his finger squarely at Butler: "At the present time there sits on the Supreme Bench of the United States a judge, one of the ablest members of that court, who is committed to the doctrine of 'reproduction cost.'"

69. HFS to John Bassett Moore (November 20, 1926) (Stone papers). Stone wrote his son that *McCardle* "may have very far-reaching consequences if the Court should ultimately hold that the present time reproduction cost is the proper value on which to base a rate for all public service companies." HFS to Lauson Stone (November 26, 1926) (Stone papers).
70. 124 I.C.C. Reports 3 (February 15, 1927) ("St. Louis & O'Fallon Excess Income").
71. *Id.* at 26. "In important aspects it is a problem which has never before been presented to either a commission or a court. We must carefully review the significance to the Nation of the decision which we make in this case in its bearings on the relation between all the railroads and all the people of the United States. It may well be that the valuation of railroads on a national scale requires the beginning of a new chapter in valuation." *Id.* at 26–27.
72. 41 Stat. 489.
73. St. Louis & O'Fallon Excess Income, *supra* note 70, at 27, 30. For an excellent account of the purposive nature of the ICC's reasoning, see John Bauer, *Interstate Commerce Commission Adopts Actual Investment at Cost Basis*, 16 NATIONAL MUNICIPAL REVIEW 454 (July 1927).
74. St. Louis & O'Fallon Excess Income, *supra* note 70, at 28–30; Hugh Willis, *St. Louis & O' Fallon Case*, 5 INDIANA LAW JOURNAL 120 122 (1929).
75. St. Louis & O'Fallon Excess Income, *supra* note 70, at 28, 30, 32. Between 1919 and 1920, the aggregate value of railroad property – and consequently railroad rates – "would have been increased ... by a sum greater than the present national debt ... and the transportation burden upon the people of the country would have been correspondingly increased without the investment of a single dollar by those who would reap the benefits." *Id.*
76. *Id.* at 34–35. "The conception of a rate base and returns thereon fluctuating up and down with changes in the level of general prices is a conception which, if carried into actual operation, could have no appeal except to stock-market speculators." *Id.* at 35.
77. Moreover railroad property "since the price revolution brought about by the World War" had never been valued using a cost reproduction new methodology, and yet, the Commission noted, "the market for railroad securities since the passage of [the Transportation Act of 1920] has steadily improved" and the "credit of the railroads in general is now excellent."

> With exceptions in certain sections of the country it will be conceded that the railroads are now in better credit and financial condition, in all probability, than at any time in their history. The standard of service is clearly better than ever before. ... Under such circumstances can it be said with any show of reason that the private owners of this property devoted to the public service are suffering confiscation? Yet the current cost of reproduction doctrine would lead to that conclusion.

Id. at 33–34.
78. *Id.* at 36, 39.
79. ARI HOOGENBOOM & OLIVE HOOGENBOOM, A HISTORY OF THE ICC: FROM PANACEA TO PALLIATIVE 91 (New York: W.W. Norton & Co. 1945). See I.L. SHARFMAN, THE INTERSTATE COMMERCE COMMISSION: A STUDY IN ADMINISTRATIVE LAW AND PROCEDURE 33 (New York: The Commonwealth Fund 1931).

80. "The land-value doctrine followed in this case apparently means that when land has been donated by the State or by individuals to a railroad in aid of construction, the carrier from the moment it begins operation is entitled to exact from the public served a full return upon the value of that land based on the then market value of adjoining lands. I am unwilling to believe that the Constitution is an instrument of public oppression." St. Louis & O'Fallon Excess Income, *supra* note 70, at 58–59 (Commissioner Eastman, concurring). Comparing *McCardle* with *Georgia Power Ry. & Power Co.*, Eastman half-heartedly claimed that the Taft Court had "very wisely avoided a crystallization of the law with respect to the limits set by the Constitution to the public regulation of undertakings affected with a public interest." *Id.* at 49, 52. But he then went on to argue that even assuming that the Taft Court were settled in its view, the question of ICC valuation was fundamentally a question "of public policy," and in such matters reasoning ought not to "be confined to deductions from past judicial utterances. The vital thing is the essential purpose of the law in its relation to the public interest." *Id.* at 50. The ICC ought not to "neglect the illumination which is thrown upon the law by its own intimate knowledge of transportation affairs and problems. I feel sure that the Supreme Court is itself desirous that we should speak both frankly and fully on these matters. . . . After the court has heard what we have to say it may decide that our conclusions as to the fundamental law are erroneous, and that will end the matter; but certainly we ought not to deprive the court of the help which it may gain from the special knowledge which it is our duty under the law to acquire." *Id.* at 51.
81. *Id.* at 62 (Commissioner Hall, dissenting).
82. *Id.* at 64 (Commissioner Aitchison, dissenting). The judgment of the ICC was controversial in the popular press. *See, e.g., Railroad Valuation on the 1914 Basis*, 93 LITERARY DIGEST 76 (April 16, 1927).
83. St. Louis & O'Fallon Ry. Co. v. United States, 22 F.2d 980, 983–84 (E.D. Mo. 1927).
84. John J. Daley, *The Greatest Lawsuit in History*, WASHINGTON POST (December 30, 1928), at SM1. "It is no exaggeration to say that this case is one of the most important – if not the most important – ever to come before the United States Supreme Court. Its decision may have a stupendous effect upon the stock market. Financial houses throughout the country are sending broadcast to their clients pamphlets and brochures discussing the probable effects of this case upon the future value of railroad securities." *Id. See* Thomas Gammack, *What Is a Railroad Worth?*, 150 OUTLOOK AND INDEPENDENT 1420 (1928).
85. Bonbright, *supra* note 34, at 182. "The importance of the case can hardly be exaggerated. There could be no clearer joining of issues." Bauer, *supra* note 73, at 459.
86. 69 CONG. REC. 7856–59 (May 7, 1928). The Conference was a progressive institution organized to advocate for the interests of shippers and the public. Richberg had participated in the ICC proceedings; he had been permitted to file an amicus brief but not to argue before the district court. In March he wrote Norris, who was the president of the Conference, asking for the backing of "a large group of Senators and Representatives" to increase the likelihood of his participating in the case before the Supreme Court. Donald R. Richberg to George W. Norris (March 20, 1928) (Norris papers). *See* 69 CONG. REC. 7951 (May 7, 1928); George W. Norris to Donald R. Richberg (March 26, 1928) (Norris papers); Donald R. Richberg to George

Ratemaking & Judicial Legitimacy

W. Norris (May 6, 1928) (Norris papers). The railroads refused to consent to Richberg's participation. *See* 69 CONG. REC. 7951 (May 7, 1928). The Senate debated the propriety of the resolution for two hours and finally voted 46–31 in its favor. *Senate "Advises" The Supreme Court*, NEW YORK TIMES (May 8, 1928), at 45.

87. Stone 1928 Docket Book. In November, Taft wrote Holmes to summarize the results of a Court conference: "131 and 132 were the cases in which the Senate desired . . . to allow a man named Richberg to file a brief and make an oral argument. He represented a farmers' association. We have concluded to allow him to file the brief and to make an oral argument as amicus curiae, at a time to be set later." WHT to OWH (November 24, 1928) (Taft papers). Richberg was eventually granted "an hour and a quarter" of oral argument. WHT to Charles Elmore Cropley (December 15, 1928) (Taft papers). Later Taft wrote his brother that in *O'Fallon* "the Senate requested that we hear argument from a counsel for farmers' associations and consider how little the railroads ought to be valued in order to lower their rates. The request of the Senate that we hear this man, with a statement by it that the Senate is entirely impartial in the matter, was enough to make the Court laugh, but we let him in, and he made a very good argument from the standpoint of his side." WHT to Horace D. Taft (January 24, 1928) (Taft papers). *See* WHT to Robert A. Taft (December 30, 1928) (Taft papers).

88. Charles G. Ross, *Railroads Win O'Fallon Case in Supreme Court*, ST. LOUIS POST-DISPATCH (May 20, 1929), at 1 ("Justice Butler, however, because of his connection with valuation cases on the side of the railroads before going on the Supreme bench, did not participate in the decision."). *See The Supreme Court's O'Fallon Decision*, 86 RAILWAY AGE 1213 (May 25, 1929).

89. St. Louis & O'Fallon Ry. Co. v. United States, 279 U.S. 461, 484, 488 (1929). Brandeis published a long, detailed dissent, in which Holmes and Stone joined. Stone authored a shorter, more pithy dissent, in which Holmes and Brandeis joined.

90. *Id.* at 485.

91. *Id.* at 486. This precise claim was false. *See supra* text at note 78. It could even be said "that the Commission did give 'due consideration' to reproduction costs, although it did not use them, and severely criticized their use, as an exclusive measure of value." Robert E. Cushman, *Constitutional Law in 1928–1929*, 24 AMERICAN POLITICAL SCIENCE REVIEW 67, 85 (1930).

92. *O'Fallon*, 279 U.S. at 487.

93. *Id.* at 495–96 (Brandeis, J., dissenting). Brandeis's point is that society values the service provided by a utility, not the physical property of the utility.

94. *Id.* at 538 (Brandeis, J., dissenting). In drafting his dissent, Brandeis engaged in extensive correspondence with ICC Commissioner Joseph Eastman. *See* Joseph B. Eastman to LDB (February 16, 1929) (Brandeis papers); Joseph B. Eastman to LDB (March 6, 1929) (Brandeis papers); Joseph B. Eastman to LDB (March 8, 1929) (Brandeis papers); Joseph B. Eastman to LDB (March 16, 1929) (Brandeis papers); Joseph B. Eastman to LDB (March 26, 1929) (Brandeis papers); Joseph B. Eastman to LDB (April 4, 1929) (Brandeis papers); Joseph B. Eastman to LDB (April 10, 1929) (Brandeis papers); Joseph B. Eastman to LDB (April 13, 1929) (Brandeis papers); Joseph B. Eastman to LDB (April 15, 1929) (Brandeis papers); Joseph B. Eastman to LDB (April 18, 1929) (Brandeis papers); Joseph B. Eastman to LDB (April 29, 1929) (Brandeis papers); Joseph B. Eastman to LDB (April 30, 1929) (Brandeis papers); Joseph B. Eastman to LDB (May 1, 1929) (Brandeis

papers); Joseph B. Eastman to LDB (May 9, 1929) (Brandeis papers); Joseph B. Eastman to LDB (May 10, 1929) (Brandeis papers); Joseph B. Eastman to LDB (May 14, 1929) (Brandeis papers). Throughout Eastman used the resources of the ICC to provide research for Brandeis's dissent.

95. *See* WHT to Charles P. Taft 2nd (May 12, 1929) (Taft papers).
96. This is a note in Brandeis's handwriting on the draft paragraph eventually inserted at page 487 of McReynolds's opinion. The draft paragraph may be found in the Brandeis papers.
97. It would have led, as Stone succinctly observed in his dissent, directly to the "economic paradox that the value of the railroads may be far in excess of any amount on which they could earn a return." 279 U.S. at 552 (Stone, J., dissenting). Charles Burlingham wrote Stone that "I have just read your short dissenting opinion in the O'Fallon case. It seems to me unanswerable." Charles C. Burlingham to HFS (May 27, 1929) (Stone papers). Stone replied, "Thank you ... for your comments on my dissent in the O'Fallon case. It is always good for the dissenter to know that there are a few who agree with him." HFS to Charles C. Burlingham (May 28, 1929) (Stone papers). Stone's former clerk Milton Handler also wrote Stone praising his dissent. "Your dissent seems so clear that one wonders how the majority could have decided the case the way it did. It is quite apparent from the late cases that a fascinating battle is now being waged." Milton Handler to HFS (May 24, 1929) (Stone papers).
98. *See, e.g.*, Charles B. Elder, *The St. Louis and O'Fallon Decision – What Does it Mean?*, 24 ILLINOIS LAW REVIEW 296, 309 (1929).
99. After announcement of the opinion, Taft wrote his son that in *O'Fallon* "you will find an enormous dissenting opinion well drawn, but it seems to me to miss the point." WHT to Charles P. Taft 2nd (May 19, 1929) (Taft papers). *See* WHT to Robert A. Taft (May 19, 1929) (Taft papers).
100. Consider this angry passage from McReynolds's opinion: "The report of the Commission is long and argumentative. Much of it is devoted to general observations relative to the method and purpose of making valuations; many objections are urged to doctrine approved by us; and the superiority of another view is stoutly asserted." *O'Fallon*, 279 U.S. at 485. Stone pointed out in his dissent that "Had the Commission not turned aside to point out in its report the economic fallacies of the use of reproduction cost as a standard of value for rate making purposes, which it nevertheless considered and to some extent applied, I suppose it would not have occurred to anyone to question the validity of its order." *Id.* at 550 (Stone, J., dissenting). *See* Cushman, *supra* note 91, at 86 ("Whatever uncertainties may have been injected into the valuation situation by this decision, we are at least fairly certain that it is unsafe for an administrative commission to try to criticize the economic theory of the Supreme Court.").
101. *Railroad Valuation*, 152 OUTLOOK AND INDEPENDENT 216 (1929).
102. *Railways Victors in Valuation Case in Supreme Court*, PHILADELPHIA INQUIRER (May 21, 1929), at 1 ("The decision is regarded as a great victory for the railroads of the country. ... The railroads generally are contending that the cost of reproduction must be the basis of valuation of their properties, or at least that it must be an important element in reckoning any valuation of their properties."). *See* Ross, *supra* note 88.

Ratemaking & Judicial Legitimacy

103. *Railroads Win Suit Involving Billions*, CHICAGO DAILY TRIBUNE (May 21, 1929), at 1. Realizing the potential for this consequence, Taft on the morning of the decision's announcement "took the extraordinary step of ordering the doors closed so that the court room would not be confused by eager correspondents rushing from the place to get bulletins on the wires." *Railways Victors in Valuation Case in Supreme Court*, supra note 102, at 4.
104. *The Railroad Victory in the Supreme Court*, 101 LITERARY DIGEST 8 (June 1, 1929). *See* Robinson, *supra* note 57, at 6–9. "Railroad stocks shot up when tickers announced the Supreme Court's decision in the O'Fallon test case, but eased down as it became better understood." *Railroad Valuation*, supra note 101, at 216. "A day's consideration of the Supreme Court's ruling in the railway valuation case has served to show that hastily predicted and sensational results of it will hardly follow." *Effect of the Decision*, NEW YORK TIMES (May 22, 1929), at 26. "What the court actually held appears to be that the Interstate Commerce Commission must give 'due consideration' to reproduction cost now in making its railroad valuation. It does not say, as some have hastily assumed, that reproduction cost shall be controlling. It is to be one of the factors, but not the only one. ... The decision seems to open the door to another controversy likely to be bitterly fought – the question of how much weight the commission must assign to reproduction cost. The court meticulously refrained from giving even a hint of its view on this highly important point." *The O'Fallon Decision*, LOS ANGELES TIMES (May 22, 1929), at A4. "Views held by Wall Street ... underwent considerable revision last week. Announced at a time when trading was proceeding on the Stock Exchange, the first news of the decision caused a sharp upturn in the carrier stocks. ... More extended study of the decision ... was accompanied by a return of the carrier stocks to near their former levels. While described as a victory for the carriers, the decision of the Supreme Court failed to sustain their methods of evaluation. ... It did not give positive direction as to what would be the right way to value a railroad, and, instead left that to the interpretation of the commission." *O'Fallon Decision Seen as Not Final*, NEW YORK TIMES (May 26, 1929), at N9. "The decision is a stimulus to litigation. The Supreme Court will be flooded with railroad valuation cases, as it has been with local utility valuation cases. Every railroad with recapturable income will want to appeal to the courts, in the hope of getting a higher valuation." *The Value of Railroads*, 128 THE NATION 662 (1929).
105. Donald R. Richberg, *After the O'Fallon Decision*, 59 NEW REPUBLIC 62 (1929). *See* William L. Ransom, *Undetermined Issues in Railroad Valuation under the O'Fallon Decision*, 44 POLITICAL SCIENCE QUARTERLY 321 (1929) ("[T]he present decision left to the future nearly all of the vital and controverted issues as to what this valuation should be and how it should be reached."). As prices tumbled during the Great Depression in the ensuing decade, a cost of reproduction theory of valuation became less and less attractive to railroads.
106. *Value and Recapture*, 86 RAILWAY AGE 1543, 1544 (June 29, 1929). "It is clear, then, that the ruling of the court did not sustain the contention of the carriers that the primary consideration in any determination of values must be cost of reproduction." *What the Railroads Have Won*, NEW YORK WORLD (May 22, 1929), at 14.
107. *O'Fallon Case to Help Roads*, WALL STREET JOURNAL (May 22, 1929), at 3.

909

108. *What the Railroads Have Won*, supra note 106, at 14. *See The O'Fallon Case*, DAILY BOSTON GLOBE (May 22, 1929), at 18. It is in this context that Brandeis's subsequent remark to Frankfurter about Brandeis's *O'Fallon* dissent should be understood: "I am glad you think well of the O'Fallon opinion. I guess no one of the majority knows the RR's plight, but I guess P.B. understands." LDB to Felix Frankfurter (May 24, 1929) in BRANDEIS-FRANKFURTER CORRESPONDENCE, at 375. Butler, recall, was perfectly clear that rates could not be based only upon value. *See supra* note 17.
109. *Hoover Confident Rates Won't Rise; Rail Chiefs Agree*, NEW YORK TIMES (May 22, 1929), at 1. It was generally agreed, therefore, that the "outstanding significance of the St. Louis & O'Fallon decision of the Supreme Court is that it limits and defers recapture liability under the Transportation Act of 1920." *O'Fallon Case to Help Roads*, supra note 107, at 1. "The chief effect of the decision it now appears will be the safeguarding of a portion of the earnings of the more prosperous roads from recapture by the government. That, however, is a matter of a few hundred millions, and not of the billions over whom the commission and the carriers have been contending." *What the Railroads Have Won*, supra note 106, at 14. "The ruling will have the effect of largely nullifying the recapture provisions of the Transportation Act of 1920. The number of roads with recapturable income, and the amount of recapturable income, may be very small." *The Value of Railroads*, supra note 104, at 662. *See O'Fallon Decision Seen as Not Final*, supra note 104, at N9 ("The chief importance of the O'Fallon decision is regarded now as being its effect on the recapture of earnings by the government."); *Says O'Fallon Case Will Not Raise Rates*, NEW YORK TIMES (September 3, 1929), at 39. The recapture provision, having never worked, was repealed in 1933. RICHARD D. STONE, THE INTERSTATE COMMERCE COMMISSION AND THE RAILROAD INDUSTRY: A HISTORY OF REGULATORY POLICY 34 (New York: Praeger 1991).
110. "Criticism of the decision lies in the fact that the majority of the Court did not inquire into the basic purpose of Congress of which valuation was merely an instrument of administration and did not consider that purpose in its bearing on fair value. The 'law of the land' was looked upon as distinct from these underlying policies and the basis of value was treated as a matter of inherent property right not subject to modification to meet the requirements of public policy." Julia Arthur Burrell, *Interstate Commerce – Recapture under Transportation Act*, 8 TEXAS LAW REVIEW 566, 573 (1930).
111. *O'Fallon*, 279 U.S. at 501 (Brandeis, J., dissenting).
112. The Commission "knew that the value for rate making purposes could not be more than that sum on which a fair return could be earned by legal rates; and that the earnings were limited both by the commercial prohibition of rates higher than the traffic would bear and the legal prohibition of a rates higher than are just and reasonable." *Id.* at 501–2 (Brandeis, J., dissenting).
113. *A Notable Decision*, HARTFORD COURANT (May 22, 1929), at 8. For a good example of the confusion cast by *O'Fallon* on traditional conservative understandings of valuation, see Wherry, *supra* note 50, at 702:

> As to the effect on railroad rates ... [c]ompetitive factors also enter into consideration. Because of this the railroads have little chance of increasing their

rates to what would be theoretically possible, as was done by other public utilities after the *Bluefield, Southwestern Bell,* and the *Indianapolis Water Company* cases. On the other hand, although an immediate increase in the rates of railroads may be doubtful, at least the decision should make a reduction of rates increasingly difficult.... The importance of this decision is that a new stability is added to the railroads. This should strengthen their credit and greatly aid the reconstruction of transportation facilities, which has been rapidly progressing in this country since the War.

The tepid conclusion that *O'Fallon* added "stability" to railroads assumed the continuation of price inflation, which the onset of the Depression would immediately disprove. It was uncontroversial that valuations based upon cost of reproduction would be disastrous for the railroads during periods of price deflation.

114. Taft's old nemesis, Amos Pinchot, see *supra* Chapter 8, at 302, registered this message loud and clear. Pinchot stressed that *O'Fallon* applied to "all public utilities regulated by commissions," and that in many contexts would serve as "a precedent for a general boosting of rates, thereby increasing the concentration of wealth, already a serious enough problem in this country." He offered a class-based account of the decision's provenance. "It is possible," he said, that

> the public will look at the decision of the court realistically, seeing in it, not so much the echo of the law of the land, as the reflection of the background and consequent bias of five individuals who may be described respectively as (1) an ex-attorney of the Northern Pacific Railroad Company; (2) an ex-attorney of the Southern Pacific Railway Company; (3) an able conservative lawyer, once Attorney General of the United States, who has, on the bench, shown at least ordinary zeal in defending corporate interests; (4) a member of the Republican old guard of Tennessee, the selection of President Harding. This justice's father was principal owner of the Knoxville and Ohio Railroad, later bought by the Southern Railway; and his own law firm was counsel for the East Tennessee, Virginia and Georgia, as well as the Knoxville and Ohio. And finally, the Chief Justice, Mr. William Howard Taft, an amiable Ohioan....

Amos Pinchot, *The Railroads Win the O'Fallon Case*, 128 THE NATION 666, 667 (1929).

115. It was observed by economists that "public service regulation has come close to a complete breakdown under the incubus of rate control by valuation." Bonbright, *supra* note 10, at 76. *See id.* at 79.

116. 280 U.S. 234 (1930).

117. WHT to OWH (January 6, 1930) (Taft papers). *See infra* Epilogue, at 1502.

118. Holmes, Brandeis, and Stone dissented. Stone's docket book suggests that in conference McReynolds had initially voted with the three dissenters.

119. *West*, 280 U.S. at 254. Sutherland used this premise to conclude that, as a matter of constitutional law, allowances for annual depreciation must be made "based upon present value," rather than upon initial cost. *Id.* at 253. "Manifestly, this allowance cannot be limited by the original cost, because, if values have advanced, the allowance is not sufficient to maintain the level of efficiency.... This naturally calls for expenditures equal to the cost of the worn out equipment at the time of replacement; and this, for all practical purposes, means present value. It is the settled rule of this Court that the rate base is present value, and it would be wholly

illogical to adopt a different rule for depreciation." *Id.* at 254. This prompted a long, scholarly, outraged dissent from Brandeis, who, joined by Holmes, demonstrated that it was the universal practice of businesses and accountants to base depreciation allowances on initial cost. Brandeis considered Sutherland's rule to be "a pervasion of this business device." *Id.* at 278 (Brandeis, J., dissenting). "No method for ascertainment of the amount of the charge yet invented is workable if fluctuating present values be taken as the basis. ... To use as a measure of the year's consumption of plant a depreciation charge based on fluctuating present values substitutes conjecture for experience." *Id.* Brandeis noted that "If the contention now urged by the Railways is sound, the management misrepresented by its published accounts its financial condition and the results of operation of the several years; and it paid dividends in violation of law." *Id.* at 288. In a short dissent, Stone observed that "what amounts annually carried to reserve will be sufficient to replace all the elements of a composite property purchased at various times, at varying price levels, as they wear out or become obsolete, is a question, not of law but of fact." *Id.* at 289 (Stone, J., dissenting).

120. The Court refused to consider whether it had been proper to include in the company's costs of reproduction easements to use city streets, freely given to the railway company by the city. Counting these easements would add $5 million to the company's rate basis. The Court considered this question waived. 280 U.S. at 248–49. In dissent, Brandeis disagreed. "Franchises to lay pipes or tracks in the public streets ... are not donations to a utility of property by the use of which profit may be made. They are privileges granted to utilities to enable them to employ their property in the public service and make profit out such use of that property." *Id.* at 257–58 (Brandeis, J., dissenting).

121. Bluefield Waterworks & Imp. Co. v. Public Service Commission, 262 U.S. 679, 692–93 (1923). *Compare* Butler, *supra* note 17, at 31–32. Butler's formulation has remained highly influential. *See, e.g., In re* Permian Basin Area Rate Cases, 390 U.S. 747, 806 (1968).

122. *West,* 280 U.S. at 249, 251, 252.

123. 41 Stat. 488–89. Taft had effectively sidestepped the issue of a constitutionally mandated fair rate of return in *Dayton-Goose Creek Railway Co.*:

> The [Transportation] act fixes the fair return for the years here involved, 1920 and 1921, at 5½ per cent. and the Commission exercises its discretion to add one-half of 1 per cent. The case of Bluefield Waterworks & Improvement Co. v. Public Service Commission is cited to show that a return of 6 per cent. on the property of a public utility is confiscatory. But 6 per cent. was not found confiscatory in Willcox v. Consolidated Gas Co., in Cedar Rapids Gas Light Company v. Cedar Rapids, or in Des Moines Gas Co. v. Des Moines. Thus the question of the minimum of a fair percentage on value is shown to vary with the circumstances. Here we are relieved from considering the line between a fair return and confiscation, because under the provisions of the act and the reports made by the appellant the return which it will receive after paying one-half the excess to the Commission will be about 8 per cent. on the reported value. This can hardly be called confiscatory. Moreover, the appellant did not raise the issue of confiscation in its bill and it cannot properly be said to be before us.

263 U.S. at 486.

124. As Holmes had observed in 1912, "[I]f the franchise is taken to mean that the most profitable return that could be got, free from competition, is protected by the 14th

Amendment, then the power to regulate is null." Cedar Rapids Gas Light Co. v. City of Cedar Rapids, 223 U.S. 655, 669–70 (1912).

125. Carlisle Bargeron, *Hughes Confirmed, 52 to 26, as Senate Hits Supreme Court*, WASHINGTON POST (February 14, 1930), at 1; *Hughes Is Attacked by Borah and Glass; Foes Force a Delay*, NEW YORK TIMES (February 12, 1930), at 1 ("Not in a century have such attacks been made upon confirmation of a chief justice."); *Senate Confirms Hughes, 52 to 26*, DAILY BOSTON GLOBE (February 14, 1930), at 1; M. Farmer Murphy, *Opposition to Hughes Mounts to Formidable Proportions in Senate*, BALTIMORE SUN (February 13, 1930), at 1. The attack on Hughes "began slowly, but gathered unexpected momentum as it progressed." Carlisle Bargeron, *Hughes Fight Breaks Out on Senate Floor*, WASHINGTON POST (February 12, 1930), at 1. "The struggle to prevent confirmation centered chiefly around the so-called conservative majority decisions of the United States Supreme Court, which the opposition contended elevated property rights above human rights, and with which view, it was alleged, Mr. Hughes was aligned." *Hughes Confirmed by Senate*, NEW YORK TIMES (February 14, 1930), at 1.

126. ERNST, *supra* note 24, at 49–50.

127. "[T]he Supreme Court has been taking the control of public service corporations and compelling high rates in order that their owners might earn big money. The latest was in the Baltimore Street Car case. ... The Hughes nomination, the culmination of entrenching monopoly and privilege, was but the match that caused the fire to break out. Hughes was not worse than the others. ... But the Supreme Court having become the 'dictator' of public service corporations and Mr. Hughes having ... been attorney for privilege seeking corporations, senators saw in that appointment the fixed policy of the alchemists' dream – converting base metal into gold – by decree of court, the people paying in rates and fares." *Justice Hughes Is a Typical Republican*, RALEIGH NEWS AND OBSERVER (February 17, 1930), at 4.

128. LDB to Felix Frankfurter (May 8, 1930), in BRANDEIS-FRANKFURTER CORRESPONDENCE, at 424–25.

129. Remarks of Senator Norris, 72 CONG. REC. 3565–81 (February 13, 1930) (extensively commenting on and reprinting the Court's opinion in *West*).

130. "During the debate yesterday and today much was said about the Supreme Court decision in the United Railways fare case from Baltimore. It was mentioned by almost every speaker as a striking example of the tendency to exalt the rights of property above those of individuals and the public." Murphy, *supra* note 125, at 1. *See* Josephus Daniels, *Turning Calcium Light on Judicial Nominations*, RALEIGH NEWS AND OBSERVER (April 13, 1930), at 10.

131. Remarks of Senator La Follette, 72 CONG. REC. 3564 (February 13, 1930).

132. Remarks of Senator Borah, 72 CONG. REC. 3448–49 (February 11, 1930). *See* Remarks of Senator Dill, 72 CONG. REC. 3499–503 (February 12, 1930) ("The views of Mr. Hughes on economic questions are just as important as his legal ability. Why do I say that? Because the Supreme Court has seen fit ... to go into the question of the valuation of public utilities. ... When you allow a court to write into its decisions a valuation upon franchises given by the people for the right to serve the people, you then enable those corporations to pick the pockets of the common men and women of America of unjustified profits under the guise of a constitutional right. ... Those who have studied the history of the fight of the progressives of this country ... know that to-day the last resort of organized capital

that plunders the common people of America is the Supreme Court of the United States.... [B]y writing their economic theories of the supremacy of property rights into the decisions of the highest court of this land, they are gradually building up a tremendous valuation of public utilities upon which the American people must pay literally hundreds of millions of dollars of tribute annually that never could be collected otherwise. So I say the decisions of the judges of the Supreme Court themselves are to blame for our being compelled to bring into this discussion the economic views of men who are presented to us to be confirmed as members of the Supreme Court."); Remarks of Senator Blaine, 72 CONG. REC. 3518 (February 12, 1930) ("[T]o whom did the railroad corporations go when they desired to have set aside and made null and void the legislation of Congress providing for a valuation of the railroads and their properties for purpose of fixing rates? They went to Mr. Hughes."); Remarks of Senator George, 72 CONG. REC. 3587 (February 13, 1930) ("If the decision of the Supreme Court which has been commented upon here for two days [*West*] is to stand, the recapture clause in the transportation act is not worth the paper upon which it is written; for there provision is made for the recapture of all over and above 6 per cent of the net earnings of the carriers of this country, and the court solemnly says that 6.26 per cent is confiscatory!").

133. Remarks of Senator Dill, 72 CONG. REC. 3499 (February 12, 1930). *See* Remarks of Senator Brookhart, 72 CONG. REC. 3505 (February 12, 1930) ("[T]he Supreme Court of the United States is now divided into two political parties. The progressive party is headed by that grand old humanitarian, Oliver Wendell Holmes. He is followed by Mr. Justice Brandeis and Mr. Justice Stone. The other members of the court belong to the conservative or reactionary party. This division more truly represents the political situation in the United States than any other party alignment at this time. We have so-called Republicans and so-called Democrats, but the vote on this confirmation will determine their real alignment. It will determine whether the progressive party wants to increase the progressive strength in the United States or the conservative or reactionary party wants to continue the rule of that court.... [When the Court says in *West*] that there will be confiscation unless [a public utility is] granted as much as 7.44 per cent as the rate of return ... then that court itself becomes the greatest confiscator of property in the history of this world.... The confiscations of the earnings of farmers alone are five or six billion dollars per year since 1920.... Party alignment will soon divide upon that question. The present illogical division must cease as the people realize and find out that in this way their earnings and their substance are being taken from them and transferred to the pockets of the few who control the corporate interests of the country."); Remarks of Senator Wheeler, 72 CONG. REC. 3516–17 (February 12, 1930) ("No man who is familiar with the decision of the Supreme Court of the United States in the recent case decided with reference to the street-railway lines in Baltimore, no man who has studied the decision of the court in the O'Fallon case, can fail to come to the solemn conclusion that the Supreme Court of the United States of America has to-day assumed to decide not only legal questions but is deciding economic questions.... As far as I am concerned, I am not going to vote against Mr. Hughes because of the fact that he is a Republican; that is not my view about it. I am voting against him because of the economic views he holds.").

Ratemaking & Judicial Legitimacy

134. Remarks of Senator Dill, 72 CONG. REC. 3501 (February 12, 1930). *See* Remarks of Senator Brookhart, 72 CONG. REC. 3508 (February 12, 1930); Remarks of Senator Glass, 72 CONG. REC. 3553 (February 13, 1930).
135. Butler's appointment had occasioned the "only near heated" argument between Brandeis and Taft; the chief justice had insisted that the legitimacy of the Court depended upon representation from both political parties rather than representation from those with different "creeds on property." *Brandeis-Frankfurter Conversations*, at 318 (July 3, 1923). *See supra* Chapter 2, at 61–62.
136. *Compare* Arthur T. Hadley, *Property in America*, 64 THE INDEPENDENT 837 (1908): "The fundamental division of powers in the Constitution of the United States is between voters on the one hand and property owners on the other. The forces of democracy on one side, divided between the executive and the legislature, are set over against the forces of property on the other side, with the judiciary as arbiter between them.").
137. *See supra* notes 132 and 133. "With national attention once more attracted to the Supreme Court, new understanding has been given to the clear-cut and deep cleavage existing between two elements within the court on economic, rather than judicial grounds. ... In the past there has been some effort to retain a balance between Republicans and Democrats in the membership of the august body. Decisions in certain recent cases ... indicate that it will be far more important to maintain a balance between two conflicting terms of economic thought which have nothing to do with politics as they have been expressed up to the present by current parties. In general the difference between the two groups involves issues between Property and Persons, with the Holmes-Brandeis group on the latter side." Richard L. Strout, *President Hoover and the Supreme Court*, CHRISTIAN SCIENCE MONITOR (March 11, 1930), at 16.
138. *See supra* Chapter 20, at 649–52.
139. Remarks of Senator Dill, 72 CONG. REC. 3502 (February 12, 1930).
140. Appalled, Stone wrote his former law clerk Milton Handler: "I wonder if you read the debates in the Congressional Record over the Hughes nomination. There were some pretty severe things said about the Court and for the first time since the Dred Scott decision there were extended debates over the opinions of the Court. The O'Fallon case and the Baltimore Railways case seem to incite the most interest. The latter was printed at length in the record." HFS to Milton Handler (April 8, 1930) (Stone papers). Ironically, Frankfurter had written Stone just after the Court's opinion in *West*:

> I have just finished the reading of the January 6th batch of opinions, and I find I'm deeply in your debt – all of us are, who really care about our constitutional system & your Court and are apprehensive over the prevailing trend to read personal limitations of outlook or economics into the Constitution. Hughes, in his Lecture on the Court, speaks of the "self-inflicted wounds" of the Court. Clearly such dissenting disavowals as the youngest and the two oldest members have been giving will help to soften the mischief of those "wounds." Your dissent in the United Railways case ... [is] the kind of utterance that will help – I hope – to confine the mischievous doctrines from undue growth.

Felix Frankfurter to HFS (January 13, 1930) (Stone papers). Stone replied, "I am bound to say that I feel a good deal of concern over some of our recent decisions, but I suppose that is the natural state of one who finds himself playing the role of dissenter." HFS to Felix Frankfurter (January 16, 1930) (Stone papers).

141. Bargeron, *Hughes Confirmed, supra* note 125. "'The underlying motive, in fact, the frequently expressed motive of the attack, was to 'teach the court a lesson.'" *Id.* The press noted "a tendency by some speakers to criticize not only Mr. Hughes but the Supreme Court itself. This criticism pointed out the fact that the court today not only interprets law but lays down policies and it was objected that this exceeds the intended authority of the court." *See Warning Contained in Hughes Fight,* HARTFORD COURANT (February 14, 1930), at 2.

142. 72 CONG. REC. 3642 (February 14, 1930). Invoking *Dred Scott*, Dill charged that the Court was creating a "system of law that is fast bringing economic slavery in this country." *Id.*

143. 72 CONG. REC. 3643 (February 14, 1930).

> When the people in their homes all over America find, as they are finding and will find, that their telephone bills are going up, and they go to their councilmen, to their legislators, to their Congressmen and their Senators and ask for legislation for relief and are told that there is no way to relieve them because of the valuation decisions of the Supreme Court that have read valuations into telephone properties that never were heretofore known in this system of American government and have read into these decisions a rate of return as being confiscatory that has heretofore been looked upon as amply compensatory, they are going to begin to think about the Supreme Court. When they find that the street-car fares are up and are being raised, and they appeal to local officials to help them [and] are told that it is because of a valuation system established by Supreme Court decision, and it can not be helped, they are going to begin to want to know about the Supreme Court. . . . [T]hey are going to begin to ask, "What is this Supreme Court, and who are these men that are saddling upon the American people these billions of dollars of valuations upon which we are compelled to pay this added return?" Then the Supreme Court will be in politics.

Id. at 3642–43.

144. *Supreme Court Idolatry*, WASHINGTON DAILY NEWS (February 13, 1930), at 12.

145. For a discussion of the authority of finality, see *supra* Chapter 20, at 654–55.

PART VI
THE POSITIVE LAW
OF PROHIBITION

Speaking before the Boston Bar Association in December 1914, a week after the first unsuccessful effort to induce Congress to approve a constitutional amendment imposing national prohibition,[1] Taft condemned the proposed amendment as a "dangerous proposition."[2] "It would revolutionize the national government," he said. "It would put on the shoulders of the government the duty of sweeping the doorsteps of every home in the land. If national prohibition legislation is passed, local government will be destroyed."[3] "How many do you think you will need to enforce that national prohibition in New York and Boston," Taft asked his audience. "What are you going to do if you pass that law?"[4]

Prohibition was all but inconceivable from the perspective of those who, like Taft, decried the "Evil of Multiplicity of Laws" caused by "the erroneous belief that any reform could be accomplished merely by legislation."[5] But World War I "changed everything."[6] The war galvanized prohibition supporters and "centralized authority in Washington."[7] Spurred by "the new janissaries of the Anti-Saloon League"[8] – probably the first and certainly the most powerful single-issue lobbying group in the nation's history[9] – Congress on December 22, 1917, submitted to the states the proposed Eighteenth Amendment, which prohibited "the manufacture, sale, or transportation of intoxicating liquors within, the importation thereof into, or the exportation thereof from the United States ... for beverage purposes." The amendment provided, obscurely, that "The Congress and the several States shall have concurrent power to enforce this article by appropriate legislation."

Supported by the "Baptist and Methodist clergy, the progressive party and its allies; the women of the suffrage movement, the western populists; most southern Democrats," and even by the Industrial Workers of the World,[10] the amendment was ratified on January 16, 1919, passing into the Constitution "more quickly than any other amendment in United States history."[11] Contemporaries were amazed.

"It is as if a sailing ship on a windless ocean were sweeping ahead, propelled by some invisible force. ... The whole swift and hurried process defies analysis or explanation. It stands [as] ... one of the wonders of our political history."[12]

We now make light of prohibition; we consign it to a fabled world of speakeasies and flappers, a world where, as Edmund Wilson marveled in 1927, "fierce protracted drinking has now become universal, an accepted feature of social life."[13] But during the 1920s prohibition was deadly serious business. It was "the most avidly discussed question of the day."[14] Inspiring fierce national polarization, prohibition continuously provoked "the emotions of the masses of the people."[15] Prohibition was also disorienting. It represented the greatest expansion of federal administrative responsibility since the days of Reconstruction. At a stroke, the federal government assumed responsibility for regulating the manufacture, sale, and transportation of alcohol throughout the nation.

Prohibition was Taft's worst nightmare come to pass.[16] It triggered an ongoing crisis about the nature and meaning of law. Enshrined in the Constitution and in solemn federal legislation, prohibition was nevertheless openly flouted, as urban populations shamelessly resisted its requirements. The federal government turned to criminal law to force compliance with the puritanical and bone-dry Volstead Act,[17] a shift that would permanently affect the orientation of the American state.

The challenge facing the Taft Court was how to sustain the authority of law in the face of such widespread and explicit defiance. Enveloped in a vicious culture war that undermined plausible appeals to a shared and crystallized public sentiment, prohibition would make Holmes's positivism seem suddenly and unexpectedly attractive, even to justices whose inclinations were otherwise conservative.

The Positive Law of Prohibition

Notes

1. 52 CONG. REC. 495–616 (December 22, 1914). Although it did not pass, the proposed amendment was nevertheless a "triumphant failure" because it received such unexpectedly strong support. DANIEL OKRENT, LAST CALL: THE RISE AND FALL OF PROHIBITION 76 (New York: Scribner 2010).
2. *Taft Is Against Federal Prohibition*, BRATTLEBORO REFORMER (December 29, 1914), at 1.
3. *National Prohibition Dangerous, Says Taft; Would Result in Destruction of Local Government*, HARTFORD COURANT (December 29, 1914), at 8.
4. *Plea for Local Option Made by Prof. Taft*, CHRISTIAN SCIENCE MONITOR (December 29, 1914), at 18. A month later, Taft reiterated his view that national prohibition "would destroy the balance of power between the Central Government and the State Government; that it was a direct blow at local self-government and at the integrity of our Federal system, which depended on preserving the control by the States of parochial and local matters; that the regulation or prohibition of the liquor traffic was essentially a local matter, because opinions with reference to how it should be treated varied with every community. Secondly, it was dangerous because the exercise of jurisdiction to prohibit the liquor traffic would call for a horde of Federal officials in addition to the hundreds of thousands now representing the United States Government, and would give to an unscrupulous manipulator in national politics, with Federal authority, a power that would be dangerous to the Republic whenever candidates were to be selected by his party, or whenever an election was to be had." *For Local Option, Mr. Taft Explains*, NEW YORK TIMES (January 24, 1915), at 10. Taft later explained that his opposition was based in part on the view that "prohibition could not be enforced effectively among our numerous population of foreign origin, especially when they are living in congested centers in large cities." WHT to Francis Peabody (July 12, 1923) (Taft papers).
5. *For Local Option, Mr. Taft Explains*, *supra* note 4.
6. LISA MCGIRR, THE WAR ON ALCOHOL: PROHIBITION AND THE RISE OF THE AMERICAN STATE 32 (New York: W.W. Norton & Co. 2016). *See* L. Ames Brown, *Nation-Wide Prohibition*, 115 ATLANTIC MONTHLY 735, 736 (1915) (the war "had the effect of imparting to the anti-alcohol movement what is perhaps the greatest impetus it has received in all the ages").
7. CHARLES MERZ, THE DRY DECADE 25 (Garden City: Doubleday, Doran & Co. 1932).
8. H.L. Mencken, *Politics*, in CIVILIZATION IN THE UNITED STATES: AN INQUIRY BY THIRTY AMERICANS 29 (New York: Harcourt, Brace & Co. 1922). *See* MCGIRR, *supra* note 6, at 21–23. The Anti-Saloon League was commonly recognized as "the amazing agency through which has been achieved what many consider the greatest change ever made in the customs of a country.... It is also plain that as it was the Anti-Saloon League that made and won the fight for the adoption of the Eighteenth Amendment, it will be the Anti-Saloon League which will make the long fight to prevent its nullification." Frank R. Kent, *Battle to Rage around Liquor for Generation*, BALTIMORE SUN (November 21, 1921), at 1. The League, as Taft delicately put it in 1917, "has learned where to touch by political threats the tender spots of legislators so as to awaken them by its power." William Howard Taft, *Prohibition: Pro and Con* (November 15, 1917), in VIVIAN, at 5.

9. The Anti-Saloon League "is unquestionably the most compact, concrete, effective and efficient political force in the country today. It can deliver more votes at a given place with less effort and at smaller expense than any other agency. It is a nonpartisan, interdenominational political machine that runs on a single track. ... It is a one-idea organization which never permits itself to be deflected from the pursuit of that idea. ... It has an annual income of approximately $2,500,000 and is actively supported by more than 700,000 extremely earnest persons, who believe in it as they believe in themselves. Upward of 60,000 churches are behind it. These 60,000 churches really are the Anti-Saloon League; the Anti-Saloon League simply is 60,000 churches. ... The way they like to express it is that the League is 'the church in action.'" Frank R. Kent, *Church Backing Gives Strength to Dry League*, BALTIMORE SUN (November 22, 1922), at 1.
10. OKRENT, *supra* note 1, at 76.
11. MCGIRR, *supra* note 6, at 35. "From the moment of submission it had taken 394 days to meet the approval of thirty-six state legislatures – less than half as long as it had taken eleven of the first fourteen states to approve the Bill of Rights." OKRENT, *supra* note 1, at 106. Only Connecticut and Rhode Island refused to ratify the Amendment. *See* Henry S. Cohn & Ethan Davis, *Stopping the Wind that Blows and the Rivers that Run: Connecticut and Rhode Island Reject the Prohibition Amendment*, 27 QUINNIPIAC LAW REVIEW 327 (2009).
12. *The Great Dry Mystery*, NEW YORK TRIBUNE (January 16, 1919), at 10.
13. EDMUND WILSON, THE AMERICAN EARTHQUAKE 91 (New York: Da Capo Press 1996) (originally published 1927).
14. WILLIAM E. LEUCHTENBURG, THE PERILS OF PROSPERITY, 1914–1932, at 235 (University of Chicago Press 1958).
15. WALTER LIPPMANN, MEN OF DESTINY 27 (New York: MacMillan Co. 1927).
16. *See Prophet Taft*, 150 THE OUTLOOK 974 (1928).
17. National Prohibition Act, Pub. L. 66-66, 41 Stat. 305 (October 28, 1919).

CHAPTER 28

Prohibition, the Taft Court, and the Authority of Law

THE RADICAL REACH of prohibition had been made possible by the "frenzy" of World War I.[1] Taft characterized prohibition as "an outgrowth of the reforming and religious enthusiasm engendered during the war."[2] But unlike other wartime innovations, prohibition remained entrenched in the Constitution as a grim avatar of the war's ideological fervor,[3] "something out of the normal."[4] In Richard Hofstadter's memorable phrase, it was "the skeleton at the feast."[5] Notwithstanding Harding's gilded broom, prohibition remained ensconced throughout the decade as something glaringly "abnormal."[6]

Prohibition initially enjoyed broad support. Its roots lay in evangelical protestant moralism, so much so that Hofstadter could dismiss it as "a pseudo-reform" produced by a "rural-evangelical virus" capable of transmuting "the reforming energies of the country ... into mere peevishness."[7] But prohibition was also "the logical result of the tendency of the times toward a government under which the people may protect themselves from evils and wrong, one of which being the organized liquor traffic of our Nation."[8] Prohibition was in this sense a legitimate child of the progressive movement.[9] It expressed middle-class aspirations to use "government action to protect or advance the public interest."[10] It was advocated to promote health,[11] workplace effectiveness,[12] "war efficiency,"[13] crime reduction,[14] and efforts to Americanize new immigrants and control African-Americans in the South.[15]

The anomalous political status of prohibition was rooted in its unique capacity to serve as a "bridge between the old and the new, between those who wanted to reform individuals and those who wanted to reform society."[16] As one astute observer remarked, "[w]hile the propaganda of prohibition still is pre-eminently a moral one, ... the conclusion is inescapable ... that the extra-religious support which vitalizes it today has been gained through its attempted assimilation of the gospel of mental and physical efficiency which now stands so firmly embodied in our national character."[17] Prohibition was supported because of its pietistic moralism,[18] its hostility to large unruly urban populations,[19] its nativism,[20] its convenience as a vehicle of social control,[21] its association with moral uplift,[22] its affirmation of efficiency,[23] and its use of social engineering to achieve social mastery.[24]

Despite this broad base of support, prohibition dominated political attention and debate during the 1920s.[25] It was "the largest political issue ... since the Civil War."[26] In his 1922 State of the Union Address, President Harding was moved to complain "that many voters are disposed to make all political decisions with reference to this single question. It is distracting the public mind and prejudicing the judgment of the electorate."[27] In contrast to the enforcement of state and local prohibition laws that predated prohibition,[28] federal efforts to implement the Eighteenth Amendment were so obviously ineffectual that widespread defiance of prohibition became, in Harding's words, a "nation-wide scandal" that was "the most demoralizing factor in our public life."[29]

"Conspicuous and flagrant violations"[30] of prohibition were so common that they provoked a vigorous discussion about the extent to which federal law could be used "to effect a radical change in the personal habits of a large part of the population, under the compulsion of the combined executive and judicial branches of the government of the United States."[31] Contemporaries of all political stripes recognized prohibition as "the most radical political and social experiment of our day"[32] and as "one of the most extensive and sweeping efforts to change the social habits of an entire nation recorded in history."[33] "Arguably the most radical and significant constitutional reform ever adopted,"[34] prohibition was in this sense a profoundly disorienting legal innovation.

Support for prohibition came at a price for both conservatives and progressives. For conservatives the price was commitment to a social reform that unabashedly deployed state compulsion to improve society. Prohibition was in many ways the apotheosis of the administrative state, for it summoned a vast governmental apparatus to control the most intimate details of personal consumption. Princeton philosopher Warner Fite, asked to comment at a symposium on the role of individualism "just after a majority of the United States have voted for a bone-dry amendment," commented dryly that he felt "like an Eskimo at the Peace Conference," because "his presence in the discussion appears to be a mere formality. On a superficial view, at least, one may doubt whether the individual has ever been estimated more cheaply. . . . The point seems to be that an individualistic social order has been tried and found wanting. 'Individualism' and 'laissez faire' . . . stand for ideas for which few respectable persons now wish to be responsible."[35]

Prohibition was especially galling to many conservatives because it was imposed by the federal government. Even if it were tolerable for states to regulate liquor, responsibility for enforcing prohibition was firmly located in a national government that was required to issue uniform rules preempting all local variation.[36] Conservatives who supported prohibition were thus forced to affirm "an experiment in federal centralization, which, if successful, would radically alter the customary and the appropriate distribution of responsibility for social welfare between Washington and the state capitals."[37] Nothing could be more inconsistent with traditional conservative commitments to localism.

Prohibition, the Taft Court, & the Authority of Law

The price was more subtle for progressives. Progressives had long aspired to endow the federal government with the kind of democratic legitimacy necessary to sustain extensive social regulations like those imposed by prohibition. But progressives in the 1920s were in fact ambivalent about prohibition,[38] because the Eighteenth Amendment was a legal cataclysm of such unimaginable proportions that it potentially undermined faith in the possibility of a national administrative state. As the *New Republic* reported, "[n]ational prohibition" was ratified "on the supposition that the American people would on the whole support its enforcement," but "this calculation ... prove[d] to be entirely false." The Eighteenth Amendment instead

> provoked a stubborn and widespread violation of the law, and as the years have come and gone this resistance has increased rather than diminished. ... [I]t has provoked dogged resistance on the part of several states .... The resistance has attained at the present time almost the dignity and importance of an organized insurrection against the authority of the federal government. ... It is certain now that the rules of conduct prescribed for all American citizens by the Eighteenth Amendment and the Volstead act will be disobeyed by a minority of the American people so large and so segregated that they cannot be forced to obey without some huge expenditure of money and police power by the federal government.[39]

The success of prohibition depended upon massive national coercive power that risked making the federal government "feared, disliked and suspected by many millions of American citizens."[40] To the extent that enforcing prohibition "brought [the national government] into suspicion, disrepute and even contempt,"[41] it contradicted "[t]he first condition of a progressive revival," which was "the restoration of the federal government in the esteem, the loyalty and the obedience of the American people." Prohibition thus provoked progressives to rethink the normative foundations of American federalism. It forced liberals to consider whether certain forms of "social behavior" should "in any well balanced federal system ... be treated at least partly as a matter of local rather than of national responsibility."[42]

Prohibition also prompted some progressives to question the proper boundaries of the administrative state. The "volume, the stubbornness and the unscrupulousness of the existing resistance to the law"[43] by millions of citizens who were "in other respects law-abiding," and who included "all the business, artistic, professional, labor and political leaders of the larger cities,"[44] raised for progressives the "totally new question" of whether law could "exterminate a habit of popular conduct to which people are so stubbornly attached."[45] To the extent that progressivism aspired to express "the collective conscience of the community in its effort to make for more and better human life,"[46] prohibition required progressives to think anew about the relationship between traditional mores and positive law.

The *New Republic*, for example, concluded that government "must expect to have its authority flouted" when "it forbids its citizens to perform innocent and inoffensive acts of private conduct."[47] The dependence of legal legitimacy on the brute fact of popular custom carried with it the startling idea that progressives may previously have "over-emphasized the importance of government as the instrument of human amelioration," because the "moral authority of the government does not rest on its legal right to issue commands."[48] Prohibition exposed the many ways in which legal legitimacy was dependent upon custom, even as progressives otherwise sought to use positive law to reform traditional mores.

It was of course possible for conservatives and liberals to debate prohibition in more predictable ways. Conservatives could condemn prohibition because it was "a gross outrage upon personal liberty"[49] that represented a giant stride toward socialism, and because it entailed "the suppression of individuality, the exaltation of the collective will and the collective interest, the submergence of the individual will and the individual interest." "The cause of Prohibition has owed its rapid success in no small measure to the support of great capitalists and industrialists bent upon the absorbing object of productive efficiency; but they have paid a price they little realize. For in the attainment of this minor object, they have made a tremendous breach in the greatest defense of the existing order of society against the advancing enemy. To undermine the foundations of Liberty is to open the way to Socialism."[50]

Progressives could counter by reaffirming the necessity for proactive state intervention to achieve desirable social reform. In 1927 the president of the National Conference of Social Work invoked "the great progressive movement of 1910 to 1914" as a platform from which to lambaste "[t]he anti-prohibitionists" who, "with their cry of personal liberty, . . . have about wrecked the true conception of government control of evils." "To be consistent those same destructionists go so far as to condemn any and all control of conduct. . . . What may the government regulate, control, or prohibit if not such human destroyers as . . . intoxicating liquors? . . . No previous time in our history has seen such a concerted movement to break the confidence of the people in their government as an instrument for human betterment."[51]

Framed in this way, prohibition merely prompted an old and familiar debate that ran through the progressive era and that would continue throughout the twentieth century. But there was something unique about prohibition that forced sophisticated Americans to transcend this tired framework. This may have been because the Anti-Saloon League, led by the astute Wayne B. Wheeler, "perhaps the most feared man" in American politics,[52] was uncannily adept at using the force of a massive single issue pressure group to compel American politicians to vote more dryly than their constituents.[53] Although Wheeler had insisted that the Eighteenth Amendment contain ambiguous language referring to "intoxicating liquors,"[54] after the Amendment was ratified he successfully pressed Congress to pass the Volstead Act[55] which defined liquor as "intoxicating" whenever it contained more than 0.5 percent alcohol.[56] It is highly unlikely that a majority of ordinary Americans actually supported such virulently bone-dry legislation.[57]

In the context of prohibition, the high-pressure tactics of the Anti-Saloon League forced positive law to grow increasingly detached from popular sentiment. The gap undermined the legitimacy of prohibition legislation. Stone, for one, considered the Volstead Act a prime example of attempting "to carry legislation too far."[58] As the *San Francisco Chronicle* astutely commented in 1920, "The drastic constitutional amendment proposed to be drastically enforced seems to have been so far in advance of public sentiment that it has in it the seeds of great trouble. The minority is too large to submit as Americans are accustomed to submit."[59] Suddenly and unexpectedly deprived of their "wholesome beer," the American Federation of Labor, which had supported the Eighteenth Amendment, turned on "the drastic Volstead Law."[60] Cities and immigrants went into open revolt.[61] Elites brazenly flouted the law.[62]

Pushed by the relentless Anti-Saloon League, which in effect was "the political arm of the evangelical churches in the small communities,"[63] prohibition became by mid-decade entangled in a full-fledged culture war.[64] As Walter Lippmann saw it, on the one side lay "the authentic expression of the ... social outlook and the religion of the older American village civilization," which strongly supported prohibition and was associated with "the Ku Klux Klan, fundamentalism, and xenophobia," while on the other side lay "the emergence of the cities as the dominant force in America," with an associated "metropolitan spirit."[65]

On the day that Massachusetts ratified the Eighteenth Amendment, prohibitionist Elizabeth Tilton described supporters as in "ecstasy": "Urbanization had not yet laid its material, beer-soaked claws on the Vote of America.... The Mold of the Frontier was conquering the City, and that meant to us a Virile Nation. We were not degenerate even in a State where 90% of the vote was urban. We were still strong in the Anglo-Saxon sense of race-survival."[66] The conflict between what Tilton called "the Mold, the old American type," and what she called the "Mass"[67] – urban ethnic immigrants – grew so fierce that Congress simply refused to reapportion its membership based upon the 1920 census, which for the first time pushed rural inhabitants from their dominant position.[68] Contemporaries well appreciated the entanglement of prohibition in the one and only failure of the nation to reapportion the House of Representatives based upon a decennial census.[69]

The clash provoked by prohibition would eventually transform the basic political alignment of the nation. The Democratic Party nominated the notoriously wet Al Smith for president in 1928. He was opposed by the dry Herbert Hoover, who declared that prohibition was "a great social and economic experiment, noble in motive and far-reaching in purpose."[70] The upshot was "a breakthrough moment" when "urban ethnic workers shifted loyalties decisively to the Democratic Party, reshaping the political landscape for Franklin Roosevelt's 1932 victory four years later."[71]

In this toxic context, the "eruption of law-breaking"[72] that accompanied prohibition was not simply about the success or failure of an ambitious social experiment. It was about "the most alarming" prospect of "nullification,"[73] which challenged the very possibility of using law to govern a divided society. The fear was that prohibition "in operation ... has led to more violation of and contempt for law, both by private individuals and public officials, and to more hypocrisy than anything else in our national life."[74] "[I]n the more conspicuous circles of our large cities, it is a social asset to ignore the law and a social dereliction to obey it.... Where the public approves the law, its penalties can be enforced; where it disapproves, they cannot.... Under the old local-option plan a community decided whether or not it would have liquor. Under the new it decides whether or not it will have law."[75]

Prohibition produced a genuine crisis of positive law.[76] "[I]t may be said ... without contradiction, that no law has ever been on the statute books that has been so freely and openly violated as have the prohibition laws in every State in the Union. There is not a county in any State in the Union where alcoholic beverage is not sold in violation of the law, and in many States it is sold more freely and openly than in the days of the saloon."[77] The question was whether a deeply polarized society could ever produce law democratically legitimate enough to inspire obedience. "Most of our people assumed that the adoption of the eighteenth amendment meant the elimination of the question from our politics," Harding mused, but to the contrary "it has ... intensified" the issue.[78] In the words of Pauline Sabin, head of the Women's Organization for National Prohibition Reform, supporters of prohibition "thought they could make prohibition as strong as the Constitution but instead have made the Constitution as weak as prohibition."[79]

The Taft Court lay at the storm center of this cultural, political, and jurisprudential maelstrom. Despite his earlier opposition to prohibition, Taft held the Court foursquare for strict enforcement of the law.[80] "I was opposed to prohibition for several reasons," he wrote, "but we adopted it into the Constitution and now we must enforce it. A republic is where the majority must rule and the minority must bend to the laws made by the majority."[81] Two weeks after Taft's death, the press could report that "Opinions today vary widely as to whether the prohibition experiment is a gradually increasing success or whether it is on the high road to failure. But no person at all cognizant of the attitude of the Supreme Court of the United States for the last decade and familiar with its decisions which have a bearing on enforcement can fail to recognize that this court by its decisions has been an unfailing tower of strength to the prohibition cause."[82]

Taft's leadership came at a high cost. Like the country, the Court was deeply divided over the interpretation and administration of prohibition. Taft remarked to his son that "[i]t would seem as if more feeling could be engendered over the Prohibition Act than almost any other subject that we have in the Court."[83] "There is something about the issue that seems to engender bitterness,"[84] Taft observed two years later. "We have had two five to four decisions, Brandeis writing the majority opinion in each case. Our dear friends Pierce Butler and George Sutherland are most sensitive on the subject of the Volstead law, but Holmes, Van Devanter, Brandeis, Sanford and I are still steady in the boat. Stone wobbles a good deal on the subject, and I don't quite see where he stands, and I am not quite sure that he does."[85]

Figure VI-1 illustrates the division that prohibition inflicted upon the Taft Court. During the 1921–1928 terms, the Court's opinions were 85 percent unanimous in nonprohibition cases, but only 74 percent unanimous in prohibition related cases. Figures VI-2 and VI-3 demonstrate that prohibition inspired disagreements that cut across the usual divide separating the conservative from the liberal wing of the Court. The alignment of justices in a typical prohibition case does not at all resemble the alignment in opinions addressing ordinary social and economic legislation. Sutherland,[86] Butler,[87] and McReynolds[88] were less likely to join or author an opinion for the Court in cases involving prohibition than they were in cases generally, whereas the reverse was true for Taft, Holmes, Van Devanter, and Sanford.

Prohibition, the Taft Court, & the Authority of Law

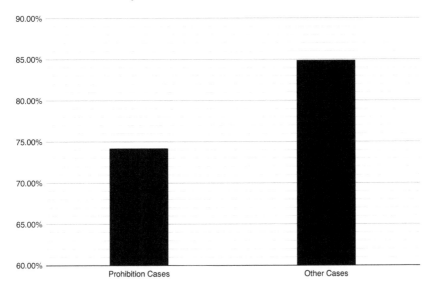

Figure VI-1 Percentage of full opinions that are unanimous in prohibition decisions versus in nonprohibition decisions, 1921–1928 terms

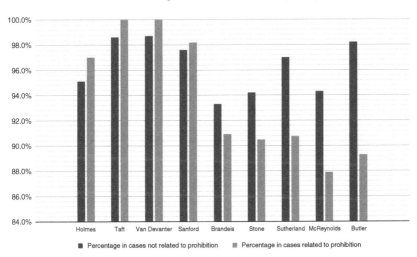

Figure VI-2 Percentage of decisions in which a justice participates and joins or authors an opinion for the Court, prohibition decisions versus nonprohibition decisions, 1921–1928 terms

Prohibition forced the Court to decide whether it would uphold purely positive law, especially criminal law, even when that law, as Stone delicately put it in 1925, "did not rest on a normally developed public opinion and is not the product of observed experience rather than of propaganda and emotionalism."[89] Throughout

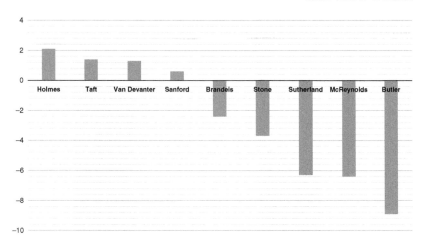

Figure VI-3 Number of percentage points by which a justice is more likely to join or author an opinion for the Court in a prohibition decision than in a nonprohibition decision

the 1920s, Taft was able to forge a consistent majority to sustain the Court's support for prohibition. He combined the votes of Van Devanter and Sanford to pioneer an innovative fusion of conservatism and positivism. This fusion would disappear after the repeal of prohibition and would not again reemerge on the Court until William Rehnquist a half century later.[90] McReynolds, Sutherland, and Butler, by contrast, maintained a traditional conservative allegiance to the customary practices of ordinary life. Not only did they seek to safeguard a protected realm of liberty,[91] but they also opposed the aggrandizement of national power required by prohibition. Prohibition thus split conservative justices on the Court into two distinct blocs.

Holmes joined with Taft in vigorously upholding prohibition, a stance that reflected both Holmes's deference to the enactments of positive law and his embrace of federal authority. But Brandeis was more divided. Despite his commitment to a decentralized federalism, Brandeis's basic inclination was to uphold national authority. Yet by the end of the decade the yawning gulf between positive law and fundamental social norms had become so sharp that Brandeis was prompted to revisit the essential question of legal legitimacy. In his famous and influential dissent in *Olmstead v. United States*,[92] Brandeis sketched constitutional protections for privacy that would foreshadow the eventual emergence of a liberal appeal to social norms to check the potential abuses of positive state law. The repeal of prohibition and liberal support for the New Deal would defer the emergence of this kind of liberalism until the 1960s and cases like *Griswold v. Connecticut*.[93]

Prohibition, in short, sparked new forms of jurisprudential thinking for both conservatives and liberals. These developments would be short lived; they would vanish with the Twenty-First Amendment and they would not reappear until many years later, when the existence *vel non* of the national American administrative state had come to seem inevitable and irrevocable.

Prohibition, the Taft Court, & the Authority of Law
Notes

1. *Progressivism and Prohibition*, 46 NEW REPUBLIC 261, 262 (1926). "Without the war, the nation might have been spared 'Prohibition,' the divisive 14-year national ban on the sale of alcoholic beverages that has become a byword for widespread lawlessness and louche morality." WILLIAM G. ROSS, WORLD WAR I AND THE AMERICAN CONSTITUTION 186 (Cambridge University Press 2017). *See id.* at 186–24; RICHARD F. HAMM, SHAPING THE EIGHTEENTH AMENDMENT: TEMPERANCE REFORM, LEGAL CULTURE, AND THE POLITY, 1880–1920, at 240 (Chapel Hill: University of North Carolina Press 1995) ("The frenzied emotions of war mobilization carried over into the drive for national constitutional prohibition."). The Eighteenth Amendment was introduced in Congress two days after Woodrow Wilson urged that war be declared on Germany. *Compare* 55 CONG. REC. 102–4 (April 2, 1917) *with* 55 CONG. REC. 197–98 (April 4, 1917). Congress proposed the amendment eight months later. *See* 40 Stat. 1050 (December 19, 1917).

After Congress declared war, "it was universally recognized that one of the most essential steps in winning the war was to suspend the liquor traffic." *Enforcement of the Prohibition Laws of the United States: A Report of the National Commission on Law Observance and Enforcement Relative to the Facts as to the Enforcement, the Benefits, and the Abuses under the Prohibition Laws, Both Before and Since the Adoption of the Eighteenth Amendment to the Constitution*, H.R. Doc. No. 71-722, 71st CONG. 3rd SESS. (January 20, 1931), at 5. A month after the country entered the war, therefore, Congress prohibited the sale to soldiers of all intoxicating liquor, including beer, ale, or wine. Pub. L. 65-12, 40 Stat. 76, 82–83 (May 18, 1917).

> By the Act of August 10, 1917, 40 Stat. 276, 282, known as the Lever Act, Congress prohibited the use after September 9, 1917, of food materials or feeds in the production of distilled spirits for beverage purposes and authorized the President to limit or prohibit their use in the production of malt or vinous liquors for beverage purposes, so far as he might, from time to time, deem it essential to assure an adequate supply of food, or deem it helpful in promoting the national security or defense. Under the power so conferred, the President, by proclamation of December 8, 1917, 40 Stat. 1728, prohibited the production after January 1, 1918, of any "malt liquor except ale and porter" containing more than 2.75 per centum of alcohol by weight. By proclamation of September 16, 1918, 40 Stat. 1848, the prohibition was extended to "malt liquors, including near beer, for beverage purposes, whether or not such malt liquors contain alcohol."

Jacob Ruppert v. Caffey, 251 U.S. 264, 278–79 (1920). On November 21, 1918, ten days after the Armistice, Congress passed the War-Time Prohibition Act, which, "for the purpose of conserving the man power of the Nation, and to increase efficiency in the production of arms, munitions, ships, food, and clothing for the Army and Navy," provided that until the termination of demobilization, which did not occur until after the Eighteenth Amendment became operative, "no grains, cereals, fruit, or other food product shall be used in the manufacture or production of beer, wine, or other intoxicating malt or vinous liquor for beverage purposes. ... [N]o beer, wine, or other intoxicating malt or vinous liquor shall be sold for beverage purposes except for export." Pub. L. 65-243, 40 Stat. 1045, 1046 (November 21, 1918). *See* Hamilton v. Ky. Distilleries & Warehouse Co., 251 U.S. 146, 153 (1919). Virtually the entire ratification process for the Eighteenth Amendment thus occurred during various forms of emergency national wartime prohibition. For a good discussion of wartime prohibition, see CHRISTOPHER N. MAY, IN THE NAME OF WAR: JUDICIAL REVIEW AND THE WAR POWERS SINCE 1918, at 60–93 (Cambridge: Harvard University Press 1989). For a chronology of wartime prohibition enactments, see Robert Post, *Federalism, Positive Law, and the Emergence of the American Administrative State: Prohibition in the Taft Court Era*, 48 WILLIAM & MARY LAW REVIEW 1, 175–76 (2006).

2. William Howard Taft, Foreword to LORD SHAW OF DUNFERMLINE, THE LAW OF THE KINSMEN 10 (London: Hodder & Stoughton 1923). See *War Breaking Down the Barriers to Prohibition and Woman Suffrage*, 64 CURRENT OPINION 82, 83 (1918) (attributing the Eighteenth Amendment "in large measure to the influence of the war"); JAMES H. TIMBERLAKE, PROHIBITION AND THE PROGRESSIVE MOVEMENT 1900–1920, at 178 (Cambridge: Harvard University Press 1963) ("In speeding the [Eighteenth] Amendment through Congress and the state legislatures, the war undoubtedly played an important part."); *The Problem of Prohibition in War Time*, 119 THE OUTLOOK 515 (1918) ("The sentiment in favor of National prohibition is due primarily to the growing belief that the evils of the liquor traffic can be overcome only by National action. But it has received a great impulse from the growing conviction that it is necessary as a war measure."); *Report of the National Commission on Law Observance and Enforcement*, supra note 1, at 45; WALTER THOMPSON, FEDERAL CENTRALIZATION: A STUDY AND CRITICISM OF THE EXPANDING SCOPE OF CONGRESSIONAL LEGISLATION 183 (New York: Harcourt, Brace & Co. 1923) ("Prohibition became associated with winning the war."); A. Lawrence Lowell, *Reconstruction and Prohibition*, 143 ATLANTIC MONTHLY 145 (February 1929); *The Prohibition Amendment and Its Outlook*, 108 COMMERCIAL AND FINANCIAL CHRONICLE 1212 (1919) ("It is probable that when we have had ten years of perspective ... it will be freely acknowledged that the reformers pressed their advantage (the advantage of an admission that the war measure was best) at a time when the thought of the people was engrossed with war, peace, and reconstruction."); RONALD SCHAFFER, AMERICA IN THE GREAT WAR: THE RISE OF THE WELFARE STATE 96–108 (New York: Oxford University Press 1991). At the time the Eighteenth Amendment was proposed, William H. Anderson, state superintendent for New York of the Anti-Saloon League, declared that "If an emergency, by opening a short cut which avoids the necessity for settling a lot of technical questions, enables the doing of certain desirable things with less delay and less friction than would be possible under normal conditions, that is one of the compensations of such a catastrophe as war." William H. Anderson, *Prohibition or War? The Views of the Anti-Saloon League*, 117 THE OUTLOOK 46, 46 (1917).

3. "[U]nfortunately the coincidence of the War, the misconception of what was going on in Europe in respect to the prohibition of intoxicating liquor, and the temporary spirit of self-restraint and sacrifice, put the measure through, and it is now working like a ratchet wheel, so that there is not the slightest chance, for a great many years, of repealing the 18th Amendment, and we are put in a situation where we must fight it through and must enforce it, if we can." WHT to Francis Peabody (July 12, 1923) (Taft papers). As late as 1930, prohibitionist Senator Morris Sheppard of Texas could pronounce that "There is as much of a chance of repealing the eighteenth amendment as there is for a humming bird to fly to the planet Mars with the Washington Monument tied to its tail." *Senator Sheppard Says Country Will Stay Dry*, WASHINGTON POST (September 25, 1930), at 5.

4. Martin Conboy, *Has the Volstead Act Nullified the Eighteenth Amendment?*, 16 GEORGETOWN LAW JOURNAL 348, 353 (1928). *See* THOMPSON, *supra* note 2, at 361–62 ("Perhaps what makes the enforcement of federal liquor laws especially difficult is that prohibition is a standard adopted under an agitated and abnormal condition of the public mind created by war psychology and prematurely imposed."); *see also* FREDERIC LYMAN COBB, PROHIBITION! THE CROWNING FOLLY OF THE GREAT WAR'S AFTERMATH 1 (New York: Peter G. Boyle 1922) ("During the war anything that had the slightest bearing on helping to 'win the war' was proposed and put in operation. Some of these energies were sane and necessary – many others were nothing but rampant hysteria, and should have ceased as soon as the war ended. But the momentum was so great most of them were swept over into peacetime. What, during the fever of war, seemed perfectly natural and sensible is entirely out of place now that the war is over. In this class Prohibition leads them all.").

5. RICHARD HOFSTADTER, THE AGE OF REFORM: FROM BRYAN TO F.D.R. 289 (New York: Vintage Books 1955).

6. WHT to Allen B. Lincoln (September 2, 1918) (Taft papers) ("We are acting now under the heroic impulse of a war, which stirs our feelings and makes us think that we can have a millennium of virtue and self-sacrifice for the future. This is a fundamental error. I profoundly deprecate having our constitutional structure seriously amended by a feverish enthusiasm, which will abate to neglect and laxity in many states as the years go on. If, through the abnormal psychology of war, the thirty-six states are induced to approve a national prohibition amendment now, we can never change it, though a great majority of the people may come later to see its utter failure.").

7. HOFSTADTER, *supra* note 5, at 289–90, 292. Hofstadter stressed the extent to which prohibition in the 1920s was associated with anti-immigrant prejudice, most especially that associated with the Ku Klux Klan. *Id.* at 293–95.

8. Statement of Mr. Wayne B. Wheeler, National Counsel for the Anti-Saloon League, and State Superintendent of the State of Ohio (December 11, 1913), in *Intoxicating Liquors*, Hearings before the House Committee on the Judiciary, 63rd CONG. 2nd SESS., at 41.

9. TIMBERLAKE, *supra* note 2, at 100. *See* DEWEY W. GRANTHAM, SOUTHERN PROGRESSIVISM: THE RECONCILIATION OF PROGRESS AND TRADITION 160, 173 (Knoxville: University of Tennessee Press 1983) (arguing that prohibition "enlisted the strong support of most southern progressives" and was "the manifestation of a desire for social uplift of the poor and of a zeal to promote social justice"); J.C. Burnham, *New Perspectives on the Prohibition "Experiment" of the 1920's*, 2 JOURNAL OF SOCIAL HISTORY 51, 52–53 (1968); Robert A. Hohner, *The Prohibitionists: Who Were They?*, 68 SOUTH ATLANTIC QUARTERLY 491, 500–1 (1969) ("Both prohibitionists and progressives reflected a moral idealism; both had great faith in progress, efficiency, and science; both attempted to curb the arrogance and power of big business, to eliminate political corruption, and to reduce crime, poverty, and disease; both sought to uplift the masses by direct legislation.").

10. THOMAS R. PEGRAM, BATTLING DEMON RUM: THE STRUGGLE FOR A DRY AMERICA, 1800–1933, at 30 (Chicago: Ivan R. Dee 1998); TIMBERLAKE, *supra* note 2, at 152.

11. *See* Henry Smith Williams, *Alcohol and the Individual*, 31 MCCLURE'S MAGAZINE 704, 712 (1908):

> So, I am bound to believe, on the evidence, that if you take alcohol habitually, in any quantity whatever, it is to some extent a menace to you. I am bound to believe, in the light of what science has revealed: (1) that you are tangibly threatening the physical structures of your stomach, your liver, your kidneys, your heart, your blood-vessels, your nerves, your brain; (2) that you are unequivocally decreasing your capacity for work in any field, be it physical, intellectual, or artistic; (3) that you are in some measure lowering the grade of your mind, dulling your higher esthetic sense, and taking the finer edge off your morals; (4) that you are distinctly lessening your chances of maintaining health and attaining longevity; and (5) that you may be entailing upon your descendants yet unborn a bond of incalculable misery.
>
> Such, I am bound to believe, is the probable cost of your "moderate" indulgence in alcoholic beverages. Part of that cost you must pay in person; the balance will be the heritage of future generations.

See also Eugene Lyman Fisk, *The Relationship of Alcohol to Society and to Citizenship*, 109 ANNALS OF THE AMERICAN ACADEMY OF POLITICAL AND SOCIAL SCIENCE 1, 5 (1923).

12. "Perhaps the most important new support that has come to the prohibition movement in recent years has come through its assimilation of the great American doctrine of mental and physical efficiency. This war against waste has had the effect of steeling the hearts of thousands of employers against the use of liquor by themselves or their employees during work hours, and to any extent which may have an appreciable influence upon the efficiency of the workmen." *See* L. Ames Brown, *Nation-Wide Prohibition*, 115 ATLANTIC MONTHLY 735, 743 (1915). The arguments of corporate employers were "seen to be increasingly unlike the fanatical creations of sentiment which formerly had so large a place in the prohibition propaganda." *Id.* at 744. *See* Edward Alsworth Ross, *Prohibition as the Sociologist Sees It*, 142 HARPER'S MAGAZINE 186, 188 (1921) ("The factory system supplanted the handicrafts, and a new class, the employers, came to realize how drink plays havoc with production. As workers became machine tenders the damage from the liquor habit in impairment of efficiency and in injury to delicate and costly machinery became ever more unmistakable. More and more employers came to look upon prohibition as a labor-efficiency policy and it was largely these men who financed the movement which brought the liquor interests to grief, despite their millions for propaganda."); Roy A. Haynes, *Says Business Man Upholds Prohibition; Haynes Convinced that Industry Is Won Over by Reason of More Efficiency*, NEW YORK TIMES (August 23, 1923), at 17.

13. There was much agitation for wartime prohibition because "human efficiency must be saved to win the war." *To Win the War*, 90 THE INDEPENDENT 486, 487 (1917). "We must not forget that when efficiency is concerned any drink, beer as well as whiskey, is bad." *Id. See* Hamilton v. Kentucky Distilleries & Warehouse Co., 251 U.S. 146, 157 (1919) ("[P]rohibition of the liquor traffic is conceded to be an appropriate means of increasing our war efficiency."); Jacob Ruppert v. Caffey, 251 U.S. 264, 282 (1920).

14. George Elliott Howard, *Alcohol and Crime: A Study in Social Causation*, 24 AMERICAN JOURNAL OF SOCIOLOGY 61, 79–80 (1918) ("Without doubt the saloon is the chief laboratory of the vice and crime attributable to the use of intoxicating

drinks. The closing of the saloon is the indispensable condition of any successful effort to eliminate the evils caused by alcohol. Wherever the saloon has been closed, whether by local option or by state-wide prohibition, drunkenness and therefore vice and crime have been lessened. Everywhere 'dry' towns compare favorably with license towns in this regard. Why stop with local or state action? Why not demand nation-wide prohibition? Are not the American people ready to empower and to require the federal government to outlaw a traffic so destructive of the moral and vital resources of the nation?"); *see also* Richard J. Hopkins, *Prohibition and Crime*, 222 NORTH AMERICAN REVIEW 40, 41 (1925) ("The liquor traffic has been the dominant cause of crime, misery and pauperism. Intoxicants, directly or indirectly, have sent more people to the jails, penitentiaries and insane asylums than any other cause.").

15. GRANTHAM, *supra* note 9, at 176; TIMBERLAKE, *supra* note 2, at 115–24.
16. GRANTHAM, *supra* note 9, at 173.
17. L. Ames Brown, *Is Prohibition American?*, 203 NORTH AMERICAN REVIEW 413, 414 (1916).
18. GRANTHAM, *supra* note 9, at 173–74; Brown, *supra* note 17, at 416–18; Frank Crane, *The Little Church on Main Street*, 72 CURRENT OPINION 736, 741 (1922); Jeremiah Hevenward, *Upholding the Constitution*, 153 HARPER'S MAGAZINE 476 (1926); Hohner, *supra* note 9, at 494–95; *"Prohibition Anderson" Answers Pertinent Questions on the Battle against Alcohol*, 62 THE FORUM 68, 68–70 (1919).
19. *See* JOSEPH R. GUSFIELD, SYMBOLIC CRUSADE: STATUS POLITICS AND THE AMERICAN TEMPERANCE MOVEMENT 97–98 (Urbana: University of Illinois Press 1963); Hohner, *supra* note 9, at 495.
20. PEGRAM, *supra* note 10, at 169–73. *See* Haynes, *supra* note 12 ("The foreign element in our population ... especially in the large cities, perhaps will be a problem always. Through all our history we have shown the world that foreign standards of life, types of citizenship, ideals and customs are not sufficient for us. Continued violation of, and contempt for, our prohibition laws have brought many loyal Americans to this definite conviction: If any of our ... un-American sons of Europe revolt against the very forces from which has sprung our greatness, then let them leave our shores. America is working out her destiny in her own American way. There is no place for the foreigner, or the native born, who ... sets himself against or apart from American tradition, American institutions.").
21. This is a major thesis of LISA MCGIRR, THE WAR ON ALCOHOL: PROHIBITION AND THE RISE OF THE AMERICAN STATE (New York: W.W. Norton & Co. 2016). *See, e.g., The Economics of War Prohibition*, 38 THE SURVEY 143 (1917) ("The public is far better advised today than ever before concerning the effects of the habitual use of intoxicants in producing criminal, insane and untrustworthy men and women and degenerate children. Prisons, asylums and public reformatories furnish continuous and abundant evidence along these lines. The increasing undiscipline of Americans has been observed and noted by investigators and students for many years. This is evidenced in lack of respect for parents, for the aged, for officers of the law and for the law itself. It has also been a uniform observation that these conditions become aggravated whenever and wherever intoxicating liquors are habitually used."); GRANTHAM, *supra* note 9, at 176–77.
22. GRANTHAM, *supra* note 9, at 173.

23. See TIMBERLAKE, *supra* note 2, at 67 (noting that the 1899 Committee of Fifty, which undertook an investigation of alcohol's role in poverty and crime, believed that the increased speed, precision, and danger of industrial machinery, as well as the greater intensity and length of the workday, necessitated workers' sobriety); *id.* at 80–81 (both the middle class and labor unions identified a relationship between sobriety and efficiency).
24. See PEGRAM, *supra* note 10, at 169 ("From its origins in the nineteenth century, temperance reform had developed as a forward-looking, optimistic social movement. Its proponents had been modernizers, those who looked forward to social, economic, and moral improvement."). Prohibition, it was said, "was bound to come as the inevitable consequence of technical and scientific progress." Henry W. Farnam, *Law, Liberty, and Progress*, 15 YALE REVIEW 433, 441 (1926).
25. Prohibition "has been marked by controversy, nation-wide in scope and almost unparalleled in intensity." Fabian Franklin, *Prohibition Ten Years After*, 83 THE FORUM 209, 209 (1930).
26. HOWARD LEE MCBAIN, PROHIBITION LEGAL AND ILLEGAL 14 (New York: MacMillan Co. 1928). Prohibition was "the livest and biggest political issue before the country." KANSAS CITY STAR (November 29, 1927), at 30. In 1929, Mabel Walker Willebrandt, the assistant attorney general in charge of prohibition enforcement, could write that it cannot "be denied that prohibition enforcement remains the chief and in fact the only real political issue of the whole nation. No political, economic or moral issue has so engrossed and divided all the people of America as the prohibition problem, except the issue of slavery.... It is no more possible to avoid prohibition discussion than to avoid breathing. In every newspaper every day of the year, on every street corner where people stop to talk, at every afternoon tea party, in every social gathering of any kind involving any class of society, one subject recurs time after time and is of universal interest: Prohibition." MABEL WALKER WILLEBRANDT, THE INSIDE OF PROHIBITION 15–17 (Indianapolis: Bobbs-Merrill Co. 1929).
27. *Address of the President*, 64 CONG. REC. 212 (December 8, 1922).
28. See *Report of the National Commission on Law Observance and Enforcement*, *supra* note 1, at 39 ("At the time of the adoption of the Eighteenth Amendment, thirty-three states had adopted prohibition by law or constitution.... In many of... [these] states the laws were quite generally enforced before national prohibition."); W.H. Stayton, *Our Experiment in National Prohibition: What Progress Has It Made?*, 109 ANNALS OF THE AMERICAN ACADEMY OF POLITICAL & SOCIAL SCIENCE 26, 26 (1923) ("[U]ntil the outbreak of the World War, the only prohibition known in this country was state or district prohibition – something resting on home rule and local self-government. ... State prohibition laws ... were well known and in some states were favored by a majority of the voters. ... [T]hey were fairly well obeyed and respected, – about as other laws were; they required for their execution no separate and expensive enforcement divisions, but were administered by the regular judicial and police forces; they brought no great scandals, and were reasonably free from corrupting effects. None of these things can, as yet, fairly be said for the Volstead Act.").

The prevalence of state prohibition laws increased dramatically in the years before the United States entered World War I. At the turn of the century there were only five states with "state-wide laws prohibiting the manufacture and sale of intoxicating beverages," but by April 1917 that number had increased to twenty-six. TIMBERLAKE, *supra* note 2, at 149–66. Of these, only thirteen – all in the southern or western regions of the country – "had sought to anticipate on a state-wide basis the drastic bone-dry legislation of the Eighteenth Amendment." CHARLES MERZ, THE DRY DECADE 22 (Garden City: Doubleday, Doran & Co. 1932). The remaining "dry" states allowed the importation and/or manufacture of alcohol for personal use, although some restricted the type of alcohol permitted and many limited the amount that could be imported during any given period. *See id.* at 20–22. Virtually all of the "wet" states had local option laws that allowed localities to vote themselves dry or refuse liquor licenses. *See generally* WAYNE B. WHEELER, FEDERAL AND STATE LAWS RELATING TO INTOXICATING LIQUOR (2d ed., Westerville: American Issue Publishing Co. 1918). It is noteworthy that the effect of the 1917 Reed Amendment, Pub. L. 64-380, 39 Stat. 1058, 1069 (March 3, 1917), was to transform states that forbade the sale and manufacture of liquor, but that permitted the importation of liquor for personal use, into bone-dry states. It was observed in 1930:

> It is not generally known that bone-dryness is an absolutely new thing in this country. It did not exist at all before 1914, and substantially not at all before 1917, when the Reed Amendment (a Federal Statute), as a war-time measure, made it unlawful to ship intoxicants into "dry" states. Before the Reed Amendment went into effect on July 1, 1917, it was lawful in almost every dry state for residents to have liquor shipped to them from wet states. Many of these dry states also permitted residents to make their own alcoholic beverages. It was, accordingly, the fact that before 1914 all, and before 1917 substantially all, of the dry states were merely partially dry, – the idea being to abolish the saloon, not to force total abstinence on everyone. These semi-dry laws commanded a large public support and respect and accordingly did not cause the resentment which the bone-dry Volstead Act has since aroused. They appear, accordingly, to have worked much better in practice than the more recent bone-dry law.

THE MODERATION LEAGUE, A NATIONAL SURVEY OF CONDITIONS UNDER PROHIBITION 1930 at 5–6 (New York: The Moderation League 1930). For a survey of state prohibition regulation regimes in 1918, see Post, *supra* note 1, at 177–83.

It is difficult to gauge the effectiveness of state prohibition in the years immediately preceding the Eighteenth Amendment. For a good discussion, see Harry M. Cassidy, *Liquor Control in the United States*, 1928 EDITORIAL RESEARCH REPORTS 683, 693–705. In 1917, the *Literary Digest* offered a useful and detailed survey of conditions under state prohibition. *Nation-wide Prohibition as a War Measure: The Story of Prohibition in States Dry for at Least a Year Told by Their Newspapers*, 54 LITERARY DIGEST 1573 (May 26, 1917). One Maine newspaper observed that state prohibition was sometimes undermined by "weak and nullifying officials" but nonetheless concluded that in rural areas "the law has 'fulfilled its high purpose in a degree that is admirable beyond measure.'" *Id.* at 1576. Newspapers in Kansas, a state with a long history of prohibition regulation, thought highly of state prohibition laws. The editor of the *Topeka State Journal* esteemed them "a great success ... and would recommend [them] to other States." *Id.* at 1603. Many newspapers noted that although prohibition had achieved desirable effects, it had also spawned an underground trade in alcohol that was difficult to eliminate. The *Tulsa World* in Oklahoma, for example, declared that while prohibition had succeeded in eliminating the licensed saloon, "instead we have the 'blind tiger' [i.e., the speakeasy] and the bootlegger. . . . The irony of the new condition is that the new evils are not amenable to regulation, are outlaws from start to finish, yet because of popular demand they remain and flourish 'in spite of police activity and religious crusades.'" *Id.* at 1613. The *Courier News* of Fargo, North Dakota, interpreted this shift as a sign of progress. Believing that "antiprohibition sentiment is losing ground rather than gaining, with the result that enforcement makes constant progress," the paper noted that the consumption of alcohol had moved "from marble-front and beveled-glass interior locations on the best business corners" to "low dives, and nauseating places" where "the social element of drinking" had been eliminated. *Id.* at 1607. Several newspapers expressed the view that the success of enforcement depended upon popular opinion. A Georgia paper asserted that "[t]he drink habit is not going by enforcement until more people believe it is wrong to drink. . . . So long as a fairly large number of individual citizens want it, liquor will continue to come to Georgia." *Id.* at 1610. Supporters of state prohibition efforts expressed optimism on this score. *Id.* at 1619. In sum, as the *Fayetteville Observer* of North Carolina noted, "prohibition has prohibited as much as most other laws, for all laws are violated." *Id.* at 1620. What this success portended for national prohibition, however, was unclear, for, as the *Cocino Sun* of Arizona presciently warned, "[g]radually, the United States is going 'dry,' by education and by a general inclination of the people, but a nation-wide prohibition law would seem at this time so drastic that a revolution of feeling might result in undoing the good work already done by the States." *Id.* at 1633.

29. *Address of the President, supra* note 27, at 215.
30. John Grier Hibben, *Our National Moral Issue: What the 18th Amendment Has Done to Us*, 87 FORUM & CENTURY 215 (1932).
31. Conboy, *supra* note 4, at 350.
32. *Progressivism and Prohibition, supra* note 1, at 262.
33. *Report of the National Commission on Law Observance and Enforcement, supra* note 1, at 10. Prohibition "marks what is perhaps the most radical change that has ever taken place in the history of a nation." Crane, *supra* note 18, at 736.
34. David E. Kyvig, *Sober Thoughts: Myths and Realities of National Prohibition after Fifty Years*, in LAW, ALCOHOL, AND ORDER: PERSPECTIVES ON NATIONAL PROHIBITION 6 (David E. Kyvig, ed., Westport: Greenwood Press 1985).
35. Walter Fite, *Individualism in the New Social Order*, in AMERICA AND THE NEW ERA: A SYMPOSIUM ON SOCIAL RECONSTRUCTION 95 (Elisha M. Friedman, ed., New York: E.P. Dutton & Co. 1920).
36. *See, e.g.*, OSCAR W. UNDERWOOD, DRIFTING SANDS OF PARTY POLITICS 52–57 (New York: The Century Co. 1928). In a remarkable series of editorials, for example, the *New York Times*, objecting to the "imposition of the prohibition amendment by the Anti-Saloon League and all the pragmatical busybodies who have bulldozed Congress and are now seeking to bulldoze the State Legislatures," charged southern dry conservative Democrats with hypocrisy:

> When so many Democrats are more Hamiltonian than Hamilton, when they miss no chance to add to the overgrown powers of the central Government, who could blame the Republicans if they should seek to regulate Federal elections in the Southern States? If "white supremacy" and local self-government are threatened at any time in the South, whose fault will it be? The fault of

Democrats who have forgotten or renounced the historic and cardinal doctrines of the Democratic Party.

State Rights Democrats, NEW YORK TIMES (April 15, 1918), at 14. Three months earlier the *Times*, apropos of Southern Democrats, had made the same point:

> The old ragers against "centralization" have become its devotees. To speak of "State rights" is almost like speaking of an ancient world, of the Kentucky and Virginia resolutions. Yet the preservation to the several States of their undelegated and unprohibited ... powers ... should be striven for by every man who wants the American form of government to retain something of its original principles, who believes in local initiative and self-government, who is not willing to sacrifice the power of the State to the all-swallowing Federal monster.

State Rights and Prohibition, NEW YORK TIMES (January 9, 1918), at 12. In 1922, Fabian Franklin confirmed the accuracy of the *Times's* prediction. He caustically observed that after 1919

> Southern Senators and Representatives and Legislaturemen who, forgetting about their cherished doctrine of State rights, had fallen over themselves in their eagerness to fasten the Eighteenth Amendment upon the country, suddenly discovered that they were deeply devoted to that doctrine when the Nineteenth Amendment came up for consideration. But nobody would listen to them.

FABIAN FRANKLIN, WHAT PROHIBITION HAS DONE TO AMERICA 30–31 (New York: Harcourt, Brace & Co. 1922).

37. *The Progressive Attitude towards Prohibition?*, 56 NEW REPUBLIC 166, 167 (1928). See MCBAIN, *supra* note 26, at 168: "The eighteenth amendment has profoundly altered our federal system of government. In comparison, the commerce clause is a frail instrument of potential centralization. If Congress ever casts off hypocrisy and sets up the necessary machinery for adequate federal enforcement, we shall enjoy a national bureaucracy worthy of our boasted 'bigness' in other respects. No wonder Congress pauses before the plain logic of the amendment."

38. The *New Republic* reported that prohibition

> divides the progressives one from another just as sharply and irreconcilably as it does the Democrats and the Republicans. The western progressives outside of Wisconsin are for the most part dry, but there are many exceptions to this rule particularly among labor-union groups. The eastern progressives who live for the most part in large cities are more likely to be wet, but there is probably a larger proportion of dry progressives in the east than of wet progressives in the west. The social workers, for instance, who tend to be progressive are usually convinced supporters of prohibition, and while this group is not numerous, it is composed of unusually disinterested and intelligent voters. There is no consensus of opinion in any part of the country among progressives as to what attitude as progressives they should adopt toward prohibition.

Progressivism and Prohibition, *supra* note 1, at 261. On the support of social workers for prohibition, see *Prohibition as Seen from Hull House*, 103 LITERARY DIGEST 22 (October 19, 1929).

39. *Progressivism and Prohibition*, *supra* note 1, at 262–63.
40. *Id.* at 263.
41. *The Progressive Attitude towards Prohibition?*, *supra* note 37, at 167.
42. *Id.* at 166–67.
43. *Progressivism and Prohibition*, *supra* note 1, at 263.

44. *The Progressive Attitude towards Prohibition?*, supra note 37, at 167.
45. *Progressivism and Prohibition*, supra note 1, at 263.
46. *The Progressive Attitude towards Prohibition?*, supra note 37, at 166.
47. *Id.* at 167.
48. *Id.* at 166–67.
49. Franklin, *supra* note 36, at 98.
50. *Id.* at 117–18, 120. The *Commercial & Financial Chronicle* opposed prohibition as part of its general hostility to what it called "reform":

> The moral of it all is, and it is a very big moral, that we cannot preserve either our liberties, our institutions, or our peculiar form of government, if we are to let self-appointed guardians of the public weal seek the cover of general law for the purpose of obtaining their self-satisfying ends. This prohibition measure and mandate is but one of these ends. It is, whether good or bad, a theory of the proper social life. In precisely the same manner theorists are seeking to control individual life in commerce. ... And, it is worth repeating, while we are saving the world we are sleeping on our own rights.

The Prohibition Amendment and Its Outlook, supra note 2, at 1212–13.
51. John A. Lapp, *Justice First: Presidential Address at the National Conference of Social Work* (May 11, 1927), in Proceedings of the National Conference of Social Work 3, 5, 7 (University of Chicago Press 1927).
52. Sean Beienburg, Prohibition, the Constitution, and States' Rights 5 (University of Chicago Press 2019). Wheeler was generally regarded as "the most powerful political figure in the nation." Justin Steuart, Wayne Wheeler: Dry Boss 189 (Westport: Greenwood Press 1928). "Wayne B. Wheeler controlled six Congresses, dictated to two Presidents of the United States, directed legislation in most of the states of the Union, picked the candidates for the most important elective state and federal offices, held the balance of power in both Republican and Democratic parties, distributed more patronage than any dozen other men, supervised a federal bureau from outside without official authority, and was recognized by friend and foe alike as the most masterful and powerful single individual in the United States." *Id.* at 11. No friend of prohibition, H.L. Mencken was profuse in his praise of Wheeler: "In fifty years the United States has seen no more adept political manipulator. He was worth a whole herd of United States Senators, with all the sachems of Tammany thrown in. He was as good as three Presidents in a row. Yet he will probably get less space in the books than even Harding. It is almost as if Goethe should get less space than Karl August von Wettin, Grand Duke of Saxe-Weimar. ... [Wheeler] had the innocent delight in politicians that foxhunters have in horses and dogs. It was his joy to arise of a bright and frosty morning, and set them to leaping and yowling over the landscape. ... Nine-tenths of those who flourished in his time bear his brand to this day." H.L. Mencken, *What Is Going on in the World*, 27 American Mercury 385, 390–91 (December 1932).
53. Wheeler pioneered the art of single-issue pressure politics. He did not care whether a politician was a Republican or a Democrat. He did not care whether a politician personally drank or not. He did not "ask any questions about a man's religion, complexion or general political principles." Steuart, *supra*

note 52, at 303. He cared only that they vote in support of dry measures. Wheeler explained his approach to "fellow reformer" Lincoln Steffans:

> I will do it the way the bosses do it, with minorities. There are some anti-saloon voters in every community. I and other speakers increase the number and the passion of them. I list and bind them to vote as I bid. I say, "We'll all vote against the men in office who won't support our bills. We'll vote for candidates who will promise to. They'll break their promise. Sure. Next time, we'll break them." And we can. We did. Our swinging, solid minorities, no matter how small, counted. The pols came to us, volunteered promises, which, by and by, were kept. We are teaching these crooks that breaking promises to us is surer of punishment than going back on their bosses, and some day they will learn that all over the United States – and we'll have national prohibition.

LINCOLN STEFFANS, THE AUTOBIOGRAPHY OF LINCOLN STEFFENS 860 (Chautauqua: The Chautauqua Press 1931). Wheeler relished his reputation as "the biggest legislative bully the country has produced." STEUART, *supra* note 52, at 184, 302–4. He discussed his theory of "Pressure Groups" in an address on practical politics at Columbia University in October 1923. *Id.* at 209. On the resulting disparity between legislative outcomes and popular sentiment, see Mencken, *supra* note 52, at 390 (The League "demonstrated with horrible clarity and a richness of instructive detail how a small pressure group, operating with competent leaders and a sufficient war-chest, may force its ideas, however idiotic, upon the witless and helpless bulk of the people."); DANIEL OKRENT, LAST CALL: THE RISE AND FALL OF PROHIBITION 105 (New York: Scribner 2010). In 1919, the *New Republic* observed that "Nobody supposes that the remarkable progress of the eighteenth amendment through Congress and the state legislatures represents a corresponding fervency of purpose in the body of the people. Would a universal referendum on federal prohibition yield even a majority vote? We doubt it." *Prohibition as a Warning*, 17 NEW REPUBLIC 359, 360 (1919).
54. OKRENT, *supra* note 53, at 94.
55. The official name for the Volstead Act was the National Prohibition Act, Pub. L. 66-66, 41 Stat. 305 (October 28, 1919), repealed by Liquor Law Repeal and Enforcement Act, Pub. L. 74-347, 49 Stat. 872 (August 27, 1935).
56. 41 Stat. at 305. *See* The National Prohibition Cases, 253 U.S. 350, 387–88 (1920); Jacob Ruppert v. Caffey, 251 U.S. 264, 280 (1920). On Wheeler's role, see OKRENT, *supra* note 53, at 110–12. The Volstead Act "was designed as 'a 1920 model of efficiency and speed.'" HAMM, *supra* note 1, at 251. The Act defined intoxicating beverages by reference to the standard previously used in the application of the War-Time Prohibition Act. *See supra* note 1.

> On February 6, 1919, the Commissioner of Internal Revenue ruled ... that a beverage containing as much as one-half of one per centum of alcohol by volume would be regarded as intoxicating within the intent of the Act of November 21, 1918.... [S]ince 1902 ... fermented liquor containing as much as one-half of one per centum of alcohol had been treated as taxable under Rev. Stats. §§ 3339 and 3242; and this classification was expressly adopted in the War Revenue Act of October 3, 1917, c. 63 § 307, 40 Stat. 311.

Jacob Ruppert, 251 U.S. at 279–80. In *Jacob Ruppert*, the Court, speaking through Brandeis, prominently cited *Purity Extract Co. v. Lynch*, 226 U.S. 192 (1912), for the proposition that it was permissible for a national statute to sweep broadly in order "to be capable of effective enforcement." *Id.* at 283, 289–92. "Since Congress has the power to increase war efficiency by prohibiting the liquor traffic, no reason appears why it should be denied the power to make its prohibition effective." *Id.* at 301. *Jacob Ruppert* thus relied upon the very argument that the liberal wing of the Court would soon be advancing in dissent in cases like *Jay Burns* and *Weaver*. See *supra* Chapter 23, at 739. It is in fact highly instructive to compare *Jacob Ruppert* with *Jay Burns*. Throughout the 1920s there were efforts to amend the Volstead Act to permit the sale and manufacture of light wines and beer. Taft considered such efforts as attempts to "nullify the practical effectiveness of the law and the amendment." WHT to Gertrude Ely (December 22, 1923) (Taft papers).

57. The Wickersham Commission offered this diagnosis of the dislocation caused by national prohibition: "It was only when the Eighteenth Amendment was adopted that total abstinence was sought to be established by fiat of law throughout the territory of the United States or even in many of those states which had adopted limited prohibition laws. There are obvious differences, both as to individual psychology and legal principle, between temperance and prohibition. ... Prohibition makes no distinction between moderate and excessive use. It is predicated upon the theory that any use of alcoholic liquors for beverage purposes, however moderate and under any conditions, is anti-social and so injurious to the community as to justify legal restraint." *Report of the National Commission on Law Observance and Enforcement*, *supra* note 1, at 89. The Anti-Saloon League's demand for bone-dry prohibition reflected the influence of its protestant evangelical constituency.

58. HFS to Huger W. Jervey (December 6, 1926) (Stone papers).

59. *Prohibition Troubles*, SAN FRANCISCO CHRONICLE (January 27, 1920), at 20.

60. *Resolution of the American Federation of Labor*, in REPORT OF PROCEEDINGS OF THE FORTY-FIRST ANNUAL CONVENTION OF THE AMERICAN FEDERATION OF LABOR 361 (Washington D.C.: Law Reporter Printing Co. 1921) ("The drastic Volstead Law has brought about the wholesale illicit manufacture of whiskey and other strong alcoholic liquors or concoctions, which has resulted in the deaths of hundreds of our citizens .... This deplorable condition has made the Volstead Enforcement Law unpopular with the vast majority of our citizens."). See *Report of A.F. of L. Executive Council*, in REPORT OF PROCEEDINGS OF THE FORTY-THIRD ANNUAL CONVENTION OF THE AMERICAN FEDERATION OF LABOR 48 (Washington D.C.: Law Reporter Printing Co. 1923) ("We do not protest against the eighteenth amendment to the constitution which now is a part of the fundamental law of the land. ... It is our contention that the eighteenth amendment under a reasonable and proper legislative interpretation would be beneficial to our country and would have the support of the great majority of our people. The eighteenth amendment, however, under the present drastic and unreasonable legislative interpretation has a destructive and deteriorating effect and influence in every direction. ... We urge, therefore, that all citizens in every walk of life demand from their representatives and senators in Washington immediate relief from the unwarranted restriction contained in the Volstead act."). See REPORT OF PROCEEDINGS OF THE FORTY-SEVENTH ANNUAL CONVENTION OF THE AMERICAN FEDERATION OF LABOR 92–93, 321 (Washington D.C.: Law Reporter Printing Co. 1927).

61. "[T]here were large numbers of people who failed to accept this law as binding.... In the large cities opposition was particularly stubborn, as the result both of

a prevailing set of moral values different from moral values in the smaller towns and the influence of a rich strain of recent European immigration." MERZ, *supra* note 28, at 71. "I think it can be said, without contradiction, that in practically all the big cities, like New York, Boston, Philadelphia, Baltimore, Chicago, St. Louis, New Orleans, San Francisco, and dozens of others, there is a distinct opposition to the enforcement of the law. In the main this opposition comes from people whose customs and society for generations past have been opposed to sumptuary laws, and who have drunk their wine and beer without acquiring intemperate habits." UNDERWOOD, *supra* note 36, at 385. *See Dry Votes in Wettest Washington*, 100 LITERARY DIGEST 8 (March 2, 1929).

62. The classic illustration is Sinclair Lewis's portrait of Babbitt mixing cocktails for the elite of Zenith while hosting a dinner party: "Well, folks, do you think you could stand breaking the law a little?" SINCLAIR LEWIS, BABBITT 112 (New York: Harcourt, Brace & World 1922). *See* Barton W. Currie, *Soft Morals*, LADIES' HOME JOURNAL (March 1923), at 32 ("The prohibition embroilment is shaping its course as an inevitable class issue. The fashionable rich demand their rum as an inalienable class privilege."); William H. Borah, *Shall the Constitution of the United States be Nullified?*, in LAW VS. LAWLESSNESS: ADDRESSES DELIVERED AT THE CITIZENSHIP CONFERENCE, WASHINGTON D.C. 176 (Fred B. Smith, ed., New York: Fleming H. Revell Co. 1924) ("The hotbed, the flouting, noisy rendezvous of lawlessness, of cynical defiance, to the Eighteenth Amendment, are among those of social standing, of large property interests, and in the wealthier homes. Without their patronage, their protection, and their example, the bootlegger could easily be brought within the control of the law."). Taft emphatically shared this same sentiment:

> My impatience at the present situation is toward the well-to-do class, the intelligent part of the community, who are not willing to give up something that isn't essential to their life or happiness, and insist upon violating the law because they don't like it. They are very much troubled over the lawlessness of somebody else – the lawlessness of the labor unions and the weakness of legislatures, and of Congress in dealing with questions of that sort, but the minute that their convenience or comfort or tastes are interfered with by a law declared to be valid, according to the only machinery that we have for that purpose, then they settle back and connive at the violation of law and make fun of it, and have no sympathy with its enforcement, naturally, because they are engaged in violating it, or at the least in encouraging bootleggers to violate it. This shows such inconsistency on the part of persons who are intelligent enough to see the necessary trend of their conduct toward a demoralization of all law, that I have no sympathy with them at all. ... [B]ecause the wealthy classes, those who consult their own comfort before anything else, as other people possibly do, don't like this limitation upon what they regard as their personal liberty, but which is not personal liberty under the Constitution, they are seizing on every little technicality to attack the law. I opposed the constitutional amendment. I felt that it would meet a lack of sympathy with the law by a lot of foreigners of the lower classes who would violate it if they could, but I confess I did not expect to find that spirit of lawlessness among the intelligent and wealthy which now exists. ... The truth is the attitude of the New Yorkers and of people on the seaboard is one which ignores the opinion of the country west of Hoboken, and that illustrates the evil of the amendment, which gives the National Government power over the parochial matters in each State that should be managed by the State itself.

WHT to James R. Sheffield (July 8, 1923) (Taft papers). *See* WHT to Francis Peabody (July 12, 1923) (Taft papers) ("The present feature of the situation most alarming is the attitude of intelligent and well-to-do people toward the law and its enforcement.... The tendency now is to limit the use of liquor and beer and wine ... to the well-to-do – a situation calculated to promote bitter class feeling, and to demoralize all law, for which the responsibility of the educated and well-to-do is plain."). Taft knew whereof he spoke. In 1924, for example, he reported to his brother about a dinner given in his honor by Eugene Meyer, "a successful Jew, who has done some very good work for the Government. ... Out of what I regard as proper respect, they did not have any liquor at all, and Alice [Roosevelt] was making fun of Nick [Longworth, Speaker of the House and Alice's husband] because he could not get anything to drink. His hostess was engaged in the same thing. Apparently it is necessary for Nick to liquor up at every dinner. It is that sort of thing that encourages the youth." WHT to Horace D. Taft (March 10, 1924) (Taft papers).

63. WALTER LIPPMANN, MEN OF DESTINY 30 (New York: MacMillan Co. 1927). *See* Frank R. Kent, *Church Backing Gives Strength to Dry League*, BALTIMORE SUN (November 22, 1922), at 1; Frank R. Kent, *Drys Ascribe Prohibition to Small Church*, BALTIMORE SUN (November 25, 1922), at 1.

64. The federal prohibition commissioner, hand-picked by Wayne Wheeler, declared that opposition to the Eighteenth Amendment displays "tendencies" that "have come to us out of the World War" and that are "in the direction of lowered and degenerated forms of literature, art, and the teachings of religion, disguised and nurtured under the cloak of 'modernism.'" ROY A. HAYNES, PROHIBITION INSIDE OUT 303–4 (New York: Doubleday, Page & Co. 1923). Opposing prohibition, Clarence Darrow argued that it was foisted on the country by "Superstitious bigots, religious fanatics, pleasure-hating lineal descendants of the Puritan witch-hunters." *Violate Dry Act, Darrow's Appeal to People of U.S.*, BROOKLYN DAILY TIMES (December 8, 1926), at 1.

65. LIPPMANN, *supra* note 63, at 28–31. "It is curious," wrote journalist Frank Kent, "how closely this struggle between the evolutionists and the anti-evolutionists parallels that between the wets and the drys.... [T]he great bulk of fundamentalists are dry and the vast majority of evolutionists are wet." Frank R. Kent, *Evolution War Similar to Wet and Dry Fight*, BALTIMORE SUN (July 14, 1925), at 1. In the countryside, prohibition was commonly associated with "100% Protestant Americanism." MCGIRR, *supra* note 21, at 135–36. On the connection between the Anti-Saloon League and the Ku Klux Klan, see Thomas R. Pegram, *The Anti-Saloon League and the Ku Klux Klan in 1920s Prohibition Enforcement*, 7 JOURNAL OF THE GILDED AGE AND PROGRESSIVE ERA 89 (2008). In 1926, Taft could remark to a close friend that "both parties are torn with the prohibition issue, with the religious issue, or, properly speaking, the Klan issue." WHT to Charles D. Hilles (July 7, 1926) (Taft papers).

Charles W. Eagles's careful study of voting patterns in the 1920s demonstrates that urban/rural tension was more pronounced in the Democratic party than in the Republican Party. Charles W. Eagles, *Congressional Voting in the 1920s: A Test of Urban–Rural Conflict*, 76 JOURNAL OF AMERICAN HISTORY 528, 532–33 (1989). The famously deadlocked 1924 Democratic Convention illustrates the extreme division between rural and urban forces that split the Democratic Party during the

1920s. In that convention "the progressives tended to be prohibitionists and Klan supporters from the South and West favoring McAdoo, whereas the more eastern-oriented libertarian wing was both wet and anti-Klan" and favored Smith. BEIENBURG, *supra* note 52, at 145. *See The Democratic Wet-And-Dry Donnybrook*, 92 LITERARY DIGEST 5 (February 12, 1927). Established eastern, wet libertarians would in 1927 form the Association Against the Prohibition Amendment ("AAPA"). OKRENT, *supra* note 53, at 295–96. As journalist Charles Merz observed, "In 1917 the chief spokesman of the opposition was the president of the United States Brewers' Association. In 1927 leadership of the opposition had passed to the president of the Pennsylvania Railroad or to the chair of the board of the General Motors Corporation or to the president of the Western Union Telegraph Company." MERZ, *supra* note 28, at 215. Eventually the AAPA would evolve into the Liberty League that vigorously opposed Roosevelt's New Deal. BEIENBURG, *supra* note 52, at 231.
66. ELIZABETH TILTON, RETAKE THE HEIGHTS 161 (n.p. 1960).
67. *Id.* at 12.
68. CHARLES W. EAGLES, DEMOCRACY DELAYED: CONGRESSIONAL REAPPORTIONMENT AND URBAN–RURAL CONFLICT IN THE 1920S (Athens: University of Georgia Press 1990); MARGO J. ANDERSON, THE AMERICAN CENSUS: A SOCIAL HISTORY 133–55 (2d ed., New Haven: Yale University Press 2015). Advocates of the Eighteenth Amendment stressed the importance of ratifying the amendment before the 1920 census when "the urban population was almost certain to be a majority." OKRENT, *supra* note 53, at 80–81.
69. It was plain to all that "Reapportionment, no matter how carefully made, would inevitably tend to shift power from the country to the city, because most of the people live in cities. It would thus tend to reduce the influence of the drys in Congress." *Congress Evades Reapportionment*, 92 LITERARY DIGEST 13 (February 19, 1927). *See, e.g.,* Robert B. Smith, *"What's the Constitution among Friends?"*, 116 THE INDEPENDENT 542 (May 8, 1926); *The Row over Reapportionment*, 101 LITERARY DIGEST 10 (June 22, 1929); *Reapportionment – Danger!*, WASHINGTON POST (February 6, 1929), at 6.
70. *Text of Herbert Hoover's Acceptance of Republican Nomination*, DAILY BOSTON GLOBE (August 12, 1928), at A18. *See Hoover's Stand for Prohibition*, 96 LITERARY DIGEST 5 (March 10, 1928).
71. MCGIRR, *supra* note 21, at 163. "Though the 1932 landslide election is often identified as the moment of realignment, the movement of urban working-class voters to the Democrats happened earlier. The war on alcohol cemented a broader sense of shared identity among immigrant ethnic workers." *Id.* The eastern establishment that made up the AAPA "feared the 'tyranny of federal power,' particularly its regulatory power over business and the economy, [whereas] urban ethnic voters feared the cultural tyranny of the Anti-Saloon League and its hold on policy makers." *Id.* at 172. *See supra* note 65.
72. Gifford Pinchot, *The State Government and Law Enforcement*, in LAW VS. LAWLESSNESS, *supra* note 62, at 104.
73. Louis Marshall, *Preservation of Law and Its Significance to American* Democracy, in LAW VS. LAWLESSNESS, *supra* note 62, at 158. *See* OKRENT, *supra* note 53, at 336; WILLEBRANDT, *supra* note 26, at 183 ("Those who favor nullification of the prohibition law are in effect denying the validity of the whole basis on which our

system of government rests: the right of majority rule."). "Nullification," in Senator Borah's dramatic words, was "the stiletto that goes to the very heart of the constitutional government." 77 CONG. REC. 512 (March 16, 1933). Yet that is exactly what opponents of prohibition openly advocated. They compared prohibition to the Fugitive Slave Law of the previous century. As Arthur Twining Hadley, the ex-president of Yale, explained, "nullification ... is not revolution. It is the safety valve which helps a self-governing community avoid the alternative between tyranny and revolution. It reduces the tension; it gives a warning to those in authority which they disregard at their own peril. ... [I]f a law lacks the authority of conscience and public opinion, it lacks precisely the qualities which are necessary to make it effective in a self-governing commonwealth." Arthur Twining Hadley, *Law Making and Law Enforcement*, 151 HARPER'S MAGAZINE 641, 646–47 (1925).

Taft, for one, was not pleased by Hadley's position. Taft wrote the president of the Unitarian Laymen's League: "Of course I realize that there is a great deal of violation of the law, especially by the luxury loving rich, who are represented by Nicholas Murray Butler and Arthur T. Hadley, who boldly announced that the way to defeat the law is to disobey it. I should very much deprecate the use of the Unitarian Laymen's League to uphold such a campaign as that to which Butler and Hadley are contributing." WHT to Charles H. Strong (July 1, 1925) (Taft papers). Taft's old nemesis, Gifford Pinchot, lately governor of Pennsylvania and a strict prohibitionist, see Gifford Pinchot, *The State Government and Law Enforcement*, in LAW VS. LAWLESSNESS, *supra* note 62, at 94–106, was asked to speak at the 1925 Yale Commencement. Although Taft claimed that the weakness of his heart required him to miss the graduation, WHT to Robert A. Taft (April 12, 1925) (Taft papers); WHT to Robert A. Taft (April 19, 1925) (Taft papers), he nevertheless commented to an old friend that he would very much have enjoyed the opportunity to hear Pinchot speak about prohibition "in Hadley's presence." WHT to George D. Seymour (July 1, 1925) (Taft papers). See *Deny Taft Fled Pinchot*, BOSTON DAILY GLOBE (June 25, 1925), at A22.

74. Mrs. Charles H. Sabin, quoted in *Mrs. Sabin Sounds Call for Wet Fight*, NEW YORK TIMES (April 4, 1929), at 1.

75. Samuel Hopkins Adams, *On Sale Everywhere*, 68 COLLIERS 7, 24 (July 16, 1921). As *The Nation* put the question in 1929:

> It is a simple matter to say categorically, Obey the law, or Enforce the law at whatever cost. Either command involves certain implications that are abhorrent to American ideals of justice. For America was founded on the notion that an unpopular law, a law that thousands upon thousands of Americans believe to be unwarranted and unjust, is better broken than obeyed. From the day when the tax on tea resulted in a ship's load of it being dumped – by an irresponsible crowd of hotheads – into Boston Harbor, this has been so. ...
>
> What, then, is this prohibition? Is it a simple law that must be enforced like any other law? Or is it as mixed up with emotions and mores and principles and behavior as was the Stamp Tax a hundred and fifty years ago? It is broken daily, hourly; it is enforced by violence, murder, and the expenditure of hundreds of millions of dollars yearly – where it is enforced at all.

This Prohibition, 128 THE NATION 443 (1929).

76. "The Eighteenth Amendment and the statutes, orders and regulations purporting to be adopted thereunder, and the abuses practiced in the alleged enforcement thereof, have brought about conditions of crime, fraud, corruption and lawlessness in such proportions and to such extent as to inculcate a general lack of respect and contempt for law." George Westervelt, quoted in *State Bar to Fight to Modify Dry Law*, NEW YORK TIMES (December 11, 1927), at 22.
77. UNDERWOOD, *supra* note 36, at 386.
78. *Address of the President*, *supra* note 27, at 215.
79. Quoted in *Four Women Lead Attack on Dry Law; Referendum Urged*, NEW YORK TIMES (February 14, 1930), at 18. Compare the 1928 Platform of the Republican Party: "The people through the method provided by the Constitution have written the Eighteenth Amendment into the Constitution. The Republican Party pledges itself and its nominees to the observance and vigorous enforcement of this provision of the Constitution." 1928 Platform of the Republican Party, available at www.presidency.ucsb.edu/documents/republican-party-platform-1928.
80. "The truth is that I was one of the foremost in opposing the 18th Amendment, chiefly for the reason that I thought its enforcement would be full of difficulty and present problems that we ought not to undertake. But I was overborne, and the 18th Amendment has become the law of the land, and like a loyal American, obedient to the Constitution, I am in favor of enforcing the Amendment in every possible and reasonable way." WHT to Louis A. Cuvillier (November 9, 1926) (Taft papers).
81. WHT to J.H. Kelley (December 7, 1923) (Taft papers).
82. John Snure, *Supreme Court's Rulings in Liquor Law Test Cases Have Been Uniformly Dry*, NEW YORK HERALD TRIBUNE (March 23, 1930), at B1. Mabel Walker Willebrandt, the assistant attorney general in charge of prohibition enforcement, praised the Court for "issuing so steadily opinions so helpful in the orderly and vigorous administration of the prohibition law." Quoted in DOROTHY M. BROWN, MABEL WALKER WILLEBRANDT: A STUDY OF POWER, LOYALTY, AND LAW 78 (Knoxville: University of Tennessee Press 1984). Willebrandt was a conscientious but controversial figure during her tenure at the Justice Department. In the end she was forced out by Hoover because "she made the dry cause a holy cause" and preferred "the big stick to persuasion." *A Dry Crusader Takes to the Air*, 101 LITERARY DIGEST 8 (June 8, 1929).
83. "[U]nless," Taft continued, "it be the technical questions of jurisdiction, the excited feelings over which among the members of the Court amaze me." WHT to Charles P. Taft 2nd (December 28, 1924) (Taft papers).
84. WHT to Horace D. Taft (December 12, 1926) (Taft papers). "There are certain members of our Court," Taft remarked, "who I dislike to say are becoming a bit raw in their opposition to the Volstead Act." *Id.*
85. *Id.* The two decisions to which Taft refers are Lambert v. Yellowley, 272 U.S. 581 (1926), and United States v. One Ford Coupe Automobile, 272 U.S. 321 (1926). *Lambert* addressed the constitutionality of federal laws regulating the medicinal uses of hard liquor. It was decided on November 29 and was authored by Brandeis, with McReynolds, Sutherland, Butler, and Stone dissenting. For a discussion of *Lambert*, see *infra* Chapter 30, at 974–76. *One Ford Coupe Automobile*, which addressed the constitutionality of private property seizures pursuant to the enforcement of prohibition, was decided on November 22. The decision was authored by

Brandeis, with McReynolds, Sutherland, and Butler dissenting. Stone filed a special and limited concurrence.

86. From the time he was appointed to the Court until the end of the 1928 term, Sutherland either joined or authored the opinion for the Court in 97 percent of the nonprohibition related cases in which he participated. During that same period, he either joined or authored the opinion for the Court in only 90.7 percent of cases involving prohibition. *See* Figure VI-2. For examples of Sutherland's discomfort with the Court's support of prohibition, see Lambert, 272 U.S. at 597 (Sutherland, J., dissenting); One Ford Coupe Automobile, 272 U.S. at 335 (Butler, J., dissenting); Carroll v. United States, 267 U.S. 132, 163 (1925) (McReynolds & Sutherland, JJ., dissenting); and Cunard Steamship Co. v. Mellon, 262 U.S. 100, 133 (1923) (Sutherland, J., dissenting). Sutherland nevertheless authored the Court's unanimous opinion in Grosfield v. United States, 276 U.S. 494 (1928), which upheld the use of civil injunctive padlocking as a remedy against properties used to violate prohibition, which was by far the law's most efficient and effective remedy.

87. From the time he was appointed to the Court until the end of the 1928 term, Butler either joined or authored the opinion for the Court in 98.2 percent of the nonprohibition related cases in which he participated. During that same period he either joined or authored the opinion for the Court in only 89.3 percent of cases involving prohibition. *See* Figure VI-2. For examples of Butler's opposition to prohibition, see Lambert, 272 U.S. at 597, 605 (Sutherland, J., dissenting); Port Gardner Investment Co. v. United States, 272 U.S. 564, 567 (1926) (Butler, J., concurring); One Ford Coupe Automobile, 272 U.S. at 335 (Butler, J., dissenting); and Samuels v. McCurdy, 267 U.S. 188, 200 (1925) (Butler, J., dissenting).

88. In a 1922 conversation with Frankfurter, Brandeis remarked that "Day & Clarke & Mc[Reynolds] are quite wild about prohibition." *Brandeis-Frankfurter Conversations*, at 306 (July 1, 1922). From the time of Taft's appointment as chief justice until the end of the 1928 term, McReynolds either joined or authored the opinion for the Court in 94.3 percent of the nonprohibition related cases in which he participated. During that same period he either joined or authored the opinion for the Court in only 87.9 percent of cases involving prohibition. *See* Figure VI-2. For examples of McReynolds's opposition to prohibition, see Lambert, 272 U.S. at 597, 605 (Sutherland, J., dissenting); One Ford Coupe Automobile, 272 U.S. at 335, 351 (Butler, J., dissenting); Carroll, 267 U.S. at 163 (McReynolds, J., dissenting); Cunard Steamship Co., 262 U.S. at 132 (McReynolds, J., dissenting); Vigliotti v. Pennsylvania, 258 U.S. 403, 409 (1922) (McReynolds, J., dissenting); and Corneli v. Moore, 257 U.S. 491, 499 (1922) (McReynolds, J., dissenting).

89. Harlan Fiske Stone, *Obedience to Law and Social Change*, 5 PROCEEDINGS OF THE BAR ASSOCIATION OF THE STATE OF NEW HAMPSHIRE 27, 34 (November 3, 1925). "Certain it is," Stone observed, "that never before in history has any people exhibited such a child-like and implicit faith in the efficacy of legislation to bring about the social Utopia as have our own people in our own time. Forgetting that social custom and the average moral standards of the community are more potent in the control of human conduct than formal law, we nevertheless seem to regard statute making as the chief and only ultimate agency of social reform and the never failing means for the minute regulation and control of all human activities. The vice of this procedure is that it leaves out of account the evils which inevitably flow from

the attempt to impose rules of conduct by legal command which do not have the moral support of the great mass of the community or which are not of sufficient importance to arouse active public interest in their behalf. ... [W]hatever advantages we gain from a partial or inadequate enforcement of the rule we adopt we pay a high price in loss of respect for law and law enforcement agencies, and in the danger of breakdown of our administrative machinery." *Id.* at 27.

90. On Rehnquist's positivism, see William H. Rehnquist, *The Notion of a Living Constitution*, 54 TEXAS LAW REVIEW 693, 704 (1976); SUE DAVIS, JUSTICE REHNQUIST AND THE CONSTITUTION 152 (Princeton University Press 1989); Robert Post, *Foreword: Fashioning the Legal Constitution: Culture, Courts, and Law*, 117 HARVARD LAW REVIEW 4, 30 (2003); Brad Snyder, *What Would Justice Holmes Do (WWJHD)?: Rehnquist's Plessy Memo, Majoritarianism, and* Parents Involved, 69 OHIO STATE LAW JOURNAL 873 (2008)
91. *See supra* Chapter 26.
92. 277 U.S. 438, 471 (1928) (Brandeis, J., dissenting).
93. 381 U.S. 479, 486, 494 (1965) (Goldberg, J., concurring).

CHAPTER 29

Prohibition and Dual Sovereignty

PROHIBITION STRAINED RECEIVED ideals of federalism. The Eighteenth Amendment suddenly made the federal government responsible for suppressing the manufacture and trade of liquor throughout the United States, a task for which it was utterly unprepared.

Over the opposition of the secretary of the treasury and the commissioner of internal revenue, Congress specified in the Volstead Act that prohibition was to be enforced by the Bureau of Internal Revenue.[1] Fearing backlash, prohibition advocates had all along refused to offer a realistic assessment of enforcement costs,[2] with the predictable result that the nation soon discovered that the actual implementation of the Volstead Act would require "an army of enforcement agents far larger than it would be practicable to assemble or obtain an appropriation for."[3] The commissioner of internal revenue immediately announced that the Bureau could fulfill its responsibility only by securing "the closest cooperation between the Federal officers and all other law-enforcing officers – State, county, and municipal."[4]

The striking fact about prohibition was that this cooperation was not forthcoming, even though virtually every state eventually passed its own version of a prohibition statute.[5] By 1923 President Harding was complaining that although "the Federal government is not equipped with the instrumentalities to make enforcement locally effective," because "it does not maintain either a police or a judicial establishment adequate or designed for such a task," the states were nevertheless "disposed to abdicate their own police authority in this matter, and to turn over the burden of prohibition enforcement to the Federal authorities. It is a singular fact that some States which successfully enforced their own prohibition statutes before the eighteenth amendment was adopted have latterly gone backwards in this regard."[6]

Prohibition & Dual Sovereignty

Throughout the decade, federal officials were appalled by "the sleeping sickness which seemed to have descended on local law enforcement" when it came to enforcing prohibition.[7] In 1927, Lincoln Andrews, the assistant secretary of the Treasury in charge of prohibition enforcement, grumbled that "[s]tate, county and municipal law officers tended to overlook their own civic responsibilities under their community laws, and to pass the responsibility for prohibition law enforcement to the Federal law and its agents. The citizens of the country generally ... looked to the national law in Federal hands for the enforcement of prohibition."[8] Andrews observed that citizens "resented this exercise of police power on the part of the Federal agents within their own communities ... in previously dry states, as well as in those that had never previously accepted state prohibition."[9]

Without the active and willing assistance of state police, the only realistic option for effective federal prohibition enforcement was, as Taft had predicted in 1915, a "horde of Federal officials."[10] But this alternative was unacceptable. "[S]uch a superimposed Federal police power," said Andrews, "is to my mind absolutely unthinkable in America, and bad enough in Russia. Such a solution is predicated upon so false a conception of our government as to offend the very fundamentals of our institutions, and I believe it could never be accepted by a thoughtful public."[11]

Congress refused to fund federal prohibition enforcement at anything close to levels that would be required to ensure compliance with the Volstead Act.[12] National prohibition enforcement was understaffed,[13] with agents who were underpaid[14] and unprofessional.[15] The federal judicial system was completely unprepared to deal with the huge influx of cases generated by prohibition.[16] H.L. Mencken famously quipped that "[p]erhaps the chief victims of Prohibition, in the long run, will turn out to be the Federal judges," whose "typical job today, as a majority of the plain people see it, especially in the big cities, is simply to punish men who have refused or been unable to pay the bribes demanded by Prohibition enforcement officers."[17]

The massive numbers of minor prohibition prosecutions[18] forced federal courts "to perform the function of petty police courts."[19] Federal judge J.F. McGee, known as the "bootleggers' terror" because he had once "sentenced 112 liquor law violators in 193 minutes," ultimately shot himself in the heart, declaring in a suicide note that "The fact is the United States District Court has become a Police Court for the trial of whisky and narcotic cases. ... Those cases occupy 85 per cent. of the court's time ... with the end not in sight. I started, in March, 1923, to rush that branch of litigation and thought I would end it, but it has ended me."[20] It was in fact the need to reform federal judicial processing of prohibition cases that in the end propelled Harding to accelerate his nomination of Taft to be chief justice.[21]

Coolidge sought to solve the excruciating dilemmas of federal prohibition enforcement by declaring that the Eighteenth Amendment "puts a concurrent duty on the States. We need their active and energetic cooperation, the vigilant action of their police, and the jurisdiction of their courts to assist in enforcement."[22]

Coolidge appealed to the enigmatic second section of the Eighteenth Amendment, which stated that "[t]he Congress and the several States shall have concurrent power to enforce this article by appropriate legislation."[23] Section 2 of the Eighteenth Amendment raised a deep question about the constitutional structure of American federalism, for it forced contemporaries to theorize the relationship between independent state sovereignty and the affirmative constitutional requirements of prohibition.

Speaking before a conference of state governors convened "to consider co-operation between the State and Federal Governments in the enforcement of the Eighteenth Amendment," Coolidge argued that the amendment imposed on states "a joint responsibility to enact and execute enforcement laws."[24] Throughout the decade, federal officials and supporters of prohibition maintained that the Eighteenth Amendment created affirmative state obligations to enforce the Constitution.[25] In 1929, for example, James M. Doran, commissioner of prohibition, proclaimed that there was "no doubt" that states were required "to exercise in their appropriate sphere of action the full police powers of the State, in order to properly discharge their obligations under the Eighteenth Amendment."[26] Idaho Senator William E. Borah, whose "ambition to be the Moses of the dry movement [was] unmistakable,"[27] wrote a long article for the *New York Times* arguing that even though "[w]e cannot mandamus a State to pass a State law, to execute or enforce a law," a state was nevertheless under a "legal obligation ... to support the law under which it lives."[28]

Maryland Governor Albert C. Ritchie argued against this interpretation of state responsibilities, contending that "the Eighteenth Amendment ... does not mean that the States are legally or morally obliged to exercise" their concurrent power of enforcement.[29] "No State is called upon to provide enforcement machinery for the Federal income tax law or the narcotic law or the Mann act or any other Federal enactment that I know of.... Why, then, should any State be obligated to set up State machinery to enforce just one out of all the thousands of Federal laws – the Federal prohibition law – merely because the Eighteenth Amendment says that it has the power to do so?"[30]

The idea that states were obligated independently to enforce the Eighteenth Amendment would seem to imply that states were also constitutionally required to enact statutes prohibiting the sale and transportation of liquor. But in 1923 a defiant New York repealed its antiliquor statute, the Mullan-Gage law.[31] In explaining his decision not to veto the repeal,[32] Governor Al Smith essentially adopted Ritchie's position. He asserted that he was "entirely unwilling to admit the contention that there was put upon the State, either by the Eighteenth Amendment [or] the Volstead act ... any obligation to pass any law adopting into the State law the provisions of the Volstead act."[33] The Eighteenth Amendment was "not a command but an option. It does not create a duty." Any other conclusion, Smith contended, would be inconsistent with "the supremacy of the Federal Government in its own sphere and the sovereignty of the several States in theirs," which is "one of the great elements in the strength of our democracy."[34]

Prohibition & Dual Sovereignty

The Taft Court brushed against the implications of New York's repeal of the Mullan-Gage statute in *Gambino v. United States*. The defendants in the case were arrested and searched by New York State troopers while transporting intoxicating liquor in an automobile in violation of the Volstead Act. "[T]he liquor and other property taken were immediately turned over to a federal deputy collector of customs for prosecution in the federal court for northern New York." The defendants moved to suppress the evidence on the ground that "the arrest, the search and the seizure were without a warrant and without probable cause, in violation" of the Fourth and Fifth Amendments. The Court agreed that the search and seizure lacked probable cause.[35] Yet the restrictions of the Fourth and Fifth Amendments did not apply to states,[36] and evidence acquired by the federal government through "the wrongful act of a stranger"[37] would not be suppressed in federal courts.[38]

As the Court framed the question, the issue was whether New York State troopers were in effect federal agents, even though there was no evidence that the troopers had "acted under the directions of ... federal officials in making the arrest and seizure."[39] If "the search and seizure was made solely for the purpose of aiding the United States in the enforcement of its laws," the evidence would be suppressed; but if the New York troopers were acting to enforce "state law," the evidence would be admitted.

After the repeal of the Mullan-Gage law, New York had no state statute prohibiting the sale and transportation of liquor. But if Coolidge and Borah were correct that states were nevertheless under an affirmative obligation to enforce the Eighteenth Amendment, the defendants' arrest might have been in the service of fulfilling New York's independent legal responsibilities. In *Gambino*, the Court, speaking unanimously through Justice Brandeis, evaded this issue.[40] Instead the Court concluded that the evidence should be suppressed because Governor Smith had "declared that ... state troopers are required to aid in the enforcement of the federal law 'with as much force and as much vigor as they would enforce any state law or local ordinance'; and that the repeal of the Mullan-Gage law should make no difference in their action, except that thereafter the peace officers must take the offender to the federal court for prosecution."[41]

In *Gambino*, the Taft Court sidestepped the deep questions of federalism raised by New York's repeal of its Mullan-Gage law. But the Court had in fact indirectly addressed these questions in an earlier decision, *United States v. Lanza*,[42] which concerned the seemingly unrelated subject of the Fifth Amendment's proscription of double jeopardy. The issue in *Lanza* was whether the proscription immunized defendants, who had been convicted of violating a state statute forbidding the possession, manufacture, and transportation of liquor, from subsequent federal prosecution under the Volstead Act for the identical acts that had formed the basis of their state law convictions. The Court, in a unanimous opinion authored by Taft, concluded that although the Double Jeopardy Clause protected citizens against successive prosecutions for the same offense, a state government and the federal government were "two sovereignties, deriving power from different sources" and hence that the defendants had for constitutional purposes "committed two different offenses by the same act."[43] Successive prosecutions for distinct offenses, even for offenses committed by the very same acts, does not constitute double jeopardy for purposes of the Constitution. *Lanza* offered a "classic formulation" of what would later become known as the "dual sovereignty" concept of double jeopardy,[44] a concept that has ever since remained valid constitutional law.[45]

Lanza was the first decision "in which the Supreme Court, faced with an actual instance of double prosecution, failed to find some remedy, consistent with the law, to avoid it."[46] In the popular press the decision was blasted as "repulsive to believers in justice"[47] and as nullifying "a fundamental American principle ... in order to impose a measure of discipline on the American people."[48] In New York, opposition to the possibility of successive prosecutions became a major rallying cry for the repeal of the Mullan-Gage law.[49] *Lanza* was regarded by contemporaries as "a sweeping victory" for "dry enforcement."[50] It meant "that prisoners charged with breaking the dry laws may be severely penalized by more than one tribunal."[51] Historians have interpreted *Lanza* as evidence of "the inclination of the Court – and the public – to support enforcement authorities during the early years of prohibition."[52]

But *Lanza* should also be understood as a contribution to the debate about the nature of state duties under the Eighteenth Amendment. If the "concurrent power" provision of the Eighteenth Amendment were itself to obligate states to enforce prohibition, state prohibition statutes would be implementing a single national, constitutional imperative.[53] *Lanza* specifically rejected this interpretation of the Amendment. It affirmed that "To regard the Amendment as the source of the power of the States to adopt and enforce prohibition measures is to take a partial and erroneous view of the matter." State prohibition measures did not "derive their force" from the Eighteenth Amendment, "but from power originally belonging to the States, preserved to them by the Tenth Amendment, and now relieved from the restriction heretofore arising out of the Federal Constitution." "We have here two sovereignties, deriving power from different sources, capable of dealing with the same subject matter within the same territory. Each may, without interference by the other, enact laws to secure prohibition, with the limitation that no legislation can give validity to acts prohibited by the Amendment. Each government in determining what shall be an offense against its peace and dignity is exercising its own sovereignty, not that of the other."[54]

Contemporaries recognized that this reasoning effectively settled the debate about the existence of affirmative state obligations to enforce the Eighteenth Amendment. Howard Lee McBain, Ruggles Professor of Constitutional Law at Columbia, characterized the implications of *Lanza* as of "the highest importance. For manifestly if the states derive from the amendment no power to enact prohibition laws, they are of a certainty under no obligation, moral or legal, to enact such laws because of the amendment.... [A] state has today ... complete option to adopt or decline to adopt prohibition as a state policy."[55] His logic was widely cited[56] and accepted,[57] with the consequence that those who sought seriously to defend state

Prohibition & Dual Sovereignty

obligations to enforce prohibition were forced to confront or distinguish Taft's opinion in *Lanza*.[58]

Lanza effectively neutralized the potential for the Eighteenth Amendment radically to restructure the American polity. The Court refused to conceptualize states as mere instrumentalities of national prohibition. But it also for the first time explicitly legitimated successive prosecutions by federal and state entities for the same act, even though such double prosecutions were widely regarded as unjust and repugnant. *Lanza* signified that the Court would sustain the "discipline"[59] that effective prohibition enforcement demanded, even if that discipline was inconsistent with traditional conceptions of fairness. Faced with a choice between customary norms and the need effectively to enforce prohibition, the Taft Court opted for the latter. *Lanza* in this regard set a pattern that would continue throughout the 1920s. The Taft Court would be widely and correctly perceived as a "bone dry" institution grimly committed to the success of the positive law of prohibition.[60]

Notes

1. Volstead Act, ch. 85, tit. 1, § 2, Pub. L. 66-66, 41 Stat. 305 (October 28, 1919). Evidently, said the commissioner of internal revenue in his report for 1919, Congress was impressed by "the similarity of some phases of the work of internal-revenue agents in the field who are assigned to secure evidence and aid in the prosecution of persons who have evaded the taxes imposed by law on the manufacture and sale of alcoholic beverages with the police function of prohibition enforcement officers." ANNUAL REPORT OF THE COMMISSIONER OF INTERNAL REVENUE 62 (Washington D.C.: Government Printing Office 1919). The Anti-Saloon League vigorously advocated locating prohibition enforcement in the Treasury Department, likely because the League anticipated that an overworked IRS commissioner would rely on League advice in decisions involving personnel and enforcement policy. THOMAS R. PEGRAM, BATTLING DEMON RUM: THE STRUGGLE FOR A DRY AMERICA, 1800–1933, at 153–54 (Chicago: Ivan R. Dee 1998); ANDREW SINCLAIR, PROHIBITION: THE ERA OF EXCESS 273–76 (New York: Brown, Little, Brown 1962).
2. CHARLES MERZ, THE DRY DECADE 82 (Garden City: Doubleday, Doran & Co. 1932).
3. *No Way to Execute Harding Dry Order; Enforcement Officials Declare Army of Agents Is Necessary to Stop Bootlegging*, NEW YORK TIMES (November 28, 1922), at 6.
4. ANNUAL REPORT OF THE COMMISSIONER OF INTERNAL REVENUE, *supra* note 1, at 62. Plainly daunted by the task imposed upon him, the commissioner declared:

> The Bureau naturally expects unreserved cooperation also from those moral agencies which are so vitally interested in the proper administration of this law. Such agencies include churches, civic organizations, educational societies, charitable and philanthropic societies, and other welfare bodies. The Bureau further expects cooperation and support from all law-abiding citizens of the United States who may have been opposed to the adoption of the constitutional amendment and the law, which in pursuance of that amendment makes unlawful certain acts and privileges which were formerly not unlawful. Thus, it is the right of the Government officers charged with the enforcement of this law to expect the assistance and moral support of every citizen in upholding the law, regardless of personal conviction.

Id. Federal pleas for civilian assistance would continue throughout the decade. *See* U.S. TREASURY DEPARTMENT, BUREAU OF PROHIBITION, PUBLIC COOPERATION IN PROHIBITION LAW ENFORCEMENT 50, 53 (Washington D.C.: Government Printing Office 1930) ("A highly important factor in establishing enforcement support and a more general observance of the prohibition law has been the active and friendly contact between Federal prohibition enforcement officials and leaders in civic, fraternal, welfare, business, and professional groups. . . . Unfortunately, too many local civic agencies in past years have shown a disposition to wait for the Federal Government to do all the prohibition enforcement work. They have not realized that it is humanly impossible for the Federal Government to do police duty in every city, town, and hamlet in the United States. . . . The active sympathy and support of groups of law-abiding citizens organized for civic and community betterment is at all times an asset of tremendous importance in the enforcement of the law."). The active enlistment of civilian groups in law enforcement continued

Prohibition & Dual Sovereignty

a pattern set during World War I. In the 1920s this produced a notorious alignment of federal prohibition agents with the Ku Klux Klan. It has been argued that "The Eighteenth Amendment and the Volstead Act in fact enabled the Klan's rise to power." LISA MCGIRR, THE WAR ON ALCOHOL: PROHIBITION AND THE RISE OF THE AMERICAN STATE xix–xx (New York: W.W. Norton & Co. 2016). *See id.* at 122–25, 140–41.

5. "If one fact was abundantly clear by 1930 it was the failure of the federal government, after ten years of earnest exhortation, to persuade the states to make a realistic effort to enforce prohibition in the United States." MERZ, *supra* note 2, at 279.

> Parsimonious state legislatures, even the ultra-dry Oklahoma General Assembly, refused to allocate sufficient funds for implementation of prohibition on the grounds that the national government should pay for enforcement. Officials in thirsty states did as little as they could and let federal officials bear the brunt of their constituents' hostility to the enforcement of prohibitory laws. In 1926 the state legislatures allocated eight times more to implement fish and game laws than to enforce prohibition.

RICHARD F. HAMM, SHAPING THE EIGHTEENTH AMENDMENT: TEMPERANCE REFORM, LEGAL CULTURE, AND THE POLITY, 1880–1920, at 266 (Chapel Hill: University of North Carolina Press 1995). *See* J.C. Burnham, *New Perspectives on the Prohibition "Experiment" of the 1920's*, 2 JOURNAL OF SOCIAL HISTORY 51, 58 (1968) ("[I]n 1927 only eighteen of the forty-eight states were appropriating money for the enforcement" of prohibition.). In 1927, total state expenditure for the enforcement of prohibition was about $690,000. PEGRAM, *supra* note 1, at 159.

6. Quoted in *Dry Law to Be Enforced, With or Without States' Help, Says President*, WASHINGTON POST (June 26, 1923), at 9. Harding observed that "[c]ommunities in which the policy was frankly accepted as productive of highly beneficial results, and in which there was no widespread protest so long as it was merely a State concern, report that since the Federal government became in part responsible there has been a growing laxity on the part of State authorities about enforcing the law." *Id.* Harding warned that "If the burden of enforcement shall continue to be increasingly thrown upon the Federal government, it will be necessary, at large expense, to create a Federal police authority, which in time will inevitably come to be regarded as an intrusion upon and interference with the right of local authority to manage local concerns. The possibilities of disaster in such a situation hardly need to be suggested." *Id.* Leading prohibitionists acknowledged the "embarrassment to enforcement" caused by "the indifference of State and local officials in many sections who shifted to the Federal Government the entire responsibility for ferreting out violators of the law and seeing that it was enforced. It had never been expected that State and local authorities would abdicate their duties and responsibilities and place on the national authorities the enormous task of policing our entire territory." Edwin C. Dinwiddie, *Is National Prohibition a Success?*, 4 CONGRESSIONAL DIGEST 26, 26 (1924).

7. Mabel Walker Willebrandt, *The Department of Justice and Some Problems of Enforcement*, in LAW VS. LAWLESSNESS: ADDRESSES DELIVERED AT THE CITIZENSHIP CONFERENCE, WASHINGTON D.C. 80 (Fred B. Smith, ed., New York: Fleming H. Revell Co. 1924). Willebrandt scored the "mistaken notion that Uncle Sam can shoulder this whole burden, which is not possible. Uncle Sam can, and will, shoulder the importing end and the sources of internal supplies, but

955

prohibition will never be satisfactorily enforced until you see that there is a rebirth of responsibility in your local communities, until you grease the wheels of the machinery of justice there, and start running morning, noon and night, – then, and only then, will this blot of lawlessness that exists in certain communities be removed." *Id.* at 92.

8. Lincoln C. Andrews, *Prohibition Enforcement as a Phase of Federal versus State Jurisdiction in American Life*, 129 ANNALS AMERICAN ACADEMY POLITICAL AND SOCIAL SCIENCE 77, 82 (1927). *See* John Grier Hibben, *Our National Moral Issue: What the 18th Amendment Has Done to Us*, 87 FORUM & CENTURY 215, 217 (1932) ("The states cannot be compelled to exercise concurrent power and corresponding legislation; this, according to the decision of the United States Supreme Court. Many states have refused to do so. Their attitude for the most part, and this is true also even of the states which had prohibition laws before the National Prohibition Act, is in a way a natural one: that the enforcement of prohibition is now a federal concern in which the state has no further responsibility and that many states do not care to assume the financial obligation thus necessitated.").

9. Andrews, *supra* note 8, at 82–83. For a good history of failed federal efforts to stimulate state enforcement of prohibition, see MERZ, *supra* note 2, at 257–81.

10. *For Local Option, Mr. Taft Explains*, NEW YORK TIMES (January 24, 1915), at 10.

11. Andrews, *supra* note 8, at 84. "No one knows," observed Andrews, "how many policemen would be necessary, and how many Federal police courts would be required, but the numbers certainly would be tremendous, and the political and social effects of their daily contact with the intimate affairs of the citizens of the communities might easily be most disastrous to democratic institutions." *Id.*

12. MERZ, *supra* note 2, at 75–157, 265. "Congress has never seen fit to set up the machinery for" the "complete enforcement" of prohibition. HOWARD LEE MCBAIN, PROHIBITION LEGAL AND ILLEGAL 32 (New York: MacMillan Co. 1928).

> That would entail a vast increase in the number of prohibition agents, of prosecuting attorneys, and of courts. The cost would be staggering. ... The monetary cost, however, would be as nothing compared to the cost to our system of government. ... If Congress should create the machinery for its up-to-the-hilt enforcement, it must of necessity spread a veritable army of federal policemen over the land. It must set up a giant bureaucracy emanating from Washington. ... Why does Congress hesitate? No doubt its motives are mixed. To plead poverty is to hide behind a shadow. ... A gigantic national police force is antipathetical to our federal scheme of things. Such a force is nevertheless the plain logic of national prohibition. ... To enact a stringent enforcement law, such as the Volstead Act, and to provide enforcement machinery that is notoriously far short of adequacy, is a gesture of sheer hypocrisy.

Id. at 32–34. "[M]eager allocations guaranteed only token federal enforcement, carried on by a skeleton force unequal to the task." HAMM, *supra* note 5, at 267. Between 1921 and 1926, annual congressional appropriations for the Prohibition Bureau were between six and ten million dollars. PEGRAM, *supra* note 1, at 159.

13. MERZ, *supra* note 2, at 119–21.

14. *Id.* at 79.

15. Until 1927, prohibition agents were not in the regular civil service and were thus appointed largely through political patronage. MERZ, *supra* note 2, at 94–97, 106–7, 189–90. The ranks of federal enforcement officials were filled by "party hacks and patronage hunters. The National Civil Service League, along with many Americans,

thought that most federal prohibition officers were at best incompetent and untrained and at worst venal and dishonest." HAMM, *supra* note 5, at 267.
16. "The condition of the American judiciary in the twenties was such that there was no hope of enforcing the Volstead Act." SINCLAIR, *supra* note 1, at 211. *See id.* at 209–14.
17. H.L. Mencken, *Editorial*, 1 AMERICAN MERCURY 161 (1924).
18. Prosecutions for violations of the Volstead Act increased from 29,114 in 1921 to 74,723 in 1929. MERZ, *supra* note 2, at 332–33.
19. *Prohibition and Federal Judges*, NEW YORK TIMES (May 29, 1925), at 16. *See Enforcement of the Prohibition Laws of the United States: A Report of the National Commission on Law Observance and Enforcement Relative to the Facts as to the Enforcement, the Benefits, and the Abuses under the Prohibition Laws, Both Before and Since the Adoption of the Eighteenth Amendment to the Constitution*, H.R. Doc. No. 71-722, 71st CONG. 3rd SESS. (January 20, 1931), at 56:

> Lawyers everywhere deplore, as one of the most serious effects of prohibition, the change in the general attitude toward the federal courts. Formerly these tribunals were of exceptional dignity, and the efficiency and dispatch of their criminal business commanded wholesome fear and respect. . . . The effect of the huge volume of liquor prosecutions, which has come to these courts under prohibition, has injured their dignity, impaired their efficiency, and endangered the wholesome respect for them which once obtained. Instead of being impressive tribunals of superior jurisdiction, they have had to do the work of police courts and that work has been chiefly in the public eye. These deplorable conditions have been aggravated by the constant presence in and about these courts of professional criminal lawyers and bail-bond agents, whose unethical and mercenary practices have detracted from these valued institutions.

Id. A more offensive assessment was offered in 1924 in a private letter by federal district judge Martin J. Wade:

> When I came on the Bench ten years ago in March next, the position was one of dignity and honor, to-day, if one stepped into a Federal Court during more than fifty per cent of each Session, he would think he was in a police court, swarming with Italians and Poles, and Greeks, Chinamen, "niggers", and samples of nearly all the races, with weeping wives and bawling children, bootleggers, dope fiends, dope peddlers, White Slavers, etc. etc. The work, the worry, the responsibility, are more than double what they were in 1915.

Martin J. Wade to Senator Thomas Walsh (December 30, 1924) (Walsh papers). Wade was writing in support of an increase in pay for federal judges.
20. *Federal Judge J.F. McGee Shoots Himself*, NEW YORK TIMES (February 16, 1925), at 1. When Emory Buckner was appointed U.S. attorney for the Southern District of New York, he was appalled by the conditions of the court:

> I found the great United States Court in the Southern District of New York had degenerated not into a police court (oh, no, not at all) but into whatever is in the subcellar under a police court; because the United States Court was attempting to run a police court without the necessary background, without the railing, without the traditions, without the attendants, without the clerks, without the stenographers, without anything at all that gives some semblance of order and some dignity, and makes these people in New York City or the nether world crouch under the pressure of the city laws they have violated. All that was gone. I found that the Police Department and the prohibition agents were bringing into that Federal Building every year 75,000 people under arrest for violation of the liquor law – not 7,500, but 75,000 people – in fifty-two weeks. I found one United

States Commissioner, who acts as a police magistrate, sitting there without a stenographer because one is not provided under the federal system, and I found perjury was so rotten that it stank.

Of the 75,000 cases the Commissioner told me himself that 95 or 98 percent were thrown out by him when the police officers or the prohibition agents testified, because, although the arrests were made the night before, it seemed they had been somewhat mistaken, or they didn't exactly recall the circumstances. Bondsmen told me, judges told me, lawyers told me, that in this vast swarming crowd of 1,500 to 2,000 and 2,500 men and women the place was full of fixers and bond-runners and bond-crooks, and lawyer crooks; that money was passed freely; and there sat the Commissioner without any stenographer to verify the perjury of witnesses. He was throwing them out like this and that, and holding others, and there he was without any power to punish the perjurers.

Quoted in MARTIN MAYER, EMORY BUCKNER 186 (New York: Harper & Row 1968).

21. *See supra* Prologue, at 5. The recommendation of the 1923 Judicial Conference to authorize commissioners to receive guilty pleas when jury trials had been waived, see *supra* Chapter 12, at note 52, was an effort to alleviate the crushing prohibition business of federal trial courts.

22. *President's Annual Message*, 67 CONG. REC. 457, 463 (December 8, 1925). In 1926, Coolidge once again urged that

[o]fficers of the Department of Justice throughout the country should be vigilant in enforcing the law, but local authorities, which had always been mainly responsible for the enforcement of law in relation to intoxicating liquor, ought not to seek evasion by attempting to shift the burden wholly upon the Federal agencies. Under the Constitution the States are jointly charged with the Nation in providing for the enforcement of the prohibition amendment.

President's Annual Message, 68 CONG. REC. 29, 34 (December 7, 1926). *See President's Annual Message*, 70 CONG. REC. 25 (December 4, 1928) ("Under the terms of the Constitution, however, the obligation is equally on the States to exercise the power which they have through the executive, legislative, judicial, and police branches of their governments in behalf of enforcement."). Herbert Hoover reaffirmed this position in his inaugural address, stressing that "the undoubted abuses which have grown up under the Eighteenth Amendment" were in part "due to the failure of some States to accept their share of responsibility for the concurrent enforcement and to the failure of many State and local officials to accept the obligation under their oath of office zealously to enforce the laws." Herbert Hoover, *Inaugural Address*, 71 CONG. REC. 5 (March 4, 1929).

23. The Court discussed the puzzling nature of the concurrent power granted by Section 2 of the Eighteenth Amendment in the Prohibition Cases, 253 U.S. 350 (1920), in which the Court held, over the dissents of McKenna and Clarke, that Congress's power to enforce the Amendment did not require the "concurrence" of the states, and that Congress had the power to define "intoxicating liquors" in the bone-dry manner of the Volstead Act. *Id.* at 387. In dissent, Clarke, invoking the *Slaughterhouse Cases*, 83 U.S. 36 (1872), argued that this construction of the Eighteenth Amendment would "radically" change "the whole constitutional theory of the relations of our state and federal governments by transferring to the general government that police power, through the exercise of which the people of the various States theretofore regulated their local affairs in conformity with the widely differing

standards of life, of conduct and of duty which must necessarily prevail in a country of so great extent as ours, with its varieties of climate, of industry and of habits of the people." 253 U.S. at 411 (Clarke, J., dissenting). On the obscure meaning of "concurrent power" in the Eighteenth Amendment, see Noel T. Dowling, *Concurrent Power under the Eighteenth Amendment*, 6 MINNESOTA LAW REVIEW 447 (1922).

24. *Governors Accept Coolidge Program to Back Up Dry Law*, NEW YORK TIMES (October 21, 1923), at 1. Coolidge's conclusions were seconded by Attorney General Daugherty, who asserted that "[t]he States owe to the Federal Government a reciprocal loyalty to support and enforce the Constitution of the United States and the laws enacted by Congress pursuant thereto." *Id.* Noting "the congestion of the dockets of the Federal courts ... from prohibition cases pending," Daugherty proposed that "larger conspiracies" be prosecuted in federal courts, whereas "smaller offenses ... be handled by local, State or Police Courts." *Id.* For a lively description of the conference, see SEAN BEIENBURG, PROHIBITION, THE CONSTITUTION, AND STATES' RIGHTS 139 (University of Chicago Press 2019); and *Governors Pledge Full Cooperation to Aid Prohibition*, WASHINGTON POST (October 20, 1923), at 1.

Three years later, on May 8, 1926, Coolidge issued Executive Order No. 4439, which provided that to "more efficiently function in the enforcement of the National Prohibition act, any state, county or municipal officer may be appointed, at a nominal rate of compensation, as prohibition officer of the Treasury Department to enforce the provisions of the National Prohibition act, and acts supplemental thereto." *Coolidge's Dry Order Amends Grant's Decree Issued in 1873 and in Force Since Then*, NEW YORK TIMES (May 22, 1926), at 2. The order provoked "a flood of bitter criticism in the Senate," and was "denounced as illegal and unconstitutional and as an encroachment on State rights." *Coolidge Dry Order Attacked in Senate as Unconstitutional*, NEW YORK TIMES (May 22, 1926), at 1. See BEIENBURG, *supra*, at 156–57; *Andrews to Try Out Coolidge Dry Order First in California*, NEW YORK TIMES (May 23, 1926), at 1; *Congress Renews Assault on Order*, NEW YORK TIMES (May 25, 1926), at 1; *Storm Grows on Coolidge Dry Order; Give State Rights Views*, NEW YORK TIMES (May 25, 1926), at 1; *House Wets to Push Bill to Let States Fix Alcohol Ratio*, NEW YORK TIMES (May 27, 1926), at 1; *House Body Denies Action to Nullify Coolidge Dry Order*, WASHINGTON POST (June 11, 1926), at 4. For a discussion of the order, see James Hart, *Some Legal Questions Growing Out of the President's Executive Order for Prohibition Enforcement*, 13 VIRGINIA LAW REVIEW 86 (1927). In the end "[n]o state officials were appointed as agents of the federal government.... No change was made in the enforcement of the law. Mr. Coolidge's order was filed away ... and the whole question was forgotten." MERZ, *supra* note 2, at 193.

For a fascinating survey of the various forms of state and federal cooperation that developed during prohibition, see J.P. Chamberlain, *Current Legislation: Enforcement of the Volstead Act through State Agencies*, 10 AMERICAN BAR ASSOCIATION JOURNAL 391, 394 (1924):

> [The Eighteenth Amendment] has brought into strong relief the inadequacy of the organization of the federal government, especially its judicial branch, to deal with so widespread a question as prohibition; it has shown that state and national government machines must operate harmoniously to put into effect a police policy declared to be national, but affecting individuals so widely,

and it has brought into the open the inconvenience of a double system of police regulations of the same article in the same country. The attempts made by the states and the nation to meet the situation constitute a chapter in our constitutional development well worth watching.

25. *See Haynes Answers Pinchot's Attack; Says State Officers Must Do Their Share to Enforce Prohibition Laws*, NEW YORK TIMES (November 5, 1923), at 3.

26. Quoted in *Ritchie and Doran Clash at Institute*, NEW YORK TIMES (August 16, 1929), at 8. *See also Dry Law Needs Help of State Says Dr. Doran*, CHRISTIAN SCIENCE MONITOR (December 13, 1929), at 1 ("'I am of the opinion,' he said, 'that the obligation to enact enforcement laws under the concurrent clause of the Eighteenth Amendment is equally obligatory upon the states, as well as upon the Federal Government.'"). Arthur J. Davis, state superintendent for Massachusetts of the Anti-Saloon League, made a similar argument: "The Eighteenth Amendment ... imposes on the states the same obligation to enforce prohibition by appropriate legislation that it imposes upon Congress." *Ritchie's Attack on Prohibition Challenged by State Dry Leader*, CHRISTIAN SCIENCE MONITOR (December 11, 1929), at 2.

27. *Borah's Fight to Make Prohibition the Big Issue*, 95 LITERARY DIGEST 5 (November 26, 1927).

28. William E. Borah, *The State's Duty under Prohibition*, NEW YORK TIMES (July 28, 1929), § 9 at 1. The article developed ideas Borah had earlier presented in William E. Borah, *Civic Righteousness: Lawlessness the Insidious Disease of Republics*, 114 CENTURY MAGAZINE 641, 644–46 (1927), and in William E. Borah, *Shall the Constitution of the United States be Nullified?*, in LAW VS. LAWLESSNESS, *supra* note 7, at 163–80. For similar positions, see WILLIAM GIBBS MCADOO, THE CHALLENGE: LIQUOR AND LAWLESSNESS VERSUS CONSTITUTIONAL GOVERNMENT 65–79 (New York: Century Co. 1928); *M'Adoo Sees a Wet Plot by Corrupt City Machines to Gain Federal Control*, NEW YORK TIMES (January 29, 1927), at 1 ("[T]he same affirmative duty rests upon the State Governments as upon Congress to provide for effective enforcement [of the Eighteenth Amendment].").

29. *Politics Institute Debates Dry Law*, NEW YORK TIMES (August 15, 1929), at 48.

30. *Id. See also* F.F. Lauriston Bullard, *Boston Is Stirred by Ritchie Speech*, NEW YORK TIMES (December 15, 1929), at E1; Austen G. Fox, *Not a State Duty; Reasons Why No State Would Trample under Foot Its Own Bill of Rights*, NEW YORK TIMES (April 30, 1931), at 22.

31. Act of June 1, 1923, ch. 871, 1923 N.Y. Laws 1690. Although New York had ratified the Eighteenth Amendment, it had also passed in 1920 the "so-called Walker Act," *Ex parte* Finegan, 270 F. 665, 665 (N.D.N.Y. 1921), which "purported to make it lawful ... for persons who" paid a state liquor tax "to traffic in liquor containing" less than "2.75 per centum of alcohol by weight." People v. Cook, 188 N.Y.S. 291, 293 (N.Y. App. Div. 1921). *See also* Act of May 24, 1920, ch. 911, §§ 2, 8, 1920 N.Y. Laws 2276, 2277, 2282. Because the Volstead Act prohibited transporting and selling beverages having in excess of 0.5 percent alcohol, the Walker Act was declared *pro tanto* unconstitutional. 188 N.Y.S. at 296. In 1921, therefore, the New York Legislature enacted the Mullan-Gage Act, which "put into the penal statutes substantially all of the provisions of the Volstead act, but accompanied them by even more rigorous provisions as to search and seizure." Alfred E. Smith, *The Governor's Statement*, NEW YORK TIMES (June 2, 1923), at 1. The Mullan-Gage

Prohibition & Dual Sovereignty

Act proved impossible to enforce. MERZ, *supra* note 2, at 203–5. On the enactment of the Mullan-Gage Act, see BEIENBURG, *supra* note 24, at 97–98 (Republican New York Governor Nathan Miller passed the act to "implement state concurrent enforcement.").

32. Smith was under enormous pressure to veto the repeal. Responding to a letter from a private citizen arguing that "[e]very State official who voted" for the repeal of the Mullan-Gage law "is subject to the law of treason, having taken the oath to sustain the Constitution of the United States," President Harding announced that

> [w]ith much of what you say I am fully in accord. ... The executives of the nation and equally the executives of the States are sworn to enforce the Constitution. It is difficult to believe that public approval will ever be given to any other than a policy of fully and literally discharging this duty. ... The States are equipped with police organizations and judicial establishments adequate to deal with such problems. The Federal Government is not thus equipped.

Harding Sees Clash if Gov. Smith Signs Dry Law Repealer, NEW YORK TIMES (May 17, 1923), at 1. See SINCLAIR, *supra* note 1, at 296–97. Smith's decision to sign the repeal marked the beginning of the alignment of the national Democratic Party with antiprohibitionism. See JAMES M. BECK, THE REVOLT AGAINST PROHIBITION 12 (New York: The Association Against the Prohibition Amendment 1930) ("The Republican Party cannot longer afford to sell its soul to the fanatical Drys and if it does, and thus becomes the party of Prohibition, it may have a like fate.").

33. Smith, *supra* note 31, at 1. Smith directly answered Harding's suggestion "that, because the States have a larger police force than the Federal Government has, and because the Federal Government has at this time what the President describes as an inadequate machinery for the enforcement of the Volstead act, therefore the States are obligated severally to enact statutes duplicating the Volstead act. I am unable to understand from what source he believes this obligation to be derived and he does not disclose it. The President might, with equal force, suggest that at any time Congress in its wisdom saw fit to withhold adequate appropriation for the enforcement of any Federal law that there immediately devolved a duty upon each State to enact that Federal law into a State statute and make every offense against Federal law not enforced a duty upon the States to punish it as a State offense and at State expense." *Id.*

34. *Id.* With something less than analytic consistency, Smith also stated that New York "peace officers" would nevertheless retain "the sacred responsibility of sustaining the Volstead act with as much force and as much vigor as they would enforce any State law or local ordinance and I shall expect the discharge of that duty in the fullest measure by every peace officer in the State. ... Let it be understood at once and for all that this repeal does not in the slightest degree lessen the obligation of peace officers of the State to enforce in its strictest letter the Volstead act, and warning to that effect is herein contained as coming from the Chief Executive of the State of New York." *Id.* Either Smith meant to argue that state legislatures had no obligation to enforce federal law, whereas state executive officials did have such an obligation, or he meant to argue that the "obligation" of state police officers to enforce the Volstead Act depended entirely on the discretionary policy of the Governor. For a discussion, see BEIENBURG, *supra* note 24, at 106–9.

35. 275 U.S. 310, 312–13 (1927). The Court refused to explain this conclusion, stating simply that "[w]e are of opinion on the facts, which it is unnecessary to detail, that there was not probable cause." *Id.* Kenneth M. Murchison calls *Gambino* an "enigmatic" decision, because the Court's holding that the officers lacked probable cause was reached "without explaining why the facts known to the investigating officers were insufficient" and because the holding was inconsistent with the Court's earlier explication of probable cause in Carroll v. United States, 267 U.S. 132 (1925). KENNETH M. MURCHISON, FEDERAL CRIMINAL LAW DOCTRINES: THE FORGOTTEN INFLUENCE OF NATIONAL PROHIBITION 62–63 (Durham: Duke University Press 1994). We know that Holmes was quite troubled by this aspect of the case. *See infra* note 41.
36. Weeks v. United States, 232 U.S. 383, 398 (1913).
37. Silverthorne Lumber Co. v. United States, 251 U.S. 385, 391 (1920). *See* Burdeau v. McDowell, 256 U.S. 465, 475 (1921).
38. Because of the obvious advantages "of basing a case even in a United States court upon a search beyond the condemning reach of the federal rule," United States attorneys began routinely to use "evidence secured by local police. Indeed, it has been said that, because of the rigidly narrow grounds upon which a federal search will be declared reasonable, the activity of the state officers is indispensable." *Prohibition Searches by New York State Police*, 37 YALE LAW JOURNAL 784, 785 (1928). "The number of prosecutions based upon searches by state officers has rapidly increased and it is now the admitted policy of the federal authorities to rely wherever possible upon the activity of the local peace officers for the arrest and prosecution of the typical bootlegger and inland rumrunner." *Id.* Federal use of evidence gathered by state actors in violation of constitutional norms applicable only to the federal government later became known as the "silver platter doctrine." *See, e.g.*, Elkins v. United States, 364 U.S. 206, 252 (1960) (Harlan, J., dissenting); Lustig v. United States, 338 U.S. 74, 79 (1949).
39. *Gambino*, 275 U.S. at 316. "[T]he rights guaranteed by the Fourth and Fifth Amendments may be invaded as effectively by ... co-operation, as by the state officers' acting under direction of the federal officials." *Id.*
40. Brandeis held that "[w]hether the laws of the state actually imposed upon the troopers the duty of aiding the federal officials in the enforcement of the National Prohibition Act we have no occasion to inquire." *Id.* at 317. The New York Court of Appeals was similarly disinclined to determine whether state police officers were independently obliged to enforce federal prohibition law. *See, e.g.*, People v. Lafaro, 165 N.E. 518, 519–20 (N.Y. 1929); *The Duty of the States in Respect of Prohibition*, 63 UNITED STATES LAW REVIEW 561 (1929).
41. *Gambino*, 275 U.S. at 315. *See supra* note 34. Brandeis stressed that "[a]id so given was accepted and acted on by the Federal officials." 275 U.S. at 315. Stone's docket book reveals that at conference only Butler and Stone initially voted to suppress the evidence. Taft, Holmes, Van Devanter, Brandeis, and Sanford voted to affirm the defendants' conviction. (McReynolds passed, and Sutherland was absent.) The opinion was assigned to Brandeis, who apparently changed his mind and carried the Court with him for his new conclusion.

The initial draft of Brandeis's proposed opinion survives. In that draft, there is a long footnote detailing Smith's oft-repeated desire for New York peace officers to enforce the Volstead Act. Brandeis also included a long footnote detailing the extensive cooperation between federal and state police in New York and the consequent urgency of clarifying whether "such a system of cooperation constitutes the New York City police a Federal agency which makes its officers amenable to the Fourth amendment." (Brandeis papers). When Taft concurred in Brandeis's opinion, he wrote: "I don't think it either necessary or proper to make the Governor's remarks a basis of this opinion. I think that ought to be stricken out. It will be the occasion of great comment." *Id.* Van Devanter concurred with Brandeis's altered judgment, but noted his agreement "with suggestion of others that it would be well to omit" the footnotes referring to Governor Smith and to the New York City police. *Id.* Butler also concurred in the opinion "subject to elimination of the footnote as suggested by Justice Van Devanter." *Id.* Sanford concurred with the thought "that certain of the notes should be omitted." *Id.* Stone also suggested the elimination of the footnotes discussing the relationship between New York police and federal authorities. He wrote Brandeis: "I think this will ameliorate the mistakes made in Burdeau v. McDowell [256 U.S. 465 (1921)] and like cases and I am for it." *Id.* Brandeis omitted the two footnotes in his published opinion. Of all the justices, only Holmes seemed to retain his initial reservations about the ultimate disposition of the case. He wrote Brandeis: "Is this consistent with Hester v. United States, 265 U.S. at 57? It is a model of research and thoroughness and I admire it – but I should like to see the Const. protection limited." *Id.*

The Court's decision in *Gambino* was "far reaching," because it rendered "the enforcement of liquor laws in New York much more difficult, and in many instances impossible." *Prohibition Searches by New York State Police, supra* note 38, at 790. It rapidly became grounds for mobilization for New York prohibitionists:

> Assemblyman Jenks indicated that in their fight this year the Drys would stress the recent decision of the United States Supreme Court which held that State police cannot search for liquor unless armed with a search warrant.
>
> "I think the recent decision of the Supreme Court . . . has shown the fallacy of Governor Smith's claim that State officers can enforce prohibition," said Assemblyman Jenks.
>
> "We have got to have a State enforcement law to make State agencies really effective in the enforcement of prohibition. Events of the last few years have shown that the State officers cannot aid very materially in the enforcement of prohibition without a State law."

Dry Bills Start Battle in Albany; State Parallel to Volstead Act Offered by Jenks in Two Assembly Measures, NEW YORK TIMES (January 10, 1928), at 4.

42. 260 U.S. 377 (1922).
43. *Id.* at 379–80, 382. Four years later, in Hebert v. Louisiana, 272 U.S. 312 (1926), the Court unanimously reaffirmed the holding of *Lanza* in an opinion by Van Devanter:

> [O]ne who . . . commits two distinct offenses, one against the United States and one against the State . . . may be subjected to prosecution and punishment in the federal courts for one and in the state courts for the other without any infraction of the constitutional rule against double jeopardy, it being limited to repeated prosecutions "for the same offense."

Id. at 314. *See Dry Law's Teeth Whetted; Supreme Court Holds Same Offense Punishable by Both State and Federal Agencies*, LOS ANGELES TIMES (November 2, 1926), at 2.

44. Note, *Double Prosecution by State and Federal Governments: Another Exercise in Federalism*, 80 HARVARD LAW REVIEW 1538, 1540–41 (1967).

45. *See, e.g.*, Gamble v. United States, 139 S.Ct. 1960 (2019); United States v. Lara, 541 U.S. 193, 199 (2004); Heath v. Alabama, 474 U.S. 82, 88 (1985); Abbate v. United States, 359 U.S. 187 (1959); Bartkus v. Illinois, 359 U.S. 121 (1959). The concept came under immediate attack after it was enunciated. *See, e.g.*, J.A.C. Grant, *The Lanza Rule of Successive Prosecutions*, 32 COLUMBIA LAW REVIEW 1309, 1331 (1932) ("Shall we fritter away our liberties upon a metaphysical subtlety, two sovereignties?"). It has remained academically unpopular ever since. *See, e.g.*, Erin M. Cranman, *The Dual Sovereignty Exception to Double Jeopardy: A Champion of Justice or a Violation of a Fundamental Right?*, 14 EMORY INTERNATIONAL LAW REVIEW 1641 (2000); Kevin J. Hellmann, *The Fallacy of Dueling Sovereignties: Why the Supreme Court Refuses to Eliminate the Dual Sovereignty Doctrine*, 2 JOURNAL OF LAW & POLICY 149 (1994).

46. Grant, *supra* note 45, at 1311. *Lanza* was in tension with the legislative history of the Eighteenth Amendment, as well as with the explicit representations of major pro-prohibition lobbying groups, like the Anti-Saloon League, who were responsible for the Amendment's passage. *Id.* at 1311 & n.13. The Eighteenth Amendment's reference to "concurrent power" was drafted by a House committee, whose chair stated that the reference meant that the federal government could not prosecute for an offense based upon an act "if the state government does." 56 CONG. REC. 424–25 (December 17, 1917). *See* MURCHISON, *supra* note 35, at 109–11.

47. *Double Dry Enforcement*, NEW YORK TIMES (March 13, 1923), at 20. Three years later, after the Court's decision in *Hebert*, see *supra* note 43, the *New York Times* could find consolation only in the thought that "each fresh reminder of how much liberty has been thrown away in an attempt to repeal custom and to enact the morality of the Anti-Saloon League is helpful for the return of common sense and something at least of earlier freedom." *Double Jeopardy*, NEW YORK TIMES (November 3, 1926), at 22. Public reaction to *Hebert* was particularly violent. The decision was widely held to evidence a "sinister departure from American fairness" caused by the fact that "Prohibition destroys not only the written but the unwritten law of the land. It is a solvent in which the letter and the spirit alike are blended into the current cure-all reform." *Double Jeopardy*, ST. LOUIS POST-DISPATCH (November 2, 1926), at 18. The *Baltimore Sun* opined that "[i]t is inconceivable that a Supreme Court ... should have made such a decision only a few years back. But since Volsteadism became the law of the land many things have changed. ... [I]t is not surprising that legal doctrines which have no place in justice or in common sense should be enunciated and supported." Quoted in *Bad News for Bootleggers*, 91 LITERARY DIGEST 18 (November 20, 1926).

48. *Double Jeopardy*, CHICAGO DAILY TRIBUNE (April 15, 1923), at 8. The possibility of multiple prosecutions for the identical act was widely regarded as "manifestly unjust." Anthony A. Goerner, *Constitutional Law: Double Jeopardy: Double Liability*, 12 CORNELL LAW QUARTERLY 212, 213 (1927). *See Smashing Another American Principle*, CHICAGO DAILY TRIBUNE (March 12, 1923), at 8; *Double Jeopardy*, 27 LAW NOTES 4 (1923).

49. Because the implication of *Lanza* was that the only way for a state to avoid the potential for double prosecutions was to repeal its own prohibition law, it was noted

at the time that "the most startling immediate result" of *Lanza* "was the repeal of the New York state prohibition act." Grant, *supra* note 45, at 1310. "In 1923 ... in New York the cry of double jeopardy was the most important slogan of the campaign for repeal. This was due to the fact that in December, 1922, the Supreme Court [in *Lanza*] had laid down the law in no unequivocal terms." McBAIN, *supra* note 12, at 146. As Governor Smith noted, the repeal of the Mullan-Gage law would "do away entirely with the possibility of double jeopardy for violation of the laws enforcing the Eighteenth Amendment.... Under the United States Supreme Court decision in the Lanza case, a citizen is today subjected to double trial and even to double punishment for a single offense .... This is an unwarranted and indefensible exception to the fundamental constitutional guarantee contained in both the Federal and State Constitutions that no person shall be twice tried or punished for the same offense." Smith, *supra* note 31, at 1. *See* Austen G. Fox, *Concurrent Enforcement: Neither Conviction nor Acquittal in the State Courts a Bar to Federal Prosecution*, New York Times (March 13, 1923), at 20.

In his private correspondence, Taft refused to acknowledge the moral force of the argument against double jeopardy. He insisted that the argument was merely a makeweight for opposition to prohibition itself:

> Austen Fox has risen in his majesty and thinks that the [Mullan-Gage] law ought to be abolished, that the State ought to take no part in enforcing the law because of the danger of double jeopardy. If it had not been through opposition to the principle of the law altogether, double jeopardy would not have been mentioned. The instances in which people have been punished twice for the same act are so few, and the danger from them is so slight, that the use of that as an argument to a practical man is ridiculous. In other words ... because the wealthy classes, those who consult their own comfort before anything else, as other people possibly do, don't like this limitation upon what they regard as their personal liberty, but which is not personal liberty under the Constitution, they are seizing on every little technicality to attack the law.

WHT to James R. Sheffield (July 8, 1923) (Taft papers). Austen Fox was a leader in the opposition to Brandeis's confirmation. *See supra* Chapter 8, at note 39.

50. *2 Prison Terms for One Drink Upheld by U.S.; Supreme Court Decision Big Victory for Drys*, CHICAGO DAILY TRIBUNE (December 12, 1922), at 2.

51. *Double Penalties in Dry Law Cases; Supreme Court Holds the Same Offense Punishable by State and Nation*, NEW YORK TIMES (December 12, 1922), at 5. In a prewar tract written for the Anti-Saloon League, Wayne Wheeler had advised prohibitionists to "draft your laws so that you can secure cumulative penalties. In other words, with the same evidence you can make a law violator pay the federal tax, and also the state liquor tax. ... By the above method you can hit a law violator from three to five times successively and it usually puts them out of commission." WAYNE B. WHEELER, FEDERAL AND STATE LAWS RELATING TO INTOXICATING LIQUOR 95–96 (2d ed., Westerville: American Issue Publishing Co. 1918).

52. MURCHISON, *supra* note 35, at 121. *See* DAVID E. KYVIG, REPEALING NATIONAL PROHIBITION 32–33 (2d ed., Kent State University Press 2000).

53. Thus, in repudiating the conclusion of *Lanza*, one commentator argued:

> The Eighteenth Amendment, if it is a law at all, is one law – a law for the whole Union. It has, indeed, appointed several agents ... to wit, the Congress and

The Taft Court

> the several States, to enforce its prohibitions, but it begins and ends with being one law.
>
> The thesis that one act which violates one law can be two crimes is shocking and false. The misconception has come about through failure to perceive the degraded position to which the States have been reduced by the Eighteenth Amendment. In legislating under it they are not acting as legislative sovereignties; they are acting as Federal agents. The Mullan-Gage act, for example, is ... the act of a legislative agent who is deputized under the second section of the amendment to exert what is there described as a "concurrent power." ...
>
> The Fifth Amendment, prohibiting double jeopardy for the same offense ... forbids double jeopardy for one offense against the Eighteenth Amendment, even when the act is punished both by the Congress and the States.

Lex Talionis, *No Double Jeopardy; Contention that Mullan-Gage Act Is Not a State but a Federal Law*, NEW YORK TIMES (May 26, 1923), at 14. *See* Alexander Sidney Lanier, *Prohibition and Double Jeopardy*, 8 VIRGINIA LAW REGISTER 740, 740 (1923); Note, *Prohibition and Double Jeopardy*, 8 VIRGINIA LAW REGISTER 774, 776 (1923).

54. *Lanza*, 260 U.S. at 381–82. *See* Hebert v. Louisiana, 272 U.S. 312, 314–15 (1926).
55. McBAIN, *supra* note 12, at 30–31. For an example of the influence of McBain's book, see *Text of Speech by Charles E. Hughes at Worcester, Urging the Election of Hoover*, NEW YORK TIMES (October 31, 1928), at 18.
56. Emerson T. Anthony, *The Veto Message Analyzed*, CHICAGO DAILY TRIBUNE (April 17, 1931), at 12; Fox, *supra* note 30.
57. "Since the states do not derive their power to legislate from the eighteenth amendment, it follows that the amendment imposes no obligation upon the states to adopt a policy of state prohibition." Karl Huston, *A Survey of All Laws at Present Affecting Intoxicating Liquors in Oregon and a Consideration of the Proper Enforcing Agents for Such Laws*, 12 OREGON LAW REVIEW 293, 295 (1933). *Lanza* suggests "that the 18th Amendment itself imposes no obligations upon the states to aid in its enforcement. Such enforcement laws as a state may choose to pass derive their validity, not from the Amendment, but from the original police power of the state." *The Duty of the States in Respect of Prohibition*, *supra* note 40, at 562.
58. *See, e.g.*, Borah, *Civic Righteousness*, *supra* note 28; *M'Adoo Sees a Wet Plot by Corrupt City Machines to Gain Federal Control*, *supra* note 28; Jesse F. Orton, *State Enforcement Acts; Mr. Orton Holds Eighteenth Amendment Places Mandate on Commonwealths*, NEW YORK TIMES (November 23, 1930), § 3 at 2; *Ritchie and Doran Clash at Institute*, *supra* note 26.
59. *See supra* text at note 48.
60. Herbert Little, *The Omnipotent Nine*, The AMERICAN MERCURY 48, 54 (September 1928) ("The Supreme Court is bone dry. ... The validity of the Eighteenth Amendment and of the enforcement acts has been upheld completely"); *see* KYVIG, *supra* note 52, at 32–35; *Dry Law Stands Firm against All Assaults; The Eighteenth Amendment and Volstead Act Have Won an Unbroken Series of Victories in the Federal Courts over a Period of Nearly Eight Years*, NEW YORK TIMES (November 20, 1927), § 10 at 9; ROY A. HAYNES, *High Court's Stand Praised by Haynes; Decisions on Prohibition Pointed to as Bulwark of Enforcement*, NEW YORK TIMES (August 21, 1923), at 19; John E. Monk, *Observations from Times Watch-Towers; Drys Eye High Court; Count Possible Retirement in Fear Successors Might Incline to Wet Views*, NEW YORK TIMES

Prohibition & Dual Sovereignty

(July 1, 1928), § 3 at 1 ("The Supreme Court, as at present constituted, uniformly has upheld the Eighteenth Amendment and the Volstead act in all cases brought before it."); A.H. Ulm, *New Dry Enforcement Code Slowly Evolved*, NEW YORK TIMES (February 21, 1926), § 8 at 22 ("'The Supreme Court has been very strict in construing the Eighteenth Amendment and the Volstead act favorably to the contentions of those who have been charged with enforcement,' said a lawyer who has had a good deal to do with the handling of the Government's side in many cases. 'The Court at times has been stricter than we expected it would be.'"). The decisions of the Court were in fact regarded as so important to the maintenance of prohibition that "the politicians of the Anti-Saloon League" insisted in 1928 "that the composition of the court is one of the great issues of this campaign. ... The inference is drawn that if the next President is personally and politically dry, he will make sure that only thorough-going prohibitionists are put on the bench. But if the next President is not himself a believer in the prohibition theory then he will make it his business to nominate wets only for the court." *Packing the Supreme Court*, HARTFORD COURANT (July 4, 1928), at 6. *See* Monk, *supra*.

For examples of Taft Court decisions upholding prohibition, see Olmstead v. United States, 277 U.S. 438 (1928); Dugan v. Ohio, 277 U.S. 61 (1928); Grosfield v. United States, 276 U.S. 494 (1928); United States v. Lee, 274 U.S. 559 (1927); Maul v. United States, 274 U.S. 501 (1927); Ford v. United States, 273 U.S. 593 (1927); McGuire v. United States, 273 U.S. 95 (1927); Murphy v. United States, 272 U.S. 630 (1926); Lambert v. Yellowley, 272 U.S. 581 (1926); Port Gardner Investment Co. v. United States, 272 U.S. 564 (1926); Dodge v. United States, 272 U.S. 530 (1926); Van Oster v. Kansas, 272 U.S. 465 (1926); United States v. One Ford Coupe Automobile, 272 U.S. 321 (1926); Ma-King Products Co. v. Blair, 271 U.S. 479 (1926); Maryland v. Soper, 270 U.S. 9 (1926); Druggan v. Anderson, 269 U.S. 36 (1925); Selzman v. United States, 268 U.S. 466 (1925); Dumbra v. United States, 268 U.S. 435 (1925); Samuels v. McCurdy, 267 U.S. 188 (1925); Carroll v. United States, 267 U.S. 132 (1925); James Everard's Breweries v. Day, 265 U.S. 545 (1924); Hester v. United States, 265 U.S. 57 (1924); Cunard Steamship Co. v. Mellon, 262 U.S. 100 (1923); Grogan v. Hiram Walker & Sons, 259 U.S. 80 (1922); Vigliotti v. Pennsylvania, 258 U.S. 403 (1922); Hawes v. Georgia, 258 U.S. 1 (1922); and Corneli v. Moore, 257 U.S. 491 (1922). *But see* Commercial Credit Co. v. United States, 276 U.S. 226 (1928); Gambino v. United States, 275 U.S. 310 (1927); Marron v. United States, 275 U.S. 192 (1927); United States v. Berkeness, 275 U.S. 149 (1927); Tumey v. Ohio, 273 U.S. 510 (1927); Byars v. United States, 273 U.S. 28 (1927); United States v. Katz, 271 U.S. 354 (1926); Agnello v. United States, 269 U.S. 20 (1925). In 1926, Taft wrote his prohibitionist brother Horace that "I don't think you need worry about our Court and the Volstead Act. We have decided most of the questions so that they are fixed." WHT to Horace D. Taft (December 16, 1926) (Taft papers).

CHAPTER 30

Prohibition and Normative Dualism

IN 1920, THE White Court construed the Eighteenth Amendment to invest the federal government with the full authority of the Supremacy Clause, so that federal statutes preempted all inconsistent state law.[1] Because federal prohibition statutes regulated intimate details of personal conduct normally associated with the exclusive jurisdiction of state law, this interpretation of the Eighteenth Amendment offended justices like Sutherland and McReynolds, who believed that decentralization was a fundamental constitutional principle that carried inherent normative force. In the context of prohibition, the Taft Court chose to override this normative commitment to localism in ways that strikingly anticipate the ruthless nationalism of the New Deal.

In 1923, Woodrow Wilson asked Brandeis to draw up a "statement of principles" about prohibition for the Democratic Party.[2] Brandeis replied with a plan that expressed an entirely functional account of federalism. Brandeis interpreted the Eighteenth Amendment's reference to "concurrent power" to signify that the American people "recognized fully that the law could not be enforced without the co-operation of the States with the Nation. ... The intention was that each government should perform that part of the task for which it was peculiarly fitted."[3]

Brandeis postulated that "[t]he Federal Government's part is to protect the United States against illegal importation of liquor from foreign countries and to protect each State from the illegal introduction into it of liquor from another State." Brandeis observed that "[t]o perform that part of the task effectively requires centralized, unified action and the employment of the large federal powers and resources." The job of a state, by contrast, was to police "the illegal sale within it of liquor illegally manufactured in it," for that "is a task for which the State Governments are peculiarly fitted; and which they should perform. That part of the task involves diversified governmental action and adaptation to the widely varying conditions in, and the habits and sentiments of the people of, the several

Prohibition & Normative Dualism

States. It is a task for which the Federal Government is not fitted."[4] "To relieve the States from the duty of performing" this task, said Brandeis, "violates our traditions; and threatens the best interests of our country." For the fulfillment of that duty, "the people of each State must look to their state governments."[5]

Brandeis's account of federalism turned on principles of institutional design. It postulated that national and state governments should each be assigned duties commensurate with their institutional competence. Brandeis interpreted the "concurrent power" provision of the Eighteenth Amendment to divide state from federal authority along lines of instrumental capacity.[6] He assumed that the constitutional question was not whether prohibition should be enforced, but which level of government could best enforce it.[7] In the context of prohibition, however, this assumption was spectacularly misplaced, as evidenced by the repeal of the Mullan-Gage law in New York.

The vulnerability of Brandeis's account of federalism became evident in 1929 when George Wickersham, newly appointed chair of Herbert Hoover's National Commission on Law Observance and Enforcement, proposed to the Conference of Governors a plan essentially identical to that crafted by Brandeis.[8] Noting that "open disrespect for the Volstead law" was a "great source of demoralizing and pecuniarily profitable crime," and noting that "[t]hus far the Federal Government alone has borne the brunt of enforcement," Wickersham suggested that the "burden" of implementing prohibition be shared between the federal government and the states. "If the National Government were to attend to preventing importation, manufacture and shipment in interstate commerce of intoxicants, the State undertaking the internal police regulations to prevent sale, saloons, speakeasies and so forth, national and State laws might be modified so as to become reasonably enforceable."[9]

Wickersham's proposal was immediately attacked on the ground that it would negate a major purpose of the Eighteenth Amendment, which was to create a national policy against liquor. The proposal was said to "nullify the Eighteenth Amendment"[10] because suspension of federal enforcement would "in effect repeal the Eighteenth Amendment in wet localities."[11] Because Wickersham's plan meant "the virtual substitution of local option by States in place of national prohibition,"[12] it set off an explosive and politically fatal controversy.[13] The lesson was that the division of authority between the national government and the states could not be constructed along merely functional lines so long as there was no agreement about fundamental objectives. Functionalism was not a viable option under conditions of deep polarization.

The widely divergent attitudes toward prohibition held by different localities forced contemporaries instead to address the quite different question of whether federal authority to regulate liquor *ought* to be limited by principles of federalism that reserved to states the undisturbed exercise of their police power. We shall call this account of federalism "normative dualism." In 1918 in *Hammer v. Dagenhart*[14] the White Court invoked principles of normative dualism to strike down a federal statute prohibiting the transportation in interstate commerce of goods manufactured by child labor. Although the federal government was acting squarely within its own designated sphere of authority, normative dualism nevertheless prevented the federal government from regulating in ways that would unduly diminish state police power. There were many important Taft Court decisions that explicitly embraced normative dualism, most prominently *Bailey v. Drexel Furniture Co.*,[15] which struck down the federal child-labor tax statute as beyond the constitutional power of the national government.[16]

Opponents of prohibition mobilized on the basis of normative dualism from the moment the Eighteenth Amendment was ratified. In the *National Prohibition Cases*, for example, they used it audaciously to attack the constitutionality of the Eighteenth Amendment itself. They advanced the seemingly paradoxical claim that by regulating personal conduct the amendment so deeply invaded "the police powers of the States," and so violently undermined the status of states "as true local, self-governing sovereignties," that it constituted a "complete subversion of our dual and federal system of government."[17] As used by advocates in the *National Prohibition Cases*, the concept of "the dual sovereignty in our federal system of Nation and State each supreme within its own sphere" did not signify a merely functional division of labor between state and federal governments, nor did it express a merely objective description of separate spheres of federal and state power. It instead represented a fundamental constitutional commitment, symbolized by the Tenth Amendment, that "state control over local affairs" was to remain immune from improper interference by the federal government.[18]

This kind of normative dualism resonated widely throughout the 1920s.[19] Even *The Nation* opined that if the Eighteenth Amendment were overthrown, "the right of self-government which the Constitution guarantees to the people of all the States will continue unimpaired," but that if the Amendment were sustained, "that right will perhaps disappear so far as the police power is concerned, and the way be opened for a Federal centralization practically complete."[20] There was widespread concern that prohibition imposed a "rigid uniformity"[21] that was "in essence a complete repudiation of the spirit of our federal system of self-governing states."[22] The Eighteenth Amendment was said to introduce "a radical change in the organic structure" of the country by commissioning the national government "to legislate upon the purely local and domestic affairs of every community in every state of the Union," while simultaneously denying states "the power all communities have been accustomed to exercise for more than a century and a quarter," which was "to regulate their conduct according to their own conceptions of propriety."[23]

From the perspective of normative dualism, the failure of prohibition was a predictable consequence of Congress's effort to enact "morals legislation for such a vast area as the United States."[24] Prohibition was tolerable when enacted by a state because "[t]he people of a state are vitally interested in its legislative and administrative policies" and "subconsciously feel that these policies, in a way, are theirs and for this reason they submit to them more readily."[25] "Such intimacy between the government and the governed," however, "is not possible with a centralized control

Prohibition & Normative Dualism

at Washington."[26] The leader of the Association Against the Prohibition Amendment stressed that the "Marylander is quite willing to yield even respect and obedience to a law he believes oppressive, provided it was passed by his own people, but his innate sense of independence resents the effort of Kansans to impose a law on him through what he believes to be a smug piece of sanctimonious humbuggery."[27]

This attack on national prohibition essentially charged federal police legislation with being antidemocratic. Opponents of prohibition did not deny that positive law could transform custom, but they stressed that it could do so only if clothed with democratic legitimacy. Democratic legitimacy requires that those affected by a law identify with the governmental unit enacting the law. National prohibition lacked democratic legitimacy to the extent that Marylanders experienced it as a law imposed upon Maryland by Kansas, rather than as the democratic will of the single unified people of the United States, of which Maryland formed a part.[28]

Normative dualism prompted prohibition's critics to condemn the Eighteenth Amendment as a form of domestic "imperialism."[29] Although the super-majoritarian ratification procedures of Article V were designed to preclude the possibility of such imperialism, inhabitants of wet states continued throughout the 1920s to attack prohibition as a national imposition.[30] The fierce controversy enveloping prohibition highlighted a strange and unsettling gap between the positive rule of recognition established by Article V and the brute sociological fact of democratic identification.

Normative dualism sought to close this gap by immunizing a local sphere of state police power from federal regulations. States could appropriately enact police regulations because they were imagined as natural units of self-government that could endow police regulations with democratic legitimacy.[31] It was commonly said in the 1920s that the transfer of state authority to Washington threatened the very value of self-government because national lawmaking was "too far removed from the people who are affected by its regulations" and hence perennially in danger of becoming merely "bureaucratic."[32]

An essential challenge of progressivism was to foster a countrywide identification with the federal government that could endow national legislation with the same quality of democratic legitimacy as that enjoyed by state legislation. The Great Depression is often taken as the moment when this identification solidified in the context of general police power. The fierce resistance to national prohibition during the 1920s, however, starkly reveals how precarious was the federal government's claim to the resource of democratic identification during the preceding decade. Throughout the 1920s prohibition was relentlessly attacked as a form of domestic imperialism that exemplified "[t]he despotism of absolute democracy."[33]

On the Taft Court, Sutherland was the most eloquent spokesman for normative dualism.[34] In 1920, Sutherland remarked to William D. Guthrie, who was slated to challenge the constitutionality of the Eighteenth Amendment before the Court in *The Prohibition Cases*,[35] that when Sutherland was in the Senate nobody "in either house of Congress had the slightest idea what was intended by" the idea of "concurrent power" in Section 2 of the Eighteenth Amendment.[36] Sutherland proposed that Section 2 be interpreted in light of "the general plan and purpose of the constitution as a whole, which clearly is to commit to the general government control over the inter-relations of the states and their peoples, while leaving to the states control over individuals and individual interests, and over local and internal matters of police."[37]

Unlike Brandeis, however, Sutherland did not conceive this division as merely functional. He instead imagined the division between state and federal power as intrinsically normative. Sutherland interpreted Section 2 "as authorizing Congress to enforce [prohibition] by *appropriate* legislation" and "as authorizing the several States to enforce it by *appropriate* legislation," so that Section 2 confined Congress and the states to legislating "within their respective and historic fields of jurisdiction."[38]

Construed in this way, the Eighteenth Amendment did not authorize Congress to invade "the field of state jurisdiction,"[39] because the "framers of the Amendment . . . did not desire to interfere with the internal powers of the States to deal with the subject in its local as distinguished from its national import."[40] Sutherland rejected as improper Congress's use of the Volstead Act to preempt the meaning of "intoxicating beverages" in Section 1 of the Amendment, because the Act made "the power of the state . . . not 'concurrent' but subordinate and, in effect, really no power at all."[41]

In the *National Prohibition Cases*, the Court decisively rejected Sutherland's reading of Section 2. Speaking through Justice Van Devanter, the Court held:

> The words "concurrent power" . . . do not mean joint power, or require that legislation thereunder by Congress, to be effective, shall be approved or sanctioned by the several States or any of them; nor do they mean that the power to enforce is divided between Congress and the several States along the lines which separate or distinguish foreign and interstate commerce from intrastate affairs. . . .
>
> The power confided to Congress . . . while not exclusive, is territorially coextensive with the prohibition of the first section, embraces manufacture and other intrastate transactions . . . and is in no wise dependent on or affected by action or inaction on the part of the several States or any of them.[42]

The Court thus authorized Congress to legislate "on the subject of intoxicants for the whole country, and . . . any inconsistent state legislation would be annulled by such federal enactments."[43]

The Court refused to interpret the Eighteenth Amendment through the lens of normative dualism, and as a result prohibition became associated with overreaching national regulation and enforcement. This in turn intensified the tension between prohibition and local customary norms, producing in some contexts outright defiance, as for example in the repeal of the Mullan-Gage law. The extent to which prohibition prompted the Taft Court to abandon the tenets of normative dualism is strikingly evident in two decisions interpreting congressional power to enforce the Eighteenth Amendment.

Prohibition & Normative Dualism

The first is *James Everard's Breweries v. Day*, in which the Taft Court upheld the authority of Congress to forbid "physicians from prescribing intoxicating malt liquors for medicinal purposes."[44] In a unanimous opinion authored by Sanford,[45] the Court reasoned that although the Eighteenth Amendment prohibited the manufacture and sale of intoxicating liquors only "for beverage purposes," Congress could nevertheless ban the medicinal use of beer in order "to make that prohibition effective."[46] Sanford cited for support *Purity Extract Co. v. Lynch*,[47] the very decision that Holmes feared that the Court was implicitly overruling in the context of social and economic regulation.[48]

Deliberately invoking the expansive construction of federal power in *McCulloch v. Maryland*,[49] *Everard's Breweries* held that Congress had power to achieve the purposes of the Eighteenth Amendment by "any means, appearing to it most eligible and appropriate, which are adapted to the end to be accomplished and consistent with the letter and spirit of the Constitution." The Court "may not inquire into the degree" of necessity, "as this would be to pass the line which circumscribes the judicial department and to tread upon legislative ground." The only question for the Court was whether "prohibiting traffic in intoxicating malt liquors for medicinal purposes has no real or substantial relation to the enforcement of the Eighteenth Amendment, and is not adapted to accomplish that end." In answering that question, the judgment of Congress "must be given great weight." The Court would extend "every possible presumption ... in favor of the validity" of a federal statute.[50]

The Court's reasoning in *Everard's Breweries* is in sharp tension with its refusal to authorize overbroad restrictions in the context of economic regulation in cases like *Jay Burns* or *Schlesinger*.[51] It is also in sharp tension with the Court's insistence on second-guessing the instrumental rationality of state statutes in cases like *Baldridge* or *Fairmont Creamery*.[52] Apparently there was something different about prohibition. It brought out a jurisprudential streak in the Court that was highly deferential to the prerogatives of government regulation. The opinion in *Everard's Breweries* could have been written by Holmes.

Everard's Breweries was a brutally nationalistic opinion. If the proscription "is within the authority delegated to Congress by the Eighteenth Amendment," Sanford wrote, "its validity is not impaired by reason of any power reserved to the States. ... And if the act is within the power confided to Congress, the Tenth Amendment, by its very terms, has no application, since it only reserves to the States 'powers not delegated to the United States by the Constitution.'"[53] Anticipating the Court's dismissal of the Tenth Amendment as a mere "truism" two decades later,[54] *Everard's Breweries* reads strikingly like post-New Deal decisions ceding to Congress virtually unfettered authority.

The Court's opinion in *Everard's Breweries* effectively meant that Congress could "do just about anything it wants to under" the Eighteenth Amendment.[55] It appears "that Congress might have saved the space which the word 'beverage' takes up in the printed Amendment," quipped Thomas Reed Powell.[56] *Everard's Breweries* gave to the national government a breadth of power that prompted pervasive disquiet in the popular press, testimony to national prohibition's threat to entrenched ideas of normative dualism. The *Literary Digest* could discover only a single newspaper "approving the ruling."[57]

Almost as an afterthought, Sanford concluded his opinion with the assertion that the statute could not be characterized as "an arbitrary and unreasonable prohibition of the use of valuable medicinal agents" because beer and malt liquor "are not generally recognized as medicinal agents" and the question of their medical value is, "at the most, debatable."[58] The afterthought was to prove highly significant when the Taft Court decided its second and far more controversial case about the nature of federal power under the Eighteenth Amendment.[59]

In *Lambert v. Yellowley*[60] the Court upheld Congress's authority to regulate medical prescriptions of vinous and spirituous liquors,[61] which at the time was a far more common and accepted medical practice than prescriptions for beer and malted liquor.[62] The decision was 5–4. Brandeis wrote the opinion for the Court, and he was joined by Taft, Holmes, Van Devanter, and Sanford.[63] Sutherland authored a spirited dissent, joined by McReynolds, Butler, and Stone.[64] The plaintiff in the case was Dr. Samuel W. Lambert, "a distinguished physician,"[65] who alleged that federal regulation interfered with his practice of medicine because he was presently caring for patients whose treatment required prescriptions of alcohol that Congress prohibited.[66]

The Court essentially treated *Everard's Breweries* as dispositive.[67] "If Congress may prohibit the manufacture and sale of intoxicating malt liquor for medicinal purposes by way of enforcing the Eighteenth Amendment, it equally and to the same end may restrict the prescription of other intoxicating liquor for medicinal purposes. In point of power there is no difference; if in point of expediency there is a difference, that is a matter which Congress alone may consider."[68] Congressional limitations on medical prescriptions of liquor "must be taken as embodying an implicit congressional finding that such liquors have no such medicinal value as gives rise to a need for larger or more frequent prescriptions. Such a finding, in the presence of the well-known diverging opinions of physicians, cannot be regarded as arbitrary or without a reasonable basis."[69] The Court concluded:

> High medical authority being in conflict as to the medicinal value of spirituous and vinous liquors taken as a beverage, it would, indeed, be strange if Congress lacked the power to determine that the necessities of the liquor problem require a limitation of permissible prescriptions, as by keeping the quantity that may be prescribed within limits which will minimize the temptation to resort to prescriptions as pretexts for obtaining liquor for beverage uses.[70]

In dissent, Sutherland sardonically noted that he was "very certain" that *Everard's Breweries* "would not have been a unanimous" decision if it had stood for what the Court now interpreted it to mean. Sutherland construed *Everard's Breweries* to rest "upon the ground that Congress, upon conflicting evidence, had determined that malt liquors possessed no substantial medicinal value and judicial inquiry upon that question was, therefore, foreclosed." In *Lambert*, by contrast,

Prohibition & Normative Dualism

Congress had concluded that vinous and spirituous liquors were "of medicinal value," and yet Congress had nevertheless insisted on laying down rules for their proper use.[71]

Because there were no congressional findings about proper prescription dosages for alcohol, the "only fact in this record bearing upon that subject" was Lambert's allegation that the statutory regulations were contrary to his medical judgment.[72] In such circumstances, essentially unlimited deference to congressional judgment would "deprive the states of the exclusive power, which the Eighteenth Amendment has not destroyed, of controlling medical practice and transfer it in part to Congress."[73] "[U]nder the pretense of adopting appropriate means, a carefully and definitely limited power" of prohibiting intoxicating liquors for beverage purposes "will have been expanded into a general and unlimited power" of prohibiting such liquors for all purposes, including medicinal ones. This would contradict "the letter and spirit of the Constitution ... and especially of the Tenth Amendment." "Because this statute by fixing inadequate prescriptions prohibits to the extent of such inadequacies the legitimate prescription of spirituous and vinous liquors for medicinal purposes, it exceeds the powers of Congress, invades those exclusively reserved to the states, and is not appropriate legislation to enforce the Eighteenth Amendment."[74]

Sutherland's dissent expresses the same concept of normative dualism that had informed his earlier interpretation of "concurrent power."[75] In contrast to the legislation at issue in *Everard's Breweries*, the law in dispute in *Lambert* explicitly regulated the practice of medicine and therefore directly intruded upon the reserved police power of the states.[76] Federal legislation circumscribing that power was to be allowed only if truly necessary. Sutherland regarded the law at issue in *Lambert* as a "transfer" of police power to the federal government and a consequent loss to the democratic legitimacy of local self-government.[77]

It is striking, however, that in both *Everard's Breweries* and *Lambert* the Taft Court decisively rejected Sutherland's vision of normative dualism, which is perhaps most conspicuously signified by Sanford's explicit repudiation of the Tenth Amendment as a symbol of the constitutional value of local self-government.[78] Although the Taft Court was, on the whole, a highly nationalist institution,[79] *Everard's Breweries* and *Lambert* contrast sharply to the normative dualism that infused some of the Court's most important decisions, like *Bailey v. Drexel Furniture Co.*[80] or *United Mine Workers of America v. Coronado Coal Co.*,[81] which were closer in spirit to the perspective expressed in Sutherland's *Lambert* dissent.[82]

In *Linder v. United States*,[83] for example, the Taft Court unanimously held that the Harrison Narcotic Act,[84] which imposed a penal tax on the dispensation of narcotic drugs, could not constitutionally be applied to a physician who in the course of his practice had given four tablets containing morphine and cocaine to a patient (who happened to be an addict). Speaking unanimously through McReynolds, the Court held that "Obviously, direct control of medical practice in the states is beyond the power of the federal government. Incidental regulation of such practice by Congress through a taxing act cannot extend to matters plainly inappropriate and unnecessary to reasonable enforcement of a revenue measure."[85]

Prohibition was somehow special. The pressure to uphold the Eighteenth Amendment led the Court in *Everard's Breweries* and *Lambert* to a purely positive account of national power. The manifest tension between the normative dualism implicit in a decision like *Linder*, and the blunt positivism of opinions like *Everard's Breweries* and *Lambert*, disconcerted contemporaries. They asked: Shall there "be two constitutions, one for prohibition and one for all other matters whatsoever?"[86]

Prohibition & Normative Dualism
Notes

1. The Prohibition Cases, 253 U.S. 350 (1920). In dissent McKenna disputed this conclusion, arguing that the Supremacy Clause "is not a declaration of the supremacy of one provision of the Constitution or laws of the United States over another, but of the supremacy of the Constitution and laws of the United States over the Constitutions and laws of the States. The Eighteenth Amendment is part of the Constitution of the United States, therefore of as high sanction as article VI. ... Section 2 [of the Eighteenth Amendment], therefore, is a new provision of power, power to the States as well as to Congress, and it is a contradiction to say that a power constitutionally concurrent in Congress and the States, in some way becomes constitutionally subordinate in the States to Congress." *Id.* at 401–2 (McKenna, J., dissenting). McKenna justified his interpretation in terms of the basic postulates of federalism:

    > From these premises the deduction seems inevitable that there must be united action between the States and Congress, or, at any rate, concordant and harmonious action; and will not such action promote better the purpose of the Amendment – will it not bring to the enforcement of prohibition, the power of the States and the power of Congress, make all the instrumentalities of the States, its courts and officers, agencies of the enforcement, as well as the instrumentalities of the United States, its court and officers, agencies of the enforcement? Will it not bring to the States as well, or preserve to them, a partial autonomy, satisfying, if you will, their prejudices, or better say, their predilections; and it is not too much to say that our dual system of government is based upon them. And this predilection for self-government the Eighteenth Amendment regards and respects, and by doing so sacrifices nothing of, the policy of prohibition.

    Id. at 405–6 (McKenna, J., dissenting).
2. Woodrow Wilson to Frank I. Cobb (April 18, 1923) (Woodrow Wilson papers). *See* ALFRED LIEF, BRANDEIS: THE PERSONAL HISTORY OF AN AMERICAN IDEAL 427–28 (New York: Stackpole 1936); ALPHEUS THOMAS MASON, BRANDEIS: A FREE MAN'S LIFE 567 (New York: Viking Press 1946). The Brandeis statement, attributed to Woodrow Wilson, together with an account of its submission to the platform committee of the 1924 Democratic Convention, may be found in Carter Glass, *New Light on Wilson and Prohibition; In a Challenge to Wets, Senator Glass Reveals Inner History of the Late President's Attitude and Shows How He Devised a Different Enforcement Policy for the States and the Federal Government*, NEW YORK TIMES (March 3, 1929), § 9 at 1.
3. Woodrow Wilson to Frank I. Cobb (April 18, 1923) (Woodrow Wilson papers). In 1916, Wilson's nomination of Brandeis as associate justice had been opposed by the Anti-Saloon League, because Brandeis had represented the Massachusetts Protective Liquor Dealers' Association in 1891, and Brandeis had then argued against prohibition. 2 THE SUPREME COURT OF THE UNITED STATES: HEARINGS AND REPORTS ON SUCCESSFUL AND UNSUCCESSFUL NOMINATIONS OF SUPREME COURT JUSTICES BY THE SENATE JUDICIARY COMMITTEE, 1916–1972, at 1054–72 (Roy M. Mersky & J. Myron Jacobstein, eds., Buffalo: W.S. Hein 1975). Brandeis had taken the position that "Liquor drinking is not a wrong; but excessive drinking is. Liquor will be sold; hence the sale should be licensed. Liquor is dangerous; hence the business should be regulated. No regulation can be enforced which is not reasonable." *Id.* at 1057. Brandeis had urged the Massachusetts

Legislature to "[t]ake the community in which you live; do not imagine one very different from your own, where men will not drink because you say they shall not." *Id.* at 1059.

4. Woodrow Wilson to Frank I. Cobb (April 18, 1923) (Woodrow Wilson papers). Later that year Frankfurter would use almost exactly this language to argue the identical position. *See* Felix Frankfurter, *A National Policy for Enforcement of Prohibition*, 109 ANNALS OF THE AMERICAN ACADEMY OF POLITICAL & SOCIAL SCIENCE 193, 193 (1923). Frankfurter explained that "[c]entralized nation-wide enforcement is impossible of achievement. It will either break or corrupt the federal machinery that attempts it." *Id.* at 194. Brandeis praised Frankfurter's article:

> Do not change the Volstead Law in any respect. Leave the percentage of alcohol where it is. Merely provide in the annual appropriation bills that the prohibition money shall be used for protection against smuggling from abroad & from one state or territory into another, and the suppression in the District of Columbia & any government reservation, etc.

LDB to Felix Frankfurter (October 24, 1923), in BRANDEIS-FRANKFURTER CORRESPONDENCE, at 146.

5. Woodrow Wilson to Frank I. Cobb (April 18, 1923) (Woodrow Wilson papers). It is hard to know whether Brandeis actually expected this political duty to be fulfilled. *Compare supra* note 3, *with* LDB to Felix Frankfurter (May 20, 1921), in BRANDEIS-FRANKFURTER CORRESPONDENCE, at 76 (commenting that "the Prohibition Amendment is perhaps serving ... a good purpose" in making manifest "the State's obligation to police itself").

6. At one point even Calvin Coolidge seemed to echo this functional view of federalism. *See To Put Local Dryness Up to Local Officers*, 85 LITERARY DIGEST 7 (April 4, 1925).

7. *But see* Glass, *supra* note 2.

8. The similarity between Wickersham's plan and Wilson's proposal to the 1924 Democratic Convention was widely noted. *See, e.g., Bishop Cannon Hits Wickersham's View*, NEW YORK TIMES (July 23, 1929), at 11; *Dry Foes to Oppose Wickersham Board in Obtaining Funds*, NEW YORK TIMES (July 20, 1929), at 1; *Holds Wickersham Should Quit Post*, NEW YORK TIMES (July 18, 1929), at 1.

9. Wickersham's letter, which was sent to New York Governor Franklin Roosevelt for presentation to the Conference of Governors, is reproduced in *Wickersham Would Change Dry Law, States Taking Over Local Enforcement*, NEW YORK TIMES (July 17, 1929), at 1. Wickersham argued that "Every State Executive has sworn to support and defend the Constitution of the United States. The Eighteenth Amendment is a part of the Constitution, just as much as any other part of it. Surely it is pertinent to their conference to suggest and consider how they may best carry out their solemn undertaking." *Id.*

10. *Dry Foes to Oppose Wickersham Board in Obtaining Funds*, *supra* note 8, at 1.

11. *Wickersham Views Attacked by Volstead; Proposal Would in Effect Repeal 18th Amendment, Dry Leader Contends*, NEW YORK TIMES (July 17, 1929), at 2. This was because "State enforcement will depend on the local attitude toward prohibition." *Wickersham Plan Splits Governors*, NEW YORK TIMES (July 18, 1929), at 1.

12. *The Wickersham Letter*, 129 THE NATION 107 (1929) ("Mr. Wickersham's plan is not a scientific solution of the liquor problem; it is not even a strictly honest one. But in the light of ten years' experience with the Volstead Act, and in the midst of the hypocrisy and failure of present methods of enforcement, one is compelled to consider results rather than technique.").
13. *Governors Shelve Wickersham's Plan and Drys' Motions*, NEW YORK TIMES (July 19, 1929), at 1; *Mr. Wickersham's Bomb*, NEW YORK TIMES (July 17, 1929), at 24. Wickersham's letter appeared to offer wet states the implicit option of modifying the national Volstead Act to make enforcement of prohibition more locally palatable. The possibility of this option outraged prohibition advocates. *See Bishop Cannon Hits Wickersham's View, supra* note 8, at 11. Cannon charged that the possibility of modifying the Volstead Act "seems to intimate the necessity for some kind of bargaining by means of which certain states would be persuaded to perform their prohibition enforcement duties, should they be given certain concessions, which concessions, however, are not indicated." *Id.* For an overview of the controversy, see *The Wickersham Scheme of Divided Enforcement*, 102 LITERARY DIGEST 5 (July 27, 1929).
14. 247 U.S. 251 (1918).
15. Bailey v. Drexel Furniture Co., 259 U.S. 20 (1922).
16. For a full account, see *infra* Chapter 36, at 1126–32.
17. The National Prohibition Cases, 253 U.S. 350, 366–67 (1920) (Argument of Elihu Root). "It is submitted that the authority conferred in Article V to amend the Constitution carries no power to destroy its federal principle in a most fundamental aspect." *Id.* at 367. Pressing his case against the amendment, Elihu Root, Taft's close friend, was nothing short of histrionic. An eyewitness described his summation:

> Mr. Root put his glasses in his pocket, and, drawing himself up to his full height, pointing his finger at the Chief Justice, with the whole nine Justices fixing their eyes upon him, he concluded his argument with these memorable words, which have burned themselves forever into my memory: "If Your Honors ... shall find a way to uphold the validity of this amendment, the government of the United States, as we have known it, will have ceased to exist. ... Your Honors will have found a legislative authority hitherto unknown to the Constitution and untrammeled by any of its limitations. ... In that case, Your Honors, John Marshall need never have sat upon your Bench."

PHILIP C. JESSUP, 2 ELIHU ROOT 479–80 (Hamden: Archon Books 1938) (quoting Nicholas Murray Butler, Address at the Odeon, St. Louis, Missouri (December 14, 1927)).

Despite his life-long friendship with Elihu Root, Taft was scathing in his denunciation of Root's argument:

> I think that the claims made by the Wets in the higher courts were the most extraordinary collection ever put forward by serious-minded men. It only shows how bitter they were. ... I cannot believe that any Supreme Court would read into any Amendment a change in the Amendment article of the constitution, the subject of Amendment not being mentioned in the article. If ever an instrument was plain the constitution is plain in regard to the method of Amendment. Any alteration of it seems so utterly gratuitous that it is hard to see where a Supreme Court would stop if it accepted such a thing. Any limitation of that power seems equally preposterous. Think of the reductio ad absurdum. The Supreme Court has

been under fire and in great danger a number of times owing to the discovery that the power of interpretation of the constitution is so great. ... The friends of the Court have said that if the interpretation put upon the constitution at any point by the Court does not suit the people they can amend it. The angry answer is that everybody knows that to amend the constitution is practically impossible, it has been made so difficult. Now come these gentlemen and propose that when an Amendment has been put through the very difficult process outlined by the constitution itself and has the support of two-thirds by both houses of Congress and the ratification by forty-six states that nine elderly gentlemen on a Bench shall pat the people on the head and say, "We think this is not good for little boys". They must reach up into the air or into their inner consciences or somewhere and without any limitation whatever except their own fitness of things decide that this Amendment does not belong in the constitution. It is the most extraordinary gift of absolute power that can be imagined and something that the court has never dreamed of claiming.

WHT to Jesse F. Orton (November 28, 1928) (Taft papers).

18. *National Prohibition Cases*, 253 U.S. at 370–71 (argument of William D. Guthrie). "The Eighteenth Amendment must be read in connection with the Tenth Amendment." *Id.* at 377.

19. *See, e.g.*, Nicholas Murray Butler, *The Constitution One Hundred and Forty Years After*, 12 CONSTITUTIONAL REVIEW 121, 123 (1928):

> It is the complete departure from the fundamental principles of the Constitution ... that makes the Eighteenth Amendment so objectionable and so offensive to everyone who understands American government and who believes in it. The incorporation in the Constitution for the first time of definite legislation and the attempted transfer by amendment to the Federal Government of the police power of the States, which can not be taken away without shaking the very foundations of the Constitution itself, are the real cause of the nation-wide dissatisfaction and revolt against the Eighteenth Amendment and the legislation built upon it.

James Beck, solicitor general of the United States from 1921 to 1925, was particularly exercised by this point:

> Certainly, the leaders of prohibition showed scant respect for the Constitution when they wrote this illegitimate amendment into that noble instrument and thus destroyed its perfect symmetry and turned a wise compact of government into a mere police code. Certainly, they had scant respect for the Constitution when they thus destroyed its basic principle of local self government and in this matter of daily habit, relegated the sovereign States to the ignominious position of mere police provinces.

JAMES M. BECK, THE REVOLT AGAINST PROHIBITION 14–15 (New York: Association Against the Prohibition Amendment 1930). *See id.* at 23.

20. *Prohibition and the Supreme Court*, 109 THE NATION 818, 819 (1919). The appeal of this argument was quite broad. *See, e.g.*, Charles K. Burdick, *Is Prohibition Lawful?*, 21 NEW REPUBLIC 245 (1920).

21. *The Supreme Court*, NEW YORK TIMES (October 14, 1932), at 18.

22. Fabian Franklin, *What's Wrong with the Eighteenth Amendment?*, 109 ANNALS OF THE AMERICAN ACADEMY POLITICAL & SOCIAL SCIENCE 48, 49 (1923).

23. Henry S. Priest, *The Eighteenth Amendment an Infringement of Liberty*, 109 ANNALS OF THE AMERICAN ACADEMY POLITICAL & SOCIAL SCIENCE 39, 44 (1923). Under the Eighteenth Amendment "the right of local self-government is torn from the individual states, whose people are made subject, even in the small

routine affairs of their daily lives, to those living in far distant localities and under other conditions." W.H. Stayton, *Our Experiment in National Prohibition: What Progress Has It Made?*, 109 ANNALS OF THE AMERICAN ACADEMY OF POLITICAL & SOCIAL SCIENCE 26, 30 (1923). See Seymour C. Loomis, *The Legal and Constitutional Aspects of the Proposed Prohibition Amendment to the Federal Constitution*, 8 SCIENTIFIC MONTHLY 335, 336–37 (1919) (the amendment was an unprecedented inclusion of police regulation in a document previously limited to a statement of principles).

24. WALTER THOMPSON, FEDERAL CENTRALIZATION: A STUDY AND CRITICISM OF THE EXPANDING SCOPE OF CONGRESSIONAL LEGISLATION 378 (New York: Harcourt, Brace & Co. 1923). The essential difficulty with Congress passing "sumptuary laws controlling the private life and conduct of affairs in local communities" is that "our local governments will grow weaker and the central government stronger in control of local affairs until local government is dominated from Washington by the votes of distant majorities indifferent to local customs and needs." Elihu Root, *Address of the President: Public Service by the Bar*, 2 AMERICAN BAR ASSOCIATION JOURNAL 736, 752 (1916).

25. THOMPSON, *supra* note 24, at 366. In opposing the Eighteenth Amendment, Massachusetts Senator Henry Cabot Lodge argued that it "will have a very bad effect on the public morals by creating a widespread indifference to law." Lodge predicted that prohibition would

> fail, and my own belief is that in a very short time we shall settle down to a condition like that presented by the amendments which attempted to confer full political rights upon the negroes of the United States, where the constitutional provision is entirely disregarded. They remain a dead letter in the Constitution.... This question is better dealt with by the States than by the National Government. The responsibility is more concentrated and there is greater harmony among the population of the smaller area inclosed within the State boundaries. ... The prohibition of liquor is essentially a police power, and ... I think we are taking a long step on a dangerous path when we take this police power from the States. The tendency now is to strip the States of one power after another that are conferred upon the National Government, forgetful of the fact that the strength and stability of our Government have depended upon the principle of local self-government embodied in the States.

55 CONG. REC. 5587 (July 31, 1917).

26. THOMPSON, *supra* note 24, at 367.

> The danger is that we will burden Washington with a mass of powers, – growing out of undigested ideas, relating to controversial matters not fundamental in character, and about which no real consensus of opinion exists, – that, in most instances, properly belong to the several states, where they can be more effectively, because more sympathetically, handled than by what, of necessity, must always seem a comparatively distant national government.

Robert von Moschzisker, *Dangers in Disregarding Fundamental Conceptions when Amending the Federal Constitution*, 11 CORNELL LAW QUARTERLY 1, 13 (1925).

27. Stayton, *supra* note 23, at 33. "One who studies the psychology of the subject is inevitably struck by the anomaly that while state prohibition laws were generally obeyed and respected, people seem to feel it a sort of duty to flout the Volstead Act. And inquiry quickly reveals at least one reason – a belief that the law was

passed not by a man's neighbors, who had an interest in him and his affairs, but by some one living at a distance, by strangers acting in a spirit of meddlesomeness." *Id.*

> Feeling that they have had a part in making the regulations, people will submit more readily to local restrictive legislation. But if the regulations are made by Congress, which is far removed from local interests, they are apt to be resented as being superimposed. Violations of these regulations then become justified by a local public opinion. This breeds a disrespect for federal law and for the government that attempts to enforce it.

THOMPSON, *supra* note 24, at 384. *See Should We Obey the Prohibition Laws? A Socratic Dialogue*, 81 THE FORUM 328, 331 (1929):

> Mr. [George] Martin: [T]he Fifteenth Amendment has been nullified, as everyone knows; and the very fact that an amendment can be nullified and that the country can forget about it, provides a needed safety valve for a constitution that can't be amended. If you tried to get a repeal of the Fifteenth Amendment to-day, you couldn't do it. So the only way out is for the South to nullify it and let the rest of the country forget about it.
>
> Mr. [Irving] Fisher: But this isn't the Fifteenth Amendment. That amendment really affected just the South.
>
> Mr. [George] Martin: It seems to me that this Prohibition question is another sectional issue pretty much of the same kind. Eventually the West and the South, which are aridly dry, will forget that the East is wet and will grow tired trying to enforce their will upon it.

28. It was argued that "[t]he exercise of police power was withheld from the United States" because "[i]n the Federal system the people cannot act collectively as a single nation." ARCHIBALD E. STEVENSON, STATES' RIGHTS AND NATIONAL PROHIBITION 80–81 (New York: Clark Boardman 1927). Only "[i]n each of the States" do "the people [act] collectively as a single unit." *Id.* Prohibitionists, of course, denied this argument. "[W]hat is good democracy in a small area is just as good in a large area . . . ." NOLAN R. BEST, YES, "IT'S THE LAW" AND IT'S A GOOD LAW 40 (New York: George H. Doran Co. 1926).

29. "Every restriction of the authority of local self-government must show cause in the interest of the liberties and opportunities of all and not in the mere desire of one or more communities or groups to govern the life of others, albeit for their own good. There may be an imperialism at home as well as abroad." Charles Evans Hughes, *Address of the President at the Annual Meeting of the American Bar Association: Liberty and Law*, 11 AMERICAN BAR ASSOCIATION JOURNAL 563, 565 (1925).

30. The absence of any national community capable of endowing national prohibition with democratic legitimacy is the essential thrust of the complaint of mathematician and *New York Post* associate editor Fabian Franklin:

> The population of the United States is, in more than one respect, composed of parts extremely diverse as regards the particular subject of this legislation. The question of drink has a totally different aspect in the South from what it has in the North; a totally different aspect in the cities from what it has in the rural districts or in small towns. . . . How profoundly the whole course of the Prohibition movement has been affected by the desire of the South to keep liquor away from the negroes, needs no elaboration; it would not be going far beyond the truth to say that the people of New York are being deprived of their right to the harmless enjoyment of wine and beer in order that the negroes of Alabama and

Prohibition & Normative Dualism

> Texas may not get beastly drunk on rotgut whiskey. ... [T]he Prohibitionist tyranny is in no small measure a sectional tyranny, which is of course an aggravated form of majority tyranny.
>
> But what needs insisting on even more than this is the way in which country districts impose their notions about Prohibition upon the people of the cities, and especially of the great cities. ... Could the tyranny of the majority take a more obnoxious form than that of sparse rural populations, scattered over the whole area of the country from Maine to Texas and from Georgia to Oregon, deciding for the crowded millions of New York and Chicago that they shall or shall not be permitted to drink a glass of beer?

FABIAN FRANKLIN, WHAT PROHIBITION HAS DONE TO AMERICA 72–75 (New York: Harcourt, Brace & Co. 1922).

Those concerned to defend prohibition sought to evoke precisely the kind of national community denied by Franklin. *See, e.g.*, WILLIAM GIBBS MCADOO, THE CHALLENGE: LIQUOR AND LAWLESSNESS VERSUS CONSTITUTIONAL GOVERNMENT 214–15 (New York: Century Co. 1928) ("The National Government, like the state governments, is not an alien and external force imposed upon the people by some outside agency. The National Government, like the state governments, is the people's government."); Jeremiah Hevenward, *Upholding the Constitution*, 153 HARPER'S MAGAZINE 476, 478 (1926) ("The issue of battle is drawn! On the one side are those who for the satisfaction of their own ungodly purposes, set themselves against what they presumptuously call 'the encroachments of Federal authority.' These men are bent on sapping and mining our national solidarity and making their liberty a cloak for detestable license. They would reduce the Constitution to a form of words devoid of force or meaning, and so manipulate the smaller political units as to bring forth confusion and every evil work. On the other side are those upon whom rests the spirit of our godly ancestors who through the agency of the Constitution welded the colonies together into a unity that should be then and forever indissoluble.").

The contestable nature of the national community in the context of prohibition was particularly evident in congressional antagonism to Taft's proposal to assign district court judges to sit temporarily wherever in the country the needs of the docket were greatest. *See supra* Chapter 12, at 449–52; Act of September 14, 1922, Pub. L. 67-298, 42 Stat. 837 (1922). Taft's proposal was opposed by those who deplored the possibility of a "flying squadron ... of the judiciary – a perambulatory crowd of judges to be floating in space throughout the entire United States." 62 CONG. REC. 5106–7 (April 6, 1922) (Remarks of Mississippi Senator John Sharp Williams). It was feared, for example, "that the Anti-Saloon League, finding some judge in some district to be perhaps lenient toward those who offend against the prohibition laws, will be able to transfer a judge from a remote section of the country who harbors different views upon that subject and thus displace the local judge in the administration of the law." 62 CONG. REC. 5154–55 (April 7, 1922) (Remarks of Montana Senator Thomas Walsh). Of course, this form of national discipline was exactly what some supporters of the Act had in mind. Representative William J. Graham, a Republican from Illinois, explicitly linked the bill to prohibition enforcement: "The [national prohibition] law is being openly flouted.... I want to see additional judges appointed on the bench of the United States ... who will inject some fear of God into the breasts of lawbreakers in this country." 62 CONG. REC. 203 (December 10, 1921). Opposition to Taft's proposed judicial reform rested on the implicit assumption that national federal law depended for its legitimacy upon a dialectical reconciliation with local values, so that it could be said without contradiction that "it is absolutely contrary to the principles of our Government to assign a judge from a distant territory to preside over cases arising in another community." 62 CONG. REC. 4847 (March 31, 1922) (Remarks of Louisiana Senator Edwin Broussard). Southerners in particular viewed the 1922 Act within a larger context of regional hostility: "[T]his is merely a provision which is an entering wedge to having what once was called a lot of 'carpetbag judges' transported from one section of the country to another." 62 CONG. REC. 204 (December 10, 1921) (Remarks of South Carolina Representative William Stevenson).

31. According to this view, states could effectively and democratically exercise the police power because "there is more likelihood of a general community of opinion in most of the states than in the country as a whole, and that is of no small importance in the enforcement of a law." A. Lawrence Lowell, *Reconstruction and Prohibition*, 143 ATLANTIC MONTHLY 145, 147–48 (1929). *See* STEVENSON, *supra* note 28, at 82–83 ("State sovereignty has been the main bulwark against the bureaucracy and absolutism of centralization. The States . . . respect local customs and habits. They authorize the exercise of sectional prejudices in both social and political matters. Such local prejudices are created by long established custom in which the history of the people, their climatic, economic and social conditions play an important part. The right of our citizens to satisfy these prejudices has been considered an essential in our conception of civil liberty. . . . In a country covering such wide geographical area as the United States, local interests and prejudices will inevitably be widely divergent. Laws enacted in one part of the country may be offensive or serve no useful purpose in another where the people live under vastly different circumstances.").

32. THOMPSON, *supra* note 24, at 366. *See* CHARLES W. PIERSON, OUR CHANGING CONSTITUTION 47–48 (Garden City: Doubleday, Page & Co. 1922) ("Advocates of the old order see in the change a breaking down of the principle of local self-government. To their minds the danger of majority tyranny, made possible by a centralization of power in a republic of such vast extent and varied interests, outweighs all the advantages of national uniformity and efficiency. Advocates of the new order think otherwise. They argue, moreover, that the states have become too great and populous to serve as units for purposes of home rule; that their boundaries are for the most part artificial and correspond to no real distinctions in the ordinary life of men.").

33. Priest, *supra* note 23, at 43. The insight of normative dualism was that legislation enacted according to democratic procedures could nevertheless be experienced as tyrannical if passed in ways that did not respect "[t]he feeling among the citizens that the government is their government in which they have a vital interest." THOMPSON, *supra* note 24, at 369. That feeling "is the soul of democracy." *Id.* Prohibition was on this account "an act of tyranny because it is felt as an act of tyranny." *Should We Obey the Prohibition Laws? A Socratic Dialogue*, *supra* note 27, at 331. *See* James E. Beck, *Should the Eighteenth Amendment be Respected?*, 9 CONGRESSIONAL DIGEST 83 (March 1930) (referring to "this system of tyranny and hypocrisy").

34. Sutherland complained to the Cleveland Chamber of Commerce in 1914 about the growing tendency "to enlarge the powers and responsibilities of the

Prohibition & Normative Dualism

national government at the expense or to the relief of the state governments, the danger of which is that we may overload the national government and correspondingly weaken the vigor and self-helpful qualities of the state governments."

> In the framework of our political institutions nothing, in my judgment, is wiser than the dual system of government, under which matters which concern the states as a political union are left to the general government and things which concern the states as political units are left to the state governments. . . .
>
> I am a believer in a strong national government and in the liberal interpretation of its powers, but I am also a believer in a strong state government with its powers jealously guarded from invasion; for I think it is only by maintaining the powers of each and holding each to the full measure of its separate responsibilities that we shall escape the weakness of over-distribution upon the one side and the dangers of over-centralization upon the other.

GEORGE SUTHERLAND, SUPERFLUOUS GOVERNMENT: AN ADDRESS BY SENATOR SUTHERLAND OF UTAH 14–15 (Cleveland: Cleveland Chamber of Commerce 1914).

35. 253 U.S. 350 (1920).
36. GS to William D. Guthrie (March 15, 1920) (Sutherland papers).
37. GS to William D. Guthrie (March 18, 1920) (Sutherland papers). Sutherland sent his thoughts to Guthrie as the latter was preparing his brief in the National Prohibition Cases, 253 U.S. 350 (1920). Guthrie incorporated into his brief Sutherland's ideas and even Sutherland's language. William D. Guthrie to GS (March 25, 1920) (Sutherland papers).
38. GS to William D. Guthrie (March 15, 1920) (Sutherland papers) (emphasis added).
39. GS to William D. Guthrie (March 18, 1920) (Sutherland papers).
40. GS to William D. Guthrie (March 15, 1920) (Sutherland papers).
41. GS to William D. Guthrie (March 18, 1920) (Sutherland papers).
42. *National Prohibition Cases*, 253 U.S. at 387.
43. CHARLES K. BURDICK, THE LAW OF THE AMERICAN CONSTITUTION: ITS ORIGIN AND DEVELOPMENT 616 (New York: G.P. Putnam's Sons 1922). In dissent McKenna adopted Sutherland's perspective. *See supra* note 1.
44. 265 U.S. 545, 554, 560 (1924). At issue was the Supplemental Prohibition Act, Pub. L. 67-96, 42 Stat. 222 (November 23, 1921). The statute was enacted to prevent the issuance of permits authorizing the manufacture and sale of beer for medicinal purposes. Attorney General A. Mitchell Palmer ruled in 1921 that such permits were not prohibited by the Volstead Act. 32 OPINIONS OF THE ATTORNEY GENERAL 467 (1921). *See Beer as Medicine, 2 Gallons at Time; New Regulations Issued by Revenue Bureau Cause Consternation in Dry Camp*, NEW YORK TIMES (October 25, 1921), at 1; *Under the Whip*, NEW YORK TIMES (June 29, 1921), at 14 ("Another triumph of discipline has been achieved by the Anti-Saloon League."). The story is well told in Jacob M. Appel, *"Physicians Are Not Bootleggers": The Short, Peculiar Life of the Medicinal Alcohol Movement*, 82 BULLETIN OF THE HISTORY OF MEDICINE 355, 358–79 (2008).
45. Butler's docket book shows that McReynolds dissented in conference.
46. *Everard's Breweries*, 265 U.S. at 560. Taft regarded *Everard's Breweries* as a "pretty important" case. WHT to Charles P. Taft 2nd (March 9, 1924) (Taft papers).

47. 226 U.S. 192 (1912). *See Everard's Breweries*, 265 U.S. at 560.
48. *See supra* Chapter 23, at 739; *infra* note 68.
49. 17 U.S. 316 (1819).
50. *Everard's Breweries*, 265 U.S. at 559–60.
51. *See supra* Chapter 23, at 739; *supra* Chapter 26, at 825 and note 19. In his dissent in *Schlesinger v. Wisconsin*, Holmes cited *Everard's Breweries* for the proposition that "with the States as with Congress when the means are not prohibited and are calculated to effect the object we ought not to inquire into the degree of the necessity for resorting to them." 270 U.S. 230, 242 (1926) (Holmes, J., dissenting). *See* David P. Currie, *The Constitution in the Supreme Court: 1921–1930*, 1986 DUKE LAW JOURNAL 65, 120 ("It remains striking, however, that under the influence of the popular uprising that culminated in the adoption of the amendment, a Court so strict in its scrutiny of legislative means under the innocuous-looking due process clauses would assume such a relaxed attitude in determining the appropriateness of means to achieve limited congressional goals – especially since nothing in the opinions suggested that the Court's principles of broad construction applied only to Prohibition cases.").
52. *See supra* Chapter 23, at 740–41; Chapter 26, at 822–23.
53. *Everard's Breweries*, 265 U.S. at 558. Compare Sanford's treatment of the Tenth Amendment with STEVENSON, *supra* note 28, who contended that the Tenth Amendment is "an express restrictive clause, protecting forever the reserved powers of the States" in a manner that "expressly modifies and limits Article V of the Constitution," and hence which renders the Eighteenth Amendment "void in so far as it purports to give to the United States authority over intra-state business." *Id.* at 130. T.R. Powell dryly commented on Stevenson's argument: "Such a straight-jacket Tenth Amendment as Mr. Stevenson invents would afford an even sadder spectacle of constitution-making than the Eighteenth Amendment itself." Thomas Reed Powell, *Book Review*, 41 HARVARD LAW REVIEW 413, 414 (1928).
54. United States v. Darby, 312 U.S. 100, 123–24 (1941) (Opinion by Stone, J.) ("Our conclusion is unaffected by the Tenth Amendment which provides: 'The powers not delegated to the United States by the Constitution, nor prohibited by it to the States, are reserved to the States respectively, or to the people.' The amendment states but a truism that all is retained which has not been surrendered.").
55. *Supreme Court Decision Mops Last Wet Hope*, CHICAGO DAILY TRIBUNE (June 10, 1924), at 5.
56. Thomas Reed Powell, *Umpiring the Federal System, 1922–1924*, 40 POLITICAL SCIENCE QUARTERLY 101, 104 (1925).
57. *The Supreme Court's Ban on Beer*, 81 LITERARY DIGEST 17 (June 28, 1924). The response of the *New York Times* was typical:

> Apparently, there is no limit to the power of Congress in the enforcement of the Eighteenth Amendment.... As Dr. George David Stewart, President of the Academy of Medicine, said:
>
>> Only the doctor knows how necessary alcohol is in certain cases, and how much should be used. In diphtheria cases, for example, especially where secondary infection has set in, nothing on God's earth will cure them but alcohol.
>
> Let them die, then! What is the judgment of mere physicians compared with the judgment of Congress?

Prohibition & Normative Dualism

Dr. Congress, NEW YORK TIMES (June 10, 1924), at 20. See *Prescription by Legislation?*, WASHINGTON POST (June 12, 1924), at 6 ("It would be interesting to know how far the process of prescription by legislation can be carried.... Is the pharmacopoeia to be embodied in the revised statutes, and is Congress to enact what medicines may and may not be prescribed, and what surgical operations may and may not be performed?"). It is striking that at the very moment that *Everard's Breweries* was provoking such controversy, "many States" were routinely – and apparently noncontroversially – banning medical uses of beer pursuant to local prohibition laws. *Everard's Breweries*, 265 U.S. at 562. The disparity well illustrates the ideological force of normative dualism.

58. *Everard's Breweries*, 265 U.S. at 561–62. In 1922, the *Journal of the American Medical Association* had sent a survey about the medicinal uses of alcohol "to 53,900 physicians, representing 37 per cent. of the physicians of the United States, and 31,154 or 58 per cent. were returned." *The Referendum on the Use of Alcohol in the Practice of Medicine*, 78 JOURNAL OF THE AMERICAN MEDICAL ASSOCIATION 210, 210 (1922). The survey asked, "Do you regard beer as a necessary therapeutic agent in the practice of medicine?" According to the *Journal*: "The total number of votes cast for beer was 30,597, and of these 22,663, or 74 per cent. were negative, and 7,934, or 26 per cent., were affirmative." *Id*. In contrast, 51 per cent of respondents thought that whiskey was "a necessary therapeutic agent in the practice of medicine," whereas 49 per cent thought that it was not.

59. I should mention, in this context, Selzman v. United States, 268 U.S. 466 (1925), in which the Court, per Chief Justice Taft, unanimously upheld federal power under the Eighteenth Amendment to regulate denatured alcohol, stating:

> The power of the Federal Government, granted by the Eighteenth Amendment, to enforce the prohibition of the manufacture, sale and transportation of intoxicating liquor carries with it power to enact any legislative measures reasonably adapted to promote the purpose. The denaturing in order to render the making and sale of industrial alcohol compatible with the enforcement of prohibition of alcohol for beverage purposes is not always effective. The ignorance of some, the craving and the hardihood of others, and the fraud and cupidity of still others, often tend to defeat its object. It helps the main purpose of the Amendment, therefore, to hedge about the making and disposition of the denatured article every reasonable precaution and penalty to prevent the proper industrial use of it from being perverted to drinking it.

Id. at 468–69. This reasoning is significantly in tension with the logic of the cases discussed in Chapter 23. It is important to note that Taft does not in *Selzman* cite Purity Extract Co. v. Lynch, 226 U.S. 192 (1912). *See supra* text at notes 46–48; *infra* note 68.

60. 272 U.S. 581 (1926).

61. At issue were the provisions of two statutes. The first was chapter 85, title 2, section 7 of the National Prohibition Act, Pub. L. 66-66, 41 Stat. 305 (October 28, 1919), which provided:

> No one but a physician holding a permit to prescribe liquor shall issue any prescription for liquor.... Not more than a pint of spirituous liquor to be taken internally shall be prescribed for use by the same person within any period of ten days and no prescription shall be filled more than once.

Lambert, 272 U.S. at 587. The second was chapter 134, section 2 of the Supplemental Prohibition Act, Pub. L. 67-96, 42 Stat. 222 (November 23, 1921), which provided:

> No physician shall prescribe nor shall any person sell or furnish on any prescription, any vinous liquor that contains more than 24 per centum of alcohol by volume, nor shall any one prescribe or sell or furnish on any prescription more than one-fourth of one gallon of vinous liquor, or any such vinous or spirituous liquor that contains separately or in the aggregate more than one-half pint of alcohol, for use by any person within any period of ten days. No physician shall be furnished with more than one hundred prescription blanks for use in any period of ninety days, nor shall any physician issue more than that number of prescriptions within any such period unless on application therefor he shall make it clearly apparent to the commissioner that for some extraordinary reason a larger amount is necessary whereupon the necessary additional blanks may be furnished him.

Lambert, 272 U.S. at 591. Almost from the start these statutes were attacked as violating the rights of physicians and the needs of patients. *See, e.g.*, *Medical Liberty Chained*, NEW YORK TIMES (August 10, 1921), at 12:

> Here we are beyond any question of the merits or demerits of prohibition in itself. Here, as some of the most distinguished physicians of this city have written, "the point at issue is the right of the physician to select his remedies and to decide what doses of these remedies each patient requires." That right, so far as the use of alcohol as a remedy is concerned, Dr. Congress proposes to take away.... [T]his Federal prescription of prescriptions will force conscientious physicians who believe in the therapeutic use of alcohol to break the law. The health, the life, of their patients will necessarily outweigh in their minds the ignorant interference of fanatical or fanatic-frightened laymen with medical practice.

62. *See supra* note 58. *Lambert* was "regarded as one of the most important tests to which the Volstead Act has been subjected." *Liquor Rule Sustained; Prescriptions to Retain Limit*, LOS ANGELES TIMES (November 30, 1926), at 1. The banner headline over the story in the *Chicago Tribune* read: "High Court Upholds 'Dr.' Volstead." CHICAGO TRIBUNE (November 30, 1926), at 1.

63. The Brandeis papers indicate that he initially circulated a brief and abrupt opinion that cited *Everard's Breweries*, documented extensive state regulation of the prescription of alcoholic beverages for medicinal purposes in order to enforce municipal prohibition laws, and then peremptorily concluded that "[t]here is no right to practice medicine which is not subordinate to the police power ... or to the power of Congress to make laws necessary and proper for carrying into execution the command of the Eighteenth Amendment." (Brandeis papers). Holmes and Sanford signed on to the draft, but Taft and Van Devanter were apparently dissatisfied, and Van Devanter drafted everything between what is now footnote 2 of the published opinion and its last paragraph, which Van Devanter also extensively edited. *Id*. Brandeis mostly accepted these changes and circulated the new draft with the notation: "Additions and Changes made at the suggestion of the Chief Justice and Mr. Justice Van Devanter are indicated in pencil on the margin." *Id*. Taft wrote Van Devanter that "I am perfectly delighted that you made your addition to B's opinion. It shows up the weakness of the dissent." WHT to WVD (November 30, 1926) (Van Devanter papers).

64. There is a note in the Brandeis papers to the effect that "McR. B & Su. say one of them will write a dissent & ask that it go over to the next term so that it can be done. St[one] says he will await dissent to see whether they can get away from the per cent case. If not he will go with the majority." (Brandeis papers). Stone wrote Sutherland that, while he "entirely" agreed with Sutherland's dissent,

> the point in the case with which I have great difficulty is the aspect given this whole question by the decision of the Court in the half per cent case, which is Ruppert v. Caffrey [251 U.S. 264 (1920)] ... if I remember correctly. There the Court held that conceding that half per cent beer was not intoxicating and that there was no general power lodged with the federal government to regulate or prohibit the consumption of non-intoxicating beverages, nevertheless the power to prohibit this particular type of non-intoxicating beverage was incidental to the general power to prohibit intoxicating beverages. Had I been on the Court at that time I should have voted with the minority, but I now find difficulty in distinguishing the reason adopted by the majority from that applicable to the present case.
>
> In the foregoing I am indicating, not a conclusion, but a doubt, which I think should be dealt with in your dissent.

HFS to GS (September 30, 1926) (Stone papers). Several months later, Stone wrote Sutherland asking if he would incorporate the following passage in his dissent:

> The question whether a state has power to regulate or prohibit the use of intoxicating liquor as a medicine is different from the question presented here. A state has plenary power in that respect, save only as it is limited by the Fourteenth Amendment. Linder v. United States. But here the question is whether that power was transferred from the state to the national government by the adoption of the Eighteenth Amendment, not whether its exercise is unreasonable or arbitrary. It is insisted that the power is incidental to the granted power to prohibit the use of intoxicating liquor as a beverage and that by the grant of the incident the power of the state to regulate the practice of medicine, so far as the use of intoxicating liquor as a medicine is concerned, has been destroyed notwithstanding the limitation of the Tenth Amendment.

HFS to GS (November 27, 1926) (Stone papers). Stone continued, "I think this comes a little closer to the real vice of the argument of the majority than your statement that the authority of Congress is here exercised not as ancillary to the power granted, etc. etc." *Id. Lambert* was decided on November 29, and Sutherland's dissent does not contain Stone's proposed paragraph that so strikingly invokes the Tenth Amendment in a manner that sharply contrasts with Stone's later opinion in United States v. Darby, 312 U.S. 100, 124 (1941), which dismisses the Tenth Amendment as "but a truism."

65. *Lambert*, 272 U.S. at 588. Lambert was the "president of the Association for the Protection of Constitutional Rights, which was organized ... by 105 physicians" to challenge federal control of the authority of doctors to prescribe liquor. *Unlimited Liquor Prescriptions*, 77 LITERARY DIGEST 10 (May 26, 1923). From 1904 to 1919, Lambert was dean of the Columbia College of Physicians and Surgeons, and he was president of the New York Academy of Medicine from 1927 to 1929. For a full biography, see 37 NATIONAL CYCLOPEDIA OF AMERICAN BIOGRAPHY 281–82 (New York: J.T. White 1951).

Lambert was a close personal acquaintance of Taft and served as a physician to Taft's relatives in the New York area. *See* Horace D. Taft to WHT (November 2,

1922) (Taft papers); WHT to Horace D. Taft (November 9, 1922) (Taft papers) ("I am very glad that Sam thinks you have gained in the last eight months. It seemed to me, when I saw you in New York, that you looked much better."); WHT to Horace D. Taft (October 26, 1922) (Taft papers); WHT to Mrs. William A. Edwards (November 17, 1922) (Taft papers) ("I am glad to think that Horace is better. The trace of albumen hasn't disappeared, but his diet has evidently done him good, and Sam Lambert has now [illegible] him to eat some eggs but no meat.").

After the decision in *Lambert*, Taft wrote his brother:

> Sam Lambert's wife was here as one of Nellie's Colonial Dames and when I saw her I told her that if she had managed the case, with her direct methods, because she appealed to me, as I told you, by seizing my coat lapel and saying that I must decide for Sam, the case might have gone what she thought was the right way. I told her to tell Joe Auerbach that if she had been employed as counsel, the result might have been different.

WHT to Horace D. Taft (May 24, 1927) (Taft papers). Joseph S. Auerbach was Lambert's counsel of record in the case. After the Court's decision, Lambert filed a petition for rehearing, arguing that the Court had in its opinion mistakenly believed that the majority of physicians were "opposed to the use of alcohol as a therapeutic." *Liquor as Medicine Ruling under Fire; Committee of Doctors to Seek Reversal of Limiting Decision by Supreme Court*, NEW YORK TIMES (December 14, 1926), at 17. *See Medicinal Liquor Up in Court Again; Dr. Lambert Asks Supreme Bench to Reopen Case Rejected Five to Four*, NEW YORK TIMES (January 6, 1927), at 3. Taft wrote his brother Horace:

> I don't see just how Sam Lambert can try again on the question, for we intended to make an end of him, and I think we have done so. If he thinks we are going back to try over the question whether a majority of doctors are in favor or opposed to larger liberality in the matter of the use of whiskey as a medicinal agent, he is greatly mistaken. I used to think that the prohibitionists were the craziest people in the landscape, but I really think their opponents are more nearly lunatics than they.

WHT to Horace D. Taft (January 16, 1927) (Taft papers). After the Court's denial of Lambert's petition, Horace replied, "I see that you have turned down Sam Lambert and I hope that now he can get some sleep." Horace D. Taft to WHT (January 18, 1927) (Taft papers).

Lambert, however, continued to press his case, arguing for the medicinal value of liquor "in the treatment of many diseases and nervous conditions, particularly those of the aged." *Advocates Liquor as Benefit to Aged; Lambert of Medical Academy Urges Doctors to Force New Dry Law from Congress*, NEW YORK TIMES (October 5, 1928), at 27; *Says Dry Act Curbs Medical Practice; Dr. Samuel W. Lambert Asserts Definition of Intoxicants Invades Doctors' Rights*, NEW YORK TIMES (January 28, 1927), at 3. *See* Horace D. Taft to WHT (October 19, 1928) (Taft papers) ("Another piece of delicious absurdity comes from a quotation by the Wets of Sam Lambert. Nothing is so firmly fixed in the minds of the Wets or so loudly trumpeted as that we are drinking more than ever under prohibition. Now comes Sam in an address and states that there has been a dreadful increase in diabetes, because alcohol is needed to burn up the sugar in the human system and now that people have so largely given up alcoholic drinks the increase in diabetes occurs. The Wets rejoice over this decision by a high medical

Prohibition & Normative Dualism

authority and are quite capable of citing in parallel columns the two arguments against prohibition, one that we are drinking more than ever and the other that the fact that we are drinking so little is destroying us."). "After 1926, the partisans of medicinal beer and spirits were increasingly marginalized. The doctors' lobby had entered the political arena and, by any measure, they had been soundly defeated." Appel, *supra* note 44, at 383. *See The Doctor's Right to Give Whisky*, 93 LITERARY DIGEST 13 (June 11, 1927).

66. Lambert v. Yellowley, 291 F. 640, 640–41 (S.D.N.Y. 1923).
67. *Lambert*, 272 U.S. at 594 ("We have spoken of that case at length because the decision was by a unanimous court and if adhered to disposes of the present case.").
68. *Id.* at 595. This language was actually written by Van Devanter. *See supra* note 63. In his original draft, Brandeis had specifically cited Purity Extract Co. v. Lynch, 226 U.S. 192 (1912), to support the need for judicial deference to government in matters of enforcement. But at precisely this time *Lynch* was becoming a controversial precedent in *Weaver*, see *supra* text at notes 47–48, and Van Devanter deliberately removed the citation. *See supra* note 63.
69. *Lambert*, 272 U.S. at 595. This language was also written by Van Devanter. *See supra* note 63.
70. *Lambert*, 272 U.S. at 597. In Brandeis's original draft, this sentence had read: "High medical authority is in conflict as to the medicinal value of spirituous and vinous liquors taken as a beverage. It would, indeed, be strange if Congress lacked the power to determine that the necessities of the liquor problem require a reasonable limitation of the permissible doses." (Brandeis papers). Van Devanter drafted the changes in the paragraph. The Court's reference to conflict of medical authority referred to a 1917 resolution of the American Medical Association declaring "that the use of alcoholic liquor as a therapeutic agent was without 'scientific basis' and 'should be discouraged.'" *Lambert*, 272 U.S. at 591. In *Lambert* itself, however, the American Medical Association filed an amicus brief disavowing its previous resolution and arguing that the "limitations on dosage of which complaint is now made ... have no foundation in scientific observation or in experience. ... They are, it is believed, arbitrary and unreasonable." Brief for American Medical Association as Amicus Curiae Supporting Appellant, Lambert v. Yellowley, No. 47 October Term 1925.
71. *Lambert*, 272 U.S. at 600, 602 (Sutherland, J., dissenting).
72. *Id.* at 601–2 (Sutherland, J., dissenting). Congress had also failed to make findings linking dosage limitations to the necessities of enforcement. *Id.* at 603 (Sutherland, J., dissenting).
73. *Id.* at 604 (Sutherland, J., dissenting). That state prohibition statutes were accorded deference in their regulation of medical prescriptions of vinous and spirituous liquors, a fact extensively documented by Brandeis's opinion, was thus irrelevant for Sutherland, because state regulations did not undermine the constitutional values protected by normative dualism. *Id.* at 603 (Sutherland, J., dissenting).
74. *Id.* at 604–5 (Sutherland, J., dissenting).
75. As Sutherland expressed the point in his presidential address to the American Bar Association:

> I believe in the most liberal construction of the national powers actually granted, but I also believe in the rigid exclusion of the national government from

those powers which have been actually reserved to the states. The local government is in immediate contact with the local problems and should be able to deal with them more wisely and more effectively than the general government having its seat at a distance. The need of preserving the power and enforcing the duty of local self-government is imperative, and especially so in a country, such as ours, of vast population and extent, possessing almost every variety of soil and climate, of greatly diversified interests and occupations, and having all sorts of differing conditions to deal with.

George Sutherland, *Address of the President: Private Rights and Government Control*, in REPORT OF THE FORTIETH ANNUAL MEETING OF THE AMERICAN BAR ASSOCIATION 212 (Baltimore: Lord Baltimore Press 1917).

76. *See, e.g.*, Linder v. United States, 268 U.S. 5, 18 (1925).
77. *Lambert*, 272 U.S. at 604 (Sutherland, J., dissenting).
78. *See supra* text at note 53. Sanford's opinion in *Everard's Breweries* may instructively be contrasted with Hammer v. Dagenhart, 247 U.S. 251 (1918), which affirmed:

> The grant of power to Congress over the subject of interstate commerce was to enable it to regulate such commerce, and not to give it authority to control the States in their exercise of the police power over local trade and manufacture.
> The grant of authority over a purely federal matter was not intended to destroy the local power always existing and carefully reserved to the States in the Tenth Amendment to the Constitution.

247 U.S. at 273–74. *Hammer* ruled that the value of local self-government was to be protected by ensuring that congressional authority was exercised in a manner consistent "with constitutional limitations and not by an invasion of the powers of the States." *Id.* at 276. Sutherland's dissent drew direct inspiration from this passage. *See Lambert*, 272 U.S. at 604 (Sutherland, J., dissenting).

79. EDWARD A. PURCELL, JR., LITIGATION AND INEQUALITY: FEDERAL DIVERSITY JURISDICTION IN INDUSTRIAL AMERICA, 1870–1958, at 192 (New York: Oxford University Press 1992).
80. 259 U.S. 20 (1922).
81. 259 U.S. 344 (1922).
82. *See infra* Chapter 36, at 1130–34; Chapter 40, at 1313–19.
83. 268 U.S. 5 (1925).
84. Pub. L. 63-223, 38 Stat. 785 (December 17, 1914).
85. *Linder*, 268 U.S. at 18.
86. Forrest Revere Black, *An Ill-Starred Decision – Lambert v. Yellowley*, 15 CORNELL LAW QUARTERLY 243, 253 (1930).

CHAPTER 31

Prohibition and Positive Law

THE EXPANSION OF federal power in America is usually explained by the consolidation of national markets, "as a natural development and outgrowth of modern industry."[1] The debacle of prohibition, however, suggests that a precondition for the legitimacy of federal authority is the belief that the nation, as distinct from individual states, is the natural unit of democratic self-determination.[2] Because this belief may apply to some spheres of federal competence – war, foreign affairs, railroads – but not to others – liquor, marriage, education – we can conceptualize the remarkable advance of federal authority in the twentieth century in terms of the multiplying domains of government action to which this belief has attached.

The Eighteenth Amendment was a proleptic leap of faith that the American people were ready to accept federal regulation of intimate habits of consumption as democratically legitimate.[3] This faith was misplaced, for the "light-hearted contempt with which the Eighteenth Amendment" was "treated by millions of good citizens – citizens who in other things are as law-abiding as anybody" – proved to be a "phenomenon" that was entirely unanticipated.[4] It was not merely that prohibition was flouted, it was rather that "great centers of population" were "wet in practice and wet in principle."[5] "The real problem of prohibition enforcement turns on the intensity of the conviction in certain communities not merely that the law is a failure, but that it ought to be a failure."[6] The widespread and flagrant defiance of prohibition[7] signaled a calamitous collapse of the law's legitimacy.[8]

Contemporaries understood the source of this collapse to lie in the fact that prohibition had "no sanction in common sense or morals. ... The preposterous Volstead act, with all its unforeseen consequences ... is not and can not be enforced in great reaches of the country because it has no hold on the reason or the moral sense of the majority."[9] It was endlessly reiterated that prohibition was a *malum prohibitum* rather than a *malum in se*,[10] for prohibition sought to interdict long-standing "traditions of habit and mind."[11]

If an essential insight of federalism was that law, particularly ordinary police regulations, should be kept as decentralized as possible to ensure the legitimacy of self-governance, the spectacular failure of national prohibition seemed to confirm that legal authority depended upon the law's being the "creation of historical growth ... supported in reality not so much by organized force as by that sense of mutual obligation and respect for the rights of others which lies at the root of, and forms the foundation of, those settled rules of conduct among individuals which alone make law and order in the community possible."[12] This was the perspective that conservative legal theorists had long brought to bear on law, which they imagined as the spontaneous self-ordering of society. Law could grow only when nourished by the soil of customary mores and values.

By losing touch with customary beliefs, national prohibition was said to succumb to the "viciousness" characteristic of all "laws which express excellent views of conduct but which run counter to the settled habits or fixed desires of a part of the community."[13] John Hessin Clarke observed in 1922 that "[t]he Eighteenth Amendment required millions of men and women to abruptly give up habits and customs of life which they thought not immoral or wrong, but which, on the contrary, they believed to be necessary to their reasonable comfort and happiness." The inevitable consequence was that "respect not only for that law, but for all law, has been put to an unprecedented and demoralizing strain in our country, the end of which it is difficult to see."[14] In its unrelenting support for prohibition in the teeth of widespread attraction to the value of normative dualism and general repugnance at the possibility of double jeopardy, the Taft Court contributed to a growing fear that the positive law of prohibition was somehow incompatible with deeply held traditional values.

This fear was amplified by a pervasive anxiety, spurred by the legal hypertrophy of World War I, that law itself was spinning out of control, wildly proliferating and increasingly detached from tradition and custom.[15] In an influential article, Arthur Twining Hadley, a former president of Yale, complained that "[o]ne of the greatest dangers which now confronts us is the increasing demand for ill-considered legislation, and the increasing readiness of would-be reformers to rely on authority rather than on public sentiment for securing their ends."[16] Hadley was one of a myriad of writers in the popular press who protested "the torrent of new laws which are deluging the country to the confusion of everyone, lawmakers included."[17]

Contemporaries believed they were witnessing the "greatest outpouring of statutory law the world has ever seen. Statute is piled upon statute, administrative agency upon administrative agency, and to the great body of statutory law has been added a mass of administrative orders ... until in the general confusion we have almost lost our place."[18] "We have hundreds of thousands of laws that should have no place upon the statute books and that come to be disregarded as a matter of course and merely stimulate a disregard of all law of whatever character," observed one commentator. "The Eighteenth Amendment and its enforcing Act are a conspicuous type of such frivolous enactments."[19] Prohibition was repeatedly cited as "an extreme case" of the kind of "legislative turpitude" that enacted laws without regard to public sentiment[20] and that sought to alter longstanding customs by "constitutional and legislative fiat alone."[21]

To stalwart progressives, of course, the general "cry to the uninformed against excessive legislation" was simply an "effort to destroy confidence in public action, and especially in legislation," with the "purpose" of discrediting government as "the only agency that can effectually protect human beings in their essential integrity. . . . If confidence in legislation and in government is destroyed exploitation will go unchecked."[22] Positive law was essential for the emerging American administrative state. Yet the debacle of prohibition undercut confidence in legislation and especially in legislation that did not embody "inherited customs . . . fortified by long public acquiescence," but that resulted instead "from the vehemence of some cult, bloc, class, or an economic or social 'ism'; – all statutory and all frankly designed to further or coerce, control, favor or suppress a minority, a business, or the social conduct of private citizens in a new and unaccustomed manner."[23]

The distinction between law as the positive enactment of the state and law as the spontaneous and organic expression of traditional social norms was exactly the point of George Sutherland's presidential address to the American Bar Association in September 1917.[24] Sutherland asserted that the most distinguishing characteristic of "our present-day political institutions" was an ill-advised "passion for making laws."[25] Sutherland cited the example of prohibition to illustrate the contemporary "mania for regulating people." "To put the consumer of a glass of beer in the penitentiary along with the burglar and the highwayman," he said, "is to sacrifice all the wholesome distinctions which for centuries have separated debatable habit from indisputable crime."[26] Prohibition was bound to fail, Sutherland predicted,[27] because "[t]he successful enforcement of the law in a democracy must always rest primarily in the fact that on the whole it commends itself to a universal sense of justice, shared even by those who violate it."[28]

The Taft Court's revival of the Due Process Clause was meant to protect a sphere of freedoms that were traditional and hence that were presumed to enjoy widespread support. That is why the Court repeatedly stressed tropes of the "normal" and the "ordinary." Prohibition, the sole major wartime initiative remaining unaltered and in force throughout the 1920s, served as a constant, corrosive example of ill-advised government intrusion into this sphere. Prohibition exemplified the evils of positive legislation, and it was in the popular mind juxtaposed to the organic principles of the common law. If statutes were produced by political pressure and lobbying, common law was made by judges whose task it was to recognize "long-accepted custom, proved by experience."[29]

It was generally acknowledged that a modern state needed both kinds of law, because in many contexts "rapid changes of conditions," moving "too rapidly for customs to form," were "the chief reason why we are bombarded by such a multitude of statutes, good, bad, and indifferent, seeking to accomplish changes by express prohibitions, commands, and statutory remedies."[30] An important question, therefore, was how aggressively courts ought to supervise "this mass of ill considered, badly drawn, experimental, first impression legislation with which the country is flooded from year to year,"[31] and how forcefully courts ought to interpret such statutes in light of their understanding of "the customs and needs of the community to be affected."[32]

These questions arose in various nonconstitutional contexts, of which perhaps the most prominent was the issue of how far courts should go in incorporating statutory principles into their judicial reasoning. More than a decade before prohibition, Roscoe Pound had presciently identified as a "notable" characteristic "of American law today ... the excessive output of legislation in all our jurisdictions and the indifference, if not contempt, with which that output is regarded by courts and lawyers."[33] Professional hostility was justified on the ground that "common law was superior to legislation because it was customary and rested upon the consent of the governed."[34] A particularly pointed expression of the presumed superiority of common law to statutory law could be found in the maxim that "statutes in derogation of the common law are to be construed strictly."[35] The Taft Court adhered to this maxim in at least one decision, *Panama Railroad Co. v. Rock*,[36] authored, not accidentally, by Sutherland.

Writing for a five-justice majority, Sutherland overturned a verdict in favor of a husband seeking damages for the wrongful death of his wife on the ground that the meaning of the article of the Civil Code of Panama authorizing recovery for "damage" caused by "fault" was "to be determined by the application of common law principles," which did not create a "private cause of action ... from the death of a human being."[37] No doubt Sutherland understood his decision as expressing a commitment to the continuity of custom and tradition embodied by the common law. The decision was roundly criticized, however, not only for misunderstanding the meaning of Panama's civil law code,[38] but also for its failure to accord any weight at all to the fact that "substantially every State in the Union" had modified the common law by adopting a wrongful death statute.[39]

By interpreting the Panama Code in a manner that deliberately ignored the force of relevant statutes, Sutherland in effect refused to recognize state legislation as evidence of evolving moral commitments. In a dissent joined by Taft, McKenna, and Brandeis, Holmes was explicit that "courts in dealing with statutes sometimes have been too slow to recognize that statutes even when in terms covering only particular cases may imply a policy different from that of the common law, and therefore may exclude a reference to the common law for the purpose of limiting their scope."[40] Roscoe Pound wrote Holmes congratulating him on his dissent, sadly noting that Sutherland's opinion "would have been fine ammunition for the Populists a generation ago."[41]

International Stevedoring Co. v. Haverty[42] is a good example of the tension within the Taft Court between legislation and traditional common law principles. The question in the case was whether the Act of June 5, 1920,[43] which extended to "seamen" a "common-law right or remedy in cases of personal injury" in the same manner as would be available to "railway employees," should apply to stevedores.

Prohibition & Positive Law

The plaintiff in the case, who was employed by a stevedore, was a longshoreman injured due to the negligence of a hatch tender, who was also employed by the stevedore. The defendant sought the benefit of the fellow servant rule, a traditional common law principle adopted in admiralty, which held that a worker injured by the negligence of a fellow worker could not recover in negligence from a common employer. The fellow servant rule had been abolished by federal statute with respect to railway employees.

Holmes received the assignment to draft the Court's decision on the Saturday after argument. By the following Monday he had drafted an opinion holding for the plaintiff on the ground that

> [t]he policy of the statute is directed to the safety of the men and to treating compensation for injuries to them as properly part of the cost of the business.... In view of the broad field in which Congress has disapproved and changed the rule introduced into the common law within less than a century, we are of opinion that a wider scope should be given to the words of the act, and whether it be said that in this statute "seamen" is to be taken to include stevedores engaged as the plaintiff was, or that the enactment shows that the policy supposed to justify the common law no longer applies to such a case the action of the Court below was right.[44]

By explicitly suggesting that common law reasoning might be informed by federal legislation abolishing the fellow servant rule for railroad employees, Holmes knew he was courting trouble. That same day he wrote a friend: "I have got the proofs of the case that was assigned to me Saturday evening (I bet they will make me cut out the best three lines)."[45]

And, of course, they did. Sutherland was adamant. "I think the judgment should be put squarely on the point alone that the word 'seamen' as used in this statute includes the respondent."[46] In the end Holmes was forced to accept Sutherland's suggestion, changing the conclusion of his opinion to read: "In view of the broad field in which Congress has disapproved and changed the rule introduced into the common law within less than a century, we are of opinion that a wider scope should be given to the words of the act, and that in this statute 'seamen' is to be taken to include stevedores employed in maritime work on navigable waters as the plaintiff was, whatever it might mean in laws of a different kind."[47] In his own private notebook of published opinions, Holmes took the unusual step of noting about *Haverty* that "I was required to strike out what I thought the true ground – that the act showed a changing policy in this class of cases."[48]

Panama Railroad and *Haverty* should be contrasted to *Gleason v. Seaboard Air Line Railroad Co.*,[49] in which Stone, writing for a unanimous Court, overruled the venerable and influential precedent of *Friedlander v. Texas & Pacific Railroad Co.*[50] to hold that a carrier could be liable for a fraudulent bill of lading issued by an employee for his own benefit. Stone crafted his opinion to reflect "accepted notions of social policy," which in his view included the idea that even an innocent principal ought to be liable for the torts of its agents. In stark contrast to *Panama Railroad* and

Haverty, Stone explicitly deduced this principle from "[t]he tendency of modern legislation in employers' liability and workmen's compensation acts and in the [federal] Bills of Lading Act... and of judicial decision as well."[51] Stone's opinion, which accepted statutes as evidence of evolving norms, brought the Court's jurisprudence into conformity with the Uniform Bills of Lading Act, which had been adopted by "a large number of states."[52]

Sutherland refused to join Stone's opinion in *Gleason*. It was not that Sutherland objected to the outcome of the Court's decision, for he specifically noted his concurrence in the Court's judgment. Sutherland's disagreement turned instead entirely on questions of method. Sutherland wrote Stone insisting that the Court put its opinion "squarely and explicitly upon" the common law maxim that "wherever one of two innocent persons must suffer by the acts of a third, he who has enabled such third person to occasion the loss must sustain it."[53] Sutherland would join an opinion that drew its premises from common law principles, but not an opinion that sought to identify relevant social norms from evolving statutory policies.

Sutherland's opinion in *Lambert* shares with his approach in *Panama Railroad*, *Haverty*, and *Gleason* the premise that legislation should be judicially interpreted in light of longstanding social values. Sutherland viewed this approach as indispensable to the legitimation of positive law, and he viewed courts as authoritative conservators of such values. Sutherland's outlook was an important contributing factor to the Taft Court's revival of *Lochnerism*.[54] Sutherland was "raw" in his "opposition to the Volstead Act" because prohibition was the very archetype of positively enacted law profoundly at odds with custom and tradition.[55]

The puzzle is why conservatives like Taft, Van Devanter, and Sanford, who supported the revival of *Lochnerism*,[56] were nevertheless so willing to embrace positive law in the context of prohibition. It is easy to understand why Holmes, even though he was personally impatient with prohibition[57] and expressed a "genial skepticism" about banning liquor,[58] supported the positive law of prohibition. Holmes's commitment to judicial restraint, his strong belief "that my agreement or disagreement has nothing to do with the right of a majority to embody their opinions in law,"[59] derived from his firm conviction that there was no "transcendental body of law" to which judges might appeal to restrict positive statutory and constitutional enactments.[60] The innovation of Holmes's jurisprudence lay precisely in the realization that "[c]ustom was no longer the buffer between consent and coercion."[61] The job of the judge was simply to enforce positive law. Holmes was clear that those who drafted and ratified the "Eighteenth Amendment meant a great revolution in the policy of this country, and presumably and obviously meant to upset a good many things on as well as off the statute book."[62] His duty was therefore to interpret the Eighteenth Amendment and its implementing legislation in ways designed to effectuate that revolution.[63]

Although Taft, Van Devanter, and Sanford exercised no such deference to positive law in the context of social and economic legislation, they most certainly did in the context of prohibition.[64] Why was this so? Van Devanter and Sanford

Prohibition & Positive Law

have not left us a documentary record which might reveal an answer to this question.[65] But Taft has bequeathed us a rich trove of letters and publications that allow us to understand why he consistently sought, like Holmes, to effectuate the objectives and authority of prohibition. Taft's behavior is particularly puzzling because prior to 1919 he had vigorously opposed prohibition on grounds very similar to those of Sutherland.

Like Sutherland, Taft repudiated prohibition as a symptom of the larger "evil" of "excess of legislation,"[66] which was caused by "the erroneous belief that any reform could be accomplished merely by legislation."[67] Taft worried that prohibition did not necessarily reflect the sentiments and morals of the community, because it tended to be passed by legislators "prone to enact laws ... only because their votes would profit them politically."[68] Indirectly referring to the Anti-Saloon League, Taft explained the passage of an early version of the Eighteenth Amendment in the House of Representatives on the ground that congressmen had been frightened into voting for prohibition by well-organized minority groups "whose votes [congressmen] feared might defeat them if they voted their own convictions."[69]

Taft maintained his public opposition to the Eighteenth Amendment right up to the moment of its ratification.[70] Calling national prohibition "an irretrievable national blunder" that would "hang a permanent millstone around our necks,"[71] his analysis was eloquent, forceful, and remarkably prescient:

> A national prohibition amendment to the Federal Constitution will be adopted against the views and practices of a majority of the people in many of the large cities.... The business of manufacturing alcohol, liquor and beer will go out of the hands of law-abiding members of the community, and will be transferred to the quasi-criminal class. In the communities where the majority will not sympathize with a Federal law's restrictions, large numbers of Federal officers will be needed for its enforcement....
>
> [T]he pressure for violation and lax execution in communities where the law is not popular, will be constant and increasing. The reaching out of the great central power to brush the doorsteps of local communities, far removed geographically and politically from Washington, will be irritating in such states and communities, and will be a strain upon the bond of the national union. It will produce variation in the enforcement of the law. There will be loose administration in spots all over the United States, and a politically inclined National Administration will be strongly tempted to acquiesce in such a condition. Elections will continuously turn on the rigid or languid execution of the liquor law....
>
> The theory that the National Government can enforce any law will yield to the stubborn circumstances and a Federal Law will become as much a subject of contempt and ridicule in some parts of the Nation as laws of this kind have been in some states....
>
> The regulation of the sale and use of intoxicating liquor should be retained by the states. They can experiment and improve.... If the power of regulation is irrevocably committed to the General Government, the next generation will live deeply to regret it.

For these reasons, therefore, first, because a permanent National liquor law in many communities will prove unenforceable for lack of local public sympathy, second, because attempted enforcement will require an enormous force of Federal policemen and detectives, giving undue power to a sinister and partisan subordinate of the National Administration, and third, because it means an unwise structural change in the relations between the people of the States and the Central Government, and a strain to the integrity of the Union, I am opposed to a national prohibition amendment.[72]

Within a week of the Eighteenth Amendment's ratification, however, Taft swallowed his antagonism and announced that "[i]t is now the duty of every good citizen in the premises, no matter what his previous opinion of the wisdom or expediency of the amendment, to urge and vote for all reasonable and practical legislative measures by Congress adapted to secure the enforcement of this amendment." "This is a democratic government," Taft pleaded, "and the voice of the people expressed through the machinery provided by the Constitution for its expression ... is supreme. Every loyal citizen must obey. This is the fundamental principle of free government."[73] "A citizen who is in favor of the enforcement of only the laws for which he has voted, and in the principle and wisdom of which he agrees," Taft argued, "is not a law-abiding citizen of a democracy. He has something of the autocratic spirit. He is willing to govern, but not to be governed. He is not willing to play the game according to the rules of the game. Therefore, whatever my previous view, I am strongly in favor now of putting the amendment to a test as favorable as possible for its successful operation."[74]

Taft stuck to this attitude throughout the 1920s.[75] In 1923, he lamented the "present lack of respect for law in this country," tracing its origins to prohibition, which was "at variance with the habits of many of our people, especially in the large cities." Acknowledging that his own "fears" about prohibition "have been realized only too fully," he nevertheless concluded that "there is nothing to be done ... except to set ourselves to the serious task of enforcing the law and to cease protesting against its enactment and by such an attitude encouraging its violation."[76] That same year he addressed Yale alumni and roundly condemned the tendency of "the intelligent and the well-to-do" to treat prohibition "with contempt."[77] Defending prohibition on the ground that it had been fairly enacted under "the rules of the game of popular government," he argued that "it is not patriotic, it is not sportsmanlike to evade or disobey." "You can say it is parochial and that there ought not to have been a constitutional amendment of that sort because it is parochial, but it is on the statute books and we can't get rid of it, and it is there by a vote according to the form of the Constitution."[78]

Strict compliance with prohibition was necessary, in other words, because prohibition was the positive law of the nation; the Eighteenth Amendment had been ratified according to the rules of recognition established in Article V. This was a position indistinguishable from the positivism of Holmes, which in the 1920s was associated with judicial progressivism.[79] But Taft was no progressive, and his commitment to strict enforcement of prohibition did not derive from any simple dedication to the rules of democratic decision-making. Taft was in fact concerned about something quite different.

Although Taft had originally "opposed the constitutional amendment" because he "felt that it would meet a lack of sympathy ... by a lot of foreigners of the lower classes who would violate it if they could," what shocked him after ratification was the extent of the "spirit of lawlessness among the intelligent and wealthy which now exists."[80] The "attitude of intelligent and well-to-do people toward the law and its enforcement" was "most alarming," because "[t]hey should know that demoralization is the necessary consequence of the attitude which they are now taking in the patronizing of bootlegging and in their general contemptuous attitude toward the law."[81]

This suggests that Taft strongly supported prohibition because he was alarmed that prohibition was a "conspicuous" law under sustained attack by influential sectors of the population. The "intelligent and wealthy" classes mattered because their actions could "impair the influence of the Constitution and laws of the country" and thereby "wreck the future of the society whose basis must rest upon them."[82] For Taft, the question of the enforcement of prohibition was "fundamental"[83] because it was the front line in the battle for the legal order itself.[84] At risk was "traditional Anglo-Saxon respect for the administration of the law."[85] Resistance to prohibition threatened "a demoralization of all law."[86]

Prohibitionists had initially argued for ratification of the Eighteenth Amendment on the ground of its substantive merits, but, after 1919, as resistance to prohibition and the Volstead Act began to swell, arguments in favor of prohibition shifted decisively toward the rule-of-law themes that so moved Taft.[87] Senator William E. Borah, for example, argued: "Important as the question of prohibition is, the question that is now presented is ... the higher and bigger and broader question of whether we, as a free people, can maintain and enforce the provisions of the Constitution as they have been written. That involves the whole question of constitutional integrity, of constitutional morality – indeed, of the ultimate success of free government itself."[88]

As early as 1921 the Judicial Section of the American Bar Association distributed "A Warning to the American People" that stressed the importance of obedience to positive law, especially among the intelligent and wealthy:

> Reverence for law and enforcement of law depend upon the ideals and customs of those who occupy the vantage ground of life in business and society. The people of the United States by solemn constitutional and statutory enactment, have undertaken to suppress the age-long evil of the liquor traffic. When, for the gratification of their appetites, or the promotion of their interests, lawyers, bankers, great merchants and manufacturers, and social leaders both men and women disobey and scoff at this law, or any other law, they are aiding the cause of anarchy and promoting mob violence, robbery and homicide. They are sowing dragon's teeth, and they need not be surprised when they find that no judicial or police authority can save our country or humanity from reaping the harvest.[89]

The idea that defiance of prohibition threatened the authority of all law became a pervasive feature of pro-prohibition rhetoric.[90] Calvin Coolidge proclaimed that "for any of our inhabitants to observe such parts of the Constitution as they like, while disregarding others, is a doctrine that would break down all protection of life and property and destroy the American system of ordered liberty."[91] Herbert Hoover branded "disregard and disobedience of law" as "[t]he most malign" of the "dangers" facing the country.[92] Hoover explained that "Our whole system of self-government will crumble either if officials elect what laws they will enforce or citizens elect what laws they will support. The worst evil of disregard for some law is that it destroys respect for all law. For our citizens to patronize the violation of a particular law on the ground that they are opposed to it is destructive of the very basis of all that protection of life, of homes and property which they rightly claim under other laws."[93]

Wayne Wheeler put this argument in especially garish tones: "For officers or the people to permit laws to be violated is a deadly attack upon the Government. Its contagion spreads from one law to another. It distills its deadly poison into the arteries of our jurisprudence. ... It assassinates the vital processes of orderly control. It is a prolific source of disease to the whole social order, and jeopardizes the life of the race."[94] Debating Wheeler in Carnegie Hall, Clarence Darrow scoffed at this logic. He challenged Wheeler to go South and preach a gospel of law-obedience to southern prohibitionists: "Dare he go down among the Southern constituents and tell them to give the negroes the rights that are guaranteed by at least three provisions? ... For sixty years every Federal provision in reference to the constitutional rights of the negroes and every law has been notoriously violated in every Southern prohibition State, and no prohibitionist dare raise his voice, and you daren't."[95] During the 1920s it was no small irony that while the requirements of the Fifteenth Amendment were openly and deliberately nullified in the South, Southern prohibitionists were among the loudest proponents of the need strictly to enforce the Eighteenth Amendment.

Taft was certainly as aware as anyone of "the inherent difficulties in enforcing a law which changes the habits of a great many people."[96] But he came to believe that the "solution requires a great deal of time and patience. The habits of an important section of a congested part of the country can not be changed over night or in years. The reform and the adaptation of society to that at which the Amendment aims must be gradual."[97] Although before 1919 Taft had "despaired of any success," by 1928 Taft had come to "really think that it is possible ... to achieve a satisfactory result." Forgetting his own past insight into the distorting effect of a powerful single-issue lobbying group like the Anti-Saloon League, Taft wrote that the "persistence with which the people maintain in Congress a two-thirds majority in both Houses gives me much hope, and I am inclined to think that this will wear down the moderate wets to a consciousness that the only solution is pressure in favor of enforcement."[98]

This conclusion separated Taft from Sutherland,[99] with whom Taft otherwise shared a conservative jurisprudence. If Sutherland believed that his judicial role was to soften prohibition to align it more closely with underlying social norms,[100] Taft took it as his responsibility to harden the teeth of prohibition so as to "wear down the recklessness of those who would try to defeat the law by disobeying it."[101] "It sometimes seemed as though there were no lengths to which [Taft] would not go, and along which he would not attempt to lead the court, in his determination to uphold prohibition enforcement."[102] In that crusade, Taft, and we can speculate also Van Devanter and Sanford, committed judicial conservatism to a policy of respect for positive law in the context of what was surely the most controversial and momentous public issue of their time.

Prohibition splintered judicial conservatism on the Supreme Court into two blocs. The first, associated with Sutherland, Butler, and McReynolds, believed that their obligation was to maintain legal legitimacy by ameliorating the positive law of prohibition through the infusion of customary social values. The second, associated with Taft, Van Devanter, and Sanford, believed that defiance of prohibition so threatened the survival of the legal order that it was necessary to override customary social values in the name of effective law enforcement. By taking this stance, they may well have helped smooth the way for the nation's eventual repudiation of a jurisprudence that privileged custom over the positive authority of social and economic legislation. Their invention of conservative positivism may paradoxically have paved a path for the full-blown emergence of an American administrative state in the subsequent era of the New Deal.

Notes

1. WALTER THOMPSON, FEDERAL CENTRALIZATION: A STUDY AND CRITICISM OF THE EXPANDING SCOPE OF CONGRESSIONAL LEGISLATION 10 (New York: Harcourt, Brace & Co. 1923). "[P]rogress toward the unitary state is not an accident but a logical development, once national unity has been attained. The system of concurrence of powers subject to national supremacy is the one to which the future belongs. States will have to be content with what cities enjoy under constitutional home rule." Ernst Freund, *The New German Constitution*, 35 POLITICAL SCIENCE QUARTERLY 177, 184 (1920).
2. Consider the forms of democratic identification that implicitly underlie the following characteristic objection to federal centralization: "Shall the conduct of citizens of Mississippi be prescribed by vote of congressmen from New York, or supervised at the expense of New York taxpayers? Will an educational system suitable for Massachusetts necessarily fit the young of Georgia? Such suggestions carry their own answer. In the very nature of things there is bound to be a reaction against centralization sooner or later." CHARLES W. PIERSON, OUR CHANGING CONSTITUTION 145 (Garden City: Doubleday, Page & Co. 1922).
3. *See, e.g.*, Wesley L. Jones, *Is Nation Ready to Respect Prohibition Law?*, 4 CONGRESSIONAL DIGEST 20 (1924): "It was the great body of our people who represent the homes and firesides and who comprise the bone and sinew of our body politic that made prohibition possible. These people, through long years of observation of the evils of the liquor traffic and experience of the benefits obtained through applying the principle of prohibition to small communities by local option and State-wide laws, came to believe its application to the Nation as a unit would be to the best interests of our national welfare."
4. Fabian Franklin, *What's Wrong with the Eighteenth Amendment?*, 109 ANNALS OF THE AMERICAN ACADEMY POLITICAL & SOCIAL SCIENCE 48, 50 (1923).
5. Walter Lippmann, *Our Predicament under the Eighteenth Amendment*, 154 HARPER'S MAGAZINE 51, 52 (1926). "The grave and dangerous fact is that to a long habit of national indifference toward all laws has now been added a definite moral revolt against one law.... No figures can express the present spirit of defiance. But certainly in a community like New York City it is intense, prevailing and increasing." *The War against Crime*, NEW YORK HERALD TRIBUNE (April 23, 1929), at 26.
6. Lippmann, *supra* note 5, at 53. To violate the law "even secretly should be a burden of shame to be undertaken by no respectable person; and yet all of us are well aware of the pride which many otherwise excellent citizens take in breaking the Volstead Act." George S. Buck, *The Crime Wave and Law Enforcement*, 131 THE OUTLOOK 16, 17 (1922).
7. "Prohibition in the United States, under the provisions of the eighteenth amendment and the Volstead Act has proved a disastrous, tragic failure." William Cabell Bruce, *U.S. Senators Discuss Prohibition Issue*, 5 CONGRESSIONAL DIGEST 191 (1926). "It has brought about close working relations between the bootlegger and thousands of the most intelligent and virtuous members of American society who feel no more compunction about violating the Volstead Act than the free-soiler did about violating the fugitive slave law, or the southern white did about nullifying ignorant negro suffrage; the Federal Constitution in each instance to the contrary notwithstanding." *Id.* "Any law that has brought in its

Prohibition & Positive Law

trail the havoc, the defiance, and the corruption which has followed the Volstead Act can not be successfully defended.... Today we have ... a general disrespect for all law that threatens the very foundation of the Republic." Walter E. Edge, *U.S. Senators Discuss Prohibition Issue*, 5 CONGRESSIONAL DIGEST 191, 193 (1926).

As early as 1922, Charles H. Strong, the president of the Unitarian Laymen's League, wrote Taft that "[e]verybody knows that the Prohibition Amendment and the Volstead Act have probably been more persistently and flagrantly violated than any other law ever adopted in this country." Charles H. Strong to WHT (October 31, 1922) (Taft papers). In an engrossing firsthand account of conditions in Pennsylvania, for example, the state was described as "[s]uffering from 'a liquor deluge,' where practically every city is 'wet as the Atlantic Ocean,' ... a 'bootleggers' Elysium,' brazen in its defiance of Prohibition laws, where 'there are far more wide-open saloons than ever flourished in pre-Prohibition days.'" *How Wet Is Pennsylvania?*, 79 LITERARY DIGEST 38 (November 10, 1923). By contrast, J.C. Burnham reports that "local enforcement in many Southern and Western areas was both severe and effective." J.C. Burnham, *New Perspectives on the Prohibition "Experiment" of the 1920's*, 2 JOURNAL OF SOCIAL HISTORY 51, 58 (1968).

For fascinating data on arrests for intoxication and death rates from alcoholism in both wet states and dry states, see The Moderation League, A NATIONAL SURVEY OF CONDITIONS UNDER PROHIBITION 1930 (New York City: 1930). The League concluded that "in wet states – that is, the states which had no state prohibition before national prohibition – the low point of drunkenness was in 1920, the first year of national prohibition." *Id.* at 4. By 1929, however, arrests for intoxication had "risen substantially to the level of pre-prohibition or saloon days." *Id.* Dry states reached the low point for intoxication arrests in 1919, but by 1929 arrests were "39% above the 1914 level," which "indicates that conditions of intemperance in these 'dry' states are worse today than before national prohibition." *Id.* at 5. Examining death rates from alcoholism (excluding deaths from wood or poison alcohol, which virtually did not occur before national prohibition, *id.* at 13), the League found that the low point in such death rates in wet states was in 1920, but that by 1929 "the death rate from alcoholism is now as high as it formerly was in the saloon days." *Id.* at 11. In dry states "more persons per capita are dying now from intemperate use of liquor than under state prohibition." *Id.* at 13.

8. The "widespread and scarcely or not at all concealed contempt for the policy of the National Prohibition Act" was generally acknowledged. *Enforcement of the Prohibition Laws of the United States: A Report of the National Commission on Law Observance and Enforcement Relative to the Facts as to the Enforcement, the Benefits, and the Abuses under the Prohibition Laws, Both Before and Since the Adoption of the Eighteenth Amendment to the Constitution*, H.R. Doc. No. 71-722, 71st CONG. 3rd SESS. (January 20, 1931), at 22. The most arresting formulation of the point was by Walter Lippmann:

> No law is enforced absolutely. The penal law is broken by murderers and thieves. The tariff law is broken by smugglers. The commercial law is broken by swindlers. The tax laws are broken by tax-dodgers. Is a breach of the Volstead Act in the same category of law breaking? Well, Harper's Magazine does not publish articles by murderers, thieves, smugglers, swindlers, and tax-dodgers discussing the policy of the law they break. The

opponents of capital punishment do not form associations of murderers. The free traders do not hold banquets attended by smugglers. The Secretary of the Treasury does not make speeches to tax-dodgers. But cabinet officers, senators, congressmen, governors, mayors, judges, chiefs of police, bankers, editors, and other pillars of society are openly convivial with men who make no bones about their defiance of the Volstead Act. Now a law which can be violated openly and without shame by men who are normally law-abiding may fairly be called a law which is not enforced.

Lippmann, *supra* note 5, at 52. *See* John Grier Hibben, *Our National Moral Issue: What the 18th Amendment Has Done to Us*, 87 FORUM & CENTURY 215, 218 (1932):

> Men and women in significantly large and increasing numbers who command the respect and confidence of their communities and who are naturally expected to be supporters of law are in possession of liquor, serve it in their homes on public as well as private occasions, and do so with no attempt whatsoever at concealment, exactly as if there were no such thing as the Eighteenth Amendment and the National Prohibition Act. They not only do not regard the law seriously, they go further; the law has become in many social circles the butt for ridicule and poor outworn jokes.
>
> No law can be effectually enforced when the normal law-abiding citizens of the community do not lend it their approval and support both in pronounced opinion and practice.... When I speak of normally law-abiding citizens ... I have in mind judges of our courts, members of Congress, lawyers, men of public-spirited citizenship and the leaders in their communities of every good cause.

9. *Prohibition, as Usual*, NEW YORK TIMES (December 2, 1926), at 26. "A law, to be enforced, must find its justification in the conscience of the American people." JAMES M. BECK, THE REVOLT AGAINST PROHIBITION 19 (New York: Association Against the Prohibition Amendment 1930). "And why is the Volstead Act unenforceable? It is because the idea that it is a criminal thing at all times and under all circumstances to make, sell, or use an intoxicating beverage is a purely artificial conception, at war with the fundamental facts of human existence, and untenable in the forum of sound human reasoning." William Cabell Bruce, *Is Nation Ready to Respect Prohibition Law?*, 4 CONGRESSIONAL DIGEST 20, 20 (1924).

10. 61 CONG. REC. 4039 (July 19, 1921) (statement of Senator Thomas E. Watson); A. Lawrence Lowell, *Reconstruction and Prohibition*, 143 ATLANTIC MONTHLY 145, 148–49 (1929); Henry Samuel Priest, *Prohibition and Respect for Law*, 221 NORTH AMERICAN REVIEW 596, 599–600 (1925); Victor S. Yarros, *Law and Law Enforcement*, 129 THE NATION 60, 61 (1929).

11. Martin Conboy, *Has the Volstead Act Nullified the Eighteenth Amendment?*, 16 GEORGETOWN LAW JOURNAL 348, 359 (1928).

> Only when public spirit is on the side of the law is the law generally obeyed. Enforcement is always difficult, but when the law declares that conduct widely practiced and widely regarded as innocent is a crime, enforcement is impossible....
>
> Prohibition aims directly at ... a social custom, the indulgence of which is not in and of itself morally wrong. Constitutional and legislative fiat alone do not and cannot restrain this custom or modify the mental attitude toward it.

David I. Walsh, *Can Prohibition Be Enforced?*, 9 CONGRESSIONAL DIGEST 81 (1930). *See Prohibition Is Dying Natural Death: Darrow*, CHICAGO DAILY

Prohibition & Positive Law

TRIBUNE (September 25, 1927), at 2 ("Mr. Darrow believes that to try to enforce a law in which the masses obviously do not believe and intend to avoid is asking trouble. He said in many cities the authorities had ceased trying to enforce prohibition.").

12. Conboy, *supra* note 11, at 354–55. *See* Struthers Burt, *The Sense of Law*, 80 SCRIBNER'S MAGAZINE 157, 158–61 (1926) ("Law ... is man's sense of fair play. ... [I]t is a common thing, an ordinary thing, a daily thing; it is not even preserved for Sundays or illnesses. ... To the lay mind, which conceived law and which must live by law, a law is not a law if it offends the sense of law, and millions of misguided experts cannot prove otherwise. The sense of law stands above all law and all laws are subject to it and refer back to it. ... There were, for instance, laws against drunkenness; there were not, before war with its false legal values blurred the sense of all civilian law, laws against drinking, for drinking is not in itself antisocial; to the contrary, it may frequently be social. ... We are witnessing to-day ... the curious spectacle of the law being punished by the sense of law, and this punishment will continue, with all its disastrous consequences, until the law reforms itself."). This form of analysis essentially replayed the views of James Coolidge Carter, whose appeal to the normative value of custom had set the terms for conservative legal elites. *See* JAMES COOLIDGE CARTER, LAW: ITS ORIGIN, GROWTH AND FUNCTION 241–49 (New York: G.P. Putnam's Sons 1907); *supra* Chapter 5, at 169. Indeed, one can understand normative dualism as itself inspired by the conviction that state law was more likely than federal law to express the living experience of customs and traditions. See *supra* Chapter 30, at note 31.
13. Buck, *supra* note 6, at 16.
14. John H. Clarke, *Observations and Reflections on Practice in the Supreme Court*, 8 AMERICAN BAR ASSOCIATION JOURNAL 263, 267 (1922). On Clarke's "wild" opposition to prohibition, see *supra* Chapter 28, at note 88. For reactions to Clarke's intervention, see *Justice Clarke Warns of Perils*, NEW YORK TIMES (February 5, 1922), at 1. Clarke was promptly criticized by Senator Harris of Georgia, who said that "[t]he Supreme Court should look after its own affairs." *Criticizes Justice Clarke; Senator Harris Says He Should Attend to Duties in Supreme Court*, NEW YORK TIMES (February 15, 1922), at 2. Harris specifically criticized Clarke's reference to prohibition. 62 CONG. REC. 2582 (February 15, 1922). For examples of Clarke's hostility to prohibition, see Grogan v. Hiram Walker & Sons, 259 U.S. 80 (1922); The National Prohibition Cases, 253 U.S. 350 (1920); and Jacob Ruppert v. Caffey, 251 U.S. 264 (1920).
15. "Like Caligula of ancient Rome who posted his laws on pillars so high that the people could not read them, Congress and the Legislatures of the various states daily grind out laws and go to the other extreme by entombing them in bulky volumes. ... And yet the citizen is presumed to know *all* the law. Is it strange that, realizing the futility of such a presumption, he begins to look lightly upon all laws?" R.E.L. Saner, *Governmental Review*, in REPORT OF THE FORTY-SEVENTH ANNUAL MEETING OF THE AMERICAN BAR ASSOCIATION 127, 138–39 (Baltimore: Lord Baltimore Press 1924).
16. Arthur Twining Hadley, *Law Making and Law Enforcement*, 151 HARPER'S MAGAZINE 641, 643 (1925). Hadley identified self-government with voluntary obedience to the law: "Conscience and public opinion enforce the laws; the police suppress the exceptions." *Id.* at 641. Therefore, laws enforceable only by

compulsion substitute "autocracy" for "self-government." *Id.* at 643. Hadley declared that "[t]o-day it is from the law maker rather than from the law breaker that our American traditions of self-government have most to fear." *Id.* "What can we do to protect ourselves," Hadley asked, "against this spirit of over-regulation which seeks to place under official control not only the organization of industry and commerce but the conduct and even the thought of the people themselves?" *Id.* at 644. It is in this context that Hadley proposed that prohibition should be met by "nullification," a "process of blocking the law by disobedience." *Id.* at 645. See *supra* Chapter 28, at 925 and note 73. "The Fugitive Slave Law was thus nullified by the people of the North; the Reconstruction Acts were thus nullified by the people of the South." Hadley, *supra*, at 645.

17. *Excessive Lawmaking the Bane of America*, 74 CURRENT OPINION 461 (1923). "The people," it was said, "are genuinely disturbed by the flood of lawmaking which each year engulfs our country." *Laws upon Laws*, 200 SATURDAY EVENING POST 26 (August 6, 1927). "Railing at law and law-makers has become of late one of our popular national sports." Henry W. Farnam, *Law, Liberty, and Progress*, 15 YALE REVIEW 433 (1926). For examples, see Philos Cooke, *Anarchy in the Law: Throughout the United States Average of 2,123 Laws Passed Each Month upon Which Citizen Must Inform Himself*, 14 LA FOLLETTE'S MAGAZINE 172 (November 1922); *Epidemic of Insane Lawmaking*, 110 THE INDEPENDENT 307 (1923); *The Rain of Law*, 77 LITERARY DIGEST 15 (April 7, 1923).

18. Marvin B. Rosenberry, *Law and the Changing Order*, 220 NORTH AMERICAN REVIEW 18, 22–23 (1924). "Each year upwards of 12,000 new statutes are ground out, and the highest courts supplement these with 13,000 interpretive decisions. It is little wonder if in this maze of legal entanglements justice wanders helplessly." *Current Comment*, 8 FREEMAN 601 (1924). The law has become "so complex and extensive that no living man can hope to learn its provisions or observe it in full." William P. Helm, Jr., *The Plague of Laws*, 10 AMERICAN MERCURY 10, 16 (1927). "Ten thousand law-mills have submerged America beneath their grist. No living man can hope to know the law, and he who claims to do so is deserving only of long hairy ears and a bale of hay." *Id.* at 10. See *The March of Events; Too Many Laws!*, 54 WORLD'S WORK 8, 9 (May 1927) ("Legislation, taken as a remedy, has itself become an ill."). "Is our Republic in danger of becoming a bureaucracy like that of Russia under the Czars by reason of too many laws and too much centralizing of governmental power in Washington? That such a danger exists – that it is real and imminent – seems to be the almost unanimous opinion of the press." *"The Cancer of Too Much Government"*, 92 LITERARY DIGEST 14 (February 19, 1927).

19. Priest, *supra* note 10, at 600.

20. Katharine Fullerton Gerould, *Our Passion for Lawmaking: An Exploration of the American Mind*, 157 HARPER'S MAGAZINE 700 (1928). "I do not doubt that many of the people who supported Prohibition actually believed that the inclusion of it in the Constitution would turn a nation sober – not merely by the aid of guns and poisons, but by some miracle involved in the words of the amendment." *Id.* at 702. But "[w]e cheapen law itself, the whole principle of self-government, by enacting laws that public opinion will not sanction." *Id.* at 704.

21. Walsh, *supra* note 11, at 81. See James Truslow Adams, *Hoover and Law Observance*, 82 THE FORUM 1, 1–7 (1929).

Prohibition & Positive Law

22. John A. Lapp, *Justice First: Presidential Address at the National Conference of Social Work* (May 11, 1927), in PROCEEDINGS OF THE NATIONAL CONFERENCE OF SOCIAL WORK 12–13 (University of Chicago Press 1927).
23. Charles M. Hough to Charles S. Whitman (June 16, 1923), in AMERICAN BAR ASSOCIATION SPECIAL COMMITTEE ON LAW ENFORCEMENT, REPORT OF THE SPECIAL COMMITTEE ON LAW ENFORCEMENT 31 (New York: The Evening Post Job Printing Office, Inc. 1923).
24. Sutherland had explored this ground in 1914 when he observed that "There seems to be always at work a mysterious, sometimes inarticulate, but always compelling, sort of community conscience which makes for righteous inter-relations, enforced by public opinion often far better and far more permanently than by the arbitrary, rigid rules of legislation." GEORGE SUTHERLAND, SUPERFLUOUS GOVERNMENT: AN ADDRESS BY SENATOR SUTHERLAND OF UTAH 6–7 (Cleveland: Cleveland Chamber of Commerce 1914).
25. George Sutherland, *Address of the President: Private Rights and Government Control*, in REPORT OF THE FORTIETH ANNUAL MEETING OF THE AMERICAN BAR ASSOCIATION 198 (Baltimore: Lord Baltimore Press 1917). Sutherland observed, "Throughout the country the business world has come to look upon the meeting of the legislature as a thing to be borne rather than desired, and to regard with grave suspicion pretty much everything that happens, with the exception of the final adjournment." *Id.* at 199. Sutherland added:

> The difficulty which confronts us ... is that we are going ahead so fast – so many novel and perplexing problems are pressing upon us for solution – that we become confused at their very multiplicity. Evils develop faster than remedies can be devised. Most of these evils, if left alone, would disappear under the powerful pressure of public sentiment, but we become impatient because the force of the social organism is not sufficiently radical and the demand goes forth for a law which will instantly put an end to the matter.

Id. at 200. Taft, Stone, and Butler were publicly associated with a similar position. *See For Local Option, Mr. Taft Explains*, NEW YORK TIMES (January 24, 1915), at 10; Harlan Fiske Stone, *Obedience to Law and Social Change*, 5 PROCEEDINGS OF THE BAR ASSOCIATION OF THE STATE OF NEW HAMPSHIRE 27 (November 3, 1925); Pierce Butler, *Some Opportunities and Duties of Lawyers*, 9 AMERICAN BAR ASSOCIATION JOURNAL 583, 586 (1923) ("A passion for new enactments prevails. The enormous number of bills introduced in the legislatures shows the extent to which it is thought that welfare can be promoted by lawmaking."). Taft said in a letter to a friend that "our need is not so much legislation as it is stability and common sense in suppressing fool propositions embodied in legislation." WHT to Henry C. Coe (September 17, 1924) (Taft papers).
26. Sutherland, *supra* note 25, at 201.
27. "It does not require a prophet to foresee that laws of this character exacting penalties so utterly disproportionate to the offense, can never be generally enforced, and to write them into the statutes to be cunningly evaded or contemptuously ignored will have a strong tendency to bring just and wholesome laws dealing with the liquor question into disrepute." *Id.* at 202. It was said of Sutherland that he personally approved "of abstinence from alcoholic beverages and of prohibition by local option." *Proceeding in the Supreme Court of the United States in Memory of Mr. Justice Sutherland*, 323 U.S. v, xii (1944) (remarks of Attorney General Biddle).

28. Sutherland, *supra* note 25, at 203. "Any attempt, therefore, to curtail the liberties of the citizen, which shocks the sense of personal independence of any considerable proportion of the community is likely to do more harm than good, not only because a strong feeling that a particular law is unjust lessens in some degree the reverence for law generally, but because such a law cannot be successfully enforced, and a law that inspires neither respect for its justice nor fear for its enforcement is about as utterly contemptible a thing as can be imagined." *Id.* at 203–4.

    It is likely that Stone's attraction to this premise explains why he was more willing than either Holmes or Brandeis to join McReynolds and Sutherland to constrain prohibition. *See* Figures VI-2 and VI-3; *supra* Chapter 28, at 927–28. Stone's son reported that although "Father recognized the validity and binding effect of the 18th Amendment and the laws passed pursuant thereto and enforced them vigorously as Attorney General, he thought they were bad laws and were an undue infringement of individual freedom. He thought the prohibitionists were 'do-gooders' and referred to the WCTU as the 'We-see-to-you-ers.' He did not care for 'hard liquor' and rarely took any, but he did enjoy and saw no harm in table wines, sherry and the like." Lauson H. Stone, *My Father the Chief Justice*, 1978 YEARBOOK OF THE SUPREME COURT HISTORICAL SOCIETY 7, 12. According to Alpheus Mason, Stone was an avid and educated collector of fine wines. ALPHEUS THOMAS MASON, HARLAN FISKE STONE: PILLAR OF THE LAW 726–33 (New York: Viking 1956); David P. Currie, *The Constitution in the Supreme Court: 1921–1930*, 1986 DUKE LAW JOURNAL 65, 120 & n.302.

29. Barrett Wendell, *Law and Legislation*, 65 SCRIBNER'S MAGAZINE 177 (1919). Wendell associated respect for custom with "the English conception of the Common Law," and a misplaced faith in statutes with the "Continental type of mind." *Id.* at 178. He warned that "[i]n regarding legislation as inherently absolute ... we are at least perilously near the danger of forgetting that it cannot safely stray too far from the limits of custom." *Id.* at 179.

30. Elihu Root, *Address of the President: Public Service by the Bar*, 2 AMERICAN BAR ASSOCIATION JOURNAL 736, 748–49 (1916). *See* Elihu Root, *The Layman's Criticism of the Lawyer*, in REPORT OF THE THIRTY-SEVENTH ANNUAL MEETING OF THE AMERICAN BAR ASSOCIATION 386, 391–94 (Baltimore: Lord Baltimore Press 1914) ("Undoubtedly there is much reason in these later days for new legislation. Our social and industrial conditions are changing very rapidly. New relations, new rights, new obligations are being created for the regulation of which the old laws and customs of the country are inadequate, and there must be new laws to prevent injustice."); Farnam, *supra* note 17, at 437 ("New inventions and new methods have led to new evils, economic, sanitary, and social, which do not cure themselves and which have come so suddenly that there has been no time for the creation of a customary law, still less of social conventions, to deal with them.").

31. Root, *Layman's Criticism*, *supra* note 30, at 393.

32. *Id.* at 392. The implicit assumption, of course, was that, left to their own devices, "courts wish to do justice, and they will if they are permitted to." *Id.* at 399.

33. Roscoe Pound, *Common Law and Legislation*, 21 HARVARD LAW REVIEW 383, 383 (1908). *See* WILLIAM HOWARD TAFT, THE ANTI-TRUST ACT AND THE SUPREME COURT 114–15 (New York: Harper & Bros. 1914).

34. Pound, *supra* note 33, at 406. Pound had no patience with this justification:

> Today we recognize that the so-called custom is a custom of judicial decision, not a custom of popular action. We recognize that legislation is the more truly democratic form of law-making. We see in legislation the more direct and accurate expression of the general will.... Courts are fond of saying that they apply old principles to new situations. But at times they must apply new principles to situations both old and new. The new principles are in legislation. The old principles are in common law. The former are as much to be respected and made effective as the latter – probably more so as our legislation improves.

Id. at 406–7. Pound argued that "modern statutes are not to be disposed of lightly as off-hand products of a crude desire to do something, but represent long and patient study by experts, careful consideration by conferences or congresses or associations, press discussions in which public opinion is focused upon all important details, and hearings before legislative committees." Id. at 384. "Courts," by contrast, "are less and less competent to formulate rules for new relations which require regulation. They have the experience of the past. But they do not have the facts of the present.... Judicial law-making for sheer lack of means to get at the real situation, operates unjustly and inequitably in a complex social organization." Id. at 403–4.

35. Id. at 387. Pound attacked this principle as assuming "that legislation is something to be deprecated. As no statute of any consequence dealing with any relation of private law can be anything but in derogation of the common law, the social reformer and the legal reformer, under this doctrine, must always face the situation that the legislative act which represents the fruit of their labors will find no sympathy in those who apply it, will be construed strictly, and will be made to interfere with the status quo as little as possible." Id.

36. 266 U.S. 209 (1924).

37. Id. at 211, 214. For a similar example of Sutherland interpreting statutes in light of common law precedents, see American Steel Foundries v. Robertson, 269 U.S. 372 (1926).

38. See Death by Wrongful Act in the Civil Law-Common Law Technique and Civil Authorities, 38 HARVARD LAW REVIEW 499 (1925).

39. Thomas W. Shelton, A Deserving Dissenting Opinion, 98 CENTRAL LAW JOURNAL 109, 109 (1925). The decision "was immediately repudiated by congressional action." James McCauley Landis, Statutes and the Sources of Law, in HARVARD LEGAL ESSAYS (Cambridge: Harvard University Press 1934), reprinted in 2 HARVARD JOURNAL ON LEGISLATION 7, 20 (1965). See Pub. L. 69-534, 44 Stat. 924, 927 (December 29, 1926). Landis attacked the Court's decision in Panama Railroad for demonstrating "neglect of the significance to be attached to legislation." Landis, supra, at 20. See J.M. Landis, American Family Laws, 45 HARVARD LAW REVIEW 952, 953 (1932).

40. Panama Railroad, 266 U.S. at 216 (Holmes, J., dissenting). Panama Railroad was later repudiated in Moragne v. State Marine Lines, Inc., 398 U.S. 375, 390–93 (1970) ("This legislative establishment of policy carries significance beyond the particular scope of each of the statutes involved."). See Gooch v. Or. Short Line R.R. Co., 258 U.S. 22, 24 (1922) ("For although courts sometimes have been slow to extend the effect of statutes modifying the common law beyond the direct operation of the words, it is obvious that a statute may indicate a change in the policy of the law, although it expresses that change only in the specific cases most likely to occur to the mind.").

THE TAFT COURT

41. Roscoe Pound to OWH (January 13, 1925) (Holmes papers). "The spectacle of a great court astute to find reasons for holding that a railroad company in 1924 is not liable for death by wrongful act committed under the jurisdiction of the civil law unless an express text so declaring in so many words can be found, is not edifying." *Id.* Sutherland's opinion, wrote Pound, "gives much aid and comfort to the adherents of an extreme economic interpretation. It is not easy to find any other ratio decidendi, unless it be an assumption that Anglo-American common law is the jural order of the universe." *Id.*
42. 272 U.S. 50 (1926).
43. Pub. L. 66-261, 41 Stat. 988, 1007 (June 5, 1920).
44. Holmes papers. At conference all had supported affirmance except McReynolds, who would have reversed the plaintiff's judgment.
45. OWH to ? (October 11, 1926) (Holmes papers). Stone also saw the difficulty coming. He wrote Holmes about his draft opinion: "I think some of the brethren may not like to go as far as the last paragraph." (Holmes papers).
46. Holmes papers. McReynolds did not dissent, but he groused to Holmes, "Rather direct legislation by the Court."
47. *Haverty*, 272 U.S. at 52.
48. Holmes papers. For a case in which Taft, McKenna, and Clarke were willing to go further in extending statutory policy than Holmes, see Gooch v. Oregon Short Line R. Co., 258 U.S. 22 (1922).
49. 278 U.S. 349 (1929).
50. 130 U.S. 416 (1889).
51. *Gleason*, 278 U.S. at 356–57. *See* Pub. L. 64-239, 39 Stat. 542 (August 29, 1916).
52. George S. Koles, *Principal and Agent: Fraudulent Acts of Agent for Own Benefit*, 14 CORNELL LAW QUARTERLY 363, 367 (1929). It also conformed the Court's jurisprudence with the so-called "New York" rule, which had previously been a minority position. *See Carriers – Agency – Bills of Lading – Liability for Fraudulent Act of Agent in Issuing Bill of Lading*, 15 VIRGINIA LAW REVIEW 670, 673 (1929).
53. GS to HFS (December 28, 1928) (Sutherland papers); Return of GS to HFS (Stone papers). Sutherland also pressed Stone "expressly" to overrule *Friedlander, id.*, a step which the original draft of Stone's opinion had tactfully avoided. Stone eventually modified his opinion to meet Sutherland's request. HFS to GS (December 19, 1928) (Stone papers). When Frankfurter later wrote Stone to congratulate him "for frankly rejecting an untenable authority rather than refining it away," Felix Frankfurter to HFS (January 5, 1929) (Stone papers), Stone was quite willing to accept credit for the boldness of the act. "It is quite impossible to ever completely overtake such an error, but the old practice of overruling in silence or by attempting to get around the difficulty by refinements and thin distinctions is almost as mischievous as the original fault." HFS to Felix Frankfurter (January 8, 1929) (Stone papers).

In contrast to Sutherland, and in keeping with his vote in *Panama Railroad*, Taft professed himself quite pleased with Stone's draft opinion: "Good. I am very glad you have cleaned this up so well." WHT to HFS (Stone papers). Holmes dissented from the Court's holding in conference, later writing Stone about the first draft of his opinion that "you make out very handsomely the liability of the Ry. Co. for the representation that the cotton had been received. But the fact that the railroad had

Prohibition & Positive Law

received the cotton does not make it liable to a party paying on the faith of a forged bill of lading. This bill of lading stands like one forged by a third person." OWH to HFS (December 15, 1928) (Stone papers). Stone sought to placate the elder justice in a note arguing that the jury in the case had specifically found inducement and reliance. HFS to OWH (December 19, 1928) (Stone papers). Holmes, however, was implacable: "Non obstante your letter I don't see how a representation that goods had been received could warrant or induce payment on a forged bill of lading – whatever the jury found. I do not see how the representation could have more effect because false than if it had been true." OWH to HFS (December 20, 1928) (Stone papers). Stone eventually withdrew from the field:

> Sorry we are not in entire accord about the cotton bill of lading case. We are so seldom on opposite sides of the fence that I hate to break a good precedent, but I suppose the pleadings, the facts and the verdict in this case establish what is in accord with common experience, that the payor on a draft drawn against a casual shipment of merchandise would not pay the draft until he knew that there were goods represented by the documents and that they had in fact arrived, however fair the documents might be on their face. I don't suppose that a false representation has to be the sole cause of the injury. It is enough that it is a contributing cause and that the injury would not have happened without it. However, I withdraw from the debate before I am beaten, but as is the way of humankind, cling to my error.

HFS to OWH (December 21, 1928) (Stone papers). Eventually Holmes joined Stone's opinion, noting that "I doubt if I shall dissent – but I don't think my objection was answered the other day and I doubt if it can be logically." OWH to HFS (Stone papers).

Oddly, in the original draft of his opinion, Stone included a passage to the effect that "[a] good many years ago Mr. Justice Holmes pointed out that the arguments in favor of creating such an exception [to the rule of principal liability for the fraud of an agent] are equally objections to the rule itself. Holmes, The Common Law, 231 n.3." (Stone papers). Butler flagged the passage, commenting "I doubt whether this should be done. It is not necessary and I am not sure that it is in the best taste." (Stone papers). McReynolds also objected to the passage, writing "I think this is badly stated & I do not like the reference to a book by a living member of this court." (Stone papers). McReynolds, tactless as usual, went on to comment: "I am with the result you reach. But I think you would be wise to revise the opinion and put it into more carefully chosen words. It is important & should show great care." (Stone papers). Eventually Stone revised the passage to read: "The arguments in favor of creating such an exception are equally objections to the rule itself. Holmes, The Common Law (1882) 231 n. 3." *Gleason*, 278 U.S. at 357.

54. In the context of prohibition, Solicitor General Beck put the matter concisely: "To the American the law is but the reasoned adjustment of human relations and its true sanction is largely in its reasonableness and not in the fiat of the State.... A law, to be enforced, must find its justification in the conscience of the American people." BECK, *supra* note 9, at 18–19. "Reasonableness," of course, was the measure of constitutionality under the Due Process Clause. *See supra* Chapter 26, at 824.

55. This is not to deny that Sutherland also disliked prohibition because he regarded it as an egregious violation of personal liberty:

> The liberty of the individual to control his own conduct is the most precious possession of a democracy and interference with it is seldom justified except where necessary to protect the liberties or rights of other individuals or to safeguard society....
>
> In passing legislation of this character doubts should be resolved in favor of the liberty of the individual and his power to freely determine and pursue his own course in his own way should rarely be interfered with, unless the welfare of other individuals or of society clearly requires it.

Sutherland, *supra* note 25, at 202.

56. Taft and Sanford were sometimes slightly less willing to abandon the presumption of validity of positive legislation than was Sutherland. *See, e.g.*, Adkins v. Children's Hospital of the District of Columbia, 261 U.S. 525 (1923); Tyson & Brothers v. Banton, 273 U.S. 418 (1927).

57. In Hamilton v. Kentucky Distilleries & Warehouse, Co., 251 U.S. 146 (1919), Brandeis, writing for a unanimous Court, upheld a wartime ban on the sale of liquor against the claim that the ban constituted an unconstitutional taking of private property. Four years later, in conversation with Felix Frankfurter, Brandeis explained: "At first went the other way 5 to 4, the Chief (White) was with me, Holmes against.... Holmes balked on 'Due Process' – the thing that prevailed with him in the Mahon case later. I told him Mugler [v. Kansas, 123 U.S. 623 (1887)] governed but he never has liked that case. *Undoubtedly his impatience with prohibition explains this.*" *Brandeis-Frankfurter Conversations*, at 324 (April 10, 1923) (emphasis added).

58. Zechariah Chafee, Jr., *Ill Starred Prohibition Cases: A Study in Judicial Pathology*, 45 HARVARD LAW REVIEW 947, 949 (1932). *See* Tyson v. Banton, 273 U.S. 418, 446 (1927) (Holmes, J., dissenting) ("Wine has been thought good for man from the time of the Apostles until recent years."); Knickerbocker Ice Co. v. Stewart, 253 U.S. 149, 169 (1920) (Holmes, J., dissenting) ("I cannot for a moment believe that apart from the Eighteenth Amendment special constitutional principles exist against strong drink."). In response to her inquiries about prohibition, Holmes wrote his friend Charlotte Moncheur that

> [m]y way of thinking is that whatever may have been the defects in knowledge and forethought when the experiment was launched it must be given fifty years or a century before we can be sure whether it is a great social improvement or a mistake. Of course it has banished much fog and much poetry from life, but it may pay in the long run. I don't like to hear of people who should set an example buying from bootleggers and giving dinners in the old form. On the other hand I still have a little whiskey that I had before the 18th Amendment and on rare occasions give a friend a glass. And when a friend has sent me a bottle as a Christmas present I have not felt bound to return it, although I should prefer that it should not be done.

OWH to Baroness Moncheur (January 27, 1928) (Holmes papers). In his private correspondence, Holmes reported telling "a casual unknown dame who came in here one Monday" that "alas the exquisite vanished in this Country with the 18th Amendment." Holmes "told her that abuses were the parents of the exquisite – and then remembered that she might be a reporter,

Prohibition & Positive Law

for all I know. But no headlines have exposed my cynicism." OWH to Nina Gray (March 25, 1922) (Holmes papers). *See* OWH to Felix Frankfurter (December 23, 1921), in HOLMES-FRANKFURTER CORRESPONDENCE, at 132–33. Holmes wrote Lady Leslie Scott that he was "rather amused that two men have each sent me a present of a bottle of whiskey, which I fear is an infringement of the law on their part, if not on mine. ... At all events, as I wrote to one of them, I have not forgotten the prayer 'Lead us into temptation.'" OWH to Lady Leslie Scott (December 24, 1927) (Holmes papers). Earlier that year Holmes's close friend Frederick Pollock wrote Holmes recounting "lurid reports ... about the demoralizing effects of Prohibition in the Middle Western States. ... Bolshevism is not the only alarming product of half-educated sentimentalism." Frederick Pollock to OWH (March 17, 1927), in 2 HOLMES-POLLOCK CORRESPONDENCE, at 195.

59. Lochner v. New York, 198 U.S. 45, 75 (1905) (Holmes, J., dissenting).
60. Black & White Taxicab & Transfer Co. v. Brown & Yellow Taxicab & Transfer Co., 276 U.S. 518, 533 (1928) (Holmes, J., dissenting).
61. MORTON J. HORWITZ, THE TRANSFORMATION OF AMERICAN LAW 1870–1960: THE CRISIS OF LEGAL ORTHODOXY 140–42 (New York: Oxford University Press 1992). "[J]udicial restraint," Horwitz writes, "follows from the collapse of [Holmes's] search for immanent rationality in customary law." *Id.* at 142.
62. Grogan v. Hiram Walker & Sons, 259 U.S. 80, 89 (1922). Holmes's observation in *Grogan* was immediately recognized as signifying "the earnest desire of the Supreme Court to aid the government generally in its attempt to carry out a 'noble experiment.'" Forrest Revere Black, *An Ill-Starred Prohibition Case: Olmstead v. United States*, 18 GEORGETOWN LAW JOURNAL 120, 124–25 (1930). *See* Wayne B. Wheeler, *Enforcing the Dry Law*, 68 THE FORUM 747, 747–48 (1922).
63. *See, e.g.*, United States v. Sullivan, 274 U.S. 259 (1927) (Holmes opinion upholding the requirement that bootleggers file tax returns reporting their illegal income). The decision was controversial in the press, where it was asked "How can society question the bootlegger's activities when it takes its due share of his profits?" *Bootleggers Not Tax Exempt*, 93 LITERARY DIGEST 10 (May 28, 1927).
64. *See supra* Part V. It was said of Sanford that he "displayed a marked zeal for prohibition enforcement." Allen E. Ragan, *Mr. Justice Sanford*, 15 EAST TENNESSEE HISTORICAL SOCIETY'S PUBLICATIONS 74, 81 (1943).
65. Sanford's views on prohibition are discussed in STEPHANIE L. SLATER, EDWARD TERRY SANFORD: A TENNESSEAN ON THE US SUPREME COURT 175–78, 247–50 (Knoxville: University of Tennessee Press 2018).
66. *For Local Option, Mr. Taft Explains, supra* note 25. *See Taft Hits Prohibition; National Legislation, He Says, Would Revolutionize Government*, NEW YORK TIMES (December 29, 1914), at 4; *Misunderstood on Prohibition, Says Prof. Taft*, CHRISTIAN SCIENCE MONITOR (January 6, 1915), at 5; *The Question of Prohibition*, WASHINGTON POST (January 4, 1915), at 6. Taft had publicly attacked statewide prohibition as early as 1906. *See* WILLIAM HOWARD TAFT, FOUR ASPECTS OF CIVIC DUTY 46–47 (New York: C. Scribner's Sons 1906):

> It is, of course the duty of the legislator in the enactment of laws to consider the ease or difficulty with which, by reason of popular feeling or popular prejudice, laws after being enacted can be enforced. Nothing is more foolish, nothing more utterly at variance with sound public policy

than to enact a law which, by reason of the conditions surrounding the community in which it is declared to be law, is incapable of enforcement. Such an instance is sometimes presented by sumptuary laws, by which the sale of intoxicating liquors is prohibited under penalty in localities where the public sentiment of the immediate community does not and will not sustain the enforcement of the law. In such cases the legislation is usually the result of agitation by people in the country who are determined to make their fellow-citizens in the city better. The enactment of the law comes through the country representatives, who form a majority of the legislature; but the enforcement of the law is among the people who are generally opposed to its enactment, and under such circumstances the law is a dead letter.

It is noteworthy that as early as 1891 Brandeis had also attacked statewide prohibition on similar grounds. *See supra* Chapter 30, at note 3; see also *infra* Chapter 33, at note 78.
67. *For Local Option, Mr. Taft Explains*, *supra* note 25.
68. *Id. See, e.g.*, Butler, *supra* note 25, at 586 ("In many places legislative method is imperfect. ... Lawmakers are influenced by powerful groups and yielding to pressure – and often to manufactured public opinion – pass laws and yet more laws. Leaders of selfish organizations control large numbers of votes. Their power continues after election day and their determinations, made without regard to any interest save their own, communicated sometimes in the form of orders, unduly affect the conduct of legislators and other public officers.").
69. *For Local Option, Mr. Taft Explains*, *supra* note 25. Taft later observed that a "weakness" in American government "that has proved at times to be serious" was that a

> faction, a minority, a class group, seeks legislation. It is in respect to some social or economic phase of conditions upon which public opinion has not been aroused and upon which the great parties have not expressed themselves. The group is a minority in every district, but it has votes enough in each district or in many districts to convince the members of the legislative body that it can wield a balance of power as between the two evenly matched parties and elect or defeat a candidate. In this way, in times past, first the liquor men and then the Prohibitionists wielded an undue weight of influence.

WILLIAM HOWARD TAFT, REPRESENTATIVE GOVERNMENT IN THE UNITED STATES 29 (New York University Press 1921). Taft himself declared in favor of local option, "by which the sale of liquor is forbidden in communities that by the expression of a majority of the voters show that public opinion will sustain the enforcement of such a law. To pass laws forbidding the manufacture and sale of liquor and then have large parts of a State where liquor is sold freely and in defiance of the law is a demoralization of all law that is most detrimental to the interest of the whole community." *For Local Option, Mr. Taft Explains*, *supra* note 25. For expressing these sentiments, Taft was briefly advanced as a "wet" candidate for president. *See Wets Want Taft for President*, CHICAGO TRIBUNE (June 4, 1915), at 17. He was also opposed by the National Anti-Saloon League as a potential nominee for the Supreme Court. *See Protest on Lehmann or Taft for Supreme Bench; National Anti-Saloon League Urges Wilson Not to Name Either Man-Labeled Foes of Prohibition*, CHICAGO DAILY TRIBUNE (January 28, 1916), at 7.
70. In November 1917, Taft observed that "The real objection to prohibition must be recognized in those communities where it would not prohibit. Nothing is so demoralizing as sumptuary laws which are not enforced. They become the tools

Prohibition & Positive Law

of politicians. They create a criminal class of those who carry on the traffic, and enable unscrupulous municipal and state officers by intermittent enforcement to use them as an active and sinister political agency." William Howard Taft, *Prohibition: Pro and Con* (November 15, 1917), in VIVIAN, at 6. Taft believed it doubtful "whether prohibition could be maintained in any large city." *Id.*

71. WHT to Allen B. Lincoln (September 2, 1918) (Taft papers).
72. *Id. See* WHT to Allen B. Lincoln (June 8, 1918) (Taft papers). Taft's letters to Lincoln were published in the *New Haven Journal-Courier*. They were revived and republished in October 1928, and trumpeted as an "amazingly accurate forecast of what would result after the enactment of the amendment, and the passage of the Volstead act." *Taft Condemned National Dry Law; Letters Written in 1918 Show His Views Were as Smith's Now; Made Striking Prediction; Foresaw Contempt for Law and Rise of Bootlegging*, NEW YORK WORLD (October 2, 1928), at 1, 4. The letters were republished in the *Baltimore Sun* and the *St. Louis Post-Dispatch*, and also in *The Outlook*, which called Taft "a prophet and a seer." *Prophet Taft*, 150 THE OUTLOOK 974, 975 (October 17, 1928). The republication put Taft "in a very awkward situation." WHT to Irving Fisher (November 21, 1928) (Taft papers). Taft's letters were used by Al Smith as part of his presidential campaign. *See Stenographic Report of Gov. Smith's Speech in Philadelphia Last Night; Quotes Taft and Wilson against Dry Law*, NEW YORK TIMES (October 28, 1928), at 2; *Text of Smith's Speech over Radio*, WASHINGTON POST (October 28, 1928), at M6; WHT to Gerald Fitz Gibbon (October 29, 1928) (Taft papers); WHT to Mrs Frederick J. Manning (October 28, 1928) (Taft papers); WHT to Charles P. Taft 2nd (October 28, 1928) (Taft papers); WHT to Horace D. Taft (October 28, 1928) (Taft papers). Taft thought it "very unfair to quote those letters to indicate my present attitude in respect to the enforcement of the law." WHT to Frederick H. Gillett (October 24, 1928) (Taft papers); WHT to I.M. Ullman (October 11, 1928) (Taft papers) ("What I said was said ten years ago, but the situation has greatly changed, and since I said those things I harangued the Alumni at Yale with all the force I could, to say to them that they violated their duty and were ignoring the country by ignoring the National Prohibition law."). *See also Taft Won't Discuss 1918 Dry Law Letters; Says Place on Bench Precludes Talking on Views Held Then that Opposed Federal Legislation*, NEW YORK TIMES (October 4, 1928), at 5.
73. William Howard Taft, *Enforce Prohibition* (February 5, 1919), in VIVIAN, at 172–73.

> One who, in the matter of national prohibition, holds his personal opinion and his claim of personal liberty to be of higher sanction than this overwhelming constitutional expression of the people, is a disciple of practical Bolshevism....
>
> The only proper and effective plan ... is to unite with the advocates of prohibition in a real bona fide effort to enforce the law. If it is successful and improved morality follows, let the opponents of the amendment confess themselves wrong and rejoice in a real reform in the welfare of society. If, on the other hand, in spite of the best teamwork, the hopes of those responsible for the amendment are blasted and only failure and demoralization follow, the case for a retracing of steps is made.

Id. See Taft on the Liquor Question; Prohibition Amounts to Confiscation in Some Cases, But It Must Be Enforced with a Heavy Hand – No Use to Talk of Knocking Out the Law, LOS ANGELES TIMES (February 9, 1919), at III3.

74. William Howard Taft, *Is Prohibition a Blow at Personal Liberty?*, LADIES HOME JOURNAL 78 (May 1919). Taft rejected "the argument against prohibition based on the postulate that in a free government like ours, in which no man is to be deprived of life, liberty and property except after due process of law, it is contrary to the spirit of our civilization and constitution to enforce upon people such a curtailment of their freedom of action in their diet." *Id.* at 31. He explained:

> How far we should go in limiting liberty for the welfare of all is, of course, a constantly recurring question. ... Reasonable restraint of personal liberty of action for the common welfare is really a matter of degree. It is to be settled by the general and dominant opinion of all the people in a community of common purpose, common ideals and the common enjoyment of the blessings of liberty and justice. This crystallizes into a kind of moral code based on the vicious effect of practices sufficiently serious to affect the welfare of the community.
>
> Our courts recognize this crystallization of public sentiment. When it is manifested in constitutional amendment and statute, they enforce it as part of the law of the land. They hold that it is not a forbidden restriction of personal liberty, but it is only the curtailment of complete freedom of action that is necessary in the interest of society. ...
>
> [The] array of the immoral and vicious effects of the free manufacture and sale of liquor upon the community can leave no doubt that the curtailment of personal freedom in effective prohibition is small as compared with its benefit to society. This settles its conformity to true principles of personal liberty.

Id. at 78.

75. Upon Taft's resignation from the bench in 1930, the *New York Herald Tribune* said of him: "Chief Justice Taft, though outspokenly opposed to the Eighteenth Amendment and the Volstead act, long before he went to the bench, took the position that these enactments being law they should be enforced. All his decisions consistently upheld the letter and spirit of the prohibition laws." *Retiring Chief Justice First to Be Honored by Two Highest Offices within Gift of Republic*, NEW YORK HERALD TRIBUNE (February 4, 1930), at 12.

76. William Howard Taft, *Foreword* to LORD SHAW OF DUNFERMLINE, THE LAW OF THE KINSMEN 10 (London: Hodder & Stoughton 1923). *See Report of the National Commission on Law Observance and Enforcement*, *supra* note 8, at 10–12.

77. William H. Taft, Address Delivered at the Yale Alumni Luncheon in New Haven, Connecticut (June 20, 1923) (Taft papers). *See Taft Warns at Yale on Breaking Laws*, NEW YORK TIMES (June 21, 1923), at 10; *Mr. Taft Demands Obedience to Law; Tells Yale Alumni Prohibition Observance and Enforcement Is Test of All Law*, CHRISTIAN SCIENCE MONITOR (June 21, 1923), at 5. "The people whom I have in mind are the first to complain of mob law, lawless violence of laborites and other disturbances of the peace, but when it comes to a violation of the 18th Amendment, and the Volstead law, they seem to feel no obligation to protest." Taft, Address Delivered at the Yale Alumni Luncheon, *supra*, at 2. "It is most discouraging," Taft wrote in a letter, "that those who are educated and ought to know the vice of a disregard of law should be willing to violate it and set an example for others to do so." WHT to Clement G. Clarke (March 20, 1925) (Taft papers). Excerpts of Taft's remarks to the Yale Alumni were later republished in 150 THE OUTLOOK 1156 (1928).

Prohibition & Positive Law

78. Taft, Address Delivered at the Yale Alumni Luncheon, *supra* note 77, at 3–4.
79. In such moods Taft struck the same note of judicial restraint and personal self-denial that characterized Holmes. "I was opposed very much to prohibition because of the difficulties of its enforcement, and I utterly deny the principle that the drinking of whiskey or wine or beer is in itself, aside from the law, immoral," he once wrote a close friend. WHT to Gertrude Ely (December 22, 1923) (Taft papers). "But," Taft continued, "the people of the United States differed from me and amended the Constitution and made this law. Now I believe in popular government, and the only method by which popular government can be made useful and effective is that when one is beaten at the polls or in the Legislature, to bow to the result and lend all his efforts to the maintenance of the dignity of law and the preservation of its strength, else we shall have demoralization of all law, and that means anarchy." *Id. See* WHT to Louis A. Cuvillier (November 9, 1926) (Taft papers): "The truth is that I was one of the foremost in opposing the 18th Amendment, chiefly for the reason that I thought its enforcement would be full of difficulty and present problems that we ought not to undertake. But I was overborne, and the 18th Amendment has become the law of the land, and like a loyal American, obedient to the Constitution, I am in favor of enforcing the Amendment in every possible and reasonable way."
80. WHT to James R. Sheffield (July 8, 1923) (Taft papers). Taft's concern was widely shared. *See, e.g., Report of the National Commission on Law Observance and Enforcement, supra* note 8, at 39: "Not the least demoralizing feature of enforcement of national prohibition, is the development of open or hardly disguised drinking winked at by those in charge in respectable places where respectable people gather. People of wealth, professional and business men, public officials and tourists are drinking in hotels, cafes and tourist camps." It was commonly believed that "[o]ur highest officials violate the law privately when there is no danger of discovery or publicity. We heard one remark not so very long ago that he had built one of the most marvelous cellars in America and stocked it with more than enough to last him a lifetime – at least six varieties of wine were served at his table – but he is viciously against all 'reds' and laboring men and anybody else who 'will not obey our laws, by heaven, sir.' Inveighing against those who would undermine our Constitution, he himself does his uttermost to bring it into contempt and to prove the theory that those sworn to uphold this particular law are our worst lawbreakers." *Who Undermines Prohibition?*, 116 THE NATION 736, 736 (1923).
81. WHT to Francis Peabody (July 12, 1923) (Taft papers).
82. Taft, Address Delivered at the Yale Alumni Luncheon, *supra* note 77, at 7–8. *See* WHT to Mrs. George H. Stanlidge (January 24, 1923) (Taft papers) ("Everyone I think who sees clearly deprecates the contemptuous tone toward the prohibition law which so many affect. I was opposed to prohibition because I was afraid of the difficulties of the enforcement and the demoralization of all law by the neglect to enforce such an important measure as that of prohibition, but now that the amendment has been adopted, the laws passed in pursuance of it should be obeyed and all good citizens should preserve an attitude of obedience toward it and respect for its enforcement.").
83. WHT to Clarence H. Kelsey (May 18, 1923) (Taft papers).
84. Taft believed that the alternative to strict enforcement of prohibition was "anarchy." WHT to Gertrude Ely (December 22, 1923) (Taft papers). He feared that efforts to ameliorate prohibition to accommodate community sentiment would undermine the law. It is fascinating that when a reporter misinterpreted Taft to have proposed

amending the Volstead Act to allow for beer and light wine, *Taft Stops Here, Pours Out Hopes for Dry Throats*, CHICAGO DAILY TRIBUNE (June 26, 1920), at 4, Taft was quick to disavow the proposal: "As a matter of fact, I am not in favor of amending the Volstead act in respect to the amount of permissible alcohol in beverages. I am not in favor of allowing light wines and beer to be sold under the eighteenth amendment. I believe it would defeat the purpose of the amendment. No such distinction as that between wines and beer on the one hand, and spirituous liquors on the other, is practical as a police measure. ... Any such loophole as light wines and beer would make the amendment a laughing stock." *Mr. Taft on the Dry Law*, CHICAGO DAILY TRIBUNE (July 27, 1920), at 6; *Taft Would Not Amend the Volstead Act*, NEW YORK TIMES (July 27, 1920), at 13. Taft did concede, however, that the Volstead Act "could be better enforced by moderate penalties and reasonable provisions than by draconian severity, and that harshly inquisitorial measures and heavy penalties, sought by fanatics, would obstruct rather than aid the law and would stir protest and turn the people against prohibition." *Id.*

85. Taft, Address Delivered at the Yale Alumni Luncheon, *supra* note 77, at 1. *See* William Howard Taft, The Attacks on the Courts and Legal Procedure: Address before the Economic Club of Worcester Massachusetts, May 13, 1914 (Taft papers) ("One great difficulty that is facing us in this country is the lack of respect for law and the weakened supremacy of the law. The idea seems to be growing that any small class that has some particular reform which it wishes to effect in its own interest may accomplish that by force and by threats of force against the whole body politic and social. In other words, physical force and lawless violence under this government of law is growing to be a calculated element in the winning of political and social issues."); William H. Taft, *The Attacks on the Courts and Legal Procedure*, 5 KENTUCKY LAW JOURNAL 3, 22 (1916).

86. WHT to James R. Sheffield (July 8, 1923) (Taft papers). *See* WHT to Francis Peabody (July 12, 1923) (Taft papers). For a flavor of the phenomenon to which Taft was responding, see *supra* note 8.

87. *See* Charles H. Brent, *Law and Order*, 42 WORLD'S WORK 267, 268–69 (1921) ("The most alarming feature of the situation just now is not merely disregard for the laws but also symptoms of disregard for the Constitution. The Eighteenth Amendment is just as much a part of the Constitution as any of the original articles. I am not concerned with the character of this amendment. I am viewing it solely as an integral part of the most sacred and binding obligation governing American citizenship. The only possible excuse for disobeying it is self-indulgence. ... The fact of the matter is that successful democracy presupposes individual self-respect and self-restraint for the sake of the commonwealth. ... There can be no corporate self-control where every citizen is part of the Government unless there is personal self-control. Towering above all public measures and mass movements to-day, stands the need of a new steadiness and a new determination to discipline our tastes, our customs, our recreations."). This shift of emphasis was noticed by the opponents of prohibition. *See, e.g.*, Stephen Leacock, 5 CONGRESSIONAL DIGEST 200 (1926) ("[Prohibitionists] are putting their trust in coercion, in the jail, in the whip and the scourge. They are done with the moral appeal. They are finished with persuasion. They want, however, authority. They want to say 'Thou shalt' and 'Thou shalt not,' and when they say it, to be obeyed under the fear of the criminal law. ... What they propose is virtually to send all people to jail who dare to drink beer, and to send them

again and again for each new offense, to break them into compliance as people were once broken upon the wheel."); *Temperance?*, 126 THE NATION 6 (1928) ("The truth of the matter is that in the bitterness provoked by the efforts to defy and to enforce the Eighteenth Amendment its original purpose has been lost sight of. . . . [M]any of its protagonists . . . forgetting their humanitarian purpose, have allowed their zeal for good to pass the proper bounds.").

88. William E. Borah, *Civic Righteousness: Lawlessness the Insidious Disease of Republics*, 114 CENTURY MAGAZINE 641, 644 (1927). Borah asserted that "there can be no more vital problem presented to a free people than the problem of whether or not they can hold and maintain the Constitution of which they have deliberately written." *Id.* Borah continued:

> We all know from a review of history that lawlessness is the insidious disease of republics. It is the one great malady against which every true patriot will ever be on guard. It is but a short step from the lawlessness of the man of means who scouts some part of the fundamental law because forsooth it runs counter to his wishes, to the soldier who may be called into the street to protect property, but who, taking counsel of his sympathies, fraternizes with the mob. The great question, therefore, before the American people now is, not that of prohibition, because that as a policy, has been settled. The supreme question is: after we have determined as a people on prohibition, whether we have the moral courage, the high determination, and the unwavering purpose to enforce that which we have written into the Constitution.

Id. at 647. In another setting, Borah proclaimed: "Whether prohibition stays or goes, the Constitution should be maintained and supported as it is written by all law-abiding people until it is changed in the manner pointed out by the Constitution. Obedience to the law is the rock foundation upon which our whole structure rests. To disregard it is to strike at the life of the Nation." William E. Borah, *U.S. Senators Discuss Prohibition Issue*, 5 CONGRESSIONAL DIGEST 191, 192 (1926).

89. *Sections and Allied Bodies*, 7 AMERICAN BAR ASSOCIATION JOURNAL 483, 484–85 (1921).

90. *See, e.g., M'Adoo's Ohio Talk Fails to Disclose His Plans for 1928*, WASHINGTON POST (January 29, 1927), at 3 ("He declared the United States, in continued flouting of prohibition laws, is approaching 'the slippery path to anarchy.'").

91. *President's Annual Message*, 68 CONG. REC. 29, 34 (December 7, 1926). In his first State of the Union Message, Coolidge announced that "[f]ree government has no greater menace than disrespect for authority and continual violation of law. It is the duty of a citizen not only to observe the law but to let it be known that he is opposed to its violation." *Address of the President*, 65 CONG. REC. 96, 98 (December 6, 1923). See WILLIAM GIBBS MCADOO, THE CHALLENGE: LIQUOR AND LAWLESSNESS VERSUS CONSTITUTIONAL GOVERNMENT 259 (New York: Century Co. 1928).

92. *Inaugural Address of President Hoover*, 71 CONG. REC. 4, 4 (March 4, 1929).

93. *Id.* at 5. Criminologist George W. Kirchwey argued that Hoover was incorrect to assert that defiance of prohibition automatically implied anarchic disrespect for all law: "That in this period of 'lawlessness' and 'demoralization' incident to the attempted enforcement of the prohibition law, the offenses of assault, fraud, vagrancy, prostitution and larceny . . . should all have fallen off by 50 per cent or more and burglary by 10 per cent or more should give pause to our Jeremiahs." George W. Kirchwey, *Our Lawlessness that Alarms Hoover*, NEW YORK TIMES

(May 26, 1929), § 5 at 5. Kirchwey concluded: "Our flippant attitude with respect to prohibition does not in the slightest degree affect our abhorrence of crime. We may not believe, as [Hoover] does, in the sanctity of 'law as law' (there are pernicious and foolish laws as well as wise and good ones)." *Id.* Analogous arguments were made on the constitutional level:

> I would venture to make a ... suggestion to the Hoover commission. ... [W]hy not invite Messrs. Taft, Coolidge, and Hoover to appear ... and state why they have done nothing, while in the White House, to enforce the Negro suffrage provisions of the Constitution? What President has sent a special message earnestly recommending reduction of the representation of the South in Congress? If no such message has ever been sent, why has a part of the sacrosanct Constitution been treated as a dead letter? And what has the President or either of the living ex-Presidents to say about the example they set to the nation by their indifference and hostility to that part of the Constitution?

Yarros, *supra* note 10, at 60–61.

94. Wayne B. Wheeler, *Law and Order*, 124 THE OUTLOOK 146, 146 (1920). "There is only one way for this Nation to avert the disaster that was visited on Rome, on France, on Russia, on all nations that sowed the seed of anarchy," Wheeler wrote. "Every loyal, Christian patriot, every hundred per cent American, must stand for law and order. Every officer of the law who deserts his office should be treated like the soldier who deserts his country in a war. We can have treason in times of peace as well as in days of national warfare." *Id.* at 146–47.

95. *Wheeler Clashes with Darrow Here in Dry Law Debate*, NEW YORK TIMES (April 24, 1927), at 1. *See, e.g.*, Adam Coaldigger, *Uplift by Force and Violence*, 40 STONE CUTTERS' JOURNAL 6 (June 1925) ("If, for instance, our congress, president, and supreme court should develop any symptoms of enforcing, or even of recognizing the existence of the fourteenth amendment, I may yet reconcile myself to the eighteenth.").

Eventually Wheeler began to lose credibility with the public when he took the question of enforceability to its logical conclusion. In 1926 the federal government began to infuse alcohol with toxic ingredients, so that those buying illegal alcohol began literally to die. The practice erupted in scandal when it caused a raft of deaths during the holiday season at the end of 1926. Treasury Secretary Mellon announced that his department would plan "to discontinue alcohol denaturing formulas which might cause death or serious illness." *Mellon Opposes Killing by Poison to Enforce Law*, NEW YORK TIMES (December 31, 1926), at 1. Wheeler vigorously opposed the move.

> "When the Government proceeds on the theory," Mr. Wheeler countered, "that its laws will be disobeyed, it cannot stand. It will decay within a year.
>
> "The Government has warned its citizens that there is poison in most bootleg alcohol. If the citizen goes ahead and drinks it he is in the same position as a man who walks into the drugstore and buys a bottle carrying a poison label and drinks it."

Wayne Wheeler Protests Elimination of Poison, BOSTON DAILY GLOBE (December 31, 1926), at A10. *See "Murder" by Poison Bootleg Liquor*, 92 LITERARY DIGEST 5 (January 15, 1927). The controversy caused intense debate in Congress, see *Congress Wets Denounce Deaths by Poison Alcohol as Government Murders*, NEW YORK TIMES (January 4, 1927), at 1, and Wheeler's reputation took a severe hit.

Prohibition & Positive Law

96. WHT to Charles H. Strong (July 1, 1925) (Taft papers).
97. WHT to Irving Fisher (November 21, 1928) (Taft papers).
98. *Id.*
99. The disparity between Taft and Sutherland may have been even more stark than the public record discloses. In Byars v. United States, 273 U.S. 28 (1927), for example, Sutherland wrote an opinion for a unanimous court reversing the judgment below and excluding evidence found as a result of a warrant to search for liquor that had not been based upon probable cause. Stone's docket book indicates that Taft, Holmes, and McReynolds had voted to affirm in conference. In Agnello v. United States, 269 U.S. 20 (1925), there was a similar disparity between Taft's public and private views. *Agnello* was a unanimous decision authored by Butler addressing the question, as Butler put it in his docket book, "Is a search warrant necessary to search a man's house for drugs? Lower court held not in the circumstances here." Butler's docket book records that all members of the Court at conference voted to reverse the lower court decision except for Holmes and Taft, who voted to affirm. Although *Agnello* concerned a prosecution for cocaine rather than liquor, it had plain and obvious implications for prohibition.
100. Prohibition created strange political bedfellows. Sutherland, for example adopted a stance that almost exactly coincided with the position of Walter Lippmann. Lippmann argued that because in the case of prohibition "we are faced with a law which cannot be enforced and which cannot be repealed," the only solution was for the Supreme Court, "bowing to public opinion, to find by the proper reasoning that the States are not violating the Eighteenth Amendment.... [T]he Constitution, thank heavens, means whatever a living Supreme Court says it means. And the Supreme Court, thank heavens, is composed on the whole not of worshippers of a sacred text, but of jurists and statesmen and human beings." Lippmann, *supra* note 5, at 54, 56. Adverting to the example of the Fifteenth Amendment, Lippmann argued that whenever the Supreme Court has faced a constitutional provision generally defied by "orderly disobedience" – "a disobedience which is open, frankly avowed, and in conformity with the general sense of what is reasonable" – it has reinterpreted the Constitution to align it with dominant public sentiment. *Id.* at 56. "When the Constitution has come into conflict with the living needs of the nation, and when amendment was impossible, the method of changing the Constitution has been to change it and then get the very human Supreme Court to sanction it.... If the test of loyalty to the laws were loyalty to the original intent of each law, we should have to confess that we are a thoroughly lawless people." *Id.* at 55–56.
101. WHT to Moses Strauss (April 1, 1929) (Taft papers). The full passage reads: "We must be patient. We can not change the habits of a whole nation all at once, and we have got to go through a trying experience in the non-enforcement of the law, but if we keep up the strength of the conscience of the majority of the people, which we now enjoy, I am quite sure that we shall wear down the recklessness of those who would try to defeat the law by disobeying it."
102. Henry F. Pringle, 2 The Life and Times of William Howard Taft 989 (New York: Farrar & Rinehart, Inc. 1939).

CHAPTER 32

Prohibition and Law Enforcement

IN THE 1920s, Americans believed that they were swept up in a crime wave of awful proportions.[1] "Few subjects occupy more space in contemporary literature," one author observed, "than analyses of the crime wave, its extent, causes and possible remedies."[2] Solicitor General James M. Beck remarked in 1921 "that the present wave of crime had no parallel since the eighteenth century."[3] A 1926 poll named "[l]awlessness or disrespect for law" as "the greatest problem confronting this country at this time."[4] Herbert Hoover made lawlessness a major theme of his new administration, announcing in his Inaugural Address that "[c]rime is increasing. Confidence in rigid and speedy justice is decreasing."[5] Hoover pledged to meet the challenge by appointing "a national commission for a searching investigation of the whole structure of our Federal system of jurisprudence"; the commission would "make such recommendations for re-organization of the administration of Federal laws and court procedure as may be found desirable."[6] Eventually the commission would become the pathbreaking National Commission on Law Observance and Enforcement.

Although Hoover was careful to stress that in his view prohibition "was not the main source of the lawlessness" afflicting the country,[7] his urgent plea for law and order was nevertheless interpreted "as an appeal to respect the Volstead act."[8] Yet Hoover was surely correct to perceive that Americans in the 1920s were anxious about the problem of lawlessness in registers that went far beyond prohibition. Apart from the anxiety generated by what Taft called "[t]he great wave of crime that we have been facing," which involved not merely liquor but also an "increase of violence" like "murder and robbery,"[9] the problem of "law and order" in the 1920s was also associated with issues of labor unrest,[10] as well as with various forms of racial violence like lynching[11] and extralegal organizations like the Ku Klux Klan.[12] Embedded in this atmosphere of anxiety, the Taft Court was, as historians have noted, "preoccupied" by "law and order issues."[13]

Prohibition & Law Enforcement

We owe to Robert Cover the insight that the Taft Court managed to achieve an "extraordinary area of consensus" about the need to uphold the rule of law and eliminate "private violence."[14] Although the Court split badly on the question of whether labor violence should be regulated by courts or by legislatures,[15] it was nevertheless united in its ambition to inaugurate "a new era in the effort to extend the rule of law into the field of industrial controversy."[16] In decisions like *American Steel Foundries v. Tri-City Central Trades Council*[17] and *United Mine Workers v. Coronado Coal Co.*,[18] the Court sought to substitute legal proceedings for what everyone regarded as private industrial warfare.[19] In *New York ex rel. Bryant v. Zimmerman*,[20] the Court upheld a New York statute designed to clamp down on the Ku Klux Klan, an organization that was "taking into its own hands the punishment of what some of its members conceived to be crimes."[21] The Court upheld New York's requirement that the Klan disclose the identity of its members.[22] In *Moore v. Dempsey*,[23] the Court used federal authority to set limits on lynching and race violence. Essentially overruling the recently minted precedent of *Frank v. Mangum*,[24] *Moore* held that federal courts could use the writ of habeas corpus to review state trials that had been rendered lawless by a mob.[25] In effect, the Court declared "lynch law as little valid when practiced by a regularly drawn jury as when administered by one elected by a mob intent on death."[26]

The Taft Court maintained this commitment to legality even in the context of prohibition. In *Tumey v. Ohio*,[27] the Court sought to define, as it had in *Moore*, the "content of the concept of the fair trial required by due process of law."[28] Ohio had by statute authorized tiny villages to create small magistrate courts, popularly known as liquor courts,[29] in which the judge, who might also be the village mayor, received as supplementary income a percentage of the fees and costs that convicted defendants were required to pay.[30] Ohio law empowered villages to receive one-half of all fines assessed by its liquor court.[31] This allocation of funds cleverly created incentives for villages entrepreneurially to enforce prohibition, for the jurisdiction of liquor courts ran to the entire county in which a village was situated.

The facts of *Tumey* illustrate these incentives. *Tumey* involved the small village of North College Hill, which had a population of 1,104 but which was situated in Hamilton County near the "very 'wet' city"[32] of Cincinnati. By prosecuting and fining residents of neighboring Cincinnati, the liquor court of tiny North College Hill could generate significant income for the village, as well for the North College Hill mayor who presided over its liquor court.[33] To sustain such prosecutions, North College Hill provided by ordinance that one half of the income generated by its liquor court would be reinvested in a "Secret Service Fund to be used for the purpose of securing the enforcement of any prohibition law."[34] In this way Ohio, the original home of the Anti-Saloon League, created a "reign of terror"[35] in which dry villages used their liquor courts to fund self-sustaining squads that would raid adjacent wet cities to enforce prohibition legislation.[36]

Writing for a unanimous Court, Taft in *Tumey* held that the Ohio statute was unconstitutional because it "vested the judicial power in one who by reason of his interest, both as an individual and as chief executive of the village, is disqualified to exercise it in the trial of the defendant."[37] "[I]t certainly violates the Fourteenth Amendment," wrote Taft, to subject a defendant's "liberty or property to the judgment of a court the judge of which has a direct, personal, substantial, pecuniary interest in reaching a conclusion against him in his case."[38]

Taft knew that *Tumey* was "a very important"[39] decision that would "rejoice the hearts of the anti-prohibitionists,"[40] but his first fidelity was to the rule of law.[41] "The fact is that the prohibitionists controlling the Legislature of Ohio have been so fierce that they have transgressed the Constitution of the United States, and we have to say so."[42] Taft was "very anxious that it shall not interfere with the efficient enforcement of law, but it does not help to enforce law by methods involved in the procedure which we condemned."[43] "The rejoicing of violators of the law over our decision ... gives me some concern," Taft wrote his son, "but I hope it will all be straightened out so that the effect of our decision will be seen to be just what it is and not to mean a general jail delivery."[44]

Tumey lay at the intersection of Taft's commitment effectively to enforce prohibition and his equally deep commitment to maintain the forms of legality essential to the rule of law. Taft wished to maintain the distinction between legal state violence and mere official lawlessness. This tension was most conspicuously and persistently played out in the Taft Court's lively Fourth Amendment jurisprudence of search and seizure. Because prohibition had flooded federal courts with criminal defendants, because many of these defendants could afford lawyers,[45] because most prohibition prosecutions required evidence of liquor,[46] and because the Taft Court was committed to the exclusionary rule as a means of enforcing the Fourth Amendment,[47] prohibition sparked a virtual "doctrinal explosion"[48] of Fourth Amendment law.[49]

The perceived difficulty of enforcing prohibition within the constitutional restraints of the Fourth Amendment[50] led some to advocate that federal courts "recognize frankly that the 4th Amendment is inconsistent with the 18th" and "that the 4th Amendment has actually been repealed, where enforcement of the Volstead Act is concerned."[51] At least one federal court reasoned that "[t]he Eighteenth Amendment must be considered in determining the question of what is an unreasonable search and seizure as prescribed by the Fourth Amendment. If there were no Eighteenth Amendment to the Constitution to be enforced, the court might have an entirely different idea of what is an unreasonable search or seizure."[52]

The Taft Court, however, was not tempted by this path. Instead, it vigorously affirmed its commitment both to the Fourth Amendment and to the exclusionary rule,[53] and it insisted on interpreting these commitments in ways that were formally independent of the Eighteenth Amendment. But at the same time the Taft Court reconfigured the structure of search and seizure law to render it more compatible with the "many situations of prohibition enforcement."[54]

The Taft Court decision that most exemplifies this approach, and that has had the most "lasting influence,"[55] is unquestionably *Carroll v. United States*.[56] *Carroll* addressed the question of whether prohibition agents could constitutionally conduct a warrantless search of an automobile suspected of carrying illegal liquor.[57] The issue of automobile searches involved "one of the most important practical

Prohibition & Law Enforcement

difficulties in the enforcement of prohibition," because, as contemporaries well understood, "the passage of automobiles in pleasant weather with their tops and curtains closed and of trucks apparently loaded with furniture or other harmless freight is now so common on certain main roads in some parts of the country as to excite little comment, and the procuring of a search warrant to stop such traffic is manifestly impossible. If the officers cannot stop and search vehicles which they strongly suspect of illegal transportation they cannot stop the traffic at all and the law will be made nugatory."[58]

The Court's opinion in *Carroll* was authored by Taft; McReynolds penned a dissent joined by Sutherland.[59] The case presented a new and exceedingly difficult problem that was "most important,"[60] because there was a pressing need to control criminal use of that "instrument of evil the automobile."[61] In its supplemental brief, the federal government argued that "the invention, the rapid development, and the general use of automobiles" had so disturbed the "proper balance between the necessities of public authority, on the one hand, and the demands of personal liberty, on the other," that the Court needed to act to end "the unprecedented 'crime wave.'"[62]

Received constitutional doctrine did not seem adequate to cope with the challenge of the automobile. The transportation of stolen liquor in cars could not be intercepted if searches required warrants, because cars would disappear by the time a warrant could be obtained. It was generally assumed that warrantless searches were constitutional only if they were incident to a legitimate arrest.[63] The legitimacy of an arrest was determined by reference to the common law, which allowed a police officer to arrest a suspect without warrant only if there was probable cause that the suspect had committed a felony, or if the suspect had, in the presence of the officer, committed a misdemeanor amounting to a breach of the peace.[64]

The Volstead Act made transportation of illegal liquor a misdemeanor, unless the accused had been guilty of two previous violations of the Act, in which case he was guilty of a felony.[65] Because the concealed transportation of liquor in a car was neither a "breach of the peace" committed "in the presence" of an officer, nor was it in most cases a felony, it did not seem possible to justify the warrantless search of a car as incident to a lawful arrest, even if there was probable cause to believe that the car contained unlawful liquor. Yet "the impossibility of enforcing the Eighteenth Amendment"[66] was the obvious consequence of failing to find some constitutional way to allow effective searches of automobiles.[67] Lower courts splintered badly on how to handle this problem.[68]

Taft constructed a solution that turned on recognizing the authority of positive statutory law to modify traditional common law understandings. Taft began with the premise that "the main purpose" of the Volstead Act was "to reach and destroy the forbidden liquor in transportation"; "provisions for forfeiture of the vehicle and the arrest of the transporter were incidental." It did not matter whether the transporter was guilty of a misdemeanor (for his first two offenses), or of a felony (for his third offense), because the object of federal intervention was "to forfeit and suppress the liquor." The validity of the seizure, therefore, depended upon the constitutionality of congressional authorization of the "seizure and forfeiture" of illegal liquor. Taft rejected the theory, advanced by the defendants, that the "validity of the seizure" depended "wholly on the validity of the arrest without a seizure," holding instead that "[t]he right to search and the validity of the seizure" depended upon "[t]he rule for determining what may be required before a seizure may be made by a competent seizing official."[69]

To determine the nature of that rule, Taft turned to a string of federal statutes beginning in the first Congress in 1789 that authorized searches of ships and other vehicles for contraband goods.[70] Taft argued that these statutes implied

> that the guaranty of freedom from unreasonable searches and seizures by the Fourth Amendment has been construed, practically since the beginning of the Government, as recognizing a necessary difference between a search of a store, dwelling house or other structure in respect of which a proper official warrant readily may be obtained, and a search of a ship, motor boat, wagon or automobile, for contraband goods, where it is not practicable to secure a warrant because the vehicle can be quickly moved out of the locality or jurisdiction in which the warrant must be sought.[71]

Acknowledging that it "would be intolerable and unreasonable if a prohibition agent were authorized to stop every automobile on the chance of finding liquor and thus subject all persons lawfully using the highways to the inconvenience and indignity of such a search,"[72] Taft read the Volstead Act to authorize only seizures in which "the seizing officer shall have reasonable or probable cause for believing that the automobile which he stops and seizes has contraband liquor therein which is being illegally transported."[73]

Sliding easily from the statute to the Constitution, Taft moved to the conclusion that under the Fourth Amendment "the true rule is that if the search and seizure without a warrant are made upon probable cause, that is, upon a belief, reasonably arising out of circumstances known to the seizing officer, that an automobile or other vehicle contains that which by law is subject to seizure and destruction, the search and seizure are valid."[74] Taft self-consciously reached this interpretation of the Fourth Amendment so that he could "conserve public interests as well as the interests and rights of individual citizens."[75] Taft's heroic effort to reinterpret Fourth Amendment doctrine in light of the pragmatic needs of law enforcement,[76] balanced against the interests of citizens to be free from arbitrary interference, essentially set the framework for modern search and seizure jurisprudence.[77]

In order to sustain this resolution of the case, Taft was forced to offer a very strained reading of the Volstead Act. Unlike the historical statutes upon which Taft based his discussion, which had explicitly authorized officials to search for contraband if they had reasonable cause, the Volstead Act provided merely that "[w]hen the commissioner, his assistants, inspectors, or any officer of the law shall discover any person in the act of transporting in violation of the law, intoxicating liquors in any wagon, buggy, automobile, water or air craft, or other vehicle, it shall be his duty to seize any and all intoxicating liquors found therein being transported contrary to law."[78] Taft was thus put in the awkward position of reading the term "shall discover" to mean "shall have probable cause to believe."[79]

This was precisely the point at which McReynolds, joined by Sutherland, aimed his forceful dissent.[80] Objecting strenuously that "[c]riminal statutes must be strictly construed and applied, in harmony with rules of the common law," McReynolds argued that "[t]he Volstead Act contains no provision which annuls the accepted common law rule or discloses definite intent to authorize arrests without warrant for misdemeanors not committed in the officer's presence." "Certainly, in a criminal statute, always to be strictly construed, the words 'shall discover ... in the act of transporting in violation of the law' cannot mean, shall have reasonable cause to suspect or believe that such transportation is being carried on. To discover and to suspect are wholly different things."[81] The Court ought to be extraordinarily cautious, McReynolds urged, before inferring that "Congress intended to remove ancient restrictions" that circumscribed the discretion of police to arrest for misdemeanors.[82]

In the absence of specific congressional authorization, the defendants' arrests were undoubtedly illegal under common law principles, and because "the seizure followed an unlawful arrest, and therefore became itself unlawful,"[83] McReynolds concluded that the evidence ought to be suppressed. "If an officer, upon mere suspicion of a misdemeanor, may stop one on the public highway, take articles away from him and thereafter use them as evidence to convict him of crime," McReynolds asked, "what becomes of the Fourth and Fifth Amendments?"[84]

The disagreement between Taft and the dissent turned most fundamentally on the generosity with which the Court was willing to interpret legislative revisions of the common law,[85] which McReynolds associated with "ancient" customs believed to mark significant constitutional values. Using an early version of an explicit statement rule, McReynolds believed that his judicial obligation was to conserve these values from the predations of merely positive legislation.[86] Taft, by contrast, was willing to give prohibition the benefit of every doubt. He sought to uphold the forces of law enforcement, which in his eyes were valiantly struggling to maintain the legitimacy of the legal order.

To sustain the convictions in *Carroll*, Taft was required to find that the arresting prohibition officers had probable cause to stop defendants' automobile. Essentially the only evidence of probable cause was that the defendants had once offered to sell illegal liquor to the officers, and that three months later these same officers saw the defendants, driving in the same car in which they had offered to sell liquor, traveling from Detroit to Grand Rapids. The officers knew that Detroit was "one of the most active centers for introducing illegally into this country spirituous liquors for distribution into the interior."[87] From this, Taft concluded: "That the officers when they saw the defendants believed that they were carrying liquor we can have no doubt, and we think it is equally clear that they had reasonable cause for thinking so."[88]

This was, to say the least, a "very loose definition of 'probable cause.'"[89] In dissent McReynolds could only ask: "Has it come about that merely because a man once agreed to deliver whisky, but did not, he may be arrested whenever thereafter he ventures to drive an automobile on the road to Detroit!"[90] To which the answer, according to political scientist Robert Cushman, was "that it certainly has, and ... most of us are not sensitive enough to feel that such a result violates the requirements either of justice or of common sense."[91]

Carroll seemed to imply "that a common reputation in the community of being a 'bootlegger' would justify prohibition agents in stopping and searching automobiles driven by persons thus suspected by their neighbors."[92] It appeared to award "discretionary carte blanche" to prohibition officers to stop and search automobiles,[93] and it was therefore attacked in the press as placing the highways "in the power of reckless prohibition agents. A moral bad effect will be to encourage the attitude of mental lawlessness already spreading through the country like a plague. The further we go with the eighteenth amendment and the Volstead act, the deeper we get into the jungle of danger and lawlessness."[94] *Carroll* was fiercely condemned as condoning "a more reprehensible practice than that exercised by British officials in colonial times," asking Americans to "surrender ... hard-earned liberties ... in order to carry on a 'noble experiment.'"[95]

Zechariah Chafee believed that Holmes and Brandeis joined *Carroll* because they "probably thought that the wise course for the Court was not to hamper prohibition but to give it almost every chance for effective operation which the government officials wished. Then if the Eighteenth Amendment failed, it would fail because of its inherent defects and not because of judicial hamstringing."[96] Chafee's speculation is consistent with the commitment of pre-New Deal progressivism to accord enlarged scope to legislative innovation and experimentation. But it significantly understates the austere depth of Holmes's positivism or the intensity of Brandeis's commitment to enforcing prohibition.[97]

Both were on vivid display a year later in *United States v. Katz*,[98] in which the Court was called upon to interpret Section 10 of the Volstead Act. Section 10 required persons who manufactured and sold liquor to keep detailed and readily available records. The question was whether Section 10 applied only to those authorized by the Volstead Act legally to manufacture and sell liquor (for religious and other purposes), or whether it applied to *all* persons, so that bootleggers who failed to document their sales committed the independent crime of violating Section 10 by failing to keep records of their illegal transactions. The latter interpretation would be most far-reaching and unusual, and the district court accordingly quashed an indictment against a bootlegger for violating Section 10.

Holmes's attitude came through loud and clear at the oral argument of the case, when he "observed that it seemed the prohibition act was designed to permit the use of every weapon by the prosecution, even to the extent of poison and entrapment, in enforcing the law, and also remarked that defense counsel was attributing to the law a sportsman-like character which it did not possess."[99] With their commitment to strict prohibition enforcement, Holmes, Brandeis, Taft, and Van Devanter voted in conference to reverse the district court. Stone, representing a majority of five, was assigned to write an opinion affirming the trial court by narrowly interpreting Section 10. His opinion, heavily edited by Van Devanter, held

Prohibition & Law Enforcement

that "General terms descriptive of a class of persons made subject to a criminal statute may and should be limited where the literal application of the statute would lead to extreme or absurd results, and where the legislative purpose gathered from the whole Act would be satisfied by a more limited interpretation."[100] In the end almost the entire Court agreed to join Stone's opinion. Only Brandeis insisted on noting a lonely dissent.[101]

The following year Brandeis and Holmes showed just how far they were prepared to go in *Maul v. United States*, a case involving Coast Guard seizures of vessels on the high seas. In a separate opinion joined by Holmes, Brandeis broadly asserted that the seizure was constitutional because "[t]here is no limitation upon the right of the sovereign to seize without a warrant vessels registered under its laws, similar to that imposed by the common law and the Constitution upon the arrest of persons and upon the seizure of 'papers and effects.'"[102] Brandeis and Holmes were willing to hold that the Coast Guard could seize liquor-laden U.S. vessels on the high seas even in the absence of a warrant and even in the absence of specific statutory authorization. In a dramatic behind-the-scenes confrontation, however, the Court refused to accept this conclusion.

Brandeis was originally assigned the opinion in *Maul*. But after Brandeis's proposed opinion was circulated, Van Devanter objected to its premise. He preferred instead to rest the resolution of the case on the ground that the Coast Guard's seizure had been authorized by statute. The Court ultimately opted for Van Devanter's approach.[103] Despite its enthusiasm for unleashing law enforcement, the Taft Court was unwilling altogether to jettison legal restraints on searches and seizures, even of U.S. ships on the high seas.

The historian Lisa McGirr has observed that prohibition "left a powerful impression on the federal state, tilting it toward policing, surveillance, and punishment."[104] The Taft Court played a dual role with regard to this tilt. While insisting on maintaining important forms of legality, it also authored decisions that transformed Fourth Amendment jurisprudence to enhance police control over civilian behavior. By so doing, the Court gave powerful but legally inflected support to the emerging needs of the administrative state to manage the conduct of its population.

Notes

1. For a sampling of the myriad of articles about the crime wave in the 1920s, see *Huge Crime Drive Planned; Authorities Here Unite Forward on Underworld*, LOS ANGELES TIMES (November 21, 1929), at A1; *War on Crime*, WASHINGTON POST (December 25, 1928), at 6; *Lawlessness: The Shame of America*, 77 CURRENT OPINION 15 (1924); *Mothers Blamed for Painted Faces and Daring Dress*, WASHINGTON POST (October 29, 1924), at 3; C.P. Connolly, *America – Land of the Lawbreaker*, MCCLURE'S MAGAZINE (July 1923), at 40; W.A. Shumaker, *Probation and the Crime Wave*, 26 LAW NOTES 123 (1922); *Crime Wave Fills Prisons*, NEW YORK TIMES (May 15, 1922), at 20; *Remedy for Rising Crime Wave Essential to National Welfare, Bar Inquiry Shows*, NEW YORK TIMES (March 12, 1922), at 1; *Governor Sees Crime Wave Due to "Living Fast"*, NEW YORK TIMES (January 20, 1922), at 1; *Crime Wave Now Greatest in Secret Service Records*, NEW YORK TIMES (December 30, 1920), at 1; *Chicago Crime Wave Still Sweeps On*, NEW YORK TIMES (December 24, 1920), at 2; *Judges Draft Bills To End Crime Wave; Measures Would Increase Penalties and Deal with Bail of Past Offenders*, NEW YORK TIMES (December 22, 1920), at 2; *Simon Says Drugs Cause Crime Wave; Declares Prohibition Has Driven Criminals from Whisky to Narcotics*, NEW YORK TIMES (December 19, 1920), at 2; *200 Police Chiefs Meet; Crime Wave as By-Product of War Cited by Convention Speaker*, NEW YORK TIMES (June 8, 1920), at 11; *Our Criminals Are New Ones; National Crime Wave Due to Them, Says Pinkerton*, LOS ANGELES TIMES (January 6, 1920), at II5.
2. Harry Elmer Barnes, *Reflections on the Crime Wave*, BOOKMAN (September 1926), at 44. Often the crime wave was linked to the overproduction of statutory law. See, e.g., James Truslow Adams, *Hoover and Law Observance*, 82 THE FORUM 1, 2–5 (1929). The linkage was well expressed in a letter to the *New York Times*:

    > Lawlessness is rampant throughout the country today as never before . . . and it is no idle statement to say that America is the most lawless nation on earth. Nowhere is there such utter disrespect and contempt of law as here, and the question naturally arises, What is the cause of it?
    >
    > It can be summed up briefly: Too much law by stupid legislation and a general indifference and apathy by the people toward public officials. The adherents of prohibition promised us a sort of millennium which was to follow the adoption and enforcement of the Eighteenth Amendment. Results speak for themselves, and instead of a utopian Sahara we have a land where crime and acts of violence fill the first page of every daily newspaper.
    >
    > Laws that cannot be enforced only breed contempt and hypocrisy, and should be wiped off the statute books. Eliminate 50 per cent. of the existing laws and give honest enforcement to the rest of them.

    Henry Engleken, *Letter to the Editor, Lawlessness*, NEW YORK TIMES (August 17, 1924), at 12. See *Laws and More Laws*, WASHINGTON POST (June 19, 1928), at 6.
3. *Beck on the Crime Wave*, NEW YORK TIMES (January 23, 1921), at 14. See WILLIAM GIBBS MCADOO, THE CHALLENGE: LIQUOR AND LAWLESSNESS VERSUS CONSTITUTIONAL GOVERNMENT 41 (New York: Century Co. 1928) ("The transcendent problem before the country today is the problem of law and order.").

Prohibition & Law Enforcement

4. *Vote Lawlessness Gravest Problem; Plurality of Leading Citizens in National Economic League Rank It First*, NEW YORK TIMES (November 29, 1926), at 21. The poll interrogated the National Council of the National Economic League:

> [T]he members of the council were asked if they believed an abnormal amount of lawlessness and disrespect for law existed in this country at present, and 1489 answered in the affirmative and 105 in the negative. This question was then propounded:
> "If so, what in your opinion is most to blame ... ?"

These causes were given:

Improper laws	649
Lax enforcement	895
Condition of public sentiment	1,065

The question "If you think it is due, wholly or in part, to improper laws, what specific laws in your opinion are most responsible?" brought the following replies:

Prohibition laws, Volstead act, Eighteenth Amendment	507
Too many laws	105
Laws relating to personal liberty	84
Laws governing courts and criminal procedure	75

Id. See Lawlessness Our Greatest Problem, 92 LITERARY DIGEST 24 (January 1, 1927); Richard Lee Strout, *Why Are We Lawless?*, WOMAN'S JOURNAL (December 1930), at 12 ("An increasing number of people" consider the problem of criminality "the most serious one before the American nation. They read daily reports of lawlessness, of rampant crime, of police impotency, of corruption in office, of alliance between authorities and underworld, of men shot down in cold blood, of no subsequent arrests.").

5. *Inaugural Address of President Hoover*, 71 CONG. REC. 4 (March 4, 1929). *See Hoover's Call to Battle against Crime*, 100 LITERARY DIGEST 5 (March 16, 1929) ("[Our new President's predominating purpose would seem to be to lead the nation in fighting that spirit of lawlessness which he considers 'the most malign' of all dangers confronting our democracy. Part of this problem, as he sees it, is the enforcement of the Eighteenth Amendment, and, by emphasizing this at the very outset, he plunges immediately into our hottest and most controversial domestic perplexity."). According to Taft, this part of Hoover's inaugural was "suggested and contributed" by Stone, to whom Hoover was very close. WHT to Samuel H. Fisher (May 2, 1929) (Taft papers); ALPHEUS THOMAS MASON, HARLAN FISKE STONE: PILLAR OF THE LAW 271 (New York: Viking 1956). In a speech that Taft believed "was largely the result" of Hoover's "conference with Stone," WHT to Samuel H. Fisher (May 2, 1929) (Taft papers), Hoover declared that "the enforcement and obedience to the laws of the United States, both Federal and State" was "the dominant issue before the American people." *Text of President Hoover's Speech on Law Observance*, NEW YORK TIMES (April 23, 1929), at 2. *See Hoover Demands Respect for Law; Calls It Nation's "Dominant Issue" in Speech Before Publishers Here*, NEW YORK TIMES (April 23, 1929), at 1. It is quite striking that if these were Stone's views, he was nevertheless an unreliable partner to Taft, Van Devanter, Holmes, Brandeis, and Sanford in their

relentless support of prohibition. In the press it was reported that Hoover's speech was "encouraged by Chief Justice Taft," who had urged the president "to curb lawlessness" and to show that "in the face of a widespread belief that government authorities themselves consider prohibition enforcement efforts futile," the new Hoover administration was nevertheless "determined to show" that it "means business." Theodore C. Wallen, *Foundations of Nation Menaced by Lawlessness, Mr. Hoover Tells Country in Plea for Observance*, NEW YORK HERALD TRIBUNE (April 23, 1929), at 16.
6. *Inaugural Address of President Hoover*, supra note 5, at 5.
7. *Hoover Demands Respect for Law*, supra note 5.

> In order to dispel certain illusions in the public mind on this subject, let me say at once that while violations of law have been increased by inclusion of crimes under the Eighteenth Amendment and by the vast sums that are poured into the hands of the criminal classes by the patronage of illicit liquor by otherwise responsible citizens, yet this is only one segment of our problem. I have purposely cited the extent of murder, burglary, robbery, forgery and embezzlement, because only a small percentage of these can be attributed to the Eighteenth Amendment. In fact, of the total number of convictions for felony last year, less than 8 per cent came from that source. That is, therefore, but a sector of the invasion of lawlessness.
>
> What we are facing today is something far larger and far more fundamental – the possibility that respect for law as law is fading from the sensibilities of our people.

Text of President Hoover's Speech on Law Observance, supra note 5. See *Inaugural Address of President Hoover*, supra note 5, at 4 ("The problem is much wider than [prohibition]."). Hoover's claim that crime was increasing apart from prohibition was vigorously disputed. See J.C. Burnham, *New Perspectives on the Prohibition "Experiment" of the 1920's*, 2 JOURNAL OF SOCIAL HISTORY 51, 61 (1968) ("During the 1920's there was almost universal public belief that a 'crime wave' existed in the United States. . . . [T]here is no firm evidence of this supposed upsurge in lawlessness."); George W. Kirchwey, *Our Lawlessness that Alarms Hoover*, NEW YORK TIMES (May 26, 1929), § 5 at 5; *The "New Hoover's" War-Cry against Crime*, 101 LITERARY DIGEST 5 (May 4, 1929) ("The part of the President's speech that arouses the most controversy is his argument that Prohibition plays but a small part in the general reign of lawlessness."); *Crime and the Bootlegger*, 98 LITERARY DIGEST 13 (August 25, 1928) ("The spider in the center of the American web of crime is the bootlegger."). The general popular belief was nevertheless that Hoover meant to initiate a strong drive to enforce prohibition, so that, "for the first time in its life, a thoroughgoing effort to enforce the Prohibition law is to be made." *Start of the Great Hoover Dry Drive*, 100 LITERARY DIGEST 5 (March 30, 1929). A popular theory was that "Hoover is at once too much of a realist to believe people can be made dry by legislation, and too much of a doer to be satisfied with the present situation. Assuming that this correctly represents his attitude, . . . the only way he can effectively move to correct this situation is by first satisfying even the most enthusiastic drys that he has done everything possible to enforce the law." *Id.* at 6. See *Making Bootleggers Felons*, 100 LITERARY DIGEST 11 (March 23, 1929).
8. *A Long Task*, NEW YORK TIMES (May 11, 1929), at 18. As Senator George Wharton Pepper once observed, "The question of law enforcement is popularly thought of just now in connection with prohibition enforcement." 64 CONG. REC. 389

Prohibition & Law Enforcement

(December 13, 1922). "We cannot agree, however, with the implication by Mr. Hoover that the Eighteenth Amendment has played only an insignificant role in the present growth of lawlessness. ... In any long view of American lawlessness the passage of the Eighteenth Amendment must be taken as marking an abrupt turn for the worse." *The War against Crime*, NEW YORK HERALD TRIBUNE (April 23, 1929), at 26.

9. WHT to Percy L. Edwards (January 28, 1927) (Taft papers). Taft understood, as Richard Nixon later understood, that support for law enforcement could create a powerful political platform. Taft was concerned to transform anxiety over crime into pressure "to stir up Legislatures to an effort to furnish machinery for the better apprehension of criminals." *Id*. Like Nixon, who claimed to speak for the "silent majority," Taft purported to speak for "the forgotten man, the victim of the murderer and robber and the criminal." Quoted in *Eighty-Third Annual Report of the Prison Association of New York*, reprinted in E. R. CASS, REVIEW OF NATIONAL CRIME COMMISSION CONFERENCE 9 (Albany: J.B. Lyon Co. 1928). "[S]omebody or some organization," Taft argued, ought "to look after the Forgotten Man – that is, society at large" – in order "to have an improvement in the administration of the criminal law as we ought to have." *American Law Institute Holds Fifth Annual Meeting*, 13 AMERICAN BAR ASSOCIATION JOURNAL 243, 246 (1927). Taft's plea was received as "stirring." *National Clearing House of Criminal Statistics Urged*, WASHINGTON POST (November 4, 1927), at 1. It was said that Taft, "in a speech delivered recently, packed into a single phrase his criticism of American justice as it is now directed. This phrase was: 'The forgotten man.'" *The Forgotten Man*, CHICAGO DAILY TRIBUNE (December 14, 1927), at 10.

In 1905, Taft had issued his famous challenge that "the administration of the criminal law in all the states in the Union ... is a disgrace to our civilization." William Howard Taft, *The Administration of Criminal Law*, 15 YALE LAW JOURNAL 1, 11 (1905). The challenge became a rallying cry for reform and was later deemed "one of the most beneficent utterances in American history." *What's Wrong with the Law?*, NEW YORK WORLD (November 11, 1926), at 14. As chief justice, Taft continued to campaign to rouse "the people to demand that an improvement be made in stiffening the powers of criminal prosecution, in enlarging the police, and in giving the Judges in the Courts more power to control the trials." WHT to George W. Burton (August 4, 1925) (Taft papers). Taft believed that the best way to diminish "crime ... is to make more efficient your laws for prosecuting it. ... [W]e can not abandon the police force in the thorough prosecution of crime as we find it, and hope that general causes will then take the place of prosecution to restrain it. They won't do it." WHT to Moses Strauss (March 5, 1928) (Taft papers). Taft displayed real violence of feeling on the subject, writing, for example, to his son Charles, who was a public prosecutor:

> I don't agree with the opponents of capital punishment at all. I think that those who commit crimes of violence in robbery are directly affected by the fear of capital punishment, and that it leaves the public helpless to abolish that as the extreme penalty. ... This man Darrow, who came very near being convicted of suborning perjury, is a great advocate of the abolition of the death penalty. I can not understand what the vogue is which makes him so popular a lecturer. ... I think the escape of those two young Jews who tortured that other young Jew to death is one of the greatest miscarriages of justice that we have had, in that it did not result in their execution.

WHT to Charles P. Taft 2nd (July 9, 1927) (Taft papers). As the decade progressed, Taft's campaign for efficient law enforcement reached a crescendo. *See, e.g.,* Basil Manly, *Chief Justice Taft Replies to Three Vital Questions,* BOSTON GLOBE (January 9, 1929), at 32; William Howard Taft, *Some Possible Reforms in Our Criminal Law,* ST. LOUIS POST-DISPATCH (December 9, 1928) (Supplement), at 2; Oliver P. Newman, *Stop Helping the Criminal: An Authorized Interview with the Chief Justice William Howard Taft,* COLLIER'S WEEKLY (January 22, 1927), at 8.

10. Felix Frankfurter, *Law and Order,* 9 YALE REVIEW 225, 226 (1920) ("Were the proverbial messenger from Mars to visit this country he would find ... a veritable devil's dance, with 'law and order' emblazoned on the banners."). At the beginning of the 1920s, the country was rocked by coal and railway strikes that produced what Harding, in an address to Congress on the industrial crisis, called "a state of lawlessness shocking to every conception of American law and order. ... In these strikes ... rights have been denied by assault and violence, by armed lawlessness ... until liberty is a mockery and the law a matter of common contempt." *The President's Address to Congress on Industrial Crisis,* NEW YORK TIMES (August 19, 1922), at 2. Harding's "remarks condemnatory of lawlessness growing out of the coal and railway strikes were commended heartily by Democrats as well as Republicans." *Harding's Stand on Strike; Will Use All Power to Keep Roads Running and Let Men Work,* NEW YORK TIMES (August 19, 1922), at 1. It also received editorial approval. *See The President to Congress,* NEW YORK TIMES (August 19, 1922), at 10. Taft believed that "the lawlessness of the trades-unions must be restrained." WHT to Mrs. Frederick J. Manning (October 6, 1922) (Taft papers). *See* William Howard Taft, *Gompers and the Law* (January 12, 1921), in VIVIAN, at 525 ("[T]he labor unions have lost much of their influence for good by their arbitrary abuse of their power and by their spirit of lawlessness.").

11. "The epidemic of lawlessness that has swept the United States in the last few years is held by many influential southern papers to be a direct result of the lynching bees and the fact that the participants in these go practically unpunished." *Law Breaking,* LOS ANGELES TIMES (October 3, 1923), at II4. In Congress, debates over the Dwyer antilynching bill turned on the need to combat "contempt for law and order." 62 CONG. REC. 547 (December 19, 1921) (statement of Representative Ansorge). "Whenever anyone excuses an act that is not lawful, no matter what the provocation may be, he invites the collapse of all authorized government. He is opening a door to lawlessness, the extent of which no man can see." 62 CONG. REC. 543 (December 19, 1921) (statement of Representative Fess). "[L]awlessness of this character allowed to go unchecked and unpunished will eventually seek out as its victims any against whom there may be a local prejudice." 62 CONG. REC. 1700 (January 25, 1922) (statement of Representative Mondell). Taft had been one of several prominent Republicans who, at the request of the National Association for the Advancement of Colored People, had petitioned Senators for an investigation of lynching and race riots. ARTHUR I. WASKOW, FROM RACE RIOT TO SIT-IN, 1919 AND THE 1960S, at 205 (Garden City: Anchor Books 1966). Taft publicly branded lynching as a cause of lawlessness equal to that of organized crime:

> [L]ynch law, prompted by the same lawlessness and a sense of cheapness of human life, and often a real race cruelty, has been until very recently looked

upon as an outbreak not under control. It has rarely been made the subject of investigation and prosecution because supported by neighborhood sympathy.

Quoted in Newman, *supra* note 9, at 9.

12. The Klan was widely understood to be a symptom of "the penetration" into the North of a "Southern spirit of lawlessness." *Lawlessness as an American Tradition*, 74 AMERICAN REVIEW OF REVIEWS 653, 654 (1926). It was also excoriated as a form of "organized lawlessness," Arthur Sears Henning, *Frown Would End Volstead Terror Reign*, CHICAGO DAILY TRIBUNE (March 30, 1929), at 1, as an instrument "of terror, oppression, and violence." Knights of the Ku Klux Klan v. Strayer, 26 F.2d 727, 728 (W.D. Pa. 1928). Ironically, the Klan was also regarded as "the shock troops of the prohibition forces," because "many of its atrocities the klan commits in the name of unofficial enforcement of the Volstead act." Henning, *supra*. Prohibition helped fuel the revival of the Klan in the 1920s:

> With prohibition came the bootlegger, and many anxious parents, seeing their sons and daughters going in for "petting parties," all-night automobile escapades and bad gin, sincerely thought the foundations of society were being undermined by the vicious elements identified in their minds with the illegitimate traffic in liquor. In town after town, all over the country, the first act of the newly formed Klan was to horsewhip the proprietor of the most notorious local speakeasy, and no inconsistency was felt because in the party which did so there might be men who themselves drank.

The Rise and Fall of the K.K.K., 53 NEW REPUBLIC 33, 34 (1927). Taft himself believed that "[t]he progress of the Klu Klux Klan [sic] in our country of course is a subject that should cause us humiliation and arouse in us an earnest wish to suppress such lawlessness as it evidently encourages." WHT to Mrs. Bellamy Storer (September 20, 1923) (Taft papers). *See* WHT to Mrs. Bellamy Storer (November 13, 1923) (Taft papers) (predicting that the popularity of the Klan would subside. "The absurdities and the extent of the lawlessness for which it is responsible create opposition. It carries its own antidote.").

The confluence of prohibition, excessive lawmaking, labor unrest, lynching, and the Klan, formed a witches' brew of anxiety over the rule of law. A typical example is this editorial in the *Newark Evening News*:

> That today in this country the fundamental principle underlying all Anglo-Saxon political order, "the rule of law," is threatened is no idle foreboding. Forces from without and within the law are at work with their undermining influences.
>
> Legislators at both the National Capitol and at the state capitols have enacted a mass of legislation which in complexity and volume is without parallel in the ancient or modern world. They have attempted to uplift society by the mere passage of a statute.
>
> The inevitable results in the fabric of society itself have made themselves felt. Flagrant violations of the prohibition amendment, an integral part of the supreme law of the land, furnish an incontrovertible evidence of the growing disrespect for the rule of law. Growing forces of lawlessness are to be seen in the advocates of direct action among the extremists in labor circles. Lynching furnishes another conspicuous example. The misguided efforts of thousands of well-meaning citizens in the Ku Klux Klan are employed to accomplish outside the law results which in themselves and if effected by other than extra-legal means would win the respect of their fellow citizens.

Promise of Bettering Law and Legal Procedure, NEWARK EVENING NEWS (February 26, 1923), at 8. For similar observations by vice president-to-be Charles G. Dawes, see *Dawes Turns Scorn on National Faults*, NEW YORK TIMES (February 23, 1923), at 5.

13. M. Browning Carrott, *The Supreme Court and Law and Order in the 1920s*, MARYLAND HISTORIAN (Fall/Winter 1985), at 12, 22. See *Taft Says States Must Curb Crime and Lawlessness*, WASHINGTON POST (January 18, 1927), at 4. At the very outset of the decade, Taft noted that "The wave of crime which is sweeping over the country is an aftermath of the war, a feature of the present unrest, and it is aggravated by the demoralization in the enforcement of prohibition of the manufacture and sale of liquor." William Howard Taft, *The Inauguration* (March 4, 1921), in VIVIAN, at 552. For Pierce Butler's discussion of the dangers of "the spirit of lawlessness that threatens now," see Pierce Butler, *Some Opportunities and Duties of Lawyers*, 9 AMERICAN BAR ASSOCIATION JOURNAL 583, 585–87 (1923).

14. Robert M. Cover, *The Left, the Right and the First Amendment: 1918–1928*, 40 MARYLAND LAW REVIEW 349, 352–54 (1981). Taft expressed this precise point in 1919, when he exhorted the newly formed American Legion to remember that it was "their obedience to orders and law which made them the efficient force they were. It was their self-restraint that made them effective. ... Liberty regulated by law is their only safe guide. ... The disposition of small local groups of American Legion men to take the law into their own hands, to regulate by force what shall appear upon the stage in opera or in a play, and to suppress by threatened or actual violence speech of which they do not approve should be discountenanced and restrained. It is lawlessness awakening the sympathy of the people that is most dangerous to the state and our liberties." William Howard Taft, *The American Legion* (December 2, 1919), in VIVIAN, at 316.

15. *See, e.g.*, Truax v. Corrigan, 257 U.S. 312 (1921); *infra* Chapter 42.
16. Edward S. Corwin, *Constitutional Law in 1921–1922*, 16 AMERICAN POLITICAL SCIENCE REVIEW 612, 628 (1922).
17. 257 U.S. 184 (1921) See *infra* Chapter 39, at 1239–54.
18. 259 U.S. 344 (1922). See *infra* Chapter 40, at 1304–17.
19. For a discussion, see Cover, *supra* note 14, at 358–63. *See also* Dorchy v. Kansas, 272 U.S. 306 (1926); Pa. R.R. Co. v. U.S. R.R. Labor Bd., 261 U.S. 72 (1923). Taft had long associated "lawlessness and anarchy" with labor strikes. William Howard Taft, *Court Injunctions* (November 15, 1919), in VIVIAN, at 308.
20. 278 U.S. 63 (1928).
21. *Zimmerman*, 278 U.S. at 77. *Zimmerman* should be read in light of Taft Court decisions upholding state efforts to crack down on left-wing incendiary speech. *See, e.g.*, Whitney v. California, 274 U.S. 357 (1927); Gitlow v. New York, 268 U.S. 652 (1925). *Zimmerman* arose in the context of a habeas petition challenging the constitutionality of the New York statute under which the defendant had been imprisoned. In dissent, McReynolds charged:

> [O]ver and over again this Court has asserted that it will not permit habeas corpus to perform the office of a writ of error.

Prohibition & Law Enforcement

>It must now be accepted as settled doctrine in this Court that one is not deprived of any federal right merely by being put on trial for violating a state statute which conflicts with the Federal Constitution. Nor is one deprived of his federal right solely because he may be imprisoned after conviction of violating a state statute admittedly in conflict with the Federal Constitution.
>
>It follows that when the petition for habeas corpus alleged that plaintiff in error was imprisoned under a charge of violating a state statute said to be unconstitutional and void, no real federal question was raised.

278 U.S. at 83–84 (McReynolds, J., dissenting). In a note to Van Devanter, who authored *Zimmerman*, Holmes wrote that he agreed with McReynolds that a habeas petition could not be used to "assail ... the constitutionality of the law upon which the judgment was based. The judgment is no less valid when based on bad than when on good law. This I think sound doctrine." OWH to WVD (November 15, 1928) (Van Devanter papers). Holmes added, however, that "if a State chooses to say that the validity of the judgment shall depend on the validity of their statute or for any other reason that the constitutional question may be raised by habeas corpus, the state has power to do so, and the question will be raised and we shall have to deal with it. That I understand is the case in New York, and it seems to me something to the above effect should be said." *Id.* According to Stone's docket book, Taft had at conference initially voted with McReynolds to reverse the judgment below.

22. On the controversial origins of the New York statute, see *The Klan Defies a State*, 77 LITERARY DIGEST 12–13 (June 9, 1923). On the sordid details of the case before the Court, see DAVID M. CHALMERS, HOODED AMERICANISM: THE HISTORY OF THE KU KLUX KLAN 1865-1965, at 258–59 (2d ed., Garden City: Doubleday 1981). *Zimmerman* was authored by Van Devanter, who later remarked to a confidante: "Personally I should be very loathe to stigmatize the general membership of the old Klan and equally loathe to stigmatize the general membership of the present order. Indeed, I have some near relatives who were members of the former Klan and for whom I entertain a high and affectionate regard." WVD to Joseph M. Hill (November 29, 1928) (Van Devanter papers).

23. 261 U.S. 86 (1923). For a discussion of *Moore*, see Eric M. Freedman, *Milestones in Habeas Corpus: Part II – Leo Frank Lives: Untangling the Historical Roots of Meaningful Federal Habeas Corpus Review of State Conviction*, 51 ALABAMA LAW REVIEW 1467, 1497–530 (2000); James Weldon Johnson & Herbert J. Seligmann, *Legal Aspects of the Negro Problem*, 140 ANNALS OF THE AMERICAN ACADEMY OF POLITICAL AND SOCIAL SCIENCE 90, 94–96 (1928).

24. 237 U.S. 309 (1915). The opinion for the Court in *Moore* was authored by Holmes, who had dissented in *Mangum*. The Court in *Mangum*, speaking through Pitney, essentially affirmed the proposition "that a man is entitled only to the justice which the community gives him and that the federal government cannot undertake the task of civilizing the whole country in spite of the wishes of the local communities." *Legal Lynching and the Constitution*, 34 NEW REPUBLIC 84, 85 (1923). McReynolds and Sutherland dissented from *Moore's* effective overruling of *Mangum*. *Moore*, 261 U.S. at 92–102 (McReynolds and Sutherland, JJ., dissenting). For a discussion of the appalling events leading up to the trial in *Moore*, see RICHARD C. CORTNER, A MOB INTENT ON DEATH: THE NAACP AND THE ARKANSAS RIOT CASES (Middletown: Wesleyan University Press 1988);

THE TAFT COURT

W. Langley Biegert, *Legacy of Resistance: Uncovering the History of Collective Action by Black Agricultural Workers in Central East Arkansas from the 1860s to the 1930s*, 32 JOURNAL OF SOCIAL HISTORY 73 (1998). On the aftermath of *Moore*, see J.S. Waterman & E.E. Overton, *The Aftermath of Moore v. Dempsey*, 18 ST. LOUIS LAW REVIEW 118 (1933).

25. Cover attributes the reversal of *Mangum* to the personal influence of Taft. *See* Cover, *supra* note 14, at 355–57. Taft himself said of *Moore* that "I would have written the opinion in a different way and would have dwelt more on our hesitation at interfering with the state court's decision and the state rule that subsequently discovered evidence is not receivable as a basis for a rehearing etc. But I doubt whether the opinion as now framed will make an uncomfortable precedent. No state officers will ever again be fools enough to let the defendants make an uncontestable case by affidavits and then demur." WHT to WVD (February 13, 1923) (Van Devanter papers). In response to Frankfurter's inquiry about how *Mangum* "was departed from," Brandeis answered: "Well – Pitney was gone, the late Chief was gone, Day was gone – the Court had changed." *Brandeis-Frankfurter Conversations*, at 316 (July 3, 1923).

26. *Mangum*, 237 U.S. at 350 (Holmes, J., dissenting). T.R. Powell summarized the lesson of *Moore* to be that "in criminal proceedings a court must behave like a court and not like a vigilance committee." Thomas Reed Powell, *The Supreme Court and State Police Power, 1922–1930 – VIII*, 18 VIRGINIA LAW REVIEW 481, 505 (1932). The significance of *Moore* should not be overstated. In 1927, the lawyers for Sacco and Vanzetti, in a last-ditch effort to save their clients from execution, cited *Moore* in a petition for an emergency writ of habeas corpus which they argued in front of Holmes at his summer home in Massachusetts. Holmes reported to Laski that the lawyers

> were here two hours and a half and said all that they had to say and I declined to issue the writ. I said that I had no authority to take the prisoners out of the custody of a State Court having jurisdiction over the persons and dealing with a crime under State law – that the only ground for such an interference would be want of jurisdiction in the tribunal or, as according to the allegations in the negro case that I wrote where a mob in and around the court ready to lynch the prisoner, jury, counsel and possibly the judges if they did not convict, made the trial a mere form. They said these facts went only to motives ... and what was the difference whether the motive was fear or the prejudices alleged in this case. I said most differences are differences of degree, and I thought that the line must be drawn between external force, and prejudice – which could be alleged in every case. I could not feel a doubt, but the result has been already some letters telling me that I am a monster of injustice – in various forms of words, from men who evidently don't know anything about the matter, but who have the customary readiness to impute evil for any result that they don't like. The house of one of the jurymen was blown up two or three nights ago.

OWH to Harold Laski (August 18, 1927), in 2 HOLMES-LASKI CORRESPONDENCE, at 971. Two weeks later Holmes wrote:

> So far as one who has not read the evidence has a right to an opinion I think the row that has been made idiotical, if considered on its merits, but of course it is not on the merits that the row is made, but because it gives the extremists a chance to yell. If justice is the interest why do they not talk about the infinitely worse cases of the blacks? My prejudices were all with

Prohibition & Law Enforcement

>Felix's book. But after all, it's simply showing, if it was right, that the case was tried in a hostile atmosphere. I doubt if anyone would say that there was no evidence warranting a conviction .... I held that I had no power to grant a *habeas corpus* and that I ought not to grant a stay, if I had power, on the application for *certiorari*, as I thought there was no case for the writ. I wrote an opinion on the spot, but left it open to apply to another Justice. They then went to Brandeis who declined to act on the ground that he had been too closely connected with the case. My secretary says that thereafter a N.Y. paper called *The Worker* had in its window "Brandeis, Pontius Pilate," and followed the analogy describing him as washing his hands of innocent blood, etc., etc. How can one respect that sort of thing? It isn't a matter of reason, but simply shrieking because the world is not the kind of a world they want – a trouble that most of us feel in some way.

OWH to Harold Laski (September 1, 1927), *id.* at 975–76. Sacco and Vanzetti's lawyers also sought to obtain stays from Taft and Stone, who each refused. Taft commented to his brother: "Brandeis, who is near Boston at Chatham, avoided action by saying that he was in some way affiliated with some of the persons that were interested in trying to secure a commutation or pardon. This is quite characteristic of Brandeis when he does not wish to decide a case that he knows he ought to decide in the proper way. It is true that his wife had lent a house she owned to take care of Mrs. Sacco, and as Brandeis and Frankfurter are very close to each other, perhaps his justification was genuine. Holmes stood up like a rock and gave his reasons, which he has often strongly expressed in the court on a similar issue." WHT to Horace D. Taft (August 25, 1927) (Taft papers).

27. 273 U.S. 510 (1927).
28. James L. Magrish, *Due Process of Law and a Fair Trial: The Tumey Case*, 1 UNIVERSITY OF CINCINNATI LAW REVIEW 338, 339–41 (1927).
29. *Tumey*, 273 U.S. at 521.
30. *Tumey* involved a village that authorized its mayor to receive $12 in costs for each conviction. *Id.* at 523.
31. Fines for the violation of Ohio's prohibition statute were between $100 and $1,000 for the first offense, between $300 and $2,000 for the second offense, and for a third and each subsequent offense between $500 and $2,000, as well as a year's imprisonment. *Id.* at 516.
32. WHT to James R. Angell (December 12, 1927) (Taft papers).
33. Between May 11, 1923, and December 31, 1923, the liquor court of the tiny village of North College Hill had assessed "upwards of $20,000" in fines, from which the village had received a little more than half. The mayor, who was the chief executive of the village and responsible for its budget, had also received for his personal income $696.35 from the "fees and costs" of convicted liquor defendants. *Tumey*, 273 U.S. at 521–22.
34. *Id.* at 518. The village used the income to fund marshals, inspectors, and detectives. *Id.*
35. *Dry League's Pet Measure in Ohio Faces Disaster*, CHICAGO DAILY TRIBUNE (October 17, 1927), at 4.
36. *See Outrageous*, CLEVELAND PLAIN DEALER (November 8, 1926), at 10 ("It would be difficult to imagine a more deplorable perversion of justice than the Ohio law which gives county wide jurisdiction to township justices of the peace. ...

A township justice who is elected by a mere handful of votes is, under the Ohio law, given authority to carry on liquor raiding operations in any part of a county having a population of over a million.... Under this provision the country justices establish permanent raiding squads.... It is, of course, wholly needless to remark that many of these agents are in no degree interested in the enforcement of the prohibition laws. It is seldom that this type goes after bootleggers or rum runners. Its activities are largely confined to violent raids on private dwellings, preferably in districts inhabited by foreign-born residents. Unfortunate victims are dragged before venal justices, heavy fines imposed, and the money thus obtained so split that the raiders themselves obtain greater remuneration than they could possibly hope for in any respectable bread-winning activity. In some cases villages and townships are enriched; in most cases the rural magistrates are rewarded with copious fees. In every case fees depend upon convictions, a condition so obviously unsound as to warrant no discussion.").

37. *Tumey*, 273 U.S. at 535. *Tumey* was regarded as "a case of considerable significance," Robert E. Cushman, *Constitutional Law in 1926–1927*, 22 AMERICAN POLITICAL SCIENCE REVIEW 70, 101 (1928), because it shook "the very foundation upon which rests the Justice of the Peace system in the United States." *Constitutional Law – Officers Acting in Judicial Capacity Are Disqualified by Interest in Controversy – Due Process of Law*, 13 VIRGINIA LAW REVIEW 584, 585 (1927). See *Justice – Above and Below*, 13 AMERICAN BAR ASSOCIATION JOURNAL 266 (1927); John M. Pfiffner, *The Mayor's Court and Due Process*, 12 IOWA LAW REVIEW 393, 393–403 (1927); *The Constitutionality of Fee Compensations for Courts*, 36 YALE LAW JOURNAL 1171 (1927). In Dugan v. Ohio, 277 U.S. 61 (1928), Taft, also writing for a unanimous court, upheld a magistrate court in a different Ohio village, because, although the mayor presided as judge, he was paid a salary from the general fund that was independent of the outcome of particular cases, and because the mayor had judicial functions but no executive functions. *Id.* at 65. For modern development of the *Tumey* doctrine, see Ward v. Village of Monroeville, 409 U.S. 57 (1972); *Safeguarding the Litigant's Constitutional Right to a Fair and Impartial Forum: A Due Process Approach to Improprieties Arising from Judicial Campaign Contributions from Lawyers*, 86 MICHIGAN LAW REVIEW 382, 392–96 (1987).
38. *Tumey*, 273 U.S. at 523.
39. WHT to Horace D. Taft (March 7, 1927) (Taft papers). The *Cincinnati Times-Star*, which was owned by Taft's elder brother Charles, proclaimed that the decision was "one of the most momentous in America's legal history." Quoted in *A Blow at "Speed-Trap" Courts*, 92 LITERARY DIGEST 13 (March 26, 1927). The "sweeping" importance of the decision was widely noted in the press. *Id.*
40. WHT to Mrs. Frederick J. Manning (March 6, 1927) (Taft papers).
41. Taft hoped that *Tumey* "will not greatly embarrass the Legislature of Ohio.... They will have to spend some more money to pay the compensation of their justices of the peace and inferior judges, and they will have to separate the office of mayor of a village from that of the judge in prohibition cases where the fines are permitted." WHT to Moses Strauss (March 8, 1927) (Taft papers). Taft sadly noted that "We could not avoid declaring the law in respect to such trials to be contrary to due process. It is one of those instances in which an enthusiastic Attorney General anxious to secure the proper enforcement of the

prohibition law forgot the rights of individual defendants as secured by the Constitution." *Id.*

42. WHT to Mrs. Frederick J. Manning (March 6, 1927) (Taft papers). Taft noted that "Wayne Wheeler was counsel in the case, but we have to distribute our favors equally and justly." *Id.* In fact the powerful Anti-Saloon League did not take *Tumey* lightly. It immediately caused the Ohio Legislature to submit to Ohio voters a substitute act, known as the Marshall Bill, which would maintain the financial incentives for village courts to try prohibition cases, but which would compensate magistrates only for time actually spent in court. The bill was soundly defeated by a two-to-one vote, and it constituted the first major legislative setback for the Anti-Saloon League. *See Ohio Kills the "Kangaroo Courts"*, 95 LITERARY DIGEST 12 (November 19, 1927); W.C. Howell, *Project to Revive J.P. Fee Courts Defeated in Supposed Strongholds*, CLEVELAND PLAIN DEALER (November 9, 1927), at 1. The *Cleveland Plain Dealer* opined:

> Defeat of the Marshall bill Tuesday by the amazing margin of more than 450,000 votes is not a defeat for prohibition. It is merely a defeat for an organization which crammed the measure down the throat of a none too willing Legislature and then sought to justify the enactment on the ground that it was a dry measure and essential to successful liquor enforcement. ... The very emphatic result should teach the much-needed lesson that Ohio stands unequivocally for decency and justice in prohibition enforcement.

The Marshall Bill, CLEVELAND PLAIN DEALER (November 10, 1927), at 20.

43. WHT to Moses Strauss (March 21, 1927) (Taft papers).
44. WHT to Charles P. Taft 2nd (March 24, 1927) (Taft papers). Fear that the opinion might be misinterpreted was a major theme in Taft's correspondence:

> I hope it will do good and will make the Legislature of Ohio understand that when they establish a court, they shall see to it that the Judge is a man who will be indifferent between the parties and do justice without a motive for doing injustice. I fear that the approval of our opinion grows more out of the feeling against prohibition than it does against the maintenance of an unjust system. That is the difficulty when you get to the liquor question – it is very hard to find anybody who does not become a partisan.

WHT to Charles P. Taft 2nd (March 20, 1927) (Taft papers).

45. Glenn Roberts, for example, writing from "the practical standpoint of a prosecuting official" trying to enforce prohibition, noted that those he sought to investigate "were generally reasonably well off as a result of their unlawful activities, and they resisted our efforts to destroy their business to the very limit. Counsel was employed to take advantage of every single defense that was available, and scarcely a single search warrant went unchallenged." Glenn D. Roberts, *Does the Search and Seizure Clause Hinder the Proper Administration of the Criminal Justice?*, 5 WISCONSIN LAW REVIEW 195, 195, 197 (1929). Roberts attributed the explosion of Fourth Amendment law in the 1920s to the presence of well-paid counsel willing and able to contest searches. *Id.* at 202–3.
46. John B. Wilson, *Attempts to Nullify the Fourth and Fifth Amendments to the Constitution*, 32 WEST VIRGINIA LAW QUARTERLY 128, 128 (1926). In Wilson's view: "Until the 'National Prohibition Act' came into effect, the average citizen had, if any, a very hazy conception of his rights under the fourth amendment. And ... many lawyers were in the same fix because of the infrequent use of the

Federal search and seizure warrant. ... But, with the coming of prohibition, the situation has changed, and the fourth has come to the front with a rush, and search and seizure has become the almost universal means of enforcing the law, and especially the prohibition law." *Id.*

47. *See generally* Weeks v. United States, 232 U.S. 383 (1914). Zechariah Chafee believed that "[t]he Fourth Amendment would be a dead letter if the United States Supreme Court had not since the decision in *Weeks v. United States* adopted the exclusion theory." Zechariah Chafee, Jr., *The Progress of the Law, 1919–1922: Evidence*, 35 HARVARD LAW REVIEW 673, 695 (1922). In 1920 only one state, Michigan, agreed with *Weeks* that constitutional restrictions against unreasonable searches and seizures should be enforced by an exclusionary rule. By 1928, however, there could "be counted in support of the federal rule eighteen states, in opposition nineteen, non-committal six, the remaining five not having reviewed the new rule but having approved the old. It can no longer be said that there is weight of authority against the federal rule, especially in view of the fact that in many of the cases opposing the rule the question was not necessary to the decision and often the result depended on one judge's vote." Osmond K. Fraenkel, *Recent Developments in the Law of Search and Seizure*, 13 MINNESOTA LAW REVIEW 1, 6 (1928). Sarah Seo offers a somewhat different count. She writes that "While thirty state courts rejected the exclusionary rule, sixteen adopted it by 1927. All but two of those sixteen did so in prohibition cases." SARAH A. SEO, POLICING THE OPEN ROAD: HOW CARS TRANSFORMED AMERICAN FREEDOM 121 (Cambridge: Harvard University Press 2019). *See* ASHER L. CORNELIUS, THE LAW OF SEARCH AND SEIZURE § 7 (2nd ed., Indianapolis: Bobbs-Merrill Co. 1930); Roberts, *supra* note 45, at 204. John Wigmore was a famous opponent of the exclusionary rule. *See, e.g.*, JOHN HENRY WIGMORE, 4 A TREATISE ON THE SYSTEM OF EVIDENCE IN TRIALS AT COMMON LAW §§ 2183–84, § 2264 (2nd ed., Boston: Little Brown 1923); John H. Wigmore, *Using Evidence Obtained by Illegal Search and Seizure*, 8 AMERICAN BAR ASSOCIATION JOURNAL 479, 479–84 (1922). His witty attack – "justice tampered with mercy" – was commonly cited in the 1920s. JOHN HENRY WIGMORE, 3 A TREATISE ON THE SYSTEM OF EVIDENCE IN TRIALS AT COMMON LAW § 2251 (1st ed., Boston: Little Brown 1904). *See* Chafee, *supra*, at 699; *Search, Seizure, and the Fourth and Fifth Amendments*, 31 YALE LAW JOURNAL 518, 522 (1922).

It was commonly observed that state courts began adopting the exclusionary rule in the 1920s because of "the personal reaction of judges to the prohibition law." *Search and Seizure – Wire Tapping – Judicial Method*, 27 MICHIGAN LAW REVIEW 78, 81 (1929). *See* Margaret Lybolt Rosenzweig, *The Law of Wire Tapping*, 32 CORNELL LAW QUARTERLY 514, 525 (1947) ("The indiscriminate raids of the prohibition agents and the fact that many defendants were erstwhile law-abiding citizens rather than hardened criminals led court after court to adopt the rule of the Weeks case."). State courts had first adopted rudimentary forms of the exclusionary rule in response to nineteenth-century prohibition laws. These laws established victimless crimes and sought to facilitate government enforcement by authorizing government searches upon the application of bystanders. State courts became suspicious of the potentially over-zealous enforcement of these laws in a manner that would affect large numbers of otherwise law-abiding persons, and so developed rough forms of the exclusionary rule. Wesley

M. Oliver, *Prohibition's Anachronistic Exclusionary Rule*, 67 DePaul Law Review 473 490–94 (2018).

48. Kenneth M. Murchison, Federal Criminal Law Doctrines: The Forgotten Influence of National Prohibition 47, 71 (Durham: Duke University Press 1994). The perception of a doctrinal explosion was common at the time. *See, e.g.*, Cornelius, *supra* note 47, at iii ("The wide-spread violations of the state and national prohibition laws and the increasing use of the raid as a means of procuring evidence by police officers; the frequent arrests and holding of suspected persons for 'investigation,' and the incidental searches in connection with such arrests have caused the subject of search and seizure to assume an importance scarcely dreamed of a few years ago. Legal problems involving search and seizure are now presented before the courts with astonishing frequency."). *See* Morgan Cloud, *The Fourth Amendment during the Lochner Era: Privacy, Property, and Liberty in Constitutional Theory*, 48 Stanford Law Review 555, 602 n.218 (1996); Orin S. Kerr, *The Fourth Amendment and New Technologies: Constitutional Myths and the Case for Caution*, 102 Michigan Law Review 801, 842–43 (2004) ("The National Prohibition Act of 1919 changed everything . . . . The federal courts began to hear a regular run of Fourth Amendment cases as federal agents investigated illegal alcohol schemes.").

49. *See* John P. Bullington, *Constitutional Law – Searches and Seizures – A New Interpretation of the Fourth Amendment*, 3 Texas Law Review 460, 461 (1925). Bullington concluded that although since *Boyd* "relatively few cases have reached the Supreme Court involving the Fourth Amendment . . . the adoption of the Eighteenth Amendment and the passing of statutes directed towards enforcing the provisions of that amendment elevated the Fourth Amendment to a place of prime importance, and presented the lower federal courts with problems which have resulted in considerable diversity of opinion." *Id.* One student comment observed that before prohibition "[c]ases in which evidence had been procured by unconstitutional searches and seizures were relatively infrequent. ... But an entirely different situation prevails today. The courts in jurisdictions" with an exclusionary rule "are crowded with prohibition cases and the most popular mode of defense is to seek the suppression of evidence on the ground that it was unreasonably seized." *The Meaning of the Federal Rule on Evidence Illegally Obtained*, 36 Yale Law Journal 536, 537 (1927). The student comment counted approximately 575 reported opinions dealing with the admissibility of illegally obtained evidence in prohibition cases in the period since 1920, of which 490 were in federal court. *Id.* at 537 n.2. *See* Howard Lee McBain, Prohibition Legal and Illegal 81–82 (New York: MacMillan Co. 1928). A federal magistrate writing in 1924 remarked on the extent to which prohibition had changed the constitutional landscape:

> The century-old formulas about inviolable homes and persons against searches and seizures began to be cherished – though largely by men who two years before could not have quoted one of them accurately. The entire aspect of the dockets of the criminal magistrates changed. I served nearly twenty years in Boston as a Federal criminal magistrate and was then made familiar with substantially all that was done in the Federal repression of crime and the application of the Federal Constitution. I had practically

nothing to do with the Fourth Amendment against unreasonable searches and seizures and against general warrants. It was as strange to me as the Second Amendment about the right to keep and bear arms would be to a liquor magistrate of to-day.

Richard W. Hale, *Liberty and Liquor*, 48 WORLD'S WORK 417, 421 (1924). By 1930 a federal commissioner could observe "that eighty per cent of the United States Commissioner's business is liquor work, and of this, by far the greater number of cases begin with a search warrant as a foundation." Robert H. Alcorn, *Search Warrants and Prohibition Enforcement*, 3 DAKOTA LAW REVIEW 171, 171 (1930). The Fourth Amendment problems posed by prohibition bear a notable resemblance to those that would later arise in the "war on drugs." *See* Craig S. Lerner, *The Reasonableness of Probable Cause*, 81 TEXAS LAW REVIEW 951, 986 (2003); Thomas Regnier, *The "Loyal Foot Soldier": Can the Fourth Amendment Survive the Supreme Court's War on Drugs?*, 72 UNIVERSITY OF MISSOURI-KANSAS CITY LAW REVIEW 631, 631 (2004).

50. "Great natural difficulties oppose the possibility of enforcement in a manner compatible with constitutional guarantees. Violations are widespread and difficult of detection, for a chemical analysis is necessary for the recognition of intoxicating liquor. And yet an arrest or search to be lawful must be based on facts, not unfounded suspicion." *Legal Search and Arrest under the Eighteenth Amendment*, 32 YALE LAW JOURNAL 490, 494 (1923). "Hence it follows that in certain jurisdictions the federal authorities rely almost wholly on state discoverers. This is not legal theory; it is fact. In more than one jurisdiction it is the daily practice." MCBAIN, *supra* note 49, at 98.

51. Frederic A. Johnson, *Some Constitutional Aspects of Prohibition Enforcement*, 97 CENTRAL LAW JOURNAL 113, 122–23 (1924).

52. United States v. Bateman, 278 F. 231, 233 (S.D. Cal. 1922). The court added:

> If an automobile, a suit case, satchel, tin container, jug, or bottle could not be searched and seized without a search warrant, they could not be seized at all, as a search warrant, under the law, can only be obtained upon affidavit showing that such automobile or other container had intoxicating liquor in it. . . . Under those circumstances the Eighteenth Amendment would have been stillborn. The act of more than two-thirds of the House of Representatives, more than two-thirds of the United States Senate, in passing such Eighteenth Amendment, and all the states of the Union, with the exception of the two smallest, in approving the Eighteenth Amendment, would have been utterly futile, and would have brought about only chaos and confusion.

Id. at 234. *See* Milam v. United States, 296 F. 629, 631 (4th Cir. 1924) ("The constitutional expression, 'unreasonable searches,' is not fixed and absolute in meaning. The meaning in some degree must change with changing social, economic and legal conditions. The obligation to enforce the Eighteenth Amendment is no less solemn than that to give effect to the Fourth and Fifth Amendments.").

53. *See* MCBAIN, *supra* note 49, at 97:

> The intrusive and pervasive character of prohibition enforcement might actually have reinforced the Court's dedication to the exclusionary rule. In the context of prohibition, illegal searches would not involve an occasional blundering constable. The state rule positively invites illegal searches. The searching officer knows that he is relatively safe . . . . He knows that he can do a lot of searching on mere suspicion. And he does. And whenever he turns up evidence it

Prohibition & Law Enforcement

is used, whether he had the legal right to turn it up or not. He is not blundering. He is following the line pointed to him by the courts.

Everyone understood that remitting the victims of illegal searches to civil remedies in damages or to criminal prosecutions of offending officers was to offer "remedies so remote as practically not to threaten or restrain at all." *Id.* at 96. The only way citizens, including influential and "erstwhile law-abiding citizens," Rosenzweig, *supra* note 47, at 525, could actually be protected from systematic illegal searches was by an exclusionary rule.

54. *The Meaning of the Federal Rule on Evidence Illegally Obtained*, *supra* note 49, at 542. "It is only natural to find that some courts desirous of enforcing prohibition efficiently, should seek to deny, distinguish or limit the" exclusionary rule of *Weeks*. Thomas E. Atkinson, *Prohibition and the Doctrine of the Weeks Case*, 23 MICHIGAN LAW REVIEW 748, 748 (1925). The upshot was that Fourth Amendment jurisprudence emerged from the prohibition era in what has now become its familiar "highly chaotic state." MCBAIN, *supra* note 49, at 82. As one student commentator complained, "[t]he generalization in the *Boyd* case has been found incompatible with prohibition enforcement. In an attempt to adapt it to the new conditions courts have lost sight of its function as a constitutional safeguard. . . . So frequently are courts shaping exceptions to the rule, so rapidly is an unwieldy mass of precedent growing, that an exact definition of the rule no longer is possible. The original federal rule against illegally seized evidence has been broken down; confusion and uncertainty remain." *The Meaning of the Federal Rule on Evidence Illegally Obtained*, *supra* note 49, at 542.

55. Lerner, *supra* note 49, at 987.

56. 267 U.S. 132 (1925). For a good study of *Carroll's* historical context, see SEO, *supra* note 47, at 113–42. Other Fourth Amendment decisions involving prohibition decided by the Taft Court include Dumbra v. United States, 268 U.S. 435 (1925), in which the Court in a unanimous opinion by Stone held that the application for a warrant alleging personal experience of an illegal sale of liquor met constitutional standards even though the application failed to disclose that the target of the warrant was legally licensed to produce religious wine. *Id.* at 437–38, 440–41. In the original draft of his opinion, Stone had written that the circumstances disclosed by the affidavits "gave rise to a reasonable *suspicion* that the liquors possessed on the suspected premises were possessed for the purpose and with the intent of selling them unlawfully to casual purchasers. Absence of a well-grounded suspicion that such was the fact could be ascribed only to a lack of intelligence or a singular lack of practical experience on the part of the officer." (Stone papers) (emphasis added). Brandeis wrote Stone: "Would it not be desirable to avoid misapprehension that the word 'suspicion' ... be deleted. Its presence will, I fear, lead officials to assume that well grounded suspicion is enough – despite what you say" elsewhere (Stone papers). Brandeis suggested that the word "belief" be substituted, which Stone did.

In the original draft of his opinion, Stone had also written that "the resort to the summary procedure of search and seizure, without disclosing, in the affidavit submitted to the judge issuing the warrant, that a permit had been granted *authorizing the possession of wine on the premises* was, to say the least, dangerous, and would seem to have been a harsh and unnecessary exercise of governmental power by the officials concerned." (Stone papers) (emphasis added). Butler suggested removing the italicized words and substituting the word "disingenuous" for the word "dangerous," changes which Stone made. Stone had also originally written that "Under such circumstances search and seizure are not unauthorized or unconstitutional *and under the law, holders of Government permits must rely for protection from the harsh and unreasonable resort to that procedure, on the self restraint and sense of moral responsibility of law enforcement officers rather than on constitutional limitations*." (Stone papers) (emphasis added). Butler starred the italicized words and suggested their removal: "Does not this tend to assure such officers that their own self restraint is the limit? Can't we avoid that? Disingenuousness in some circumstances might evidence malice, want of probable cause, and the like." *Id.* Stone obligingly removed the offending language.

In 1927 the Court decided Byars v. United States, 273 U.S. 28 (1927), which featured a unanimous opinion by Sutherland holding that a search warrant based upon mere belief did not meet the standards of probable cause. *Id.* at 29. *Byars* also held that the requirements of the Fourth Amendment would apply to a search conducted by state police if a federal official had participated in the search "under color of his federal office and ... the search in substance and effect was a joint operation of the local and federal officers." *Id.* at 33. This holding later became the basis for rejecting the so-called "silver platter" doctrine. Lustig v. United States, 338 U.S. 74, 78–79 (1949) (opinion by Justice Frankfurter). *See* Elkins v. United States, 364 U.S. 206, 211 (1960). Stone's docket book indicates that at conference Taft, Holmes, and McReynolds had initially voted in *Byars* to affirm the defendant's conviction.

In 1927 the Court also decided Marron v. United States, 275 U.S. 192 (1927), which nicely illustrates the Taft Court's complex effort to maintain fidelity to Fourth Amendment standards and yet also to allow ample room for prohibition enforcement. *Marron* was a unanimous opinion by Butler. On the one hand, it held that a warrant authorizing the seizure of liquor could not constitutionally justify the seizure of books and ledgers used in a bootlegger's business: "The requirement that warrants shall particularly describe the things to be seized makes general searches under them impossible and prevents the seizure of one thing under a warrant describing another. As to what is to be taken, nothing is left to the discretion of the officer executing the warrant." *Id.* at 196. *But see* Steele v. United States, 267 U.S. 498 (1925) (upholding an ambiguous warrant). But *Marron* also held, on the other hand, that the books and ledgers could nevertheless constitutionally be introduced into evidence because they had been seized incident to a lawful arrest, having been discovered by prohibition agents when entering the defendants' premises and witnessing an ongoing illegal enterprise for the sale of liquor. *Marron*, 275 U.S. at 199.

> The officers were authorized to arrest for crime being committed in their presence .... They had a right without a warrant contemporaneously to search the place in order to find and seize the things used to carry on the criminal enterprise. The closet in which liquor and the ledger were found was used as a part of the saloon. And, if the ledger was not as essential to the maintenance of the establishment as were bottles, liquors and glasses, it was none the less a part of the outfit or equipment actually used to commit the offense. And, while it was not on [the

defendant's] person at the time of his arrest, it was in his immediate possession and control. The authority of officers to search and seize the things by which the nuisance was being maintained, extended to all parts of the premises used for the unlawful purpose.

Id. at 198–99. The authority of police to search without warrant incident to a valid arrest was not a new rule invented by the Taft Court. It had been strongly reaffirmed in *Weeks*, which had asserted that "the right on the part of the Government ... to search the person of the accused when legally arrested to discover and seize the fruits or evidences of crime ... has been uniformly maintained in many cases." Weeks v. United States, 232 U.S. 383, 392 (1914). But *Marron* interpreted that authority in an extremely generous way, which more than compensated for its strict interpretation of the requirements for a formal search warrant.

57. *Carroll*, 267 U.S. at 134.
58. ARTHUR W. BLAKEMORE, NATIONAL PROHIBITION § 25 (2d ed., Albany: M. Bender 1925). The conclusion was a common one. *See, e.g.*, Milam v. United States, 296 F. 629, 631 (4th Cir. 1924) ("In view of the difficulties of enforcing the mandate of the Eighteenth Amendment and the statutes passed in pursuance of it, we cannot shut our eyes to the fact known to everybody that the traffic in intoxicating liquors is carried on chiefly by professional criminals in motor cars. Robberies and other crimes are committed, and criminals escape by their use. To hold that such motor cars must never be stopped or searched without a search warrant would be a long step by the courts in aid of the traffic outlawed by the Constitution. ... Objections to such searches made by officers with due courtesy and judgment generally come, not from citizens interested in the observance of the law, but from criminals who invoke the Constitution as a means of concealment of crime."); United States v. Bateman, 278 F. 231, 234 (S.D. Cal. 1922) ("There is now and has been ever since this amendment went into effect almost a continuous stream of automobiles from at or near the Mexican border to Los Angeles and other parts of the country. If these automobiles could not be stopped and searched without a search warrant, the country, of course, would be flooded with intoxicating liquors, unlawfully imported."); People v. Case, 190 N.W. 289, 292 (Mich. 1922) ("The automobile is a swift and powerful vehicle of recent development, which has multiplied by quantity production and taken possession of our highways in battalions, until the slower, animal-drawn vehicles, with their easily noted individuality, are rare. Constructed as covered vehicles to standard form in immense quantities, and with a capacity for speed rivaling express trains, they furnish for successful commission of crime a disguising means of silent approach and swift escape unknown in the history of the world before their advent. The question of their police control and reasonable search on highways or other public places is a serious question .... The baffling extent to which they are successfully utilized to facilitate commission of crime of all degrees, from those against morality, chastity, and decency to robbery, rape, burglary, and murder, is a matter of common knowledge. Upon that problem a condition and not a theory confronts proper administration of our criminal laws.").
59. *Carroll*, 267 U.S. at 143, 163. *Carroll* was originally argued on December 4, 1923. *Id.* at 132. It was reargued on March 14, 1924, and not decided until March 2, 1925. *Id.* We know that the Court first voted to affirm the judgment below admitting the evidence seized without a warrant. Taft assigned the opinion to McReynolds, who

"in the course of writing the opinion ... changed his mind and concluded that the judgment should be reversed." C. Dickerman Williams, *The 1924 Term: Recollections of Chief Justice Taft's Law Clerk*, 1989 YEARBOOK OF THE SUPREME COURT HISTORICAL SOCIETY 40, 47. McReynolds's change of mind evidently caused the case to be reargued. Butler's docket book for the 1923 term shows a vote taken in *Carroll*, most likely at the conference of March 29, 1924, after reargument, in which McReynolds, Sutherland, Butler, and Sanford voted for reversal, against the votes of Taft, McKenna, Holmes, Van Devanter, and Brandeis to affirm. Butler's docket book contains some tantalizing clues about the discussion at conference: "O.W.H. Different principles. W.H.T. suggests automobile differs from house." "Common law right of peace officer to arrest. [Park v. United States, 294 F. 776 (1st Cir. 1924).] What are reasonable grounds for belief of present commission. Must have ascertained facts. 'In presence of = immediate knowledge.' O.W.H. 'Probable cause to surmise.'" There is an ambiguous reference to Brandeis:

> L.D.B. Court could find business[.]
> Stopping & Arrest misdemeanor on suspicion.

Whether the second line refers to Brandeis's comments is not clear. It is probable that after this conference Taft reassigned the opinion to himself. Almost a year later he wrote his brother:

> I have had ready for delivery an important opinion in respect to the right of Govt officers to seize automobiles which they have reasonable ground for thinking contain unlawful liquor. We have had the case for two years. I gave the case to McReynolds. He brought it back saying he could not write for the validity of the seizure. On a vote we lost once but McKenna came over so that I was able to assign it to myself. I have been working on the thing since October. I brought in an opinion the last of the year. I succeeded in winning over all but McR and Sutherland. McR has written a dissent and a strong one. I don't know whether Sutherland will go with him or not. Van Devanter thinks not. At any rate we carry the day and I am rejoiced because I think it important to establish the correct principle in respect to the search of this instrument of evil the automobile.

WHT to Horace D. Taft (March 1, 1925) (Taft papers). *See* WHT to Robert A. Taft (March 8, 1925) (Taft papers) ("I am especially interested in the opinion with reference to seizure of liquor in automobiles. I was once outvoted in the Conference, but by dint of argument and opinion writing I got all votes but two.").

The date of McKenna's switch is of some importance, because, as we saw in Chapter 4, his mental deterioration by the 1924 term was such that on November 9, 1924, eight justices of the Court voted formally not to "decide any case in which there were four on one side and four on the other, with Mr. Justice McKenna's casting the deciding vote." Memorandum, November 10, 1924 (Taft papers), reprinted in WALTER MURPHY & C. HERMAN PRITCHETT, COURTS, JUDGES, AND POLITICS: AN INTRODUCTION TO THE JUDICIAL PROCESS 199–201 (3d ed., New York: Random House 1979). The published opinion of *Carroll* states, most unusually, "Mr. Justice McKenna, before his retirement, concurred in this opinion." 267 U.S. at 163. Six weeks after November 9, however, Taft was still apparently unsure of his majority. On December 22, 1924, Taft wrote his son Robert, "I have

Prohibition & Law Enforcement

got a case in which the Court is not agreed, and I am very doubtful of my majority after I get the opinion written. I am not at all sure that I can hold it, a result that entitles one to no credit so far as the known work of the Court is concerned." WHT to Robert A. Taft (December 22, 1924) (Taft papers). *See* WHT to Charles P. Taft 2nd (December 22, 1924) (Taft papers) ("[I am] preparing myself to write an opinion in a case in which I may not succeed in winning the majority after I have got it written, although we have a vote of that kind. It is a most important case, and I am greatly interested, but I don't know that I shall succeed. It is a good deal easier to write an opinion when the Court is all with you than where the distinctions are narrow, the record is badly made and some rather new principle is to be established against a vigorous opposition.").

During December, Taft corresponded with Van Devanter about *Carroll*. On December 22, 1924, Van Devanter sent Taft a dictated memorandum on how the opinion could be drafted, together with "some suggestions of things to avoid." WVD to WHT (December 22, 1924) (Taft papers). Van Devanter wrote: "I ... am still of opinion that our vote was right. ... I really think Beck's substituted brief a good one.... That it has not had a better effect is to be regretted.... I am at a loss to understand why its better parts have not carried conviction to others. The more I think of the case the more I think the view we entertain is right and that the other view would be productive of harmful results in many ways." *Id*. Taft replied that he had already "blocked out an opinion" which "noted the very distinction, which you emphasize, between the searching of houses and the searching of ships." WHT to WVD (December 23, 1924) (Taft papers). Apparently, Taft learned from Van Devanter's memorandum, which does not now survive, about the Acts of May 1822 and June 1834, dealing with searches and seizures of liquor in Indian territory. *See Carroll*, 267 U.S. at 152–53.

Most important, Taft's letter to Van Devanter suggests something of Taft's strategy to convince Butler to join the majority opinion: "I note what you say about brother Butler," Taft wrote Van Devanter, "and I shall try to steer away from the suggestion that we are introducing any new law and new principle of constitutional construction, but are only adapting old principles and applying them to new conditions created by the change in the National policy which the 18th Amendment represents." WHT to WVD (December 23, 1924) (Taft papers). It is noteworthy that the previous day Taft had in a letter to his son referred to his *Carroll* opinion as having to establish "some rather new principle." WHT to Charles P. Taft 2nd (December 22, 1924) (Taft papers).

It is possible that the wavering fifth vote in *Carroll* in December 1924 was not McKenna, but Brandeis, for on December 26, 1924, Taft wrote his brother Horace:

> I have been working for nearly ten days on an opinion of much importance, upon which the Court is divided, and with which I have had a good deal of trouble. I sent the opinion to the printer to-day, and hope to get back the first copy this evening. I would like to get a majority of the Court because of the importance of the principle, but I don't know that I shall. Brandeis was with me strongly before the summer vacation, but he went up to Cambridge and must have communed with Frankfurther [sic] and that crowd, and he came back with a notice to me that he was going to change his vote. Brandeis tries as hard as he can to be a good fellow, and in many respects he is, but when he gets into the field of politics and political economics, his judgment is all awry and his methods are not above criticism.

The Taft Court

WHT to Horace D. Taft (December 26, 1924) (Taft papers). The only plausible case to which this letter might refer is *Carroll*. But we do not know the grounds of Brandeis's dissatisfaction, if any. *See* LDB to WHT (January 15, 1925) (Taft papers).

It does appear, however, that at least by December 28 Taft no longer regarded the vote in *Carroll* as five-to-four. At that time, he wrote his son Charles: "I have finished one opinion. It took me a full two weeks to prepare and write it. It is on a very important phase of the National Prohibition Act. Our Court is going to be divided, but I am quite hopeful that I may command six of the Court. It is a case that came over from last year and has given me a great deal of trouble, so that I feel somewhat relieved for getting as far as I have with it, although I shall probably encounter considerable discussion tomorrow when we hold our Conference." WHT to Charles P. Taft 2nd (December 28, 1924) (Taft papers).

60. WHT to Charles P. Taft 2nd (December 22, 1924) (Taft papers).
61. WHT to Horace D. Taft (March 1, 1925) (Taft papers). Taft was convinced that "the automobile is the greatest instrument for promoting immunity of crimes of violence that I know of in the history of civilization." WHT to Francis Peabody (July 12, 1923) (Taft papers). In Taft's view:

> The statistics of crime are ... most disheartening, and yet a large percentage of the increase, so far as crimes of larceny and robbery are concerned, is due to the automobile. That is the greatest instrument to promote immunity from punishment for crime that we have had introduced in many, many years, and we haven't as yet neutralized its effect. Whether we can do so or not is a question for men engaged in the detection of crime. When we see how much crime there is, and with what immunity criminals commit murder in order to further their crimes of robbery, it makes one gag with indignation to think of the milk and water people who with their philanthropies are engaged in trying to make our penitentiaries sweet homes for the luxurious betterment of murderers and robbers.

WHT to Horace D. Taft (November 16, 1923) (Taft papers). In 1927, Taft gave an interview in which he remarked that "There is the greatest incentive to crime in the automobile and the fine roads that we build, because of the immunity from punishment achieved by the quickness with which crime can be committed and escape be had, making detection most difficult. This not only increases crime in the city, because criminals may escape to the country, but it also gives opportunity to city criminals to enlarge their sphere of action and much increases crime in the country, which, in times past, was largely immune." Quoted in Newman, *supra* note 9, at 9.

62. Substituted Brief for the United States on Reargument, Carroll v. United States, No. 15 October Term 1923, at 20–21. The brief was submitted by Solicitor General James M. Beck. The government frankly conceded "the novelty of the question" presented by *Carroll. Id.* at 21. For Beck's view on the crime wave, see *supra* note 3 and accompanying text. Van Devanter considered Beck's brief to be "really ... a good one." WVD to WHT (December 22, 1924) (Taft papers).

63. Cornelius, *supra* note 47, at § 35; Jacob W. Landynski, Search and Seizure and the Supreme Court: A Study in Constitutional Interpretation 87 (Baltimore: Johns Hopkins Press 1966); H.C. Underhill, A Treatise on the

Prohibition & Law Enforcement

LAW OF CRIMINAL EVIDENCE § 746 (3rd ed., Indianapolis: Bobbs-Merrill Co. 1923) ("The right to seize intoxicating liquor without a warrant is coextensive with the right to arrest without a warrant."); Hugh E. Willis, *Unreasonable Searches and Seizures*, 4 INDIANA LAW JOURNAL 311, 313–15 (1929). For arguments challenging this assumption, see AKHIL REED AMAR, THE BILL OF RIGHTS: CREATION AND RECONSTRUCTION 64–77 (New Haven: Yale University Press 1998); TELFORD TAYLOR, TWO STUDIES IN CONSTITUTIONAL INTERPRETATION: SEARCH, SEIZURE AND SURVEILLANCE AND FAIR TRIAL AND FREE PRESS (Columbus: Ohio State University Press 1969).

64. *Carroll*, 267 U.S. at 155–56. *See* Snyder v. United States, 285 F. 1 (4th Cir. 1922); WILLIAM E. MIKELL, HANDBOOK OF CRIMINAL PROCEDURE 8 (2nd ed., St. Paul: West Publishing Co. 1918); FRANCIS WHARTON, 1 A TREATISE ON CRIMINAL PROCEDURE 69–77 (10th ed., San Francisco: Bender-Moss 1918); ELIJAH N. ZOLINE, 1 FEDERAL CRIMINAL LAW AND PROCEDURE §§ 19–24 (Boston: Little, Brown 1921).

65. *Carroll*, 267 U.S. at 154. The Volstead Act provided that offenders were to be punished by a fine of not more than $500 for the first offense, by a fine of not more than $1,000 or by not more than ninety days' imprisonment for the second offense, and "by a fine of $500 or more and by not more than 2 years' imprisonment for the third offense." *Id.* Thus an offender "is to be arrested for a misdemeanor for his first and second offenses and for a felony if he offends a third time." *Id.* In 1929, in an effort to ratchet up prohibition enforcement, these penalties were changed by the Jones Act, which provided that the penalty for a first violation of the National Prohibition Act "shall be a fine not to exceed $10,000 or imprisonment not to exceed five years, or both: Provided, That it is the intent of Congress that the court, in imposing sentence hereunder, should discriminate between casual or slight violations and habitual sales of intoxicating liquor, or attempts to commercialize violations of the law." Jones Act, Pub. L. 70-899, 45 Stat. 1446 (March 2, 1929). The harsh penalties of the Jones Act proved a strategic error for prohibitionists because it augmented simmering resentments against the harshness of prohibition enforcement.

66. United States v. Hilsinger, 284 F. 585, 588 (S.D. Ohio 1922).

67. "If the Eighteenth Amendment is to be enforced at all, the courts should be permitted to consider the practical necessities of the particular situations." *Search and Seizure: Constitutional Prohibition Applied to Transportation of Contraband Liquor in Automobile*, 12 VIRGINIA LAW REGISTER 236, 238–39 (N.S.) (1926).

68. BLAKEMORE, *supra* note 58, at 476; *Search of Automobile without Warrant – When Reasonable*, 23 MICHIGAN LAW REVIEW 891, 894–97 (1925). Some courts held that old understandings of the Fourth Amendment would have to bend because courts were "under the duty of deciding what is an unreasonable search of motor cars, in the light of the mandate of the Constitution that intoxicating liquors shall not be manufactured, sold, or transported for beverage purposes." Milam v. United States, 296 F. 629, 631 (4th Cir. 1924). *See* United States v. Bateman, 278 F. 231 (S. D. Cal. 1922). Others held that it was "a breach of the peace to transport intoxicating liquors." Hughes v. State, 238 S.W. 588, 596 (Tenn. 1922). Still other courts effaced the common law distinction between felonies and misdemeanors. *See, e.g.*, United States v. Vatune, 292 F. 497, 499 (N.D. Cal. 1923) ("In these days of widespread

violation of the law, due to large temptation, big profits, and unrestrained appetites, together with the facile employment of the automobile in aid of successful consummation thereof, an officer ought not to be censured nor society penalized by a meticulous refusal to support a prosecution, if the officer, even in the absence of a warrant, and even with respect to a mere misdemeanor, acting upon the appearances, determines that the law may be maintained only by the 'immediate apprehension' of the offender, providing, always, of course, that the officer acts in good faith and upon reasonable grounds of suspicion."); Lambert v. United States, 282 F. 413, 417 (9th Cir. 1922). Other courts expanded the concept of "in the presence of," so that police officers could search automobiles if they had (in effect) probable cause to believe that illegal liquor was being transported. *See* Park v. United States, 294 F. 776, 783 (1st Cir. 1924); United States v. Hilsinger, 284 F. 585, 588–89 (S.D. Ohio 1922) ("The federal courts seem generally to have recognized the right to apprehend, search, and seize an automobile truck in transit with contraband liquor, when the officers have reasonable and probable cause . . . ."). Yet other courts held that because liquor was contraband, which was forfeit and in which there was no right of private property, a defendant had "no right to return of the property, nor to object to its use in evidence." United States v. Fenton, 268 F. 221, 222 (D. Mont. 1920). *See* Boyd v. United States, 286 F. 930 (4th Cir. 1923). This last rationale provoked particular outrage, for it seemed to imply that no remedy would lie whenever a search, however illegal, turned up contraband: "[I]t is not and cannot be the law in criminal cases that an illegal arrest or search could be legalized by the finding of evidence that a crime had been committed, for a search or arrest illegal to begin with remains illegal, and no injury should be allowed to flow to the defendant by reason of his submission to it." United States v. Rembert, 284 F. 996, 1003–4 (S.D. Tex. 1922). The holding in *Fenton* was described as a fine example

> of precisely what the law is not . . . . Forfeiture proceedings are necessary to determine the disposition of things seized as contraband. For a seizure for forfeiture is not in itself a complete proceeding. It must be followed by judicial proceedings, wherein the government must prove its title to forfeiture.
>
> Moreover, the legality of the arrest of [sic] search must be determined by the facts as they were known to the officer at the moment the arrest was made or the search instituted, and can never be justified by what has been found. A search that is unlawful when it begins is not made lawful when it ends by the discovery and seizure of liquor.

WILLIAM J. MCFADDEN, THE LAW OF PROHIBITION 226–27 (Chicago: Callaghan & Co. 1925).

69. *Carroll*, 267 U.S. 154–55, 157–58. That rule, said Taft, is "not to be determined by the character of the penalty to which the transporter may be subjected," *id.*, nor is it to be determined by the common law "right to arrest." *Id.* at 158. "The character of the offense for which, after the contraband liquor is found and seized, the driver can be prosecuted does not affect the validity of the seizure." *Id.* at 159.
70. Taft's use of the earliest of these statutes has been criticized as seriously misconstruing the history of the Fourth Amendment. *See generally* LANDYNSKI, *supra* note 63, at 90; Thomas Y. Davies, *Recovering the Original Fourth Amendment*, 98 MICHIGAN LAW REVIEW 547 (1999).
71. *Carroll*, 267 U.S. at 153.

Prohibition & Law Enforcement

72. *Id.* at 153–54. "Travelers may be so stopped in crossing an international boundary because of national self protection reasonably requiring one entering the country to identify himself as entitled to come in, and his belongings as effects which may be lawfully brought in." *Id.* at 154.
73. *Id.* at 156. Taft reached this conclusion by noting that the Volstead Act refers to Section 970 of the revised statutes, which immunizes seizing officers from damage suits if "there was reasonable cause of seizure." *Id.* at 155. Taft assimilated the statutory standard of "reasonable cause" to the common law standard of "probable cause," which determined the legality of "arrests without warrant for past felonies, and in malicious prosecution and false imprisonment cases." *Id.* at 161.
74. *Id.* at 149. Taft's careful statement of the rule seemed to imply that the constitutional legitimacy of warrantless searches and seizures required a "law" that made goods "subject to seizure and destruction." *Id.*
75. *Id.* One commentator deemed the outcome "a very practical desirable result [that] gives vitality to the eighteenth amendment and its enforcement while still staying within and complying with the spirit and requirements of the fourth amendment." *Search of Automobile without Warrant – When Reasonable*, supra note 68, at 898. "The decision and reasoning in the Carroll case represent a sensible interpretation of the Fourth Amendment, and should enable federal prohibition officers to do their duty without undue risk and hindrance." James Parker Hall, *Constitutional Law – Search and Seizure – Contraband Liquor in Automobile*, 20 ILLINOIS LAW REVIEW 162, 165 (1925).
76. *Carroll* has been termed "the leading *Lochner* era example" of "pragmatist reasoning." Cloud, *supra* note 48, at 602. "Certain it is that the Carroll Case presented the court with a balance of interests of unusual importance. On the one hand, to hold that the Fourth Amendment inhibited the search of an automobile without a search warrant, unless circumstances warranting a common-law arrest existed, would have seriously crippled the enforcement of the Eighteenth Amendment; while on the other hand, the old conservative opinions of the court had to be gotten rid of, and a burden of unknown weight be put upon the individual for the benefit of a newly appended amendment." Bullington, *supra* note 49, at 469.
77. Davies, *supra* note 70, at 733–34.
78. *Carroll*, 267 U.S. at 144, 150–53.
79. *See, e.g., id.* at 158.
80. At the announcement of the case,

> McReynolds delivered himself without reference to his written opinion in such a way that Holmes remarked (as Holmes told me) to our new member Stone that there were some people who could be most unmannerly in their dissenting opinions, but as I had seven-two, I was not particularly affected by McReynolds' appeal to the galleries.

WHT to Robert A. Taft (March 8, 1925) (Taft papers).
81. *Carroll*, 267 U.S. at 164, 166 (McReynolds, J., dissenting).

> Since the beginning apt words have been used when Congress intended that arrests for misdemeanors or seizures might be made upon suspicion. It has studiously refrained from making a felony of the offense here charged; and it did not undertake by any apt words to enlarge the power to arrest. It was not ignorant

of the established rule on the subject, and well understood how this could be abrogated.

Id.

82. *Id.* at 168 (McReynolds, J., dissenting).
83. *Id.* This point struck at another vulnerability in Taft's opinion. Taft argued that the Volstead Act itself contemplated that "[t]he seizure ... comes before the arrest." *Carroll*, 267 U.S. at 159. But this was an obvious non sequitur. It did not follow that, because Congress authorized a seizure without warrant, it either could or did also authorize an arrest without warrant. Taft's argument, if accepted, established only that the Volstead Act rendered constitutional seizures justified by probable cause in the absence of a warrant. This conclusion would certainly justify seizure of liquor without warrant in circumstances where there was no need to arrest, as for example from an unoccupied car. In *Carroll*, by contrast, prohibition agents could not search the defendants' vehicle until they had first stopped a moving car and placed the drivers "into custody under and by virtue of the authority of the law," JOHN G. HAWLEY, THE LAW OF ARREST ON CRIMINAL CHARGES 13 (3rd ed., Chicago: T.H. Flood 1919), which is to say that they could not seize until they had, in the understanding of the time, first arrested a vehicle's driver. *See* Henry v. United States, 361 U.S. 98, 103 (1959) (stopping of car deemed an "arrest"); Brinegar v. United States, 338 U.S. 160 (1949) (same); Forrest R. Black, A CRITIQUE OF THE CARROLL CASE, 29 COLUMBIA LAW REVIEW 1068, 1077–87 (1929); *Constitutional Law – Search and Seizure – Search of Automobile for Intoxicating Liquor*, 4 NEBRASKA LAW BULLETIN 171, 172–73 (1925); *Scope of the Government's Privilege of Search and Seizure without a Warrant*, 27 COLUMBIA LAW REVIEW 300, 306 n.38 (1927); *cf.* Robert Meisenholder, *Arrest – Stopping and Questioning as an Arrest – Reasonable Suspicion from Facts Disclosed by Questioning as Justification*, 37 MICHIGAN LAW REVIEW 311, 311–13 (1938). That is why McReynolds forcefully argued that the defendants "were first brought within the officers' power, and, while therein, the seizure took place." *Carroll*, 276 U.S. at 169 (McReynolds, J., dissenting). In the face of McReynolds's challenge, Taft's bland assertion that the arrest came "after" the seizure simply assumes what needed to be demonstrated.

Taft might have argued that the search and seizure were valid, because legislatively authorized, even if the arrest of the defendants was illegal. An "illegal arrest" was not thought to have any "effect on the evidence or upon the jurisdiction of the court in a criminal case." Thomas E. Atkinson, *What Is an Unreasonable Search?*, 24 MICHIGAN LAW REVIEW 277, 280 (1926). In such circumstances, however, the defendants "would have at least a technical right to recover damages for the illegal arrest, even though the subsequent search be held valid." *Id.* at 279. (Atkinson was the attorney of record for the defendants in *Carroll*.)

Taft might also have argued that stopping a moving vehicle was not equivalent to arresting its occupants. It is noteworthy, however, that Taft specifically did not make this argument, nor can I find any contemporary author who did. *See, e.g.*, Terry v. Ohio, 392 U.S. 1, 16 (1968) ("It must be recognized that whenever a police officer accosts an individual and restrains his freedom to walk away, he has 'seized' that person."). Taft might also have

Prohibition & Law Enforcement

argued that a statutory authorization to seize without warrant was also a statutory authorization to arrest without warrant. Brandeis came close to advancing this logic in United States v. Lee, 274 U.S. 559 (1927), which involved the authority of the Coast Guard to seize and search vessels suspected of violating revenue laws. Brandeis argued that

> [o]fficers of the Coast Guard are authorized, by virtue of Revised Statutes, to seize on the high seas ... an American vessel subject to forfeiture for violation of any law respecting revenue. From that power it is fairly to be inferred that they are likewise authorized to board and search such vessels when there is probable cause to believe them subject to seizure for violation of revenue laws, and to arrest persons thereon engaged in such violation.

Id. at 562. If the Coast Guard had probable cause to suspect illegal liquor, Brandeis wrote, "search and seizure of the vessel, and arrest of the persons thereon ... is lawful, as like search and seizure of an automobile, and arrest of the persons therein, by prohibition officers on land is lawful. Compare Carroll v. United States, 267 U.S. 132, 149." *Id.* at 563. Brandeis did not quite claim that arrest of persons before the discovery of the contraband is lawful, but he came very close, and his argument appeared to contemplate what would be warrantless arrests on the basis of probable cause. There is a memorandum to Brandeis from his clerk stating that the opinion in *Lee* could be written to argue that "without a search, there was plainly enough to excite suspicion. The cases show that is sufficient to justify an arrest, and a search following an arrest, of a boat within the U.S., or of an auto." Memorandum from R.G.P. to LDB (April 3, 1927) (Brandeis papers). In *Carroll*, however, Taft made no such argument. He simply blurred the relationship between the search and the arrest.

84. *Carroll*, 267 U.S. at 169 (McReynolds, J., dissenting). Note that in this rhetorical question McReynolds slides from the proposition that Congress has not in fact authorized seizures on probable cause, to the intimation that Congress cannot, consistent with the Fourth and Fifth Amendments, do so.

85. Taft's opinion was constructed on the premise that the Volstead Act authorized searches and seizures made with probable cause although without warrant, and that this statutory authorization did not contravene the Fourth Amendment. He did not reach or address the question of whether warrantless searches and seizures with probable cause would also be constitutional in the absence of statutory authorization. *See* Brinegar v. United States, 338 U.S. 160, 183 (1949) (Jackson, J., dissenting); United States v. Di Re, 332 U.S. 581, 584–87 (1948); Eldon D. Wedlock, Jr., *Car 54 – How Dare You!: Toward a Unified Theory of Warrantless Automobile Searches*, 75 MARQUETTE LAW REVIEW 79, 86 (1991) ("[I]n Brinegar v. United States, the statutory limits of the Carroll rule were surpassed for the first time."). Two years after *Carroll*, in Maul v. United States, 274 U.S. 501 (1927), the Court explicitly refused to accept a proposed opinion circulated by Brandeis that would have held that the Coast Guard could constitutionally conduct searches and seizures on the high seas without warrants and without statutory authorization. The Court instead chose to affirm an alternative opinion drafted by Van Devanter holding that warrantless searches and seizures by the Coast Guard on the high seas were authorized by statute. *See infra* text at notes 101–2.

86. Butler was apparently induced to join the majority opinion on the ground that the opinion was faithful to original common law principles. *See supra* note 59. It is noteworthy that seven months after *Carroll*, Butler authored the Court's unanimous opinion in Agnello v. United States, 269 U.S. 20 (1925), which reversed a lower court judgment admitting evidence seized in a defendant's house. It is also noteworthy that Butler's docket book shows that at conference Holmes and Taft had voted to affirm. *Agnello*, which concerned cocaine rather than liquor, squarely held for the first time that "[t]he search of a private dwelling without a warrant is in itself unreasonable and abhorrent to our laws." *Id.* at 32. Butler wrote: "Save in certain cases as incident to arrest, there is no sanction in the decisions of the courts, federal or state, for the search of a private dwelling house without a warrant. ... Belief, however well founded, that an article sought is concealed in a dwelling house furnishes no justification for a search of that place without a warrant. And such searches are held unlawful notwithstanding facts unquestionably showing probable cause." *Id.* at 33. Butler also held in *Agnello* that a search of a defendant's dwelling that was "several blocks distant" from the site of an arrest, and which was searched when "the conspiracy was ended and the defendants were under arrest and in custody elsewhere," could not "be sustained as an incident of the arrests." *Id.* at 31. *Agnello* was read as showing "clearly that the Supreme Court considers the problem of the search of vehicles to be an exceptional one, and that it intends no relaxation of the strict protection, under the Fourth Amendment, of dwellings and buildings from unreasonable searches." Sterling C. Holloway, *Search and Seizure – The Carroll Case Viewed in the Light of Later Decisions*, 4 TEXAS LAW REVIEW 241, 241 (1926). *See The Exclusion of Evidence Illegally Obtained*, 2 ST. JOHN'S LAW REVIEW 196, 201 (1928) (*Carroll* "represents the widest departure from the Weeks case thus far attempted. Whatever doubts may have been raised by the Carroll case were shortly dispelled by Agnello v. United States.").
87. *Carroll*, 267 U.S. at 160. Michigan was a primary route for smuggling illegal liquor into the United States from Canada. During prohibition the state waged a fierce ongoing battle against motor vehicles carrying illegal contraband. *See, e.g.*, *The Rum War on the Detroit Front*, 102 LITERARY DIGEST 5 (July 6, 1929). This is probably why the *Michigan Law Review* published so many articles addressing questions of search and seizure.
88. *Carroll*, 267 U.S. at 160.
89. Regnier, *supra* note 49, at 645. *See* Lerner, *supra* note 49, at 987.
90. *Carroll*, 267 U.S. at 174 (McReynolds, J., dissenting).
91. Robert E. Cushman, *Constitutional Law in 1924–1925*, 20 AMERICAN POLITICAL SCIENCE REVIEW 80, 89 (1926) ("[I]t is submitted that the court's decision is a sensible one if the prohibition law is to be enforced, and does not involve any essential injustice.").
92. Hall, *supra* note 75, at 165. "Does not the Court fail to distinguish between believing upon a basis of specific facts and merely suspecting upon a basis of general facts? The Volstead Act as differentiated from the ordinary revenue act does not permit seizure or arrest on suspicion. The officers knew not a single specific fact upon which they could base actual belief. It was mere suspicion. ... Does [*Carroll*] mean that the officers had a general license to stop the defendants every time they were on the road? Such a general license would be more atrocious than the use of the general or blanket warrant against which James Otis made his impassioned protest." Black, *supra* note 83, at 1088.

Prohibition & Law Enforcement

93. *Search and Seizure: Constitutional Prohibition Applied to Transportation of Contraband Liquor in Automobiles*, 13 CALIFORNIA LAW REVIEW 351, 352 (1925). "As a practical matter, it is very probable that the power given by this rule to the police may be abused and every automobile stopped, under the theory that the end justifies the means employed. It is obvious that one law should not be broken in order to help enforce another. The probable cause may be 'meagre.'" *Search and Seizure without a Warrant*, 73 UNIVERSITY OF PENNSYLVANIA LAW REVIEW 413, 418 (1925).
94. *The More Volstead, the Less Law*, WASHINGTON POST (March 9, 1925), at 6 (quoting the *Baltimore Sun*). The reasonableness standard, Sarah Seo writes, "'clothed' the police with 'discretion or judiciary power' as a matter of constitutional law." SEO, *supra* note 47, at 140. Just as Taft insisted that ordinary people trust the discretion of the equitable judge, see *infra* Chapter 41, at 1380, so he insisted that street level law enforcement officers receive the benefit of analogous trust.
95. Black, *supra* note 83, at 1098.
96. Zechariah Chafee, Jr., *Ill Starred Prohibition Cases: A Study in Judicial Pathology*, 45 HARVARD LAW REVIEW 947, 949 (1932).
97. In November 1922, Brandeis wrote Frankfurter assessing the results of the off-year election. In Massachusetts, Democrats had recaptured many seats in the legislature but, in a referendum, voters had defeated a bill that would have required the state to enforce prohibition. Brandeis commented to Frankfurter, "[B]ut for the Anti-Dry vote Mass. did very well." LDB to Felix Frankfurter (November 14, 1922), in BRANDEIS-FRANKFURTER CORRESPONDENCE, at 125.
98. 271 U.S. 354 (1926).
99. *Plea to Punish Liquor Buyers Heard by Court*, WASHINGTON POST (March 12, 1926), at 4. On Holmes's reference to poison, see *supra* Chapter 31, at note 95.
100. *Katz*, 271 U.S. at 362.
101. *Id.* at 364. Brandeis wrote Stone, "I have held this for calmer re-reading – but remain unconvinced. Please note my dissent." (Stone papers). Holmes wrote that he would "not dissent unless strong dissent is written." (Stone papers).
102. 274 U.S. 501, 524–25 (1927) (Brandeis, J., concurring). Holmes joined Brandeis's concurrence.
103. *Maul* was argued on January 19, 1927. Stone's docket book indicates that the Court voted unanimously on January 22 to uphold the legality of the Coast Guard's seizure of the vessel on the high seas. Brandeis was assigned the opinion, which he circulated in April. On April 5, Taft wrote Brandeis to say:

> I called at Van Devanter's last night to see him about another matter, and he brought up the seizure case that he you and I discussed, and in which you have written an opinion. He told me that he had said to you that he could not concur in your opinion. I suggested to him then that he write an opinion and that then the two opinions be submitted for a vote as to which shall represent the opinion of the Court. He said he could not do it this week but he would next. He has studied so much of the case that I think he might do it promptly. This is the only solution that I see of the present situation. It would only mean an opinion and a concurring opinion.

WHT to LDB (April 5, 1927) (Taft papers). *See* WHT to the Brethren (April 22, 1927) (Taft papers). In his opinion in United States v. Lee, 274 U.S. 559 (1927), decided on the same day as *Maul*, Brandeis explicitly built his argument around Van Devanter's conclusion in *Maul*. Brandeis wrote:

> Officers of the Coast Guard are authorized, by virtue of Revised Statutes, to seize on the high seas beyond the 12-mile limit an American vessel subject to forfeiture for violation of any law respecting the revenue. Maul v. United States (The Underwriter) No. 655, decided this day. From that power it is fairly to be inferred that they are likewise authorized to board and search such vessels when there is probable cause to believe them subject to seizure for violation of revenue laws, and to arrest persons thereon engaged in such violation. . . . In the case at bar, there was probable cause to believe that our revenue laws were being violated by an American vessel and the persons thereon, in such manner as to render the vessel subject to forfeiture. Under such circumstances, search and seizure of the vessel, and arrest of the persons thereon, by the Coast Guard on the high seas is lawful, as like search and seizure of an automobile, and arrest of the persons therein, by prohibition officers on land is lawful. Compare Carroll v. United States, 267 U.S. 132, 149.

274 U.S. at 562–63.
104. LISA MCGIRR, THE WAR ON ALCOHOL: PROHIBITION AND THE RISE OF THE AMERICAN STATE 221 (New York: W.W. Norton & Co. 2016).

CHAPTER 33

Olmstead v. United States

THE TROPE OF lawlessness in the 1920s was volatile and unstable. It applied not merely to those who defied prohibition, but also to prohibition officials who broke the law in their efforts to enforce it. For the bulk of the decade, national prohibition enforcement officers were political appointees who were zealous, ill-trained, incompetent, and unprofessional.[1] Prohibition enforcement was often allied to lawless civilian groups like the Ku Klux Klan.[2] It became commonplace to remark on "the curious lawlessness which prohibition breeds in its official bosom."[3]

Prohibition was said to have created "a new crime, unusual in America. . . . It is the crime of official lawlessness."[4] "[T]he disregard of law by enforcement officials has been increasing alarmingly . . . in an effort to prevent the illegal sale of alcoholic liquors."[5] Observers remarked that "Homes and places of business are invaded by officials without search warrants or with warrants improperly issued and served. Property is seized or destroyed without warrant of law. Persons are assaulted on the barest suspicion of guilt or are arrested and booked at police headquarters for 'investigation' – a charge for which there exists no lawful authority. . . . Suspects are held incommunicado from relatives and lawyers. The 'third degree' is familiar to all."[6]

On the floor of the Senate "[f]ederal officers involved in dry-law killings and other attacks were scathingly arraigned by Senators Copeland of New York, Hawes of Missouri and Tydings of Maryland."[7] If prohibitionists charged those who defied the Eighteenth Amendment with lawlessness, the epithet was returned with interest by those who were appalled by "the utter disregard for law and personal rights which has become the almost invariable accompaniment of the efforts on the part of our enforcement officers to compel compliance" with prohibition.[8] "[N]othing," it was said, "breeds disrespect for all law so much as its violation by those charged with upholding it."[9]

1061

The widespread phenomenon of zealously overreaching prohibition officials propelled a wave of state courts independently to adopt the exclusionary rule.[10] As the Supreme Court of Florida opined in 1922 when opting for the exclusionary rule:

> For one to acquire illegally, or illegally to possess, intoxicating liquors is a crime; but it is a crime that generally affects a few persons in a restricted locality. To permit an officer of the state *to acquire evidence illegally* and in *violation of sacred constitutional* guaranties, and to use the *illegally acquired* evidence in the prosecution of the person who illegally acquired the intoxicants, strikes at the very foundation of the administration of justice, and where such practices prevail make law enforcement a mockery.
>
> In this era, when earnest-thinking men and women are ardently trying to arouse public sentiment on the subject of strict law enforcement, it would seem most meet and proper for the courts to set the example, and not sanction lawbreaking and constitutional violation in order to obtain testimony against another law-breaker. Better the mob and the Ku-Klux, than a conviction obtained in a temple of justice by testimony illegally acquired by agents of the government and officers of the law. . . . The liberties of the people cannot safely be intrusted to those who believe that violation of prohibition laws is more heinous than violations of the Constitution.[11]

The need simultaneously to enforce prohibition and yet also to cabin official lawlessness came to a head in the monumental and explosive case of *Olmstead v. United States*,[12] "[t]he last major Supreme Court decision concerning prohibition enforcement" and "in many ways the most controversial and significant."[13] *Olmstead* held in 1928 that wiretapping did not constitute a search or seizure under the Fourth Amendment, and that the exclusionary rule would not apply to evidence illegally obtained, as distinct from unconstitutionally obtained.[14] "Led by Chief Justice Taft . . . whose crusade for stricter enforcement of prohibition reached its zenith in this case,"[15] the Court in *Olmstead* violently split 5–4, with Taft writing a majority opinion joined by Van Devanter, McReynolds, Sutherland, and Sanford.[16] Holmes, Brandeis, Butler, and Stone each dissented separately.[17]

Why would McReynolds and Sutherland, who detested prohibition, join Taft in this controversial decision, and why would Holmes and Brandeis, who had all along supported vigorous prohibition enforcement, dissent? The puzzle deepens because both Holmes and Brandeis had earlier in the decade authored opinions that would seem to sustain Taft's position. In *Hester v. United States*,[18] Holmes held for a unanimous court that the seizure of liquor in plain view in a defendant's open fields after police trespassed onto the defendant's land did not constitute a search or seizure for purposes of the Fourth Amendment. And in *United States v. Lee*[19] Brandeis drew on *Hester* to hold that the use by the Coast Guard of a searchlight to examine the deck of a ship on the high seas did not constitute a search.[20]

Everything about *Olmstead* was dramatic and riveting.[21] The defendant in the case, Roy Olmstead, was in 1920 the youngest and most charismatic lieutenant in the Seattle police department. He eventually quit his day job to develop a huge and

Olmstead v. United States

sophisticated smuggling operation that imported Canadian liquor into the State of Washington.[22] Known as the "king of the rumrunners,"[23] he was a popular hero in Seattle because

> [h]e never corrupted his merchandise. People could trust it. He never allowed his employees to arm themselves, lecturing to them sternly that no amount of money was worth a human life. His business arrangements were conducted with a firm integrity, for he was, in his own way, a moralist. Because Olmstead was so attractive personally and because he scrupulously avoided the sordid behavior of others in the same business – no murder, no narcotics, no rings of prostitution or gambling – many people could not regard him as an authentic criminal.[24]

Olmstead was convicted in federal court in 1925 largely on the basis of evidence gathered by wiretaps.[25] At the time, wiretapping was a misdemeanor under the laws of the State of Washington.[26] In 1924 Attorney General Stone was said to have sent "a directive to the newly formed Federal Bureau of Investigation" that announced, "under the heading 'Unethical Tactics,' that 'Wiretapping ... will not be tolerated.'"[27] But this directive did not govern the Treasury Department, where prohibition enforcement was located, so that wiretapping was a "principal method used ... to catch [prohibition] offenders."[28] The upshot was that federal use of wiretapping was associated almost exclusively with the enforcement of prohibition.[29]

Olmstead challenged the admissibility of the wiretap evidence. His challenge was rejected by the Ninth Circuit Court of Appeals on May 9, 1927.[30] Six months later, on November 21, 1927, the Taft Court denied Olmstead's petition for a writ of *certiorari*;[31] Stone's docket book records that only Brandeis voted in conference to consider the case.[32] But after a petition for rehearing the Court met again on January 7 and reversed itself, issuing a writ of *certiorari* that limited "consideration ... to the question whether the use of evidence of private telephone conversations, between the defendants and others, intercepted by means of wire tapping, is a violation of the Fourth and Fifth Amendments and, therefore, not permissible in the federal courts."[33] After the grant of *certiorari*, Assistant Attorney General Mabel Walker Willebrandt, who was in charge of prohibition enforcement at the Justice Department, withdrew from the case in protest at what she regarded as the government's unethical use of wiretapping.[34]

During the two weeks before the case was argued on February 20–21, Brandeis, who was vehement on the question of preserving the integrity of law enforcement practices, prepared a memorandum that would eventually become his dissent.[35] In its earliest versions, the memorandum began with the argument that courts ought not to admit illegally procured evidence because redress should be denied to one who has "unclean hands."[36] This argument, as Brandeis explicitly recognized, was distinct from the constitutional question of whether wiretapping was a search or seizure for purposes of the Fourth Amendment.[37] When the Court met in conference on February 25, Taft, joined by Van Devanter, McReynolds,

Sutherland, and Sanford, voted to affirm Olmstead's conviction; Holmes, Brandeis, Butler, and Stone voted to reverse. Taft assigned the opinion to himself.[38]

On March 21, Brandeis circulated to the Court the part of his memorandum that dealt with the admission of illegally obtained evidence, together with a note: "In this case, the non-constitutional ground for reversal, which I suggested, was not discussed at the conference. Several of the brethren stated that they had not considered it. For this reason it seems to me appropriate that I should circulate now this memorandum in which I have stated somewhat fully the reasons of the view expressed."[39]

Sutherland, who had been sick with colitis throughout most of fall 1927,[40] sailed for Europe to recuperate on May 18, 1928.[41] He left behind a memorandum for Taft concerning his views on undecided cases. About *Olmstead* he said:

> This is the wire tapping case in which there probably will be a vigorous dissent. In a general way my view is that the conversations which were heard as a result of the wire tapping did not relate to a past crime but were part of a crime then being committed. The question is whether there was an unlawful search and seizure; and plainly there was not. Neither papers nor information was surrendered under any form of compulsion. Consequently, the evidence was admissible however we may condemn the manner of obtaining it. I am inclined to think the opinion should squarely meet the proposition that there was probably a violation of the state law which we do not in any way attempt to excuse. That however is a matter for the state, and the federal courts cannot refuse to receive evidence plainly relevant and material because the state law may have been violated in obtaining it. The point made, that there was an unlawful search and seizure, being negatived, that is the end of the matter so far as we are concerned.[42]

On May 25, Taft sent a first draft of his opinion to Van Devanter and Sanford, seeking suggestions.[43] He noted that "I have talked over this case a good deal with Justice Sutherland, and he has left authority with me to consent to what I shall write."[44] On May 31, Taft sent the draft of his opinion to McReynolds, stressing that "I have adopted all of your suggestions."[45] Apparently, Butler had complained that Brandeis discussed issues not encompassed within the narrow grant of *certiorari*, and Taft had asked McReynolds how the majority should respond. Should it abide by the restrictions in the grant of *certiorari* and leave Brandeis's attack unanswered, or should the majority itself go beyond the limitations in the grant of *certiorari* and discuss the question of illegally procured evidence?

> The question has now arisen whether we ought to allow Brandeis, after consenting to a limitation on the discussion to be had under the certiorari, to introduce the question of the Washington statute and his own ethical view. I think that Pierce Butler thinks we ought not to allow it, but I am rather inclined to let it go as it is. Butler thinks that if we let this in, we ought also to take in the discussion on the question whether the evidence of the intercepted conversations was properly admissible under the general rules of evidence. But we did distinctly agree that that should not be taken up, and it was strenuously argued in

Olmstead v. United States

Conference that the interception of messages was contrary to law. Indeed it was on that ground that Holmes changed his vote. I feel, therefore, that we ought to let it go as it is and not raise the question now as to the limitation of the discussion of certioraris.[46]

Olmstead came down on June 4, 1928, the last day of the 1927 term. In his opinion, Taft first addressed the constitutional question of the search and seizure.[47] He began with the claim that "[t]he well known historical purpose of the Fourth Amendment ... was to prevent the use of governmental force to search a man's house, his person, his papers and his effects; and to prevent their seizure against his will." The Fourth Amendment, therefore, attached only to "material things – the person, the house, his papers or his effects." Because the wiretapping in this case did not involve "trespass upon any property of the defendants,"[48] because the government did not appropriate any thing or effect of the defendants, as for example their letters, the Fourth Amendment "does not forbid what was done here. There was no searching. There was no seizure. The evidence was secured by the use of the sense of hearing and that only. There was no entry of the houses or offices of the defendants."[49]

Taft denied that the defendants owned or controlled the "telephone wires reaching to the whole world from the defendant's house or office."[50] "The reasonable view is that one who installs in his house a telephone instrument with connecting wires intends to project his voice to those quite outside, and that the wires beyond his house and messages while passing over them are not within the protection of the Fourth Amendment. Here those who intercepted the projected voices were not in the house of either party to the conversation." Congress could of course ban the use of wiretap evidence by statute, "[b]ut the courts may not adopt such a policy by attributing an enlarged and unusual meaning to the Fourth Amendment."[51]

Taft's argument deployed two metaphors: appropriation and trespass. Fourth Amendment protection could be triggered by the appropriation – the forceful taking – of a thing. Appropriation was constitutionally suspect because it interfered with a person's control over things that belonged to him. Consent was required before the state could take or seize a person's property. In *Olmstead*, Taft seemed to argue that the eye does not appropriate what it sees, nor does the ear appropriate what it hears. That is the significance of Taft's observation that wiretapping involved "hearing and that only."[52]

The second metaphor used by Taft's opinion was that of trespass. Trespass – unlawful entry – onto some property owned by a defendant could render a search or seizure incompatible with the Fourth Amendment. Trespass violated the exclusive dominion required by property, even if an unlawful government intrusion did not result in the actual seizure of property. It is for this reason that Taft repeatedly stressed that the government had never entered the defendants' houses, nor had the defendants owned the telephone wires into which the wiretaps were inserted.

Either appropriation or trespass constituted an independently sufficient ground to justify Fourth Amendment protection. Fourth Amendment protection could be triggered by an appropriation without a trespass, as for example if the government were to inspect mail within its custody.[53] Or Fourth Amendment protection could be triggered by a trespass without an appropriation, as for example if government officials were to break into a house and use their eyes to search its contents.[54] But in Olmstead's case there was neither appropriation nor trespass; there was neither a seizure nor a search.[55] This suggests that Sutherland and McReynolds may have been willing to join Taft's opinion because it was constructed entirely in terms of constitutional concepts with which they were sympathetic, like consent and property.[56] As his memorandum to Taft indicates, Sutherland imagined that Fourth Amendment protections turned on issues of "compulsion."[57]

One could, of course, construct a rationale for excluding the wiretap evidence in *Olmstead* within the paradigm of appropriation and trespass. That is exactly the basis of Butler's dissent. Butler argued that "The communications belong to the parties between whom they pass. During their transmission the exclusive use of the wire belongs to the persons served by it. Wire tapping involves interference with the wire while being used. Tapping the wires and listening in by the officers literally constituted a search for evidence."[58] Butler invoked the metaphor of trespass, of unwarranted intrusion into a domain under the rightful control of a person, to justify the conclusion that wiretapping constituted a search triggering Fourth Amendment protection.[59] Butler could make this move only by using the metaphor of trespass in ways that transcended the strict confines of positive property law.[60]

In his opinion for the Court, Taft never explained why he rejected this more expansive notion of trespass.[61] To justify restricting the reach of the Fourth Amendment to "the possible practical meaning of houses, persons, papers, and effects," he quoted, cryptically and without elaboration, the crucial premise of his *Carroll* opinion: "The Fourth Amendment is to be construed in the light of what was deemed an unreasonable search and seizure when it was adopted and in a manner which will conserve public interests as well as the interests and rights of individual citizens."[62]

Taft had written this passage in *Carroll* to underscore the practical necessity of authorizing warrantless searches of automobiles. In *Olmstead*, however, he did not offer an analogous justification for the necessity of wiretapping.[63] That was left to Sutherland in an opinion a decade later. Dissenting from a decision holding that the Communications Act of 1934[64] had prohibited wiretapping by federal law enforcement officials, Sutherland made an explicitly pragmatic argument:

> The decision just made will necessarily have the effect of enabling the most depraved criminals to further their criminal plans over the telephone, in the secure knowledge that even if these plans involve kidnapping and murder, their telephone conversations can never be intercepted by officers of the law and revealed in court. ... My abhorrence of the odious practices of the town gossip, the Peeping Tom, and the private eavesdropper is quite as strong as that of my brethren. But to put the sworn officers of the law, engaged in the detection and apprehension of organized gangs of criminals, in the same category, is to lose all sense of proportion.[65]

Olmstead v. United States

Taft's opinion was constructed within a strict framework of appropriation and trespass. The difficulty with this framework is that it could not explain relevant precedents, even those cited in Taft's opinion itself. In *Hester v. United States*, for example, the Court had held that the Fourth Amendment did not apply to liquor found in a defendant's open fields as a result of an official trespass onto the defendant's land. Holmes had held for the Court in *Hester* that "the special protection accorded by the Fourth Amendment to the people in their 'persons, houses, papers, and effects,' is not extended to the open fields. The distinction between the latter and the house is as old as the common law."[66] But if it is asked why the Fourth Amendment ignores a trespass onto open fields, but not a trespass into a house, the answer cannot be given by the concept of trespass itself. The answer requires instead a theory of what the concept of trespass is meant to protect, which presumably would explain why the word "houses" in the Fourth Amendment ought not to be interpreted to include the open fields owned by a homeowner that surround his house.

Brandeis's dissent in *Olmstead* would prove to be a profound and generative source of law because it offered just such a theory of the "underlying purpose"[67] of the Fourth Amendment. "The makers of our Constitution," argued Brandeis, "undertook to secure conditions favorable to the pursuit of happiness. They recognized the significance of man's spiritual nature, of his feelings and of his intellect. They knew that only a part of the pain, pleasure and satisfactions of life are to be found in material things." They therefore "sought to protect Americans in their beliefs, their thoughts, their emotions and their sensations. They conferred, as against the Government, the right to be let alone – the most comprehensive of rights and the right most valued by civilized men. To protect that right, every unjustifiable intrusion by the Government upon the privacy of the individual, whatever the means employed, must be deemed a violation of the Fourth Amendment."[68]

Brandeis attributed to the Fourth Amendment the same purpose that nearly four decades previously he had attributed to the common law in his famous and influential article on *The Right to Privacy*:

> The intense intellectual and emotional life, and the heightening of sensations which came with the advance of civilization, made it clear to men that only a part of the pain, pleasure, and profit of life lay in physical things. Thoughts, emotions, and sensations demanded legal recognition, and the beautiful capacity for growth which characterizes the common law enabled judges to afford the requisite protection, without the interposition of the legislature.
>
> Recent inventions and business methods call attention to the next step which must be taken for the protection of the person, and for securing to the individual what Judge Cooley calls the right "to be let alone." Instantaneous photographs and newspaper enterprise have invaded the sacred precincts of private and domestic life; and numerous mechanical devices threaten to make good the prediction that "what is whispered in the closet shall be proclaimed from the house-tops." ... [T]he question whether our law will recognize and protect the

right to privacy in this and in other respects must soon come before our courts for consideration.[69]

The reason why the Fourth Amendment protects a house against trespass, but not open fields, is because the purpose of the Fourth Amendment is to protect "reasonable expectations of privacy," and there are no such expectations in open fields, regardless of ownership.[70] It would take thirty-nine years, but eventually in *Katz v. United States*[71] the Court would overrule Taft's opinion in *Olmstead* and adopt instead the theory of Brandeis's dissent.[72]

The interesting question is why "the privacy of the individual" should for a progressive like Brandeis trump the law-enforcement demands of the administrative state. What exactly was the *constitutional* status of privacy? When post-New Deal liberalism began to theorize the civil rights and civil liberties that ought to circumscribe the discretion of the administrative state, it typically turned to theories of democracy. It was well understood that democratic legitimacy was necessary to underwrite the authority of the administrative state. This is essentially the approach taken in footnote four of Stone's opinion in *United States v. Carolene Products Co.*[73] Brandeis was himself an early pioneer of this form of reasoning.[74] But the odd point about Brandeis's *Olmstead* dissent is that it does not purport to advance a theory of democratic legitimacy. Instead Brandeis appeals to the same customary, social values that he had defended in his earlier article on the right of privacy.

It is no surprise, then, that in his separate dissent Holmes refused to join Brandeis's interpretation of the Fourth Amendment.[75] The whole point of Holmes's positivism was to constrain courts from using traditional values to limit positive law.[76] Brandeis's *Olmstead* dissent is startling because it appeals precisely to such values. It embraces the customary norms ordinarily protected by the common law, and it even postulates that these norms are necessary for human flourishing. The fiasco of federal prohibition enforcement evidently caused some progressives, like Brandeis, to repudiate strict Holmesian positivism by acknowledging that the "moral authority of the government does not rest [merely] on its legal right to issue commands," but also on "the collective conscience of the community in its effort to make for more and better human life."[77]

In 1890, in *The Right to Privacy*, Brandeis had sought to demonstrate how the common law expressed and protected the collective conscience of the community. In 1928, under the relentless pressure of prohibition, Brandeis sought to transform the Constitution into an instrument for the expression and protection of that same collective conscience. He would in this way pioneer a distinctively liberal appeal to social mores as necessary limitations on the administrative state.[78]

Brandeis's posture in *Olmstead* was structurally analogous to the judicial conservatism of Sutherland in *Adkins*, or Butler in *Jay Burns Baking*, or McReynolds in *Fairmont Creamery*. No less than they, Brandeis in *Olmstead* appealed to fundamental social norms as a ground from which judges could constitutionally constrain positive law. The distinction between Brandeis and his three conservative colleagues lay not so much in the form of constitutional authority to which each laid claim, as in the content of the social values that each sought to use

Olmstead v. United States

the Constitution to enforce. Brandeis aspired to identify and defend values that could not be encompassed by traditional ideals of autonomy, consent, and property. He sought to protect what we would now call "dignity." In the context of the Fourth Amendment, Brandeis feared that "[t]he progress of science" would furnish "the Government with means of espionage" that would crush individual personality.[79]

Brandeis did not explain why he chose to invoke the value of privacy to limit wiretapping rather than the warrantless searches of automobiles. From a biographical perspective, the explanation would no doubt lie in the violent, almost visceral disgust that Brandeis felt at the "espionage"[80] of wiretapping.[81] The question of which social values should be so fundamental as to trump positive law would of course become a central problem for post-New Deal liberal constitutionalism. Brandeis's *Olmstead* dissent neither anticipates nor contributes to that question. But it does demonstrate that a progressive jurisprudence can root itself in social norms and speak from their authority, and this demonstration pointed the way toward a communitarian liberalism that would ultimately flower in decisions like *Katz* and *Griswold v. Connecticut*.[82]

Apart from the question of whether wiretapping was a search and seizure under the Fourth Amendment, *Olmstead* also contained a second issue, which was not constitutional, and which had been specifically excluded by the limited grant of *certiorari*. It was the issue, however, that from the first had most concerned Brandeis and that had caused Holmes to author a separate dissenting opinion. It was the issue of official lawlessness, which lay at the bottom of the question whether federal courts ought to admit evidence procured in violation of law.[83] Wiretapping was a misdemeanor under Washington law, and so the evidence that convicted Olmstead was secured through what was, literally, a crime.

In a short but pungent opinion, Holmes argued that the Court was not "bound" by any "body of precedents" and that therefore it had "to choose, and for my part I think it a less evil that some criminals should escape than that the Government should play an ignoble part." Breaking the law by wiretapping was a "dirty business"[84] and federal courts ought not "to allow such iniquities to succeed."[85]

Brandeis made the same point, although more elaborately and to more brilliant rhetorical effect.[86] He argued that by ratifying the crimes of its agents, the government and its judiciary had itself become "a lawbreaker," and that federal courts should use the doctrine of clean hands to protect themselves from this danger. The court ought to exclude such evidence "in order to maintain respect for law; in order to promote confidence in the administration of justice; in order to preserve the judicial process from contamination." He concluded with an eloquent peroration that evoked the widespread popular anxiety about official lawlessness and that deftly turned the tables on Taft's often-stated conviction that prohibition should be enforced to maintain the rule of law:

> Decency, security and liberty alike demand that government officials shall be subjected to the same rules of conduct that are commands to the citizen. In a government of laws, existence of the government will be imperiled if it fails to observe the law scrupulously. Our Government is the potent, the omnipresent

teacher. For good or for ill, it teaches the whole people by its example. Crime is contagious. If the Government becomes a lawbreaker, it breeds contempt for law; it invites every man to become a law unto himself; it invites anarchy. To declare that in the administration of the criminal law the end justifies the means – to declare that the Government may commit crimes in order to secure the conviction of a private criminal – would bring terrible retribution. Against that pernicious doctrine this Court should resolutely set its face.[87]

If Taft was concerned that defiance of prohibition would lead to "anarchy,"[88] Brandeis would expose the real roots of legal legitimacy. If Taft worried about the growth of a "contemptuous attitude toward law,"[89] Brandeis would explain how the foundations of "a government of law" were actually maintained. If Taft insisted that "intelligent and well-to-do people" exemplify respect and obedience to law,[90] Brandeis would emphasize whose "example" really mattered. For Brandeis, and perhaps also for Holmes, these questions turned on the necessity of maintaining the very rule of law that legitimated the administrative state itself.

Taft was rhetorically defenseless in the face of this relentless assault. He could in his opinion only argue that the Court "must apply in the case at bar" the common law rule in effect in the State of Washington in 1889, the year when Washington was admitted to the Union.[91] This common law rule, Taft asserted, was that "the admissibility of evidence is not affected by the illegality of the means by which it was obtained."[92] Although Taft did not seek to justify this rule, he did intimate its underlying utilitarian calculation in favor of law enforcement: "A standard which would forbid the reception of evidence if obtained by other than nice ethical conduct by government officials would make society suffer and give criminals greater immunity than has been known heretofore. In the absence of controlling legislation by Congress, those who realize the difficulties in bringing offenders to justice may well deem it wise that the exclusion of evidence should be confined to cases where rights under the Constitution would be violated by admitting it."[93]

The upshot was that in the name of upholding the sanctity of the legal order, Taft and the Court had been maneuvered into ratifying official lawbreaking.[94] And in the name of suppressing those who would defy the law of prohibition, they had been forced to condone a practice that was forbidden to FBI officers as "unethical" and that was at the federal level associated almost entirely with prohibition enforcement.[95] Taft was well within his rights to complain that it was "bizarre" to interpret *Olmstead* as reflecting "an interest in convicting bootleggers,"[96] because "the men who voted with the majority and carried the case included men who have in a good many instances taken a view of the law which would be regarded as anti-prohibition, like Sutherland, Butler and McReynolds, and the other side includes Holmes and Brandeis, who have been voting to sustain the 18th Amendment vigorously in many cases."[97] But the Court was nevertheless in an impossible position, and it made Taft unusually bitter.[98]

It was all but inevitable that *Olmstead* would be read as an opinion carrying "still further the process of creating a governmental bureaucracy equipped with almost unlimited powers of espionage for the purpose of attempting to enforce

Olmstead v. United States

Prohibition."[99] The Court was said to be "bewitched by Prohibition,"[100] and *Olmstead* was blasted as "the Dred Scott decision of prohibition."[101] Most damaging, however, was the perception, hammered home by *Olmstead*, that prohibition could be imposed on a recalcitrant population only by such "detestable" practices as the "dirty business" of wiretapping.[102] The impression left by *Olmstead* was that "the heaviest load which prohibition has to carry is the shocking lawlessness that has been employed to enforce it."[103]

In *Olmstead*, the Taft Court opted for law enforcement over the rule of law. The decision was received as confirming the view that prohibition would be sustained by all means necessary. Attempting to explain the demise of prohibition, the historian David Kyvig has observed that "[d]uring the 1920s the Supreme Court did more than either Congress or the president to define the manner in which national prohibition would be enforced."[104] Kyvig argues that decisions like *Olmstead*, *Lanza*, *Carroll*, and *Lambert* created "[t]he image of a government prepared to engage in more aggressive and intrusive policing practices than ever before in order to enforce" prohibition. These cases confirmed the "disenchanted" perception "that government, unable to cope with lawbreakers by using traditional police methods, was assuming new powers in order to accomplish its task."[105]

The Taft Court's relentless efforts to sustain prohibition thus accentuated the disparity between the positive law of prohibition and traditional values. The Taft Court's unyielding positivism fed the perception that "prohibition destroys not only the written but the unwritten law of the land as well."[106] Prohibition displaced "fundamental American principle" to impose "discipline on the American people."[107] The perception was most acute in the context of law enforcement, in which Americans increasingly concluded that the "experience of the last decade has shown that if we keep nationwide prohibition we shall continue to have with it summary haltings of automobiles at night, regulation of non-intoxicants, wire tapping, invasions of the home, and indiscriminate fatal shootings. These are the price we pay for prohibition."[108] And, increasingly, Americans concluded, as did Zechariah Chafee, that "the price is too high."[109]

By exposing and sharpening the administrative teeth necessary to sustain the noble experiment, the Taft Court contributed to the growing national sense that prohibition was simply not worth the costs of its enforcement. Taft had been right in the years before 1918. A sumptuary law disconnected from the conscience of the community, and obeyed only because of an escalating spiral of repressive enforcement, was simply not sustainable. The lesson was that not even the Constitution itself can retain authority if its mandates are regarded as illegitimate. The catastrophe of prohibition demonstrated that constitutional legitimacy does not flow merely from the ratification procedures of Article V. It does not flow solely from any rule of recognition, however onerous. The positive law of the Constitution must also be answerable, in some measure, to the people and to their beliefs.

In 1933, five years after *Olmstead*, Americans ratified the Twenty-First Amendment, which repealed the Eighteenth. They acted to reconnect their actual convictions to the positive law of the Constitution.

The Taft Court

Notes

1. *See supra* Chapter 29, at 948–49 and note 15. In 1925, Assistant Attorney General Mabel Willebrandt, who was in charge of prohibition enforcement at the Justice Department, complained:

    > At present we haven't had the right kind of investigators. Many of them are well-meaning, sentimental and dry, but they can't catch crooks. The sole object of others has been to appropriate all the graft in sight, and they won't catch crooks. These two classes have obtained their positions largely because prohibition enforcement officers have been appointed at the instance of Senators, Congressmen and political leaders. The average Senator or Congressman recommends a man because he has been useful politically or because he is an Anti-Saloon Leaguer, a confirmed dry or a widely known Sunday school teacher; but that kind of man doesn't often make a good detective.

    Quoted in A.H. Ulm, *A Woman Directs the Dry Battle*, NEW YORK TIMES (January 25, 1925), § 4 at 1. See MABEL WALKER WILLEBRANDT, THE INSIDE OF PROHIBITION 111–41 (Indianapolis: Bobbs-Merrill Co. 1929). "When in 1927 Congress finally got around to requiring professional examinations for field agents, the results were disastrous. The Commissioner of Prohibition admitted that almost three-quarters of his men had failed the test." WALTER F. MURPHY, WIRETAPPING ON TRIAL: A CASE STUDY IN THE JUDICIAL PROCESS 11–12 (New York: Random House 1965). "During the first six years of prohibition, one of every twelve [prohibition] agents was fired" for some form of corruption. THOMAS R. PEGRAM, BATTLING DEMON RUM: THE STRUGGLE FOR A DRY AMERICA, 1800–1933, at 159 (Chicago: Ivan R. Dee 1998).
2. LISA MCGIRR, THE WAR ON ALCOHOL: PROHIBITION AND THE RISE OF THE AMERICAN STATE 83–88, 124–41 (New York: W.W. Norton & Co. 2016).
3. *More Prohibition Zeal*, NEW YORK TIMES (May 3, 1928), at 19.
4. 71 CONG. REC. 3141 (June 19, 1929) (statement of Sen. Harry Hawes). "Federal and local officers seldom shoot in the enforcement of any law except the commandment that 'thou shalt not drink an alcoholic beverage.' To compel obedience to the prohibition law they shoot upon the slightest provocation, and invariably they go scot free. Why? Because the prohibitionists are in the saddle and, so far from being shocked by the carnage of prohibition enforcement, they condone the crimes committed in its name. If it were not so, there would be no prohibition murders, for murderers in uniform would be punished, and red-handed zealotry would become unpopular." Arthur Sears Henning, *Frown Would End Volstead Terror Reign*, CHICAGO DAILY TRIBUNE (March 30, 1929), at 1.
5. Austin Haines, *The Crimes of Law Enforcement*, 33 NEW REPUBLIC 316, 317 (1923). *See Prohibition Killings*, 95 LITERARY DIGEST 12 (October 8, 1927).
6. Haines, *supra* note 5, at 316. It should be noted that in an opinion by Butler, with Sutherland and Sanford dissenting, the Taft Court came down hard on corrupt prohibition officials. *See* Donnelley v. United States, 276 U.S. 505 (1928). According to Stone's docket book, the case was voted on three times in conference. Originally, Holmes was assigned to write an opinion for Sutherland, Brandeis, McReynolds, and Sanford reversing the conviction of a prohibition agent, but

Olmstead v. United States

eventually Butler persuaded the Court to hold instead that the Volstead Act made it a crime for prohibition agents intentionally to fail to report the illegal transportation of liquor.

An important Taft Court decision dealing with the issue of what the press called "police terrorism" was Ziang Sung Wan v. United States, 266 U.S. 1, 14–17 (1924), in which the Court, in a unanimous opinion by Brandeis, found that the use of the "third degree" rendered a confession involuntary and hence inadmissible. *Unto the Least of These*, 119 THE NATION 459, 459 (1924). On the day of the argument, Taft wrote his wife that he had just submitted an

> important ... murder case. One Chinaman is charged with killing three others at an educational mission here in Washington and the question we have to decide is whether the method by which his confession was secured was such that it ought not to have been admitted in evidence. There are several members of the Court perhaps a majority thinking the confession should not have been admitted. ... If the confession goes out it is doubtful whether he could be convicted a second time. There has been unreasonable delay in the trial. The murder was committed in 1919. I am inclined to think that the defendant was guilty.

WHT to Helen Herron Taft (April 8, 1924) (Taft papers). Butler's docket book shows that at conference McKenna, Van Devanter, and Sutherland had originally voted to admit the confession. Taft wrote Brandeis about his opinion, "I concur. I think this case as you conclusively show is so exceptional that it can not return to plague us in other cases where confessions are most useful evidence." Holmes wrote, "Yes siree. I suppose you are right not to show disgust or wrath. I don't know whether I could have held in." McReynolds, who had equivocated in conference, wrote, "I shall not oppose." Sutherland said, "This is well done. I voted the other way but probably shall acquiesce." Van Devanter returned, "I shall assent." (Brandeis papers). Brandeis later wrote Frankfurter about the "third degree" that "Our police practices – and the attitude of most prosecutors & the bar thereto carry us back to the age of torture on the continent." LDB to Felix Frankfurter (November 4, 1928), in BRANDEIS-FRANKFURTER CORRESPONDENCE, at 350. Brandeis believed that "few tasks in connection with the Criminal Law are so important as a thorough enquiry into, & exposition of, the practices of the police in connection not only with 3rd degree, but generally re the interrogation of persons arrested." LDB to Felix Frankfurter (September 28, 1927), *id.* at 308–9.

On reaction to *Ziang Sung Wan*, see, for example, *The Third Degree*, 40 NEW REPUBLIC 272 (1924); Zechariah Chafee, Jr., *Compulsory Confessions*, 40 NEW REPUBLIC 266, 267 (1924) ("The Supreme Court's opinion forcibly proves the need of a thorough-going investigation of the extent to which the 'third degree' prevails in American cities, and a careful consideration of the circumstances under which interrogation of the accused by government officials should be permitted, if at all."); *Torture Is Again Condemned*, NEW YORK TIMES (October 15, 1924), at 22 ("There will be general approval – which Supreme Court decisions do not always get – with the decision in which the Justices this week condemned a conviction for murder based on a confession obtained by what they call duress."). *The Nation* strongly affirmed the Court's opinion:

> In a decision which ought to strike at the roots of police terrorism the United States Supreme Court has just granted Ziang Sung Wan a new trial,

on the ground that the alleged confession was extorted. ... It is time that something was done to make police officials remember that they too are required to obey the law. Doubtless it is true, as they allege, that some valid confessions are extorted by the third degree; doubtless the inquisitors of the middle ages, too, could point to some honest successes of their methods. But the defense is not justification.

Unto the Least of These, supra, at 459. *The Outlook* opined: "Here is a clearer decision from a higher authority than has appeared before holding the 'third degree' to be in violation not merely of American statute law but of the whole spirit of Anglo-Saxon judicature. It ought to have the effect of ending definitely and for all time this barbaric practice. But unaided it will not." *Police Take Notice,* 138 THE OUTLOOK 318, 319 (1924). Concern with the "third degree" became so great that the Wickersham Commission devoted substantial attention to the subject. *See* National Commission on Law Observance and Enforcement, REPORT ON LAWLESSNESS IN LAW ENFORCEMENT (Washington D.C.: U.S. Government Printing Office 1931).

7. *Glass Charges President "Submerges" Prohibition; Senate Clash on Killings,* NEW YORK TIMES (June 20, 1929), at 1. *See* James W. Wadsworth, Jr., *The Death Toll of Enforcement,* 229 NORTH AMERICAN REVIEW 257, 261-62 (1930); *Enforcement's Innocent Victims,* 101 LITERARY DIGEST 5 (June 29, 1929); *Senate Rebels at Dry Slaughter,* CHICAGO DAILY TRIBUNE (June 20, 1929), at 1; *The Aurora Killing,* 101 LITERARY DIGEST 8 (April 13, 1929); *Dry Agents' Bullets Make Big Casualty List of U.S. Citizens,* CHICAGO DAILY TRIBUNE (September 25, 1927), at 6; Oswald Garrison Villard, *Official Lawlessness: The Third Degree and the Crime Wave,* 155 HARPER'S MAGAZINE 605 (1927) ("[T]he most dangerous criminals we have in America are the officials who in growing number openly disregard or violate the laws.").

The Wickersham Commission later remarked on the tendency to regard "the attempt to enforce the National Prohibition Act as something on another plane from the law generally; an assumption that it was of paramount importance and that constitutional guarantees and legal limitations on agencies of law enforcement and on administration must yield to the exigencies or convenience of enforcing it." *Enforcement of the Prohibition Laws of the United States: A Report of the National Commission on Law Observance and Enforcement Relative to the Facts as to the Enforcement, the Benefits, and the Abuses under the Prohibition Laws, Both Before and Since the Adoption of the Eighteenth Amendment to the Constitution,* H.R. Doc. No. 71-722, 71st CONG. 3rd SESS. (January 20, 1931), at 81-82.

> Some advocates of the law have constantly urged and are still urging disregard or abrogation of the guarantees of liberty and of sanctity of the home which had been deemed fundamental in our policy. ... [T]he federal field force as it was at first, was largely unfit by training, experience, or character to deal with so delicate a subject. High-handed methods, shootings and killings, even where justified, alienated thoughtful citizens, believers in law and order. Unfortunate public expressions by advocates of the law, approving killings and promiscuous shootings and lawless raids and seizures and deprecating the constitutional guarantees involved, aggravated this effect. Pressure for lawless enforcement, encouragement of bad methods and agencies of obtaining evidence, and crude methods of investigation and seizure on the part of

Olmstead v. United States

> incompetent or badly chosen agents started a current of adverse public opinion in many parts of the land.

Id. at 82.

8. Henry Hasley, *Criminal Law – Searches and Seizures – Tapping of Telephone Wires – Admissibility of Evidence*, 4 NOTRE DAME LAW 202, 205 (1928).
9. Haines, *supra* note 5, at 318.
10. See *supra* Chapter 32, at note 47. In the words of one contemporary treatise writer:

> If, for example (as has frequently been the case), an over-zealous officer should station himself on one of our trunk highways, over which thousands of automobiles travel every day, stop every car and search the occupants, greatly to the annoyance and humiliation of many innocent people, would not such a practice tend to bring unnecessary prejudice and odium upon the law itself? ...
>
> Faced with a startling increase in illegal searches and seizures which affected not only the guilty but the innocent as well, many of the courts came to a realization that practical measures would have to be adopted or the constitutional provisions against unreasonable searches and seizures would become a dead letter, as it now is in those states where the federal rule has been rejected.

ASHER L. CORNELIUS, THE LAW OF SEARCH AND SEIZURE 42 (2nd ed., Indianapolis: Bobbs-Merrill Co. 1930).

11. Atz v. Andrews, 84 Fla. 43, 52 (1922).
12. 277 U.S. 438 (1928).
13. DAVID E. KYVIG, REPEALING NATIONAL PROHIBITION 34 (2nd ed., Kent State University Press 2000).
14. *Olmstead*, 277 U.S. at 464–69.
15. KYVIG, *supra* note 13, at 34.
16. *Olmstead*, 277 U.S. at 455.
17. *Id.* at 469, 471, 485, 488.
18. 265 U.S. 57 (1924).
19. 274 U.S. 559 (1927).
20. The original draft of Brandeis's opinion in *Lee* had excited some concern over its broad claims about the searchlight. In its original form, Brandeis's opinion had read:

> The testimony of the boatswain shows that he examined the motor-boat by means of a searchlight. ... For aught that appears, the presence of the cans of liquor, as well as of the defendants, was discovered before the motor-boat was boarded. To pry into the secrets of a motor-boat by means of a searchlight is not prohibited by the Constitution. Compare Hester v. United States.

(Brandeis papers). Van Devanter explicitly objected to this language: "Please note me as concurring in the result. I am not prepared to accept the full statement as to what may be done with searchlight, nor do I feel sure that it is not necessary in this case." WVD to LDB (Brandeis papers). Brandeis's clerk commented on Van Devanter's objection:

> I see no possibility of omitting a statement as to what can be done with the searchlight. ... If the evidence is admissible though obtained by a trespass as in the Hester case, it certainly ought to be admissible though obtained by turning

> a searchlight upon a boat, which is very doubtful legal wrong if any [sic]; I should hate to attempt to persuade your court that damages could be recoverable for it. ...
>
> The Carroll case is conclusive against the contention that there is any constitutional limitation upon the right to look, for there was certainly probable cause for suspicion.

Memorandum to LDB (April 14, 1927) (Brandeis papers). In Brandeis's published opinion, the offending passage was amended to read:

> The testimony of the boatswain shows that he used a searchlight. ... For aught that appears, the cases of liquor were on deck and, like the defendants, were discovered before the motorboat was boarded. Such use of a searchlight is comparable to the use of a marine glass or a field glass. It is not prohibited by the Constitution. Compare Hester v. United States.

Stone's docket book shows that at conference Butler had voted in *Lee* to affirm the judgment below suppressing the seized evidence. Taft wrote Brandeis, "I am going to acquiesce although I have qualms." WHT to LDB (Brandeis papers). Taft's opinion in *Olmstead* cites and relies on both *Hester* and *Lee*. *Olmstead*, 277 U.S. at 465. David Currie describes Taft's use of these opinions by Holmes and Brandeis as the chickens coming "home to roost." David P. Currie, *The Constitution in the Supreme Court: 1921–1930*, 1986 DUKE LAW JOURNAL 65, 105.

21. The decision has received excellent book-length treatment. See MURPHY, *supra* note 1.
22. Olmstead's story is well told in NORMAN H. CLARK, THE DRY YEARS: PROHIBITION AND SOCIAL CHANGE IN WASHINGTON 161–78, 218–19 (Seattle: University of Washington Press 1965). Clark reports that during his time in prison Olmstead became converted to Christian Science and "to the proposition that liquor is bad for man and society." *Id*. at 218.
23. *Id*. at 161. He was also called in the newspapers "'the booze baron,' or 'the good bootlegger' who 'had served a social purpose.'" *Id*.

> [Olmstead's] organization had some fifty employees – salesmen, telephone operators, watchmen, warehousemen, deliverymen, truck drivers, bookkeepers, a lawyer, and even an official fixer, though Olmstead himself remained on intimate terms with some of his old police colleagues. The liquor was brought from England to Vancouver in three small ocean-going freighters which Olmstead chartered. These ships would stay well outside of American territorial waters and would be met by one or more of Olmstead's three fast motorboats. ... The list of customers was long and impressive. ... The organization might move as many as 200 cases a day, and gross receipts usually ran between $150,000 and $200,000 a month, with a net profit of about $4,000. With his share of the proceeds Olmstead lived in a huge house which reporters were later to describe as "palatial."

MURPHY *supra* note 1, at 16–17.

24. CLARK, *supra* note 22, at 166.
25. *Olmstead*, 277 U.S. at 456–57.
26. "Every person ... who shall intercept, read or in any manner interrupt or delay the sending of a message over any telegraph or telephone line ... shall be guilty of a misdemeanor." *Id*. at 468 (quoting Remington Compiled Stat. § 2656-18 (1922)). At least twenty-five other states had similar statutes. *See id*. at 479 n.13 (Brandeis,

Olmstead v. United States

J., dissenting). Olmstead knew that he was being wiretapped by federal agents; "a free-lance wire tapper" hired by the prohibition bureau had offered to sell him the transcript of his conversations. CLARK, *supra* note 22, at 168. But Olmstead "replied that he knew something about the rules of evidence, that such a transcript could never be used in court against him, that wire tapping was against state law, and that [the wire tapper] could go to hell." *Id.* Brashly, Olmstead took only minimal precautions. *Id.*

27. William S. Fairfield & Charles Clift, *The Wiretappers*, 7 REPORTER 10 (December 23, 1952). "For 'many years' prior to 1929" the "FBI's Manual of Rules and Regulations, under the heading 'unethical tactics,' banned wire-tapping and provided for the dismissal of anybody who engaged in it." ALEXANDER CHARNS, CLOAK AND GAVEL: FBI WIRETAPS, BUGS, INFORMERS, AND THE SUPREME COURT 20 (Urbana: University of Illinois Press 1992). I have been unable to locate an original copy of this directive or manual in Justice Department files, but it seems clear that wiretapping was forbidden within the Stone Justice Department. *See* MURPHY, *supra* note 1, at 13; WILLIAM ALLEN WHITE, A PURITAN IN BABYLON, THE STORY OF CALVIN COOLIDGE 274 (New York: MacMillan Co. 1938); Richard C. Donnelly, *Comments and Caveats on the Wire Tapping Controversy*, 63 YALE LAW JOURNAL 799, 799–800 (1954); *Justice Department Bans Wire Tapping; Jackson Acts on Hoover Recommendation*, NEW YORK TIMES (March 18, 1940), at 1; 86 CONG. REC. APP. 1471–72 (March 18, 1940).

On August 7, 1924, Roger Baldwin recorded a memorandum describing an interview with Attorney General Stone and J. Edgar Hoover. Memorandum of an Interview between Roger Baldwin and Harlan Fiske Stone and J. Edgar Hoover, August 7, 1924 (American Civil Liberties Union Archives). Baldwin wrote:

> Both the Attorney General and Mr. Hoover say that any illegal methods of getting evidence would result in disciplinary measures against agents using them, Mr. Hoover going so far as saying that they could be fired without a hearing, upon proof that such methods have been used. He referred specifically to tapping telephones, placing dictagraphs in offices and homes, opening mail without warrants, engaging in provocative work and employing third-degree methods. ... He furthermore said that the control of expenditures of local offices were so close and in his hands personally, that it would be impossible to put in telephone-tapping devices without his knowing it. He says the Department welcomes any information tending to show that any agent has violated these instructions and that such agents will be dismissed at once. The Attorney General says the same thing, asking us for specific evidence on which to base any further instructions to the men.

Id.

In 1928, Stone's 1924 policy was apparently reaffirmed by Attorney General Sargent. *See Wire Tapping in Law Enforcement*, Hearings before the House Committee on Expenditures in the Executive Departments, 71st CONG. 3rd SESS. (1931), at 2 (statement of William D. Mitchell); David M. Helfeld, *A Study of Justice Department Policies on Wire Tapping*, 9 LAWYERS GUILD REVIEW 57, 59 (1949). On December 2, 1929, J. Edgar Hoover testified before a Subcommittee of the House Appropriations Committee that "[w]e have a very definite rule in the bureau that any employee engaging in wire tapping will be dismissed from the service of the bureau." *Department of Justice Appropriation Bill for 1931*, Hearing before the Subcommittee of the House Committee on Appropriations, 71st CONG. 2nd SESS. (1929), at 63. Hoover contended that "government agents had 'no ethical right' to tap, even though the Olmstead ruling had given them that right." CHARNS, *supra*, at 20.

28. JACOB W. LANDYNSKI, SEARCH AND SEIZURE AND THE SUPREME COURT: A STUDY IN CONSTITUTIONAL INTERPRETATION 200 (Baltimore: Johns Hopkins Press 1966). The tension between prohibition enforcement and other forms of law enforcement continued even after the Bureau of Prohibition was transferred to the Justice Department in 1930. On January 19, 1931, Attorney General Mitchell entered a new directive, because "[t]he present condition in the department can not continue. We can not have one bureau in which wiretapping is allowed and another in which it is prohibited. The same regulations must apply to all." *Wire Tapping in Law Enforcement*, *supra* note 27, at 2 (statement of William D. Mitchell). Essentially Mitchell's new regulations allowed wiretapping if approved by a chief of a bureau in consultation with an assistant attorney general. *Id.* In 1933, for a single year, Congress added a proviso to an appropriations bill for the Department of Justice to the effect that "no part of this appropriation shall be used for or in connection with 'wire tapping' to produce evidence of violations of the National Prohibition Act, as amended and supplemented." Pub. L. 72-387, 47 Stat. 1371, 1381 (March 1, 1933). *See* Louis Fisher, *Congress and the Fourth Amendment*, 21 GEORGIA LAW REVIEW 107, 128–29 (1986).

29. About half the states prohibited the use of wiretapping with respect to all law enforcement. *See supra* note 26.

30. 19 F.2d 842, 847 (9th Cir. 1927).

31. Olmstead v. United States, 275 U.S. 557 (1927).

32. Stone 1927 Docket Book, at 84.

33. Olmstead v. United States, 276 U.S. 609, 609–10 (1928). Stone's docket book is unclear about exactly what happened at the Court's January 7 meeting. Stone 1927 Docket Book, at 343. It records a vote in which the Court split 4–4, with Taft, Holmes, McReynolds, and Sanford voting "No," and Van Devanter, Brandeis, Butler, and Stone voting "Yes." (Sutherland was absent). There is an "X" placed by Taft's name, which was Stone's characteristic method of designating the justice assigned to draft an opinion.

One interpretation of this docket entry is that it records a 4–4 split on the question of whether admission of evidence procured through wiretapping violates the Fourth Amendment. It would be odd to record a vote on the merits before the oral argument of the case, which did not occur until February 20–21. But if the docket entry does in fact record such a vote, it indicates that some time after the oral argument Holmes and Van Devanter switched their votes. *See* Stone 1927 Docket Book, at 402. Given that Holmes would eventually refuse to reach the Fourth Amendment question, his vote at the January 7 meeting is not surprising. Van Devanter's vote is more puzzling, but he might have had the same Fourth Amendment concerns as those he expressed to Brandeis in *United States v. Lee*. *See supra* note 20. After the decision, however, Van Devanter, at least to Taft, expressed confidence in its result. *See infra* note 96. A different interpretation of Stone's January 7 docket entry,

Olmstead v. United States

however, is that it instead records a vote on whether *certiorari* should be granted. But on this interpretation the "X" by Taft's name is inexplicable.

On the day after the conference, Taft wrote his daughter: "We held a Conference yesterday in which the Court did something that I did not like, but which resulted in bringing before us a question which I hope a majority of the Court can be induced to decide the right way. I find it odd how absorbed one becomes in the merits or demerits of a question, and that old as I am and long has been my experience, defeat colors the rest of the day which follows and one despairs of the Republic." OWH to Mrs. Frederick J. Manning (January 8, 1928) (Taft papers).

34. WILLEBRANDT, *supra* note 1, at 231–32. *See The Inside of Prohibition*, NEW YORK TIMES (August 19, 1929), at 14 ("I certainly approved of apprehending Olmstead ... but didn't approve the way the prohibition agents obtained their evidence. Practically all their testimony consisted of things they overheard on tapped telephone wires. Now, I thoroughly disapprove of the practice of tapping telephone wires. Irrespective of its legality, I believe it a dangerous and unwarrantable policy to follow in enforcing law. Many of the States of the Union have State laws against it. ... I indicated to the Solicitor General my unwillingness to argue the case and try to justify the prohibition agents' wire-tapping tactics when I so thoroughly disapproved of them. Consequently, Mr. Mitchell employed distinguished counsel, a man formerly associated with his firm in Minnesota.").

35. LEWIS J. PAPER, BRANDEIS 307–14 (Englewood Cliffs: Prentice-Hall 1983).

36. Brandeis papers. *See* Olmstead v. United States, 277 U.S. 438, 483 (1927) (Brandeis, J., dissenting).

37. By February 17, Brandeis's memorandum had begun to assume a form roughly similar to that of his published dissent. On February 23, three days after oral argument, Brandeis circulated the memorandum to Holmes for comment. At that time the memorandum addressed, first, the question of whether a wiretap was a search or seizure for purposes of the Fourth Amendment, and, second, the question of whether the federal government ought to admit evidence secured by criminal conduct. Holmes replied:

> I think this is a fine discourse. I agree with the last point. I still wobble on the illegal search and regrettably but categorically disagree with the notion that the use of the knowledge gained by wiretapping is contra Am. V. I fear that your early stated zeal for privacy carries you too far.

Brandeis papers. Alongside the sentence "Can it be that the Constitution affords no protection against such invasions of individual security?", which appears at page 474 of Brandeis's published dissent, Holmes commented, "This would not be invasions of personal liberty in any sense that I can understand. It is the personal liberty of the other fellow that you want to restrict." Alongside the sentence in which Brandeis observes that *Boyd* "reviewed the history that lay behind the Fourth and Fifth Amendments," *Olmstead*, 277 U.S. at 474 (Brandeis, J., dissenting), Holmes commented: "My impression was that Wigmore had thrashed the history" set forth in *Boyd*. When Brandeis wrote, "[t]here is, in essence, no difference between the sealed letter and the private telephone message," *Olmstead*, 277 U.S. at 475, Holmes noted in the margin, "I think there is a good deal of difference." When Brandeis argued that the use "in any criminal proceeding" of material obtained through "unjustified" wiretaps in violation of the Fourth Amendment "constitutes a violation of the Fifth Amendment," *Olmstead*, 277 U.S. at 478 (Brandeis, J., dissenting), Holmes wrote, "I think this wrong," as he also did next to Brandeis's sentence: "And the use, as evidence in a criminal proceeding, of facts ascertained by such intrusion must be deemed a violation of the Fifth." *See Olmstead*, 277 U.S. at 478–79 (Brandeis, J., dissenting). Holmes's comments are contained in the draft of the memorandum that is located in the Brandeis papers.

38. Stone 1927 Docket Book, at 402. Taft wrote his son that he did not look forward to drafting the opinion. WHT to Robert A. Taft (February 26, 1928) (Taft papers). In truth Taft had just experienced a difficult personal situation that, given his increasingly violent feelings about the need for strict law enforcement, see *supra* Chapter 32, at note 9, must have made *Olmstead* an especially exasperating case. Taft's younger son Charles was at that time a prosecuting attorney for Cincinnati, Taft's hometown. During the entire fall and early winter of 1927–28, Charles was involved in the high-profile prosecution of George Remus, the "king of the bootleggers," who was on trial for the murder of his estranged wife. Remus had shot his wife in plain daylight as she was driving to court to divorce him. Remus was an ex-lawyer who chose to defend himself, pleading temporary insanity because, while he was in prison serving time for prohibition offenses, his wife had cuckolded him with Franklin Dodge, an ace federal prohibition investigator. Remus alleged that Dodge and Remus's wife had become lovers and robbed him of all his assets while he was in prison. *See* Orville Dwyer, *Remus Good or Remus Bad Next Move in Trial*, CHICAGO DAILY TRIBUNE (December 6, 1927), at 13; *Remus Tells Why He Shot Wife to Death; Had Moral Right to Kill Her, He Says*, CHICAGO DAILY TRIBUNE (October 7, 1927), at 1. During the trial Charles and Remus nearly came to blows on several occasions. When Charles alleged that Remus had been disbarred for reasons other than his prohibition conviction, Remus returned:

> "A nice statement to make by the son of the Chief Justice of the United States, if the Court pleases. He knows that the defendant is charged with murder, and he knows that he makes these statements for no other purpose than to cause prejudice as a result of these newspaper men that are here.
> He knows that in no court of justice that kind of treatment would be taken for granted. He knows that the only record admissible in this court of law, or any other court of law, not only in this county but in the Supreme Court of which this young man's father is the lord high Chief Justice.
> It has been the pleasure of this defendant to appear before that high Chief Justice, but the specimen as given by this offshoot of that great renowned character is pitiful . . . .
> Five hundred judges and members of the Chicago bar have volunteered to come down here as character witnesses, and just because the son of the Chief Justice in this wonderful United States makes that kind of an assertion – man, if I had you in the corridor I would wreck you physically. I will tell you the truth – "
> Mr. Taft's cheeks were red as he listened. Remus had stamped his way over to the State's Attorney's table and was shaking his fist under Mr. Taft's nose.

Remus Near Blows with Prosecutors, NEW YORK TIMES (November 19, 1927), at 19. *See* Orville Dwyer, *Judge Warns Remus to Abide by Court Rules*, CHICAGO DAILY TRIBUNE (November 18, 1927), at 8; *Remus Tells Jury He Defended Home*,

Olmstead v. United States

NEW YORK TIMES (December 20, 1927), at 13 (reporting that Remus declared to the jury that "[t]his defendant . . . started in life at $5 a month . . . we could not all be born with a golden spoon in our mouths like Charles P. Taft the second"). After deliberating for only thirty minutes, the jury acquitted Remus on grounds of insanity. Orville Dwyer, *Remus Free if Found Sane*, CHICAGO DAILY TRIBUNE (December 21, 1927), at 1. Remus painted himself as a "martyr" to the "awful mistake" of prohibition, Orville Dwyer, *Remus Paints Self to Jury as Home Defender*, CHICAGO DAILY TRIBUNE (December 20, 1927), at 12, which in his view had created a corps of corrupt officials like Dodge. He was suffering, as F.H. La Guardia said, of "dementia Volsteadia." *La Guardia Believes Remus Is Victim of Dementia Volsteadia*, CHICAGO DAILY TRIBUNE (October 16, 1927), at 3. Dodge was in fact eventually convicted on perjury charges. *Dodge, Foe of Remus, Is Given Prison Sentence*, CHICAGO DAILY TRIBUNE (October 27, 1931), at 20. The connection between Taft and his son excited public commentary. *See Father Taft Must Think Much About Remus Case*, NEWARK EVENING NEWS (November 25, 1927).

During the trial William Howard Taft received word that Remus "was looking for a weapon to use it on Charlie." WHT to Robert A. Taft (December 11, 1927) (Taft papers). "We seem to be surrounded by bootlegging atmospheres," he wrote his brother Horace. WHT to Horace D. Taft (December 12, 1927) (Taft papers). "Remus is a bad man and I rather think a dangerous man. The bootlegging seems to develop an indifference to murder and to make people think that murder can be committed with immunity." *Id*. The thought that Remus "was seeking a weapon in order to attack Charlie and kill him," *id*., made Taft "anxious and concerned." WHT to James R. Angell (December 12, 1927) (Taft papers). He wrote his son to take extra precautions in the courtroom. WHT to Robert A. Taft (December 11, 1927) (Taft papers). Taft despaired of the "sympathetic feeling for Remus throughout the community. The desperation of these wets is such that mere murder seems not a matter for comment, especially if it grows out of bootlegging. . . . However, there must be somebody to fight for the people and for society, and if Charlie is doing his work well, as I hope he is, and suffers in the doing of it, it is a sacrifice that must be made in the discharge of his duty." WHT to Horace D. Taft (December 12, 1927) (Taft papers).

These circumstances could not but affect Taft's perspective on the prosecution of the major bootlegger of Seattle in February 1928.

39. Brandeis papers. Brandeis wrote Holmes: "Don't spend time on this. It is part of what you have already seen. The others have not." To this Holmes replied, "Count me in." *Id*. Stone responded to Brandeis's circulation with a short letter:

> I quite agree with you that we should lay it down as a rule to be applied in the federal courts that evidence procured by violations of the criminal law should be excluded. I would not, however, be inclined to place this result on the analogy to ratification or to the maxim that equity will not aid one who comes into court with unclean hands, applicable in the field of private law. I don't think that those analogies really apply to the acts of government agents.
>
> I would say that the evidence should be placed on broad grounds of public policy similar, if not identical, to those which have led the court to exclude evidence procured in violation of constitutional provisions. It seems to me quite as offensive to policy and morals for the federal government to secure convictions through its sending its agents into the state and there

The Taft Court

> violating the state law by its officers [as] to secure convictions through the violation of its own constitution.

HFS to LDB (March 22, 1928) (Stone papers).

40. Thomas R. Brown to WHT (December 22, 1927) (Taft papers) (Sutherland was suffering from "chronic colitis, associated with some disturbance in his gastric and pancreatic secretions, and very much affected by the condition of his nervous apparatus, so that worry, strain and fatigue manifest themselves rather strikingly in this portion of his body"). According to Dr. Brown, Sutherland's physician, Sutherland could start "work the first of the year if he can be spared some of the routine wear and tear. ... I feel, however, he should have this summer a long holiday, preferably beginning about the middle of May so that he can not only consolidate his gain, but markedly improve his condition so that there may be a complete freedom from his symptoms by the fall." *Id.* *See* WHT to Thomas R. Brown (December 26, 1927) (Taft papers) ("I can save him some of the usual work, and I shall do it conscientiously.").

41. WHT to Robert A. Taft (April 15, 1928) (Taft papers) ("Sutherland is going abroad for his health on the 18th of May, and the Court is very anxious to get through."). *See* WHT to GS (May 17, 1928) (Sutherland papers) ("I have been delighted to see how strong you are now and how much work you have done of the hard kind of opinion writing that consumes thinking energy. I am looking forward with satisfaction to greeting you both in the full bloom of youthful health. And what pleasure you will have in the consciousness that you are not a slave to a lot of opinions the thought of which would continue to cloud your summer. I felicitate you. But don't try to do too much. ... Practice the Italian saying '*Dolce fier nient*.' I don't think it is always sweet to do nothing. But under the beautiful Italian skies you can show that some times it applies and add to the sweetness the recurring thought of the hard useful work you have done and leave behind. There is nothing quite so satisfying as that thought. And then know too you carry with you the loving thoughts and hopes of all your colleagues. They are real and sincere and awaken fervor."); GS to WHT (May 18, 1928) (Taft papers) ("That was a very sweet going away letter and Mrs. Sutherland and I appreciate it beyond expression. I shall think of you always as my good Chief for whom my admiration and affection run a close race."). While in Europe, Sutherland wrote Taft occasional letters about his travels. *See, e.g.*, GS to WHT (July 3, 1928) (Taft papers) ("Italy has every appearance of prosperity. Mussolini has done marvelous things. He has made the strike a thing of the past and has almost gotten rid of the beggar and the petty thief – though it is still well to insure your trunks.").

42. Memorandum from GS to WHT (May 15, 1928) (Sutherland papers).

43. WHT to ETS (May 25, 1928) (Taft papers); WHT to WVD (May 25, 1928) (Taft papers).

44. WHT to WVD (May 25, 1928) (Taft papers). On May 30, Taft wrote McReynolds and Van Devanter asking if Taft could insert this sentence into the opinion: "The Gouled case [255 U.S. 298 (1921)] is an extreme case, was not elaborately considered, and is not to be extended beyond its own facts by implication." WHT to JCM (May 30, 1928) (Taft papers); WHT to WVD (May 30, 1928) (Taft papers). "I ought to say," Taft added, "that I talked the matter over with Justice Sutherland before he left, and he approved exactly such a reference to the Gouled case." *Id.* In

Olmstead v. United States

his published opinion, Taft wrote that "Gouled v. United States carried the inhibition against unreasonable searches and seizures to the extreme limit. Its authority is not to be enlarged by implication, and must be confined to the precise state of facts disclosed by the record." *Olmstead*, 277 U.S. at 463.

45. WHT to JCM (May 31, 1928) (Taft papers). "[E]xcept," Taft added, "that I left out a part of the written portion of your memorandum, not because I did not approve it, but because it seemed wiser to make it a little shorter." *Id.*

46. *Id.* Taft invited Van Devanter, McReynolds, and Sanford to his home on Friday, June 1, for a conference to "settle" the question of the limits of the grant of *certiorari*. *Id.* Aware of the tension between McReynolds and Brandeis, Taft was a good deal less discreet in venting his exasperation at Brandeis in his letter of May 31 to Sanford:

> Pierce Butler wants to confine our discussion in the wire tapping case to the constitutional questions that were specially reserved, and I would be quite content to do that but my recollection is that we did discuss very vigorously in Conference the question whether the fact that Washington had a criminal statute making intercepting of telephone messages a misdemeanor should not prevent the admission of such messages thus overheard. I agree that there was a specific limitation in the certiorari and that Brandeis in writing his first opinion violated the limitation, but as Holmes bases his dissent not on the unconstitutional feature but on the crime, as he calls it, we can not very well throw those two men out. I concede that where we make a limitation we ought to stick to it, and I think anyone would have done so but the lawless member of our Court. Nevertheless, I think we might as well meet the issue as it is, and provide hereafter for making people shinny on their own side.

WHT to ETS (May 31, 1928) (Taft papers). Apparently the Friday conference did not produce much change, for on June 1 Taft recirculated his opinion to the whole Court, saying that "I think there is nothing of substance that has been changed, except an added comment on the Gouled case and a more elaborate explanation of the discussion of the question of the alleged unethical conduct of the Government witnesses in intercepting the messages, and the effect of the Washington statute." WHT to the Members of the Court (June 1, 1928) (Taft papers). We don't have the date on which Brandeis circulated his full dissenting opinion to the Court, but we do know that Holmes replied, "I agree on the last ground – I am not quite ready to accept the constitutional one although I agree that the policy established by a law is not to be confined to the words. Gooch v. Oregon Short Line R.R. Co. 258 U.S. 22, 24." (Brandeis papers). Conversely, Stone wrote Brandeis, "I am with you in the constitutional point. . . . I have some doubts about your second ground but will let you know." *Id.* In his final published opinion, Stone nevertheless concurred in Brandeis's dissent, as well as with the dissent of Holmes and the dissent of Butler ("so far as it deals with the merits"). *Olmstead*, 277 U.S. at 488 (Stone, J., dissenting).

47. Taft disposed of the Fifth Amendment claim at the outset of his opinion: "There is no room in the present case for applying the Fifth Amendment, unless the Fourth Amendment was first violated. There was no evidence of compulsion to induce the defendants to talk over their many telephones. They were continually and voluntarily transacting business without knowledge of the interception. Our consideration must be confined to the Fourth Amendment." *Olmstead*, 277 U.S. at 462.

48. *Id.* at 463–64, 457. The wiretapping occurred because of the insertion of wires "in the streets near the houses." *Id.*
49. *Id.* at 464. The maxim that the Fourth Amendment was "to be liberally construed to effect the purpose of the framers of the Constitution in the interest of liberty" could not "justify enlargement of the language employed beyond the possible practical meaning of houses, persons, papers, and effects, or so to apply the words search and seizure as to forbid hearing or sight." *Id.* at 465.
50. *Id.* at 465. "The intervening wires are not part of his house or office any more than are the highways along which they are stretched." *Id.*
51. *Id.* at 465–66.
52. *Id.* at 464.
53. *Id.* ("It is plainly within the words of the Amendment to say that the unlawful rifling by a government agent of a sealed letter is a search and seizure of the sender's papers or effects. The letter is a paper, an effect, and in the custody of a Government that forbids carriage except under its protection.").
54. Silverman v. United States, 365 U.S. 505, 509–11 (1961) ("Eavesdropping accomplished by means of ... a physical intrusion is beyond the pale of even those decisions in which a closely divided Court has held that eavesdropping accomplished by other electronic means did not amount to an invasion of Fourth Amendment rights. ... The absence of a physical invasion of the petitioner's premises was ... a vital factor in the Court's decision in Olmstead."). On the ongoing importance of the metaphor of trespass to Fourth Amendment jurisprudence, see Utah v. Streiff, 579 U.S. 232, 237 (2016).
55. This is perhaps why Holmes refused to find that wiretapping constituted a search and seizure under the Fourth Amendment. In his dissent he said only that, "While I do not deny it, I am not prepared to say that the penumbra of the Fourth and Fifth Amendments covers the defendant, although I fully agree that Courts are apt to err by sticking too closely to the words of a law where those words import a policy that goes beyond them. Gooch v. Oregon Short Line R. R. Co., 258 U.S. 22, 24." *Olmstead*, 277 U.S. at 469 (Holmes, J., dissenting). See *supra* note 46.
56. That neither Sutherland nor McReynolds conceived the issue in *Olmstead* as a prohibition question is suggested by Nardone v. United States, 302 U.S. 379 (1937), in which long after prohibition the Court construed chapter 652, section 605 of the Communications Act of 1934, Pub. L. 73-416, 48 Stat. 1064, 1103 (June 19, 1934), which prohibited "any person" from intercepting telephone messages, as applying to federal law enforcement officials. Both Sutherland and McReynolds dissented. *Nardone*, 302 U.S. at 385–87. It is noteworthy that Van Devanter, who may have initially voted to suppress the evidence in *Olmstead*, did not dissent in *Nardone*. This suggests that Van Devanter's change of heart in *Olmstead*, if indeed he had such a change of heart, see *supra* note 33, may have been produced by his loyalty to Taft. But see *infra* note 96.
57. See *supra* text at note 42. Sutherland would later write Taft that the *Olmstead* opinion "will stand as good law and good sense. My only regret is that Pierce Butler dissented, though he did not go along with Brandeis, which helps some. My secretary sent me a copy of the opinion and I read it with care. It is as clear as crystal and in no way met by the dissenting opinions. To me it seems so entirely obvious that I marvel that the question could be seriously considered from the opposite point of view." GS to WHT (September 2, 1928) (Taft papers).

Olmstead v. United States

58. *Olmstead*, 277 U.S. at 487 (Butler, J., dissenting).
59. In a letter to Holmes, Frederick Pollock seemed to take the alternative position, that wiretapping was a form of appropriation:

> The point of substance, apart from any question of construction, is whether tapping telephone messages is mere eavesdropping, or on the same footing as intercepting and reading a closed letter. Common sense appears to favour the latter view.
>
> Was it ever doubted that a telegram follows the analogy of a letter in this respect? . . .
>
> As to the Fourth Amendment, it seems that even if you are bound to the letter, effects is a word of large import and may well be held to cover interests not falling within any recognized denomination of property.

Frederick Pollock to OWH (July 2, 1928), in 2 HOLMES-POLLOCK CORRESPONDENCE, at 225. Holmes likely disagreed with Pollock. *See supra* note 37.
60. In Silverman v. United States, 365 U.S. 505 (1961), the Court would later choose to make an analogous move:

> [T]he officers overheard the petitioners' conversations only by usurping part of the petitioners' house or office – a heating system which was an integral part of the premises occupied by the petitioners, a usurpation that was effected without their knowledge and without their consent. In these circumstances we need not pause to consider whether or not there was a technical trespass under the local property law relating to party walls. Inherent Fourth Amendment rights are not inevitably measurable in terms of ancient niceties of tort or real property law.

Id. at 511.
61. Brandeis later wrote Frankfurter: "I suppose some reviewer of the wire tapping decision will discern that in favor of property the Constitution is liberally construed – in favor of liberty, strictly." LDB to Felix Frankfurter (June 15, 1928), in BRANDEIS-FRANKFURTER CORRESPONDENCE, at 333.
62. *Olmstead*, 277 U.S. at 465.
63. In his private correspondence, however, Taft was more explicit: "The truth is we have to face the problem presented by new inventions. Many of them are most useful to the criminals in their war against society and are at once availed of, and these idealistic gentlemen urge a conclusion which facilitates the crime by their use and furnishes immunity from conviction by seeking to bring its use by government officers within the obstruction of the bill of rights and the 4th amendment." WHT to Horace D. Taft (June 12, 1928) (Taft papers).
64. Pub. L. 73-416, 48 Stat. 1064 (June 19, 1934).
65. Nardone v. United States, 302 U.S. 379, 385, 387 (1937) (Sutherland, J., dissenting). McReynolds joined Sutherland's dissent.
66. 265 U.S. 57, 59 (1924).
67. *Olmstead*, 277 U.S. at 476 (Brandeis, J., dissenting).
68. *Id.* at 478 (Brandeis, J., dissenting).
69. Samuel D. Warren & Louis D. Brandeis, *The Right to Privacy*, 4 HARVARD LAW REVIEW 193, 195–96 (1890). *Compare* Brandeis's *Olmstead* dissent: "Subtler and more far-reaching means of invading privacy have become available to the Government. Discovery and invention have made it possible for the Government,

by means far more effective than stretching upon the rack, to obtain disclosure in court of what is whispered in the closet." 277 U.S. at 473 (Brandeis, J., dissenting). The connection between Brandeis's *Olmstead* dissent and his earlier article has been widely noted. *See, e.g.*, Ken Gormley, *One Hundred Years of Privacy*, 1992 WISCONSIN LAW REVIEW 1335, 1360–69; Daniel J. Solove, *Conceptualizing Privacy*, 90 CALIFORNIA LAW REVIEW 1087, 1099–102 (2002); Silas J. Wasserstrom & Louis Michael Seidman, *The Fourth Amendment as Constitutional Theory*, 77 GEORGETOWN LAW JOURNAL 19, 63–66 (1988).

70. Katz v. United States, 389 U.S. 347, 362 (1967) (Harlan, J., concurring). *See id.* at 361: "[C]onversations in the open would not be protected against being overheard, for the expectation of privacy under the circumstances would be unreasonable. Cf. *Hester v. United States*."

71. 389 U.S. 347 (1967).

72. The Court stated: "We conclude that the underpinnings of *Olmstead* ... have been so eroded by our subsequent decisions that the 'trespass' doctrine there enunciated can no longer be regarded as controlling. The Government's activities in electronically listening to and recording the petitioner's words violated the privacy upon which he justifiably relied while using the telephone booth and thus constituted a 'search and seizure' within the meaning of the Fourth Amendment." *Id.* at 353.

73. 304 U.S. 144, 152 n.4 (1938). *See generally* JOHN HART ELY, DEMOCRACY AND DISTRUST (Cambridge: Harvard University Press 1980).

74. *See supra* Chapter 8, at 312–15, 320.

75. *Olmstead*, 277 U.S. at 469 (Holmes, J., dissenting). *See supra* note 37.

76. *See supra* Chapter 5, at 169–70.

77. *The Progressive Attitude towards Prohibition?*, 56 NEW REPUBLIC 166, 166–67 (1928).

78. Particularly noteworthy in this regard is that by 1926 Brandeis had come to stress "the limits of the mala prohibited [sic], as distinguished from the mala in se. It seems to me we were rather presumptuous in brushing away the distinction – another bit of really shallow rationalization; that there is, moreover, an essential difference between a crime and a delict; & that there are few acts or omissions which ought to be treated as crimes which do not arouse righteous indignation. For these some other solution should be found than existing penalties." LDB to Felix Frankfurter (July 2, 1926), in BRANDEIS-FRANKFURTER CORRESPONDENCE, at 245–46. The distinction between *mala prohibita* and *mala in se* was frequently drawn in discussions of prohibition. *See supra* Chapter 31, at 993–94. Brandeis had himself stressed the essential distinction between positive law and community sentiment as early as 1891, when he argued against prohibition in Massachusetts. *See supra* Chapter 30, at 993–94. Brandeis had testified before a committee of the Massachusetts legislature:

> MR. BRANDEIS. You cannot make a law which will be effectual that has not the moral support of a majority of the people unless you establish a despotism; and, on the other hand, you cannot disregard a law which expresses the will of the majority unless you invite anarchy.
>
> MR. JOHNSON. Isn't the existence of a statute proof of the will of the majority?
>
> MR. BRANDEIS. No. It is evidence which creates presumption; but the presumption may be rebutted by the facts.

Olmstead v. United States

2 THE SUPREME COURT OF THE UNITED STATES: HEARINGS AND REPORTS ON SUCCESSFUL AND UNSUCCESSFUL NOMINATIONS OF SUPREME COURT JUSTICES BY THE SENATE JUDICIARY COMMITTEE, 1916–1972, at 1064 (Roy M. Mersky & J. Myron Jacobstein, eds., Buffalo: W.S. Hein 1975). Brandeis testified that "No law can be effective which does not take into consideration the conditions of the community for which it is designed; no law can be a good law – every law must be a bad law – that remains unenforced. That is a fundamental truth in legislation." *Id.* at 1059. *Compare* the Court's unanimous decision in United States v. Balint, 258 U.S. 250, 251–52 (1922): "While the general rule at common law was that the scienter was a necessary element in the indictment and proof of every crime, and this was followed in regard to statutory crimes even where the statutory definition did not in terms include it, there has been a modification of this view in respect to prosecutions under statutes the purpose of which would be obstructed by such a requirement. ... Many instances of this are to be found in regulatory measures in the exercise of what is called the police power where the emphasis of the statute is evidently upon achievement of some social betterment rather than the punishment of the crimes as in cases of mala in se."

79. *Olmstead*, 277 U.S. at 474 (Brandeis, J., dissenting). Recall in this context that *The Right to Privacy* was also a massive (and successful) effort to transform the common law so that it might protect traditional values against new threats posed by "[r]ecent inventions and business methods." Warren & Brandeis, *supra* note 69, at 195.

80. "As a means of espionage, writs of assistance and general warrants are but puny instruments of tyranny and oppression when compared with wire-tapping." *Olmstead*, 277 U.S. at 476 (Brandeis, J., dissenting). Many years later, in congressional debates about the banning of wiretapping, Brandeis's dissent in *Olmstead* would be quoted in support of a statutory ban on the "despicable system of espionage under the wire-tapping practice." 76 CONG. REC. 2691 (January 27, 1933) (statement of Representative Charles John Schafer). *See* Pub. L. 72-387, 47 Stat. 1371, 1381 (March 1, 1933); 76 CONG. REC. 2693 (January 27, 1933) (statement of Representative George Holden Tinkham) (referring to the "flaming language" of Brandeis's *Olmstead* dissent, "the language of the spirit of America against espionage").

81. In 1920 Brandeis had written Frankfurter:

> I told Charles Merz the other day that the N[ew] R[epublic] ought to take up a continuous campaign against espionage. ...
>
> [I]t seems to me important that the attack on espionage be not confined to industrial espionage. That is merely one bad application of a practice. The fundamental objection to espionage is (1) that espionage demoralizes every human being who participates in or uses the results of espionage; (2) that it takes sweetness & confidence out of life; (3) that it takes away the special manly qualities of honor & generosity which were marked in Americans.
>
> It is like the tipping system an import from Continental Europe & the Near East only a thousand times worse. ... [T]he immorality, the ungentlemanliness, should be made the keynote, & not the industrial wrong or infringement of liberty as in the Red Campaign.
>
> It is un-American. It is nasty. It is nauseating.

The Taft Court

LDB to Felix Frankfurter (November 26, 1920), in BRANDEIS-FRANKFURTER CORRESPONDENCE, at 48.

Several years later Brandeis urged the *New Republic*'s Herbert Croly to "struggle to uproot the detective system root and branch-in government and in industry." LDB to Felix Frankfurter (March 15, 1924), *id.* at 161. Brandeis proclaimed: "Let him vow to strive without ceasing until the system is driven out or his own death release him. If the detective system lives, our ideals cannot survive. If I were dictator, I should abolish the system today without reserve, in every department of life and take all chances." *Id.* In 1926, upon learning of Frankfurter's plan to conduct a survey of the effectiveness of the criminal law in Boston, Brandeis wrote:

> I suggest that, as an incident of the current survey, special care be taken to ascertain and record: (a) The character (ethical) of the evidence through which it is sought to obtain a conviction – e.g. to what extent it is of the character held legal in Burdeau v McDowell 256 U.S. 465, & the many cases where fed crimes were prosecuted in U.S. courts with evidence illegally procured by state officials. . . .
>
> I have grave doubt whether we shall ever be able to effect more than superficial betterment unless we undertake to deal fundamentally with the intangibles; and succeed in infusing a sense (A) of the dignity of the law among a free, self-governing people and (B) of the solemnity of the function of administering justice. Among the essentials is that the government must, in its methods, & means, & instruments, be ever the gentleman. Also we must recognize the fallacy . . . that the main function of Courts is to settle controversies. This view seems to me a bit of that finite 19th century wisdom of the Militarians which has brought so much evil as well as good. There are times of ease & prosperity when the pressing danger is somnolence rather than litigiousness.

LDB to Felix Frankfurter (July 2, 1926), *id.* at 245. In 1927, Brandeis sought to instigate a "needed investigation of the government prostitutes – sometimes called spies, and euphemistically known as detectives, inspectors, special agents & intelligence officers." LDB to Felix Frankfurter (February 4, 1927), *id.* at 272.

There was in fact widespread indignation that prohibition had "created a bureaucracy in Washington to enforce the law that has filled the States with spies and enforcement officers who have invaded the sacred precincts of the home, walked roughshod over the rights of the people, destroyed confidence in the Federal Government, and accomplished no material results thereby." OSCAR W. UNDERWOOD, DRIFTING SANDS OF PARTY POLITICS 388 (New York: Century Co. 1928).

82. 381 U.S. 479, 494 (1965) (Goldberg, J., concurring).
83. During the Court's consideration of the case, Butler forcefully argued that it ought to say nothing about this issue because it had been excluded by the order granting *certiorari*. *See supra* text at note 33; *supra* note 46. In his dissent, Butler stated: "The order allowing the writs of certiorari operated to limit arguments of counsel to the constitutional question. I do not participate in the controversy that has arisen here as to whether the evidence was inadmissible because the mode of obtaining it was unethical and a misdemeanor under state law. I prefer to say nothing concerning those questions because they are not within the jurisdiction taken by the order." *Olmstead*, 277 U.S. at 486 (Butler, J., dissenting). For a discussion of *Olmstead* and the Court's power to use the writ of *certiorari* to limit the consideration of questions

Olmstead v. United States

in a case, see Benjamin B. Johnson, *The Origins of Supreme Court Question Selection*, 122 COLUMBIA LAW REVIEW 793, 840–44 (2022).

84. *Olmstead*, 277 U.S. at 470 (Holmes, J., dissenting). Holmes's law clerk, Arthur E. Sutherland, recalled: "I sat in the courtroom and heard the old man read his dissent. His words and voice and manner were disdainful. It seemed as though he were obliged to hold something unpleasant in his hands. I can still hear his careful voice speaking of 'this dirty business'." David M. O'Brien, *Sutherland's Recollections of Justice Holmes*, 1988 YEARBOOK OF THE SUPREME COURT HISTORICAL SOCIETY 18, 25.

85. *Olmstead*, 277 U.S. at 470 (Holmes, J., dissenting). "[I]t makes no difference," Holmes argued,

> that in this case wire tapping is made a crime by the law of the State, not by the law of the United States. It is true that a State cannot make rules of evidence for Courts of the United States, but the State has authority over the conduct in question, and I hardly think that the United States would appear to greater advantage when paying for an odious crime against State law than when inciting to the disregard of its own. I am aware of the often repeated statement that in a criminal proceeding the Court will not take notice of the manner in which papers offered in evidence have been obtained. But that somewhat rudimentary mode of disposing of the question has been overthrown by Weeks v. United States, 232 U.S. 383, and the cases that have followed it.

Id. at 470–71 (Holmes, J., dissenting). Holmes's opinion infuriated Taft, who regarded it as nasty. WHT to Horace D. Taft (June 12, 1928) (Taft papers).

86. Taft later wrote his brother: "Holmes has written the nastiest opinion in dissent and Brandeis is fuller of eloquence and idealism. . . . The truth is that Holmes voted the other way till Brandeis got after him and induced him to change on the ground that the state law in Washington forbade wiretapping. Holmes in his opinion really admits that the 4th Amendment does not cover wiretapping. If it does not, then the law is all against his conclusion on which he rests his case but he is a law unto himself if Brandeis says yes." WHT to Horace D. Taft (June 12, 1928) (Taft papers).

87. *Olmstead*, 277 U.S. at 483–85 (Brandeis, J., dissenting). Stone wrote separately to argue that the grant of *certiorari* did not restrain the Court from considering the question of the admissibility of the evidence, which was fairly presented by the record on appeal. *Id.* at 488 (Stone, J., dissenting). See *supra* note 83. In his last days as attorney general, after his nomination to the Court had been confirmed by the Senate, Stone wrote Frankfurter that he had reorganized the Bureau of Investigation of the Justice Department to impress upon agents of the Bureau

> that the real problem of law enforcement is in trying to obtain the cooperation and sympathy of the public and that they cannot hope to get such cooperation until they themselves merit the respect of the public. The Agents of the Bureau of Investigation have been impressed with the fact . . . that they must not be guilty of violations of law in gathering evidence upon violations of law, for the respect to which they are entitled as law enforcement officers can only be obtained by their strictly observing the rights of citizens and the law of the land.

HFS to Felix Frankfurter (February 9, 1925) (Stone papers). Stone was "firmly of the opinion that officials of the Department of Justice can more effectively perform their duties by acting the part of gentlemen than by resorting to tactics of a different character. The work of gathering evidence and of conducting litigation should be done in a gentlemanly way. Agents of the Bureau of Investigation in the past may have been inclined to place emphasis on the end rather than on the means." *Id. See* HFS to Roger Baldwin (January 20, 1925) (American Civil Liberties Union Archives: The Roger Baldwin Years: 1917–1950, vols. 271–272) ("I am coming around to the view that law administration would be imensely [sic] improved in the United States not only by strict obedience to law by all law enforcement officers, but by insistence that the United States and its law enforcement officials should play the roll [sic] of gentlemen in the difficult task of law administration.").

88. *See supra* Chapter 31, at note 79.
89. *See supra* Chapter 31, at 1001.
90. *See supra* Chapter 31, at 1000.
91. *Olmstead*, 277 U.S. at 468. Taft's appeal to the common law was in truth ambiguous, because the nature of the law that determined the admission of evidence in federal criminal prosecutions was at the time unclear. In 1851, the Court had held that evidentiary rules in federal criminal prosecutions were to be determined by the law in effect in the state of prosecution in 1789. United States v. Reid, 53 U.S. 361, 362–63 (1851). In 1892, in Logan v. United States, 144 U.S. 263, 303 (1892), the Court applied the logic of *Reid* to decide that federal courts should in criminal trials apply the law of evidence in effect in the state of prosecution as of the date of the state's admission to the Union. As the law of evidence evolved, this approach produced increasingly intolerable results. By 1918, therefore, the Court in Rosen v. United States, 245 U.S. 467 (1918), was prepared to invoke "the light of general authority and of sound reason" explicitly to discard "the dead-hand of the common-law rule of 1789." *Rosen* fashioned its own rule of evidence that reflected "the conviction of our time." *Id.* at 470–71. *See* Greer v. United States, 245 U.S. 559, 561 (1918). Two years later, however, the Court without explanation returned to the original regime of *Reid. See* Jin Fuey Moy v. United States, 254 U.S. 189, 195 (1920). The upshot was that at the time of *Olmstead* the law of evidence for federal criminal trials was in a state of "perplexity." W. Barton Leach, *State Law of Evidence in the Federal Courts*, 43 HARVARD LAW REVIEW 554, 565 (1930).

In *Olmstead*, Taft chose to ignore *Rosen* and to follow *Logan*, holding that Olmstead's trial should be governed by the evidentiary law of Washington in effect in 1889, the year of Washington's admission to the Union:

> While a Territory, the English common law prevailed in Washington and thus continued after her admission in 1889. The rules of evidence in criminal cases in courts of the United States sitting there, consequently are those of the common law. United States v. Reid, 12 How. 361, 363, 366; Logan v. United States, 144 U.S. 263, 301; Rosen v. United States, 245 U.S. 467.... The common law rule is that the admissibility of evidence is not affected by the illegality of the means by which it was obtained.

Olmstead, 277 U.S. at 466–67. *See* Leach, *supra*, at 564–65. In 1944, Rule 26 of the Federal Rules of Criminal Procedure overruled this approach on the ground that "since all Federal crimes are statutory and all criminal prosecutions in the Federal

Olmstead v. United States

courts are based on acts of Congress, uniform rules of evidence appear desirable if not essential in criminal cases, as otherwise the same facts under differing rules of evidence may lead to a conviction in one district and to an acquittal in another." Fed. R. Crim. P. 26, Notes to the Rules of Criminal Procedure for the District Courts of the United States, reprinted in 7 DRAFTING HISTORY OF THE FEDERAL RULES OF CRIMINAL PROCEDURE 225, 260 (Madeleine J. Wilken & Nicholas Triffin, eds., Buffalo: William S. Hein & Co. 1991). The approach of Rule 26 was based on the Court's decisions in Funk v. United States, 290 U.S. 371, 379 (1933), and Wolfe v. United States, 291 U.S. 7, 12 (1934), which held that rules of evidence in criminal cases should be determined "by common law principles as interpreted and applied by the federal courts in the light of reason and experience." Id.

Taft's use of Logan allowed him to ignore the inconvenient fact that Washington law at the time of the Olmstead trial was to the effect that "it is beneath the dignity of the state and contrary to public policy for the state to use for its own profit evidence that has been obtained in violation of the law." State v. Buckley, 258 P. 1030, 1031 (Wash. 1927). See State v. Gibbons, 203 P. 390, 396 (Wash. 1922). Oddly, neither Holmes nor Brandeis challenged Taft's choice of law in their dissent.

92. Olmstead, 277 U.S. at 467. In his private correspondence Taft elaborated the point:

> Holmes says the misdemeanor of the State of Washington is a crime but he does not realize or consider that the admissibility of evidence in the federal courts is determined not by a statute but by the common law. More than this, a large majority of the states supreme Courts refuse to follow the Weeks case decided by our Court as to the admissibility of evidence secured by violation of the Fourth Amendment. Chief Judge Cardozo speaking for the Court of Appeals of New York writes an opinion showing that 31 State Supreme Courts are against it and only 14 for it. They have had in New York a case decided by their Appellate Division following the same principle in which the evidence of the police man who listened in by wiretapping was held to be admissible although the law of New York forbids wiretapping as a misdemeanor.

WHT to Horace D. Taft (June 12, 1928) (Taft papers). See *supra* note 91.

93. Olmstead, 277 U.S. at 468. Holmes would later take exception to this formulation of the question:

> The C. J. who wrote the prevailing opinion, perhaps as a rhetorical device to obscure the difficulty, perhaps merely because he did not note the difference, which perhaps I should have emphasized more, spoke of the objection to the evidence as based on its being obtained by "unethical" means (horrid phrase), although he adds & by a misdemeanor under the laws of Washington. I said that the State of Washington had made it a crime and that the Government could not put itself in the position of offering to pay for a crime in order to get evidence of another crime. Brandeis wrote much more elaborately, but I didn't agree with all that he said. I should not have printed what I wrote, however, if he had not asked me to.

OWH to Frederick Pollock (June 20, 1928), in 2 HOLMES-POLLOCK CORRESPONDENCE, at 222. Taft's pragmatic calculus has apparently proved convincing to later generations, because, in the absence of statutory authorization, the acquisition of evidence through the violation of criminal law (as distinct from evidence acquired through the violation of the Constitution) has not been thought to warrant exclusion. See, e.g., United States v. Powell, 847 F.3d 760, 771 (6th Cir.), cert. denied, 138 S.Ct. 143 (2017); United States v. Kontny, 238 F.3d 815, 818 (7th Cir.), cert. denied, 532 U.S. 1022 (2001); United States v. Thompson, 936 F.2d 1249 (11th Cir. 1991), cert. denied, 502 U.S. 1075 (1992); but see State v. Scalera, 393 P.3d 1005, 1008 (Haw. 2017); People v. Hawkins, 668 N.W.2d 602, 609 (Mich. 2003).

94. The position clearly made Taft uncomfortable and defensive:

> Of course one does not like to be held up as one who favors the worst morals but we have to put up with such attacks in our efforts to follow the old time common law recognized by all authorities English and American that if evidence is pertinent it is admissible however obtained. Cardozo argues that this view is the proper one in defense of society. We have a hard enough time to convict without presenting immunity to ... criminals. I shall continue to be worried by attacks from all the academic lawyers who write college law journals but I suppose it is not a basis for impeachment. We pointed out that Congress can change the rule if it sees fit. It will be of interest to see whether Congress will do it. Here it may be that the prohibitionists in Congress will oppose such legislation not because of their sensitiveness as to the scope of the Fourth Amendment but just because they are in favor of convicting bootleggers. Indeed many of the opposing views are and will be due to that issue solely.

WHT to Horace D. Taft (June 12, 1928) (Taft papers). Taft was particularly exercised at the "outcry" in the "New York papers." WHT to WVD (June 13, 1928) (Van Devanter papers). The "feeling about bootleggers and prohibition is so strong among the wealthy in the East" that they do not "seem to realize that this decision is exactly in accord with the law of their state defended as it is more broadly even in an attack on the Weeks case by another Jew Cardozo and by the Appellate Division case cited in the last page of the opinion." Taft confided to Van Devanter that Taft's brother Horace "writes me that the Springfield Republican ... defends the opinion, pointing out that there was no such outcry as these New York papers make when wiretapping was used against anarchists as there would not be if murderers were caught by it but bootleggers are a different matter." Id.

95. See Frown on Wire-Tapping, NEW YORK TIMES (June 7, 1928), at 29 ("Attorney General Sargent has instructed agents of the Department of Justice not to resort to this measure for running down criminals and Commissioner Doran has discouraged its use by prohibition agents. ... 'Although wire-tapping is legal, it is not ethical,' the Department of Justice holds.").

96. Taft would persistently resist the effort to categorize Olmstead as a prohibition opinion. He wrote his brother, "It has an element of humor for me that the public seems to be affected by the fact that it is against the bootleggers and assumes that it was that which carried the day. Of course that had nothing to do with the conclusion. The telephone might just as well have been used to carry on a conspiracy to rob, to murder, to commit treason." WHT to Horace D. Taft (June 12, 1928) (Taft papers). Taft wrote Van Devanter that, "I suppose you have seen the criticisms of my opinion and our decision in the wire tapping case. We'll have to stand it of course, without answer or demur. ... It can't be gotten out of the heads of the public that it is a decision on the Prohibition law. I doubt if the indignation of critics would be so great if it were a conspiracy to murder that was carried on that way." WHT to WVD (June 12, 1928) (Van Devanter papers). Van Devanter replied:

Olmstead v. United States

> I have seen many of the public comments on the wire-tapping decision and have observed, as you have, that some of the comments treat the decision as though it was peculiar to prohibition cases. Had the decision related to evidence in a case involving a scheme to defraud the United States or to corrupt some of its officers the press and public would have given it undivided approval. The real nature of the question and of the decision will gradually come to be appreciated and understood. As with any important constitutional decision it must be judged by its working through a period of time and not by its accidental application in a similar case. No doubt other cases will be arising in which the principle will have application to other kinds of crime and in other surroundings. When this happens the vision of those who are talking about it now will expand to a larger range and views will be readjusted accordingly. I am quite content to leave the outcome to experience. A man named Lowman or something like that who was once Lieutenant Governor of New York and is now an Assistant Secretary of the Treasury or in some other position of prominence in the prohibition administration, gave out an interview – am told it is authentic – to the effect that in the enforcement of the prohibition law "the practice of wire-tapping will be followed wherever deemed expedient." This is an unfortunate statement made at an inappropriate time. For other reasons I have come to think that Lowman is quite unfit for his job. More than half the agitation about prohibition is due to the actions and declarations of incompetents in places of authority. A wise man in such a place would talk little, would work hard and endeavor to exercise a wide supervision and devote himself to securing results which will speak for themselves.

WVD to WHT (June 15, 1928) (Van Devanter papers). "Time and experience will demonstrate that the decision is right," Van Devanter wrote Taft. "Part of the opposition comes from men who look on the decision as merely relating to the detection of liquor transactions. Another part look on it as likely to interfere with socialistic and communistic efforts. The publication called 'The Nation' has come to be distinctly socialistic and in its last issue it published an ugly criticism of the decision on its first page. . . . From beginning to end it lends itself to tearing down, not building up. Every communist in the country and every sympathizer with communism naturally will be against the decision, and so will those who call themselves reformers but in truth are infected with communism. We do not have to go far to see that this is so." WVD to WHT (June 16, 1928) (Van Devanter papers).

Taft replied:

> I hope with you that consideration of the question will justify our conclusion in the minds of fair men who understand the exact issue. I anticipate that there will be an immediate effort by legislation to negative the effect of the decision but I am hoping that a discussion will clarify the real issue. I have no objection to a provision that no evidence secured by wire tapping or intercepting messages over telephone systems shall be admissible in courts of the United States in the trial of criminal cases provided that the act shall not apply in any indictment for treason, murder, anarchy, robbery, conspiracy against the United States where there is evidence tending to show that the telephone is being used to promote such treason, murder, anarchy, robbery or conspiracy. I am not troubled about the liquor law. That can take care of itself but in the crimes above mentioned and others society would be at the mercy of the most dangerous criminals if they could use the telephone to carry on such crimes and be immune from using the telephone to discover or offset its use for such criminal purpose. Otherwise such immunity would be making the telephone a Frankenstein.

WHT to WVD (June 22, 1928) (Van Devanter papers). Van Devanter promptly wrote back to Taft, "I seriously doubt the propriety of making any concessions respecting the need for legislation restraining the use of evidence of the kind considered in the wire-tapping cases. To my mind there is no need for such legislation; nor is there any sound basis for making a legislative distinction in this regard between different classes of crime. The agitation which followed the decision will gradually exhaust itself and the decision will come to be accepted as sound in principle and needed in practice." WVD to WHT (June 25, 1928) (Taft papers).

97. WHT to M.S. Sherman (July 11, 1928) (Taft papers).
98. Taft complained to his brother that the *Olmstead* dissenters

> abused us as encouragers of criminals in receiving the evidence of the wiretapping as proper. Brandeis was especially severe in his strictures on our lack of dignity and morality and I have no doubt he will find a good many followers. It is rather trying to be held up as immoral by one who is full of tricks all the time. But he can become full of eloquent denunciation without great effort. . . . His claques in the law school contingent will sound his praises and point the finger of scorn at us, but if they think we are going to be frightened in our effort to stand by the law and give the public a chance to punish criminals, they are mistaken, even though we are condemned for lack of high ideals. . . . Stone has become entirely subservient to Holmes and Brandeis – I am very much disappointed in him. I urged Coolidge to appoint him but he hungers for the applause of the law school professors and the admirers of Holmes. If Holmes' dissents in constitutional cases had been followed, we should have had no constitution. . . . Holmes has very little knowledge of governmental principles.

WHT to Horace D. Taft (June 8, 1928) (Taft papers). By July, however, Taft had acquired some philosophical distance from the controversy. He wrote Sutherland, "You may have seen the severe criticisms of our judgment in the wire tapping case, but I think the more that the case is read and understood, the less effective will be the eloquence and denunciation of Brandeis and Holmes. I feel quite sure that we are right, and that this will be ultimately recognized." WHT to GS (July 25, 1928) (Sutherland papers).

99. *The Court on Wire-Tapping*, New York World (June 6, 1928), at 12.
100. *Wire-Tapping Held Legal*, 97 Literary Digest 10 (June 16, 1928) (quoting the *New York Evening Post*).
101. *A New Dred Scott Decision*, 149 The Outlook 293, 293 (1928). Even the Anti-Saloon League refused unequivocally to support the decision:

> The Anti-Saloon League "deplores" the recent Supreme Court decision legalizing "wire-tapping" in Prohibition cases, if the ruling is to apply to the Prohibition law only, according to Dr. S.E. Nicholson, National Secretary and State Superintendent of the dry organization. . . . It is feared by the dry forces that prohibition will fall into "disrepute" and suffer "irreparable harm" if the American public concludes that "universal snooping" is favored for enforcing the Eighteenth Amendment.
>
> "The wet opposition would say we are menacing the privacy and the rights of Americans if we relied on 'wire-tapping' to get prohibition enforcement," Dr. Nicholson declared. . . . "We do not favor the decision, unless it is to be interpreted as applying to all criminal cases of every kind, in which case the decision is sound and necessary."

Olmstead v. United States

    Dr. Nicholson Backs Dry Wire-Tapping, NEW YORK TIMES (June 24, 1928), at N3.
102. *Judge-Made Law*, BARRON'S WEEKLY (June 11, 1928), at 11.
103. *Editorial*, 126 THE NATION 679 (1928). For Van Devanter's attack on this article, see *supra* note 96.
104. KYVIG, *supra* note 13, at 132.
105. *Id.* at 35.
106. *Double Jeopardy*, ST. LOUIS POST-DISPATCH (November 2, 1926), at 18.
107. *Double Jeopardy*, CHICAGO DAILY TRIBUNE (April 15, 1923), at 8.
108. Zechariah Chafee, Jr., *Ill Starred Prohibition Cases: A Study in Judicial Pathology*, 45 HARVARD LAW REVIEW 947, 949 (1932).
109. *Id.*

Plate 7 The Taft Court inspects a plaster model of the proposed new Supreme Court Building in the Russell Senate Office Building on May 17, 1929. From left to right are Louis D. Brandeis, Willis Van Devanter, William Howard Taft, Oliver Wendell Holmes, Pierce Butler, Edward T. Sanford, and Harlan Fiske Stone. Photograph by Underwood & Underwood, Collection of the Supreme Court of the United States.

Plate 8 The Taft Court pays a courtesy call on President Hoover on October 7, 1929. Photograph by P&A Photos, Collection of the Supreme Court of the United States.

Plate 9 Oliver Wendell Holmes and Louis Dembitz Brandeis arrive at Court on March 8, 1930, Holmes's eighty-ninth birthday. Later in the day they would learn of the deaths of Taft and Sanford. Photograph by Handy Studios, Collection of the Supreme Court of the United States.

Plate 10 Cartoon depicting the effect of the *Coronado* decision and injunctions on organized labor, originally published in *Labor* and republished at 74 LITERARY DIGEST 21 (July 1, 1922).

Plate 11 Cartoon attacking judicial review after the announcement of *Adkins*, published in THE CINCINNATI POST (April 19, 1923), clipped by Taft and kept in his papers. The bones in the dish are labeled "Minimum Wage" and "Child Labor" Laws.

Plate 12 Cartoon lampooning Sutherland's opinion in *Adkins*, originally published in the *New York World* and republished at 13 AMERICAN LABOR LEGISLATION REVIEW 130 (June 1923).

Plate 13 Cartoon praising *Pierce*, published in the NEWS TRIBUNE (Tacoma) (June 2, 1925), at 1.

PART VII
FEDERALISM AND THE AMERICAN PEOPLE

The shock of World War I lay not only in its vast extension of government regulatory power, but also in its concentration of authority in the federal government. Prohibition entrenched this disorienting tilt toward national power. If a divided Taft Court consistently upheld the extraordinary exercise of national legislative power established by the Eighteenth Amendment, its response to the expansion of federal authority in other contexts was more nuanced and ambivalent.

In some areas, like railroad regulation, the Taft Court was highly supportive of an enlarged national presence, but in other contexts, like intergovernmental tax immunity, the Court pursued and expanded *Lanza*'s vision of dual sovereignty. The trauma of the war and prohibition seemed to spur the Court to seek an ever-sharper separation between the distinct spheres of national and state jurisdiction. In matters involving congressional power, the Taft Court would sometimes reassert the very normative dualism that its own prohibition decisions radically undermined. The Court was especially suspicious of federal efforts to regulate ordinary property, as distinct from property affected with a public interest.

The upshot was a muddle that reflected the confusion of postwar American society. The country valued the manifest efficiencies of national regulation and yet was dogged by a nagging sense that precious values of federalism were losing influence and importance. The jagged jurisprudence of the Taft Court illustrates how imperatives of federal control were asserted, resisted, and transformed in the turbulent 1920s.

An important theme that consistently shines through the Taft Court's jurisprudence is its recognition of, and solicitude for, the national market. The theme is plainly visible in the Court's dormant Commerce Clause doctrine, even though that doctrine vigorously reasserted traditional tropes of dual sovereignty. The theme is also on display in the Court's use of diversity jurisdiction to fashion a general federal common law designed to sustain the vigor and integrity of the national market.

It is striking that in developing general common law the Taft Court imagined federal courts as speaking for the values of the entire American people. When the Court declared general common law, it lost all track of metaphors of dual sovereignty. The Court spoke for neither federal nor state law, but for all the people of the United States. The Court often spoke in this same oracular voice when it interpreted the Constitution. When construing the Fourteenth Amendment, the Court imagined itself as formulating principles that transcended the positive law of the national government and of the states, and that instead expressed the crystallized public sentiments of the entire American people.

In 1938 the epochal case of *Erie Railroad Co. v. Tompkins*[1] sharply undermined this vast authority by stripping the Court of its jurisdiction to function as a common law court. In modern times, at least as a theoretical matter, the Court is authorized to pronounce only the positive law of the national government. This makes it quite difficult for us to imagine the very different authority invoked by the Taft Court in its constitutional decisions. We still quarrel among ourselves about what it might mean for the Court to interpret a Constitution that represents only federal positive law. The Taft Court, by contrast, easily assumed the prerogative to speak in ways that altogether transcended the boundaries of any positive law. It spoke in a voice quite lost to many twenty-first century observers.

Note

1. 304 U.S. 64 (1938).

CHAPTER 34

Federalism and World War I

IN 1908 WOODROW WILSON noted that although federalism was "the cardinal question of our constitutional system," "the balance of powers between the States and the federal government now trembles at an unstable equilibrium."[1] Within a decade Wilson would lead the nation into a war that would shatter that fragile equilibrium. The war entailed a "vast extension of centralized national authority"[2] and a total commitment to "highly centralized"[3] planning that required the country "to think and act on the scale of a nation."[4] The mobilization demanded by the war "radically" transgressed "the principle of dual sovereignty which has hitherto underlain our federal system."[5]

The transformation carried enormous implications for the landscape of federalism. "In the great World War the thoughts of the entire country were turned for years to a common purpose," recalled Attorney General Harry Daugherty in 1922: "The Government regulated our food, our fuel and our means of communication. Taxes were greatly increased.... It is only natural, therefore, that local government should now appear to be much less important than it was before the war and that there should be an ever-increasing tendency toward the centralization of governmental power and governmental activities in Washington."[6]

When during the war Taft publicly wondered how the Court's controversial decision in *Hammer v. Dagenhart*,[7] which struck down the Keating-Owen Child Labor Law,[8] could possibly have "roused public criticism," he concluded that the "absorption of unusual governmental power at Washington under the war power of Congress makes people forget the importance of maintaining local self-government.... [E]nthusiasts ... have no patience with constitutional restriction of Congress' power."[9]

Conversely, when Taft's own 1922 decision in *Bailey v. Drexel Furniture Co.*,[10] which struck down the child-labor tax statute,[11] was praised on the floor of Congress as restoring the proper balance between federal and state governments,

Congressman Henry St. George Tucker emphasized that Taft's opinion pierced "the confusion incident to the war ... with the Federal Government functioning in every direction under continuing war powers, with the people accustomed during the war to look to Washington for all things as the speediest avenue of relief. It was natural for them to forget on the return of peace that their State governments were the natural channels through which their local needs were to be supplied."[12]

The question faced by the Court in the 1920s was how to render traditional understandings of federalism compatible with the "revolutionary changes"[13] in federal power spawned by the war. The almost unseemly haste with which the Wilson administration dismantled the centralized regulatory apparatus of the war,[14] together with Harding's declared intention of returning to "normalcy," suggest the distrust inspired by the wartime eruption of centralized federal power.[15] Coolidge expressed the national unease when he acknowledged that "[o]ur generation has recently lived through times still so vivid as to seem but as yesterday, which have taught us deeply to appreciate the value of union in purpose and effort," and yet simultaneously cautioned that the spirit of "our Federal system, distributing powers and responsibilities between the States and the National Government" means that "more centralization ought to be avoided."[16]

Thoughtful assessments of federalism throughout the 1920s were pervasively inflected with similar ambivalence. On the one hand, the conduct of the war made manifest the effectiveness and efficiency of centralized federal control. It was obvious to all that such control might be necessary for survival in the dangerous world of the twentieth century. It was also increasingly evident that in many ways "the states are antiquated political areas – they are no longer social and economic units."[17] The Interstate Commerce Commission's management of state and national railroads, for example, was universally accepted as a necessary instance of centralized federal control. It was also commonly acknowledged that "[t]he centralization of American business and the standardizing of American culture are proceeding with prodigious momentum."[18]

Yet, on the other hand, the country had suffered "a surfeit of Federal administration during the war."[19] The 1920s witnessed a powerful backlash, so that the "doctrine of state rights" was "revived and restored to the vigor of former times."[20] The Taft Court era was, as Brandeis put it, a time "of revulsion against federal control."[21] The "vast extension of the Federal police power"[22] implicit in national prohibition stood as a standing testament to federal excess.[23] So it was that "[t]he chief cause of the opposition to the Child Labor Amendment is unquestionably the reaction against the extension of Federal police control secured by the Eighteenth Amendment."[24]

The upshot was a messy uncertainty about questions of national authority. *The Outlook*, which had once been a vehicle for Theodore Roosevelt's unabashed nationalism,[25] could observe that although "[t]here are few thinking men to-day who would say that, in the abstract, there should be any further centralization of power in Washington," yet "never a session of Congress passes but that some addition is made to the bureaucracy of the National Capital."[26] Having tasted the apple of national efficiency, the nation could not easily return to the old boundaries

Federalism and World War I

separating federal from state power.[27] "We worship Jefferson," noted one observer, "but more and more come to obey Hamilton ... because ... interests find through Federal force a potent way to carry out their plans."[28]

The resulting confusion produced anxiety and concern. Writing in 1922, for example, New York lawyer Charles W. Pierson expressed the "gravest misgivings" about the "impressive phenomenon of federal encroachment upon state power." Pierson was fully aware that the "most potent" cause of this encroachment was "internal economic development." "The invention of railways drew the different sections of the country together in a common growth, and tended to make the barriers interposed by state lines and state laws seem artificial and cumbersome. In fact, they sometimes came to be regarded as intolerable and destructive of progress." Notwithstanding their inevitability, however, Pierson found these transformations profoundly distressing. "Are the states to be submerged and virtually obliterated in the drift toward centralization? ... The integrity of the states was a cardinal principle of our governmental scheme. Abandon that and we are adrift from the moorings which to the minds of statesmen of past generations constituted the safety of the republic."[29]

The Taft Court was forced to construct a jurisprudence of federalism for a country afflicted with apprehension and self-doubt. Not surprisingly, its decisions reflected the confusion of the national mind.

Notes

1. WOODROW WILSON, CONSTITUTIONAL GOVERNMENT IN THE UNITED STATES 173, 191 (New York: Columbia University Press 1921) (originally published in 1908).
2. *After the War – Reaction or Reconstruction*, 13 NEW REPUBLIC 331, 332 (1918).
3. *Republican Resurrection*, 9 NEW REPUBLIC 172, 173 (1916).
4. Walter Lippmann, *How to Integrate America*, 6 NEW REPUBLIC 157, 158 (1916).
5. Edward S. Corwin, *War, the Constitution Moulder*, 11 NEW REPUBLIC 153, 154 (1917).
6. Harry M. Daugherty, *The Co-operative Duties of the States and the Federal Government*, 71 UNIVERSITY OF PENNSYLVANIA LAW REVIEW 1, 3–4 (1922). See Horace J. Fenton, *Federal Encroachments on State Rights*, 22 CURRENT HISTORY 613, 614 (1925): "The World War gave ... tremendous emphasis [to] a strong national pride which martial and diplomatic successes have assisted not a little in swelling. We think in terms of the nation rather than of the States, which in the minds of many now mean little more than administrative sections of a great country."
7. 247 U.S. 251 (1918).
8. Pub. L. 64-249, 39 Stat. 675 (September 1, 1916).
9. William Howard Taft, *Child-Labor Legislation* (June 20, 1918), in VIVIAN, at 69. *See, e.g.*, Raymond G. Fuller, *A Quest for Constitutionality*, 6 CHILD LABOR BULLETIN 210 (November 1918):

    > The first child-labor laws were passed by the states because everybody used to look to the states alone for social legislation. But before this war the people were thinking nationally and were coming more and more to look to the nation for protection and the promotion of public health, morals and general welfare. Not only were they thinking nationally, but more things were coming to be looked upon as matters of national concern. The war has strengthened these tendencies of American thought.

    A good example of how the exigencies of war overrode ordinary perceptions of federalism is that the War Labor Policies Board, under Taft himself, decided to ignore the spirit of the Court's recent decision in *Dagenhart*. A month after the decision, the Board

    > adopted a resolution making the Secretary of Labor responsible "for the enforcement of the contract clause with reference to the employment of children by which all government contracts are to contain a clause providing that the contractor shall not directly or indirectly employ any child under the age of fourteen years, or permit any child between the ages of fourteen and sixteen to work more than eight hours in any one day, more than six days in any one week."

    A Reprieve for Children, 16 NEW REPUBLIC 7 (1918). The *New Republic* observed that the Board's resolution "is only the last of a lengthening series of cases in which the executive branch of the government, responsive to prevailing public opinion and the critical needs of the nation, has found itself compelled to contravene the spirit of the law as interpreted by the Supreme Court."

    > The patent fact is that in matters of fundamental public policy, we are rapidly becoming a nation divided against ourselves at the fountain heads of authority. Each executive act, however essential to the defense of the nation,

that circumvents a solemn decree of the Supreme Court tends to bring not only the Supreme Court but the entire judiciary into contempt among the great masses of the people. It would seem obvious that unless there is a redefinition of authority by which the conduct of the Supreme Court is brought into harmony with the spirit of the times, the end of the war will find us facing domestic anarchy.

Id. at 8. The specter of that domestic anarchy alarmed Taft, who urged that the "conduct of the war" not become an occasion to "completely upset the balance between the federal and state governments." William Howard Taft, *The Constitution in Wartime* (October 18, 1918), in VIVIAN, at 103, 105.

10. 259 U.S. 20 (1922). Following the practice of the 1920s, I shall sometimes refer to this case as the Child Labor Tax Case.
11. Pub. L. 65-254, 40 Stat. 1057, 1138–40 (February 24, 1919).
12. 62 CONG. REC. 7595 (May 24, 1922). The historian Stephen B. Wood interprets Brandeis's joining of Taft's opinion in the Child Labor Tax case as reflecting "the tremendous psychological and philosophical shock Americans (especially those attached to the Jeffersonian democratic persuasion) suffered as a result of the unprecedented centralization that was necessary to put the nation on a war footing in World War I."

The immense bureaucracy, the coercive power of gathered sovereignty, and the restrictions imposed publicly and privately upon mind and expression indelibly influenced men who were sensitive – as Brandeis and Frankfurter were – to the libertarian credo that power corrupted and paralyzed local responsibility but that a wide dispersion of political and economic authority fostered democratic virtues and militated against arbitrary assaults upon individuals. There had never before been such far-reaching national control, and many persons hoped it would never again be necessary.

STEPHEN B. WOOD, CONSTITUTIONAL POLITICS IN THE PROGRESSIVE ERA: CHILD LABOR AND THE LAW 291–92 (University of Chicago Press 1968).

13. *After the War, supra* note 2, at 331–32.
14. By the beginning of December 1918, *The Survey* could observe that "[a]lready, in the short time since the armistice has been declared, there has been a noticeable lessening of that centralization of plans and of direction which is necessary to pass safely over this difficult period of change." *The Carrying Forward of War-Time Industrial Standards*, 41 THE SURVEY 308, 309 (1918).
15. *See, e.g., Federalism Now Too Aggressive*, 71 AMERICAN REVIEW OF REVIEWS 5 (January 1925):

The States in recent years have had to submit to a devastating invasion of their resources by a national Government that knows no check when the war power is invoked. No ruler or government, having once seized great and unusual spheres of authority under exceptional circumstances, is ever willing to retire to its own proper place when the emergency is passed. It is now for the citizen to decide to what extent he finds it beneficial to him to aggrandize the Government at Washington at the expense of his State Government.

16. *Full Text of President Coolidge's Memorial Day Address at Arlington*, NEW YORK TIMES (May 31, 1925), at 2. Coolidge concluded, "We must maintain a proper measure of local self-government while constantly making adjustments to an increasing interdependence." *Id. See* Clyde A. Beals, *State Governors Challenge*

Federal Encroachments, 22 CURRENT HISTORY 793, 793 (1925) (describing the seventeenth annual Governors' Conference, in which "President Coolidge's call for a revival of responsibility on the part of the State Governments was in every one's mind").

17. John Ely Briggs, *State Rights*, 10 IOWA LAW BULLETIN 297, 308 (1925). See William D. Riter, *Constitutional Conceptions: A Contrast*, 216 NORTH AMERICAN REVIEW 637, 639 (1922) ("To-day there is a wide-spread feeling that the States have outgrown their usefulness. And as a necessary corollary there is an alarming tendency to insist that the Constitution be interpreted in such a way as to impose no limits on Federal activities whatever.").

18. *The Revival of Anti-Federalism*, 41 NEW REPUBLIC 211, 212 (1925).

19. William A. Robinson, *A Constitutional Retrospect*, 11 AMERICAN BAR ASSOCIATION JOURNAL 32 (1925). "People tell anecdotes about the stupidity, incompetence, or high-handedness of tax collectors. The honesty of Federal administration has been discredited by the scandalous conditions discovered in the Veterans' Bureau and the Prohibition Enforcement service." *Id.* at 32–33.

20. Briggs, *supra* note 17, at 297. *See* Fenton, *supra* note 6, at 613 ("Many American citizens are terribly alarmed today at the prospect, as it seems to them, of the absolute extinction of State authority, government of all local affairs by bureau chiefs in Washington, the end of individual liberty and political chaos."); *The Revival of Anti-Federalism*, *supra* note 18, at 212:

> Since ... the passage of the Eighteenth Amendment and the experiences of the Great War, the protests against proposed increases of federal authority have become comparatively weighty and sincere. The deplorable effects of the attempt to accomplish a desirable social purpose by the absolute federal proscription of alcoholic drinks have aroused the old suspicions of proposed increases in federal authority. Many intelligent and disinterested citizens are afraid that, if the process of centralizing the socializing and regulative activities of government in Washington continues, the American people will ultimately be ruled by a necessarily irresponsible federal bureaucracy which will dry up the sources of local initiative and responsibility. They consider the United States too large, populous and diversified a country to be wholesomely or even safely governed by one dominant political machine. The process of centralization has in their opinion already proceeded so far that it has enfeebled the state governments. The only way to restore them to vitality is to resist the easy but dangerous alternative of calling in the federal authority as the solve-all of American politics, and to force on social reformers the duty and necessity of accomplishing their purposes through agitation within the states and action by them.

21. LDB to Felix Frankfurter (May 5, 1925), in BRANDEIS-FRANKFURTER CORRESPONDENCE, at 201.

22. *The Conference of Governors*, NEW YORK TIMES (July 1, 1925), at 22.

23. *See supra* note 20; Briggs, *supra* note 17, at 310:

> The revolt against national prohibition has been most effective as expressed in terms of federal usurpation. A great many people who have no sympathy for intemperance and no taste for alcoholic beverages are nevertheless bitterly opposed to the Eighteenth Amendment. They regard it as a dangerous encroachment upon state rights – the entering wedge for further interference by the national government.

24. Edward A. Harriman, *The Twilight of the States*, 16 AMERICAN BAR ASSOCIATION JOURNAL 128, 130 (1930). There was a fear of "[a] Volstead child-labor law" that "would produce a legal situation similar to that respecting prohibition under the Eighteenth Amendment." Bentley W. Warren, *Destroying Our "Indestructible States"*, 133 ATLANTIC MONTHLY 370, 374–75 (1924). In the words of John Ely Briggs, "The reaction against the increasing authority of the national government is widespread. As reflected in newspaper comment and periodical literature there seem to be two outstanding causes: first, the national control of state activities through the system of 'federal aid'; and second, the character of the Eighteenth Amendment and the proposed child labor amendment." Briggs, *supra* note 17, at 308–9.
25. *See* IRA V. BROWN, LYMAN ABBOTT 210 (Cambridge: Harvard University Press 1953); FRANK L. MOTT, 3 A HISTORY OF AMERICAN MAGAZINES, 1865–1885, at 430–32 (Cambridge: Harvard University Press 1967).
26. *Coolidge, the Jeffersonian*, 143 THE OUTLOOK 529, 530 (1926). "The piling up of board upon board, bureau upon bureau, department upon department in the Federal Government must come to an end, and that shortly. And, when the Federal Government once stops gobbling up the functions of the States, it will almost certainly have to regurgitate some of those it has already swallowed." *Id.*
27. *See, e.g.*, *Pleads for State Rights*, NEW YORK TIMES (June 19, 1923), at 3 (quoting the plea of Representative Finis J. Garrett of Tennessee to "halt [this] mad rush toward centralizing of governmental functions and absorption by the Federal organism of governmental powers").
28. Don C. Seitz, *Whence Cometh Federalism*, 146 THE OUTLOOK 350, 350–51 (1927).
29. CHARLES W. PIERSON, OUR CHANGING CONSTITUTION 23, 143 (Garden City: Doubleday, Page & Co. 1922).

CHAPTER 35

Dual Sovereignty and Intergovernmental Tax Immunities

I N *UNITED STATES V. LANZA*[1] the Taft Court used the concept of dual sovereignty to interpret the Double Jeopardy Clause of the Fifth Amendment.[2] It was a concept that came easily to hand, expressing a longstanding vision of federalism that was well captured in Edward Corwin's classic description of "two mutually exclusive, reciprocally limiting fields of power, the governmental occupants of which confront each other as equals."[3] The Court had concisely summarized this concept of dual sovereignty in 1905: "There are certain matters over which the National Government has absolute control, and no action of the State can interfere therewith, and there are others in which the State is supreme, and in respect to them the National Government is powerless. To preserve the even balance between these two governments and hold each in its separate sphere is the peculiar duty of all courts."[4]

The Court had for generations conceived the constitutional value of federalism in terms of preserving separate and incompatible spheres of state and federal authority. When the national "regimentation"[5] accompanying World War I suddenly blurred the boundaries of these spheres, one response of the Taft Court was vigorously to reassert its inherited concept of federalism. This response is most apparent in the Taft Court's doctrine of intergovernmental tax immunity, which during the 1920s was inflated to reach "scarcely believable proportions and extensions."[6]

The doctrine of intergovernmental tax immunity is about the constitutionality of federal taxation applied to instrumentalities of state government, or the constitutionality of state taxation applied to instrumentalities of the federal government. The doctrine may be technical and obscure, but it uniquely presents almost purely abstract questions of constitutional structure. It does not raise issues that were during the 1920s highly fraught with ideological controversy, like the desirability of *laissez-faire* economics, the requirements of the national market, or the proper

Dual Sovereignty & Intergovernmental Tax Immunities

protections owed to private property. The doctrine of intergovernmental tax immunity instead focuses cleanly and precisely on the question of how the taxation of one governmental sovereign should be permitted to affect the operation of another. The Taft Court's development of the doctrine nicely illustrates its vision of constitutional structure in a context that is relatively undistorted by competing considerations.

Although the origins of intergovernmental tax immunity doctrine can be traced back to the Court's 1819 ruling in *McCulloch v. Maryland*,[7] which held that the State of Maryland could not tax the Bank of the United States, it was first fully articulated more than fifty years later in *Collector v. Day*, which held that the federal government could not tax "the means and instrumentalities employed by [state governments] to carry into operation the powers granted" them, and that, conversely, state governments could not tax the means and instrumentalities of the federal government.[8] *Day* summoned an image of the "general government, and the States" as "separate and distinct sovereignties, acting separately and independently of each other, within their respective spheres." Each was "supreme" in "its appropriate sphere," and mutual immunity from taxation was necessary because of "the great law of self-preservation; as any government, whose means employed in conducting its operations, if subject to the control of another and distinct government, can exist only at the mercy of that government."[9]

The framework established by *Day*, which assumed that the relationship between state and federal governments was "one of tension rather than collaboration,"[10] quickly became received constitutional wisdom.[11] Even Holmes could assert in 1922 that states should be rigorously precluded from taxing instrumentalities of the federal government, and that this proscription ought to be enforced with greater strictness than prohibitions against state regulations of interstate commerce. In *Gillespie v. Oklahoma*,[12] a case holding that Oklahoma could not apply a general income tax to oil and gas revenues derived from land leased from federally protected Indians,[13] Holmes held: "The criterion of interference by the States with interstate commerce is one of degree. It is well understood that a certain amount of reaction upon and interference with such commerce cannot be avoided if the States are to exist and make laws. . . . The rule as to instrumentalities of the United States on the other hand is absolute in form and at least stricter in substance. . . . 'A tax upon the leases is a tax upon the power to make them, and could be used to destroy the power to make them.'"[14]

Holmes would have occasion to regret these words later in the decade.[15] He came to appreciate that "the criterion of interference" of state taxation on federal instrumentalities must also be conceptualized as "one of degree."[16] During the 1920s, however, the Taft Court would embark on an increasingly frantic struggle absolutely to immunize both state and federal instrumentalities from the effects of the other's taxation.[17] The Court sought to reaffirm the very structural bifurcations the war had so thoroughly obscured.

Although the Taft Court's efforts have sometimes been characterized as formalist, as evidencing a commitment to "the logical and literal application of precedents" as distinct from "practical judicial statesmanship,"[18] in fact the Court was exquisitely sensitive to "the practical effect" of taxation.[19] The Court was determined to delve beneath the surface of tax schemes to ascertain whether they actually impinged upon the distinct spheres of federal or state instrumentalities. The Court's intolerance of such impingements escalated as the decade progressed.

The difficulty was not that the Taft Court was formalist. It was instead that the Court labored with increasing intensity to implement a conceptual schema of dual sovereignty that was hopelessly incompatible with the integrated economic reality of postwar America. The more meticulously the Court sought to apply the schema, the more its decisions were driven into intellectual incoherence.

The difficulties of the Court's project are well illustrated by the notorious 1928 case of *Panhandle Oil Co. v. Mississippi* ex rel. *Knox*, in which Butler, speaking for Taft, Van Devanter, Sutherland, and Sanford, ruled that Mississippi could not apply a general gasoline tax to sales made by a local dealer to the United States "for the use of its Coast Guard Fleet in service in the Gulf of Mexico and its Veterans' Hospital at Gulfport." Butler specifically noted that "the validity of the taxes ... is to be determined by the practical effect of enforcement." Because the amount of Mississippi's tax depended upon the quantity of gasoline sold to the United States, Butler reasoned that the state was actually taxing the "transactions by which the United States secures the things desired for its governmental purposes." The practical effect of the tax was "directly to retard, impede and burden the exertion of the United States of its constitutional powers to operate the fleet and hospital."[20]

It was breathtakingly bold to hold that the Constitution precluded any state tax that increased the cost of ordinary purchases by instrumentalities of the federal government. In effect, *Panhandle* aimed at entirely insulating federal institutions from the effects of state taxation.[21] As Holmes spelled out in a justly famous dissent, this objective was essentially quixotic:

> I am not aware that the President, the Members of Congress, the Judiciary or, to come nearer to the case in hand, the Coast Guard or the officials of the Veterans' Hospital, because they are instrumentalities of government and cannot function naked and unfed, hitherto having been held entitled to have their bills for food and clothing cut down so far as their butchers and tailors have been taxed on their sales; and I had not supposed that the butchers and tailors could omit from their tax returns all receipts from the large class of customers to which I have referred. The question of interference with Government, I repeat, is one of reasonableness and degree and it seems to me that the interference in this case is too remote.[22]

Holmes's dissent is best known for its repudiation of the very position that Holmes himself had asserted in *Gillespie* six years earlier, which is that the power to tax includes the power to destroy. In 1928, taking direct aim at Chief Justice Marshall's "often quoted proposition that the power to tax is the power to destroy," Holmes noted that "[i]n those days it was not recognized as it is today that most of the distinctions of the law are distinctions of degree. If the states had any power it

Dual Sovereignty & Intergovernmental Tax Immunities

was assumed that they had all power, and that the necessary alternative was to deny it altogether. ... But this court which so often has defeated the attempt to tax in certain ways can defeat an attempt to discriminate or otherwise go too far without wholly abolishing the power to tax. The power to tax is not the power to destroy while this court sits."[23] Because the Court could supervise the nature and extent of the burdens created by intergovernmental taxation, there was no need wholly to insulate either state or federal instrumentalities from every effect of the other's taxation. Hostile or discriminatory taxation could be blocked by the Court; trivial and uniform taxes, like those at issue in *Panhandle*, could withstand constitutional scrutiny.

Five members of the Court remained unmoved by Holmes's eloquent dissent. The next year the Court redoubled its efforts to disentangle the twin spheres of American sovereignty. Not only did the Court continue to regard the power to tax as potentially oppressive, but in *Macallen Co. v. Massachusetts*, Sutherland, speaking for a majority of six, escalated the stakes by asserting that "for one government – state or national – to lay a tax upon the instrumentalities or securities of the other is derogatory to the latter's dignity, subversive of its powers, and repugnant to its paramount authority." "These constitute special and compelling reasons," Sutherland explained, "why courts, in scrutinizing taxing acts ... should be acute to distinguish between an exaction which in substance and reality is what it pretends to be, and a scheme to lay a tax upon a nontaxable subject by a deceptive use of words."[24]

If the constitutionality of one government's taxation of another turns on the degree of inconvenience inflicted by the tax, Holmes was undoubtedly correct that courts could strike down taxation that went "too far." But if the question of constitutionality turns instead on affronts to a state's "dignity" – on derogations of its "paramount authority" – then no degree of injury at all can be tolerated. In his typically abstract way, Sutherland took the constitutional issue of intergovernmental tax immunity entirely beyond the realm of empirically ascertainable facts.

In *Macallen*, Sutherland reached out to overturn the important precedent of *Flint v. Stone Tracy Co.*,[25] which had held that a state can impose "excise" taxes on a corporate franchise, and that it could measure the value of the franchise "by income from the property of the corporation although a part of such income is derived from nontaxable property."[26] *Macallen* effectively prohibited states from assessing taxes on corporations based upon the value of, or income arising from, corporate holdings in federal securities. The constitutionality of such taxes, Sutherland reasoned, could not be determined merely by the label "excise tax," for when a state includes in the measure of a tax the value of nontaxable property, the "probability" exists that "the real purpose" of the tax is "to reach" the protected property. Pursuing a thoroughly skeptical agenda, Sutherland stressed that it was "essential to the preservation of the constitutional limitations imposed upon the taxing power of the states" that courts "look beyond the words to the real legislative purpose." If these limitations could "be evaded by the adoption of a delusive name to characterize the tax or form of words to describe it, the destruction of the vitality of these necessary safeguards will soon follow."[27]

The Court's effort to police the boundary between national and state governments reached its apogee in McReynolds's opinion for five justices in *Long v. Rockwood*,[28] which held that royalties from federal patents could not be taxed by states. In the teeth of a devastating Holmes dissent,[29] *Long* seemed to imply that income from any federally created right was immune from state taxation. This implication was so extreme that *Long* was unanimously overruled only four years later in a case involving state taxation of royalties from federal copyrights.[30]

The overreaching of *Long*, the urgency of *Macallen*, and the obsessive scrupulousness of *Panhandle*, all evidence the Taft Court's increasingly anxious effort to maintain a clean separation between the spheres of federal and of state power. Stone put his finger on the root of the problem when he observed that, following Marshall, the Court "dealt with the whole question as an infringement of sovereignty and treated the sovereignty infringed as though it were that of a government wholly foreign to the taxing government, and thus, I think, left out of account the necessity of making the two governments function together as part of one system."[31] It was clear to Stone that the whole framework of analysis had to be fundamentally reconceived.

Stone attempted the task in 1926 in his opinion for a unanimous Court in *Metcalf v. Mitchell*, which concerned the question of whether federal income tax could be applied to fees received by consulting engineers "professionally employed to advise states or subdivisions of states with reference to proposed water supply and sewage disposal systems."[32] Stone, who had been on the Court for less than a year, demonstrated the kind of originality that would eventually make him one of the Court's great justices. He sought to rethink the doctrine of intergovernmental tax immunity from the ground up.[33]

Noting, on the one hand, that "those agencies through which either government immediately and directly exercises its sovereign powers, are immune from the taxing power of the other," and, on the other hand, that "not every person who uses his property or derives a profit, in his dealings with the government, may clothe himself with immunity from taxation on the theory that either he or his property is an instrumentality of government," Stone proposed a fundamentally new framework for how constitutional doctrine might resolve this tension. "The line which separates those activities having some relation to government, which are nevertheless subject to taxation, from those which are immune" he wrote, could be ascertained only by reference "to the reason upon which the rule rests, and which must be the guiding principle to control its operation."[34]

This premise expressed the core insight of the legal realism that Stone had learned from Holmes. Like Holmes, Stone viewed law as instrumental – as existing to serve discrete purposes. Stone proposed that the purpose of intergovernmental tax immunity was not to make federal and state governments immune from the effects of each other's taxation. This purpose was unreasonable because "the taxing power of either government, even when exercised in a manner admittedly necessary and proper, unavoidably has some effect upon the other.... Taxation by either the state or the federal government affects in some measure the cost of operation of the other."[35]

Dual Sovereignty & Intergovernmental Tax Immunities

Instead, Stone said, the purpose of the doctrine was that "neither government may destroy the other nor curtail in any substantial manner the exercise of its powers. Hence the limitation upon the taxing power of each, so far as it affects the other, must receive a practical construction which permits both to function with the minimum of interference each with the other; and that limitation cannot be so varied or extended as seriously to impair either the taxing power of the government imposing the tax ... or the appropriate exercise of the functions of the government affected by it."[36] In essence, Stone proposed what in contemporary terms would be categorized as a balancing test.

Stone's reconceptualization of the doctrine of intergovernmental tax immunity would not take root until the 1930s.[37] For the remainder of its brief span, the Taft Court would not use the doctrine of intergovernmental tax immunity in the flexible manner suggested by Stone. Instead, it would remain fixated on the goal of immunizing both federal and state governments from the effects of the other's taxation,[38] an impossible goal but one that nevertheless lucidly expressed the imaginary of dual sovereignty. Dissenting in *Macallen*, Stone pleaded for the Court to adopt the new perspective advanced in *Metcalf*,[39] but to no avail. The Court was too intent on prying apart the distinct spheres of federal and state power.

Notes

1. 260 U.S. 377 (1922).
2. *See supra* Chapter 29, at 951–53.
3. EDWARD CORWIN, THE COMMERCE POWER VERSUS STATES RIGHTS 135 (Princeton University Press 1936). Deborah Jones Merritt has observed that something like this image of federalism was "[t]he first, and oldest, of the Supreme Court's concepts of federalism." Deborah Jones Merritt, *Three Faces of Federalism: Finding a Formula for the Future*, 47 VANDERBILT LAW REVIEW 1563, 1564 (1994).
4. South Carolina v. United States, 199 U.S. 437, 448 (1905). As the president of the American Bar Association instructed the lawyers assembled at its 1924 annual meeting: "The national government is supreme within the scope of its limited powers, and the state governments are supreme in *all* powers not relinquished by them to the federal government." R.E.L. Saner, *Governmental Review*, in REPORT OF THE FORTY-SEVENTH ANNUAL MEETING OF THE AMERICAN BAR ASSOCIATION 127, 134 (Baltimore: Lord Baltimore Press 1924).
5. Edward S. Corwin, *The Passing of Dual Federalism*, 36 UNIVERSITY OF VIRGINIA LAW REVIEW 1, 1 (1950).
6. WILLIAM B. LOCKHART et al., CONSTITUTIONAL LAW: CASES – COMMENTS – QUESTIONS 503 (St. Paul: West Publishing Co. 1964).
7. 17 U.S. 316 (1819).
8. 78 U.S. 113, 127 (1870). *Day* differed from *McCulloch* because the latter had specifically reserved the question of whether the federal government could tax instrumentalities of state governments. Marshall had strongly hinted in *McCulloch* that federal and state governments were not symmetrically situated. *McCulloch*, 17 U.S. at 435–36.
9. *Day*, 78 U.S. at 124, 127.
10. Corwin, *supra* note 5, at 4.
11. *See, e.g., id.* at 19 ("The doctrine of tax exemption was the climactic expression of the competitive theory of Federalism. . . ."). In dissent in Missouri *ex rel.* Burnes Nat'l Bank v. Duncan, 265 U.S. 17, 26 (1924), Sutherland offered a typically lucid account of this framework: "It is fundamental, under our dual system of government, that the Nation and the State are supreme and independent, each within its own sphere of action; and that each is exempt from the interference or control of the other in respect of its governmental powers, and the means employed in their exercise."

    In *Duncan*, Sutherland interpreted dual sovereignty to imply an anticommandeering principle analogous to that later articulated in Printz v. United States, 521 U.S. 898 (1997). *Duncan* concerned the validity of a federal statute requiring that national banks be authorized to serve as "executors if trust companies competing with them have that power." 265 U.S. at 23. The Court ruled that because Missouri allowed trust companies to act as executors, the case presented "the naked question" of "whether Congress had the power to do what it tried to do." *Id.* Holmes, speaking for seven justices, held in the affirmative. Sutherland, dissenting with McReynolds, reasoned that it

    > is settled beyond controversy, that the right of a State to pass laws, to administer them through courts of justice, and to employ agencies for the legitimate purposes of state government cannot be taxed, . . . and that rule is but an application of the

Dual Sovereignty & Intergovernmental Tax Immunities

> general and broader rule, which forbids any interference by the federal government with the governmental powers of a State. The settlement of successions to property on death is a subject within the exclusive control of the States and entirely beyond the sphere of national authority.... The duty and power of the State to provide a tribunal for the accomplishment of these ends ... it follows, cannot be abridged by federal legislation....
>
> During the process of administration the estate, in contemplation of law, is in the custody of the court exercising probate powers, and of this court the executor or administrator is an officer....
>
> The probate courts of a State have only such powers as the state legislature gives them. They are wholly beyond the jurisdiction of Congress, and it does not seem to me to be within the competency of that body, on any pretext, to compel such courts to appoint as executor or administrator one who the state law has declared shall not be appointed.
>
> The particular invasion here sanctioned may not be of great moment; but it is a precedent, which, if carried to the logical extreme, would go far toward reducing the States of the Union to the status of mere geographical subdivisions.

Id. at 27, 29 (Sutherland, J., dissenting).
12. 257 U.S. 501 (1922).
13. Holmes held for the Court that "the lessee was an instrumentality used by the United States in carrying out duties to the Indians that it had assumed." *Id.* at 504. Pitney, Clarke, and Brandeis dissented without opinion.
14. *Id.* at 505 (quoting Indian Territory Illuminating Oil Co. v. Oklahoma, 240 U.S. 522, 530 (1916)).
15. *Gillespie* was immediately controversial. *See* Jaybird Mining Co. v. Weir, 271 U.S. 609, 619 (1926) (Brandeis, J., dissenting) ("I suspect that my brethren would agree with me in sustaining this tax on ore in the bins but for *Gillespie*.... Any language in [*Gillespie*] which may seem apposite to the case at bar, should be disregarded as inconsistent with the earlier decisions."); *cf.* Thomas Reed Powell, *The Waning of Intergovernmental Tax Immunities*, 58 HARVARD LAW REVIEW 633, 641 (1945) (arguing that *Gillespie* should be consigned "to a merited limbo"); Note, 23 ILLINOIS LAW REVIEW 707, 712–13 (1929).
16. *Compare* Panhandle Oil Co. v. Mississippi *ex rel.* Knox, 277 U.S. 218, 221 (1928) (relying upon *Gillespie*), *with id.* at 223 (Holmes, J., dissenting). That state taxation impaired federal interests as a matter of degree had been sporadically recognized in previous Court opinions. *See, e.g.*, Union Pac. R.R. Co. v. Peniston, 85 U.S. 5, 30–31 (1873):

> But it is often a difficult question whether a tax imposed by a State does in fact invade the domain of the General government, or interfere with its operations to such an extent, or in such a manner, as to render it unwarranted. It cannot be that a State tax which remotely affects the efficient exercise of a Federal power is for that reason alone inhibited by the Constitution. To hold that would be to deny to the States all power to tax persons or property. Every tax levied by a State withdraws from the reach of Federal taxation a portion of the property from which it is taken, and to that extent diminishes the subject upon which Federal taxes may be laid. The States are, and they must ever be, coexistent with the National government. Neither may destroy the other. Hence the Federal Constitution must receive a practical construction. Its limitations and its implied prohibitions must not be extended so far as to destroy the necessary powers of the States, or prevent their efficient exercise.

By the 1920s, it could be said that "the Supreme Court has allowed states to tax the property of railroads either created by the federal government, or employed by it; the property of telegraph companies erected under Act of Congress on military or postroads; the property of bridge companies erected under Act of Congress across navigable rivers; and the premiums of a bonding company authorized by statute to become surety on bonds required by the United States." Note, *Exemption of Federal Instrumentalities from State Taxation*, 77 UNIVERSITY OF PENNSYLVANIA LAW REVIEW 115, 118 (1928). It could thus be concluded that the "cases seem to indicate that the Supreme Court is influenced by the closeness of the connection between the government and the alleged instrumentality claiming exemption from taxation; and by the effect of the tax on that connection.... In some of the cases the connection is close and the effect on the government is direct, and the Court rules against taxation as a matter of law. In other cases the connection is less clear and the Court considers whether as a matter of fact the tax is an unreasonable interference with the government." *Id.* at 119.

17. In the words of one commentator, the Court "materially" enlarged "the application of the doctrine, if not beyond its proper scope, certainly beyond the limits previously recognized." Note, *Taxation: State Taxation of Federal Agencies and Instrumentalities*, 13 MARQUETTE LAW REVIEW 117, 121 (1929).

18. Note, *supra* note 15, at 709.

19. *Panhandle*, 277 U.S. at 222. *See* Macallen Co. v. Massachusetts, 279 U.S. 620, 625 (1929) ("[N]either state courts nor legislatures, by giving the tax a particular name, or by using some form of words, can take away our duty to consider its nature and effect."); Nat'l Life Ins. Co. v. United States, 277 U.S. 508, 519 (1928) (holding that immunity cannot be evaded by any "device or form of words"); Northwestern Mut. Life Ins. Co. v. Wisconsin, 275 U.S. 136, 140 (1927) ("[I]f the challenged Act, whatever called, really imposes a direct charge upon interest derived from United States bonds, it is pro tanto void.").

20. 277 U.S. 218, 220–22 (1928).

21. McReynolds (joined by Stone) dissented separately. "I am unable to think that every man who sells a gallon of gasoline to be used by the United States thereby becomes a federal instrumentality, with the privilege of claiming freedom from taxation by the state." *Id.* at 225 (McReynolds, J., dissenting).

22. *Id.* at 225 (Holmes, J., dissenting). Brandeis and Stone joined Holmes's opinion. Brandeis wrote Holmes that "This is fine & I humbly join." (Holmes papers). Stone wrote his former law clerk Milton Handler that the case seemed "plain enough to me, but evidently not to others." HFS to Milton Handler (May 28, 1928) (Stone papers). Thirteen years later Stone would write an opinion overruling *Panhandle* in Alabama v. King & Boozer, 314 U.S. 1, 9 (1941).

23. *Panhandle*, 277 U.S. at 223 (Holmes, J., dissenting). Frankfurter immediately recognized a classic in the offing, writing Holmes that "the power to tax is not the power to destroy 'while this Court sits,' ought forever to reserve for the museum of judicial dicta Marshall's utterance. What hold words have on men – I sometimes suspect, particularly on our profession. These are really exciting opinions of yours – like sparkling wine in a dry age." Felix Frankfurter to OWH (May 22, 1928), in HOLMES-FRANKFURTER CORRESPONDENCE, at 227. Holmes wrote back to acknowledge the power of "phrases – they put water under the boat and float it over dangerous obstacles." OWH to Felix Frankfurter (May 26,

1928), *id.* at 228. As early as 1923, Frankfurter had discussed with Brandeis "Marshall's dictum 'power to tax, is power to destroy.' [Frankfurter] [s]aid 'that was dreadful. Holmes always snorts at that. Marshall's dicta raised hell in all sorts of ways – taken terribly seriously.'" *Brandeis-Frankfurter Conversations,* at 326 (August 11, 1923).
24. 279 U.S. 620, 628–29 (1929). Holmes, Brandeis, and Stone dissented.
25. 220 U.S. 107 (1911).
26. *Macallen,* 279 U.S. at 628. In dissent, Stone, writing also for Holmes and Brandeis, queried the urgency of the Court's judgment:

> For seventy years this Court has consistently adhered to the principle that either the federal or state governments may constitutionally impose an excise tax on corporations for the privilege of doing business in corporate form, and measure the tax by the property or net income of the corporation, including the tax-exempt securities of the other or income derived from them. ...
>
> It would seem that only considerations of public policy of weight, which appear to be here wholly wanting, would justify overturning a principle so long established. It has survived a great war, financed by the sale of government obligations, and it has never even been suggested that in any practical way it has impaired either the dignity or credit of the national government.

Id. at 636, 637 (Stone, J., dissenting). Stone wrote Noel Dowling that a recent decision "in effect overruling Flint v. Stone Tracey Co." was one of "the notable cases of the year." HFS to Noel T. Dowling (June 4, 1929) (Stone papers). Stone wrote Milton Handler that he found *Macallen* a "startling innovation." HFS to Milton Handler (May 29, 1929) (Stone papers).
27. *Macallen,* 279 U.S. at 629–31. This reasoning is discussed in Thomas Reed Powell, *An Imaginary Judicial Opinion,* 44 HARVARD LAW REVIEW 889, 901–4 (1931).
28. 277 U.S. 142 (1928). Brandeis, Sutherland, and Stone joined a dissent by Holmes.
29. After the argument of the case, Holmes wrote Frederick Pollock that "I shall try to smash" the notion "that patents can't be taxed." OWH to Frederick Pollock (February 17, 1928), in 2 HOLMES-POLLOCK CORRESPONDENCE, at 215.
30. Fox Film Corp. v. Doyal, 286 U.S. 123, 131 (1932). Arguably *Macallen* had in effect been overruled the year before in Educational Film Corp of America v. Ward, 282 U.S. 379 (1931), in an opinion written by Stone to which Sutherland dissented. For the subsequent history of *Macallen,* see Dennis Rimkunas & Benjamin S. Jacobs, *Corporate Franchise and Income Taxes,* 27 JOURNAL OF MULTISTATE TAXATION AND INCENTIVES 8, 8–9 (2017).
31. HFS to Thomas Reed Powell (January 30, 1931) (Stone papers). Edward Corwin would later coin the term "Cooperative Federalism" to describe the vision implicit in Stone's observation. Corwin, *supra* note 5, at 19–21.
32. 269 U.S. 514, 518 (1926). According to Stone's docket book, only Sutherland had voted the other way in conference. Sutherland wrote on his return to Stone's circulated opinion that "I felt rather strongly the other way, but I shall yield. You have written a good opinion and if we are to draw what seems to me to be a rather arbitrary line, perhaps this is good as any." GS to HFS (Stone papers). Brandeis commented to Stone, "As already stated I shall abide the view of the Conference on your statement

of the point discussed by us." LDB to HFS (Stone papers). Van Devanter wrote, "I quite agree," adding some excellent editing suggestions. WVD to HFS (Stone papers).

33. Stone later wrote Noel Dowling at Columbia that "[t]he cases are in a very great state of confusion and I doubt whether there is any way of reducing them into a semblance of order except along the lines indicated in [*Metcalf*]." HFS to Noel T. Dowling (January 22, 1926) (Stone papers).
34. *Metcalf*, 269 U.S. at 522–23.
35. *Id.* at 523.
36. *Id.* at 523–24.
37. For Stone's subsequent development of the conceptual framework of *Metcalf*, see Helvering v Gerhardt, 304 U.S. 405 (1938); and Graves v. New York *ex rel.* O'Keefe, 306 U.S. 466 (1939). On the significance of *Metcalf*, see Noel T. Dowling, Elliott E. Cheatham, & Robert L. Hale, *Mr Justice Stone and the Constitution*, 36 Columbia Law Review 351, 353 (1936); and Kyle Richard, *Towards a Standard for Intergovernmental Tax Immunity between the Several States*, 70 Tax Lawyer 869, 878 (2017).
38. In 1930, Frankfurter wrote Stone observing that "Your Court has certainly been tearing up what one had supposed were rather deep-rooted foundations in the law of taxation. ... [O]ur federalism is dependent on leaving sources of taxation open to both states and nation without too many artificial restrictions, and particularly restrictions as rigid and iron as constitutional adjudications involve ... . I believe that the expression of your individual views upon these matters is profoundly important in the ultimate development of the Court's ideas." Felix Frankfurter to HFS (May 22, 1930) (Stone papers).
39. *Macallen*, 279 U.S. at 637 (Stone, J., dissenting).

CHAPTER 36

Normative Dualism and Congressional Power

WORLD WAR I demonstrated that issues of national consequence required federal regulation, whether or not these issues had previously been allocated to the traditional sphere of state sovereignty. The war accelerated the continental integration of the American market, which in turn emphasized the need for federal control. The Taft Court responded to these changes by authorizing pragmatic expansions of congressional power. By sanctioning hitherto unexercised forms of national legislative authority, the Taft Court itself further blurred the theoretically separate spheres of state and federal sovereignty.

In the context of congressional power, the Taft Court inherited a version of dual sovereignty that we have called normative dualism.[1] A classic statement of normative dualism may be found in *United States v. E.C. Knight Co.*, which in 1895 struck down the application of the Sherman Anti-Trust Act to sugar manufacturing:

> It cannot be denied that the power of a State to protect the lives, health, and property of its citizens, and to preserve good order and the public morals, "the power to govern men and things within the limits of its dominion," is a power originally and always belonging to the States, not surrendered by them to the general government, nor directly restrained by the Constitution of the United States, and essentially exclusive. ... On the other hand, the power of Congress to regulate commerce among the several States is also exclusive. ...
>
> It is vital that the independence of the commercial power and of the police power, and the delimitation between them, however sometimes perplexing, should always be recognized and observed, for while the one furnishes the strongest bond of union, the other is essential to the preservation of the autonomy of the States as required by our dual form of government; and acknowledged evils, however grave and urgent they may appear to be, had better be borne, than the risk be run, in the effort to suppress them, of more serious consequences by resort to expedients of even doubtful constitutionality....

Slight reflection will show that if the national power extends to all contracts and combinations in manufacture, agriculture, mining, and other productive industries, whose ultimate result may affect external commerce, comparatively little of business operations and affairs would be left for state control.[2]

E.C. Knight held that it was "vital" to maintain separate spheres of state and federal jurisdiction, and hence that the Constitution itself prohibited Congress from legislating in ways that might unduly constrict the authority and effectiveness of state police power. A quarter century later, in *Hammer v. Dagenhart*,[3] the Court held that this principle of normative dualism was so powerful that it could preclude the federal government from legislating even in its own exclusive sphere of interstate commerce if its regulations threatened to undermine local state police power.

E.C. Knight intimated, however, that federal power could reach transactions otherwise within the exclusive jurisdiction of state police power if the parties involved possessed the "intention to put a restraint upon trade or commerce."[4] Subsequent decisions, like *Swift & Co. v. United States*, explicitly confirmed that federal anti-trust law could regulate intrastate transactions so long as the relevant actors evidenced an "intent ... to aid in an attempt to monopolize commerce among the states."[5] Taft himself had first proposed this innovative analytic framework in his pioneering anti-trust decision in *United States v. Addyston Pipe & Steel Co.*,[6] written while he was a judge on the Sixth Circuit.[7] The *Addyston Pipe* formula allowed federal anti-trust enforcement to respect the values articulated by *E.C. Knight* and yet to escape an impractical division of economic life into strictly separated spheres of state and federal sovereignty.[8]

As chief justice, Taft scrupulously maintained the *Addyston Pipe* formula in interpreting the constitutional reach of federal anti-trust law. In *United Mine Workers v. Coronado Coal Co.*, for example, Taft spoke for a unanimous Court in reversing a trial court judgment holding a union liable for violations of the Sherman Act. He concluded that because "[c]oal mining is not interstate commerce, and the power of Congress does not extend to its regulation as such," the federal government could not penalize a union for striking against the production of coal destined for interstate commerce "unless the obstruction to mining is intended to restrain commerce."[9]

In other contexts, however, the Taft Court expressed an enhanced nationalism that seemed difficult to reconcile with the normative dualism of *E.C. Knight*. Prohibition is an outstanding example.[10] Another is the Court's treatment of federal grants to states. Such grants are now an essential component of federal–state relations, but in the 1920s they were relatively new and regarded with deep suspicion, as "an exceedingly potent and insidious influence, leading state officials to surrender voluntarily state prerogatives in exchange for appropriations of federal money."[11] President Coolidge characterized conditional federal grants as an "insidious practice which sugar-coats the dose of Federal intrusion." "The ardent States' rights advocate," said Coolidge, "sees in this practice a vicious weakening of the State system. The extreme Federalist is apt to look upon it in cynical fashion as bribing the States into subordination. The average American, believing in our dual-sovereignty system, must feel that the policy of national doles to the States is bad and may become disastrous."[12]

The Taft Court did not hesitate to approve conditional federal grants. The issue came before the Court in the form of a challenge to the Sheppard-Towner Act,[13] which established an innovative federal program authorizing annual grants to states meeting conditions for the improvement of maternal and infant health.[14] The Act was condemned as "a usurpation of power not granted to Congress by the Constitution – an attempted exercise of the power of local self-government reserved to the states by the 10th Amendment."[15] It was charged that the Act deployed federal spending power "for purposes not national, but local to the States," and was therefore unconstitutional because it constituted "an effective means of inducing the States to yield a portion of their sovereign rights."[16] In *Massachusetts v. Mellon*,[17] however, the Taft Court repulsed this attack and crafted standing and political question doctrines that to this day have strictly limited judicial oversight over the federalism implications of the congressional spending power.

The Taft Court's nationalism was on particularly clear display in its decisions concerning federal regulatory power over railroads. The Transportation Act of 1920[18] essentially nationalized railroad regulation in the United States.[19] American railroads had been in dire financial straits before the war. A decade of Interstate Commerce Commission ("ICC") "resistance to rate increases, along with the roads' mismanagement and earlier overcapitalization, impeded the modernization of trackage and rolling stock."[20] After seizing and operating the roads during the war, Congress decided to hand them back to private ownership under the care of an ICC charged with facilitating an efficient nationwide rail service.[21]

The 1920 Act "rewrote railroad regulatory policy and for the first time created a single, national railroad system."[22] The Act authorized "sweeping," "pervasive," and "detailed" forms of "federal control"[23] that explicitly extended to intrastate railway transportation, so long as the purpose of federal regulation was to "maintain an adequate railway service for the people of the United States."[24] The Act was premised squarely on the view that railroad transportation was a comprehensive, integrated system that provided a necessary infrastructure for the national market.

Almost as soon as he became chief justice, Taft inherited a "very important case"[25] from Wisconsin that challenged the authority of the ICC to preempt intrastate railroad rates on the ground that these rates were too low to ensure the financial health of the nation's interstate railroad system.[26] At issue was the capacity of state railroad commissions to maintain control over local rates, a matter of great significance. The power of the ICC under the Act was "assailed, not only by Wisconsin but also twenty other states, whose attorneys general filed briefs as amici curiae."[27]

Taft promptly authored a unanimous[28] and starkly nationalist[29] opinion, which asserted the principle that "[c]ommerce is a unit and does not regard state lines."[30] The Court held that Congress had authority to enact the "new departure" of the Transportation Act of 1920 because plenary federal control was necessary "to maintain an adequate railway service for the people of the United States."[31] It was immediately recognized that the "practical effect" of the *Wisconsin Rate Case* was virtually to sweep "state regulatory powers out of existence," at least "to the extent necessary to protect interstate carriers in the enjoyment of such revenues as the federal commission finds necessary to them in the public interest."[32]

In a private letter to Taft, Van Devanter argued that national authority should be justified as necessary to safeguard the structural integrity of the national market. "It would tend to commend the new enactment and the decision to the public mind," Van Devanter wrote,

> [i]f, instead of indicating that the chief purpose of the new enactment is to put the carriers on their feet and to benefit them, it were also indicated that this is a means to an end and that the real end is to bring about efficient transportation highways and instrumentalities whereby the present and the increasing needs of the public will be met and satisfied, whereby the means will be at hand for readily transporting the products of the farms, mines and forests to the centers of consumption and use in this country and to the seaboard, of carrying the products of mills, factories and industrial plans from the place of fabrication to the place of use, and so on and so on.[33]

Throughout the 1920s, the Taft Court would pursue a relentlessly nationalist agenda with respect to railroads, consistently supporting the purpose of the Transportation Act "affirmatively to build up a system of railways prepared to handle promptly all the interstate traffic of the country" by putting "the railroad systems of the country more completely than ever under the fostering guardianship and control" of the ICC.[34] The "power of the states over traffic charges" was accordingly reduced "to a shadow."[35] State regulation was permitted only in the insignificant interstices of the rail system.[36] State railroad commissions were rendered powerless even to prevent ICC-sanctioned abandonments of intrastate traffic along "physically detached" lines entirely within a state, so long as the lines were "operated in both intrastate and interstate commerce as a part of the system by means of connections with other railroads."[37] The Taft Court announced that federal power was justified because the "[e]fficient performance" of either interstate or intrastate commerce "is dependent upon the efficient performance of the transportation system as a whole."[38]

The ferocious nationalism of the Court's treatment of railroads,[39] a nationalism that far exceeded the narrow bounds of the Transportation Act,[40] no doubt reflected the experience of mobilization during World War I. The country learned then that rail transportation within the country was essentially one integrated system.[41] The Taft Court explicitly acknowledged that "[i]n solving the problem of maintaining the efficiency of an interstate commerce railway system which serves both the States and the Nation, Congress is dealing with a unit in which state and interstate operations are often inextricably commingled."[42] The conclusion that interstate and intrastate railroad transportation were fused into a single "unit" precluded the possibility of carving railroad transportation into distinct and exclusive spheres of state and federal sovereignty, as the Court insisted upon doing with respect to commercial transactions in the context of anti-trust law.

Normative Dualism & Congressional Power

The Taft Court was willing to approve broad congressional commerce power whenever it perceived an analogous need for national integration, which in the rapidly consolidating economy of the 1920s was not confined to railroads. A good example is *Stafford v. Wallace*,[43] which upheld the Packers and Stockyards Act of 1921[44] that provided for "the supervision by federal authority of the business of the commission men and of the live-stock dealers in the great stockyards of the country."[45]

Explicitly drawing on the "close analogy" to the Transportation Act of 1920,[46] the Court, speaking through Taft, concluded that "it was one of the chief purposes of the Constitution to bring under national protection and control" the "ever flowing" "streams of commerce" that connect "one part of the country to another."[47] Although *Stafford* is sometimes dismissed as a mere extension of the "current of commerce" approach of *Swift & Co. v. United States*,[48] it in fact marked a significant departure from *Swift*. *Swift* created doctrine to determine whether the Sherman Act could be applied to particular transactions. It held that federal power was appropriate whenever specific persons intended to restrain and monopolize interstate commerce. By contrast *Stafford* addressed the facial constitutionality of a statute regulating broad categories of transactions, regardless of the intent of the particular persons involved.[49]

Many of the transactions regulated by the Packers and Stockyards Act had heretofore been assigned to the exclusive domain of state police power. But *Stafford* concluded that this was irrelevant. *Stafford* held that "[t]he reasonable fear by Congress" that a course of conduct "usually lawful and affecting only intrastate commerce when considered alone, will probably and more or less constantly be used in conspiracies against interstate commerce or constitute a direct and undue burden on it," could serve "the same purpose as the intent charged in the Swift indictment to bring acts of a similar character into the current of interstate commerce for federal restraint."[50]

Stafford was a highly nationalist decision.[51] It explicitly declared that the Court ought to defer to Congress's judgment about whether a pattern of intrastate transactions should be characterized as burdening interstate commerce. "Whatever amounts to more or less constant practice, and threatens to obstruct or unduly to burden the freedom of interstate commerce is within the regulatory power of Congress under the commerce clause, and it is primarily for Congress to consider and decide the fact of the danger and meet it. This court will certainly not substitute its judgment for that of Congress in such a matter unless the relation of the subject to interstate commerce and its effect upon it are clearly non-existent."[52]

Stafford effectively ceded to Congress discretion to determine when interstate and intrastate commerce were so intermingled as to be regarded as a single "unit."[53] It thus broke in at least two respects with the basic thrust of the normative dualism of *E.C. Knight*. First, it authorized congressional regulation of spheres of economic life previously reserved for the "exclusive" regulation of state police power. The intrastate transactions controlled by the Packers and Stockyard Act had heretofore been beyond the reach of federal authority. Second, it authorized Congress to determine when such regulation was justified. *Stafford* was explicit in its ambition to assure the adequacy of federal power to safeguard a national market characterized by "modern conditions,"[54] in which intrastate and interstate transactions were thoroughly integrated.

Yet even as the Taft Court expanded the reach of congressional power, it refused entirely to abandon the logic of normative dualism. Taft himself vigorously affirmed that the "essence" of "our whole Federal System" was in "giving through the states local control to the people over local affairs and confining national and general subjects to the direction of the central government.... A centralized system of government ... would break up the Union in a short time."[55] In his very first term, Taft authored a highly controversial opinion – *Bailey v. Drexel Furniture Co.*[56] – that forcefully reaffirmed the logic of normative dualism in the context of the combustible subject of child labor.

In 1918, the Court had in *Hammer v. Dagenhart*[57] narrowly struck down the Keating-Owen Child Labor Act,[58] which prohibited the transportation in interstate commerce of the products of child labor. Although the regulation of interstate commerce was within the distinct sphere of federal authority, the Court in *Dagenhart*, speaking through Day, held that the effects of the Act on state police power would nevertheless violate the tenets of normative dualism by unacceptably constricting the scope of state police power. Congress responded by enacting the child-labor tax act, which imposed an excise tax of 10 percent on most employers who used child labor.[59] The statute drew on the Court's 1904 decision in *McCray v. United States*, which had upheld a congressional tax that effectively drove oleomargarine out of the interstate market. Speaking for six justices, Edward White in *McCray* forcefully affirmed "that the judiciary is without authority to avoid an act of Congress exerting the taxing power, even in a case where, to the judicial mind, it seems that Congress had, in putting such power in motion, abused its lawful authority by levying a tax ... the enforcement of which might ... indirectly affect subjects not within the powers delegated to Congress."[60]

Refusing to be bound by *McCray*, Taft in *Bailey* authored a decision for eight justices[61] striking down the child labor tax act on the ground that the statute's use of the taxing power would usurp an authority "reserved" to the "States ... by the Tenth Amendment" and would "break down all constitutional limitation of the powers of Congress and completely wipe out the sovereignty of the States."[62] Taft distinguished *McCray* on the ground that the child labor tax act, unlike the tax on oleomargarine, was a "detailed ... regulation of a state concern."[63] Although Taft declined to overrule *McCray*'s refusal to second-guess congressional motive, he nevertheless insisted that "there comes a time in the extension of the penalizing features of the so-called tax when it loses its character as such and becomes a mere penalty, with the characteristics of regulation and punishment. Such is the case in the law before us."[64]

"The good sought in unconstitutional legislation," Taft observed, "is an insidious feature, because it leads citizens and legislators of good purpose to promote it, without thought of the serious breach it will make in the ark of our covenant, or the harm which will come from breaking down recognized standards. In the maintenance of local self-government, on the one hand, and the national power, on the other, our country has been able to endure and prosper for near a century and a half."[65]

What Florence Kelley condemned as the "inhuman decision of the Supreme Court"[66] in *Bailey* sparked instant and fierce opposition,[67] prompting not only calls for a constitutional amendment authorizing federal regulation of child labor,[68] but also for a constitutional amendment to strip the Supreme Court of the power to declare congressional statutes unconstitutional.[69] Senator Robert La Follette delivered a fiery keynote to the 1922 annual convention of the American Federation of Labor discussing *Bailey* and proposing an amendment to give Congress power to override judicial decisions holding federal statutes unconstitutional.[70] Branding judicial review "a Frankenstein which must be destroyed," La Follette declared that "We cannot live under a system of government where we are forced to amend the Constitution every time we want to pass a progressive law."[71]

In the press it was reported that "Hoots, jeers and hisses greeted the name of Chief Justice Taft of the Supreme Court today in the convention of the American Federation of Labor, which, in a wild demonstration, approved an address by Senator La Follette attacking and condemning what he termed the 'judicial oligarchy.'" "The Senator was greeted with a storm of applause and cheering when he appeared as the principal speaker.... Delegates stood on chairs, pounded tables and shouted at the top of their voices as he attacked the Federal courts which, he said, had 'wrested the sovereignty from the people.' Time and again he was interrupted by shouts of agreement. His suggestion for a Congressional veto on the decisions of the Supreme Court was uproariously acclaimed."[72] The popular wave of opposition to judicial review in the early 1920s was inspired not merely by opposition to the Court's pinched view of government regulation, but also by the Taft Court's reassertion of normative dualism to restrict federal legislative power in *Bailey*.[73]

In the ambivalent 1920s, however, *Bailey* was also vigorously defended by those who opposed the transformation of "our Federal system ... into a centralized governmental machine, with the States of little more significance than counties are now."[74] Many praised *Bailey's* eloquent admonition that attempts to unduly expand congressional power, even to achieve good ends, risked undermining the essential constitutional structure of the nation. "The decision is far more important than it seems," proclaimed the *Wall Street Journal*.

> In nothing has the feebleness of character of those we send to Congress been shown more conclusively than in the attempt to abrogate states' rights. This country is a Union. Apart from its "territories" it is made up of forty-eight states, each, in accepting the federal Constitution, reserving definite rights of self-government. It is not too much to say that this system of government has made the United States possible. With all its conflicting interests, its varying living conditions, its racial extremes, its diversities of crop and climate, its almost capricious distribution of population, a centralized government, such as some of our short-cut politicians find so simple, would have proved unworkable long ago.[75]

We might ask how *Bailey*'s passionate commitment to normative dualism could possibly be reconciled with decisions like *Stafford* or the *Wisconsin Rate Case*. In the latter cases, the Court conceived the national market as an indivisible unit that Congress was authorized to regulate as a single interdependent entity. In *Bailey*, by contrast, the Court conceived the market as divided into separate spheres corresponding to the distinct contours of federal and state authority. When was the Taft Court inclined to take one view or the other? Two lines of explanation suggest themselves. The first emphasizes the *form* of congressional power, the second the *substance*. A focus on form is suggested by *Bailey's* companion case, *Hill v. Wallace*.[76]

Decided on the same day as *Bailey*, *Hill* struck down the Future Trading Act,[77] which used federal taxing power to impose a detailed regulatory scheme on boards of trade. The Court unanimously concluded that the Act was unconstitutional, although Brandeis wrote separately to explain his "doubt" that "the plaintiffs are in a position to require the court to pass upon the constitutional question in this case."[78] Speaking through Taft, and in plain tension with *McCray*, the Court reasoned that because "[t]he manifest purpose of the tax" was to "compel boards of trade to comply with regulations" addressed to matters "wholly within the police power of the State,"[79] the Act could "not be sustained as an exercise of the taxing power of Congress conferred by § 8, Article I."[80] The Court also held that the Act could not be "sustained under the commerce clause of the Constitution" because there was "not a word in the act from which it can be gathered that it is confined in its operation to interstate commerce."[81]

> The transactions upon which the tax is to be imposed ... are sales made between members of the Board of Trade in the City of Chicago for future delivery of grain, which will be settled by the process of offsetting purchases or by a delivery of warehouse receipts of grain stored in Chicago. Looked at in this aspect and without any limitation of the application of the tax to interstate commerce, or to that which the Congress may deem from evidence before it to be an obstruction to interstate commerce, we do not find it possible to sustain the validity of the regulations as they are set forth in this act. A reading of the act makes it quite clear that Congress sought to use the taxing power to give validity to the act. It did not have the exercise of its power under the commerce clause in mind and so did not introduce into the act the limitations which certainly would accompany and mark an exercise of the power under the latter clause.[82]

This language rather broadly intimated that Congress could constitutionally reimpose the very regulations at issue in *Hill* if only they were properly justified as protections of interstate commerce.[83] In less than three weeks Congress took the hint, and a bill was introduced in the House "for the prevention and removal of obstructions and burdens upon interstate commerce in grain by regulating transactions on grain future exchanges."[84] By the end of the summer Congress enacted the Grain Futures Act,[85] which imposed rules "substantially identical" to those of the Future Trading Act,[86] but which instead invoked Congress's power to regulate interstate commerce.

Normative Dualism & Congressional Power

A year later the Court upheld the Grain Futures Act in *Board of Trade v. Olsen*,[87] in which Taft, writing for seven justices,[88] explained that the Act contained "the very features the absence of which we held in ... somewhat carefully framed language ... prevented our sustaining the Future Trading Act."[89] Taft stressed that in the Grain Futures Act Congress purported "to regulate interstate commerce and sales of grain for future delivery on boards of trade because it [found] that by manipulation they have become a constantly recurring burden and obstruction to that commerce."

> In the act we are considering, Congress has expressly declared that transactions and prices of grain in dealing in futures are susceptible to speculation, manipulation and control which are detrimental to the producer and consumer and persons handling grain in interstate commerce and render regulation imperative for the protection of such commerce and the national public interest therein.
> It is clear from the citations, in the statement of the case, of evidence before committees of investigation as to manipulations of the futures market and their effect, that we would be unwarranted in rejecting the finding of Congress as unreasonable, and that in our inquiry as to the validity of this legislation we must accept the view that such manipulation does work to the detriment of producers, consumers, shippers and legitimate dealers in interstate commerce in grain and that it is a real abuse.[90]

Olsen upheld the very regulations that *Hill* had struck down as invading the regulatory domain of the states. As an interpretation of Congress's power under the Commerce Clause, *Olsen* expressed the same appreciation of the integrated nature of the national market as did *Stafford*. Like *Stafford*, *Olsen* was willing to grant substantial deference to Congress's justification of the need for federal regulation to protect an integrated national market.[91] *Olsen* ceded Congress ample discretion to protect an interstate commerce that was imagined as a "great interstate movement,"[92] a "current" that "flows ... from the West to the East, and from one State to another,"[93] as though it were so many railway lines spanning the nation.[94]

The contrast between *Hill* and *Olsen* suggests that the Taft Court was concerned about the *form* of congressional legislation. The Court did not seem as concerned to reserve a distinct economic sphere for the exclusive regulation of the states as it was insistent that Congress exercise only limited forms of power. The essential thought, which had been emphasized in *Bailey*, was that if the national taxing power became an unrestrained platform for regulation, there would be virtually no limit to federal authority.[95] The Court was determined to prevent federal taxing power from becoming a blank check for federal legislation. But the very regulations struck down in *Hill* could be upheld once they were reconceptualized as an exercise of a commerce power inherently limited by the commercial currents of the national market.

This explanation has force, so far as it goes. Yet it fails to explain why later in the decade the Taft Court was willing to uphold Congress's use of the taxing power to regulate narcotics in *Nigro v. United States*.[96] At issue in *Nigro* was the Anti-Narcotic Act of December 17, 1914, popularly known as the Harrison Narcotics

Act.⁹⁷ The Act used the taxing authority of Congress to impose detailed national regulations on the intrastate and interstate production and sale of narcotics. In an opinion authored by Taft, from which McReynolds, Sutherland, and Butler dissented, the Court affirmed the holding of *Bailey* "that Congress, by merely calling an act a taxing act, cannot make it a legitimate exercise of taxing power under section 8 of article 1 of the Federal Constitution, if in fact the words of the act show clearly its real purpose is otherwise."⁹⁸ But if in the Court's view the regulatory features of the Act were "genuinely calculated to sustain the revenue features," then "Congress does not exceed its power if the object is laying a tax and the interference with lawful purchasers and users of the drug is reasonably adapted to securing the payment of the tax. Nor does it render such qualification or interference with the original state right an invasion of it because it may incidentally discourage some in the harmful use of the thing taxed."⁹⁹ As applied to the Harrison Narcotics Act, this reasoning verged on the credulous. In dissent, McReynolds could only sputter:

> The plain intent is to control the traffic within the States by preventing sales except to registered persons and holders of prescriptions, and this amounts to an attempted regulation of something reserved to the States. . . . The suggestion to the contrary is fanciful. Although disguised, the real and primary purpose is not difficult to discover, and it is strict limitation and regulation of the traffic. Whether, or how far, opium, tobacco, diamonds, silk, etc., may be sold within their borders is primarily for the States to decide; the federal government may not undertake direct regulation of such matters.¹⁰⁰

We may ask, therefore, why the Taft Court was willing to countenance virtually unlimited congressional taxation of narcotics, but not of child labor. The answer requires us to look past the mere form of congressional legislation. Plainly other factors were influencing the Court's delineation of federal power. In seeking to identify these factors, it is helpful to begin by focusing on the object of congressional legislation.

In *Dagenhart*, the White Court considered a federal effort to regulate ordinary employment relationships. It conceptualized jurisdiction over these relationships as divided into two distinct spheres of national and state sovereignty. It rejected the contention that the national market in goods manufactured with child labor was a single indivisible unit that effaced the distinction between these spheres. *Dagenhart* explicitly repudiated the claim that individual states were effectively disempowered from prohibiting child labor because of exposure to "unfair competition"¹⁰¹ from states marketing less expensive goods produced by cheap child employees.¹⁰² *Dagenhart* held that the possibility of interstate competition "does not give Congress the power to deny transportation in interstate commerce to those who carry on business where the hours of labor and the rate of compensation . . . have not been fixed by a standard in use in other states. . . . The grant of power of Congress over the subject of interstate commerce was to enable it to regulate such commerce, and not to give it authority to control the states in their exercise of the police power over local trade and manufacture."¹⁰³

Faced with a renewed congressional effort to regulate these same ordinary employment relationships, the Taft Court in *Bailey* accepted *Dagenhart*'s assumption that the national manufacturing market was divided into separate state and federal spheres. At no point did the Taft Court imagine the market for manufactured goods as a single cohesive "unit." It is worth asking, therefore, why the Taft Court could so readily accept the fact of an integrated national market in the context of railroad rates, stockyards, and boards of trade, but refuse to recognize any such integration in the context of child labor, or indeed in the context of employment regulation generally.[104]

The question allows us to see that the Taft Court's support for expansive federal commerce power was largely articulated in the context of property "affected with a public interest,"[105] which the Court regarded as legitimately subject "to a more intimate public regulation."[106] Child labor did not involve property affected with a public interest. The Taft Court regarded "freedom in the making of contracts of personal employment, by which labor and other services are exchanged for money or other forms of property," as "an elementary part of the rights of personal liberty and private property, not to be struck down directly or arbitrarily interfered with."[107] Contracts of employment, including the child-labor contracts at issue in *Bailey*, were ordinary property, the regulation of which was suspect from the start.

The puzzle is that the Court had held in 1913 that prohibitions of child labor did not violate the Fourteenth Amendment.[108] If states could regulate child labor, then why could not the federal government? A second dimension of the problem must thus be thematized. As the debate over prohibition made clear, it was commonplace in the 1920s to associate the value of democracy with local state government. Even sophisticated observers would pose the challenge of federalism as "reconciling centralization with self-government."[109] The "bureaucratic hypertrophy"[110] of a "remote ... government"[111] was typically contrasted with "the true ideals of liberty and Democracy" exemplified in the "local self-government" of the states.[112] The 1924 Platform of the Democratic Party, for example, declared: "We condemn the efforts of the [R]epublican [P]arty to nationalize the functions and duties of the states. We oppose the extension of bureaucracy, the creation of unnecessary bureaus and federal agencies and the multiplication of offices and office-holders. We demand a revival of the spirit of local self-government essential to the preservation of the free institutions of our republic."[113]

To those who defended the necessity of decentralization, the scope and diversity of the country implied "that no one central authority can supervise the daily lives of a hundred million people, scattered over half a continent, without becoming top-heavy" with "the burden of federal bureaucracy."[114] There was a pervasive fear that national legislation was always on the verge of devolving into "a centralized governmental machine."[115] Henry Wade Rogers, dean of the Yale Law School, neatly summarized this perspective when he inveighed against federal centralization in the pages of the *North American Review*:

> The writers on political institutions have pointed out many times the advantages of local government over centralized government. They have taught us that local self-government develops an energetic citizenship, and centralization an enervated one; ... that under local self-government officials exist for the

benefit of the people, and that under centralization the people exist for the benefit of the officials; that local self-government provides for the political education of the people, and that centralization, based upon the principle that everything is to be done for the people rather than by the people, creates a spirit of dependence which dwarfs the intellectual and moral faculties and incapacitates for citizenship; ... that under local self-government every individual has a part to perform and a duty to discharge in public affairs, while under a centralized government one's affairs are managed by others.[116]

Taft's opinion in *Bailey* gestures toward this account of federalism when it explicitly contrasts "national power" to "the maintenance of local self-government."[117]

Congressional statutes were for this reason intrinsically more dangerous to liberty than was state legislation. Even if the substance of federal and state regulations were otherwise identical, the former would pose a more powerful threat to constitutional freedom than the latter. This is because the restrictions of state law were conceived as self-imposed restraints, whereas national legislation was always at risk of degenerating into external coercion by an alien and distant bureaucracy.[118] This stereotypic dichotomy was daily reinforced by the clumsy, overbearing federal enforcement of prohibition.

It follows from this view of federalism that congressional regulations of ordinary property, like the employment contracts of child labor, were more suspect than state regulations of ordinary property. This may explain why the Taft Court was willing to accept massive and intimate federal regulation of property affected with the public interest in the context, say, of railroads or stockyards, while nevertheless insisting that federal efforts to regulate ordinary business transactions be cabined by doctrines that sharply constrained federal power in the name of normative dualism.

This pattern is plainly observable in the Court's interpretation of federal antitrust law,[119] as it is in the context of the Court's treatment of the Federal Employers' Liability Act,[120] or the Federal Trade Commission Act.[121] In all such cases of federal regulation of ordinary property, the Taft Court was concerned to enforce normative dualism in ways notably absent from decisions like *Stafford* or *Olsen*. In the latter context, the Court could experience the national market as a single unified entity, whereas in the former the Court insisted on dividing the market into distinct national and local components. The Court's structural decisions about the limits of federal power, in other words, were intimately fused with its understanding of individual rights.

It is noteworthy that when the Taft Court encountered federal legislation unambiguously aimed at sustaining, rather than regulating, ordinary property, it was not tempted to invoke normative dualism to limit federal authority. Consider, for example, the Court's 1925 decision in *Brooks v. United States*,[122] which unanimously upheld the National Motor Vehicle Theft Act ("NMVTA").[123] The Act prohibited the knowing transportation in interstate commerce of stolen cars. From a structural point of view, the NMVTA was indistinguishable from the Keating-Owen Child Labor Law that the Court had struck down in *Dagenhart*. Both closed interstate commerce to certain goods in order to affect behavior in the states where the goods had originated.

Taft, who wrote the opinion, was a strong supporter of *Dagenhart*.[124] Yet when in *Brooks* he sought to distinguish *Dagenhart*, the best he could do was to argue that the Keating-Owen Child Labor Law was "a congressional attempt to regulate labor in the State of origin, by an embargo on its external trade," banning from interstate commerce goods that "were harmless, and could be properly transported without injuring any person who either bought or used them." But exactly the same characterization could be applied to the NMVTA, which was a congressional effort to discourage theft in states of origin by banning from interstate commerce vehicles that were harmless in themselves.[125]

What really seems to have distinguished *Brooks* from *Dagenhart* is that the latter involved legislation restricting ordinary contracts of employment, whereas the former involved a statute unambiguously seeking to protect "the property rights of those whose machines against their will are taken into other jurisdictions."[126] The NMVTA, as distinct from the Keating-Owen Child Labor Law, was an effort to use national power to combat what all regarded as an "immorality"[127] endangering ordinary property. Even though the NMVTA was a federal effort to regulate local crime, which is ordinarily conceived as within the distinct police power of the states,[128] it did not trigger the Court's instinct to preserve an exclusive sphere of state sovereignty.[129] The same might be said of the Court's willingness to uphold national narcotic legislation in *Nigro*.

It is telling that *Brooks* does not cite cases like *Stafford* or *Olsen* for support. Instead it self-consciously aligns itself with a well-developed line of precedents upholding "the authority of Congress to keep the channels of interstate commerce free from immoral and injurious uses."[130] These precedents took pains to stress that such federal regulation could extend only to "illicit articles"[131] not included in "the liberty protected by the Constitution,"[132] for "surely it will not be said to be a part of anyone's liberty, as recognized by the supreme law of the land, that he shall be allowed to introduce into commerce among the States an element that will be confessedly injurious to the public morals."[133] If *Stafford* and *Olsen* upheld congressional authority in part because constitutional values associated with liberty of contract were not immediately implicated by the regulation of property affected with a public interest, so the cases cited by *Brooks* explicitly stood for the proposition that these values were also not implicated by the regulation of indisputably immoral conduct, like theft.

The cases cited by *Brooks* reveal a good deal about the Taft Court's sense of constitutional authority. In upholding the Transportation Act of 1920, or federal regulations of stockyards or of boards of grain, the Taft Court portrayed Congress as authorized to speak for a specifically national interest – the protection of interstate commerce. But in the precedents cited by *Brooks*, which upheld federal regulation of "illicit" or "immoral" conduct, the Court did not imagine Congress as speaking for a distinctly national interest. It imagined Congress as instead speaking for common values shared by *both* federal and state governments. Thus, in *Hoke & Economides v. United States*,[134] which upheld the White-Slave Traffic Act prohibiting the transportation of women across state lines for "immoral purposes,"[135] the Court explained: "Our dual form of government has its perplexities, State and Nation having different spheres of jurisdiction ... but it must be kept in mind that we are one people; and the powers reserved to the States and those conferred on the Nation are adapted to be exercised, whether independently or concurrently, to promote the general welfare, material and moral."[136]

This image of an overarching unity – of a "general welfare, material and moral" that spanned both state and federal governments – authorized federal courts to sustain federal legislation that might otherwise be thought to efface the boundary between state and federal power. It is striking that in neither *Bailey* nor *Dagenhart* did the Court imagine Congress as speaking for "one people" who shared common values.[137] Although progressives struggled to characterize Congress as expressing a shared American democratic will[138] – in somewhat the same manner that Taft in *Myers* had hesitantly characterized the president as speaking for the authentic will of the whole country[139] – the Court refused in *Bailey* and *Dagenhart* to equate congressional condemnation of child labor with the expression of "public morals." Apparently, the brutality of child labor did not raise issues of the "general welfare, material and moral," as did the transportation of women across state lines. In vain did Congress expressly condemn child labor in the most explicit terms as "a national evil, a blot upon the fair name of our Republic" in which "the child is wronged, the Nation is wronged and the Nation's industry."[140] In *Bailey* and *Dagenhart*, the Court imagined the prohibition of child labor as a distinctively federal interest. Federal regulation to eliminate child labor was thus subject to the restraints of normative dualism.

The contrast between *Bailey* and *Brooks* illustrates the care taken by the Taft Court to classify only some government interests as transcending the distinction between federal and state governments. Taft himself characterized shared interests that escaped the dichotomies of dual sovereignty as the "crystallization of public sentiment."[141] Prohibiting the immoral transportation of women was such a shared interest, but prohibiting the degradation of children in factories was not. The Court, not Congress, had authority to discern when public sentiment was truly crystallized in a way that obliterated the distinction between state and federal interests. In classifying interests in this way, the Taft Court understood itself as articulating the fundamental values of the entire American people.

When a federal court today engages in constitutional interpretation, we conceptualize it as speaking solely for national law. But when the Taft Court interpreted the Constitution in light of the "public morals" of the country, it instead imagined itself to be speaking directly for the entire American people in their capacity as neither state nor federal citizens. This was a form of judicial authority traditionally associated with common law courts. It was the same kind of authority asserted by the Court when it insisted on its capacity to declare general common law in diversity cases.

Normative Dualism & Congressional Power

Notes

1. *See supra* Chapter 30, at 969–70.
2. 156 U.S. 1, 11, 13, 16 (1895).
3. 247 U.S. 251 (1918).
4. *E.C. Knight*, 156 U.S. at 17, 19.
5. *Swift*, 196 U.S. 375, 398 (1905).
6. 85 F. 271, 297–99 (6th Cir. 1898), aff'd, 175 U.S. 211 (1899).
7. Taft held that Congress was constitutionally authorized "to strike down any combination which had for its object the restraint and attempted monopoly of trade and commerce among a given number of states in specified articles of commerce." *Id.* at 298.
8. Stanley I. Kutler, *Chief Justice Taft, Judicial Unanimity, and Labor: The* Coronado *Case*, 24 THE HISTORIAN 68, 81 (1961).
9. 259 U.S. 344, 407, 411 (1922). *See id.* at 408:

   > In Hammer v. Dagenhart, we said: "The making of goods and the mining of coal are not commerce, nor does the fact that these things are to be afterwards shipped, or used in interstate commerce, make their production a part thereof." Obstruction to coal mining is not a direct obstruction to interstate commerce in coal, although it, of course, may affect it by reducing the amount of coal to be carried in that commerce. We have had occasion to consider the principles governing the validity of congressional restraint of such indirect obstructions to interstate commerce in *Swift & Co. v. United States.*

   In *Coronado*, Taft vacated a judgment against a defendant union because there "was no evidence submitted to the jury upon which they could properly find" intent "to restrain or monopolize interstate commerce." *Id.* at 413. Throughout the decade the Taft Court consistently held federal anti-trust prosecutions to the *Swift* criterion of intent. *See, e.g.*, United Leather Workers' Int'l Union v. Herkert & Meisel Trunk Co., 265 U.S. 457, 468–70 (1924); Indus. Ass'n of S.F. v. United States, 268 U.S. 64, 66 (1925). For further discussion, see *infra* Chapter 40, at 1313–19.
10. *See supra* Chapter 30.
11. CHARLES W. PIERSON, OUR CHANGING CONSTITUTION 22 (Garden City: Doubleday, Page & Co. 1922); *see also* John Ely Briggs, *State Rights*, 10 IOWA LAW BULLETIN 297, 308–9 (1925).
12. *Full Text of President Coolidge's Memorial Day Address at Arlington*, NEW YORK TIMES (May 31, 1925), at 2.
13. Pub. L. 97-67, 42 Stat. 224 (November 23, 1921).
14. For a discussion of the Act, see THEDA SKOCPOL, PROTECTING SOLDIERS AND MOTHERS: THE POLITICAL ORIGINS OF SOCIAL POLICY IN THE UNITED STATES 480–524 (Cambridge: Harvard University Press 1992).
15. Massachusetts v. Mellon, 262 U.S. 447, 479 (1923). *See Governors Divide over Federal Aid*, NEW YORK TIMES (July 1, 1925), at 1; *Those 'Dangerous' Federal Doles*, 86 LITERARY DIGEST 12 (July 18, 1925); *State Rights and Baby Welfare*, 85 LITERARY DIGEST 37 (April 8, 1922); *Fears Federal Grip: Maine Governor Sees National Government Encroaching on State's Activities*, NEW YORK TIMES (December 21, 1921), at 16. It was almost a cliché to denounce the Sheppard-Towner Act as a federal usurpation of state power. *See, e.g.*, William Cabell Bruce, *Recent Strides of Federal Authority*, 77 SCRIBNER'S MAGAZINE 639, 643 (1925);

Bentley W. Warren, *Destroying Our "Indestructible States"*, 133 ATLANTIC MONTHLY 370, 375 (1924); William D. Riter, *Constitutional Conceptions: A Contrast*, 216 NORTH AMERICAN REVIEW 637, 645 (1922); *Back to the Constitution*, NEW YORK TIMES (January 23, 1922), at 10. In the words of the President of the American Bar Association: "Is it not true that there is a spirit abroad in the land, which prompts no man to do for himself what he can get the government to do for him? So that thus through paternalistic legislation, we hear the faint cry of maternalistic bureaus and other bureaus which are insidiously destroying our resourcefulness, our self-sufficiency and our very independence itself." R.E.L. Saner, *Governmental Review*, in REPORT OF THE FORTY-SEVENTH ANNUAL MEETING OF THE AMERICAN BAR ASSOCIATION 137–38 (Baltimore: Lord Baltimore Press 1924).
16. Massachusetts v. Mellon, 262 U.S. 447, 479 (1923).
17. 262 U.S. 447 (1923).
18. Pub. L. 66-152, 41 Stat. 456 (February 28, 1920).
19. *See supra* Chapter 21, at 693–94.
20. MORTON KELLER, REGULATING A NEW ECONOMY: PUBLIC POLICY AND ECONOMIC CHANGE IN AMERICA, 1900–1933, at 50 (Cambridge: Harvard University Press 1990).
21. James M. Beck, *Federal Power over Intrastate Railroad Rates*, 71 UNIVERSITY OF PENNSYLVANIA LAW REVIEW 11, 12 (1922).
22. HERBERT HOVENKAMP, ENTERPRISE AND AMERICAN LAW 1836–1937, at 166 (Cambridge: Harvard University Press 1991).
23. *The "Return" of the Railroads*, 22 NEW REPUBLIC 6 (1920).
24. *Federal Control of Intrastate Railroad Rates*, 35 HARVARD LAW REVIEW 864, 865 (1922).
25. WHT to Horace D. Taft (December 24, 1921) (Taft papers).
26. R.R. Comm'n v. Chi., Burlington & Quincy R.R. Co., 257 U.S. 563 (1922) (this case is also known as the *Wisconsin Rate Case*). The case differed from the so-called *Shreveport Case*, because *Shreveport* addressed only the ICC's power to remedy discrimination caused by particular intrastate rates. Houston, E. & W. Tex. Ry. Co. v. United States, 234 U.S. 342 (1914). The *Wisconsin Rate Case*, in contrast, involved a blanket ICC order raising all intrastate rates, regardless of whether any particular rate "work[ed] a discrimination against interstate travelers," 257 U.S. at 580, on the ground that a general increase in rates was necessary "to make the system adequate to the needs of the country by securing for it a reasonably compensatory return for all the work it does." *Id.* at 589. *See also id.* at 585–86: "Intrastate rates and the income from them must play a most important part in maintaining an adequate national railway system. ... The effective operation of the [Transportation] act will reasonably and justly require that intrastate traffic should pay a fair proportionate share of the cost of maintaining an adequate railway system." Thomas Reed Powell observed that the *Wisconsin Rate Case* "seems to go beyond the doctrine of the Shreveport Case in that in effect it requires local commerce to help interstate commerce and not merely to refrain from hindering it." Thomas Reed Powell, *The Supreme Court's Review of Legislation in 1921–1922*, 37 POLITICAL SCIENCE QUARTERLY 486, 489 (1922).
27. Edward S. Corwin, *Constitutional Law in 1921–1922*, 16 AMERICAN POLITICAL SCIENCE REVIEW 612, 619 (1922).

Normative Dualism & Congressional Power

28. We have in the Van Devanter papers an undated, handwritten note from Taft asking Van Devanter to review his opinion "before I circulate it. I would like your judgment on it and especially on the last part of it where I briefly discuss the validity of the act. Am I too abrupt or sweeping in my hypothetical generalizations?" At the time there was apparently in circulation a memorandum by Brandeis proposing that the case be decided on narrower and more technical grounds, which did not explicitly embrace the goal of ensuring the financial health of the railroads. *See* LDB, Memorandum (September 24, 1921) (Taft papers). Van Devanter wrote back to Taft disapproving Brandeis's memorandum because it entailed "too much straining to keep a large conveyance in a narrow path." WVD to WHT (n.d.) (Taft papers). "There is also an entire failure to recognize ... other new provisions which are designed to secure a fair revenue to the carriers so that they may appropriately discharge their functions and be of real service to commerce and the public." *Id.* By contrast, Van Devanter "thoroughly" agreed with Taft's "strong opinion," suggesting only that it could be "strengthened by a short statement at an appropriate place of how closely interstate and intrastate commerce are intertwined." *Id.*

    There also exists an undated letter from McReynolds to Taft stating that McReynolds did not "want to fail in my obligation of frankness with you," and informing Taft that "I do not like yr. opinion." JCM to WHT (n.d.) (Taft papers). McReynolds thought the opinion hard "to follow and ... almost sure to produce confusion and add to our difficulties. The subject is of tremendous importance and should be put in the clearest possible way with no non-essential matter." *Id.* Taft's opinion was announced on February 27, 1922. As late as February 11, Taft was still worrying to Van Devanter that there was "no word from Brandeis or McReynolds. ... They are forging thunderbolts, I suppose." WHT to WVD (February 11, 1922) (Van Devanter papers). Eventually Taft put together a unanimous court on the ground, as he later wrote his brother, that the ICC has power

    > to require state authorities to keep up their intrastate rates so as to contribute a fair share to the cost of running the railroad system. The agricultural bloc will not like the decision and there will probably be some effort to amend the law, and I think it may be successful, but the law is a good one, and I hope any attempt to amend it may be defeated. We had a unanimous judgment in that case, which gives it a good deal of weight. I worked hard on the case and wrote and rewrote the opinion, and finally got it into fair shape.

    WHT to Horace D. Taft (February 28, 1922) (Taft papers). Almost a year later, Brandeis complained to Frankfurter that more ICC cases ought to be assigned to him, "like [the] Wisconsin Rate Cases ... but first White and then Taft took it. Both asked me to talk with them about the cases. White's opinion was so bad I had it go over – then Taft took it, & though he knew practically nothing about it he felt he ought to write it. He was very nice in the suggestions he took from me." *Brandeis-Frankfurter Conversations*, at 322 (August 6, 1923). It is in this context that Brandeis observed to Frankfurter that Van Devanter "would make an ideal Cardinal," because he was so useful to his masters, like White and Taft. *Id.*

29. Early in his career as a federal circuit judge, Taft declared that "[t]he railroads have become as necessary to life and health and comfort of the people of this country as

are the arteries on the human body." Thomas v. Cincinnati, N.O. & T.P. Ry. Co., 62 F. 803, 821 (C.C.S.D. Ohio 1894). In 1917, Taft argued that the best method to improve the health of the railway system was by incorporating the "railways under federal law and taking them out from under the nagging supervision of state commission supervision." William Howard Taft, *Our Railway Situation* (December 20, 1917), in VIVIAN, at 20. Taft believed that the poor condition of the railroads was due to "the hostile blundering, greed, and jealousy of state legislatures," and he advocated "the complete taking over of the interstate commerce business of the country into the regulation of the Interstate Commerce Commission." William Howard Taft, *Wise and Unwise Extension of Federal Power*, 1 CONSTITUTIONAL REVIEW 67, 72–73 (1917) ("*Federal Power*"). He fully anticipated that such a solution would "cause a great deal of local opposition by the enormous machinery that has now been created for the intra-state regulation. . . . The state [railroad] commissioners have already organized with a view to protection of their jurisdiction." *Id.* at 72.

30. *Wisconsin Rate Case*, 257 U.S. at 588. Taft strongly supported the Transportation Act of 1920 and the consequent amplification of ICC regulatory power. William Howard Taft, *The Cummins Railway Bill* (January 15, 1920), in VIVIAN, at 333; William Howard Taft, *The Esch Railway Bill* (January 16, 1920), *id.* at 336; William Howard Taft, *The Railroad Bill* (January 30, 1920), *id.* at 345; William Howard Taft, *The New Railroad Bill* (March 18, 1920), *id.* at 366. Taft believed that railroads should be independent of "state nagging" because they "are the arterial system of the whole country." William Howard Taft, *The Cummins Railway Bill, supra,* at 335.

31. *Wisconsin Rate Case*, 257 U.S. at 585. Taft's opinion rested on the "far-reaching" conclusion "that the transportation systems of the country are not divided by the boundaries of the states but are nation-wide institutions to be dealt with in the interest of the country as a whole." Parker McCollester, *Regulation of Intrastate Commerce under the Commerce Clause*, 31 YALE LAW JOURNAL 870, 878 (1922). The loss of state power sparked a backlash in the traditionally states' rights-oriented Democratic Party, which declared in its 1924 Platform that the Transportation Act of 1920 "has unnecessarily interfered with the power of the states to regulate purely intrastate transportation." 1924 Platform of the Democratic Party, available at www.presidency.ucsb.edu/documents/1924-democratic-party-platform. The Platform demanded "that the states of the union shall be preserved in all their vigor and power. They constitute a bulwark against the centralizing and destructive tendencies of the republican party." *Id.*

32. *States' Rights and Railroad Rates*, WALL STREET JOURNAL (March 1, 1922), at 1. The *Wall Street Journal* considered the decision "one of the most important that the Supreme Court has rendered in recent years." *Supreme Court Upholds Federal Rate-Making Power*, WALL STREET JOURNAL (February 28, 1922), at 6.

33. WVD to WHT (n.d.) (Taft papers). Van Devanter told Taft that he regarded "the opinion as a vital one, as of more importance than we now realize and as calculated to be a great factor in adjusting our present unbalanced and ill regulated transportation system to the increasing needs of the country and in ultimately placing it on a footing where it can serve all sections and all patrons at a minimum of cost, inconvenience and delay. . . . [W]hen once it becomes well organizes [sic] and rightly disciplined,

Normative Dualism & Congressional Power

I apprehend that the rates will become less than anyone now would venture to predict." *Id.*

34. Dayton-Goose Creek Ry. Co. v. United States, 263 U.S. 456, 478 (1924).
35. *The Waning Power of the States over Railroads: Curtailment of State Regulatory Activities by the Transportation Act*, 37 HARVARD LAW REVIEW 888, 890 (1924). *See* Chi., Milwaukee & St. Paul Ry. Co. v. Pub. Utils. Comm'n, 274 U.S. 344, 350–52 (1927) (holding that a state commission, without any evidentiary foundation, improperly based its decision to reduce intrastate railroad rates on a decision by the ICC to lower interstate rates it found to be too high); N.Y. Cent. R.R. Co. v. N.Y. & Pa. Co., 271 U.S. 124, 125–26 (1926) (deciding that state authorities could not grant reparations to a railroad when a federal statute forbade the reduction of railroad rates for six months after the end of federal controls unless approved by the ICC); R.R. Comm'n v. E. Tex. R.R. Co., 264 U.S. 79, 84, 90 (1924) (determining that attempts by the state to prohibit a failed railroad from dismantling its salvageable property because the railroad still had four and a half years of state incorporation left were impermissible under the applicable statute); Nashville, Chattanooga & St. Louis Ry. v. Tennessee, 262 U.S. 318, 320, 323 (1923) (permitting the ICC to authorize a general increase in railway shipping rates, while denying the Railroad and Public Utilities Commission of Tennessee permission to decrease the rates for carriers of materials to build public roads). Brandeis, however, was intermittently concerned to search for procedural and political accommodations that might ease the tension between paramount federal power and local state interests. *See supra* Chapter 8, at 319–20; Ark. R.R. Comm'n v. Chi., Rock Island, & Pac. R.R. Co., 274 U.S. 597, 599, 603 (1927):

> The railroad concedes that states have the exclusive right to fix intrastate rates, subject to the limitation that such rates must not unduly discriminate against interstate commerce; that a mere difference in rate does not constitute an undue discrimination; that the question whether discrimination exists is one for the Interstate Commerce Commission; that to justify federal interference there must be substantial disparity resulting in real discrimination; and that the extent of the alleged discrimination must be found in the federal commission's order. It contends that the Interstate Commerce Commission found that the existing intrastate class and commodity tariff discriminated unjustly against interstate commerce; that it ordered the removal of the discrimination; and that the railroad had, therefore, the right and the duty to substitute a new non-discriminating tariff. The answer of the state commission is a denial that the federal commission made such finding or order. . . .
>
> The intention to interfere with the state function of regulating intrastate rates is not to be presumed. Where there is a serious doubt whether an order of the Interstate Commerce Commission extends to intrastate rates, the doubt should be resolved in favor of the state power. If, as the railroad believed, the federal commission intended to include the intrastate Arkansas rates within its order, it should have taken action, through appropriate application, to remove the doubt by securing an expression by that commission of the intention so to do.

Taft commented on a draft of Brandeis's opinion in *Chicago, Rock Island, & Pacific Railroad Co.* that "[w]e are teaching" three-judge courts "a little sense of propriety as to dealing with state courts." (Brandeis papers).

36. *See, e.g.*, Mo. Pac. R.R. v. Boone, 270 U.S. 466 (1926) (allowing states some latitude to determine railroad rates and fares); W. & Atl. R.R. v. Ga. Pub. Serv. Comm'n, 267 U.S. 493 (1925) (giving states the right to require railroads to furnish

switching service for shippers); Norfolk & W. Ry. Co. v. Pub. Serv. Comm'n, 265 U.S. 70 (1924) (permitting states to require railroad carriers to provide the necessary facilities to allow shippers to remove freight carried on the railroad). For an example of the Court earnestly wrestling with the question of whether a state-ordered grade crossing was too expensive, see Lehigh Valley R.R. Co. v. Bd. of Pub. Util. Comm'rs, 278 U.S. 24, 35 (1928):

> The care of grade crossings is peculiarly within the police power of the states, Railroad Comm'n v. Southern Pacific Co., 264 U.S. 331, 341; and if it is seriously contended that the cost of this grade crossing is such as to interfere with or impair economical management of the railroad, this should be made clear. It was certainly not intended by the Transportation Act to take from the States, or to thrust upon the Interstate Commerce Commission, investigation into parochial matters like this, unless, by reason of their effect on economical management and service, their general bearing is clear. Railroad Commission v. Southern Pacific Co., 264 U.S. 331. The latter case makes a distinction between the local character of the usual elimination of grade crossings and the vital character from the standpoint of finance of the investment of large sums in the erection of a union station.

37. Colorado v. United States, 271 U.S. 153, 159–60 (1926).
38. *Id.* at 164. Concerned to preserve a space for local initiative, Brandeis nevertheless insisted that "nice adjustments" would be required to reconcile federal and state regulatory power over railroads. *See, e.g.,* Lawrence v. St. Louis-S.F. Ry. Co., 274 U.S. 588, 594–95 (1927):

> [T]he fact is important that the controversy concerns the respective powers of the nation and of the states over railroads engaged in interstate commerce. Such railroads are subject to regulation by both the state and the United States. The delimitation of the respective powers of the two governments requires often nice adjustments. The federal power is paramount. But public interest demands that, whenever possible, conflict between the two authorities and irritation be avoided. To this end it is important that the federal power be not exerted unnecessarily, hastily, or harshly. It is important also that the demands of comity and courtesy, as well as of the law, be deferred to. It was said in Western & Atlantic R. R. v. Georgia Public Service Commission, 267 U.S. 493, 496, that a law of a state may be valid which prohibits an important change in local transportation conditions without application to the state commission, although the ultimate authority to determine whether the change could or should be made may rest with the federal commission. And it was there said that the "action of the company in discontinuing the service without a petition" to the state body was "arbitrary and defiant." Compare Henderson Water Co. v. Corporation Commission, 269 U.S. 278. To require that the regulating body of the State be advised of a proposed change seriously affecting transportation conditions is not such an obvious interference with interstate commerce that, on application for a preliminary injunction, the act should lightly be assumed to be beyond the power of the state.

See also St. Louis-S.F. Ry. Co. v. Ala. Pub. Serv. Comm'n, 279 U.S. 560 (1929) (holding that an interstate railroad must first comply with the terms of an Alabama statute before it could challenge in federal court those provisions requiring railroads to petition the state before discontinuing any railroad service within the state).

39. *See, e.g.,* United States v. Ill. Cent. R.R. Co., 263 U.S. 515, 525 (1924) (upholding the ICC's decisions on the ground that the interests of individual carriers must yield to the public need); St. Louis-S.F. Ry. Co. v. Pub. Serv. Comm'n, 261 U.S. 369, 372

Normative Dualism & Congressional Power

(1923) (cautioning that any exercise of state authority which directly regulated interstate commerce was repugnant to the Constitution); The New England Divisions Case, 261 U.S. 184, 189–90 (1923) (highlighting Congress's unequivocal purpose in passing the Transportation Act of 1920 to preserve the financial integrity of national railway transportation); Pa. R.R. Co. v. U.S. R.R. Labor Bd., 261 U.S. 72, 79–80 (1923) (emphasizing that Congress has deemed it of high public importance to prevent labor disputes from interrupting interstate commerce). In Alabama & Vicksburg Railway Co. v. Jackson & Eastern Railway Co., 271 U.S. 244 (1926), the Court, in an opinion by Brandeis, held that state courts were without power to authorize a railroad to exercise eminent domain for the purpose of creating a junction with another railroad, even if a state court had held that "the proposed connection was a proper one" and that "the authority granted by the state law to secure junctions did not interfere with interstate commerce to an appreciable degree, if at all." *Id.* at 247. Brandeis conceded that the Court had earlier permitted such state determinations in Wisconsin, Minnesota & Pacific Railroad Co. v. Jacobson, 179 U.S. 287 (1900), but noted that "[s]ince then the authority of the Interstate Commerce Commission has been greatly enlarged and the power of the States over interstate carriers correspondingly restricted." Ala. & Vicksburg Ry. Co., 271 U.S. at 248. "The only limitation set by Transportation Act, 1920, upon the broad powers conferred upon the Commission over the construction, extension and abandonment of the lines of carriers in interstate commerce, is that introduced as paragraph 22 of § 1, which excludes from its jurisdiction 'spur, industrial, team, switching or side tracks, located wholly within one State, or of street, suburban, or interurban electric railways, which are not operated as a part or parts of a general steam railroad system of transportation.' It is clear that the connection here in question is not a track of this character." *Id.* at 249. The Court accordingly held that the jurisdiction of the ICC was "exclusive." *Id.* at 250. Responding to Brandeis's draft opinion, Taft wrote, "I concur. After a while you will get into the minds of state courts that the I.C.C. really exercises some authority." WHT to LDB (Brandeis papers).

40. *See, e.g.*, Midland Valley R.R. v. Barkley, 276 U.S. 482, 487 (1928) (declaring that when Congress chose to regulate the distribution of coal cars it abrogated state rules in this field); Davis v. Wechsler, 263 U.S. 22, 24 (1923) (emphasizing that state courts may not allow local rules to defeat a federal right); Am. Ry. Express v. Levee, 263 U.S. 19, 21 (1923) (holding that a local rule regarding the burden of proof contravened federal law and was therefore invalid). Particularly striking is the line of cases developed by Brandeis that prohibited under the dormant Commerce Clause state courts from assuming jurisdiction over tort suits against interstate railroads when the cause of action does not arise within the forum state, when the defendant does not own or operate a railroad within the forum state, and when the plaintiff is also a nonresident of the forum state. *See* Davis v. Farmers' Co-Operative Equity Co., 262 U.S. 312, 317 (1923). *See also* Mich. Cent. R.R. Co. v. Mix, 278 U.S. 492, 495 (1929) (holding that a plaintiff cannot subject a nonresident corporation to suit in a state where she has acquired residence after the accident has occurred); Atchison, Topeka & Santa Fe Ry. Co. v. Wells, 265 U.S. 101, 103 (1924) (declaring invalid a Texas statute which permitted a nonresident to prosecute an out-of-state railroad corporation for an accident occurring in another state). *But see* Hoffman v. Missouri *ex rel.* Foraker, 274 U.S. 21, 22–23 (1927)

(holding that a railroad company must comply if it is sued where it owns, operates, and carries on its business); Chicago & Northwestern Ry. Co. v. Alvin R. Durham Co., 271 U.S. 251, 258 (1924) (holding that the liability of a garnishee is fixed by state, not federal, law); Missouri ex rel. St. Louis, Brownsville & Mex. Ry. Co. v. Taylor, 266 U.S. 200, 207 (1924) (ruling that, where a railway carrier has a usual place of business in a state and the alleged negligence occurs there, it is amenable to suit in that state); EDWARD A. PURCELL, JR., LITIGATION AND INEQUALITY: FEDERAL DIVERSITY JURISDICTION IN INDUSTRIAL AMERICA, 1870–1958, at 193-96 (New York: Oxford University Press 1992) (discussing Brandeis's support of devices like the Commerce Clause venue doctrine to pursue practical considerations); Bernard C. Gavit, *Jurisdiction over Causes of Action against Interstate Carriers*, 3 INDIANA LAW JOURNAL 130, 137 (1927) (concluding that federal legislation may be needed to govern the venue of actions against interstate carriers).

The Taft Court also frequently interpreted federal statutes regulating railroads as preempting and displacing state law. In Napier v. Atlantic Coast Line Railroad Co., 272 U.S. 605 (1926), for example, Brandeis held for a unanimous Court that the Boiler Inspection Act, Pub. L. 61-383, 36 Stat. 913 (February 17, 1911), had "occupied the field of regulating locomotive equipment used on a highway of interstate commerce, so as to preclude state legislation." *Napier*, 272 U.S. at 607. Even though federal regulators had not ruled under the Act that interstate railroads had to obtain "a particular type of fire box door or a cab curtain," id. at 609, Brandeis nevertheless upheld a federal court injunction prohibiting enforcement of state statutes requiring these safety devices, even assuming that "there [was] no physical conflict between the devices required by the State and those specifically prescribed by Congress or the Interstate Commerce Commission" and that the required state devices actually "promote [d] safety." *Id.* at 610–11. "[R]equirements by the States are precluded, however commendable or however different their purpose. ... If the protection now afforded by the Commission's rules is deemed inadequate, application for relief must be made to it." *Id.* at 613. One local paper complained that the decision "seems to us going a bit too far, and is just another example of the startling and over-mastering incursion of Federal power in this land. If we must depend upon the Congress to regulate the equipment of the B. & O. yards in Grafton, we have come to a dangerous place in American law and its administration." *A Real Danger*, GRAFTON (WEST VIRGINIA) SENTINEL (December 2, 1926), at 4. Brandeis, however, wrote Frankfurter the day after the decision: "In [*Napier*] I have endeavored to make clear, as a matter of statutory construction, the 'occupying the field' doctrine. I think the states could be taught, by a similar ABC article that, if they wish to preserve their police power, they should, through the 'state block' in Congress, see to it in every class of Congressional legislation that the state rights which they desire to preserve be expressly provided for in the acts." LDB to Felix Frankfurter (November 30, 1926), in BRANDEIS-FRANKFURTER CORRESPONDENCE, at 263. *See also* Chesapeake & Ohio Ry. Co. v. Stapleton, 279 U.S. 587, 593 (1929) (declaring that, where the field is relations between an interstate carrier and its interstate employees, it is exclusively a federal question); Mo. Pac. R.R. Co. v. Porter, 273 U.S. 341, 346 (1927) (holding that, where Congress has entered a field of regulation, state laws have no application); Chi., Milwaukee & St. Paul Ry. Co. v. Coogan, 271 U.S. 472, 474 (1926) (stating that the

Normative Dualism & Congressional Power

Federal Employers' Liability Act preempts state law with respect to employers' liability to employees engaged in interstate transportation by rail).

41. *See* Marvin B. Rosenberry, *Development of the Federal Idea*, 218 NORTH AMERICAN REVIEW 145, 158 (1923):

> During the World War, the Federal Government took over the operation of the railway and telegraph systems as a war measure. It is already apparent that this step is to have a far-reaching effect upon the transportation systems of the country. The advantages of unified control, direct routing and free exchange of equipment are so manifest.... The decision of the United States Supreme Court in [the *Wisconsin Rate Case*] ... indicates quite clearly that every transportation agency in the country is likely to be drawn into the Federal system, with the power and authority of the agents of the Federal Government vastly extended. Already the power of the States to regulate intra-state transportation is greatly limited.

Many of the Taft Court's opinions include direct references to the period when the federal government took control of the nation's rail system. *See, e.g.*, United States v. Reading Co., 270 U.S. 320, 330 (1926) (holding the federal government liable for charges it erroneously collected from railway carriers under the Federal Control Act); Marion & Rye Valley Ry. Co. v. United States, 270 U.S. 280, 282 (1926) (stating that no compensation was due where the taking of a railroad under the Federal Control Act was not implemented); Davis v. Wechsler, 263 U.S. 22, 24 (1923) (holding that state courts may not defeat federal rights by applying local rules); Wabash Ry. Co. v. Elliott, 261 U.S. 457, 463 (1923) (ruling that no liability can attach for personal injury where a railway company is under federal control); Davis v. L.N. Dantzler Lumber Co., 261 U.S. 280, 289 (1923) (holding that a railroad under federal control could not be subject to garnishment in state court); N.C. R.R. Co. v. Lee, 260 U.S. 16, 17 (1922) (holding that the federal government was operating a North Carolina railway not as a lessee but by right of eminent domain).

42. Dayton-Goose Creek Ry. Co. v. United States, 263 U.S. 456, 485 (1924).
43. 258 U.S. 495 (1922). McReynolds dissented without opinion; Day did not participate in the case.
44. Pub. L. 67-51, 42 Stat. 159 (August 15, 1921).
45. *Stafford*, 258 U.S. at 497.
46. *Id.* at 522–23. The Court cited the *Wisconsin Rate Case* for the proposition that "intrastate transactions that affect prejudicially interstate commerce" can be regulated by Congress. *Id.* at 523.
47. *Stafford*, 258 U.S. at 518–19. Taft sent a draft of his opinion to Van Devanter and Clarke for review, "because we are very clear in our judgment, and I would like the benefit of your criticism before I send it on to other members of the Court who are more doubtful." WHT to WVD (April 20, 1922) (Van Devanter papers); WHT to JHC (April 20, 1922) (Taft papers). When Taft circulated his draft more generally Brandeis replied, "This is very strongly put and has converted me." LDB to WHT (Taft papers). Holmes responded to Taft's draft with an admiring comment: "Admirable and big." OWH to WHT (Taft papers). Holmes thought the opinion "expressed the movement of interstate commerce in a large and rather masterly way." OWH to Frederick Pollock (May 21, 1922), in 2 HOLMES-POLLOCK CORRESPONDENCE, at 96; *see also* OWH to Felix Frankfurter (May 4, 1922), in

HOLMES-FRANKFURTER CORRESPONDENCE, at 140 ("I think the C.J.'s opinion as to commission merchants and dealers in stock yards is fine. It has a sort of march, like the movement of interstate commerce that it describes."). *See* OWH to Harold Laski (May 3, 1922), in 1 HOLMES-LASKI CORRESPONDENCE, at 423: "Taft continues to give me great satisfaction as C.J. He delivered a decision last Monday on the power of Congress to deal with commission merchants and dealers in the Stock Yards that had a kind of big movement in it parallel to the interstate trade he sought to portray. Also he is amiable and comfortable." Clarke had similarly complemented Taft about an early draft of the opinion: "You are exceedingly happy I think in describing the movement involved as in substance a single one from the producing farmers in the west to the consuming and expecting cities in the East. That is what it really is and it will be an addition to the law to have it clearly stated & recognized in practice. This [illegible] character of the movement subordinates separate incidents which seem local to the main purpose or intent." JHC to WHT (n.d.) (Taft papers).

48. 196 U.S. 375, 398–99 (1905). *See, e.g.*, Vanue B. Lacour, *The Misunderstanding and Misuse of the Commerce Clause*, 30 SOUTHERN UNIVERSITY LAW REVIEW 187, 227 (2003); Earl L. Shoup, *The Life and Times of William Howard Taft by Henry F. Pringle*, 26 WASHINGTON UNIVERSITY LAW QUARTERLY 142, 146 (1940) (book review).

49. Clarke was quite clearly troubled by this difference. He wrote Taft:

> I really doubt the soundness of the expression ... that the Act of Congress can supply the equivalent of intent in the conduct of the parties themselves which led to the conclusion in the Swift case. Must not the intent be found in the conduct dealt with? That binds it together so that the courts will not dissect it and affirm or condemn its separate elements but will deal with the transaction as a comprehensive whole. The fact is there's something of finessing to be done in this case and you are so much more capable of that kind of thinking than I am that I am sure I couldn't be of service if I should try by writing a volume.

JHC to WHT (n.d.) (Taft papers).

50. *Stafford*, 258 U.S. at 520–21.

51. It has been said that Taft's opinions staking out liberal interpretations of congressional power under the Commerce Clause mark "his most successful and influential work as Chief Justice." Stanley I. Kutler, *Chief Justice Taft, National Regulation, and the Commerce Power*, 51 JOURNAL OF AMERICAN HISTORY 651, 651 (1965). *See* Alpheus T. Mason, *William Howard Taft, 1857–1930*, 34 ILLINOIS LAW REVIEW 884, 886 (1940). Taft repeatedly expressed his admiration for John Marshall, "the greatest Judge that America or the World has produced," WILLIAM HOWARD TAFT, POPULAR GOVERNMENT: ITS ESSENCE, ITS PERMANENCE AND ITS PERILS 131 (New Haven: Yale University Press 1913), because Marshall set the course of the Court toward a "liberal construction of the Constitution in conferring powers upon the National Government" and against "the school of Jefferson" that would have "emphasize[d] unduly the sovereignty of the States." *Id.* at 133–37. *See* William Howard Taft, *Address before the National Civic Federation at the Belasco Theatre in Washington D.C.* (January 17, 1910), in 1 PRESIDENTIAL ADDRESSES AND STATE PAPERS 550 (New York: Doubleday, Page & Co. 1910); William Howard Taft, *Criticisms of the Federal Judiciary*, 29 AMERICAN LAW REVIEW 641, 645 (1895).

Normative Dualism & Congressional Power

52. *Stafford*, 258 U.S. at 521. Thirteen years later, and over the dissenting votes of McReynolds, Van Devanter, Sutherland, and Butler, Chief Justice Hughes would quote this passage in his opinion in NLRB v. Jones & Laughlin Steel Corp., 301 U.S. 1, 37 (1937), in an effort to justify the Court's acceptance of the vast new regulatory powers claimed by the federal government during the New Deal. Taft himself summarized the holdings of *Stafford* and the *Wisconsin Rate Case* this way: "It is clear . . . that if Congress deems certain recurring practices, though not really part of interstate commerce, likely to obstruct, restrain or burden it, it has the power to subject them to national supervision and restraint." United Mine Workers v. Coronado Coal Co., 259 U.S. 344, 408 (1922). For a discussion of *Stafford*, see Barry Cushman, *Continuity and Change in Commerce Clause Jurisprudence*, 55 ARKANSAS LAW REVIEW 1009, 1026–29 (2003).

53. Several years later, in Atlantic Coast Line Railroad Co. v. Standard Oil Co., 275 U.S. 257 (1927), which concerned the question of whether shipments of oil should be charged at interstate or intrastate rates, the Court, speaking through Taft, was quite explicit that the "stream of commerce" metaphor of *Stafford* should not be taken as a literal definition of the scope of interstate commerce. Instead, the Court explained, *Stafford* "held that a reasonable fear upon the part of Congress, that acts usually affecting only intrastate commerce when occurring alone, would probably and more or less constantly be performed in aid of conspiracies against interstate commerce, or constitute a direct and undue obstruction and restraint of it, would serve to bring such acts within lawful Federal statutory restraint." *Id.* at 272. Thus *Stafford* "can not be cited to show what is interstate and what is intrastate commerce in a controversy over rates to determine whether they come normally within the regulation of Federal or State authority." *Id.* at 273. *See* United Leather Workers Int'l Union v. Herkert & Meisel Trunk Co., 265 U.S. 457, 469 (1924) (noting that *Stafford* does not establish "that a strike against the manufacturer of commodities intended to be shipped in interstate commerce is a conspiracy against that commerce" and that *Stafford* held that Congress can regulate what it finds to be "abusive practices . . . usually only within state police cognizance" that threaten to "obstruct or unduly to burden" interstate commerce). *Stafford* is thus an opinion addressed to congressional authority to define the boundaries of its own power.

54. *Stafford*, 258 U.S. at 518.

55. WILLIAM HOWARD TAFT, OUR CHIEF MAGISTRATE AND HIS POWERS 52–53 (New York: Columbia University Press 1916).

56. 259 U.S. 20 (1922). For a summary of press reactions, see *The Child-Labor Law Quashed*, 73 LITERARY DIGEST 11 (May 27, 1922).

57. 247 U.S. 251 (1918). Taft opposed the Keating-Owen Law, arguing that "the use by Congress of the power of interstate commerce as a club to control the states, in the character of the police measures that they shall adopt in their own internal affairs, is a departure from its previous course that may well give great concern." Taft, *Federal Power*, *supra* note 29, at 75. Taft reasoned that although Congress ought to be able to regulate interstate commerce "for the purpose of promoting or limiting commerce as a vehicle to proper objects," it should not be permitted to regulate interstate commerce "for the purpose of putting the states under duress to adopt a police policy in matters over which they have by the Constitution complete control." *Id.* at 76. Although the Court in *Dagenhart* did not accept Taft's invitation to delve into the motives of Congress, Taft nevertheless applauded the decision. *See*

William Howard Taft, *Child-Labor Legislation* (June 20, 1918), in VIVIAN, at 69–70 ("In matters intrusted to the states by the Constitution, we must look to the states for proper laws and their effective enforcement. To do otherwise is to confess our national system a failure."). In his book on popular government, Taft wrote: "Child labor in the State of the shipment has no legitimate or germane relation to the interstate commerce of which the goods thus made are to form a part, to its character or to its effect. Such an attempt of Congress to use its power of regulating such commerce to suppress the use of child labor in the State of shipment would be a clear usurpation of that State's rights." TAFT, POPULAR GOVERNMENT, *supra* note 51, at 142–43. *See* Taft, *Address before the National Civic Federation*, *supra* note 51, at 552; Robert C. Post, *Chief Justice William Howard Taft and the Concept of Federalism*, 9 CONSTITUTIONAL COMMENTARY 199, 205–8 (1992).

58. Pub. L. 64-249, 39 Stat. 675 (September 1, 1916).
59. Pub. L. 65-254, 40 Stat. 1057, 1138–40 (February 4, 1919). After *Dagenhart*, the Senate sought to revive the Keating-Owen prohibitions "as a war measure," *A New Campaign against Child Labor*, 120 THE OUTLOOK 518 (1918), but the Armistice caused the Act's supporters instead to formulate a federal tax law that applied to the use of child labor. *Id.* The full story is told in STEPHEN B. WOOD, CONSTITUTIONAL POLITICS IN THE PROGRESSIVE ERA: CHILD LABOR AND THE LAW (University of Chicago Press 1968); Mark E. Herrmann, *Looking Down from the Hill: Factors Determining the Success of Congressional Efforts to Reverse Supreme Court Interpretations of the Constitution*, 33 WILLIAM & MARY LAW REVIEW 543, 547–64 (1992).
60. 195 U.S. 27, 63–64 (1904).
61. Taft's opinion was joined by all justices except Clarke, who dissented without opinion. Clarke would later observe to Woodrow Wilson that the case was "unfortunately ... considered and decided when one of my sisters was dying and I could not write a dissenting opinion. I am sure a dissent based on the decisions from the oleomargarine to the Narcotic Drug Cases could have been made very convincing." JHC to Woodrow Wilson (September 9, 1922) (Woodrow Wilson papers).
62. *Bailey*, 259 U.S. at 38. Brandeis told Taft that *Bailey* was "a very good opinion," "clear and forceful," and that Taft had "done all that can be done to distinguish the earlier cases." LDB to WHT (Taft papers). Brandeis wrote Frankfurter that

> The N[ew] R[epublic], The Survey & like periodicals should not be permitted to misunderstand yesterday's decision on The Child Labor and Board of Trade cases, & should be made to see that holding these Acts void is wholly unlike holding invalid the ordinary welfare legislation.
> That is – that we here deal
> (1) With distribution of functions between State & Federal Governments
> (2) With the attempt at dishonest use of the taxing powers.

LDB to Felix Frankfurter (May 16, 1922), in BRANDEIS-FRANKFURTER CORRESPONDENCE, at 100–1. Brandeis's condemnation of the "dishonest use of the taxing powers" should be contrasted to his prewar recommendation that Congress use its taxing power to regulate state banks and insurance companies. *See* LOUIS D. BRANDEIS, OTHER PEOPLE'S MONEY AND HOW THE BANKERS USE IT 88 (New York: Frederick A. Stokes Co. 1914) ("While Congress has not been granted power to regulate *directly* state banks, and trust or life insurance companies ... except in respect to interstate commerce, it may do so *indirectly* by virtue either of its control of the mail privilege or through the taxing power."). Brandeis's mention of the "Board of Trade cases" refers to the fact that *Bailey* was decided on the same day as Hill v. Wallace, 259 U.S. 44 (1922), which struck down a section of the Future Trading Act, 1921, Pub. L. 67-66, 42 Stat. 187 (August 24, 1921). For a discussion of Brandeis's vote in *Bailey*, see WOOD, *supra* note 59, at 292–93.

After *Bailey* was announced, James M. Beck, the solicitor general who had defended the child-labor tax law, and who was personally a strong defender of states' rights, see JAMES M. BECK, THE VANISHING RIGHTS OF THE STATES 14 (New York: George H. Doran Company 1926), wrote Taft to confess that "none who heard you deliver the opinion may have welcomed the decision more than I. Had the Court adhered tenaciously to the views of the late Chief Justice White in McCray v. United States, our form of Government would have sustained a serious injury." James M. Beck to WHT (May 16, 1922) (Taft papers). Taft replied, "I had an impression that your soul was not wrapped up in the Child Labor cases." WHT to James M. Beck (May 17, 1922) (Taft papers). Taft later remarked that he "hoped that the judgment supported by the opinion of eight Judges would have some effect to stop the tendency of Congress to seek to give to the Federal Government that which under the Constitution really belongs to the States." WHT to Henry St. George Tucker (September 27, 1922) (Taft papers).

63. *Bailey*, 259 U.S. at 42. For a good discussion, see Thomas Reed Powell, *Child Labor, Congress, and the Constitution*, 1 NORTH CAROLINA LAW REVIEW 61 (1922).

64. *Bailey*, 259 U.S. at 38.

65. *Id.* at 37. Taft had long opposed federal regulation of child labor as "a clear usurpation of ... State's rights." *See, e.g.*, TAFT, POPULAR GOVERNMENT *supra* note 51, at 142–43.

66. *Address of Miss Florence Kelley*, in REPORT OF PROCEEDINGS OF THE FORTY-SECOND ANNUAL CONVENTION OF THE AMERICAN FEDERATION OF LABOR 248 (Washington D.C.: Law Reporter Printing Co. 1922).

67. *See, e.g.*, W.B. Rubin, *The Constitution and the Supreme Court*, 29 AMERICAN FEDERATIONIST 675, 678 (1922) ("When the Supreme Court declared the child labor law unconstitutional it assumed a power, first, which it was never intended it should have by the framers of our Constitution, and second it continued a usurpation of power initiated in that court by Chief Justice Marshall. . . . Our Court is not a Czar or a monarch over the people."). Taft was inclined to dismiss this opposition. Three months after *Bailey*'s release, he wrote Van Devanter, "I suppose you have noted the yawping of Gompers and Lafollette over the child labor and Coronado [259 U.S. 344 (1922)] cases, but I have not heard much of an echo. I think we did good work in those cases." WHT to WVD (August 19, 1922) (Van Devanter papers).

68. REPORT OF PROCEEDINGS OF THE FORTY-SECOND ANNUAL CONVENTION OF THE AMERICAN FEDERATION OF LABOR, *supra* note 66, at 372–73. President Harding subsequently proposed a constitutional amendment authorizing federal regulation of child labor. *Address of the President*, 64 CONG. REC. 212, 215 (December 8, 1922). The following year Coolidge also recommended that Congress pass such a constitutional amendment. *Address of the President*, 65 CONG. REC. 96, 99 (December 6, 1923). The Republican Party Platform of 1924 endorsed "the

recommendation of President Coolidge for a constitutional amendment authorizing congress to legislate on the subject of child labor." Platform of the Republican Party, 1924, available at www.presidency.ucsb.edu/documents/republican-party-platform-1924. The platform of the Progressive Party in 1924 was similarly enthusiastic. Platform of the Progressive Party available at www.presidency.ucsb.edu/documents/progressive-party-platform-1924 ("We favor prompt ratification of the Child Labor amendment."). The 1924 Platform of the Democratic Party, by contrast, merely provided that "Without the votes of democratic members of congress the child labor amendment would not have been submitted for ratification." 1924 Platform of the Democratic Party available at www.presidency.ucsb.edu/documents/1924-democratic-party-platform.

Taft himself opposed the effort to enact a constitutional amendment authorizing federal regulation of child labor:

> I don't know how you feel about the child labor amendment, but the more I have thought of it, the more convinced I have been that it would be a mistake to pass it. I think the southern States are getting into better shape with reference to child labor laws, and that the two centers of activity in favor of adopting the amendment are the labor unions and those good people who have no hesitation in changing the Constitution and shifting all the burdens of executing laws to the National Government whenever there is any doubt as to their enforcement, and whenever they happen to be particularly interested in enforcement. I think the centralization that has been going on has been greatly detrimental to our constitutional structure.

WHT to Robert A. Taft (December 22, 1924) (Taft papers). *See* WHT to Mrs. Frederick J. Manning (December 20, 1925) (Taft papers). The effort to ratify a constitutional amendment giving the federal government authority to regulate child labor eventually failed. In the opinion of *The Outlook*, "Opposition to the proposed Child Labor Amendment ... is based in part upon the belief that, in spite of their failure, State governments are worth preserving. Every State government is a laboratory. Its unsuccessful experiments can be rejected by the other States. Its successful experiments can be imitated or improved. The very differences between State laws on the same subject are a source of strength for our Federal Republic. ... It is a mistake to think that all opposition to the Child Labor Amendment is based on the self-interest of those who wish to exploit the labor of children." *The Child Labor Amendment*, 137 THE OUTLOOK 496 (1924).

Taft's opposition to federal child-labor regulation did not express a latent libertarian streak, for he was quick to approve state regulation of child labor. *See* Chesapeake & O. Ry. Co. v. Stapleton, 279 U.S. 587, 593 (1929) ("That the state has power to forbid such employment and to punish the forbidden employment when occurring in intrastate commerce, and also has like power in respect of interstate commerce so long as Congress does not legislate on the subject, goes without saying."); William Howard Taft, *Address of the President*, in REPORT OF THE THIRTY-SEVENTH ANNUAL MEETING OF THE AMERICAN BAR ASSOCIATION 370 (Baltimore: Lord Baltimore Press 1914) ("The hours-of-labor statutes, child-labor statutes, the tenement-housing statutes, the statutes requiring wholesome surroundings for labor, are legislation paternal but useful.").

69. *Is the Supreme Court Too Supreme?*, 74 LITERARY DIGEST 21 (July 1, 1922).

70. *Address of Senator Robt. M. La Follette*, in REPORT OF PROCEEDINGS OF THE FORTY-SECOND ANNUAL CONVENTION OF THE AMERICAN FEDERATION OF LABOR, *supra* note 66, at 241–42; *La Follette Lashes Federal Judiciary*, NEW YORK TIMES (June 15, 1922), at 1; Robert M. La Follette, *Supreme Court Ruler of Nation: Highest Tribunal Has Usurped Power to Nullify Laws*, LA FOLLETTE'S MAGAZINE (June 1922), at 83.
71. *Address of Senator Robt. M. La Follette*, *supra* note 70, at 241–42.
72. *La Follette Lashes Federal Judiciary*, *supra* note 70. La Follette's speech was reprinted in the *Locomotive Engineers Journal*, see Senator Robert M. La Follette, *The Usurped Power of the Supreme Court*, 56 LOCOMOTIVE ENGINEERS JOURNAL 497 (July 1922), which endorsed his proposed constitutional amendment. *See Respect for Supreme Court*, 56 LOCOMOTIVE ENGINEERS JOURNAL 492–93 (July 1922) ("Why should the workers accept as divine law the decrees of the same 'Injunction Bill' Taft, who, first among federal judges, nailed the engineer to his locomotive and denied him the right to quit work when the job and pay dissatisfied him? . . . Perhaps Mr. Debs is right when he says, in his article in this issue of THE JOURNAL, that Mr. Taft was appointed to administer this kind of justice.").
73. *See, e.g.*, George W.P. Hunt, *Ridiculous Reasoning*, 50 THE SURVEY 217 (1923).
74. Fabian Franklin, *Why the Supreme Court Rejected the Child-Labor Law*, 108 THE INDEPENDENT 507, 508 (1922).

> That that system is worth preserving is not a dictate of mere conservatism; nor is it recommended solely by the sentiment which attaches to the tradition of State individuality, or aversion to unlimited centralized control in a vast and varied country like ours. For the initiative of the separate States has been a fruitful source of our social and governmental progress. . . .
>
> If, however, anything like the traditional autonomy of our States in their home affairs is to be preserved, it will not do to look to the Supreme Court to save it from destruction. . . . If the people, or the Congress which the people choose as their representative, don't care a fig for the fundamental principles of the Constitution, ways will be found a-plenty to undermine those principles. . . . When the Prohibition amendment was adopted by Congress, many Representatives and Senators were perfectly aware of its monstrous impropriety as part of our Federal Constitution, but few had the courage and manliness to vote against it. . . . [W]e must be thankful to the Supreme Court not only for maintaining those principles when the Constitution warrants its interposition, but also for directing the nation's attention to their vital importance, as Chief Justice Taft has done upon the present occasion.

Id.
75. *Victory for States' Rights*, WALL STREET JOURNAL (May 17, 1922), at 1.
76. 259 U.S. 44 (1922).
77. Pub. L. 67-66, 42 Stat. 187 (August 24, 1921).
78. *Hill*, 259 U.S. at 72 (Brandeis, J., concurring). Brandeis's doubt, however, did not prevent him from pronouncing "that the Future Trading Act is unconstitutional." *Id.*
79. *Hill*, 259 U.S. at 66–67.
80. *Id.* at 68. In Trusler v. Crooks, 269 U.S. 475 (1926), the Court later struck down other provisions of the Future Trading Act on the same grounds as in *Hill*. *Id.* at 482.
81. *Hill*, 259 U.S. at 68. On May 18, 1922, Brandeis sent his daughter copies of the Court's opinions in *Bailey* and *Hill*, commenting "To see the full import – study the Child Labor and Future Trading Act opinions, in connection with the Stockyard

THE TAFT COURT

case [*Stafford*]. . . . I am convinced that the immediate loss will result in great gain later. If we may hope to carry out our ideals in America, it will be by development through the State and local Governments. Centralization will kill – only decentralization of social functions can help. In the 19th Century nationalization was the keynote & the 20th should bring local development in States & cities." LDB to Susan Brandeis (May 18, 1922), in BRANDEIS FAMILY LETTERS, at 379–80.

82. *Hill*, 259 U.S. at 68–69. We have extant virtually identical letters sent by Taft to Van Devanter and Brandeis, describing that he had reached in his opinion "a different conclusion from that which was voted at conference." WHT to LDB (May 12, 1922) (Taft papers); WHT to WVD (May 12, 1922) (Van Devanter papers). To Brandeis, Taft wrote:

> [W]e voted first that there was equitable jurisdiction by a vote of 7 to 1, you voting "No", and Justice Holmes being doubtful. On the question whether it could be sustained as a taxing act, the vote stood 7 to 1, Justice McKenna casting the negative vote, and you not voting. Later we took a vote as to whether the act could be sustained as a regulation of interstate commerce. At first, by a vote of 5 to 4, it was held that it could not be sustained. Later there was a change, and by a vote of 5 to 3, you not voting, its validity as a regulation of interstate commerce was sustained. On a close examination of the case, the law and the record, I have reached the conclusion stated in this opinion, namely that we have jurisdiction, that the law is invalid as a taxing law, and that it can not be sustained as a valid regulation of interstate commerce.

WHT to LDB (May 12, 1922) (Taft papers). That same day Brandeis wrote Taft that "Your argument that the law cannot be sustained either as a taxing act or as a regulation of interstate commerce is strong and convincing. I still feel grave doubt whether there is equity jurisdiction . . . and am not yet certain what I ought to do. Probably I should concur & state my doubt as to cause of action etc." LDB to WHT (May 12, 1922) (Taft papers). The question of whether *Hill* created a precedent for suits restraining the collection of taxes in violation of 26 U.S.C. § 7421 would cause embarrassment for the Court the following year in Graham v. Du Pont, 262 U.S. 234, 257–58 (1923). We have a letter from Taft to Brandeis, discussing the difficulties he faced in drafting *Graham* in light of his own opinion in *Hill*:

> Your suggestion that the tax in Hill vs. Wallace was in effect a penalty, because prohibitive and intended to stop, appeals to me, and I shall try and add something to the opinion of that sort so as to relieve us from embarrassment in the future. In other words, I might add something like this:
> Perhaps it would be better to include Hill vs. Wallace in the class of cases represented by Lipke vs. Lederer, [259 U.S. 557 (1922)], in that the tax imposed was really in the nature of a penalty to enforce a regulation than a tax in the proper sense.
> Do you think that would be sufficient and give us a chance in the future to avoid the use of Hill vs. Wallace as an uncomfortable precedent?

WHT to LDB (May 18, 1923) (Taft papers).

83. Taft stated explicitly that because "sales for future delivery on the Board of Trade are not in and of themselves interstate commerce," they

> can not come within the regulatory power of Congress as such, unless they are regarded by Congress, from the evidence before it, as directly interfering with interstate commerce so as to be an obstruction or a burden thereon. . . . It was upon

Normative Dualism & Congressional Power

> this principle that, in Stafford v. Wallace ... we held it to be within the power of Congress to regulate business in the stockyards of the country, and include therein the regulation of commission men and of traders there, although they had to do only with sales completed and ended within the yards, because Congress had concluded that through exorbitant charges, dishonest practices and collusion they were likely, unless regulated, to impose a direct burden on the interstate commerce passing through.

Hill, 259 U.S. at 69. This language pointed rather directly to the purpose of Congress and the evidence before it as the measures of constitutional power.

84. 62 CONG. REC. 7987 (June 1, 1922).
85. Pub. L. 67-331, 42 Stat. 998 (September 21, 1922).
86. *Two Attempts to Regulate the Grain Trade: Findings of Fact by Congress*, 37 HARVARD LAW REVIEW 136, 138 (1923) ("Congress quickly grasped the inferential suggestion that a similar statute might be upheld if based on the commerce clause, and passed the Grain Futures Act."). *See Grain Futures Act Is Upheld*, LOS ANGELES TIMES (April 17, 1923), at 22: "Promptly Congress met the issue by reenacting substantially all the regulatory features of the law, but based its new exercise of authority on its control over interstate commerce, declaring that trading in grain futures, unless properly regulated by the Federal government, could be made a restraint upon interstate shipments of grain."
87. 262 U.S. 1 (1923). On the day of the decision, Taft wrote his brother:

> I deliver an important opinion this morning sustaining the validity of an act of Congress putting the Chicago Grain Board under federal control and compelling them to admit ... representatives of cooperative farmers' associations on payment of regular dues and compliance with rules. I delivered a similar opinion in the matter of the Chicago Stockyards Act last year. I have carried the Court in both cases against considerable opposition not apparent in the vote. ... If there ever was real interstate and foreign commerce it is that which is transacted on these two boards. It affects and dominates the consumers of the world in food products. It is just what our ancestors were seeking to have Congress regulate. Whether the legislation will do any good is another question but it does this good that the farmers have their own secretary of agriculture to supervise these two markets which they have always denounced as the chief sources of their woe.

WHT to Horace D. Taft (April 16, 1923) (Taft papers). On that same day, Taft wrote his son:

> To-day I decide one of the most important cases that I have had to dispose of, and that is the constitutionality of the Chicago Board of Trade case. I decided the stock yards case last year, and now this comes up this year, and I think I have carved out a view of interstate commerce which is useful for the purpose of bringing within Congressional control the real centers of our interstate and foreign commerce. How valuable in results that control by Congress may be we can not guarantee – that is not our business – but we shall have put the power where in substance and real effect under the Constitution it ought to be.

WHT to Robert A. Taft (April 16, 1923) (Taft papers). The decision was regarded by the press as "a nationally important case" that represented "a staggering victory" for "the farm bloc." *The Supreme Court Fences the Pit*, 77 LITERARY DIGEST 16 (May 5, 1923) (quoting the *Norfolk Virginian-Pilot*).

88. McReynolds and Sutherland dissented without opinion. Butler's docket book indicates that at conference Holmes had voted to strike down the Act, while McKenna

was uncertain about his view of the question. Taft first circulated his opinion privately to Van Devanter and to Brandeis. In the Van Devanter papers, there is a note from Taft stating: "I send this opinion in the Board of Trade case for your overhauling without mercy. I know that you are busy but you are too good natured for your own good. . . . I have not circulated it. I have sent it to Brandeis, J." WHT to WVD (April 4, 1923) (Van Devanter papers).

89. *Olsen*, 262 U.S. at 32. Taft, as he had in *Stafford*, paid elaborate homage to Holmes's opinion in *Swift*:

> [*Stafford*] was but the necessary consequence of the conclusions reached in the case of Swift & Co. v. United States, 196 U.S. 375. That case was a milestone in the interpretation of the commerce clause of the Constitution. It recognized the great changes and development in the business of this vast country and drew again the dividing line between interstate and intrastate commerce where the Constitution intended it to be. It refused to permit local incidents of great interstate movement, which taken alone were intrastate, to characterize the movement as such. The Swift Case merely fitted the commerce clause to the real and practical essence of modern business growth. It applies to the case before us just as it did in Stafford v. Wallace.

Id. at 35. Actually, however, as in *Stafford*, the problem facing the Court in *Olsen* concerned the facial constitutionality of a rule, as distinct from the constitutionality of particular applications of a rule. *Olsen* thus concerned quite different issues from those that confronted the Court in *Swift*. *See supra* text at notes 48–49. It is possible that Taft's focus on *Swift* in *Olsen* was a deliberate effort to capture Holmes's vote, which in conference had been against the Act's constitutionality.

90. *Olsen*, 262 U.S. at 32, 37–38.

91. In the last years of his life Taft stressed "the all-inclusiveness of the regulation of interstate commerce entrusted to Congress." WHT to HFS (August 31, 1928) (Taft papers):

> In Gibbons v. Ogden, and in other cases following it, the breadth and scope of the Congressional power can hardly be made greater. The power of Congress in this respect is described as exactly what it would be in a government without states, and to include all that the legislature of such a government could do in regulating commerce and navigation, except a violation of the Fifth Amendment.

This is a very encompassing account of federal power over interstate commerce. It is, however, in considerable tension with Taft's own consistent support for the Court's decision in *Hammer v. Dagenhart*. In the 1920s, *Dagenhart* stood for the proposition that the Court can examine the purposes of congressional regulation of interstate commerce to determine whether they are pretextual; that is, whether Congress has tried to achieve ends not otherwise within its authority. *See* Linder v. United States, 268 U.S. 5, 17 (1925). Such scrutiny of congressional purpose is inconsistent with conceptualizing congressional commerce power as the equivalent of plenary state police power, limited only by the subject matter of "commerce and navigation."

92. *Olsen*, 262 U.S. at 35.

93. *Stafford*, 258 U.S. at 516.

94. For an example of popular linkage of federal power over railroads and federal power over aspects of national economic life like grain, see *Overlapping Regulations*, NEW YORK TIMES (June 12, 1922), at 14; SARAH H. GORDON, PASSAGE TO UNION: HOW THE RAILROADS TRANSFORMED AMERICAN LIFE, 1829–1929, at

Normative Dualism & Congressional Power

347–48 (Chicago: Ivan R. Dee 1996) ("By 1900 the social order that had emerged in the United States was overwhelmingly based on the principle of national commercial exchange. ... [T]he railroads held a prominent position in defining the social order, a position threatened only by the introduction of an even better system of transportation.").

95. *See, e.g., Bailey,* 259 U.S. at 37–38:

> Out of a proper respect for the acts of a co-ordinate branch of the Government, this court has gone far to sustain taxing acts as such, even though there has been ground for suspecting from the weight of the tax it was intended to destroy its subject. But, in the act before us, the presumption of validity cannot prevail, because the proof of the contrary is found on the very face of its provisions. Grant the validity of this law, and all that Congress would need to do, hereafter, in seeking to take over to its control any one of the great number of subjects of public interest, jurisdiction of which the States have never parted with, and which are reserved to them by the Tenth Amendment, would be to enact a detailed measure of complete regulation of the subject and enforce it by a so-called tax upon departures from it. To give such magic to the word "tax" would be to break down all constitutional limitation of the powers of Congress and completely wipe out the sovereignty of the States.

If the potentially limitless scope of the taxing power rendered it particularly susceptible to possible abuse, and hence in need of constitutionally restrictive interpretation, the more narrow scope of relatively specific grants of power, like the Eighteenth Amendment or the Spending Clause, rendered them correspondingly less dangerous to the principles of dual sovereignty.

96. 276 U.S. 332 (1928).
97. Pub. L. 63-223, 38 Stat. 785 (December 17, 1914), as amended in, Pub. L. 65-254, 40 Stat. 1057, 1130 (February 24, 1919). Earlier in the decade, the Taft Court had dropped dark hints about the constitutionality of Congress's use of its taxing power to regulate narcotics in the Harrison Act. So, for example, McReynolds stated in *dicta* in his unanimous opinion for the Court in United States v. Daugherty, 269 U.S. 360, 362–63 (1926) that "The constitutionality of the Anti-Narcotic Act, touching which this Court so sharply divided in United States v. Doremus, was not raised below and has not been again considered. The doctrine approved in Hammer v. Dagenhart; Child Labor Tax Case; Hill v. Wallace; and Linder v. United States, may necessitate a review of that question if hereafter properly presented." Just one year before McReynolds had announced in his opinion for a unanimous Court in Linder v. United States, 268 U.S. 5, 17 (1925): "Congress cannot, under the pretext of executing delegated power, pass laws for the accomplishment of objects not entrusted to the Federal Government. And we accept as established doctrine that any provision of an act of Congress ostensibly enacted under power granted by the Constitution, not naturally and reasonably adapted to the effective exercise of such power, but solely to the achievement of something plainly within power reserved to the states, is invalid and cannot be enforced."
98. *Nigro,* 276 U.S. at 353. *See also* Alston v. United States, 274 U.S. 289, 294 (1927) (holding that the first section of the Harrison Act was a valid exercise of the taxation power). When Federal District Judge George M. Bourquin accused "a couple of Supreme Court judges" of getting "cold feet" when the Court declined to declare the Harrison Act unconstitutional, *Federal Judge Again Scores Narcotic Law,* SAN FRANCISCO CHRONICLE (October 6, 1928), at 3, Taft dashed off a note to Van

The Taft Court

Devanter: "Bourquin seems to be something of an ass." WHT to WVD (October 22, 1928) (Taft papers). Van Devanter responded, "I concur." *Id.*

99. *Nigro*, 276 U.S. at 354. It is probable that although Brandeis joined the Court's decision in *Nigro*, he disapproved of the policy of the Harrison Act. He had earlier remarked to Frankfurter:

> Charles Warren, who is much concerned by drugs (He had the narcotic cases under him while in the Dept.), thinks the Act has been practically futile; and that conditions have grown infinitely worse since. Cannot someone be found who will really enquire into the results of the Federal police legislation (other than liquor) & exhibit the balance sheet? I am disposed to think that it does grave harm to a great degree otherwise than in centralization. i.e. in misleading the community into the belief that the fed. Govt (or any government) can help, instead of turning folk back to themselves for the remedy in self-mastery.

LDB to Felix Frankfurter (March 12, 1925), in BRANDEIS-FRANKFURTER CORRESPONDENCE, at 198–99.

100. *Nigro*, 276 U.S. at 356–57 (McReynolds, J., dissenting). McReynolds continued:

> The habit of smoking tobacco is often deleterious. Many think it ought to be suppressed. The craving for diamonds leads to extravagance, and frequently to crime. Silks are luxuries, and their use abridges the demand for cotton and wool. Those who sell tobacco, or diamonds, or silks may be taxed by the United States. But, surely, a provision in an act laying such a tax which limited sales of cigars, cigarettes, jewels, or silks to some small class alone authorized to secure official blanks would not be proper or necessary in order to enforce collection. The acceptance of such a doctrine would bring many purely local matters within the potential control of the federal government. The admitted evils incident to the use of opium cannot justify disregard of the powers "reserved to the States respectively, or to the people."

Id.

101. *Dagenhart*, 247 U.S. 251, 273 (1918). "So long as there is a single State which for selfish or other reasons fails to enact effective child-labor legislation, it is beyond the power of every other State to protect effectively its own producers and manufacturers against what may be considered unfair competition of the producers and manufacturers of that State." *To Prevent Interstate Commerce in the Products of Child Labor*, Sen. Rep. No. 358, 64th CONG. 1st SESS. (April 19, 1916), at 21.

102. Virtually the same argument would be made at the time of *Bailey. See, e.g.*, Medill McCormick, *Child Labor Must Go*, 29 AMERICAN FEDERATIONIST 644 (1922): "The country has become an economic unit; production in one state is intimately affected by costs and conditions of production in another state. The country is becoming increasingly a social and political unit. Its citizens everywhere in the union must suffer from a continuing injury to its citizens in any part of the union."

103. *Dagenhart*, 247 U.S. at 273–74.

104. Thus, writing fourteen years later in Carter v. Carter Coal Co., 298 U.S. 238 (1936), which threw down the gauntlet to the New Deal, Sutherland was explicit that "The relation of employer and employee is a local relation. At common law, it is one of the domestic relations. The wages are paid for the doing of local work. Working conditions are obviously local conditions. The

employees are not engaged in or about commerce, but exclusively in producing a commodity. And the controversies and evils, which it is the object of the act to regulate and minimize, are local controversies and evils affecting local work undertaken to accomplish that local result." *Id.* at 308–9. Sutherland's peroration moved Edward Corwin to comment: "Just as the primary purpose before the Civil War of the doctrine of powers exclusively reserved to the States was the protection of the relationship between master and slave from interference by the National Government, so its primary purpose nowadays is to protect similarly the relationship of employer and employee, except in the case of interstate carriers." EDWARD CORWIN, THE COMMERCE POWER VERSUS STATES RIGHTS 208–9 (Princeton University Press 1936).

105. *See* BARRY CUSHMAN, RETHINKING THE NEW DEAL COURT: THE STRUCTURE OF A CONSTITUTIONAL REVOLUTION 141–53 (Oxford University Press 1998); Barry Cushman, *Formalism and Realism in Commerce Clause Jurisprudence*, 67 UNIVERSITY OF CHICAGO LAW REVIEW 1089, 1128–29 (2000).
106. Charles Wolff Packing Co. v. Kansas Court of Industrial Relations, 262 U.S. 522, 538–39 (1923).
107. Prudential Ins. Co. v. Cheek, 259 U.S. 530, 536 (1922).
108. Sturges & Burn Mfg. Co. v. Beauchamp, 231 U.S. 320, 325–26 (1913).
109. Briggs, *supra* note 11, at 311.
110. Bruce, *supra* note 15, at 644.
111. Warren, *supra* note 15, at 377.
112. Albert C. Ritchie, *Give Us Democracy: A Plea for Freedom from Federal Transgression in the Domain of the State*, 230 NORTH AMERICAN REVIEW 400, 400, 402 (1930). Even so shrewd an observer as Woodrow Wilson could advance this line of analysis, as when he argued "that centralization is not vitalization. Moralization is by life, not by statute; by the interior impulse and experience of communities, not by fostering legislation which is merely the abstraction of an experience which may belong to a nation as a whole or to many parts of it without having yet touched the thought of the rest anywhere to the quick." WOODROW WILSON, CONSTITUTIONAL GOVERNMENT IN THE UNITED STATES 197 (New York: Columbia University Press 1921) (originally published in 1908). "Deliberate adding to the powers of the federal government by sheer judicial authority," Wilson concluded, would "certainly mean ... by degrees to do away with our boasted system of self-government." *Id.* at 195–96.
113. Available at www.presidency.ucsb.edu/documents/1924-democratic-party-platform#:~:text=.
114. PIERSON, *supra* note 11, at 144. *See also The Revival of Anti-Federalism*, 41 NEW REPUBLIC 211, 212 (1925).
115. Franklin, *supra* note 74, at 508.
116. Henry Wade Rogers, *The Constitution and the New Federalism*, 188 NORTH AMERICAN REVIEW 321, 334–35 (1908). Progressives who viewed as "absurd" those who professed "to see the approaching extinction of the American democracy in what they call the drift toward centralization," argued that "a measure of Federal centralization" merely bestowed "on the Federal government powers necessary to the fulfillment of its legitimate responsibilities," in the exercise of which the national government served as an authentic instrument of popular will.

HERBERT CROLY, THE PROMISE OF AMERICAN LIFE 277–79 (Cambridge: Harvard University Press 1965) (1909). Taking aim at "[t]he majority of Americans" who "still shrink from removing the legal obstacles to the organization of an all-powerful national government, because they have no confidence in the ability of popular opinion to employ discreetly or to control sufficiently such a formidable engine of political authority," progressives issued a powerful challenge: "A nation without sufficient self-confidence to organize and operate a government capable of being flexibly adapted to the serious practical emergencies of its own career, is trying to dispense with the spiritual foundation of all thoroughgoing democracy.... And as a consequence of proving false to the spirit of democracy ... its legal machinery will break down unless it is moulded and informed by the democratic principle of ultimate popular control of all the machinery and instruments of government." *Government According to Law*, 5 NEW REPUBLIC 4, 4–5 (1915).

117. *Bailey*, 259 U.S. at 37.
118. It is noteworthy that Taft's opinion in *Bailey* describes the child-labor tax law as "a penalty to *coerce* people of a State to act as Congress wishes them to act in respect of a matter completely the business of the state government under the Federal Constitution." *Id.* at 39 (emphasis added). For another example of Taft explicitly appealing to the potentially oppressive and managerial nature of federal power, see Taft, *Federal Power*, *supra* note 29, at 78 ("No one who has been familiar with the working of the conservation system in the West can be unacquainted with the difficulty that has arisen from Washington management of matters that are really of a local nature."). For a discussion of Taft's various views on federalism, see Post, *supra* note 57.
119. *See, e.g.*, Ramsay Co. v. Associated Billposters, 260 U.S. 501, 511 (1923) (distinguishing between business practices that "directly affect[] local business only" and "those designed and probably adequate materially to interfere with the free flow of commerce among the States and with Canada"); Fed. Baseball Club v. Nat'l League of Prof'l Baseball Clubs, 259 U.S. 200, 208 (1922) (holding that, although players travel to different states for games, professional baseball is not interstate commerce because exhibitions of baseball are "purely state affairs"). In Moore v. New York Cotton Exchange, 270 U.S. 593 (1926), the Court refused to apply federal anti-trust laws to a commodities exchange, declaring that "The New York exchange is engaged in a local business. Transactions between its members are purely local in their inception and in their execution.... If interstate shipments are actually made, it is not because of any contractual obligation to that effect.... The most that can be said is that the agreements are likely to give rise to interstate shipments. This is not enough." *Id.* at 604. *See* United States v. N.Y. Coffee & Sugar Exch., 263 U.S. 611, 621 (1924) (holding that the Court, unlike Congress, cannot legislatively determine that intrastate transactions systematically burden interstate commerce and hence become properly subject to federal jurisdiction).
120. Pub. L. 60-100, 35 Stat. 65 (April 22, 1908). *See, e.g.*, Balt. & Ohio Southwestern R.R. Co. v. Burtch, 263 U.S. 540, 543 (1924) (holding that there must be incontrovertible evidence of interstate shipment before the Federal Employers' Liability Act ("FELA") would apply); Indus. Accident Comm'n v. Davis, 259 U.S. 182, 187–88 (1922) (holding that an employee who was injured while making a repair

Normative Dualism & Congressional Power

on an interstate train was not covered by FELA because the train was stationary at the time of the accident); Shanks v. Del., Lackawanna & W. R.R. Co., 239 U.S. 556, 557 (1916) (same); The Second Employers' Liability Cases, 223 U.S. 1, 48–49 (1912) ("Congress, in the exertion of its power over interstate commerce, may regulate the relations of common carriers by railroad and their employés, while both are engaged in such commerce, subject always to the limitations prescribed in the Constitution, and to the qualification that the particulars in which those relations are regulated must have a real or substantial connection with the interstate commerce in which the carriers and their employés are engaged."); *cf.* The Employers' Liability Cases, 207 U.S. 463, 504 (1908) (holding the original Employers' Liability Act unconstitutional as beyond federal power). Although FELA sought to regulate railways, it regulated an aspect of the railroad business that was not ordinarily considered property affected with a public interest – namely, the employment relationship.

121. Pub. L. 63-203, 38 Stat. 717 (September 26, 1914). *See, e.g.*, FTC v. Pac. States Paper Trade Ass'n, 273 U.S. 52, 66 (1927) ("[A]s the contracts between the wholesaler and the retailer constitute a part of commerce among the States, the elimination of competition as to price by the application of the uniform prices fixed by the local association was properly forbidden by the order of the commission.").

122. 267 U.S. 432 (1925).

123. Pub. L. 66-70, 41 Stat. 324 (October 29, 1919).

124. *See supra* note 57.

125. *Brooks*, 267 U.S. at 438. In Taft's papers is a long, undated memorandum entitled BROOKS v. UNITED STATES, which is presently to be found in Reel 614 of the Taft papers. In the memorandum Taft struggles to reconcile the NMTVA with *Dagenhart*:

> If the result of interstate transportation will be to spread some harmful matter or product Congress may interfere without violating the Tenth Amendment. The facilities of interstate commerce may be withdrawn from those who are using it to corrupt others physically or morally. But if the transportation is being used to transport something harmless in itself and not calculated to spread evil, like cotton cloth, Congress may not prohibit its interstate transportation, although its inception may have been in some evil which is the legitimate object of the police power, such as child labor. But the interstate carriage of lottery tickets will communicate the gambling fever, of obscene literature will communicate moral degeneracy, of impure food will endanger health, of diseased will infect local cattle, of prostitutes will demoralize and tempt to immorality the conscience of the community. Transporting women merely for the purpose of private enjoyment is harder to justify, and might have been decided differently later, but the law may be said to save states from having persons without morals coming to their localities and carrying on their immorality.
>
> At first I had a little difficulty with stolen automobiles as the chief evil in connection therewith is the stealing and that of course is over before the machine takes on its character as a stolen automobile. This makes it look something like Hammer v. Dagenhart. But a stolen automobile is a canker. It attracts shady and disreputable individuals and leads to secret and underhanded dealings. Certainly it is not ultra vires for Congress to prohibit the interstate communication of this canker.
>
> Of course there is the argument that it is the facilities of interstate transportation that make the suppression of automobile thefts so difficult. If each state were an island detection would be much simpler. But for that

matter it is the facilities of interstate transportation that makes the suppression of child labor so difficult. If child labor made goods were confined to the domestic state market, child labor manufacturing would soon be abandoned.

I think the justification must be that Congress can prohibit the interstate spread of an evil thing, although it cannot prohibit the spread of something harmless in itself in order to suppress an evil which is properly the object of state police regulation.

Taft's conclusion that stolen cars were a "canker," but that the products of child labor were mere cotton cloth, seems to modern eyes largely an unconvincing *post hoc* rationalization. As had been vigorously pointed out at the time of *Dagenhart*:

> In point of fact the products of child labor are not harmless, and there is a definite evil in their transportation across state lines. The evil is involved in the movement itself, and its effects are felt both in the state of production and in the state of destination. Transportation of child-made goods encourages the ruin of the lives of future citizens in the state of production. It directly aids this immorality quite as much as the transportation across state lines of girls for the purpose of prostitution. ... Moreover, the interstate transportation of child-made goods unfairly discriminates against citizens of the state of destination. It tends to lower their standards of child-labor protection. It is the same effect sought to be avoided by the prohibition of importation of convict-made goods from foreign countries.

Thurlow M. Gordon, *Child Labor Law Case*, 32 HARVARD LAW REVIEW 45, 55 (1918).

126. *Brooks*, 267 U.S. at 439. *See* Post, *supra* note 57, at 220. Barry Cushman has hypothesized that the best interpretation of *Brooks* turns "on issues of vested rights and substantive due process." Barry Cushman, *Carolene Products and Constitutional Structure*, 2012 SUPREME COURT REVIEW 321, 323. Cushman contends that the Court's decisions concerning congressional power to prohibit the interstate transportation of items are most convincingly understood as turning on whether persons have a legitimate vested interest in the items. If there were no such interest, as in *Brooks*, congressional prohibitions would be permitted. But if there were legitimate vested interests, as in the case of the products of child labor, congressional prohibitions are proscribed by "a principle of substantive due process." *Id.* at 334. This principle, Cushman contends, quoting William Sutherland, prohibits "arbitrarily" depriving a person "of liberty and property" "in violation of the fifth amendment." *Id.* at 340. *See* William A Sutherland, *The Child Labor Cases and the Constitution*, 8 CORNELL LAW QUARTERLY 338, 343 (1923). The difficulty with this interpretation is that states could and did prohibit child labor. *See supra* text at note 108 and note 68; Chesapeake & O. Ry. Co. v. Stapleton, 279 U.S. 587, 593 (1929). If such items could be banned consistent with the Due Process Clause of the Fourteenth Amendment, why could they not also be banned consistent with the Due Process Clause of the Fifth Amendment? Sutherland's argument proves too much. Not surprisingly, understanding the pattern of Taft Court federalism decisions requires theorizing the constitutional difference between federal and state regulations.

127. *Brooks*, 267 U.S. at 436–37.

128. United States v. Lopez, 514 U.S. 549 (1995).

Normative Dualism & Congressional Power

129. Indeed, the Court announced: "Congress can certainly regulate interstate commerce to the extent of forbidding and punishing the use of such commerce as an agency to promote immorality, dishonesty or the spread of any evil or harm to the people of other States from the State of origin. In doing this it is merely exercising the police power, for the benefit of the public, within the field of interstate commerce." *Brooks*, 267 U.S. at 436–37. NMVTA, however, was not meant to prevent "the spread of any evil or harm to the people of other States from the State of origin," but instead, like *Dagenhart*, to prevent harms within the state of origin. *Id.* at 436. And, of course, the child-labor regulations at issue in *Dagenhart* were certainly an exercise of "the police power, for the benefit of the public, within the field of interstate commerce." *Id.* at 436–37. The gross inaccuracy of Taft's characterizations is telling, because they graphically illustrate the Court's difficulty in distinguishing *Dagenhart* in a manner that does not turn on the substantive rights affected by the regulations at issue.
130. Caminetti v. United States, 242 U.S. 470, 491 (1917). *See Brooks*, 267 U.S. at 437 (listing cases in which the Court upheld interstate regulations that prohibited various types of immorality).
131. Hipolite Egg Co. v. United States, 220 U.S. 45, 57 (1911).
132. The Lottery Case, 188 U.S. 321, 356 (1903).
133. *Id.* at 357.
134. 227 U.S. 308 (1913).
135. Pub. L. 61-277, 36 Stat. 825 (June 25, 1910). The title of the legislation was "An Act to further regulate interstate and foreign commerce by prohibiting the transportation therein for immoral purposes of women and girls, and for other purposes." *Id.*
136. *Hoke & Economides*, 227 U.S. at 322.
137. By contrast, the Senate Committee Report that recommended the Keating-Owen Child Labor Law specifically invoked *Hoke*. *To Prevent Interstate Commerce in the Products of Child Labor*, *supra* note 101, at 21.
138. *See, e.g.*, CROLY, *supra* note 116.
139. *See supra* Chapter 11, at 417.
140. *To Prevent Interstate Commerce in the Products of Child Labor*, H.R. Rep. No. 46, 64th CONG. 1st SESS. (January 17, 1916), at 6.
141. William Howard Taft, *Is Prohibition a Blow at Personal Liberty?*, LADIES HOME JOURNAL (May 1919), at 78.

CHAPTER 37

The Dormant Commerce Clause and the National Market

"**D**ORMANT COMMERCE CLAUSE" doctrine authorizes courts constitutionally to invalidate state regulations that impede the free operation of interstate commerce. Dormant Commerce Clause doctrine is a supple and flexible instrument for protecting the integrity of the national market, and the Taft Court found it irresistibly attractive.

The Taft Court staked out its position in the early and dramatic case of *Pennsylvania v. West Virginia*,[1] which concerned a West Virginia statute prohibiting the interstate transportation of locally produced natural gas until the reasonable requirements of West Virginia residents had first been satisfied.[2] Most unusually, the case was brought in the Court's original jurisdiction. The states of Ohio and Pennsylvania sued West Virginia directly in the Supreme Court to enjoin enforcement of the statute. Existing precedents held that states were constitutionally authorized to prevent natural resources like wild game[3] or fresh running water[4] from entering interstate commerce.

Over the objection of Holmes that "nothing in the commerce clause" prevented a state "from giving a preference to its inhabitants in the enjoyment of its natural advantages,"[5] and over vehement dissents by McReynolds and Brandeis that the case did not present a "justiciable controversy,"[6] Van Devanter, whose nationalism found dormant Commerce Clause doctrine extremely congenial, authored an opinion for six justices declaring: "By the Constitution the power to regulate interstate commerce is expressly committed to Congress and therefore impliedly forbidden to the States. The purpose in this is to protect commercial intercourse from invidious restraints, to prevent interference through conflicting or hostile state laws and to insure uniformity in regulation."[7]

Van Devanter's stress on the need for "uniformity in regulation" in the governance of interstate commerce expressed an important post-Reconstruction theme in the Court's constitutional jurisprudence.[8] The ideal of uniformity was integral to Republican efforts to protect the national market from what they

The Dormant Commerce Clause & the National Market

perceived to be the depredations of irresponsible states, mostly in the South and West. The Taft Court repeatedly emphasized that ideal.[9] Taft himself had explicitly invoked the theme of uniformity when as president he vetoed the Webb-Kenyon Act,[10] which prohibited the shipment of liquor into any state where it was intended to be used in a manner illegal under state law.

"One of the main purposes of the union of the States under the Constitution was to relieve the commerce between the States of the burdens which local State jealousies had in the past imposed upon it," President Taft had explained. The intention of the Commerce Clause was "to secure uniformity in the regulation of commerce between the States. To suspend that purpose and to permit the States to exercise their old authority before they became States, to interfere with commerce between them and their neighbors, is to defeat the constitutional purpose."[11] Taft forcefully construed the Commerce Clause as designed to protect the free flow of interstate goods.[12]

In *Pennsylvania v. West Virginia*, Van Devanter was similarly purposive in his explication of dormant Commerce Clause doctrine. He emphasized the need for a single integrated national market. In matters of interstate commerce, Van Devanter stressed, "we are a single nation – one and the same people."[13] Van Devanter quoted extensively from McKenna's eloquent 1911 opinion in *West v. Kansas Natural Gas*. If states were authorized to restrict the export of natural goods, McKenna had written, "a singular situation might result."

> Pennsylvania might keep its coal, the Northwest its timber, the mining states their minerals. And why may not the products of the field be brought within the principle? Thus enlarged, or without that enlargement, its influence on interstate commerce need not be pointed out. To what consequences does such power tend? If one state has it, all states have it; embargo may be retaliated by embargo, and commerce will be halted at state lines. And yet we have said that "in matters of foreign and interstate commerce there are no state lines." In such commerce, instead of the states, a new power appears and a new welfare, a welfare which transcends that of any state. But rather let us say it is constituted of the welfare of all of the states, and that of each state is made the greater by a division of its resources, natural and created, with every other state, and those of every other state with it. This was the purpose, as it is the result, of the interstate commerce clause of the Constitution of the United States.[14]

The purpose of dormant Commerce Clause doctrine was to create an uninhibited common market among the states.

Pennsylvania v. West Virginia was first argued on December 8–9, 1921. It was reargued on February 28–March 1, 1922, and then argued for a third time on April 20, 1923. The case stood at 5–4 after its second reargument, with Holmes, Pitney, McReynolds, and Brandeis dissenting. Worried about the impending retirement of Day, Taft wrote Van Devanter in August to urge him to complete his draft opinion by the beginning of the 1922 term. "We ought to decide the West Virginia gas case before [Day] goes off," Taft said, "because we need his vote and we ought not to have the case reargued a second [sic] time. You said that you expected to stay in Washington a few weeks and work on that case, but I know how easy it is in vacation to ignore resolutions made before. I write now to ask whether you think you could have the opinion for circulation when we meet."[15]

Van Devanter replied that "I shall have the opinion in the interstate gas case ready, but we must remember that there probably will be two dissents – one by Holmes or Brandeis, for the two and one by Pitney for himself. I therefore sincerely wish Day will not leave so soon but will remain two to three weeks after the Term begins. I shall so write to him." But there was also a second and more ominous difficulty. Van Devanter informed Taft that Clarke "expects to resign on Sept 18, his 65th birthday." Van Devanter explained that Clarke "is one of the five in the interstate gas case. I am taking out a telegram asking him to await a letter from me and a letter asking him to make his resignation effective two weeks or so after the Term begins or to withhold it until then, because of that and other cases, petitions for rehearing etc."[16]

Two weeks later, Van Devanter reported to Taft that Day "approves and assents to my suggestion about the time of his going," but that "Clarke's leaving before the court convenes will leave us evenly divided in the gas cases unless we can gain a vote or the others lose one. ... Possibly there will have to be another reargument, but that ought not to be."[17] *Pennsylvania v. West Virginia* was restored to the docket for reargument on November 13, 1922, Day's last day on the Court. Ultimately, Van Devanter's opinion for the Court was announced on June 11, 1923. The next day Brandeis commented to Frankfurter that "The most terrible thing the Ct did was assumption of jurisdiction in West Virginia Natural Gas case. Van D. by general phrases glides over total absence of jurisdictional bases in Record. I don't care much about natural gas – it will soon all be gone – but the decision is very important to hydroelectric. It means rich states can withdraw power from poor states – N[ew]. H[ampshire]. and N[orth]. C[arolina]. Water power can be demanded by surrounding states through high power transmission lines."[18]

After the announcement of Van Devanter's decision, Clarke penned a personal note of congratulations. "It's one of the great cases and your handling of it all that can be desired. ... I was anxious about the case from fear that the changes in the court might change the result as we arrived at it."[19] The Court subsequently granted West Virginia's petition for reargument, which was held on November 20, 1923. Brandeis reported the scene at the fourth argument of the case:

> The W.Va. natural gas cases were argued, if possible, more badly than ever before. The questions of substantive constitutional law and of procedural constitutional law involved are as important as any now conceivable. Neither the bar, the public or the interests great or small indicated in any way that they cared in the least. Charles Warren, who was present, could tell a strange tale of the lack of interest as compared with that which he described as having been taken on similar occasions a century & less ago. The court room was empty, even the lawyers awaiting later assigned cases not being in attendance. One might have supposed that a default judgment was being entered in a police court on the promissory note of an insolvent.[20]

The Dormant Commerce Clause & the National Market

Almost immediately after the fourth argument, the Court released a short opinion reaffirming its initial decision.[21] Taft recused himself from the rehearing.[22] There is an undated, unattributed press clipping in the Taft papers entitled *The Gas Case Reopened*, which observes: "It has been suggested that, since Hon. Charles P. Taft, a brother of the Chief Justice, is a director in the Columbia Gas & Electric Company, one of the corporations affected by the West Virginia law, the Chief Justice, with this fact brought to his attention, might hesitate to participate in the further hearing of the case."[23] With Taft recused, the vote at the final rehearing was 5–3. Brandeis noted sardonically to Frankfurter: "The W.Va. gas case are [sic] decided by vote of McKenna J."[24] It is notable that Taft had not recused himself in earlier iterations of the case, when the vote stood at 5–4. His recusal at that time would have been decisive for the outcome of the decision.

The drama of *Pennsylvania v. West Virginia* underscores the importance of dormant Commerce Clause doctrine, which establishes the ground rules for the national market in America. At the heart of this doctrine lies a deep and complex conundrum: How can the Court distinguish constitutional exercises of state police power from impermissible restraints on interstate commerce? To solve this puzzle, the Taft Court turned to the conceptual schema of dual sovereignty, with its sharp division between separate spheres of federal and state authority. The Court distinguished a domain of *interstate* commerce, which required national uniformity, from a domain of *intrastate* commerce, which could be subject to diverse local regulations.

Sometimes the Taft Court conceptualized these two domains as factually distinct, as though one could simply point to an economic transaction and know from the state of the world whether it lay in interstate or in intrastate commerce. States could regulate the latter but not the former. In *Heisler v. Thomas Collier Co.*, for example, the Court was faced with a dormant Commerce Clause challenge to a Pennsylvania tax on anthracite coal.[25] Because Pennsylvania had a virtual monopoly on anthracite, and because Pennsylvania shipped 80 percent of its production out of state,[26] the tax would almost certainly be paid by out-of-state consumers. But the Court was moved neither by these facts, nor by the circumstance that the tax was imposed upon anthracite that was intended for interstate shipment. It did not even matter that the specific coal that was taxed may already have been purchased by out-of-state customers.[27]

Speaking unanimously through McKenna, the Court held that the Pennsylvania tax was constitutionally legitimate because it was assessed before the coal had actually entered interstate commerce. Although the coal was taxed after it had been "washed, screened, or otherwise prepared for market," the tax applied while the coal was still "part of the general mass of property of the State, and subject to its jurisdiction."[28] The tax was therefore within the scope of the state's police power. Any other rule, the McKenna said, would have unacceptable consequences:

> If the possibility, or, indeed, certainty of exportation of a product or article from a State determines it to be in interstate commerce before the commencement of its movement from the State, it would seem to follow that it is in such commerce from the instant of its growth or production, and in the case of coals,

as they lie in the ground. The result would be curious. It would nationalize all industries, it would nationalize and withdraw from state jurisdiction and deliver to federal commercial control the fruits of California and the South, the wheat of the West and its meats, the cotton of the South, the shoes of Massachusetts and the woolen industries of other States, at the very inception of their production or growth, that is, the fruits unpicked, the cotton and wheat ungathered, hides and flesh of cattle yet "on the hoof," wool yet unshorn, and coal yet unmined, because they are in varying percentages destined for and surely to be exported to States other than those of their production.[29]

Heisler imagined the boundary between intrastate and interstate commerce as a precise frontier that was crossed when goods began their interstate journey.[30] "[T]here must be a point of time," the Court noted, when goods "cease to be governed exclusively by the domestic law and begin to be governed and protected by the national law of commercial regulation, and that moment seems to us to be a legitimate one for this purpose, in which they commence their final movement for transportation from the State of their origin to that of their destination."[31]

Heisler held that the distinct spheres of federal and state jurisdiction were to be kept as constitutionally separate as possible. So long as state regulations were applied to intrastate commerce, their effects on interstate commerce were constitutionally irrelevant. The constitutionality of state laws under the dormant Commerce Clause depended only on whether they were applied in their proper sphere. A contrary conclusion, the Court reasoned, would "nationalize all industries" and deprive states of the capacity for local self-government.[32]

On this account, the function of dormant Commerce Clause jurisprudence was to chart the location of the physical boundary separating intrastate from interstate commerce.[33] State regulations that breached this boundary and touched transactions in interstate commerce were categorically unconstitutional. "The action of the State as a regulation of interstate commerce does not depend upon the degree of interference; it is illegal in any degree."[34]

Heisler offers a relatively simple framework for dormant Commerce Clause doctrine. The problem is that the framework, like the schema of dual sovereignty used by the Taft Court in the context of intergovernmental tax immunities,[35] was incompatible with the complex economy of the 1920s. In cases like *Stafford* and *Olsen*, the Taft Court recognized that interstate commerce was an ongoing stream that swept within its current many transactions that were otherwise entirely intrastate. In such circumstances, how was interstate commerce to be distinguished from intrastate commerce? Consider, for example, *Missouri* ex rel. *Barrett v. Kansas Natural Gas*,[36] which involved the efforts of state public utility commissions to regulate prices charged by an interstate supplier of natural gas to local distributors. The gas flowed in a continuous stream from the site of its production to its ultimate consumers, traversing pipelines owned by various intermediary companies.

As in *Heisler*, the Court assumed that the constitutionality of the state regulation turned on whether it was applied to interstate or to intrastate commerce. But in *Kansas Natural Gas*, the Court puzzled about exactly how to make this distinction. "The line of division between cases where, in the absence of

The Dormant Commerce Clause & the National Market

congressional action, the state is authorized to act, and those where state action is precluded by mere force of the commerce clause of the Constitution," the Court mused, "is not always clearly marked." The Court solved the problem by concluding that the boundary between interstate and intrastate commerce ought to be placed at the point at which title to the gas passed from an interstate supplier to a local distributor:

> With the delivery of the gas to the distributing companies ... the interstate movement ends. Its subsequent sale and delivery by these companies to their customers at retail is intrastate business and subject to state regulation. In such case the effect on interstate commerce, if there be any, is indirect and incidental. But the sale and delivery here is an inseparable part of a transaction in interstate commerce – not local but essentially national in character, – and enforcement of a selling price in such a transaction places a direct burden upon such commerce inconsistent with that freedom of interstate trade which it was the purpose of the commerce clause to secure and preserve. It is as though the Commission stood at the state line and imposed its regulation upon the final step in the process at the moment the interstate commodity entered the State and before it had become part of the general mass of property therein.[37]

Speaking unanimously through an opinion by Sutherland,[38] the Court held that the transfer of title in the gas to local distributors was the frontier that fundamentally altered the constitutional character of the gas. State regulation was permitted on one side of the frontier but not on the other. This was true even if Congress had not in fact "seen fit to regulate" the interstate flow of the gas. In such circumstances, Congress's

> silence, where it has the sole power to speak, is equivalent to a declaration that that particular commerce shall be free from regulation.... [H]ere the sale of gas is in wholesale quantities, not to consumers, but to distributing companies for resale to consumers in numerous cities and communities in different States. The transportation, sale and delivery constitute an unbroken chain, fundamentally interstate from beginning to end, and of such continuity as to amount to an established course of business. The paramount interest is not local but national, admitting of and requiring uniformity of regulation. Such uniformity, even though it be the uniformity of governmental nonaction, may be highly necessary to preserve equality of opportunity and treatment among the various communities and States concerned.[39]

As in *Heisler*, the Court in *Kansas Natural Gas* postulated a sharp boundary that partitioned state from federal power. In *Heisler*, this border was marked by the physical movement of goods. In *Kansas Natural Gas*, by contrast, the border was set at the line where the gas was transferred to local distributors. At this boundary the "paramount interest" shifted from the "national" to the "local."[40] *Heisler* was content to demarcate intrastate from interstate commerce based upon facts in the physical world, and it accordingly did not employ the language of "interests."

Kansas Natural Gas was by contrast prompted to use the language of "interests" because gas in interstate commerce was not separated from gas in intrastate commerce by any feature of the physical world.

The language of "interests," however, does not easily mesh with the sharp boundaries required by the analytic framework of dual sovereignty. Federal and state "interests" do not simply disappear at some precisely marked frontier. Governments have reasons for regulating goods that do not suddenly vanish merely because goods pass from one pipeline into another, or because they begin, or cease, what is characterized as an interstate journey. Government interests are persistent and continuous, with extension and weight, and they therefore do not fit well within a paradigm of separate and exclusive spheres of state and federal sovereignty that require abrupt and discontinuous transitions of jurisdiction.

This mismatch explains why the Court in *Kansas Natural Gas* made no effort to explain why the "paramount" interests of federal and state governments switched at precisely the moment when gas was transferred to local distributors. Sutherland's conclusion is especially puzzling because the federal government had not actually attempted to regulate the interstate transportation of gas. In *Kansas Natural Gas*, therefore, the Court was proposing a national interest in a "uniformity of governmental nonaction"[41] that was purely hypothetical. It was an interest postulated and enforced by courts, not by Congress. But exactly how did the Court know that this hypothetical interest outweighed concrete and palpable state interests in the local price of natural gas when title to the gas had not yet been transferred to local distributors?

It is apparent that in *Kansas Natural Gas* the Court was not concerned carefully to examine this question. Sutherland was instead content to allow his evaluation of government interests to remain formal and abstract. We can infer that his use of the metaphor of "interests" was simply a conclusory label applied *post hoc* to justify the constitutional consequences of an essentially arbitrary line separating state from federal sovereignty. *Kansas Natural Gas* is, in this sense, a transitional decision. It uses the modern language of "interests" to rationalize what is in fact a traditional application of the schema of dual sovereignty.

This schema, however, was fast unraveling. *Stafford* and *Olsen* both stressed that the legal definition of interstate commerce must reflect "practical"[42] concerns. No practical account of commerce would break it into two separate spheres, with intrastate transactions in one category and interstate transactions in the other. The very image of a "stream" of commerce summoned a picture of economic life in which local and national economic transactions were so intermingled as to fuse into a single "unit." That is why *Olsen* could simultaneously hold that the grain traded at the Chicago Board could properly be subject to "local taxing ... while in Chicago," and yet also hold that this did "not take it out of interstate commerce in such a way as to deprive Congress of the power to regulate it."[43] The underlying thought was that transactions could be characterized as interstate for some purposes, but as intrastate for other purposes.

It is striking that in the context of congressional power the Taft Court could at times flatly deny the existence of distinct and exclusive spheres of interstate and

The Dormant Commerce Clause & the National Market

intrastate commerce, and yet in the context of dormant Commerce Clause doctrine the Court could earnestly seek to locate and enforce a metaphysical boundary separating these two incompatible spheres. *Heisler* stood for the stark proposition that a state was free to act as it wished so long as it regulated only intrastate commerce; conversely, *Pennsylvania v. West Virginia* held that state interference with the exclusively federal realm of interstate commerce was flatly impermissible. This simple logic expressed the schema of dual sovereignty, which governed the imagination of many Taft Court dormant Commerce Clause decisions.

Consider, for example, *Public Utilities Commission v. Attleboro Steam & Electric Co.* The case concerned a local Rhode Island power utility, the Narragansett Company, which was charging such low rates to a Massachusetts corporation, the Attleboro Company, that it was endangering its own financial health. The Rhode Island Public Utilities Commission sought to raise these rates, arguing that it could not

> effectively exercise its power to regulate the rates for electricity furnished by the Narragansett Company to local consumers, without also regulating the rates for the other service which it furnishes; that if the Narragansett Company continues to furnish electricity to Attleboro Company at a loss this will tend to increase the burden on the local consumers and impair the ability of the Narragansett Company to give them good service at reasonable prices; and that, therefore, the order of the Commission prescribing a reasonable rate for the interstate service to the Attleboro Company should be sustained as being essentially a local regulation, necessary to the protection of matters of local interest, and affecting interstate commerce only indirectly and incidentally.[44]

The argument of the Rhode Island Public Utilities Commission relies on the same logic that the Taft Court had itself adopted in the *Wisconsin Rate Case*, which authorized federal regulation of intrastate railroad rates on the theory that higher intrastate rates were necessary to maintain the health of the interstate rail system.[45] The Rhode Island Commission advanced the analogous contention that higher rates on interstate electricity were necessary to maintain the health of the intrastate electricity system.

Speaking through Sanford, the Taft Court refused to accept the analogy.[46] Sanford said:

> The test of the validity of a state regulation, is not the character of the general business of the company, but whether the particular business which is regulated is essentially local or national in character. Plainly, however, the paramount interest in the interstate business carried on between the two companies is not local to either State, but is essentially national in character. The rate is therefore not subject to regulation by either of the two States in the guise of protection to their respective local interests; but, if such regulation is required it can only be attained by the exercise of the power vested in Congress.[47]

Like *Kansas Natural Gas*, *Attleboro Steam & Electric* seeks to marry the language of "interests" to the dichotomous schema of dual sovereignty. Yet in both cases the language of "interests" is mere window dressing. *Attleboro Steam & Electric* turns on the premise that Rhode Island simply has no business regulating the interstate transmission of electricity. The Court invokes the language of "interests" only to rationalize this conclusion. The *Wisconsin Rate Case*, by contrast, stands for the proposition that the allocation of paramount government interests does not fall neatly along the boundary between interstate and intrastate commerce. If the logic of *Attleboro Steam & Electric* had been applied to the Interstate Commerce Commission ("ICC") in the *Wisconsin Rate Case*, the Court would have found that states possessed a "paramount interest" in intrastate rates and consequently that the ICC was forbidden from interfering with intrastate railroad fares.

The asymmetry between the *Wisconsin Rate Case* and *Attleboro Steam & Electric* reveals not only the conclusory use of the metaphor of "interests" in the Court's dormant Commerce Clause cases, but also the highly nationalist tilt of the Taft Court.[48] In the context of the dormant Commerce Clause, this tilt had profoundly deregulatory implications. The Court's solicitude for the national market created an ever-expanding "uniformity of governmental nonaction." No doubt that is one reason why the Taft Court found the requirement of uniformity so attractive. In *Attleboro Steam & Electric*, Rhode Island was constitutionally disabled from protecting the interests of Rhode Island residents in the name of entirely putative national interests in uniformity. These interests were not embodied in any actual regulatory scheme that might balance the competing needs of Rhode Island and Massachusetts residents.[49]

The lesson of *Attleboro Steam & Electric* is that states need to stay on their own side of the interstate/intrastate commerce divide. No matter what their actual interests in regulation, states cannot stray into the exclusively federal domain of interstate commerce. Many Taft Court decisions taught this same simple lesson. *Dahnke-Walker Milling Co. v. Bondurant*, for example, considered the application of a Kentucky statute "prescribing the conditions on which corporations of other States might do business" to purchase wheat in Kentucky that was to be shipped out of state. Speaking through Van Devanter, the Court ruled that the application of the statute was constitutionally invalid because a "corporation of one state may go into another, without obtaining the leave or license of the latter, for all the legitimate purposes of [interstate] commerce; and any statute of the latter state which obstructs or lays a burden on the exercise of this privilege is void under the commerce clause."[50]

Similarly, in *Real Silk Hosiery Mills v. Portland* the Court unanimously struck down as applied to a foreign corporation a nondiscriminatory ordinance requiring any salesman who takes "orders for goods for future delivery and receives payment . . . in advance" to "secure a license and file a bond." Speaking through McReynolds, the Court held "that the ordinance materially burdens interstate commerce and conflicts with the Commerce Clause. . . . Nor can we accept the theory that an expressed purpose to prevent possible frauds is enough to justify legislation which really interferes with the free flow of legitimate interstate commerce."[51]

In *Texas Transport & Terminal Co. v. New Orleans*, Sutherland spoke for seven justices in striking down the application of a nondiscriminatory license tax to a steamship agent who exclusively represented steamship companies engaged in interstate or foreign commerce. The Court relied upon "the general and well established rule, which is that a state or state municipality is powerless to impose a tax upon persons for selling or seeking to sell the goods of a nonresident within the state prior to their introduction therein ... or to impose a tax upon persons for securing or seeking to secure the transportation of freight or passengers in interstate or foreign commerce."[52]

In each of these cases the Court conceptualized interstate commerce as a forbidden zone for state regulation. The consequence of this approach was to shrink the permissible scope of state police regulation as local markets became increasingly saturated with national companies and products. Brandeis found this logic alarming. He repeatedly sought to protect local state police power from the encroaching imperialism of the national market.[53]

In *Texas Transport & Terminal*,[54] for example, Brandeis dissented on the ground that interstate and intrastate commerce were far too intermingled for any such simple and blunt rule as the Court proposed.[55] There were, for example, many precedents holding that states could tax the property of interstate railroads.[56] The question, therefore, was not whether a state trespassed into the federal sphere of interstate commerce, but rather the nature and consequences of that trespass. The issue, as Brandeis saw it, was whether state regulations *directly* burdened interstate commerce. "The validity of a state tax under the commerce clause," he wrote, "does not depend upon its character or classification. It is not void merely because it affects or burdens interstate commerce. The tax is void only if it directly burdens such commerce, or (where the burden is indirect) if the tax discriminates against or obstructs interstate commerce."[57]

Although the distinction between "direct" and "indirect" burdens sounds "strangely formal" coming from Brandeis,[58] it was in fact a common trope in the black-letter doctrine of the dormant Commerce Clause.[59] The Court appealed to the distinction whenever the necessity of allowing both local and national regulations was obvious and unavoidable.[60] The distinction derived from a venerable line of cases conventionally said to originate in 1851 in *Cooley v. Board of Wardens*.[61] *Cooley* and its sequelae held that certain aspects of interstate commerce were so intrinsically local that states could regulate them in the absence of preemptive congressional legislation.[62]

Cooley itself concerned a Pennsylvania statute, explicitly approved by federal law, that regulated pilots in local harbors. Although conceding that the statute reached interstate commerce, *Cooley* nevertheless squarely held that "the power to regulate commerce embraces a vast field, containing not only many, but exceedingly various subjects ... some imperatively demanding a single uniform rule ... and some, like the subject now in question, as imperatively demanding that diversity, which alone can meet the local necessities of navigation." In the absence of contrary federal legislation, state laws governing matters that were "local and not national," matters that did not "admit only of one uniform system," were constitutional, even though applied to interstate commerce.[63]

The Taft Court applied the *Cooley* doctrine in the context of the newly developing area of automobile regulation.[64] By the 1920s, everyone understood that highways and vehicles were arteries of interstate commerce. But everyone also understood that states were primarily responsible for the regulation of roads and vehicles, so that it would be disastrous if the Court were to attempt to impose the "uniformity of governmental nonaction" that it willingly embraced in other contexts. The Court concluded that "in the absence of federal legislation covering the subject, [a] State may impose, even upon vehicles using the highways exclusively in interstate commerce, non-discriminatory regulations for the purpose of insuring the public safety and convenience,"[65] and that "a state may impose, even on motor vehicles engaged exclusively in interstate commerce, a reasonable charge as their fair contribution to the cost of constructing and maintaining the public highways."[66]

During the 1920s, states could require motor vehicles "engaged exclusively in interstate commerce" to obtain liability insurance, so long as the required insurance was "limited to damages suffered within the State by persons other than the passenger."[67] They could impose maximum weight limits on trucks, even if these limits prevented interstate trucking firms from realizing a profit.[68] But states could not extend or withdraw permission to engage in interstate commerce based upon judgments about whether an interstate route "is already being adequately served" by other common carriers.[69] In the context of automobile cases, the Taft Court explicitly refused to apply the principle of *Heisler* that "[w]hether any statute or action of a State impinges upon interstate commerce depends upon the statute or action, not upon ... the motive which impelled it."[70] In determining the constitutionality of state regulations of interstate vehicular traffic, the Court evaluated many factors, including the purpose and effect of state regulations, the balance of national and state interests, and so forth.[71]

The doctrine of direct burdens applied in contexts other than automobiles. Its significance lay in its acknowledgment of situations where the complex interpenetration of local and national markets rendered inapplicable the simple schema of dual sovereignty. The doctrine offered shorthand labels to express a conclusion about the constitutionality of state regulations that unambiguously touched interstate commerce.[72] State actions constituting "a real and direct invasion" of interstate commerce were said to be unconstitutional, whereas state actions with effects on interstate commerce that were "something incidental or remote"[73] would withstand constitutional scrutiny.[74]

The Court was never clear, however, about how to distinguish direct from indirect burdens on interstate commerce. "The line of division between cases where, in the absence of congressional action, the State is authorized to act, and those where state action is precluded by mere force of the commerce clause of the Constitution," observed the Court in *Kansas Natural Gas*, "is not always clearly marked. In the absence of congressional legislation, a State may constitutionally impose taxes, enact inspection laws, quarantine laws and, generally, laws of internal police, although they may have an incidental effect upon interstate commerce.... But the commerce clause of the Constitution, of its own force, restrains the States from imposing direct burdens upon interstate commerce."[75]

The Dormant Commerce Clause & the National Market

"Considerations of policy" were plainly at issue in the decision to characterize some burdens on interstate commerce as direct and others as indirect.[76] Courts needed to assess both the weight of federal interests in uniformity and the significance of countervailing state interests in promoting local welfare.[77] To explicitly evaluate these competing considerations, however, meant abandoning the schema of dual sovereignty and frankly acknowledging that the Court was fashioning economic policy for the nation. This the Court was reluctant to do.[78]

Helson v. Kentucky is a revealing example. *Helson* concerned the application of Kentucky's general sales tax to gasoline used by a ferryboat engaged in "an exclusively interstate business."[79] Speaking through Sutherland, the Court in *Helson* reasoned in much the same way that the Court had reasoned the year before in *Panhandle*.[80] Just as Butler in *Panhandle* had concluded that as a practical matter Mississippi's gasoline tax was on the federal government itself, so Sutherland concluded in *Helson* that as a practical matter Kentucky's gasoline tax was on interstate commerce.[81] "Is not the fuel consumed in propelling the boat an instrumentality of commerce no less than the boat itself? A tax, which falls directly upon the use of one of the means by which commerce is carried on, directly burdens that commerce."[82] The Kentucky tax, Sutherland declared, was unconstitutional because it intruded upon a sphere "of interstate and foreign commerce" that was "committed exclusively to the control of Congress."[83]

Insofar as *Helson* holds that any state tax on the realm of interstate commerce is "direct" and therefore unconstitutional, it uses the distinction between direct and indirect burdens to advance the simple analytic structure of dual sovereignty. Stone, joined by Holmes and Brandeis, was prepared to "acquiesce in the result" of *Helson*, but he refused to "assent to the reasoning by which the present forbidden tax on the use of property in interstate commerce is distinguished from a permissible tax on property, measured by its use or use value in interstate commerce."[84] Stone could not discern "any practical justification" for "an interpretation of the commerce clause which would relieve those engaged in interstate commerce from their fair share of the expense of government of the states in which they operate by exempting them from the payment of a tax of general application, which is neither aimed at nor discriminates against interstate commerce. It 'affects commerce among the states and impedes the transit of persons and property from one state to another just in the same way, and in no other, that taxation of any kind necessarily increases the expenses attendant upon the use or possession of the thing taxed.'"[85]

Stone's critique was essentially identical to the one he had expounded in *Metcalf* in the context of intergovernmental tax immunities:[86] Just as states could not be hermetically insulated from the effects of general nondiscriminatory federal taxation, so interstate commerce could not be hermetically insulated from the effects of general nondiscriminatory state taxation. Interstate and intrastate commerce were intermingled and interdependent, as were national and state interests, and no doctrine could be adequate that failed to acknowledge this fact. The simple invocation of a dichotomous distinction, whether it was that between direct and indirect burdens, or that between interstate and intrastate commerce, was not remotely capable of unpacking the complex policy questions posed by dormant Commerce Clause doctrine.

Stone's most sustained critique of the Court's dormant Commerce Clause doctrine was contained in his justly famous dissent in *Di Santo v. Pennsylvania*.[87] In *Di Santo*, the Court struck down a law requiring nonsteamship companies selling steamship tickets for transportation to or from foreign countries to obtain a license. The object of the law was to prevent fraud. The Court's opinion by Butler was a blunt and unselfconscious iteration of the premises of dual sovereignty.[88] It held that the "soliciting of passengers and the sale of steamship tickets . . . constitute[s] a well-recognized part of foreign commerce," and that a "state statute which by its necessary operation directly interferes with or burdens foreign commerce is a prohibited regulation and invalid, regardless of the purpose with which it was passed."[89]

Stone's dissent is celebrated for its frontal attack on the categorical distinction between direct and indirect burdens on commerce. "In this case the traditional test of the limit of state action by inquiring whether the interference with commerce is direct or indirect seems to me too mechanical, too uncertain in its application, and too remote from actualities, to be of value. In thus making use of the expressions, 'direct' and 'indirect interference' with commerce, we are doing little more than using labels to describe a result rather than any trustworthy formula by which it is reached."[90] Stone's innovative and powerful analysis of the Court's failure of judicial craft was widely praised.[91]

Just as Stone had sought in *Metcalf* to orient intergovernmental tax immunity doctrine to the actual effects of taxation on government functioning, so in *Di Santo* he sought to orient dormant Commerce Clause doctrine to "a consideration of all the facts and circumstances, such as the nature of the regulation, its function, the character of the business involved and the actual effect on the flow of commerce." Stone's point was that only a comprehensive analysis of this kind could ascertain whether a "regulation concerns interests peculiarly local and does not infringe the national interest in maintaining the freedom of commerce across state lines."[92] In both *Metcalf* and *Di Santo*, Stone urged courts candidly to consider all relevant circumstances and government interests, trusting that a sufficiently shared sense of relevant purposes would somehow produce correct, or at least satisfactory, decisions. The assumption underlying Stone's approach was that courts should deploy constitutional law as an explicit and purposive instrument for the implementation of forward-looking policies.

Despite Stone's protestations, the Taft Court did not abandon the opaque distinction between direct and indirect burdens on commerce.[93] Stone was the only member of the Taft Court prepared frankly to repudiate the distinction. Perhaps this was because Stone wanted the Court candidly to acknowledge its own role as a policymaker,[94] a role that could be vindicated only by the authority of expertise. Stone alone seemed inclined explicitly to embrace that authority.[95] The appeal to this form of authority is the deep but implicit significance of the Court's later adoption of such modern judicial techniques as balancing. During the 1920s, however, Stone was quite isolated in his effort to repudiate the disintegrating fiction

The Dormant Commerce Clause & the National Market

of dual sovereignty and undertake a radical reworking of the Court's dormant Commerce Clause doctrine.

It also seems plausible to suppose that the Taft Court refused to abandon the categorical distinction between "direct" and "indirect" burdens on interstate commerce in part because the very opacity of the distinction allowed the Court covertly to impose substantive economic views that had little to do with the abstract architecture of dual sovereignty. It is easy to see why a court that believed that "[t]he world is not going to be saved by legislation"[96] would welcome a national "uniformity of governmental nonaction."[97] Dormant Commerce Clause doctrine offered a tactful vehicle for returning the country to normalcy without the political inconvenience of having to announce controversial justifications sounding explicitly in due process rights.

Consider, for example, a decision like *Michigan Public Utilities Commission v. Duke*, in which the Court struck down as applied to an interstate trucker a Michigan statute that in essence required that any person "transporting persons or property by motor vehicle for hire upon the public highways of the State" must become a common carrier.[98] It is worth quoting at length from the Court's unanimous opinion by Butler:

> This Court has held that, in the absence of national legislation covering the subject, a State may rightfully prescribe uniform regulations necessary for public safety and order in respect to the operation upon its highways of all motor vehicles – those moving in interstate commerce as well as others; that a reasonable, graduated license fee imposed by a State on motor vehicles used in interstate commerce does not constitute a direct burden on interstate commerce, and that a State, which, at its own expense, furnishes special facilities for the use of those engaged in intrastate and interstate commerce may exact compensation therefor, and if the charges are reasonable and uniform, they constitute no burden on interstate commerce. Such regulations are deemed to be reasonable and to affect interstate commerce only incidentally and indirectly. But it is well settled that a State has no power to fetter the right to carry on interstate commerce within its borders by the imposition of conditions or regulations which are unnecessary and pass beyond the bounds of what is reasonable and suitable for the proper exercise of its powers in the field that belongs to it. One bound to furnish transportation to the public as a common carrier must serve all, up to the capacity of his facilities, without discrimination and for reasonable pay. The act would put on plaintiff the duty to use his trucks and other equipment as a common carrier in Michigan, and would prevent him from using them exclusively to perform his contracts. This is to take from him use of instrumentalities by means of which he carries on the interstate commerce in which he is engaged as a private carrier and so directly to burden and interfere with it. And it is a burden upon interstate commerce to impose on plaintiff the onerous duties and strict liability of common carrier, and the obligation of furnishing such indemnity bond to cover the automobile bodies hauled under his contracts as conditions precedent to his right to continue to carry them in interstate commerce. Clearly, these requirements have no relation to public safety or order in the use of motor vehicles upon the highways, or to the collection of compensation for the use of the

highways. The police power does not extend so far. It must be held that, if applied to plaintiff and his business, the act would violate the commerce clause of the Constitution.[99]

Butler's argument is essentially that to convert an interstate trucker into a common carrier would be to transform the ordinary property of his business into a form of property affected by the public interest. Butler's concern to safeguard the trucker's liberty of contract manifestly propelled his conclusion that the Michigan statute constituted a direct burden on interstate commerce.[100] The Court's substantive views about proper economic regulation were inseparable from its structural judgment about the allocation of national and state power.

The same phenomenon is equally apparent in cases like *Lemke v. Farmers' Grain Co.*[101] and *Shafer v. Farmers' Grain Co.*,[102] in which the Court struck down North Dakota statutes imposing uniform grading standards for grain, on the ground that the grain was destined for shipment to other states and hence beyond the regulatory power of the state of origin.[103] The tension with decisions like *Heisler*[104] is obvious. Indeed, Alexander Bickel has charged that the Taft Court's hijacking of the federalism values of the Commerce Clause to express "the same social and economic theories as in its Due Process decisions" ultimately "brought into disrepute the fair and hopeful idea of federalism," which was the Court's "gravest transgression. ... By comparison the evil of the Court's due-process holdings may seem ephemeral."[105]

What Bickel perhaps did not sufficiently appreciate is that the Taft Court did not seek merely to protect the national market. It sought to protect a national market that was endowed with all the individual economic freedoms that the Court regarded as essential to the maintenance of American civilization. For the Taft Court, structure and individual rights were indissolubly fused.

The Dormant Commerce Clause & the National Market
Notes

1. 262 U.S. 553 (1923).
2. For a discussion of the case, see Thomas Reed Powell, *Current Conflicts between the Commerce Clause and State Police Power, 1922–1927*, 12 MINNESOTA LAW REVIEW 321, 331–33 (1928); Thomas Reed Powell, *Umpiring the Federal System, 1922–1924*, 40 POLITICAL SCIENCE QUARTERLY 101, 118–19 (1925); Note, 24 COLUMBIA LAW REVIEW 64 (1924); Note, 10 VIRGINIA LAW REVIEW 233 (1924); Note, 22 MICHIGAN LAW REVIEW 138 (1923); *cf.* Thomas Porter Hardman, *The Right of a State to Restrain the Exportation of Its Natural Resources*, 26 WEST VIRGINIA LAW QUARTERLY 1 (1919); William N. Eskridge Jr. & John Ferejohn, *The Elastic Commerce Clause: A Political Theory of Federalism*, 47 VANDERBILT LAW REVIEW 1355, 1384 (1994).
3. Greer v. Connecticut, 161 U.S. 519 (1896).
4. Hudson County Water Co. v. McCarter, 209 U.S. 349 (1908). *See* Trenton v. New Jersey, 262 U.S. 182 (1923).
5. *Pennsylvania*, 262 U.S. at 602 (Holmes, J., dissenting). Brandeis in his dissent signified his agreement with the substantive grounds of Holmes's dissent.
6. *Pennsylvania* 262 U.S. at 603 (1923) (McReynolds, J., dissenting). McReynolds asserted that "the freedom of interstate commerce is not committed to any state as parens patriae." *Id.* at 604. McReynolds reasoned: "If West Virginia should prohibit the drilling of new gas wells, I hardly suppose complainants could demand an injunction here even if it were admitted that their supplies would be cut off.... And suppose West Virginia should repeal the charters of all her public service corporations now transporting gas and thereby disable them, could we interfere upon the demand of another state who claimed that she would suffer?" *Id.* On the tension between *Pennsylvania* and *Massachusetts v. Mellon*, 262 U.S. 447 (1923), see Ann Woolhandler & Michael G. Collins, *State Standing*, 81 VIRGINIA LAW REVIEW 387, 467–75, 492 (1995). In a separate dissent, Brandeis strenuously argued that there was no standing because neither Ohio nor Pennsylvania sought "to protect some right of property or personal right." *Pennsylvania*, 262 U.S. at 610 (Brandeis, J., dissenting). On the importance of *Pennsylvania* for standing doctrine, see Daniel A. Fiedler, *Standing Underwater*, 85 GEORGE WASHINGTON LAW REVIEW 1554, 1564–65 (2017); Kenneth Culp David, *Ripeness of Governmental Action for Judicial Review*, 68 HARVARD LAW REVIEW 1326, 1365 (1955); *Threat of Enforcement – Prerequisite of a Justiciable Controversy*, 62 COLUMBIA LAW REVIEW 106, 114–15 (1962).
7. *Pennsylvania*, 262 U.S. at 596. The profound lesson, as distilled by one commentator, was that "If the interstate commerce clause, as has so often been reiterated, was intended to make the United States a single nation in their trade relations, it must follow that the natural resources of the states above all should be made available to the whole country. If the states are one nation, then there can be no reason why people who happen to be geographically located in a particular state should have the exclusive benefit of its peculiar natural products." Note, *State Statutes Limiting Export of Natural Resources*, 33 YALE LAW JOURNAL 185, 188–89 (1923).
8. *See, e.g.*, United States v. E.C. Knight Co., 156 U.S. 1, 32 (1895) (Harlan, J., dissenting) ("Commerce among the States, as this court has declared, is a unit, and in respect of that commerce this is one country, and we are one people."); Bowman v. Chi. & Northwestern Ry. Co., 125 U.S. 465, 508 (1888); W. Union Tel. Co. v. Pendleton, 122 U.S. 347, 358 (1887); Robbins v. Shelby County Taxing Dist., 120

U.S. 489, 494 (1887) ("[I]n the matter of interstate commerce the United States are but one country, and are and must be subject to one system of regulations and not to a multitude of systems."); Walling v. Michigan, 116 U.S. 446, 456–57 (1886) (Congressional nonaction with regard to "the transportation, purchase, sale, and exchange of commodities [between states] is a declaration of its purpose that the commerce in that commodity . . . shall be free. There would otherwise be no security against conflicting regulations of different states, each discriminating in favor of its own products or citizens and against the products and citizens of other states."); Mobile v. Kimball, 102 U.S. 691, 697 (1880) ("[I]t is a matter of public history that the object of vesting in Congress the power to regulate commerce with foreign nations and among the States was to insure uniformity of regulation against conflicting and discriminating State legislation."); Inman S.S. Co. v. Tinker, 94 U.S. 238, 245 (1876).

9. The theme of uniformity resonated in many areas of Taft Court jurisprudence, most especially in its admiralty decisions. Consider, for example, Washington v. W.C. Dawson & Co., 264 U.S. 219 (1924), which struck down federal legislation authorizing state workmen's compensation laws to apply to injured seamen. Over a masterful dissent by Brandeis, the Court, speaking through McReynolds, held that:

> Without doubt Congress has power to alter, amend or revise the maritime law by statutes of general application embodying its will and judgment. This power, we think, would permit enactment of a general employers' liability law or general provisions for compensating injured employees; but it may not be delegated to the several States. The grant of admiralty and maritime jurisdiction looks to uniformity; otherwise wide discretion is left to Congress. . . . Exercising another power – to regulate commerce – Congress has prescribed the liability of interstate carriers by railroad for damages to employees . . . and thereby abrogated conflicting local rules. . . .
>
> This cause presents a situation where there was no attempt to prescribe general rules. On the contrary, the manifest purpose was to permit any State to alter the maritime law and thereby introduce conflicting requirements. To prevent this result the Constitution adopted the law of the sea as the measure of maritime rights and obligations. The confusion and difficulty, if vessels were compelled to comply with the local statutes at every port, are not difficult to see. Of course, some within the States may prefer local rules; but the Union was formed with the very definite design of freeing maritime commerce from intolerable restrictions incident to such control. The subject is national. Local interest must yield to the common welfare. The Constitution is supreme.

Id. at 227–28. Although *Dawson* was inconsistent with Clark Distilling Co. v. Western Maryland Railway Co, 242 U.S. 311 (1917), in which the Court had upheld Congress's power to splinter the uniformity of interstate commerce by authorizing states to prevent the importation of out-of-state liquor, it nevertheless carried forward the jurisprudence of such controversial decisions as Southern Pacific Co. v. Jensen, 244 U.S. 205, 215 (1917), and Knickerbocker Ice Co. v. Stewart, 253 U.S. 149, 163–64 (1920). *Compare* State Industrial Commission v. Nordenholt Corp., 259 U.S. 262 (1922); Red Cross Line v. Atlantic Fruit Co., 264 U.S. 109 (1924); Panama Railroad Co. v. Johnson, 264 U.S. 375 (1924); Alaska S.S. Co. v. McHugh, 268 U.S. 23 (1925). By the end of the Taft Court, this jurisprudence had assumed almost parodic proportions.

In London Guarantee & Accident Co. v. Industrial Accident Comm'n of CA, 279 U.S. 109 (1929), for example, which concerned the question of whether California's Workmen's Compensation Act could constitutionally be applied to the death of an apprentice seaman who had drowned while in a small boat that had set forth from a pier to board an anchored fishing vessel that had broken free from its anchor and was drifting into shore. Taft, speaking for eight justices, held:

> Workmen's compensation acts will apply unless their application would interfere with the uniformity of the general maritime law in interstate and foreign commerce, and there is neither here. But this omits one of the grounds for making an exception – that it shall not be prejudicial to the characteristic features of the maritime law. That is just what it would be here, for here we have a transaction on the navigable waters of the United States which in every respect covers all the characteristic features of maritime law and has no other features but those. To apply to such a case a state Compensation Law would certainly be prejudicial to those features. We must hold, therefore, that it was a violation of the exclusive maritime jurisdiction conferred by the Constitution to apply in this case the California Compensation Act.

Id. at 125. A week before Taft's opinion came down, Stone objected to this paragraph on the ground that the conclusion "that the local remedy cannot be applied if it interferes with any of the characteristic features of the maritime law, each independently of its uniformity in interstate and foreign commerce" was a virtually meaningless criterion.

> If you mean this literally, then I cannot see how there could ever be any local remedy where there is admiralty jurisdiction, for a local remedy, like that of a workman's compensation law in any case, does interfere with characteristic features of maritime law to the extent that it applies a different rule and allows a different recovery from admiralty. If the phrase "characteristic features of maritime law," then used in this connection, refer, as I had always supposed was the case, to those features which give it uniformity in interstate and international relations, then certainly the local remedy in the present case does not interfere with such characteristic features .... As it stands, this paragraph leaves the reader uncertain under what circumstances the local remedy may be applied without interfering with the characteristic features of maritime law.
>
> I note, too, that in this paragraph you use the phrase "characteristic features of maritime law", as synonymous with the "characteristic features of maritime jurisdiction", but do they mean the same thing and, when you speak of characteristic features of maritime jurisdiction, are there any such except those which are essential to giving admiralty jurisdiction which, by assumption, are present in every case dealing with this subject?

HFS to WHT (April 2, 1929) (Stone papers). It is noteworthy that Stone did not dissent even though Taft does not seem to have altered his opinion. We know that Holmes disapproved of this whole line of cases, yet he also did not dissent. Only Brandeis dissented, and that without opinion.

10. Pub. L. 62-398, 37 Stat. 699 (February 18, 1913).
11. 49 CONG. REC. 4292 (February 28, 1913). It is worth noting that then-Senator George Sutherland also believed that the Webb-Kenyon Act was unconstitutional, arguing that "[s]ince the purpose of conferring authority to regulate interstate commerce upon Congress was to prevent a multiplicity of diverse and conflicting rules made by the separate States, it would seem to follow that the regulation of any given article must be uniform in character, and that varying regulations could not be justified upon the varying desires or opinions of the several States." 49 CONG. REC. 2910 (February 10, 1913). Sutherland observed that as a direct consequence of the Court's decisions holding that

insurance was not commerce, see Paul v. Virginia, 75 U.S. 168, 183 (1868), "[m]any of the States have ... passed laws in effect discriminating against insurance companies of sister States and in favor of their own." 49 CONG. REC. at 2905.

12. Congress overrode Taft's veto, and the Webb-Kenyon Act became law. Although the Court had previously held that state prohibitions on the importation of liquor violated the dormant Commerce Clause, Leisy v. Hardin, 135 U.S. 100, 124–25 (1890), it upheld the Webb-Kenyon Act in Clark Distilling Co. v. Western Maryland Railway Co., 242 U.S. 311, 337–38 (1917). For good discussions of the interplay between state and federal regulation, see Henry Wolf Biklé, *The Silence of Congress*, 41 HARVARD LAW REVIEW 200, 205–9 (1927) (suggesting that Congress's affirmative indication that interstate commerce may be subject to state restrictions may allow such restrictions even in areas of national concern); and Barry Cushman, Lochner, *Liquor and Longshoremen: A Puzzle in Progressive Era Federalism*, 32 JOURNAL OF MARITIME LAW & COMMERCE 1, 21–35 (2001). Cushman accurately observes that the Taft Court in its admiralty jurisprudence, see *supra* note 9, adopted policies that were in tension with *Clark Distilling*.
13. *Pennsylvania*, 262 U.S. at 596.
14. *Id.* at 599–600 (quoting from West v. Kansas Natural Gas, 221 U.S. 229, 255 (1911)).
15. WHT to WVD (August 19, 1922) (Van Devanter papers).
16. WVD to WHT (August 27, 1922) (Taft papers).
17. WVD to WHT (September 10, 1922) (Taft papers).
18. *Brandeis-Frankfurter Conversations*, at 312–13 (June 12, 1923).
19. JHC to WVD (June 30, 1923) (Van Devanter papers).
20. LDB to Felix Frankfurter (November 20, 1923), in BRANDEIS-FRANKFURTER CORRESPONDENCE, at 148.
21. Pennsylvania v. West Virginia, 263 U.S. 350 (1923).
22. *Id.* at 351.
23. Taft papers, Reel 656. Taft wrote his son: "I don't expect to sit in the case. I agree with you that there is no real reason for withdrawal, but it is better a good deal to avoid cavil on that subject by a defeated party. We have to be very careful these days because the enemies of the Court are up and doing and seizing every sort of excuse for attacking it. La Follette has now arrived and expects to exploit his views tomorrow. I suppose he will have something to say about the Court and perhaps something to say about me personally. It isn't going to be a pleasant winter in that respect." WHT to Robert A. Taft (November 4, 1923) (Taft papers).
24. LDB to Felix Frankfurter (December 3, 1923), in BRANDEIS-FRANKFURTER CORRESPONDENCE, at 149.
25. 260 U.S. 245 (1922). The tax was for 1.5 percent of the market value of the anthracite, assessed "at the time when the coal has been subjected to ... preparation 'and is ready for shipment or market.'" *Id.* at 253.
26. As the Court stated:

> Anthracite coal ... is asserted to be found in only nine counties in [Pennsylvania], and practically nowhere else in the United States. The fact, it is further said, gives the State a monopoly of it, and that a tax upon it is levying a tribute upon the consumption of other States, and nine of them have appeared by their attorneys general to assail it as illegal and denounce it as an attempt to

> regulate interstate commerce. In emphasis of the contention, the Governor of the State is quoted as urging the tax because of that effect. The fact, tribute upon the consumers of the coal in other States, is pronounced inevitable, as, it is the assertion, 80% of the total production is shipped to other States, and that this constitutes its "major 'market.'" And the dependency upon Pennsylvania is represented as impossible of evasion or relief. Anthracite coal, is the assertion, has become a prime necessity of those States, "particularly for domestic purposes" and even "municipal laws and ordinances have been passed forbidding the use of other coal for heating purposes."

   Id. at 258.
27. *Id.* at 260. *See* Thomas Reed Powell, *State Production Taxes and the Commerce Clause*, 12 CALIFORNIA LAW REVIEW 17, 17–18 (1923).
28. *Heisler*, 260 U.S. at 253, 261. *See* Lacoste v. Dep't of Conservation, 263 U.S. 545, 550–51 (1924) (upholding Louisiana's right to regulate the taking of its wild animals and their subsequent use).
29. *Heisler*, 260 U.S. at 259–60.
30. *See, e.g.,* Carson Petroleum Co. v. Vial, 279 U.S. 95, 101 (1929); Hughes Bros. Timber Co. v. Minnesota, 272 U.S. 469, 475 (1926) ("Mere intention ... does not put [goods] in interstate commerce, nor does preparatory gathering, for that purpose, at a depot. It must appear that the movement for another State has actually begun and is going on."); Champlain Realty Co. v. Brattleboro, 260 U.S. 366, 376 (1922): "The interstate commerce clause ... does not give immunity to movable property from local taxation which is not discriminative unless it is in actual continuous transit in interstate commerce. When it is shipped by a common carrier from one state to another, in the course of such an uninterrupted journey, it is clearly immune. The doubt arises when there are interruptions in the journey, and when the property, in its transportation, is under the complete control of the owner during the passage. If the interruptions are only to promote the safe or convenient transit, then the continuity of the interstate trip is not broken."
31. *Heisler*, 260 U.S. at 260–61.
32. For a good example of the Court reasoning in this vein in the context of congressional legislative power, see Hammer v. Dagenhart, 247 U.S. 251, 272–73 (1918):

   > [T]he production of articles, intended for interstate commerce, is a matter of local regulation. When the commerce begins is determined, not by the character of the commodity, nor by the intention of the owner to transfer it to another state for sale, nor by his preparation of it for transportation, but by its actual delivery to a common carrier for transportation, or the actual commencement of its transfer to another state.... If it were otherwise, all manufacture intended for interstate shipment would be brought under federal control to the practical exclusion of the authority of States.

   Reasoning like this, of course, is exceedingly hard to reconcile with a decision like Stafford v. Wallace, 258 U.S. 495 (1922). *See supra* Chapter 36, at 1125–26.
33. The Taft Court was frequently called upon to decide exactly when goods had begun their interstate journey "from the place of their production or preparation," *Heisler*, 260 U.S. at 259, and this task could sometimes take on surprisingly metaphysical dimensions. In Oliver Iron Mining Co. v. Lord, 262 U.S. 172 (1923), for example, a unanimous Court, speaking through Van Devanter, upheld a Minnesota tax on mining as applied to an open pit where the ore was loaded "directly into" railroad cars that promptly began their "interstate journey." *Id.* at 178. The Court refused to

acknowledge any ambiguity in the boundary between interstate and intrastate commerce.

> Mining is not interstate commerce, but, like manufacturing, is a local business subject to local regulation and taxation. Its character in this regard is intrinsic, is not affected by the intended use or disposal of the product, is not controlled by contractual engagements, and persists even though the business be conducted in close connection with interstate commerce. The ore does not enter interstate commerce until after the mining is done, and the tax is imposed only in respect of the mining. ... The tax may indirectly and incidentally affect such commerce, just as any taxation of railroad and telegraph lines does, but this is not a forbidden burden or interference.

Id. at 178–79.
34. *Heisler*, 260 U.S. at 259.
35. *See supra* Chapter 35.
36. 265 U.S. 298 (1924).
37. *Id.* at 308. In Sonneborn Bros. v. Cureton, 262 U.S. 506 (1923), by contrast, the Court found that goods shipped into a state could be taxed only after their "interstate transportation was at an end," by which it meant that the goods had "come to a state of rest" and were indistinguishable from other goods within the state. *Id.* at 508.
38. Butler's docket book shows that the case was also unanimous in conference.
39. *Kansas Natural Gas*, 265 U.S. at 308–10. Conversely, the Court also concluded that "[t]he business of supplying, on demand, local consumers is a local business, even though the gas be brought from another State and drawn for distribution directly from interstate mains; and this is so whether the local distribution be made by the transporting company or by independent distributing companies. In such case the local interest is paramount, and the interference with interstate commerce, if any, indirect and of minor importance." *Id.* at 309.
40. *Id.*
41. *Id.* at 310.
42. *See* FTC v. Pac. States Paper Trade Ass'n., 273 U.S. 52, 63–64 (1927) ("Commerce among the States is not a technical legal conception, but a practical one, drawn from the course of business."); Stafford v. Wallace, 258 U.S. 495, 518–19 (1922); Board of Trade v. Olsen, 262 U.S. 1, 35 (1923). The Court would repeat this point even in the context of the dormant Commerce Clause. *See, e.g.*, Foster-Fountain Packing Co. v. Haydel, 278 U.S. 1, 10 (1928) ("In determining what is interstate commerce, courts look to practical considerations and the established course of business."); Eureka Pipe Line Co. v. Hallanan, 257 U.S. 265, 272 (1921) ("As has been repeated many times, interstate commerce is a practical conception.").
43. *Olsen*, 262 U.S. at 33. *See* Binderup v. Pathe Exch., Inc., 263 U.S. 291, 311 (1923) ("It does not follow that because a thing is subject to state taxation it is also immune from federal regulation under the Commerce Clause.").
44. 273 U.S. 83, 87 (1927).
45. For a discussion, see *supra* Chapter 36, at 1123–24.
46. Reiterating views he had privately expressed to Frankfurter in the context of *Pennsylvania v. West Virginia*, see *supra* text at note 18, Brandeis dissented. He reasoned:

> The power of the state to regulate the selling price of electricity produced and distributed by it within the state and to prevent discrimination is not affected

> by the fact that the supply is furnished under a longterm contract. If the commission lacks the power exercised, it is solely because the electricity is delivered for use in another state. That fact makes the transaction interstate commerce, and Congress has power to legislate on the subject. It has not done so, nor has it legislated on any allied subject, so there can be no contention that it has occupied the field. Nor is this a case in which it can be said that the silence of Congress is a command that the Rhode Island utility shall remain free from the public regulation – that it shall be free to discriminate against the citizens of the state by which it was incorporated and in which it does business. That state may not, of course, obstruct or directly burden interstate commerce. But to prevent discrimination in the price of electricity wherever used does not obstruct or place a direct burden upon interstate commerce. Such regulation or action is unlike the burden imposed where a transportation rate is fixed, or where property moving in interstate commerce is taxed. The burden resulting from the order here in question resembles more nearly that increase in the cost of an article produced and to be delivered which arises by reason of higher taxes laid upon plant, operations or profits, or which arises by reason of expenditures required under police regulations. It is like the regulation sustained in Pennsylvania Gas Co. v. Public Service Commission, 252 U.S. 23, where an order of the New York Public Service Commission fixed the rates at which gas piped from without the state and delivered directly to the consumers might be sold.

Attleboro Steam & Electric, 273 U.S. at 91–92 (Brandeis, J., dissenting). According to Stone's docket book, Taft passed in conference. After Brandeis circulated his dissent, Holmes sent him back a note saying: "I don't see it." OWH to LDB (Brandeis papers).

47. *Attleboro Steam & Electric*, 273 U.S. at 90. About such cases and reasoning, the *New Republic* worried that "There is real danger that a utility engaged in the transmission of electric power from one state to another and there distributing it to homes, offices and factories may be completely freed from state regulation by the courts, even though there be no federal regulation. . . . The immediate goal of the interstate power interests is to escape regulation and so in Congress they will oppose federal regulation and in the courts they will oppose state regulation. Some day when the public will no longer tolerate the failure to regulate, probably the power interests, like the railroads, will favor the broadest displacement of state power by the federal." William Boyd Hunter, *One Gap in Rate Regulation*, 47 NEW REPUBLIC 34, 36 (1926).

48. Peter Fish has observed that "Taft, Willis Van Devanter, Pierce Butler, George Sutherland, and Edward T. Sanford constituted a majority bloc decidedly antagonistic to exercises of state authority." Peter G. Fish, *William Howard Taft and Charles Evans Hughes: Conservative Politicians as Chief Judicial Reformers*, 1975 SUPREME COURT REVIEW 123, 135. Writing in 1933, Felix Frankfurter and Henry M. Hart, Jr. thought they detected "a trend toward decreasing interference with state court judgments, a weakening in the impulse to invoke federal law to invalidate state legislative and administrative action. Just as this impulse was rampant, both in bar and bench, in the prosperous years of the middle twenties, so it may be, in these times of economic dislocation, relatively quiescent." Felix Frankfurter & Henry M. Hart, Jr., *The Business of the Supreme Court at October Term, 1932*, 47 HARVARD LAW REVIEW 245, 274 (1933).

49. *See supra* note 47. The Court's decision in *Attleboro Steam & Electric* might perhaps be justified without appealing to metaphors of dual sovereignty. If Rhode Island were empowered to raise Narragansett's rates, Massachusetts might equally

be authorized to lower them. The interstate transmission of power might thus become subject to incompatible state regulations. Although the Court mentioned this possibility, see *Attleboro Steam & Electric*, 273 U.S. at 90, it is significant that the Court did not rely on policy considerations of this kind to justify its conclusion. Instead, it flatly asserted the "essentially national" character of interstate commerce, holding that this character rendered interstate commerce altogether immune from regulation "in the guise of protection to ... local interests." *Id.*

50. 257 U.S. 282, 286, 291 (1921). The Court held that "[w]here goods are purchased in one state for transportation to another the commerce includes the purchase quite as much as it does the transportation." *Id.* at 290. This account of interstate commerce is in tension with the view of interstate commerce taken in *Heisler*, for in that case the Court considered it irrelevant whether the coal had already been purchased for interstate delivery. See *supra* text at note 27. Edward Corwin thus characterized the holding of *Bondurant* as "[a] new extension to the 'commerce' clause as a restriction on state power.... [I]t is an important development of the law, as the later application of it, in Lemke v. Farmers' Grain Co. [258 U.S. 50 (1922)], to set aside a vital part of North Dakota's plan for controlling the marketing of grain in the interest of the growers, strikingly demonstrates." Edward S. Corwin, *Constitutional Law in 1921–1922*, 16 AMERICAN POLITICAL SCIENCE REVIEW 612, 630–31 (1922). Corwin concluded that "this new extension of the 'commerce' clause probably takes away from the states much more valuable 'sovereignty' than the Child Labor decision saves to them; and this is done by judicial interpretation alone." *Id.* at 631 n.85. Brandeis dissented in *Bondurant* on jurisdictional grounds. *Bondurant*, 257 U.S. at 293 (Brandeis, J., dissenting).

51. 268 U.S. 325, 335–36 (1925).

52. 264 U.S. 150, 152–53 (1924).

53. In a letter to Frankfurter, Brandeis suggested that Frankfurter "start the Webb Kenyon idea as to Foreign Corp[oration]s," which would essentially involve congressional legislation authorizing local regulations of interstate commerce. LDB to Felix Frankfurter (May 13, 1925), in BRANDEIS-FRANKFURTER CORRESPONDENCE, at 202. Mentioning *Texas Transport & Terminal* by name, as well as other Taft Court decisions, Brandeis observed that "many more communities dismayed at amendment of their license fee taxation, would surely be glad to join & with the Back to the State Movement on the rise, Congress might do some work on these lines." *Id.* Taft and Sutherland, of course, held very contrary views of "the Webb Kenyon idea." See *supra* note 11 and accompanying text.

54. *Texas Transport & Terminal*, 264 U.S. at 155 (Brandeis, J., dissenting). Holmes joined Brandeis's dissent. Butler's docket book indicates that Sanford had voted with Brandeis and Holmes in conference. Brandeis dissented in a great many of the Court's dormant Commerce Clause decisions. *See, e.g.*, Dahnke-Walker Milling Co. v. Bondurant, 257 U.S. 282 (1921); Lemke v. Farmers' Grain Co., 258 U.S. 50 (1922); Pennsylvania v. West Virginia, 262 U.S. 553 (1923); Ozark Pipe Line Corp. v. Monier, 266 U.S. 555 (1925); Shafer v. Farmers' Grain Co., 268 U.S. 189 (1925); Alpha Portland Cement Co. v. Massachusetts, 268 U.S. 203 (1925); Fidelity & Deposit Co. v. Tafoya, 270 U.S. 426 (1926); Di Santo v. Pennsylvania, 273 U.S. 34 (1927); Public Utilities Commission v. Attleboro Steam & Electric Co., 273 U.S. 83 (1927); Cudahy Packing Co. v. Hinkle, 278 U.S. 460 (1929).

55. Brandeis argued:

> It is settled law that interstate commerce is not directly burdened by a tax imposed upon property used exclusively in interstate commerce, or by a tax upon net income derived exclusively from interstate commerce, or by an occupation tax, fixed in amount, although the business consists exclusively of selling goods brought from another State. On the other hand, the burden is deemed direct, where the tax is upon property moving in interstate commerce, or where it lays, like a gross-receipts tax, a burden upon every transaction in such commerce "by withholding, for the use of the State, a part of every dollar received in such transactions," or where an occupation tax is laid upon one who, like a drummer or delivery agent, is engaged exclusively in inaugurating or completing his own or his employer's transaction in interstate commerce.
>
> The New Orleans tax is obviously not laid upon property moving in interstate commerce. Nor does it, like a gross-receipts tax, lay a burden upon every transaction. It is simply a tax upon one of the instrumentalities of interstate commerce. It is no more a direct burden, than is the tax on the other indispensable instrumentalities; upon the ship; upon the pilot boat, which she must employ; upon the wharf at which she must load and unload; upon the office which the owner would have to hire for his employees, if, instead of engaging the services of an independent contractor, he had preferred to perform those duties himself.

Texas Transp. & Terminal, 264 U.S. at 156–57 (Brandeis, J., dissenting).

56. *Id.* at 156 (Brandeis, J., dissenting). *See* St. Louis & Southwestern Ry. Co. v. Nattin, 277 U.S. 157, 159 (1928) ("Without doubt a local legislative body ... may lay general ad valorem taxes upon all property within its jurisdiction, including that of common carriers engaged in interstate commerce, without violating the Federal Constitution. That such taxation does not amount to regulation of interstate commerce is settled doctrine."); Citizens Nat'l Bank v. Durr, 257 U.S. 99, 110 (1921) ("Ordinary property taxation imposed upon property employed in interstate commerce does not amount to an unconstitutional burden on the commerce itself.").

57. *Texas Transport & Terminal*, 264 U.S. at 155 (Brandeis, J., dissenting).

58. ALEXANDER M. BICKEL, THE UNPUBLISHED OPINIONS OF MR. JUSTICE BRANDEIS: THE SUPREME COURT AT WORK 118 (Cambridge: Harvard University Press 1957). Bickel notes that Brandeis nevertheless adhered "unfalteringly to the concept of direct and indirect burdens." *Id.* This is not entirely true. For example, Brandeis authored the Taft Court's unanimous decision in Davis v. Farmers' Co-op. Equity Co., 262 U.S. 312 (1923), which considered the constitutionality of a Minnesota statute providing that "Any foreign corporation having an agent in this state for the solicitation of freight and passenger traffic or either thereof over its lines outside of this state, may be served with summons by delivering a copy thereof to such agent." *Id.* at 313–14. A Kansas railroad company that did not own or operate any railroad in Minnesota, but that maintained an agent in the state for solicitation of traffic, was sued for a loss of grain that occurred in Kansas. Apart from the jurisdictional statute, nothing in the cause of action connected the Kansas railroad to Minnesota. Although the company challenged the constitutionality of the statute under both the Due Process and Equal Protection Clauses, Brandeis chose to find it unconstitutional as applied under the dormant Commerce Clause. He wrote:

> It may be that a statute like that here assailed would be valid, although applied to suits in which the cause of action arose elsewhere, if the transaction out of which it arose had been entered upon within the state, or if the plaintiff was, when it arose, a resident of the state. These questions are not before us, and we

express no opinion upon them. But orderly effective administration of justice clearly does not require that a foreign carrier shall submit to a suit in a state in which the cause of action did not arise, in which the transaction giving rise to it was not entered upon, in which the carrier neither owns nor operates a railroad, and in which the plaintiff does not reside. The public and the carriers are alike interested in maintaining adequate, uninterrupted transportation service at reasonable cost. This common interest is emphasized by the Transportation Act 1920, which authorizes rate increases necessary to ensure to carriers efficiently operated a fair return on property devoted to the public use. Avoidance of waste, in interstate transportation, as well as maintenance of service, have become a direct concern of the public. With these ends the Minnesota statute, as here applied, unduly interferes. By requiring from interstate carriers general submission to suit, it unreasonably obstructs, and unduly burdens, interstate commerce.

Id. at 316–17. Without explicitly invoking the direct/indirect dichotomy, Brandeis effectively balanced burdens on interstate commerce against the advantages to Minnesota in asserting virtually universal jurisdiction, and he determined that Minnesota's statute was unconstitutional as applied. Butler, who had specifically asked to be noted as not participating in the decision, nevertheless wrote Brandeis to say that "I think it an excellent opinion." Van Devanter wrote, "I think this is good doctrine convincingly and very clearly stated." And Taft wrote, "You have threaded your way to the end with great success and with convincing reason." Holmes returned, "Nicely laid out." McKenna, oddly, wrote, "Narrow treading but there is only one result when one opposes or tries to oppose, a majority. Besides by yielding one gets the praise of being susceptible to reason." (Brandeis papers). *See* Atchison, T. & S.F. Ry. Co. v. Wells, 265 U.S. 469 (1924); Michigan Cent. R. Co. v. Mix, 278 U.S. 492 (1929).

Four years later a Missouri railroad cited *Davis* to support its claim that a negligence suit brought against it in Missouri should be dismissed as inconsistent with the dormant Commerce Clause because the accident had occurred in Kansas and the witnesses necessary to adjudicate the suit were in Kansas. Brandeis spoke for a unanimous Court in rejecting the claim: "Here, the railroad is not a foreign corporation; it is sued in the state of its incorporation. It is sued in a state in which it owns and operates a railroad. . . . It is sued in a state in which it carries on doubtless intrastate as well as interstate business. Even a foreign corporation is not immune from the ordinary processes of the courts of a state, where its business is entirely interstate in character. It must submit, if there is jurisdiction, to the requirements of orderly, effective administration of justice, although thereby interstate commerce is incidentally burdened." Hoffman v. Missouri *ex rel.* Foraker, 274 U.S. 21, 22–23 (1927). Taft commented on Brandeis's draft opinion, "I concur. Give these R. R. lawyers an inch and they'll take an ell." (Brandeis papers). *See* Missouri *ex rel.* St. Louis, B. & M. Ry. Co. v. Taylor, 266 U.S. 200 (1924).

59. The trope had a venerable history. *See* Austin v. Tennessee, 179 U.S. 343, 349 (1900) (upholding a Tennessee law prohibiting the importation and sale of cigarettes): "We have had repeated occasion to hold, where state legislation has been attacked as violative . . . of the power of Congress over interstate commerce, . . . that, if the action of the state legislature were a bona fide exercise of its police power, and dictated by a genuine regard for the preservation of the public health or safety, such legislation would be respected, though it might interfere indirectly with interstate commerce." *See* Barry Cushman, *Formalism and Realism in Commerce Clause Jurisprudence*, 67 UNIVERSITY OF CHICAGO LAW REVIEW 1089, 1111–14 (2000).

The Dormant Commerce Clause & the National Market

60. As the *New Republic* pointed out, the assumption that there was "an incompatibility between state and federal regulation," and the aspiration to carve out "mutually exclusive spheres of action for each," will "not work in a highly organized society such as the United States of today. The two functions are really supplementary. The success of a federal system depends upon an assignment of powers and responsibilities to the central and local governments which varies at different times in response to changing conditions, but which always assumes coöperation rather than antagonism." *The Revival of Anti-Federalism*, 41 NEW REPUBLIC 211, 212 (1925).
61. 53 U.S. 299 (1851).
62. *See* Cushman, *supra* note 59, at 1114–16.
63. *Cooley*, 53 U.S. at 319.
64. *See* Bernard C. Gavit, *State Highways and Interstate Motor Transportation*, 21 ILLINOIS LAW REVIEW 559 (1926); George Vaughn Strong, *Constitutional Aspects under the Commerce Clause of State Regulation and Taxation of Interstate Motor Carriers*, 3 TEMPLE LAW QUARTERLY 17 (1928).
65. Sprout v. City of South Bend, 277 U.S. 163, 169 (1928). The Court observed:

> A State may ... require payment of an occupation tax from one engaged in both intrastate and interstate commerce. ... But in order that the fee or tax shall be valid, it must appear that it is imposed solely on account of the intrastate business; that the amount exacted is not increased because of the interstate business done; that one engaged exclusively in interstate commerce would not be subject to the imposition; and that the person taxed could discontinue the intrastate business without withdrawing also from the interstate business. ... The privilege of engaging in [interstate] commerce is one which a State cannot deny. ... A State is equally inhibited from conditioning its exercise on the payment of an occupation tax.

Id. at 170–71 (citations omitted).

66. *Id.* at 170. In Clark v. Poor, 274 U.S. 554 (1927), an interstate trucking company challenged the application of an Ohio law that required motor transportation companies operating within the state to obtain a certificate and to pay a fee "graduated according to the number and capacity of the vehicles used." *Id.* at 555–56.

> The plaintiffs claim that, as applied to them, the Act violates the commerce clause of the Federal Constitution. They insist that, as they are engaged exclusively in interstate commerce, they are not subject to regulation by the State; that it is without power to require that before using its highways they apply for and obtain a certificate; and that it is also without power to impose, in addition to the annual license fee demanded of all persons using automobiles on the highways, a tax upon them ... for the maintenance and repair of the highways and for the administration and enforcement of the laws governing the use of the same. The contrary is settled. The highways are public property. Users of them, although engaged exclusively in interstate commerce, are subject to regulation by the State to ensure safety and convenience and the conservation of the highways.

Id. at 556–57.

67. *Sprout*, 277 U.S. at 172.
68. Morris v. Duby, 274 U.S. 135, 144 (1927). "In the absence of national legislation especially covering the subject of interstate commerce, the State may rightly prescribe uniform regulations adapted to promote safety upon its highways and the conservation of their use, applicable alike to vehicles moving in interstate commerce and those of its own citizens. Of course the State may not discriminate against interstate commerce." *Id.* at 143.

The Taft Court

69. Buck v. Kuykendall, 267 U.S. 307, 313 (1925). McReynolds dissented in *Buck*, authoring an opinion published in the companion case of George M. Bush & Sons Co. v. Maloy, 267 U.S. 317 (1925):

> The problems arising out of the sudden increase of motor vehicles present extraordinary difficulties. As yet nobody definitely knows what should be done. Manifestly, the exigency cannot be met through uniform rules laid down by Congress.
>
> Interstate commerce has been greatly aided – amazingly facilitated, indeed – through legislation and expenditures by the States. The challenged statutes do not discriminate against such commerce, do not seriously impede it, and indicate an honest purpose to promote the best interests of all by preventing unnecessary destruction and keeping the ways fit for maximum service.
>
> The Federal Government has not and cannot undertake precise regulations. Control by the States must continue, otherwise chaotic conditions will quickly develop. The problems are essentially local, and should be left with the local authorities unless and until something is done which really tends to obstruct the free flow of commercial intercourse.
>
> The situation is similar to the one growing out of the necessity for harbor regulations. State statutes concerning pilotage, for example, have been upheld although they amounted to regulation of interstate and foreign commerce. "They fall within that class of powers which may be exercised by the States until Congress has seen fit to act upon the subject."

267 U.S. at 325–26 (McReynolds, J., dissenting). *See* United States v. Hubbard, 266 U.S. 474, 480, 481 (1925) (McReynolds, J., dissenting) (concluding that states may control until Congress indicates its intent to regulate).

The Taft Court's automobile cases are analogous to its decisions dealing with interstate ferries. The Court was willing to grant states authority to "fix reasonable rates applicable to ferriage from [their] river front[s] or ... prescribe reasonable regulations calculated to secure safety and convenience in the conduct of the business," but it was not willing to grant states power to "make [their] consent and license a condition precedent to a right to engage" in interstate ferriage. Mayor of Vidalia v. McNeely, 274 U.S. 676, 683 (1927). The Court thus distinguished, as with highways, "power to license and therefore to exclude from the business" from "power to regulate it." *Id.* at 680.

70. *Heisler*, 260 U.S. at 259. Compare the observation of Holmes in his opinion for the Court in *Gillespie*, "It is well understood that a certain amount of reaction upon and interference with [interstate] commerce cannot be avoided if the States are to exist and make laws." Gillespie v. Oklahoma, 257 U.S. 501, 505 (1922).

71. For an example of this approach outside the automobile context, see St. Louis-S.F. Ry. Co. v. Pub. Serv. Comm'n, 261 U.S. 369 (1923), in which the Court was required to decide whether an order of the Missouri Public Service Commission requiring an interstate train to stop at a certain city violated the dormant Commerce Clause. The Court, speaking unanimously through McKenna, held that "the primary principle is that, although interstate commerce is outside of regulation by a State, there may be instances in which a State, in the exercise of a necessary power may affect that commerce. There is, however, no inevitable test of the instances; the facts in each must be considered." *Id.* at 371. The Court accordingly balanced the state's interests in ordering the stops against the resulting impact on interstate commerce.

Id. at 372–73. *Cf.* Lake Shore & Mich. S. Ry. Co. v. Ohio *ex rel.* Lawrence, 173 U.S. 285, 308 (1899) (acknowledging the Court's adoption of a case-by-case inquiry and declining an "attempt to lay down any rule that would govern every conceivable case").

72. F.D.G. RIBBLE, STATE AND NATIONAL POWER OVER COMMERCE 221 (New York: Columbia University Press 1937).
73. United Leather Workers Int'l Union v. Herkert & Meisel Trunk Co., 265 U.S. 457, 466 (1924); Anderson v. Shipowners Ass'n, 272 U.S. 359, 364 (1926).
74. Foster-Fountain Packing Co. v. Haydel, 278 U.S. 1, 10 (1928); Pub. Utils. Comm'n v. Attleboro Steam & Elec. Co., 273 U.S. 83, 87–88 (1927); Interstate Busses Corp. v. Holyoke St. Ry. Co., 273 U.S. 45, 52 (1927); Shafer v. Farmers' Grain Co., 268 U.S. 189, 199 (1925); Indus. Ass'n v. United States, 268 U.S. 64, 81–82 (1925); Buck v. Kuykendall, 267 U.S. 307, 315 (1925); Hygrade Provision Co. v. Sherman, 266 U.S. 497, 503 (1925); Sonneborn Bros. v. Cureton, 262 U.S. 506, 515 (1923); Lemke v. Farmers' Grain Co., 258 U.S. 50, 59 (1922).
75. Missouri *ex rel.* Barrett v. Kan. Natural Gas Co., 265 U.S. 298, 307 (1924). *See* Or.-Wash. R.R. & Navigation Co. v. Washington, 270 U.S. 87, 101 (1926): "In the relation of the States to the regulation of interstate commerce by Congress there are two fields. There is one in which the State can not interfere at all, even in the silence of Congress. In the other, (and this is the one in which the legitimate exercise of the State's police power brings it into contact with interstate commerce so as to affect that commerce), the State may exercise its police power until Congress has by affirmative legislation occupied the field."
76. Powell, *Current Conflicts, supra* note 2, at 323. *See* Cushman, *supra* note 59, at 1101–26.
77. Thus, in a case in which natural gas was "transmitted directly from the source of supply in Pennsylvania to the consumers in the cities and towns of New York," without the intervention of any local distributors, the Court nevertheless decided that New York could regulate the local price of the gas, even though it was regulating interstate commerce, because "[i]n dealing with interstate commerce it is not in some instances regarded as an infringement upon the authority delegated to Congress, to permit the States to pass laws indirectly affecting such commerce, when needed to protect or regulate matters of local interest. Such laws are operative until Congress acts under its superior authority by regulating the subject-matter for itself." Pennsylvania Gas Co. v. Pub. Serv. Comm'n, 252 U.S. 23, 28–29 (1920). The contrast between the logic of *Pennsylvania Gas* and that of *Missouri v. Kansas Natural Gas Co*, 265 U.S. 298 (1924), is a measure of the Taft Court's escalating commitment to the priority of perceived national interests.
78. In 1897 Holmes theorized one possible source of this reluctance:

> The training of lawyers is a training in logic. The processes of analogy, discrimination, and deduction are those in which they are most at home. The language of judicial decision is mainly the language of logic. And the logical method and form flatter that longing for certainty and for repose which is in every human mind. But certainty generally is illusion, and repose is not the destiny of man. Behind the logical form lies a judgment as to the relative worth and importance of competing legislative grounds, often an inarticulate and unconscious judgment, it is true, and yet the very root and nerve of the whole proceeding.

Oliver Wendell Holmes, *The Path of the Law*, 1 BOSTON LAW SCHOOL MAGAZINE 1, 8 (1897).

79. 279 U.S. 245, 248 (1929).
80. *See supra* Chapter 35, at 1112–13. *Helson* is effectively the equivalent in dormant Commerce Clause jurisprudence of the Taft Court's *Panhandle* decision in intergovernmental tax immunity doctrine. Analogously, Alpha Portland Cement Co. v. Massachusetts, 268 U.S. 203 (1925), which involved a state's taxation of the assets of a foreign corporation involved in interstate commerce, is effectively the equivalent in dormant Commerce Clause jurisprudence of the Taft Court's *Macallen* decision in intergovernmental tax immunity doctrine. *See supra* Chapter 35, at 1113. In *Alpha Portland Cement*, the Taft Court, speaking through McReynolds, and with only Brandeis dissenting, held that a state could not "impose upon a foreign corporation which transacts only interstate business within her borders an excise tax measured by a combination of two factors – the proportion of the total value of capital shares attributed to transactions therein, and the proportion of net income attributed to such transactions." 268 U.S. at 216–17. Speaking for the Court, McReynolds opined that "a state may not burden interstate commerce or tax property beyond her borders under the guise of regulating or taxing intrastate business. So to burden interstate commerce is prohibited by the commerce clause; and the Fourteenth Amendment does not permit taxation of property beyond the state's jurisdiction. The amount demanded is unimportant when there is no legitimate basis for the tax." *Id.* at 218. *See* T.R. Powell, *State Taxation Controversies*, 76 UNIVERSITY OF PENNSYLVANIA LAW REVIEW 773, 791–93 (1928). Just as *Macallen* had shrunk the effective base of local state taxation to extend immunity to income produced by federal fiscal instrumentalities, so *Alpha Portland Cement* shrunk the effective base of local state taxation to extend immunity to income produced by interstate commerce. Just as *Macallen* overruled the controlling precedent of *Flint v. Stone Tracy Co.*, so *Alpha Portland Cement* overruled the controlling precedent of Baltic Mining Co. v. Massachusetts, 231 U.S. 68 (1913). As Van Devanter later wrote Taft, "Experience tends to make me believe that when a tax which may be imposed (as a franchise or occupational tax) is measured by something beyond the reach of the particular taxing power, there is a real transgression of constitutional principles." WVD to WHT (November 11, 1927) (Van Devanter papers).

The day after *Alpha Cement* was decided, Brandeis wrote Frankfurter, "The Shaffer [sic] Case (North Dakota farm Act – Van Devanter) and the Alpha Cement Case (Mass. Foreign Corp Tax) McReynolds, show that relief can be had only through the application of the Webb-Kenyon Act theory (Clark Dist. Co. Case). Wouldn't it be well to start that idea? It might take in these days of revulsion against federal control." LDB to Felix Frankfurter (May 5, 1925), in BRANDEIS-FRANKFURTER CORRESPONDENCE, at 201. *See supra* notes 11, 12, and 53 (discussing the "Webb-Kenyon theory"); *infra* text at notes 101–3 (discussing *Shafer*).

Alpha Portland Cement was extended in Cudahy Packing Co. v. Hinkle, 278 U.S. 460 (1929). *See* BICKEL, *supra* note 58, at 125–26. Speaking for seven justices, McReynolds held that the State of Washington could not impose graduated filing fees and license taxes based upon the authorized stock of a foreign corporation, even though the state's exactions were capped at $3,000, and even though the corporation did more than $600,000 of intrastate business in Washington. Brandeis conceded that if Washington "sought to impose a tax on corporations engaged wholly in interstate commerce, or if the taxes laid a direct burden upon interstate commerce, or if they were laid upon property without the state, or if they were unjustly discriminatory, the fact that they are small in amount would, of course, be immaterial." *Hinkle*, 278 U.S. at 467 (Brandeis, J., dissenting). Holmes joined Brandeis in his dissent. At one point, Brandeis argued:

> I am aware that it has been said by this court that a license fee of a given per cent. of the entire authorized capital of a foreign corporation doing both a local and interstate business is essentially a tax on the entire business, interstate as well as intrastate; and a tax upon property outside the state. But that was said in cases where the statute did not fix any maximum. The statement seems to me legally unsound. If it were true, that every tax imposed generally upon a foreign corporation doing both interstate and intrastate business taxed its interstate business and its property outside the state then most of such corporations would largely escape taxation. By the same process of reasoning all taxes laid by a state upon property within its borders, which is used in both intrastate and interstate commerce, would be a tax on interstate commerce. But such taxes have been universally upheld.

Id. at 469–70 (Brandeis, J., dissenting). Holmes underlined this passage and wrote Brandeis: "Good. I have been wanting to have this said." (Brandeis papers). Stone's docket book suggests that he had been uncertain about how to vote in conference. After reading Brandeis's circulated dissent, however, he wrote Brandeis to say:

> In your dissent ... you took a sustainable position and present it with great force. But the other position, so far as it relates to making capital used outside the state a measure of the tax imposed within the state is also a workable rule. In one way it has an advantage over the one which you prefer, in that it is capable of more definite and certain application, for it seems to me that under the rule you lay down as the tax becomes larger it is always open for the taxpayer to come here to have us pass on the question whether the tax is too large or too substantial.... These considerations, and my general disposition not to dissent unless I feel strongly on the subject, lead me to stand by my vote, although I can say very frankly that I could not affirm that your position is in any sense unsound.

HFS to LDB (February 16, 1929) (Brandeis papers). For a discussion of the subsequent history of *Alpha Portland Cement* and *Cudahy*, see BICKEL, *supra* note 58, at 152–63.

81. "While a state has power to tax property having a situs within its limits, whether employed in interstate commerce or not, it cannot interfere with interstate commerce through the imposition of a tax which is, in effect, a tax for the privilege of transacting such commerce." *Helson*, 279 U.S. at 249. *See* New Jersey Bell Tel. Co. v. State Board of Taxes, 280 U.S. 338 (1930).
82. *Helson*, 279 U.S. at 252.
83. *Id.* at 248. McReynolds dissented without opinion.
84. *Id.* at 252–53 (Stone, J., concurring). Brandeis had written Stone, "I think the reasoning in Sutherland's opinion is, in view of the Court's decisions, worse than the result. Perhaps concurring in the result – with a few well chosen words would be the most effective blow for a right rule." LDB to HFS (April 4, 1929) (Stone papers).
85. *Helson*, 279 U.S. at 253 (Stone, J., concurring).
86. *See supra* Chapter 35, at 1114–15.
87. 273 U.S. 34 (1927).
88. With characteristic acerbity, Thomas Reed Powell noted that "[f]or a reasoned consideration of the problem before the court we must go to the minority opinions."

1189

Thomas Reed Powell, *Current Conflicts between the Commerce Clause and State Police Power, 1922–1927*, 12 MINNESOTA LAW REVIEW 470, 479 (1928). Brandeis, joined by Holmes, dissented, arguing that the licensing requirement did not "directly burden interstate or foreign commerce" because it was "in essence an inspection law." *Di Santo*, 273 U.S. at 39, 41–42 (Brandeis, J., dissenting). Brandeis's opinion is notable for its famous plea: "[T]he logic of words should yield to the logic of realities." *Id.* at 43. Stone's separate dissent was joined by both Holmes and Brandeis.

89. *Di Santo*, 273 U.S. at 36–37. "The Congress has complete and paramount authority to regulate foreign commerce and, by appropriate measures, to protect the public against the frauds of those who sell these tickets and orders." *Id.* at 37.

90. *Id.* at 44 (Stone, J., dissenting).

91. Noel T. Dowling, *Interstate Commerce and State Power*, 27 VIRGINIA LAW REVIEW 1, 27–28 (1940). *See e.g.*, Powell, *Current Conflicts, supra* note 88, at 491:

> The notable dissent of Mr. Justice Stone in the Di Santo Case should be pinned on the wall of the study of every Justice of the Supreme Court to serve as a guide in the writing of opinions even in cases where no one has any doubt that the interests of unimpeded commerce outweigh the local need for regulation. Unless the competing considerations which must have been voiced in the conference room are made explicit in the opinions, counsel may not be forewarned of the factors that induce judgment and so may continue to write briefs and make arguments that exalt excessive generalizations at the expense of concrete analysis.

Stone's dissent sparked sustained criticism of the Court's "formalistic jurisprudence." *See, e.g., Mechanical Jurisprudence and Constitutional Law*, 124 THE NATION 253–54 (1927):

> [Justice Stone deals] with his problem realistically, in the light of modern ideas of logic and of human reasoning, and abandons the formalistic jurisprudence with which the majority apparently deceive themselves. Whatever one may think of the present-day reluctance to concentrate additional power in the federal government, it seems clear that the matter with which the State statutes deal can best be left for regulation by State officials rather than by remote government officials in Washington. Obvious also is it that in the present state of the public mind Congress will be unlikely to undertake federal regulation of the problem involved, and the sole practical effect of the decision will probably be to allow the defrauding of ignorant immigrants to go on unchecked. It is to be regretted that, perhaps because of a failure of some of its members to appreciate that they are in the last analysis dealing not with questions of pure logic but of policy, the majority of our highest judicial tribunal have once more shown an inability to grapple with the social realities which lie behind all legal rules.

92. *Di Santo*, 273 U.S. at 44 (Stone, J., dissenting). Fourteen years later, Stone would have the pleasure of authoring an opinion overruling *Di Santo* on exactly these grounds. California v. Thompson, 313 U.S. 109, 116 (1941).

93. So, for example, in Buck v. Kuykendall, 267 U.S. 307 (1925), the Court held that a state could constitutionally regulate interstate traffic on its highways so long as it did so for a proper purpose. *Id.* at 314. Yet in other contexts the Court was prepared to announce that "a state statute which by its necessary operation directly interferes with or burdens [interstate] commerce is a prohibited regulation and invalid, regardless of the purpose with which it was enacted." Shafer v. Farmers' Grain Co., 268 U.S. 189, 199 (1925). This was true in *Di Santo* itself, which asserted that

a statute imposing a direct burden is unconstitutional "regardless of the purpose with which it was passed." *Di Santo*, 273 U.S. at 37.
94. On the Court's reluctance to adopt this role, see *supra* note 78.
95. See *supra* Chapter 20, at 661–62.
96. WILLIAM HOWARD TAFT, OUR CHIEF MAGISTRATE AND HIS POWERS 13 (New York: Columbia University Press 1916). Taft believed that he inhabited "an age and generation when ... the danger to the best interests of the country, is in the overwhelming mass of ill-digested legislation. ... The value of the legislation seems not to be in the good of its operation, but in its vote-getting quality, and its use as molasses for the catching of political flies. Therefore, a system in which we may have an enforced rest from legislation for two years is not bad." *Id*. at 12. On the similar views of Sutherland, see *supra* Chapter 23, at 740–41.
97. The influence of political ideology on federalism jurisprudence is a staple of contemporary political science. *See, e.g.*, Frank B. Cross & Emerson H. Tiller, *The Three Faces of Federalism: An Empirical Assessment of Supreme Court Federalism Jurisprudence*, 73 SOUTHERN CALIFORNIA LAW REVIEW 741, 745–46 (2000) (arguing that political ideology, among other factors, contributes to the way individual justices decide federalism cases).
98. 266 U.S. 570, 574 (1925).
99. *Id*. at 576–77.
100. Just so that no one would miss the point, Butler devoted his penultimate paragraph to a brief statement of the conclusion that "it is beyond the power of the State by legislative fiat to convert property used exclusively in the business of a private carrier into a public utility, or to make the owner a public carrier, for that would be taking private property for public use without just compensation, which no State can do consistently with the due process of law clause of the Fourteenth Amendment." *Id*. at 577–78. The Court devoted greater attention to the due process point the following year in Frost & Frost Trucking Co. v. Railroad Commission, 271 U.S. 583, 592 (1926) (holding that a private carrier cannot be transformed into a public entity by legislative command).
101. 258 U.S. 50 (1922).
102. 268 U.S. 189 (1925).
103. For a discussion of these decisions, see BICKEL, *supra* note 58, at 164–201; Powell, *Current Conflicts*, *supra* note 88, at 472–75. *Lemke* and *Shafer* both relied heavily on *Bondurant*. Thomas Reed Powell commented on the *Lemke* decision that "[i]t is not unlikely" that it, like *Bondurant*, "was influenced by a disrelish of the particular state requirement involved." Thomas Reed Powell, *The Supreme Court's Review of Legislation in 1921–1922*, 37 POLITICAL SCIENCE QUARTERLY 486, 499 (1922).

North Dakota legislation had long been the bête noir of conservatives. *See, e.g.*, William Howard Taft, *North Dakota Politics* (December 13, 1920), in VIVIAN, at 509–12 ("There is much general interest in the politics of North Dakota, akin to that which there is in Russian affairs. North Dakota has been a laboratory for the trying out of novel political, social and economic experiments, and the people are paying the price."); Horace D. Taft to WHT (February 19, 1921) (Taft papers) ("The North Dakota situation is very diverting. The North Dakota people will be like the boy who was kicked by the mule. You know his father told him he would never be so handsome again, but he would know a great deal more. All the votes in the world can't make bankers lend the money even at nine per cent."); James F. Vivian, *"Not A Patriotic Party": William Howard Taft's Campaign against the Nonpartisan League, 1920-1921*, 50 NORTH DAKOTA HISTORY 4 (No. 4) (1983).

Taft was in fact sued for defamatory falsehood for his hostile comments on the North Dakota Nonpartisan League, and he was forced to issue a public retraction. *Mr. Taft Apologizes to Macdonald*, NONPARTISAN LEADER (March 7, 1921), at 18; *Mr. Taft Finds League Enemies Deceived Him*, NONPARTISAN LEADER (March 7, 1921), at 1 ("We want to thank Mr. Taft for the manly spirit he has shown in admitting his mistake."). Taft, however, persisted in his views, charging in his James Stokes Lectureship at New York University on April 30, 1921, that the Nonpartisan League "is not a patriotic American party. It has been made possible by the insistence of a number of unsuccessful and in many instances foreign born farmers in North Dakota, who were aroused by a real grievance, as to grain classification and rates, and who conceived the idea that through a political combination they could exclude every other class and every other interest and run the state for the farmers alone." WILLIAM HOWARD TAFT, REPRESENTATIVE GOVERNMENT IN THE UNITED STATES 27-28 (New York University Press 1921). *See Democracy Losing Prestige, Says Taft*, NEW YORK TIMES (May 1, 1921), at 19; *Taft Denounces Radical Parties*, WASHINGTON POST (May 1, 1921), at 7. Only a month before his nomination to be chief justice, Taft was attacked on the floor of the Senate for his hostility to the League. 61 CONG. REC. 917-22 (May 2, 1921) (statement of Senator Ladd):

> Ex-President Taft has during the past year gone out of his way repeatedly to cast reflections upon the farmers' aspirations as represented by the Nonpartisan League.... It is clearly evident Mr. Taft knows very little of the real problems of the practical farmer who tills his own land, but has depended upon information largely furnished by that group who have for ages and in North Dakota for the past 40 years farmed the farmers, and from which group the tillers of the soil are determined to break away in their own orderly fashion and as loyal American citizens, not, as Mr. Taft would have you believe, as hoodlums and anarchists.

The Nation even opposed Taft's appointment to the Court in part on the ground that "it must be perfectly plain that Mr. Taft will not be able to divest himself of an acquired prejudice in any case coming before him because of the activities" of the Nonpartisan League. *The Chief Justice – a Mistaken Appointment*, 113 THE NATION 32 (1921).

104. 260 U.S. 245 (1922); *see supra* text at note 27.
105. BICKEL, *supra* note 58, at 165.

CHAPTER 38

National Judicial Power and the American People

THE ORIGINS OF what is now called substantive due process doctrine are commonly said to lie in the 1897 decision of *Allgeyer v. Louisiana*, which involved a Louisiana statute that forbade Louisiana citizens from entering into contracts of insurance outside the state with foreign insurance companies that did not comply with Louisiana law.[1] Although *Allgeyer* spoke generally about the "liberty" protected by the Due Process Clause of the Fourteenth Amendment,[2] it explicitly acknowledged the right of Louisiana to prohibit contracts with noncomplying foreign insurance companies if made within the state.[3] The actual issue decided by the case concerned only Louisiana's authority to forbid contracts made outside the jurisdiction of the state:

> In the privilege of pursuing an ordinary calling or trade and of acquiring, holding and selling property must be embraced the right to make all proper contracts in relation thereto, and although it may be conceded that this right to contract in relation to persons or property or to do business within the jurisdiction of the State may be regulated and sometimes prohibited when the contracts or business conflict with the policy of the State as contained in its statutes, yet the power does not and cannot extend to prohibiting a citizen from making contracts of the nature involved in this case outside of the limits and jurisdiction of the State, and which are also to be performed outside of such jurisdiction; nor can the State legally prohibit its citizens from doing such an act as writing this letter of notification, even though the property which is the subject of the insurance may at the time when such insurance attaches be within the limits of the State. The mere fact that a citizen may be within the limits of a particular State does not prevent his making a contract outside its limits while he himself remains within it.[4]

Allgeyer held that a state could regulate insurance contracts made within its jurisdiction, but not those made outside its jurisdiction. Its holding was thus less about abstractly protecting liberty of contract than about protecting the access of citizens to the national market. Although federal courts normally sought to protect the integrity of the national market by using dormant Commerce Clause jurisprudence, that jurisprudence did not in 1897 apply to the insurance industry. Since the 1860s the Court had adhered to the position that "[t]he business of insurance is not commerce."[5] Protecting the national insurance market, therefore, required the Court to turn to the Due Process Clause instead of the dormant Commerce Clause.

We now distinguish the individual rights protected by the Due Process Clause from the structural concerns addressed by the dormant Commerce Clause. But this distinction did not exist during the Taft Court era. Just as the Taft Court used the dormant Commerce Clause to safeguard individual rights, so it also used the Due Process Clause to preserve the structural integrity of the national market. The Court willingly followed in *Allgeyer*'s footsteps. In *St. Louis Cotton Compress Co. v. Arkansas*, for example, Holmes relied on *Allgeyer* for the proposition that the Due Process Clause prohibited Arkansas from imposing a 5 percent tax on premiums paid by an out-of-state company for insurance on its Arkansas properties to insurance companies not authorized to do business in Arkansas. Holmes read *Allgeyer* to stand for the proposition that although "the State may regulate the activities of foreign corporations within the State," it "cannot regulate or interfere with what they do outside."[6]

In *Compañia General de Tabacos de Filipinas v. Collector of Internal Revenue*, the Taft Court considered a Philippine statute imposing a tax on extrajurisdictional contracts with foreign insurance companies not licensed to do business in the Philippines. Because federal legislation imposed "upon the Legislature of the Philippine Islands the same limitation by which the Fourteenth Amendment restrains the states of the Union," the Court read *Allgeyer* to stand for the proposition that a state "may not compel any one within its jurisdiction to pay tribute to it for contracts or money paid to secure the benefit of contracts made and to be performed outside of the state."[7]

Allgeyer, *St. Louis Cotton Compress* and *Compañia General de Tabacos de Filipinas* all advance the same nationalist agenda as that pursued by the Court in its dormant Commerce Clause jurisprudence. They seek to preserve the integrity of the national insurance market. But there is nevertheless an important difference between cases that rely on the Due Process Clause and cases that rely on the dormant Commerce Clause. When using the dormant Commerce Clause, the Court speaks in the name of Congress, even if Congress is in fact silent.[8] When using the Due Process Clause in decisions like *Allgeyer*, *St. Louis Cotton Compress*, or *Compañia General de Tabacos de Filipinas*, by contrast, the Court speaks directly for the Constitution. The Court takes it upon itself, as an exercise of Article III power, to use the Fourteenth Amendment to fashion a jurisprudence of individual rights that insulates the national market from balkanization.

The Taft Court went to great lengths to deploy individual rights under both the Due Process Clause and the Equal Protection Clause to prevent local discrimination against foreign corporations. In *Fidelity & Deposit Co. v. Tafoya*, for example, the Court used the Due Process Clause to strike down a New Mexico statute forbidding foreign insurance companies from paying nonresidents of New Mexico "for the obtaining, placing or writing of any policy ... of insurance covering risks" within the state.[9] Over the dissents of McReynolds, Brandeis, and Sanford, who thought that the case was moot, Holmes held that although a "State has the power and constitutional right arbitrarily to exclude" a foreign corporation, it could not do so "as part of a scheme to accomplish a forbidden result."[10] "Thus the right to exclude a foreign corporation cannot be used to prevent it from resorting to a federal court, or to tax it upon property that by established principles the State has no power to tax, or to interfere with interstate commerce. . . . A State cannot regulate the conduct of a foreign railroad corporation in another jurisdiction, even though the Company has tracks and does business in the State making the attempt."[11]

In *Hanover Fire Insurance Co. v. Harding*, the Court acknowledged "that foreign corporations can not do business in a State except by the consent of the State; that the State may exclude them arbitrarily or impose such conditions as it will upon their engaging in business within its jurisdiction," yet at the same time the Court held that "a number of decisions of recent years" demonstrated that "the State may not exact as a condition of the corporation's engaging in business within its limits that its rights secured to it by the Constitution of the United States may be infringed."[12] The Court in *Harding* invalidated as violative of the Equal Protection Clause a discriminatory tax on foreign corporations.[13]

In *Power Manufacturing Co. v. Saunders*, the Court struck down as inconsistent with the Equal Protection Clause an Arkansas statute that required suits against domestic corporations to be brought "in a county where it has a place of business or in which its chief officer resides," but that allowed suits against foreign corporations to be brought "in any county in the State."[14] Arkansas defended the statute on the ground that foreign corporations "impliedly assented to the venue provisions," but the Court rejected this argument, citing Taft Court precedents to the effect "that a foreign corporation by seeking and obtaining permission to do business in a State does not thereby become obligated to comply with or estopped from objecting to any provision in the state statutes which is in conflict with the Constitution of the United States."[15]

The elite bar in Arkansas applauded *Saunders*, because in their view the venue statute had kept "foreign capital out of Arkansas."[16] The Taft Court was deeply concerned with establishing, to the extent possible, a single continental market for national corporations. Exemplifying this "increasingly nationalistic outlook"[17] are the Court's determined efforts to ensure that national corporations would have access federal courts. As Taft remarked in 1922:

> Another test of the trained self-restraint of the American people is the constitutional and statutory provisions enabling non-residents to avoid the assumed local prejudice of state courts against them by trying their controversies with home people in Federal Courts. . . . It is not too much to say . . . that few factors in the rapid growth of the newer parts of the country have been more effective than the knowledge by those whose confidence and capital were needed to build up that new country that the Constitution and the laws of the nation furnished a national court wholly impartial between citizens of all the states in which their contracts and property rights, though they were non-residents, could be adjudged and protected. Such courts have in an indirect but most strikingly effective way united the sections of the country in a common effort to develop our great resources.[18]

In his first term as chief justice, Taft induced the Court in *Terral v. Burke Construction Co.*[19] to unanimously overturn longstanding precedents to ensure that foreign corporations would have unrestricted access to a federal forum. It was common practice before the 1920s for states legislatively to restrict the access of foreign corporations to federal courts.[20] The roots of the practice went back to a strongly pro-states' rights decision in 1868 holding that states had a virtually free hand in regulating foreign corporations.[21] Because states could exclude foreign corporations altogether, the Court had originally approved statutes allowing foreign corporations to operate in a state only upon condition that they refrain from suing in diversity in federal court or from removing cases to federal courts.[22] But the Court soon had second thoughts, and the result was a stream of waffling precedents that could not "be reconciled."[23]

Terral swept the deck clean by establishing the unambiguous principle "that a State may not, in imposing conditions upon the privilege of a foreign corporation's doing business in the State, exact from it a waiver of the exercise of its constitutional right to resort to the federal courts."[24] Taft enthusiastically announced:

> The principle does not depend for its application on the character of the business the corporation does, whether state or interstate, although that has been suggested as a distinction in some cases. It rests on the ground that the Federal Constitution confers upon citizens of one State the right to resort to federal courts in another, that state action, whether legislative or executive, necessarily calculated to curtail the free exercise of the right thus secured is void because the sovereign power of a State in excluding foreign corporations, as in the exercise of all others of its sovereign powers, is subject to the limitations of the supreme fundamental law.[25]

At stake in *Terral* was whether a foreign corporation could sue state residents in diversity jurisdiction or remove to federal court suits initially filed against it in state court. Foreign corporations sought the shelter of federal courts because of what the historian Edward Purcell has called "the system of corporate diversity litigation,"[26] which both in its doctrine and operation strongly favored corporate interests over those of employees and ordinary persons.[27] The system was for this reason quite controversial, and indeed it was one of the chief causes of the dissatisfaction with federal courts that Taft had long been concerned to allay.[28] Several months after *Terral*, for example, Senator Walsh of Montana gave a long and well-publicized speech looking "forward to the eventual abolition of the jurisdiction of the Federal courts in civil causes because of diversity of citizenship or alienage or because the controversy involves a Federal question."[29]

Taft rejected Walsh's position in part because Taft strongly believed that federal diversity jurisdiction was essential to underwrite national financial markets. As he told the American Bar Association in 1922:

> I venture to think that there may be a strong dissent from the view that danger of local prejudice in state courts against non-residents is at an end. Litigants from the eastern part of the country who are expected to invest their

capital in the West or South will hardly concede the proposition that their interests as creditors will be as sure of impartial judicial consideration in a western or southern state court as in a federal court. The material question is not so much whether the justice administered is actually impartial and fair, as it is whether it is thought to be so by those who are considering the wisdom of investing their capital in states where that capital is needed for the promotion of enterprises and industrial and commercial progress. No single element – and I want to emphasize this because I don't think it is always thought of – no single element in our governmental system has done so much to secure capital for the legitimate development of enterprises throughout the West and South as the existence of federal courts there, with a jurisdiction to hear diverse citizenship cases.[30]

Brandeis, who was close to Senator Walsh, opposed the system of corporate diversity litigation, and hence was hostile to diversity jurisdiction itself.[31] Brandeis noted that Taft "speaks feelingly" on the subject of diversity "whenever it [comes] up."

I think his point is theoretical, like much of the economists mouthing of the "rational man." Of course, the bankers & still less the investors, do not give the subject of litigation any thought when they make loans. What rate they get depends mainly on the money market, and the credit of the State or municipality. And we are reminded frequently that it is not the federal courts of the West and South, but those of New York in which the bankers' counsel are mainly interested. Moreover, they & everybody within every State ought to be made to care whether the State tribunals are worthy & not seek the "easier way."[32]

The Taft Court, however, followed Taft, not Brandeis, systematically seeking to protect the access of foreign corporations to federal diversity jurisdiction. The year after *Terral*, for example, it reached out in *Lee v. Chesapeake & Ohio Railway Co.*[33] to unanimously overturn another precedent, Ex parte *Wisner*.[34] *Wisner* had held that cases brought in a state court jurisdiction in which neither party resided could not be removed to federal district courts under diversity jurisdiction, because venue would have been improper as an original matter.[35] Aggressively settling "a much disputed question,"[36] Van Devanter in *Lee* pronounced *Wisner* "essentially unsound" and announced that "we feel constrained ... definitely to overrule it."[37]

Central to the Taft Court's understanding of the importance of federal courts was the doctrine of *Swift v. Tyson*,[38] which declared that federal courts could in diversity cases reach decisions on the basis of federal common law, or what at the time was called "general law, not based on any legislation of the State or local law or usage."[39] National corporations frequently invoked federal diversity jurisdiction, and in response federal common law established a distinct and generally pro-business legal regime[40] that served as the instrument of "a uniform policy toward interstate business."[41]

Federal common law was driven by the perceived needs of the national market. As one opponent of federal diversity jurisdiction argued in Congress, federal common law constituted the "centralization of power in the Federal Government" and the "obliteration of State lines."[42] Just as the Taft Court was willing to countenance national uniformity established by Congress in the Packers and Stockyards Act or the Grain Futures Act, so it was itself willing to impose such uniformity by establishing federal common law. Although *Bailey* and the Court's decisions interpreting federal anti-trust law strongly suggest that federal regulation of local and ordinary property aroused anxiety to preserve a separate and exclusive sphere of sovereign state police power, the Court strangely failed to experience any of this anxiety when federal courts applied general common law to local and ordinary transactions. The Court did not worry that the application of federal common law would impose the dead hand of national uniformity on local self-government.

It is true that congressional legislation flatly preempted state law, whereas federal common law could itself be displaced by explicit state legislation. Yet federal common law, coupled with federal diversity jurisdiction, was a powerful instrument of national integration that pushed aside ordinary state judicial decision-making. It is important to understand why federal common law did not provoke concerns about sacrificing state autonomy at the altar of a distant and bureaucratic national state. Although Article III courts and Congress were equally branches of the federal government, judicially constructed federal common law apparently stood in a different relationship to local self-government than did congressional legislation.

This is likely because the dominant view in the 1920s regarded common law as "springing from custom" that embodied "the experience of free men."[43] As Taft put it in 1905, whereas "under the civil law the state seems a separate entity, different from the people who constitute it, ... at the common law the theory is that the state is ... a great partnership in which [the individual] has a voice."[44] When the Taft Court announced rules of common law, therefore, it imagined itself as speaking for the fundamental values of the entire American people, and not merely for distinct values associated specifically with the federal government. The entire conceptual apparatus of dual sovereignty simply dropped away in the context of common law adjudication.

This allows us to glimpse a fundamental, but to modern eyes almost invisible, dimension of the Taft Court's authority. We have now so thoroughly assimilated the positivism of Holmes that we implicitly and inevitably imagine federal courts as speaking specifically for national law. But in the prepositivist 1920s, the Court frequently imagined itself as speaking for a law that came neither from the federal government nor from a state government. It sought instead to directly express the customs and beliefs of the American people. The Taft Court was in this respect like a common law court for the entire nation.

Understanding this source of authority is relevant not merely for the somewhat obscure subject of federal common law, but also for the Court's power to declare constitutional law. Although today we sharply distinguish between constitutional and common law courts, in the 1920s these two forms of judicial power were conceptually and jurisprudentially connected. One cannot begin to appreciate the nature of constitutional law during the Taft Court era without grasping that when the Court pronounced the meaning of the Constitution, it could speak in a register that transcended the reach of merely federal authority. When the Court construed the Fourteenth Amendment, it conceived itself as speaking for the American people as a whole, just as it did when establishing federal common law.[45] As McReynolds once put it, "In the last analysis it is for us to determine what is arbitrary or oppressive upon consideration of the natural and inherent principles of practical justice which lie at the base of our traditional jurisprudence and inspirit our Constitution."[46]

It is for this reason that the Supreme Court, in the years before the constitutional crisis of the New Deal, felt at liberty to use its constitutional authority to discern the "public morals" of the country, even in defiance of a contrary congressional judgment, as was the case in the context of child labor.[47] It is why the Court could so confidently fuse the Constitution with "those privileges long recognized at common law as essential to the orderly pursuit of happiness by free men," as in *Meyer*.[48] To understand constitutional law before the New Deal, in other words, is to appreciate that when the Court interpreted the Constitution it did not necessarily conceive itself as merely an arm of the federal government. It could speak for an American ethos that swept aside distinctions between state and national sovereignties. This is precisely the transcendent authority that the Court would formally renounce a decade later in *Erie Railroad Co. v. Tompkins*.[49] The positivism theorized by Holmes during the 1920s would cut very deeply indeed.

Consider the Taft Court's most controversial application of federal common law – *Black & White Taxicab & Transfer Co. v. Brown & Yellow Taxicab & Transfer Co.*[50] The facts of the case were particularly embarrassing. The Brown & Yellow Taxicab Company had entered into a contract with the Louisville & Nashville Railroad Company for the exclusive privilege of servicing the road's depot at Bowling Green. Such exclusive contracts, however, were unenforceable under Kentucky law; they were deemed monopolistic and contrary to public policy.[51] Not to be deterred, the Brown & Yellow Company, with the support of the railroad, reincorporated itself in Tennessee and invoked diversity jurisdiction to bring suit against the railroad and a competitive taxicab company in federal district court in Kentucky. Because federal common law would enforce monopolistic contracts, the company won a decree preventing any interference with its exclusive privileges.

Speaking for six justices, Butler, upheld this disposition of the case. He took the occasion to issue a ringing endorsement of federal common law:

> For the discovery of common law principles applicable in any case, investigation is not limited to the decisions of the courts of the State in which the controversy arises. State and federal courts go to the same sources for evidence of the existing applicable rule. The effort of both is to ascertain that rule. ... As respects the rule of decision to be followed by federal courts, distinction has always been made between statutes of a State and the decisions of its courts on questions of general law. The applicable rule sustained by many

decisions of this Court is that in determining questions of general law, the federal courts, while inclining to follow the decisions of the courts of the State in which the controversy arises, are free to exercise their own independent judgment.[52]

It is noteworthy that Butler's defense of federal common law explicitly turns on the notion that the common law can be assigned to neither state nor federal spheres of sovereignty. The "sources" of the common law were understood to be deeper than any such artificial governmental distinctions.

Holmes authored one of his most brilliant and influential dissents,[53] contending that federal recourse to general law constituted "an unconstitutional assumption of powers by the courts of the United States which no lapse of time or respectable array of opinion should make us hesitate to correct."[54] Holmes argued that there was no "transcendental body of law outside of any particular State but obligatory within it unless and until changed by statute."[55] Unpacking the implications of his positivist jurisprudence, Holmes explained that law "does not exist without some definite authority behind it,"[56] and that "the common law so far as it is enforced in a State ... is not the common law generally but the law of that State existing by the authority of that State without regard to what it may have been in England or anywhere else."[57] "[I]t is a question of the authority by which certain particular acts, here the grant of exclusive privileges in a railroad station, are governed. In my opinion the authority and only authority is the State, and if that be so, the voice adopted by the State as its own should utter the last word."[58] Holmes advocated that *Swift* be left "undisturbed," but that it should not be allowed to spread its "assumed dominion into new fields."[59]

Black & White Taxicab sparked fierce controversy.[60] The stakes of the debate cannot be understood, however, until it is noticed that the Court interpreted federal common law to reflect exactly the same preoccupations as the Court's due process jurisprudence. Butler specifically justified the federal rule upholding monopolistic contracts on the ground that:

> Care is to be observed lest the doctrine that a contract is void as against public policy be unreasonably extended. Detriment to the public interest is not to be presumed in the absence of showing that something improper is done or contemplated. ... And it is to be remembered, as stated by Sir George Jessel, M.R., in Printing Company v. Sampson, that public policy requires that competent persons "shall have the utmost liberty of contracting, and that their contracts, when entered into fairly and voluntarily shall be held sacred, and shall be enforced by Courts of justice." The station grounds belong to the railroad company and it lawfully may put them into any use that does not interfere with its duties as a common carrier.[61]

Butler's celebration of freedom of contract could have been lifted directly from *Adkins*.[62]

Protecting economic liberty was a policy that the Taft Court pursued *both* in its due process doctrine *and* in its articulation of federal common law. In each context the policy had profound structural implications for the distribution of power between federal and state governments. In interpreting the Fourteenth Amendment, the Court understood itself to be articulating "the fundamental principles of liberty and justice which lie at the base of all our civil and political institutions" and which "are applicable alike in all the States and do not depend upon or vary with local legislation."[63] These principles flowed directly from the deepest mores of the American people.

The Taft Court sought to protect economic liberty in the context of both common and constitutional law.[64] Both forms of law served as powerful instruments of centralization.[65] A constitutional decision like *Adkins* impressed a dead uniformity on the states, rendering "invalid . . . any State minimum wage law which might come before the Court."[66] The Taft Court's robust expansion of due process doctrine would eventually provoke Thomas Reed Powell to protest that "[f]or one interested in local self government the work of the Supreme Court of the United States in applying the Fourteenth Amendment to state legislation must raise the question whether judicial centralization is not pushed to an extreme under our federal system."[67] "The due process clauses ought to go," argued the *New Republic*, because "the centralizing authority lodged with the Supreme Court over the domestic affairs of forty-eight widely different states is an authority which it simply cannot discharge with safety either to itself or to the states."[68]

The Taft Court, however, was unmoved by fears of over-centralization. Its allegiance to normative dualism seemed simply to vanish in the context of both constitutional law and general federal common law. This was because in each context the Taft Court arrogated to itself the authority to speak for the one united people of America. Despite the strenuous protests of Holmes and Brandeis,[69] the Court exercised its authority in a manner that was largely unchecked by countervailing considerations of local self-government. The Taft Court imagined the federal judiciary as altogether beyond the logic of federalism.[70] The mandate of Article III courts was to conserve "the general welfare, material and moral," of the "one people" who inhabited the United States of America.[71] It would take the existential controversies of the New Deal to unsettle this grand and innocent mandate.[72]

The deepest significance of *Erie Railroad Co. v. Tompkins* lay in the Court's theoretical renunciation of the generalized moral authority of a common law court. Henceforth the Court's role would be to enforce merely positive federal law. But what exactly was the "positive" law of the Constitution? In Holmes's view, the minimal content of the Constitution lay chiefly in the compulsion of its few words. In Brandeis's view, by contrast, the content of the Constitution lay in the richer ideals of a national democratic state. In the view of Taft and other conservatives, the Constitution was primarily about protecting the property rights essential for economic prosperity. This view was largely repudiated in the furnace of the New Deal.

In the decades after *Erie*, the challenge of ascertaining the positive law of the Constitution would shape the Court's frantic search for a source of authority adequate to its constitutional ambitions. The full force of this constitutional crisis would not become evident until the Court had repudiated its traditional common law authority to speak for the diffuse mores of the people themselves.[73] The 1920s was probably the last moment when the Court could unself-consciously assume the imperial authority of that lost voice.

The Taft Court

Notes

1. 165 U.S. 578, 588 (1897): "We have then a contract which it is conceded was made outside and beyond the limits of the jurisdiction of the State of Louisiana, being made and to be performed within the State of New York, where the premiums were to be paid and losses, if any, adjusted."
2. *Id.* at 589:

    > The liberty mentioned in that amendment means not only the right of the citizen to be free from the mere physical restraint of his person, as by incarceration, but the term is deemed to embrace the right of the citizen to be free in the enjoyment of all his faculties; to be free to use them in all lawful ways; to live and work where he will; to earn his livelihood by any lawful calling; to pursue any livelihood or avocation, and for that purpose to enter into all contracts which may be proper, necessary and essential to his carrying out to a successful conclusion the purposes above mentioned.

3. *Id.* at 590–91:

    > Has not a citizen of a State, under the provisions of the Federal Constitution above mentioned, a right to contract outside of the State for insurance on his property – a right of which state legislation cannot deprive him? We are not alluding to acts done within the State by an insurance company or its agents doing business therein, which are in violation of the state statutes. Such acts come within the principle of the Hooper case [155 U.S. 648 (1895)], and would be controlled by it. When we speak of the liberty to contract for insurance or to do an act to effectuate such a contract already existing, we refer to and have in mind the facts of this case, where the contract was made outside the State, and as such was a valid and proper contract.

4. *Id.* at 591–92.
5. Hooper v. California, 155 U.S. 648, 655 (1895); Paul v. Virginia, 75 U.S. 168, 183 (1868) ("Issuing a policy of insurance is not a transaction of commerce."). In *Allgeyer*, therefore, the Court started from the premise that "[t]here is no doubt of the power of the State to prohibit foreign insurance companies from doing business within its limits. The State can impose such conditions as it pleases upon the doing of any business by those companies within its borders, and unless the conditions be complied with the prohibition may be absolute. The cases upon this subject are cited in the opinion of the court in Hooper v. California." 165 U.S. at 583. It would not be until 1944 that the Supreme Court would overrule almost seventy years of doctrine to hold that Congress could regulate insurance as a consequence of its authority to control interstate commerce. United States v. South-Eastern Underwriters Ass'n, 322 U.S. 533, 553 (1944). On the special circumstances of the insurance industry in the 1920s, see EDWARD A. PURCELL, JR., LITIGATION AND INEQUALITY: FEDERAL DIVERSITY JURISDICTION IN INDUSTRIAL AMERICA, 1870–1958, at 205–13 (New York: Oxford University Press 1992).
6. 260 U.S. 346, 348–49 (1922).
7. 275 U.S. 87, 91, 94–95 98 (1927). Taft authored the Court's opinion, which was for seven justices. Holmes, Brandeis, and Sanford had dissented in conference. No vote is recorded for Sutherland. Sanford eventually switched his vote. We have extant a letter from Van Devanter to Taft, arguing that even "[g]ranted that the property as such was taxable while in the Philippines, that affords no ground for saying that the Philippine government may tax transactions and business done outside the

jurisdictional limits of that government." WVD to WHT (November 11, 1927) (Taft papers). Taft replied, "I send you herewith my opinion. . . . I wish you would look this over and let me know what you think about the solution here suggested. I am sending this to Pierce and to Mac, and I am sending it also to Stone, because you know he voted with us, before I circulate it." WHT to WVD (November 16, 1927) (Taft papers). On that same day, Taft wrote McReynolds that "Brandeis and Holmes have been talking with Stone, and I don't know whether he will stay put or not." WHT to JCM (November 16, 1927) (Taft papers).

Holmes authored a dissent in the case, joined by Brandeis. Holmes distinguished *Allgeyer* and *St. Louis Cotton Compress Co.* on the ground that the taxes in those cases were penalties rather than true taxes. The distinction between taxes and penalties had formed the foundation of Taft's own opinion in Bailey v. Drexel Furniture Co., 259 U.S. 20, 38 (1922). Although the point is a little obscure, a modern account of Holmes's dissent would stress his observation that when government "taxes domestic insurance it reasonably may endeavor not to let the foreign insurance escape. If it does not discriminate against the latter it naturally does not want to discriminate against its own." *Compañía General*, 275 U.S. at 101 (Holmes, J., dissenting). Holmes and Brandeis contended that it did not matter that the Philippines taxed domestic insurance contracts by laying the tax "upon the company," whereas in the case of foreign insurance the Philippines imposed the same tax by laying it "upon the insured." What mattered was only that "the rule of taxation" imposed upon domestic and foreign insurance companies was "uniform." *Id.* Holmes's dissent is notable for its famous aperçu that "Taxes are what we pay for civilized society, including the chance to insure." *Id.* at 100. Holmes's clerk at the time recalls that when Holmes

> was working on the opinion, the Justice (presumably to amuse himself) asked me what the difference was between a tax and a penalty. I said it was a question of moral feeling; if the discouraged act carried general moral condemnation, the exaction was a penalty. He condemned this suggestion with some scorn. The law, he said, must not be confused with morals. I suspect that the vigor of his rejection of the suggestion hid a doubt. His own definition of a penalty depends on the state of mind of the legislators, which probably has an origin in some general public feeling of social condemnation. I suspect that the impost in question disclosed an intention in the minds of the island legislators to stop purchases of foreign insurance.

David M. O'Brien, *Sutherland's Recollections of Justice Holmes*, 1988 YEARBOOK OF THE SUPREME COURT HISTORICAL SOCIETY 18, 24.

Compañía General was understood in the literature to have very broad implications. "To say that this tax results in some prohibition of foreign business and so is invalid, amounts to saying that no tax on foreign contracts is legal. So the case seems necessarily to decide that a tax on acts outside the state is unconstitutional." *Taxation – May a State Levy a Tax on Acts Done Outside the State?*, 26 MICHIGAN LAW REVIEW 803, 804 (1928). *See State Regulation of Foreign Made Contracts under the Fourteenth Amendment*, 41 HARVARD LAW REVIEW 390, 393 (1928) ("The doctrine of the *Allgeyer* case must, therefore, rest on the idea that the due process clause incorporated the common law notion that a state's jurisdiction extends no further than its borders."). For a general discussion of the cases, see Nathan Greene, *The Allgeyer Case as a Constitutional Embrasure of*

Territoriality, 2 St. John's Law Review 22 (1927); Thomas Reed Powell, *The Supreme Court and State Police Power, 1922–1930* (pt. 5), 18 Virginia Law Review 131, 150–57 (1931).
8. Hence Congress could overrule judgments of the Court rendered under the dormant Commerce Clause. *See* Clark Distilling Co. v. Western Maryland Railway Co., 242 U.S. 311 (1917).
9. 270 U.S. 426, 433, 436 (1926). New Mexico sought to justify the law as a prophylactic

> to prevent the use of dummy agents in the State. It was suggested that agents were paid by commissions at well known conventional rates, and that the statute meant to forbid the dividing of these commissions, and in that way to prevent the work being done and paid for elsewhere, while nominal agents in New Mexico were paid small sums for the use of their names. In short, it is said the purpose was to secure responsible men to represent the Company on the spot.

Id. at 435. In the original draft of his opinion, Holmes continued after this passage: "We are far from saying that such a purpose was not legitimate or that the State might not use all its powers to accomplish it." (Holmes papers). Butler, however, objected to the sentence. "I think the State without power to forbid payment for work done outside to secure business within, and that the Company and its 'agents' in New Mexico may make their own arrangements as to compensation. At any rate, the statements and implications indicating the contrary seem unnecessary. Is it not enough to take the statute at what it says & condemn it?" *Id.* Van Devanter agreed with Butler: "I am not prepared to go so far. An agent who does only half the work cannot be entitled to full commission by mere legislative edict – at least I should not want to say ... that now." *Id.* Taft also chimed in: "I suggest that it is not wise for us to decide in this case more than we have to decide. I hesitate to intimate what our views might be on a statute differently drawn. It might return to plague us." *Id.* Taft also wrote separately to Sutherland to report that: "Van Devanter is disposed to criticise the language ... that I have marked ... as intimating an opinion as to what we might think of the statute if it made another provision. I agree with him that it is wiser not to give our opinion on another act than the one we have before us." WHT to GS (January 13, 1926) (Sutherland papers). Holmes eventually removed the sentence.
10. *Tafoya*, 270 U.S. at 434. *See* Palmetto Fire Ins. Co. v. Connecticut, 272 U.S. 295, 304 (1926) (citing *Tafoya* for the principle that the state may not use the power to exclude to accomplish an unconstitutional result).
11. *Tafoya*, 270 U.S. at 434–35.
12. 272 U.S. 494, 507 (1926). In Bothwell v. Buckbee, Mears Co., 275 U.S. 274 (1927), by contrast, the Court, speaking through a unanimous Brandeis opinion, held that a foreign corporation's access to a state court could properly be conditioned on its complying with registration requirements before doing business in the state. Brandeis distinguished *Allgeyer* and *St. Louis Cotton Compress* on the ground that those cases merely held "that a state may not prohibit either a citizen or a resident from making a contract – in other words, doing an act – in another state," whereas in this case what was involved was a state's power to prohibit a foreign corporation "from doing business within the state without first complying with the prescribed conditions," and denying to a foreign corporation "the aid of its courts in enforcing a contract which involved violation of its laws." *Id.* at 276–77.

McReynolds, who had voted the other way in conference, responded to the draft of Brandeis's opinion with the comment, "I feel quite uncertain but do not care to say anything." (Brandeis papers).

13. The opinion was unanimous. Brandeis wrote Taft, "I hope you will consent to delete so much of [your opinion] as finds discrimination in the immunity of foreign casualty corporations from the tax. I think this is not shown to be an arbitrary classification. . . . You have threaded your way skillfully through a labyrinth beset with dangers; and I should be sorry to have to withhold assent to your opinion." LDB to WHT (November 2, 1926) (Taft papers).
14. 274 U.S. 490, 491–92 (1927). *See* Ky. Fin. Corp. v. Paramount Auto Exch. Corp., 262 U.S. 544, 551 (1923).
15. *Saunders*, 274 U.S. at 496–97. The Court cited *Harding* and Frost & Frost Trucking Co. v. Railroad Commission, 271 U.S. 583 (1926). *Saunders*, 274 U.S. at 497. In dissent, Holmes, joined by Brandeis, refused to extend the logic of *Tafoya* to the question of equal protection:

> In order to enter into most of the relations of life people have to give up some of their Constitutional rights. If a man makes a contract he gives up the Constitutional right that previously he had to be free from the hamper that he puts upon himself. Some rights, no doubt, a person is not allowed to renounce, but very many he may. So we must go further than merely to point to the Fourteenth Amendment. I see nothing in it to prevent a foreign corporation agreeing with the State that it will be subject to the general law of torts and will submit to a transitory action wherever it may be sued. . . . While we adhere to the rule that a State may exclude foreign corporations altogether it seems to me a mistake to apply the inequality clause of the Fourteenth Amendment with meticulous nicety. The Amendment has been held not to overthrow ancient practices even when hard to reconcile with justice. I think there are stronger grounds for not reducing the power of the States to attach conditions to a consent that they have a right to refuse, when there is no attempt to use the conditions to invade forbidden fields.

Id. at 497–98 (Holmes, J., dissenting). Van Devanter, who authored *Saunders*, was appalled by Holmes's dissent. He sent a copy of the opinion to his close friend Walter Sanborn, chief judge of the Eighth Circuit, commenting "I particularly ask you to look at the dissenting opinion. I hardly know what would be left if it were the prevailing opinion." WVD to Walter H. Sanborn (June 4, 1927) (Van Devanter papers). Sanborn answered, "I am very glad that you and your associates who agree with you in this opinion and others like it control the Supreme Court of the United States. If instead of Justices Sutherland, Butler and Stone there had been placed upon the Supreme Court gentlemen whose minds naturally run in accord with the views of the dissenters in this case, it seems to me that the personal rights and property rights of the citizens and corporations of the United States would have been without protection." Walter H. Sanborn to WVD (June 15, 1927) (Van Devanter papers).
16. George B. Rose to WVD (June 8, 1927) (Van Devanter papers). Rose, a prominent Arkansas attorney, wrote Van Devanter to praise *Saunders*: "The decision . . . is not only right in principle; but it is one of the greatest blessings that ever came to our State. Petty lawyers interested in damage suits against foreign corporations have kept this infamous statute upon the books and have harrassed [sic] such corporations by bringing suits in the most remote counties, and often in counties where the cards had been stacked against the defendant; and nothing has done so much to keep

foreign capital out of Arkansas. It is the honest people of the State who will be the greatest beneficiaries of this epoch-making decision; but no doubt its benefits will be felt in many other jurisdictions." *Id.* Van Devanter was so pleased with the Rose letter that he sent an excerpt of it to Taft. WVD to WHT (June 13, 1927) (Van Devanter papers).

17. PURCELL, *supra* note 5, at 192.
18. William Howard Taft, *At the Cradle of Its Greatness, Address at the Rededication of the Old Supreme Court Building in Philadelphia*, 8 AMERICAN BAR ASSOCIATION JOURNAL 333, 335 (1922).
19. 257 U.S. 529 (1922).
20. About half of the states imposed such restrictions. PURCELL, *supra* note 5, at 205.
21. Paul v. Virginia, 75 U.S. (8 Wall.) 168, 181 (1868):

> Now a grant of corporate existence is a grant of special privileges to the corporators, enabling them to act for certain designated purposes as a single individual, and exempting them (unless otherwise specially provided) from individual liability. The corporation being the mere creation of local law, can have no legal existence beyond the limits of the sovereignty where created. . . . The recognition of its existence even by other States, and the enforcement of its contracts made therein, depend purely upon the comity of those States – a comity which is never extended where the existence of the corporation or the exercise of its powers are prejudicial to their interests or repugnant to their policy. Having no absolute right of recognition in other States, but depending for such recognition and the enforcement of its contracts upon their assent, it follows, as a matter of course, that such assent may be granted upon such terms and conditions as those States may think proper to impose. They may exclude the foreign corporation entirely; they may restrict its business to particular localities, or they may exact such security for the performance of its contracts with their citizens as in their judgment will best promote the public interest. The whole matter rests in their discretion.

22. Doyle v. Cont'l Ins. Co., 94 U.S. 535, 542 (1876).
23. *Terral*, 257 U.S. at 532.
24. *Id.* Edward Purcell writes that after *Terral*, "[f]or the first time since the corporate system developed in the 1870s . . . insurers had unrestricted and unproblematic access to federal courts across the nation. They wasted no time in taking advantage of the opportunity." PURCELL, *supra* note 5, at 205. Former congressman George K. Denton wrote Taft that "by reason of the recent holding of the United States Supreme Court that foreign corporations may remove causes into the Federal Court even though they are not engaged in Interstate Commerce," he expected "that almost all insurance cases where the amount involved is more that [sic] $3,000 will be removed by one party or the other and this is true I think of corporation cases generally." George K. Denton to WHT (December 27, 1922) (Taft papers). He predicted that federal dockets would soon be clogged.

Terral was understood to revive the doctrine of "unconstitutional conditions," which the Court had initially developed to regulate state prohibitions on foreign corporations. For a discussion of the doctrine, see GERARD CARL HENDERSON, THE POSITION OF FOREIGN CORPORATIONS IN AMERICAN CONSTITUTIONAL LAW 132–47 (Cambridge: Harvard University Press 1918). The Taft Court experienced great difficulties in establishing a clear or consistent account of this doctrine. *Compare* Packard v. Banton, 264 U.S. 140, 144 (1924) ("The streets belong to the public and are primarily for the use of the public in the ordinary way. Their use

National Judicial Power & the American People

for the purposes of gain is special and extraordinary and, generally at least, may be prohibited or conditioned as the legislature deems proper."), *with* Frost & Frost Trucking Co. v. R.R. Comm'n, 271 U.S. 583, 593–94 (1926) ("It would be a palpable incongruity to strike down an act of state legislation which . . . seeks to strip the citizen of rights guaranteed by the federal Constitution, but to uphold an act by which the same result is accomplished under the guise of a surrender of a right in exchange for a valuable privilege which the state threatens otherwise to withhold. . . . [The state] may not impose conditions which require the relinquishment of constitutional rights.").

The prominent St. Louis corporate attorney Frederick N. Judson had theorized as early as 1891 the relationship between constitutional protections for freedom of contract and unconstitutional conditions doctrine as applied to nonresident corporations: "It is clear that if the power of the State to fix the conditions upon which nonresident corporations are permitted to engage in business in the State with its citizens is construed as including the regulation of the terms of the private contracts which they are permitted to make, it will necessarily follow that in the departments of business, constantly becoming more numerous, which, under modern conditions, are necessarily transacted through organized and concentrated capital, the right of private contract may be effectually abolished and the system of 'official contracts' substituted therefor." Frederick N. Judson, *Liberty of Contract under the Police Power*, in REPORT OF THE FOURTEENTH ANNUAL MEETING OF THE AMERICAN BAR ASSOCIATION 249–50 (Philadelphia: Dando Printing & Publishing Co. 1891).

25. *Terral*, 257 U.S. at 532–33. Within the year the Court, speaking unanimously through Sutherland, was forced explicitly to correct Taft's odd implication that there was a constitutional right to resort to federal courts, whether by filing a cause of action or by removal. In Kline v. Burke Construction Co., 260 U.S. 226 (1922), the Court backtracked, saying that there was no such right "derived from the Constitution of the United States, unless in a very indirect sense. Certainly it is not a right granted by the Constitution." *Id.* at 233. The Constitution merely authorized Congress to create or withdraw access to lower federal courts. "The Constitution simply gives to the inferior courts the capacity to take jurisdiction in the enumerated cases, but it requires an act of Congress to confer it." *Id.* at 234. *See* PURCELL, *supra* note 5, at 207. Four years later, however, Taft reasserted for a unanimous Court that the right "to remove suits . . . from the state courts to the federal courts" was a "constitutional right." Hanover Fire Insurance Co. v. Harding, 272 U.S. 494, 507 (1926). On the importance of *Terral*, see Frost & Frost Trucking Co. v. R.R. Comm'n, 271 U.S. 583, 594–95 (1926).

26. PURCELL, *supra* note 5, at 8–9.
27. On the procedural advantages of a federal forum, see *supra* Chapter 15, at 509–11.
28. *See* William Howard Taft, *Criticisms of the Federal Judiciary*, 29 AMERICAN LAW REVIEW 641, 659 (1895).
29. 62 CONG. REC. 8549 (June 12, 1922).
30. William Howard Taft, *Possible and Needed Reforms in Administration of Justice in Federal Courts*, 8 AMERICAN BAR ASSOCIATION JOURNAL 601, 604 (1922). Taft had been expressing this same view since 1895. *See, e.g.*, Taft, *supra* note 28, at 658–59.
31. LDB to Felix Frankfurter (April 2, 1925), in BRANDEIS-FRANKFURTER CORRESPONDENCE, at 200.

32. LDB to Felix Frankfurter (May 10, 1928), in BRANDEIS-FRANKFURTER CORRESPONDENCE, at 331–32. In August 1924, Brandeis argued to Frankfurter that "claims as to what investors will do, what will or won't frighten [them] off" were grossly exaggerated. *Brandeis-Frankfurter Conversations*, at 331 (August 2, 1924). The "truth" is, Brandeis asserted, that "pressure of money & pressure of its manipulation (bankers) lead to investment & no causal connection between decisions & legislation & refusal to invest." *Id.* Frankfurter later published an article reasserting Brandeis's position: "[I]t is urged that eastern investments in the west and south are exposed in state tribunals to the risks of unfairness toward non-resident capital. This is an old claim, and has the momentum of constant repetition. But, surely, the argument is theoretical. Bankers, and still less investors, do not contemplate litigation for default when they make loans. What rate they get depends mainly on the money market and the credit of borrowers." Felix Frankfurter, *Distribution of Judicial Power between United States and State Courts*, 13 CORNELL LAW QUARTERLY 499, 521 (1928). Tony Freyer, however, argues that federal courts were in fact "instrumental in overcoming local resistance to national business during the late nineteenth century." Tony A. Freyer, *The Federal Courts, Localism, and the National Economy, 1865–1900*, 53 BUSINESS HISTORY REVIEW 343, 344 (1979).

33. 260 U.S. 653 (1923). Butler's docket book shows that *Lee* was unanimous in conference.

34. 203 U.S. 449 (1906).

35. *Id.* at 460–61. For a discussion of *Lee* and *Wisner*, see PURCELL, *supra* note 5, at 191–93. *Wisner* had caused endless difficulties. *See, e.g., In re* Moore, 209 U.S. 490, 507 (1908) (noting that the *Wisner* holding did not apply where the parties consented to the jurisdiction of a federal district court); *Removal of Causes When Neither Party Is a Resident of the State in which Suit Is Brought*, 71 UNIVERSITY OF PENNSYLVANIA LAW REVIEW 242, 246 (1923) (arguing that "[t]he Wisner case and those Federal cases following it have confused general jurisdiction with venue, and cannot be supported in reason").

36. *Current Decision, Lee v. Chesapeake & Ohio Ry. Co.*, 32 YALE LAW JOURNAL 747, 747 (1923).

37. *Lee*, 260 U.S. at 660. Shortly after *Lee* was announced, Van Devanter wrote a friend to explain the import of the decision:

> Of recent years there has been very great difficulty about the jurisdiction of District Courts on removals from state courts, and the matter reached a stage of intolerable uncertainty and diverging opinions. Some of the District Courts were remanding cases which others retained. Removals were made from state courts such as Washington and Montana to the District Courts in New Jersey and Maryland. A District Court in New York declined to remand a cause which had been removed into it from a state court in Vermont. Some of the District Judges said the matter was very plainly settled one way and others asserted with equal confidence that it was settled the other way. Some were frank enough to tell the truth and say that the whole matter was in great confusion. All of this was due to two very unfortunate decisions in our court. The first was the Wisner case, in 203 U.S., and the second was the Moore case, in 209 U.S. There were later decisions following both in an indulgent way and attempting to explain them, although logically that was impossible. The Wisner case was dead wrong, but was consistent with itself. The Moore case was a miserable straddle and not really in accord with anything. It tried to correct the Wisner case and did so in a degree, but it did

not strike it down. I wrote a couple of opinions this term which I believe have untangled the subject and substituted order for chaos.

WVD to A.C. Campbell (March 6, 1923) (Van Devanter papers). John Clarke, retired from the Court at the time of *Lee*, wrote Van Devanter after the decision that it was "in your best vein and does what should have been done years ago. It was one of those unfortunate straddles which some men persuade themselves are very astute & which others let pass rather than oppose. You clean it up nicely & make me more confident even than your letter did that all is well." JHC to WVD (March 2, 1923) (Van Devanter papers).

38. 41 U.S. 1 (1842).
39. Salem Trust Co. v. Mfrs.' Fin. Co., 264 U.S. 182, 191 (1924). Although there were a few narrow exceptions, federal courts generally viewed themselves as bound by state statutes and state interpretations of such statutes. Keith v. Johnson, 271 U.S. 1, 8 (1926); Risty v. Chi., Rock Island, & Pac. Ry. Co., 270 U.S. 378, 387 (1926); Edward Hines Yellow Pine Trs. v. Martin, 268 U.S. 458, 462, 464 (1925); Mason v. United States, 260 U.S. 545, 557 (1923).
40. Freyer, *supra* note 32, at 355 ("[I]t was fairly well acknowledged that federal courts favored national business – which was usually corporate business.").
41. *Id.* at 362. "The virtues of the Swift v. Tyson idea as a device for achieving national uniformity," remarked Grant Gilmore, "are obvious." GRANT GILMORE, THE AGES OF AMERICAN LAW 34 (New Haven: Yale University Press 1977). As noted at the annual meeting of the American Bar Association in 1882, federal common law was the law "not of one state, but of all the states; not of a section, but of the entire people; not of local interests, but of the general welfare. It is the only homogeneous law we have." *Special Comm., Am. Bar Ass'n, Minority Report on the Relief of the United States Courts*, in REPORT OF THE FIFTH ANNUAL MEETING OF THE AMERICAN BAR ASSOCIATION 378 (Philadelphia: George S. Harris & Sons 1883). *See* TONY FREYER, HARMONY & DISSONANCE: THE SWIFT & ERIE CASES IN AMERICAN FEDERALISM 81–82 (New York University Press 1981) (discussing the report's support for *Swift*). In 1932, Judge John J. Parker passionately asserted that "[n]o power exercised under the Constitution has, in my judgment, had greater influence in welding these United States into a single nation" than federal diversity jurisdiction. John J. Parker, *The Federal Jurisdiction and Recent Attacks Upon It*, 18 AMERICAN BAR ASSOCIATION JOURNAL 433, 437 (1932). "[N]othing has done more to foster interstate commerce and communication and the uninterrupted flow of capital for investment into the various parts of the Union; and nothing has been so potent in sustaining the public credit and the sanctity of private contracts." *Id.* Diversity jurisdiction, Parker argued, created a "uniformity of decision throughout the United States in matters of general law." *Id.* at 438.
42. 10 CONG. REC. 1278 (March 3, 1880) (statement of Representative Richard W. Townshend). *See* FREYER, *supra* note 41, at 79–80. Read in full, Townshend's observations invoke classic themes of federalism: "What does all this mean? It is easily to be seen that it means centralization of power in the Federal Government. It means a distrust of the capacity of the people for self-government. ... It means a strong government. It means an obliteration of State lines and the degradation of the State judiciary." 10 CONG. REC. 1278 (March 3, 1880). Harry Scheiber

characterizes the development of federal common law as a "centralizing doctrine of major import." Harry N. Scheiber, *Federalism and the American Economic Order, 1789–1910*, 10 LAW & SOCIETY REVIEW 56, 102 (1975). On the scope of federal common law, see Erie R.R. Co. v. Tompkins, 304 U.S. 64, 75–76 (1938) (discussing the diverse topics addressed within "general law").

43. Charles Evans Hughes, *American Lawyers Welcomed in Historic Westminster Hall, Response on Behalf of the American Bar Association*, 10 AMERICAN BAR ASSOCIATION JOURNAL 567, 569 (1924).

44. William Howard Taft, *The Administration of Criminal Law*, 15 YALE LAW JOURNAL 1, 2 (1905). Taft regarded the common law as a form of "customary law handed down from one generation to another," and therefore as growing out of the people themselves. William Howard Taft, *The Selection and Tenure of Judges*, in REPORT OF THE THIRTY-SIXTH ANNUAL MEETING OF THE AMERICAN BAR ASSOCIATION 419–20 (Baltimore: Lord Baltimore Press 1913).

45. The Taft Court's jurisprudence of judicial comity is an important exception to this generalization. The conceptual framework of dual sovereignty was highly influential in the Court's understanding of issues of judicial comity. The Taft Court persistently showed great sensitivity to the fact that "[i]n this country, in which in every state we have courts of concurrent jurisdiction under the federal and state authority, it is of the highest importance that conflict of jurisdiction should be avoided. It can only be avoided by forbearance and comity." Harkin v. Brundage, 276 U.S. 36, 55 (1928). *See, e.g.*, Rhea v. Smith, 274 U.S. 434, 441–45 (1927) (reconciling the applicability of state and federal statutes concerning liens upon real estate); Fenner v. Boykin, 271 U.S. 240, 243–48 (1926) (declining to apply Ex parte *Young* to enjoin a state court proceeding); Harrigan v. Bergdoll, 270 U.S. 560, 564–65 (1926) (enforcing a state statute of limitations); Cent. Union Tel. Co. v. Edwardsville, 269 U.S. 190, 195 (1925) (upholding a state-law procedural waiver of the plaintiff's federal constitutional claims); United States *ex rel.* Kennedy v. Tyler, 269 U.S. 13, 19 (1925) (vindicating New York's judicial power over Native American lands); Kline v. Burke Constr. Co., 260 U.S. 226 (1922). The Taft Court sought to maintain a delicate balance between national supremacy and respect for state courts. In Davis v. Corona Coal Co., 265 U.S. 219 (1924), for example, the Court, in an opinion by Holmes, refused to accept a state law procedural defense to the assertion of a federal claim. Holmes observed that "[p]erhaps it was not quite fully remembered that the laws of the United States are a part of the *lex fori* of a state." *Id.* at 222. Taft wrote Holmes in response to this opinion that "I don't mind a little lecture to state courts that they are still within the United States." WHT to OWH (Holmes papers). In Lion Bonding & Surety Co. v. Karatz, 262 U.S. 77 (1923), by contrast, the Court, through Justice Brandeis, scolded a lower federal court for seeking to divest a state court of jurisdiction in the context of a receivership. "Lower federal courts," Brandeis wrote, "are not superior to state courts." *Id.* at 90. Taft wrote Brandeis about this sentence that it "would seem to state the obvious, but whatever many District & Circuit Judges would assent in this regard, the fact is that in their hearts they feel otherwise. The opinion will do a world of good." WHT to LDB (Brandeis papers). Brandeis was always quite clear that "questions of jurisdiction are really questions of power between States and Nations." *Brandeis-Frankfurter Conversations*, at 313 (June 28, 1923).

46. Arizona Copper Co. v. Hammer, 250 U.S. 400, 450–51 (1919) (McReynolds, J., dissenting).

47. *See supra* Chapter 36, at 1132–34.
48. Meyer v. Nebraska, 262 U.S. 390, 99 (1923). *See supra* Chapter 26, at 827–28.
49. 304 U.S. 64 (1938).
50. 276 U.S. 518 (1928). *See Erie R.R. Co.*, 304 U.S. at 73 ("Criticism of the doctrine became widespread after the decision of Black & White Taxicab Co."). "Outraging opponents of diversity and embarrassing its supporters, the Taxicab case quickly became a symbol of corporate exploitation of federal jurisdiction." EDWARD A. PURCELL, Jr., BRANDEIS AND THE PROGRESSIVE CONSTITUTION: ERIE, THE JUDICIAL POWER, AND THE POLITICS OF THE FEDERAL COURTS IN TWENTIETH-CENTURY AMERICA 78 (New Haven: Yale University Press 2000).

There had been a sharp exchange about federal common law in the Taft Court during the preceding year in Empire Trust Co. v. Cahan, 274 U.S. 473 (1927). *Cahan* came up in diversity and concerned the standard of liability to which a bank should be held for honoring fraudulent checks. The Second Circuit had virtually imposed strict liability upon the bank, but the Supreme Court, in a unanimous opinion by Holmes, reversed, articulating a standard close to that created by New York law. Holmes reasoned:

> It is very desirable that the decision of the Courts of the United States and that of the highest Court of the State where the business was done, should agree, as was recognized by the Circuit Court of Appeals. The result to which we come restores that agreement, at least when the checks are certified or accepted by the banks upon which they are drawn, as was the case here with all but two. Whiting v. Hudson Trust Co., 234 N.Y. 394. ... As the Court remarks in the case cited "The transactions of banking in a great financial center are not to be clogged, or their pace slackened, by over-burdensome restrictions." 234 N.Y. 406.

Cahan, 274 U.S. at 480. In its original draft, this paragraph had read:

> It is very desirable, to say the least, that the decision of the Courts of the United States and that of the highest Court of the State where the business was done, should agree, as was recognized by the Circuit Court of Appeals. The result to which we come restores that agreement, at least when the checks are certified or accepted by the banks upon which they are drawn, as was the case here with all but two. Whiting v. Hudson Trust Co. ... *We should expect that when necessary the Court of Appeals would take the further step of applying the same principle to uncertified checks.* ... As the Court remarks in the case cited "The transactions of banking in a great financial center are not to be clogged, or their pace slackened, by over-burdensome restrictions."

(Holmes papers) (emphasis added). Butler marked the paragraph and commented: "It seems to me better to omit the implication that the decision ought to be bound by the decisions of the State Court. The rule that this Court is not so bound is so well known and has been followed so long that we would better adhere to it. Moreover, no expression on the point is necessary in this case." (Holmes papers). Taft marked the same paragraph and commented, "Swift v. Tyson is too deeply embedded in our reports however one might differ from it were the question an open one." (Holmes papers). Taft also asked, "Why should we adopt this prophecy or hope about the view of another Court?"

51. *Black & White Taxicab*, 276 U.S. at 523, 526. *See* Palmer Transfer Co. v. Anderson, 115 S.W. 182, 187 (Ky. 1909) (holding that a railroad may not grant exclusive use of a certain part of its grounds to a single common carrier); McConnell v. Pedigo, 18

S.W. 15, 15–16 (Ky. 1892) (holding that under Kentucky law a railroad could not grant to one carrier the exclusive right to come on depot grounds to transport railroad passengers to their final destinations).

52. *Black & White Taxicab*, 276 U.S. at 529–30. *See* Salem Trust Co. v. Manufacturers' Finance Co., 264 U.S. 182, 191–92 (1924) ("The question is one of general law, not based on any legislation of the state, or local law or usage, and the lower court rightly decided that it was not bound by the rule applied in the decisions of the highest court of Massachusetts.").

53. Holmes's dissent was joined by Brandeis and Stone. Brandeis wrote Holmes, "The gem of the Term. I'm a joiner." LDB to OWH (Holmes papers). Brandeis later wrote Frankfurter, "Holmes's dissent in Black & White Taxi Cab Case will stand among his notable opinions. It was delivered with fervor." LDB to Felix Frankfurter (April 10, 1928), in BRANDEIS-FRANKFURTER CORRESPONDENCE, at 330. Frankfurter later called the opinion "the term's masterpiece." Felix Frankfurter to OWH (September 9, 1928), in HOLMES-FRANKFURTER CORRESPONDENCE, at 233. Stone wrote Holmes, "It seems to me shocking that we should allow our jurisdiction to be used to have set aside a well settled local policy like this." HFS to OWH (April 2, 1928) (Stone papers). According to Stone's docket book, McReynolds voted at conference to dissent alongside of Holmes, Brandeis, and Stone. About a month after the case was argued, Holmes wrote Frederick Pollock:

> [T]here have been two cases on which I have got excited.... It is a time-honored practice for the U.S. judges when a case between citizens of different states is tried before them and the question is one that depends, according to the common phrase, on "the general law," to say that the parties are entitled to their independent opinion, and, if so minded, to decline to follow the Supreme Court of the State. I say that this is a pure usurpation founded on a subtle fallacy. They say the question is a question of the common law and that they must decide what the common law is. I hit at this once in a dissent by saying that the common law is not a brooding omnipresence in the sky. [S. Pac. Co. v. Jensen, 244 U.S. 205, 222 (1917).] The question of what is the law of Massachusetts or of Louisiana is a matter that Mass. or La. has a right to determine for itself, and that being so, the voice of the state should be obeyed as well when it speaks through its Supreme Court as it would if it spoke through its Legislature. It all comes from Story in Swift v. Tyson who declined to follow New York law upon a commercial question.... The decision was unjustifiable in theory but did no great harm when confined to what Story dealt with, but under the influence of Bradley, Harlan, et al. it now has assumed the form that upon questions of the general law the U.S. courts must decide for themselves – of course expressing a desire to follow the state courts if they can. I doubt if I can carry a majority, for the tradition is old, and some ex-circuit judges will not have forgotten the arrogant assumption to which they have been accustomed.

OWH to Frederick Pollock (February 17, 1928), in 2 HOLMES-POLLOCK CORRESPONDENCE, at 214–15. Pollock replied that "[t]he Kentucky judgment is in English eyes, antediluvian, but that does not matter." Frederick Pollock to OWH (May 7, 1928), *id.* at 219. There is a tantalizing letter from Stone to Herman Oliphant, stating, "I think Holmes' dissent in the Black & White Taxi case is a very remarkable document. Sometime I should like to tell you some of the circumstances attending its production. It must seem very heretical to some of our Harvard friends." HFS to Herman Oliphant (April 23, 1928) (Stone papers).

54. *Black & White Taxicab*, 276 U.S. at 533 (Holmes, J., dissenting). In *The Nation*, Heywood Broun immediately recognized the states' rights implications of Holmes's position:

> [I]t is largely through the seizure of authority that the Supreme Court has done its bit to sweep away the noxious theory of States' rights. I suppose the justices have done as much as ever Union soldiers did to batter down the sovereignty of the particular units as opposed to the federal whole. By a curious quirk Justice Holmes who himself bore arms in the conflict is now among the States'-rights wing of the court upon certain occasions.

Heywood Broun, *It Seems to Heywood Broun*, 126 THE NATION 479 (1928). For a defense of *Swift* that frankly rests on the theory that diversity jurisdiction carries with it the power of federal courts to make substantive law, see Henry Schofield, *Swift v. Tyson: Uniformity of Judge-Made State Law in State and Federal Courts*, 4 ILLINOIS LAW REVIEW 533, 537–41 (1910).

55. *Black & White Taxicab*, 276 U.S. at 533 (Holmes, J., dissenting). Thus when Stone circulated a draft of his proposed opinion in Risty v. Chicago, R.I. & P. Ry. Co., 270 U.S. 378 (1926), which involved diversity actions turning on the construction of South Dakota legislation, he had written that "It is the duty of the federal courts, in suit brought in or removed to the district courts, to decide for themselves all relevant questions of state law, and while they will *ordinarily* follow the decisions of state courts as to the interpretation of a state statute. . . ." (Stone papers) (emphasis added). Holmes marked the word "ordinarily" and wrote, "I think they ought always to follow state decisions on interpretation of a state statute. I should pay no attention to wobbly phrases in that matter." In his published opinion Stone removed the adverb.

56. *Black & White Taxicab*, 276 U.S. at 533 (Holmes, J., dissenting). As Holmes had written to Morris Cohen in 1919: "As long as law means force – (and when it means anything else I don't care who makes it and will do as I damn choose) – force means an army and this army will belong to the territorial club. Therefore the territorial club will have the last word." OWH to Morris Cohen (November 23, 1919) (Holmes papers).

57. *Black & White Taxicab*, 276 U.S. at 533–34 (Holmes, J., dissenting). After reading the opinion, Frankfurter wrote Holmes:

> I have just read your dissent in the Black & White Taxicab case and I'm all stirred with delight. You have written, if I may say so, a landmark opinion. To think that it has taken a century to expose the fallacy of one of the most obstinate doctrines of your Court! And you have done it with such ineluctable lucidity that only the pertinacity of error can explain persistence in it. . . . I'm particularly aroused, because I've been delving a bit into Swift v. Tyson and its sequelae, and the more I study the applications of that doctrine the less respect I have for it. My betters tell me to revere Story, but I cannot escape a strong scepticism about his intellectual greatness, much as I admire his energy, and his powers of formulation, which gave substance to scattered materials.

Felix Frankfurter to OWH (April 14, 1928), in HOLMES-FRANKFURTER CORRESPONDENCE, at 225. Holmes answered, "I hoped that you would share my views in the Taxicab case. It is the only one that has stirred me much lately." OWH to Felix Frankfurter (April 21, 1928), *id.* at 226.

58. *Black & White Taxicab*, 276 U.S. at 535 (Holmes, J., dissenting). For a clear example of the jurisprudential implications of this kind of positivism, see Ingenohl v. Walter E. Olsen & Co., Inc., 273 U.S. 541, 544 (1927) ("A trade-mark started elsewhere

would depend for its protection in Hongkong upon the law prevailing in Hongkong and would confer no rights except by the consent of that law. When then the judge who, in the absence of an appeal to the Privy Council, is the final exponent of that law, authoritatively declares that the assignment by the Custodian of the assets of the Manila firm cannot and will not be allowed to affect the rights of the party concerned in Hongkong, we do not see how it is possible for a foreign Court to pronounce his decision wrong. It will be acted on and settles the rights of the parties in Hongkong and in view of that fact it seems somewhat paradoxical to say that it is not the law. If the Alien Property Custodian purported to convey rights in English territory valid as against those whom the English law protects he exceeded the powers that were or could be given to him by the United States.").
59. *Black & White Taxicab*, 276 U.S. at 535 (Holmes, J., dissenting). As has been noted, however, when it came to common law issues that Holmes himself felt passionate about, as for example tort liability and juries, Holmes was not above authoring opinions explicating general federal common law in ways that contradicted local state law. See *supra* Chapter 5, at 173.
60. About two weeks after the decision, Brandeis wrote Frankfurter:

> 1. I think it would be an excellent idea to draft a bill to correct the alleged rule acted on as to general law in the Black & White case. The draft bill should go to Sen. Tom Walsh. He sat through the reading of the opinions, seated in a front seat, & seemed much interested.
> 2. Another bill should be drawn, correcting the court's error in construction of the Fed Statutes as to what is a fraud on its jurisdiction. Such action as was taken in the Black & White Case, ought to be prohibited whether strictly a fraud or not. That bill should go to Judge Moore.
> 3. Another bill should be drafted to put an end to removals, where there is a several controversy. That provision is being construed as removing the whole cause – an obvious injustice to those defendants who want to remain in the State Court, & to the pl[ainti]ff. That bill also should go to Judge Moore.

LDB to Felix Frankfurter (April 21, 1928), in BRANDEIS-FRANKFURTER CORRESPONDENCE, at 330. A "several controversy" was one involving both federal and state questions.

On May 3, Senator Walsh introduced S. 4333, 70th CONG. 1st SESS. (1928), which provided "[t]hat the decisions of the highest court of a State shall govern the courts of the United States in the ascertainment of the common law or general jurisprudence of such State." See S. 96, 71st CONG. 1st SESS. (1929) (same); PURCELL, *supra* note 50, at 224–25; Henry W. Taft to WHT (May 15, 1928) (Taft papers) ("I suppose you have also heard of the bill introduced by Walsh which compels the federal courts to adopt the common law or general jurisprudence of a state as laid down by the highest court of such state. This is to meet the situation created by the court in the Black and White Taxicab case, decided April 9, 1928."). Walsh's bill came at a particularly awkward time, for S. 3151 had just passed the Senate Judiciary Committee. Sponsored by Senator George Norris of Nebraska, S. 3151 deprived federal district courts of both diversity and federal question jurisdiction. For Taft's response to S. 3151, see *supra* Chapter 15, at 516–18. Taft regarded S. 3151 as a direct assault on the Court's efforts to create an integrated national financial market. *See* WHT to George Wickersham (March 29, 1928) (Taft papers):

> I think the question ought to be brought to the attention of the public through the newspapers. The western States don't realize the value to them of having Federal Courts to which eastern capital may recur for the adjustment of the rights of its owners. The necessary effect of such legislation in requiring every person in the East who lends any money in the West to subject himself to the delays and injustices against non-residents in litigation in the West will certainly increase the cost of borrowing money in the West and send up the rates of interest. For those people who are interested in helping the farmer to redeem his mortgages, this is the worst thing that could happen.... I think the American Bar Association might well act on the subject, though its influence is not so great, but I think you might well in a deft way bring the attention of the New York press to the radical nature of this Bill.... [T]he Senate ... is a most Bolshevik body, and the House is the only one that retains any conservatism at all.... I think if you could you might stir up members of your Bar representing the great lending element of the country to an agitation on this subject, just to have it understood what the purpose and effect will be.

In Taft's eyes, diversity jurisdiction was

> the source of the greatest usefulness in avoiding injustice due to sectional prejudice in the administration of justice. Such litigation has made up a large part of the dockets of the existing trial Federal courts, and always has ... engendered financial confidence on the part of the States where capital comes from in the justice to be rendered in other States to which the capital goes. If this bill were to pass, I should think it would strike the worst blow against the farmers that could be imagined.... Thoughtless people have not appreciated how cheap money has been secured for all the enterprises through the West because of the jurisdiction of the trial Federal courts in these diverse citizenship questions.

WHT to Casper Yost (April 5, 1928) (Taft Papers). On May 3, 1928, Senator Norris amended his bill to reinstate federal question jurisdiction, but he remained adamant that diversity jurisdiction should be eliminated. S. 3151, 70th CONG. 1st SESS. (May 3, Calendar Day May 8, 1928). Senator Norris specifically pointed to *Black & White Taxicab & Transfer Co.* in defending his bill. George W. Norris to Lewis A. Gannett (April 28, 1928) (Taft papers).

61. *Black & White Taxicab*, 276 U.S. at 528.
62. 261 U.S. 525 (1923).
63. Herbert v. Louisiana, 272 U.S. 312, 316–17 (1926).
64. "The expanding scope and shifting orientation of the federal common law roughly paralleled the rise of substantive due process in the 1890s, and both developments expanded the role and lawmaking power of the federal judiciary." PURCELL, *supra* note 5, at 61–62.
65. The Framers of the Fourteenth Amendment were quite aware of its centralizing effects. Consider, for example, Senator Charles Sumner's paean to the "imperialism of Equal Rights":

> The Nation will not enter the State, except for the safeguard of rights national in character, and then only as the sunshine, with beneficent power, and, like the sunshine, for the equal good of all. As well assail the sun because it is central – because it is imperial. Here is a just centralism; here is a generous imperialism. Shunning with patriotic care that injurious centralism and that fatal imperialism, which have been the Nemesis of France, I hail that other centralism which supplies an equal protection to every citizen, and that other imperialism

which makes Equal Rights the supreme law, to be maintained by the national arm in all parts of the land. Centralism! Imperialism! Give me the centralism of Liberty. Give me the imperialism of Equal Rights.

44 CONG. GLOBE 651 (April 13, 1871).

66. *The Minimum Wage Law Unconstitutional*, 133 THE OUTLOOK 694 (1923). *See* John A. Ryan, *A Deplorable Court Decision*, CATHOLIC CHARITIES REVIEW 170, 172 (May 1923) ("It should be remembered that all of the twelve minimum wage statutes in that many states are certain to be annulled as soon as actions can be brought against them in the various federal district courts."); *The Minimum Wage*, LA FOLLETTE'S MAGAZINE (May 1923), at 68.
67. Thomas Reed Powell, *The Supreme Court and State Police Power, 1922–1930*, 17 VIRGINIA LAW REVIEW 529, 531 (1931).
68. *The Red Terror of Judicial Reform*, 40 NEW REPUBLIC 110, 113 (1924).
69. On Brandeis's unhappiness with the doctrine of federal common law, see PURCELL, *supra* note 50, at 133–40. On Brandeis's unhappiness with the centralizing implications of substantive due process doctrine, see New State Ice Co. v. Liebmann, 285 U.S. 262, 311 (1932) (Brandeis, J., dissenting): "It is one of the happy incidents of the federal system that a single courageous State may, if its citizens choose, serve as a laboratory; and try novel social and economic experiments without risk to the rest of the country. This Court has the power to prevent an experiment. . . . We have power to do this, because the due process clause has been held by the Court applicable to matters of substantive law as well as to matters of procedure." For an example of the intersection between Holmes's theoretical opposition to substantive due process and his localism, see New York, Philadelphia & Norfolk Telegraph Co. v. Dolan, 265 U.S. 96, 98 (1924).
70. *But see supra* note 45.
71. Hoke & Economides v. United States, 227 U.S. 308, 322 (1913).
72. The Court did not abandon its commitment to federal common law until 1938 in Erie Railroad Co. v. Tompkins, 304 U.S. 64 (1938), at a time when it was simultaneously ending its efforts to use the Due Process Clause to endow freedom of contract with constitutional protections.
73. For a modern effort to reclaim for the federal judiciary the generalized authority of a common law court, see DAVID A. STRAUSS, THE LIVING CONSTITUTION (Oxford University Press 2010).

PART VIII
LABOR, EQUAL PROTECTION, AND RACE

Writing to Congress from Versailles in May 1919, President Wilson apologized for his inability to attend the opening of an "extraordinary session of the Congress." It was "my duty," he said "to take part in the counsels of the peace conference and contribute what I can to the solution of the innumerable questions" upon whose settlement "the peace of the whole world" depends. Yet the president also felt obliged to direct Congress's attention to significant pending issues in the United States, and, standing "at the front of all others... is the question of labour." "We cannot go any further in our present direction," Wilson said. "We cannot live our right life as a nation or achieve our proper success as an industrial community if capital and labour are to continue to be antagonistic instead of being partners."[1]

Wilson's concern was widely shared. "Today we all see clearly that the war between capital and labor," the eminent and unimpeachable Charles W. Eliot had declared the previous month, "is getting to a stage or condition which seriously endangers the existing industrial and social structures."[2] The conflict, he later added, was "rapidly becoming [a] civil war."[3] By the end of the year, Ray Stannard Baker could complain that "We are facing dangerous days in America, in many ways the most dangerous in our history. A tendency exists among great numbers of our people to take violent sides upon the chief problem confronting us – the relationship of capital and labor."[4]

The labor shortages created by World War I, combined with the Wilson administration's solicitude for organized labor, had created favorable conditions for the growth of unions. Membership rose from 2,582,600 in 1915 to 3,467,300 in 1918. It would rise another 19 percent to 4,125,200 in 1919, and yet another 22 percent to 5,047,800 in 1920.[5] The spurt in union membership prompted a sharp increase in labor militancy. Matters would come to a head in the years immediately after the war when American employers, freed from the oversight of wartime regulation, launched a coordinated campaign to restore prewar control over their workforce.[6]

Labor and capital violently collided in 1919, as the nation was rocked by a massive succession of strikes. More than 4,160,348 workers were involved in industrial disputes.[7] "One of every five employed workers was involved in a strike during 1919, a record that has never been surpassed, or even approached, in American history."[8] There was a general strike in Seattle; the police walked out in Boston; there was a massive, nationwide effort to organize United States Steel. The country was afflicted by a brooding sense of social breakdown, a fear that civilization itself was dissolving into a brutal and unforgiving conflict between workers and employers.[9]

The stakes of the confrontation seemed almost existential. In 1917 the Bolsheviks had seized power in Russia, and many feared that America might be next in line for a genuine revolution. "Republican Senator Joseph Frelinghyusen of New Jersey voiced the thoughts of many of his party colleagues when he declared in 1919 that ... [i]f labor agitation continued unchecked, ... 'Sovietism' would overthrow American institutions."[10] The *Literary Digest* summarized the widespread belief that "The epidemic of strikes that has been sweeping over the United States since the signing of the Armistice ... has resulted in a marked loss of public sympathy by organized labor. ... The reason for this, many witnesses aver, is the growing fear that the rank and file of American unionism is turning away from the conservative leadership represented by Samuel Gompers ... and giving ear to the revolutionary teachings of 'red' agitators. ... 'The radicals are in the saddle within the ranks of organized labor, and strikes and threats of strikes are merely the prelude to a reign of lawlessness whose object is the overthrow of the American Government and the substitution of the Soviet form of government.'"[11] Taft was among those who added fuel to these fears. He proclaimed in 1919:

> One of the phases of the reaction from the war has been the intoxication of power of the extremists of the labor group. These persons in every country have been caught by the Lenine plan of ruling by the Soviets of workingmen. The war emphasized the special dependence of society on labor as a group and the Russian debacle gave opportunity to exploit that dependence as a means of subjecting all other groups, however much more numerous, to the dictation of labor. ... It can only be cured by some striking instances of successful resistance to this rapidly growing tyranny by those against whom it is immediately directed. ... The feverish labor enthusiasts need object lessons to bring them to reason. They do not realize the strength of the conservative forces in this country, which will rise to meet persistence in Soviet methods.[12]

American employers struck back hard at the postwar labor insurgency.[13] They created and pushed the "American plan," which aggressively combined an antiunion commitment to the open shop with new techniques of personnel management, including various forms of welfare capitalism.[14] Employers redoubled their efforts to use courts to suppress strikes, which were labor's chief weapon in the struggle for industrial recognition. The "labor injunction ... reached its apogee in

Labor, Equal Protection, and Race

the 1920's."[15] Courts enjoined about 3–5 percent of all recorded strikes in the first two decades of the twentieth century, whereas they issued injunctions in 25 percent of all recorded strikes in the 1920s. All in all, we know of about 2,800 injunctions during the Taft Court era.[16]

The assault devasted union membership, which fell 5% in 1921, another 16% in 1922, and a further 10% in 1923. By 1929, union membership would stand at only 3,442,600, a decline of 32% from 1920.[17] Losses in membership were accompanied by a "tremendous lessening in both number and extent of the industrial disputes for 1922–1930."[18] If the period 1916–21 averaged 3,508 disputes a year, the years between 1922 and 1925 averaged only 1,304 disputes. That number declined by half during the period 1926 to 1930, when the nation averaged only 791 disputes per year. If we account for the actual number of workers involved in these disputes, the drop from the first period to the last was about 90%.[19]

The Taft Court was in the thick of these developments. During its very first term, the Court issued a quartet of far-reaching labor decisions,[20] each authored by Taft himself, that aroused instant and profound hostility.[21] By June 1922 a special committee of the American Federation of Labor ("AFL") reported to the annual convention that the Supreme Court has "all but outlawed the activities of organized labor, which alone can protect the workers from the oppression and aggression of the greedy and cruel interests. This despotic exercise of a usurped power by nine men, or a bare majority of them, over the lives and liberties of millions of men, women and children, is intolerable." The country's "very existence as a democracy and a government of law is at stake. A judicial oligarchy is threatening to set itself up above the elected Legislatures, above the people themselves."[22]

Matters reached such a fever pitch that the AFL resolved to secure a constitutional amendment to prohibit child labor; a constitutional amendment to prohibit "the enactment of any law or the making of any judicial determination which would deny the right of the workers of the United States ... to organize for the betterment of their conditions; to deal collectively with employers; to collectively withhold their labor and patronage and induce others to do so"; and a constitutional amendment to overturn the institution of judicial review.[23] By the conclusion of Taft's first term, the Court's handling of what was commonly characterized as "industrial warfare"[24] had earned the Court the mortal enmity of organized labor.

The tension between the Taft Court and organized labor continued throughout the decade. Three issues were at the heart of the ongoing struggle. The first concerned whether the function of constitutional law was to protect the rights of individual employees or whether it was instead to create a market in which employers and employees could deal with each other under conditions of roughly equal bargaining power. At root, this question turned on the legal status of unions, which depended upon the status of groups in constitutional law. Although as a co-chair of the National War Labor Board during World War I, Taft fully understood the practical need for what he called a "group system" in the labor market,[25] he could not bring himself to repudiate a constitutional commitment to individualism that tilted the Court decisively in management's favor. The Court's decisions left in their turbulent wake a national industrial labor policy that was paralyzed and ineffective.

The second issue involved the Taft Court's insistence on using anti-trust law to discipline the employment relationship. The Court interpreted anti-trust law to prevent industrial disputes from disrupting national markets and to impose what the Court regarded as an appropriate balance of power between employers and unions. In these efforts the Court arrogated to itself the authority to speak for the fundamental economic policy of the country. The Court deemed it essential to protect managerial initiative, which, like property, it regarded as indispensable for the progress of civilization. The Court's use of anti-trust law to control labor relations provoked an intense and ultimately successful backlash.

The third issue concerned the use of labor injunctions to regulate industrial conflict. Federal equitable power both established the substantive law that governed labor controversies and enforced that law through harsh sanctions, including criminal punishments, which bypassed basic protections of the criminal process, like juries. Organized labor denounced federal equity as "government by injunction." In truth, courts regulating industrial disputes assumed an unusual combination of legislative, executive, and judicial power. Federal equity epitomized what labor regarded as the false pretention to speak directly for the values and commitments of the entire American people. Taft had personally participated in the development of the labor injunction in the closing decade of the nineteenth century, and he led a Court that was deeply invested in its deployment.

Intense controversies over these questions persisted throughout the 1920s. By the conclusion of the decade, the Taft Court had so overreached that labor was able to convince the nation that the Court was not to be trusted to express national commitments. With the passage of the Norris-LaGuardia Act of 1932,[26] the country enacted positive legislation that virtually banished federal equity from the scene of employer–employee conflicts. The federal judiciary had ignominiously lost its bid to speak for the American community.

If labor relations were one scene of violent conflict in the 1920s, the other was race relations. In the tribal 1920s, the impulse to 100 percent Americanism exaggerated tensions in a society that was already highly racist. The fragile reconciliation that ended Reconstruction had been purchased at the price of a convenient agreement between North and South to suppress questions of racial justice. Southern Democrats sought to entrench white dominance, while Northern Republicans sought to entice Southern whites without disturbing basic structures of racial subordination. This configuration hardened during the progressive era when Southern states developed new techniques to enforce racial hierarchy. The first decades of the twentieth century witnessed the perfection of institutions of Southern segregation, as well as the almost complete exclusion of Southern Blacks from the franchise. By 1917, it was openly acknowledged that the Fifteenth Amendment was "entirely disregarded" and a "dead letter in the Constitution."[27]

World War I transformed the racial question from a largely sectional issue into a conflict of national scope. Blacks began to escape from the stifling oppression of the South when the war in Europe increased demand for higher-paying work in

Labor, Equal Protection, and Race

the North, even as the war cut off the supply of white, immigrant, European labor.[28] Leaving the apartheid of the South for the subtler racism of the North, Blacks began to create great urban communities in border and Northern states. Interracial relations, which had heretofore been largely a Southern question, suddenly became a pressing issue throughout the entire country.

Its national dimensions became apparent when America entered the war and inducted 368,000 Black men.[29] Woodrow Wilson, receiving a deputation of Black clergy at the White House, set aside his customary denigration of African Americans to declare: "I have always known that the negro has been unjustly and unfairly dealt with; your people have exhibited a degree of loyalty and patriotism that should command the admiration of the whole nation. In the present conflict your race has rallied to the nation's call . . . . [O]ut of this conflict you must expect nothing less than the enjoyment of full citizenship rights – the same as are enjoyed by every other citizen."[30]

Black soldiers fought valiantly in Europe. In France they experienced – many for the first time – genuine respect and equality. Having fought for democracy abroad, they expected to participate in democracy when they returned home. The thought was well captured by W.E.B. Du Bois, the brilliant editor of the National Association for the Advancement of Colored People's ("NAACP") *The Crisis*:

> [B]y the God of Heaven, we are cowards and jackasses if now that war is over, we do not marshal every ounce of our brain and brawn to fight a sterner, longer, more unbending battle against the forces of hell in our own land.
> We *return*.
> We *return from fighting*.
> We *return fighting*.
> Make way for Democracy! We saved it in France, and by the Great Jehovah, we will save it in the United States of America, or know the reason why.[31]

"For three centuries we have suffered and cowered," Du Bois wrote. "No race ever gave Passive Resistance and Submission to Evil longer, more piteous trial. Today we raise the terrible weapon of Self-Defense. When the murderer comes, he shall not longer strike us in the back. When the armed lynchers gather, we too must gather armed. When the mob moves, we propose to meet it with bricks and clubs and guns."[32]

White America, however, was not prepared peacefully to abdicate its culture of repression. It refused to welcome home Black soldiers on terms of equality. As South Carolina Congressman James Byrnes, who would later join the Court as a justice in 1941, said: "For any negro who has become inoculated with the desire for political equality, there is no employment for him in the South, nor is there any room for him in the South. This is a white man's country, and it will always remain a white man's country."[33] The upshot was that 1919 became a crisis year not merely for labor, but also for race relations.

The nation was engulfed in vicious racial violence. As Figure VIII-1 illustrates, lynchings spiked. Hideous race riots swept throughout the entire country;

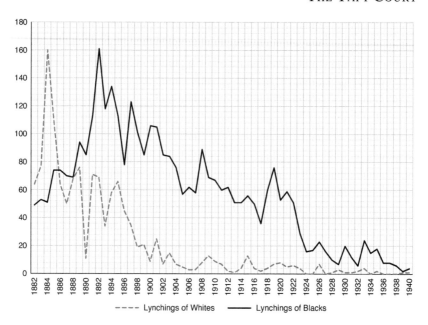

Figure VIII-1 Lynchings by year and by race, 1882–1940
Source: ROBERT L. ZANGRANDO, THE NAACP CRUSADE AGAINST LYNCHING, 1909–1950 (Philadelphia: Temple University Press 1980)

Black neighborhoods were torched and pillaged. Black victims were barbarically tortured and mutilated. "London newspapers reported that the fighting in the United States had 'now assumed the proportions of a race war.'"[34] James Weldon Johnson called the summer of 1919 "The Red Summer."[35] John Hope Franklin pronounced it "the greatest period of interracial strife the nation has ever witnessed."[36]

Taft, speaking in 1919 to the Black students of Hampton Institute, condemned the lynchings as a "horrible exhibition of inhumanity of men, growing out, first, of race prejudice, and then out of the instinctive brutality of men."[37] He denounced the riots as "temporary" manifestations "proceeding out of the stirring up of passion and of forces that rush to the front after a war."[38] But in the face of the appalling injuries inflicted on Black communities throughout the country, Taft nevertheless insisted on "patience against injustice." "We are going upward," he explained to his audience of Black students. "[E]ven the average white men in the South are coming to see the great mistakes that have been made in dealing with the Negroes, are coming to appreciate the value of the Negroes in their communities.... The Southern leaders are realizing that they must do their part."[39] Taft counseled Hampton students to put their trust in the enlightened self-interest of white Southern elites.

Taft's advice exemplified the outlook of contemporary Northern white Republicans, who typically advocated a patient faith in the evolving good sense of Southern leaders. It also well describes the jurisprudence of the Taft Court.

Labor, Equal Protection, and Race

Although the Court would occasionally strike down especially blatant examples of Southern racism that used explicit racial classifications, as for example the Texas white primary statutes[40] or various overt schemes of racialized zoning,[41] it was for the most part content to validate the pervasive humiliations of Southern apartheid[42] as well as the equally virulent racism of Western anti-Asian laws.[43]

The Taft Court explicitly sanctioned all this in the name of the racial instincts of the common American man.[44] The Court did not acknowledge any judicial obligation to protect "discrete and insular minorities."[45] In contrast to the Court's labor decisions, Taft Court opinions about racial justice did not provoke backlash, perhaps because they accurately reflected the rampant racism of the 1920s. It is nevertheless striking that the Court's equal protection jurisprudence had nothing whatever to say about explicitly apartheid institutions like segregated education. The silence illuminates the extent to which equal protection jurisprudence during the Taft Court era was a lost doctrine. It drifted from case to case, absorbing the larger agendas of the Court, like the protection of national markets, the promotion of economic growth, or the safeguarding of commercial corporations. But the Equal Protection Clause itself was not associated with any particular constitutional values or commitments.

It is difficult now to appreciate just how shapeless equal protection doctrine was during the Taft Court era. The doctrine would not begin to assume its contemporary orientation until the 1930s. By that time, African American organizations had emerged on the political scene. They had begun to exert the kind of political influence that organized labor had long asserted. It is a disturbing but nevertheless powerful paradox that in the 1920s American constitutional law did not accord African Americans the rights necessary to protect political and economic agency because at that time neither the Court nor the country perceived African Americans as political and economic agents.

Blacks as a group did not begin to break out of the stifling jaws of this paradox until the very end of the Taft Court, when the NAACP waged an epic and precedent-shattering battle to defeat the nomination of John J. Parker to succeed Edward T. Sanford. The NAACP's stunning success made white elites sit up and take notice. As a political matter, Black votes could no longer safely be ignored. In the next decade the Court would conclude that as a constitutional matter Blacks could also no longer be ignored. Within twenty years the Court would transform the Equal Protection Clause into a vehicle for assimilating discrete and insular minorities into the mainstream of the American constitutional order.

Notes

1. *Message of the President*, 58 CONG. REC. 40, 41 (May 20, 1919).
2. Charles W. Eliot, *Labor in a Democratic Society*, 42 THE SURVEY 73, 73 (1919).
3. Charles W. Eliot, PROCEEDINGS OF THE FIRST INDUSTRIAL CONFERENCE, OCTOBER 6 TO 23, 1919, at 63 (Washington D.C.: Government Printing Office 1920).
4. Ray Stannard Baker, *Industrial Unrest Near Point of Inevitable Head-On Crash*, BALTIMORE SUN (December 28, 1919), at 4.
5. Statistics on union membership may be found in Irving Bernstein, *The Growth of American Unions*, 44 JOURNAL OF ECONOMIC REVIEW 301, 303 (1954). "For the first time in United States history, union membership approached 20 percent of the civilian nonagricultural labor force, a level more than twice as high as any previous peak." MELVYN DUBOFSKY, THE STATE AND LABOR IN MODERN AMERICA 74 (Chapel Hill: University of North Carolina Press 1994).
6. In Samuel Gompers's words, "Throughout the whole period that has elapsed since November 11, 1918, the American political and industrial bourbons have laid a course of plunder, restriction and coercion." Samuel Gompers, *Labor's Protest against Rampant Tragedy*, 27 AMERICAN FEDERATIONIST 521, 529 (1920).
7. H.M. Douty, *The Trend of Industrial Disputes, 1922–1930*, 27 JOURNAL OF THE AMERICAN STATISTICAL ASSOCIATION 168, 171 (1932). For a vivid description of the resulting explosion, see the opinion of the Kansas Supreme Court quoted in *supra* Chapter 25, at 795.
8. DAVID BRODY, LABOR IN CRISIS: THE STEEL STRIKE OF 1919, at 129 (Urbana: University of Illinois Press 1987).
9. Haggai Hurvitz, *Ideology and Industrial Conflict: President Wilson's First Industrial Conference of October 1919*, 18 LABOR HISTORY 509, 512–13 (1977). In 1919 Warren Harding wrote his old friend Frank Edgar Scobey that "I really think we are facing a desperate situation. It looks to me as if we are coming to a crisis in the conflict between the radical labor leaders and the capitalistic system under which we have developed the republic. . . . I think the situation has to be met with exceptionable [sic] courage." Warren G. Harding to Frank Edgar Scobey (October 25 & November 3, 1919) (Harding papers), quoted in DUBOFSKY, *supra* note 5, at 77. On the massive steel strike of 1919, see BRODY, *supra* note 8. On the Boston police strike, which brought Calvin Coolidge, then governor of Massachusetts, to national attention, see Richard L. Lyons, *The Boston Police Strike of 1919*, 20 NEW ENGLAND QUARTERLY 147 (1947). To nearly universal approval, Coolidge famously proclaimed that "There is no right to strike against the public safety by anybody, anywhere, anytime." *Id.* at 165. On the general strike in Seattle, in which labor established a council that appeared to many to be modeled after a Bolshevist soviet, see Robert L. Friedheim, *The Seattle General Strike of 1919*, 52 PACIFIC NORTHWEST QUARTERLY 81 (1961); Robert L. Friedheim & Robin Friedheim, *The Seattle Labor Movement, 1919–20*, 55 PACIFIC NORTHWEST QUARTERLY 146 (1964).
10. Robert H. Zieger, *From Hostility to Moderation: Railroad Labor Policy in the 1920s*, 9 LABOR HISTORY 23, 25 (1968). *See, e.g., Public Opinion Turning against Steel Strikers: Sympathy of the American Press Rapidly Alienated by Radical Talk of Industrial Revolution*, NEW YORK TRIBUNE (September 28, 1919), at C7.
11. *Red Forces Disrupting American Labor*, 63 LITERARY DIGEST 11 (October 25, 1919).
12. William Howard Taft, *Taft Condemns Union Heads for Refusal of Request to Defer Calling Steel Strike*, WASHINGTON POST (October 13, 1919), at 1.

13. Samuel Gompers, *The Conspiracy against Labor*, 29 AMERICAN FEDERATIONIST 721 (1922).
14. RONALD L. FILIPPELLI, LABOR IN THE USA: A HISTORY 152–54 (New York: Alfred A Knopf 1984).
15. ARNOLD M. PAUL, CONSERVATIVE CRISIS AND THE RULE OF LAW: ATTITUDES OF BAR AND BENCH, 1887–1895, at 229 n.18 (Ithaca: Cornell University Press 1960).
16. WILLIAM E. FORBATH, LAW AND THE SHAPING OF THE AMERICAN LABOR MOVEMENT 98 n.4 (Cambridge: Harvard University Press 1991).
17. Bernstein, *supra* note 5, at 303.
18. Douty, *supra* note 7, at 169.
19. *Id.* at 169–70.
20. American Steel Foundries v. Tri-City Central Trades Council, 257 U.S. 184 (December 5, 1921); Truax v. Corrigan, 257 U.S. 312 (December 19, 1921); Bailey v. Drexel Furniture Co., 259 U.S. 20 (May 15, 1922); United Mine Workers v. Coronado Coal Co., 259 U.S. 344 (June 5, 1922).
21. "Within a year the Court has handed down four decisions of major importance to the labor movement and in each of these decisions it has delivered a blow at labor and at the normal, natural, constructive progress which the labor movement seeks to achieve within the law." *Executive Council Supplemental Report No. 2*, in REPORT OF PROCEEDINGS OF THE FORTY-SECOND ANNUAL CONVENTION OF THE AMERICAN FEDERATION OF LABOR 295 (Washington D.C.: Law Reporter Printing Co. 1922).
22. *Report of Special Committee*, in REPORT OF PROCEEDINGS OF THE FORTY-SECOND ANNUAL CONVENTION OF THE AMERICAN FEDERATION OF LABOR, *supra* note 21, at 371–72.
23. *Id.* at 372–73. The Committee also proposed a constitutional amendment to make it "easier" to amend the Constitution, so that the Constitution might become "more flexible to meet the needs of the people." *Id.* at 373.
24. *Labor and the Public*, NEW YORK TIMES (December 8, 1921), at 17. *See Nation in Industrial War, Sterling Asserts*, WASHINGTON POST (July 28, 1922), at 2. The metaphor of "industrial war" had a long history. *See, e.g.*, W.G. Sumner, *Industrial War*, 2 THE FORUM 1 (1886).
25. William Howard Taft, *National War Labor Board* (November 26, 1918), in VIVIAN, at 125–26.
26. Pub. L. 72-65, 47 Stat. 70 (March 23, 1932).
27. 55 CONG. REC. 5587 (July 31, 1917) (remarks of Massachusetts Senator Henry Cabot Lodge). A good statement of the reconciliation Northern Republicans sought to forge between North and South may be found in Taft's speech as chair of the Lincoln Memorial Commission when he presented the Lincoln Memorial to the nation on May 30, 1922. Taft praised the memorial as marking "the restoration of the brotherly love of the two sections," and he celebrated Lincoln as "one who is as dear to the hearts of the South as to those of the North. The Southerner knows that the greatest misfortunate in all the trials of that section was the death of Lincoln. Had he lived, the consequences of the war would not have been as hard for them to bear, the wounds would have been more easily healed, the trying days of reconstruction would have been softened." ADDRESS OF WILLIAM HOWARD TAFT, CHAIRMAN OF THE LINCOLN MEMORIAL COMMISSION IN PRESENTING THE MEMORIAL TO THE PRESIDENT OF THE UNITED STATES, at 9–10, available at https://archive.org/details/addressofwilliootaft/page/n1/mode/2up.

28. John Hope Franklin, From Slavery to Freedom: A History of Negro America 472 (New York: Knopf 1967). Coincidentally, there was also a severe depression in southern agriculture during the early years of the war. The migration north was the result of both pull and push.
29. Robert Whitaker, On The Laps of Gods: The Red Summer of 1919 and the Struggle for Justice that Remade a Nation 41 (New York: Crown Publishers 2008).
30. Quoted in Rollin Lynde Hartt, *The New Negro*: *"When He's Hit, He Hits Back!"*, 105 The Independent 59, 60 (January 15, 1921).
31. W.E.B. Du Bois, *Returning Soldiers*, 18 The Crisis 13, 14 (May 1919).
32. W.E.B. Du Bois, *Let Us Reason Together*, 18 The Crisis 231 (September 1919).
33. Quoted in Whitaker, *supra* note 29, at 45.
34. Whitaker, *supra* note 29, at 53.
35. Franklin, *supra* note 28, at 480. *See* Cameron McWhirter, Red Summer: The Summer of 1919 and the Awakening of Black America 480 (New York: Henry Holt & Co. 2011).
36. Franklin, *supra* note 28, at 480.
37. William Howard Taft, *Hampton's Gift to the Nation*, 48 Southern Workman 299, 301 (1919).
38. *Id.* "Mob violence," Taft wrote in an editorial, "is disgraceful to American civilization. Lynching is dreadful and there is no justification for it. . . . Every man with a sense of responsibility and with a pride in American civilization should deprecate such violence. Those who take part in it ought to be severely punished." William Howard Taft, *Lynch Law* (April 11, 1918), in Vivian, at 50. Taft was perfectly aware of the deep disappointment that underlay the turmoil of 1919:

> The war, which the Negroes eagerly accepted as an opportunity with which to demonstrate their patriotic citizenship and their right to equality of treatment, has not proved to be as useful in this regard as they hoped. Circumstantial accounts of the ill-advised efforts of American white officials, with greater or less authority, to create among our allies a sense of the inferiority of the Negro soldier and officer that must be maintained in American military circles have made the Negro soldiers feel that they were not permitted even to die on equal terms with white soldiers. That feeling is intensified by the complete lack of race prejudice they found among the French against the Negro, whether French or American.

William Howard Taft, *Racial Prejudice* (June 2, 1919), in Vivian, at 221. Taft also knew that "The lynchings, those horrible exhibitions of blood lust against which all good people are joining in apparently hopeless protest, have led to desperation among the blacks. The returned Negro soldier, used to arms, returning from the war environments, resenting the ingratitude he sees in all of this, is prompted to 'direct action' to remedy his wrongs. He has heard much of 'direct action' from other groups seeking redress of their grievances. The general unrest is in harmony with his impulses." William Howard Taft, *Tolerance and Sympathy Needed* (August 4, 1919), in Vivian, at 250.
39. Taft, *supra* note 37, at 302.
40. Nixon v. Herndon, 273 U.S. 536 (1927); Nixon v. Condon, 286 U.S. 73 (1932).
41. Buchanan v. Warley, 245 U.S. 60 (1918); Harmon v. Tyler, 273 U.S. 668 (1927).
42. Gong Lum v. Rice, 275 U.S. 78 (1927).
43. Terrace v. Thompson, 263 U.S. 197 (1923).
44. United States v. Bhagat Singh Thind, 261 U.S. 204 (1923).
45. United States v. Carolene Products Co., 304 U.S. 144. 152 n.4 (1938).

CHAPTER 39

Labor and the Jurisprudence of Individualism

IN 1842, THE great Massachusetts Chief Justice Lemuel Shaw held that a union could not be indicted for criminal conspiracy unless "the purpose to be accomplished by the combination, or the concerted means of accomplishing it, be unlawful or criminal."[1] Unions could act to advance the economic interests of their members so long as they used only lawful means. Standing alone, therefore, an agreement to strike for the purpose of obtaining union recognition, with the intention of damaging the business of an employer until recognition was granted, was neither unlawful nor criminal.

After the Civil War, however, American jurisprudence began to recognize and protect the right of free labor.[2] In the *Slaughterhouse Cases*, Stephen Field famously referenced Adam Smith's *Wealth of Nations* to the effect that the "property which every man has in his own labor, as it is the original foundation of all other property, so it is the most sacred and inviolable."[3] Labor organizations peacefully striking to unionize business establishments were accordingly condemned because the purpose of denying nonunion workers the opportunity to seek employment was declared illegal.

Focusing on the question of whether "the seven millions of non-union laborers have no rights which the one million union men are bound to recognize,"[4] courts began to expand judicial restrictions on union organizing. In one of the "first decisions to ban the labor boycott,"[5] a New York State trial judge explained:

> The law says that workingmen may co-operate or combine for the purpose of obtaining an increase of their wages, but they have no right to combine for the purpose of preventing other people from working who are willing to accept less wages. You see at once, that if that doctrine prevailed, we would be face to face with a species of slave labor. The workingman would be enslaved by the very forces organized and set in motion for his protection. If there is one thing in this

country which the people have ever insisted upon, it is free labor, and I sincerely trust that they may not have to add to the old war cries of free speech, free press and free men, the new war cry of free labor.... Laboring men have a right ... to combine and cooperate for the purpose of increasing their wages, of improving their condition, and of elevating their social status.... But the moment they go beyond that and seek to put their ban upon others who take a different view of what is adequate rate of wages, they forfeit sympathy and take the position of a tyrant.[6]

The right of free labor converted the "scab" into "a creditable type of nineteenth-century hero. In defense of his rights as an individual, he deliberately incurs the reprobation of many of his fellows.... He steadily asserts in action his right to work on such conditions as he sees fit to make, and in so doing he displays remarkable courage."[7] "Surely there can be no form of slavery more abhorrent to our American people," wrote American banking and railroad entrepreneur Austin Corbin in 1889, "than that in which the head of some labor union is enabled to dictate when a man may, or must not, work for his daily bread."[8]

Conceptualizing the American labor force as a mighty sea of individual workmen, each equipped with a distinct right to free labor, would prove a powerful rhetorical resource for employers who in the 1920s sought to resist union organization. The Republican Publicity Association, for example, would proclaim in 1920 that the "inherent right of every man to earn, according to his ability, is gaining the recognition that it should, and it will prevail in spite of the opposition of Mr. Gompers and his ilk.... His plans, if fully successful, would be destructive of the independence of the individual and mark the end of that competition and rivalry which are the stimulation of all industry and production."[9]

The image of the American labor market as a simple aggregation of individual workers was of course wildly out of touch with the economic realities of industrial production in twentieth-century America. As the socialist lawyer Morris Hillquit observed in 1928: "The jobs of the country are largely concentrated in the hands of a few powerful industrial concerns. The individual worker is absolutely powerless to deal with such concerns on terms of equality. It is preposterous to speak as we do of the labor contract between, say, an individual steel worker, and the United States Steel Corporation.... The only way in which labor can meet organized capital in the labor market on terms of relative equality and actually bargain for terms of employment is by collective and organized action."[10]

To create such collective and organized action, unions were forced to develop an outlook that stressed the fundamental importance of group demands. As Robert Franklin Hoxie pointed out in his pioneering work in 1919: "The economic viewpoint of unionism is primarily a group viewpoint, and its program a group program. The aim of the union is primarily to benefit the group of workers concerned, rather than the workers as a whole or society as a whole."[11] It served the interests of employers to celebrate the free labor of individual workers, because the rhetoric of individualism undermined union solidarity and so prevented unions from being able to "dictate the terms" on which employers "may be permitted" to conduct business.[12]

Labor & the Jurisprudence of Individualism

Early in their careers, Taft and Holmes had each explicitly rejected the "abstract individualism"[13] implied by the rhetoric of free labor. Neither thought it realistic to conceptualize the labor market as "the enthronement of the will" and the individual "contract as the instrument of its attainment."[14] In 1900, as chief justice of Massachusetts, Holmes bluntly asserted (in dissent) that "unity of organization is necessary to make the contest of labor effectual."[15] Six years previously, in the course of imposing a six-month jail sentence on an organizer for the American Railway Union during the great Pullman strike of 1894, Taft, writing as a Sixth Circuit judge, had articulated virtually the same thought. Taft explained that employees have

> the right to organize into or to join a labor union which should take joint action as to their terms of employment. It is of benefit to them and to the public that laborers should unite in their common interest and for lawful purposes. They have labor to sell. If they stand together, they are often able, all of them, to command better prices for their labor than when dealing singly with rich employers, because the necessities of the single employee may compel him to accept any terms offered him. The accumulation of a fund for the support of those who feel that the wages offered are below market prices is one of the legitimate objects of such an organization. They have the right to appoint officers who shall advise them as to the course to be taken by them in their relations with their employer. They may unite with other unions. The officers they appoint, or any other person to whom they choose to listen, may advise them as to the proper course to be taken by them in regard to their employment, or, if they choose to repose such authority in any one, may order them, on pain of expulsion from their union, peaceably to leave the employ of their employer because any of the terms of their employment are unsatisfactory.[16]

Taft reiterated these themes as Secretary of War in 1908, in anticipation of his successful presidential campaign. Speaking at Cooper Union in New York, Taft recognized that "the organization of capital into corporations with the position of advantage which this gives it in a dispute with single laborers over wages, makes it absolutely necessary for labor to unite to maintain itself." Taft condemned capitalists who refused to acknowledge "that the organization of labor – the labor union – is a permanent condition in the industrial world. It has come to stay. ... Under existing conditions the blindest course that an employer of labor can pursue is to decline to recognize labor unions as the controlling influence in the labor market and to insist upon dealing only with his particular employees." "I know that there has been at times a suggestion in the law that no strike can be legal," Taft said, but "I deny this."

> Men have a right to leave the employ of their employer in a body in order to impose on him as great an inconvenience as possible to induce him to come to their terms. They have the right in their labor unions to delegate to their leaders the power to say when to strike. They have the right in advance to accumulate by contributions from all members of the labor union a fund which shall enable them

to live during the pendency of the strike. They have the right to use persuasion with all other laborers who are invited to take their places, in order to convince them of the advantage to labor of united action. It is the business of courts and of the police to respect these rights with the same degree of care that they respect the rights of owners of capital to the protection of their property and business.[17]

Taft's vision, however, was distinctly at odds with that of the Supreme Court. Two weeks after Taft's address at Cooper Union, the Court implicitly ruled on the desirability of labor unions in its six-to-two decision in *Adair v. United States*.[18] *Adair* struck down as unconstitutional provisions of the Erdman Act[19] that prohibited interstate railroads from discriminating against employees on the basis of union membership. The Court placed its decision squarely on Fifth Amendment due process rights to "make contracts for the purchase of the labor of others, and equally the right to make contracts for the sale of one's own labor." The Court held that "the employer and the employee have equality of right, and any legislation that disturbs that equality is an arbitrary interference with the liberty of contract which no government can legally justify in a free land." "It cannot be ... that an employer is under any legal obligation, against his will, to retain an employee in his personal service any more than an employee can be compelled, against his will, to remain in the personal service of another."[20]

Adair exemplifies "the individualist approach"[21] that sustained free labor ideology. The implicit premise of the Court's reasoning was that individual railroad employees were symmetrically situated to the great interstate railroad corporations that dominated continental travel. Each was constitutionally protected in the exercise of their sovereign free will to contract as they chose. This perspective rendered unions merely voluntary associations of individual employees, entitled to no more government solicitude than any other purely voluntary organization. What this perspective missed, however, was the unique role played by unions in labor markets dominated by large corporations. Because in such markets labor could not hope to bargain on proximate terms of equality except through unions, unions served a distinctively public function. They offered the possibility of stability and legitimacy.

McKenna dissented in *Adair* on the ground that the purpose of the Erdman Act was to "reduce to a minimum labor strikes which affect interstate commerce." He quoted from a letter sent to Congress by the secretary of the Interstate Commerce Commission that had been included in the legislative history of the Act: "With the corporations as employers, on one side, and the organizations of railway employees, on the other, there will be a measure of equality of power and force which will surely bring about the essential requisites of friendly relation, respect, consideration, and forbearance."[22] Holmes dissented on the more abstract ground that the Constitution did not forbid the regulation of employment contracts whenever "an important ground of public policy" was at stake.[23]

Richard Olney, who had been attorney general under Cleveland, and who had crushed the massive Pullman strike of 1894,[24] was appalled by *Adair*. "It is archaic – it is a long step back into the past – to conceive of and deal with relations between employer [in great modern industries] and employee as if the parties were

Labor & the Jurisprudence of Individualism

individuals. Co-operation and combination are the characteristics of modern industrialism." It is "impossible" to expect "the individual laborer ... to cope with associated and organized capital on even terms." "Only by their united and disciplined strength," Olney wrote, could "those with labor to sell hope to make reasonable terms with the partnerships and corporations desirous to buy." "To shut a man from work because he is a member of a labor union is to deliver an attack upon labor unions of the deadliest character. If the attack cannot be prevented by being put under the ban of the law, the labor unions can hardly do otherwise than assert themselves and repel the attack through a strike." It was therefore "inexplicable" that the Court could not find "any connection between membership of a labor union and the carrying on of interstate commerce."[25]

Seven years later, over the dissents of Holmes, Day, and Hughes, the Court in *Coppage v. Kansas*,[26] speaking forcefully through Pitney,[27] once again expressed an individualistic view of the employment relationship. It struck down a Kansas statute that prohibited "yellow-dog" contracts, which were agreements signed by employees not to join a union.[28] The Court explicitly acknowledged "the full right of the individual to join the union," but insisted that "he has no inherent right to do this and still remain in the employ of one who is unwilling to employ a union man, any more than the same individual has a right to join the union without the consent of that organization." The Court characterized "the relation of employer and employee" as "a voluntary relation," and affirmed that contracts of "personal employment" were especially indispensable to both constitutional property and liberty, "as essential to the laborer as to the capitalist, to the poor as to the rich; for the vast majority of persons have no other honest way to begin to acquire property, save by working for money." "Granted the equal freedom of both parties to the contract of employment, has not each party the right to stipulate upon what terms only he will consent to the inception, or to the continuance, of that relationship?"[29]

Pitney denied that there was any policy reason to protect unionization. "[N]o attempt is made, or could reasonably be made," Pitney said, "to sustain the purpose to strengthen these voluntary organizations, any more than other voluntary associations of persons, as a legitimate object for the exercise of the police power. They are not public institutions, charged by law with public or governmental duties, such as would render the maintenance of their membership a matter of direct concern to the general welfare."[30]

Nor, Pitney explained, could the Court agree that wage contracts were less voluntary for poor laborers than for rich corporations. Pitney maintained that "normal and inevitable" differences in wealth produced by the market could not justify state interference with precious constitutional liberties of the kind at stake in employment contracts:

> [I]t is said by the Kansas supreme court to be a matter of common knowledge that "employees, as a rule, are not financially able to be as independent in making contracts for the sale of their labor as are employers in making a contract of purchase thereof." No doubt, wherever the right of private property exists, there must and will be inequalities of fortune; and thus it naturally happens that parties negotiating about a contract are not equally unhampered by

circumstances. This applies to all contracts, and not merely to that between employer and employee. Indeed, a little reflection will show that wherever the right of private property and the right of free contract coexist, each party when contracting is inevitably more or less influenced by the question whether he has much property, or little, or none; for the contract is made to the very end that each may gain something that he needs or desires more urgently than that which he proposes to give in exchange. And, since it is self-evident that, unless all things are held in common, some persons must have more property than others, it is from the nature of things impossible to uphold freedom of contract and the right of private property without at the same time recognizing as legitimate those inequalities of fortune that are the necessary result of the exercise of those rights. ...

And since a state may not strike them down directly, it is clear that it may not do so indirectly, as by declaring in effect that the public good requires the removal of those inequalities that are but the normal and inevitable result of their exercise, and then invoking the police power in order to remove the inequalities, without other object in view.[31]

Coppage held that employment contracts could not be regulated to compensate for structural disadvantages inflicted on labor by existing market practices. "[A]n interference with the normal exercise of personal liberty and property rights is the primary object of the statute, and not an incident to the advancement of the general welfare. But, in our opinion, the Fourteenth Amendment debars the states from striking down personal liberty or property rights, or materially restricting their normal exercise, excepting so far as may be incidentally necessary for the accomplishment of some other and paramount object, and one that concerns the public welfare. The mere restriction of liberty or of property rights cannot of itself be denominated 'public welfare,' and treated as a legitimate object of the police power; for such restriction is the very thing that is inhibited by the Amendment."[32]

The valorization of the "normal" functioning of the market, which would become a significant theme during the 1920s in the Taft Court's review of social and economic regulation, is plainly evident in *Coppage*. It is a theme very much in tension with the Court's nearly simultaneous approval of workmen's compensation legislation, sometimes in opinions written by Pitney himself.[33] In the workmen's compensation cases, the Court upheld restrictions on employment contracts on the ground that legislatures could alter common law rules of tort liability in ways reasonably designed to acknowledge the "different relation to the common undertaking" of employers and employees.[34]

The Court authorized government to regulate employment contracts to protect workers' safety because, as the Court delicately put it in *Holden v. Hardy*, "proprietors ... and their operatives do not stand upon an equality."[35] The Court fully understood that employees lacked sufficient market power to negotiate for adequate workplace safety. But the Court in *Coppage* refused to allow this same powerlessness to justify legislative protections for union membership. Most likely this was because recognizing unions, in contrast to increasing protections for worker safety, would redistribute power within the structure of the labor market itself. It would allow workers to join together to attempt to equalize bargaining

Labor & the Jurisprudence of Individualism

power with capital in negotiating for wages. But the Court apparently regarded the individualism of the employment market, with its attendant structural disadvantages for employees, as necessary for the "normal and inevitable" operation of economic freedom.

In focusing on the constitutional prerequisites of "essential" individual freedom, the Court plainly had very much in mind the managerial prerogatives of employers. This focus came sharply into view two years after *Coppage* when the Court decided *Hitchman Coal & Coke Co. v. Mitchell*.[36] *Hitchman* involved the question of whether a federal court could restrain a union from organizing a corporation whose employees had assented to yellow-dog contracts. In a 6–3 decision (with Brandeis, Holmes, and Clarke dissenting), the Court, again speaking through Pitney, held in December 1917 that federal courts could enjoin unionizing campaigns that involved tortious interference with contracts, including at-will yellow-dog contracts.[37] No one even pretended that federal protection of these contracts was for the benefit of individual employees. Everyone recognized that the purpose of federal intervention was to protect the managerial prerogatives of employers.[38]

Citing *Adair* and *Coppage*, Pitney explained in *Hitchman* that "[t]his court repeatedly has held that the employer is as free to make non-membership in a union a condition of employment, as the working man is free to join the union, and that this is a part of the constitutional rights of personal liberty and private property, not to be taken away even by legislation, unless through some proper exercise of the paramount police power." Conceding "the right of workingmen to form unions, and to enlarge their membership by inviting other workingmen to join," Pitney nevertheless insisted that an employer, "having in the exercise of its undoubted rights established a working agreement between it and its employés, with the free assent of the latter, is entitled to be protected in the enjoyment of the resulting status, as in any other legal right."[39]

Hitchman created a powerful new weapon for employers to resist unionization.[40] Although yellow-dog contracts could not realistically be enforced against individual workers, they could justify employers' petitions to "secure injunctions prohibiting unions from attempting to organize their employees or inducing them to join in strikes. With this development, yellow dog contracts ... came into ... widespread use."[41] *Hitchman* prepared the ground for the explosion of federal labor injunctions that would occur during the 1920s.

Even as *Hitchman* was decided, however, events were rapidly overtaking the individualist assumptions implicit in the Court's view of the labor market. In December 1917, the nation was searching for a labor policy adequate to the challenges of World War I. It had quickly become apparent that modern warfare obliterated "the old lines between soldier and civilian, between war operations and the work of production," because war had become "a contest between the industrial organization and technique of the opposing nations."[42] That is why Major-General Enoch Crowder, who oversaw the operation of the draft, announced that men "must work or fight": "This is not alone a war of military maneuver," Crowder explained. "It is a deadly contest of industries and mechanics. Germany must not be thought of merely as possessing an army, we must think of her as being an army – an army in which every factory and loom in the Empire is a recognized part in a complete machine running night and day at terrific speed. We must make of ourselves the same sort of effective machine."[43] The war, said Taft, exposed "the dependence of every nation upon the working people: labor was essential to the winning of the war. ... The nation in which labor deserted was beaten."[44]

The individualist labor market imagined by Pitney was incapable of meeting the demands of the war. Military enlistment and decreased immigration produced chronic labor shortages, yet the war demanded increased production. There was steep wartime inflation. The result was a tumultuous labor market, in which there were frequent strikes and an "extraordinary movement of workers from one industry to another or from plant to plant" in search of higher wages.[45] It quickly became clear that some form of collective representation, either through trade unions or shop committees, was necessary to stabilize labor-management relationships.

The Wilson administration commissioned a War Labor Conference Board, co-chaired by Taft and Frank P. Walsh, a prominent labor attorney who had headed Wilson's Commission on Industrial Relations, to propose a set of principles to govern national labor policy during the war. Recognizing the need for collective bargaining to steady the labor market, the Conference Board announced in March 1918:

> There should be no strikes or lockouts during the war. ...
>
> The right of workers to organize in trade-unions and to bargain collectively, through chosen representatives, is recognized and affirmed. This right shall not be denied, abridged, or interfered with by the employers in any manner whatsoever. ...
>
> Employers should not discharge workers for membership in trade unions, nor for legitimate trade-union activities.[46]

These principles were starkly inconsistent with the holdings of *Adair*, *Coppage*, and *Hitchman*.[47]

On April 8, 1918, Wilson by proclamation created the National War Labor Board ("NWLB"), which was charged with adjudicating controversies involving the application of the principles promulgated by the Conference Board.[48] Taft and Walsh were named co-chairs of the NWLB, and they functioned as an effective and amicable team.[49] They promptly swept aside the Court's holdings in *Adair*, *Coppage*, and *Hitchman*. They prohibited yellow-dog contracts and all discrimination against employees on grounds of union membership.[50] Although the NWLB had no enforcement powers, it spoke with the full authority of the federal government. When Western Union Telegraph refused to abandon its policy of dismissing workers who were union members, the Wilson administration seized control of all telegraph and telephone lines.[51] It did not go unnoticed that "the necessity of mobilizing millions of workers" required "the Taft-Walsh Labor Policies Board" to promulgate policies that were "in flat contravention of the Supreme Court's decisions."[52]

Labor & the Jurisprudence of Individualism

The NWLB required employers to bargain collectively with freely chosen representatives of employees. Although it did not impose union recognition in workplaces that had not been unionized before the war, it did mandate that employers bargain with shop committees selected by employees in the workplace. Since employers could no longer discriminate among workers based on union membership, union members quickly came to dominate shop committees throughout the country.[53] As a consequence, the NWLB "instituted a mini-legal revolution by making the right to unionize real and by requiring employers to bargain collectively."[54] In the process, the NWLB exercised "immense" "influence for improvement of industrial relations during the war" and "achieved its most pressing task, the stabilization and adjustment of industrial relationships in such a way as to maintain and increase the war production of the nation."[55]

Believing that the Board "has attained a real success," Taft after the war recommended "that a board of somewhat similar jurisdiction should be created either by the President or by law as an instrumentality for the peaceful settlement of industrial disputes during the period of readjustment after the war, if not thereafter." Because the NWLB balanced representatives of employers with representatives of organized labor, Taft understood that his recommendation effectively acknowledged that the "organization of labor has become a recognized institution in all the civilized countries of the world. It has come to stay; it is full of usefulness and is necessary to the laborer."[56]

The experience of the war made Taft impatient with the employer who was a "bourbon," who believed that "[i]t is my legal right to manage my business as I choose, to pay such wages as I choose, to exclude from my employment union men, because I don't approve of the tenets of the union . . . . I run a closed non-union shop, and I am happy and propose to continue happy." This man, Taft said,

> is far behind in the progress of our social civilization. . . . He looks to fear of courts and injunctions and police and militia as the ordinary and usual instruments for continuing his business peacefully and maintaining his rights. He is like the man who regards the threat of a divorce court as a proper and usual means of continuing domestic unhappiness. . . . He does not see that the whole public is interested in industrial peace. . . . [W]hether we will or not, the group system is here to stay, and every statesman and every man interested in public affairs must recognize that it has to be dealt with as a condition, to be favored in such a way as to minimize its abuses and to increase its utility.[57]

The success of the NWLB drew on the wide-ranging authority assumed by the federal government during the war. It was plain, however, that the national government would not assert such authority after the Armistice, and so the question was whether a system of labor–management relations such as Taft imagined, which essentially depended upon voluntary compliance, could survive the peace. That question was quickly settled by the tumultuous labor unrest of 1919. "One does not pick up a newspaper these days," it was said, "without finding anywhere from one to a dozen head-line announcements of new strikes and new developments in old ones."[58]

The strikes were in part caused by labor's new-found militancy, inspired by an environment in which, for the first time in American history, labor organizing had been protected by the federal government. The strikes were in part prompted by rampant postwar inflation, which corroded wartime wage increases. And the strikes were also in part provoked by the unleashed aggression of employers seeking to crush union organizing in postwar America. NWLB regulations had been deeply resented. Employers "who submitted to necessity during the war but whose prejudices against labor were magnified by the petty tyranny incidental to the suddenness of labor's power," were eager to reassert their traditional prerogatives. "One influential officer of a great clothing concern said recently: 'I am sick of the daily demands of labor committees or union leaders. *I am looking for the day when I can see a million men outside my office begging work: then we can teach labor some sense.*'"[59]

The chosen vehicle for "the employers' campaign to liquidate labor's wartime gains"[60] was the "American Plan," which consisted of a commitment to a shop that was in theory open to all employees, including union members, but that was in practice antiunion.[61] "To many employers," Taft observed, the "open shop . . . means . . . a shop from which union men are excluded."[62]

The "American Plan" celebrated precisely the individualist premises that Pitney had so forcefully articulated in *Coppage*. As the United States Chamber of Commerce declared in 1919, "the right of open shop operation, that is, the right of employer and employee to enter into and to determine the conditions of employment relations with each other, is an essential part of the individual right to contract possessed by each of the parties."[63] The American Bankers' Association endorsed the American Plan because "[e]very man should be free to work out his own salvation, and not be bound by the shackles of organization to his detriment."[64] "The workman," said Elbert H. Gary, chair of the Board of the United States Steel Corporation, "if he belongs to a labor union, becomes the industrial slave of the union. He has no power or initiative or opportunity to apply his natural mental and physical capacity."[65]

For a year after the Armistice the nation suffered titanic struggles between employers determined to roll back labor's wartime advances and employees equally determined to entrench and expand rights they had enjoyed during the war.[66] Employers freely played the "red" card, accusing unions of an anti-American radicalism.[67] In the heated atmosphere of the time, accusations of foreign radicalism were effective in turning public opinion against labor.[68] Rampant inflation, together with the severe inconveniences that accompanied labor stoppages in essential services like railroads and coal, further alienated public opinion.

The Wilson administration struggled to salvage the connections it had forged with organized labor. It called an Industrial Conference for October 1919 to seek solutions to the crisis, inviting representatives of employers, employees, and the public.[69] Wilson charged the Conference with finding a way to "bring capital and labor into close cooperation" and to "obviate the wastefulness caused by the continued interruption of many of our important industrial enterprises by strikes and lockouts."[70] "We have found ways of regulating all the other relations of mankind," said Secretary of Labor William Wilson. "Surely human intelligence can devise some acceptable method of adjusting the relationship between employer and employee."[71]

The conference collapsed, however, when employer representatives refused to accept a resolution that recognized the right of employees "to organize without discrimination, to bargain collectively, to be represented by representatives of their own choosing."[72] From the employers' perspective, "the principle of the open shop" was fundamental, and "the 'essential' conditions of the true open shop were that 'the representatives of the employees ... should be chosen from their own number,' (in other words, not from 'outsiders' such as union officials), and that 'no employer should be required to deal with labor unions.'... [I]t was the 'utmost freedom' of management to act without outside interference and not labor's freedom to be employed without discrimination that became the essence of the open shop."[73]

Taft was despondent. "The group of employers in the industrial conference have by one vote yielded to their bourbon members in rejecting Mr. Gompers' resolution on collective bargaining," he wrote. "The truth is that the reactionaries among them do not approve of labor unions at all, and would wish to prevent their existence and operation if they could."

> Collective bargaining is the logical result of the right of labor to organize. That is what trade unions are for. They are to enable groups of workingmen to formulate their claims for certain terms of employment. In the unions they find the strength enabling them to deal with powerful employers on an equality. As individuals, they cannot bargain. They must do it through representatives. Why should they be limited in the choice of those who are to speak for them? The only possible reason is to exclude trade unionism in its essence from its legitimate and acknowledged purpose. It is really a contradiction in terms to favor trade unions and collective bargaining and then limit choice of representation.[74]

As if on cue, the United Mine Workers ("UMW") went out on strike the week after the Conference disbanded. Breaking the tacit alliance between labor and the Democratic Party, Attorney General A. Mitchell Palmer broke the strike by securing a broad judicial injunction.[75] "We are Americans," UMW Acting President John L. Lewis conceded, "we cannot fight our Government."[76] Although Taft applauded the use of the injunction to end of the strike,[77] he cautioned that "the usefulness of the injunction in the coal strike should not mislead reactionary employers into the belief that it is a panacea for labor troubles."

> It has worked well because public opinion has sanctioned its use by the courts at the instance of the government in defense of the lives of the whole people. But it was only justified by the great emergency, and was only made necessary by the incredible sense of irresponsible power of the strike leaders. Labor troubles are not to be permanently solved in any such way. Government of the relations between capital and labor by injunction is a solecism. It is an

absurdity. Injunctions in labor troubles are merely the emergency brakes for rare use and increase of sudden danger. Frequent application of them would shake to pieces the whole machine. They should be availed of only when the soviet policy of a selfish aggregation of men pushes society against the wall into a desperate situation. ... There is no law that can be enforced against either party to compel an agreement. That which must impel both sides to come together is a social obligation which only enforces itself through public opinion and the conscience of both sides as members of society.[78]

When Wilson suffered a disabling stroke in fall 1919, control of his administration fell increasingly into the hands of the "Bourbon Southern wing of the Democratic party," which "frothed at the mouth at [Wilson's] association of the name and fortunes of the party with the interests of labor."[79] The Republican Party was of course closely associated with the interests of employers and was opposed to pro-labor legislation like the Clayton Act. As a result, labor was left without a home in either party. Neither Republicans nor Democrats wished to antagonize organized labor, but each party was plainly aware of the public's frustration at the profound inconveniences of labor unrest.[80]

Harding's landslide victory in the 1920 election was popularly perceived as catastrophic for organized labor.[81] Brandeis immediately wrote Frankfurter that "I think labor ought to be advised to look for a substitute for the closed shop and also for strikes. The courts and public opinion are closing in on both."[82] In truth, however, Harding emerged from the 1920 election "confused, prejudiced, and inconsistent"[83] in his attitude toward labor. His administration would feature policies that ranged from the savage Daugherty injunction of 1922[84] to the relatively enlightened programs of Hoover.[85] What is essential, however, is that from the moment of his nomination Harding never understood himself as a spokesman for extreme antilabor members of the Republican Party, like Senator Miles Poindexter of Washington, who stridently accused "labor leaders claiming to be conservative" of being disguised "Communist Bolsheviki" seeking the "abolishment of the wage system" and a "dictatorship of the proletariat."[86]

Remembering the decisive role played by labor in narrowly defeating Hughes in 1916, Harding was temperamentally inclined to respond "favorably to the counsel of former Senator George Sutherland of Utah and former President William Howard Taft, both of whom ... were concerned as much about antilabor extremism as about labor's 'arrogance.'"[87] So, for example, Sutherland wrote Harding in January 1921:

> I know there is sentiment in our party – I find it with some of my best friends – that the open shop is the only thing to be considered. Personally, I agree with the open shop idea, provided it means an open shop for everybody and does not mean a closed shop for the man who belongs to a labor organization. I think the latter attitude would simply be the substitution of one form of intolerance for another. I have talked with some men prominent in labor circles, and I get the very decided impression that the Unions generally recognize that they have lost, to a great degree, the sympathy of the public and they are disposed to be far less

arrogant than they were before the election. I do not think it would be wise to adopt a course of drastic opposition which would incur their enmity and deprive us of their help in case of trouble. I think the policy should be one of absolute fairness without discrimination, for or against, any class of labor so long as it conducts itself in conformity to law and the rights of others, including the general public.[88]

In the end, Harding "sought to deaden the labor issue, to render the labor vote harmless." He tried to "convince workers and their leaders that the GOP constituted no threat to collective bargaining and that the party was not in the hands of the vocal reactionaries who called loudly for an all-out attack."[89]

Harding's nomination of Taft to be chief justice was consistent with this ambivalence. Taft had successfully chaired the NWLB, earning the respect and cooperation of labor, and he had staunchly defended the right of employees to bargain collectively through representatives of their own choosing. Taft's insistent and explicit embrace of the "group system" seemed to portend a possible judicial departure from the individualism of *Adair*, *Coppage*, and *Hitchman*.[90]

Yet Taft was also "one of the early injunction judges";[91] indeed, he was known as "the 'father of injunctions.'"[92] Taft had been personally attacked in 1908 by Gompers as "the originator and specific champion of discretionary government – that is, government by injunction."[93] Taft had also firmly denounced labor's postwar aggression. "The war gave the labor unions . . . a sense of absolute power," he chided, "which they have abused, and in their abuse of it they have united the public in a determination in self-defense to prevent future abuses."[94] Taft had publicly rejoiced "in the failure" of the steel strike. "The strike was sustained only by cooperation of the alien workingmen who were unfamiliar with our institutions, many of them unable to talk our language, and all of them out of sympathy with our governmental system. They were permeated with the false doctrines of Bolshevism, intoxicated with the idea of obtaining complete control through this strike of the plants in which they were employed, and of initiating a Soviet system by which they should plunder the wealth they saw all about them."[95]

As Taft assumed the center chair, therefore, the nation waited anxiously to see how the newly constituted Taft Court would handle the contentious questions of "industrial warfare"[96] that had consumed the nation since the Armistice. The timing was not auspicious. In October 1921, the nation was threatened by a potentially calamitous strike of railroad shopmen,[97] the last great postwar strike, which personally worried and concerned Taft.[98] At the very moment that Taft was fretting about a possible railroad strike, the Court was confronted by a blockbuster case, *American Steel Foundries v. Tri-City Central Trades Council*,[99] which squarely posed the question of how courts should regulate industrial strife.

The case was difficult and complex. It had first been argued on January 17, 1919; after a year of intense industrial unrest, it had been restored to the docket for reargument on June 1, 1920, and it was reargued for a second time on October 4, 1920. After the death of White, the case was again restored to the docket. There is every reason to believe that the case bitterly divided the Court.[100] It was set for a third argument on October 4, 1921, the second day of the maiden term of the Taft

Court.[101] It was Taft's first great challenge as chief justice and, in the end, he achieved what Holmes characterized as "a happy success in uniting the Court."[102]

The facts of the case read like the story of labor relations in the United States during the first decades of the twentieth century. American Steel Foundries was a New Jersey corporation with a large plant for manufacturing steel products in Illinois. The plant employed about 1,600 men. In November 1913, tired of paying union wages and dealing with union demands, American Steel Foundries shut down the plant, reopening in April 1914 as a nonunion factory with a workforce of about 350 employees who were paid a reduced wage. The Tri-City Trades Council, a labor organization composed of about thirty-seven different trade unions in the area, called a strike to restore a union wage scale. Two employees left the plant to join the strike, only one of whom was a member of a union.

To enforce the strike, the Tri-City Trades Council formed a picket line around the plant, and there were sporadic reports of disorder and violence.[103] American Steel Foundries sought and received an injunction enjoining the defendants from, among many other things, "in any way or manner whatsoever by use of *persuasion*, threats, or personal injury, intimidation, . . . interfering with, hindering, obstructing or stopping any person engaged in the employ of the American Steel Foundries in connection with its business." Defendants were also prohibited "*from picketing* or maintaining at or near the premises of the complainant . . . any picket or pickets."[104] When the Trades Council appealed, the Seventh Circuit modified the decree by eliminating the word "persuasion" and "by inserting after the clause restraining picketing the following: 'in a threatening or intimidating manner.'"[105]

The question thus presented was "whether or not picketing is necessarily illegal – particularly picketing by mere persuasion where no violence, threats, or intimidation is directly or indirectly used."[106] There were two conflicting lines of cases facing the Court. On one side were decisions holding that during a lawful strike a "union may appoint pickets or a committee to visit the vicinity of factories for the purpose of taking note of the persons employed, and to secure, if it can be done by lawful means, their names and places of residence for the purpose of peaceful visitation."[107] On the other side were precedents holding that "[t]here is and can be no such thing as peaceful picketing, any more than there can be chaste vulgarity, or peaceful mobbing, or lawful lynching."[108] Just two weeks before the argument in *American Steel Foundries*, a New York trial judge had explicitly rejected the claim that it was permissible to engage in "peacefully picketing." "Why picket at all? Picketing and the posting of sentinels are done as war measures. Our laws and institutions will not permit of the waging of private war in such a manner."[109]

American Steel Foundries eerily revived a case that had intimately involved Taft when he was Secretary of War. A federal district judge had issued a labor injunction prohibiting the Iron Molders' union from picketing, whether by peaceful persuasion or otherwise.[110] As Theodore Roosevelt recalled the situation in 1908, just a month before Taft was elected president:

> The editor of the Iron Molders' Journal, Mr. J.P. Fry, brought the case before me, stating that the union did not know what to do; that its funds were

limited; that they felt that they were suffering from a gross injustice which they were powerless to remedy. I called in Mr. Taft and asked Mr. Fry to lay the case before him, as, of course, Mr. Taft was far more competent than I was to express his judgment as the legality and propriety of the action taken.

Mr. Taft satisfied himself of the facts and at once became exceedingly indignant at such an injunction having been issued. He stated that in his opinion the position taken by the court in issuing the injunction was clearly untenable and that what was needed was that the union should get some first-class lawyer to represent them and should bring the case before the higher courts.[111]

Taft suggested that his Yale classmate Frederick N. Judson, whom Taft would later appoint as his alternate on the NWLB,[112] be hired to handle the case. "Mr. Taft explained that one of the troubles of the labor unions was that often they did not get the best type of counsel, so that their case was not properly presented, and that in his judgment Mr. Judson would be sure to present this case aright. He stated that the decision of the court ought certainly to be in their favor."[113]

Taft proved correct in his prediction. The Seventh Circuit did indeed modify the injunction. In *Iron Molders' Union No. 125 v. Allis-Chalmers Co.*,[114] it held that "With respect to picketing as well as persuasion, we think the decree went beyond the line. . . . Under the name of persuasion, duress may be used; but it is duress, not persuasion, that should be restrained and punished. . . . Prohibitions of persuasion and picketing, as such, should not be included in the decree."[115] Now, in 1921, in *American Steel Foundries*, this case would come back to haunt Taft, for the Seventh Circuit decision below had expressly relied on *Allis-Chalmers* to modify the district court injunction.[116] *American Steel Foundries* was in federal court because of diversity jurisdiction, and the parameters of equitable relief were therefore a matter of federal common law.

In the decades after In re *Debs*,[117] organized labor had engaged in "unceasing agitation" to restrict the issuance of federal injunctions in labor disputes.[118] Labor thought it had finally achieved that goal in 1914 with the enactment of the Clayton Act,[119] which seemed on its face to restrict federal equitable intervention in labor disputes,[120] and which Gompers famously celebrated as "the Industrial Magna Carta" of labor that secures "industrial freedom and makes workers free in thought and act."[121] Gompers's interpretation of the Act was supported by Taft's former attorney general George Wickersham, who worried that "labor organizations have secured . . . the legalization of the boycott as a lawful instrument to ensure the dominance of organized labor, thus substituting Gompers' conception of liberty for that of the Declaration of Independence, the Constitution of the United States and Abraham Lincoln."[122]

But the Clayton Act had been badly drafted. Taft, in his presidential address to the American Bar Association, assured the organization "in the presence of Justices of the Supreme Court"[123] that, when closely parsed, the Clayton Act actually changed very little and was chiefly "declaratory merely of what would be law without the statute."[124] The *New Republic* concurred, concluding that "Congress has passed a law which organized labor firmly believes has exempted it from the Sherman law, but which in reality is skillfully drafted so as to do nothing of the kind."[125] Labor unions, in the view of the progressive intellectuals at the magazine, were sorely in need of "expert assistance" and "highly trained counsel," who would not have permitted "such a shabbily drawn piece of legislation as the Clayton act" to "have been put on the statute books."[126]

When the Supreme Court finally undertook to interpret the Clayton Act in January 1921, it held in a six-to-three decision in *Duplex Printing Press Co. v. Deering*, authored by Pitney, that Taft was correct and that the Act was "but declaratory of the law as it stood before."[127] There is nothing in the Act, Pitney wrote, that exempts unions from federal injunctions when they depart from their "normal and legitimate objects and engage in an actual combination or conspiracy in restraint of trade. And by no fair or permissible construction can it be taken as authorizing any activity otherwise unlawful, or enabling a normally lawful organization to become a cloak for an illegal combination or conspiracy in restraint of trade as defined by the anti-trust laws."[128] In vain did Brandeis, joined by Holmes and Clarke, dissent on the ground that it ought to be "Congress, not the judges" who "should declare what public policy in regard to the industrial struggle demands."[129] The result was that the Clayton Act, "a statute full of words that seemed a balm to labor, turned out upon interpretation to be chiefly a bane."[130] The Act actually *expanded* federal equitable jurisdiction, because it authorized private parties to apply for injunctions which previously could have been issued only at the behest of the federal government.[131]

In *American Steel Foundries*, Taft took the occasion explicitly and forcefully to reaffirm *Duplex Printing Press*. "It is clear," Taft said, "that Congress wished to forbid the use by the federal courts of their equity arm to prevent peaceable persuasion by employees, discharged or expectant, in promotion of their side of the dispute, and to secure them against judicial restraint in obtaining or communicating information in any place where they might lawfully be. This introduces no new principle into the equity jurisprudence of those courts. It is merely declaratory of what was the best practice always."[132]

Since the time of Lemuel Shaw's decision in *Hunt*, the "best practice" had determined the legality of concerted labor action either by its purpose or by the means through which it sought to effectuate that purpose. In *Hitchman Coal & Coke*, the Court had held that seeking to induce workers to breach their contracts "was an unlawful purpose,"[133] so that an organizing drive with that purpose could be enjoined even though a union did not engage in picketing, threats, violence, or intimidation.[134] Similarly, the purpose of the union's action in *Duplex Printing Press* was to implement a "secondary boycott," which was illegal under anti-trust laws. Consequently, the absence of threats, violence, picketing, or intimidation was irrelevant to the propriety of an injunction to shut down the boycott.[135]

The first question in *American Steel Foundries* was therefore whether the Tri-City Central Trades Council had a lawful purpose in picketing the plant, given that the Council consisted of unions that were not recognized by the plant, and that those on the picket lines were not employees or ex-employees of the plant.[136] "The argument made on behalf of the American Foundries in support of enjoining persuasion is that the Tri-City Central Trades Council and the other defendants

Labor & the Jurisprudence of Individualism

being neither employees nor strikers were intruders into the controversy, and were engaged without excuse in an unlawful conspiracy to injure the American Foundries by enticing its employees, and, therefore, should be enjoined."[137]

This kind of claim had been superbly analyzed twenty years before in Holmes's brilliant essay *Privilege, Malice, and Intent*,[138] in which he argued that law frequently privileges the intentional infliction of harm, as the Tri-City Central Trades Council's picketing no doubt was meant to cause. A simple example is the privilege extended by law to those who seek to harm their competitors in the natural operation of the market. The question of "whether, and how far, a privilege shall be allowed is a question of policy. Questions of policy are legislative questions" because unconscious "economic sympathies" might undermine merely judicial judgment.[139] Holmes illustrated his theory by reference to judicial regulation of labor boycotts, in which judges seeking to prevent harms caused by union organizing were "flying in the face of the organization of the world." Instead of applying the "very serious legislative considerations" required properly to analyze such situations, they were instead merely venting "unconscious prejudice or half conscious inclination." They were entering the "fields of battle" entailed by policy disputes without training or proper preparation, and thus frustrating the need for law to become an instrument of an "organized society knowingly seeking to determine its own destinies."[140]

Two years later, in *Vegelahn v. Guntner*, Holmes applied his theory of justified harm to a case in which a union picketed a shop to pressure it to pay union wages. Although individuals could without consequence withhold patronage from the shop for any reason, the question was whether persons could combine to engage in such actions for the purpose of establishing a shop with union wages. The majority of the Supreme Judicial Court of Massachusetts held that it was illegal for persons to conspire to interfere with an employer's "right to engage all persons who are willing to work for him, at such prices as may be mutually agreed upon," as well as with the right of "persons employed or seeking employment" to "enter into or remain in the employment of any person or corporation willing to employ them."[141] The union was therefore prohibited from using entirely peaceful means of persuasion for the purpose of altering the shop's wages.

In dissent, Holmes agreed that unions could be enjoined from any "threat of violence, either express or implied," or from interfering "with existing contracts." But the court approved an injunction that prohibited peacefully persuading others not to deal with the plaintiff. Such an injunction squarely raised the question of whether the intentional infliction of harm against the plaintiff could be justified in law. This was the precise issue that Holmes had analyzed in *Privilege, Malice, and Intent*. In *Vegelahn*, Holmes argued that the same reasons of policy that privileged the intentional infliction of harm in competition also privileged a union's use of peaceful methods to obtain higher wages.

> [T]he policy of allowing free competition justifies the intentional inflicting of temporal damage, including the damage of interference with a man's business by some means, when the damage is done, not for its own sake, but as an

instrumentality in reaching the end of victory in the battle of trade. ... We all agree, I presume, that it may be done by persuasion to leave a rival's shop, and come to the defendant's. ... It may be done by the withdrawal of, or threat to withdraw, such advantages from third persons who have a right to deal or not to deal with the plaintiff, as a means of inducing them not to deal with him either as customers or servants. ... I have seen the suggestion made that the conflict between employers and employed was not competition. But I venture to assume that none of my brethren would rely on that suggestion. If the policy on which our law is founded is too narrowly expressed in the term "free competition," we may substitute "free struggle for life." Certainly, the policy is not limited to struggles between persons of the same class, competing for the same end. It applies to all conflicts of temporal interests.[142]

Holmes explicitly rejected the conclusion that union action could be suppressed because it was the action of "a combination of persons." "It is plain from the slightest consideration of practical affairs," Holmes said, "that free competition means combination, and that the organization of the world, now going on so fast, means an ever-increasing might and scope of combination." "One of the eternal conflicts out of which life is made up is that between the effort of every man to get the most he can for his services, and that of society, disguised under the name of capital, to get his services for the least possible return. Combination on the one side is patent and powerful. Combination on the other is the necessary and desirable counterpart, if the battle is to be carried on in a fair and equal way."[143]

At least since his 1889 opinion as a young Ohio trial judge in *Moores & Co. v. Bricklayers' Union*,[144] Taft had consistently analyzed labor issues using essentially the same analytic framework as Holmes would later explicate in *Privilege, Malice, and Intent*.[145] Like Holmes, Taft did not regard the intentional infliction of harm as dispositive. Instead, the question was whether harm was "done with or without just cause or excuse."[146] In 1921, in *American Steel Foundries*, Taft applied this analytic framework to explore whether Tri-City Central Trades Council's purpose of forcing American Steel Foundries to pay union wages was sufficient to justify intentionally inflicting harm on the company.

One difficulty was that neither the Council nor its members were employees or former employees of American Steel Foundries. The Council was a stranger to the relations between American Steel Foundries and its workmen. In explaining why the Council was nevertheless justified in calling for the strike, and hence why the strike ought not be enjoined because its purpose was improper, Taft deployed rhetoric that mirrored Holmes's language – rhetoric that turned on words like "struggle," "competition," and "combination."

> It is thus probable that members of the local unions were looking forward to employment when complainant should resume full operation and even though they were not ex-employees within the Clayton Act, they were directly interested in the wages which were to be paid.
>
> Is interference of a labor organization by persuasion and appeal to induce a strike against low wages, under such circumstances without lawful excuse and

malicious? We think not. Labor unions are recognized by the Clayton Act as legal when instituted for mutual help and lawfully carrying out their legitimate objects. They have long been thus recognized by the courts. They were organized out of the necessities of the situation. A single employee was helpless in dealing with an employer. He was dependent ordinarily on his daily wage for the maintenance of himself and family. If the employer refused to pay him the wages that he thought fair, he was nevertheless unable to leave the employ and to resist arbitrary and unfair treatment. Union was essential to give laborers opportunity to deal on equality with their employer. They united to exert influence upon him and to leave him in a body in order by this inconvenience to induce him to make better terms with them. They were withholding their labor of economic value to make him pay what they thought it was worth. The right to combine for such a lawful purpose has in many years not been denied by any court. The strike became a lawful instrument in a lawful economic struggle or competition between employer and employees as to the share or division between them of the joint product of labor and capital. To render this combination at all effective, employees must make their combination extend beyond one shop. It is helpful to have as many as may be in the same trade in the same community united, because in the competition between employers they are bound to be affected by the standard of wages of their trade in the neighborhood. Therefore, they may use all lawful propaganda to enlarge their membership and especially among those whose labor at lower wages will injure their whole guild. It is impossible to hold such persuasion and propaganda without more, to be without excuse and malicious. The principle of the unlawfulness of maliciously enticing laborers still remains and action may be maintained therefor in proper cases, but to make it applicable to local labor unions, in such a case as this, seems to us to be unreasonable.[147]

It is no wonder that Holmes was moved to write Frankfurter the day after Taft announced his opinion that "I was delighted at the labor decision of the CJ yesterday."[148]

Taft's description of the essential function of labor unions was immediately canonized as "one of the most glowing paeans in the books upon the necessity of trade unionism in modern industrial society."[149] Taft's reasoning cut deeply into the received doctrinal structure of the Court's constitutional labor decisions. It decisively reaffirmed "the group system,"[150] challenging the individualist conception of the labor market that underlay decisions like *Adair* and *Coppage*. If the law favored the formation of unions because, as Taft affirmed, unions were necessary "to give laborers opportunity to deal on equality with their employer," then Holmes's dissent in *Coppage* acquired new force. Holmes had argued that prohibiting yellow-dog contracts was constitutionally permissible because "a workman not unnaturally may believe that only by belonging to a union can he secure a contract that shall be fair to him," and hence the state could legitimately seek "to establish the equality of position between the parties in which liberty of contract begins."[151]

In 1932, the House Report on the Norris-LaGuardia Act would quote Taft's language in *American Steel Foundries* to support the constitutionality of Section 2 of the proposed Act affirming a new national policy in favor of unionization.[152] To realize this policy, the Act prohibited federal courts from enforcing yellow-dog contracts.[153] Five years later, in *NLRB v. Jones & Laughlin Steel Corp*, Hughes would cite *American Steel Foundries* for the proposition that the Court had "long ago" recognized that unions were "essential to give laborers opportunity to deal on an equality with their employer."[154]

Taft's affirmation of "the group system" created serious tensions with Pitney's opinion in *Hitchman*. American Steel Foundries had in its brief specifically invoked *Hitchman* to argue that the Tri-City Central Trades Council was guilty of the "unlawful purpose" of interfering with its employment contracts. It made no difference that these contracts were "at-will," for *Hitchman* had held that even at-will contracts were valuable property, worthy of equitable protection. American Steel Foundries argued that the "illegal effort to secure the violation of the employment contract between the petitioner and its employees" was "injurious to the business and the property and the property rights of the petitioner" and hence under *Hitchman* "subject to injunction."[155]

Taft distinguished *Hitchman* on two grounds. The first was that the union in *Hitchman* had used "deception and misrepresentation" to induce breaches of contract, and that the "unlawful and deceitful means used were quite enough to sustain the decision of the court without more."[156] The second was that in *Hitchman* the UMW had sought to organize a nonunion mine in a distant state because mines paying union wages could not successfully compete in the national market against the lower labor costs of out-of-state nonunion mines. Taft argued that "the purpose of the plan" in *Hitchman* was "sufficient to show the remoteness of the benefit ultimately to be derived by the members of the International Union from its success." In *American Steel Foundries*, by contrast, Taft concluded that the Council had a "sufficient interest in the wages paid to the employees of *any employer in the community* to justify their use of lawful and peaceable persuasion to induce those employees to refuse to accept ... reduced wages and to quit their employment."[157]

Both these efforts to distinguish *Hitchman* were unconvincing. The first ignored *Hitchman*'s clear implication that an intention to induce a breach of contract was sufficient to render the purpose of a labor action illegitimate regardless of the use of "deception and misrepresentation."[158] The second perfectly illustrated the legislative "questions of policy" that Holmes theorized were at the heart of judicial regulation of labor controversies. Both the UMW and the Tri-City Central Trades Council acted on the premise that union wages in an industry cannot ultimately be sustained unless labor costs were equalized as between union and nonunion shops. In *Hitchman*, this premise led the UMW to attempt to organize nonunion coal fields in West Virginia;[159] in *American Steel Foundries*, the same premise led the Tri-City Central Trades Council to attempt to raise wages in a local plant in its own tri-city area. The Court asserted that the benefits to the union in *Hitchman* were too remote to justify efforts to interfere with contracts, whereas the Court held that the benefits to the union in *American Steel Foundries* were direct and could justify such interference. Taft offered no explanation for the

Labor & the Jurisprudence of Individualism

difference.[160] The "recognition of a solidarity of interest among the laborers in a restricted industrial area," Thomas Reed Powell dryly observed, "is of course capable of extension by one who might discover that widely-separated plants may compete with each other."[161]

The precarious way that Taft distinguished *Hitchman* apparently caused some tension with Pitney. Taft wrote Pitney two days before the announcement of *American Steel Foundries*, insisting that "There is nothing in conflict with the Hitchman case in what I say, and it seems to me that we had better let it go as it is. . . . I hope you will conclude, after thinking the matter over, that there is nothing in the opinion that interferes with what the Court has previously said, and that it is so unusual to get as many of the Court together on such an important case as this that we had better let it go, as the opinion has been approved."[162]

In fact, however, *American Steel Foundries* did come back to haunt *Hitchman*. A decade after the decision, the Senate refused to confirm Hoover's nomination of John J. Parker to fill the seat left vacant after Edward Sanford's death, in part because Parker, as a judge on the Fourth Circuit, had issued a *Hitchman* injunction preventing a union from organizing in ways that would violate yellow-dog contracts.[163] The *coup de grâce* was delivered by Senator William Borah, who boldly asserted that *Hitchman* had been overruled by *American Steel Foundries*. Taft, Borah argued, had held "that labor organizations were lawful, and that they had a right to increase their membership and that they had a right to persuade people to join them, that it was in their interest to do so, and that therefore their doing so was not accompanied by malice or ill will, and therefore subject to restraint."[164] Parker had "wholly" ignored "the Tri-City case, which had been decided in the meantime, and which, if I can understand language, had wholly modified the Hitchman case and had held definitely that persuasion, if it was not accompanied by unlawful means, such as deception and threats, was permissible. . . . The very object and purpose of the Tri-City case was to modify the holding in the Hitchman case."[165]

In one of the great ironies of history, Taft in 1930 emerged as an unlikely protector of labor, because his decision in *American Steel Foundries* was read as effectively nullifying *Hitchman*. Just as *American Steel Foundries* became a foundational precedent for those advocating for the recognition of the group system in the Norris-LaGuardia Act of 1932, so it also became a foundational precedent for those who sought to repudiate *Hitchman* and "the industrial servitude" of "indefensible injunctions" enforcing yellow-dog contracts.[166]

Back in 1921, however, at the outset of the Taft Court, *American Steel Foundries* was a far more equivocal case, and Taft was a far more ambivalent figure, than the retrospective appropriations of 1930 suggest. If Taft believed, on the one hand, that "courts cannot settle industrial controversies," he also believed, on the other hand, that courts could and should "keep the contestants in the legal field of their controversy."[167] Throughout his entire career, Taft never wavered in his conviction that courts, in the exercise of their equitable power, were ideal instruments to interpret and enforce "fixed rules of law" that prevented labor disputes from spinning out of control and descending into lawlessness.[168] As Taft had held uncontroversially in 1894 as an appellate judge, law imposed two distinct kinds of restrictions on concerted labor actions. It prohibited labor from organizing "to accomplish a criminal or unlawful purpose," and it prohibited labor from acting to achieve lawful purposes "by criminal or unlawful means."[169]

It was common ground within the Taft Court that when workmen combined to accomplish illegal purposes their concerted actions could be restrained. In *Dorchy v. Kansas*, for example, Brandeis wrote for a unanimous Court that "a strike may be illegal because of its purpose, however orderly the manner in which it conducted.... Neither the common law, nor the Fourteenth Amendment, confers the absolute right to strike."[170] Taft differed from Holmes and Brandeis in the extent of his confidence that courts, as distinguished from legislatures, were appropriate fora for distinguishing proper from improper purposes. Just as Taft deeply believed in the authority of federal courts to pronounce common law, so he believed in the authority of federal courts to control labor controversies through the exercise of their equity jurisdiction.

It was also common ground within the Taft Court that even if labor combined to achieve a legitimate purpose, it could not act in illegal ways.[171] Primarily this meant that striking workers could not intimidate or threaten or coerce. The connection between labor and unlawful violence was pervasive and deeply fraught.[172] By the 1920s, labor unrest had become associated with "a state of lawlessness shocking to every conception of American law and order."[173] It was commonly observed that "there is probably no other country in which violence is so common. Nearly all strikes of importance lead to clashes between strikers and strike sympathizers on the one hand and the strike breakers and guards and spies furnished by detective agencies on the other."[174]

The association of labor with lawlessness was multidimensional and complex. At times accusations of lawlessness were used to isolate and discredit extreme left-wing elements of the labor movement, like the Industrial Workers of the World ("IWW") or the communists. So, for example, in the years immediately after the Armistice, Taft would endlessly repeat that the "I.W.W.'s and the Bolshevists" were "in favor of direct action, which means lawless violence and overturning of government."[175] Taft argued that

> [t]he businessmen of this country cannot be told too often that the proper course for them to pursue ... is in friendship for the labor unions under the leadership of the American Federation of Labor. Failure to recognize the power of conservative patriotic labor unionism and to express sympathy with it and a willingness to classify its leaders as associates of I.W.W.ism, extreme socialism and bolshevism, weaken the power of those leaders with their fellows and tends to throw the whole labor movement under the control of the lawless extremists.[176]

At other times, accusations of lawlessness were lodged against mainstream labor organizations, as for example when they attempted to leverage the threat of strikes to obtain legislation. The controversial 1916 Adamson Act[177] is illustrative. The Act was rammed through Congress by a Wilson administration anxious to avert a potential railroad strike by the usually "conservative"[178] Railroad Brotherhoods.

Labor & the Jurisprudence of Individualism

The Act mandated an eight-hour day and higher wages for railroad employees engaged in interstate commerce. Three years later the former progressive Senator Albert Beveridge was still seething that the "ruthless" labor pressure was "intimidation," "as violently lawless as that of robbery at the mouth of a gun or the point of a dirk."[179]

Taft agreed with Beveridge, characterizing the Adamson Act as "the subordination of all national authority to the demands of one class by something equivalent to force, by a refusal to discharge the function in society which they performed, and which was essential to its life, unless laws were enacted granting all they asked. That is the principle of the Soviet."[180] This kind of thinking was prevalent in the opening years of the Taft Court. In 1921, while *American Steel Foundries* was still pending, one could read in the papers that "the public" expressed "a very special repugnance to having its throat cut" when railroad shop workers affiliated with the American Federation of Labor ("AFL") threatened a national strike. The strike was condemned as the equivalent of "a resort to force and an attempt at coercing" railroads by threatening the "unthinkable" – "to starve and freeze the public, to bring stark ruin crashing down upon millions of helpless and innocent people."[181]

The primary association of labor with lawlessness, however, stemmed from the fact that employees could maintain an equality of bargaining power only if they were able to cartelize the labor market, which meant ensuring that countless individual workingmen would not willingly sell their labor at nonunion wages to break strikes.[182] This created a structural incentive that indelibly connected organized labor with violence: "It is safe to say that there is not a single member of a labor union possessing ordinary intelligence who would consider it of any use whatever in gaining a point with his employer to leave his service quietly, individually or in company with others, and seek work somewhere else. It is his belief in his ability, in conjunction with his companions, to prevent other men taking his place that impels him to leave; and this he knows cannot be done without violence; therefore, the very existence of the institution of strikes is founded upon lawlessness."[183]

The association of strikes with violence permeated judicial reasoning and decisions.[184] In 1894, for example, a judge on the Seventh Circuit enjoined a strike on the ground that

> [a] strike is essentially a conspiracy to extort by violence; the means employed to effect the end being not only the cessation of labor by the conspirators, but the necessary prevention of labor by those who are willing to assume their places, and, as a last resort, and in many instances an essential element of success, the disabling and destruction of the property of the master; and so, by intimidation and by the compulsion of force, to accomplish the end designed. I know of no peaceable strike. I think no strike was ever heard of that was or could be successful unaccompanied by intimidation and violence.[185]

"Unions," said Jane Addams, "are constantly disgraced by acts of disorder and lawlessness."[186] "It needs no prophet," Taft remarked in 1919, "to come and tell us that in the use of the instrumentality of a strike, which is the lawful and ultimate weapon of trades-unions to accomplish their purpose, it is most difficult to avoid lawless violence. Even if the union which initiates a strike exercises every possible care to avoid lawlessness, lawlessness will, if the strike be at all extended, generally occur."[187] Judicial decisions in the 1920s could casually refer to "the usual incidents of violence and exhibitions of force," sometimes progressing to a virtual "state of war," that accompanied union strikes.[188]

In *American Steel Foundries*, Taft frankly acknowledged the strike as "a lawful instrument in a lawful economic struggle or competition." But he also carefully retained jurisdiction to distinguish lawful strikes from strikes that threatened illegal violence. If Taft was prepared to be generous with regard to accepting the necessity of concerted labor action, he was equally determined to retain firm judicial control of industrial conflict and tightly to constrain how strikes could be conducted. A central question in *American Steel Foundries* was the extent and manner in which the Tri-City Central Trades Council could picket the plant.

The function of picketing is to inform employees, potential employees, the public, and an employer about the existence of, and justification for, a strike. Having acknowledged the legality of strikes, Taft could not deny the legitimacy of this function.[189] In *American Steel Foundries* he declared it an existing "principle" of "equity jurisprudence" that federal courts should refuse to enjoin "peaceable persuasion by employees, discharged or expectant, in promotion of their side of the dispute, and to secure them against judicial restraint in obtaining or communicating information in any place where they might lawfully be." He also noted that the Clayton Act specifically forbade enjoining such behavior. It followed that the Seventh Circuit had been correct to excise that "part of the decree of the District Court which forbade [the Trade Council] by persuasion to induce employees, or would-be employees to leave, or stay out of, complainant's employ."[190] Unions legally on strike were entitled to use "lawful and peaceable persuasion" to advance their cause.[191]

Labor was not entitled, however, to engage in "intimidation or obstruction." It was not entitled even to "adopt methods" that, in the Court's judgment, "*inevitably lead* to intimidation and obstruction." "We are a social people." Taft explained, "and the accosting by one of another in an inoffensive way and an offer by one to communicate and discuss information with a view to influencing the other's action are not regarded as aggression or a violation of that other's rights. If, however, the offer is declined, as it may rightfully be, then persistence, importunity, following and dogging become unjustifiable annoyance and obstruction which is likely soon to savor of intimidation. From all of this the person sought to be influenced has a right to be free and his employer has a right to have him free."[192]

From this premise, Taft jumped to a seemingly radical conclusion. He refused to sustain that portion of the Seventh Circuit judgment that had applied "the case of *Iron Molders Union No. 125 v. Allis-Chalmers Co.*" and had "modified the order of the District Court which enjoined defendants 'from picketing or maintaining at or near the premises of the complainant or on the streets leading to the premises of said complainant, any pickets and pickets' by adding the words 'in a threatening or intimidating manner.'" The judgment of the Seventh Circuit, said

Labor & the Jurisprudence of Individualism

Taft, ignores "the necessary element of intimidation in the presence of *groups as pickets*. It does not secure practically that which the court must secure and to which the complainant and his workmen are entitled. The phrase really recognizes as legal that which bears the sinister name of 'picketing' which it is to be observed Congress carefully refrained from using in section 20" of the Clayton Act.[193]

At first glance, it appeared as if *American Steel Foundries* had taken the breathtakingly audacious step of prohibiting picketing itself. But Taft was careful to assert that "each case must turn on its own circumstances." The key point was that "courts of equity" should use their "flexible remedial power" to find ways to "reconcile the conflicting interests" of, on the one hand, "employees to work for whom they will, and, undisturbed by annoying importunity or intimidation of numbers, to go freely to and from their place of labor," and, on the other hand, "ex-employees and others properly acting with them" to "observe who are still working for the employer, to communicate with them and to persuade them to join the ranks of his opponents in a lawful economic struggle."[194]

In *American Steel Foundries*, this reconciliation required detailed regulation of the conduct of the Tri-City Central Trades Council:

> We think that the strikers and their sympathizers engaged in the economic struggle should be limited to one representative for each point of ingress and egress in the plant or place of business and that all others be enjoined from congregating or loitering at the plant or in the neighboring streets by which access is had to the plant, that such representatives should have the right of observation, communication and persuasion, but with special admonition that their communication, arguments and appeals shall not be abusive, libelous or threatening, and that they shall not approach individuals together but singly, and shall not in their single efforts at communication or persuasion obstruct an unwilling listener by importunate following or dogging his steps. This is not laid down as a rigid rule, but only as one which should apply to this case under the circumstances disclosed by the evidence and which may be varied in other cases. It becomes a question for the judgment of the chancellor who has heard the witnesses, familiarized himself with the locus in quo and observed the tendencies to disturbance and conflict. The purpose should be to prevent the inevitable intimidation of the presence of groups of pickets, but to allow missionaries.[195]

Pitney apparently objected to the stark distinction Taft drew between picketers and "missionaries." Taft defended this approach in a letter to Pitney written shortly before the opinion was released:

> It seems to me that in your objection ... to the use of the word "picketing" alone as the thing to be enjoined, you don't take quite into consideration its advantage. It puts picketing in a class by itself and disposes of it. It renders uniform the practice in the Federal Courts, and I hope will have some effect the country over, to get rid of the idea that it has suggested, of an authorized and legal arraying of one side against the other by groups. I am very glad that Justice Holmes and Justice Brandeis have consented to it, because I think it will help to

the solution of a difficult problem, and I hope you won't continue your objection. It seems to me to strike out the word "persuasion" leaves the decrees in the form in which we would have them, and that by setting over persuasion against picketing, as we do, we make the distinction which is a wise and clear one.[196]

In the end Pitney dropped his objection, and only Clarke dissented (without opinion) from the judgment. Brandeis wrote separately to say that he concurred "in substance in the opinion and the judgment of the Court."[197] The day after the decision came down, Holmes declared to Frankfurter that he "was delighted at the labor decision of the CJ yesterday – and though of course there were details as to which I should go farther I was so content to get what we got that I didn't think it wise to say any qualifying words."[198] The virtual unanimity of the Court proved a powerful signal, and *American Steel Foundries* quickly became "unquestionably the leading case upon the law of picketing and has influenced practically all subsequent decisions involving picketing."[199]

Apparently Taft was serious in his effort to suppress the word "picketing," which, as he wrote Pitney, he associated with the action of *groups*.[200] Two weeks later, for example, Taft wrote in an opinion for the Court that *American Steel Foundries* had held "that peaceful picketing was a contradiction in terms."[201] Although Taft's effort to eliminate the word "picketing" was doomed to failure,[202] *American Steel Foundries* did spark a marked "tendency ... toward minutely detailed and very strict regulations in injunctions relating to the manner in which picketing may be conducted. In the majority of injunctions issued since 1921, precisely the same number of pickets have been permitted as in the American Steel Foundries Company case, namely, one at each factory gate. This has become almost a fetish."[203] *American Steel Foundries* prompted courts to draft clearer and more precise injunctions, which were "distinctly more effective."[204]

The price of this precision was a somewhat fussy definition of intimidation, one which regarded "as primary" the right of persons to avoid "an enforced discussion of the merits of the issue between *individuals* who wish to work, and *groups* of those who do not, under conditions which subject the individuals who wish to work to a severe test of their nerve and physical strength and courage."[205] It was commonly observed that "slavish adherence to the rule of one picket per gate, which many courts have adopted since the American Steel Foundries case, often denies strikers a fair opportunity to present their case to new and prospective employees."[206] In *Vegelahn*, for example, Holmes had dissented from the proposition that "two men, walking together up and down a sidewalk, and speaking to those who enter a certain shop, do necessarily and always convey a threat of force."[207] But Taft insisted on drafting *American Steel Foundries* to give the benefit of the doubt to judicial control. He was determined to avoid vague rules that would leave "compliance largely to the discretion of the pickets" and that ignored "the necessary element of intimidation in the presence of groups as pickets."[208]

The upshot, as Clarke commented on his return to Taft's circulated draft, was that "the definite – very definite – rule you have laid down as to picketing seems to me to in fact prohibit it altogether. Very certainly it would not be safe for *one* man to attempt to approach the workers going to a manufacturing works.

Labor & the Jurisprudence of Individualism

The workers are just as much given to violence as the strikers are and we should at least permit the defenders of the strikers to have *one* witness to detail how their supporter came to his death or to receive the injuries which he certainly would receive. There are some subjects, I think this is one of them, that refuse to submit to precise definition."[209]

Samuel Gompers made the same point. *American Steel Foundries*, he said, held that "picketing is unlawful except under such restrictions as to make picketing ineffective and worthless." *American Steel Foundries* "acknowledged the lawfulness of picketing but laid down such restrictions as to make impossible anything approaching effective picketing. If the decision of the Supreme Court were to be followed in practice throughout the land, the right of striking workers to inform those seeking employment concerning the existence of strike conditions would be foreclosed forever."[210] Gompers "scored Chief Justice Taft," claiming that "courts which have been issuing injunctions against labor organizations are 'courts of iniquity' instead of 'courts of equity.'"[211] The Executive Council of the AFL reported to the Forty-Second Annual Convention of the Federation:

> In reaching this decision, the supreme court either demonstrated its misconception of industrial disputes or knowingly closed its eyes to the dangers surrounding union men who would peacefully solicit the membership and support of non-union workers. While every protection is afforded to the employer and safety is made the predominating element for the ingress and egress of non-union workmen and while the right of persuasion is hesitatingly admitted, no protection or safety is afforded to the union workmen or sympathizers who would dare singly to approach groups of non-union workers for the purpose of communicating with them. In other words every conceivable protection is given the non-union workers but no protection whatever is accorded the union worker in the exercise of his rights against the assaults of the employers' hirelings and violent methods of promoting discord.[212]

Taft's generous acknowledgment of the "group system" thus produced only "a hollow victory"[213] for labor.[214] Although *American Steel Foundries* authorized sympathetic trial courts to allow labor more effective representation if justified by particular circumstances,[215] sympathetic judges were few and far between. *American Steel Foundries* was in fact a profoundly two-faced decision: it both recognized unions and bound them tightly in cords of black judicial silk.[216] Taft's opinion unconsciously drew upon an implicit but deep-seated asymmetry: Taft perceived strikebreakers as "individuals who wish to work,"[217] but he categorized unions as a "group" or class.[218] In conflicts between the two, Taft's sympathies lay with the individual. This asymmetry lay at the root of what the AFL Executive Council condemned as the "class biased decisions of our courts."[219]

Taft's ambivalence was in fact characteristic of the 1920s. The nation simply did not know how to make sense of organized labor. It was generally recognized that organized labor, in one form or another, had become an inevitable aspect of the domestic scene, which is why employers throughout the 1920s scrambled to create domesticated company unions.[220] Yet organized labor remained an anomalous and undigested exception to the individualism that otherwise dominated the decade.[221] Taft was proud that the American workingman expressed his "views as an independent member of society" rather than adopting "the narrow interest of class to ignore ... the welfare of society."[222] Taft endorsed the Harding-Coolidge ticket because it stood "for Americanism as against Socialism. It will be for the rule of the majority as against Soviet and organized labor direction of what concerns the public .... It will be for the just interest of all the people as against the selfish and inconsiderate demands of a small but powerfully organized minority."[223]

Taft's discomfort with labor, viewed as a separate class or group, echoed the fundamental constitutional principle, enshrined in the Fourteenth Amendment since the decades after the Civil War, that "[c]lass legislation, discriminating against some and favoring others, is prohibited; but legislation which, in carrying out a public purpose, is limited in its application, if within the sphere of its operation it affects alike all persons similarly situated, is not within the amendment."[224] Republican government, Thomas Cooley had powerfully reasoned, requires "that all freemen, when they form a social compact, are equal, and no man, or set of men, is entitled to exclusive, separate public emoluments or privileges from the community, but in consideration of public services."[225] That is why Methodist Episcopal Bishop William Quayle could famously attack organized labor in 1920 as "a direct and deadly threat against popular forms of government." "Our government," said Quayle, "is for all the people, not for any one class or faction."[226]

Taft generalized this point in 1922 when he condemned political "parties based on class and faction" that would "sacrifice the general interest of the country to the achievement of a particular object." Taft asserted that "the institution and maintenance of great parties is an antidote for class consciousness and selfish factional diversion of national funds and energy into class preferment and away from the general good." Taft felt vindicated by the fact that many "workingmen" refused to vote narrowly for their interests as employees in 1920; they did not "enter the voting booth to bear a class label. They are Republicans or Democrats."[227] "Two great parties," Taft affirmed,

> mean a cleavage down through all the strata of society, the wealthy, the educated, the moderate circumstanced, the business men, the workingmen, and the farmers. The group system tends to parties with a horizontal cleavage of the strata of society, and we find the farmers in one party, the workingmen in another, the business men in another, the manufacturers in another, each contending for its special interest and ignoring the welfare of society as a whole. Normal party feeling in one of two great parties tends to neutralize this class and selfish spirit, and prompts a consideration of the interest of all classes of the people represented in the party.[228]

This vision of American political dynamics essentially branded as illegitimate political manifestations of the "group system."[229] The group system meant socialism or the soviet, as distinct from "the general good." Traditional progressive commitments to a transcendent public interest expressed this same rejection of particular group interests. So, for example, in his influential prewar progressive manifesto, *The Promise of American Life*, Herbert Croly had sharply critiqued "militant unionists" for abandoning "traditional American individualism" and for believing that "attachment" to the union was "more important" than "attachment to the American ideal and to the national interest." Unions, Croly argued, were deficient because they sought to promote "a class interest" by creating "special rights" in "favor of one class of citizens."[230]

Organized labor, for its part, denied progressives' faith in an overarching public interest. Like Holmes, labor imagined society as essentially an ongoing struggle among groups. What progressives called the "public interest" was for labor nothing more than a "desire for the worker's commodities." The "public" cares about "the continuous operation of industry so that its wants may be supplied without interruption. After these wants have been supplied, it is a matter of no concern to the community what becomes of the worker."[231] Labor therefore distrusted progressive, middle-class appeals to the "public interest," because they believed that the public primarily consisted of those who were concerned to consume the products of labor at the cheapest possible price.

This same reasoning led organized labor to oppose all schemes involving "the un-American and repugnant idea of compulsory arbitration."[232] Organized labor advocated instead for public policies based on what it called the "Voluntary Principle,"[233] by which it meant that law should empower employees to assert their collective strength and freely compete with capital in a struggle for the distribution of surplus value.[234] It did not matter to organized labor that a strike might, for example, freeze the coal supply for the entire nation. Organized labor insisted that the struggle between miners and mining companies was essentially a private economic contest.[235] The public had no right to intervene, just as it had no right to intervene if two private coal companies fought for control of particular markets.

To traditional progressives, steeped in the priority of the public interest, this denial "to the general public of any right of representation" in matters that plainly affected the public welfare was puzzling and problematic.[236] Newton Baker, for example, postulated that "the first principle in all efforts to solve controverted questions of labor relations" must be the recognition "that there are three parties to every labor controversy – the employer, the employee and the public. . . . [I]t must be recognized that this public interest cannot be left to be injured or destroyed by prolonged conflict between the other two parties."[237] The voluntary principle, however, chimed with the views of conservatives who wished to insulate from public control freedom of contract (for employers) and freedom of labor (for employees). A case like *Charles Wolff Packing Co. v. Kansas Court of Industrial Relations*[238] thus aligned with the agendas of both the Taft Court and organized labor, because each was determined to create a protected space for private transactions that would be free from public regulation.

In the rapidly consolidating and interdependent economy of the 1920s, however, it was increasingly difficult to maintain that the national labor market could plausibly remain beyond the reach of public regulation. A coal strike by a national union like the UMW could affect the fuel required by millions; a strike by a national railroad brotherhood could disable the entire economy. Even those who favored "individual liberty and the right of concerted action" were of the opinion that "a national strike paralysis of transportation, or of coal, or food supply is clearly an indefensible attack on the public safety; that is the evident judgment of the whole country."[239] During the turmoil of 1919, Taft had himself reached the conclusion that although workingmen had a right to strike, nevertheless:

> When they increase in size, so that by withdrawal from labor in which they are engaged as a whole, they can paralyze an industry, the product of which is necessary for the life of the country, and they deliberately do this for the purpose of subjecting the public to suffering, and it may be to starvation or to freezing, they are using their power of combination not against their employers but against the public who are not a party to the issue. They are deliberately doing so to compel the public to compel the employers in some way or other to yield to the demands of the combination of workingmen. In any ordinary strike, incidental annoyance to the public, which is negligible, does not render the strike illegal. But when enormous combinations of workingmen deliberately enter upon a country wide plan to take the country by the throat and compel the country to compel the employers in that particular field of industry to yield to the demands of the men, they are engaged in an unlawful conspiracy. The sacredness of their individual right to labor on such terms as they choose, and to leave their employment when they will, does not protect or justify them in such a conspiracy.[240]

Just as Taft was prepared to acknowledge the group system and its concomitant right to strike only if the efficacy of strikes were sharply curtailed by burdensome restrictions on picketing, so Taft was prepared to acknowledge the right to strike only in circumstances where the inconvenience to the public was not too great. In doctrinal terms, we might say that Taft was quick to deem the free labor rights of employees as "affected with a public interest."[241] Apparently, he could more readily perceive the paramount public interest in regulating coal miners or railroad workers than the paramount public interest in regulating the price of coal or of employment agencies.[242]

In fashioning the Transportation Act of 1920,[243] Congress had come within a hair's breadth of prohibiting strikes by railroad workers in interstate commerce.[244] In the face of furious labor opposition, Congress backed off and settled for a method of resolving industrial disputes that was roughly patterned upon the NWLB. The NWLB had been composed of equal representatives of labor and management, and it had lacked authority to enforce its decrees. The Transportation Act of 1920 established a new Railroad Labor Board ("RLB") that would arbitrate disputes between labor and management on interstate railroads.[245] Like the NWLB, the RLB was without authority to enforce its judgments, but, in contrast to the NWLB, membership on the RLB was evenly divided between representatives of labor, management, and the public.[246] Labor bitterly opposed the RLB, in part because it believed that public members would systematically align with management,[247] and in part because the Transportation Act provided that the Board "shall hear, and ... with due diligence *decide*, any dispute involving grievances, rules, or working conditions."[248] The RLB seemed too close to the "compulsory arbitration laws and industrial courts" with which labor associated the evil of "involuntary servitude."[249]

The RLB, like the NWLB before it, frankly incorporated the group system. The very design of the RLB acknowledged that railroad disputes could best be resolved through mediation and compromise among directly affected groups.[250] The RLB did not purport to speak in the name of legal rights, as would a court. The RLB declared that "It must be evident to all and beyond doubt or controversy, from the very nature of things and the character of the disputes that cause the friction between carriers and their employees which lead to interruption of traffic, that Congress did not intend or expect to limit the Labor Board to deciding these disputes according to the strict legal rights of the parties, because if it did, and both parties relied strictly and fully on their legal rights, the disputes never could be solved." The RLB considered its primary mission to be ensuring "the continued and proper functioning" of the railroad "transportation systems," which could be accomplished only by "looking to justice, equity, and fair dealing between the carriers and their employees and the greater and dominating interests of the public."[251]

This mission required the RLB to issue principles and decisions that directly contradicted the holdings of *Adair*, *Coppage*, and *Hitchman*. The RLB candidly demanded that railroads, workers, and the public acknowledge the "group system" within the railroad labor market.[252] The RLB declared in 1921 that it would decide cases on the basis of principles that, like those that had been adopted by the NWLB, required nondiscrimination against union members and mandated that workers be able to select their own representatives without management interference or obstruction.[253] The decade of the 1920s thus began with a sharp contradiction between the individualist free labor principles that had informed the Court's twentieth-century precedents, and the "group system" that was acknowledged by all as necessary for the realistic governance of interstate railroads.

The tension came to a head when the Taft Court was forced to consider decisions by the RLB imposing conditions that were inconsistent with the Court's own precedents. American railroads in 1920 were divided on the question of how militantly to invoke the managerial rights accorded them in the Court's past constitutional decisions. Among the most adamantly antilabor corporations was the large and powerful Pennsylvania Railroad.[254] In April 1921, the RLB dissolved the wartime labor agreements that the Wilson administration had negotiated with the national railroad unions. As control of railroads passed back from the federal government into the hands of prior owners, the RLB required each company to renegotiate a collective agreement with its own employees.[255] The RLB held that employees should be able freely to select the representatives who would negotiate on their behalf.[256] The Pennsylvania Railroad, however, refused to let its employees be represented by the union to which they had previously belonged, System Federation No. 90, which was affiliated with the AFL.[257] The Pennsylvania Railroad insisted that it would not negotiate with unions, but only with workers who were company employees. This was the very position that, when advanced by "bourbon" employers at Wilson's 1919 Industrial Conference, had caused labor delegates to walk out.[258] It was a direct and frontal challenge to the "group system" established by the Transportation Act of 1920.

The RLB held that the Transportation Act required carriers to negotiate with the "representatives" of employees,[259] and that "it necessarily follows, under our system of government, that a majority of such employees would have the right to designate their representatives." "There is nothing in the statute to deny the employees the privilege of belonging to an organization and being represented by that organization through its accredited officers. In fact this has been the established custom for many years and is recognized in the Transportation Act itself."[260]

The RLB was clear that "employees may vote for representatives who are not employees of the carrier, if they so desire, just as the carrier may select a representative who is neither a director nor a stockholder. It is out of line with the customary procedure in this country to contend that a party to any suit or controversy in any court or tribunal shall be denied counsel and compelled to represent himself." Although the Pennsylvania Railroad asserted managerial prerogatives that the Supreme Court had itself constitutionally awarded to employers, the RLB was appalled at what it regarded as the company's revanchist stance: "At a time when the Nation is slowly and painfully progressing through the conditions of industrial depression, unemployment, and unrest consequent upon the war, it is almost treasonable for any employer or employee to stubbornly haggle over nonessentials at the risk of social chaos."[261]

The constitutionality of the RLB's order was brought before the Taft Court in *Pennsylvania Railroad Co. v. United States Railroad Labor Board*.[262] The delicacy of the situation could not be overstated. It was manifest to the RLB, as it had been to the NWLB, as it had been to the Congress that had enacted the Transportation Act of 1920, that the individualist premises of the Court's constitutional jurisprudence were not adequate to the complexities of a modern national transportation system. A workable labor policy had to be rooted in a pluralist respect for groups. Yet decisions like *Hitchman* and *Coppage* were less than a decade old, and the individualism of these decisions underlay belief in a "public" interest that transcended the needs of particular classes or groups.

American Steel Foundries had tiptoed around these precedents with great tact. But the Pennsylvania Railroad was bent on forcing a blunt legal confrontation. It argued that the Transportation Act of 1920 was unconstitutional to the extent it authorized the RLB to interfere with management's constitutional prerogatives to determine "the administration of rules, working conditions, and wages."[263] Speaking for a unanimous Court, Taft deftly sidestepped the company's constitutional challenge.

The Pennsylvania Railroad, Taft said, insists "that the right to deal with individual representatives of its employees as to rules and working conditions is an inherent right which can not be constitutionally taken from it." But, Taft reasoned, "the decisions of the Labor Board are not to be enforced by process"; the "only sanction of its decision is to be the force of public opinion invoked by the fairness of a full hearing, the intrinsic justice of the conclusion, strengthened by the official prestige of the Board, and the full publication of the violation of such decision by any party to the proceeding." It was not the job of the Board to determine "the legal rights and obligations of railway employers and employees or to enforce or protect them. Courts can do that. The Labor Board was created to decide how the parties ought to exercise their legal rights so as to enable them to cooperate in running the railroad. It was to reach a fair compromise between the parties without regard to the legal rights upon which each side might insist in a court of law. The Board ... is to give expression to its view of the moral obligation of each side as members of society to agree upon a basis for cooperation in the work of running the railroad in the public interest."[264]

The "only limitation" on the Board's decisions, said Taft, was that they be "just and reasonable." As to that question, Taft was prepared to reassert the legitimacy of the group system that he had advanced in *American Steel Foundries*: "Congress has frequently recognized the legality of labor unions, and no reason suggests itself why such an association ... may not be regarded as among the organizations of employees referred to in this legislation."[265] But, because the Pennsylvania Railroad was free to disregard the decision of the RLB,[266] the Board's decision could not be said to violate any constitutional right of the railroad.[267]

This was a clever and lawyerly argument. Taft drove it home two years later in *Pennsylvania Railroad System and Allied Lines Federation No. 90 v. Pennsylvania Railroad Co.* Taking Taft at his word, the Pennsylvania Railroad simply ignored the Board's decision. In outright defiance of the likely wishes of the majority of its employees, the company forcibly established a company union with which to negotiate terms and conditions of employment. Taft nevertheless concluded for a unanimous Court that because there was "nothing compulsory" in the Transportation Act "as against either the Company or the employees upon the basis of which either acquired additional rights against the other which can be enforced in a court of law," Congress did not intend for courts to enforce by injunctions what the Act characterized as "the duty of all carriers and their officers, employees, and agents to exert every reasonable effort and adopt every available means to avoid any interruption to the operation of any carrier growing out of any dispute between the carrier and the employees or subordinate officials thereof."[268]

Taft's evasions came at a high cost. It was rightly observed in the press that the Court had "extracted" the "teeth of the Transportation Act."[269] The RLB was in effect rendered irrelevant and vestigial. And the Court backed itself into the embarrassing position of declaring, on the one hand, that the public policy of Congress encouraging collective bargaining was just and reasonable, but that, on the other hand, it was not legally enforceable by the parties. This was a practical and conceptual disaster. It left national labor policy exactly where it had been before World War I. As the *New Republic* pointed out, "A policy of genuine conference has been recognized as desirable by Congress, by the Labor Board and by the Supreme Court in obiter dicta. Its public desirability rests largely on the need for avoiding interruptions of transportation. Since it is not enforced by a publicly established penalty, the obvious inference is that the only way to enforce it is by action of the unions aggrieved, through the penalty of the strike. The policy of conference having failed, the purpose of avoiding interruptions of transportation is by the same token endangered."[270]

The deeper difficulty, however, was *why* the Court was forced into this embarrassing position. The Court was evidently unwilling directly to confront the jurisprudential structure of decisions like *Adair, Coppage,* and *Hitchman,* with which the policies of the RLB were so manifestly incompatible. As Ralph Easley, the director of the National Civic Federation, wrote in an editorial that Taft clipped and kept in his papers, "There is no power whatever in the [Transportation] act to prevent strikes. No such law could ever have been passed. That would mean 'putting teeth' in the bill, and 'putting teeth' in the bill means the compulsory acceptance of awards, which would require an amendment to the Constitution of the United States, since under it there is no authority for compelling a man to work against his will or for preventing him from quitting work."[271]

Although Easley stressed the free labor rights of individual employees, everyone understood that the real issue was how the constitutionally entrenched managerial prerogatives of employers could be reconciled with a coherent national labor policy. By sidestepping this question, the Court exemplified and exposed the weaknesses of the "associative state"[272] that historians now deem characteristic of America during the 1920s.[273] The country well understood the need for national policy and direction, but it could not bring itself to constrain individual freedoms in ways necessary to implement such policy. The preferred solution was voluntary co-operation guided by responsible state organizations, which was the pattern set by Hoover at the Department of Commerce. When voluntary co-operation disintegrated, as happened in the case of the Pennsylvania Railroad, this paradigm of governmentality collapsed.

The logjam would not begin to break until 1930, five months after Taft's departure, when the Court under Hughes considered provisions of the Railway Labor Act[274] ("RLA") that had been enacted a year after *Pennsylvania Railroad System and Allied Lines Federation No. 90* to replace the shattered remnants of the Transportation Act of 1920. The RLA was largely drafted through negotiations between the railroad companies and unions, which were now in agreement that the Transportation Act required reformation. Establishing a scheme for voluntary, but enforceable arbitration, the RLA provided that management and labor should make good-faith efforts to settle disputes through bargaining between representatives "designated by the respective parties . . . without interference, influence, or coercion exercised by either party over the self-organization or designation of representatives by the other."[275]

In *Texas & N.O.R. Co. v. Brotherhood of Railway and Steamship Clerks,* the Court confronted a case in which a railroad, imitating the Pennsylvania Railroad, had created its own company shop instead of bargaining with the union chosen by its employees. The railroad argued that enforcement of the RLA would violate its constitutional prerogatives to manage its own workplace. Hughes, speaking for a unanimous Court, held that the RLA's prohibition against interference with employee representation was mandatory and that it could be enforced by a judicial injunction. Citing *American Steel Foundries,* Hughes concluded that

Labor & the Jurisprudence of Individualism

"[i]t has long been recognized that employees are entitled to organize for the purpose of securing the redress of grievances and to promote agreements with employers relating to rates of pay and conditions of work." Hughes held that *Adair* and *Coppage* were inapplicable because the Act did "not interfere with the normal exercise of the right of the carrier to select its employees or to discharge them. The statute is not aimed at this right of the employers but at the interference with the right of employees to have representatives of their own choosing."[276]

Unlike the Taft Court, the Hughes Court was willing to accept the logical implications of Taft's own recognition of the "group system." No doubt there are many reasons why this might be so. As the need for an effective national labor policy became more apparent, the countervailing demands of a postulated sphere of individual liberty grew weaker. This is analogous to the dynamic that we traced in our discussion of *Euclid* in Chapter 26.

The nation had also by 1930 grown more comfortable with the insights of interest-group pluralism, in which the public values enforced by law could not be so sharply distinguished from the values of the groups that increasingly occupied public spaces.[277] The RLA frankly enlisted the public force of the state to enforce agreements reached directly through negotiation by affected groups. Implicit in this design was an equality of groups that Taft could never quite integrate into his normative image of the Republic. Although the Taft Court made major strides in pushing the country toward an acceptance of "the group system" in the context of labor markets, it remained ambivalent, always yearning for a nation founded on individual rights whose protection would produce a genuinely public interest.

Notes

1. Commonwealth v. Hunt, 45 Mass. 111, 122 (1842). *See* Walter Nelles, *Commonwealth v. Hunt*, 32 COLUMBIA LAW REVIEW 1148 (1932).
2. *See* William E. Forbath, *The Ambiguities of Free Labor: Labor and the Law in the Gilded Age*, 1985 WISCONSIN LAW REVIEW 767; Charles W. McCurdy, *The Roots of Liberty of Contract Reconsidered: Major Premises in the Law of Employment, 1867–1937*, 1984 YEARBOOK OF THE SUPREME COURT HISTORICAL SOCIETY 20.
3. The Slaughterhouse Cases, 83 U.S. 36, 110 n.39 (1872) (Field, J., dissenting). *See, e.g.*, Bogni v. Perotti, 224 Mass. 152, 155 (1916):

   > In the *Slaughter House Cases*, in the dissenting opinion of Mr. Justice Swayne, but respecting a subject as to which there was no controversy, occur these words:
   > "Labor is property and as such merits protection. The right to make it available is next in importance to the rights of life and liberty."
   > It was settled that the right to labor and to make contracts to work is a property right by *Adair v. U.S.* and *Coppage v. Kansas*. Controversy on that subject before this court must be regarded as put at rest by those decisions. The right to work, therefore, is property. One cannot be deprived of it by simple mandate of the Legislature. It is protected by the Fourteenth Amendment to the Constitution of the United States and by numerous guarantees of our Constitution. It is as much property as the more obvious forms of goods and merchandise, stocks and bonds. That it may be also a part of the liberty of the citizen does not affect its character as property.

   Summarizing received wisdom, Taft asserted in 1914 that "three important phases of what we include in the general term 'individual liberty'" are "the right of property, freedom to contract, and freedom of labor." WILLIAM HOWARD TAFT, THE ANTI-TRUST ACT AND THE SUPREME COURT 2–3 (New York: Harper & Bros. 1914).
4. H.F. Henry, Jr., *Rights of Employers*, THE SOCIAL ECONOMIST (October 1892), at 5.
5. Haggai Hurvitz, *American Labor Law and the Doctrine of Entrepreneurial Property Rights: Boycotts, Courts, and the Juridical Reorientation of 1886–1895*, 8 INDUSTRIAL RELATIONS LAW JOURNAL 307, 321 (1986).
6. People v. Kostka, 4 New York Criminal Reports 429, 434 (1886).
7. Charles E. Eliot, *Five American Contributions to Civilization*, 78 ATLANTIC MONTHLY 433, 438 (1896). *See* Jane Addams, *The Present Crisis in Trades-Union Morals*, 179 NORTH AMERICAN REVIEW 178, 178 (1904) (commenting on "the recognition of the non-union man as the 'modern hero,' and of his sufferings as those of the martyr."). For labor's perspective on the strikebreaker, see Thomas J. Walsh, *Injunctions in Labor Disputes*, 56 LOCOMOTIVE ENGINEERS JOURNAL 737, 738 (October 1922) ("The man who in these times follows a trade or pursues a calling not in the professional class, and who refuses to contribute a dollar of his means to a union, the purpose of which is to promote the interests of those engaged like him . . . exhibits a repulsive selfishness. He gets the benefit of the wage scale which, through united effort, his associates exact . . . but he contributes nothing to that end. . . . *He is in a just sense a traitor to his class in these days in which, but for organized labor, we should know both industrial and political slavery*." (emphasis in the original)).
8. Austin Corbin, *The Tyranny of Labor Organizations*, 149 NORTH AMERICAN REVIEW 413, 420 (1889). "The worker in this country at least, under the law, happily, is not a slave; he owes no permanent service to anybody; he is a free man, as he ought to be. . . .

In lieu of the individual freedom of all workmen ... a new formula was invented and enforced by these self-constituted authorities. Employees then at work were compelled to abandon their duties unless and until the requirements of the league or order were complied with. These demands included rates of wages fixed by the order; hours of labor also arbitrarily fixed; the confinement of help employed to members of the order; an arbitrary uniform scale of wages for all employees engaged in certain forms of work." *Id.* at 414–15.

9. *Republicans Start "Open Shop" Fight*, NEW YORK TIMES (November 7, 1920), at 1.
10. Morris Hillquit, *Discussion – Injunctions and Fact-Finding in Labor Disputes*, 13 PROCEEDINGS OF THE ACADEMY OF POLITICAL SCIENCE 84 (June 1928). Five years later, Senator Norris would eloquently articulate this point in arguing for the enactment of the Norris-LaGuardia Act. *See* 75 CONG. REC. 4504 (February 23, 1932) (Remarks of Senator Norris). On the asymmetry between labor and capital in the labor market, and on the need for labor to organize to bargain effectively, see Herbert Hovenkamp, *Labor Conspiracies in American Law, 1880–1930*, 66 TEXAS LAW REVIEW 919 (1988).
11. ROBERT FRANKLIN HOXIE, TRADE UNIONISM IN THE UNITED STATES 282 (New York: D. Appleton & Co. 1919).
12. Corbin, *supra* note 8, at 420.
13. Felix Frankfurter, *The President's Industrial Conference*, 22 NEW REPUBLIC 179 (1920).
14. *Id.*
15. Plant v. Woods, 176 Mass. 492, 505 (1900) (Holmes, C.J., dissenting). In his Malthusian way, Holmes then continued:

> Although this is not the place for extended economic discussion, and although the law may not always reach ultimate economic conceptions, I think it well to add that I cherish no illusions as to the meaning and effect of strikes. While I think the strike a lawful instrument in the universal struggle of life, I think it pure phantasy to suppose that there is a body of capital of which labor, as a whole, secures a larger share by that means.
>
> The annual product, subject to an infinitesimal deduction for the luxuries of the few, is directed to consumption by the multitude, and is consumed by the multitude always. Organization and strikes may get a larger share for the members of an organization, but, if they do, they get it at the expense of the less organized and less powerful portion of the laboring mass. They do not create something out of nothing.
>
> It is only by devesting our minds of questions of ownership and other machinery of distribution, and by looking solely at the question of consumption, – asking ourselves what is the annual product, who consumes it, and what changes would or could we make, – that we can keep in the world of realities.
>
> But, subject to the qualifications which I have expressed, I think it lawful for a body of workmen to try by combination to get more than they now are getting, although they do it at the expense of their fellows, and to that end to strengthen their union by the boycott and the strike.

Id.
16. Thomas v. Cincinnati, N.O. & T.P. Ry. Co., 62 F. 803, 817 (Cir. Ct. S.D. Ohio 1894). Elements of Taft's argument seem drawn from E.L. Godkin, *The Labor Crisis*, 105 NORTH AMERICAN REVIEW 177, 189–90 (1867):

> When the workman goes into the market with his labor, ... if he finds wages are lower than he thinks they ought to be, he cannot wait in order to subject them to the test of capitalists' competition. He has not the means of remaining idle or seeking employment elsewhere.... His labor all year round is

barely sufficient to support himself and those dependent on him, and a month's or a week's idleness may plunge him in want or in debt....

It has, therefore, been apparent to the working classes, that ... the only remedy was combination, the union of a body of workmen large enough, by mutual aid, to support each other in testing the market by waiting, and to subject the employer to something like the same inconvenience in waiting to which the men are subjected. It is only when these conditions are secured, that the politico-economical process for the ascertaining the true rate of wages begins. The mass of labor is then measured against the mass of capital. The laborers array themselves on one side, the capitalists on the other, and have a trial of endurance.... A strike, therefore, means simply the concerted organized abstention of the laborers in one trade and one place from work, with the view of ascertaining whether the price they have put on labor or that which the masters have put on it be the correct one, the laborers being supported out of a fund previously accumulated by themselves.

For other iterations of this argument, see George E. McNeill, *The Problem of To-Day*, in THE LABOR MOVEMENT: THE PROBLEM OF TO-DAY 454 (Boston: A.M. Bridgman & Co. 1887); and U.M. Rose, *The Law of Trusts and Strikes*, in REPORT OF THE SIXTEENTH ANNUAL MEETING OF THE AMERICAN BAR ASSOCIATION 287, 297 (Philadelphia: Dando Printing & Publishing Co. 1893) ("The laborer, by his contract of hiring, not only transfers his labor, but he surrenders a part of his personal liberty. As compared with most sellers of commodities, he is under many disadvantages. He is single, while capital ... may be said in its force to be collective. Usually the laborer's case will brook no delay – he must have work or he and his family must starve. Capital, however, can wait until approaching famine compels a surrender. The sale of the laborer is a forced sale; and at forced sales commodities usually bring only ruinous prices.").

17. Address of Hon. William H. Taft, Secretary of War, delivered before the Cooper Union, New York City, Friday, January 10, 1908, in ROBERT LEE DUNN, WILLIAM HOWARD TAFT: AMERICAN 232, 229–30, 240 (Boston: The Chapple Publishing Co. 1908). Taft readily acknowledged that "The effect of the organization of labor, on the whole, has been highly beneficial in securing better terms for employment for the whole laboring community. I have not the slightest doubt, and no one who knows anything about the subject can doubt, that the existence of labor unions steadies wages." *Id.* at 231. Taft reiterated these ideas in 1914 in his presidential address to the American Bar Association:

[T]here has been a strong movement, and a most beneficial one, to give equality of opportunity to wage-earners in their struggle for a livelihood and their pursuit of happiness, and this movement has been greatly promoted by the direct efforts of labor combinations and their political influence. Without such combinations, we may well doubt whether the present condition of the wage-earner would be near so good as it is today. The history of the common law shows beyond question that its principles were framed in the interest of the employer, and that in the mutual relations of master and servant the servant was at a disadvantage. The power of combination among wage-earners, which if not condemned was at least frowned upon at common law, has created now an equality of resources in the inevitable and continuing contest between employers and employees that has greatly made for the improvement of the latter.

William Howard Taft, *Address of the President*, in REPORT OF THE THIRTY-SEVENTH ANNUAL MEETING OF THE AMERICAN BAR ASSOCIATION 370 (Baltimore: Lord Baltimore Press 1914).

Labor & the Jurisprudence of Individualism

18. 208 U.S. 161 (1908).
19. 30 Stat. 424 (June 1, 1898).
20. *Adair*, 208 U.S. at 172, 175–76.
21. Thomas Reed Powell, *Collective Bargaining before the Supreme Court*, 33 POLITICAL SCIENCE QUARTERLY 396, 401–2 (1918).
22. *Adair*, 208 U.S. at 187–88 (McKenna, J., dissenting).
23. *Adair*, 208 U.S. at 191 (Holmes, J., dissenting).
24. See GERALD G. EGGERT, RICHARD OLNEY: EVOLUTION OF A STATESMAN (University Park: Pennsylvania State University Press 1974).
25. Richard Olney, *Discrimination against Union Labor – Legal*, 42 AMERICAN LAW REVIEW 161, 164–65 (1908).
26. 236 U.S. 1 (1915).
27. Pitney "had long condemned closed-shop unionism as a judge in New Jersey's courts." Daniel Ernst, *The Yellow-Dog Contract and Liberal Reform, 1917–1932*, 30 LABOR HISTORY 251, 253 (1989).
28. For an excellent account of the history and theory of yellow-dog contracts, see Ernst, *supra* note 27. For a fine and roughly contemporaneous account, see Edwin E. Witte, *Yellow Dog Contracts*, 6 WISCONSIN LAW REVIEW 21 (1930). "The term, 'yellow dog contract', was coined about ten years ago, has come into general use only within the last year. ... Most commonly, it is applied to written promises in which a workman as a condition of employment obligates himself not to join a labor union." *Id.* at 21. See JOEL I. SEIDMAN, THE YELLOW DOG CONTRACT (Baltimore: Johns Hopkins Press 1932).
29. *Coppage*, 236 U.S. at 12, 14, 19–20.
30. *Id.* at 16–17.
31. *Id.* at 17–18. See Sidney Post Simpson, *Constitutional Rights and Industrial Struggle*, 30 WEST VIRGINIA LAW QUARTERLY 125, 132–35 (1924).
32. *Coppage*, 236 U.S. at 18–19.
33. Arizona Copper Co. v. Hammer, 250 U.S. 400 (1919). On the drafting of *Arizona Copper Co.*, see ALEXANDER M. BICKEL, THE UNPUBLISHED OPINIONS OF MR. JUSTICE BRANDEIS: THE SUPREME COURT AT WORK 61–76 (Cambridge: Harvard University Press 1957).
34. *Arizona Copper*, 250 U.S. at 419–20, 422–23. *Arizona Copper* was a five-to-four decision. McKenna, joined by White, Van Devanter, and McReynolds, dissented on the ground that it was "the very foundation of right – of the essence of liberty as it is of morals – to be free from liability if one is free from fault." *Id.* at 436 (McKenna, J., dissenting). McReynolds wrote separately to stress that both *Adair* and *Coppage* were inconsistent with upholding a mandatory workmen's compensation scheme. *Id.* at 451–52 (McReynolds, J., dissenting). "In the last analysis," McReynolds asserted, "it is for us to determine what is arbitrary or oppressive upon consideration of the natural and inherent principles of practical justice which lie at the base of our traditional jurisprudence and inspirit our Constitution. A legislative declaration of reasonableness is not conclusive; no more so is popular approval – otherwise constitutional inhibitions would be futile. And plainly, I think, the individual's fundamental rights are not proper subjects for experimentation; they ought not to be sacrificed to questionable theorization. Until now I had supposed that a man's liberty and property – with their essential incidents – were under the protection of

our charter and not subordinate to whims or caprices or fanciful ideas of those who happen for the day to constitute the legislative majority." *Id.* at 450–51.
35. 169 U.S. 383, 397 (1898). The Court understood that metaphors of voluntary agreement were misplaced because "the proprietors lay down the rules, and the laborers are practically constrained to obey them." *Id.*
36. 245 U.S. 229 (1917). For a good discussion, see Walter Wheeler Cook, *Privileges of Labor Unions in the Struggle for Life*, 27 YALE LAW JOURNAL 779 (1918).
37. *Hitchman* was "based on the principle that it is a tort to induce a breach of contract." Simpson, *supra* note 31, at 139 n.49.
38. "The value of yellow dog contracts lies not in enforcement against the workmen who sign them, but in injunctions against attempts of unions to organize these employes or to induce them to join in strikes. ... Unlike most contracts, these are for practical purposes unenforcible against the signers; and it is solely as a restraint upon a third party, the union, that they have any significance." Witte, *supra* note 28, at 22.
39. *Hitchman*, 245 U.S. at 251, 253. "In short, plaintiff was and is entitled to the good will of its employés, precisely as a merchant is entitled to the good will of his customers although they are under no obligation to continue to deal with him. The value of the relation lies in the reasonable probability that by properly treating its employés, and paying them fair wages, and avoiding reasonable grounds of complaint, it will be able to retain them in its employ, and to fill vacancies occurring from time to time by the employment of other men on the same terms. The pecuniary value of such reasonable probabilities is incalculably great, and is recognized by the law in a variety of relations." *Id.* at 252. This reasoning was extremely odd, because the employer's contracts with its employees were *at will*, meaning that they could be broken at any time and for any reason by either party. Sometimes Pitney wrote as if the employer's right was that its employees not "leave plaintiff's service without plaintiff's consent." 245 U.S. at 262. But, as Thomas Reed Powell observed, this was "strange" reasoning: "The employes could break their contracts only by not leaving plaintiff's employ after affiliating with the union. If they joined, they were to depart, not only with plaintiff's consent, but by its express requirement. They could not both break their contracts and leave without the plaintiff's consent." Powell, *supra* note 21, at 415.
40. By 1930, Harvard Law Professor Francis Bowes Sayre could observe that "The doctrine which is being utilized to-day in American courts perhaps more extensively than any other as a weapon of attack upon labor groups is that of inducing breach of contract." Francis Bowes Sayre, *Labor and the Courts*, 39 YALE LAW JOURNAL 682, 691 (1930).
41. Witte, *supra* note 28, at 24.
42. Ernest L. Bogart, *Economic Organization for War*, 14 AMERICAN POLITICAL SCIENCE REVIEW 587, 587 (1920). "[V]ictory has been dependent not merely upon the number of men in the field and on the seas, nor upon the strategy of warfare, but to an even greater extent upon the effectiveness of the industrial organization behind the lines." *Id.* at 588.
43. *Draft Age Men are to Work or Fight*, CHRISTIAN SCIENCE MONITOR (May 23, 1918), at 6.
44. Quoted in *Ex-President Stirs Guests at Banquet*, FRANKLIN NEWS-HERALD (December 31, 1919), at 9.

Labor & the Jurisprudence of Individualism

45. *To Check Labor Unrest*, BALTIMORE SUN (October 4, 1917), at 2. "Three thousand strikes erupted during the first six months of the war, and 4 million workers went on strike during the war. Cost-plus contracts awarded by the Administration stimulated higher wages but generated inflation. Unemployment ... fell to 1.4 percent in 1918." WILLIAM G. ROSS, WORLD WAR I AND THE AMERICAN CONSTITUTION 118 (Cambridge University Press 2017).

46. UNITED STATES DEPARTMENT OF LABOR, BUREAU OF LABOR STATISTICS, NATIONAL WAR LABOR BOARD: A HISTORY OF ITS FORMATION AND ACTIVITIES, TOGETHER WITH ITS AWARDS AND THE DOCUMENTS OF IMPORTANCE IN THE RECORD OF ITS DEVELOPMENT 32 (Washington D.C.: Government Printing Office 1922) (Bulletin of the United States Bureau of Labor Statistics No. 287). The principles announced by the Board included the eight-hour day and a living wage that would "insure the subsistence of the worker and his family in health and reasonable comfort." *Id.* at 32–33. The principles also provided that existing conditions of unionization should be frozen in place:

    1. In establishments where the union shop exists the same shall continue and the union standards as to wages, hours of labor and other conditions of employment shall be maintained.
    2. In establishments where union and nonunion men and women now work together, and the employer meets only with employees or representatives engaged in said establishments, the continuance of such conditions shall not be deemed a grievance. This declaration, however, is not intended in any manner to deny the right, or discourage the practice of the formation of labor unions, or the joining of the same by the workers in said establishments, as guaranteed in the last paragraph.

    Id. at 32.

47. The basic principle that employees should not be discriminated against on the basis of union membership had first been articulated in September 1917 by a committee of employers representing "sixteen manufacturers' associations and more than 50,000 manufacturers." *Seek Pact with Labor*, WASHINGTON POST (September 7, 1917), at 5; *Changing Existing Standards*, 18 AMERICAN INDUSTRIES 33 (November 1917). The employers asserted that:

    The Nation needs the service of every citizen. Its industrial workers are as indispensable to victory as the soldier on the firing line. ... We, therefore, urge ... as [a] guiding principle the fundamental American doctrine authoritatively stated by the Anthracite Coal Strike Commission with the approval of representatives of both employers and unions included in its membership and commended as the basis of industrial adjustments by Presidents Roosevelt, Taft, and Wilson: That no person shall be refused employment or in any way discriminated against on account of membership or nonmembership in any labor organization; that there shall be no discrimination against, or interference with, any employee who is not a member of any labor organization by members of such organization.

    NATIONAL WAR LABOR BOARD, *supra* note 46, at 27–28. The manufacturers also advocated maintaining the prewar status of workplaces with respect to union organization. They affirmed that as "applied to what are commonly known as 'open' or 'closed' shop conditions, it shall be understood and agreed that every employer entering the period of the war with a union shop shall not by a lockout or other means undertake to alter such conditions for the duration of the war, nor shall any combination of workmen undertake during the like period to 'close' an 'open' shop." *Id.* at 28.

Hitchman, which was decided in the midst of these delicate negotiations, was attacked as "breaking the labor truce." *Breaking the Labor Truce*, 13 NEW REPUBLIC 197 (1917) ("[T]he Supreme Court of the United States delivered, last week, what can only be construed as a frontal attack on organized labor. . . . The decision will . . . confirm the popular feeling . . . that a majority of the Supreme Court are endeavoring to enforce their own reactionary views of public policy, in direct opposition to the more enlightened views prevailing in legislatures and among the public."). *See* Samuel Gompers, *Unwise Trouble Provoking*, 25 AMERICAN FEDERATIONIST 32, 35 (1918) ("The trade union movement is the one agency that can mobilize the good will and the ability of America's workers in support of the government. Eliminate organization and the way is prepared for an American Bolsheviki. In this practical world of work engaged in a gigantic undertaking comes an edict from the realm of legalistic reasoning. The Supreme Court chooses the hour of the nation's supreme need of organization to defend antiunionism or antiorganization and come to the aid of the capitalistic forces hostile to labor. . . . An edict can not change needs of war production and transportation. . . . The very futility of the decision will prevent the accomplishment of the full degree of harm that might result at another time. This is a time when precedents, policies, persons are swept aside by urgent national need. A new organization of society is in the making based upon new concepts of cooperation."). *See* W.B. Rubin, *A Judicial "And-You-Too-Brutus" Stab at Unionism*, 25 AMERICAN FEDERATIONIST 216 (1918); Samuel Gompers, *That Supreme Court Decision*, 25 AMERICAN FEDERATIONIST 225 (1918).

48. NATIONAL WAR LABOR BOARD, *supra* note 46, at 34.
49. Before the creation of the Board, Taft and Walsh had been locked in a highly contentious relationship. VALERIE JEAN CONNER, THE NATIONAL WAR LABOR BOARD: STABILITY, SOCIAL JUSTICE, AND THE VOLUNTARY STATE IN WORLD WAR I at 18–20 (Chapel Hill: University of North Carolina Press 1983). Their eventual cooperation, however, was essential to the Board's success. *Id.* at 184–85. The selection of Taft and Walsh as co-chairs was "a shrewd political compromise," for it "brought together the unlikely combination of an outspoken labor lawyer and Democratic partisan with a reputation for radicalism in business circles, with a former U.S. president and Republican partisan with a reputation for hostility to labor in liberal circles." Robert D. Cuff, *The Politics of Labor Administration during World War I*, 21 LABOR HISTORY 546, 560 (1980).
50. The Board held that even if the yellow-dog contracts of the Smith & Wesson Arms Co. were "lawful when made," they were "contrary to the principles of the National War Labor Board, and the practice of taking such contracts should be discontinued for the period of the war." NATIONAL WAR LABOR BOARD, *supra* note 46, at 260. For similar holdings, see *id.* at 52–56, 211–13, 332–33; EDWIN E. WITTE, THE GOVERNMENT IN LABOR DISPUTES 222 (New York: McGraw-Hill Book Co. 1932); Ross, *supra* note 45, at 126–27; Witte, *supra* note 28, at 30; and Ernst, *supra* note 27, at 254.
51. NATIONAL WAR LABOR BOARD, *supra* note 46, at 24–25. *See* William Howard Taft, *Western Union and Union Labor* (July 18, 1918), in VIVIAN, at 74. In deciding the case, Taft was forced to break with all the employers' representatives on the Board. For a detailed discussion, see CONNER, *supra* note 49, at 35–49. "It 'was something of a Pyrrhic victory for the unions,' however, since the industry was placed under

Labor & the Jurisprudence of Individualism

the jurisdiction of Postmaster General Albert S. Burleson, who was not favorable toward unions and ignored the Board's order, and a strike by telegraph workers in July 1919 was unsuccessful." Ross, *supra* note 45, at 125–26. *See* JOSEPH A. MCCARTIN, LABOR'S GREAT WAR: THE STRUGGLE FOR INDUSTRIAL DEMOCRACY AND THE ORIGINS OF MODERN AMERICAN LABOR RELATIONS, 1912–1921, at 179 (Chapel Hill: University of North Carolina Press 1997).

52. *The A.F.of L. Convention*, 15 NEW REPUBLIC 164, 165 (1918). *See A Reprieve for the Children*, 16 NEW REPUBLIC 7, 8 (1918); Note, 22 COLUMBIA LAW REVIEW 78, 79 (1922). For other examples of the War Labor Board contradicting contemporaneous Supreme Court precedent, see *supra* Chapter 34, at note 9.

53. H.M., *The War Labor Board*, 1 THE LIBERATOR 12 (December 1918). It was also the case that "In grasping the shop union the old A.F. of L. organizations have grasped industrial unionism, denounced by many of the conservative labor leaders for two years past." *Id*. at 15. No doubt this experience was influential in the AFL's postwar decision to seek to unionize the steel industry.

54. MELVYN DUBOFSKY, THE STATE AND LABOR IN MODERN AMERICA 73 (Chapel Hill: University of North Carolina Press 1994). "[L]iberals associated with the NWLB credited William Howard Taft for much of the board's pre-Armistice success. [They] recognized Taft's careful guidance in many of the board's most important decisions. Indeed, Walsh believed that the NWLB had worked only because Taft had continually checked the employer members, who in the summer of 1918 had 'sat like hawks ... [ready] to pounce down on any person making an effort to ameliorate the conditions of the workers any place.'" CONNER, *supra* note 49, at 184.

55. Richard B. Gregg, *National War Labor Board*, 33 HARVARD LAW REVIEW 39, 61 (1919). On its passing, the NWLB was mourned by "both Socialist and conservative papers." *Passing of the War-Labor Board*, 62 LITERARY DIGEST 17 (August 30, 1919). The *Washington Post*, for example, editorialized:

> Had there been no such organization to compose the differences between capital and labor, embarrassing strikes and lockouts would have ensued, to the great loss of employers and employees, and it is no exaggeration to suggest that the nation's interests would have been very seriously affected, with the probability that the war would have been prolonged.
>
> Justice for the man who toils and for capital can be secured through arbitration. Let the nation profit by the demonstration that has been given by the war labor board. Congress will do well to provide permanent machinery for accomplishing the purposes which it accomplished.

War Labor Board, WASHINGTON POST (August 14, 1919), at 6. The *New York Times* opined, "If the board had not been starved out, it might have increased the country's indebtedness to it by guiding it through the labor troubles of peace as successfully as it did through the problems of war. It is a task of even greater difficulty." *War Wages Era Ended*, NEW YORK TIMES (August 14, 1919), at 8. The Socialist *New York Call* thought the NWLB "the one emergency agency 'that was worth while, and from which workers received some substantial benefits.'" Quoted in *Passing of the War-Labor Board, supra*, at 17.

56. William Howard Taft, *National War Labor Board* (November 26, 1918), in VIVIAN, at 124, 125, 127.

57. *Id*. at 125–26. "The advantage of the group system of dealing between employers and employees," Taft subsequently said, "is one that must be fully recognized by

every one having any vision of the future, and that what is essential is that the groups should be so organized that somebody on each side shall be responsible for the justice of the action of the respective groups." William Howard Taft, *Our Industrial Victory*, 8 PROCEEDINGS OF THE ACADEMY OF POLITICAL SCIENCE IN THE CITY OF NEW YORK 353, 353 (February 1919). Taft was especially concerned to support "intelligent, conservative labor leaders," Taft, *supra* note 56, at 126, like "my dear old antagonist, Samuel Gompers," *Our Industrial Victory*, *supra* at 353, and so avert "the danger from bolshevism" arising from "their extreme constituents." Taft, *supra* note 56, at 126. Taft subsequently became even blunter about this theme:

> The day of the industrial autocrat is passing and should pass. The workingmen have learned that in organization [is] power, and through organization they have acquired the means of manifesting that power and bringing it to bear on employers. It is well for employers to realize this. It is well for them promptly to recognize the advantage of conservative elements in labor organizations. It is well for them to welcome labor leadership in such organizations which are opposed to anarchy, extreme socialism and bolshevism as it is showing itself in Europe. By strengthening the patriotic, conservative, clear-sighted leaders in organized labor, through recognition of them and dealing with them, they are helping to stabilize society and, indeed, to improve conditions.

William Howard Taft, *Industrial Democracy* (April 14, 1919), in VIVIAN, at 199–200. For an example of Taft's genuine admiration for Gompers in the immediate aftermath of the war, see Address of Mr. Taft at a Luncheon [of the Civil Federation] Given in Honor of Mr. Samuel Gompers at the Holland House, New York, April 12, 1919 (Taft papers) ("Few people realize how much we are indebted to Mr. Gompers and those associated with him in the American Federation of Labor for holding our own ranks of labor.... I want to say personally for Mr. Gompers that I read his statements in respect to the war with profound admiration and gratitude.").

58. *The High Cost of Strikes*, 62 LITERARY DIGEST 15 (August 30, 1919). "Strikes and rumors of strikes have become so much a part of our daily routine that more than half the time the average citizen doesn't even trouble himself to find what they are all about." *High Cost of Strikes*, CINCINNATI ENQUIRER (August 19, 1919), at 4.
59. Malcolm Kerr, *Post-War Causes of Labor Unrest*, 81 ANNALS OF THE AMERICAN ACADEMY OF POLITICAL AND SOCIAL SCIENCE 101, 102 (January 1919).
60. SELIG PERLMAN & PHILIP TAFT, 4 HISTORY OF LABOR IN THE UNITED STATES, 1896–1932, at 491 (New York: MacMillan Co. 1935).
61. Management associations publicly explained the American plan in this way: "In practically all of the literature issued by the open shop associations 'the American plan' is used in preference to the 'open shop.' And throughout the literature runs this note of caution to the members of such associations: 'Be fair! The American plan makes no discrimination between capable workmen; it is neither the closed union shop nor the closed nonunion shop.' Of course, it is assumed no employer purposely would employ a preponderating number of union men, for that would enable them to strike and close his shop." *Public Sponsors Open Shop Associations*, 67 IRON TRADE REVIEW 1339, 1341 (1920).

In practice, the implementation of the American plan tended to be highly antilabor. The Federal Council of Churches, for example, issued a statement condemning "the open shop policy, the so-called American plan of employment," for being "used to designate establishments that are definitely anti-union. Obviously, a shop of this kind is not an open shop, but a closed shop – closed against members of unions. We feel impelled to call public attention to the fact that a very widespread impression exists that the present open shop campaign is inspired in many quarters by this antagonism to union labor. Any such attempt must be viewed with apprehension by fair-minded people." *Protestant Church Council Denounces Open Shop Crusade*, NEW YORK TRIBUNE (December 27, 1920), at 3. *See* Samuel Gompers, *"Open Shop" Hypocrisy Exposed*, 28 AMERICAN FEDERATIONIST 109 (1921); *Open Shop Move as Blow at Unions*, NEW YORK TIMES (December 27, 1920), at 21 ("The open shop campaign in American industry was described as an attempt to destroy the organized labor movement, in a statement issued yesterday by the Commission of the Church and Social Services of the Federal Council of the Churches of Christ in America.").

For a discussion of the open shop movement, see Allen M. Wakstein, *The Origins of the Open-Shop Movement, 1919–1920*, 51 JOURNAL OF AMERICAN HISTORY 460 (1964).

62. William Howard Taft, *Collective Bargaining I* (March 1, 1921), in VIVIAN, at 544. In commenting on the "national movement among employers in favor of an open shop," Taft cautioned that "we must not be misled of the term 'open shop' to disguise a movement which has for its object not the mere defeat of those labor unions who insist on the closed shop, but the destruction of labor unions generally. There is a class of employers who believe that there is nothing but evil in the combinations of workingmen[,] who regard the strike as an unmitigated instrument of evil and who look forward to stamping out labor unions by a combination of employers who will refuse to employ union men at all, who will discharge men who join a union and who will include in their contracts of employment a clause by which the employee binds himself during his employment not to belong to a union. Such employers are within their lawful right in making such contracts ... but the shop they are conducting is not an open shop. It is a closed nonunion shop. It is just as unsocial as the closed shop of the labor union and deserves no more support or sympathy from good men or from the public than the other. It is the custom of Bourbon employers engaged in fighting labor unionism to the death to call the movement to kill unionism an open-shop movement. This is a deceitful misuse of the term." William Howard Taft, *The Open-Shop Problem* (January 22, 1921), in VIVIAN, at 529–30. Taft himself advocated instead for the kind of open shop over which he had presided at the NWLB. This was a shop that would allow "those who decide to join or form unions to do so and to act together in dealing with their employer and those who do not wish to join unions to work peacefully and to deal with their employer individually or through chosen committees, as they will. Such freedom of collective bargaining will make for a better understanding for mutual forbearance and for industrial peace." *Id.* at 531. Employers seeking "to suppress labor unions" are "attempting the unwise, the unjust and the impossible." *Id.*

63. Quoted in Savel Zimand, *Who Is Behind the Open Shop Campaign?*, 25 NEW REPUBLIC 255, 255 (1921). The vote behind the Chamber's endorsement of the plan was 1,664–4. *Id.*

64. Quoted *id.* at 256. *See* Henry Harrison Lewis, *The Great Open Shop "Conspiracy"*, 3 INDUSTRY: A SEMI-MONTHLY INTERPRETATION OF INDUSTRIAL PROGRESS 2, 4 (January 1, 1921). Rejecting the overtures of organized labor, the National Grange resolved at its annual convention to oppose "any system which denies to any individual the right to work in any place where there is need of his industry, at

any time and at any wage which is satisfactory to him." *Resolution on Right to Work*, in JOURNAL OF PROCEEDINGS OF THE NATIONAL GRANGE OF THE PATRONS OF HUSBANDRY 138 (Springfield: National Grange Monthly 1920). The AFL described the campaign for the open shop in this way:

> Reactionary employers have joined their might in a campaign which they are pleased to call a campaign for the "open shop," which they have been waging vigorously since the signing of the armistice. Compelled by the pressure of public opinion to accept Labor's cooperation during the war ... they cast off all pretense immediately upon the passing of the emergency.
>
> This entire campaign ... is in no sense a campaign for the "open shop" no matter what definition may be given to that term. The campaign is (distinctly and solely) one for a shop that shall be closed against union workmen. It is primarily a campaign disguised under the name of an "open shop" campaign, designed to destroy trade unions and to break down and eliminate the whole principle of collective bargaining.

The Challenge Accepted, 28 AMERICAN FEDERATIONIST 289, 290 (1921).

65. *Gary Defines Stand on Open and Closed Shop*, WALL STREET JOURNAL (April 19, 1921), at 3. Gary added, revealing the true source of his opposition to unionization, that "If our own shops should become thoroughly unionized.... then the management would be in the hands of the unions." *Id*. Matthew Woll, vice president of the AFL, replied to Gary: "There is a necessity for unionization of the steel industry because in the mills of the Steel Trust there is no freedom for the workers.... The steel trust will be unionized. No slavery has ever persisted forever, no slavery can persist forever." *Gompers and Woll Attack Judge Gary*, NEW YORK TIMES (April 20, 1921), at 13. "Charging that the labor policy of the United States Steel Corporation would revive serfdom," William F. Kehoe, secretary of the Central Trades and Labor Council, asserted that "No worker who joins a trade union is the slave of that trade union or of its representatives. The worker joins the trade union for the purpose of being able to express collectively his opinions and his wishes." *Labor's Reply to the Gary Speech*, CHRISTIAN SCIENCE MONITOR (April 21, 1921), at 5.

66. As Taft put it in 1920, "In all the countries engaged in the war ... industrial laborers were made to know the indispensable function that they performed in society, even more clearly in war than in peace. This war was successfully waged not alone in the trenches ... but in the workshops and mines and other places of labor in the countries which were carrying it on, and those who were engaged in this work were advised and became fully conscious of how important they were to all society in what they were doing. It gave them an unusual sense of power and filled them with the hope that as they were indispensable, they might readjust the rewards of labor so as to take all that they chose to take." William Howard Taft, Address of Wm. H. Taft before the National Geographic Society, Washington D.C., Friday, January 23, 1920, at 17 (Taft papers).

67. Henry Harrison Lewis, *An Open Letter to American Workmen*, 1 INDUSTRY 5, 6 (November 15, 1919) ("The American workman must be American first, and his unions and associations must be restored to a condition where Americanism will be the dominant feature. Americanism does not permit association with those who would confiscate and destroy, and plunge the country into riot, and misery and anarchy.").

68. DAVID BRODY, LABOR IN CRISIS: THE STEEL STRIKE OF 1919, at 128–46 (Urbana: University of Illinois Press 1987). Taft seems to have been quite susceptible to

charges that foreign radicals were infiltrating the ranks of organized labor. "Bolshevism is militant and threatening in every European country," he said. "It has penetrated to this country. Because of the presence of hordes of ignorant European foreigners, not citizens, and not intending to become citizens, with little or no knowledge of our language, with no appreciation of American civilization or American institutions of civil liberty, it has taken strong hold in many of our congested centers and is the backing of a good many of the strikes from which our whole community is suffering to-day. The radical agitators of these troubles encourage lawlessness, stimulate resistance to lawful authority and the abuse of the power of organization." Address of Hon. William H. Taft at Malden, Massachusetts, October 30, 1919, at 4 (Taft papers). See William Howard Taft, *Bolshevism and Americanism*, 2 NORTHWEST WARRIORS MAGAZINE 5, 31–32 (March 1, 1920).

69. DEPARTMENT OF LABOR, PROCEEDINGS OF THE FIRST INDUSTRIAL CONFERENCE (Washington D.C.: Government Printing Office 1920). Anticipating the conference, Taft urged both labor and capital to compromise:

> "The hope of progress in the United States today," said William Howard Taft, who, in the words of J. Hampton Moore, is America's most useful citizen, "lies in the conservative labor leader and the progressive employer."
>
> "The Bourbons of both camps are the only people who menace this country," added the former president. "There is just as great a division among business men as there is among labor leaders. The Bourbons of business are the reactionaries who will have nothing to do with labor leaders. The Bourbons of labor are the radicals, and they wish to have nothing whatever to do with business or business men. Both groups are agitators. Both injure the country....
>
> "On the war-labor board we had to fight the Bourbons of business just as much as the extremists of labor, and sometimes I thought that the greatest danger to our country was from these reactionary employers, because they really made the radicals."

Quoted in Carl W. Ackerman, *Industrial Security Threatened Only by Bourbons, Says Taft*, ATLANTA CONSTITUTION (October 17, 1919), at 12.

70. *Letter from Woodrow Wilson*, PROCEEDINGS OF THE FIRST INDUSTRIAL CONFERENCE, *supra* note 69, at 5.

71. *Address of Hon. W.B. Wilson*, PROCEEDINGS OF THE FIRST INDUSTRIAL CONFERENCE, *supra* note 69, at 9.

72. PROCEEDINGS OF THE FIRST INDUSTRIAL CONFERENCE, *supra* note 69, at 266. "I have always thought," Taft later said, "that true collective bargaining meant bargaining through any agent or representatives whom the employees or any of them might choose to select." William Howard Taft, *Collective Bargaining I*, *supra* note 62, at 545. *See* Samuel Gompers, *Call It by Its Right Name*, 28 AMERICAN FEDERATIONIST 225 (1921).

73. Haggai Hurvitz, *Ideology and Industrial Conflict: President Wilson's First Industrial Conference of October 1919*, 18 LABOR HISTORY 509, 522 (1977).

74. William Howard Taft, *Gompers' Mistake* (October 25, 1919), in VIVIAN, at 292–93. *See* William Howard Taft, *Employers' Leadership* (October 20, 1919), *id.* at 289. The conference ended when Gompers walked out after the employers' group rejected his motion. Gompers announced that the Executive Council of the AFL "had voted to devote all its moral and financial support to aid the steel strikers in enforcing their demand for collective bargaining." "You have defeated the labor

group in its declaration," he said, "but we will meet you again in conference, and when we do meet you there you will be glad to talk collective bargaining." *Gompers Leads Men Out*, NEW YORK TIMES (October 23, 1919), at 1. Taft scored Gompers for "withdrawing with a threat." *Gompers Mistake, supra*, at 293. "The real impulse of the present body of the strikers," Taft said, "is now a Bolshevistic one.... They are in favor of putting the theories of Lenin and Trotsky into practice here.... They regard this strike as a revolution against the existing social order of the United States." *Id.* "What matters it if the extremists are threatening Mr. Gompers' control of the Federation of Labor?" Taft asked. "It is vastly better he should lose it and go down fighting for his principles as an American labor unionist than that he should assume leadership and responsibility for a radical and red rebellion." *Id.* at 294. "The country is in no humor for another such humiliating episode as that of the passage of the Adamson law. The spirit of Americanism is rising. The highwayman's method will not succeed again.... If Mr. Gompers is determined to start the fight, the struggle will be a long and disastrous one for all, but the American people in the end will triumph over the soviet." *Id.* at 294–95. The best narrative of Taft's disillusionment with labor during the course of the many strikes of 1919 may be found in Address of Wm. H. Taft before the National Geographic Society, *supra* note 66.

75. PERLMAN & TAFT, *supra* note 60, at 471–72. President Wilson declared, "It is recognized that the strike would practically shut off the country's supply of its principal fuel at a time when interference with that supply is calculated to create a disastrous fuel famine.... It would involve stopping the operation of railroads, electric light and gas plants, street railway lines and other public utilities, and the shipping to and from this country .... I feel it my duty in the public interest to declare that any attempt to carry out the purposes of this strike and thus to paralyze the industry of the country with the consequent suffering and distress of all our people, must be considered a grave moral and legal wrong against the Government and the people of the United States." *President Wilson's Statement about the Coal Strike*, NEW YORK TIMES (October 26, 1919), at 1.

76. *Order Calling Off Coal Strike to Go Out Today*, ST. LOUIS POST-DISPATCH (November 11, 1919), at 1. Although the strike was officially over, "no miners returned to work. A month later the union accepted the proposal in President Wilson's name for an immediate increase of 14 per cent, further increases and other disputed points to be decided by an arbitration commission." PERLMAN & TAFT, *supra* note 60, at 472.

77. "The ending of the coal strike is a great victory for the people. It saves them from inconvenience and real suffering.... It seems ... the irony of fate that a Democratic administration, which pressed the Clayton and Adamson laws through Congress ... should be driven by its responsibility into a federal court to ask an injunction against the leaders of a union numbering hundreds of thousands of members." William Howard Taft, *Court Injunctions* (November 15, 1919), in VIVIAN, at 306–7. Taft cited his own decision in Toledo, A.A. & N.M. Ry. Co. v. Pennsylvania Co., 54 F. 730 (N.D. Ohio 1893), as precedent for the injunction against the coal miners. *Id.* Apparently Taft's theory was that the coal strike was called "for an unlawful purpose." Taft, *Court Injunctions, supra*, at 308.

78. William Howard Taft, *Labor Injunctions* (November 20, 1919), in VIVIAN, at 310.

79. Lincoln Colcord, *The Administration Adrift*, 109 THE NATION 635, 636 (1919).

80. For a good description of labor's rebuffs at the hands of each party, see ROBERT H. ZIEGER, REPUBLICANS AND LABOR 1919–1929, at 17–50 (Lexington: University of Kentucky Press 1969).
81. After his election as vice president, Coolidge observed that "in the last election the country had expressed its opinion against organized labor as it had a few years ago against organized capital." *Coolidge Declares Vote Rebuked Labor*, NEW YORK TIMES (November 24, 1920), at 1. The *Wall Street Journal* crowed: "Here is a people's victory over shirkers and grafters. . . . [T]he incoming Congress is now in a position to deal convincingly with union labor and Mr. Gompers is an optimist indeed if he believes that it will fail in that necessary task." *Will Mr. Gompers Face the Facts?*, WALL STREET JOURNAL (November 4, 1920), at 1. *See* George Rothwell Brown, *Must Reform Party*, WASHINGTON POST (November 4, 1920), at 1 ("The landslide of Republican votes in the labor centers is a body blow at the radical labor agitator. . . . [T]here is plainly forecast a more conservative attitude toward labor questions in Congress and the end of a policy which has made labor a favored class under the law."). Taft himself observed in January that "The last election should have been informing to Mr. Gompers . . . . The overwhelming election of a candidate who had as senator voted to punish as an unlawful conspiracy a combination of employees engaged in interstate commerce to strike and stop that commerce ought to be a lesson." William Howard Taft, *Gompers and the Law* (January 12, 1921), in VIVIAN, at 526.
82. LDB to Felix Frankfurter (November 26, 1920), in BRANDEIS-FRANKFURTER CORRESPONDENCE, at 48.
83. ZIEGER, *supra* note 80, at 36. For example, as discussed in *supra* Chapter 25, at 795, Harding in June 1921 seemed to propose a plan for compulsory arbitration despite the firm opposition of his own party platform. *See infra* note 248. Elbert H. Gary, chair of the United States Steel Corporation, seemed to propose something similar in response to the 1919 steel strike. *See Gary Defines Stand on Open and Closed Shop*, *supra* note 65, at 3 ("I do not believe in socialism; in governmental management or operation; but I do advocate publicity, regulation and reasonable control through Government agencies. . . . Laws – clear, well defined, practicable and easy of comprehension – covering these matters, might be passed, and if so they should apply to all economic organizations, groups or bodies exceeding certain specified numbers amounts. Both organized capital and organized labor should be placed under these laws."). Taft considered Gary's views those of an extremist. William Howard Taft, *Gary and Unionism* (April 27, 1921), in VIVIAN, at 572.

> One may fully admit that labor unionism has defects of the character elaborated by Judge Gary, without at all going to the startling conclusion that now we must substitute for it government regulation. It is a proposed surrender of the benefit of the free action of economic forces in a quarter where we would least expect it. . . . It is the putting forward of a remedy impossible in two respects: How is labor unionism to be abolished? How is governmental machinery to be created which will fix or regulate relations between labor and capital?

Id. Some virulently antilabor politicians, like Senator Miles Poindexter of Washington, also recommended the creation of "government tribunals" for "the settlement of economic disputes" that would require labor and capital "to submit to the arbitrament of the law." Miles Poindexter, *Labor and the Open Shop*, 125 OUTLOOK 17, 18 (May 5, 1920).

84. Robert M. La Follette, *Government by Injunction*, 14 La Follette's Magazine 130 (September 1922). For a description of the Daugherty injunction, see *infra* note 191.
85. Robert H. Zieger, *Herbert Hoover, the Wage-Earner, and the "New Economic System," 1919–1929*, 51 Business History Review 161 (1977).
86. Poindexter, *supra* note 83, at 17–18. During the campaign Harding "made no effort to identify organized labor with radicalism" and "largely ignored the Red issue." Zieger, *supra* note 80, at 45.
87. Zieger, *supra* note 80, at 38, 52. Several weeks after Harding received the Republican nomination, Sutherland wrote him to report on a meeting with twenty-eight businessmen, all "employers of labor on a large scale." "They are for the open shop, of course, but not hostile to organized labor, though greatly deploring certain of its tendencies. They do not expect or ask that the next administration shall be hostile to organized labor, but only that it shall stand for equality of rights and equality of burden, with the public welfare as the supreme guide."

> My own feeling is that wherever and however you deal with this question, special emphasis should be laid upon the rights of the general public, from whose pockets in the last analysis come both dividends and wages and who, while greatly outnumbering both employers and workmen, are unorganized and therefore in danger of being ground between these highly disciplined organizations. I am not sure but that one of the gravest dangers the people as a whole are facing is that of being dominated and exploited by and for the benefit of organized minorities of various kinds who know exactly what they want. The government while bound within the legitimate scope of its powers to enforce the square deal as between labor and capital, owes a peculiar, if not a paramount duty to the general public – numerically strong, but strategically weak – to see that it is not made the victim of the conscious or unconscious selfishness of both classes. I am afraid that compulsory arbitration is not the remedy. There are inherent and serious difficulties in the way of applying the coercive processes of the law to large groups of men whose offense may often consist of simply failing to recognize and discharge their economic duties to society. But I think at least we should devise some plan by which the claims of either against the other where they cannot be settled by mutual arrangement, may be heard and determined by a thoroughly impartial tribunal whose standing and character will be such that its findings will have behind them the sanction of an instructed and determined public opinion.

GS to Warren G. Harding (June 26, 1920) (Sutherland papers). After the election, Sutherland wrote Harding that the conservative labor leaders "who opposed you have been somewhat startled and chastened by the great vote you received, and they would probably welcome an opportunity of establishing themselves on a friendly footing." GS to Warren G. Harding (November 10, 1920) (Sutherland papers).
88. GS to Warren G. Harding (January 4, 1921) (Sutherland papers). Harding replied that he was in "complete accord" with Sutherland's advice. "This administration can not afford to be intolerant. On the contrary, I mean to do all I know how to promote understanding and concord." Warren G. Harding to GS (January 9, 1921) (Sutherland papers).
89. Zieger, *supra* note 80, at 46.
90. On labor's attitudes toward Taft at the time of his nomination, see *supra* Prologue, at 2–3.
91. Samuel Gompers, *Taft, The Injunction Standard Bearer*, 14 American Federationist 785, 786 (1907). To Gompers, Taft was "Injunction Judge Taft."

Labor & the Jurisprudence of Individualism

Samuel Gompers, *President Roosevelt's Attack on Labor*, 15 AMERICAN FEDERATIONIST 973, 977, 979 (1908).
92. William Howard Taft, *Judicial Decisions as An Issue in Politics*, 33 MCCLURE'S MAGAZINE 201, 209 (June 1909).
93. Samuel Gompers, *Official Circular*, 15 AMERICAN FEDERATIONIST 955, 957 (1908). "It is Mr. Taft's injunctions and other matters affecting the rights of the workers which make him an undesirable and unpopular candidate.... Mr. Taft has always been the active and energetic servant of the corporations as against the unions, as his judicial record proves." Samuel Gompers, *Candidate Taft, Take Notice!*, 15 AMERICAN FEDERATIONIST 960, 962 (1908).
94. William Howard Taft, *Prideful Labor Unions* (March 25, 1920), in VIVIAN, at 372.
95. Address of Wm. H. Taft before the National Geographic Society, *supra* note 66, at 23–24.
96. *Press Sees Strike as Public Calamity*, NEW YORK TIMES (October 17, 1921), at 3.
97. *Id*. For a full-scale treatment of the strike, see COLIN J. DAVIS, POWER AT ODDS: THE 1922 NATIONAL RAILROAD SHOPMEN'S STRIKE (Champaign: University of Illinois Press 1997).
98. A week after the 1921 term opened, Taft wrote his brother:

> The strike which the railroad men threaten is most formidable. I sincerely hope that the Administration and Congress will stand up and not run away. The 30th of October is perhaps as good a time for the fight to begin as any in the year. It is after harvest, and there has been a good deal of distribution of food, business is bad, and there are a great many unemployed. I hope that the railroads may be able, if the strike comes, to maintain some freight business so as to prevent the people from starving. It will, however, shut down almost all industries and it will throw out of employment a great many more millions of men than the railroad men. I think the railroad people are contemplating winning by reason of the fear of the consequences that they can instill in the hearts of the people generally and especially of those in authority. If we can fight this thing through, it will end that kind of a strike forever, just as Deb's failure did. It is certainly a very critical time.

WHT to Charles P. Taft (October 16, 1921) (Taft papers).
99. 257 U.S. 184 (1921). For a factual summary of the case, see ELIAS LIEBERMAN, UNIONS BEFORE THE BAR 108–17 (New York: Oxford Book Co. 1950).
100. *See, e.g.*, David Joseph Danelski, The Chief Justice and the Supreme Court 180 (Ph.D. Dissertation, University of Chicago 1961); Kevin J. Burns, *Chief Justice as Chief Executive: Taft's Judicial Statesmanship*, 43 JOURNAL OF SUPREME COURT HISTORY 47, 58 (2018). In Holmes's papers there is a draft dissent (seemingly joined by Pitney), with a note stating: "Written some years ago, when I thought that the case was to be decided the other way." On the Saturday after the third argument, Holmes wrote Laski: "Already we are in the field – a labor case that has been argued 3 times and in which I prepared what then was a dissent has now taken the form of memoranda by Pitney and me – but I don't know how the boys will go – I only circulated mine yesterday P's having been handed out two days before. What I had to say was nothing much – A repetition of the dissent in *Vegelahn v. Guntner* [167 Mass. 92, 104 (1896)] 25 years ago – noting the tendency in that direction. By good luck a decision of the English Court of Appeals – [Ware and De Freville, Ltd. v. Motor Trade Association,] 1921 3 KB 40 has just come out in which Scrutton refers to my opinion as one of the best statements and agrees with it. [Frederick Pollock] has just sent me a note of his on

it in [37] *L.Q. Review* [395 (October 1921)]." OWH to Harold Laski (October 9, 1921), in 1 HOLMES-LASKI CORRESPONDENCE, at 374.

101. The argument in *American Steel Foundries* carried over until October 5. The next day, after hearing argument on "labor cases and others of public importance," Taft wrote his brother Horace that "I look forward to our first conferences in which these cases will be discussed with much interest." WHT to Horace D. Taft (October 6, 1921) (Taft papers). Immediately after his first conference, however, Taft wrote his elder brother that "the mental effort and the clash of minds in a conference room are quite tiring." Taft to Charles P. Taft (October 16, 1921) (Taft papers).

Representing American Steel Foundries was Taft's close friend Max Pam, a Jewish Austrian émigré who was counsel and a director of American Steel Foundries, and who had also been closely connected to Elbert Gary in the formation of the United States Steel Corporation. *Max Pam Dies of Heart Attack*, NEW YORK TIMES (September 15, 1925), at 25. Pam "enjoyed the close friendship" of Taft, "at whose home in Washington and at whose Summer home at Murray Bay, Canada, he was a frequent guest." *Id*. During the entire pendency of the case, Taft was actively involved in seeking to obtain a political appointment for Pam in the Harding administration. *See* WHT to Max Pam (September 26, 1921) (Taft papers); WHT to Gus Karger (September 28, 1921) (Taft papers); Max Pam to WHT (October 6, 1921) (Taft papers) ("It made me quite happy Tuesday and Wednesday to have the pleasure and privilege to appear before the Supreme Court with you as the Chief Justice. Indeed, it made me feel not only that 'you were at home', but that it was your natural place, and that time and circumstance conspired that you should have it just when and as it came."); WHT to Charles D. Hilles (October 6, 1921) (Taft papers); WHT to Colonel I.M. Ullman (October 6, 1921) (Taft papers); WHT to Max Pam (October 9, 1921) (Taft papers); WHT to Colonel I.M. Ullman (October 9, 1921) (Taft papers); Max Pam to WHT (October 19, 1921) (Taft papers); WHT to Colonel I.M. Ullman (November 6, 1921) (Taft papers). While the case was pending, Taft hosted Pam at a private breakfast at the Willard Hotel at 8 am on November 16, and Pam offered Taft free income tax advice. WHT to Max Pam (October 20, 1921) (Taft papers); Wendell W. Mischler to Max Pam (November 23, 1921) (Taft papers); Max Pam to WHT (November 28, 1921) (Taft papers).

102. OWH to Harold Laski (December 22, 1921), in 1 HOLMES-LASKI CORRESPONDENCE, at 389. The next day Holmes commented to Frankfurter that in *American Steel Foundries* Taft "had so successfully stifled competition." OWH to Felix Frankfurter (December 23, 1921), in HOLMES-FRANKFURTER CORRESPONDENCE, at 132.

103. As Taft summarized the evidence: "It is clear ... that, from the outset, violent methods were pursued from time to time in such a way as to characterize the attitude of the picketers as continuously threatening. A number of employees, sometimes 15 or more, slept in the plant for a week during the trouble, because they could not safely go to their homes. The result of the campaign was to put employees and would-be employees in such fear that many abandoned work, and this seriously interfered with the complainant in operating the plant ... ." *American Steel Foundries*, 257 U.S. at 200.

104. *Id*. at 193–94 (emphasis added).

105. *Id*. at 194–95.

106. Francis Bowes Sayre, *The Picketing Decisions*, 47 THE SURVEY 558, 559 (1922).

Labor & the Jurisprudence of Individualism

107. Karges Furniture Co. v. Amalgamated Woodworkers' Local Union, 75 N.W. 877, 880–81 (Ind. 1905). *See* Pope Motor Car Co. v. Keegan, 150 F. 148, 150 (N.D. Ohio 1906) ("I cannot believe that, under proper circumstances, and with such a sense of self-restraint as men can exercise, picketing may not be properly conducted."); Jerome R. Hellerstein, *Picketing Legislation and the Courts*, 10 NORTH CAROLINA LAW REVIEW 158, 173–74 (1931).
108. Atchison, T. & S.F. Ry. Co. v. Gee, 139 F.582, 584–86 (S.D. Iowa 1905). "When men want to converse or persuade, they do not organize a picket line. . . . [T]he peaceful, law-abiding man can be and is intimidated by gesticulations, by menaces, by being called harsh names, and by being followed, or compelled to pass by men known to be unfriendly. . . . [A] state of serfdom shall not exist, by a so-called system of 'picketing' of one crowd of men over another. No self-respecting man will submit to it." *Id. See* Hellerstein, *supra* note 107, at 172–73; Sayre, *supra* note 40, at 701–3.
109. *Pickets a Menace Is Judge's Ruling*, NEW YORK TIMES (September 23, 1921), at 4. Justice Selah B. Strong of Brooklyn announced:

> The defendants, many of whom are foreigners, claiming that this is a free country, state that they are within their rights, admit the picketing and allege that the plaintiff has no cause for complaint. Some foreigners coming to this country have a strange idea of freedom and liberty. . . . Their cry is that, all men being equal no individual must be permitted to profit by reason of individual strength or arm or brain, that everything in life must be brought to some unknown level. Men and women of this sort come into this country in droves, and the immigration laws are insufficient to curb them. It is therefore important that they be made to realize that the American people and American institutions stand for a liberty with justice to all and with our shops open to all on a common ground of equality. Any attempt to equalize the strength of brains of individuals is an attempt to deprive the individual of the right of freedom which a free country guarantees to its citizens.

Id. Strong explicitly rejected the policies of the NWLB, explaining that during the war labor leaders had asserted that "we rule." But, said Strong, "No labor organization in any shop had a right to demand and insist that each, every and all employees shall join the organization. No such right exists in any club or social organization, and no such right exists in any free country. There is no freedom of action left to the individual when such demand is made. It is thoroughly un-American in spirit and it cannot be tolerated by American people. . . . During the war did not the labor delegates in this country hold the Government by the throat, when weak-kneed officials and public officers bent to their demands, instead of using the draft army for essentials?" *Id.* The New York Court of Appeals later modified Strong's injunction. A.L. Reed Co. v. Whiteman, 144 N.W. 885 (N.Y. 1924).
110. Allis-Chalmers Co. v. Iron Molders' Union No. 125, 150 F.155 (E.D. Wisc. 1906).
111. *Claims of Taft on Labor's Vote*, CHICAGO DAILY TRIBUNE (October 26, 1908), at 1.
112. W.B. Rubin, *Chief Justice Taft and Picketing*, 29 AMERICAN FEDERATIONIST 106, 107 (1922).
113. *Claims of Taft on Labor's Vote*, *supra* note 111, at 1. On appeal the case for the union was also argued by labor lawyer W.B. Rubin. The company was represented by James M. Beck, later to become solicitor general during the Taft Court.
114. Iron Molders' Union No. 125 v. Allis-Chalmers Co., 166 F. 45 (7th Cir. 1908).
115. *Id.* at 51. "The decree is modified by striking out 'persuasion' and 'persuading' from the 4th and 7th paragraphs; further modified by adding after 'picketing' in the 5th paragraph 'in a threatening or intimidating manner.'" *Id.* at 52.

116. Tri-City Central Trades Council v. American Steel Foundries, 238 F. 728, 731 (7th Cir. 1916). Taft would in fact use the occasion to overturn *Allis-Chalmers*, 257 U.S. at 207, much to the bafflement of his erstwhile allies. *See, e.g.*, Rubin, *supra* note 112, at 107.
117. 158 U.S. 564 (1895).
118. Duplex Printing Press Co. v. Deering, 254 U.S. 443, 484 (1921) (Brandeis, J., dissenting). *See* WITTE, *supra* note 50, at 66.
119. Pub. L. 63-212, 38 Stat. 730 (October 15, 1914).
120. Section 6 of the Act provided: "That the labor of a human being is not a commodity or article of commerce. Nothing contained in the anti-trust laws shall be construed to forbid the existence and operation of labor, agricultural, or horticultural organizations, instituted for the purposes of mutual help, and not having capital stock or conducted for profit, or to forbid or restrain individual members of such organizations from lawfully carrying out the legitimate objects thereof; nor shall such organizations, or the members thereof, be held or construed to be illegal combinations or conspiracies in restraint of trade, under the anti-trust laws." Section 20 of the Act provided:

> That no restraining order or injunction shall be granted by any court of the United States, or a judge or the judges thereof, in any case between an employer and employees, or between employers and employees, or between employees, or between persons employed and persons seeking employment, involving, or growing out of, a dispute concerning terms or conditions of employment, unless necessary to prevent irreparable injury to property, or to a property right, of the party making the application, for which injury there is no adequate remedy at law, and such property or property right must be described with particularity in the application which must be in writing and sworn to by the applicant or by his agent or attorney.
>
> And no such restraining order or injunction shall prohibit any person or persons, whether singly or in concert, from terminating any relation of employment, or from ceasing to perform any work or labor or from recommending, advising, or persuading others by peaceful means so to do; or from attending at any place where any such person or persons may lawfully be, for the purpose of peacefully obtaining or communicating information, or from peacefully persuading any person to work or to abstain from working; or from ceasing to patronize or to employ any party to such dispute, or from recommending, advising, or persuading others by peaceful and lawful means so to do; or from paying or giving to, or withholding from, any person engaged in such dispute, any strike benefits or other moneys or things of value; or from peaceably assembling in a lawful manner, and for lawful purposes; or from doing any act or thing which might lawfully be done in the absence of such dispute by any party thereto; nor shall any of the acts specified in this paragraph be considered or held to be violations of any law of the United States.

121. Samuel Gompers, *The Charter of Industrial Freedom*, 21 AMERICAN FEDERATIONIST 971, 974 (1914).
122. George W. Wickersham, *Labor Legislation in the Clayton Act*, 22 AMERICAN FEDERATIONIST 493, 498 (1915). The *New York Times* complained that the Act was "a monument of the commanding and supercongressional position of Mr. Samuel Gompers and the Federation of Labor. ... Must injunctions be pared? Must the secondary boycott be legalized? The unsleeping watchmen of organized labor know how intrepid most Congressmen are when threatened with

Labor & the Jurisprudence of Individualism

the 'labor vote.'" *The Supercongress*, NEW YORK TIMES (September 29, 1915), at 12. The *Times* charged that "the Clayton law reeks with the worst sort of politics and class legislation." *The Clayton Law*, NEW YORK TIMES (June 17, 1915), at 10.

123. Everett P. Wheeler, *Injunctions in Labor Disputes and Decisions of Industrial Tribunals*, 8 AMERICAN BAR ASSOCIATION JOURNAL 506, 508 (1922).

124. Taft, *Address of the President*, *supra* note 17, at 380. *See* WILLIAM HOWARD TAFT, JUSTICE AND FREEDOM FOR INDUSTRY: ADDRESS DELIVERED AT THE CONVENTION BANQUET OF THE NATIONAL ASSOCIATION OF MANUFACTURERS, WALDORF ASTORIA, NEW YORK CITY 9–11 (May 26, 1915) ("The power that leaders of the American Federation of Labor exercise has become excessive and detrimental to the public weal .... [T]hey have sought to make themselves and their agents a privileged class, not subject to the laws that affect every other man, and even themselves when not engaged in labor disputes."). Taft wrote his friend Gus Karger that "The labor unions are getting a gold brick as the courts will decide and Wilson will transfer the odium to them." WHT to Gus Karger (July 12, 1914) (Taft papers). The *New Republic* concurred that the Act had been drafted by "a pusillanimous Congressional committee of lawyers who were willing to draft a deceitful statute and shield themselves against the wrath of labor behind the Supreme Court of the United States." *"Labor Is Not a Commodity"*, 9 NEW REPUBLIC 112, 114 (1916).

125. *"Labor Is Not a Commodity"*, *supra* note 124, at 112. The *New Republic* took the occasion to suggest that labor needed better expert "guides and advisers," who could competently accomplish the "technical task of translating labor's yearning into a legal enactment." *Id.* "To be sure Congress *was* dishonest in the Clayton Act," Frankfurter wrote Holmes in 1921, using almost exactly the same language as had Taft in his private correspondence, *supra* note 124, "and both Congress and the Presbyterian Pope (alas! What a feeble Pope he, that dwells in the White House now, is), handed 'Labor' a gold-brick." Felix Frankfurter to OWH (January 14, 1921), in HOLMES-FRANKFURTER CORRESPONDENCE, at 100.

126. *The "Law" and Labor*, 25 NEW REPUBLIC 245, 248 (1921). "There is need of a general staff to do continuous thinking for labor, trained writers and speakers to interpret the needs and the methods of labor to the general public, and finally, skilled technicians dealing with special problems. Mr. Gompers will learn that 'intellectuals' may have as deep a social sympathy and understanding as men who work at crafts. American labor leaders will learn, as English labor is steadily learning, that one of the banes of our civilization is the cleavage between labor by hand and labor by brain." *Id.* The tension between the AFL and legal professionals and academics would continue right through the drafting of what would eventually become the Norris-LaGuardia Act. *See, e.g.*, FELIX FRANKFURTER & NATHAN GREENE, THE LABOR INJUNCTION 206–12 (New York: The MacMillan Co. 1930). On controversy over the meaning of the Clayton Act, see Stanley I. Kutler, *Labor, The Clayton Act, and the Supreme Court*, 3 LABOR HISTORY 19 (1962); Robert K. Murray, *Public Opinion, Labor, and the Clayton Act*, 21 THE HISTORIAN 255 (1959); and Alpheus T. Mason, *The Labor Clauses of the Clayton Act*, 18 AMERICAN POLITICAL SCIENCE REVIEW 489 (1924).

127. 254 U.S. 443, 470 (1921). The Court's holding in *Duplex* was foreshadowed in Paine Lumber Co. v. Neal, 244 U.S. 459 (1917). Nevertheless, the *Garment Worker* editorialized that the *Duplex* decision "was a surprise to the leaders and

members of organized labor. It was not anticipated, as the general belief was prevalent that the Clayton act specifically permitted members of unions to dissuade other people from working for employers during a labor dispute or from trading with them; in fact, permitting picketing and the secondary boycott." *An Unjust Decision*, GARMENT WORKER (January 7, 1921), at 4.

128. *Duplex Printing Press*, 254 U.S. at 469. Gompers attacked the decision as nullifying "the whole movement of 30 years to place workers and employers on a basis of equality before the law." *Samuel Gompers Attacks Supreme Court Decision*, BALTIMORE SUN (January 5, 1921), at 2. Taft, in turn, attacked Gompers, not only because Gompers brazenly "denounced opinions of the Supreme Court and other courts, but he has not hesitated to advise his fellow members of the Federation of Labor to disobey the orders of the courts made in pursuance of such decisions in causes in which such members were defendants. . . . This would set at naught the law of the land and is a vicious abuse in seeking to array a class against the whole body, politic and social. . . . [T]he labor unions have lost much of their influence for good by their arbitrary abuse of their power and by their spirit of lawlessness. . . . If the members of organized labor would make their body the useful agency and the power for good in the country which it may be, they should recognize their obligations to obey the law as interpreted by the highest court in the land, as other persons within its jurisdiction must do." William Howard Taft, *Gompers and the Law*, *supra* note 81, at 525–6.

129. *Duplex Printing Press*, 254 U.S. at 485 (Brandeis, J., dissenting).

130. Thomas Reed Powell, *The Supreme Court's Control over the Issue of Injunctions in Labor Disputes*, 13 PROCEEDINGS OF THE ACADEMY OF POLITICAL SCIENCE 37, 74 (June 1928). At the time, Holmes wrote Frankfurter: "I am bound to admit to anyone who allowed his personal preferences to affect his judgment there was [a] strong case for holding the Clayton Act to be a piece of legislative humbug – intended to sound promising and to do nothing. It seems to me, however, that although it was not an unlikely conjecture that that was what was meant, we were bound to assume the contrary and could not assume the contrary without coming to Brandeis's conclusions. But I don't think it a case for treating the majority opinion as bending the obvious to their wishes. . . . I went and go the whole hog with Brandeis but I am not inclined to be severe on the opposite view, even while I think it a public misfortune." OWH to Felix Frankfurter (January 30, 1921), in HOLMES-FRANKFURTER CORRESPONDENCE, at 103.

131. WITTE, *supra* note 50, at 69; Murray T. Quigg, *Trade Union Activities and the Sherman Law*, 147 ANNALS OF THE AMERICAN ACADEMY OF POLITICAL AND SOCIAL SCIENCE 51, 55–56 (1930). After *Duplex Printing Press*, it was commonly recognized that "the Clayton Act of 1914, as the courts were interpreting it, was more of an acceleration of, than a brake upon, strike injunction issuance." P.F. Brissenden, *The Labor Injunction*, 48 POLITICAL SCIENCE QUARTERLY 413, 417 (1933). See Osmond K. Fraenkel, *Judicial Interpretation of Labor Laws*, 6 UNIVERSITY OF CHICAGO LAW REVIEW 577, 579 (1939). At the time of the Clayton Act's passage, Andrew Furuseth, who would later become the key figure behind the enactment of the Seamen's Act of 1915, Pub. L. 63-302, 38 Stat. 1164 (March 4, 1915), and of the Jones Act of 1920, Pub. L. 66-261, 41 Stat. 988 (June 5, 1920), "went to Sam Gompers and protested. I said, 'Your injunction bill here extends the equity power and gives the equity court rights that it doesn't now have, even under the

contention of the men who are using it. You are turning yourselves into the court with hands and feet bound in passing this bill.' And Sam said: 'Well, Andy, you have got your black glasses on.' ... And then ... the courts said the Clayton Act did nothing except legalize injunctions." REPORT OF PROCEEDINGS OF THE FORTY-NINTH ANNUAL CONVENTION OF THE AMERICAN FEDERATION OF LABOR 320–21 (Washington D.C.: Law Reporter Printing Co. 1929).

132. *American Steel Foundries*, 257 U.S. at 203. In effect, Taft interpreted the Clayton Act as intended "to restrain federal courts from doing only what they would restrain themselves from doing." T.R. Powell, *Supreme Court's Review of Legislation, 1921–1922*, 37 POLITICAL SCIENCE QUARTERLY 486, 506 n.1 (1922). In *American Steel Foundries*, Taft also held that the restrictions of the Clayton Act applied only to a dispute "between an employer and employee, ... or between employees, or between persons employed and persons seeking employment, and not to such dispute between an employer and persons who are neither ex-employees nor seeking employment." 257 U.S. at 202. As a technical matter, then, the Clayton Act applied only to the dispute between the company and its two ex-employees who joined the picket line; it did not apply to the conflict between the company and the many other picketers who came from the Tri-City Central Trades Council who were neither ex-employees nor seeking employment.

133. *Hitchman*, 245 U.S. at 259.

134. *See id.* at 273–74 (Brandeis, J., dissenting).

135. *Duplex Printing Press*, 254 U.S. at 474, 478.

136. Philip Wager Lowry, *Strikes and the Law*, 21 COLUMBIA LAW REVIEW 783, 787 (1921).

137. *American Steel Foundries*, 257 U.S. at 208.

138. Oliver Wendell Holmes, *Privilege, Malice, and Intent*, 8 HARVARD LAW REVIEW 1 (1894).

139. *Id.* at 3. "Perhaps one of the reasons why judges do not like to discuss questions of policy, or to put a decision in terms upon their views as law-makers, is that the moment you leave the path of merely logical deduction you lose the illusion of certainty which makes legal reasoning seem like mathematics. But certainty is only an illusion, nevertheless. Views of policy are taught by experience of the interests of life." *Id.* at 7. It is in this essay, writes Morton Horwitz, "that a fully articulated balancing test" enters "American legal theory" for "the first time." Morton J. Horwitz, *The Place of Justice Holmes in American Legal Thought*, in THE LEGACY OF OLIVER WENDELL HOLMES, JR. 56–57 (Robert W. Gordon, ed., Stanford University Press 1992).

140. Holmes, *supra* note 138, at 7–9.

141. 167 Mass. 92, 97 (1896).

142. *Id.* at 104–7 (Holmes, J., dissenting). In his draft unpublished dissent in *American Steel Foundries*, Holmes would later write that "I perceive no difference in privileges between the rivalry in interest of employer and employed and competition in the narrower sense.... The case is not helped by speaking of the plaintiffs' rights in its business. Like most other rights they are relative. The defendants also have rights and the problem is to fix a boundary line." (Holmes papers). Later commentators would object to Holmes's analogy between competition among businesses and the struggle between unions and businesses for control of the workplace. "[E]fficient competitive practices in business" function to privilege

the "commission of harm" because such competition works "to improve service and to lower prices for all, incidental benefits which hardly follow from increased labor organization." Charles O. Gregory, *Peaceful Picketing and Freedom of Speech*, 26 AMERICAN BAR ASSOCIATION JOURNAL 709, 709 (1940). For Holmes, however, social struggle was its own end. In the absence of clear legislative direction, it was not to be confined by overarching judicial conceptions of a public good, like consumer welfare.

143. 167 Mass. at 107–8 (Holmes, J., dissenting). Holmes continued: "If it be true that workingmen may combine with a view, among other things, to getting as much as they can for their labor, just as capital may combine with a view to getting the greatest possible return, it must be true that, when combined, they have the same liberty that combined capital has, to support their interests by argument, persuasion, and the bestowal or refusal of those advantages which they otherwise lawfully control. . . . [T]he fact that the immediate object of the act by which the benefit to themselves is to be gained is to injure their antagonist does not necessarily make it unlawful, any more than when a great house lowers the price of goods for the purpose and with the effect of driving a smaller antagonist from the business." *Id.* at 108–9. In his draft dissent in *American Steel Foundries*, Holmes had said: "After long struggles it now I suppose hardly is disputed that in the making of bargains between employers and employed a combination of men on the one side is as lawful as a combination of dollars on the other. . . . Organization wherever possible seems to be the manifest destiny of the civilized world and with labor is largely an accomplished fact." (Holmes papers).

144. 10 Ohio Dec. Reprint 665 (Cincinnati Supr. Ct. 1889). Taft later told Stone that *Moores & Co.* was an opinion written with "all my youthful soul." WHT to HFS (January 26, 1927) (Taft papers).

145. *See* Daniel R. Ernst, *Free Labor, the Consumer Interest, and the Law of Industrial Disputes, 1885–1900*, 36 AMERICAN JOURNAL OF LEGAL HISTORY 19 (1992).

146. *Moores & Co.*, 10 Ohio Dec. Reprint at 671. Taft observed:

> Every man, be he capitalist, merchant, employer, laborer or professional man, is entitled to invest his capital, to carry on his business, to bestow his labor, or to exercise his calling, if within the law, according to his pleasure. Generally speaking, if, in the exercise of such a right by one, another suffers a loss, he has no ground of action. Thus, if two merchants are in the same business in the same place, and the business of the one is injured by the competition, the loss is caused by the other's pursuing his lawful right to carry on business as seems best to him. In this legitimate clash of common rights, the loss which is suffered, is *damnum absque injuria*. So it may reduce the employer's profits that his workman will not work at former prices, and that he is obliged to pay on a higher scale of wages. The loss which he sustains, if it can be called such, arises merely from the exercise of the workman's lawful right to work for such wages as he chooses, and to get as high a rate as he can. It is caused by the workman, but it gives no right of action. Again if a workman is called upon to work with the material of a certain dealer, and it is of such a character as either to make his labor greater than that sold by another, or is hurtful to the person using it, or for any other reason is not satisfactory to the workman, he may lawfully notify his employers of his objection and refuse to work it. The loss of the material man in his sales caused by such action of the workman is not a legal injury, and not the subject of action.

Labor & the Jurisprudence of Individualism

Id. at 668–69. Taft reasoned, as would Holmes:

> Assume that what is done is intentional, and that it is calculated to do harm to others. Then comes the question, was it done with or without just cause or excuse? If it was bona fide done in the use of a man's own property, in the exercise of a man's own trade, such legal justification would, I think, exist, not the less because what was done might seem to others to be selfish and unreasonable. But such legal justification would not exist when the act was done merely with the intention of causing temporal harm, without reference to defendant's own lawful enjoyment of his own rights.
>
> Malice, then, is really intent to injure another without cause or excuse.

Id. at 671.

147. *American Steel Foundries*, 257 U.S. at 208–10.
148. OWH to Felix Frankfurter (December 6, 1921), in HOLMES-FRANKFURTER CORRESPONDENCE, at 132.
149. Hellerstein, *supra* note 107, at 182. *See* JOHN A. FITCH, THE CAUSES OF INDUSTRIAL UNREST 94, 292 (New York: Harper & Bros. 1924); WITTE, *supra* note 50, at 291 n.2.
150. *See supra* note 57.
151. *Coppage*, 236 U.S. at 26–27 (Holmes, J., dissenting).
152. *Define and Limit the Jurisdiction of Courts Sitting in Equity*, H.R. Rep. No. 669, 72nd CONG. 1st SESS. (March 2, 1932), at 6. *See* WITTE, *supra* note 50, at 277. Section 2 of the Norris-LaGuardia Act provides:

> In the interpretation of this Act and in determining the jurisdiction and authority of the courts of the United States, as such jurisdiction and authority are herein defined and limited, the public policy of the United States is hereby declared as follows:
>
> Whereas under prevailing economic conditions, developed with the aid of governmental authority for owners of property to organize in the corporate and other forms of ownership association, the individual unorganized worker is commonly helpless to exercise actual liberty of contract and to protect his freedom of labor, and thereby to obtain acceptable terms and conditions of employment, wherefore, though he should be free to decline to associate with his fellows, it is necessary that he have full freedom of association, self-organization, and designation of representatives of his own choosing, to negotiate the terms and conditions of his employment, and that he shall be free from the interference, restraint, or coercion of employers of labor, or their agents, in the designation of such representatives or in self-organization or in other concerted activities for the purpose of collective bargaining or other mutual aid or protection.

Pub. L. 72-65, 47 Stat. 70 (March 23, 1932).

153. Section 3 of the Act begins:

> Any undertaking or promise ... in conflict with the public policy declared in section 2 of this Act, is hereby declared to be contrary to the public policy of the United States, shall not be enforceable in any court of the United States and shall not afford any basis for the granting of legal or equitable relief by any such court.

47 Stat. 70. For the contents of Section 2, see *supra* note 152.

154. 301 U.S. 1, 33 (1937).

155. *American Steel Foundries*, Revised Brief and Argument for Petitioner, at 75, 78–80. *See supra* note 39.
156. *American Steel Foundries*, 257 U.S. at 211. *See* Sayre, *supra* note 40, at 693 n.42.
157. *American Steel Foundries*, 257 U.S. at 211–13 (emphasis added).
158. Thus, Seventh Circuit Judge Francis E. Baker wrote Taft two weeks after the release of *American Steel Foundries* to say that the opinion was "specially valuable in restricting the Hitchman case on the question of persuasion." Francis E. Baker to WHT (December 17, 1921) (Taft papers). *See* WITTE, *supra* note 50, at 224–25. Although American Steel Foundries attempted to bring its case within the ambit of *Hitchman* by charging that the Tri-City Central Trades Council sought to induce *violations* of employment contracts, the company never made clear why this was true, given that its employment contracts were at-will. Revised Brief and Argument for Petitioner, *supra* note 155, at 78. "If either party, with or without cause, ends an employment at will, the other has no legal grounds of complaint," Baker had said in his decision in Iron Molders' Union No. 125 v. Allis-Chalmers Co., 166 F. 45, 50 (7th Cir. 1908). The fundamental difficulty was that the yellow-dog employment contracts in *Hitchman* were also at-will, and so the concept of inducing a violation of them, which was so critical to Pitney's reasoning in the case, was far from clear. This is a point that Brandeis had made crisply in his *Hitchman* dissent:

> There was no attempt to induce employés to violate their contracts. The contract created an employment at will; and the employé was free to leave at any time. The contract did not bind the employé not to join the union; and he was free to join it at any time. The contract merely bound him to withdraw from plaintiff's employ, if he joined the union....
>
> Merely persuading employés to leave plaintiff's employ or others not to enter it, was not unlawful. To induce third persons to leave an employment is actionable if done maliciously and without justifiable cause although such persons are free to leave at their own will.... As persuasion, considered merely as a means, is clearly legal, defendants were within their rights if, and only if, their interference with the relation of plaintiff to its employés was for justifiable cause. The purpose of interfering was confessedly in order to strengthen the union, in the belief that thereby the condition of workmen engaged in mining would be improved; the bargaining power of the individual workingman was to be strengthened by collective bargaining; and collective bargaining was to be insured by obtaining the union agreement. It should not, at this day, be doubted that to induce workingmen to leave or not to enter an employment in order to advance such a purpose, is justifiable when the workmen are not bound by contract to remain in such employment.

Hitchman, 245 U.S. at 272–73 (Brandeis, J., dissenting). The absence of mutuality led some courts to characterize at-will yellow-dog contracts as unenforceable. *See* Exchange Bakery & Restaurant v. Rifkin, 245 N.Y. 260 (1927); Interborough Rapid Transit Co. v. Lavin, 247 N.Y. 65 (1928); WITTE, *supra* note 50, at 224–25; Homer F. Carey & Herman Oliphant, *The Present Status of the Hitchman Case*, 29 COLUMBIA LAW REVIEW 441 (1929).
159. WITTE, *supra* note 50, at 120; Carey & Oliphant, *supra* note 158, at 442.
160. Carey & Oliphant, *supra* note 158, at 446–47. Indeed, in his unpublished draft dissent in *American Steel Foundries*, Holmes had explicitly written: "The interests of the union are nation wide. It strives to bring all labor into it and to establish national standards of reward.... [I]n view of the fact that it now is one of those

Labor & the Jurisprudence of Individualism

great powers that form themselves consistently with but independent of government, it seems to me wholly inadequate to treat its quasi legislation as impertinent interference." (Holmes papers).
161. Powell, *supra* note 130, at 56 n.30.
162. WHT to MP (December 3, 1921) (Taft papers). By contrast, Holmes wrote Frankfurter after the announcement of the decision that "it removed one ball from recent decisions of the Court." OWH to Felix Frankfurter (December 6, 1921), in HOLMES-FRANKFURTER CORRESPONDENCE, at 132.
163. United Mine Workers of America v. Red Jacket Consolidated Coal and Coke Co., 18 F.2d 839 (4th Cir.), *cert denied sub nom.* Lewis v. Red Jacket Consol. Coal & Coke Co., 275 U.S. 536 (1927). On the circumstances of the *Red Jacket* case, see Peter Graham Fish, *Red Jacket Revisited: The Case that Unraveled John J. Parker's Supreme Court Appointment*, 5 LAW & HISTORY REVIEW 51 (1987).
164. Remarks of Senator William Borah, 72 CONG. REC. 7935 (April 29, 1930). At the hearings on Parker, the president of the AFL testified that he construed *American Steel Foundries* to mean "that the late Chief Justice Taft had arrived at the conclusion that 'yellow-dog' contracts were inequitable and that employees subjecting themselves to the signing of such contracts did so under duress and compulsion. . . . Justice Taft, when he rendered his decision in the Tri-City case, believed that the time had arrived in the development of modern industry and in the expansion and growth of the Nation, that union among employees was essential, not only necessary, but essential, in order that they might deal with powerful corporations and powerful employers." Testimony of William Green, *Confirmation of Hon. John J. Parker to Be an Associate Justice of the Supreme Court of the United States* (April 5, 1930), Hearing before the Subcommittee of the Senate Committee on the Judiciary, 71st CONG. 2nd SESS., at 5–26.
165. Remarks of Senator William Borah, 72 CONG. REC. 7937 (April 29, 1930). Parker "quotes at length from the Hitchman case; not a quotation, not a line from the Tri-City case. Shall we infer that [Parker] did not know the effect of the Tri-City case, or shall we infer that [he] preferred the Hitchman case in order to sustain this outrageous and unconscionable contract?" *Id.* For discussions of the confirmation battle over Parker, see Ernesto J. Sanchez, *John J. Parker and the Beginning of the Modern Confirmation Process*, 32 JOURNAL OF SUPREME COURT HISTORY 22 (2007); Elizabeth G. McCrodden, *John J. Parker's Failed Quest for a Seat on the Supreme Court*, 7 NORTH CAROLINA STATE BAR JOURNAL 10, 16 (2002); and Ron Hirsch Mendlesohn, *Senate Confirmation of Supreme Court Appointments: The Nomination and Rejection of John J. Parker*, 14 HOWARD LAW JOURNAL 105 (1968).
166. William Green, quoted in M. Farmer Murphy, *Parker Is Rejected for Supreme Court Post by 41–39 Vote*, BALTIMORE SUN (May 8, 1930), at 1.
167. Taft, *The Open-Shop Problem, supra* note 62, at 531.
168. "The use of the injunction by a court is necessary in extreme cases to protect the business and property of the employer. This is when the employes step over the line of the law and seek by compound boycott or by violence to terrorize employers into yielding to their terms. Not infrequently the injunction has been effective to prevent such methods. But the injunction is a last resort. It is an instrument in the field where rights are determined by the fixed rules of law. It is utterly unserviceable for the regulation of the practical relations between employer and employe. It

plays a part in the legalistic field of action only." Address of Wm. H. Taft before the National Geographic Society, *supra* note 66, at 14.
169. Thomas v. Cincinnati, N.O. & T.P. Ry. Co., 62 F. 803, 818 (S.D. Ohio 1894). "A strike is concerted action. Concert of action is an illegal conspiracy if either the method of action is unlawful or its object is." William Howard Taft, *Labor Strikes* (May 16, 1919), in VIVIAN, at 213.
170. 272 U.S. 306, 311 (1926).
171. Addressing an Annual Banquet of Boston Printers, whom he had represented in resisting what he regarded as a misguided strike by the Boston Typographical Union, Brandeis emphasized in 1904 that "Lawless or arbitrary claims of organized labor should be resisted at whatever cost." LOUIS D. BRANDEIS, BUSINESS – A PROFESSION 24, 26 (Boston: Small, Maynard & Co. 1914).
172. Dianne Avery, *Images of Violence in Labor Jurisprudence: The Regulation of Picketing and Boycotts, 1894–1921*, 37 BUFFALO LAW REVIEW 1 (1988/89); ROBERT HUNTER, VIOLENCE AND THE LABOR MOVEMENT (New York: MacMillan Co. 1922).
173. *Address by the President of the United States*, 62 CONG. REC. 11539 (August 18, 1922). For a characteristic condemnation by Taft of unions as afflicted with a "spirit of lawlessness," see *supra* note 128.
174. WITTE, *supra* note 50, at 7. "It is true," Brandeis had conceded in 1903, that labor union activism "has often been attended by intolerable acts of violence, intimidation and oppression." Louis D. Brandeis, *The Incorporation of Trade Unions*, 15 GREEN BAG 11, 11 (1903).
175. William Howard Taft, *The Economic Conference* (September 8, 1919), in VIVIAN, at 270. "The contest with lawlessness, if the Reds manipulate the unions, will be attended with great losses and bloodshed, because the poison of Bolshevism is persistent and widespread in its effects." William Howard Taft, *Red Control of Labor* (October 18, 1919), in VIVIAN, at 288.
176. William Howard Taft, *Federation of Labor* (June 8, 1919), in VIVIAN, at 224.
177. Pub. L. 64-252, 39 Stat. 721 (September 3, 1916).
178. William Howard Taft, *The Crisis before Us* (August 9, 1919), in VIVIAN, at 253.
179. *Beveridge Flays Coal Settlement*, BOSTON GLOBE (December 23, 1919), at 2.
180. Address of Wm. H. Taft before the National Geographic Society, *supra* note 66, at 24.
181. *Press Sees Strike as Public Calamity*, *supra* note 96.
182. Hovenkamp, *supra* note 10.
183. Henry, *supra* note 4, at 6. For a typical evocation of labor violence, see REPORT OF THE SEVENTEENTH ANNUAL MEETING OF THE AMERICAN BAR ASSOCIATION 36–38 (Philadelphia: Dando Printing & Publishing Co. 1894).
184. The chair of the Railroad Labor Board, for example, could write in 1923 that "The people of this country know that the economic power of the strike degenerates nine times out of ten into crude, raw, naked, hideous physical force. . . . Indeed, it is known that only in rare instances can a strike succeed without the accompaniment of violence." Ben W. Hooper, *Radicalism versus Government*, 217 NORTH AMERICAN REVIEW 289, 296 (1923). As early as 1894, Taft could complain that in many unions

> [t]he turbulent are either in the majority or by mere violence of demonstration overawe the conservative element. The leaders are selected, not because of their clear judgment and intelligence, but because they are glib of tongue and intemperate of expression. The influx of foreign workmen bringing with them the

socialistic ideas which prevail among the laboring classes of Europe, has planted in many unions the seeds of sedition and discontent with the existing order. Hence it is, that whenever a controversy arises between labor and capital resulting in a strike, lawlessness too often follows any attempt of the employer lawfully to continue his business. If this lawlessness is not repressed promptly and firmly, as often it is not, the sympathies of members of the union are awakened in behalf of lawless methods, their former law-abiding disposition is blunted and they manifest an alarming indifference to the necessity for peace and order.

William H. Taft, *The Right of Private Property*, 3 MICHIGAN LAW JOURNAL 215, 227 (1894).

185. Farmers' Loan & Trust Co. v. Northern Pac. R. Co., 60 F. 803, 821 (7th Cir. 1894). "To my thinking, [an] exact definition of a strike is this: A combined effort among workmen to compel the master to the concession of a certain demand, by preventing the conduct of his business until compliance with the demand. The concerted cessation of work is but one of, and the least effective of, the means to the end; the intimidation of others from engaging in the service, the interference with, and the disabling and destruction of, property, and resort to actual force and violence, when requisite to the accomplishment of the end, being the other, and more effective, means employed. It is idle to talk of a peaceable strike. None such ever occurred. The suggestion is impeachment of intelligence. From first to last, from the earliest recorded strike to that in the state of West Virginia, which proceeded simultaneously with the argument of this motion, to that at Connellsville, Pa., occurring as I write, force and turbulence, violence and outrage, arson and murder, have been associated with the strike as its natural and inevitable concomitants. No strike can be effective without compulsion and force. That compulsion can come only through intimidation. A strike without violence would equal the representation of the tragedy of Hamlet with the part of Hamlet omitted." *Id*. at 821.

Never one to hold his tongue, Justice Brewer on the Supreme Court made this association explicit in an address to the New York Bar in 1893:

> The common rule as to strikes is this: Not merely do the employees quit the employment, and thus handicap the employer in the use of his property, and perhaps in the discharge of duties which he owes to the public; but they also forcibly prevent others from taking their places. It is useless to say that they only advise – no man is misled. When a thousand laborers gather around a railroad track, and say to those who seek employment that they had better not, and when that advice is supplemented every little while by a terrible assault on one who disregards it, every one knows that something more than advice is intended. It is the effort of the many, by the mere weight of numbers, to compel the one to do their bidding. It is a proceeding outside of the law, in defiance of the law, and in spirit and effect an attempt to strip from one that has that which of right belongs to him – the full and undisturbed use and enjoyment of his own.

David J. Brewer, *The Movement of Coercion*, An Address Before the New York State Bar Association, January 17, 1893, at www.minnesotalegalhistoryproject.org/assets/Brewer%20-%20Coercion%20(1893)-CC.pdf.

186. Jane Addams, *The Present Crisis in Trades-Union Morals*, 179 NORTH AMERICAN REVIEW 178, 182 (1904). Employers, aware of this disgrace, would not infrequently seek to instigate violence in order to discredit strikes. *See* FITCH, *supra*

note 149, at 213–16; Brandeis, *supra* note 174, at 13; Samuel Gompers, *Gompers' Reply, The Incorporation of Trade Unions*, 1 GREEN BAG 2ND 306, 311 (1998)(1902). And, of course, violence was also a technique used by employers to outright intimidate striking workers. *See* Address of Hon. William H. Taft, Secretary of War, *supra* note 17, at 245–46; BRODY, *supra* note 68, at 132–33. In 1903, Brandeis observed that "Nearly every large strike is attended by acts of flagrant lawlessness. The employers, and a large part of the public, charge these acts to the unions. In very many instances, the unions are entirely innocent. Hoodlums, or habitual criminals, have merely availed themselves of a convenient opportunity for breaking the law, in some instances even incited thereto by employers desiring to turn public opinion against the strikers." Brandeis, *supra* note 174, at 13.

187. Address of Hon. William H. Taft at Malden, Massachusetts, October 30, 1919, *supra* note 68, at 12. *See* William H. Taft, *Recent Criticism of the Federal Judiciary*, in REPORT OF THE EIGHTEENTH ANNUAL MEETING OF THE AMERICAN BAR ASSOCIATION 266 (Philadelphia: Dando Printing & Publishing Co. 1895). On Taft's state of mind in the early 1920s, see WHT to George Harvey (July 21, 1922) (Taft papers). Harvey was the American ambassador to Great Britain. Seven months after drafting *American Steel Foundries*, Taft wrote Harvey to complain about strikes in the coal and railroad industries: "The situation in the United States now is . . . quite critical in respect to the coal strike and the railway strike. . . . The war and general lawlessness everywhere stimulate bloody, murderous violence on the part of the strikers and their sympathizers, . . . Debs has now rushed in with a general declaration of war, while Gompers continues his vaporizings, but I don't think they help the labor people. They rather tend to solidify conservative public opinion, which, with the President's enforcement of peace, will be quite likely to determine the controversy as it has in the past."

188. Borderland Coal Corp. v. International Organization of Mine Workers of America, 275 F. 871, 872–73 (D. Ind. 1921), *rev'd sub nom.* Gasaway v. Borderland Coal Corp., 278 F. 56 (7th Cir. 1921).

189. In his draft unpublished dissent in *American Steel Foundries*, Holmes had written that "As a competitor might persuade a servant in the employ of his rival to come to him when the term of service should have expired, I suppose that strikers could persuade others to join them, when free from contract obligations, in order to make it harder for the employer to get along without them and so induce him to grant the desired increase." (Holmes papers). In joining Holmes's proposed dissent, Pitney had insisted that this passage be omitted.

190. *American Steel Foundries*, 257 U.S. at 203, 208. As a matter of technical doctrine, the Clayton Act forbade enjoining "persuasion" in the decree addressed to the two employees who were out on strike, whereas general federal equitable practice prohibited enjoining "persuasion" in the decree addressed to the other defendants.

191. *Id.* at 212–13. The importance of this seemingly anodyne point was tested when in September 1922 Attorney General Daugherty prompted newly appointed federal District Judge James H. Wilkerson to hand "down one of the most sweeping federal injunctions in U.S. history," DAVIS, *supra* note 97, at 130–31, to end the nationwide strike of railroad shopmen. The injunction is reproduced in FRANKFURTER & GREENE, *supra* note 126, at 243–63. Wilkerson's injunction prohibited, *inter alia*, "in any manner by letters, printed or other circulars, telegrams, telephones, word of mouth oral persuasion, or suggestion, or through

Labor & the Jurisprudence of Individualism

interviews to be published in newspapers or otherwise in any manner whatsoever, encourage ... any person ... to abandon the employment of said railway companies." *Id.* at 258. The "astonishing Daugherty injunction," David E. Lilienthal, *Labor and the Courts*, 34 NEW REPUBLIC 314 (1923), was instantly controversial, even within Harding's Cabinet, where it "outraged" both Hoover and Hughes. HERBERT HOOVER, THE MEMOIRS OF HERBERT HOOVER: THE CABINET AND THE PRESIDENCY 47–48 (New York: MacMillan Co. 1951). "American labor has had much experience with injunctions," Gompers wrote, "but it has never known any other injunction as drastic, as cynically oblivious to the Constitution and the law of the land as the Daugherty injunction." Samuel Gompers, *Tyranny Must Be Balked at Any Cost*, 29 AMERICAN FEDERATIONIST 766, 767 (1922). Taft wrote his brother:

> I can say to you confidentially that I don't think Harding has been well advised in instituting his injunction suit in Chicago and in securing an injunction apparently so wide in its effect. I don't want to intimate any opinion as to its validity, which is doubtful because of its sweeping character, for that may come before us, but I think he might have secured just as effective an injunction and made it less wide, and might have omitted those features of it which awaken your surprise and doubts. I must think, however, that there is a deep-seated protest in the minds of the people against the assumptions of the labor unions, and that the more loudly they roar, the less response they are likely to have from the body of the people, who feel the pinch from their autocratic attitude. The talk of a general strike in protest against the injunction is of course exploited in the newspapers. ... but I can not think that the heads of unions, whose members are in regular service and earning good wages, propose to precipitate any such condition and challenge the country to a life struggle as this would be, because the country would then be with its back against the wall, and in a contest between 96 per cent of the people or more and these would-be strikers, there would be suffering, but there would be a conclusive victory which would make unions seem reasonable in the future for a long time.

WHT to Horace D. Taft (September 7, 1922) (Taft papers). For Daugherty's defense of the injunction, see HARRY M. DAUGHERTY, THE INSIDE STORY OF THE HARDING TRAGEDY 132–38 (New York: Churchill Co. 1932); *Address by the Attorney General*, 64 CONG. REC. 983 (December 28, 1922).

192. *American Steel Foundries*, 257 U.S. at 203–4 (emphasis added). The Court showed itself to be exquisitely sensitive to the possibility of intimidation:

> In the present case the 3 or 4 groups of picketers, were made up of from 4 to 12 in a group. They constituted the picket line. Each union interested, electricians, cranemen, machinists and blacksmiths, had several representatives on the picket line, and assaults and violence ensued. They began early and continued from time to time during the 3 weeks of the strike after the picketing began. All information tendered, all arguments advanced and all persuasion used under such circumstances were intimidation. They could not be otherwise. It is idle to talk of peaceful communication in such a place and under such conditions. The numbers of the pickets in the groups constituted intimidation. The name "picket" indicated a militant purpose, inconsistent with peaceable persuasion. The crowds they drew made the passage of the employees to and from the place of work, one of running the gauntlet. Persuasion or communication attempted in such a presence and under such conditions was anything but peaceable and lawful. When one or more assaults or disturbances ensued, they characterized the whole campaign, which became effective because of its intimidating character, in spite of the admonitions given by the leaders to their followers as to lawful methods to be pursued, however sincere. Our conclusion

is that picketing thus instituted is unlawful and can not be peaceable and may be properly enjoined by the specific term because its meaning is clearly understood in the sphere of the controversy by those who are parties to it.

Id. at 204–5.
193. Id. at 207 (emphasis added).
194. Id. at 206. See WITTE, supra note 50, at 224–25.
195. *American Steel Foundries*, 257 U.S. at 206–7. "'Singly or in concert', says the Clayton Act. 'Not together, but singly,' says the Chief Justice in interpreting it." Powell, supra note 130, at 56. For the text of the Clayton Act, see supra note 120. Taft's proposed injunction should be contrasted to what Holmes had proposed in his draft unpublished dissent. Holmes had concluded that the Seventh Circuit opinion should be affirmed, but that the number of picketers be limited to two: "Bearing in mind that the strikers are under injunction against all violence or threats of violence expressed or implied I think that picketing when not in numbers that of themselves imply a threat of violence is a lawful means to a lawful end. To avoid all questions I should be willing to limit the number of pickets at any given point to two. See Trades Disputes Act, 1906, 6 Edw. VIII, c. 47." (Holmes papers).
196. WHT to MP (December 3, 1921) (Taft papers). Two weeks later, Taft wrote Francis Baker, the Seventh Circuit judge who had written *Iron Molders Union No. 125*: "So far as picketing is concerned, we thought we might as well step on that particular term, which has always grated me in connection with labor controversies, because it indicates a character of attitude that I think ought to be discouraged. Of course it is a question of definition, as many issues are, but I thought I would like to indicate the proper spirit in which the advocates of the labor side should approach those whom they wish to convince." WHT to Francis E. Baker (December 20, 1921) (Taft papers). See supra note 192.
197. 257 U.S. at 213. About a year after the opinion came down, Brandeis wrote Frankfurter to say that "Trade unionism should be frankly accepted and all war upon it, direct and indirect, by employers must cease. Unions should be free, at all times and under all circumstances, to use any form of persuasion (as distinguished from coercion) upon other workers to join their unions. Non-union workers should be protected against coercion; but never by or through the employer, or by any act or proceeding brought or done in his interest. Protection may be afforded unto the non-union man only by action or proceeding instigated and conducted by himself or on his behalf by the state." LDB to Felix Frankfurter (September 4, 1922), in BRANDEIS-FRANKFURTER CORRESPONDENCE, at 106.
198. OWH to Felix Frankfurter (December 6, 1921), in HOLMES-FRANKFURTER CORRESPONDENCE, at 132.
199. WITTE, supra note 50, at 36. State courts also "accepted" *American Steel Foundries* "as stating the correct rule of law." Id. See FRANKFURTER & GREENE, supra note 126, at 181–82; Keuffel & Esser v. International Ass'n of Machinists, 93 N.J. Eq. 429, 430 (1922) ("The authority of that high tribunal is of such weight as to be practically controlling on us."). Seventh Circuit Judge Francis Baker predicted as much, writing Taft that "the decision will stand as the leading case and also, I believe, the ending case. Counsel for employers and counsel for labor unions will now be able to point out for their clients the clearly defined line, which must always abide because it is the true line, and good faith advocates of

the non-union shop and of the union shop ought never to come into actionable collision. Injunctions ought not to be necessary except to enforce the restraints which each side now knows it should enforce for itself." Francis E. Baker to WHT (December 17, 1921) (Taft papers). The *New York Tribune* praised *American Steel Foundries* for very much the same reason: "The fine sanity and common sense of Chief Justice Taft have seldom shone to better advantage than in clarifying opinion concerning the rights and wrongs of picketing. ... In a word, a picket must display good manners. ... The court makes its doctrine clear. The rules are sufficiently specific for any one to understand. There will not be a picket in doubt as to what he may do." *Legal Picketing*, NEW YORK TRIBUNE (December 7, 1921), at 12.
200. Taft's "logophobia" about the word "picketing," T.R. Powell later said, "might have asked that the Progressive Convention in 1912 should sing 'Abide with Me' rather than 'Onward Christian Soldiers.'" Powell, *supra* note 130, at 57. *See supra* notes 192 & 196.
201. Truax v. Corrigan, 257 U.S. 312, 340 (1921). Brandeis, by contrast, wrote in dissent in *Truax* that *American Steel Foundries* "held that peaceful picketing is not unlawful." *Truax*, 257 U.S. at 371 (Brandeis, J., dissenting).
202. A decade later, the magisterial Edwin E. Witte would summarize the holding of *American Steel Foundries* in this way: "With regard to the law of picketing, the controlling principle stated in the American Steel Foundries case cannot be improved upon. Persuasion is legitimate, intimidation unlawful; and the dividing line depends upon the facts in each case. This is a sound principle, but it does not automatically decide whether picketing should be permitted in a particular question." WITTE, *supra* note 50, at 295.
203. *Id.* at 37. *See id.* at 54. *American Steel Foundries* "dealt a death blow to the legality of mass picketing in this country. Before the *Tri-City* decision, few cases made any reference at all, either in opinion or in injunctions which were granted against violent or intimidating picketing but which permitted peaceful conduct, to the actual number of workers who might be placed on the picket line. Since the *Tri-City* case, however, it is almost universal practice carefully to limit the number of pickets." Hellerstein, *supra* note 107, at 182–83.
204. WITTE, *supra* note 50, at 118.
205. *American Steel Foundries*, 257 U.S. at 206 (emphasis added). "The treatment of the matter by the courts," observed one commentator, "takes on a ludicrous aspect."

> It is industrial struggle with which the courts are dealing. If the strikers observe the law under the rules which have been laid down, the picket line must be carried on with the decorum of a college debate, with one or two men at each entrance representing the workers, registered, and even limited in the hours in which they may exhort, the tone of voice they may use, and the gestures they may make in addressing workers in a plant which may employ a thousand workers.

Hellerstein, *supra* note 107, at 183–84.
206. WITTE, *supra* note 50, at 295. As one commentator observed, "I wonder how far woman's suffrage would have gotten if the suffragists had been obliged to face a decision of this kind." Rubin, *supra* note 112, at 108.

207. *Vegelahn*, 167 Mass. at 105 (Holmes, J., dissenting). Undoubtedly this was one of the "details as to which I should go farther" to which Holmes referred in his letter to Frankfurter. *See supra* text at note 198. In his own draft unpublished dissent, Holmes had proposed limiting the number of picketers to two. *See supra* note 195.
208. *American Steel Foundries*, 257 U.S. at 207. Senator Thomas J. Walsh later remarked on "the absurdity of holding picketing to be lawful or unlawful dependent upon whether one or more than one picket is posted at any particular place." Walsh, *supra* note 7, at 737.
209. JHC to WHT (Taft papers). By contrast, Day commented to Taft: "This opinion is absolutely fair to both sides. It *establishes* rules which will govern such controversies, and I am glad to concur." WRD to WHT (return on draft opinion) (Taft papers).
210. Samuel Gompers, *The Supreme Court at It Again*, 29 AMERICAN FEDERATIONIST 44, 45 (1922). Local labor leaders interviewed by the *New York Times* after the decision construed Taft's opinion "as legalizing 'peaceful picketing,'" and, in contrast to Gompers, proclaimed themselves "satisfied" because "the legitimate labor movement does not tolerate [force or violence] within its ranks." *Pickets Must Not Molest Workers*, NEW YORK TIMES (December 6, 1921), at 21.
211. *Gompers Raps Judge Taft and "Iniquity Courts"*, NEW YORK TRIBUNE (April 17, 1922), at 5.
212. *Report of A.F. of L. Executive Council*, in REPORT OF PROCEEDINGS OF THE FORTY-SECOND ANNUAL CONVENTION OF THE AMERICAN FEDERATION OF LABOR 44–45 (Washington D.C.: Law Reporter Printing Co. 1922). The committee concluded that *American Steel Foundries* "has practically taken the life blood out of section 20 of the Clayton law." *Id.* at 49.
213. Calvert Magruder, *A Half Century of Legal Influence upon the Development of Collective Bargaining*, 50 HARVARD LAW REVIEW 1071, 1081 (1937). *See* Sayre, *supra* note 40, at 703 ("[B]y limiting the unions to a single picket at each gate in a plant employing at the time some 350 men, the practical exercise of the right was very seriously curtailed if not denied.").
214. "What a mockery upon the acknowledged rights of workers on strike to win over would-be strike-breakers by pleading and persuasion!" *Report of Special Committee*, in REPORT OF PROCEEDINGS OF THE FORTY-SECOND ANNUAL CONVENTION OF THE AMERICAN FEDERATION OF LABOR, *supra* note 212, at 372. It is perhaps most accurate to say that "[t]he Tri-City case itself was a compromise decision pleasing neither side." Note, 10 CALIFORNIA LAW REVIEW 237, 237 (1922).
215. *See, e.g.*, Great Northern R. v. Brosseau, 286 F. 414, 418 (D.N.D. 1923) ("The impartial history of strikes teaches that there is as much danger to strikers on the picket line from private detectives and sometimes from new employés, as there is of the same kind of wrong on the part of strikers against new employés. . . . The strikers on the picket line are entitled to have enough present to shield them against the temptation of their adversaries to resort to violent methods. They also need the same protection against trumped-up charges or unfair evidence relative to any assaults that may occur on either side.").
216. As Sayre properly said, "The legal battleground has shifted from a fight over the right of labor unions to exist to a contest as to what means may lawfully be used by labor organizations in the economic struggle over the price of labor." Sayre, *supra* note 106, at 558.

Labor & the Jurisprudence of Individualism

217. *American Steel Foundries*, 257 U.S. at 206.
218. Thus, in editorializing in favor of an injunction against striking miners, the *New York Tribune* put the matter this way: "The strikers do not come as individuals, but as an organized army.... The law here acts entirely in defence [sic] of the individual freedom of the workers and those for whom they wish to work, against the organized and coercive interference of a powerful body." *The Injunction against Strikers*, NEW YORK TRIBUNE (August 16, 1897), at 6. Taft's personal sympathy for strikebreakers is evident in St. Louis-San Francisco Ry. Co. v. Mills, 271 U.S. 344 (1926), in which a strikebreaker during the railroad shopmen's strike of 1922 was shot to death by strikers while returning home from work. The estate of the worker sued the railroad under the Federal Employers' Liability Act. Speaking unanimously through Stone, the Court held that under the circumstances the railroad company did not owe the strikebreaker a duty of protection. Taft, however, commented on his return to the circulated draft of Stone's opinion: "I concur, but I think you might add that if in the contract of employment there had been a term that the railroad company would safely guard the men to their homes and back again, different questions might have arisen. I have a feeling that the R.R. Company owed something morally under conditions like this to their strike breakers and that such men may protect themselves by such a contract." (Stone papers). Stone later interpolated this sentence into his draft: "Nor is there any evidence of such an undertaking in the contract of employment." 271 U.S. at 346. The sentence was suggested by Van Devanter. Sanford wrote on his return, "Yes, with regret that we must come to this conclusion, but it seems to be inevitable." (Stone papers). This Stone opinion is a good example of Van Devanter's extensive editing of Stone's early work.
219. *Report of A.F. of L. Executive Council* (June 12, 1922), *supra* note 212, at 40. As the associate director of the fledgling American Civil Liberties Union observed: "It of course goes without saying that threats and intimidation are not proper, but the line between heated persuasion and intimidation is a shadowy one at best.... In the decision of such questions the personal equation and opinions of the judge must of necessity play a considerable part, and it is not surprising that the results have been confusion.... It is small wonder... that many in the ranks of organized labor have come to feel that the cards are stacked against them when once their dispute comes into the courts." Albert de Silver, *The Injunction – A Weapon of Industrial Power*, 114 THE NATION 89–90 (1922).
220. "The 'company union' was almost wholly a post-war development, and by 1926 some 1,400,000 workers were covered by employee representation. This weak substitute for genuine trade unionism was the chief issue at the 1926 convention of the American Federation of Labor." H.M. Douty, *The Trend of Industrial Disputes, 1922–1930*, 27 JOURNAL OF THE AMERICAN STATISTICAL ASSOCIATION 168, 171 (1932). "The company union is another method of combating unionism which has gained great impetus in recent years. A conservative estimate places the membership of company unions at not less than one-third that of all labor unions.... The entire growth is a development of the last decade." WITTE, *supra* note 50, at 218–19. *See* CLARENCE E. BONNETT, EMPLOYERS' ASSOCIATIONS IN THE UNITED STATES 30–32 (New York: MacMillan Co. 1922); Daniel Nelson, *The Company Union Movement, 1900–1937: A Reexamination*, 56 BUSINESS HISTORY REVIEW 335 (1982); David Montgomery, *Thinking about American Workers in the 1920s*, 32

INTERNATIONAL LABOR AND WORKING CLASS HISTORY 4, 6 (Fall 1987); CHRISTOPHER L. TOMLINS, THE STATE AND THE UNIONS: LABOR RELATIONS, LAW, AND THE ORGANIZED LABOR MOVEMENT IN AMERICA, 1880–1960, at 93–94 (Cambridge University Press 1985).

221. *See, e.g.*, HERBERT HOOVER, AMERICAN INDIVIDUALISM 41–43 (Garden City: Doubleday, Page & Co. 1923) ("There has been in the last thirty years an extraordinary growth of organizations for advancement of ideas in the community of mutual cooperation and economic objectives – the chambers of commerce, trade associations, labor unions, bankers, farmers, propaganda associations, and what not. These are indeed variable mixtures of altruism and self-interest. Nevertheless, in these groups the individual finds an opportunity for self-expression and participation in the moulding of ideas, a field for training and the stepping stones for leadership.... At times these groups come into sharp conflict.... If they develop into warring interests, if they dominate legislators and intimidate public officials, if they are to be a new setting of tyranny, then they will destroy the foundation of individualism. Our Government will then drift into the hands of timorous mediocrities dominated by groups until we shall become a syndicalist nation on a gigantic scale.").

222. William Howard Taft, *Prideful Labor Unions* (March 25, 1920), in VIVIAN, at 372. It was un-American, said Taft, "to array a class against the whole body, politic and social." William Howard Taft, *Gompers and the Law*, supra note 81, at 525.

223. William Howard Taft, *The Harding-Coolidge Ticket* (June 18, 1920), in VIVIAN, at 428.

224. Barbier v. Connolly, 113 U.S. 27, 32 (1884). For a discussion, see *supra* Chapter 24, at 757–58; *infra* Chapter 42, at 1404–6.

225. THOMAS M. COOLEY, TREATISE ON CONSTITUTIONAL LIMITATIONS 35 (Boston: Little, Brown & Co. 1868).

226. "In the past years," said Quayle, "I have noticed with great care the operation of Union Labor, and have seen their power or compulsion brought to bear on Legislation and Presidents, to enact class legislation.... As an American Citizen I have a right to hold that a law should be made for all American people and not for one class of American People. That is Americanism." LETTERS TO A BISHOP: CORRESPONDENCE BETWEEN SAMUEL GOMPERS, PRESIDENT OF THE AMERICAN FEDERATION OF LABOR, AND BISHOP WILLIAM A. QUAYLE, OF THE METHODIST EPISCOPAL CHURCH 3, 7 (American Federation of Labor 1920). Samuel Gompers objected to Quayle's remarks and sought to engage him in an epistolary debate. Gompers eventually published their exchange in a pamphlet.

227. WILLIAM HOWARD TAFT, LIBERTY UNDER LAW: AN INTERPRETATION OF THE PRINCIPLES OF OUR CONSTITUTIONAL GOVERNMENT 33, 37 (New Haven: Yale University Press 1922). "They look at the election from a broad American standpoint and vote their judgment. The man who carries the labor vote in his pocket is a bogy." *Id.* at 37–38.

228. *Id.* at 33–34. See WILLIAM HOWARD TAFT, REPRESENTATIVE GOVERNMENT IN THE UNITED STATES 25–26 (New York: New York University Press 1921):

> The striking advantage ... which our democracy and representative system gain by reason of these two large parties, is in the fact that they are each made up of all classes and conditions. Their cleavage is vertical and not horizontal. Each includes well to do, the moderate circumstanced, and the poor.

> Each includes the capitalist and the working man, the educated and the ignorant. Each views questions and politics from the standpoint of all the people. In order that each may command support from each class and group of people, each must shape its policies to be fair to each class, and not to exclude consideration of other classes. They can not be selfish in seeking the welfare of one group, because their constituent elements, if they would hold them together, forbid. Party success thus bids them to take an obviously patriotic course, having the interests of all in view.
>
> The danger to the body politic in these days is the attempt of a class to use the government for itself and to ignore altogether the rights and benefits of the rest of society. The Socialist party is engaged in seeking to arouse discontent against the well to do, and to create a class war. A great many laborers and extremists in the labor unions would constitute, if they could, a class party, having the interests of no others in mind except the laborers. Witness the bitter fight waged by organized labor against the creation of state constabularies to maintain law and order in the sparsely settled communities of our states.

229. In his presidential address to the American Bar Association, Taft observed:

> We are living in an age of what I may call factionalism, an age in which classes are disposed to think that the happiness of each class is more important than the general sum of happiness of the entire community, and that the members of each class, denied what they wish, may properly violate the law, destroy property and even lives in order to secure it. Such a spirit is dangerous. It is an evidence of lack of that self-restraint without which the bonds of society will necessarily be loosed. We see it in the wild ravings and action of the militant suffragettes in England. We see it in the resistance to lawful authority in Idaho and Colorado by the Western Federation of Miners. We see it in the dynamite plots of the bridge workers and the iron workers at Los Angeles and at Indianapolis. We see it in opposition to federal legislation to protect aliens' treaty rights. Such a spirit flouts the law, does not regard order and peace as essential to social and political happiness, but exalts the supreme selfishness of a class and is willing to pull down the structures of society in order to secure the granting of its particular demands.

Taft, *Address of the President, supra* note 17, at 372–73.
230. HERBERT CROLY, THE PROMISE OF AMERICAN LIFE 126–31 (New York: MacMillan Co. 1911). *See* Stanley Shapiro, *The Great War and Reform: Liberals and Labor, 1917–19*, 12 LABOR HISTORY 323 (1971).
231. Frank Morrison, quoted in *Labor's Ultimatum to the Public*, NEW YORK TIMES (July 18, 1920), at 40. Morrison was the secretary of the AFL. He explained: "When we read in the daily newspapers that 'the people will not approve of such and so' of plans of the workers to help themselves; when it is said that 'the great American public will not permit *this or that to be done*'; when we are told that 'the community has rights which must be respected,' we know that the class variously referred to as 'the people,' 'the great American public' and 'the community' comprise those persons in whose interest the newspapers are published, by whom they are owned and under whose direction the views are given expression. They do not embrace the workers *now any more* than they have ever done since the beginning of history." *Id*. The community, Morrison asserted, uses force to impose its will, deploying "existing agencies" like "the army" and "the courts." *Id*.
232. *The Challenge Accepted: Labor Will Not Be Outlawed or Enslaved*, 28 AMERICAN FEDERATIONIST 289, 294 (1921). The AFL defined "compulsory labor" as "work for wages, hours and under any conditions that may be determined by governmental court or board," and it equated such labor with "involuntary servitude." REPORT

OF PROCEEDINGS OF THE FORTY-THIRD ANNUAL CONVENTION OF THE AMERICAN FEDERATION OF LABOR 50 (Washington D.C.: Law Reporter Printing Co. 1923). The AFL's opposition to compulsory arbitration underlay its hostility to both fascism and communism. Thus William Green, as AFL president, denounced Mussolini's "Charter of Labor":

> The so-called Fascist "Charter of Labor" is a proclamation of enslavement in that it reduces the working people subject to it to a condition of industrial servitude. It is a blow at human freedom and sets up compulsory methods in industry for private initiative and freedom of contract. It completely destroys the principle and processes of collective bargaining.
>
> The world has never witnessed a greater exhibition of autocracy gone mad. The principles underlying the so-called "Charter of Labor" are the same as the principles underlying the industrial and political policies pursued by the Soviet Government in Russia. Each of them seeks to establish the superiority and domination of the State over the individual and over individual liberty and human freedom. . . .
>
> There can be no freedom in any nation except where the people are industrially free. This applies to both employers and employes. Government regulation and Government control of industry and the relationship between employers and employes such as is proposed is most reprehensible and is resented by all those associated with industry. It discourages capital and makes the workers slaves.

Green Denounces Fascist Labor Plan, NEW YORK TIMES (April 23, 1927), at 6. *See Mussolini's New Grip on Industry,* 93 LITERARY DIGEST 10 (May 7, 1923).

233. *The Challenge Accepted, supra* note 232, at 295. "Voluntarism," said William Green, president of the AFL, "is of the new order of democracy and self-rule." William Green, *Another Board Splintered,* 32 AMERICAN FEDERATIONIST 245 (1925).

234. "The right to free contract, the right to work or not to work . . . marks the boundary line between slavery and freedom. . . . Free labor permits of no exception. Whether the same be in public or private service, whether the laborer act as an individual or en masse." *Kansas Industrial Law Dismembered,* in REPORT OF PROCEEDINGS OF THE FORTY-THIRD ANNUAL CONVENTION OF THE AMERICAN FEDERATION OF LABOR, *supra* note 232, at 56–57.

235. "We reaffirm that industry is and must remain industrial, and that it is not and should never be political." REPORT OF PROCEEDINGS OF THE FORTY-THIRD ANNUAL CONVENTION OF THE AMERICAN FEDERATION OF LABOR, *supra* note 232, at 72.

236. Walter Lippmann, *Can the Strike Be Abandoned,* 21 NEW REPUBLIC 224, 225 (1920). Other progressives, like Croly himself, when faced with the postwar collapse of the progressive movement, began in the 1920s to abandon the ideal of an abstract public interest, with its concomitant vision of "a classless democracy," and instead to embrace "the need of collective class action" in a form roughly modeled on the British Labour Party. Herbert Croly, *The Eclipse of Progressivism,* 24 NEW REPUBLIC 210, 213 (1920). *See* Herbert Croly, *The Outlook for Progressivism in Politics,* 41 NEW REPUBLIC 60 (1924). As organized labor began to score legislative victories under the Wilson administration, it was also forced into a posture of seeking government support and action. *See, e.g., Recognition of Labor,* 13 NEW REPUBLIC 84, 85 (1917) ("Mr. Gompers himself, the arch-opponent of union participation in politics, is as much a state servant as if he

were himself a member of the Cabinet. . . . The wage-earners require a corporate policy, expressive both of their own common class interest and of a serviceable, harmonious relation to the other classes in the community; and such a policy can be worked out, but only as it is being worked out in Great Britain – that is, by attaching to labor unionism political methods and outlook."); *The Predicament of Organized Labor*, 9 NEW REPUBLIC 114, 114–15 (1916) ("Year after year the Federation under the leadership of Mr. Gompers has gone on record as vehemently opposed to the eight-hour day by legislative enactment and in favor of direct action as the exclusive means of securing a shorter work day. . . . But if the Federation is finally compelled by the Adamson law to accept the principle of legislative enactment they will find general denunciation of further governmental intervention utterly futile. The question will no longer be whether or not the labor movement will accept arbitration, but what form arbitration shall take. The organized labor movement will have to learn to look upon itself as an integral part of the social structure of the nation rather than as a state within a state.").

237. Newton D. Baker, *Labor Relations and the Law*, 8 AMERICAN BAR ASSOCIATION JOURNAL 731, 736 (1922).
238. 262 U.S. 522 (1923). *See supra* Chapter 25, at 793–99.
239. *State Control of Strikes*, 108 THE INDEPENDENT 192, 192–93 (February 25, 1922).
240. Address of Hon. William H. Taft at Malden, Massachusetts, October 30, 1919, *supra* note 68, at 8. *See* Address of Wm. H. Taft before the National Geographic Society, *supra* note 66, at 27; TAFT, *supra* note 3, at 26. The passage quoted in text seems to assert that a large strike by workers essential to the public interest is actually an illegal secondary boycott, because it is designed to force the public to pressure employers. But this is merely wordplay, since such a strike is in the first instance directed against the employer to improve the working conditions of union members.
241. *See supra* Chapter 25. Taft could point to Wilson v. New, 243 U.S. 332 (1917), as precedent for this conclusion in the context of employees who worked on interstate railroads. *See id.* 352–53: "[W]hatever would be the right of an employee engaged in a private business to demand such wages as he desires, to leave the employment if he does not get them, and, by concert of action, to agree with others to leave upon the same condition, such rights are necessarily subject to limitation when employment is accepted in a business charged with a public interest and as to which the power to regulate commerce possessed by Congress applied, and the resulting right to fix, in case of disagreement and dispute." *See* Marjorie Jean Bonney, *Federal Intervention in Labor Disputes*, 7 MINNESOTA LAW REVIEW 467, 482 n.74 (1923). But insofar as Taft had in mind injunctions aimed at striking coal miners, see *infra* note 244, Taft assumed an asymmetry between state regulation of the market in coal and state regulation of the market for labor to mine coal. The sale of coal was deemed not to involve property affected with a public interest, *supra* Chapter 22, at 722, whereas an injunction aimed at striking miners would have to assume that their labor was affected with a public interest. *See* Samuel Gompers, *The Coal Commission or the Constitution*, 30 AMERICAN FEDERATIONIST 651 (1923); Marjorie Jean Bonney, *Federal Intervention in Labor Disputes*, 7 MINNESOTA LAW REVIEW 550, 566–68 (1923); *Wants Board to End Coal Mine Disputes*, NEW YORK TIMES (December 9, 1921), at 1.
242. Ribnik v. McBride, 277 U.S. 350 (1928); *supra* note 241; *supra* Chapter 25, at 801–2.
243. Pub. L. 66-152, 41 Stat. 456 (February 28, 1920).

244. William Howard Taft, *The Anti-Strike Clause* (February 19, 1920), in VIVIAN, at 355 ("We have now more clearly developed than ever before . . . the formidable danger to the public welfare that unrestrained freedom of combination to strike gives to railway employees as a unit."). *See Ex-President Stirs Guests at Banquet, supra* note 44, at 9: "If a man does not want to be a coal miner, Mr. Taft said, he can do something else. But the principle of striking and making a third party, the public, suffer untold misery, is not provided for in the free liberty guaranteed by the Constitution. In the Senate, he declared, is a bill drawn along lines that makes a strike of 2,000,000 railroad men an offense against the United States. 'This is opposed by the labor circles on Constitutional rights. That is a great mistake. Every man who has a right to labor, has the right to give up that place if he chooses, but he has no right through conspiracy – for that is what it amounts to – to encroach upon the rights and welfare of the third party – the public.'"
245. *See* JOSHUA BERHNARDT, THE RAILROAD LABOR BOARD: ITS HISTORY, ACTIVITIES AND ORGANIZATION (Baltimore: Johns Hopkins Press 1923); H.D. WOLF, THE RAILROAD LABOR BOARD (University of Chicago Press 1927).
246. 41 Stat. at 470 (1920).
247. *Remarks of Samuel Gompers*, in REPORT OF PROCEEDINGS OF THE FORTY-SECOND ANNUAL CONVENTION OF THE AMERICAN FEDERATION OF LABOR, *supra* note 212, at 348.
248. 41 Stat. at 470 (1920) (emphasis added). In August 1922, President Harding called for Congress to make "the decisions of the board . . . enforceable and effective against carriers and employees alike." *Address by the President of the United States, supra* note 173, at 11539. *See One Law for All*, THE OUTLOOK (September 6, 1922), at 9.
249. Matthew Woll, *Laws Faithless to Our Forefathers*, 67 THE FORUM 201, 218 (1922). *See* Samuel Gompers, *The Issues that Face America*, 27 AMERICAN FEDERATIONIST 422, 427–28 (1920); Samuel Gompers, *Labor's Protest against Rampant Tragedy*, 27 AMERICAN FEDERATIONIST 521, 528 (1920); *Report of A.F. of L. Executive Council*, in REPORT OF PROCEEDINGS OF THE FORTY-SECOND ANNUAL CONVENTION OF THE AMERICAN FEDERATION OF LABOR, *supra* note 212, at 70. The AFL opposed "compulsory arbitration" as an "unwarranted interference with the rights of free men, a restriction of the right to the freedom of contract, a denial of liberty, and a return to involuntary *servitude* – industrial serfdom." Matthew Woll, *Compulsion Destroys Liberty*, 26 AMERICAN FEDERATIONIST 156, 157 (1919). Enforceable voluntary arbitration, by contrast, was an entirely different matter. *See, e.g., A New Effort to End Strikes*, 96 LITERARY DIGEST 11, 12 (March 3, 1928).
250. The Transportation Act of 1920 provided:

> It shall be the duty of all carriers and their officers, employees, and agents to exert every reasonable effort and adopt every available means to avoid any interruption to the operation of any carrier growing out of any dispute between the carrier and the employees or subordinate officials thereof. All such disputes shall be considered and, if possible, decided in conference between representatives designated and authorized so to confer by the carriers, or the employees or subordinate officials thereof, directly interested in the dispute.

41 Stat. 469.
251. Decision # 224, 2 RLB 251, 253, 255 (1921).

Labor & the Jurisprudence of Individualism

252. In Decision #224, for example, the RLB held that an employee could not be discharged because of union membership, which directly contradicted the Court's constitutional decision in *Adair*. The RLB was quite aware that "For this Board to hold that the discharge of these men for the reason that they do belong to a union was wrongful might at first glance appear to be either a willful or an ignorant disregard of the carrier's constitutional right as declared by the Supreme Court of the United States." Decision # 224, 2 RLB 251, 252 (1921).

253. The RLB declared that certain principles would guide its decision-making. These included:

> 4. The right of railway employees to organize for lawful objects shall not be denied, interfered with, or obstructed.
> 5. The right of such lawful organization to act toward lawful objects through representatives of its own choice, whether employees of a particular carrier or otherwise, shall be agreed to by management.
> 6. No discrimination shall be practiced by management as between members and nonmembers of organizations.

Decision # 119, Exhibit B, 2 RLB 87, 96 (1921).

254. *The Pennsylvania's Lost Case*, 33 NEW REPUBLIC 85, 86 (1923) ("General Atterbury, Vice President of the Pennsylvania in charge of labor policy, had almost single-handed converted some of the more important railroad executives to an anti-union policy. It was he who prevented the formation of National Boards of Adjustment, which would have embodied genuine collective bargaining and would have relieved the Labor Board of the heaviest part of its burden. It was he who raised the slogan 'Make no contracts whatever with labor organizations,' and secured the abrogation of the national agreements. It is hardly too much to say that if it had not been for Mr. Atterbury's labor policy on the Pennsylvania and elsewhere, the shop strike would not have occurred.").

255. Decision # 119, 2 RLB 87 (April 14, 1921). Taft very much advocated for this decision. *See* William Howard Taft, *Collective Bargaining I*, *supra* note 62; William Howard Taft, *Collective Bargaining II* (March 2, 1921), in VIVIAN, at 546; William Howard Taft, *Collective Bargaining III* (March 3, 1921), in VIVIAN, at 548. The RLB enunciated the general principles cited in *supra* note 253 to guide the company-by-company negotiations required by Decision No. 119.

256. *See supra* note 253.
257. Decision # 218, 2 RLB 207, 208 (1921).
258. *See supra* text at notes 72–73.
259. *See supra* note 250.
260. Decision # 218, 2 RLB 207, 210–11 (1921).
261. *Id*. at 211–12.
262. 261 U.S. 72 (1923).
263. Brief of Appellant, Pennsylvania Railroad Co. v. United States Railroad Labor Board, 261 U.S. 72, 74, 81–82 (1923). The Transportation Act of 1920 "authorizes a board to fix rules, working conditions and wages, not temporarily but permanently, a power which, under the opinion in *Wilson v. New*, Congress itself does not possess." *Id*. at 83. In Wilson v. New, 243 U.S. 332 (1917), the Court had approved emergency federal action to regulate wages and hours of interstate railroad employees. *See supra* Chapter 25, at 793–94.
264. *Pennsylvania Railroad*, 261 U.S. at 79, 84.

265. *Id.* at 82, 84.
266. "The statute does not require the Railway Company to recognize or deal with, or confer with labor unions. It does not require employees to deal with their employers through their fellow employees. But we think it does vest the Labor Board with power to decide how such representatives ought to be chosen with a view to securing a satisfactory cooperation and leaves it to the two sides to accept or reject the decision." *Id.* at 85.
267. The Court's decision was announced on February 19, 1923. We have a letter from Brandeis to Taft dated January 27, in which Brandeis states:

> I think the decision clearly right, the argument on the merits sound and persuasive, indeed unanswerable.
>
> But I think it would be very unfortunate to decide that Barton et al., as individuals, could, under any circumstances, be enjoined from expressing their opinions on a matter which they believe is properly before them.
>
> I think the Board qua board is suable – perhaps an injunction or prohibition may lie to prevent the board from exceeding its jurisdiction. But we ought not to say that it may not publish its opinion, and we don't have to do so, to approve the judgment below.
>
> I hope we can talk this over.

LDB to WHT (January 27, 1923), in 5 LETTERS OF LOUIS D. BRANDEIS, at 86. Brandeis's reference to "Barton" is likely to Judge R.M. Barton of Tennessee, a Democrat appointed to the RLB as its first Chair by Wilson. Harding reappointed Barton to the RLB on May 11, 1923. *Barton Reappointed to Rail Labor Board*, NEW YORK TIMES (May 12, 1923), at 5. In his published opinion Taft clearly holds that the Board has jurisdiction over the controversy, and it is therefore difficult to reconstruct what might have prompted Brandeis's letter.
268. 267 U.S. 203, 215 (1925). For the text of the Transportation Act, see *supra* note 250. Taft was crystal clear about the obstructionist tactics deployed by the Pennsylvania Railroad:

> The Pennsylvania Company is using every endeavor to avoid compliance with the judgment and principles of the Labor Board as to the proper method of securing representatives of the whole body of its employees, it is seeking to control its employees by agreements free from the influence of an independent trade union, it is, so far as its dealings with its employees go, refusing to comply with the decisions of the Labor Board and is thus defeating the purpose of Congress. Appellants charge that the company is attempting by threats to discharge its employees to secure their consent to the agreement of July 1, 1921, as to wages and working conditions agreed to by the representatives of its employees it declared elected. This is denied, though there is some evidence tending to support the charge. All these things it might do and remain within its strict legal rights after it came fully into control of its railroad property subsequent to September 1, 1920. We do not think Congress, while it would deprecate such action, intended to make it criminal or legally actionable. Therefore the bill of complaint does not aver a conspiracy, and without that equitable relief cannot be granted.

267 U.S. at 217. On the recalcitrance of the Pennsylvania Railroad Co., see *Railroad Adjustment and Arbitration*, 38 NEW REPUBLIC 327, 328 (1924) ("As is well known, during the shop strike the example of the Pennsylvania

encouraged a large number of other systems to substitute company unions for recognition of the employes' own organizations.").

269. *The Transportation Act's Teeth Out*, 84 LITERARY DIGEST 12 (March 26, 1925). *See Ominous for the Labor Board*, WALL STREET JOURNAL (March 4, 1925), at 1.

270. 42 NEW REPUBLIC 85 (1925). William Green, president of the AFL, editorialized that the RLB "is now nothing more than an empty show. . . . The unions always have contended that the law gave the board no power of compulsion and they have contended likewise that compulsion was wrong in any event. . . . The American labor movement has pinned its faith on voluntarism." Green, *supra* note 233, at 245.

271. *Toothless Bodies*, NEW YORK HERALD TRIBUNE (March 8, 1925) (Taft papers). In 1936, Alpheus Thomas Mason could observe, "The attempt of government . . . to force agreements between employers and organized labor is not very different from enforcing a statute outlawing strikes. Both proceedings smack of compulsory arbitration, and this method of dealing with the industrial problem has found little favor among our judges. Compulsory arbitration involves unusual restrictions on both liberty and property." Alpheus Thomas Mason, *Labor and Judicial Interpretation*, 184 ANNALS OF THE AMERICAN ACADEMY OF POLITICAL AND SOCIAL SCIENCE 112, 121 (1936).

272. TOMLINS, *supra* note 220, at 91. *See* BRIAN BALOGH, THE ASSOCIATIONAL STATE: AMERICAN GOVERNANCE IN THE TWENTIETH CENTURY (Philadelphia: University of Pennsylvania Press 2015).

273. Hoover's work at the Department of Commerce with trade associations exemplifies the framework of the associative state. *See supra* Chapter 21, at 695–96. For Hoover's views on the regulation of labor, see Zieger, *supra* note 85.

274. Pub. L. 69-257, 44 Stat. 577 (May 20, 1926).

275. 44 Stat. 578. Two days after *Pennsylvania Railroad System and Allied Lines Federation No. 90*, the *Wall Street Journal* predicted that labor and management would ultimately agree that employees should have "a free hand in choosing their representatives for negotiation." *Ominous for the Labor Board, supra* note 269.

276. 281 U.S. 548, 570–71 (1930).

277. On the transition from progressivism to pluralism, see MARK V. TUSHNET, THE HUGHES COURT: FROM PROGRESSIVISM TO PLURALISM, 1930–1941 (Cambridge University Press 2021).

CHAPTER 40

Labor and the Construction of the National Market

TWO WEEKS AFTER Taft's confirmation as chief justice, the *New Republic* observed that there were nine significant pending cases. The most important of these was "that of the Coronado Coal Company, which involves the right of a corporation to collect from a labor union in consequence of damage suffered during a strike." The *New Republic* feared that *Coronado* would pose a terrible challenge to the new chief justice, because immediately upon taking office he would be faced with "a decision as important as that in the Dred Scott case."[1]

United Mine Workers of America v. Coronado Coal Co.[2] was indeed a dramatic case. It would create "a profound sensation."[3] In the words of one newspaper, *Coronado* was "without doubt one of the most important [cases] ever decided by" the Supreme Court.[4] Its riveting facts embodied "industrial warfare in the literal sense of the term."[5] *Coronado* challenged the Court to lift "union-made strikes out of the category of guerrilla warfare"[6] and subject them to the "reign of law."[7]

The case involved the Bache-Denman Company, which had been organized in 1903 to mine coal in western Arkansas.[8] About 75 percent of the company's coal was shipped out of state.[9] In March 1914, the company decided that to increase profitability it would convert to an open shop and avoid the high cost of union labor.[10] The difficulty was that one of the company's mines had contracted with the local chapter of the United Mine Workers of America ("UMW"), agreeing to hire only union employees. The company contrived to lease the mine to a dummy out-of-state corporation, which promptly broke the contract, shut down the mine, and fired all employees. The company's plan was to reopen the mine a month later as an open shop.

The company used the month to prepare for what it knew would be "a bitter fight."[11] It hired armed guards. "Rifles and ammunition were bought, searchlights were put on the shaft and tipple, and a contract was made with the Burns Detective Agency to send 'four or five reliable watchmen.'"[12] Operations resumed on April 4

Labor & the Construction of the National Market

with nonunion labor. A crowd gathered two days later. It overpowered and beat the guards and new employees, hoisting on the tipple a banner reading "This is a union man's country."[13] The company responded by obtaining a federal court injunction and increasing the detectives "to sixty or seventy – all armed with long-distance rifles and supplied with many thousands of rounds of ammunition."[14] Matters grew more tense, until in July a large crowd attacked the mine. "The guards and nonunion employes resisted for a while, but were outflanked and fled. In the course of the battle the tipple was fired and the mine dynamited."[15] Nonunion miners were murdered. Eventually federal troops entered to restore order, remaining until 1915.[16]

The company went bankrupt, but its receiver sued the UMW, as well as the local division of the UMW known as District 21, for treble damages under the Sherman Anti-Trust Act.[17] The receiver sought damages for injuries to the company's property and business. This was an audacious move because at the time "the decisions were unanimous to the effect that it was improper for an unincorporated association to be a party plaintiff or defendant."[18] There was a "well established rule that a trade union is not a legal entity for the purposes of being sued and bringing suit."[19] The rule was controversial. There had been many unsuccessful but nevertheless "insistent demands" for legislation to overrule it.[20]

In 1902, for example, Brandeis had famously and publicly debated Samuel Gompers at the Economic Club of Boston about whether trade unions should be "incorporated," meaning in the parlance of the time whether they should be made suable as parties for damages.[21] Although Brandeis made clear his appreciation of trade unions, because they "have accomplished much, and because their fundamental principle is noble," he nevertheless advocated for "the incorporation of labor unions" to "protect them from their own arbitrariness. The employer and the community also require this protection."[22] Gompers politely declined the invitation to make unions suable in damages. "Do you blame us," Gompers asked, "if we fear to place further power in the courts and judges of our country. . . . What chance has labor, the laborers, for fair play when the whole history of jurisprudence has been against the laborer?"[23]

In *Coronado*, the federal district court in Arkansas permitted the UMW to be sued for damages, and a trial resulted in a verdict of $200,000 for the plaintiffs, which was trebled. To the verdict was added attorneys' fees amounting to $25,000, as well as interest of $120,000. The Eighth Circuit vacated the judgment as to interest, but otherwise affirmed the verdict.[24] The decision was regarded as "of vital importance to the organized labor movement. If the decision of the Circuit Court is affirmed by the Supreme Court of the United States and stands as a principle of law, the existence of every national and international union is endangered."[25]

As the case came to the Court, the UMW was facing a judgment of $625,000, about $10 million in contemporary dollars. The case posed three major legal questions: (1) Whether unions could properly be sued as parties in actions for damages; (2) Whether the national UMW, as distinct from local District 21, could appropriately be held liable for the union riots; and (3) Whether the Sherman Act applied to a strike of coal miners against a mine that shipped most of its product to interstate markets.[26]

The case was argued on October 15, 1920. It was so important that the UMW procured the services of former Justice Charles Evans Hughes to represent it.[27] We know from Taft's correspondence that the Court voted 5–4 to affirm the verdict, with Holmes, Day, Brandeis, and Clark dissenting.[28] The opinion was assigned to Van Devanter, who characteristically delayed drafting an opinion.[29] Taft later wrote his brother that "White did not press Van to a decision. ... White was a man for procrastination in questions likely to call out attack."[30] The upshot was that when Taft ascended to the bench in June 1921, it was necessary to set the case for reargument, which occurred on March 22–23, 1922.[31]

All recognized the vital importance of the case. Taft published his opinion on June 5, 1922. A week later Taft sent a long, handwritten letter to his brother to recount the Court's deliberations after the March argument. Taft sought to explain how he had come to decide that although the UMW was suable as an entity, the judgment of the district court should nevertheless be reversed because the Sherman Act reached only interstate commerce and the union riot had involved only intrastate commerce:

> I determined to have the thing decided and gotten out of the way. We voted to affirm. There were four principal questions. First, could trade unions be sued as such, second was the National union responsible for what was done, and third was the District Union No. 21 conspiring against interstate commerce in what was done so as to bring their outrageous act within the Antitrust statute and fourth was the supplementary charge to the jury a coercion of the jury into the verdict rendered. On the first issue Holmes & Day voted with us, making seven, Brandeis & Clarke dissenting. On the second and third issues, Holmes, Brandeis and Clarke dissented. On the fourth Day, Brandeis, & Clarke dissented. I took the case and read the record of 3000 pages and made full notes. I became convinced that the strike was only a local strike for which the Nat. Union was not responsible and that it did not concern and was not intended to interfere with interstate commerce. Although I was doubtful at first about the suability of unions I became convinced on that subject. So I wrote a very long opinion taking up every question to satisfy my colleagues. I supposed that Brandeis and Clarke would dissent from the conclusion as to suability but to my surprise Brandeis came in with emphasis Clarke more hesitatingly. Holmes was full of praise for the opinion. ... Holmes who hates long opinions said when I apologized ... "but it is interesting."[32]

The Court had initially voted to affirm the Eighth Circuit, with Holmes, Day, Brandeis, and Clarke again dissenting. But sometime during April or May Taft changed his mind and decided to reverse the Eighth Circuit, vacating the judgment against the unions. Despite Taft's very informative letter, much concerning the Court's deliberations remains obscure.[33]

Taft's recollection that Brandeis initially dissented on the suability question, for example, seems implausible. Not only had Brandeis been publicly advocating for the incorporation of labor unions for two decades,[34] but we have in the Brandeis papers an unpublished draft dissent explicitly beginning with the concession that "I agree" that "labor unions, if guilty of participating in such acts cannot escape liability on the ground that they are unincorporated."[35] Brandeis was very much on record that "[t]he plea of trades unions for immunity, be it from injunction or from liability for damages, is as fallacious as the plea of the lynchers. If lawless methods are pursued by trades unions, whether it be by violence, by intimidation, or by the more peaceful infringements of legal rights, that lawlessness must be put down at once and at any cost."[36]

Brandeis's draft dissent instead rested on the same ground as that ultimately adopted by Taft – that the strike was beyond the jurisdiction of federal anti-trust legislation. Citing *Hammer v. Dagenhart*,[37] Brandeis argued that the riot's "relation to interstate commerce lacked that direct connection which this Court has held to be necessary to bring the transaction within the scope of federal concern."[38] It is probable that Brandeis was working on this dissent as late as May 1922.[39] We have no way of knowing whether it was seen by Taft, or whether it influenced his final opinion,[40] although Taft's striking misattribution of Brandeis's vote on the suability question suggests that he probably did not very carefully read Brandeis's eloquent manuscript.[41]

What is clear is that Taft was aware that he was working on a "great case"[42] whose announcement would likely meet with a tumultuous reception. We know that Taft was at this time very much concerned with the effect of dissent on the reputation of the Court.[43] And we also know that in late April and early May, the press was filled with headlines like: 'God Save Labor from the Courts,' Exclaims Gompers. They Are 'Most Unfair' in Industrial Cases."[44] Testifying before the famed Lockwood Housing Commission of New York, which was investigating union abuses,[45] Gompers attacked "court decisions," including *Hammer v. Dagenhart*, in an effort "to show that the courts had trespassed on the rights of labor."[46] Gompers opposed judicial review, affirming that "courts should not have the power to declare unconstitutional any statute passed by congress or a state legislature."[47]

These reports are no doubt why Taft wrote his brother on May 7, plainly with *Coronado* in mind, that

> [t]he only class which is distinctly arrayed against the Court is a class that does not like the courts at any rate, and that is organized labor. That faction we have to hit every little while, because they are continually violating the law and depending on threat and violence to accomplish their purpose. They are not content to depend only on organization, and the background of lawless trouble is always presented to give them an undue influence. Every decision, therefore, of the Court that indicates a means of minimizing this influence or preventing violence is heralded as a destruction of their liberties. It seems to fall to my lot to have to be the protagonist against them in this regard, although I think I am a good deal more friendly to organized labor than most people who have to deal with them. But in doing one's duty one must expect to be misunderstood by those who are unfavorably affected by the enforcement of the law.[48]

In the end, we shall never know when or why Taft changed his mind about whether to affirm the Eighth Circuit. It might have been because, as he wrote his brother, a close reading of the 3,000-page record had changed Taft's mind. Or it might have been because Taft came under the sway of Brandeis's brilliant draft dissent. Or it might have been because Taft realized that, having delivered the highly controversial *Bailey* decision striking down the child-labor tax on May 15,[49] he desperately needed a unanimous Court before releasing yet another explosive opinion.[50] Whatever the reason, at some time between the end of March and the end of May Taft altered course and decided to reverse the Eighth Circuit, and he managed to persuade his colleagues to join his long, well-crafted opinion that elegantly split the baby.[51]

Taft first took up the question of whether "unincorporated associations," like the UMW and District No. 21, were "suable in their names." He acknowledged at the outset that "[u]ndoubtedly at common law an unincorporated association of persons was not recognized as having any other character than a partnership in whatever was done, and it could only sue or be sued in the names of its members, and their liability had to be enforced against each member." But Taft then argued that, as a matter of policy,

> [i]t would be unfortunate if an organization with as great power as this International Union has in the raising of large funds and in directing the conduct of 400,000 members in carrying on, in a wide territory, industrial controversies, and strikes out of which so much unlawful injury to private rights is possible, could assemble its assets to be used therein free from liability for injuries by torts committed in course of such strikes. To remand persons injured to a suit against each of the 400,000 members, to recover damages and to levy on his share of the strike fund, would be to leave them remediless.[52]

Taft adduced as precedent the English case of *Taff Vale Co. v. Amalgamated Society of Railway Servants*,[53] in which an English court, in a decision ultimately affirmed by the House of Lords, had altered the common law to hold a trade union suable in its own name.[54] Taft notably failed to mention that the outrage sparked by *Taff Vale* contributed to the formation of the British Labour party, and that the case itself had subsequently been specifically overridden by the Trade Disputes Act of 1906, the famous history of which Taft knew well.[55] Most striking was Taft's elaborate reference in an unusual footnote[56] to the many state and federal laws that recognized labor unions as distinct entities entitled to appear in processes like "statutory arbitrations" or "official labor boards."[57]

Two aspects of Taft's approach deserve special emphasis. First, Taft's conclusion follows naturally from the "group system" that Taft had explicitly recognized in *American Steel Foundries*. Endowing unions with legal personality acknowledged the official role in public life that Taft had been willing to grant unions since (at least) his days as co-chair of the National War Labor Board. As Frankfurter immediately saw in praising the opinion, "it would have been a distinct departure from reality for the Supreme Court solemnly to hold" that the union, which "is an entity for all the affairs of life, the law, for some mystical reasons of its own, cannot so recognize. ... The real problem, then, is not to deny the fact that a trade union *is*, but to work out the legal scope of its activities."[58]

Labor & the Construction of the National Market

Second, Taft altered traditional common law precedents by explicitly recognizing positive legislation as a generative source of authority for the development of common law policy, an approach that was highly controversial during the 1920s.[59] Taft's "emphasis on the existence of statutes giving 'affirmative legal recognition'" to unions,[60] as well as his conclusion that "in this state of federal legislation, we think that such organizations are suable in the federal courts for their acts,"[61] was specifically noted by commentators interested in the development of common law methods of adjudication.[62]

The upshot was that by modifying the common law to impose entity liability on trade unions and thus inflict what was widely "regarded as one of the heaviest blows union labor ever has sustained,"[63] the Court laid itself open to charges of "judicial legislation."[64] The *New York World*, for example, editorialized: "The matter of forcing incorporation on unions is a matter which only the legislative power of the States or Nation can determine. Judges are entitled to a personal opinion on this question, but to act officially in treating the unions as incorporated bodies is to assume for themselves the exercise of legislative powers barred by the fundamental law."[65] The much-noticed fact of judicial unanimity was helpful in this regard.[66] "Since the opinion was unanimous," editorialized the normally pro-labor *Baltimore Sun*, "there can hardly be any doubt as to the accuracy of its interpretation of the law."[67]

Because *Coronado* would ultimately hold that the strike did not involve interstate commerce and so liability did not attach under the Sherman Act, Taft's elaborately reasoned holding about the suability of unions was also vulnerable to the accusation of being mere *dicta*. The Executive Committee of the American Federation of Labor ("AFL"), for example, charged that *Coronado*'s conclusions about entity liability were to an "astounding extreme" "purely gratuitous."[68] La Follette pointedly noted that a "six-line decision was all that was required to dispose of the case on its merits," yet the Court "went out of its way to change the law as it has existed in this country since the beginning of the Government, that unincorporated associations, such as are involved here, could not be sued as an entity."[69] Many commentators have agreed with this judgment.[70]

Taft himself, however, was convinced to the contrary. In his long, handwritten letter to his brother, Taft observed that "[t]his history will show you that the decision is not properly obiter dictum at all. It disposes of the questions logically and in order and one of those is the suability of trades unions."[71] Brandeis was apparently also sensitive to the charge of *dicta*, for he took the time to write an extended and closely reasoned letter to Frankfurter defending the need to reach the question of entity liability.[72]

Coronado's conclusions about entity liability were generally received favorably by the press.[73] Public acceptance of unions as legitimate organizations was paired with the thought that unions must "answer to the law."[74] The *St. Louis Post-Dispatch*, for example, reasoned:

> To recognize in law the right of labor to organize and to exert great powers affecting the interests of employers and the public, to provide for collective bargaining and for settlement of disputes through labor organizations and yet

hold them exempt from the operation of laws for the protection of public and private rights and exempt from liability for damages perpetrated under their direction, would be abnormal. It would set up a privileged class exercising power, collecting and expending large funds, having rights and privileges and protection under the laws, but free from all legal obligations, responsibilities and liabilities.[75]

The *St. Louis Globe-Democrat* predicted that "[t]he results of this decision will be a larger sense of responsibility on the part of labor leaders, and a greater care for the protection of property rights. If the unions can be made to pay for damages done by them, they will be slow to incur such a liability. This in the long run will tend to establish better relations between labor and capital. It will help to remove one of the greatest sources of friction and of animosity, and promote a better understanding between the two elements of industry."[76]

It was widely asserted that by making labor unions answerable in damages *Coronado* had actually reduced the need for judicial injunctions, since employers now had access to an adequate remedy at law.[77] This was the thesis of a *New York Times* editorial that Taft clipped and kept in his papers. The editorial condemned La Follette and Gompers who "cry out against legality as 'slavery.' Eventually they will learn that in civilized life law is the only sure instrument of freedom."[78] Former Secretary of War Newton Baker speculated that *Coronado*, "which has been widely denounced as the hardest blow Labor has yet received, may well turn out to be a disguised blessing, first by decreasing the resort to injunctive remedies and second, by giving these great labor organizations a new sense of their dignity and responsibility."[79] The underlying thought was that *Coronado* would deter only "lawless acts" and "attempts to hinder, restrain or monopolize interstate trade."[80] *Coronado* can in this sense be understood as a step toward fulfilling the larger agenda of the Taft Court, which was to bring private violence within the control of the legal system.[81]

Some in the labor movement professed to find *Coronado* empowering. The UMW, for example, which regarded *Coronado* as "the most important and far-reaching court decision ever rendered in a labor case,"[82] took a positive view of the decision.[83] "If a labor union can be sued," it said, then "it can also sue. If a labor union can sue, then there is no good reason why it should not utilize the law and the courts for the protection of itself, its members and their welfare against oppression, damage or outrage."[84] Most in the labor movement, however, found this perspective naïve:

> There is no use blinking the fact that the great majority of the judges on the bench generally ascend to their positions after faithful service to big corporations. ... These judges have a coal owners' and a steel owners' philosophy. They carry their views upon the bench. For example, imagine a union suing for damages before a court presided over by a man like Judge Taft. Is there any doubt that the cards would be stacked against the union before the trial opened? These judges belong to the enemy, and the records of the labor movement for two generations leave no room for any other opinion. To accept the servile status which the

Supreme Court has assigned to the unions of the country without a determined struggle would be to deliver the unions bound hand and foot to the enemy.[85]

The key issue was one of agency.[86] Taft had himself once publicly noted that "Even if the union which initiates a strike exercises every possible care to avoid lawlessness, lawlessness will, if the strike be at all extended, generally occur."[87] The question, as *The Nation* immediately observed, was thus whether "even in a strike which is itself lawful," unions would "be held liable for the lawless acts of their most irresponsible members." *The Nation* feared that "courts will be quick to find a theory of agency by which the act of each member during a strike will be held to be the act of the union."[88] Gompers was quite explicit on this point. *Coronado*, he charged, "amounts to the denial of the right to strike" and reestablishes "slavery and involuntary servitude," because if there were an approved strike and if "one or two, or one-half dozen of the men ... should commit some overt act, and the organization of the international would be held responsible in treble damages, it would simply mean that the organization, national or international, would never approve, would never dare to approve" the strike. "Otherwise they would be compelled to be in constant litigation and be driven out of existence."[89] Gompers vigorously denounced *Coronado* as "a blow at the 'very foundation of the organized labor movement of America,'" as "the climax of decisions of the United States Supreme Court in the last few months against labor since the ascension to the Chief Justiceship of Mr. Taft."[90]

Taft had been careful in *Coronado* to hold that under ordinary principles of agency law the national UMW could not be held responsible for the local strike in Arkansas.[91] But he did find that District 21 was responsible, and he did so using rather loose language that "excited much comment":[92] "[T]he authority is put by all the members of the District No. 21 in their officers to order a strike, and if in the conduct of that strike unlawful injuries are inflicted, the district organization is responsible, and the fund accumulated for strike purposes may be subjected to the payment of any judgment which is recovered."[93] Harvard Law Professor Francis Bowes Sayre, citing this sentence, observed that it was surely "bad law as well as a serious error of judgment gratuitously to suggest that the district organization is necessarily responsible for violence unauthorized by its members in the conduct of authorized strikes."[94] As one commentator put it, if during an authorized strike "fifty odd members commit acts of lawlessness resulting in damage to the plaintiff's property," should the union "as an entity be held responsible for the damage done? Should the tens of thousands of other members, in their group character, be made insurers for the good conduct of every member?"[95]

Uncertainty attending the agency question fueled the ferocity of labor's response. Labor's suspicions were especially aroused by the last paragraph of Taft's *Coronado* opinion, in which, having found that there was insufficient evidence to show that the strike was within the prohibition of the Sherman Act, Taft nevertheless went out of his way to remark that "The circumstances are such as to awaken regret that, in our view of the federal jurisdiction, we cannot affirm the judgment."[96] That sentence, said Gompers, was "gratuitous, bitter and unforgivable."[97] In its report on *Coronado*, the AFL Executive Committee remarked that the sentence showed "how eager the Supreme Court was to inflict injury upon labor."[98]

Not only did labor vow to seek legislative redress by attacking "that legislative monstrosity known as the Sherman anti-trust law,"[99] but in its 1922 annual convention the AFL resolved to seek a constitutional amendment "providing that if the United States Supreme Court decides that an act of Congress is unconstitutional, or by interpretation asserts a public policy at variance with the statutory declaration of Congress, then if Congress by a two-thirds majority re-passes the law, it shall become the law of the land."[100] Senator La Follette spoke eloquently for the amendment at the convention, arguing, strangely, that if the Constitution were so amended, "Congress could by statute speedily correct the indefensible policy, asserted by the Supreme Court in the Coronado case, with respect to labor unions, farmers' associations and other voluntary organizations."[101]

Of course, *Coronado*'s holding on entity liability was not a constitutional decision but instead an interpretation of either federal common law or federal antitrust legislation, depending upon how one reads the decision. What was palpable, however, was labor's animus against the Court. Senator Frank Kellogg was moved to write a correspondent: "The other day Senator La Follette went out to Cincinnati to the annual meeting of the American Federation of Labor and made a terrific onslaught on the Supreme Court, the Constitution, and everything else. ... The discouraging thing is that he was enthusiastically received and wildly cheered at the meeting in Cincinnati. There is getting to be such a bitter feeling in this country between the labor unions and everybody else that I do not know what it is coming to."[102]

We know that Taft was preoccupied with the backlash to *Coronado* throughout the summer of 1922. Five days after announcing the decision, Taft was scheduled to sail for England to study reforms in civil procedure.[103] Before leaving he dashed off a quick handwritten note to Van Devanter: "I am rather looking forward to the sea trip with the hope of rest. ... I hope to escape having to read Gompers' diatribes on me while on the sea."

> I have not seen many of the papers but I presume from an editorial in The World that my opinion in the Coronado case will come in for great attack in Congress and the journals inclined to stir up labor against the courts. There will be an effort made to destroy the effect of the ruling by act of Congress just as they did by act of Parliament in the Taff Vale case. But I am hopeful that the Judiciary Committees will delay consideration of such a bill to the short session and then they will be unable to pass it. Moreover I think Harding would veto it but after him one can not tell. I should think that labor could not excite the farmers on such a subject and that the agricultural bloc will not take it up.[104]

Almost immediately upon landing, Taft wrote his brother that "The Federation of Labor will be in session all the time I am in England and I expect to hear denunciations from Gompers and in resolutions reported in the dispatches from time to time but I hope it is too late to get the thing up in Congress seriously before election and time helps in such cases."[105] As late as August, Taft was writing Day:

"You have doubtless noted the onslaught on the Court by Gompers and La Follette. ... They attack the Child Labor judgment but they are more troubled by the Coronado decision. They don't dare test the feeling over the latter decision by attempting to reverse it by legislation. At least I have not seen any proposal to do what Parliament did in England to the Taff-Vale decision."[106]

In the end, labor's fears of *Coronado*'s ominous consequences proved exaggerated. A review of labor law in 1932 reports that "Damage suits have not destroyed labor unions nor driven them into secrecy, nor have they proved by any means as serious as have injunctions. The reasons why the dire predictions have not come true are mainly two: (1) procedural difficulties in suing labor unions and (2) inability under the established principles of agency law to connect unions or their members with alleged unlawful acts."[107] Taft's hope that damage actions would bring industrial warfare under legal supervision would thus prove unavailing.[108]

In retrospect, we can see that an important factor was that *casus belli* declined sharply; the years after 1922 witnessed a steep drop in labor activism.[109] After the collapse of the Railroad Shopmen's strike, the AFL retreated from its postwar militancy and decided on a radically new direction. In 1923, it adopted a policy of "cooperation and collaboration," affirming that "the true role of industrial groups ... is to come together, to legislate in peace, to find the way forward in collaboration."[110] Without cooperation, the AFL cautioned, "political bureaucracy will gain the ascendancy."[111] The AFL sought to advance a "change" in the "understanding of the trade union."[112] The union "not only cares for the interests of the workers, but is an agency through which the workers cooperate in production and contribute the experience of those who handle tools and machinery."[113] The premise was that "wage earners can benefit only through prosperous industries."[114] As AFL President William Green announced in 1927: "Partnership ... must be the basis of constructive relations between employers and employed."[115]

Despite the thunderclap that accompanied *Coronado*'s publication, therefore, the actual overhang of the case during the 1920s lay mainly in the normative dualism that justified Taft's reversal of the Eighth Circuit. Taft reasoned that the "obstruction of coal mining, though it may prevent coal from going into interstate commerce, is not a restraint of that commerce, unless the obstruction to mining is intended to restrain commerce in it, or has necessarily such a direct, material, and substantial effect to restrain it that the intent reasonably must be inferred. In the case at bar there is nothing in the circumstances or the declarations of the parties to indicate that" the officers of District No. 21 "had in mind interference with interstate commerce or competition when they entered upon their unlawful combination" to assault the company.[116] Under the circumstances, said Taft, it was "of far higher importance" than the punishment of District No. 21 "that we should preserve inviolate the fundamental limitations in respect to the federal jurisdiction."[117]

Coronado came down just three weeks after Taft's opinion in *Bailey*[118] strongly reaffirmed the normative dualism of *Hammer v. Dagenhart*. Like *Bailey*, *Coronado* was very much in tension with the unbounded nationalism implicit in other early Taft Court decisions like the *Wisconsin Rate Case*[119] or *Stafford v. Wallace.*[120] Taft attempted to bridge this tension by carefully explaining in *Coronado* that where "Congress deems certain recurring practices though not really part of interstate commerce, likely to obstruct, restrain or burden it," Congress had the undoubted "power to subject" such practices "to national supervision and restraint."[121] But Congress had made no such finding in the Sherman Act, which instead required judges to determine in each individual case whether a defendant's actions are part of a "plan to hinder, restrain, or monopolize interstate commerce." In answering this question, "the intent to injure, obstruct, or restrain interstate commerce must appear as an obvious consequence of what is to be done, or be shown by direct evidence or other circumstance."[122]

This criterion of federal jurisdiction left ample room for judicial discretion.[123] Taft in effect invited federal courts to use anti-trust legislation to determine the legal boundaries of permissible union activism. As one commentator put it, "The result depends on how each judge weights the interests of organized labor, employer, and public, and how grievous he considers the malfeasances for which each is responsible."[124] In *Coronado*, Taft sought to strike a balance, just as he had in *American Steel Foundries*. And, as in *American Steel Foundries*, Taft sought to commit the arbitration of that balance to the discretion of federal judges.

In October 1921, District Judge Albert Barnes Anderson, whom La Follette later singled out to the AFL annual convention as a petty tyrant and arrogant despot,[125] had held that the effort of the UMW to unionize West Virginia coal production to protect organized mines in the central competitive field from the cheaper costs of nonunionized labor was "in direct contravention of the Sherman Anti-Trust Act," because it sought to prevent "competition in the sale of bituminous coal throughout the several states."[126] Although Anderson's decree had been quickly reversed by the Seventh Circuit, its rationale posed a mortal threat to national labor organizations. If national unions could be prevented from organizing nonunion shops in order to prevent price competition, "the very life of organized labor" would be threatened.[127] As Samuel Gompers put it, "control of all the workers in a trade . . . protects the fair employer from competition with producers who care not how they grind their employes so long as they also grind out profits."[128]

In *Coronado*, Taft explicitly discussed the abstract theory of the Anderson injunction. He wrote:

> What really is shown by the evidence in the case at bar, drawn from discussions and resolutions of conventions and conference, is the stimulation of union leaders to press their unionization of nonunion mines, not only as a direct means of bettering the conditions and wages of their workers, but also as a means of lessening interstate competition for union operators, which in turn would lessen the pressure of those operators for reduction of the union scale or their resistance to an increase. *The latter is a secondary or ancillary motive*, whose actuating force in a given case necessarily is dependent on the particular circumstances to which it is sought to make it applicable. If unlawful means had here been used by the national body to unionize mines whose product was important,

actually or potentially, in affecting prices in interstate commerce, the evidence in question would clearly tend to show that that body was guilty of an actionable conspiracy under the Anti-Trust Act. This principle is involved in the decision of the case of *Hitchman Coal Co. v. Mitchell*, and is restated in *American Steel Foundries v. Tri-City Central Trades Council*.[129]

Taft made clear that a miner's union could be held liable if it were shown that it struck with the intent "to restrain commerce" *or* if "the obstruction to mining ... has necessarily such a direct, material and substantial effect to restrain it that the intent reasonably must be inferred." Every judicial factfinder would have to consider "the particular circumstances" of "a given case."[130] This framework of analysis invited courts to infer intent differently in the context of strikes called by international unions like the UMW, whose "direct, material and substantial" effects on interstate commerce would likely be considerable, than in the context of strikes called by local unions like District No. 21. Taft thus created a framework that could be used to box out national unions from efforts to organize non-union shops to protect unionized establishments from cheap, non-union competition.[131] Taft was explicit that if the international UMW had used "the same unlawful means" as District 21, and if the coal affected by the international union was actually or potentially "important" in "affecting prices in interstate commerce," the UMW would be "guilty of an actionable conspiracy under the Anti-Trust Act."[132]

In *Coronado* itself, however, Taft went out of his way to emphasize that because the UMW had not ratified the strike, it "was in fact a local strike, local in its origin and motive, local in its waging, and local in its felonious and murderous ending."[133] A court could draw no inference of an intent to restrain interstate commerce from the "5,000 tons" of coal per week produced by the Company's mines, since they would "have no appreciable effect upon the price of coal or non-union competition." Taft concluded that in the *Coronado* case "there was no evidence submitted to the jury upon which they properly could find that the outrages, felonies, and murders of District 21 and its companions in crime were committed by them in a conspiracy to restrain or monopolize interstate commerce. The motion to direct the jury to return a verdict for the defendants should have been granted."[134]

Coronado left considerable "liberty to the opinions and estimates of the individual judge"[135] about whether the Sherman Act would apply to any particular strike. *The Nation* was astute to observe that "in practice this will mean that the union must estimate in advance the chances of judicial approval or condemnation of its purposes and strike at its peril if it has guessed wrong. Judges, however incorruptible are almost always drawn from a class which by interest, education, and environment is little fitted to appreciate the realities of the industrial struggle from the standpoint of the workers. Yet a judicial decision may leave labor with no alternative but acquiescence in exploitation or open revolt."[136]

The elasticity of the *Coronado* approach was vividly illustrated three years later when the case returned to the Court in *Coronado Coal Co. v. United Mine Workers of America* (*Coronado II*).[137] *Coronado I* had remanded the case to the district court. The company then located new evidence and new witnesses. One such witness was a disaffected former local union official named James K. McNamara, who testified that John Phillip White, president of the UMW, had assured striking miners that the UMW would reimburse them for their expenses.[138] McNamara's testimony also contained "much, if credited, from which the jury could reasonably infer that the purpose of the union miners in District No. 21 and the local unions engaged in the plan was to destroy the power of the owners and lessees of the Bache-Denman mines to send their output into interstate commerce to compete with that of union mines in Oklahoma, in Kansas, in Louisiana markets and elsewhere." Another former local union official testified "that he made speeches all through District No. 21" and that in each he mentioned "the danger from non-union coal in taking the markets of union coal and forcing a non-union scale, and that it was a constant subject of discussion among the officers and members." There was also testimony that the potential output of the company's mines, if hypothetically worked to full capacity, was not the 5,000 tons a week that *Coronado I* had calculated, but 5,000 tons a day.[139]

Despite this new evidence, the trial court directed a verdict for the defendants, and this judgment was affirmed by the Eighth Circuit.[140] Butler's docket book indicates that in conference Holmes and Brandeis voted to affirm the Eighth Circuit; McReynolds voted to reverse it; and four other justices (McKenna having stepped down two days before the oral argument in the case) voted to follow Taft and affirm the Eighth Circuit with regard to the UMW, but to reverse it with regard to District No. 21 and the local unions.[141] As published, Taft's opinion was unanimous.

In affirming the directed verdict in favor of the UMW, Taft explained that "[g]iving the fullest credence to all that McNamara says, it is clear that White did not intend by what he did to make" the strike "a national affair. The International Board had not approved as the constitution required that they should do in order to make it so." Although White might have incurred personal liability, the UMW itself, as an organization, had not done so. "[C]ertainly it must be clearly shown in order to impose such a liability on an association of 450,000 men that what was done was done by their agents in accordance with their fundamental agreement of association."[142]

District No. 21, by contrast, had acted through its elected officers in endorsing the strike and in perpetuating the riots. A jury could conclude from the new evidence that its "outrages, destruction and crimes" were "intentionally directed toward a restraint of interstate commerce." Taft concluded his opinion with this explanation of *Coronado*'s "intent" standard:

> The mere reduction in the supply of an article to be shipped in interstate commerce by the illegal or tortious prevention of its manufacture or production is ordinarily an indirect and remote obstruction to that commerce. But when the intent of those unlawfully preventing the manufacture or production is shown to be to restrain or control the supply entering and moving in interstate commerce, or the price of it in interstate markets, their action is a direct violation of the Anti-Trust Act. We think there was substantial evidence at the second trial in this case tending to show that the purpose of the destruction of the mines was to stop the

production of nonunion coal and prevent its shipment to markets of other states than Arkansas, where it would by competition tend to reduce the price of the commodity and affect injuriously the maintenance of wages for union labor in competing mines, and that the direction by the District Judge to return a verdict for the defendants other than the International Union was erroneous.[143]

The "celebrated case"[144] of Coronado Coal was then remanded for further proceedings, where it slowly dwindled to an inglorious end in 1927. After two subsequent mistrials, the company, which had once been awarded $745,000 in damages, agreed to settle for $27,500.[145]

What survived was a jurisdictional test for the application of the Sherman Act that was so "unreal" as to come "near to being judicial hocus-pocus."[146] Wherever there was any appreciable interpenetration of interstate and local markets, which by the 1920s meant virtually everywhere, it was impossible to know whether any seemingly local strike could be swept into the maws of the Sherman Act.[147] The definition of "intent" offered by *Coronado II*, were it to be found by a jury, could easily sustain the notorious Anderson injunction.[148]

As a matter of hard logic, "the fundamental limitations in respect to the federal jurisdiction," which Taft had sought in *Coronado I* to "preserve inviolate," were built on sand. The *symbolic* importance of those limitations, however, should not be underestimated; they carried the full freight of the Court's commitment to normative dualism. In the term before *Coronado II*, for example, the issue of normative dualism had arisen in the context of a strike by a local leather workers union against five corporations that manufactured trunks and leather goods. The strike was for union recognition. Ninety percent of the goods manufactured by these corporations was shipped out of state, and the local union was aware of this fact as it shut the corporations down.[149] The Eighth Circuit, speaking through Van Devanter's good friend Walter Henry Sanborn, effectively seized on the ambiguity of *Coronado* to hold that if a strike "necessarily" has the "direct, material and substantial effect" of shutting down interstate commerce, "the intent" to restrain interstate commerce "must be inferred."[150] Federal jurisdiction would then attach under the Sherman Act.

Taft was not amused. He wrote his son that "[i]t seems to me to be a case where Federal Judges in the 8th Circuit think they ought to amplify their jurisdiction and make a case of interstate commerce out of something we have declared not to be interstate commerce many a time."[151] But Butler's conference notes show something most unusual. Taft spoke first, declaring that there was "no evidence of restraint of interstate commerce." But Van Devanter flatly contradicted him, saying that there was a "direct" restraint. Disagreements between Taft and Van Devanter were *very* rare. Butler records that Holmes, Brandeis, Sutherland, and Butler voted with Taft; McKenna, McReynolds, and Sanford with Van Devanter. Ultimately McKenna, Van Devanter, and Butler would dissent without opinion.[152]

In his opinion, Taft was firm in his support for fundamental limitations of federal jurisdiction. He frankly acknowledged the "practical conception of interstate commerce ... as a flowing stream," but he also insisted that "the mere reduction in the supply of an article to be shipped in interstate commerce by the illegal or tortious prevention of its manufacture is ordinarily an indirect and remote obstruction to that commerce."

> It is only when the intent or the necessary effect upon such commerce in the article is to enable those preventing the manufacture to monopolize its supply or control its price, or discriminate as between its would-be purchasers, that the unlawful interference with its manufacture can be said directly to burden interstate commerce. The record is entirely without evidence or circumstances to show that the defendants in their conspiracy to deprive the complainants of their workers were thus directing their scheme against interstate commerce. It is true that they were, in this labor controversy, hoping that the loss of business in selling goods would furnish a motive to the complainants to yield to demands in respect to the terms of employment; but they did nothing which in any way directly interfered with the interstate transportation or sales of the complainants' product.[153]

Taft quoted with approval the observation of Judge Kimbrough Stone, who had dissented in the Eighth Circuit, that Sanborn's opinion would effectively invoke "federal jurisdiction" over every strike in every factory that sends an "appreciable amount of its product" into interstate commerce. Taft acidly noted that "[w]e can not think that Congress intended any such result in the enactment of the Anti-Trust Act or that the decisions of this Court warrant such construction."[154] The preservation of a symbolic line between federal and state authority, however elastic and manipulable, was important to Taft.

In the right circumstances, the maintenance of normative dualism could serve a distinctly conservative agenda. *Industrial Association of San Francisco v. United States*, for example, involved an association of San Francisco builders devoted to promoting the open shop. The Association refused to sell "certain specified kinds of materials" to builders who would not pledge themselves to an open shop.[155] Builders who made the pledge received a permit that authorized them to purchase building materials. With the exception of plaster, the building materials subject to the permit system were produced in California.[156]

A central question was whether including plaster in the scheme subjected the builders to federal anti-trust liability. Sutherland ruled for a unanimous Court that it did not, because the permit system did not apply to plaster until it "had been brought into the state and commingled with the common mass of local property, and in respect of which, therefore, the interstate movement and the interstate commercial status had ended." If the permitting system did interfere "with the free movement of materials and supplies from other states," the "effect upon, and interference with, interstate trade, if any, were clearly incidental, indirect and remote, precisely such an interference as this court dealt with in" *Coronado I* and *Heckert*.[157] The Court therefore vacated an injunction that had been issued against the builders' association.[158]

Industrial Association of San Francisco was argued on March 10, 1925. It was announced on April 13, 1925. At conference, Taft took the position that the San Francisco builders ought to be liable under the Sherman Act, but he was the only member of the Court to do so. In the end Taft "acquiesced" in Sutherland's opinion.[159] It is noteworthy that although *Coronado II* had been argued on January 7, 1925, it was not voted on in conference until April 11, two days before the Court announced its decision in *Industrial Association of San Francisco*.[160] Taft did not release his opinion in *Coronado II* until May 25. It is not implausible to speculate that the rather loose language in *Coronado II* might have originated in Taft's effort to cabin what he regarded as the unduly stringent constriction of federal jurisdiction in *Industrial Association*.[161]

Whatever the explanation, the violent swings in the Court's conceptualization of the "intent" necessary to trigger federal anti-trust jurisdiction, from *Heckert* to *Industrial Association of San Francisco* to *Coronado II*, left the law in state of tattered confusion.[162] By the end of the decade, astute commentators could conclude:

> In labor cases, the courts do not apply the distinctions between direct and incidental interferences with interstate commerce . . . by which the intra-state activity of business enterprises is saved from subjection to the anti-trust laws. By the loose use of familiar forms of words the federal courts may bring within their net every activity of organized labor affecting products which in whole or part are destined for interstate commerce or which at some time may have been within its stream. Such a conception of the overruling scope of interstate commerce, were it applied in other fields of commercial regulation, would largely dislocate the present balance of adjustments between states and nation. Labor finds itself outside of these adjustments.[163]

The Taft Court's elastic concept of jurisdiction was not accidental. It empowered federal courts to use anti-trust law to protect national markets from the predations of organized labor. In other circumstances, the Taft Court used dormant Commerce Clause doctrine or due process doctrine to defend national markets. But in the context of labor activism the Court's doctrine of choice was anti-trust law. Federal anti-trust legislation depended upon such a vague and pliable distinction between reasonable and unreasonable restraints of trade[164] that the Taft Court found it a useful and flexible instrument for constructing national labor markets according to its own vision of proper economic policy.

From its inception, the Sherman Act endowed federal courts with powerful forms of discretion. The Act contained what seemed like an impossibly broad and absolute prohibition against "[e]very contract . . . or conspiracy, in restraint of trade or commerce among the several States."[165] Because the statute could not possibly mean what it literally said, federal courts were forced to search for some method to interpret it in a plausible way. As a Sixth Circuit judge in 1898, Taft pioneered what would become the dominant approach. Taft held that the Sherman Act prohibited anticompetitive combinations that were voidable at common law.[166] In effect, therefore, federal anti-trust legislation functioned as an open invitation for federal courts to interpret and apply general principles of common law. Federal courts construed the Sherman Act to elevate "the old common-law doctrines of conspiracy and restraint of trade to the status of modern Federal law."[167] In interpreting the Act, Taft later said, "there being several possible interpretations of its language, the court adopts that which conforms to prevailing morality and predominant public opinion."[168]

Although there is no doubt that the Sherman Act had originally been enacted to control the wave of industrial consolidation that swept the American economy in the last decades of the nineteenth century, Taft's interpretation of the Act quickly transformed it into an effective instrument for curbing organized labor.[169] So long as labor actions affected interstate commerce, the Sherman Act essentially authorized federal courts to invoke common law doctrines to regulate combinations of workingmen. The statute empowered federal judges to prohibit what they regarded as socially undesirable labor conspiracies.

Taft had long advocated for the view that the common law forbade secondary boycotts. In 1889, in *Moores & Co. v. Bricklayers' Union*, Taft considered a case in which the Bricklayers' Union was engaged in a labor dispute with the firm of Parker Brothers. The Union demanded that Parker Brothers "reinstate one apprentice . . . and discharge another." When Parker Brothers refused, the Union declared a boycott, refusing to work with the materials of any firm that supplied materials to Parker Brothers. When Moores & Co. continued to supply lime to Parker Brothers, the Union decreed that its members, who comprised "nine-five per cent. of the building trade" in Cincinnati, should refuse to work on any job using lime from Moores & Co. The company promptly brought suit "to recover damages for loss occasioned" to their business "by a wrongful and malicious conspiracy" of the Union. The trial resulted in a verdict of $2,250 for Moores & Co.[170]

Using reasoning that explicitly invoked the image of a "normally" functioning market, Taft concluded that secondary boycotts of this kind were actionable under the common law.

> The normal operation of competition in trade is the keeping away or getting away patronage from rivals by inducements offered to the trading public. The normal operation of the right to labor is the securing of better terms by refusing to contract to labor except on such terms. . . . If the workmen of an employer refuse to work for him except on better terms at a time when their withdrawal will cause great loss to him, and they intentionally inflict such loss to coerce him to come to their terms, they are bona fide exercising their lawful right to dispose of their labor for the purpose of lawful gain. But the dealings between Parker Bros. and their material men, or between such material men and their customers, had not the remotest natural connection, either with defendants' wages or their other terms of employment. There was no competition or possible contractual relation between plaintiffs and defendants, where their interests were naturally opposed. The right of the plaintiffs to sell their material was not one which, in its exercise, brought them into legitimate conflict with the right of defendants to dispose of their labor as they chose. The conflict was brought about by the effort of defendants to use plaintiffs' right of trade to injure Parker Bros. and upon failure of this, to use plaintiffs' customers' right of trade to injure plaintiffs. Such effort cannot be in the bona fide exercise of trade, is without just cause, and is, therefore, malicious. The immediate motive of defendants here was to show to the building world what punishment and disaster necessarily followed

a defiance of their demands. The remote motive of wishing to better their condition by the power so acquired, will not, as we think we have shown, make any legal justification for defendants' acts. . . . We are of opinion that even if acts of the character and with the intent shown in this case, are not actionable when done by individuals, they become so when they are the result of combination, because it is clear that the terrorizing of a community by threats of exclusive dealing in order to deprive one obnoxious member of means of sustenance will become both dangerous and oppressive.[171]

The Bricklayers' Union refused to work with the lime of Moores & Co. to pressure the latter to encourage Parker Brothers to settle favorably with the Union. It is therefore plain that the Union had an entirely self-interested justification for boycotting Moores & Co.[172] Yet in Taft's view this justification was too "remote" to constitute a legal excuse for the injury inflicted upon Moores & Co. The question, of course, is why this might be so.

In 1900, as chief justice of Massachusetts, Holmes had in *Plant v. Woods* considered a case in which a union headquartered in Baltimore had peacefully notified employers of members of a rival union (headquartered in Lafayette) that the employers could expect "strikes and boycotts" if they did not either fire members of the Lafayette union or induce them to join the Baltimore union. All of Holmes's colleagues on the Massachusetts Supreme Judicial Court held that the actions of the defendant Baltimore union were "without justification" and hence "malicious and unlawful." "The necessity that the [members of the Lafayette union] should join this association is not so great, nor its relation to the rights of the defendants, as compared with the right of the [members of the Lafayette union] to be free from molestation, such as to bring the acts of the defendant under the shelter of the principles of trade competition."[173]

Holmes dissented. He conceded that the purpose of the Baltimore union "was not directly concerned with wages. It was one degree more remote. The immediate object and motive was to strengthen the defendants' society as a preliminary and means to enable it to make a better fight on questions of wages or other matters of clashing interests." Yet Holmes did not believe that it was properly his judicial function to second-guess the necessity of actions that plainly served the economic interests of a union, however indirectly: "I differ from my Brethren in thinking that the threats were as lawful for this preliminary purpose as for the final one to which strengthening the union was a means. I think that unity of organization is necessary to make the contest of labor effectual, and that societies of laborers lawfully may employ in their preparation the means which they might use in the final contest. . . . I think it lawful for a body of workmen to try by combination to get more than they now are getting, although they do it at the expense of their fellows, and to that end to strengthen their union by the boycott and the strike."[174]

The contrast between *Moores & Co.* and *Woods* illustrates the essential difference between Taft and Holmes. Holmes, who had brilliantly demonstrated in *Privilege, Malice, and Intent* that limitations on the self-interested economic actions of labor unions were at root judgments of legislative policy, insisted on judicial modesty in seeking to control what was essentially a Darwinian struggle for economic power. But Taft experienced no such hesitation. He believed it necessary and proper for courts to use common law principles to prohibit secondary boycotts because he regarded them as "both dangerous and oppressive." They were a vehicle for "terrorizing" a community.[175]

Underlying Taft's conclusion lay a puzzle. Everyone agreed that individuals were free to do business with whomever they chose. Why then should a peaceful boycott, which involves nothing more than the simple refusal to do business, be stigmatized as illegal?[176] In Taft's eyes, the answer was that boycotts were "combinations" to inflict harm that were without legal justification and hence illegal conspiracies. But this reasoning was circular. Boycotts were obviously undertaken to improve the bargaining position of unions. Why did this not constitute a legal justification? Why were the benefits of a boycott too "remote" to justify the boycott?

One possible answer is that labor boycotts were proving all too successful in the waning years of the nineteenth century. In the 1880s, organizations like the Knights of Labor began to deploy boycotts as a powerful tactic in the ongoing economic struggle between capital and labor.[177] The spectacular effectiveness of the tactic aroused fierce moral, political, and legal opposition.[178] William Graham Sumner, for example, whom Taft noted "had more effect on me mentally than any man with whom I came in contact either at college or at school,"[179] condemned the boycott as a "monstrous" innovation.

> The boycott consists in cutting a man out of the organization of society. If a man can be so extruded from human society, without process of law, that he cannot buy or sell, hire, let, beg, borrow, lend, employ or be employed, what becomes of the security of life, liberty, or property? Of course, no such result could be brought about unless the boycotters could bring terrorism to bear on the whole community, including, at last, jurors, judges, and witnesses, to force people who are not parties to the quarrel to depart from the legal and peaceful enjoyment of their own will and pleasure to take part in the boycott.[180]

The future educator Sherman Thacher summarized public opposition to the boycott in this way: "Just what the boycott means is this: Do whatever we demand or we will injure you in every possible way. ... The threats have been made by a vast secret organization of unknown power. ... To grant any such power would mean the overthrow of society for a class in society. ... It is essentially inhuman as it is un-American."[181] Taft succinctly restated these views in his inaugural address as president. "The secondary boycott," he asserted, "is an instrument of tyranny, and ought not to be made legitimate."[182]

After the enactment of the Sherman Act in 1890, Taft held on the Sixth Circuit that secondary boycotts were proscribed by the new anti-trust statute because they were unlawful under the common law. In 1894, in *Thomas v. Cincinnati, N.O. & T.P. Railway Co.*, Taft considered a boycott called by Eugene Debs's American Railway Union ("ARU") against the Pullman Palace Car Company. The Pullman Company was engaged in a dispute with its employees about the payment of wages. Members of the ARU resolved to support Pullman's

Labor & the Construction of the National Market

employees by refusing to work for any railroad that used Pullman cars. Citing his own opinion in *Moores & Co.*, Taft concluded that the purpose of the ARU strike was unlawful because "it was a boycott."

> The employees of the railway companies had no grievance against their employers. Handling and hauling Pullman cars did not render their services any more burdensome. They had no complaint against the use of Pullman cars as cars. They came into no natural relation with Pullman in handling the cars. He paid them no wages. He did not regulate their hours, or in any way determine their services. Simply to injure him in his business, they were incited and encouraged to compel the railway companies to withdraw custom from him by threats of quitting their service, and actually quitting their service. This inflicted an injury on the companies that was very great, and it was unlawful, because it was without lawful excuse. All the employees had the right to quit their employment, but they had no right to combine to quit in order thereby to compel their employer to withdraw from a mutually profitable relation with a third person for the purpose of injuring that third person, when the relation thus sought to be broken had no effect whatever on the character or reward of their service. It is the motive for quitting, and the end sought thereby, that makes the injury inflicted unlawful, and the combination by which it is effected, an unlawful conspiracy. The distinction between an ordinary lawful and peaceable strike entered upon to obtain concessions in the terms of the strikers' employment and a boycott is not a fanciful one, or one which needs the power of fine distinction to determine which is which. Every laboring man recognizes the one or the other as quickly as the lawyer or the judge. The combination under discussion was a boycott. It was so termed by Debs, Phelan, and all engaged in it. Boycotts, though unaccompanied by violence or intimidation, have been pronounced unlawful in every state of the United States where the question has arisen, unless it be in Minnesota; and they are held to be unlawful in England.[183]

Taft held that because the ARU strike was improper under common law, it also constituted an unlawful "conspiracy in restraint of trade" under the newly enacted Sherman Act.[184]

When he ran for president, Taft was forced to account for his labor decisions. He stressed that he had striven to elucidate "with all the clearness of which I was capable, the distinction between the strike and boycott."[185] That distinction, it turned out, expressed a particular vision of how "normal" markets should function.[186] As Taft would later explain: "A secondary boycott has such possibilities in the way of injuring the whole community, of bringing into contests that are none of their own making so many indifferent and innocent persons, that ethics and law and public policy all require the recognition of the distinction which makes lawful the combination of working-men against employers in their natural controversies over wages and terms of employment, but condemns the use of combination by either party to compel third persons against their will to come into the fight."[187]

The central point for Taft was that law should, to the extent feasible, segregate the parties to a labor dispute "from the rest of the community," so that individual companies and unions could engage in tests of economic strength while neutral economic actors could remain insulated from the economic fall-out.[188] Secondary boycotts were illegitimate because they violated this principle of compartmentalization. Secondary boycotts escalated industrial disagreements so that they affected the entire market and hence harmed innocent third parties. They were thus, as the employers at Wilson's first Industrial Conference would collectively assert in 1919, "indefensible, anti-social, and immoral."[189]

Taft's view was officially endorsed by the Court in 1921 in *Duplex Printing Press Co. v. Deering*. Speaking through Pitney, the Court enjoined the International Association of Machinists ("IAM") from using a boycott to pressure a manufacturer of printing presses that had insisted on running an open shop. The IAM had warned the manufacturer's "customers that it would be better for them not to purchase, or, having purchased, not to install, presses made by complainant, and threatening them with loss should they do so." This was a forbidden "secondary boycott," Pitney said, because it was "a combination not merely to refrain from dealing with complainant, or to advise or by peaceful means persuade complainant's customers to refrain ('primary boycott'), but to exercise coercive pressure upon such customers, actual or prospective, in order to cause them to withhold or withdraw patronage from complainant through fear of loss or damage to themselves should they deal with it."[190]

Secondary boycotts of this kind were prohibited by the Sherman Act even if they consisted entirely of "peaceable persuasion," and even if the refusal to deal with customers of the manufacturer was for the purpose of attaining "some object beneficial" to the union. In essence, said Pitney, the object of a secondary boycott was to threaten "to inflict damage upon the immediate employer, between whom and his employees no dispute exists, in order to bring him against his will into a concerted plan to inflict damage upon another employer who is in dispute with his employees."[191] Even if workingmen were legally entitled to use strikes to inflict deliberate harm on their own employers to better their own working conditions, they were not legally justified in seeking to attain this same end by deliberately inflicting harm on neutral third parties.

The Sherman Act condemned secondary boycotts as malicious and without justification because, as Pitney put it pithily, such boycotts threatened "a general class war."[192] The Court feared that the involvement of "neutrals" in secondary boycotts would escalate "industrial war to a point one degree removed from the employer–employee relation"; the Court resolved to use the Sherman Act to confine industrial struggles within "close limits."[193] This was a policy choice. *Duplex Printing Press* was a hard blow to organized labor, for boycotts had long been one of its most important and effective weapons.[194] It was surely no accident that the Court embraced a view of properly functioning markets in which organized labor was decisively disadvantaged.

The boundary between permissible strikes and impermissible boycotts was far from clear.[195] "No part of the law is in a more formless or chaotic condition than the law of boycotts," observed Sayre. "[A]mong judges there is utter failure to agree how to draw the line between the primary and secondary boycott."[196] The issue

Labor & the Construction of the National Market

would come to a head for the Taft Court in 1927 in the pivotal and inflammatory case of *Bedford Cut Stone Co. v. Journeymen Stone Cutters' Ass'n*,[197] which would quickly earn a reputation as the Taft Court's "most extreme anti-organized labor decision."[198]

In *Bedford Cut Stone*, members of the Journeymen Stone Cutters' Association of North America refused to work on limestone that had been quarried and (at least) partially fabricated by certain corporations in Indiana. The Association had a membership of about 5,000 workers, "divided into over 150 local unions, located in various states and in Canada."[199] The Indiana corporations shipped about 70 percent of all cut stone in the country;[200] and about 75 percent of their product was sent to out-of-state markets.[201] In 1921, the corporations, as part of the general postwar movement toward the open shop, collectively refused to renew contracts with the Association and instead insisted upon creating a company union. The Association struck. It invoked a provision in its rules forbidding union members from working on "unfair" stone, meaning any "stone 'that has been started – planed, turned, cut, or semifinished – by men working in opposition to our organization.'"[202]

"The rule requiring members to refrain from working on 'unfair' stone was persistently adhered to and effectively enforced against [the corporations'] product, in a large number of cities and in many states. The evidence shows many instances of interference with the use of [the corporations'] stone by interstate customers, and expressions of apprehension on the part of such customers of labor troubles if they purchased the stone."[203] The corporations brought suit in federal court to enjoin the enforcement of the union rule against working unfair stone, claiming that the rule created a secondary boycott that was illegal under the Sherman Act.

The refusal of stonecutters throughout the United States to work on the corporations' unfair stone was entirely peaceful. "It does not appear that the quarrying of stone, or sawing it into blocks, or the transportation of it, or setting it in the buildings, or any other building operation, was sought to be interfered with, and no actual or threatened violence appears, no picketing, no boycott, and nothing of that character."[204] The question was thus cleanly posed whether members of a union could refuse to work on stone produced by corporations that were trying to break their own union.

District Judge Albert Barnes Anderson, whose record was "not one of squeamishness in granting labor injunctions,"[205] refused to enjoin the implementation of the union's rule, and his decision was affirmed by a unanimous panel of the Seventh Circuit. The union was within its "rights to induce members of [its] craft to refrain from further cutting upon stone which had before been partly cut by nonunion labor," the panel declared, "notwithstanding such refusal might have tended in some degree to discourage builders from specifying appellants' stone, and thus to reduce the quantity of their product which would enter interstate commerce." Speaking for himself alone, Judge Samuel Alschuler also reasoned that union members refused to work on the unfair stone only after it had come to rest subsequent to its interstate journey, so that under the holdings of *Coronado*

I and *Herkert*, "interstate commerce within the purview of the statute is not here involved." Alschuler also noted the absence of evidence "of any purpose to restrain commerce."[206] He therefore concluded that federal courts were without jurisdiction under the Sherman Act to enjoin the Association's work stoppages.

Bedford Cut Stone was argued at the Court on January 18, 1927. Four days later, the Court discussed the case in conference. In a "sharp difference of opinion,"[207] Holmes, Brandeis, Sanford, and Stone voted to affirm the Seventh Circuit,[208] whereas the remaining five justices voted to reverse. Although Taft assigned the opinion to Sutherland, he nevertheless retained an intense personal interest in the case. Two days after conference, Taft made a note to himself to "get up" his opinions in *Moores & Co.* and *Thomas* "for Sandford [sic] and for George Sutherland."[209] He wrote, and then scrapped, a four-page memorandum to Sanford,[210] which the next day he rewrote as an extended seven-page argument to the effect that the outcome in *Bedford Cut Stone* was determined by *Duplex Printing Press*.

In his discussion, Taft explained in detail his old opinions in *Moores & Co.* and *Thomas*.[211] Sanford was apparently concerned "that equity could not enjoin men from quitting work upon material which had been partially prepared by non-union manufacturers."[212] Taft agreed that equity could not compel men to work, but he used his earlier opinions to show that equity could enjoin a union, or the officers of a union, from directing members "to strike for the purpose of enforcing the boycott."[213] He then argued that in *Duplex Printing Press* the Court had conclusively held that a strike against materials was an illegal secondary boycott for purposes of federal anti-trust law.

Taft concluded his long memorandum with a passionate plea: "If we were to hold that 5,000 men constituting the great bulk of all the stone cutters of the United States may by refusing to work material shipped to the great centers of building throughout the country, compel the shipper either to give up his sales, or to subject himself to the control of the union, we should be imposing on interstate trade a burden that would be intolerable, and every National labor union could at once adopt it as a means of establishing a closed shop instead of an open shop in every center of business activity in the country. I beg of you to think this over."[214] Taft sent a copy of his Sanford memorandum to Sutherland, commenting: "I am doing what I can to convince Sanford that he is very much out of plumb in respect to the Bedford Stone Company" case.[215]

Taft's memorandum is most illuminating. In public, Taft had long advocated that the Sherman Act be interpreted to construct "normal" markets, which meant markets that would confine "industrial warfare"[216] to discrete, compartmentalized controversies between individual employers and their employees.[217] This was a pragmatic use of law,[218] designed to minimize the possibility that industrial conflicts might escalate into a "class war"[219] that would paralyze interstate commerce. Yet it was also readily foreseeable that concentrated capital in large firms would render these restrictions decisively disadvantageous to labor. As the facts of *Bedford Cut Stone* illustrated, labor could exert effective market power only when it could unite across firms.

Labor & the Construction of the National Market

Taft's memorandum to Sanford surfaces the extent to which crude considerations of class advantage were also driving Taft's aversion to secondary boycotts. At root, Taft feared union control and the closed shop.[220] He sought to protect "the indispensable element of individual initiative and enterprise" upon which he believed that economic progress depended.[221] Although Taft in 1919 had well understood that "[i]njunctions in labor troubles are merely the emergency brakes for rare use and increase of sudden danger,"[222] and although in *Coronado* he may have sought to substitute damage actions for injunctions, nevertheless by the latter half of the decade Taft was fully on board with using the Sherman Act to sustain comprehensive federal equitable control of labor controversies. An important goal of this control was to prevent union domination.

At the Court's conference on *Bedford Cut Stone*, Brandeis reiterated arguments he had originally asserted in dissent in *Duplex Printing Press* in 1921, to the effect that the common law did not regard union refusals to work on nonunion materials as impermissible secondary boycotts.[223] These arguments apparently unsettled Stone. Taft therefore suggested to Sutherland that "you might set your Law Clerk to looking up other cases on the common law question" raised by Brandeis's *Duplex Printing Press* dissent. "Sanford seemed to be more troubled about the remedy in equity," Taft observed, "while Stone seemed to be troubled by the cases that Brandeis insisted fixed the common law. Both of them of course are wide of the mark, but we have to approach them according to their difficulties.... I don't think we ought to let up in seeking to have them take the proper view." "I am inclined to think that it is better not to have the case rushed through," Taft added, "but to give time enough to let us discuss with these people carefully what the issues are – in other words, to let the matter grow cold and take it up again. I suppose Brandeis has his dissenting opinion already drafted. I never have seen him in such a state of rejoicing after getting Sanford and Stone apparently into his army and into his plan of weakening the Court by boring from within."[224]

The next day, Taft wrote Stone to emphasize the need for judicial unity and consistency. "I am quite anxious," Taft said, "as I'm sure we all are, that the continuity and weight of our opinions on important questions of law should not be broken any more than we can help by dissents." Taking a not-so subtle jab at Brandeis, and playing on Stone's insecurity as a recently seated justice, Taft continued:

> Of course there are some who have deep convictions on the subject of the law governing the relations between employer and employee, whether it involves interstate commerce or not, and I suppose it is to be expected that in their attitude of protest in the past they should find distinctions enabling them to continue their attitude in cases presenting what are substantially the same issues, but with respect to those Judges who have come into the Court since these decisions were rendered, I am sure it is not their purpose to depart from what has been declared to be accepted law.[225]

Taft argued that *Duplex Printing Press* had settled the question of whether a union's refusal to work with nonunion materials was an impermissible secondary boycott under the Sherman Act, regardless of whether some state courts, like those of New York, California, or North Carolina, had decided that as a matter of common law such refusals were legal.[226] "Whatever you might think of this issue, freed from authority as a matter of common law, it here is affected by the Anti Trust law and the construction put upon it by us with reference to what constitutes a burden or restraint of interstate commerce, and I think it is impossible to read Pitney's opinion in the Duplex case without perceiving that the majority of the Court took the attitude" that the refusal to work on nonunion materials was impermissible under the Sherman Act.[227] "I hope you will look into this matter with care," Taft added, "because differences of the court, while they must sometimes occur, don't help the weight of its judgment."[228]

Stone thanked Taft for his letter, promising to "go over the whole matter afresh, reading particularly the citations which you give in your letter." Evidently taken aback and on the defensive, Stone added:

> I, of course, appreciate the importance of avoiding dissents which do not seem necessary, and I am sure that you know me well enough now to know that I am not disposed to be opinionated or over "cocky" about the opinions which I do hold. My vote should not be taken to have the finality which perhaps it appeared to have. It was dictated by the fear that our decision in its practical operation, if followed, would preclude all strikes against non-union material under all circumstances except within the state of origin. I dislike to see the Court take this stand without facing squarely the facts. Moreover, it seemed to me that this case was controlled by that part of Mr. Justice Sutherland's case, Industrial Ass'n v. United States, which deals with plaster produced outside the state of California and shipped into California. Although the reasons assigned for the result in that case did not seem to me valid as they amounted practically to a revival of the reasoning in the now discredited sugar refining case, I agreed with the result.[229]

Taft forwarded his correspondence with Stone to Sutherland "to keep you advised of his attitude of mind."[230]

Sutherland did not retain his case files, so we have no record of preliminary drafts of his opinion in *Bedford Cut Stone*. But we do have a letter Taft sent him on March 11 that characterizes his draft opinion "admirable." Taft suggested, however, that Sutherland's manuscript did not "quite meet the second phase of Stone's difficulties."

> Of course you do in your general description of the findings and conclusions in the Duplex case, but Stone's second difficulty was that a strike against material was not actionable at common law, and that those cases led him to think, therefore, that this did not present a case under the Anti Trust law. The truth is, as you can see by reading Brandeis' opinion, that this was one of the chief arguments against the conclusion reached in the Duplex case, and I think it would add force to what you have to say in the Duplex case if you were to insert something like the enclosed. . . . [I]f you put this in, I think I would cut down your reference to the Thomas case and the quotation therefrom to a mere citation of it among other

cases. This is only a suggestion, but I am anxious to meet what will trouble Stone, and I think, too, will trouble Sanford. ... Stone said to me that he hoped you would not wish to bring the opinion up for announcement until he had another week in which to examine it, and this will give you an opportunity to change it yourself, if you think it wise.[231]

It seems that Taft had drafted suggested language, no longer available to us, stressing that *Duplex Printing Press* had itself already addressed and settled the question whether a union's refusal to work on nonunion goods was an impermissible secondary boycott under the Sherman Act. Perhaps in his original draft Sutherland had emphasized Taft's 1894 Circuit Court opinion in *Thomas* to establish that the Sherman Act prohibited secondary boycotts disallowed by the common law.[232] All we can say for certain is that in the end Sutherland's published opinion handled the question by emphasizing the precedent of *Duplex Printing Press*, even though in the process Sutherland paid elaborate homage to Taft by citing three of his old labor opinions:

> In cases arising outside the Anti-Trust Act, involving strikes like those here under review against so-called unfair products, there is a sharp conflict of opinion. On the one hand, it is said that such a strike is justified on the ground of self-interest; that the injury to the producer is inflicted, not maliciously, but in self-defense; that the refusal of the producer to deal with the union and to observe its standards threatens the interest of all its members and the members of the affiliated locals; and that a strike against the unfair material is a mere recognition of this unity of interest, and in refusing to work on such material the union is only refusing to aid in its own destruction. The opposite view is illustrated by such cases as Toledo, etc., Ry. Co. (C. C.) 54 F. 730; Thomas v. Cincinnati, etc. Ry. Co. (C. C.) 62 F. 803, 817; Moores v. Bricklayers' Union, 23 Wkly. Law Bul. (Ohio) 48 (affirmed by the Supreme Court of Ohio without opinion, 51 Ohio St. 605); Burnham v. Dowd, 217 Mass. 351; Purvis v. United Brotherhood, 214 Pa. 348; Booth & Bro. v. Burgess, 72 N. J. Eq. 181; Piano & Organ Workers v. P. & O. Supply Co., 124 Ill. App. 353.
> But with this conflict we have no concern in the present case. The question which it involves was presented and considered in the Duplex Co. Case, as the prevailing and the dissenting opinions show; and there it was plainly held that the point had no bearing upon the enforcement of the Anti-Trust Act, and that, since complainant had a clear right to an injunction under that act as amended by the Clayton Act, it was "unnecessary to consider whether a like result would follow under the common law or local statutes."[233]

It is no small irony that, apparently at Taft's urging, Sutherland emphasized the distinction between federal anti-trust legislation and the very common law doctrine that defined impermissible labor combinations which Taft himself had imported into federal anti-trust jurisprudence. Sutherland held that it did not matter whether the common law prohibited union refusals to work on nonunion products because the Sherman Act independently required that such combinations be prohibited. The question was therefore why federal anti-trust legislation, independent of the common law, prohibited union members from refusing to work on nonunion products in circumstances like those at issue in *Bedford Cut Stone*. Sutherland's opinion does not discuss this question. It neither cites evidence of congressional intent, nor points to specific statutory language, nor adduces general reasons of policy. Sutherland in fact fails to offer any explanation at all.

The opinion announced by Sutherland on April 11[234] stresses only the blunt precedential authority of *Duplex Printing Press*: "With a few changes in respect of the product involved, dates, names and incidents, which would have no effect upon the principles established, the opinion in *Duplex Co. v. Deering*, might serve as an opinion in this case." The Association was guilty of an illegal "secondary boycott," Sutherland argued, because refusing to work on nonunion stone "had no purpose other than that of coercing or inducing the local employers to refrain from purchasing" limestone produced by the Indiana corporations. Sutherland conceded that "the product against which the strikes were directed, it is true, had come to rest in the respective localities to which it had been shipped, so that it had ceased to be a subject of interstate commerce." But the relevant precedents were not *Coronado I* or *Herkert*, but instead *Coronado II*, because the purpose of the strikers was to restrain "the interstate sale and shipment of the commodity." "In the present case, ... the strikes were directed against the use of the product in other states, with the immediate purpose and necessary effect of restraining future sales and shipments in interstate commerce."[235] The utter, meaningless plasticity of *Coronado II*'s intent standard was painfully manifest.

Taft's intense lobbying paid off, in the sense that Sanford wrote separately to concur "upon the controlling authority of *Duplex Co. v. Deering*, which, as applied to the ultimate question in this case, I am unable to distinguish."[236] And Stone also concurred "for that reason alone," noting that "as an original proposition" he would not have interpreted the Sherman Act from prohibiting "a labor union from peaceably refusing to work upon material produced by non-union labor or by a rival union, even though interstate commerce were affected. In light of the policy adopted by Congress in the Clayton Act, with respect to organized labor, and in the light of *Standard Oil Co. v. United States* ... I should not have thought that such action as is now complained of was to be regarded as an unreasonable and therefore prohibited restraint of trade."[237] Taft wrote his son that both Sanford and Stone concurred "grudgingly, Stone with a kind of kickback that will make nobody happy. I am not always sure how experience as the head of a Law School and supervising a Law Journal helps in making a first class Judge. Stone is a good Judge, but he will need longer experience, but he is well fitted to his task."[238]

Brandeis dissented, authoring what Taft characterized as "one of his meanest opinions,"[239] but which was nevertheless joined by Holmes, who regarded the dissent as "Ripping – A-1."[240] As early as 1913 Brandeis had declared that "[a] proper application of the anti-trust law would permit of a 'reasonable' restraint of trade by the unions in the promotion of their proper interests. What is reasonable is to be determined by public policy. Public policy, in turn, will not declare that labor shall be prohibited from taking whatever action may prove to be essential to the preservation of its rights, the legitimate advancement of its cause."[241] In *Bedford Cut Stone*, Brandeis argued that a union's refusal to work on unfair stone was "a reasonable" restraint on trade and hence permissible under the Sherman Act.[242]

Brandeis noted that the local stonecutters unions were, standing alone, "weak"; they could not counteract the power of the Indiana corporations except by combining into a national union capable of coordinating stonecutters throughout the country.[243] The refusal of the Association to work on unfair stone, therefore, should be conceptualized simply as the refusal of a union to work on the product of an employer with whom it was in serious conflict.[244]

> The manner in which the journeymen's unions acted was also clearly legal. The combination complained of is the co-operation of persons wholly of the same craft, united in a national union, solely for self-protection. No outsider – be he quarrier, dealer, builder, or laborer – was a party to the combination. No purpose was to be subserved except to promote the trade interests of members of the Journeymen's Association. There was no attempt by the unions to boycott the plaintiffs. There was no attempt to seek the aid of members of any other craft, by a sympathetic strike or otherwise. The contest was not a class struggle. It was a struggle between particular employers and their employees.[245]

In Brandeis's view, this clearly distinguished *Bedford Cut Stone* from *Duplex Printing Press*:

> The combination there condemned was not, as here, the co-operation for self-protection only of men in a single craft. It was an effort to win by invoking the aid of others, both organized and unorganized, not concerned in the trade dispute. The conduct there condemned was not, as here, a mere refusal to finish particular work begun "by men working in opposition to" the union. It was the institution of a general boycott, not only of the business of the employer, but of the businesses of all who should participate in the marketing, installation, or exhibition of its product. The conduct there condemned was not, as here, action taken for self-protection against an opposing union installed by employers to destroy the regular union with which they long had had contracts.... The serious question on which the court divided in the Duplex Case was not whether the restraint imposed was reasonable. It was whether the Clayton Act had forbidden federal courts to issue an injunction in that class of cases.[246]

Brandeis concluded his dissent with a sentence that invoked the Thirteenth Amendment and that served, and that was meant to serve, as a clarion call to organized labor: "If, on the undisputed facts of this case, refusal to work can be enjoined, Congress created by the Sherman Law and the Clayton Act an instrument for imposing restraints upon labor which reminds one of involuntary servitude."[247] On the very day that the Court's decision was announced, Brandeis wrote Frankfurter that "[i]f anything can awaken Trade Unionists from their lethargy, this should. And perhaps it needs a jolt of this kind to arouse them in this era of friendly cooperation."[248] Three days later he reiterated his "hope that our new Dred Scott decision will help another cause in a Sumter way."[249]

Frankfurter took up the cudgel and two weeks later published *"Reminds of Involuntary Servitude"* in the *New Republic*.[250] It began with Brandeis's theme that "Labor has now for long been subdued by the siren propaganda of 'prosperity.' A severe jolt was needed to awaken the more innocent even of trade unionists from the illusions of the Civic Federation, of dinners with the mighty, of all the prattle of 'identity of interest.' And the jolt was administered on April 11 by the Supreme Court in its decision in the Bedford Cut Stone case." "It is idle to seek an explanation for the division of the Supreme Court Justices ... in any specific authority," Frankfurter explained. "The opinion of the majority reflects the outlook on economic policy and on the coercive function of law in industrial conflicts entertained by the men who compose the majority – Sutherland, Taft, Van Devanter, McReynolds, and Butler. Law did not compel the views of these men in this case; their views made the law."[251]

Frankfurter charged that although the Court was prepared to acknowledge "the legitimacy of trade unions in the abstract," it was nevertheless determined "to deny workers that unity of organization which is necessary to make the contest of labor effectual."[252] The decision thus "commits a grave wrong against labor," and "[i]t is for labor to make reply to this doctrine," perhaps "through political action."[253]

Press coverage of the decision was largely muted. The Court's opinion was characterized as "a major victory for the pro-Sutherland or anti-Brandeis viewpoint"[254] which established "no new principle"[255] and which "will pretty well represent the common sense view of the people of the United States."[256] "Under prosperity and high wages," it was noted, "labor unions are gradually losing power, just as they gradually gained power in the last century. An important milestone in labor's downhill journey is last Monday's decision by the United States Supreme Court" in *Bedford Cut Stone*.[257]

Sutherland's facile conclusion that the union intended to restrain interstate commerce in the manner prohibited by *Coronado II*,[258] in stark contrast to his refusal to find any such intent with regard to employers in his own recent opinion in *Industrial Association*,[259] "led many men to the conclusion that strikes in interstate commerce are now practically illegal, and will be enjoined by the courts and that unless legislative relief is forthcoming from Congress, the organization of labor in interstate commerce is practically without value."[260] In the eyes of the *New York Herald Tribune*, this was a very good thing. "The interstate commerce power is a special and formidable barrier against sympathetic strikes and secondary boycotts," the paper opined. "We have outgrown devices like the ... secondary boycott through which minorities seek to hold up the public and even terrorize the nation. The Supreme Court's latest decision fortifies the existing prohibitions against such violations of the security of commerce and the peace of the state."[261]

In effect, *Bedford Cut Stone* made it virtually impossible for "national trade unions" to "protect the standards they have achieved against regional attacks which organized groups of employers can successfully wage."[262] This was a mortal thrust, and it galvanized organized labor.[263] Marveling at the reaction, the prominent labor

Labor & the Construction of the National Market

scholar Edwin Witte noted that "[a]fter having remained dormant for several years, the ever-smouldering volcano of resentment which organized labor entertains against courts over the use of injunctions in labor disputes has suddenly again burst forth into glaring flame."[264]

William Green, president of the AFL, announced that the federation would seek to exempt trade unions from the reach of the Sherman Anti-Trust Act, whose application "to labor and labor organizations as thus interpreted by the Supreme Court, renders the condition of working people to the point where it approximates involuntary servitude. ... Compulsion in either giving or withholding service is contrary to the ideals of American citizenship."[265] "In plain terms," Green said, "hundreds of men are being forced to work, by order of the Court, against their will and in spite of their protest. The Court's order serves to strip them of the use of their economic strength, the only power workingmen may exercise as a means of protection against injustice and oppression. It means forced labor in a free country."[266] Labor was put in essentially the same position as in Mussolini's recently released Charter of Labor for fascist Italy.[267]

Because the decision "denies labor one of its strongest weapons, the direct boycott,"[268] organized labor fought back as though "the very future of effective trade unionism in the United States of America" was at stake.[269] "The decision has thoroughly aroused organized labor to the danger of being completely stopped by courts from carrying on their activities in a manner which has until now been considered in full accordance with the law of the land."[270] "It looks," Brandeis wrote Frankfurter, "as if the A.F. of L. were really alive to the danger."[271]

Advocates of labor took their cue from Brandeis's eloquent dissent. "Justice Brandeis ... has armed free men in their fight against the court's opinion," declared the *Stone Cutters Journal*.[272] "Justice Brandeis warns workers what is in store for them. He says it will enslave them; that it will take from them the right to elect under what conditions they will labor."[273] "Justice Brandeis has said the last word in his approach to an institution that is supposed to guard the liberties of citizens but which ... would enslave workers," declared the *Garment Worker*.[274] At the AFL national convention in October 1927, the Committee on Resolutions echoed Brandeis's rhetoric of involuntary slave labor:

> The sinister significance of the decision against the Journeymen Stonecutters' Union compels the most thoughtful attention. The fundamental difference between the free man and the slave is that the man who is free has the legal right to withhold his labor and to join with his fellows in applying the principle of mutual aid to improve conditions under which they live and work. The slave is a slave only because he is by law denied such rights.
>
> In the Journeymen Stonecutters' case the Supreme Court holds that under the circumstances presented in that case the law will not permit American workers to agree to withhold themselves from the service of the employer. Thus, the court has denied a very substantial portion of the essential rights the possession of which marks the free man from the serf and slave.[275]

From Taft's point of view, the rhetoric of involuntary servitude was seriously misplaced. Taft quite agreed that no court could issue a "mandatory injunction to compel the enforcement of personal service against either the employer or the employed,"[276] but, as he pointed out to Sanford, the court's injunction in *Bedford Cut Stone* applied to the union's enforcement of its own rules, not to individual workingmen.[277] So far as equity was concerned, individual workingmen were free to quit.[278] Judicial equitable power bound only the union.[279]

Ironically, however, this defense of *Bedford Cut Stone* depended precisely upon the individualism that Taft's own recognition of the "group system" had supposedly rendered obsolete.[280] Because modern concentrations of capital stripped individual workers of the freedom effectively to bargain for conditions of their own employment,[281] it was only through the combined force of a union that meaningful freedom could be underwritten.[282] Insofar as court decrees bound unions, therefore, they also undermined the only power that could actually be effectively exercised by workers.[283] The Court's injunction in *Bedford Cut Stone*, although addressed in formal terms only to the union, in fact compelled individual employees to work under conditions in respect of which the actuality of voluntary consent was impossible.

Brandeis understood this with great clarity. "Men are not free if dependent industrially upon the arbitrary will of another," he said. "Industrial liberty on the part of the worker cannot, therefore, exist if there be overweening industrial power. Some curb must be placed upon capitalistic combination. Nor will even this curb be effective unless the workers coöperate, as in trade unions. Control and coöperation are both essential to industrial liberty."[284] It was to this economic reality that Brandeis referred when in the context of secondary boycotts he called for courts to acquire "a better realization of the facts of industrial life."[285] The Taft Court's entrenched inability to appreciate this reality, its insistence on transforming into a criminal conspiracy the agreement to engage in behavior that would be perfectly legal if conducted by individuals, confirmed labor's belief that judges were prejudiced by their corporate backgrounds.[286] It cemented labor's characterization of the Court as speaking for those who sought to preserve the prerogatives of capital and not for the public interest or for the shared views of the American people. In labor's eyes, the Taft Court did not declare law, but instead imposed the class prejudices of the justices.

The outrage sparked by *Bedford Cut Stone* fueled the resurgence of militant labor resistance for which Brandeis longed.[287] The AFL Executive Council announced at the annual convention in October 1927, a full two years before the beginning of the Great Depression, that "in order to give the trade unions not only legal existence but the right to exercise their normal functions, two legislative remedies must be enacted: amendment of anti-trust and anti-combination legislation to prevent restriction of normal union activity ... and definition of the jurisdiction of equity courts. ... We shall submit to Congress legislative drafts and shall give these measures priority in our legislative efforts."[288]

Two resolutions were submitted to the convention, and each was unanimously adopted. The first argued that because "any continued vitality" of the Sherman Act "must result in the abolition of all trade Unions organized for mutual aid and protection of the working people," it was necessary to seek "the immediate repeal of the Sherman anti-combination law."[289] Speaking in favor of the resolution, Andrew Furuseth, longtime president of the International Seamen's Union, remarked that *Bedford Cut Stone* fell "like a whip on the scourged back." "Enforce the Sherman Anti-trust law in all its vigor," he said, "and there will be no conventions of the American Federation of Labor unless they meet in the cellar somewhere in secrecy."[290]

Although the AFL's effort to repeal the Sherman Act would prove futile, the second AFL resolution, which proposed "legislation to properly define and thus limit the equity power of the courts,"[291] ultimately led, through a fascinating and circuitous path, to the passage of the Norris-LaGuardia Act of 1932.[292] Three months after the convention, Green declared that judicial injunctions like those issued in *Bedford Cut Stone* are "a real grievance ... against which labor emphatically complains, smarting under a deep sense of wrong and injustice. Labor is determined to seek legislative redress."[293] "We did not at first consider the injunctions a serious problem," Green said, "but today we find ourselves hampered in our legitimate activities by the frequent and broadening use of the court injunction. The extent to which it is used now reduces working men and women to a condition of involuntary servitude. ... The point has been reached as in the Bedford cut stone case ... where workers are compelled to work against their will. ... This abuse must stop. We must rouse the American people to a realization of the situation and will take a more active part in the coming political contest in order to secure a remedy."[294]

Labor's renewed urgency to restrict labor injunctions originated in its opposition to *Bedford Cut Stone*, in which the Taft Court, in the guise of interpreting federal anti-trust legislation, had effectively assumed the customary prerogative of a common law court to distinguish proper from improper restraints on trade. In aspiring to speak for the shared mores of the American people, however, the Court unwittingly unleashed a backlash in which the Court would itself be discredited. The Norris-LaGuardia Act should be understood as a successful assault on the Court's authority to speak for American values. The legislation was a major step toward preparing the ground for the positive law of the federal administrative state.

Labor's struggle against the labor injunction would challenge an entrenched instrument of social control with roots stretching back to the last decades of the nineteenth century. These roots had been planted by Taft himself in his own pioneering decisions as a circuit judge. Uprooting them would prove no easy task, because the authority of a court sitting in equity was thought to epitomize the inherent power and majesty of the judicial branch. Labor's attack on the labor injunction was, in effect, an attack on the authority of the federal judiciary itself.

Notes

1. 27 NEW REPUBLIC 177 (1921).
2. 259 U.S. 344 (1922).
3. Robert Cushman, *Constitutional Law in 1924–25*, 20 AMERICAN POLITICAL SCIENCE REVIEW 80, 93 (1926).
4. *Mine Workers Case Is Important One*, HARTFORD COURANT (June 12, 1922), at 11. It was, said the *Wall Street Journal*, the "most important" decision "ever handed down by the court in labor and capital matters." *Liability of Unions*, WALL STREET JOURNAL (June 6, 1922), at 10.
5. *The American Taff Vale Case*, 114 THE NATION 736, 736 (1922).
6. *The Virginia-Pilot*, quoted in *Labor Unions Liable to Pay for Strike Damages*, 72 LITERARY DIGEST 8, 9 (June 17, 1922).
7. *Labor and the Supreme Court*, NEW YORK TIMES (June 7, 1922), at 15.
8. David Y. Thomas, *Blanket Liability for Labor Unions*, 16 CURRENT HISTORY 769, 769 (1922).
9. *Coronado Coal*, 259 U.S. at 412.
10. Thomas, *supra* note 8, at 769.
11. Draft Opinion of LDB, in ALEXANDER M. BICKEL, THE UNPUBLISHED OPINIONS OF MR. JUSTICE BRANDEIS: THE SUPREME COURT AT WORK 85 (Cambridge: Harvard University Press 1957).
12. Thomas, *supra* note 8, at 769.
13. Draft Opinion of LDB, *supra* note 11, at 86.
14. *Id.*
15. Thomas, *supra* note 8, at 770.
16. *Id.* In a brilliant unpublished dissent, Brandeis bitterly summarized these facts:

> Throughout these trying months the operators acted strictly within their legal rights. The unionists, on the other hand, had been lawless aggressors, violating grievously the laws of Arkansas .... To destroy a business is illegal. It is not illegal to lower the standard of working men's living or to destroy the union which aims to raise or maintain such a standard. A business is property; the law protects it .... A man's standard of living is not property; and the law does not protect by injunction or otherwise.... Such being the law every citizen should obey it; and the court must enforce it. It may be morally wrong to use legal processes, great financial resources and a high intelligence to lower miners' standards of living; but so long as the law sanctions it, economic force may not be repelled by physical force. If union members deem the law unwise or unjust, they may, like other American citizens, exercise their political right to change it by new legislation, and, if need be, by constitutional amendment. But no government may tolerate willful disobedience to its laws.

Draft Opinion of LDB, *supra* note 11, at 86–88.

17. *Coronado Coal*, 259 U.S. at 347. Also named as defendants were "27 local unions in District No. 21, and 65 individuals."
18. E. Merrick Dodd, Jr., *Dogma and Practice in the Law of Associations*, 42 HARVARD LAW REVIEW 977, 1000 (1929). *See* Note, 10 CALIFORNIA LAW REVIEW 506, 507–9 (1922).
19. Note, *The Coronado Coal Case*, 32 YALE LAW JOURNAL 59, 60 (1922). On the equity side of their jurisdiction, by contrast, courts had long used the concept of representative parties effectively to make unincorporated associations amenable to

lawsuits. *See* Wesley A. Sturges, *Unincorporated Associations as Parties to Actions*, 33 YALE LAW JOURNAL 383, 387 (1924); *Coronado Coal*, 259 U.S. at 387.
20. *The Coronado Mine Case*, 8 AMERICAN BAR ASSOCIATION JOURNAL 353 (1922). "Many unsuccessful attempts" had been made "to change the law so that unions could be sued." *Supreme Court Usurps Legislative Power*, WICHITA PLAINDEALER (June 22, 1922), at 1 (quoting the National Catholic Welfare Council). In 1920, for example, the *Wall Street Journal* editorialized that if the incoming Harding administration had any "backbone," the "repeal of the Clayton law, the incorporation of labor unions, and an enforced secret ballot for strike votes" would be "on the program of the coming session of Congress." *Some Simple Lessons*, WALL STREET JOURNAL (November 4, 1920), at 1. Yet legislative initiatives making unions suable had been successful in only a very few states, although, "on the other hand, statutes have been passed in a few jurisdictions expressly codifying the common-law rule to the effect that unincorporated associations may not bring an action in the association name." Note, *supra* note 19, at 61.
21. The debate is today most easily accessed in Louis D. Brandeis & Samuel Gompers, *The Incorporation of Trade Unions*, 1 GREEN BAG 2ND 306 (1998). The debate was originally recounted in *"No Thank You!" Says Gompers*, BOSTON DAILY GLOBE (December 5, 1902), at 4.
22. Brandeis & Gompers, *supra* note 21, at 306–7.
23. *Id.* at 312–14.
24. United Mine Workers of America v. Coronado Coal Co., 258 F. 829 (8th Cir. 1919).
25. *Coronada* [sic] *Coal Company vs. United Mine Workers of America*, 26 AMERICAN FEDERATIONIST 613, 615 (1919). This was because "the tendency of the employing interests today is to hold trade unions responsible financially for whatever alleged ill-advised or wrongful act any one of its members or sympathizers may commit, inadvertently or by design, on the theory that the trade union movement is obligated to discipline and to direct the conduct of its members. . . . Whenever an officer of an incorporated financial industrial or commercial enterprise exceeds the power specially delegated to him, the courts declare his act ultra-vires and the company is absolved from all responsibility. But when a labor man at a trade union meeting makes ill-advised utterances, even when such utterances are condemned by those in authority, then the union and its members may nevertheless be robbed of their funds and savings." *Coronado Coal Company vs. United Mine Workers*, in REPORT OF PROCEEDINGS OF THE THIRTY-NINTH ANNUAL CONVENTION OF THE AMERICAN FEDERATION OF LABOR 362 (Washington D.C.: Law Reporter Printing Co. 1919). *See* Matthew Woll, *Labor Menaced by Courts*, 26 AMERICAN FEDERATIONIST 511, 512 (1919) (The decision of the Eighth Circuit not only outlaws "the right to strike but also attacks the right of the workers to combine in order to deal collectively with their employers. . . . This decision must be reversed and if the United States Supreme Court fails to do so, then Congress must again be asked to put an end to the peculiarly warped opinions and judgments of our judiciary.").
26. A fourth issue was argued, which concerned the trial judge's potentially coercive charge to the jury, but in the end this issue was not discussed by the Court. *Coronado Coal*, 259 U.S. at 413. We know, however, that in Clarke's mind this issue was essential. JHC to WHT (n.d.) (Taft papers).
27. Brandeis would later tell Frankfurter that "Since I've been on Bench only one labor case well argued, Hughes' argument on first hearing of Coronado case."

The Taft Court

Brandeis-Frankfurter Conversations, at 306 (July 1922). At one point in the litigation, the UMW had also been represented by Democratic presidential candidate and New York Court of Appeals Judge Alton B. Parker. *See* Note, 9 VIRGINIA LAW REVIEW 52, 53 (1922).

28. WHT to Horace D. Taft (June 16, 1922) (Taft papers). *See* BICKEL, *supra* note 11, at 91.
29. WHT to Horace D. Taft (June 16, 1922) (Taft papers); WHT to JHC (January 1, 1922) (Taft papers).
30. WHT to Horace D. Taft (June 16, 1922) (Taft papers).
31. By the time of reargument Hughes had become secretary of state, and he was replaced by William A. Glasgow Jr., a prominent Philadelphia attorney who, like Hughes, was normally associated with corporate interests. *W.A. Glasgow Dies; Noted Attorney*, NEW YORK TIMES (March 15, 1930), at 14.
32. WHT to Horace D. Taft (June 16, 1922) (Taft papers).
33. Stanley I. Kutler, *Chief Justice Taft, Judicial Unanimity, and Labor: The Coronado Case*, 24 THE HISTORIAN 68 (1961).
34. *See supra* text at notes 21–23.
35. Draft Opinion of LDB, *supra* note 11, at 84. Brandeis's law clerk at the time was Dean Acheson. BICKEL, *supra* note 11, at 91–93. Acheson's first draft of Brandeis's dissent, dated January 1921, begins with the sentence: "I agree with the majority of the court that had the defendant association inflicted the damaged [sic] here sued for in the course of a conspiracy to restrain interstate commerce it would be liable under the terms of the Sherman Act." (Brandeis papers).
36. LOUIS D. BRANDEIS, BUSINESS – A PROFESSION 26 (Boston: Small, Maynard & Co. 1914).
37. "As the Court said in *Hammer v. Dagenhart*: 'The making of goods and the mining of coal are not commerce, nor does the fact that these things are to be afterwards shipped or used in interstate commerce, make their production a part thereof.'" Draft Opinion of LDB, *supra* note 11, at 85.
38. *Id.* at 89. *See* Note, *Labor Organizations and the Anti-Trust Laws*, 35 HARVARD LAW REVIEW 459, 460 n.4 (1922) ("If the distinction between commerce and manufacture set forth in the case of *United States v. E.C. Knight Co.* were accepted at face value to-day it would be hard to find a restraint on commerce.... The United Mine Workers have no connection with the coal industry aside from the mining operations and the restraint on labor supply is a step back of actual manufacture in the productive process.").
39. BICKEL, *supra* note 11, at 97. There is a note attached to Brandeis's draft opinions in *Coronado* that reads: "Revised M[ar]ch 26,/21; May 20/22; Revised May 23." It is not clear whether May 23 refers to 1922 or 1921. We know that Brandeis assented to Taft's opinion on May 28, 1922. LDB to WHT (May 28, 1922) (Taft papers).
40. We do not have much evidence of Taft's drafting process. On May 30, Taft, who was chair of the Memorial Commission that designed and built the Lincoln Memorial, presented the Memorial to the nation. *See Harding Dedicates Lincoln Memorial*, NEW YORK TIMES (May 31, 1922), at 3. The week before Taft had written his wife that "The arrangements for the Lincoln Memorial are pressing now and the preparations of my speech when I am trying to write an opinion in a great case is a great interruption." WHT to Helen Herron Taft (May 23, 1922) (Taft papers). In an undated letter to Taft

joining the *Coronado* opinion, *infra* note 41, Clarke wrote: "Permit me to congratulate you on your address to day. You rose to the occasion admirably. It was finely conceived & worded and delivered – and in striking contrast with some of the others which made me who hopes he is of the 'judicious' in such matters 'grieve.' You know I wouldn't flatter Neptune for his trident." JHC to WHT (n.d.) (Taft papers).

41. Kutler, *supra* note 33, at 74. On May 28, Brandeis wrote Taft to say that "Your memo opinion is eminently satisfactory to me." LDB to WHT (May 28, 1922) (Taft papers). Brandeis offered a "few" suggestions, including the quotation from *Hammer v. Dagenhart* that had been in Brandeis's draft opinion and that Taft subsequently incorporated into his opinion. *Coronado Coal*, 259 U.S. at 408. *See* WHT to LDB (May 29, 1922) (Taft papers) ("I have yours of May 28th, and thank you for the suggestions you make, all of which I shall adopt."). In his letter, Brandeis wrote: "I heartily agree that unions are suable in the federal Courts independently of the Anti-trust Law." In an undated letter, Clarke wrote Taft to say:

> I have just completed an attentive reading of your memorandum in [*Coronado*]. I was so impressed with the fictitious character of this case when I studied it carefully after the first argument, that I haven't gone minutely into it since. Of course the unions were not seeking to restrain, restrict or [?] interstate commerce in coal. As you well say, to affect interstate commerce incidentally is not sufficient. The greater interstate should be the better for them if they could have the wages and working conditions they desired. It is pure lawyer fiction to extend the statute to such a case & I readily agree with your result without rereading the testimony. I don't mean that I read it as carefully as you have done before writing but I went through it with sufficient care to feel very confident of the result. ... P.S. I have grave doubts as to suability but shall suppress them if this result can be accomplished.

JHC to WHT (n.d.) (Taft papers).

42. WHT to Helen Herron Taft (May 23, 1922) (Taft papers).
43. On May 2, Taft (along with Pitney and Clarke) represented the Court at the rededication of the old Supreme Court Building in Philadelphia. Taft clearly had potential controversy on his mind. He proclaimed that "A judiciary whose judgments must be made to follow popular clamor and the inconstancy of mob opinion indicates a people lacking that conservative and conserving self-restraint without which popular government is foredoomed to failure." *Chief Justice Taft's Address*, 8 AMERICAN BAR ASSOCIATION JOURNAL 333, 333 (1922). Taft fretted about the baleful influence of dissents on public opinion. "It has been impossible for the court in the exercise of its unusual jurisdiction to avoid decisions of issues which from time to time figure in the politics of the country. ... The questions decided are often close ones, and develop conscientious differences of view by the different members of the court, and lead to strong dissents by a minority. These fan the flame of criticism by those unfavorably affected by the judgment. Such incidental results are inseparable from the institution. The court has lived down temporary unpopularity so produced in the past. Let us hope it may in the future." *Id.* at 334–35. *See Taft Extols Value of Supreme Court*, NEW YORK TIMES (May 3, 1922), at 7. At the time, Taft was preparing to release his opinion in Bailey v. Drexel Furniture Co., 259 U.S. 20 (1922), which would be announced on May 15, and which Taft knew would ignite a firestorm of protest. *See supra* Chapter 36, at 1126–27.

44. *"God Save Labor from the Courts," Exclaims Gompers*, NEW YORK TIMES (April 22, 1922), at 1. *See No Laws Can Curb Labor. . . . Insists Wrongs Are Preferable to Court Regulation of Cases*, NEW YORK TRIBUNE (April 23, 1922), at 1.

45. *See* Joint Legislative Committee on Housing, Intermediate Report, Legislative Document No. 60 (Albany: J.B. Lyon Co. 1922), at https://ia802609.us.archive.org/21/items/intermediaterepoolockgoog/intermediaterepoolockgoog.pdf. The Lockwood Committee uncovered corruption in New York's developers, lenders, and construction unions. The lead attorney for the Committee was Samuel Untermeyer. The notoriety of Gompers's exchanges with Untermeyer may be seen in Newton D. Baker, *Labor Relations and the Law*, 8 AMERICAN BAR ASSOCIATION JOURNAL 731, 734 (1922) ("The extent of the distrust of legal remedies enforceable by the courts, on the part of Labor is best shown by the extended examination of Mr. Samuel Gompers by Mr. Untermeyer before the Lockwood Investigating Committee in April of this year."). The week before his testimony to the Lockwood Committee, Gompers had in New Haven specifically scored Taft's decision in *American Steel Foundries* because it "practically annulled the Clayton Act." *Gompers Raps Judge Taft and "Inequity Courts"*, NEW YORK TRIBUNE (April 17, 1922), at 5. *See Gompers Says Taft Voided Labor Act*, COURIER-JOURNAL (April 17, 1922), at 2. Gompers said that "courts which have been issuing injunctions against striking labor organizations are 'courts of inequity' instead of courts of equity." *Gompers Sends Broadside at Foes of Labor*, CHICAGO DAILY TRIBUNE (April 17, 1922), at 10.

46. *Gompers Defiant of Union Labor Curb*, NEW YORK TIMES (May 5, 1922), at 3. Taft was certain to be alert to Gompers assault on *Hammer* because the announcement of Taft's own controversial opinion in Bailey v. Drexel Furniture Co., 259 U.S. 20 (May 15, 1922), was only one week away.

47. *Make Congress Supreme Court, Gompers Says*, CHICAGO DAILY TRIBUNE (May 5, 1922), at 11. Gompers was merely restating existing AFL policy. As early as February 1919, in its program for reconstruction after the war, the AFL had declared that "An insuperable obstacle to self-government in the United States exists in the power which has been gradually assumed by the Supreme Courts of the Federal and State governments to declare legislation null and void upon the ground that, in the court's opinion, it is unconstitutional. It is essential that the people, acting directly or through Congress or state legislatures, should have final authority in determining which laws shall be enacted." *American Federation of Labor Reconstruction Program*, 26 AMERICAN FEDERATIONIST 129, 133 (1919). *See Judicial Construction of Law*, in REPORT OF PROCEEDINGS OF THE THIRTY-NINTH ANNUAL CONVENTION OF THE AMERICAN FEDERATION OF LABOR, *supra* note 25, at 361; *The Challenge Accepted*, in REPORT OF THE PROCEEDINGS OF THE FORTY-FIRST ANNUAL CONVENTION OF THE AMERICAN FEDERATION OF LABOR 61 (Washington D.C.: Law Reporter Printing Co. 1921) (call for "Removal by congress of the usurped power of courts to declare unconstitutional laws enacted by congress"). *Dagenhart* was very much on the AFL's mind in 1919. *See* Matthew Woll, *Protect the Children*, 26 AMERICAN FEDERATIONIST 155, 155 (1919) (attacking the *Dagenhart* majority as expressing a "pseudo-legal-economic science . . . of unrestrained competition" that "teaches the extermination of the weak by the strong."); Matthew Woll, *Judges Autocratic Power Must Go*, 26 AMERICAN FEDERATIONIST 508, 509–10 (1919) ("[T]he American people now find

Labor & the Construction of the National Market

their path barricaded by the assumed right of our judges to veto whatever legislation the people demand and by injunctive decree enact legislation that the people do not want. It is inconceivable that such an autocratic power can long survive in a democracy.... [N]ow that the war is over and the principles of democracy have come to be accepted the world over, the American Federation of Labor proposes that adequate steps be taken to bring into existence the rule which will provide that in the event of a supreme court declaring an act of Congress or of a state legislature unconstitutional and the people acting directly or through Congress or a state legislature should re-enact the measure, that it shall then become the law without being subject to annulment by any court.").

48. WHT to Horace D. Taft (May 7, 1922) (Taft papers).
49. Bailey v. Drexel Furniture Co., 259 U.S. 20 (1922). For the controversy surrounding *Bailey*, see *supra* Chapter 36, at 1127.
50. *See* Laurence Todd, *The Newberry Case in the United States Senate*, 72 BROTHERHOOD OF LOCOMOTIVE FIREMEN AND ENGINEMEN'S MAGAZINE 11 (February 1, 1922) ("Chief Justice Taft has announced that the Coronado Coal Company case ... must be re-argued.... During the past year many writers have referred to the anticipated decision, which would destroy the foundations of the organized labor movement. Since his recent decisions curtailing the right to picket – in the Steel Foundries case and the Truax case – Mr. Taft was expected to hand down the Coronado decision without further delay. Labor representatives are inclined to look upon this new move as a sign that the Supreme Court is at least worried by the criticism aroused by its recent anti-Labor decisions, and that it now will move with more caution in this field. Possibly the decision prepared a year ago and now abandoned without ever having seen the light was too easily assailable. Possibly Mr. Taft disagreed with some of its terms.").

Taft's correspondence at that time suggests that he was both conscious of potential threats to the Court and confident of the Court's ability to weather any potential storm. So, for example, Taft wrote the chief judge of the New York Court of Appeals in April: "My last eight years have been spent in going about the country, to the small towns in almost every State ... which convinces me that the controlling public opinion of this country is to be found in moderately-circumstanced patriotic American people who live in these towns and who are staunch in support of the Constitution and the present social order, and who can be roused by any real threat of socialism or communism. Of course they have a certain degree of inertia growing out of their confidence in things as they are, and it needs some sharp warning to arouse them to united effort, but they are there and will stay there to preserve the country. I think that politicians, and even judges, are not entirely conscious of the existence of this conservative backbone of the country, and are sometimes made timorous by the fear that we are facing a cataclysm and living on a volcano, all of which to me is ridiculous." WHT to Frank H. Hiscock (April 12, 1922).

51. Brandeis later recalled that "As to Coronado, passed from week to week, once considered by Taft then brought in conclusions – (1) liable under Sherman Law (2) evidence to hold & (2) interstate commerce. I expressed views (1) liable at c[ommon]. L[aw]. And no evidence of conspiracy & (2) no interstate commerce. When Taft came to write changed his views & then carried Court with him. I pounded on jurisdictional observance." *Brandeis-Frankfurter Conversations*, at 305 (June 18, 1922). Two weeks later Brandeis added, "They will take from Taft [but] wouldn't from us. If

good enough for Taft good enough for us – they say, & a natural sentiment." *Id.* at 307 (July 1, 1922).

Taft preserved in his papers some of his colleagues' returns on his draft. Brandeis wrote, "Yes. This is a most valuable piece of work." Holmes said, "I think this is fine. Yes." There is a return from Holmes on a revised draft that reads, "I like this as much on the second reading as I did on the first." Pitney jotted, "Too true to be good; otherwise most excellent! ... A great constructive opinion. I envy you your capacity for work. How do you manage it? Look out, lest you overdo it." McReynolds, true to form, returned: "I am sorry you can't make the scoundrels pay." Day commented, "I agree, and regret that this gross outrage by the local union cannot be reached by federal authority."

52. *Coronado Coal*, 259 U.S. at 383, 385, 388–89.
53. [1901] A.C. 426.
54. The difficulty with this reference, of course, was that "There is a great mass of authority in this country holding contra to the Taff Vale case." Note, 2 Wisconsin Law Review 51,52 (1922).
55. 6. Edw. 7 c 47. *See* William Howard Taft, *Address of the President*, in Report of the Thirty-Seventh Annual Meeting of the American Bar Association 372 (Baltimore: Lord Baltimore Press 1914); WHT to WVD (n.d.) (Van Devanter papers); WHT to WRD (August 18, 1922) (Taft papers); *The American Taff Vale Case, supra* note 5; *Executive Council Supplemental Report No. 2*, in Report of Proceedings of the Forty-Second Annual Convention of the American Federation of Labor 291–92 (Washington D.C.: Law Reporter Printing Co. 1922) ("It is astounding that the court should have sought a precedent in ancient and outlawed British court findings, ignoring entirely the modern British law upon which all modern British court decisions have been founded."); Leon Fink, *Labor, Liberty, and the Law: Trade Unionism and the Problem of the American Constitutional Order*, 74 Journal of American History 904, 916 (1987).

Two months after delivering *Coronado*, Taft wrote his son from England that he had had a conversation with F.E. Smith, the lord chancellor, "about the decision in the Coronado case, in which we held that an unincorporated labor union could be sued as such, and referred to the Taff-Vale case. He said that case was rightly decided, and that it was a shameless surrender to the trades unions to pass the law of 1901, I think it is – the trades unions dispute act, by which actions against trades unions for a tort were forbidden and the effect of the decision negatived. They are now agitating a change of that sort so as to make the unions responsible. Lord Haldane told me that although he had appeared on behalf of the unions in the Taff-Vale case and had been beaten, he thought the decision was a right one. Sir Willys Chitty told me that he had a friend, who was the Attorney General at the time that it was proposed to pass the trades dispute act and destroy the effect of the Taff-Vale case, and that his friend refused to advocate such legislation and resigned his office rather than to do so." WHT to Robert A. Taft (July 29, 1922) (Taft papers).

56. *Coronado Coal*, 259 U.S. at 386 n.1. Taft very rarely used footnotes of this kind in his opinions. *See supra* Chapter 5, at note 215.
57. *Coronado Coal*, 259 U.S. at 386.
58. Felix Frankfurter, *The Coronado Case*, 31 New Republic 328, 330 (1922). At Wilson's first Industrial Conference in October 1919, the employer group had submitted a "Statement of Principles Which Should Govern the Employment

Relation in Industry." This Statement included the proposition: "The public safety requires that there shall be no exercise of power without corresponding responsibility. Every association, whether of employers or employees, must be equally subject to public authority and legally answerable for its own conduct or that of its agents." DEPARTMENT OF LABOR, PROCEEDINGS OF THE FIRST INDUSTRIAL CONFERENCE 82 (Washington D.C.: Government Printing Office 1920).

59. *See supra* Chapter 31, at 996–98.
60. Dodd, *supra* note 18, at 1003.
61. *Coronado Coal*, 259 U.S. at 391.
62. In an excellent article, Katherine B. and Roswell F. Magill noted the "steady legislative trend toward treating labor organizations as distinct entities, capable of unified group action, and entitled to certain rights and privileges as such. Some authorities argue quite convincingly that a series of legislative enactments may be just as helpful in determining a proper legal policy as judicial opinions or decisions." Katherine B. Magill & Roswell F. Magill, *The Suability of Labor Unions*, 1 NORTH CAROLINA LAW REVIEW 81, 86 (1922). See W. Lewis Roberts, *Labor Unions, Corporations – The Coronado Case*, 5 ILLINOIS LAW QUARTERLY 200, 203–4 (1923); D.F.L., *The Coronado Case*, 5 ILLINOIS LAW QUARTERLY 126, 128 (1923). In a note praised by Brandeis as "a worthy discussion," LDB to Felix Frankfurter (November 22, 1922), in BRANDEIS-FRANKFURTER CORRESPONDENCE, at 125, the author observed that "It is only fair to state that the court was influenced in reaching its result by an interpretation of several acts of Congress, believed by the court to have altered the common law piecemeal." Note, *supra* note 19, at 62 n.14.
63. *Union Held Suable for Strike Damage by Supreme Court*, NEW YORK TIMES (June 6, 1922), at 1. *See* Baker, *supra* note 45, at 735. The *New York Call* branded *Coronado* "The most staggering blow ever aimed at the organized working class." Quoted in *Labor Unions Liable to Pay for Strike Damages*, *supra* note 6, at 8.
64. Edward Corwin, *Constitutional Law in 1921–1922*, 16 AMERICAN POLITICAL SCIENCE REVIEW 612, 627 (1922). *See Report of A.F. of L. Executive Council*, in REPORT OF PROCEEDINGS OF THE FORTY-THIRD ANNUAL CONVENTION OF THE AMERICAN FEDERATION OF LABOR 94 (Washington D.C.: Law Reporter Printing Co. 1923) (The Court's conclusion is "at variance ... with prior holdings of responsible courts and basic conceptions of law" and hence manifested "the fact that courts rather than the legislatures are the real rulers of the country.").
65. Quoted in *Labor Unions Liable to Pay for Strike Damages*, *supra* note 6, at 9. *See* Note, *supra* note 19, at 63 ("For a court to legislate judicially upon a political question of such vital importance to so large a percentage of the population is daring conduct. ... The Supreme Court ... chose to face the matter frankly and courageously.").
66. *Union Held Suable for Strike Damage by Supreme Court*, *supra* note 63; *The American Taff Vale Case*, *supra* note 5; *Labor and the Supreme Court*, *supra* note 7. Even the communist *The Worker* stressed that "The Supreme Court under Taft's guidance, was united in a unanimous decision on these class issues." *When Labor Really Wins*, THE WORKER (June 24, 1922), at 2.
67. *Labor Unions Suable*, BALTIMORE SUN (June 7, 1922), at 8. The *Cincinnati Times-Star*, which was owned by Taft's brother, pointedly noted that a "fact that seems to have escaped Mr. Gompers's attention is that the decision of the Supreme Court is unanimous. Among the Justices of the present Court are men who are regarded as liberals as well as men who are regarded as conservatives. If the decision was as bad

as Mr. Gompers thinks, how does it happen that we hear of no dissenting opinion by Justices Brandeis or Clarke?" Quoted in *Labor Unions Liable to Pay for Strike Damages, supra* note 6, at 8.
68. *Executive Council Supplemental Report No. 2, supra* note 55, at 291. *See id.* at 295.
69. *La Follette Scores Coronado Decision*, NEW YORK TIMES (June 8, 1922), at 37. "While the Coronado Coal Company decision therefore sets aside the money judgment rendered against the defenders, it is mostly ominous in what it foreshadows for the future of union labor in this country." *Id.* La Follette's remarks were delivered to the annual AFL convention. *See* REPORT OF PROCEEDINGS OF THE FORTY-SECOND ANNUAL CONVENTION OF THE AMERICAN FEDERATION OF LABOR, *supra* note 55, at 234, 240.
70. *See, e.g.*, BICKEL, *supra* note 11, at 98 ("Taft dealt at great length with the question whether the union, though an incorporated association, was a suable entity. There was no need to do so, since the suit was to be dismissed anyway."); Thomas, *supra* note 8, at 772; Note, *supra* note 27, at 52 ("It was mere dictum; but it was so expressly declared that and so clearly demonstrated why such bodies should be liable, that the dictum will likely be followed in the future."); Note, *supra* note 18, at 507 ("[T]he Chief Justice went on to say, by way of dictum, that for wrongful acts of its members an unincorporated union is suable as a legal entity separate and apart from its members."); but see *Labor Unions Not Exempt from the Sherman Law*, THE OUTLOOK (June 14, 1922), at 286.
71. WHT to Horace D. Taft (June 16, 1922) (Taft papers).
72. LDB to Felix Frankfurter (August 31, 1922), in BRANDEIS-FRANKFURTER CORRESPONDENCE, at 104–5:

> [L]iability for an alleged wrong can be enforced, only if:
> 1. The defendant is properly before the court. This involves
>   (a) going before a court with jurisdiction over subject matter and party
>   (b) joining proper necessary parties ...
> 2. The plaintiff is proven to have suffered a legal wrong.
> 3. The defendant is proven to have committed a legal wrong.
> 4. The pleadings are appropriate to recovery for the wrong proven.
>
> The courts ... had to decide (as a matter of procedure) whether the unions had been legally brought into court. And it properly decided this (namely 1. above) before taking up any other question. [H]olding that the unions ... were legally before the Court, it necessarily proceeded to the determination of the other three questions. It found, then, that the plaintiffs had suffered legal wrongs; that the International Union had committed no wrong whatsoever; that the District and local union had committed wrongs; but that these wrongs proved were not those sued on; that is, were not violations of federal law.
>
> To have proceeded first to the determination of questions 2, 3 or 4 *supra* would have been, at least, bad judicial practice; for the Court should not have enquired into them, unless it had decided that unions were ... as matter of procedure, properly before the Court.
>
> The liability sought to be enforced was not the joint and several liability of the members of the union. It was the liability of the unions as entities. If the judgment below had been affirmed, no person would have been liable *qua* member. Only the property of the entity, present and thereafter to be acquired could have been reached to satisfy that judgment. There were joined as defendants 66 natural persons, but not *qua* members. As to these only questions 2, 3 and 4 actually arose.

> If the judgment had been affirmed and had not been satisfied by, or out of the property of the Union, a question might have arisen whether by any proceeding the individual members could be made to satisfy the judgment. That is, whether there is a members' liability akin to a stockholders' liability; and also whether there is, otherwise, an individual liability for the wrongs proven. But no such question could arise or was discussed in that case.

Brandeis's elaborate explanation should be compared to his own draft dissent, see *supra* text at note 35, in which Brandeis seems to give only conditional and hypothetical assent to entity liability.

73. *Labor Unions Liable to Pay for Strike Damages*, *supra* note 6, at 9 ("Turning from the views of the press of the workers and the press of the employers to the daily newspapers of the country, we find an opinion almost unanimously favorable to the court.").
74. *Law and Union Labor*, ST. LOUIS POST-DISPATCH (June 6, 1922), at 14.
75. *Id.* See *Labor Unions Not Exempt from the Sherman Law*, *supra* note 70, at 286.
76. *The Labor Decision*, ST. LOUIS GLOBE-DEMOCRAT (June 7, 1922), at 14. The editorial begins with a remarkable paragraph: "Is Mr. Taft to be another John Marshall? In the short time that he has been Chief Justice of the United States Supreme Court he has written and handed down a series of decisions of outstanding importance in the definition of constitutional authority, marked by clear and vigorous utterance of elemental principles of law and a careful adjustment of the scales of justice." *Id.* The editorial specifically mentions the Wisconsin Rate Case, 257 U.S. 563 (1922), Hill v. Wallace, 259 U.S. 44 (1922), and Bailey v. Drexel Furniture Co., 259 U.S. 20 (1922). *See supra* Chapter 36 for a discussion of these cases.

Taft subsequently wrote Casper Salathiel Yost, the editor of the *Globe-Democrat*, to thank him "for giving such a clear statement as to what the decision covers."

> I am very much pleased with the fact that the decision is a unanimous one and that, I hope, will give force to its effect. I observe that Mr. Gompers and Senator La Follette are engaged in a raid on the Supreme Court because of that decision and the one in the child labor tax case. I also observe that the viciousness, arising from a certain immunity that labor unions feel in violating the law, has precipitated the massacre in Illinois of fourteen or fifteen people or more, in a most cold-blooded way, and possibly this will show more clearly the necessity and the justification for our interpretation of the law and keep Mr. Gompers and others explaining something that cannot fail to shock the American people.

WHT to C.W. Yost (June 26, 1922) (Taft papers). Taft was referring to the notorious Herrin Massacre, which occurred on June 22, in which striking miners massacred nineteen strikebreaking employees who had surrendered to union workers. Frederick D. Schwarz, *The Time Machine*, 48 AMERICAN HERITAGE 107 (May/June 1997); SELIG PERLMAN & PHILIP TAFT, 4 HISTORY OF LABOR IN THE UNITED STATES, 1896–1932, at 483–84 (New York: MacMillan Co. 1935). The UMW had been on strike since April 1922, in both anthracite and bituminous fields, in an effort to maintain the union contract in the Central Competitive Field. Tensions were running high. *Id.* at 482. The Herrin Massacre colored the public reception of *Coronado*. *The Coronado Mine Decision*, 6 CONSTITUTIONAL REVIEW 170, 171 (1922) ("And just at this very juncture comes a most impressive object lesson of the consequences to which strikes may and too often do lead, which makes the American people wish that this system of private warfare, a relic of barbarism, could be abolished forever. We refer, of course, to the unspeakable horror at Herrin, Illinois, when striking union miners most brutally murdered more than a score of non-union men."); Frankfurter, *supra* note 58, at 329. The employer of the mine involved in the Herrin Massacre vowed to sue the UMW in damages based upon *Coronado*. *Company to Sue County and Miners' Union for Million*, ST. LOUIS GLOBE-DEMOCRAT (June 22, 1922), at 2. *See* EDWIN E. WITTE, THE GOVERNMENT IN LABOR DISPUTES 140 (New York: McGraw-Hill Book Co. 1932).

77. *See* Corwin, *supra* note 64, at 635. Many papers quoted Henry S. Drinker, Jr., who had represented the Coronado Coal Company: "'Now that labor unions are legally liable for damages which they cause,' says Mr. Drinker, 'it would seem that the courts would be much less likely to grant injunctions, since after the commission of the act there is a ready and adequate remedy.'" *Upholds Coronado Ruling*, NEW YORK TIMES (June 19, 1922), at 5. *See Coal Decision Held to Put Curb on Injunctions*, NEW YORK TRIBUNE (June 19, 1922), at 16; *Harding Will Fight Strike*, LOS ANGELES TIMES (June 19, 1922), at I4. Edward Corwin noted that taken together *Coronado* and *American Steel Foundries* "signalize a new era in the effort to extend the rule of law into the field of industrial controversy. 'Government by injunction,' which sprang full-panoplied from the judicial bosom in the decision in the Debs case, has not proved a success in all respects; yet the only tolerable escape from it was the one which the Coronada [sic] decision opens up, to wit, legal responsibility on the part of organized labor." Corwin, *supra* note 64, at 628. Taft, of course, was well aware of the limitations of equitable power as a routine framework for the governance of labor relations. *See* William Howard Taft, *Labor Injunctions* (November 20, 1919), in VIVIAN, at 310, quoted in *supra* Chapter 39, at 1237–38.

78. *A Gain for Labor*, NEW YORK TIMES (August 13, 1922), at 36.

79. Baker, *supra* note 45, at 735.

80. *The Coronado Decision*, LOUISVILLE COURIER-JOURNAL (June 9, 1922), at 6. *See Labor and the Supreme Court*, 108 THE INDEPENDENT 539 (June 24, 1922) ([T]*he Supreme Court did not deny, limit, or restrict in any way the right to strike*. What the court *did* decide . . . is that a labor union can not . . . escape financial liability for offences committed by it *against the laws of the United States*."); *The Coronado Mine Case*, *supra* note 20, at 353 ("No rights of any law-abiding labor organization can be infringed or impaired by reason of the doctrine here established. Only those who set themselves up in opposition to the law are affected thereby.").

81. *See supra* Chapter 32, at 1025.

82. *The Coronado Decision*, 33 UNITED MINE WORKERS JOURNAL 6, 7 (June 15, 1922). *See Union Held Suable for Strike Damage by Supreme Court*, *supra* note 63 (*Coronado* is "one of the most important pieces of labor litigation ever before the Supreme Court").

83. *See Union Officials Call Decision "Great Victory"*, WASHINGTON POST (June 6, 1922), at 8.

84. *The Coronado Decision*, *supra* note 82, at 6. The future president of the AFL, William Green, took a much more negative view of *Coronado* when he represented the UMW as a delegate to the annual AFL national convention. *See* REPORT OF PROCEEDINGS OF THE FORTY-SECOND ANNUAL CONVENTION OF THE AMERICAN

FEDERATION OF LABOR, *supra* note 55, at 373. Labor did in fact begin to test the symmetry of the *Coronado* holding. *See, e.g., Suit Filed to Test Coronado Decision*, ST. LOUIS POST-DISPATCH (June 17, 1922), at 2 (describing a suit in a union's name alleging the misuse of a union label).

85. *Unions before the Courts*, NEW YORK CALL (June 19, 1922), at 8.
86. "Even in a strike which is itself lawful, the unions are to be held liable for the lawless acts of their most irresponsible members unless they can prove that such acts are contrary to their explicit intent and instructions. In other words, while strikes are not forbidden, yet the Supreme Court has presented unscrupulous employers with a way to keep unions from financing strikes. In the numerous suits just filed by employers to take advantage of this decision, it is now suggested that every member of a labor union during a strike is an agent of the union, and that regardless of instructions, the union is responsible for his acts. The remedy for this intolerable situation" consists "in securing the enactment of a statute by Congress, similar to the British Trade Disputes Act." *The Coronado Decision*, 56 LOCOMOTIVE ENGINEERS JOURNAL 491 (July 1922).
87. Address of Hon. William H. Taft at Malden, Massachusetts, October 30, 1919, at 12 (Taft papers).
88. *The American Taff Vale Case*, *supra* note 5, at 736.
89. *Gompers Assails Supreme Court*, NEW YORK TIMES (June 10, 1922), at 10. Notably the UMW celebrated how *Coronado* dealt with the actual question of agency that was before it. "Union-busting employers have all along contended that the international was responsible for every act of every member, and they have been supported in that position by many courts. But the rule laid down by the Supreme Court puts a crimp in that policy. A union can now be held for those things for which it is directly responsible, but nothing more." *The Coronado Decision*, *supra* note 82, at 6.
90. *Gompers Attacks Coronado Decision*, NEW YORK TIMES (June 7, 1922), at 4.
91. *Coronado Coal*, 259 U.S. at 393–95. Taft wrote:

> A corporation is responsible for the wrongs committed by its agents in the course of its business, and this principle is enforced against the contention that torts are ultra vires the corporation. But it must be shown that it is in the business of the corporation. Surely no stricter rule can be enforced against an unincorporated organization like this. Here it is not a question of contract, or of holding out an appearance of authority, on which some third person acts. It is a mere question of actual agency, which the constitutions of the two bodies settle conclusively. If the International body had interfered, or if it had assumed liability by ratification, different questions would have arisen.

Id. at 395. In the press, the "apparent holding that an international union cannot be held responsible for a strike which it does not call or ratify" was deemed of great importance. John J. Leary, Jr., *Labor Hard Hit by Decision in Coronado Case*, BALTIMORE SUN (June 6, 1922), at 1.

92. Note, *supra* note 18, at 510.
93. *Coronado Coal*, 259 U.S. at 403. It is quite possible that the sentence was merely careless draftsmanship. Taft did take pains to offer a detailed reading of the record explicitly to conclude that "The overwhelming weight of the evidence establishes that this was purely a union attack, under the guidance of District officers." *Id.* at 401. But the Executive Committee of the AFL nevertheless read the sentence quoted

in text to mean that "in any strike sanctioned by national or international officials or supported by funds from the national treasury ... the national organization as such may be held responsible in damages for whatever act may be held unlawful and which may be committed by individuals about whom the national may have no knowledge or of whose action the national may be entirely uninformed. ... For a national union of workers to be held responsible for the acts of some of its members or of a local union, no matter how remote, is an injustice, the enormity of which is difficult to comprehend." *Executive Council Supplemental Report No. 2, supra* note 55, at 294–95. Uncertainty over the agency question ultimately led to the enactment of Section 6 of the Norris-LaGuardia Act, Pub. L. 72-65, 47 Stat. 71 (March 23, 1932), which provides: "No officer or member of any association or organization, and no association or organization participating or interested in a labor dispute, shall be held responsible or liable in any court of the United States for the unlawful acts of individual officers, members, or agents, except upon clear proof of actual participation in, or actual authorization of, such acts, or of ratification of such acts after actual knowledge thereof." On the Act's alteration of traditional agency law, see *Define and Limit the Jurisdiction of Courts Sitting in Equity*, Sen. Rep. No. 1060, 71st CONG. 2nd SESS. (June 18, 1930), at 10.

94. Francis Bowes Sayre, *The Coronado Decision*, 48 THE SURVEY 385, 386 (June 15, 1922). "Even a corporation," Sayre wrote, "although responsible for the wrongful acts of its servants and agents committed within the scope of their authority, is not liable for acts of unauthorized violence on the part of their agents outside of the scope of their authority. Authorization to order a strike is surely not authorization to commit such acts of violence as were proved in the Coronado case." *Id. Compare supra* note 91.

95. Note, *supra* note 19, at 63. Some commentators, putting the sentence in the context of the entire opinion, concluded that "It is more reasonable to suppose that the court really had in mind that the liability in each instance should be tested by the ordinary rules of agency." Magill & Magill, *supra* note 62, at 83. *See* Note, *supra* note 18, at 510–11. In a private letter to his son, Taft characterized *Coronado* as involving "the right to sue labor unions, although unincorporated, *for torts committed by their authorized management.*" WHT to Robert A. Taft (July 29, 1922) (Taft papers) (emphasis added). Brandeis was murky about the exact agency principles invoked by *Coronado*. He wrote Frankfurter:

> It is not true that a union can be liable only if every member authorized or ratified the alleged wrong deed or that a union cannot be liable unless every member is liable. Entities are often liable for acts which were neither actually authorized nor ratified, as a railroad for the conductor's negligence or wanton act. And, of course, a person who is a member may be liable, although the union is not. To hold that a union could be liable only if every member authorized or ratified the act would involve treating the union not as entity but merely as the joint agent of the several members.

LDB to Felix Frankfurter (August 31, 1922), in BRANDEIS-FRANKFURTER CORRESPONDENCE, at 105.

96. *Coronado Coal*, 259 U.S. at 413. Brandeis later cryptically remarked to Frankfurter that "I pounded on the jurisdictional observance & glad to get Taft to say what he did in last P[aragraph]." *Brandeis-Frankfurter Conversations*, at 305 (June 18, 1922).

97. *Gompers Attacks Coronado Decision*, *supra* note 90. Reporters noted that Gompers "appeared to be particularly bitter against Chief Justice Taft." *Id*. Gompers commented

that "Now the Supreme Court has practically swept aside the provisions of the Clayton act." *"Clayton Act Is Swept Aside," Says Gompers*, ST. LOUIS POST-DISPATCH (June 6, 1922), at 2.
98. *Executive Council Supplemental Report No. 2, supra* note 55, at 295.
99. *Report of the Executive Council*, in REPORT OF PROCEEDINGS OF THE FORTY-THIRD ANNUAL CONVENTION OF THE AMERICAN FEDERATION OF LABOR, *supra* note 64, at 32. *See Gompers Attacks Coronado Decision, supra* note 90 ("It goes without saying that the convention of the Federation of Labor will take steps seeking legislation to remedy the effect of the Coronado decision."); *Gompers Says Workers Will Ask for New Laws*, BALTIMORE SUN (June 10, 1922), at 2; *Labor to Seek Law to Protect Funds of Union*, CHICAGO DAILY TRIBUNE (June 18, 1922), at 2. At its 1922 annual convention, the AFL resolved to seek "an act repealing the Sherman Anti-Trust Law, which ... through judicial misinterpretation and perversion has been repeatedly and mainly invoked to deprive the toiling masses of their natural and normal rights." See REPORT OF PROCEEDINGS OF THE FORTY-SECOND ANNUAL CONVENTION OF THE AMERICAN FEDERATION OF LABOR, *supra* note 55, at 373, 398. This was not the first time that the AFL had opposed the Sherman Act. *See, e.g.*, Samuel Gompers, *Official Circular*, 15 AMERICAN FEDERATIONIST 955, 956 (1908).
100. REPORT OF PROCEEDINGS OF THE FORTY-SECOND ANNUAL CONVENTION OF THE AMERICAN FEDERATION OF LABOR, *supra* note 55, at 373, 398. *See Report of A.F. of L. Executive Council*, in REPORT OF PROCEEDINGS OF THE FORTY-THIRD ANNUAL CONVENTION OF THE AMERICAN FEDERATION OF LABOR, *supra* note 64, at 35–36; John P. Frey, *Shall the People or the Supreme Court Be the Final Voice in Legislation?*, 29 AMERICAN FEDERATIONIST 629, 631, 634–35 (1922) ("The American trade union movement has definitely opposed the power exercised by the United States Supreme Court in declaring federal legislation unconstitutional. It has taken this position because it believes that such power is an insufferable obstacle to self-government. ... A government of free men does not, and can not, admit the existence of some superior power, an authority beyond their control, which can, at will, nullify the legislation which they, or their duly elected representatives, have enacted. To admit the existence of such a power is to acknowledge that popular sovereignty is a theory instead of a fact."); W.B. Rubin, *The Constitution and the Supreme Court*, 29 AMERICAN FEDERATIONIST 675, 678 (1922) ("When the Supreme Court declared the child labor law unconstitutional it assumed a power, first, which it was never intended it should have by the framers of our Constitution, and second it continued a usurpation of power initiated in that court by Chief Justice Marshall."). The chair of the Railroad Labor Board condemned the AFL resolution as "revolutionary in its nature" and equivalent to "the complete wiping out of our written Constitution." Ben. W. Hooper, *Radicalism versus Government*, 217 NORTH AMERICAN REVIEW 289, 295 (1923).
101. *Address of Senator Robt. M. La Follette*, in REPORT OF PROCEEDINGS OF THE FORTY-SECOND ANNUAL CONVENTION OF THE AMERICAN FEDERATION OF LABOR, *supra* note 55, at 242.
102. Frank B. Kellogg to Robert E. Olds (July 1, 1922) (Kellogg papers at the Minnesota Historical Society).
103. Taft sailed on June 10. *See Taft Sails for England*, NEW YORK TIMES (June 12, 1922), at 14 ("In view of the congested condition of the American judicial dockets,

Mr. Taft hopes to be able to obtain some impressions from the British judicial system suggestive of changes in the American procedure calculated to improve conditions. He has been interested in reports of comparatively recent innovations in British procedure, especially those calculated to speed the processes of the law."). *See* WHT to Horace D. Taft (April 17, 1922) (Taft papers) ("My purpose to go abroad is become more and more confirmed. ... I am determined to push a movement for the betterment of the procedure in the Federal courts. I suppose I weigh down such reform by my advocacy of it, in arousing the opposition of certain elements, especially in the Senate, but I don't know why that should prevent my initiating matters when nobody is likely to do so, and perhaps one exaggerates the influence of those who are blatant in their opposition, if one has a good cause."). Taft's visit was breathlessly covered in the press. *See, e.g., Taft to Meet King at Harvey Dinner*, NEW YORK TIMES (June 15, 1922), at 6; *Fetes for Taft in Britain*, NEW YORK TIMES (June 17, 1922), at 12; *British and American Admirers Give Taft Warm Welcome on His Arrival in London*, NEW YORK TIMES (June 19, 1922), at 1; *Taft Asks Britons Not to Be Misled by Factions Here*, NEW YORK TIMES (June 20, 1922), at 1; *"Hic et Ubique"*, NEW YORK TIMES (June 21, 1922), at 12; *Taft Calls on King, Lunches with Harvey and Visits the English Law Courts*, NEW YORK TIMES (June 21, 1922), at 1; *Taft Visits Law Courts*, NEW YORK TIMES (June 23, 1922), at 4; *Taft Made a Bencher of Middle Temple*, NEW YORK TIMES (June 24, 1922), at 3; *Taft Visits Commons*, NEW YORK TIMES (June 27, 1922), at 14; *Oxford Makes Taft Doctor of Civil Law*, NEW YORK TIMES (June 29, 1922), at 10; *Bench and Bar Dine Taft in Famous Hall*, NEW YORK TIMES (July 6, 1922), at 4; *Cambridge Degree Conferred on Taft*, NEW YORK TIMES (July 7, 1922), at 18; *Taft Sails for Home*, NEW YORK TIMES (July 9, 1922), at 21.

104. WHT to WVD (n.d.) (Van Devanter papers). La Follette had been active in seeking to arouse farmers to the implications of *Coronado*, arguing that it would impose entity liability on farmers' cooperatives. *See* Robert M. La Follette, *The Coronado Coal Company Decision and the Farmer*, 14 LA FOLLETTE'S MAGAZINE 31 (June 1922) ("The challenge in the Coronado Coal Company decision is to the laborer and the farmer alike. It is a challenge to all the people who desire to protect their ancient and inalienable right to organize with their associates in societies for mutual protection and benefit without subjecting themselves and their property to the restraints and liability which the law intended to impose only upon the great corporations and trusts organized solely for profit.").

105. WHT to Horace D. Taft (June 16, 1922) (Taft papers). In July, Taft wrote his son that the "opinion seems to have called forth great denunciation by Gompers and La Follette and other demagogues, and to have suggested a movement to deprive the Court of the power of holding laws unconstitutional. I don't know how formidable such a movement may be, but certainly in the past, especially in Marshall's time, threats against the Court were quite as menacing as they are now. The outrages committed by labor unions in the coal business in Illinois and in West Virginia have not I think given any particular force to such a movement. I have an abiding conviction that when the issue is squarely presented, the supporters of an amendment to the Constitution will find arrayed against them a conservative strength that in their blatant mouthings they do not realize the existence of. The daily vaporings of Gompers and the open declaration of war by Debs are calculated to arouse all

Labor & the Construction of the National Market

the conservative feeling that there is in the country." WHT to Robert A. Taft (July 29, 1922) (Taft papers).

106. WHT to WRD (August 18, 1922) (Taft papers). The next day Taft wrote Van Devanter, "I suppose you have noted the yawping of Gompers and La Follette over the Child Labor and Coronado cases, but I have not heard much of an echo. I think we did good work in those cases." WHT to WVD (August 19, 1922) (Taft papers). In December, George Wharton Pepper declared in an address to a bar association:

> It really should not surprise us if there are multitudes today who stand aghast when suddenly they realize the opinions of a bare majority of nine justices may nullify the expressed will of the national legislature.
>
> Two facts stare these earnest men in the face. One is that the Supreme Court recently declared the Federal Child Labor law unconstitutional. The other is that the Supreme Court recently declared the consequences of civil liability for torts attach to unincorporated labor unions in the same way in which such liability would attach to groups of people associated for business purposes.
>
> Such judicial decisions seem to many honest people symptoms of a judicial tyranny. Multitudes of people personify the judiciary and honestly think its functioning in some cases a usurpation as unjustified as any king ever attempted to do to a Parliament.

Quoted in *Butler's Nomination to U.S. Supreme Court*, SAN FRANCISCO EXAMINER (December 20, 1922), at 32. *See* H.M. Crist to WHT (December 12, 1922) (Taft papers). Taft was furious. He wrote his daughter the day after learning of Pepper's remarks: "Pepper is a Jesuit. He is running for the Presidency now. He is cultivating the labor party. . . . He hopes to gain strength as a candidate for the party by winking at the labor element, and that leads him to say some things that are quite disloyal to our Court. I don't resent this on the part of a radical, but on the part of a man like Pepper it is most exasperating." WHT to Mrs. Frederick J. Manning (December 13, 1922) (Taft papers).

107. WITTE, *supra* note 76, at 142. On the first point, Witte notes that in 1932 only fourteen states and the federal courts authorized entity liability against unions. Witte observes that although "the prestige of the U.S. Supreme Court is such" that "state courts might reasonably be expected to follow" *Coronado's* holding, "no such tendency . . . has been discernible to date." *Id.* at 144. Apparently under established principles of agency law, "employers have been able to collect substantial damages from unions or their members in comparatively few cases. Employers have spent far more in attorneys' fees and court costs in trying to collect damages from unions and their members than they have realized in damages. . . . The prospect that employers will find damage suits the most powerful of all weapons against labor unions seems as remote as ever." *Id.* at 148–49.

108. Damage suits against unions did increase, however, after the federal government prohibited courts from issuing injunctions in labor disputes. *See* THURMAN W. ARNOLD, THE BOTTLENECKS OF BUSINESS 247 (New York: Reynal & Hitchcock 1940). *See, e.g.*, Apex Hosiery Co. v. Leader, 310 U.S. 469 (1940).

109. *See supra* Part VIII, at 1219.

110. *Report of the Executive Council, Industry's Manifest Duty*, in REPORT OF PROCEEDINGS OF THE FORTY-THIRD ANNUAL CONVENTION OF THE AMERICAN FEDERATION OF LABOR, *supra* note 64, at 31–32. On the significance of this

policy statement, see *Report of Executive Council*, in REPORT OF PROCEEDINGS OF THE FORTY-EIGHTH ANNUAL CONVENTION OF THE AMERICAN FEDERATION OF LABOR 23 (Washington D.C.: Law Reporter Printing Co. 1928); Worth M. Tippy, *Injunction Abuse*, 35 AMERICAN FEDERATIONIST 287, 289 (1928).

111. *Industry's Manifest Duty, supra* note 110, at 33. "The continuing clamor for extension of state regulatory powers under the guise of reform and deliverance from evil, can but lead into greater confusion and more hopeless entanglements." *Id.* at 31. "The threat of state invasion of industrial life is real. Powerful groups of earnest and sincere persons constantly seek the extension of state suzerainty over purely industrial fields. Such ignorant encroachments as the Esch-Cummins act, the Kansas Court of Industrial relations and the Colorado Industrial Commission act, each a blundering gesture of government acting under the spur of organized propaganda or of political appetite for power, are examples of what all industry has to fear." *Id.*

112. *Report of Executive Council*, in REPORT OF PROCEEDINGS OF THE FORTY-SEVENTH ANNUAL CONVENTION OF THE AMERICAN FEDERATION OF LABOR 34 (Washington D.C.: Law Reporter Printing Co. 1927).

113. *Id.* at 34. "This change in understanding of the trade union will do much to show that it is a better business policy to have the cooperation of trade unions than it is to fight them. It will also secure a more favorable public opinion in support of remedial labor legislation. In no small degree is this changing understanding due to the new emphasis Labor has put upon its constructive work.... By shifting attention from problems of defense or aggression to those of constructive building, the relative importance of the sustained work of the union becomes more obvious.... The business advantage of unionization has become more generally accepted." *Id.* at 34–35. The 1927 AFL Convention unanimously approved a report stressing "the usefulness of trade union organization in relation to such problems as that of efficiency and economical production." *Id.* at 288.

114. *Report of Executive Council*, in REPORT OF PROCEEDINGS OF THE FORTY-EIGHTH ANNUAL CONVENTION OF THE AMERICAN FEDERATION OF LABOR, *supra* note 110, at 115. Because "standards of living can be permanently raised only by increasing production," the AFL recognized that "organized labor has a basis of common interests with management and therefore find cooperation an advantage." *Id.* at 23. In 1927, the AFL Executive Council announced a new policy of using "government statistics" to determine in collective bargaining "whether wages paid to wage earners will enable them to share in advances in material civilization." *Report of Executive Council, supra* note 112, at 37. The proposal was widely praised as "the beginning of a new era in the relations between labor and capital," one which would substitute "fact-finding" for "war." *Labor's Plan to Get Its Share of the Profits*, 95 LITERARY DIGEST 8 (October 22, 1927).

115. William Green, *Mutual Responsibility*, 34 AMERICAN FEDERATIONIST 529, 529 (1927). "The American Federation of Labor has declared that the materials of increased productivity are essential to sustained increases in standards of living and that the union holds itself ready to do its part in working out better methods and plans for production. Where employers are ready to make cooperation possible, trade unionists are ready to do their part." *Id.* at 530. In his first campaign speech as a presidential candidate, Hoover singled out this policy for special praise. "American labor has been the first labor body in the world that has

had the intelligence and courage to realize and express the fact that increased wages and salaries must in the long run be based upon a sharing of labor in the savings made through industrial and commercial efficiency." *Text of Herbert Hoover's Opening Campaign Speech Last Night at Newark*, BALTIMORE SUN (September 18, 1928), at 13. "The whole relationship between employer and employe has shown great improvement in these past seven years," Hoover declared, because "there has been a revolution through shifting of basic ideas on the part of both business and labor. The large majority of both sides today willingly accept the fundamental principle that the highest possible wages are the road to increased consumption of goods and thereby to prosperity. Both accept the fundamental fact that greater efficiency, large application of mechanical devices and full personal effort are the road to cheaper costs, lower prices and thus again to wider consumption and larger production of goods.... Both realize that labor is entitled to participation in the benefits of increased efficiency by increased wage, either directly or through the decrease in living costs. Both have joined in repelling socialism and other subversive movements." *Id.* Hoover's speech was praised by John L. Lewis as "a whole-hearted recognition of the rights and ideals of Labor." Quoted in *Hoover's Appeal to the Workers*, 94 LITERARY DIGEST 10, 11 (October 6, 1928).

116. *Coronado Coal*, 259 U.S. at 410–11. *See* Oliver Iron Mining Co. v. Lord, 262 U.S. 172, 178–79 (1923). Taft was frank to detail the blatant provocations of the company that might have provided "a full local motive for the conspiracy" to invade the mine. 259 U.S. at 411. Taft observed:

> Bache's breach of his contract with the District No. 21, in employing nonunion men three months before it expired, his attempt to evade his obligation by a *manipulation* of his numerous corporations, his advertised anticipation of trespass and violence by warning notices, by inclosing his mining premises with a cable and stationing guards with guns to defend them, all these, in the heart of a territory that had been completely unionized for years, were calculated to arouse a bitterness of spirit entirely local among the union miners against a policy that brought in strangers, and excluded themselves or their union colleagues from the houses they had occupied and the wages they had enjoyed.

Id. (emphasis added). In his original draft, Taft had written: "to evade his obligation by a *hugger-mugger* of his numerous corporations." John W. Davis, who at the time represented Bache personally, wrote a letter to Ernest Knaebel, the Court Reporter, reporting that his client was "deeply stung by the term 'hugger-mugger.'" Believing that it had "an unpleasant connotation," Davis asked the Reporter to "substitute 'some less dubious' word before publication of the report." Ernest Knaebel to WHT (October 27, 1922) (Taft papers). Taft replied that he thought "the word 'huggermugger' is a pretty good word, and I think in a way that Bache deserved it. But I don't want to give pain where I can avoid it, or, where I have given it, to fail to ameliorate it, if it can be done without a sacrifice of principle or judicial necessity. What word would you suggest?" WHT to Ernest Knaebel (October 28, 1922) (Taft papers). Eventually Taft substituted the word "manipulation." The version of the case in West's Supreme Court Reporter, however, still carries the word "huggermugger."

117. *Coronado Coal*, 259 U.S. at 413.

118. Bailey v. Drexel Furniture Co., 259 U.S. 20 (May 15, 1922).
119. 257 U.S. 563 (1922). *See supra* Chapter 36, at 1123–24.
120. 258 U.S. 495 (1922). *See supra* Chapter 36, at 1125–26.
121. *Coronado Coal*, 259 U.S. at 408. Fifteen years later, Chief Justice Hughes would cite this passage, as well as the general reasoning of *Coronado*, to sustain the exercise of federal power in N.L.R.B. v. Jones & Laughlin Steel Corp., 301 U.S. 1, 39–40 (1937).
122. *Coronado Coal*, 259 U.S. at 408.
123. For a discussion of the indeterminacy if not downright irrationality of this standard, see G.W. Terborgh, *The Application of the Sherman Law to Trade-Union Activities*, 37 JOURNAL OF POLITICAL ECONOMY 203 (1929).
124. Note, *Organized Labor and Restraints on Interstate Commerce*, 43 HARVARD LAW REVIEW 459, 462 (1930). "Labor law is a field in which emotion runs high and prejudices are strong; these factors will inevitably play a large part in decisions." *Id*. In this regard Brandeis once remarked to Frankfurter that the "Court is malleable almost on everything except trade unions. There its prejudices become active. Can never tell what court will do – what its mood will be when case reaches it." *Brandeis-Frankfurter Conversations*, at 322 (August 6, 1923).
125. *Address of Senator Robt. M. La Follette*, in REPORT OF PROCEEDINGS OF THE FORTY-SECOND ANNUAL CONVENTION OF THE AMERICAN FEDERATION OF LABOR, *supra* note 55, at 233. Anderson was promoted to the Seventh Circuit by Coolidge in 1925.
126. Borderland Coal Corp. v. UMW, 275 F. 871, 872 (D. Ind. 1921), *reversed sub nom*. Gasaway v. Borderland Coal Corp., 278 F. 56 (7th Cir. 1921).
127. Albert de Silver, *The Injunction – A Weapon of Industrial Power*, 114 THE NATION 89 (1922). *See* Note, *supra* note 38, at 461–62 (The right of a labor union "to exist must include the right to increase its membership. Certainly a legitimate object of a labor union is to win recruits. ... It seems paradoxical that the existence of a union cannot be attacked, but that when it once approaches a national scope it may not peaceably urge others to join the organization.").
128. Samuel Gompers, *Antitrust Law and Labor*, 21 AMERICAN FEDERATIONIST 35 (1914).
129. *Coronado*, 259 U.S. at 408–9 (emphasis added). *The United Mine Workers Journal* stressed this aspect of *Coronado*. *See United States Supreme Court Decides the Coronado Case in Favor of United Mine Workers of America*, 33 UNITED MINE WORKER'S JOURNAL 3 (June 15, 1922).
130. *Coronado Coal*, 259 U.S. at 409, 411.
131. It was said in the press that "The organizations of capital are localized; trade unions should be localized. Organizations of capital are forbidden to create artificial monopolies; trade unions should be forbidden to create monopolies." *One Law for All*, 132 THE OUTLOOK 9 (September 6, 1922).
132. *Coronado Coal*, 259 U.S. at 409.
133. *Id.* at 412.
134. *Id.* at 412–13.
135. John A. Ryan, *Relation of Recent Supreme Court Decisions to Labor Unions and Industrial Legislation*, in PROCEEDINGS OF THE NATIONAL CONFERENCE OF SOCIAL WORK 287 (University of Chicago Press 1922).
136. *The American Taff Vale Case*, *supra* note 5, at 736–37.

137. 268 U.S. 295 (1925).
138. *Id.* at 303. McNamara was aggrieved because he claimed that the UMW had not made good on this promise.
139. *Id.* at 307–9.
140. Finley v. United Mine Workers of America, 300 F. 972 (8th Cir. 1924).
141. On May 17, Taft wrote his son that "This last week I have been spending in a leisurely way writing an opinion in an important case that involved the examination of a great deal of evidence." WHT to Robert A. Taft (May 17, 1925) (Taft papers). Three days later Taft sent Van Devanter a note: "I enclose the opinion in the Coronado case. Pass your eye over it and if you see any breaks note them by just criticism but please do not take your time from your own work." WHT to WVD (May 20, 1925) (Van Devanter papers). Taft's opinion was announced on May 25.
142. *Coronado II*, 268 U.S. at 304.
143. *Id.* at 305, 310. This exact passage was cited by Parker in his notorious opinion in International Organization, United Mine Workers of America v. Red Jacket Consol. Coal & Coke Co., 18 F.2d 839, 845–46 (4th Cir. 1927):

> We think there can be no question that the case at bar falls within the rule just quoted from the second Coronado decision. Here it appears that the total production of the mines of complainants is in excess of 40,000,000 tons per year, more than 90 per cent. of which is shipped in interstate commerce. Interference with the production of these mines as contemplated by defendants would necessarily interfere with interstate commerce in coal to a substantial degree. Moreover, it is perfectly clear that the purpose of defendants in interfering with production was to stop the shipments in interstate commerce. It was only as the coal entered into interstate commerce that it became a factor in the price and affected defendants in their wage negotiations with the union operators. And, in time of strike, it was only as it moved in interstate commerce that it relieved the coal scarcity and interfered with the strike. A conspiracy is in violation of the statute, where there exists an intent to restrain interstate trade and commerce and a scheme appropriate for that purpose, even though it does not act directly upon the instrumentalities of commerce. And where the necessary result of the things done pursuant to or contemplated by the conspiracy is to restrain trade between the states, the intent is presumed. Defendants must be held "to have intended the necessary and direct consequences of their acts and cannot be heard to say the contrary."

Parker's opinion in *Red Jacket* opinion used the formulations of the two *Coronado* cases in a predictable and lawyerly way to reinstate the reasoning of the notorious Anderson injunction against the national UMW. *See supra* text at notes 125–29.
144. Walter H. Saunders, *A Review of Recent Decisions Affecting Labor and Employment*, 15 GEORGETOWN LAW JOURNAL 361, 362 (1927).
145. *Coronado Coal Suit Ended after 13 Years*, WASHINGTON POST (October 14, 1927), at 3.
146. Terborgh, *supra* note 123, at 224. For a good discussion, see CHARLES O. GREGORY, LABOR AND THE LAW 200–22 (New York: W.W. Norton & Co. 1949).
147. On the potentially radical implications of *Coronado II*, see Charles O. Gregory, *The Sherman Act v. Labor*, 8 UNIVERSITY OF CHICAGO LAW REVIEW 222, 226–28 (1941). *But see* Apex Hosiery Co. v. Leader, 310 U.S. 469, 512–13 (1940). As T.R. Powell noted: "[T]he miners were aware that if they lost their fight, their neighbors in other states would be likely to lose theirs. This awareness, however, seems

a slim basis for an assumption that the miners were animated by the altruism of helping their neighbors through keeping up their own wages and thereby keeping up the price of coal sent by their mine to extra-state markets, when the advantage of keeping up their own wages might well be deemed the only end directly in view." T.R. Powell, *II Commerce, Congress, and the Supreme Court, 1922–1925*, 26 COLUMBIA LAW REVIEW 521, 546 (1926). *See, e.g.,* Thomas Reed Powell, *The Supreme Court's Control over the Issue of Injunctions in Labor Disputes*, 13 PROCEEDINGS OF THE ACADEMY OF POLITICAL SCIENCE 37, 58–59 (June 1928); Note, 34 WEST VIRGINIA LAW QUARTERLY 176, 176 (1928) ("Is not the primary purpose – the direct object, benefit of the labor members, rather than a malicious or even willful desire or intent to interfere with interstate trade?").

148. On the distinction between a jury finding of such intent after full presentation of evidence, and a judge finding of such intent on the basis of affidavits filed to support the issuance of a temporary restraining order, see Note, *supra* note 147, at 182. In 1940, the Court in an opinion by Stone over the dissent of McReynolds and Hughes, explicitly held that "Since, in order to render a labor combination effective it must eliminate the competition from non-union goods, an elimination of price competition based on differences in labor standards is the objective of any national labor organization. But this competition has not been considered to be the kind of curtailment of price-competition prohibited by the Sherman Act." *Apex Hosiery*, 310 U.S. at 504. To support this conclusion, Stone strikingly reached back for authority to *American Steel Foundries*, not to *Coronado*.

149. United Leather Workers International Union, Local Lodge or Union No. 66 v. Herkert & Meisel Trunk Co., 265 U.S. 457, 463 (1924).

150. United Leather Workers' International Union, Local Lodge or Union No. 66 v. Herket & Meisel Trunk Co., 284 F. 446, 453 (8th Cir. 1922). The AFL was appalled by Sanborn's opinion. It would, said Gompers, create "an entirely new and confiscatory principle ... for the oppression of labor." Samuel Gompers, *Where Judges Make the Law*, 30 AMERICAN FEDERATIONIST 69 (1923). Gompers cited Heisler v. Thomas Collier Co., 260 U.S. 245 (1922), for the importance of maintaining the separation of interstate commerce from mining and manufacturing. *See supra* Chapter 37, at 1163–64. Sanborn's opinion threatened "to nationalize all industries." *Where Judges Make the Law*, *supra*, at 71.

151. WHT to Robert A. Taft (June 8, 1924) (Taft papers).

152. The day before the decision was due to be announced, Taft wrote his son that "the Court divides five to four.... Van Devanter dissents with McReynolds, McKenna and Butler." On Taft's account, McReynolds switched his vote at the last moment to join Taft. If Butler's account of the conference votes is correct, Sanford switched his vote to join Taft, whereas Butler switched his vote to join Van Devanter.

153. *Herkert & Meisel Trunk Co.*, 265 U.S. at 466, 471.

154. *Id.* at 471–72. One observer was moved to remark that "The second Coronado decision shakes the authority of the Herkert & Meisel decision." Saunders, *supra* note 144, at 364.

155. Industrial Association of San Francisco v. United States, 268 U.S. 64, 75 (1925). The materials were "cement, lime, plaster, ready-mixed mortar, brick, terra cotta and clay products, sand, rock and gravel." *Id.* Plaster was also restricted. *Id.* Builders could not obtain these materials unless they received a permit, and a permit was not

Labor & the Construction of the National Market

forthcoming unless a builder pledged itself to adopt "the 'American plan.'" *Id. See supra* Chapter 39, at 1236. The pledges were enforced "upon shops and building jobs by inspectors, and daily reports were made as to whether the plan was being observed." *Id.* at 76. There was in the United States a long history of employers banding together to enforce antiunion policies. *See, e.g.*, HARRY W. LAIDLER, BOYCOTTS AND THE LABOR STRUGGLE: ECONOMIC AND LEGAL ASPECTS 36–39 (New York: John Lane Co. 1914).

156. "The thing aimed at and sought to be attained was not restraint of the interstate sale or shipment of commodities, but was a purely local matter, namely, regulation of building operations within a limited local area, so as to prevent their domination by the labor unions." *Industrial Association of San Francisco*, 268 U.S. at 77.

157. *Id.* at 78–80. Sutherland wrote that the case was "controlled by" the reasoning of *Heckert*:

> If an executed agreement to strike, with the object and effect of closing down a mine or a factory, by preventing the employment of necessary workmen, the indirect result of which is that the sale and shipment of goods and products in interstate commerce is prevented or diminished, is not an unlawful restraint of such commerce, it cannot consistently be held otherwise in respect of an agreement and combination of employers or others to frustrate a strike and defeat the strikers by keeping essential domestic building materials out of their hands and the hands of their sympathizers, because the means employed, whether lawful or unlawful, produce a like indirect result. The alleged conspiracy and the acts here complained of, spent their intended and direct force upon a local situation – for building is as essentially local as mining, manufacturing or growing crops – and if, by a resulting diminution of the commercial demand, interstate trade was curtailed either generally or in specific instances that was a fortuitous consequence so remote and indirect as plainly to cause it to fall outside the reach of the Sherman Act.

Id. at 82. Stone later wrote that he disagreed with Sutherland's reasoning in *Industrial Association* because it "amounted practically to a revival of the reasoning in the now discredited sugar refining case [United States v. E.C. Knight Co., 156 U.S. 1 (1895)]." HFS to WHT (January 26, 1927) (Taft papers). But Stone conceded that he "agreed with the result" in *Industrial Association. Id.*

158. Sutherland acknowledged that in "some three or four sporadic and doubtful instances, during a period of nearly two years," the interstate shipment of materials was suppressed by the permitting system. But, said Sutherland, "when we consider that the aggregate value of the materials involved in these few and widely separated instances, was, at the utmost, a few thousand dollars, compared with an estimated expenditure of $100,000,000 in the construction of buildings in San Francisco during the same time, their weight, as evidence to establish a conspiracy to restrain interstate commerce or to establish such restraint in fact, becomes so insignificant as to call for the application of the maxim, '*de minimus non curat lex*.'" 268 U.S. at 84.

159. Butler Docket Book. Two years later Taft would write Stone that "I voted against the decision of the Court in Industrial Association vs. the United States, but I acquiesced because I considered it, on the statement of Justice Sutherland, a mere difference on my part in the matter of the significance of evidence, rather than any difference in principle between us. When the case is carefully read, it will

be seen that it is a case of *de minimis* and a mere yielding to the opinion of the court below in its conclusions of fact." WHT to HFS (January 27, 1927) (Stone papers).
160. Butler Docket Book. So far as one can infer from Stone's docket book, Stone, who was confirmed in February, did not participate in the Court's deliberations or decision in *Coronado II*.
161. The following year, in Anderson v. Shipowners Ass'n of the Pacific Coast, 272 U.S. 359 (1926), the Court unanimously ruled that an agreement by owners of merchant vessels to control the hiring of seamen violated the Sherman Act because "ships and those who operate them are instrumentalities of commerce and within the Commerce Clause." *Id.* at 363. Speaking for the Court, Sutherland reasoned that no allegations of intent were required because "that is the necessary and direct consequence of the combination and the acts of the associations under it, and they cannot be heard to say the contrary." *Id.* Neither *Industrial Association*, nor *Herkert*, nor *Coronado I*, were "in point," because "the conspiracies or combinations in all three related to local matters.... Here, however, the combination and acts complained of ... related to the employment of seamen for service on ships, both of them instrumentalities of, and intended to be used in, interstate and foreign commerce; and the immediate force of the combination, both in purpose and execution, was directed toward affecting such commerce. The interference with commerce, therefore, was direct and primary, and not, as in the cases cited, incidental, indirect and secondary." *Id.* at 363–64. On remand, however, the Ninth Circuit found that the actions of the Shipowner's Association were reasonable and hence permissible under the anti-trust statute. Andersen v. Shipowners' Ass'n of the Pacific Coast, 31 F2d 539 (9th Cir. 1929), *cert. denied*, 279 U.S. 864 (1929). Stone, who had taken no part in the Taft Court's decision in the case, nevertheless presciently wrote Sutherland while the case was under submission that "A whole body of state case law recognizes the validity of employer's associations, with certain limits, where employers find it necessary to combine in order to attain a parity of position with powerful labor unions in the bargaining struggle. The tendency of the state courts apparently is to sustain the validity of such combinations. Similarly combinations fixing scales of wages and hours of employment are upheld." HFS to GS (November 17, 1926) (Stone papers).
162. In 1940, Thurman Arnold, as assistant attorney general in charge of anti-trust enforcement, was categorical that the test of "intent" was "impossible to apply. The conception of the 'intent' of a large organization is a pure fiction." ARNOLD, *supra* note 108, at 247–48.
163. Felix Frankfurter & Nathan Greene, *Congressional Power over the Labor Injunction*, 31 COLUMBIA LAW REVIEW 385, 391–92 (1931).
164. Standard Oil Co. of New Jersey v. United States, 221 U.S. 1, 60 (1911).
165. 26 Stat. 209 (1890).
166. United States v. Addyston Pipe & Steel Co., 85 F. 271 (6th Cir. 1898). "It is certain that, if the contract of association which bound the defendants was void and unenforceable at the common law because in restraint of trade, it is within the inhibition of the statute if the trade it restrained was interstate. Contracts that were unreasonable restraint of trade at common law were not unlawful in the sense of being criminal, or giving rise to a civil action for damages in favor of one prejudicially affected thereby, but were simply void, and were not enforced by the court. The effect of the act of 1890 is to render such contracts unlawful in an affirmative or

positive sense, and punishable as a misdemeanor, and to create a right of civil action for damages in favor of those injured thereby, and a civil remedy by injunction in favor of both private persons and the public against the execution of such contracts and the maintenance of such trade restraints." *Id.* at 278–79.

167. Alpheus Thomas Mason, *Labor and Judicial Interpretation*, 184 ANNALS OF THE AMERICAN ACADEMY OF POLITICAL AND SOCIAL SCIENCE 112, 115 (1936).
168. WILLIAM HOWARD TAFT, THE ANTI-TRUST ACT AND THE SUPREME COURT 47 (New York: Harper & Brothers 1914).
169. *Id.* As early as 1896 it was common to observe that the use of the Sherman Act to enjoin strikes "is one of the grievances most bitterly resented by the laboring classes. This statute was passed for the avowed purpose of putting a restraint upon great corporations and monopolies. Not a single corporation has been interfered with under it, nor a single monopoly restrained. . . . This law . . . has emphatically been proved to be one which cannot be enforced against the rich, and which can be enforced against the poor." *Government by Injunction*, 54 THE OUTLOOK 953 (1896). In 1906, the AFL complained that "The anti-trust and interstate commerce law enacted to protect the people against monopoly in the products of labor . . . have been perverted, so far as the laborers are concerned, so as to invade and violate their personal liberty as guaranteed by the constitution." *Labor's Bill of Grievances*, 13 AMERICAN FEDERATIONIST 294, 295 (1906). In 1914, Gompers declared the Sherman Anti-Trust law "the most serious menace to the labor movement." Gompers, *supra* note 128, at 37.
170. Moores & Co. v. Bricklayers' Union, 10 Ohio Dec. Reprint 665, 666 (Ohio Superior Ct. 1889).
171. *Id.* at 672–73.
172. Commentators sometimes distinguished illegal boycotts from legitimate strikes on the ground that the latter sought to improve the wages and working conditions of the strikers, whereas the former were "for the general benefit of laborers of the same class" in a context "where the persons striking have no personal grievance." Frederic J. Stimson, *The True Attitude of Courts and Legislatures upon Labor Questions*, 10 GREEN BAG 103, 104 (1898). But, in the words of the noted Catholic theologian John A. Ryan, "While the courts with practical unanimity recognize that labor unions have a right to better the conditions of their members, as to wages, hours, etc., they declare that the unions have no right to seek an end which involves merely injury to others. As a matter of fact, this distinction has no genuine basis. A labor union never aims at injuring others as an ultimate end. The final end sought . . . is always the welfare of the workers." John A. Ryan, *The Labor Injunction in the Light of Justice*, 35 AMERICAN FEDERATIONIST 290, 292 (1928).
173. Plant v. Woods, 176 Mass. 492, 494, 496, 502 (1900).
174. *Id.* at 505 (Holmes, C.J., dissenting).
175. *Bricklayers' Union*, 10 Ohio Dec. Reprint at 672–73.
176. Jackson H. Ralston, *Government by Injunction*, 5 CORNELL LAW QUARTERLY 424, 429 (1920).
177. *See* NORMAN WARE, THE LABOR MOVEMENT IN THE UNITED STATES 1860–1895, at 334–45 (New York: Vintage 1929).
178. "The use of the word 'boycott' is in itself a threat. In popular acceptation, it is an organized effort to exclude a person from business relations with others by

persuasion, intimidation, and other acts which tend to violence, and thereby to coerce him, through fear of resulting injury, to submit to dictation in the management of his affairs." Brace Brothers v. Evans (Pa. Ct. Common Pleas 1888), in 3 RAILWAY AND CORPORATION LAW JOURNAL 561, 564 (1888). The boycott "is one of the most heartless and brutal manifestations of private revenge recorded in history, and is calculated to call forth the abhorrence and just reprehension of all men who respect law and love liberty." Charles Claflin Allen, *Injunction and Organized Labor*, in REPORT OF THE SEVENTEENTH ANNUAL MEETING OF THE AMERICAN BAR ASSOCIATION 307 (Philadelphia: Dando Printing & Publishing Co. 1894). *See* Crump v. Virginia, 84 Va. 927 (1888); Connecticut v. Glidden, 55 Conn. 46 (1887).
179. WHT to Hamilton Holt (November 25, 1927) (Taft papers).
180. W.G. Sumner, *Industrial War*, 2 THE FORUM 1, 7 (1886).
181. Sherman D. Thacher, *Boycotting*, 201 NEW ENGLANDER AND YALE REVIEW 1038, 1040–41 (1886).
182. William Howard Taft, *Inaugural Address*, 44 CONG. REC. 1, 5 (March 4, 1909).
183. 62 F. 804, 818–19 (6th Cir. 1894). Because "there was no natural relation between Pullman and the railway employees," the efforts of the latter to injure railroads because they would not injure Pullman was "without cause, and malicious, and is unlawful, even though the injury is inflicted merely by quitting employment." *Id.* at 820.
184. *Id.* at 821. The year before Taft had explained the distinction between a strike and a boycott in his opinion in Toledo, A.A. & N.M. Ry. Co. v. Pennsylvania Co., 54 F. 730, 737–38 (Cir. Ct. N.D. Ohio 1893):

> Herein is found the difference between the act of the employes of the complainant company in combining to withhold the benefit of their labor from it and the act of the employes of the defendant companies in combining to withhold their labor from them; that is, the difference between the strike and the boycott. The one combination, so far as its character is shown in the evidence, was lawful, because it was for the lawful purpose of selling the labor of those engaged in it for the highest price obtainable, and on the best terms. The probable inconvenience or loss which its employes might impose on the complainant company by withholding their labor would, under ordinary circumstances, be a legitimate means available to them for inducing a compliance with their demands. But the employes of defendant companies are not dissatisfied with the terms of their employment. So far as appears, those terms work a mutual benefit to employer and employed. What the employes threaten to do is to deprive the defendant companies of the benefit thus accruing from their labor, in order to induce, procure, and compel the companies and their managing officers to consent to do a criminal and unlawful injury to the complainant. Neither law nor morals can give a man the right to labor or withhold his labor for such a purpose.

185. William Howard Taft, *Judicial Decisions as an Issue in Politics*, 33 MCCLURE'S MAGAZINE 201, 206 (June 1909). Theodore Roosevelt vigorously agreed with this distinction. "The heartiest encouragement should be given to the wageworkers to form labor unions and to enter into agreements with their employers; and their right to strike, so long as they act peaceably, must be preserved. But we should sanction neither a boycott nor a blacklist which would be illegal at common law." *Special Message from the President of the United States*, 42 CONG. REC. 5327, 5328 (April 28, 1908). For a roughly contemporaneous account of boycotting, see LAIDLER, *supra* note 155.

186. Taft, *supra* note 182, at 5.
187. TAFT, *supra* note 168, at 24.
188. In his 1914 presidential address to the ABA, Taft argued that the Clayton Act should be interpreted to authorize judicial injunctions against boycotts that threatened to undermine the compartmentalization of industrial controversies. The Act, said Taft,

> segregates the parties to the controversy from the rest of the community and says in effect that acts committed singly or in concert by the parties on either side against the other which do not amount to violence or crime or a threat of either, and which do not involve peaceful moral coercion of outsiders, are legal in the trade warfare and shall not be enjoined. Recommendation and persuasion of others to help either side in the warfare are declared to be legal, but not so moral coercion. The real and great danger from boycotts in such disputes is the use of them to drag into trade disputes against their will all classes of the community not normally related to the issue. It is the embarrassment and injury they would thus inflict upon the forgotten man, the entity called the "public," that creates the illegality. This was actionable before the new statute and remains so.

Taft, *Address of the President*, *supra* note 55, at 377.
189. PROCEEDINGS OF THE FIRST INDUSTRIAL CONFERENCE, *supra* note 58, at 82. Employers formed "the belligerent American Anti-Boycott Association" in 1902. The Association eventually became the League for Industrial Rights. *See* CLARENCE E. BONNETT, EMPLOYERS' ASSOCIATIONS IN THE UNITED STATES 24 (New York: MacMillan Co. 1922); *The League for Industrial Rights*, 1 INDUSTRY 11 (November 15, 1919).
190. Duplex Printing Press Co. v. Deering, 254 U.S. 443, 463, 466 (1921).
191. *Id.* at 467–68, 474.
192. *Id.* at 472. *Duplex* drew upon the Court's precedent in Loewe v. Lawlor, 208 U.S. 274 (1908), in which the Court declared that individual union members engaged in a secondary boycott against a nonunion hat manufacturer were subject to treble damages under the Sherman Act. The *New York Tribune* editorialized in favor of *Duplex*:

> The Clayton act ... dealt with limited, concrete two-party disputes. It didn't contemplate licensing what the Marxians call "the universal class war." The secondary boycott is a natural instrument in warfare of that kind. ...
>
> Such running amuck practices would make the anti-trust laws meaningless. They would leave the individual no freedom at all to do business. The secondary boycott is, in fact, an unlimited conspiracy to restrain trade – to involve lookers-on in a dispute with which they have nothing to do. In the public interest such molestation should be made impossible. It is viciously unfair and un-American.

No Secondary Boycotts, NEW YORK TRIBUNE (January 5, 1921), at 10.
193. *Strikes and Boycotts*, 34 HARVARD LAW REVIEW 880, 887 (1921).
194. *Id.* at 880.
195. *See* Hopkins v. Oxley Stave Co., 83 F. 912, 917 (8th Cir. 1897); Truax v. Corrigan, 257 U.S. 312, 364 n.28 (1921) (Brandeis, J., dissenting).
196. Francis Bowes Sayre, *Labor and the Courts*, 39 YALE LAW JOURNAL 682, 699–700 (1930). "The definitions of 'boycott,' as the word has been defined in the many cases, are nearly as varied as the cases defining the term." Truax v. Bisbee Local, No. 380, 19 Ariz. 379, 387–88 (1918). *See* Felix Frankfurter &

Nathan Greene, *Use of the Injunction in American Labor Controversies*, 44 LAW QUARTERLY REVIEW 164, 187 (1928); EDWIN STACEY OAKES, THE LAW OF ORGANIZED LABOR AND INDUSTRIAL CONFLICTS 601 (Rochester: Lawyers Co-Operative Publishing Co. 1927); WITTE, *supra* note 76, at 38–45; Jerome R. Hellerstein, *Secondary Boycotts in Labor Disputes*, 47 YALE LAW JOURNAL 341, 341–42 (1938); *Strikes and Boycotts, supra* note 193, at 885. For an example of Taft stigmatizing as a "secondary boycott" what to all intents and purposes would seem to be an ordinary strike against a primary employer, on the ground that union pickets sought to discourage consumers from patronizing the employer, see Truax v. Corrigan, 257 U.S. 312, 330 (1921). See *also supra* Chapter 39, at note 240.
197. 274 U.S. 37 (1927).
198. Herbert Little, *The Omnipotent Nine*, 15 AMERICAN MERCURY 56, 57 (September 1928). *See* PAUL L. MURPHY, THE CONSTITUTION IN CRISIS TIMES 1918–1969, at 62 n.64 (New York: Harper & Row 1972).
199. *Bedford Cut Stone*, 274 U.S. at 41.
200. *Id.* at 59 (Brandeis, J., dissenting).
201. *Bedford Cut Stone*, 274 U.S. at 41.
202. *Id.* at 41–43.
203. *Id.* at 43.
204. Bedford Cut Stone Co. v. Journey Stone Cutters' Ass'n, 9 F.2d 40, 40 (7th Cir. 1925).
205. Felix Frankfurter, *"Reminds of Involuntary Servitude"*, 50 NEW REPUBLIC 262 (1927). On Frankfurter's authorship of this article, see LDB to Felix Frankfurter (April 26, 1927), in BRANDEIS-FRANKFURTER CORRESPONDENCE, at 287.
206. *Bedford Cut Stone*, 9 F.2d at 40–41.
207. HFS to WHT (January 26, 1927) (Taft papers).
208. Stone 1926 Docket Book
209. Memorandum (January 24, 1927) (Taft papers).
210. WHT to ETS (January 24, 1927) (Taft papers) (Marked "not sent").
211. WHT to ETS (January 25, 1927) (Taft papers). Taft also discussed his opinion in Toledo, A.A. & N.M. Ry. Co. v. Pennsylvania Co., 54 F. 730 (Cir. Ct., N.D. Ohio 1893), although it did not technically involve an alleged violation of the Sherman Act.
212. WHT to ETS (January 24, 1927) (Taft papers).
213. WHT to ETS (January 25, 1927) (Taft papers). In the unsent version of his memorandum, Taft added, "As we held in the Coronado case, the unions are entities and may themselves be enjoined I suppose. Certainly they could be enjoined through those who represent them. Certainly their officers could be enjoined from directing or enforcing a rule requiring a strike which should be an illegal step in a conspiracy, so long as it did not compel an individual by the process of contempt to do work." WHT to ETS (January 24, 1927) (Taft papers). Taft's reasoning rests on a distinction between individual journeymen and the union as an entity. Evidence had been introduced in *Bedford Cut Stone* that "the journeyman stonecutter, if left to himself and satisfied with his own arrangements with his local contractor, did not care what the stone was or where it came from. If he quit work on Bedford limestone, he only did so because he was under threat of penalty enforced by the national union." Murray T. Quigg, *Trade Union Activities and the Sherman Law*, 147 ANNALS OF THE AMERICAN ACADEMY OF POLITICAL AND SOCIAL SCIENCE 51, 56 (1930).

214. WHT to ETS (January 25, 1927) (Taft papers).
215. WHT to GS (January 25, 1927) (Taft papers).
216. Quoted in Basil Manly, *Chief Justice Taft Replies to Three Vital Questions*, BOSTON GLOBE (January 9, 1929), at 32.
217. *See supra* note 188.
218. As Max Radin pointed out, "What we may say of Justice Taft and his brethren in spirit is that they are convinced of the value of a certain social theory and are determined to judge cases according to the measure in which they do or do not further that theory. This, I make bold to say, is quite unexceptionable. Indeed, it is inevitable." Max Radin, *The Ancient Grudge*, 7 THE FREEMAN 381, 382 (1923).
219. WILLIAM HOWARD TAFT, REPRESENTATIVE GOVERNMENT IN THE UNITED STATES 25 (New York University Press 1921).
220. In their conversations, Brandeis and Frankfurter agreed on the Court's "fear of power of labor & redistribution of economic power." *Brandeis-Frankfurter Conversations*, at 325 (August 10, 1923).
221. Taft believed that the nation must preserve "in our business the indispensable element of individual initiative and enterprise and reward, for upon that is dependent in the last analysis, our progress to better things." *Taft Tells Minneapolitans What Constitutes True and Ideal Americanism*, MINNEAPOLIS MORNING TRIBUNE (February 12, 1920), at 6. The early boycott cases were remarkably candid about the need to preserve the entrepreneurial initiative of management. In *Moores & Co.*, for example, Taft cited a pivotal decision by the Connecticut Supreme Court prohibiting a union boycott of the Carrington Publishing Company for refusing to unionize:

> It seems strange that in this day and this free country – a country in which law interferes so little with the liberty of the individual – that it should be necessary to announce from the bench that every man may carry on his business as he pleases, may do what he will with his own so long as he does nothing unlawful, and acts with due regard to the rights of others; and that the occasion for such an announcement should be, not an attempt by government to interfere with the rights of the citizen, nor by the rich and powerful to oppress the poor, but an attempt by a large body of working-men to control, by means little if any better than force, the action of employers. The defendants and their associates said to the Carrington Publishing Company: "You shall discharge the men you have in your employ, and you shall hereafter employ only such men as we shall name. It is true, we have no interest in your business, we have no capital invested therein, we are in nowise responsible for its losses or failures, we are not directly benefited by its success, and we do not participate in its profits; yet we have a right to control its management, and compel you to submit to our dictation." The bare assertion of such a right is startling. The two alleged rights cannot possibly co-exist. One or the other must yield. If the defendants have the right which they claim, then all business enterprises are alike subject to their dictation. No one is safe in engaging in business, for no one knows whether his business affairs are to be directed by intelligence or ignorance,—whether law and justice will protect the business, or brute force, regardless of law, will control it; for it must be remembered that the exercise of the power, if conceded, will by no means be confined to the matter of employing help. Upon the same principle, and for the same reasons, the right to determine what business others shall engage in, when and where it shall be carried on, etc., will be demanded, and must be conceded. The principle, if it once obtains a foothold, is aggressive, and is not easily checked. It thrives on what it feeds, and is insatiate in its demands. More requires more. If a large body of irresponsible men demand and receive power outside of law, over and above law, it is not to be expected that they will be satisfied with a moderate and reasonable use of it. All

history proves that abuses and excesses are inevitable. The exercise of irresponsible power by men, like the taste of human blood by tigers, creates an unappeasable appetite for more. Business men have a general understanding of their rights under the law, and have some degree of confidence that the government, through its courts, will be able to protect those rights. This confidence is the corner-stone of all business; but if their rights are such only as a secret and irresponsible organization is willing to concede to them, and will receive only such protection as such an organization is willing to give, where is that confidence which is essential to the prosperity of the country?

Connecticut v. Glidden, 8 A. 890, 894 (Ct. 1887). *See* Percy L. Edwards, *The Right of Equity to Interfere in the Strife between Labor Organizations and the Corporations*, 57 ALBANY LAW JOURNAL 377, 379 (1898).

222. William Howard Taft, *Labor Injunctions* (November 20, 1919), in VIVIAN, at 310. *See supra* Chapter 39, at 1237–38.

223. Brandeis had written:

> When centralization in the control of business brought its corresponding centralization in the organization of workingmen, ... a single employer might, as in this case, threaten the standing of the whole organization and the standards of all its members; and when he did so the union, in order to protect itself, would naturally refuse to work on his materials wherever found. When such a situation was first presented to the courts, judges concluded that ... the strike against the material was considered a strike against the purchaser by unaffected third parties. Burnham v. Dowd, 217 Mass. 351; Purvis v. United Brotherhood, 214 Pa. 348; Booth v. Burgess, 72 N. J. Eq. 181. But other courts, with better appreciation of the facts of industry, recognized the unity of interest throughout the union, and that, in refusing to work on materials which threatened it, the union was only refusing to aid in destroying itself. Bossert v. Dhuy, 221 N. Y. 342; Cohn & Roth Electric Co. v. Bricklayers, 92 Conn. 161; Gill Engraving Co. v. Doerr (D. C.) 214 Fed. 111; State v. Van Pelt, 136 N. C. 633; Grant Construction Co. v. St. Paul Building Trades, 136 Minn. 167; Pierce v. Stablemen's Union, 156 Cal. 70.
>
> So, in the case at bar, deciding a question of fact upon the evidence introduced and matters of common knowledge, I should say, as the two lower courts apparently have said, that the defendants and those from whom they sought co-operation have a common interest which the plaintiff threatened. This view is in harmony with the views of the Court of Appeals of New York. For in New York, although boycotts like that in Loewe v. Lawlor, 208 U.S. 274, are illegal because they are conducted, not against a product, but against those who deal in it, and are carried out by a combination of persons, not united by common interest, but only by sympathy, it is lawful for all members of a union by whomever employed to refuse to handle materials whose production weakens the union.

Duplex Printing Press, 254 U.S. at 482–83 (Brandeis, J., dissenting).

224. WHT to GS (January 25, 1927) (Taft papers).
225. WHT to HFS (January 26, 1927) (Taft papers).
226. Two months previously the Court had decided United States v. Brims, 272 U.S. 549 (1926), in which it had unanimously held that a tripartite agreement among "manufacturers of millwork in Chicago, building contractors who purchase and cause such work to be installed," and the local Chicago carpenters' union, to refuse to work with nonunion millwork, much of which was produced in "mills located outside of Illinois – mostly in Wisconsin and the South," and which sold "in the Chicago market

cheaper than local manufacturers who employed union labor could afford to do," was a violation of the Sherman Act. *Id.* at 552. Speaking through McReynolds, and citing *Coronado II*, the Court ruled that "It is a matter of no consequence that the purpose was to shut out nonunion millwork made within Illinois as well as that made without. The crime of restraining interstate commerce through combination is not condoned by the inclusion of intrastate commerce as well." *Id.* at 552–53. In conference, both Brandeis and Holmes had passed, although they eventually joined McReynolds's published opinion. Stone 1926 Docket Book. Stone did not participate in the case. Taft did not so much as mention *Brims* in his memorandum to Stone. Sutherland did cite the case in his eventual opinion for the Court. *Bedford Cut Stone*, 274 U.S. at 52. In dissent, Brandeis sought to distinguish *Brims*:

> In United States v. Brims the combination complained of was not the co-operation merely of working men of the same craft. It was a combination of manufacturers of millwork in Chicago with building contractors who cause such work to be installed and the unions whose members are to be employed. Moreover the purpose of the combination was not primarily to further the interests of the union carpenters. The immediate purpose was to suppress competition with the Chicago manufacturers.

Bedford Cut Stone, 274 U.S. at 64 (Brandeis, J., dissenting).
227. WHT to HFS (January 26, 1927) (Taft papers). On disagreement in state courts about whether a union's refusal to work on nonunion materials was an illegal boycott, see WITTE, *supra* note 76, at 28–30.
228. WHT to HFS (January 26, 1927) (Taft papers). Taft included his memorandum to Sanford in his letter to Stone.
229. HFS to WHT (January 26, 1927) (Taft papers). On Taft's effort to distinguish *Industrial Association*, see *supra* note 159. Taft, with typical tact, knew well enough when to leave Stone alone. Taft replied: "Now that I have ... pointed out what seemed to me to be the controlling considerations that should govern in the decision of this case, I shall not bother you further, unless, as you say, you come and talk with me about it when I shall be glad to continue our discussion." WHT to HFS (January 27, 1927) (Stone papers).
230. WHT to GS (January 27, 1927) (Taft papers).
231. WHT to GS (March 11, 1927) (Taft papers). It is ironic that Taft would seek to justify the holding of *Bedford Cut Stone* not in terms of the common law, but by reference to the positive legislative mandate of the Sherman Act. It had been Taft himself who had so influentially demonstrated that the Act was literally without meaning unless interpreted in light of common law precedents. *See supra* note 166.
232. *See supra* text at note 183.
233. *Bedford Cut Stone*, 274 U.S. at 53. Sutherland was in fact accurate to note that in *Duplex Printing Press* Pitney had held that secondary boycotts violated federal anti-trust law "irrespective of whether" they were "lawful or unlawful at common law." *Duplex Printing Press*, 254 U.S. at 466.

Ironically, it was Taft's son Robert who several decades later as a United States senator would revive judicial restrictions against secondary boycotts in the Taft-Hartley amendments to the original NLRA. *See* 29 U.S.C. § 158(b)(4); National Woodwork Manufacturers Ass'n v. NLRB, 386 U.S. 612, 624 (1967); *see generally* Megan Slater Shaw, *"Connote No Evil": Judicial Treatment of the Secondary Boycott before Taft-Hartley*, 96 NEW YORK UNIVERSITY LAW REVIEW 334 (2021).

234. On April 9, Taft wrote Sutherland "to report to you what we did. Your three cases are ready for announcement on Monday. Stone in the Bedford Stone Company case said that that he might modify what he had written. Sanford said what he expected to do, which was merely to say that he thought the case was covered by the Duplex case and therefore followed it." WHT to GS (April 9, 1927) (Taft papers).
235. *Bedford Cut Stone*, 274 U.S. at 45–50. On April 23, 1927, the Executive Board of the Association revoked the rule requiring members to refrain from finishing work started by men working in opposition to the union. STONE CUTTERS JOURNAL (May 1927), at 2.
236. *Bedford Cut Stone*, 274 U.S. at 55 (Sanford, J., concurring). One contemporary commentator observed that "An interesting and profitable study ... might be to determine the effect upon his colleagues of the strong nationalistic outlook and broad statesmanship of Mr. Chief Justice Taft, who was with the majority in the instant case." Note, 22 ILLINOIS LAW REVIEW 444, 446 n.4 (1927).
237. *Bedford Cut Stone*, 274 U.S. at 55–56 (Stone, J., concurring). "[T]here is a difference," Stone later wrote Walter Wheeler Cook about his concurring opinion, "between being one of five and one of six to uphold an earlier opinion with which the Judge does not agree." HFS to Walter Wheeler Cook (May 4, 1927) (Stone papers).
238. WHT to Robert A. Taft (April 10, 1927) (Taft papers). Stone believed that Taft's "enthusiasm for me seems to have waned after my opinion in [Bedford Cut Stone Co. v. Journey Stone Cutters' Ass'n of North America], in which I expressed the view that under the Clayton Act labor unions could not be held to violate the Sherman Anti-Trust law by merely refusing to work on nonunion material which had been the subject of interstate commerce. After that he seems to have thought that, like Holmes and Brandeis, I was 'hopeless'." HFS to Children (November 24, 1939) (Stone papers). For a discussion of the intracourt politics underlying *Bedford Cut Stone*, see ALPHEUS THOMAS MASON, HARLAN FISKE STONE: PILLAR OF THE LAW 254–60 (New York: Viking 1956).
239. WHT to Robert A. Taft (April 10, 1927) (Taft papers).
240. Brandeis papers.
241. Quoted in *Brandeis on the Labor Problem: How Far Have We Come on the Road to Industrial Democracy?*, 15 LA FOLLETTE'S WEEKLY MAGAZINE 5, 15 (May 24, 1913).
242. *Bedford Cut Stone*, 274 U.S. at 58 (Brandeis, J., dissenting). "[I]n Mr. Justice Sutherland's opinion for the majority not one word is said as to the reasonableness – or unreasonableness – of the restraint." Alexander B. Royce, *Labor, the Federal Anti-Trust Laws, and the Supreme Court*, 5 NEW YORK UNIVERSITY LAW REVIEW 19, 27 (1928). Fourteen years later, Robert Jackson was moved to observe:

> A failure to enforce the antitrust laws against the real offenders would have been bad enough, but they were turned to strengthen the forces bearing down upon labor as it tried to find through self-organization and with legislative aid the voice with which to bargain on equal terms with masters of industry. In 1908, the Supreme Court averred that labor unions were illegal combinations in restraint of trade if they attempted to boycott the goods of any firm that sold its product in interstate commerce. Those who enjoy comparative studies of the judicial process will find it suggestive to note that restraint placed by labor upon interstate commerce, without weighing its reasonableness in the circumstances, was held to be an illegal restraint. Yet restraints by industrialists were illegal only when "unreasonable."

Labor & the Construction of the National Market

ROBERT JACKSON, THE STRUGGLE FOR JUDICIAL SUPREMACY 63 (New York: Alfred A. Knopf, Inc. 1941).

243. *Bedford Cut Stone*, 274 U.S. at 59 (Brandeis, J., dissenting). In language that would later be much referenced, Brandeis noted:

> The Sherman Law was held in United States v. United States Steel Corporation to permit capitalists to combine in a single corporation 50 per cent. of the steel industry of the United States dominating the trade through its vast resources. The Sherman Law was held in United States v. United Shoe Machinery Co. to permit capitalists to combine in another corporation practically the whole shoe machinery industry of the country, necessarily giving it a position of dominance over shoe manufacturing in America. It would, indeed, be strange if Congress had by the same act willed to deny to members of a small craft of workingmen the right to cooperate in simply refraining from work, when that course was the only means of self-protection against a combination of militant and powerful employers. I cannot believe that Congress did so.

274 U.S. at 65 (Brandeis, J., dissenting).

244. Immediately after the decision, the *New Republic* remarked that "Interpretation of the anti-trust laws by the Supreme Court seems to describe two divergent curves, one constantly enlarging the scope of combination in profit-seeking business, the other constantly restricting the powers of self-defensive organizations of labor. To say that Congress never intended these laws to be applied to labor is perhaps beside the point. The Supreme Court's judgment is informed by its preconceptions concerning public policy, and as to good public policy in economic matters the education of most of the justices is woefully deficient." 50 NEW REPUBLIC 233 (1927).

245. *Bedford Cut Stone*, 274 U.S. at 60 (Brandeis, J., dissenting). In his unsent memorandum to Sanford, Taft had gone out of his way to argue that "The union which is made up of a good many men all over the United States in itself is a conspiracy, if its object is a step in an illegal conspiracy. You don't have to have two unions in order to make a conspiracy. The fact that you have two or more persons in a union may make their joint action a conspiracy." WHT to ETS (January 24, 1927) (Taft papers). Taft refrained from such inflammatory language in the actual memorandum he eventually sent to Sanford. It is noteworthy that Taft did not analogously find that the combination of many individuals into a single corporation was also a conspiracy.

246. *Bedford Cut Stone*, 274 U.S. at 63 (Brandeis, J., dissenting). *See* Note, 40 HARVARD LAW REVIEW 1154 (1927) ("The two cases are clearly distinguishable. The *Duplex* case involved a general boycott which extended outside the industry in question. There was no boycott in the principal case, simply a refusal by members of a crafts union to work on any products which had been manufactured by persons fighting against fellow-members.... The same factor distinguished this case from the cases of secondary boycott."). A later commentator distinguished *Duplex Printing Press* from *Bedford Cut Stone* on the ground that "in the earlier case there had been a psychological reason for the majority decision in that, in order to achieve a closed shop, a powerful union had taken the offensive against a single manufacturer. In the late case no such element was present, since the members of a single craft merely sought to protect themselves against anti-union action by a powerful organization of employers." Osmond K. Fraenkel, *Judicial*

Interpretation of Labor Laws, 6 UNIVERSITY OF CHICAGO LAW REVIEW 577, 580 (1939).

247. *Bedford Cut Stone*, 274 U.S. at 65 (Brandeis, J., dissenting). Justice Harlan had been an early and influential proponent of the rhetoric of involuntary servitude. *See* Arthur v. Oakes, 63 F. 310, 317–18 (7th Cir. 1894) (Opinion by Harlan, J.) ("[T]he vital question remains whether a court of equity will, under any circumstances, by injunction, prevent one individual from quitting the personal service of another? An affirmative answer to this question is not, we think, justified by any authority to which our attention has been called or of which we are aware. It would be an invasion of one's natural liberty to compel him to work for or to remain in the personal service of another. One who is placed under such constraint is in a condition of involuntary servitude, – a condition which the supreme law of the land declares shall not exist within the United States, or in any place subject to their jurisdiction."). Taft had himself occasionally used the rhetoric of involuntary servitude. *See, e.g.*, Address of Hon. William H. Taft, Secretary of War, delivered before the Cooper Union, New York City, Friday, January 10, 1908, in ROBERT LEE DUNN, WILLIAM HOWARD TAFT: AMERICAN 236 (Boston: Chapple Pub. Co. 1908): "It is a very serious question whether under our Constitution a decree of a tribunal under a compulsory arbitration law could be enforced against the side of the laborers. It would come very close to the violation of the thirteenth amendment, which forbids involuntary servitude."

Throughout the 1920s organized labor appealed continuously to the Thirteenth Amendment's prohibition on involuntary servitude as a constraint on the power of states to prohibit strikes. *See, e.g., The Challenge Accepted: Labor Will Not be Outlawed or Enslaved*, 28 AMERICAN FEDERATIONIST 289, 294 (1921); *Gompers Assails Supreme Court, supra* note 89; James Gray Pope, *Labor's Constitution of Freedom*, 106 YALE LAW JOURNAL 941 (1997); sources cited in *supra* Chapter 39, at note 232. To those who approved the Court's decision, however, "Involuntary servitude cannot be claimed here on justifiable constitutional grounds. The individual stone cutter or workingman is free to quit or to state upon what terms he will sell his services – for good reason, a bad one, or none at all; the important point is that he cannot join with others, 'conspire' with them, to do so when as a result, directly and unreasonably, the interstate channel of that industry is clogged." Note, *supra* note 236, at 447. Not surprisingly, therefore, one's view of the question very much depended upon whether the injunction was seen through the lens of the "individual" workingman, see *supra* note 213, or instead through the lens of the "group system." *See* Note, 14 VIRGINIA LAW REVIEW 112, 120 (1927). As one contemporary commentator noted, "The instant case is another example ... of the increasing tendency of the courts to limit the action of workingmen when acting *in unison*." Note, *supra* note 236, at 448 (emphasis added). It was said that the "case exemplifies the progressive tendencies of the courts to recognize the facts that a large co-operating body of men must have some limit placed on their actions in procuring their ultimate ends." Note, 3 NOTRE DAME LAWYER 104, 105 (1927).

248. LDB to Felix Frankfurter (April 11, 1927), in BRANDEIS-FRANKFURTER CORRESPONDENCE, at 283–84.

249. LDB to Felix Frankfurter (April 14, 1927), in BRANDEIS-FRANKFURTER CORRESPONDENCE, at 284.

250. Frankfurter, *supra* note 205. Brandeis wrote Frankfurter that the article was "a stirring document. It looks as if the A.F. of L. were really alive to the danger." LDB to Felix Frankfurter (April 26, 1927), in BRANDEIS-FRANKFURTER CORRESPONDENCE, at 287.
251. Frankfurter, *supra* note 205, at 262–63. Frankfurter continued, "A strange deference to authority moved Mr. Justice Sanford and Mr. Justice Stone." *Id.* Compare Taft: "I presume that the division of the Court will arouse the labor people as usual and they will proceed to damn the Court, but the principle of the case has been covered by so many of our decisions, although only one seems to be in the mind of Stone and Sanford that it seems like harking back to controversies that had long been settled." WHT to Robert A. Taft (April 10, 1927) (Taft papers).
252. Frankfurter, *supra* note 205, at 263–64. As the *New Republic* would opine six months later, injunctions like those at issue in *Bedford Cut Stone*, which enforce "the whip of the Sherman Act," "virtually prohibit unions from defending their very existence so long as the products of their labor are sold in interstate commerce." *Anti-Trust Laws, or Anti-Labor?*, 52 NEW REPUBLIC 276, 277–78 (1927).
253. Frankfurter, *supra* note 205, at 264. As one commentator observed, "The extreme position which the federal courts have now reached in condemning secondary economic pressure in labor cases is likely to produce an extreme reaction if organized labor and its sympathizers regain political strength." Note, 4 WISCONSIN LAW REVIEW 250, 255 (1927). Realizing the important political implications of the decision, Taft immediately wrote Coolidge: "In pursuance of my promise, I enclose herewith Mr. Justice Sutherland's opinion in the Bedford Cut Stone case." WHT to Calvin Coolidge (April 12, 1927) (Taft papers).
254. *Strike Injunction Upheld in Highest Court*, BROOKLYN STANDARD UNION (April 14, 1927), at 8.
255. David Lawrence, *Blow to Labor Boycott in Stone Cutters' Decision*, ASHBURY PARK PRESS (April 14, 1927), at 6. "The majority opinion ... rests squarely upon the law and the evidence, and this is the place where it should rest. The Supreme Court is not a legislative but a judicial body. It interprets but does not make the laws. If any relief is sought it must be by an appeal to Congress." *Supreme Court on the Boycott*, LEXINGTON HERALD-LEADER (April 16, 1927), at 4. The eminent and sympathetic authority Edwin Witte observed that "While there is really little that is new in the Bedford Cut Stone Company decision, the doctrines therein announced have never been accepted by labor as being the law, and, consequently, have aroused widespread alarm and resentment." Edwin E. Witte, *The Journeymen Stonecutters' Decision and other Recent Decisions against Organized Labor*, 17 AMERICAN LABOR LEGISLATION REVIEW 139, 140 (1927).
256. *The Bedford Stone Case*, LANSING STATE JOURNAL (April 15, 1927), at 6. "The reasoning of the Supreme Court is absolutely concurrent with commonsense. Labor unions and business concerns should stand before the law on the same footing and neither should be allowed to use force against the other. The elements of justice in a case of this kind seem too clear and obvious even to warrant a judicial opinion." *Busting a Labor Union Trust*, GREENVILLE NEWS (April 16, 1927), at 4. The *Des Moines Register*, however, noted that the decision was "evidence of the slant of the court as now constituted." "If the logic of this decision is followed," the *Register* reasoned, "it will outlaw strikes. ... [I]t is expressive of a desire and reflective of a tendency to give free rein to open shop employers and to

check unions." *The Right to Strike*, DES MOINES REGISTER (April 23, 1927), at 4. See Royce, *supra* note 242, at 27 ("There is no doubt that the decision in the *Bedford Stone* case goes further to limit organized labor in its struggle for existence than a large section of the population thinks fair or necessary.").

257. MIAMI HERALD (April 13, 1927), at 13.

258. It was observed that it was "equally consistent with the facts ... to say that the 'sole purpose' was not to interfere with the distribution of plaintiff's product, and even less with interstate commerce as such. The defendant union was not interested in that of itself, but was rather trying to get the plaintiffs to operate their shops again on a union basis. ... In reiterating that the general order to strike against the petitioners' product could have no purpose other than that of coercing or inducing the local employers to refrain from purchasing such product, the court seems to minimize the importance of the re-organization of the petitioners' shops and quarries, although in a later part of the decision, it conceded that this was the ultimate end in view." Note, 37 YALE LAW JOURNAL 84, 86–87 (1927).

259. "Many acute thinkers have been unable to discover any substantial difference in principle between ... the *Bedford Cut Stone* case on the one hand, and the *San Francisco Industrial Association* case on the other. The truth of the matter seems to be that under recent interpretations of the Sherman and Clayton Acts the limits of what constitutes restraint of trade and commerce among the several states are even more illusory than those of the common law doctrine; as a result, decisions under the Sherman Act especially in the field of labor law have come to depend very largely upon the underlying philosophies and social beliefs of individual judges. ... It is high time that the anti-trust laws, designed to prevent the monopolization of trade, should be amended so as to prevent their being utilized as a weapon for attack upon the principle of collective bargaining." Sayre, *supra* note 196, at 690–91. For a trenchant analysis, see Powell, *The Supreme Court's Control over the Issue of Injunctions*, *supra* note 147, at 59–60.

260. Note, 1 ST. JOHN'S LAW REVIEW 189, 189 (1927). Thus in 1930 the chair of the Committee on the Study of Anti-Trust Legislation of the National Civil Federation reported a consensus conclusion that *"every strike, no matter how peaceful, if it interfered with commodities in interstate commerce, is unlawful."* Wheeler P. Bloodgood, *The Effects of the Administration of the Anti-Trust Laws Upon Labor and Services*, 147 ANNALS OF THE AMERICAN ACADEMY OF POLITICAL AND SOCIAL SCIENCE 111, 112 (1930) (emphasis in the original).

261. *The Barrier against Boycotts*, NEW YORK HERALD TRIBUNE (April 15, 1927), at 20.

262. Note, *supra* note 258, at 96.

263. Royce, *supra* note 242, at 19 ("It was apparent from the newspaper reports of the Convention of the American Federation of Labor at Los Angeles that efforts will be made to obtain Congressional action making the Anti-Trust laws inapplicable to labor activities, even if repeal of those laws is necessary to that end. This agitation is clearly the direct result of the decision of the United States Supreme Court on April 11, 1927, in the case of *Bedford Cut Stone*.").

264. Witte, *supra* note 255, at 139.

265. *Asks Labor Relief from Sherman Act*, NEW YORK TIMES (April 13, 1927), at 27. See *Labor Expected to Act against Injunction Law*, CHRISTIAN SCIENCE MONITOR

(April 13, 1927), at 1; *Labor Seeks Exemption from Law*, PITTSBURGH PRESS (April 22, 1927), at 15.

266. *Labor Plans War in Injunction Case*, NEW YORK TIMES (May 26, 1927), at 28. See *Labor Plans to Restrict Injunctions*, HARTFORD COURANT (May 26, 1927), at 23; *Injunctions on Labor Opposed and Defended*, NEW YORK TIMES (August 28, 1927), at XXII.

267. Mussolini released his Charter of Labor the week after *Bedford Cut Stone* was announced. The Charter prohibited "strikes, lockouts, sabotage, and boycotts," and it provided for compulsory arbitration. *Italy Puts Boss and Worker in Grip of State*, CHICAGO DAILY TRIBUNE (April 22, 1927), at 14. Green denounced the Charter in virtually the same terms as he condemned *Bedford Cut Stone*: "The so-called fascist 'charter of labor' is a proclamation of enslavement in that it reduces the working people subject to it to a condition of industrial servitude. It is a blow at human freedom and sets up compulsory methods in industry for private initiative and freedom of contract." *Green Warns Labor Fascism Kills Liberty*, CHICAGO DAILY TRIBUNE (April 24, 1927), at 1. "Makes us think of the old days when we were fighting the Kansas Industrial Court Law, doesn't it?" asked the *Stone Cutters Journal*. Adam Coaldigger, *All to the Bad*, STONE CUTTERS JOURNAL (June 1927), at 4. *See, e.g., Fascism's Latest*, BALTIMORE SUN (April 23, 1927), at 8. Directly drawing the connection between fascist Italy and the *Bedford Cut Stone* decision, the A.F. of L. Weekly News Bulletin observed, "If workers must give their labor lest others be inconvenienced, where is the difference between this and Mussolini's system that outlaws strikes and sets wages by arbitrary compulsion?" Quoted in Coaldigger, *supra*, at 5–6. *See "Brandeis and Holmes Dissenting"*, 51 GRANITE CUTTERS' JOURNAL 7 (June 1927).

268. STONE CUTTERS JOURNAL (May 1927), at 10. *See Strikes and Boycotts, supra* note 193, at 880; Note, 26 MICHIGAN LAW REVIEW 198, 201 (1927). "The Supreme Court of the United States has again given evidence that it is no friend of labor. Its members, attorneys for corporations, usually, before their appointment to judicial offices, carry their prejudices to the bench with them. And when opportunity offers they declare those prejudices to be the law of the land. . . . The latest pronouncement of the court takes from organized labor one of its most effective weapons. It is now declared unlawful for the members of a union to agree together that they will not handle work which has been produced in part by non-union men of their own craft." William H. Holly, *The Stone Cutters and the Supreme Court*, 51 GRANITE CUTTERS' JOURNAL 24 (June 1927). On the consequences of the decision for union practices, see Edwin E. Witte, *Social Consequences of Injunctions in Labor Disputes*, 24 ILLINOIS LAW REVIEW 772, 779 (1930).

269. *Another Judicial Assault*, 26 GARMENT WORKER 4 (April 22, 1927). The president of the National Founders' Association countered that "no union shall have the power to destroy an industry which [it] cannot dominate. They want unlimited power and immunity from their own destructive efforts. . . . It is strange that the simple right in property, which would seem to be easily understood, is so strongly attacked by the union leaders while they so strongly defend their own inherent rights and property. The lesson from this whole case is that unionism is as dangerous today as it ever was, and its sheep's clothing does not completely cover the aggressive wolf of destruction." *Says Unions Would Retain Power to Destroy Industry*, HARTFORD COURANT (May 2, 1927), at 19.

270. I. Weinzweig, *Anti-Labor Decision*, 12 THE ADVANCE 4 (April 29, 1927).
271. LDB to Felix Frankfurter (April 26, 1927), in BRANDEIS-FRANKFURTER CORRESPONDENCE, at 287.
272. Coaldigger, *supra* note 267, at 4 (quoting from A.F. of L. Weekly News Bulletin).
273. *Id.*
274. *Justice Brandeis Arms Court Opponents*, 26 GARMENT WORKER 4 (April 29, 1927). See *"Brandeis and Holmes Dissenting"*, *supra* note 267.
275. REPORT OF PROCEEDINGS OF THE FORTY-SEVENTH ANNUAL CONVENTION OF THE AMERICAN FEDERATION OF LABOR, *supra* note 112, at 320.
276. Toledo, A.A. & N. M. Ry. Co. v. Pennsylvania Co., 54 F. 730, 743 (Cir. Ct. N.D. Ohio 1893).
277. "There is no prayer to enjoin the members of the union from quitting. The injunction is against the union, which of course means the officers of the union and against the entity, which would direct the men through their officers, and in this case the President of the National Union, to strike for the purpose of enforcing the boycott. A union of men engaged together is in itself, if engaged in something that illegally injures another, a conspiracy. The fact that the union itself is an entity does not prevent the combination of the members from constituting a conspiracy." WHT to ETS (January 25, 1927) (Taft papers). See *supra* note 213.
278. Taft also knew, however, that individual workingmen who quit for the wrong reasons – who quit to inflict unjustified injury on their employers – were also individually "liable in damages to the complainant if any injury is thereby inflicted." Toledo, A.A. & N. M. Ry. Co. v. Pennsylvania Co., 54 F. 730, 743 (Cir. Ct. N.D. Ohio 1893).
279. "[T]he act of the union officers in calling a strike deserves careful consideration. Although ... laborers can never be directly forbidden to quit work, ... yet under the modern aspect of trade organizations, a strike may in reality be effectually blocked by placing certain inhibitions upon these officers." James Wallace Bryan, *Injunctions against Strikes*, 40 AMERICAN LAW REVIEW 42, 50–51 (1906).
280. See *supra* Chapter 39, at 1235.
281. In dissent in Hopkins v. Oxley Stave Co., 83 F. 912, 932 (8th Cir. 1897), one of the early and most influential cases to enjoin a labor boycott, Eighth Circuit Judge Henry Clay Caldwell wrote: "While laborers, by the application to them of the doctrine we are considering, are reduced to individual action, it is not so with the forces arrayed against them. A corporation is an association of individuals for combined action; trusts are corporations combined together for the very purpose of collective action and boycotting; and capital, which is the product of labor, is in itself a powerful collective force."
282. As William Green testified before a Senate subcommittee in February 1928:

> [W]e are not attempting to interfere with the rights of any individuals; ... but we are living in an age of organization, an age when practically everything worth while is being accomplished through organized efforts. ... [I]n this day of organization of corporations and powerful employing interests, how is it possible for the individual workingman to promote his own economic, social, and individual interest through independent effort or individual action? There is no opportunity for the individual to cope with these large corporations. ... [I]s it right in this modern age that working men should be rendered voiceless through the use of these injunctions; that they must be told that they can not talk to their fellow men,

tell them when a grievance is on and where a strike is in effect? Must we be denied the right of free speech and free press and free assemblage?

Statement of William Green, President American Federation of Labor, in *Limiting Scope of Injunctions in Labor Disputes* (February 11, 1928), Hearings before a Subcommittee of the Senate Committee on the Judiciary on S. 1482 70th CONG. 1st SESS., at 92–93. *See* ROBERT FRANKLIN HOXIE, TRADE UNIONISM IN THE UNITED STATES 232 (New York: D. Appleton & Co. 1919): "[T]he law, built on the individualistic basis, refuses to recognize that one group of workers in a union is vitally affected by or interested in the conditions of another group even in the same union, and in this it fails to recognize the interrelationship of the modern evolving industrial situation. It cannot do so, while it is based on the absolutistic assumptions of individual freedom and free competition. On the basis of these assumptions, it has little capacity for dealing with developed and developing machine industry."

283. *See To Define and Limit the Jurisdiction of Courts Sitting in Equity*, Sen. Rep. No. 1060, Pt. 2 (Minority Views), 71st CONG. 2nd SESS. (June 18, 1930), at 7:

> It is obvious that existing conditions under which large employers of labor possess unprecedented power to dictate contract and conditions of employment have been developed through governmental grants of authority to form corporations and organizations of corporations. . . . Such a power, unrestrained by the organization of labor, would permit employers arbitrarily to fix the wages and conditions of labor under which millions of men and women would find their only opportunity to earn a living.
>
> A single laborer, standing alone, confronted with such far-reaching, overwhelming concentration of employer power, and compelled to labor for the support of himself and family, is absolutely helpless to negotiate or to exert any influence over the fixing of his wages or the hours and conditions of his labor. A man must work in order to live. If he can exercise no control over his conditions of employment, he is subjected to involuntary servitude.

284. LOUIS D. BRANDEIS, BUSINESS – A PROFESSION 369 (Boston: Hale, Cushman & Flint 1933).
285. *Duplex Printing Press*, 254 U.S. at 481 (Brandeis, J., dissenting).
286. "A judge, inevitably, takes with him to the bench the same slant at economic and social questions which he had as a member of the bar. . . . If his early years were spent in an individualistic community – any small city or town in the seventies or eighties for instance – it will be difficult for him to have an intelligent understanding of collectivist ideas or the problem of present-day industrial centres." DAVID E. LILIENTHAL, *Labor and the Courts*, 34 NEW REPUBLIC 314, 316 (1923).
287. At the 1927 Annual AFL Convention, delegates were treated to the firebrand oratory of Chicago labor attorney Hope Thompson, whose remarks "were greeted with prolonged applause." John J. Leary, *Proposes Labor Unite on Judges*, BOSTON DAILY GLOBE (October 8, 1927), at 7.

> Legislation is more friendly to labor than the courts, and the reason is clear. The legislators are elected and come among us with frequent short terms. They are more human. Many of them are not lawyers. You can get a lot through a legislature, but as a rule, if that law is humanitarian to any considerable extent, if it really protects workingmen, the courts will take a butcher knife and cut it all to pieces.
>
> Why do they do it? . . . In almost all cases the judges are lawyers who have served capital and capitalist interests. They have had a lifetime of training in that

point of view. It is not a matter of dishonesty with them, it is not a matter of any intention to be unfair, but it is a bias that has been born and trained into them through the years of their early life.

Hope Thompson, *Address*, in REPORT OF PROCEEDINGS OF THE FORTY-SEVENTH ANNUAL CONVENTION OF THE AMERICAN FEDERATION OF LABOR, *supra* note 112, at 225. Interstate commerce, said Thompson, is "the god of the courts!" *Id.*

288. *Report of A.F.of L. Executive Council*, in REPORT OF PROCEEDINGS OF THE FORTY-SEVENTH ANNUAL CONVENTION OF THE AMERICAN FEDERATION OF LABOR, *supra* note 112, at 40.

289. REPORT OF PROCEEDINGS OF THE FORTY-SEVENTH ANNUAL CONVENTION OF THE AMERICAN FEDERATION OF LABOR, *supra* note 112, at 154–55. See *id.* at 307.

290. *Id.* at 293. *See* Matthew Woll, *Organized Labor Demands Repeal of the Sherman Act*, 147 ANNALS OF THE AMERICAN ACADEMY OF POLITICAL AND SOCIAL SCIENCE 185 (1930) ("Repeal or modification of the anti-combination and anti-conspiracy provisions of existing laws, specifically of the Sherman and the Clayton Acts, is regarded by American organized labor as a national necessity in the interest of progress, freedom, justice and democracy.").

291. REPORT OF PROCEEDINGS OF THE FORTY-SEVENTH ANNUAL CONVENTION OF THE AMERICAN FEDERATION OF LABOR, *supra* note 112, at 320.

292. Pub. L. 72-65, 47 Stat. 70 (March 23, 1932). Testifying before the first Senate hearings that would eventually lead to the enactment of the Norris-LaGuardia Act, Green offered *Bedford Cut Stone* as Exhibit A to illustrate the need for legislative reform. Statement of William Green, *supra* note 282, at 42–60. For the tumultuous story of the Act's design, see WITTE, *supra* note 76, at 273–79; and GEORGE I. LOVELL, LEGISLATIVE DEFERRALS: STATUTORY AMBIGUITY, JUDICIAL POWER, AND AMERICAN DEMOCRACY 161–216 (Cambridge University Press 2003).

293. *Labor Injunctions Assailed by Green in Chicago Speech*, HARTFORD COURANT (January 14, 1928), at 2. "In the last few years injunctions against organized labor have increased, not only in number but in extent. Some are so sweeping that members of trade unions are forbidden to organize other workers, to strike to withhold service from unfair employers or to exercise normal trade-union functions. There is scarcely any trade-union activity which has not been restrained or denied through the ever-broadening use of the writ of injunction. Because of this tendency, labor reasons that in many instances, the courts either consciously or unconsciously place themselves on the side of corporations and big business in their attempts to destroy labor organizations. The question of economic freedom is involved in this court injunction problem." William Green, *Injunctions before the Senate*, 35 AMERICAN FEDERATIONIST 145 (1928).

294. *Labor Starts Drive against Injunction*, NEW YORK TIMES (February 6, 1928), at 6.

CHAPTER 41

Government by Injunction

O N JULY 2, 1894, the very day on which Taft was asked to consider the legality of the Pullman boycott of Eugene Debs and his American Railway Union ("ARU"),[1] the administration of Grover Cleveland entered federal court in Chicago and sought definitively to resolve the exploding railroad crisis.[2] The 150,000-member ARU had managed to bring rail traffic within the United States to a terrifying halt, blocking "shipment of the nation's vital supplies, including food, fuel, and livestock."[3] The country experienced the disruption as "the greatest strike, inaugurating the most tremendous, as well as the most disastrous labor agitation of the nineteenth century . . . [,] the fiercest, most stupendous battle ever waged between capital and labor."[4]

Cleveland's attorney general, Richard Olney, decided to use an innovative legal tactic to end the strife. He prayed for "an injunction of so broad and sweeping a character that interference with the railroads, even of the remotest kind, will be made practically impossible without incurring penalties for contempt of court."[5] The federal court did not even wait a day before issuing an omnibus injunction addressed to Debs and several named defendants, as well as to "all persons combining and conspiring with them, and all persons whosoever," ordering them to "desist and refrain from," *inter alia*, interfering with rail traffic, and from "compelling or inducing . . . by threats, intimidation, persuasion, force or violence, any" railroad employees "to refuse or fail to perform any of their duties as employés . . . in connection with the interstate business or commerce" of the railroads.[6]

It was a pivotal moment in the history of equity jurisprudence in the United States. Two months later, at the annual meeting of the American Bar Association ("ABA"), lawyers spent an entire day discussing the startling implications of this groundbreaking use of federal equitable power. They listened to a long scholarly paper by St. Louis attorney Charles Claflin Allen, who sought to grasp the recent "revolution . . . of equity jurisdiction." "What is the purpose," Allen asked, "of issuing injunctions against great masses of men? ... Is it intended that the mere issuing of the writ should act *in terrorem* over the entire body of men engaged in the strike? Or is it expected, by posting copies in public places, to establish a novel method of service by publication?" Surely "the real purpose" of the injunction, Allen suggested, is to call "forth the power of the court to punish for contempt; to make of a court of equity in practical effect a criminal court."[7]

The corporate lawyers who commented on Allen's paper tended to praise the court's bold intervention.[8] Conceding that the injunction "was an unprecedented exercise of power," they stressed that it was a "great advantage" of "judge-made law" that it could "mould itself to the exigencies of society and to the requirements of the occasion."[9] "Equity has always recognized the right to enjoin irreparable injuries to property. The chancellor did not consider whether or not there might also be a punishment for that offence if it should be committed. He sought by injunction to prevent it. He did not seek to prevent it because it was a crime."[10] It was generally agreed that although summary trials for criminal contempt "placed" a "grave responsibility" on judges, we could nevertheless "safely trust the courts" to execute their new duties.[11]

When the Debs injunction was upheld by a Circuit Court in December,[12] John Peter Altgeld, Illinois's fiery governor, elevated these seemingly technical questions into a white-hot political controversy. He accused the federal court of having staged a deadly "usurpation" by creating "government by injunction, whereby a Federal Judge not content with deciding controversies brought into his court ... proceeds to legislate and then to administer. He issues a ukase which he calls an injunction forbidding whatever he pleases and what the law does not forbid and thus legislates for himself without limitation and make things penal which the law does not make penal ... and he deprives men of the right of trial by jury when the law guarantees this right, and he then enforces this ukase in a summary and arbitrary manner by imprisonment, throwing men into prison, not for violating a law, but for being guilty of a contempt of court in disregarding one of these injunctions." Altgeld asserted that federal courts were not to be trusted with this immense and novel power, because they were "special guardians of corporations ... determined to crush labor organizations."[13] Courts purported to speak for the public interest, but in fact they spoke only for their corporate masters.

The Supreme Court upheld the injunction in May in an epic opinion captioned In re *Debs*.[14] Altgeld immediately charged that the Court had marked "a turning-point in our history, for it establishes a new form of government: that is, government by injunction. The provision of the Constitution that no man shall be deprived of his liberty without a trial by an impartial jury is practically wiped out by this decision of the Supreme Court ... and the theory that ours is a government of law is now at an end, for every community is now subject to any whim or caprice which any Federal judge may promulgate."[15] "For a number of years," Altgeld later said, "the great corporations and trusts and syndicates have carefully looked after the matter of appointments to the Federal bench, and so great was their influence that few could be appointed who were not satisfactory to them. In many cases men were taken out of the corporation offices and put on the Federal bench. These men brought with them all of the bias and prejudice that takes possession of men who have long been subject to corporate influence and environment."[16]

Altgeld's attack struck a political nerve. The following year the Democratic Party included in its 1896 platform a plank objecting "to government by injunction as a new and highly dangerous form of oppression by which Federal Judges, in contempt of the laws of the States and rights of citizens, become at once legislators, judges and executioners."[17] The phrase "government by injunction" quickly became "a synonym of modern tyranny."[18] Only three years after *Debs*, the *Albany Law Journal* could observe that "the exercise of no function of the judiciary of this country to-day is receiving so much adverse criticism as that of the exercise of the power to stay acts or the assumed acts of any number of persons by the writ of injunction, so that the term, 'government by injunction,' has become a term very familiar to ears and eyes" as a "term of reproach."[19] Even the *Wall Street Journal* was prepared to concede that there were many legitimate "objections" to the deployment of injunctions "in the case of a dispute between employer and employe."[20]

The most thoughtful and precise critique of the new-fangled labor injunctions was offered by Brandeis's law partner, William H. Dunbar, who carefully detailed how "federal courts . . . have shown a disposition to extend their powers beyond any limits heretofore recognized."[21] Equitable decrees, Dunbar reasoned, drew their authority from the *in personam* jurisdiction of a court over parties to a controversy. But injunctions seeking to control the behavior of "all other persons whomsoever" far exceeded this authority. "The right to lay down general rules for the government of the community, to declare *ex cathedra*, in advance of any contentious proceedings in which the question arises, what may and what may not lawfully be done, to impose on the whole community a duty to refrain from doing a certain act, is in its nature a legislative right."[22] Courts were, in effect, enacting statutes and displacing duly elected legislators.

Cutting to the heart of the matter, Dunbar asked what equity could possibly add to the effectiveness of the state acting "through its police and, if necessary, its military force," to control what otherwise would be the crimes of striking employees. The obvious answer was that criminal prosecutions required jury trials, whereas criminal contempt could be summarily punished by a single federal judge. Because strikers were generally supported by their communities, it was difficult to induce juries to convict.[23] Everyone assumed that Chicago juries would refuse to find ARU members guilty.

It was black-letter law that a court could grant extraordinary equitable relief like an injunction only if a litigant lacked an adequate remedy at law. An adequate remedy might in theory include a criminal prosecution. "It is difficult to believe," Dunbar wrote, "that jurisdiction in equity can be supported on the ground that a judge in chancery will probably . . . reach one conclusion, while a jury at law on the same state of facts is likely to reach a contrary conclusion." Could it be possible, Dunbar asked, that the "likelihood that a jury will deny punishment affords a ground for seeking relief in equity?"[24]

Because labor injunctions effectively promulgated rules for the governance of future conduct, and because the enforcement of such injunctions displaced juries as a limitation on the application of criminal sanctions, federal equity threatened to bypass institutions long believed essential to check raw official coercion. Dunbar feared that the exercise of unrestrained judicial power in the context of virulent labor controversies might undermine the legitimacy required by courts to perform their essential function, which was to resolve disputes between litigants. Courts could not successfully adjudicate disputes if they came to be perceived as political organs of repression.

Dunbar's apprehension proved prophetic. At the turn of the century, federal courts aggressively expanded their equitable jurisdiction, seeking to tame the most violent and heated controversies of the day, controversies that Thomas Cooley in his 1894 ABA Presidential Address likened to "civil war."[25] Judicial efforts to control that war were without legislative warrant, and plainly courts could not justify their decisions by drawing upon a common reservoir of crystallized public sentiment. Courts were thus left exposed and vulnerable. The predictable consequence was that labor injunctions rapidly frayed the authority of federal courts in the eyes of working people, who came to despise courts as "engines of government for the coercion of labor."[26] Labor condemned the injunction as "a despotic government vested in the judiciary."[27] Organized labor came to believe that injunctions were not expressions of law at all, but were instead illegitimate efforts to impose the political views of judges.[28]

Professor William Draper Lewis, who would eventually help create the American Law Institute, thought that labor injunctions undermined "that respect for the court[s] which is the rich product of our civilization, and which is the very force which makes these injunctions a success at the present time. One cannot come in contact with the class adversely affected by these orders without at once perceiving that we are rapidly undermining one of the props of that social order which is necessary for the continuation of any civilization."[29] Far preferable, said an author in the *Albany Law Journal*, to "keep the Federal judiciary as free as possible from taint of partiality or forwardness in mixing into matters of a social-political character. These questions and struggles growing out of the critical relations of capital and labor have assumed, to an extent, a political issue; and it is better policy that the Federal courts should avoid as much as possible, and as much as consistent with the proper exercise of their duties, the assuming of jurisdiction over the questions involved."[30]

The labor injunction that emerged from the maelstrom of the 1890s nevertheless "became the principal legal instrument for governing industrial conflict and a major obstacle to unionism for the next four decades."[31] Organized labor thought that it had solved the problem of the labor injunction by the enactment of the Clayton Act in 1914, but *Duplex Printing Press* in 1921 made clear that labor was mistaken.[32] The Clayton Act in fact enlarged the availability of injunctions, making them for the first time accessible to private parties. In 1917, *Hitchman* authorized injunctive relief to prevent union organizing if employees had signed yellow-dog contracts,[33] thus opening a path to federal equitable jurisdiction to virtually any employer with foresight whose business could claim the shelter of federal diversity jurisdiction or a sufficient connection to interstate commerce.

As the decade of the 1920s began, therefore, the problem of labor injunctions loomed larger than ever.[34] "The judiciary of the United States, federal and state,"

Government by Injunction

Gompers dryly noted in 1923, "has gone injunction mad."[35] Throughout the decade courts issued labor injunctions in ever-increasing numbers.[36] In 1927 alone, some 700 injunctions were levied against labor.[37]

Dunbar was proved correct that the "effectiveness of the injunction to break strikes was found to lie in the speed with which labor men of high and low rank who might violate an order given in an *ex parte* hearing might be sent to jail."[38] An efficient "instrument of police in labor struggles,"[39] the injunction was experienced by working people as "a 'most elastic instrument of tyranny,'"[40] and its reform became "labor's foremost legislative demand."[41] If progressives objected to the invalidation of economic and social regulations under the Due Process Clause, "the principal ground for dissatisfaction" among workers was the labor injunction, "defining and limiting the rights of organizations of labor, particularly in connection with strikes."[42] "On no other issue is labor so united; conservatives and radicals alike regard injunctions as an outrage and in strongest terms denounce the courts which issue them."[43]

In 1930, Felix Frankfurter and Nathan Greene reported that "the extraordinary remedy of injunction" had in fact become "the ordinary legal remedy, almost the sole remedy."[44] The labor injunction inspired intense "bitterness" because it made "infraction of a criminal statute also a contempt of court," and so essentially evaded "the safeguards of criminal procedure."[45] By addressing injunctions to "all persons whomsoever," federal equitable power transformed a "particular controversy between particular parties – which is the limited sphere of judicial power," into "the occasion for a code of conduct governing the whole community."[46] The result was a judiciary with manifestly "weakened prestige."[47] As federal courts reached out to govern the civil war between capital and labor, their impartiality and authority grew increasingly suspect.

Even so impeccable a white-shoe lawyer as Senator George Wharton Pepper could unambiguously attribute "the growing bitterness of organized labor toward the federal courts" to the malign influence of labor injunctions.[48] "Respect for courts is not the least valuable part of our English inheritance," Pepper cautioned in 1924. "Under such a system of government as ours the maintenance of well-nigh universal confidence in the judiciary is pretty nearly essential to national safety. Is it not worth our while to place elsewhere than upon our federal judges" the burden of absorbing "the shock of our industrial warfare?"[49]

Taft was at the very center of these developments. He ascended to the Court trailing a long, influential connection to the development of federal equity jurisdiction. His 1893 decision in *Toledo, A.A. & N. M. Ry. Co. v. Pennsylvania Co.*[50] was an early and consequential discussion of the capacity of federal courts equitably to intervene in labor disputes. Only three months after the Court's announcement of In re *Debs*, Taft celebrated the decision before the annual meeting of the ABA as "a great judgment of a great court."[51] As a presidential candidate, Taft firmly defended the need for contempt prosecutions to be tried before judges rather than juries. "It would greatly weaken the authority and force of an order of court if it were known that it was not to be enforced except after a verdict of jury."[52] Displaying the deep distrust of juries that was a constant theme in his career,[53] Taft explained that "the uncertainties and digressions and prejudices that are injected into a jury trial ... would ... make the order of the court go for nothing."[54]

In his inaugural address as president, Taft acknowledged that "the power of the federal courts to issue injunctions in industrial disputes" was a topic "which has awakened the most excited discussions." He agreed to press for technical changes in the issuance of temporary restraining orders, which were often decisive in breaking the momentum of a strike and yet which were frequently issued *ex parte* on the basis of unexamined affidavits. But Taft also unambiguously announced that "my convictions are fixed. Take away from the courts, if it could be taken away, the power to issue injunctions in labor disputes, and it would create a privileged class among the laborers and save the lawless among their number from a most needful remedy available to all men for the protection of their business against lawless invasion."[55]

In 1911, Brandeis, together with other luminaries like Jane Addams, wrote President Taft to stress the "serious distrust which has come to be felt by great masses of workers toward the fabric of our law and the structure and control of the machinery through which we apply it."[56] The letter had little effect. In accepting the Republican Party nomination for a second term, Taft remained adamantly opposed to all efforts "to weaken the courts by forbidding the use of the writ of injunction to protect a lawful business against the destructive effect of a secondary boycott and by interposing a jury in contempt proceedings brought to enforce the court's order and decrees."[57]

Two years later, Taft explained that the inadequacy of ordinary criminal sanctions was due precisely to the disparity between legal rights and community values. The criminal law was an inadequate instrument of social control, Taft argued, because of "the inertia or political timidity of the officers of the law or the prejudice of voters and juries growing out of sympathy with the cause, in supposed furtherance of which, such offenses are committed."[58] Speaking to the graduating class of Cincinnati Law School in May 1914, Taft attacked the pending Clayton Act on the ground that it gave "reign to lawlessness" and weakened "the power of courts" by providing "that no court can enforce its deliberate judgment made after full hearing against a defiant and disobedient defendant, until a jury has been called after judgment to decide that he is disobedient. This gives a defeated litigant the opportunity to have a judgment or decree carefully rendered, reviewed by a jury with every opportunity to appeal to emotion, prejudice and irrelevant circumstances. This is a recall of judicial decisions in miniature, but in its way quite as dangerous an innovation."[59]

Taft's defense of equitable power foreshadows the position he would later adopt in the context of prohibition. As chief justice, Taft would seek to uphold the dignity of the Eighteenth Amendment by insisting on harsh enforcement measures to impose prohibition in the teeth of entrenched popular opposition. Taft's case for strict enforcement of labor injunctions advanced a similar argument. Swift and certain punishment was necessary to sustain the requirements of legality, especially when legality diverged from community mores.

Government by Injunction

In the context of prohibition, however, Taft sought to vindicate the legal authority of the Constitution. In the context of labor injunctions, by contrast, Taft sought to uphold merely the discretionary decrees of individual judges. Sometimes these decrees enforced the requirements of general common law, as in *American Steel Foundries*, and sometimes, as in *Bedford Cut Stone*, they enforced federal anti-trust legislation, which, as Taft himself had explained, meant reading common law precedents into the vague and opaque words of the Sherman Act.[60] If the authority of common law derived from its representation of "public sentiment ... crystallized in general custom,"[61] it is surely curious that federal labor injunctions were so detested that juries refused to enforce them.

The unpopularity of labor injunctions poses an important conceptual puzzle. If labor injunctions could draw authority neither from common and traditional values, nor from positive legislation, exactly what principle of legality was Taft so concerned to defend? Taft's memorandum to Sanford in Bedford Cut Stone suggests that Taft's determined support for labor injunctions ultimately derived from his commitment to protecting the property and prerogatives of employers.[62] For Taft, labor injunctions protected employers in the exercise of that "initiative and enterprise of capital necessary to the real progress of all."[63] His intense lifelong advocacy for labor injunctions, in other words, was almost certainly motivated by the same principles as those that led Taft to invest property rights with such powerful constitutional protection.

As chance would have it, Taft, sitting as chief justice, would decide an important case dealing with the requirement of a jury trial for criminal contempt, *Michaelson v. United States*,[64] as well as a major case dealing with a wholesale restriction on the judicial labor injunctions, *Truax v. Corrigan*.[65] In *Michaelson*, Taft demonstrated his great capacity for political flexibility and compromise, whereas in *Truax* he evinced his determination to preserve what he regarded as constitutional essentials.

An important requirement of the Clayton Act was its provision that defendants in cases for contempt could choose to be tried by a jury instead of by a judge, so long as their contempt had not been "committed in the presence of the court, or so near thereto as to obstruct the administration of justice," and so long as the alleged contemptuous act was "of such character as to constitute also a criminal offense under any statute of the United States, or under the laws of any State in which the act was committed."[66] This provision of the Clayton Act, which was "most hotly contested in Congress,"[67] did not specify whether the contempt at issue was civil or criminal. From labor's point of view, the provision was needed to prevent federal equity judges from becoming "at once legislators, judges and executioners."[68] The interposition of the jury was intended to impose an "element of popular cooperation" before punishment, which it was hoped would result in "public confidence, in the enforcement of law."[69]

During the Railroad Shopmen's strike of 1922, federal courts issued approximately 300 injunctions to control labor protests.[70] Workmen who were convicted of criminal contempt for violating these injunctions, and whose contempt consisted of acts that might otherwise have been prosecuted as crimes, argued that the Clayton

Act entitled them to a jury trial, which they had been denied. But in *Michaelson v. United States* their convictions were upheld by "a most powerful Circuit Court of Appeals in an opinion written by a very able judge,"[71] Francis E. Baker.

Baker reasoned that it was an inherent attribute of the "judicial power" granted by Article III of the Constitution for a federal judge who was otherwise seized with jurisdiction to hear a case in equity to punish an offender for criminal contempt. Once a federal court acquired jurisdiction, it automatically and irrevocably possessed this inherent power. Congress "can, as a potter, shape the vessel of jurisdiction, the capacity to receive; but, the vessel having been made, the judicial power of the United States is poured into the vessel, large or small, not by Congress, but by the Constitution." The judicial power included the right to "enforce" an equitable decree through "the deterrent effect of fine, or imprisonment for a definite period"; "the vindication or enforcement of the decree must be held to be an inherent power of the equity court, a power within the power to render the decree."[72] The Clayton Act was therefore unconstitutional to the extent that it stripped federal judges of the inherent Article III power to punish criminal contempt without a jury.

Michaelson was argued at the Supreme Court on April 9–10, 1924. Given the intensity and persistence of Taft's articulated opposition to "interposing a jury in contempt proceedings," it comes as something of a surprise to read in Butler's notes that on April 12 Taft spoke first at conference and announced that "Congress has power to give jury trial in a punitive case – criminal."[73] Although McKenna disagreed, all other members of the Court concurred, McReynolds doing so "tentatively." Taft assigned the opinion to Sutherland, who carried the case over the summer and announced a clear, compact, and forceful opinion the following October.

The essential question to be answered, Sutherland said, is whether the Clayton Act "infringes any power of the courts vested by the Constitution and unalterable by congressional legislation."[74] Invoking the avoidance canon and quoting previous case law, Sutherland explained that it was the duty of the Court to construe the statute "if fairly possible, so as to avoid, not only the conclusion that it is unconstitutional, but also grave doubts upon that score." By interpreting the statute to apply only to criminal contempt, as distinct from civil contempt, Sutherland was "at once relieved of the doubt which might otherwise arise in respect of the authority of Congress to set aside the settled rule that a suit in equity is to be tried by the chancellor without a jury," since "the proceeding for criminal contempt, unlike that for civil contempt, is between the public and the defendant, is an independent proceeding at law, and no part of the original cause." Hence the "discretion given the court in this respect is incidental and subordinate to the dominating purpose of the proceeding which is punitive to vindicate the authority of the court and punish the act of disobedience as a public wrong."[75]

Sutherland insisted that "the power to punish for contempts is inherent in all courts," and hence that federal courts, "when called into existence and vested with jurisdiction over any subject" possess the inherent power to punish for contempt. Although "the attributes which inhere in that power and are inseparable from it can neither be abrogated nor rendered practically inoperative," nevertheless in the

Government by Injunction

context of "inferior federal courts" those attributes "may be regulated within limits not precisely defined." The Clayton Act fell on the right side of the constitutional line because it was:

> of narrow scope, dealing with the single class where the act or thing constituting the contempt is also a crime in the ordinary sense. It does not interfere with the power to deal summarily with contempts committed in the presence of the court or so near thereto as to obstruct the administration of justice, and is in express terms carefully limited to the cases of contempt specifically defined. Neither do we think it purports to reach cases of failure or refusal to comply affirmatively with a decree – that is to do something which a decree commands – which may be enforced by coercive means or remedied by purely compensatory relief. If the reach of the statute had extended to the cases which are excluded a different and more serious question would arise. But the simple question presented is whether Congress may require a trial by jury upon the demand of the accused in an independent proceeding at law for a criminal contempt which is also a crime.[76]

Sutherland's opinion is both crisp and narrow. We do not have Sutherland's case files, so we cannot trace the development of his thought, but we do have a most suggestive letter that Taft sent Sutherland on October 4, sixteen days before the announcement of Sutherland's opinion:

> In the matter of your very carefully drawn opinion ... is it not unnecessary for us in reaching the conclusion to discuss the question of the difference between judicial jurisdiction and judicial power? That the two may often mean the same thing is undoubtedly true, but that they may in the Constitution and elsewhere have different meanings, it seems to me at least, could be fairly well established. Whether this be true or not, however, I put it to you whether it isn't unwise for us, when we have a plain ground upon which to reverse the case and hold the law valid, to enter upon a discussion that leads to a conclusion that might embarrass some of us in the consideration of other cases, because we think there may have to be recognized such a distinction in certain connections. Moreover, is it not unsafe to hold in a case that does not require it that there is a limitation in the grant of judicial power to the United States which would prevent Congress providing for a jury trial in equity cases or in certain issues in equity? I don't say that this may not be the correct view, but when we can dispose of this case most satisfactorily, as you have done in the rest of the opinion, isn't it unwise to commit the Court on an issue like this? I suggest that you leave out of the opinion the passage beginning on page 2, immediately after the words "Is the provision of the Clayton Act granting right of trial by jury constitutional", and include in the omission also pages 3, 4, 5, and 6, to the middle of the latter page, where you begin with the sentence "Shortly stated, the statute provides that willful disobedience" et seq.[77]

From the published opinion, it seems as if Sutherland adopted Taft's advice. In effect, Taft recommended that Sutherland remove unnecessary *dicta* expounding limitations on congressional power to regulate equity, as well as a theoretical discussion of the relationship between jurisdiction and power, a relationship that underlay Baker's controversial opinion in the Seventh Circuit. Taft suggested that it would be sufficient for the Court to uphold the Clayton Act as written, without explaining why it might refuse to uphold other acts attempting to encroach on the inherent power of courts to punish for contempt.

Taft's wise counsels of caution are best understood in the context of the 1924 presidential election, which was very much on everyone's mind in October. As early as February 1922, the railroad unions, led by the conservative Brotherhoods who typically remained aloof from the American Federation of Labor ("AFL"), had initiated a call for a Conference on Progressive Political Action ("CPPA"), which would include aroused farmers, socialists, and the surviving remnants of Roosevelt's progressive party, the Committee of Forty Eight.[78] CPPA candidates were quite successful in the November elections in 1922,[79] and a second Conference was held in Cleveland in December. That conference endorsed a so-called "post-card platform,"[80] which included as one of its six short points: "That Congress end the practice of the courts to declare legislation unconstitutional."[81]

The third meeting of the CPPA was held in St. Louis in February 1924, two months before the Court heard arguments in *Michaelson*. The remarkable victory of the British Labor Party in November had "greatly stimulated" CPPA members to think about creating an equivalent American third party.[82] La Follette "was the one name on men's lips" as the conference pledged to seek "legal changes to establish trial by jury for alleged contempt of court, and to limit the use of injunctions in industrial disputes."[83] The hope "was to throw the election of the President into the House of Representatives," where La Follette could prevail under "the state unit rule."[84]

On July 4, 1924, the CPPA met again and endorsed La Follette as a candidate for president. The platform called for the "Abolition of the tyranny and usurpation of the courts, including the practice of nullifying legislation in conflict with the political, social or economic theories of the judges. Abolition of injunction in labor disputes and of the power to punish for contempt without trial by jury."[85] Throughout the summer and fall of 1924, La Follette's campaign focused attention squarely on the legitimacy of judicial review and federal labor injunctions.

We know that the Court sought to suppress dissents in response to "La Follette's attack on the Courts and the Constitution."[86] We also know that throughout 1924 Taft paid close attention to the presidential campaign. On April 28, 1924, only two weeks after the oral argument in *Michaelson*, Taft wrote Andrew Mellon, the secretary of the treasury, saying that "[w]ith every one who realizes the possibilities of danger to the country if in the next Presidential election such principles as those represented by the so-called Progressive element in the Democratic party, or by La Follette and his followers, prevail, I have an intense interest in the present situation . . . . It is not too much to say that the welfare of the country is critically dependent upon the success of President Coolidge."[87]

Government by Injunction

By fall 1924, Taft was directly corresponding with Coolidge himself: "Everyone who understands the situation and the exigency is praying for your triumphant victory, and I follow with intense interest every report that comes, either through the newspapers or by letter, of the progress of the campaign."[88] Taft wanted to "deal a body blow to LaFollettism, labor union tyranny and socialism." He approved the decision "to force considerations of the issue of the Constitution and the Court" because he believed that it was "in accordance with wisdom and courage."[89] Taft worried that "the danger to the country of throwing the election into Congress is so great that I pray fervently that the danger may be averted."[90] Right up to the end of October, Taft found himself "anxious about the election";[91] he longed for an outcome that would produce "rejoicing by those who believe in the existing order of things."[92]

Taft knew that the outcome in *Michaelson* would undermine La Follette's campaign against the federal judiciary, and he was likely determined that the Court's opinion seem as generous as possible to those who sought to curb abuses of equitable contempt power. Taft's instincts in this matter were sound. The outcome of *Michaelson* was received as "remarkable,"[93] in part because, as the *Garment Worker* observed, it was so "unexpected."[94] Earlier in the year the Court had unanimously declared in the context of enforcing a labor injunction that contempt proceedings were "sui generis – neither civil actions nor prosecutions for offenses, within the ordinary meaning of those terms – and exertions of the power inherent in all courts to enforce obedience, something they must possess in order properly to perform their functions."[95] State courts had very nearly uniformly invalidated statutes requiring that courts use juries to convict for criminal contempt, on the ground that such legislation unconstitutionally limited "the power of courts."[96]

In this context, *Michaelson* was seen as a surprising and genuinely liberal decision, widely praised as "epoch-making," as "the most important ruling of the Supreme Court for more than half a century."[97] "[T]he press, without regard to party, including both conservative and progressive papers," joined "in approval of the decision."[98] Labor spokesmen characterized *Michaelson* as "the most important decision from the standpoint of labor since the Dred Scott decision."[99] Donald Richberg, who argued the case, declared it of "far-reaching importance."[100] Gompers observed that "a great cloak of autocratic power is shorn away."[101]

The price of this praise, as Taft no doubt predicted, was the concomitant acknowledgment that "such a decision should give pause to all those who would destroy the Supreme Court's authority as one of the checks and balances of our system of government under the Constitution."[102] Never mind that *Michaelson* was a decision *upholding* a federal statute from constitutional attack. It was nevertheless a decision that could be used to beat back La Follette's assault on the Court. As the *Washington Post* enthusiastically but nonsensically editorialized, *Michaelson* exemplified "the indispensable value of the Supreme Court – and of its power to pass upon the constitutionality of acts of Congress – as the protector of the rights of the people against legislative oppression. ... [H]ere is an apt illustration of the value, to the individual citizen, of that very function of the Supreme Court which La Follette, with his demagogical pretense of regard for the people, is seeking to destroy."[103] Or, as more carefully and clearly explained by the *St. Louis Globe-Democrat*:

> The decision is an important one in itself, but it is of particular importance at this time, when the court is being attacked for decisions said to be unfair to labor, and when a political demand is being made, backed by the heads of the American Federation of labor, for an amendment to the Constitution depriving the court of the power to nullify unconstitutional acts of Congress, on the claim, as set forth by the La Follette platform, that the court invalidates law "in conflict with the political, social or economic theories of the judges." For this decision proves again, as has been proven many times, that the court is not swayed by the "political, social or economic theories" of the judges, but concerns itself, in this expression of authority, solely with the law and its relation to the Constitution. Often, indeed, its decisions are contrary to the personal sympathies and desires of its members.[104]

Of course the obvious political expediency of the *Michaelson* decision, timed as it was for the weeks immediately preceding the 1924 election, did not itself go unnoticed. James Landis, for example, who would clerk for Brandeis in the 1925 term, wrote in *The Survey*:

> The agitation against the judiciary in 1912, following a period of abuse of equity powers by courts in industrial disputes, brought forth the legislative response in the Clayton Act. A period of a much greater abuse of the same power in the same fashion, culminating in the famed Wilkerson Injunction of 1922, brought forth another attack against the judiciary. The decision on the Clayton Act follows. The sequence of events is not accidental. Constitutional decisions involve more than mere technical questions; they "expound" a constitution. If this process is more than the mere analytical dissection of a document, it must, like all judicial decision, give effect to the social ideals of the time and place. To ignore the formulation of these ideals, as represented in a vast popular movement, would be to attribute to the Supreme Court not judicial independence but judicial ignorance of the philosophy and end of law.[105]

Gompers, commenting on the Court's abrupt vindication of labor in the context of its prior unbroken string of antilabor decisions, puckishly asked, "Is it possible that the Supreme Court has heard of the political campaign to reform the courts' usurpation of power?"[106]

The real underlying problem, Gompers added, was the labor injunction itself, which ought to be eliminated.[107] In Frankfurter's words, "the root of the matter still remains – the use of injunction in industrial disputes. . . . There is no reason in so-called expediency for continuing our disastrous history with the injunction."[108]

But those who sought to end the regime of labor injunctions, as the AFL was to aspire to do after *Bedford Cut Stone*, were forced to confront a mysterious but towering decision that Taft had himself authored in the heady days of 1921 – *Truax v. Corrigan*.[109] *Truax* was the fourth and most inscrutable of the quartet of foundational labor cases decided by the Taft Court in its first term.

Government by Injunction

Notes

1. Thomas v. Cincinnati, N.O. & T. P. Ry. Co., 62 F. 803, 805 (Cir. Ct. S.D. Ohio 1894).
2. United States v. Debs, 64 F. 724, 726 (Cir. Ct. N.D. Ill. 1894).
3. Owen M. Fiss, Troubled Beginnings of the Modern State, 1888–1910, at 58 (New York: MacMillan Pub. Co. 1993).
4. *Labor Up in Arms*, Washington Post (July 1, 1894), at 1.
5. *Government Will Now Step In*, Chicago Daily Tribune (July 2, 1894), at 1.
6. United States v. Debs, 64 F. 724, 726–27 (Cir. Ct. N.D. Ill. 1894).
7. Charles Claflin Allen, *Injunction and Organized Labor*, in Report of the Seventeenth Annual Meeting of the American Bar Association 309, 316 (Philadelphia: Dando Printing & Publishing Co. 1894).
8. Arnold M. Paul, Conservative Crisis and the Rule of Law: Attitudes of Bar and Bench, 1887–1895, at 146–49 (Ithaca: Cornell University Press 1960).
9. Report of the Seventeenth Annual Meeting of the American Bar Association, *supra* note 7, at 40.
10. *Id.* Others, however, worried that the price of the Olney injunction "may be the sapping of the right of trial by jury in criminal cases; the drawing within the bounds of equity, under the name of contempt, of crime, and of bringing a man up before a single judge to be punished nominally for contempt, but really for a crime for which we all believe could not be punished in this country except by the sentence of a court bench or a verdict of a jury. . . . Can we suppose for a moment that the men who published the bill of rights and formed the constitution, when they provided guarantees, ever contemplated that they could be swept aside by an equitable invention which would turn crime into contempt?" *Id.* at 31–32.
11. *Id.* at 38.
12. United States v. Debs, 64 F. 724, 726–27 (Cir. Ct. N.D. Ill. December 14, 1894).
13. Quoted in *Like a Czar*, St. Louis Post-Dispatch (January 10, 1895), at 8.
14. *In re* Debs, 158 U.S. 564 (1895). The decision is well discussed in Fiss, *supra* note 3, at 53–74.
15. Quoted in *Altgeld's Blow-Off*, Los Angeles Times (June 3, 1895), at 1.
16. *What Altgeld Said*, New York Times (October 18, 1896), at 2. Altgeld wanted to use the 1896 election to pose the question "whether the people of this country, and especially the laboring masses who do not have much of a voice in the selection of Judges, shall recognize and thus perpetuate the system of governing by injunction, which does away with constitutional government, which does away with government by law, does away with trial by jury, does away with trial according to the forms of law and substitutes the caprice, whim, prejudice, or passion of a Judge for all these, making him at once legislator, Judge, and, to a certain extent, executioner." *Id.*
17. Democratic Party Platform, 1896, at www.presidency.ucsb.edu/documents/1896-democratic-party-platform. No plank in the Democratic party platform "seems to have aroused more radical difference of opinion than the one which opposes 'government by injunction.'" *"Government by Injunction"*, 13 Literary Digest 801, 801 (October 24, 1896).
18. Ronald Ellis, *The Criticism of Courts*, 10 American Lawyer 111, 113 (1902).

19. *Government by Injunction*, 57 ALBANY LAW JOURNAL 8 (1898). In 1898, the *Harvard Law Review* noted that injunctions have become "a matter of popular interest and controversy, and, as it were, a burning question." Charles Noble Gregory, *Government by Injunction*, 11 HARVARD LAW REVIEW 488, 489 (1898).
20. *"Government by Injunction"*, WALL STREET JOURNAL (April 3, 1903), at 1. *See Federal Authority and State Rights*, 54 THE OUTLOOK 719 (1896) ("In our judgment, 'government by injunction' is a dangerous form of government."); *Government by Injunction*, 54 THE OUTLOOK 1135 (1896) ("History demonstrates, beyond all peradventure, that the mere possession of arbitrary power by a judicial tribunal is certain to corrupt the tribunal and to endanger the community.").
21. William H. Dunbar, *Government by Injunction*, 13 LAW QUARTERLY REVIEW 347, 353 (1897). William Draper Lewis, who emphasized that "No one can read these cases without realizing that the Judge is upholding not what he believes to be the law, but his own personal order," also offered a trenchant critique. *See* William Draper Lewis, *Strikes and Courts of Equity*, 46 AMERICAN LAW REGISTER 1, 9 (1898). Draper reasoned that "The community must believe the judiciary are impartial. This implicit trust, and the consequent position of the judiciary which enable them to compel obedience without force, is one of the tests of advanced civilization, as it is the best guarantee for civil order. Such trust is impossible, and, we believe, properly impossible, where the judge tries not violations of law, but violations of his personal order." *Id*. at 9–10. Lewis was also concerned that using equitable jurisdiction to punish behavior that was otherwise criminal "is in direct conflict with a principle ... vital to the well being of any people. This principle is that no citizen shall be accused of criminal acts, or have the fact of his having committed a criminal act determined, by anyone connected with, or selected by, the government." *Id*. at 8. Also noteworthy was F.J. Stimson, *The Modern Use of Injunctions*, 10 POLITICAL SCIENCE QUARTERLY 189 (1895).
22. Dunbar, *supra* note 21, at 362. Dunbar reasoned that "the order of the Court restraining a defendant from doing an act imposes no obligation on an independent individual to refrain from doing the same act in the assertion of a right claimed by him." *Id*. at 364. Federal courts justified their jurisdiction by assuming that they had jurisdiction *in rem* over the property subject to their protection, a jurisdiction commonly asserted in admiralty proceedings. *See* REPORT OF THE SEVENTEENTH ANNUAL MEETING OF THE AMERICAN BAR ASSOCIATION, *supra* note 7, at 41; Gregory, *supra* note 19, at 489.
23. Dunbar, *supra* note 21, at 350, 356.
24. *Id*. at 361. "A community in which the jury system is still preserved and regarded as a bulwark of liberty will not tolerate encroachments on the part of courts of equity by which, in those very cases in which a large part of the community is most disposed to rely upon the jury as a check upon the supposed partiality of the courts, the process of punishment by contempt is made to take the place of trial by jury. The machinery essential to the ordinary working of the courts is in danger of being wrecked by its use in such extraordinary emergencies." *Id*. at 366. It is for this reason that equity courts came to be compared to the despised Stuart Star Chamber. *See, e.g.*, Gregory, *supra* note 19, at 503; Stimson, *supra* note 21, at 193.

25. Thomas M. Cooley, *Address of the President*, in REPORT OF THE SEVENTEENTH ANNUAL MEETING OF THE AMERICAN BAR ASSOCIATION, *supra* note 7, at 226. Thus in the *Debs* case it was argued, most probably by Clarence Darrow, that requiring workers to desist and refrain from striking was as "puerile and ridiculous" as reading "a writ of injunction to Lee's army during the late civil war." 158 U.S. at 597. *See* FISS, *supra* note 3, at 58 n.35. As late as 1936 it could be said that "In the matter of labor injunctions we are dealing with the materials of a smoldering civil war which has frequently in the past century broken into flame." Osmond K. Fraenkel, *Recent Statutes Affecting Labor Injunctions and Yellow Dog Contracts*, 30 ILLINOIS LAW REVIEW 854, 855 (1936).
26. *Government by Injunction*, 4 AMERICAN FEDERATIONIST 82 (1897). *See* Samuel Gompers, *Taft, The Injunction Standard Bearer*, 14 AMERICAN FEDERATIONIST 785, 788–89 (1907).
27. Samuel Gompers, *Official Circular*, 15 AMERICAN FEDERATIONIST 955, 957 (1908).
28. "The issuance of injunctions in labor disputes is not based upon law, but is a species of judicial legislation, judicial usurpation, in the interests of the money power against workmen innocent of any unlawful or criminal act." *President Gompers' Report*, in REPORT OF PROCEEDINGS OF THE TWENTY-SEVENTH ANNUAL CONVENTION OF THE AMERICAN FEDERATION OF LABOR 34 (Washington D.C.: National Tribune Co. 1907). In 1908, Jane Addams observed that "From my own experience I should say perhaps that the one symptom among working-men which most definitely indicates a class feeling is a growing distrust of the integrity of the courts, the belief that the present judge has been a corporation attorney, that his sympathies and experience and his whole view of life is on the corporation side." *Is Class Conflict in America Growing and Is It Inevitable?*, 13 AMERICAN JOURNAL OF SOCIOLOGY 756, 772 (1908).
29. Lewis, *supra* note 21, at 10. *See* William G. Peterkin, *Government by Injunction*, 6 AMERICAN LAWYER 5 (1898) ("The feeling of distrust of, and opposition to, all courts and particularly to the Federal courts, resulting from the hasty conclusions that they have in these matters arbitrarily assumed an authority which doesn't belong to them, and through sheer love of power and desire to favor the rich have conspired to oppress the people, is widespread enough to constitute a grave danger to our institutions.").
30. Percy Edwards, *Government by Injunction*, 57 ALBANY LAW JOURNAL 8, 12 (1898).
31. PAUL, *supra* note 8, at 139.
32. *See supra* Chapter 39, at 1241–42.
33. *See supra* Chapter 39, at 1233.
34. In September 1921, John P. Frey, editor of the *International Molder's Journal*, published this indictment of the labor injunction:

> Courts of equity have gradually widened the scope of their injunctions and extended their jurisdiction until they have in many instances invaded the field definitely set aside by the constitution for the activities and scope of the legislative branch of the government. They have become to all intents and purposes super-legislative bodies, law-makers governed by their "conscience" – Lawmakers who have set aside the basic American principle that "governments derive their just powers from the consent of the governed."

Their usurpation of legislative powers; their denial of the right of a trial by jury for acts committed outside of the court's presence, constitute a most serious menace to government by law.

John P. Frey, *Judicially-Created Class Distinctions*, 28 AMERICAN FEDERATIONIST 730, 732 (1921). *See* JOHN P. FREY, THE LABOR INJUNCTION: AN EXPOSITION OF GOVERNMENT BY JUDICIAL CONSCIENCE AND ITS MENACE (Cincinnati: Equity Publishing Co. [1923?]).

35. *Labor Must Resist Judicial Tyranny*, 30 AMERICAN FEDERATIONIST 802, 802 (1923).
36. Leon Fink, *Labor, Liberty, and the Law: Trade Unionism and the Problem of the American Constitutional Order*, 74 JOURNAL OF AMERICAN HISTORY 904, 918 (1987).
37. Worth M. Tippy, *Injunction Abuse*, 35 AMERICAN FEDERATIONIST 287 (1928).
38. John J. Leary, *Decision Granting Jury Trial in Contempt Held Vital to Labor*, BALTIMORE SUN (October 21, 1924), at 1.
39. Willam Seagle, *Misgovernment by Injunction*, 130 THE NATION 574 (1930).
40. John A. Ryan, *The Labor Injunction in the Light of Justice*, 35 AMERICAN FEDERATIONIST 290, 291 (1928).
41. EDWIN E. WITTE, THE GOVERNMENT IN LABOR DISPUTES 124 (New York: McGraw-Hill Book Co. 1932). "Indeed, from 1894 to 1914, the unions and their friends offered bills to curb equity jurisdiction in every congressional session but one." Fink, *supra* note 36, at 916.
42. JOHN A. FITCH, THE CAUSES OF INDUSTRIAL UNREST 94, 275–76 (New York: Harper & Bros. 1924).

> Decisions affecting hours of labor and other attempts to regulate the contract of employment are often given more importance by the general public than by the workers. The Lochner case, for example, has long been cited by liberal thinkers outside the labor movement as an example of judicial obstinacy and lack of enlightenment. The most unconcerned person with whom the writer has ever talked on this subject was the secretary of a local baker's union in New York, who had almost forgotten the decision. It was of no importance one way or the other, he said. Where the union was strong they could get the ten-hour day without a law to help. Where the union was weak the law did not do any good, because it would not be enforced. His whole interest, therefore, was centered on strengthening the union rather than on securing of legislation....
>
> The principal ground for dissatisfaction is to be found in the decisions of courts defining and limiting the rights of organizations of labor, particularly in connection with strikes. ... [T]he handling of labor cases by courts, more particularly inferior courts, is a matter of almost daily occurrence. This has come about largely by the extension of the use of the injunction.

Id.

43. WITTE, *supra* note 41, at vii. "Though the ranks of labor may be split into factions over almost every other question, from communism to industrial unionism, on one matter they are unanimous. Labor has a thoroughgoing distrust and suspicion of the courts.... It is difficult to imagine a condition more dangerous to the development of democratic government ... than that a large proportion of the producing class should feel a complete lack of confidence in the only orderly means of redress provided by our system." David E. Lilienthal, *Labor and the Courts*, 34 NEW REPUBLIC 314 (1923). Lilienthal believed that "There has probably never been

Government by Injunction

a time in the history of the American labor movement when the attention of Labor and its friends has been so intensely focused on the courts." *Id.*

44. FELIX FRANKFURTER & NATHAN GREENE, THE LABOR INJUNCTION 52 (New York: MacMillan Co. 1930). No other country in the world used the labor injunction in the manner of the United States. It was "America's distinctive contribution in the application of law to industrial strife." *Id.* at 53. Frankfurter and Greene's *The Labor Injunction* has long been regarded as a classic treatment of the issue. Upon receiving a copy of the book, Holmes wrote Frankfurter that he thought it "more than ever ... a first class piece of work. I think that perhaps you have a bias on the labor side and may not show quite so clearly the terrors of a mob let loose as the wrongs to the union – but you have brought out what I think most needed to be brought out, and I should think that the book ought to have great influence." OWH to Felix Frankfurter (March 25, 1930), in HOLMES-FRANKFURTER CORRESPONDENCE, at 253.

45. FRANKFURTER & GREENE, *supra* note 44, at 106–7. As Matthew Woll, vice president of the AFL, noted in mid-decade, "Under the injunction process, courts have virtually assumed the power to enact criminal legislation and to punish as crimes acts which neither law nor public opinion condemns. Contempt proceedings inherently associated with the injunction process insure conviction in an overwhelming number of cases when the constitutional right of trial by jury would mean acquittal." Matthew Woll, *Laws Faithless to Our Forefathers*, 67 THE FORUM 201, 216 (1922).

46. FRANKFURTER & GREENE, *supra* note 44, at 126. Of particular concern to Frankfurter and Greene was the fact that injunctions tended to be written in broad, encompassing and vague terms. "To sanction vague and undefined terminology in 'drag-net' clauses largely unenforceable, and certainly unenforced, is to distort the injunction into a 'scarecrow' device for curbing the economic pressure of the strike and thereby to discredit equity's function in law enforcement." *Id.* at 107–8. This was a longstanding complaint. *See, e.g.*, Stimson, *supra* note 21, at 201 ("Since the very essence of the injunction is a definite prohibition, upon which a contempt may be shown as precise as an indictment, let us beware of the mandatory injunction giving indefinite orders to an army of men to do their duties.").

47. FRANKFURTER & GREENE, *supra* note 44, at 131. *See* Note, 41 HARVARD LAW REVIEW 909, 910 n.6 (1928). In the words of Edwin E. Witte, "The great evil of the use of injunctions in labor disputes is not that it handicaps organized labor, but that it undermines our American institutions. The courts of this country can not function as they ought to function when subjected to the distrust, if not hatred, of millions of working men." E.E. Witte, *Results of Injunctions in Labor Disputes*, 12 AMERICAN LABOR LEGISLATION REVIEW 197, 201 (1922). Consider, for example, this typical editorial in the *Brotherhood of Locomotive Firemen and Enginemen's Magazine*:

> The thing we call "business" is now operating the Government through its control of politics. The business of "business" is to exploit. Because of the domination of politics by "business" America is no longer the "land of the free" which our forefathers founded. ...
>
> "Business" which includes all the owners of Big Business, finance and industry and their devotees, control government as absolutely as an engineer controls the movements of his engine. ... [W]hen either the executive or the legislative branches of the Government institute any proceeding against the

working class, no matter how flagrantly violative of the fundamental or basic law of the land such a proceeding may be – no matter how subversive of the constitutional rights of those against whom it is directed – there is always the judiciary, from the judge – often a product of the legal department of some big corporation – sitting on the Federal bench clear up to the United States Supreme Court, that can be relied upon to sustain such proceeding and make it "constitutional" irrespective of how clearly unconstitutional it may be.

Vote and Vote Right and Avert This Menace, BROTHERHOOD OF LOCOMOTIVE FIREMEN AND ENGINEMEN'S MAGAZINE (October 15, 1922), at 6.

48. George Wharton Pepper, *Injunctions in Labor Disputes*, in REPORT OF THE FORTY-SEVENTH ANNUAL MEETING OF THE AMERICAN BAR ASSOCIATION 176 (Baltimore: Lord Baltimore Press 1924). Pepper observed that it brought "emotional relief" to some "to picture the courts as the tribunals for ending industrial wars." But, said Pepper, "urgency of this sort overlooks some fundamentals."

> The first is that in a free country we cannot by governmental action compel people to work. . . . The third is that while under all conditions government must protect life and property, yet if we insist upon interpreting the courts to masses of citizens as mere obstacles to industrial justice we shall not only be undermining popular respect for our most important institution, but we shall be straining government to the breaking point. . . .
>
> *Let us put no trust in industrial coercion. Let us make no appeal to the courts beyond the barest limits of protection to life and property, and let us never make an appeal even in these cases a covert method of imposing upon the courts an impossible jurisdiction over all industrial happiness and welfare.*

GEORGE WHARTON PEPPER, MEN AND ISSUES: A SELECTION OF SPEECHES AND ARTICLES 61, 63 (New York: Duffield & Co. 1924) (emphasis in the original). As a senator from Pennsylvania with close ties to major corporate and railroad interests in the state, Pepper had considerable involvement in some of the major strikes of the decade. *See* Robert H. Zieger, *Senator George Wharton Pepper and Labor Issues in the 1920s*, 9 LABOR HISTORY 163 (1968).

49. Pepper, *Injunctions in Labor Disputes*, *supra* note 48, at 179. Wilson's secretary of war, Newton Baker, trenchantly observed in 1922:

> [I]n labor controversies each judge has in part at least his own code, and, when a labor controversy arises there is a great scurrying on both sides to get it before a judge whose code, that is to say whose personal equation, is satisfactory, and who it is thought can be relied upon out of sympathy or ambition or fears to favor one side or the other. . . .
>
> The consequences have been disastrous. Apart from the present, and, we hope temporary, disrespect for law growing out of the sudden enactment of prohibition, there is no field of legal administration which has so absolutely failed to secure public confidence and respect as the law in labor disputes. . . . The public are mystified at the spectacle of court-made crimes, enforced as contempts, without a jury trial, by a judge whose feelings are apparently offended when his orders are disobeyed, and who often seems to feel the dignity of the court as well as of the law must be vindicated by severity. Phrases like "government by injunction" capture the roving imagination of the public and are denounced in the platforms of great political parties . . . all because courts are called upon to promulgate and enforce police regulations in a field where we citizens have not yet reached ideas clear enough to legislate. Just what would have happened if the courts had not enlarged their equity powers and kept some semblance of peace

Government by Injunction

> I do not know; but the thing that has followed their assumption of the jurisdiction is a loss of prestige in the courts and a widespread distrust of law and courts.

Newton D. Baker, *Labor Relations and the Law*, 8 AMERICAN BAR ASSOCIATION JOURNAL 731, 733–34 (1922).

50. 54 F. 730 (Cir. Ct. N.D. Ohio 1893).
51. William H. Taft, *Recent Criticism of the Federal Judiciary*, in REPORT OF THE EIGHTEENTH ANNUAL MEETING OF THE AMERICAN BAR ASSOCIATION 272 (Philadelphia: Dando Printing & Publishing Co. 1895).
52. Address of Hon. William H. Taft, Secretary of War, delivered before the Cooper Union, New York City, Friday, January 10, 1908, in ROBERT LEE DUNN, WILLIAM HOWARD TAFT: AMERICAN 259 (Boston: The Chapple Pub. Co. 1908).
53. *See supra* Chapter 15, at 509–10.
54. Taft, *supra* note 52, at 259. For these views Taft was attacked during the 1908 election as "the originator and specific champion of discretionary government – that is, government by injunction," and as "upholding and extending into our country a despotic government vested in the judiciary." *Official Circular, supra* note 27, at 957. Samuel Gompers charged that Taft "has learned nothing and forgotten nothing on the subject since his career as a judge of the Federal Circuit. He was one of the early injunction judges, and as statesman and politician he is evidently determined to defend his record." Gompers, *supra* note 26, at 786. McKinley's victory in 1896, as well as Taft's own victory in 1908, both in the teeth of determined labor opposition, confirmed Taft's lifelong belief that in the crunch labor could not turn out its votes in a contested presidential election. Taft's belief was confirmed in 1920 by Harding's triumph.
55. William Howard Taft, *Inaugural Address*, 44 CONG. REC. 1, 5 (March 4, 1909).
56. Louis D. Brandeis *et al.* to WHT (December 30, 1911), in 2 LETTERS OF LOUIS D. BRANDEIS, at 532.
57. *Speech of William Howard Taft Accepting the Republican Nomination for President of the United States* (August 1, 1912), Sen. Doc. No. 902, 62nd CONG. 2nd SESS., at 10.
58. William Howard Taft, *Address of the President*, in REPORT OF THE THIRTY-SEVENTH ANNUAL MEETING OF THE AMERICAN BAR ASSOCIATION 371 (Baltimore: Lord Baltimore Press 1914).
59. William H. Taft, *The Attacks on the Courts and Legal Procedure*, 5 KENTUCKY LAW JOURNAL 3, 23 (1916).
60. *See supra* Chapter 40, at 1319–23. Taft believed that the general and opaque language of the Sherman Act invited courts to interpret it in light of "prevailing morality and predominant public opinion." WILLIAM HOWARD TAFT, THE ANTI-TRUST ACT AND THE SUPREME COURT 47 (New York: Harper & Brothers 1914).
61. T.M. Cooley, *Labor and Capital before the Law*, 139 NORTH AMERICAN REVIEW 504, 504 (1884).
62. *See supra* Chapter 40, at 1326–27.
63. William Howard Taft, *Mr. Wilson and the Campaign*, 10 YALE REVIEW 1, 19–20 (1920).
64. 266 U.S. 42 (1924).
65. 257 U.S. 312 (1921).

66. Clayton Act, Sections 21–24, 38 Stat. 738–40 (1914). Jury trials were also not required for charges of criminal contempt in cases involving injunctions brought on behalf of the United States.
67. J.M. Landis, *Labor's New Day in Court*, 53 THE SURVEY 175, 175 (1924). The provision had been stoutly defended by John W. Davis, then a member of Congress from West Virginia. *See, e.g.*, 48 CONG. REC. (APPENDIX) 313, 318 (July 9, 1912); *Davis Felicitated on Clayton Ruling*, NEW YORK TIMES (October 24, 1924), at 2.
68. *See supra* text at note 17.
69. *Injunctions and Contempt of Court*, 520 NEW REPUBLIC 287, 289 (1924). Frankfurter was the author of this article, for Brandeis wrote him the next day to say that "Your article on Injunctions & the S[upreme]. C[ourt]. is in every way admirable." LDB to Felix Frankfurter (November 20, 1924), in BRANDEIS-FRANKFURTER CORRESPONDENCE, at 182. In the course of its 1916 attack on the technical incompetence of the Clayton Act, the *New Republic* asserted:

> The only section of the Clayton act which is of any value to labor is that which gives, in a limited class of cases, trial by jury for violation of an injunction. It applies only where the thing which the workingman has done is not only a violation of the injunction, but also a crime. As far as it goes, it is a distinct gain, for one of the worst features of labor injunctions has been the fact that a violation of the injunction was tried by the judge who had issued it, and who naturally felt that anything that savored of a violation of it was a personal affront to him. But the section does not go far, and it is doubtful whether a laboring man will be very anxious to brand himself a criminal by claiming its protection.

"*Labor Is Not a Commodity*", 9 NEW REPUBLIC 112, 113 (1916). It was also feared that employers could "on the same set of facts" seek civil contempt, as distinct from criminal contempt, and hence imprison strikers while denying them "the right of trial by jury." W.B. Rubin, *Ten Years After*, 34 AMERICAN FEDERATIONIST 206, 212 (1927).
70. On the number of injunctions issued during the strike, see Pepper, *Injunctions in Labor Disputes, supra* note 48, at 176–77.
71. *Injunctions and Contempt of Court, supra* note 69, at 287.
72. Michaelson v. United States, 291 F. 940, 946–47 (7th Cir. 1923).
73. Taft first learned of Caraway's bill to prohibit federal judges from commenting on the credibility of witnesses or the weight of evidence at about the same time as the Court heard argument in *Michaelson*. Taft did not compose his memorandum arguing that the bill was unconstitutional because of the inherent powers of Article III courts until December 1924, which was after the presidential election. *See supra* Chapter 15, at 511–12 and note 30.
74. Michaelson v. United States, 266 U.S. 42, 64 (1924). The Seventh Circuit had also claimed, oddly, that the Clayton Act did not apply to employees of interstate railroads because "the rules for economic combats in private and local industries, which society tolerates, have no just application to our present-day system of railroad transportation." 291 F. at 943. Interstate railroads were so thoroughly regulated, so "bound hand and foot," *id.* at 944, that in effect the strike of a railroad's employees "was controversy with, or a strike against, the Labor Board as an instrumentality of our national government, and is to be classed with the insurrection of the Boston policemen." *Id.* at 945. Sutherland gave this argument the short shrift it deserved:

> To say that railroad employees are outside the provisions of the statute, is not to construe the statute, but to ingraft upon it an exception not warranted by its terms.

> If Congress had intended such an exception, it is fair to suppose that it would have said so affirmatively. The words of the act are plain and in terms inclusive of all classes of employment; and we find nothing in them which requires a resort to judicial construction. The reasoning of the court below really does not present a question of statutory construction, but rather an argument justifying the supposititious exception on the ground of necessity or of policy – a matter addressed to the legislative and not the judicial authority. Neither was the strike one against the Labor Board. It was a strike notwithstanding the action of the board, but against the respondent. The policemen's strike was against a governmental employer. The Labor Board was not an employer, but an arbitrator, whose determination, moreover, had only the force of moral suasion.

    Michaelson, 266 U.S. at 68–69.
75. *Id.* at 64–65. On the importance that the Taft Court attributed to the distinction between civil and criminal contempts, see *Ex parte* Grossman, 267 U.S. 87 (1925), which held that the president could pardon the latter but not the former.
76. *Michaelson*, 266 U.S. at 65–66.
77. WHT to GS (October 4, 1924) (Taft papers).
78. KENNETH CAMPBELL MACKAY, THE PROGRESSIVE MOVEMENT OF 1924, at 54–70 (New York: Octagon Books 1972).
79. REPORT OF THE PROCEEDINGS OF THE SECOND CONFERENCE FOR PROGRESSIVE POLITICAL ACTION 6–7 (1922): "Twenty-one Senators were elected who may be listed as far more responsive to the public interest than their predecessors. Of these at least ten are outspoken progressives. ... In addition, twelve undesirable Senators or candidates were defeated or retired voluntarily from the contest. ... In the opinion of your Committee, approximately one hundred and forty Representatives in the Lower House have been elected who are either unqualifiedly representative of the desires of the Conference, or are men whose past record or declaration class them as progressive minded in the people's interests. In addition to this, substantial gains were made in a number of state elections. In Wisconsin, Fighting Bob LaFollette carried with him an overwhelming progressive state administration."
80. MACKAY, *supra* note 78, at 54–71.
81. REPORT OF THE PROCEEDINGS OF THE SECOND CONFERENCE FOR PROGRESSIVE POLITICAL ACTION, *supra* note 79, at 22. In its longer version, which was not ultimately brought to the floor of the Conference, this plank read: "Abolition of the tyranny and usurpation of state and federal courts, ending the abuse of the power of injunction and the nullification of acts of Congress and state legislatures." *Id.* at 24.
82. Norman Thomas, *Progressivism at St. Louis*, 118 THE NATION 224, 224 (1924). For illustrative examples, see *What of a New Party?*, 56 LOCOMOTIVE ENGINEERS JOURNAL 809 (November 1922); *Labor Ousts Lloyd George*, 56 LOCOMOTIVE ENGINEERS JOURNAL 811 (November 1922); Frederic C. Howe, *Labor's Rise to Political Power*, 56 LOCOMOTIVE ENGINEERS JOURNAL 815 (November 1922); and George Soule, *Planks for a Labor Platform*, 56 LOCOMOTIVE ENGINEERS JOURNAL 816 (November 1922). It is fascinating to note that Soule, whose primary focus was on economic planning, included in his proposed labor platform a plank providing: "In order further to safeguard such legislation as is contemplated [elsewhere in this platform], there is needed a constitutional amendment which will prevent the Supreme Court from abrogating laws which embody the will of the people as expressed through acts of Congress. If desired, the Supreme Court may be granted a veto power such as is now held by the president, but at least it should be provided

that any law held unconstitutional by the Supreme Court shall become valid if repassed by Congress by a two-thirds majority. This would certainly provide a sufficient check on Congress to prevent it from violating the spirit of the Constitution." *Id.* at 816–17. As distinguished from the railroad brotherhoods, the AFL trade unions remained skeptical of third-party ambitions. *See, e.g., "Intellectuals" and Labor*, 46 GRANITE CUTTERS' JOURNAL 2 (April 1922).

83. Thomas, *supra* note 82, at 225. The platform approved by the conference included provisions for:

> 2. Abolition of the tyranny and usurpation of the courts, including the practice of nullifying acts of Congress and state legislatures.
> 3. The abolition of injunctions in labor disputes and of the power to punish for contempt without trial by jury.

REPORT OF THE PROCEEDINGS OF THE THIRD CONFERENCE FOR PROGRESSIVE POLITICAL ACTION 22 (1924).

84. George T. Odell, *Mr. La Follette Winning Support of Progressives*, CHRISTIAN SCIENCE MONITOR (February 12, 1924), at 1.
85. MACKAY, *supra* note 78, at 271. "The increasingly drastic use of the writ of injunction by American courts, and especially the writ by District Judge James H. Wilkerson during the strike of the railroad shop crafts in 1922, has deeply modified the traditional non-partisan attitude of organized labor and is largely responsible for the present participation of the railroad and allied unions in the third party movement." *The Common Welfare*, 52 THE SURVEY 535 (1924).
86. WHT to Pierce Butler (September 16, 1924) (Taft papers). Taft had been anticipating a challenge to the Court from La Follette since at least 1922, ever since La Follette's call for a constitutional amendment revoking judicial review. *See* WHT to GS (September 10, 1922) (Sutherland papers). On the Court's response to these challenges, see *supra* Chapter 19, at 614–17.
87. WHT to Andrew W. Mellon (April 28, 1924) (Taft papers).
88. WHT to Calvin Coolidge (September 16, 1924) (Taft papers).
89. *Id.* Van Devanter observed in a letter to Clarke that "McReynolds ... thinks Coolidge and Davis are not fitted for the Presidency and that La Follette would be impossible. So he is not altogether happy." WVD to JHC (October 2, 1924) (Van Devanter papers).
90. WHT to Mrs. Frederick J. Manning (October 20, 1924) (Taft papers). "Of course," Taft wrote his friend Gus Karger, "we must count on the vote of the lunatic fringe of intellectuals and of a lot of simple-minded people, who seem to find the statement that [La Follette] is sincere to satisfy them that they should vote for him. These include the people who read the New Republic and the dreamers without judgment, and those who expect the ideal without knowing exactly what it is in the matter of government." WHT to Gus Karger (September 22, 1924) (Taft papers).
91. WHT to Robert McDougal (October 29, 1924) (Taft papers). *See* WHT to Robert A. Taft (November 2, 1924) (Taft papers) ("I suppose you are as anxious as I am to have this election over").
92. WHT to Gus Karger (October 31, 1924) (Taft papers).
93. Note, *Jury Trial in Cases of Contempt of Court*, 4 OREGON LAW REVIEW 145, 147 (1925).

94. *Trial by Jury Rule Is Not Discussed*, 24 GARMENT WORKER 8 (November 14, 1924).
95. Myers v. United States, 264 U.S. 95, 103 (1924).
96. Walton Lunch Co. v. Kearney, 236 Mass. 310, 317 (1920). *See* Carter v. Virginia, 96 Va. 791 (1899); Smith v. Speed, 11 Okla. 95 (1901); Pacific Livestock Co. v. Ellison Ranching Co., 46 Nev. 351 (1923); but see Richardson v. Kentucky, 141 Ky 497 (1911). The provisions of the Clayton Act at issue in *Michaelson* had been found unconstitutional by a federal district court. *See In re* Atchison, 284 F. 604 (S. D. Fla. 1922).
97. Uncle Dudley, *A New Right for Labor*, BOSTON GLOBE (October 22, 1924), at 16A. "[T]he Supreme Court's sanction of the power of Congress to impose reasonable restraints upon the terrible power of courts to commit for contempt is a decision of the highest moment." *Injunctions and Contempt of Court, supra* note 69, at 288.
98. *Labor's "Magna Charta" Upheld*, 82 LITERARY DIGEST 12 (November 8, 1924).
99. Leary, *supra* note 38.
100. *Effect Far Reaching, Labor Attorney Says*, BALTIMORE SUN (October 21, 1924), at 9.
101. *Supreme Court Ruling Praised by Gompers*, NEW YORK TIMES (October 22, 1924), at 13. *See Stone Welcomes the Decision*, NEW YORK TIMES (October 22, 1924), at 13.
102. *Supreme Court Protects Labor*, ST. LOUIS POST-DISPATCH (October 21, 1924), at 16. Robert Cushman celebrated the "soothing influence" of Michaelson "upon a public opinion ... which has been watching with increasing concern the rapid expansion of 'government by injunction.' Necessary as the injunctive process and summary punishments for contempt of court may be, it is a cause for congratulation that the Supreme Court has been able to sustain on constitutional grounds such mitigations of the essentially rigorous and sometimes arbitrary nature of these acts of judicial power." Robert Cushman, *Constitutional Law in 1924–25*, 20 AMERICAN POLITICAL SCIENCE REVIEW 80, 92 (1926).
103. *Jury Trials for Contempt*, WASHINGTON POST (October 22, 1924), at 6. As the *Wall Street Journal* put it, the decision "is an answer to the representation now being made for political purposes that the court is attempting to usurp legislative power by going out of its way to declare acts of Congress unconstitutional." *Court Seeks to Uphold Statutes*, WALL STREET JOURNAL (October 24, 1924), at 9.
104. *Labor and the Supreme Court*, ST. LOUIS GLOBE-DEMOCRAT (October 22, 1924), at 16.
105. Landis, *supra* note 67, at 177. Landis's professor, Felix Frankfurter, intimated the same point four days later: "It is idle to wonder whether the revived criticism of the Supreme Court in the fields that permit of capricious exercise of discretion may not have had their subtle reflex in the present decision. Certain it is that the impregnating atmosphere of public opinion in regard to the essentially political functions exercised by the Supreme Court has in the past been known to penetrate even the conference room." *Injunctions and Contempt of Court, supra* note 69, at 288.
106. *Supreme Court Ruling Praised by Gompers, supra* note 101.

107. "But the injunction remains. It may still be issued in labor disputes where no such injunction would lie if there were no labor dispute in progress. The injunction itself, as used in labor disputes, must go before the Constitution is fully and finally vindicated and made supreme in our court system." *Id.*
108. *Injunctions and Contempt of Court, supra* note 69, at 289.
109. 257 U.S. 312 (1921).

CHAPTER 42

Truax v. Corrigan

LIKE *AMERICAN STEEL FOUNDRIES*, *Truax v. Corrigan* came to the Taft Court with a troubled history.[1] The case arose in 1916 when William Truax, owner of a restaurant known as the "English Kitchen" in Bisbee, Arizona, cut the wages of his employees, who were members of the local Cooks' and Waiters' Union. The union struck to maintain a union pay scale. It placed pickets in front of the restaurant, and they carried banners proclaiming "the English Kitchen Unfair to Cooks and Waiters."[2] Union pickets distributed handbills and circulars;[3] they "loudly advised all friends of organized labor to desist from patronizing the English Kitchen."[4] These tactics diminished the revenue of the English Kitchen by more than 75 percent.[5] There was no evidence of physical violence or intimidation.[6]

Truax claimed that the strike nevertheless constituted an illegal "secondary boycott" because the object of the union's picketing was to persuade independent third-party customers to cease patronizing the English Kitchen.[7] At the time, however, Paragraph 1464 of the 1913 Arizona Civil Code, which anticipated the Clayton Act, prohibited injunctions in peaceful labor controversies.[8] The Arizona Supreme Court reasoned that because the union had the proper purpose of improving "the working conditions of members of the organization," the question was whether the "means adopted to accomplish such purpose," the "so-called boycott of the plaintiffs' business, and the placing of pickets near the front entrance of plaintiffs' restaurant," was "lawful." The court held that a customer boycott of this kind did not violate Truax's rights. "The extent of the publicity given such dispute is unimportant and violates no right of plaintiffs, either civil or criminal. If the publicity given the existence of the dispute results in a loss of patronage and business to plaintiffs, such loss is attributable to the dispute, and not attributable to the publicity given to the dispute. Consequently the mere publication of the existence of a strike and of its causes in a thorough manner is no ground for equitable interference."[9]

The Arizona Supreme Court did conceded that in the absence of Paragraph 1464, "a serious question would likely exist in this jurisdiction whether, as a matter of law, in the nature of things 'peaceful' picketing may exist; but with paragraph 1464 on our statute books, that question is eliminated as a question of law, and expressly made a question of fact during the existence of a labor strike; and, before the courts are permitted to interfere by injunction, the necessity must appear to prevent irreparable injury to property or property rights, and picketing in a peaceful manner creates no such necessity for injunction interference by the courts." Even if the picketers conveyed defamatory messages calculated "to bring plaintiffs into disrepute, contempt, or ridicule," their communications were nevertheless peaceful, and equity would not enjoin the publication of a libel because the resulting injuries could be remedied either by "a criminal action of libel" or by "a civil action."[10]

When Truax challenged the constitutionality of Paragraph 1464, the Arizona Supreme Court acknowledged that the application of the statute allowed the union to damage the goodwill of the English Kitchen. Conceding that "good will in any business is a valuable factor to business success," the court asserted that "no man carrying on any business has a vested property right in the esteem of the public. If the business man conducts his business in such a manner as to displease his former patrons ... such loss is not in any way a loss of property to which the loser has a right. If the cause of the loss of patronage to business is attributable to the peaceable persuasion of another person, ... no right of the employer is violated if the striking employés advertise the cause of the strike. If the publicity given the facts cause a loss, such loss is attributable to the employer and his business methods as the proximate cause of the loss to him."[11] "The plaintiffs' property rights are not invaded by picketing, unless the picketing interferes with the free conduct of the business by the plaintiffs; and plaintiffs do not claim that defendants have, by using violent means with picketing, invaded their rights in this respect, by causing a loss in business."[12]

Truax came up to the Supreme Court on a writ of error. At issue were not the procedures by which labor injunctions could be enforced, which was the question that *Michaelson* would later address, but rather whether labor injunctions themselves, in the absence of violence, could be abolished by legislatures. In *Duplex Printing Press*, decided on January 3, 1921, the Court interpreted the Clayton Act to render ineffectual provisions which labor believed had deprived federal courts of jurisdiction to issue labor injunctions.[13] Stripped to its essentials, the issue in *Truax* was whether the Constitution itself required the statutory interpretation contained in *Duplex Printing Press*.

The shock of *Duplex Printing Press* dramatically escalated the stakes of *Truax*. A Conference of Representatives of National Trade Unions declared in response to *Duplex Printing Press* in February 1921 that "for six years the Clayton act, accepted on all sides as the established law of the land, to an appreciable degree checked the abuse of the writ of injunction," but now "a majority of the justices of the supreme court have swept away this strong barrier against a feudalistic legal concept and labor finds itself at the mercy of an unlimited use of judge-made law."

Truax v. Corrigan

The injunction as it is now used and abused in labor disputes is without sanction either in the constitution or in the fundamental law of the land. It is a pure usurpation of power and authority.... The workers maintain that the constitution of the United States is a living document .... The workers maintain that in their every day life and work rights which the constitution declares to be inalienable should in practice, as well as in theory, be inalienable. Among these rights is the right to liberty – freedom from involuntary servitude or compulsory labor, except as punishment for crime. This guarantee of the thirteenth amendment lives, and the workers are determined that it shall not be denied them. Nor shall this guarantee of their freedom be so distorted as to compel a group slavery in modern industry as reprehensible as was the individual, chattel slavery of old. ...

This conference proposes and urges public support for: ....

No application of the use of injunctions in industrial disputes where they would not apply in the absence of such disputes. ...

Removal by Congress of the usurped power of courts to declare unconstitutional laws enacted by Congress.[14]

Duplex Printing Press primed federal courts to issue a cascade of labor injunctions during the 1920s. At the outset of the decade *Truax* posed the question whether the power to issue these injunctions was constitutionally protected. It was feared that "should the Supreme Court reverse the action of the Supreme Court of Arizona the incidental but essential effect of the decision would be to declare the operative parts of the Clayton Act unconstitutional."[15] If *Truax* were to hold the Arizona statute barring injunctions unconstitutional, it would force labor into a bruising confrontation with the institution of judicial review itself.

Truax was initially argued before the White Court on April 29–30, 1920. After the argument, as Holmes, Brandeis, and Clarke walked home together, Holmes remarked, "Well, at least in this case no one will vote for reversal," to which Brandeis replied, "We'll be lucky if we can sustain it five to four."[16] Brandeis was of course correct. In fact the Court voted to reverse the Arizona Supreme Court. White assigned the opinion to Pitney, who had authored *Coppage* and *Hitchman*, and who at the time was writing *Duplex Printing Press*.

We know that Brandeis circulated a manuscript advocating that the decision of the Arizona Supreme Court be affirmed. We have a letter from Pitney to Brandeis on November 3, 1920, saying that he had not yet "seriously tackled the opinion," but that he would "give full consideration" to Brandeis's communication before reaching a final judgment.[17] Sometime after the beginning of the 1920 term, Pitney changed his mind about the outcome of the case. He sent a draft opinion to the entire Court stating: "At the last Term the conference voted to reverse and opinion was allotted to me. Being unable, on further examination, to write in accordance with the vote, I circulate this Memorandum as a report."[18]

Truax was reargued on October 5–6, 1921, the third and fourth days of Taft's first term as chief justice. We know almost nothing about the Court's deliberations. There is a letter from Taft to Van Devanter on December 7, two days after the Court's announcement of *American Steel Foundries*, in which Taft enclosed "a tentative opinion in the Arizona Truax case. I wish you would look it over and cut and slash as you think wise. I found on looking into the case that it seemed necessary to take up the due process feature rather more than I had anticipated. I have not sent this to the whole Court, because I want to have the benefit of your suggestions and corrections before doing so. I presume it is too late to expect to get it ready for next Monday, but if you could read it tonight and talk with me in the morning about it, I would be very much obliged."[19] The letter evidences the speed with which Taft had begun to construct a special relationship with Van Devanter.

Taft announced his opinion two weeks later, on December 19, 1921. In contrast to *American Steel Foundries*, Taft could not in *Truax* unite the Court. The final vote was 5–4, with Holmes, Pitney, Brandeis, and Clarke dissenting. Taft was determined to use his slim majority to author the strongest possible opinion. At issue in *Truax* was the existence of the labor injunction *per se*, and on this question, as Taft had been frank to acknowledge in his inaugural address as president, his "convictions" were "fixed."[20]

Taft split his opinion into two parts. He dealt first with the due process objection to Paragraph 1464. He began with the premise that "Plaintiffs' business is a property right and free access for employees, owner, and customers to his place of business is incident to such right. Intentional injury caused to either right or both by a conspiracy is a tort. . . . Intention to inflict the loss and the actual loss caused are clear. The real question here is: Were the means used illegal?"[21]

Taft characterized the picketing, even though peaceful, as intimidating and coercive. "It was not lawful persuasion or inducing. It was not a mere appeal to the sympathetic aid of would-be customers by a simple statement of the fact of the strike and a request to withhold patronage. It was compelling every customer or would-be customer to run the gauntlet of most uncomfortable publicity, aggressive and annoying importunity, libelous attacks, and fear of injurious consequences, illegally inflicted, to his reputation and standing in the community. . . . Violence could not have been more effective. It was moral coercion by illegal annoyance and obstruction." Taft read the Arizona Supreme Court as granting "complete immunity from any civil or criminal action to the defendants, for it pronounces their acts lawful."[22]

On this framing of the case, the precise issue in *Truax* was whether Arizona could constitutionally strip Truax's "property" of protections against a kind of "moral coercion" that was by hypothesis neither tortious nor criminal under Arizona law. Taft said about this issue: "To give operation to a statute whereby serious losses inflicted by such *unlawful* means are in effect made remediless, is, we think, to disregard fundamental rights of liberty and property and to deprive the person suffering the loss of due process of law."[23] The difficulty with this reasoning is that it does not explain why the means used by the union were "unlawful." Taft analyzed the due process issue on the contrary assumption that the means used by the union were lawful under Arizona law. Federal general common law, with its distinctive torts, did not apply to the case, because the case did not arise under federal diversity jurisdiction. If Taft meant to advance the unusual claim that the means were unlawful under federal constitutional law, which was the only federal law applicable to the case, he needed to make clear why that might be so.

Taft responded to this challenge by suggesting a line of thought that was both startling and radical. Taft implied that the Due Process Clause itself imposes upon

Truax v. Corrigan

states a baseline set of protections that must be extended to property. *Truax* is one of very few cases in the Court's history flatly to hold that states have affirmative constitutional obligations to protect fundamental federal rights, like property or liberty. The Due Process Clause, Taft declared, "makes a required minimum of protection for every one's right of life, liberty, and property, which the Congress or the Legislature may not withhold."[24]

Many years later, the distinguished Chicago law professor David Currie would marvel at Taft's easy assumption that it was not the picketers, but the state, "that had 'deprived' the employer of his property."[25] The implications were momentous. "A court might be tempted to conclude that a government that deprives people of life by not punishing murder also does so by declining to feed the hungry or to rescue fire victims, and ... we would have discovered a constitutional right to basic welfare services." Currie was certain that Taft himself "would have been among the last to believe that by [his *Truax* opinion] he had laid the foundation for a constitutional right to the provision of welfare."[26]

Taft's anxiety to protect the entrepreneurial initiative of employers led him to cross a line that few justices have been willing to cross – the line that separates negative from positive rights. Taft bluntly asserted that the Constitution itself entitled persons to certain minimal levels of affirmative state protection for their fundamental rights. In the century that has followed *Truax*, the Court has not only refused to expand this reasoning, it has at times explicitly rejected it.[27] It might be that Taft was so new to the Court when he authored *Truax* that he was not aware of the audacity of his logic. But it is hard to imagine that the shrewd and technically adept Van Devanter did not perceive the startling implications of Taft's opinion. He must simply have bit his lip.[28]

The practical effect of this portion of Taft's opinion was to reinforce the conclusion of *American Steel Foundries*, which had been issued two weeks before, that labor picketing was intrinsically coercive and so required close judicial supervision. *Truax* effectively constitutionalized Taft's preference for single "missionaries," as distinct from group picketing.[29] Freed from the responsibility of speaking for the entire Court, Taft felt liberated in *Truax* to characterize *American Steel Foundries* as holding "that peaceful picketing was a contradiction in terms."[30]

The premise of Taft's due process argument was that Arizona had left Truax remediless for tortious assaults on his property, denying him the option of suing for damages or enlisting the state in a criminal prosecution. An entirely different question would be presented, however, if Arizona did "not withhold from the plaintiffs all remedy for the wrongs they suffered but only the equitable relief of injunction."[31] The Clayton Act, for example, had eliminated federal equitable interventions in labor controversies, but it had not left employers otherwise remediless. To meet this possibility, Taft argued that even if Arizona provided other remedies to Truax for the tortious assault of his employees, Paragraph 1464 would nevertheless violate the Equal Protection Clause of the Fourteenth Amendment.

Taft's recourse to the Equal Protection Clause was most unusual. Equal protection jurisprudence was not well developed or theorized during the Taft Court era. In *Buck v. Bell* Holmes famously dismissed appeals to equal protection as "the usual last resort of constitutional arguments." He not inaccurately summarized the state of equal protection doctrine by affirming that "the law does all that is needed when it does all that it can, indicates a policy, applies it to all within the lines, and seeks to bring within the lines all similarly situated so far and so fast as its means allow."[32] In 1911, Van Devanter had influentially decreed in *Natural Carbonic Gas* that "[t]he equal-protection clause of the 14th Amendment does not take from the state the power to classify in the adoption of police laws, but admits of the exercise of a wide scope of discretion in that regard, and avoids what is done only when it is without any reasonable basis, and therefore is purely arbitrary.... One who assails the classification [of] a law must carry the burden of showing that it does not rest upon any reasonable basis, but is essentially arbitrary."[33]

Under the *Natural Carbonic Gas* test, the issue in *Truax* was whether Arizona lacked a reasonable basis to prohibit the remedy of an injunction in the context of peaceful labor controversies, but nevertheless to allow injunctions in other contexts. What is striking about *Truax*, however, is that Taft did not immediately turn to *Natural Carbonic Gas* to determine whether Paragraph 1464 violated the Equal Protection Clause. Instead he invoked a much older tradition, one exemplified by Justice Field's opinion in *Barbier v. Connolly*[34] to the effect that "[c]lass legislation, discriminating against some and favoring others, is prohibited, but legislation which, in carrying out a public purpose, is limited in its application, if within the sphere of its operation it affects alike all persons similarly situated, is not within the amendment."[35]

As we have discussed, this tradition ran aground in the early twentieth century when the Court acknowledged that the public as a whole could benefit from legislation that explicitly addressed only specific groups.[36] The operative question, as the Court had noted in 1898 in *Holden v. Hardy*, was "whether the legislature has adopted the statute in exercise of a reasonable discretion, or whether its action be a mere excuse for an unjust discrimination, or oppression, or spoliation of a particular class."[37] Van Devanter's formulation in *Natural Carbonic Gas* became iconic because it compressed this inquiry into the single question of whether a classification had a "reasonable basis," meaning whether it had a justification sounding in the public good.[38] A statute with such a justification was by definition not improper class legislation. The upshot was that, after *Natural Carbonic Gas*, equal protection doctrine became essentially duplicative of due process doctrine.[39]

Remnants of the older tradition nevertheless persisted,[40] and they were particularly likely to be triggered for Taft (and for Sutherland) in the context of labor regulations. Taft was frank to say that "I don't like special legislation for labor unions."[41] Accepting the Republican nomination for president in 1912, for example, Taft condemned proposals to eliminate labor injunctions as "class legislation designed to secure immunity for lawlessness in labor disputes on the part of laborers."[42] On his last day as president, Taft vetoed an appropriations bill that prohibited funds for anti-trust enforcement from being applied to labor unions or farmer cooperatives.[43] Taft declared that "[t]his provision is class legislation of the most vicious sort. If it were enacted as substantive law and not merely as a qualification upon the use of monies appropriated for the enforcement of the

Truax v. Corrigan

law, no one, I take it, would doubt its unconstitutionality."[44] The next year Taft denounced the Clayton Act as class legislation: "The great political power that labor combinations are believed to exercise has enabled them successfully to press upon legislatures the idea that they are politically a privileged class, that the interest of the community lies in making them so, and that their cause is so important that the ordinary means of enforcing the law against their violations of it should be weakened rather than strengthened."[45] Over and against such narrow "class" interests, Taft insisted that law must serve the interests of "the 'public,'" of "the general sum of happiness of the entire community."[46]

Sutherland's views on class legislation were almost identical to those of Taft. In his presidential address to the American Bar Association ("ABA"), Sutherland declared "class legislation" to be "the most odious form of legislative abuse," and it "is by no means infrequent."[47] In 1914, Sutherland unsuccessfully led the charge against the very funding proviso that Taft had vetoed the year before.[48] In 1921, Sutherland explained his opposition to the proviso on the ground that "any law which arbitrarily separates men into classes to be punished or rewarded, not according to what they do but according to the class to which they are assigned, is odious and despotic, no matter how large a majority may have approved it."

> I have personally the greatest possible sympathy for the farmers of the country who have been first to feel the hardship of falling prices, but legislation which proposes to extend special and exclusive aid to them is almost sure to be, in one way or another, at the expense of other classes of our citizenship. Apart from all other consideration, the danger of all such legislation is that it may constitute the first link in a chain of precedents which, beginning in necessity, passes from one gradation to another until, at length, it rests in mere favor.
>
> Not so long ago Congress enacted legislation which attempted to exempt combinations of farmers and horticulturists and workmen from penalties of the Sherman Anti-Trust law, while leaving combinations of business men subject to it. The right of farmers to form associations and the right of workmen to form unions for the purpose of improving their condition and advancing their legitimate interests, is beyond question. ... An organization of farmers, or an organization of workmen is, *per se*, entirely legal, but so is an organization of business men. It is only when such an organization has for its object the restraint of interstate commerce ... that it becomes amenable to the Sherman Law. ... [I]f restraint of trade be an offense when effected by a combination of lumber dealers it is, to my mind, a perversion of all logical processes to contend that restraint of trade is not an offense when effected by a combination of farmers or workmen; and no such distinction can be made unless we are prepared to incorporate into our political system the new and dangerous doctrine that the character of the actor, and not the quality of the act, shall be the test of culpability.[49]

By the time Sutherland joined the Taft Court, however, this form of legal analysis had already become vestigial. The point can be well illustrated by the Court's 1928 decision in *Liberty Warehouse Co. v. Burley Tobacco Growers' Co-Operative Marketing Ass'n*.[50] The case concerned the constitutionality of a Kentucky statute authorizing the incorporation of nonprofit agricultural cooperatives that could consist only of farmers. The law exempted these cooperatives from otherwise generally applicable anti-trust restrictions. This was exactly the kind of statute that Sutherland in 1921 had explicitly condemned as impermissible class legislation. The relevant precedent, which Taft had cited in his 1913 veto of the appropriations bill for anti-trust enforcement, was the Court's 1902 decision in *Connelly v. Union Sewer Pipe Co.*,[51] in which the Court had struck down as unconstitutional class legislation an Illinois anti-trust statute that exempted from otherwise generally applicable anti-trust restrictions agricultural products and livestock while in the hands of producers or farmers.[52]

In *Liberty Warehouse*, by contrast, both Sutherland and Taft silently joined McReynolds's opinion for the Court, which surveyed the large number of states that had established cooperative agricultural marketing acts to overcome the peculiar market disabilities facing small, dispersed, independent farmers. McReynolds easily concluded that "[t]he opinion generally accepted – and upon reasonable grounds, we think – is that co-operative marketing statutes promote the common interest. ... The liberty of contract guaranteed by the Constitution is freedom from arbitrary restraint – not immunity from reasonable regulation to safeguard the public interest. The question is whether the restrictions of the statute have reasonable relation to a proper purpose."[53] McReynolds seamlessly subsumed the issue of class legislation into a *Natural Carbonic Gas* inquiry into appropriate public purpose. McReynolds did not even bother to ask whether the statute unjustly discriminated in favor of farmers, as distinct from serving the interest of the public as a whole.[54] The two questions simply merged into a single inquiry that was virtually indistinguishable from ordinary due process analysis.

The very "group system" endorsed by Taft in the context of the National War Labor Board strongly suggested that governments had powerful reasons for classifying disputes involving labor differently from other civil disputes.[55] But in *Truax* Taft's long-held but anachronistic instincts about class legislation were somehow triggered. Taft went so far as to declare that the Equal Protection Clause's prohibition of class legislation was its one "additional guaranty of a right" that extended "beyond the requirements of due process." Citing *Union Sewer Pipe*, Taft argued in *Truax* that "[i]t is besides the point to say that plaintiffs had no vested right in equity relief, and that taking it away does not deprive them of due process of law," because the "equality clause" forbids "the granting of equitable relief to one man and the denying of it to another under like circumstances and in the same territorial jurisdiction."[56]

On Taft's own account, however, whether the Arizona statute constituted impermissible class legislation depended upon whether it was reasonably related to a proper purpose or was instead merely an undeserved windfall to striking employees. Despite his invocation of the vestigial rhetoric of class legislation, Taft in *Truax* was therefore brought inevitably back to the inquiry of *Natural Carbonic Gas*. The law of remedies is full of distinctions about when particular litigants can and cannot not obtain specific kinds of remedies. The question facing Taft was whether the limitations on employers' remedies created by Paragraph 1464 were justified by plausible reasons. The rhetoric of class legislation added nothing to this inquiry.

Truax v. Corrigan

What in retrospect is striking about *Truax* is that Taft's urgency to protect the property rights of employers pushed him to modify the *Natural Carbonic Gas* test in ways that eerily anticipate the development of modern equal protection doctrine:

> To sustain the distinction here between the ex-employees and other tortfeasors in the matter of remedies against them, it is contended that the Legislature may establish a class of such ex-employees for special legislative treatment. In adjusting legislation to the need of the people of a state, the Legislature has a wide discretion, and it may be fully conceded that perfect uniformity of treatment of all persons is neither practical nor desirable, that classification of persons is constantly necessary, and that questions of proper classification are not free from difficulty. But ... "[c]lassification ... must always rest upon some difference which bears a reasonable and just relation to the act in respect to which the classification is proposed, and can never be made arbitrarily and without any such basis." ...
>
> Classification is the most inveterate of our reasoning processes. We can scarcely think or speak without consciously or unconsciously exercising it. It must therefore obtain in and determine legislation; but it must regard real resemblances and real differences between things and persons, and class them in accordance with their pertinence to the purpose in hand. Classification like the one with which we are here dealing is said to be the development of the philosophic thought of the world and is opening the door to legalized experiment. When fundamental rights are thus attempted to be taken away, however, we may well subject such experiment to attentive judgment. The Constitution was intended – its very purpose was – to prevent experimentation with the fundamental rights of the individual. ...
>
> It is urged that this court has frequently recognized the special classification of the relations of employees and employers as proper and necessary for the welfare of the community and requiring special treatment. ... It seems a far cry from classification on the basis of the relation of employer and employee in respect of injuries received in course of employment to classification based on the relation of an employer, not to an employee, but to one who has ceased to be so, in respect of torts thereafter committed by such ex-employee on the business and property right of the employer. It is really a little difficult to say, if such classification can be sustained, why special legislative treatment of assaults upon an employer or his employees by ex-employees may not be sustained with equal reason. It is said the state may deal separately with such disputes because such controversies are a frequent and characteristic outgrowth of disputes over terms and conditions of employment. Violence of ex-employees toward present employees is also a characteristic of such disputes. Would this justify a Legislature in excepting ex-employees from criminal prosecution for such assaults and leaving the assaulted persons to suits for damages at common law?[57]

This is a rich and striking passage. It begins with a clear-headed restatement of the *Natural Carbonic Gas* test and the need to preserve government discretion to classify. But it almost immediately qualifies that discretion in important ways. Judicial review, argues Taft, should be stricter in the context of "fundamental rights." The fundamental rights at issue in *Truax* were "the ordinary business and property rights of a person."[58] Taft asserts that "attentive judgment" ought to be brought to bear whenever a legislature seeks differentially to allocate these essential rights on the basis of "experimental" ideas. The "very purpose" of the Constitution, Taft affirms, is to foreclose "experimentation with the fundamental rights of the individual."

Taft's logic would later evolve into the branch of equal protection doctrine that uses strict scrutiny to review legislation that burdens fundamental rights.[59] Taft's objections to Paragraph 1464 sound analogous to what we would now call narrow tailoring. The "attentive judgment" invoked by Taft is most conspicuously evidenced by his complaint that Paragraph 1464 is underinclusive. Taft was particularly concerned that the "necessary effect" of Paragraph 1464 was that

> the plaintiffs in error would have had the right to an injunction against such a campaign as that conducted by the defendants in error, if it had been directed against the plaintiffs' business and property in any kind of a controversy which was not a dispute between employer and former employees. If the competing restaurant keepers in Bisbee had inaugurated such a campaign against the plaintiffs in error and conducted it with banners and handbills of a similar character, an injunction would necessarily have issued to protect the plaintiffs in the enjoyment of their property and business.[60]

Although Taft did not explain precisely why the underinclusivity of Paragraph 1464 rendered it constitutionally suspicious, he plainly believed that because the statute limited fundamental rights, it should somehow be placed under an especially strict obligation of justification.

The actual doctrinal structure of *Truax* thus turned on what Taft in fact considered the most important issue in the case – the need to preserve inviolate the business and property rights of employers.[61] These were for Taft "fundamental" because they were "the corner stone of our civilization."[62] And it was exactly on this point that Holmes in his dissent chose to engage Taft. "The dangers of a delusive exactness in the application of the Fourteenth Amendment," wrote Holmes, are

> a source of fallacy throughout the law. By calling a business "property" you make it seem like land, and lead up to the conclusion that a statute cannot substantially cut down the advantages of ownership existing before the statute was passed. An established business no doubt may have pecuniary value and commonly is protected by law against various unjustified injuries. But you cannot give it definiteness of contour by calling it a thing. It is a course of conduct and like other conduct is subject to substantial modification according to time and circumstances both in itself and in regard to what shall justify doing it a harm.[63]

Holmes's point is that the goodwill of an employer may have value, but it is in no way analogous to real property. As the Arizona Supreme Court rightly concluded, the law may seek to prevent every trespass on land, but it does not seek to

Truax v. Corrigan

prohibit every impairment of goodwill.[64] Goodwill may with legal impunity be diminished by competitors or by the critical judgments of consumers. The law seeks to protect goodwill only when it is injured by illegal means. In his due process analysis, Taft may have meant that the Due Process Clause itself requires states to protect the goodwill of business employers. But this claim is implausible, and Taft fails to offer any reasons that might make it persuasive.

On the *Natural Carbonic Gas* prong of Taft's opinion, Holmes thought it obvious "that the selection of the class of employers and employees for special treatment, dealing with both sides alike" was "beyond criticism on principles often asserted by this Court. ... Legislation may begin where an evil begins. If, as many intelligent people believe, there is more danger that the injunction will be abused in labor cases than elsewhere I can feel no doubt of the power of the Legislature to deny it in such cases."[65] Under traditional equal protection doctrine, in other words, it was immaterial that Paragraph 1464 was underinclusive by prohibiting injunctions in the context of labor protesters but allowing them in the context of improper picketing by boisterous competitors. It is telling that Holmes did not discuss either fundamental rights or class legislation, nor did he even conceive the possibility that equal protection might impose a requirement of narrow tailoring.

Holmes concluded his short, four-paragraph dissent by emphasizing the tension between constitutional adjudication and basic principles of federalism: "There is nothing that I more deprecate than the use of the Fourteenth Amendment beyond the absolute compulsion of its words to prevent the making of social experiments that an important part of the community desires, in the insulated chambers afforded by the several states, even though the experiments may seem futile or even noxious to me and to those whose judgment I most respect."[66] This was a liberal form of normative dualism. It invoked the value of local self-government to check the centralizing implications of the Court's own expansive interpretation of the Fourteenth Amendment. By contrast, *Bailey* used the principles of normative dualism to check the centralizing implications of Congress's expansive interpretation of federal taxing power.

Pitney, who had long been a cutting edge of the Court's assault on organized labor, converted his internal memorandum into a long dissent, which was joined by Clarke.[67] Pitney asserted that whether a state chose to permit peaceful picketing to promote boycotts was a matter of substantive state property law, not federal constitutional right. Because states were free to change their definitions of property, Pitney could find no "ground for declaring that the state's action is so arbitrary and devoid of reasonable basis that it can be called a deprivation of liberty or property without due process of law, in the constitutional sense. In truth, the states have a considerable degree of latitude in determining, each for itself, their respective conditions of law and order, and what kind of civilization they shall have as a result."[68]

Turning to Taft's Equal Protection Clause argument, Pitney argued that Paragraph 1464 applied equally to "employers and employees, irrespective of who is the plaintiff and who defendant."[69] Because the statute "applies equally to all persons coming within its reach," it worked "no discrimination *as against*" an employer that he was legally authorized to obtain an injunction against business competitors who might initiate a similar campaign of peaceful picketing.[70] The

1409

statute's underinclusiveness, in other words, was constitutionally irrelevant. That the statute failed to cover situations "which in consistency ought, it is said, to have been covered – an omission immaterial to the plaintiffs" – was, asserted Pitney, implicitly to use the Equal Protection Clause "to transform the provision of the Fourteenth Amendment from a guaranty of the 'protection of equal laws' into an insistence upon laws complete, perfect, symmetrical."[71] Apparently Pitney would have found modern strict scrutiny doctrine, with its requirement of narrow tailoring, all but unintelligible. It is worth noting that in the 1920s commentators vigorously agreed with Pitney's critique of narrow tailoring; they forcefully argued that the underinclusivity of Paragraph 1464 was immaterial because it did not harm Truax.[72]

Pitney sought to bring equal protection doctrine back to the framework of *Natural Carbonic Gas*. The real question, Pitney said, was whether "the statute creates an arbitrary and unreasonable discrimination," which plainly it did not.

> Doubtless the Legislature, upon a review of the subject in the light of a knowledge of conditions in their own state that we do not possess, concluded that in labor controversies there were reasons affecting the public interest for preventing resort to the process of injunction and leaving the parties to the ordinary legal remedies, which reasons did not apply generally. ... In adjusting their laws to the needs of the people, the states have a wide range of discretion about classification; the equal protection clause does not require that all state laws shall be perfect and complete, nor that the entire field of proper legislation shall be covered by a single act; and it is not a valid objection that a law made applicable to one subject might properly have been extended to others.[73]

If Holmes's dissent in *Truax* perfectly displays his concise and austere style, dissecting only what he regarded as the precise theoretical errors in Taft's opinion; and if Pitney's dissent embodies his earnest, straightforward, orthodox approach; Brandeis's dissent is a moving example of his unique and original jurisprudence. It is a profound exploration of the nature of judicial review in a democracy.[74] Conceding that the "legal right to carry on ... business for profit ... – be it called liberty or property – has value; and he who interferes with the right without cause renders himself liable," Brandeis observed that the fundamental question was whether defendants were justified in damaging the right.[75]

Brandeis reasoned that what counts as justification must "necessarily change from time to time." Change was unavoidable because "the rules governing the contest" between labor and capital are "merely experiments in government," and these rules "must be discarded when they prove to be failures."[76] The nub of the matter, from Brandeis's point of view, was how this need for change should be integrated into constitutional analysis. Directly contradicting Taft's assertion that the purpose of the Constitution was to prevent experimentation, Brandeis insisted that the Constitution should instead be understood as a charter of democracy that empowered the people to govern themselves through the

Truax v. Corrigan

continuous exercise of public discussion and evaluation.[77] Constitutional doctrine must permit government to respond to ever-changing circumstances:

> Whether a law enacted in the exercise of the police power is justly subject to the charge of being unreasonable or arbitrary can ordinarily be determined only by a consideration of the contemporary conditions, social, industrial and political, of the community to be affected thereby. Resort to such facts is necessary, among other things, in order to appreciate the evils sought to be remedied and the possible effects of the remedy proposed. Nearly all legislation involves a weighing of public needs as against private desires, and likewise a weighing of relative social values. Since government is not an exact science, prevailing public opinion concerning the evils and the remedy is among the important facts deserving consideration, particularly when the public conviction is both deep-seated and widespread and has been reached after deliberation. What, at any particular time, is the paramount public need, is necessarily largely a matter of judgment. Hence, in passing upon the validity of a law charged as being unreasonable, aid may be derived from the experience of other countries and of the several states of our Union in which the common law and its conceptions of liberty and of property prevail. The history of the rules governing contests between employer and employed in the several English-speaking countries illustrates both the susceptibility of such rules to change and the variety of contemporary opinion as to what rules will best serve the public interest. The divergence of opinion in this difficult field of governmental action should admonish us not to declare a rule arbitrary and unreasonable merely because we are convinced that it is fraught with danger to the public weal, and thus to close the door to experiment within the law.[78]

It followed from this perspective that the Due Process Clause should be construed to leave ample room for the exercise of democratic "judgment." The test for a violation of the Due Process Clause ought to be whether the "statutory prohibition of the remedy by injunction is in itself arbitrary and so unreasonable as to deprive the employer of liberty or property without due process of law." Because the reasonableness of a statute is ultimately a question of fact, it was essential for courts broadly to consider "the experience of other countries and of the several states of our Union in which the common law and its conceptions of liberty and of property prevail."[79] This wide frame of reference both tempered the potentially narrow ideological attitudes of individual judges and prevented questions of constitutionality from turning on narrow and contingent factual records that might emerge from the vagaries of litigation.

Brandeis offered a long and scholarly disquisition on the treatment of labor injunctions in English-speaking countries. He particularly focused on England, where peaceful picketing was not subject to equitable control. The regulation of industrial controversies in England "has been enforced by the courts almost wholly through the criminal law or through actions for compensation."[80] In the United States, by contrast, although labor injunctions had not been used by courts until about 1888, they have since grown "extensive and conspicuous."[81] They have become embroiled in bitter controversy,[82] with employees charging "that the real motive in seeking the injunction was not ordinarily to prevent property from being injured nor to protect the owner in its use, but to endow property with active, militant power which would make it dominant over men; in other words, that under the guise of protecting property rights, the employer was seeking sovereign power." The sovereign power was embodied in the figure of the single judge, who "often usurped the functions not only of the jury but of the police department; ... in prescribing the conditions under which strikes were permissible, and how they might be carried out, he usurped also the powers of the Legislature; and ... incidentally he abridged the constitutional rights of individuals to free speech, to a free press, and to peaceful assembly."[83]

Given this history, and given the experience of English law, Brandeis concluded that it was not arbitrary for Arizona to subscribe to the view "that the law of property was not appropriate for dealing with the forces beneath social unrest; that in this vast struggle it was unwise to throw the power of the state on one side or the other, according to principles deduced from that law; that the problem of the control and conduct of industry demanded a solution of its own; and that, pending the ascertainment of new principles to govern industry, it was wiser for the state not to interfere in industrial struggles by the issuance of an injunction."[84]

Brandeis's dissent brilliantly expresses his distinctive understanding of judicial review, an understanding that in so many ways has become the modern view of the relationship between judicial review and legislation. Brandeis argued that judicial deference is justified out of respect for the practices of democratic self-government. Legislation requires popular value judgments that must be continually revised in light of evolving conditions. Courts should refrain from unduly constraining these essential democratic processes even if they believe that legislation might be unwise or economically counterproductive. Property rights are not fundamental but exist to serve the interests of democracy. Implicit in Brandeis's dissent is the genuinely innovative premise that a commitment to political self-governance is lexically prior to a commitment to economic expansion and growth. Democracy trumps prosperity.

Brandeis also argued that the denial of equitable relief was not a violation of the Equal Protection Clause. "States are free since the adoption of the Fourteenth Amendment, as they were before, either to expand or to contract their equity jurisdiction" in order "to meet the changing needs of society." Courts refuse equitable relief for all kinds of reasons: they do not, for example, "restrain actionable libels," nor do they issue mandatory injunctions to enforce "obligations involving personal service." For reasons of policy, Congress forbids federal courts from "staying proceedings in any court of a state ... and also from enjoining the illegal assessment and collection of taxes." So long as government disallows equitable relief for reasons that are not "arbitrary or unreasonable," the prohibition does not "constitute a denial of equal protection of the laws merely because some, or even the same property rights which are excluded by this statute from protection by injunction, receive such protection under other circumstances, or between persons standing in different relations. The acknowledged legislative discretion exerted in classification, so frequently applied in defining rights, extends equally to the grant of remedies."[85]

Truax v. Corrigan

Truax was a defining moment in the history of the Taft Court.[86] Taft laid down an unmistakable marker only three months after beginning his first term.[87] He might negotiate on marginal issues regarding the relationship between labor and capital, but he would aggressively safeguard what he regarded as essential judicial protections for the entrepreneurial property of employers.[88] *Truax* made it "certain that ... no effective anti-injunction laws can be passed by the states."[89] Writing to Austen Fox, the New York lawyer who had been a leader in the opposition to Brandeis's confirmation, Taft commented about *Truax* that "[t]he disposition to regard the Constitution as something that does not mean any limitation at all is a dangerous one, and I rejoice that we had a majority of the Court that took the more conservative view."[90] He later added to another correspondent, "I deprecate the latitudinarian view of the Constitution which some of our brethren seem to have in certain cases, but we must do the best we can."[91]

Truax split the Taft Court at its very inception. Holmes reported to his friend Laski that Taft's intransigence "disappointed" both Holmes and Brandeis, especially after Taft's "happy success in uniting the Court" in *American Steel Foundries*.[92] Holmes regarded "the Chief's performance" as "rather spongy – copious citations of generalities become platitudes that don't bring you any nearer to the concrete case. I always say that I will admit any general proposition that anyone wants to lay down and decide the case either way."[93]

What Holmes failed fully to appreciate was that Taft in *Truax* was groping for a new doctrinal language that would use the Equal Protection Clause to create rules of strict scrutiny to protect fundamental rights. Despite his recognition of the "group system," Taft believed that employers alone embodied "the initiative and enterprise of capital necessary to the real progress of all."[94] For this reason, Taft regarded employers' rights as fundamental and as requiring narrowly tailored legal protection.[95] He therefore rejected Brandeis's invitation to conceptualize labor and capital as groups engaged in a struggle whose outcome was a matter of indifference to constitutional jurisprudence. Chicago Law Professor Charles O. Gregory later observed that in Paragraph 1464 Arizona had essentially accepted "an economics of pressure groups evolved by the groups themselves for their own self-interest, regardless of its effect on society in general."[96] This pluralist vision of society was unacceptable to Taft, who remained throughout his judicial tenure committed to what he regarded as the public interest, which he consistently identified with the prerogatives of property.

Truax was received by the public as a "sweeping decision"[97] that was "of serious consequence to organized labor."[98] "Supreme Court again Wallops Union Picketing," the headlines screamed, "States Have No Right to Forbid Injunctions."[99] Taken together with *American Steel Foundries*, said the Buffalo *Commercial*, *Truax* "will put an end to a practice that was as odious as it was intolerable and disgraceful. ... It takes the bullets out of the picketer's cartridges, and virtually puts an end to picketing by union labor."[100] "The whole country must rejoice in the knowledge that it has a supreme tribunal that possesses at once the power and the courage to deal conclusively with a situation that year by year has grown more difficult," editorialized the *Los Angeles Evening Express*. "Neither business nor labor knew where it stood.... Therefore, the decisions of the supreme court, establishing fundamental principle and easily recognizable limitations, setting forth the law so clearly as to be understood by all concerned, must afford the very greatest relief to honest labor and honest business alike."[101]

Within the law reviews, *Truax* was recognized "as marking an epoch in constitutional law,"[102] although Taft's opinion received "practically unanimous disapproval."[103] Taft's claim that it was arbitrary to distinguish between injunctions in labor cases and injunctions in other situations excited "intellectual amazement,"[104] if not outright incredulity.[105] It was said that Taft's rejection of the classification in Paragraph 1464 contained "not one word of substantive argument," but consisted instead in "merely the reiterated dogmatic statement that" the classification "is here 'unreasonable' although admitted proper in other connections, such as Employers' Liability statutes."[106] The decision was condemned as a throwback to *Lochner*.[107]

The most sustained assault on the decision came in what Taft called the "weekly dreadfuls," the periodical magazines that "discuss social questions."[108] Francis Bowes Sayre in *The Survey* opined that *Truax* gave the Fourteenth Amendment "a wider meaning than it has ever been given before."[109] The *New Republic* condemned *Truax* as "fraught with more evil than any which [the Court] has rendered in a generation."[110] Taft's decision "justified the worst fears about him more quickly than the sturdiest sceptic was entitled to fear."[111] Taft blithely indulged in "a schoolboy's begging of the question."[112] His opinion was filled with "jejune logomachy" that dealt "with abstractions and not with the work-a-day world, its men and its struggles.... Mr. Taft, as a member of the War Labor Board, came in contact with not a little that must have informed his mind as to the industrial struggle and law's relation to it. But all those crude and sordid and unsymmetrical facts have no place in the mind of Chief Justice Taft."[113] *Truax* "is destined to become even more classic than the Lochner case," a "strait-jacket for a free people unless the Supreme Court some day sees fit to change its mind."[114]

"The simple fact of the matter," said the *New Republic*, "is that in a decision like Truax v. Corrigan, the Court, under the guise of legal form, exercises political control"[115] about "the most contentious issue which presented itself in American labor law, to wit, the use of the injunction against picketing and boycott, particularly where no violence was used and the claim of destruction of property was merely colorable."[116] By the vote of one man, observed *The Nation*, the Supreme Court once again decides "a matter of the gravest importance to the public good."[117] And that one man, "the new Chief Justice, no matter how great his attainments as a lawyer and a man, has always held to the reactionary view of the law of labor disputes."[118]

Labor is often told "to look to the legislatures for relief from the disadvantages at which it finds itself in the industrial struggle," said *The Nation*. But now the Court in *Truax* has exercised its constitutional prerogative to prohibit the country from following "the example of England in her Trade Disputes Act of 1906." What, then, was labor to do? Should it "attempt to break the power of the judiciary by direct action"? "If in future years Truax v. Corrigan comes back to plague us in terms of defiance of the courts, we shall know where to assess the blame."[119]

Truax v. Corrigan

The Nation proved prophetic. Organized labor was indeed driven to assault the courts.[120] At its Annual Meeting in June 1922, the American Federation of Labor embraced La Follette and his call for a constitutional amendment to disestablish judicial review.[121] In 1922, the powerful Railroad Brotherhoods were driven to create the Conference on Progressive Political Action and to endorse that same proposed amendment.[122] At the bottom of this turmoil lay *Truax*, often too threatening to be explicitly named in the polemics of the time, which tended instead to focus on the other three decisions in the labor quartet – *Bailey, Coronado,* and *American Steel Foundries*.

In point of fact, however, *Truax* never exerted much influence on the history of American constitutional law. It asserted a vision of due process that was too radical ever to find acceptance. Its equal protection holding, while eerily anticipating the modern development of the doctrine, was also deliberately designed to immunize the Clayton Act from constitutional scrutiny. Taft repeatedly stressed that *Truax* did not "in effect" hold "invalid § 20 of the Clayton Act. ... [T]he equality clause of the Fourteenth Amendment does not apply to congressional but only to state action."[123] The Equal Protection Clause did not apply to the federal government, and, in 1921, the Due Process Clause of the Fifth Amendment, which did so apply, had not yet been construed to contain an "equal-protection component"[124] that was "precisely the same" as the Equal Protection Clause.[125]

Truax thus had little or no relevance when organized labor began after *Bedford Cut Stone* seriously to attempt to curtail federal labor injunctions.[126] Indeed, at the first meeting of a Senate subcommittee charged with considering the ancestor of the Norris-LaGuardia Act, Senator Shipstead testified that "[t]he majority of court, headed by Chief Justice Taft, held that only Congress held this power to limit court jurisdiction in equity cases, and that the State Legislature did not have this power. The entire Supreme Court bench, as I understand, conceded the power of Congress, however, to define and limit equity jurisdiction."[127] As the Norris-LaGuardia Act began to take shape at the end of the decade, therefore, *Truax* was oddly absent from the conversation,[128] although it continued to exert some influence in the context of state anti-injunction statutes.[129]

During the Taft Court era the influence of *Truax* lay primarily in its validation of the labor injunction, and, indirectly, in its resurrection of the Equal Protection Clause as a restriction on state social and economic regulation. Taft's aggressive use of equal protection produced what Brandeis called "evil effects":[130] "There might be reason for protection of equality – of treatment of races, religion in country like ours," Frankfurter told Brandeis in 1923, "but that use made of [the Equal Protection] clause by Taft in Truax v. Corrigan was fantastic." "Dreadful," Brandeis replied.[131]

The Taft Court

Notes

1. For a discussion of the historical background of the case, see Astrid J. Norvelle, *"80 Percent Bill," Court Injunctions, and Arizona Labor: Billy Truax's Two Supreme Court Cases*, 17 WESTERN LEGAL HISTORY 163 (2004).
2. Truax v. Bisbee Local, 19 Ariz. 379, 381 (1918).
3. The Arizona Supreme Court reproduced examples of these handbills. One read, in part:

   > Billie Truax contends that it is impossible to operate a restaurant on the eight-hour basis and make it pay. Witness every other restaurant in the Warren district operating satisfactorily on the eight-hour basis.
   >
   > Why does Bill Truax employ scab Mexican painters?
   >
   > The truth is very obvious, it is cheaper and hastens the day when he "has it made," and can return to that dear Los Angeles, be a gentleman, perhaps have a Japanese valet, a Chinese cook, and an imported Jamaican chauffeur.
   >
   > Don't overlook the fact that Bill Truax's past record relative to Union Labor is not an unblemished tablet of stone, but nevertheless it is quite as enduring, and he will find it writ in letters large wherever he tries to do business in this U.S.A.
   >
   > The need and the necessity of the workers to organize and conduct their negotiations with the employers on a collective bargaining basis is denied by few. That is just where it "gets to" Bill Truax; his autocratic methods in handling his help, chasing them down the street with a butcher knife, and other stunts of a like nature will have to go, and *believe us, it hurts.*

   A second read:

   > To every man, woman, and child and all lovers of fair play:
   >
   > We are fighting the most consistent "bad actor" in the district, Wm. Truax.
   >
   > Wm. Truax fought the eighty per cent. law. (Please don't overlook this fact.)
   >
   > Wm. Truax always favored hiring foreigners almost exclusively. . . .
   >
   > Wm. Truax initiated this fight, and we are going to see it through now that it has been forced upon us. When you patronize Bill Truax you are aiding and abetting a diminutive but potential force for evil in tearing down the wages and hours in this district.
   >
   > Help us win.

   Bisbee Local, 19 Ariz. at 382–83.
4. *Id.* at 382.
5. Truax v. Corrigan, 257 U.S. 312, 327 (1921).
6. "The evidence coming from plaintiffs is that the persons placed near their place of business acted at all times peaceably. The alleged purpose for which the men were placed near plaintiffs' business entrance was to advertise the strike and influence prospective customers from patronizing plaintiffs." *Bisbee Local*, 19 Ariz. at 391. "Whatever interference with plaintiffs' business the presence of the banner carriers caused, that interference did not arise from any boisterous conduct of the carriers. Their conduct was at least peaceable. Their presence near the English Kitchen is the only ground for complaint." *Id.* at 392.
7. *Truax*, 257 U.S. at 330 ("A secondary boycott of this kind is where many combine to injure one in his business by coercing third persons against their will to cease patronizing him by threats of similar injury."). *See Bisbee Local*, at 389–90. "The

relief demanded is a writ of injunction enjoining, restraining, and prohibiting defendants, etc., 'from in any manner or by any means conspiring or combining to boycott the business of plaintiffs, and from threatening or declaring any boycott against said business, and from abetting, aiding, or assisting in any such boycott, and from, directly or indirectly, threatening, coercing, menacing, intimidating, *or persuading* any person or persons whomsoever from buying from or otherwise dealing with plaintiffs, and from printing, publishing, or displaying any sign, banner, or other device for the purpose of advertising or in furtherance of any boycott against plaintiffs' business, and from referring, either in print or otherwise, to plaintiffs as unfair, in furtherance of such boycott.'" *Id.* at 384–85 (emphasis added).

8. The Act provided:

> No restraining order or injunction shall be granted by any court of this state, or a judge or the judges thereof, in any case between an employer and employees, or between employers and employees, or between employees, or between persons employed and persons seeking employment, involving or growing out of a dispute concerning terms or conditions of employment, unless necessary to prevent irreparable injury to property or to a property right of the party making the application, for which injury there is no adequate remedy at law, and such property or property right must be described with particularity in the application . . . .
>
> And no such restraining order or injunction shall prohibit any person or persons from terminating any relation of employment, or from ceasing to perform any work or labor, or from recommending, advising, or persuading others by peaceful means so to do; or from attending at or near a house or place where any person resides or works, or carries on business, or happens to be for the purpose of peacefully obtaining or communicating information, or of peacefully persuading any person to work or to abstain from working; or from ceasing to patronize or to employ any party to such dispute; or from recommending, advising, or persuading others by peaceful means so to do.

Truax, 257 U.S. at 322.

9. *Bisbee Local*, 19 Ariz. at 387, 389.
10. *Id.* at 392–94.
11. Truax v. Corrigan, 20 Ariz. 7, 9–10 (1918). "Why should the employer be heard to question the right of the other party to the dispute to advertise the fact of the unsettled condition of the dispute?" *Id.* at 10–11.
12. *Id.* at 12.
13. *See supra* Chapter 39, at 1241–42.
14. *The Challenge Accepted*, 28 AMERICAN FEDERATIONIST 289, 293, 296 (1921). In June 1921, the AFL Annual Convention passed a resolution calling "upon all affiliated organizations . . . to inaugurate energetic campaigns against the ever-growing abuse of injunctions in labor disputes and to conduct such campaigns through meetings, publications and other avenues of publicity earnestly and unceasingly until the intolerable practice is abandoned by legislative relief or otherwise." REPORT OF THE PROCEEDINGS OF THE FORTY-FIRST ANNUAL CONVENTION OF THE AMERICAN FEDERATION OF LABOR 382–84 (Washington D.C.: Law Reporter Printing Co. 1921).
15. Jackson H. Ralston, *Government by Injunction*, 5 CORNELL LAW QUARTERLY 424, 428 (1920). *See Report of A.F. of L. Executive Council*, in REPORT OF THE PROCEEDINGS OF THE FORTY-FIRST ANNUAL CONVENTION OF THE AMERICAN FEDERATION OF LABOR, *supra* note 14, at 76 (*Truax* "indirectly involves the

constitutionality under the federal constitution of the labor provisions of the Clayton act, including particularly the right of picketing.").

16. *Brandeis-Frankfurter Conversations*, at 306 (July 1, 1922). To Brandeis the incident illustrated how "Holmes has no realization of what moves men – he is as innocent as a girl of sixteen is supposed to have been. And most of the time it doesn't matter in his position." *Id.* at 307.
17. MP to LDB (November 3, 1920) (Brandeis papers).
18. Brandeis papers.
19. WHT to WVD (December 7, 1921) (Taft papers).
20. William Howard Taft, *Inaugural Address*, 44 CONG. REC. 1, 5 (March 4, 1909).
21. *Truax*, 257 U.S. at 327–28.
22. *Id.* The harm caused by the defendants, Taft emphasized, was "not a mere libel," for that "would not have had any such serious consequences. The libel of the plaintiffs here was not the cause of the injury; it was only one step or link in a conspiracy unlawfully to influence customers." *Id.* at 328–29.
23. *Id.* at 330 (emphasis added).
24. *Id.* at 332. Just imagine, Edward Corwin immediately remarked, the "obvious bearing" of this holding "on the question of the validity of the projected Anti-Lynching law." Edward Corwin, *Constitutional Law in 1921–1922*, 16 AMERICAN POLITICAL SCIENCE REVIEW 612, 633 (1922). The Dyer Anti-Lynching Bill, which had first been introduced in Congress in 1918, and which was eventually passed by the House in 1922, declared it a federal criminal offense for state law enforcement officials to neglect or omit to make all reasonable efforts to prosecute those involved in lynch mobs. *See* H.R. 11279, 65th CONG. 2nd SESS. (April 8, 1918). The bill decreed "that the putting to death within any State of a citizen of the United States by a mob or riotous assemblage of three or more persons openly acting in concert, in violation of law and in default of protection of such citizen by such State or the officers thereof, shall be deemed a denial to such citizen by such State of the equal protection of the laws."
25. David P. Currie, *Positive and Negative Constitutional Rights*, 53 UNIVERSITY OF CHICAGO LAW REVIEW 864, 876 (1986). Compare Taft's reasoning in *Truax* with Sanford's opinion for a unanimous Court in Corrigan v. Buckley, 271 U.S. 323 (1926). *Corrigan* involved a suit by John Buckley to enjoin the conveyance of property by Irene Corrigan to Helen Curtis, who was Black, on the ground that the property contained a racially restrictive covenant that precluded the sale. Corrigan claimed the enforcement of the covenant violated the Fourteenth Amendment, but the Court rejected that argument on the ground that "the prohibitions of the Fourteenth Amendment 'have reference to State action exclusively, and not to any action of private individuals.'" 271 U.S. at 330. *See* David P. Currie, *The Constitution in the Supreme Court: 1921–1930*, 1986 DUKE LAW JOURNAL 65, 70–74.
26. Currie, *Positive and Negative Constitutional Rights*, *supra* note 25, at 877–78.
27. *See* DeShaney v. Winnebago County Department of Social Services, 489 U.S. 189 (1989); United States v. Morrison, 529 U.S. 598 (2000).
28. Van Devanter, seeking to cement his relationship with the new chief justice, merely commented on his return to Taft's draft opinion, "I very sincerely congratulate you on so wholesome an outcome in a difficult case. The dissent nicely serves to emphasize the points of your decision. They neither shake your reasoning nor raise any doubt of the propriety of its application." (Taft papers). McKenna said,

Truax v. Corrigan

"Good work. Most heartily." (Taft papers). And Day, who Brandeis later said was fiercely passionate about *Truax* – "you ought to hear Day on that opinion" – said "Certainly. No other view is permissible after this clear demonstration of the right one." (Taft papers). *See Brandeis-Frankfurter Conversations*, at 306 (July 1, 1922).

29. "True, the Tri-City case decided that 'dogging and importunity' were tortious; but it is one thing for the Federal courts to establish their own rules of tort liability – and quite another to hold that this Federal rule of tort-liability, established but yesterday, is one of fundamental right, which all jurisdictions are obliged by the Constitution to follow." Note, 10 CALIFORNIA LAW REVIEW 237, 239 (1922). "The Supreme Court in *American Steel Foundries v. Tri-City Central Trades Council* laid down the law for the federal courts, and, in *Truax v. Corrigan*, denied to the states the power to establish rules substantially less restrictive." Joseph Tanenhaus, *Picketing as a Tort: The Development of the Law of Picketing from 1880 to 1940*, 14 UNIVERSITY OF PITTSBURGH LAW REVIEW 170, 195 (1953).

30. *Truax*, 257 U.S. at 340. The *Wall Street Journal* crowed that *Truax*, together with *American Steel Foundries*, "show that 'peaceful picketing' is not synonymous with driving away customers or interfering with another man's right to conduct business, or to work for whom he pleases at any wage he chooses to accept." *Peaceful Picketing*, WALL STREET JOURNAL (December 21, 1921), at 1.

31. *Truax*, 257 U.S. at 330.

32. Buck v. Bell, 274 U.S. 200, 208 (1927). In writing for the Court in Missouri, K. & T. Ry. Co. v. May, 194 U.S. 267 (1904), Holmes had offered this account of the Equal Protection Clause: "With regard to the manner in which such a question should be approached, it is obvious that the legislature is the only judge of the policy of a proposed discrimination. The principle is similar to that which is established with regard to a decision of Congress that certain means are necessary and proper to carry out one of its express powers. *M'Culloch v. Maryland*, 4 Wheat. 316. When a state legislature has declared that, in its opinion, policy requires a certain measure, its action should not be disturbed by the courts under the 14th Amendment, unless they can see clearly that there is no fair reason for the law that would not require with equal force its extension to others whom it leaves untouched." *Id.* at 269.

33. Lindsley v. Natural Carbonic Gas Co., 220 U.S. 61, 78–79 (1911).

34. 113 U.S. 27 (1884).

35. *Id.* at 32, quoted in *Truax*, 257 U.S. at 333.

36. *See supra* Chapter 24, at 757–58.

37. 169 U.S. 366, 398 (1898).

38. This shift is plainly visible in the summary of equal protection doctrine set forth in *Ruling Case Law*. *Ruling Case Law* was a professional publication that digested existing law. In 1915, it encapsulated the requirements of the Equal Protection Clause in this way: "Although class legislation is prohibited by the federal guaranty as to the equal protection of the laws, yet this does not prohibit a reasonable classification of persons and things for the purpose of legislation, but such classification is distinctly contemplated by the amendment." 6 RULING CASE LAW § 369 (1915). "One of the essential requirements as to classification, in order that it may not violate the constitutional guaranty as to equal protection of the laws, is that the classification must not be capricious or arbitrary, but must be reasonable and natural or must be based on some natural principle of public policy." *Id.* at § 372.

39. Hence Taft's frank acknowledgment that the Equal Protection Clause "is associated in the amendment with the due process clause and it is customary to consider them together. It may be that they overlap, that a violation of one may involve at times the violation of the other." *Truax*, 257 U.S. at 331–32. As one commentator put it: "[I]n many cases, laws which have been held invalid as denying due process of law might also have been so held as denying equal protection of the laws, or *vice* versa, and that, in fact, in not a few cases the courts have referred to both prohibitions leaving it uncertain which prohibition was deemed the most pertinent and potent on the premises." WESTEL WOODBURY WILLOUGHBY, 3 THE CONSTITUTIONAL LAW OF THE UNITED STATES 1929 (New York: Baker, Voorhis & Co. 1929). For examples of the overlap between due process and equal protection analysis, see Kansas City Southern Ry. Co. v. Road Improvement Dist. No. 3, 266 U.S. 379, 386–87 (1924) ("Only where the legislative determination is palpably arbitrary, and therefore a plain abuse of power, can it be said to offend the due process of law clause of the Fourteenth Amendment. And only where there is manifest and unreasonable discrimination in fixing the benefits which the several parcels will receive can the legislative determination be said to contravene the equal protection clause of that amendment."); Lacoste v. Department of Conservation of Louisiana, 263 U.S. 545, 552 (1924).
40. This tradition is admirably explored in V.F. Nourse & Sarah A. Maguire, *The Lost History of Governance and Equal Protection*, 58 DUKE LAW JOURNAL 955, 975–78 (2009).
41. WHT to Robert A. Taft (February 23, 1925) (Taft papers).
42. *Speech of William Howard Taft Accepting the Republican Nomination for President of the United States*, Sen. Doc. No. 902, 62nd CONG. 2nd SESS. (August 1, 1912), at 10. Roosevelt had also rejected similar legislation on the ground that it was an "unconstitutional" expression of the "foul and evil" attitude of "class consciousness." *Special Message from the President of the United States*, 42 CONG. REC. 5327–28 (April 28, 1908).
43. *Sundry Civil Appropriation Bill*, H.R. 28775, 62nd CONG. 3rd SESS. (February 22, 1913), at 123. The bill stated: "Provided, however, That no part of this money shall be spent in the prosecution of any organization or individual for entering into any combination or agreement having in view the increasing of wages, shortening of hours, or bettering the condition of labor, or for any act done in furtherance thereof not in itself unlawful; Provided further, That no part of this appropriation shall be expended for the prosecution of producers of farm products and associations of farmers who cooperate and organize in an effort to and for the purpose to obtain and maintain a fair and reasonable price for their products."
44. *Veto Message*, 49 CONG. REC. 4838 (March 4, 1913). The provision was reenacted the following year and signed into law by Wilson. It was repassed each year throughout the 1920s. FELIX FRANKFURTER & NATHAN GREENE, THE LABOR INJUNCTION 141 (New York: MacMillan Co. 1930).
45. William Howard Taft, *Address of the President*, in REPORT OF THE THIRTY-SEVENTH ANNUAL MEETING OF THE AMERICAN BAR ASSOCIATION 371 (Baltimore: Lord Baltimore Press 1914).
46. *Id.* at 372.
47. George Sutherland, *Address of the President: Private Rights and Government Control*, in REPORT OF THE FORTIETH ANNUAL MEETING OF THE AMERICAN BAR ASSOCIATION 212 (Baltimore: Lord Baltimore Press 1917).

Truax v. Corrigan

48. *See* 51 CONG. REC. 11803–4 (July 8, 1914) (Discussing Pub. L. No. 63-161, 38 Stat. 609, 652 (August 1, 1914), forbidding funds to be spent to enforce anti-trust legislation against unions and farmers).
49. George Sutherland, *Principle or Expedient?*, 5 CONSTITUTIONAL REVIEW 195, 207–9 (1921). Sutherland's complaint about "the new and dangerous doctrine that the character of the actor, and not the quality of the act, shall be the test of culpability" is curious, given that Sutherland had himself eloquently defended a conception of workman's compensation that was, in his own words, premised entirely on "the status of industry and workman." *Address of Hon. George Sutherland to the Third Annual Convention of International Association of Casualty and Surety Underwriters*, Sen. Doc. No. 131, 63rd CONG. 1st SESS. (June 14, 1913). *See* Cudahy Packing Co. v. Parramore, 263 U.S. 418, 423 (1923) ("Workmen's Compensation legislation rests upon the idea of status, not upon that of implied contract.") (opinion by Sutherland, J.).
50. 276 U.S. 71 (1928).
51. 184 U.S. 540 (1902). *See Veto Message*, 49 CONG. REC. 4838 (March 4, 1913).
52. On *Connelly*, see Nourse & Maguire, *supra* note 40, at 975–78.
53. *Liberty Warehouse*, 276 U.S. at 96–97. Stone's docket book indicates that Sutherland passed in conference, so it is fair to assume that he retained lingering reservations about the kind of blatant "class legislation" at issue in *Liberty Warehouse*.
54. Stone commented to his former clerk Milton Handler that "I agree with you that McReynolds['] opinion in the Co-operative Marketing case is easily the most important decision this term, and is handled in admirable fashion. ... Of course, if its reasoning is followed it puts a different aspect on the rule of classification as announced in some of the earlier cases." HFS to Milton Handler (March 2, 1928) (Stone papers). For a good discussion of *Liberty Warehouse* in the context of older ideas of class legislation, see Matthew O. Tobriner, *The Constitutionality of Cooperative Marketing Statutes*, 17 CALIFORNIA LAW REVIEW 19 (1928).
55. *See supra* Chapter 39, at 1234–35.
56. *Truax*, 257 U.S. at 334–35.
57. *Id.* at 336–38.
58. *Id.* at 335.
59. *See, e.g.*, Shapiro v. Thompson, 394 U.S. 618, 638 (1969); Graham v. Richardson, 403 U.S. 365, 375 (1971) ("It is enough to say that the classification involved in *Shapiro* was subjected to strict scrutiny under the compelling state interest test, not because it was based on any suspect criterion such as race, nationality, or alienage, but because it impinged upon the fundamental right of interstate movement.").
60. *Truax*, 257 U.S. at 331.
61. *See supra* Chapter 40, at 1326–27. The class bias assumed in this formulation of the right should not go unnoticed. "The desire to carry on business activities and maximize profits by 'fair' means was made a legal right; the desire to obtain the largest possible return for one's labor by similar methods was not. Any interference with the rights of business had to be privileged to be legal, and the burden of proving legal justification was hoisted onto the shoulders of labor. When employees, once entreaty and bargaining broke down, resorted to bringing economic pressure to bear upon the employer by interfering with this business relationship, their activities carried a presumption of illegality." Tanenhaus, *supra* note 29, at 187.

62. WHT to Elihu Root (December 21, 1922) (Taft papers).
63. *Truax*, 257 U.S. at 342–43 (Holmes, J., dissenting). Holmes told his friend Harold Laski that "[a]t B[randeis]'s request I wrote a few words before I saw his and as he wanted me to print I did." OWH to Harold Laski (December 22, 1921), in 1 HOLMES-LASKI CORRESPONDENCE, at 389.
64. *See supra* text at note 11.
65. *Truax*, 257 U.S. at 343 (Holmes, J., dissenting).
66. *Id.* at 344 (Holmes, J., dissenting).
67. Holmes reported to Laski that Brandeis viewed it as "proof of Pitney's intellectual honesty that having taken [*Truax*] to work the other way after the first argument he changed his mind on reflection." OWH to Harold Laski (December 22, 1921), in 1 HOLMES-LASKI CORRESPONDENCE, at 389. Pitney, Brandeis later remarked to Frankfurter, "was very different – real character. He welcomed correction and discussion. In an opinion he cited *Adair*, *Coppage*, cases and I suggested that they were like *Dred Scott* and ought not to be cited. He eliminated reference!" *Brandeis-Frankfurter Conversations*, at 322 (August 7, 1923). For an indication of Taft's irritation with Pitney for his dissent in *Truax*, see WHT to WVD (December 26, 1921) (Van Devanter papers).
68. *Truax*, 257 U.S. at 348–49 (Pitney, J., dissenting). Pitney did not in fact interpret Paragraph 1464 as changing "any substantive rule of law." In Pitney's view, the law did not make legal any picketing that would otherwise be illegal. Instead he interpreted Paragraph 1464 as establishing "a new rule of evidence for determining whether picketing was peaceful and not otherwise unlawful, and that, measured by the standard thus prescribed, defendants were not subject to injunction." *Truax*, 257 U.S. at 346–47 (Pitney, J., dissenting).
69. *Id.* at 350 (Pitney, J., dissenting).
70. *Id.* Because the classification in Paragraph 1464 addressed labor disputes but not other forms of picketing, it was underinclusive. Taft viewed this underinclusivity as evidence of irrationality. Pitney countered this point by observing that "Whatever complaint the competing restaurant keepers might have, if in the case supposed they were subject to be stopped by an injunction where former employees were not, it would not be a denial of equal protection to plaintiffs. Cases arising under this clause of the Fourteenth Amendment, pre-eminently, call for the application of the settled rule that before one may be heard to oppose state legislation upon the ground of its repugnance to the federal Constitution he must bring himself within the class affected by the alleged unconstitutional feature." *Id.* Pitney's argument anticipates Justice Byron White's later claim that First Amendment overbreadth doctrine involves a form of exceptional third-party standing. *See* Broadrick v. Oklahoma, 413 U.S. 601, 612 (1973).
71. *Truax*, 257 U.S. at 351 (Pitney, J., dissenting).
72. Thomas Reed Powell, for example, was especially merciless in skewering Taft on this point. Powell observed that Taft had effectively concluded that Truax

> was denied equal protection of the laws by being deprived of an injunction against intimidating picketers who were his employees when he would not have been denied an injunction against intimidating picketers who were his competitors. He was deprived of equal protection because his desired remedy was denied him against some instead of against all. The absurdity of such a ground of decision was amply exposed in the dissenting opinion

Truax v. Corrigan

of Mr. Justice Pitney. Only an overwhelming desire to reach the result could have induced such an intellectual strain as the majority opinion indulges in.

Thomas Reed Powell, *The Supreme Court's Control over the Issue of Injunctions in Labor Disputes*, 13 PROCEEDINGS OF THE ACADEMY OF POLITICAL SCIENCE 37, 64–65 (June 1928). *See supra* note 70. For Powell's extreme disdain for this kind of reasoning, which today would be uncontroversially accepted under the rubric of "narrowly tailoring," see Thomas Reed Powell, *Alien Land Cases in United States Supreme Court*, 12 CALIFORNIA LAW REVIEW 259, 277 (1924); *see infra* Chapter 43, at note 236. The author of an excellent note in the *Yale Law Journal* wrote:

> [I]t is submitted with all deference that Justice Pitney is clearly right and that he is borne out by both the history of the amendment and the history of its enforcement. It was passed after the Civil War in order to place all people on an equality of rights, to prevent a state from *discriminating against* anyone, but not to require absolute uniformity of law. And it has been construed ... to permit attacks on state laws only by those *who are discriminated against*. If A has a right against X, B must have a similar right against X, unless differentiated by a proper and reasonable classification. But if B has a right against X, he cannot thereby claim that he must have a similar right against Y or object because Y may be privileged where X is not. Such a complaint can only be made by X. So here if the defendants are unfairly privileged as against competing employers, it is for the latter alone to complain....
>
> It is not important then that these "tort-feasors" may be unwisely privileged; the question is whether plaintiffs are denied rights which others similarly situated have. And as plaintiffs have such right as all other employers have, the question is therefore entirely one of the reasonableness of the classification which puts employers into a separate group from other plaintiffs.

Note, 31 YALE LAW JOURNAL 408, 412–13 (1922). Edward Corwin, however, was prepared to acknowledge the force in Taft's reasoning. Corwin, *supra* note 24, at 634 n.96.

73. *Truax*, 257 U.S. at 352–53 (Pitney, J., dissenting).
74. Clarke refused to join Brandeis's dissent, writing: "I am sorry I can't go with you in this but your dissent is much too discursive & expanded to please me. I shall concur in the dissent of Pitney, J." (Brandeis papers).
75. *Truax*, 257 U.S. at 354 (Brandeis, J., dissenting).
76. *Id.* at 354–55 (Brandeis, J., dissenting).
77. *See supra* Chapter 8, at 312–15.
78. *Truax*, 257 U.S. at 356–57 (Brandeis, J., dissenting). Five and a half years later, Brandeis would elaborate this vision of democracy and public opinion in his famous concurring opinion in Whitney v. California, 274 U.S. 357, 372 (1927) (Brandeis, J., concurring). Brandeis's concurrence in *Whitney* was the foundation upon which the Court in the 1930s erected the edifice of modern First Amendment doctrine. *See, e.g.,* Stromberg v. California, 283 U.S. 359 (1931); Thornhill v. Alabama, 310 U.S. 88 (1940). *Thornhill*, in particular, followed directly from Brandeis's opinion in Senn v. Tile Layers Protective Union, 301 U.S. 468 (1937), which effectively overruled *Truax* by implying that the point of peaceful picketing was "to acquaint the public with the facts" and to persuade through "publicity." *Id.* at 480–81. *See* Charles O. Gregory, *Peaceful Picketing and Freedom of Speech*, 26 AMERICAN BAR ASSOCIATION JOURNAL 709, 712–15 (1940). Brandeis distinguished *Truax* by characterizing it as applicable only to conduct that was otherwise tortious. *Senn*, 301 U.S. at 479–80.

79. *Truax*, 257 U.S. at 356–57 (Brandeis, J., dissenting).
80. *Id.* at 358–60, 366 (Brandeis, J., dissenting).
81. *Id.* at 366 (Brandeis, J., dissenting).
82. Brandeis rehearsed the more or less standard objections to labor injunctions. *Id.* at 366–68 (Brandeis, J., dissenting).
83. *Id.* at 367–68 (Brandeis, J., dissenting).
84. *Id.* at 368 (Brandeis, J., dissenting). *See id.* at 372: "A state, which despite the Fourteenth Amendment possesses the power to impose on employers without fault unlimited liability for injuries suffered by employees, and to limit the freedom of contract of some employers and not of others, surely does not lack the power to select for its citizens that one of conflicting views on boycott by peaceful picketing which its legislature and highest court consider will best meet its conditions and secure the public welfare."
85. *Id.* at 373–74, 376 (Brandeis, J., dissenting).
86. A week after the opinion's release, Brandeis wrote Woodrow Wilson, "You were so deeply interested in the labor provisions embodied in the Clayton Act that I am venturing to send you the recent opinions in the Truax Case." LDB to Woodrow Wilson (December 28, 1921), in 5 LETTERS OF LOUIS D. BRANDEIS, at 40.
87. Van Devanter's good friend, the conservative Judge Walter H. Sanborn, wrote Van Devanter on the very day that *Truax* was announced to "heartily congratulate you and Chief Justice Taft upon the decisions you are handing down, and especially upon those which sustain the constitution of the United States and declare that the means of livelihood of the citizens of this nation are protected thereby, and that they shall not be deprived thereof by violence and robbery. I am rejoiced at the decision in the Arizona case . . . . I regret that the majority of the Court is not larger, but enough is sufficient." Walter H. Sanborn to WVD (December 19, 1921) (Van Devanter papers). District Judge James D. Elliott, whom Taft had appointed in 1911, wrote Taft to say that he regarded the *Truax* opinion "as the greatest that has been filed in [the] Supreme Court in your time or mine. I say this deliberately and with no thought of exaggeration." The Arizona statute threatened "to destroy the entire fabric of Constitutional freedom and independence of individual citizenship." James D. Elliott to WHT (January 9, 1922) (Taft papers).
88. On Taft's commitment to managerial freedom, see *supra* Chapter 41, at 1381. The *Garment Worker* commented on *Truax* that Taft seemed to be taking two incompatible positions:

> First, patronage is property and can be protected against a boycott by an injunction. Second, workers have the right to take this alleged "property" from an owner if they use dancing master methods.
>
> It is clear that the chief justice looks upon his first position as a principle and his second position a merely a method to soften his blow against the boycott. Or, in other words, workers may boycott, but if the boycott is successful they can be stopped by an injunction judge.

U.S. Supreme Court Holds Void State Law Based on Clayton Act, 21 GARMENT WORKER 1 (December 30, 1921).
89. E.E. Witte, *Results of Injunctions in Labor Disputes*, 12 AMERICAN LABOR LEGISLATION REVIEW 197, 199 (1922).

Truax v. Corrigan

90. WHT to Austen G. Fox (January 31, 1922) (Taft papers).
91. WHT to G.H. Harrison (February 13, 1922) (Taft papers).
92. OWH to Harold Laski (December 22, 1921), in 1 HOLMES-LASKI CORRESPONDENCE, at 389. *See* OWH to Felix Frankfurter (December 23, 1921), in HOLMES-FRANKFURTER CORRESPONDENCE, at 132 ("The *Truax* case disappointed me after the C.J. had so successfully stifled competition the week before").
93. OWH to Harold Laski (December 22, 1921), in 1 HOLMES-LASKI CORRESPONDENCE, at 390. *See* OWH to Harold Laski (January 15, 1922), *id.* at 398 ("The C.J. disappointed us after a good start, as it seemed, in what we think the right direction in an earlier case. I thought this performance rather spongy.").
94. William Howard Taft, *Mr. Wilson and the Campaign*, 10 YALE REVIEW 1, 19–20 (1920).
95. *See supra* Chapter 40, at 1326–27.
96. Gregory, *supra* note 78, at 710.
97. *Labor Unions Lose Injunction Battle*, NEW YORK TIMES (December 20, 1921), at 4.
98. *Court's Power to Halt Labor Picket Upheld*, SAN FRANCISCO CHRONICLE (December 20, 1921), at 1.
99. CHICAGO DAILY TRIBUNE (December 20, 1921), at 13.
100. Quoted in *When Picketing Is Illegal*, 72 LITERARY DIGEST 14 (January 7, 1922). The *Fayetteville Observer* editorialized that "It is to be hoped that this decision will put an end to the mob practice of picketing. ... It strikes us that Chief Justice Taft has a very clear conception of right and justice." *Picketing Unlawful*, FAYETTEVILLE OBSERVER (December 21, 1921), at 4.
101. *"Peaceful Picketing" Restrained*, LOS ANGELES EVENING EXPRESS (December 29, 1921), at 20.
102. Note, *supra* note 29, at 237.
103. Charles E. Clark, *The Courts and the People*, 57 LOCOMOTIVE ENGINEERS JOURNAL 626, 627 (August 1923). *See* Corwin, *supra* note 24, at 632 ("No decision of the term has attracted more animadversion than that in Truax v. Corrigan."). For favorable treatments of the case, see Everett P. Wheeler, *Injunctions in Labor Disputes and Decisions of Industrial Tribunals*, 8 AMERICAN BAR ASSOCIATION JOURNAL 506 (1922); Thomas E. Shelton, *The Labor "Picketing" Opinion*, 94 CENTRAL LAW JOURNAL 55 (1922); and Note, 8 VIRGINIA LAW REVIEW 374 (1922). Wheeler, who was the chair of the ABA Committee on Jurisprudence and Law Reform, declared that "The radical objection to acts like that of Arizona is that it is class legislation. ... This is the true American principle; equal rights, equal justice for all citizens. It was to secure this principle and to prevent it from state interference that the Fourteenth Amendment was adopted. ... The American idea is to give all men equal opportunity. ... The Arizona legislation discriminates against the successful man. It snatches the prize from the hopeful and energetic. By legalizing weapons of offence, on the part of labor union, it encourages lawless labor leaders." Wheeler, *supra*, at 507–8.
104. Powell, *The Supreme Court's Control over the Issue of Injunctions in Labor Disputes*, *supra* note 72, at 65. In words that could be applied to the Court's contemporary use of strict scrutiny, T.R. Powell wrote that "The door is now open for the Supreme Court to declare that any statute of a state that limits injunctive relief is unconstitutional unless it completely abolishes equity jurisdiction. ...

Arizona's particular discrimination would be removed if it forbade injunctions against picketing generally instead of only in labor disputes, but it still might be possible to get five Justices to find that a plaintiff is discriminated against if he loses the opportunity to get an injunction against a specified act instead of against all acts." *Id.* at 65–66. It would at least have been "tenable," Powell said, though "novel," for the Court to have held that the Arizona statute violated due process. "Rights without effective remedies are not very effective rights." *Id.* at 65.

105. "It is hard to follow the Court to its conclusion that this classification is clearly unreasonable. The decision is regrettable." Note, *supra* note 72, at 414. "The decision has been sharply criticized, and it would certainly seem that Mr. Chief Justice Taft's view on the point as to equal protection of the laws is open to question. To say that while a classification based on the relation of employer and employee is a reasonable one, a classification based on the relation of employer and ex-employee on strike is beyond the bounds of reason, would seem to involve a doctrinaire insistence on a purely legal conception which does not take into account the actual facts of the situation. As an original question it would seem very doubtful as to whether a classification of this sort was not a reasonable one." Sidney Post Simpson, *Constitutional Rights and the Industrial Struggle*, 30 WEST VIRGINIA LAW QUARTERLY 125, 137–38 (1924).

106. Note, *supra* note 29, at 239–40. Corwin noted that *Truax* preceded *Coronado* "by some months," and he speculated that the outcome in the latter "may represent an attempt at compromise between the majority and minority of the court" in *Truax*. "[I]f labor unions become generally suable for their torts, the contention, today incontrovertible in fact, that the injuries they do property are irreparable, will lose force, and thus the very basis will be removed for the issuance of injunctions in labor controversies." Corwin, *supra* note 24, at 635.

107. Note, *supra* note 29, at 240 n.16.

108. Five days after announcing the decision, Taft wrote his brother that "I haven't seen much comment on the Truax case, . . . but I presume that when the legal magazines and the weekly 'dreadfuls' that discuss social questions come out, there will be no dearth of comment. There is one thing about judicial opinions that there is no stopping place. You may get into a row over one case, but other cases press on and you must continue the work without regard to any particular period in progress." WHT to Horace D. Taft (December 24, 1921) (Taft papers).

109. Francis Bowes Sayre, *The Picketing Decisions*, 47 THE SURVEY 558, 560 (1922). " In spite of the fact that no injunction was apparently ever issued by a court in a labor dispute prior to 1868 in England or to 1888 in America, in spite of the fact that the injunction remedy is an extraordinary process issued within the discretion of a court of equity only under exceptional circumstances, in spite of the fact that its issue in labor cases has led, in the opinion of many, to serious abuses and has caused storms of protest in which many thoughtful lawyers have joined, yet the right of an employer to its issue is such a 'fundamental principle of right and justice' that a state has no power to forbid its issue to prevent peaceful picketing." *Id.* It "causes one to wonder just how far the Fourteenth Amendment goes." *Id.*

110. *The Same Mr. Taft*, 29 NEW REPUBLIC 191, 192 (1922).

111. *The Political Function of the Supreme Court*, 29 NEW REPUBLIC 236, 236 (1922).

112. *The Same Mr. Taft*, *supra* note 110, at 192.

Truax v. Corrigan

113. *Id.* at 193.
114. *The Political Function of the Supreme Court, supra* note 111, at 236-37. Frankfurter records that in a conversation with Brandeis "I spoke of ... necessity of putting an end to labor injunctions & difficulty of Truax v. Corrigan, toward accomplishing latter. L.D.B.: 'Well – Court may reverse itself – I put it to them, to Taft that he has not hesitated to do so, once or twice when it mattered less than in valuation cases.'" *Brandeis-Frankfurter Conversations,* at 325 (August 10, 1923).
115. *The Political Function of the Supreme Court, supra* note 111, at 237.
116. *The Same Mr. Taft, supra* note 110, at 191.
117. *Does Mr. Taft Want Direct Action?,* 114 THE NATION 32, 32 (1922). *Truax* "decides in effect that the sovereign people cannot constitutionally change the rules of law in the field of industrial relations unless the court sanctions the change." *Id.*
118. *Id.* In response to an inquiry from a friend, Taft said that he "had not seen the article in the New York Nation in respect to my opinions in the labor cases – I do not want to see it, because I know the editor, and would regard his approval of the opinion as evidence of its wrongful tendency. I am sorry to say that I entertain a contempt for Oswald Villard that it grieves me to have to express." WHT to Frederick L. Hoffman (January 11, 1922) (Taft papers).
119. *Does Mr. Taft Want Direct Action?, supra* note 117, at 32-33.
120. Gompers was appalled at the combination of *Truax* and *American Steel Foundries.* He wrote:

> In its anxiety to protect property the Supreme Court of the United States, of which William Howard Taft is Chief Justice, is moving with unusual speed toward the destruction of liberty. Within a few weeks the Supreme Court has struck twice at liberty, both times with extreme care, deliberation and thoroughness. In both these cases the right of workers to picket is attacked until now, as a lawful right, it has substantially ceased to exist. ...
>
> It is clear beyond any manner of doubt that Chief Justice Taft is irrevocably committed to the proposition that the injunction as used in industrial disputes is to be upheld and broadened upon every occasion, be the cost to freedom and to our democratic institutions what it may.
>
> It is clear that the Chief Justice is equally committed to the proposition that picketing is to be destroyed, carrying with it to destruction the right of workers to inform others concerning conditions of employment which may obtain in establishments wherein a dispute exists over working conditions or terms of employment.
>
> Chief Justice Taft has long been known to the people of the United States as the "father of injunctions." As a jurist, immersed in the atmosphere of legal technicalities and legal precedents he is bound to give prior consideration to the precedents of the past, particularly those created by his own decisions, in fixing the limitations of human liberties for the future. ...
>
> The accident of political choice, having placed upon the Supreme bench a man committed to the vigorous use of the injunction and all that it signifies, the people of the United States may expect from the tribunal over which this man presides nothing but a continued upholding and exaltation of the injunction.

Samuel Gompers, *The Supreme Court at It Again,* 29 AMERICAN FEDERATIONIST 44, 44, 46 (1922).
121. *See supra* Chapter 40, at 1312. At the 1922 Convention a special committee reported:

> In December, 1921, the Supreme Court, by its decision in the case of Truax vs. Corrigan set aside as unconstitutional a State law which limited the power of the courts to issue injunctions in labor disputes, thus frustrating the efforts of labor in all industrial states to secure relief from the arrogated authority of the courts. . . .
>
> This despotic exercise of a usurped power by nine men, or a bare majority of them, over the lives and liberties of millions of men, women and children, is intolerable.

Report of Special Committee, in REPORT OF PROCEEDINGS OF THE FORTY-SECOND ANNUAL CONVENTION OF THE AMERICAN FEDERATION OF LABOR 372 (Washington D.C.: Law Reporter Printing Co. 1922).

122. *See supra* Chapter 41, at 1384.
123. 257 U.S. at 340. Taft also stressed that the Clayton Act had not been interpreted to immunize the kind of peaceful but intimidating picketing that the Arizona Supreme Court had declared privileged from equitable relief. *Id.* at 340–41.
124. United States v. Vaello Madero, 142 S.Ct. 1539, 1541 (2022).
125. Weinberger v. Wiesenfeld, 420 U.S. 636, 638 n.2 (1975).
126. *See* Simpson, *supra* note 105, at 144: "The unconstitutionality of simply denying the remedy of injunction, as distinguished from complete legalization of the injury, is rested by the Supreme Court upon the provision of the Fourteenth Amendment as to the equal protection of the laws, and not upon the provision as to due process of law. Mr. Chief Justice Taft, in *Truax v. Corrigan*, has pointed out that: '. . . the equality clause of the Fourteenth Amendment does not apply to congressional but only to state action.' Therefore, there would seem to be no constitutional objection to the denial of the remedy of injunction in cases arising under the judicial power of the United States, even though the statute denying the remedy applies only in labor controversies."
127. *Limiting the Scope of Injunctions in Labor Disputes*, Hearings Before a Subcommittee of the Committee on the Judiciary on S. 1482, 70th CONG. 1st SESS. (1928), at 4.
128. *See* Osmond K. Fraenkel, *Recent Statutes Affecting Labor Injunctions and Yellow Dog Contracts*, 30 ILLINOIS LAW REVIEW 854, 873, 876 (1936).
129. *See, e.g., In re* Opinion of the Justices, 275 Mass. 580, 584 (1931); *In re* Opinion of the Justices, 166 A. 640, 645 (N.H. 1933). Other state decisions sought to distinguish *Truax*, see Starr v. Laundry and Dry Cleaning Workers' Local Union, 155 Or. 634, 637–41 (1936), and American Furniture Co. v. I.B. of T.C. and H. of A., 268 N.W. 250, 260–62 (Wisc. 1936), in particular by appealing to the legality of the peaceful picketing approved in *American Steel Foundries*, see Fenske Bros., Inc. v. Upholsterers' Int'l Union, 358 Ill. 239, 251–57 (1934). For a summary of the law as of 1937, see Note, *Constitutionality of State Statutes Limiting Injunctions in Labor Disputes*, 46 YALE LAW JOURNAL 1064 (1937).

In the end, the most telling obituary of *Truax* was written in the court of common pleas in Pennsylvania, which in 1938 applied a Pennsylvania statute forbidding the issuance of injunctions in labor controversies. In response to the argument of the employer citing *Truax* for the proposition that the statute was unconstitutional, the court explained:

> [W]e cannot overlook the fact that since the Truax case, not only Congress but the legislatures of more than a score of states, including our own and leading

industrial jurisdictions such as New York, Massachusetts, and Illinois, have passed similar legislation. All of this legislation would be invalid were the Truax case still to be considered the law. This legislative interpretation of the Constitution by the law-making bodies of more than half the number of States necessary to amend the Constitution should not be disregarded. In the face of this almost overwhelming affirmation of the reasonableness and desirability of such a statute, it would be presumptuous of us to declare it a violation of the fourteenth amendment on the ground that it is unreasonable.

Lipoff v. United Food Workers Indus. Union, Local No. 107, 33 Pa. D. & C. 599, 613 (Ct. C.P., Phila. Cnty. 1938).

130. *Brandeis-Frankfurter Conversations*, at 307 (July 1, 1922).
131. *Id.* at 318 (July 14, 1923).

CHAPTER 43

The Equal Protection Clause and Race

THROUGHOUT THE 1920S, the Equal Protection Clause was a text in search of a rationale. The Taft Court used equal protection doctrine to invalidate state laws more frequently than did its predecessors,[1] but it deployed the doctrine in ways that had very little to do with protecting disadvantaged groups, which is at the heart of modern understandings of the Equal Protection Clause. Interpreting the Clause to express the traditional racial instincts of the American people, the Taft Court did not seek to uproot deeply entrenched institutions of racial and ethnic segregation. The Court instead used equal protection doctrine, as it used due process doctrine, to advance social policies that it deemed important, like safeguarding the national market from local interference, protecting corporations and employers, and promoting economic development.

By 1921 the interpretation of the Equal Protection Clause offered by *Natural Carbonic Gas* had become pretty much black-letter law. So, for example, when a litigant used the Clause to challenge the constitutionality of a Connecticut statute providing that no guest in an automobile could recover from an owner or operator for injuries negligently caused by the operation of the vehicle, the Court unanimously ruled that the "Constitution does not forbid the creation of new rights, or the abolition of old ones recognized by the common law, to attain a permissible legislative object," and that to achieve its purposes a state may use any classification it chooses so long as it is not "without basis and arbitrary." "It is enough that the present statute strikes at the evil where it is felt and reaches the class of cases where it most frequently occurs."[2]

The obvious and striking inconsistency of this reasoning with the logic of *Truax* illustrates how the justices used equal protection doctrine to advance judicial values they deemed otherwise important. The Court was content to adopt the deferential posture of *Natural Carbonic Gas* in cases that did not touch on a pressing judicial agenda,[3] but it was also prepared to stiffen the severity of its review whenever it perceived important constitutional values to be at stake. *Truax* set a pattern in this regard. Brandeis was prompted to observe to Frankfurter in 1924

The Equal Protection Clause & Race

that equal protection doctrine "now looms up even more menacingly than due process."[4] Writing Stone in 1928, Frankfurter sardonically noted that the Court would use "the requirement of 'the equal protection of the laws'" to impose restrictions "upon the discretionary power of the States over local matters" whenever the restrictions of "the due process clause" were not available.[5]

Consider, for example, the Court's 1923 decision in *Kentucky Finance Corp. v. Paramount Auto Exchange Corp.*[6] The case involved a Kentucky corporation not doing business in Wisconsin that sued a Wisconsin corporation in Wisconsin for replevin of an automobile. At issue was a Wisconsin statute providing that examination by discovery of a foreign corporation which was a party in a case "may be had ... in any county of this state," whereas examination of a nonresident party that was not a corporation could be had in the state "only if he could be personally served therein with notice and subpoena, and then only in the county where such service was had." Nonresident corporations were thus subject "to a rule much more onerous than that applicable to nonresident individuals in like situations and also more onerous than that applicable to resident suitors, whether individuals or corporations." The Wisconsin Supreme Court "justified this difference in legislative treatment and also the order for an examination in this case on the ground that they amounted to no more than a reasonable exercise of the authority of the state over a nonresident corporation coming voluntarily into the state to seek a remedy in her courts against a resident defendant."[7]

Speaking through Van Devanter, the Court refused to accept this explanation. A foreign corporation, it said, "cannot be subjected, merely because it is such a corporation, to onerous requirements having no reasonable support in that fact and not laid on other suitors in like situations. Here the statute authorized the imposition, and there was imposed, on the plaintiff a highly burdensome requirement because of its corporate origin, – a requirement which under the statute could not be laid on an individual suitor in the same situation. The discrimination was essentially arbitrary."[8]

Brandeis, joined by Holmes,[9] dissented on the ground that only twenty-five years previously the Court in *Blake v. McClung*[10] had explicitly held that a foreign corporation not doing business in a state was not "within the jurisdiction" of the state within the meaning of the Equal Protection Clause, which prohibits a state from denying "to any person *within its jurisdiction* the equal protection of the laws."[11] "In my opinion," Brandeis wrote, "the equal protection clause does not prevent Wisconsin from moulding, in the case of foreign corporations, the details of its judicial procedure to accord with the requirements of justice."[12] It is plain that in *Kentucky Finance* the Court used the Equal Protection Clause to advance its larger agenda of protecting the national market from local discrimination.[13]

If one important theme in *Kentucky Finance* was discrimination against *out-of-state* corporations,[14] a second was official discrimination against *corporations*, whether in-state or out of state. The Taft Court was determined to use the Equal Protection Clause to prevent discrimination of the latter kind. In *Quaker City Cab Co. v. Pennsylvania*, for example, the Court considered a tax that applied to corporations (whether in-state or foreign) that commercially transported passengers, but that did not apply to natural persons or partnerships that commercially transported passengers. Holding that a classification must not be "arbitrary, but based on real and substantial difference having a reasonable relation to the subject of the particular legislation," Butler, speaking for six justices, held that the mere fact of incorporation was irrelevant to the purpose of the legislation.[15] "In no view can it be held to have more than an arbitrary basis. As construed and applied by the state court in this case, the section violates the equal protection clause of the Fourteenth Amendment."[16]

Stone's dissent perfectly expresses the interchangeability of equal protection and due process analysis during the 1920s. Citing *Flint v. Stone Tracey Co.*, in which the Court had upheld against Fifth Amendment challenge a congressional tax imposed "upon the exercise of the privilege of doing business in a corporate capacity,"[17] Stone argued "[t]hat businesses carried on in corporate form may be taxed, while those carried on by individuals or partnerships are left untaxed, was the rule broadly applied under the Fifth Amendment . . . and I can see no reason for not applying it here under the Fourteenth Amendment as well."[18]

Holmes also dissented, and as usual he went right to the heart of the matter in a single short paragraph: "If usually there is an important difference of degree between the business done by corporations and that done by individuals, I see no reason why the larger businesses may not be taxed and the small ones disregarded, and I think it would be immaterial if here and there exceptions were found to the general rule. Furthermore if the State desired to discourage this form of activity in corporate form and expressed its desire by a special tax I think that there is nothing in the Fourteenth Amendment to prevent it."[19]

The whole point of the Court's opinion in *Quaker City Cab*, however, was to use equal protection doctrine to protect corporations from discrimination. Taft had for a very long time sought to immunize corporations from precisely such differential treatment. In 1895, for example, he had argued to the annual meeting of the American Bar Association that "corporations are indispensable both to the further material progress of this country and to the maintenance of what we have enjoyed." Yet, Taft reasoned, "so strong has the hostility to corporations become, especially in certain of the southern and western States where the agricultural community is large, life is hard, and wealth is rare, that any plan which can be contrived to diminish the property of corporations or to cripple their efficiency seems to meet with favor." These "prejudices" often take the form "of discriminating taxation." In such circumstances, Taft declared, it was the "duty" of federal courts "to declare void the legislation involved and to enjoin State officers from seizing or injuring the property of corporations."[20]

Brandeis's view of corporations was diametrically opposed to that of Taft. In *Quaker City Cab* Brandeis published a long and scholarly dissent designed to demonstrate that states were justified in discriminating against corporations.[21] "There are still intelligent, informed, just-minded, and civilized persons who believe that the rapidly growing aggregation of capital through corporations constitutes an insidious menace to the liberty of the citizen," Brandeis said. There are still citizens who believe that increasing corporate power

> tends to increase the subjection of labor to capital; that, because of the guidance and control necessarily exercised by great corporations upon those engaged in business, individual initiative is being impaired and creative power will be

lessened; that the absorption of capital by corporations, and their perpetual life, may bring evils similar to those which attended mortmain; that the evils incident to the accelerating absorption of business by corporations outweigh the benefits thereby secured; and that the process of absorption should be retarded. The court may think such views unsound. But obviously the requirement that a classification must be reasonable does not imply that the policy embodied in the classification made by the Legislature of a state shall seem to this court a wise one.[22]

Brandeis's opposition to corporations grew out of his more encompassing antagonism to the growing scale of American economic life, with its attendant concentrations of economic power.[23] Brandeis believed that "it was a great mistake to hold that corporations were citizens entitled to sue in Federal Courts on grounds of citizenship."[24] Brandeis was destined, however, to lose his struggle to contain expanding corporate power. The Court willingly followed Taft's lead to hold that government was not entitled to impose greater burdens on corporations than on natural persons merely because of the fact of incorporation. The Court believed, as Stone would put it during the following term: "It would be difficult to select any single agency of more universal use or more generally recognized as a usual and appropriate means of carrying on commerce and trade than the business corporation."[25] The Taft Court used equal protection doctrine to protect business corporations to promote economic growth.

This is a strikingly different conception of the Equal Protection Clause than that which comes readily to mind in a post-*Carolene Products* and post-*Brown* era. We now imagine that the Equal Protection Clause is designed to protect discrete and insular minorities, subordinated groups or castes. But this way of thinking about equal protection barely registered with the Taft Court. Of all the justices on the Court, one might perhaps have thought that Brandeis would have been most alert to these possible uses of the Equal Protection Clause. In the context of labor decisions, Brandeis was certainly the justice who was most clearly cognizant of the need to acknowledge the existence of group entities like unions.[26] Brandeis was also exquisitely aware of the need to recognize group ethnic identities.

As a committed Zionist, Brandeis embraced the value of cultural pluralism. By 1915, Brandeis had come to believe that the "right of development on the part of the group is essential to the full enjoyment of rights by the individual. For the individual is dependent for his development (and his happiness) in large part upon the development of the group of which he forms a part. We can scarcely conceive of an individual German or Frenchman living and developing without some relation to the contemporary German or French life and culture." Brandeis regarded liberalism as inadequate because it recognized only "individual equality before the law" and failed "to recognize the equality of whole peoples or nationalities." We must "protect as individuals those constituting a minority," Brandeis declared, "but we fail to realize that protection cannot be complete unless group equality also is recognized."[27]

In a legendary Fourth of July Address on "True Americanism" at Faneuil Hall in 1915, Brandeis celebrated "the development of the individual for his own and the common good." But Brandeis also stressed that America "has always declared herself for equality of nationalities as well as for equality of individuals. It recognizes racial equality as an essential of full human liberty and true brotherhood, and that racial equality is the complement of democracy."[28]

"America," Brandeis said, "has believed that each race had something of peculiar value which it can contribute to the attainment of those high ideals for which it is striving. America has believed that we must not only give to the immigrant the best that we have, but must preserve for America the good that is in the immigrant and develop in him the best of which he is capable. America has believed that in differentiation, not in uniformity, lies the path of progress."[29] Brandeis's address "brought repeated demonstrations from the great crowd" of 1,000 or more, "many of whom craned their necks from the crowded doorway to get a glimpse" of the famous speaker.[30] It was praised as "less chauvinistic" than the usual Fourth of July address, "and one that can be less easily perverted into a partisan, or racial, or caste appeal. . . . Never, within the memory of the generation that has come up since the civil war ... have so many component parts of the population shared equally in celebrations of the day."[31]

What Brandeis called "racial" equality likely meant something closer to what today we might call equality of "ethnicity" or "nationality."[32] Brandeis celebrated cultural diversity and pluralism. But this did not prompt him to imagine law as an instrument for the removal of stigma or the eradication of caste, in the sense that either *Carolene Products* or *Brown* might now inform our contemporary sense of the purpose of the Equal Protection Clause. Brandeis may have championed labor's efforts to form groups necessary to underwrite equality in the workplace; he may have applauded the efforts of ethnic groups at cultural self-assertion; but it is hard to find evidence that he attributed special legal significance to the systematic discrimination inflicted on race understood as a negative status category.[33]

It is ironic that in 1925 Alain Locke published a groundbreaking anthology, *The New Negro*,[34] which famously celebrated Black life in the same logic of cultural pluralism that Brandeis had articulated in 1915. Locke delineated a "Negro Renaissance" of "folk-expression and self-determination"; he portrayed African Americans as one of the "emergent nationalities" that had burst forth everywhere on the globe in the wake of the war.[35] Locke saw the poetry, art, and music of African Americans as contributing to the cultural diversity that Brandeis prized.[36] But there is no sign that Brandeis himself appreciated issues of what we would now call "race" either in this light, or in the alternative light of a status degradation requiring constitutional correction.

What is true of Brandeis is trebly so of the Court as a whole. The Taft Court typically used the Equal Protection Clause to invalidate economic regulation or taxation, rather than racial discrimination.[37] This had been true of the Court's equal protection jurisprudence since the end of Reconstruction, and the Taft Court faithfully continued this tradition. As one commentator observed in 1934, "the Fourteenth Amendment has given quite a bit more protection to corporations than it has to the Negro race."[38]

The Equal Protection Clause & Race

Yet we must also acknowledge that in 1927 the Taft Court did decide *Nixon v. Herndon*, in which it used the Equal Protection Clause to strike down a 1923 Texas statute providing that "in no event shall a negro be eligible to participate in a Democratic party primary election held in the state of Texas."[39] *Nixon* was a striking and significant case. Primary elections had first been adopted by Texas in 1905 to sidestep the evils of corrupt party nominating conventions,[40] but they soon proved fertile ground for discriminating against African Americans.

As far back as 1879, Senator William Windom of Minnesota had observed that "[t]he black man does not excite antagonism because he is black, but because he is a *citizen*, and as such may control an election."[41] When the Texas primary system was first introduced, county Democratic Executive Committee chairs were authorized to establish voting qualifications, and "it was implicitly understood that blacks would be barred from voting."[42] Enforcement was uneven, however, and in some counties Democratic politicians actively competed for the support of Black voters. The loser of one such contest in San Antonio was so angry that in 1923 he sought and attained state legislation uniformly barring Black voters in Democratic primaries throughout the state.[43] In a one-party state like Texas, exclusion from the Democratic primary was "equivalent to disfranchisement,"[44] and the Texas statute quickly became one of the "most effective techniques employed to keep blacks from voting."[45]

Dr. Lawrence A. Nixon, a Black El Paso dentist who had until 1923 regularly voted in Democratic primaries, agreed to challenge the statute in a lawsuit brought by the National Association for the Advancement of Colored People ("NAACP").[46] Nixon sought $5,000 in damages for violations of "the Fourteenth and Fifteenth Amendments."[47] The district court dismissed Nixon's action without opinion. The case was argued at the Supreme Court on January 4, 1927. At conference, the justices voted unanimously to reverse.[48] Taft assigned the opinion to Holmes, likely because in 1903 Holmes had authored *Giles v. Harris*, which had refused to enjoin violations of the Fifteenth Amendment on the ground that "traditional limits of proceedings in equity have not embraced a remedy for political wrongs,"[49] and because in 1924 Holmes had authored *Love v. Griffith*,[50] which had refused to enjoin Texas's failure to register Blacks in Texas Democratic primaries on the ground that the case was moot.

Texas unabashedly defended its 1923 statute. "It is an 'ancient and accepted doctrine,' to use the words of the Democratic platform, ... that the Democratic party of the State is a white man's party." "To deny any group of men or women, or both, the right to form such associations as they please, and to lay down such qualifications for membership as they please, would certainly be to deny a fundamental right of American citizens. White people have just as much right to organize their own private political party as either whites or negroes have to vote at the general elections."[51] The chief defense of Texas lay in its claim that the Fifteenth Amendment did not apply to party primaries.[52] In a wobbly four-person opinion by McReynolds, the Court had held in 1921 that Congress had no power to regulate primaries under Article I, Section 4. The Court reasoned that primaries "are in no sense elections for an office, but merely methods by which party adherents

1435

agree upon candidates whom they intend to offer and support for ultimate choice by all qualified electors."[53]

An important question in *Nixon* was whether primaries were part of the official election apparatus of the state, or instead merely the self-constitution of private political associations.[54] There was also a second question in the case, which concerned the relationship between the Fourteenth and Fifteenth Amendments. Did the Equal Protection Clause of the Fourteenth Amendment cover voting rights? If so, what independent role was left for the Fifteenth Amendment?[55] There had been inklings in prior Supreme Court opinions that the Fourteenth Amendment protected only "civil rights, as distinguished from those which are political."[56]

In a terse, "very plain"[57] opinion, Holmes deftly sidestepped both questions. He first dismissed the argument that the case involved a nonjusticiable political question. "The objection that the subject-matter of the suit is political is little more than a play upon words. Of course the petition concerns political action but it alleges and seeks to recover for private damage. That private damage may be caused by such political action and may be recovered for in suit at law hardly has been doubted for over two hundred years. ... If the defendants' conduct was a wrong to the plaintiff the same reasons that allow a recovery for denying the plaintiff a vote at a final election allow it for denying a vote at the primary election that may determine the final result."[58]

Having thus prepared the ground for a viable constitutional claim, Holmes simply ignored the issue of the Fifteenth Amendment,[59] which the parties had all along considered to be the heart of the case.[60] He wrote:

> We find it unnecessary to consider the Fifteenth Amendment, because it seems to us hard to imagine a more direct and obvious infringement of the Fourteenth. That Amendment, while it applies to all, was passed, as we know, with a special intent to protect the blacks from discrimination against them. ... The statute of Texas in the teeth of the prohibitions referred to assumes to forbid negroes to take part in a primary election the importance of which we have indicated, discriminating against them by the distinction of color alone. States may do a good deal of classifying that it is difficult to believe rational, but there are limits, and it is too clear for extended argument that color cannot be made the basis of a statutory classification affecting the right set up in this case.[61]

Holmes's reasoning is difficult to follow. It does not clearly delineate the relationship between the equal protection rights protected by the Fourteenth Amendment and the political rights protected by the Fifteenth Amendment.[62] But it does seem to suggest that the former prohibits what we today would call facial racial classifications, which Holmes intimates are hard to accept as "rational."

Brandeis reported that Holmes delivered his opinion in *Nixon* "with much joy."[63] After finishing the oral recitation of his opinion, Holmes is said to have remarked, "I know that our good brethren, the negroes of Texas, will now rejoice that they possess at the primary the rights which heretofore they have enjoyed at the general election."[64] The comment was understood by some, including Thurgood Marshall, as a sign of Holmes's belief that he had "laid the white primary to rest."[65]

The Equal Protection Clause & Race

But it was taken by others as an ironic but "realistic appreciation of the futility of judicial interference" with Texas's determination to exclude Black voters.[66] If the latter interpretation is correct, Holmes was prophetic. The Texas legislature, in session at the time *Nixon* was decided, was "undaunted." Within four months it simply "repealed the offending statute and granted the executive committee of the Democratic party the power to prescribe membership qualifications and voting requirements for its primaries."[67]

In his early years, Holmes had been a committed abolitionist,[68] and he apparently retained strong opinions about the "special intent" of the Fourteenth Amendment. His blunt assertion that it was meant "to protect the blacks from discrimination against them," together with his sweeping observation that classifications based upon "color alone" are "difficult to believe rational," might induce an unwary reader to imagine that the Taft Court read the Equal Protection Clause in a manner similar to the modern Court. One might be tempted to conclude that the Taft Court regarded racial classifications as intrinsically arbitrary. But this would miss Holmes's careful qualification that race "cannot be made the basis of a statutory classification *affecting the right set up in this case*."[69] In other contexts, the Taft Court, including Holmes,[70] was quite prepared to affirm the propriety of racial classifications.[71]

Only eight months after *Nixon*, for example, the Taft Court decided *Gong Lum v. Rice*,[72] in which it unanimously upheld segregated education in Mississippi. Martha Lum, the daughter of a well-to-do Chinese merchant, attempted to attend the white school in Rosedale, where she lived, but the state superintendent of education ruled that she could not attend "on the ground that she was of Chinese descent and therefore not a member of the white or Caucasian race."[73] Her mother, an "educated lady from Hong Kong," "got very angry"[74] and decided to sue. At the time, the Mississippi Constitution of 1890 provided that "[s]eparate schools shall be maintained for children of the white and colored races." It was alleged that Martha was "not a member of the colored race, nor is she of mixed blood, but that she is of pure Chinese origin and descent, and a native born citizen of the United States of the State of Mississippi."[75] The trial court accepted this argument and ordered her admitted to the white school.

The Mississippi Supreme Court reversed. It held that the constitutional provision was designed "to provide schools for the white or Caucasian race, to which schools no other race could be admitted, carrying out the broad dominant purpose of preserving the purity and integrity of the white race."[76] The Lums filed a writ of error in the Supreme Court, alleging that the classification of Martha as "colored" was a violation of the Equal Protection Clause. The case was argued on October 12, 1927. At conference, the justices voted unanimously to affirm the Mississippi Supreme Court.[77]

Taft wrote the Court's opinion. He said that the case "reduces itself to the question whether a state can be said to afford to a child of Chinese ancestry born in this country, and a citizen of the United States, equal protection of the laws by giving her the opportunity for a common school education in a school which receives only colored children of the brown, yellow or black races."[78] Taft explicitly refused to decide whether there was a nonwhite school located in an equally convenient fashion for Martha as was the white school that she wanted to attend. "Had the petition alleged specifically that there was no colored school in Martha Lum's neighborhood to which she could conveniently go," Taft said, "a different question would have been presented, and this, without regard to the State Supreme Court's construction of the State Constitution as limiting the white schools provided for the education of children of the white or Caucasian race. But we do not find the petition to present such a situation."[79]

Taft's avoidance of the question of equality is striking, for he was well aware that "[s]ince Emancipation and the horror of Reconstruction the Negroes have not been accorded the same opportunities in the Southern States for education and development as the whites. . . . The statistics show a woeful lack of a sense of justice to the Negro in the distribution of educational funds to the two races."[80] By stipulating away the question of equality, Taft narrowed the case to the precise issue of separation itself. *Gong Lum* is thus about the question of segregation, which Taft, citing precedents like *Plessy v. Ferguson*,[81] *Cumming v. Richmond County Board of Education*,[82] and *Roberts v. Boston*,[83] held "has been many times decided to be within the constitutional power of the state legislature to settle without intervention of the federal courts under the Federal Constitution."[84] If racial separation was constitutional, then so was the decision of Mississippi to classify a Chinese student as "colored."[85]

If Holmes had implied in *Nixon* that classifications based solely upon race were arbitrary, *Gong Lum* unanimously sustained such classifications. The two cases seem to inhabit distinct and incompatible constitutional universes. As historian G. Edward White notes, *Gong Lum* "treated classifications based on race as presumptively reasonable rather than presumptively suspect," and this could only have been on the ground "that race and skin color were proxies for a host of salient differences among humans."[86] But what might these differences be, especially in light of a case like *Nixon*?

Nixon and *Gong Lum* can be reconciled only by carefully examining the intensely ambivalent attitudes toward race held by Northern Republican elites during the 1920s. A perfect expression of this ambivalence may be found in President Harding's remarkable address celebrating the semicentennial of the founding of Birmingham, Alabama. Delivered on October 26, 1921, at the very outset of the Taft Court, Harding used the occasion to confront the question of race in the United States. He began with a bold claim. "If the Civil War marked the beginnings of industrialism in a South which had previously been almost entirely agricultural, the World War brought us to full recognition that the race problem is national rather than merely sectional."[87]

Harding stressed that what we now call the Great Migration,[88] which began during the European war, "has brought the question of race closer to North and West, and I believe it has served to modify somewhat the views of those sections on this question. It has made the South realize its industrial dependence on the labor of the black man and made the North realize the difficulties of the community in which two greatly differing races are brought to live side by side."[89] Harding likely had in mind the terrible nationwide race-riots of 1919, only two years before.

The Equal Protection Clause & Race

Harding then offered a stunning vision "of the true way out" of the nation's racial difficulties:

> Politically and economically there need be no occasion for great and permanent differentiation, for limitations of the individual's opportunity, provided that on both sides there shall be recognition of the absolute divergence in things social and racial. When I suggest the possibility of economic equality between the races, I mean it in precisely the same way and to the same extent that I would mean it if I spoke of equality of economic opportunity as between members of the same race. In each case I would mean equality proportioned to the honest capacities and deserts of the individual.
>
> Men of both races may well stand uncompromisingly against every suggestion of social equality. Indeed, it would be helpful to have that word "equality" eliminated from this consideration; to have it accepted on both sides that this is not a question of social equality, but a question of recognizing a fundamental, eternal, and inescapable difference.[90]

This is a startling, schizophrenic passage, which perfectly captures the inconsistent attitudes toward race typical of Northern Republican elites in the 1920s. The passage struggles to reconcile rigorous racial separation with a Jacksonian commitment to a classless society of individuals.

On the one hand, Harding expresses the same hostility to class-based perspectives that we have seen in Taft and Sutherland. He proclaims that "Coming as Americans do from many origins of race, tradition, language, color, institutions, heredity; engaged as we are in the huge effort to work an honorable national destiny from so many different elements, the one thing we must sedulously avoid is the development of group and class organizations in this country. There has been time when we heard too much about the labor vote, the business vote, the Irish vote, the Scandinavian vote, the Italian vote, and so on."[91] Instead, Harding asserts, we must celebrate "our oneness as Americans," which "has risen superior to every appeal to mere class and group. And so I would wish it might be in this matter of our national problem of races."[92] Harding even warns the South against "the menace which lies in forcing upon the black race an attitude of political solidarity. The greater hope, the dissipation of hatred, the discouragement of dangerous passions lie in persuading the black people to forget old prejudices and to have them believe that ... they would be treated just as other people are treated, guaranteed all the rights that people of other colors enjoy, and made, in short, to regard themselves as citizens of a country and not of a particular race."[93]

Yet, on the other hand, Harding also forcefully reaffirms and even celebrates racial distinction. He stands "uncompromisingly against every suggestion of social equality."[94] He wants "to have that word 'equality' eliminated" from consideration. In the context of race, Harding is prepared to acknowledge "fundamental, eternal, and inescapable difference." The question posed by Harding's remarkable speech is how this emphasis on eternal difference can be rendered compatible with the ideal of a classless, raceless society of individuals who compete on terms of perfect equality.

Harding's strategy is to reconcile these two inconsistent perspectives by allocating them to distinct spheres of national life. When Harding speaks about politics or the market, he insists that we focus on the "capacities and deserts of the individual." Harding affirms that, "politically and economically" speaking, Americans ought to to have no "class or group," only our "oneness as Americans," which is "superior to every consideration of groups or class, of race or color or section or prejudice." With regard to the duties of citizenship, or to the prerogatives of the market, "there need be no occasion for great and permanent differentiation, for limitations of the individual's opportunity"; "reward shall at last be distributed in proportion to individual deserts, regardless of race or color."[95]

It is thus no accident that a decision like *Nixon* occurs in the context of voting, in which Harding suggests that racial classifications should have no place.[96] Similarly, the Court's 1918 decision in *Buchanan v. Warley*,[97] which struck down an ordinance using racial classifications to restrict contracts for the purchase and sale of real property, involved market transactions, which Harding suggests ought also to be constructed according to the principles of a classless individualism. The week after *Nixon* was decided, the Taft Court explicitly reaffirmed *Buchanan* in *Harmon v. Tyler*,[98] which summarily invalidated a New Orleans zoning ordinance restricting the purchase and sale of houses based upon explicit racial classifications. In both *Buchanan* and *Harmon*, the Court annulled race-based government restrictions that prevented market actors from making free and individual economic decisions.[99]

We must understand, of course, that the putative individualism in political and economic matters, extolled by Harding and protected by the Taft Court in decisions like *Nixon* and *Harmon*, was in fact largely illusory. By 1921, "the Southern states by residential, literacy, and tax requirements had reduced the numbers of Negro voters to negligible proportions."[100] In his inaugural address as president in 1909, Taft had himself frankly acknowledged that "the fifteenth amendment has not been generally observed."[101] Just before becoming chief justice, Taft affirmed once again that "the Negro citizen of the United States is entitled, under the Constitution, to vote wherever he is a resident, but circumstances have made this impossible at present in the States of the South."[102] States also easily circumvented the economic freedoms formally granted by cases like *Harmon*. The schemes of residential zoning endorsed by *Euclid* were well understood to create highly effective race-neutral tools for establishing and maintaining residential segregation. Segregation could also be effectively maintained by private racially restrictive covenants commonly included in land deeds.[103]

Nevertheless, Harding's forceful (if ideological) affirmation of individualism in the political and economic spheres makes all the more puzzling his simultaneous and unequivocal declaration that our "oneness as Americans" ought to have no application *whatever* in the social sphere. Harding insists that "Men of both races may well stand uncompromisingly against every suggestion of social equality." Harding proclaims that a race-blind individualism has no place within the social sphere, where there is only "fundamental, eternal, and inescapable difference." If politics and the market are for Harding inhabited by

The Equal Protection Clause & Race

individuals who equally partake in the "oneness of Americans," the social sphere is instead inhabited by persons who are irreducibly and irrevocably assigned to distinct racial groups.

So that he would not be misunderstood, Harding explicitly adduced the need for racial separation in terms of "Mr. Lothrop Stoddard's book on *The Rising Tide of Color*, or, say, the thoughtful review of some recent literature of this question which F.D. Lugard presented in a recent Edinburg [sic] Review."[104] Stoddard and Lugard explained white (Nordic) supremacy in terms of the eugenics popularized in the writings of Madison Grant. The premise of this work was that "the basic factor in human affairs is not politics, but race."[105] Race was conceptualized as irreducible and unalterable. Races could not commingle or amalgamate; a mulatto was a degenerate mongrel, "a walking chaos, so consumed by his jarring heredities that he is quite worthless."[106] "Crossings with the negro are uniformly fatal," Stoddard asserted. "Whites, Amerindians, or Asiatics – all are alike vanquished by the invincible prepotency of the more primitive, generalized, and lower negro blood."[107] In stark contrast to Brandeis, the eugenicists invoked by Harding believed that culture was a mere manifestation of racial biology.[108]

The eugenic literature referenced by Harding in his effort to articulate a new and comprehensive settlement of the race question in America emphasized "the supreme importance of heredity and the supreme value of superior stocks," as well as the necessity of manifesting "a true *race*-consciousness (as opposed to national or cultural consciousness)."[109] This literature was rampant in America throughout the 1920s. It was influential in the enactment of the epoch-making Immigration Act of 1924.[110] As Stoddard explained, "Immigration restriction is a species of segregation on a large scale, by which inferior stocks can be prevented from both diluting and supplanting good stocks. . . . [T]he immigrant tide must at all costs be stopped and America given a chance to stabilize her ethnic being."[111]

It is plain, however, that Harding was not a eugenicist of the Grant/Stoddard stripe. The latter believed not only in the primacy of racial biology, but also in a steep hierarchy of races that made political equality unimaginable. As Grant put it bluntly in his introduction to Stoddard's book, "Democratic ideals among a homogeneous population of Nordic blood, as in England or America, is one thing, but it is quite another for the white man to share his blood with, or intrust his ideals to, brown, yellow, black, or red men. This is suicide pure and simple."[112] Stoddard explicitly asserted that we should "unlearn" the principle "that all men were equal," which was a "dangerous" fallacy: "We now know that men are not, and never will be, equal. We know that environment and education can develop only what heredity brings."[113] Southern Democrats, who believed in this kind of white supremacy, blasted Harding's Birmingham speech on exactly the ground that it implied a political equality that was and ought to be unthinkable.[114]

In his speech to Birmingham, therefore, Harding had worked himself into a difficult conceptual corner. On the one hand, he asserted traditional Republican ideals of political and economic equality, which meant that he could not endorse outright white supremacy. Yet, on the other hand, he needed to explain why there were "fundamental, eternal, and inescapable" differences that required repudiating ideals of social equality. How Northern Republicans negotiated this conceptual puzzle is at the heart of the jurisprudence of race in the Taft Court era.

The repudiation of social equality by Northern Republicans meant that they were committed to imagining the races as separate and distinct. Yet constitutional guaranties of political and economic equality required Northern Republicans also to deny the existence of racial hierarchies. The upshot was a formula – "separate but equal" – that modern readers have come to associate with the mealy rationalizations of a tainted decision like *Plessy v. Ferguson*.[115] In fact, however, this formula lay at the foundation of the entire Northern Republican strategy toward race. The fiction of "separate but equal" allowed Northern Republicans to appeal to Southern whites by emphasizing racial distinctions, yet to maintain a kind of tepid fidelity to the ideals of equality enshrined in the Reconstruction Amendments championed by Republicans after the Civil War.

At the turn of the twentieth century the most eloquent exponent of this fiction was Booker T. Washington, who famously said in his 1895 address to the Atlanta Exposition: "In all things that are purely social we can be as separate as the fingers, yet one as the hand in all things essential to mutual progress."[116] Washington did not publicly aspire to social equality; he did not publicly seek integration. Instead he worked hard to make Blacks economically independent on the assumption that actual political equality would follow from market autonomy. At least in his public announcements, Washington asserted that African Americans could exist as socially separate but also as economically and politically equal.[117] It is no accident that Washington was a favorite among elite Republicans at the outset of the twentieth century.[118] Harding's speech in Birmingham was deeply informed by Washington's vision.

Taft was an avid admirer of Washington.[119] As president, Taft remarked that "No one can read the lectures that Booker Washington has delivered to his own people without realizing that he is one of the greatest men of this century."[120] Taft, whom Du Bois once dismissed as "a Northern white man with Southern principles,"[121] was utterly committed to Washington's larger project of racial conciliation through economic independence instead of social equality. That project, however, was bitterly controversial within the Black community. Du Bois early on described it as requiring "that black people give up, at least for the present, three things, – First, political power, Second, insistence on civil rights, Third, high education of Negro youth, – and concentrate all their energies on industrial education, the accumulation of wealth, and the conciliation of the South."[122]

Taft explicitly and candidly articulated Washington's program in his inaugural address as president. Taft argued that "the colored men must base their hope on the results of their own industry, self-restraint, thrift, and business success, as well as upon the aid and comfort and sympathy which they may receive from their white neighbors of the South."[123] Taft adopted this strategy of conciliation because he believed that "[r]acial prejudice is a fact which cannot be got out of the way by merely pointing out its injustice. It must be worn away by the logic of events, by education, by stimulation of the moral sense and by the operation of economic causes and enlightened selfishness. Frontal attacks on it by argument rarely, if ever, succeed."[124]

Taft was personally committed to this strategy of conciliation. Two months after he became president, he joined the Board of Trustees of Hampton Institute.[125] Hampton was a Virginia industrial school for newly freed slaves that had been founded in 1868 by General Samuel Chapman Armstrong, who was at the time associated both with the Freedman's Bureau and with the American Missionary Association.[126] As Taft put it, "Armstrong taught the dignity of labor by teaching how much it could accomplish in material gain, in discipline of character, and in happiness. He taught the comfort and inspiration of real religion, and he united them all – practical learning, manual skill, the training and discipline of labor, and religious inspiration to make Hampton men and women the leaders of their race and missionaries of the gospel of practical and uplifting Christianity."[127]

The "most distinguished graduate of Hampton,"[128] who took its educational philosophy to Tuskegee, was Booker T. Washington. Tuskegee was the "daughter" of Hampton,[129] but Hampton was administered by whites, whereas Tuskegee was run by Blacks.[130] Both were subsidized by white philanthropy. In 1914, Taft became the president of the Hampton Institute Board of Trustees,[131] a position that he maintained throughout the remainder of his life. While he was chief justice, Taft spearheaded an ambitious and successful $7,000,000 endowment campaign for Hampton.[132]

The vocational orientation of Hampton was vigorously opposed by Black leaders like Du Bois, who objected that the school diverted resources away from true institutions of higher learning, and that a focus on vocational education "deliberately makes it impossible for [Hampton's] most promising and brilliant students to receive college training or higher technical and professional training." "We do not feel," Du Bois charged, that at present "Hampton is our school – on the contrary, we feel that she belongs to the white South and to the reactionary North, and we fear that she is a center of that underground and silent intrigue which is determined to perpetuate the American Negro as a docile peasant and peon, without political rights or social standing, working, for little wage."[133]

Taft was not one to take such criticism lying down. He explicitly defended the quietism of Hampton against the more militant stance of Du Bois. Taft wrote that there were "two classes" of Black leaders. "The first class resents so deeply the unfairness which racial prejudice leads to that they seek to end it by direct protest and frontal attacks upon it and its consequences." But the second class, which is "far wiser than the first," understands "that the way to ameliorate conditions is not by direct frontal attacks of resentment or revenge, but by the education of their people and a stimulation of them to greater industry and economic success, so that it shall be the enlightened selfish policy of the controllers of public opinion in the South to welcome the industrial development of the race for the benefit of the whole South, white and black."[134]

Taft acknowledged that the "educated, wealthier classes of the South ... are supersensitive over fear of social equality," but he believed that they nevertheless "recognize how valuable properly trained Negro labor is to the South, and they are anxious in every way to improve the condition of the race which makes up so large a part of their population."[135] In essence this meant that Taft was inclined endlessly to subordinate Black rights to Southern sensibilities in the hope that "the controllers of public opinion in the South" might become more tolerant. While they waited, Blacks were thrown into a kind of constitutional limbo, outside the normal legal order. Taft's connections to Hampton while he was chief justice made perfectly plain to him the terrible consequences of this indeterminate status.

In the 1920s, Virginia acolytes of eugenicists like Grant and Stoddard began a concerted campaign to defend the purity of the white race.[136] John Powell, a famous Virginia pianist, published a prominent article in the *Richmond Times Dispatch* arguing that "race legislation in the Southern States" was "necessary and beneficial ... in maintaining white ascendency and Anglo-Saxon civilization," and that the latter was under threat due to "the most serious and fundamental peril ... of racial amalgamation." The solution was to prevent intermarriage between whites and persons who had any "trace whatsoever of any blood other than Caucasian."[137] Powell created "Anglo-Saxon Clubs" to agitate for the enactment of Virginia's 1924 Racial Integrity Act, whose purpose was explicitly "to preserve the integrity of the white race."[138]

Hampton, which depended on the support of local Virginia white elites, was soon caught up in this whirlwind of white racial self-assertion. Matters came to a head in 1925, only two years before the Court considered *Gong Lum*. To win the goodwill of surrounding residents, Hampton had long sponsored regular public concerts and recitals at Ogden Hall, a commodious 2,000 seat auditorium built in 1919 under the leadership of Taft's fundraising.[139] Although Hampton followed an intricate "system of interracial etiquette,"[140] it did not impose segregated seating at public concerts. On February 21, 1925, the dance troop headed by Ruth St. Denis and Ted Shawn performed at Ogden Hall. The hall was packed because, "as one trustee later explained, 'the dancers were practically naked and therefore everybody went.'"[141]

The wife of the influential progressive Virginia journalist Walter Scott Copeland, editor of the Newport News *Daily Press* and four-time president of the Virginia Press Association, arrived late and was given seating next to Black members of the audience.[142] She was outraged, and Copeland promptly blasted Hampton in an editorial.[143] Entitled the "Integrity of the Anglo-Saxon Race," the editorial announced the formation of a local Anglo-Saxon Club, and it warned of "powerful influences" that were working "to wipe out the color line and place the two races upon terms of absolute equality. The ultimate aim of that movement is amalgamation."[144]

"Here in this old Virginia community," Copeland wrote, "there is an institution which teaches and practices social equality between the white and negro races." Hampton did not even make a "pretense of separating the races" in Ogden Hall; "to the contrary, the whites are informed that if they attend the entertainments they must come on the same terms as the negroes, and no distinctions made." Copeland wanted "to arouse the Anglo-Saxon to the danger which threatens. ... Amalgamation would mean the destruction of the Anglo-Saxon race in America and the substitution of a race of mulattoes. Rather than that we would prefer that every white child in the United States were sterilized and the Anglo-Saxon race left to perish in its purity."[145]

James E. Gregg, the principal of Hampton, immediately wrote Copeland to say that "for the past fifty years – there has never been encouragement of the social mingling of the races under circumstances which would lead to embarrassment on either side." Hampton, said Gregg, "has simply tried to be courteous and fair on the one hand to its white friends, both of the North and of the South, and on the other hand to its negro constituency."[146] But Copeland was in no mood to be placated. He propounded a long set of questions to Gregg, including whether or not "the officers and teachers of the institution, white and colored, meet upon terms of social equality?" Whether they did "not on occasion sit together at the same table and have a sociable meal together without racial distinction"?[147]

"Of course Dr. Gregg opposes amalgamation of the races," Copeland said. "That goes without saying, but social equality would lead to amalgamation ultimately, and that is the stern question which the white race must face. Place the two races upon terms of perfect equality; educate them both in the same manner; obliterate the color line in the social circle and make it the fashion for whites and negroes to meet in society without racial distinction or discrimination, and in spite of all that Dr. Gregg and men like him might do to prevent it, there would be 'association of a romantic nature,' and mixed marriages more and more." Hampton "has no moral right to teach and practice anything which is contrary to the Virginia spirit, and our sense of propriety, nor to ignore in any degree our time-honored customs." Were the officers of Hampton to suggest that white members of the audience who demanded segregated seating simply "stay away" from Ogden Hall, that "would be ... equivalent to saying that the officers did not care for the respect and good will of the white people of this community."[148]

The controversy put Hampton in a most uncomfortable position, which was made worse when Du Bois editorialized in *The Crisis* that Gregg should have replied to Copeland, "Yes, we do practice social equality at Hampton. We always have practiced it and we always shall. How else can teacher and taught meet but as equals. ... The results of the social equality practiced at Hampton have been fine friendships, real knowledge of human souls, high living and high thinking."[149]

Copeland was not amused.[150] He invited Gregg to publish corrections if Du Bois had "misrepresented the institution in any particular and if his interpretation be false."[151] The *Richmond Times Dispatch* also piled on, referencing Du Bois and asserting that "it is a serious charge that has been brought against the Hampton institute. It is openly said that here ... in a State where the preservation of the Anglo-Saxon race in all its purity is the fundamental principle of racial control, [it] is not only teaching the equality of the races but is putting its precepts of equality into actual practice." The controversy landed squarely in the midst of the $7,000,000 endowment campaign spearheaded by Taft, and the *Times Dispatch* implored prominent Southern members of the campaign Advisory Committee to withdraw until Hampton had answered "fully and frankly the charges that have been lodged against it."[152]

The Taft Court

Taft began to receive irate letters from members of the Advisory Committee, including one from Richard Manning, the former governor of South Carolina, demanding that Hampton respond to Copeland's questions.[153] Taft wrote Gregg:

> From what I know, I should think that the situation at Hampton was as free from the danger of promoting so-called miscegenation as any school of the kind could possibly be. I realize the delicacy with which such a statement must be made so as not to injure the just sensibilities of your students and their friends. I observe one question in which [the correspondent] asks whether the social equality between the two races is taught. I don't suppose that you have any instruction on this subject. The only equality that is taught is the political equality of the races and the equality before the law, in accord with the provisions of the 14th and 15th Amendments.[154]

It is significant that Taft's letter explicitly reiterates the separate spheres approach propounded by Harding in Birmingham. Taft insisted that the political equality guaranteed by the Fifteenth Amendment, and the civic equality guaranteed by the Fourteenth Amendment, should persist, even in the absence of social equality. He wanted Hampton to teach that its students could experience a "oneness as Americans" in politics and before the law, even as they were ripped out of the social fabric of American life. It was important to Taft that even though Blacks were set apart as socially separate, they could nevertheless be deemed politically and economically equal.[155] The humiliation of Hampton ought to have taught Taft that this aspiration was illusory.

In November 1925, the North Carolina Glee Club played at Ogden Hall to an unsegregated audience, and an infuriated Copeland charged that "Ogden Hall is a law unto itself and mixes the races indiscriminately."[156] This time John Powell and the Anglo-Saxon Clubs organized a mass meeting to protest Hampton's teaching "of social equality."[157] The crowd demanded that "their local delegate, George Alvin Massenburg, introduce a bill at the next General Assembly to require segregated seating at all public gatherings."[158] The proposed Massenburg Bill placed Hampton in the awkward position of having to choose between respecting its students and maintaining the friendship of the "educated, wealthier classes of the South."[159]

In the *Daily Press*, Copeland offered to cease his agitation for legislation were Hampton to give "assurances" that it would "yield to the sentiment of this community and discontinue those practices in the institution which have offended the whites and aroused their resentment."[160] But segregating seating in Ogden Hall would also send a degrading message to Hampton's Black students and supporters.[161] In May, for example, the Hampton choir had refused to perform at a Washington D.C. concert for the International Council of Women when the choir learned that seating in the hall was segregated.[162] The students said that they would "not be humiliated in the eyes of the foreign women who had come to believe that America was the land of the free and the home of the brave."[163] The Hampton professor accompanying the group, the composer Nathaniel Dett, had tried to call Taft for advice, but reporters could learn only that "the Chief Justice said someone

The Equal Protection Clause & Race

had called him in the matter, but as he did not know the circumstances, he would have to be excused from commenting on it in any way."[164]

Despite Taft's efforts to avoid public comment, the proposed Massenburg Bill brought the turbulence of racial segregation directly into Taft's own home. The Hampton Trustees met to discuss Hampton's dilemma at Taft's house on March 3, 1926. Present at the meeting was Jackson T. Davis, a noted Virginian educator who had helped establish the Jeanes Foundation. Davis "spoke of the 'Jim Crow' laws as the thing which the Negroes most resent; and expressed his belief that if Hampton were to attempt such segregation it might as well go out of business. Discussion of the race question is increasing: is being stimulated by the study of eugenics, race amalgamation, and other social questions in the college." The minutes of the meeting record that "The Chief Justice expressed his opinion that in the circumstances an official protest would be unwise, though such action might be desired by our colored constituency."[165] The Trustees, following Taft's advice, decided on a conciliatory stance; they opted not to lobby against passage of the bill.

The Massenburg Bill passed overwhelmingly in the Virginia Legislature, by votes of 63–3 in the House, and 30–5 in the Senate.[166] Even in the (relatively) genteel State of Virginia, no white politician could allow himself to be outflanked when it came to the "fundamental" principles of "racial control" necessary to ensure "the preservation of the Anglo-Saxon race in all its purity."[167] The only hope of stopping the Massenburg Bill was an executive veto.

Taft once again advised inaction. In matters of race, his inclination was consistently to defer to Southern white sensibilities. "I am inclined to think that the wisest thing for us to do is to say nothing. I agree that our constituents will wonder why, but I think it is better for us now not to assume that this bill was passed just to attack Hampton. The Governor is certain to sign the bill, and what we must do is to adjust ourselves to the law. It is a painful situation, but I don't think it helps to accentuate it by publicity."[168] The noted educator Mrs. Mary Cooke Branch Munford, whom Taft quite liked, nevertheless lobbied Taft to intercede with newly elected Virginia Governor Harry F. Byrd, and Taft agreed to a compromise. He would send a letter to Munford giving his reasons why, if he were the governor of Virginia, he would veto the bill. Munford would then be free to show Byrd the letter.[169]

Taft's argument in his letter exemplifies his larger strategy of appealing to the self-interest of Southern white elites. Taft noted that Hampton had

> never sought to impress upon Hampton students the desirability of promoting so-called social equality between the races. On the contrary, their attitude has been that that is not important, but that their object should be to maintain themselves and secure their rights of life, liberty and property and their prosperity and comfort by developing themselves through hard work, self-restraint, self-sacrifice and saving, and to demonstrate their usefulness to the community by their good citizenship, their character and their economic and civic usefulness. This attitude has not met with the approval of some of the leaders of the negro race whose course has tended to cultivate and render acute resentments against the white race, because of the feeling that the white race is not willing to encourage

so-called social equality between the two. The Hampton spirit, therefore, is one which accords with the spirit of high-minded Virginians in respect of the progress to be developed in the colored race.[170]

The Massenburg Bill, said Taft, was the result of "agitation by extremists who stress the impending possibility and danger of intermixture of the races, without any real basis for their fears." Hampton had been "a great co-educational school" for sixty years, and "during that time not a single scandal has disturbed the even tenor of its life, and not an instance can be cited ... among the students, or among its graduates, in which there has been any marriage or known illicit relation between members of the two races."[171]

Byrd, who had no liking for the bill, nevertheless ignored Taft's letter and allowed the bill to become law without his signature.[172] Taft was left with a bitter taste in his mouth. He wrote his daughter that he did not like to get involved because "the issue is one that may come before me on the Supreme Bench. ... One of the reasons why I dislike to be connected with any institution, other than the Supreme Court, is that in one way or another, if I am so connected, my colleagues always seek to use the influence of my position to affect measures in which the institution is interested. It is that which makes me very anxious to break off association with everything."[173]

Taft was right to be concerned, for the looming question on the agenda of the Hampton Board was whether to test the constitutionality of the Virginia Public Assemblage Act of 1926, which mandated that seating at all public assemblies be segregated. Taft was thrust to the verge of a massive conflict of interest. The question was discussed at a "strenuous meeting" of the Board on April 22,[174] at which Taft was absent. Robert R. Moton, Washington's successor as principal of Tuskegee, and the only Black member of the Hampton Board, urged that Hampton file a test case in court. Conveying his views by letter, Moton declared that if Hampton "should now retire before a deliberate attack upon its peaceful policy of conciliation, it would constitute a repudiation of all its past history as well as its most recently declared principles." A test case would spark "such a rallying of the colored people to Hampton as it has never had before, and of the large majority of the best Southern white people as well."[175]

The influential white educator James Hardy Dillard, however, "advised strongly against testing the new law in the courts, and said he thought the institute had come through the affair well by doing nothing and saying nothing; but there is unquestionably a wide spread feeling in the community that Hampton has changed in its policies and practices, a feeling which must be reckoned with. ... He counseled strongly giving up all assemblages that may be considered 'public' and admitting people outside of the Institute by invitation only."[176]

The Board ultimately followed Dillard's advice. It said nothing to protest the new legislation, but, on the advice of counsel, it closed Ogden Hall recitals to the public and permitted attendance by invitation only. The Virginia statute applied only to "public" assemblies. The upshot was that Hampton was able to preserve the dignity of its Black students by withdrawing Ogden Hall, built during Taft's

The Equal Protection Clause & Race

chairmanship, from the public sphere. This shrewd maneuver may have solved Hampton's immediate problem, but it also clearly demonstrated the intellectual bankruptcy of the Northern Republican strategy of separate spheres.

The Massenburg Bill was an obvious effort to stamp Blacks with the public stigma of social subordination. It was so understood by all involved. Public segregation, as Taft himself had observed, was "a studied effort" to make Blacks "feel a sense of social inferiority."[177] Political equality, however, requires at a minimum equality in the public sphere, for citizens who are made to feel inferior in public are not equal citizens. Du Bois thus had it exactly right when he condemned Harding's Birmingham speech on the ground that the "real meaning of 'social equality'" was "the right of a human being to accept companionship with his fellow on terms of equal and reciprocal courtesy," and that social equality in this sense "is the foundation of democracy." "Mr. Harding," Du Bois had written, "meant that the American Negro must acknowledge that it was a wrong and a disgrace for Booker T. Washington to dine with President Roosevelt."[178]

The events at Hampton were a textbook illustration of Du Bois's telling indictment. They demonstrated that Southern legislation to prevent social equality inevitably spilled over into the public sphere and was thus fundamentally incompatible with the ideal of a politically individualistic and classless society that Taft and his Court sought to realize through their jurisprudence. This was true not only in the political sphere, but also, as the brilliant young journalist Herbert Seligmann crisply put it at the outset of the decade, in the sphere of civil and economic rights:

> What does the white American mean by social equality? To take the words at their face value, one would suppose he meant association of colored and white persons in the home, personal intercourse without regard to race. In practice the denial of social equality is not confined to personal relations, but includes civil procedure. The socially inferior Negro is exploited on the farm because white lawyers will not take his case against white planters. As soon as the bar of social inferiority is broken down the Negro threatens the white man with competition. ... Every demand for common justice for the Negro, that he be treated as a human being, if not as a United States citizen, can be and is met with the retort that the demand is for social equality. Instantly every chord of jealousy and hatred vibrates among certain classes of whites – and in the resulting atmosphere of unreasoning fury even the most moderate proposals for the betterment of race relations take on the aspect of impossibilism. By the almost universal admission of white men and of white newspapers, denial of social equality does not mean what the words imply. It means that Negroes cannot obtain justice in many Southern courts; it means that they cannot obtain decent education, accommodation in public places and on common carriers; it means that every means is used to force home their helplessness by insult, which, if it is resisted, will be followed by the administration of the torch or the hempen rope or the bullet.[179]

If for no other reason than his travails at Hampton, Taft must have known all this by the time he came to write *Gong Lum* in 1927.

Even if Taft had not personally experienced the mortifications of Hampton, the bankruptcy of the formula of "separate but equal" was obvious in *Gong Lum* itself. The Mississippi Supreme Court in *Gong Lum* had frankly announced that the purpose of the relevant provision of the Mississippi Constitution was to preserve "the purity and integrity of the white race."[180] The implication was that racial purity, in the simple biological sense, was a desirable value that government could justifiably seek to protect. But if this were true, the principle of "separate but equal" meant Mississippi must afford Chinese equal access to the good of racial purity. Yet the Mississippi Supreme Court interpreted its state Constitution to protect the racial "purity" only of the white race. It made no effort to offer the good of racial purity equally to other races; and indeed it explicitly denied other races access to this good by requiring them to commingle under the expansive rubric of "colored."[181] As the Taft Court itself acknowledged, Martha Lum was required to attend a school that consisted of an amalgamation of "the brown, yellow or black races."[182] If amalgamation was harmful for the white race, it was equally harmful for these other races. Mississippi did not even purport to offer "separate but equal" access to the good of racial purity.

Stone, who would later author *Carolene Products*, recognized this precise point, writing Taft that the opinion did "not quite meet" the objection that the State of Mississippi had failed the standard of separate but equal:

> I understand that one contention made by the plaintiff is based upon a closer recognition of the supposed advantages resulting from segregation of the races – in fact, she relies on that and upon the denial of it, in that she is not given a school separate from the colored school, and she urges that is in itself a denial of equal protection. She says that to protect the white race from the dangers of race mixture and not to protect children of the Chinese race is to deny the latter the equal protection of the laws.
>
> I suppose the answer is that the State has made a beginning and that reforms do not have to be made all at once, as we have held in one or two cases. It might be well to mention the point, as the contention is different from those made in any of the other cases where negroes have resisted segregation at schools.[183]

Evidently Stone did not care enough about this argument to press it. Yet the plain implication of the Mississippi Supreme Court's frank decision to ensure only the purity of the white race is that only the purity of the white race was worth protecting.

The judgment of the Mississippi Supreme Court thus did not apply the maxim of separate but equal. It instead enforced the supremacy of the white race. Grant and Stoddard were correct that if the white race were supreme, it was delusional to imagine a society that could be equal in its political and economic spheres.[184] Given this contradiction, it is no wonder that in *Gong Lum* the Taft Court refused to acknowledge the racial subordination that was plainly laid out before its eyes. Taft, and most likely all the justices who participated in *Gong Lum*, understood the semiotics of racial separation well enough, but they chose to remain deliberately

The Equal Protection Clause & Race

oblivious to what they knew.[185] It was more convenient to ignore obvious inequality than to challenge the entire system of Southern apartheid.

No justice of the Taft Court, apart from Taft himself, sought to justify this refusal to confront Southern segregation. But, with characteristic candor, Taft did explicitly defend a strategy of deliberate ignorance. He argued that embracing Du Bois's path of confrontation would be counterproductive. As Taft wrote in 1921, "The only relief" from Black political inequality "which we can anticipate is ... the self-elevation of the Negro to such a place in the community that public opinion in those States where he is now denied the franchise, will yield it to him. This will come as his self-control, good sense, business standing, and value in the community demonstrate his power to wield it for the good of the community. In other words, when he shows his economic value to a community, and proves his good sense and usefulness, he will secure that which the law gave him years ago."[186]

In essence, Taft believed what the Court had explicitly stated in 1896 in *Plessy v. Ferguson*, which is that law "is powerless to eradicate racial instincts, or to abolish distinctions based upon physical differences, and the attempt to do so can only result in accentuating the difficulties of the present situation."[187] *Gong Lum* is thus fundamentally inconsistent with Taft's stance in the context of labor injunctions, in which he believed that popular opposition should be ruthlessly suppressed to enforce the requirements of legality. It is also inconsistent with Taft's stance in Eighteenth Amendment cases, where Taft adamantly believed that positive law should trump contrary social customs. Like the Southern prohibitionists who urged the necessity of enforcing the Eighteenth Amendment in the North, Taft was content to allow the Fourteenth and Fifteenth Amendments to remain largely fallow in the South.

In the context of prohibition, Taft believed that social mores could be modified by giving teeth to the positive requirements of the Volstead Act. In *Gong Lum*, by contrast, Taft allowed Southern social customs to override the positive rights established by the Reconstruction Amendments. His deference was based upon the view that white "racial prejudice" could in the end only be "worn away by the logic of events, by education, by stimulation of the moral sense and by the operation of economic causes and enlightened selfishness."[188] In the context of prohibition, Taft imagined that social customs were malleable to positive law; in the context of race relations, he believed that positive law was helpless in the face of entrenched social mores.

The upshot was that solicitude for Southern whites in effect exiled Southern Blacks from the protections of the Constitution. As Taft explicitly acknowledged, they would have to wait patiently for a change in Southern sensibility before they could expect legal enforcement of the rights "which the law gave [them] years ago."[189] Blacks would have to remain without the prerogatives of constitutional citizenship until white prejudice could be "worn away."[190] Taft evidently expected Blacks to accept a kind of constitutional invisibility. Booker T. Washington was so popular among Northern Republican elites because he publicly justified and sanctioned that invisibility.

It is no surprise, then, that in the South "[i]n the 1920's the new peculiar institution of Negro subordination ... reached its apogee as an established reality

THE TAFT COURT

in law, politics, economics, and folkways. ... The question was settled."[191] With the exception of an occasional decision like *Nixon* or *Harmon*, which involved limited, discrete, and explicit racial classifications in contexts that were unambiguously political or economic, the Taft Court was prepared to concede the essentials of white supremacy. Caught between directly confronting Southern segregation and abandoning its own fiction of political and economic equality, the Court chose to keep its head in the sand, affirming both separation and equality.

What remains to be explained is a second puzzle posed by Harding's Birmingham address. Given Harding's commitment to individual merit in political and economic spheres, why did he simultaneously insist on such rigorous racial separation in the social sphere? Eugenicists like Grant and Stoddard could easily explain the necessity of social separation. Race was biological, and separation was necessary for the self-preservation of the white race. But Harding could not explain his commitment to social separation in terms of this kind of biological necessity, because it was inconsistent with the economic and political equality that Northern Republican elites purported to defend.

Harding's commitment to social separation is best understood as politically, not biologically, motivated. It sprang from the hope of breaking the solidly Democratic South. Harding had taken an initial step in that direction by winning Tennessee, which was "the first of the southern states to give its electoral vote voluntarily to a republican candidate for president."[192] That triumph would lead to Harding's nomination of Sanford to replace Pitney.[193] Since Southern whites would not support the Republican Party unless it accepted segregation, Republican hopes of becoming a dominant and truly national party depended upon its accommodation of Southern racism.

One can perceive a somewhat analogous dynamic at work in the Taft Court. Unlike Holmes, Taft was not attracted to eugenics.[194] Taft's support of segregation had little to do with opposition to biological amalgamation. It was instead a purely pragmatic political accommodation. Taft wanted Article III courts to become truly national institutions, with legitimacy in all sections of the nation.[195] He believed that segregation had to be tolerated because the "educated, wealthier classes of the South" were "supersensitive over fear of social equality."[196] Taft saw no viable alternative but to accept the facts of prejudice.

Like *Plessy*, and like Harding, Taft believed that social segregation was required by the irresistible "racial instincts" of the American people.[197] It is plain from its decisions that the entire Taft Court was willing to accept this view of the matter. The point can perhaps best be illustrated by the remarkable opinion of *United States v. Bhagat Singh Thind*,[198] in which Sutherland, speaking for a unanimous Court,[199] interpreted the meaning of race in a federal statute that limited naturalization to aliens who were "free white persons." The question in *Thind* was whether "a high caste Hindu of full Indian blood" was "a white person within the meaning" of the statute.[200]

Sutherland had three months earlier issued his maiden Supreme Court opinion in *Ozawa v. United States*, ruling for a unanimous Court that the category "free

The Equal Protection Clause & Race

white persons" did not include "a person of the Japanese race."[201] In his brief, Ozawa had argued that Japanese were "particularly white-skinned. They are whiter than the average Italian, Spaniard or Portuguese."[202] George Wickersham, who represented Ozawa in oral argument, contended that a "'[w]hite person,' as construed by this Court and by the state courts, means a person without negro blood."[203]

Sutherland rejected these arguments, holding that the phrase "a free white person" was drafted in the 1790 Naturalization Act[204] "to confer the privilege of citizenship upon that class of person who the fathers knew as white, and to deny it to all who could not be so classified."[205] The phrase, in other words, should be interpreted according to the same premises of white supremacy as those expressed by the Mississippi Supreme Court. Whiteness, and only whiteness, was to be privileged. Because, as Taft had explicitly held in *Truax*, the requirements of the Equal Protection Clause did not apply to the federal government,[206] Congress was constitutionally free to legislate through racial classifications of this kind, even if they created an explicit racial hierarchy.

Sutherland held in *Ozawa* that Congress meant to impose "a racial and not an individual test." The 1790 Naturalization Act did not refer to "the mere color of the skin of each individual"; color differed "greatly among persons of the same race, even among Anglo-Saxons."[207] Instead "the federal and state courts, in an almost unbroken line, have held that the words 'white person' were meant to indicate only a person of what is popularly known as the Caucasian race."[208] Ozawa did not come within the terms of the statute because he was "clearly of a race which is not Caucasian."[209]

Bhagat Singh Thind sought to hoist the Court on its own petard. He argued that "scientific authorities" classified high-caste Hindus from the Punjab "as of the Caucasian or Aryan race."[210] Embarrassed, the Court was forced to execute an abrupt *volte face*. By the Caucasian race, Sutherland explained, *Ozawa* did not refer to a "matter of scientific classification." The reach of the statute was to be determined by "popular meaning" rather than "scientific application," for "it would be obviously illogical to convert words of common speech used in a statute into words of scientific terminology when neither the latter nor the science for whose purposes they were coined was within the contemplation of the framers of the statute or of the people for whom it was framed."[211]

Thind concluded that the meaning of "white persons" was to be determined not by science, but by the "common understanding, by unscientific men."

> The words of familiar speech, which were used by the original framers of the law, were intended to include only the type of man whom they knew as white. The immigration of that day was almost exclusively from the British Isles and Northwestern Europe, whence they and their forebears had come. When they extended the privilege of American citizenship to "any alien being a free white person" it was these immigrants – bone of their bone and flesh of their flesh – and their kind whom they must have had affirmatively in mind. The succeeding years brought immigrants from Eastern, Southern and Middle Europe, among them the Slavs and the dark-eyed, swarthy people of Alpine and Mediterranean stock, and

these were received as unquestionably akin to those already here and readily amalgamated with them."²¹²

Sutherland's account of race seems at first glance to be biological. Referring to the framers, Sutherland characterizes "white persons" as those who are "bone of their bone and flesh of their flesh." Yet, when pressed, Sutherland's biological metaphors quickly dissolve into sociological ones. Sutherland acknowledges that the "dark-eyed, swarthy people of Alpine and Mediterranean stock" could be "received as unquestionably akin to those already here."²¹³ This process of amalgamation – this assimilation to those already here – was necessarily sociological in nature, not biological. The question therefore arises why elegant, high-caste Hindus could not be similarly amalgamated.

Sutherland's answer was simply that the "children of English, French, German, Italian, Scandinavian, and other European parentage, quickly merge into the mass of our population and lose the distinctive hallmarks of their European origin. On the other hand, it cannot be doubted that the children born in this country of Hindu parents would retain indefinitely the clear evidence of their ancestry. It is very far from our thought to suggest the slightest question of racial superiority or inferiority. What we suggest is merely racial difference, and it is of such character and extent that the great body of our people instinctively recognize it and reject the thought of assimilation."²¹⁴ Like *Plessy*, then, *Thind* ultimately appeals to the racial instincts of the American people;²¹⁵ it theorizes race as an elemental and socially constructed category.²¹⁶

This understanding of race solved certain problems for the Court. It empowered the Court to speak with the authority of a common law tribunal. Questions of race, as *Plessy* had explicitly asserted, primarily involve interpreting and applying "the established usages, customs, and traditions of the people."²¹⁷ Using race in this way also explained why racial discrimination could permeate the social sphere and yet could be forbidden in the artificial and judicially constructed realms of civil and political rights, where society was constitutionally deemed to be composed of individuals who were without class or race. It involved no great conceptual leap to conclude that courts could override popular perceptions when necessary to protect constitutional rights like those at issue in *Nixon* or *Harmon*.

Yet by locating the definition of race in the instincts of the common man, the Court also risked these instincts spilling over from the social realm into the political and economic spheres where the Court was obliged to defend a classless equality. Insofar as the average American did not conceive races as equal, but instead as hierarchically ranked, the Court's ambition to construct a world of equal economic and political individuals would be perpetually threatened. Therefore in *Thind*, as in *Gong Lum*, the Taft Court was quick to invoke the fiction of formal racial equality. It affirmed that popular attitudes did not imply "the slightest question of racial superiority or inferiority"; they postulated difference, not inequality.

But, just as in *Gong Lum*, this assertion was patently false. The Court was well aware that by denying the possibility of citizenship for East and South Asians,

The Equal Protection Clause & Race

it was also sanctioning virulent racial prejudice that excluded these populations from equal participation in the market. Throughout the West, there were statutes "proscribing land ownership by persons ineligible for citizenship."[218] The Court's decision in *Thind* thus became a reason for consigning these populations to a subordinate and stigmatized economic status.[219]

The attorney general of California, for example, promptly proclaimed that *Thind* would permit the state to curtail "the menacing spread of Hindus holding our lands."[220] The *San Francisco Chronicle* greeted *Thind* with the happy recognition that it "places Hindu residents of this State, many of whom have large lease-holdings of agricultural lands, and especially the rice lands in the Sacramento and Imperial valleys, under the provisions of the alien land law, thus forbidding them from farming these lands within the State of California upon leaseholds or contracts."[221] The *Literary Digest* observed that *Thind* was "hailed for the most part with delight by the California press and that of our Western seaboard, which we find has a Hindu problem just as much as a Japanese problem."[222]

Two months after the announcement of *Thind*, the constitutionality of these Western alien land laws was debated in the Taft Court in four closely related cases.[223] Speaking through Butler, the Court upheld them all against constitutional challenge. The chief case was *Terrace v. Thompson*,[224] in which the Court considered a Washington statute that forbade aliens who could not declare in good faith that they intended to become citizens of the United States from owning agricultural land.[225] Since Japanese aliens were, after *Ozawa*, ineligible for naturalization, they could not in good faith declare their intention to become citizens.

Washington's prohibition was challenged by the Terraces, American landowners who wished to lease agricultural land to Nakatsuka, a Japanese farmer, as well as by Nakatsuka himself. The plaintiffs sought to enjoin the operation of the statute. In what amounted to a sweeping vindication of equitable jurisdiction, Butler held that injunctive remedies were appropriate so long as a statute prohibited the exercise of constitutional rights, like the Terraces's right "to use, lease and dispose" of property, or like Nakatsuka's right "to earn a livelihood by following the ordinary occupations of life," and so long as "the threatened enforcement" of the statute "deters" the exercise of those rights. Litigants ought not be "obliged to take the risk of prosecution, fines and imprisonment and loss of property in order to secure an adjudication of their rights."[226] Modern constitutional adjudication owes a great deal to the low threshold for equitable relief set by *Terrace*. McReynolds and Brandeis disagreed with this expansive view of equity and dissented (without opinion) on the ground that the litigants in *Terrace* had not presented a "justiciable question."[227]

On the substance of the case, Butler easily disposed of the claim that the statute violated the Due Process Clause. Illustrating how the Taft Court interpreted the Clause *in pari materia* with traditional common law principles, Butler reasoned that because at common law government could prohibit aliens from holding real property, "[s]tate legislation applying alike and equally to all aliens, withholding from them the right to own land, cannot be said to be capricious or to amount to an

1455

arbitrary deprivation of liberty or property, or to transgress the due process clause."[228] The trickier claim, however, was that the statute violated the Equal Protection Clause because it discriminated "arbitrarily against Nakatsuka and other ineligible aliens because of their race and color."[229]

The federal district court that had initially heard the case concluded that it was reasonable to distinguish between persons based upon race and color:

> It is obvious that the objection on the part of Congress is not due to color, as color, but only to color as an evidence of a type of civilization which it characterizes. The yellow or brown racial color is the hallmark of Oriental despotisms, or was at the time the original naturalization law was enacted. It was deemed that the subjects of these despotisms, with their fixed and ingrained pride in the type of their civilization, which works for its welfare by subordinating the individual to the personal authority of the sovereign, as the embodiment of the state, were not fitted and suited to make for the success of a republican form of Government. Hence they were denied citizenship. . . .
>
> Congress, in withholding the right to citizenship from these Oriental races, no doubt recognized, as statesmen long have done, that it was of the essence of its duty to insure the perpetuation of our own type of civilization. . . .
>
> The sympathetic and temperate view here expressed, no doubt, should restrain us from forcing our civilization upon alien types. Yet it lessens no jot or tittle the duty of the court to hold impregnable the barrier erected by Congress to preserve, in its purity, our own type of civilization. The more homogeneous its parts, the more perfect the union. It may be that the changes wrought in the Orient in the last 50 or 75 years now warrant a different policy; but there is no law or treaty that yet has said "the twain shall meet," or that, if citizenship be accorded these Orientals, the danger is past of our becoming a "mechanical medley of race fragments."[230]

Butler, however, was much too shrewd explicitly to endorse this kind of overtly racist reasoning, even though similar prejudices had effectively been sustained by the Court itself in *Ozawa* and *Thind*. The tension with the Equal Protection Clause, which applied to states but not to Congress, would simply be too great. He therefore entirely avoided the question of race.

Butler held instead that the "rule established by Congress on this subject, in and of itself, furnishes a reasonable basis for classification in a state law withholding from aliens the privilege of land ownership."[231] Because the "quality and allegiance of those who own, occupy and use the farm lands within its borders are matters of highest importance and affect the safety and power of the State itself," the distinction between those who in good faith expected to become citizens, and those who did not, was relevant to significant state interests.[232]

This was a tactful way for the Court to sidestep the manifest and ugly racial prejudices that enveloped the alien land laws. The difficulty was that this strategy of avoidance was impeached by *Terrace*'s companion case, *Porterfield v. Webb*,[233] in which the Court upheld a California statute that prohibited ineligible aliens from acquiring interests in real property, yet that allowed eligible aliens to obtain such

The Equal Protection Clause & Race

interests even if they refused to declare any intention to become United States citizens. The blunt distinction between eligible and ineligible aliens in the California statute could not plausibly be explained in terms of loyalty to the state. Unlike the Washington statute at issue in *Terrace*, California's legislation was based precisely and solely on the racial distinctions affirmed in *Ozawa* and *Thind*.

Not deterred, Butler upheld the California legislation by applying the deferential standard of *Natural Carbonic Gas*: "In the matter of classification, the States have wide discretion. Each has its own problems, depending on circumstances existing there. It is not always practical or desirable that legislation shall be the same in different States. We cannot say that the failure of the California Legislature to extend the prohibited class so as to include eligible aliens who have failed to declare their intention to become citizens of the United States was arbitrary or unreasonable."[234]

As cases like *Truax* or *Quaker City Cab* illustrate, the Taft Court was more than capable of tightening the deferential standard of review of *Natural Carbonic Gas* whenever it perceived important constitutional values to be at stake. But apparently the Court saw no such values at issue in *Porterfield*, even though the case effectively denied persons access to real property on the basis of their race. T.R. Powell mercilessly ridiculed the Court's abject deference. "'There's a Reason,' says the learned Justice, but he seems not to have it so clear in his mind at the moment as to be able to tell us what it is."[235] If the constitutional justification for denying aliens ineligible for citizenship the right to own real property was their questionable allegiance to the state, how could California permit eligible aliens to own such land despite their willful refusal to commit to citizenship?[236] The distinction drawn by California invited "inquiry whether the reason relied on to justify the discrimination and the restraint was the real reason motivating the legislation or merely a fortunate excuse."[237]

The invidious purposes of the Western alien land laws were in fact visible for all contemporaries to see.[238] They were explicitly argued to the court by California's Attorney General Ulysses Sigel Webb, who gave a remarkably frank answer when Taft asked him what the Japanese were doing "to which you take objection":

> "The white people refuse to assimilate with the Japanese," Mr. Webb replied, "and as the Japanese line advances we retreat, and we do not like to retreat.
>
> "When the Japanese occupy land in our State they exclude from it people who might become citizens. We believe our Government, State and national, will be best protected and served when our lands are occupied by those who have sympathy with our institutions and can be compelled to contribute to its preservation. I am speaking plainly."
>
> "The court wants you to speak plainly," Chief Justice Taft remarked.
>
> "We had one race problem which was settled by the Civil War," continued Mr. Webb. "There is another growing up now on the Pacific Coast that is more threatening. We have already lost the Philippines. The Japanese dominate there now. We believe this Government is a white man's government.

"I will not stop now to debate the wisdom of the settlement of the negro problem following the war. Had Lincoln lived, the outcome might have been different. We object to Japanese owning or controlling our agricultural lands through lease and cropping contracts because we want to live in California."[239]

The Taft Court turned a deliberately blind eye to the blatant racial prejudice that so obviously motivated the Western alien land laws, forms of prejudice that the Court had itself unleashed in *Ozawa* and *Thind*.[240] Although the alien land legislation at issue in *Terrace* and *Porterfield* negated fundamental property rights in ordinary markets, it seems as if the Taft Court was willing to strike down only blunt and explicit state racial classifications, like those at issue in *Nixon* or *Harmon*. Otherwise it was content to allow the nation's "racial instincts" to play themselves out in terrible and consequential ways.[241]

Caught between the Court's acceptance of racial caste and the Court's celebration of a classless society of individuals, it is no wonder that equal protection doctrine during the Taft Court era proved aimless and ineffectual. The doctrine drifted from case to case, acquiring force chiefly when caught in the current of the Court's ongoing commitments to the national market, to economic development, or to employers' rights. The Taft Court's reluctance to challenge "supersensitive" white fears "of social equality,"[242] or white Western terror at un-American Asian competition,[243] meant that racial minorities were in effect virtually exiled from constitutional protections, without legally cognizable agency.

A little-remembered incident in 1930 would spark a process that would transform this stagnant doctrinal structure. On the morning of Saturday, March 8, 1930, Edward Terry Sanford stopped by his dentist in the Farragut Apartments to have a tooth pulled. Arising from the chair after the operation, he suddenly became dizzy and began talking "incoherently about 'the court' and the conference he was to have attended."[244] Sanford was taken by ambulance to his home where he died later that morning. The diagnosis was "uremic poisoning."[245] To replace Sanford, Hoover nominated Fourth Circuit Judge John J. Parker.[246] In the course of the battle to confirm Parker, the political position of African Americans as a minority racial group entitled to constitutional rights would be transformed.

The NAACP took the most unusual step of officially opposing Parker's nomination.[247] Spearheading the fight was Walter White, the NAACP's acting secretary, who testified to a confused Senate subcommittee that when in 1920 Parker had accepted the nomination of the Republican Party to run for Governor of North Carolina, Parker had said:

> The negro as a class does not desire to enter politics. The Republican Party of North Carolina does not desire him to do so. We recognize the fact that he has not yet reached that stage in his development when he can share the burdens and responsibilities of government. This being true, and every intelligent man in North Carolina knows that it is true, the attempt of certain petty Democratic politicians to inject the race issue into every campaign is most reprehensible. I say it deliberately there is no more dangerous or contemptible enemy of the State than men who for personal or political advantage will attempt to kindle the flame of

The Equal Protection Clause & Race

racial prejudice or hatred ... [T]he participation of the negro in politics is a source of evil and danger to both races and is not desired by the wise men in either race or by the Republican party of North Carolina.[248]

White insisted that Parker's statement demonstrated that Parker gave "his full approval" to the disenfranchisement of Black voters in "an open, shameless flouting of the fourteenth and fifteenth amendments." "If Judge Parker, for political advantage, can flout two amendments to the Federal Constitution to pander to base race prejudice, we respectfully submit that he is not of the caliber which loyal, intelligent Americans have the right to expect of Justices of the Nation's highest court."[249]

White accused Parker of sacrificing Black constitutional rights at the altar of Southern sensitivities.[250] The Senate subcommittee was baffled, because the position White "attributed to Judge Parker" was "shared by a majority of white Republicans in Southern States," not to mention almost all Southern Democratic politicians.[251] It was indeed the articulated position of Taft himself, and it was most likely the driving force behind Taft Court decisions like *Gong Lum* and *Thind*. Just how far did White intend his accusations to reach?

The Senate subcommittee was "bewildered at the spectacle of the Negro stepping out of his traditional role of a meek, uncomplaining creature who submitted without question to whatever was put upon him."[252] The NAACP's "struggle against the confirmation of the North Carolina jurist ... not only revealed in a startling fashion the resentment of eleven million Negroes at a rapidly growing disregard of their political rights but showed as well that the Negro no longer intends supinely to permit the whittling down, little by little, of the constitutional rights which, theoretically, belong to him as an American citizen."[253]

White proved a stunningly effective organizer, even prompting comparison to "the Antisaloon League in the organized prohibitionists' sphere."[254] There were mass meetings in large cities with "telegraph banks ... to make it easier for individuals to send their protests. Telegrams, letters, and petitions poured into Senate offices."[255] The Great Migration had transformed Blacks into a swing voting bloc in many urban areas, so that mass national Black political mobilization in 1930 represented a new political phenomenon.[256] White adroitly tapped the potential political influence of African-Americans to produce "impressive evidences of a 'comeback' by the Negroes, as a minority voting power, on a scale that may cause them to be reckoned with more seriously than at any time since Southern reconstruction days. For Negro voters now easily can decide contests between the big parties in a half dozen or more large Northern States. All they need are political mindedness, cohesion and management. And in the result of the fight over Judge Parker there are makings for all those requirements."[257] "Whatever the outcome of the issue," said the *Christian Science Monitor*, "there can be no question that the Negro association is playing a most important role in the matter; a fact that will not be lost upon either the Negroes or the political leaders. This is the first time that the Negro in an organized campaign is making himself felt in a powerful political manner."[258]

The intervention of the NAACP, along with the determined opposition of organized labor,[259] undercut the Parker nomination as it worked its way through the Senate. The Senate Judiciary Committee voted against Parker's confirmation 10–6. It was said in the press that: "We will not stand for more yellow-dog contract and injunction judges on the Supreme Court Bench. We will not stand for more judges inclined toward unfair racial discrimination being elevated to a bench which should be above prejudice. . . . Parker is an incident. The Supreme Court is the issue."[260] On May 7, 1930, the Senate rejected Parker's nomination by a vote of 41–39.[261] It was a stunning turn of events.[262] "The Negro," observed Brandeis, "has moved a step forward."[263]

Parker's defeat marked the emergence of the NAACP as a nationally effective political pressure group whose demands could not be ignored. It was "a watershed in the maturation of black political power."[264] Not only did the Parker fight transform "the NAACP into a leading civil rights organization, it brought about the recognition that the black vote in the North and in border states was a force to be reckoned with."[265] Parker was the first Supreme Court nominee to be rejected since the Grover Cleveland administration, and, as the *Washington Post* acknowledged, "it was the Negro opposition that gave the commanding position to the movement led by the Progressives."[266] Nine years later, William Hastie remarked that Parker's defeat made America "realize that, after a long lapse following the Reconstruction, the Negro again had become a powerful and an important figure in national politics." It "probably impressed the nation more than any other single thing accomplished by the American Negro during the 20th century."[267]

Walter White's deft opposition to Parker shattered the seeming inevitability of the Northern white policy of conciliation. It countered the political strategy of Booker T. Washington by checking the instinct of Northern elites endlessly to defer to the sensibilities of white Southerners. Blacks could no longer costlessly be ignored as a group that lacked political agency or voice. By demonstrating that Blacks could exercise real political power, NAACP opposition to Parker gave teeth to the demand that the Reconstruction Amendments receive effective judicial recognition. It lent force to the insistence that Blacks be recognized as agents whose constitutional rights deserved respect. Courts would face consequences if they failed to bring African Americans back within the protective shelter of the Constitution.

Eight years later, in *Carolene Products*, the implications of this transformation would become visible in the Court's reinterpretation of the Equal Protection Clause. By acknowledging a judicial obligation to protect "discrete and insular minorities," the Court began to interpret the Clause in a way that would lift it from decades of drift and endow it with vigorous new purpose. Paradoxically, however, judicial recognition of this purpose did not occur until African Americans had first proven themselves effective participants in the political arena.

We are comfortable with the thought that political agency requires the protection of political rights. But the history of the Taft Court's jurisprudence of race suggests that the converse might also be true. Until a group is experienced as an active political agent, courts may with impunity deny it the rights that define political agency. That is what happened to African Americans during the era of

The Equal Protection Clause & Race

the Taft Court. Their rights were endlessly deferred because they were not perceived as a group capable of political agency. In his Birmingham speech, Harding had specifically identified the "labor vote, the business vote, the Irish vote," and so on, but in a speech about race relations and political equality, it is striking that he did not even mention the Black vote. In fact he warned Alabama precisely that continued repression of its Black population threatened to create the "menace" of "forcing upon the black race an attitude of political solidarity."[268] Insofar as the struggle over the Parker nomination suddenly and unexpectedly made such solidarity manifest to a dominant, white audience, it signaled a new Black political presence. The Black vote could no longer be ignored.

Members of the Taft Court were almost certainly aware of the racial injustices they condoned. It would seem to follow that they were unwilling to intervene on behalf of a minority without the political muscle to make acquiescence expensive. The Court could ignore the interests of African Americans because it was costless to do so. Southern Democrats wished to maintain apartheid; Northern Republicans wished to make inroads into the white Democratic South.[269] In this political logic, Blacks had no voice to which governing elites felt compelled to respond. The suffocating stalemate began to collapse only when the Great Migration, and access to the voting booth in northern and border states, endowed African Americans with the opportunity for political participation. During the controversy over the Parker nomination, African Americans seized that opportunity to make their voices heard in a manner that had not occurred since Reconstruction.

In contrast to African Americans, organized labor was a recognized political participant throughout the 1920s. Every literate politician knew the risks of alienating the "labor vote." Labor could sometimes make its opponents pay for their indifference. This meant that organized labor could exact costs for the Court's consistently pro-employer jurisprudence. In practical terms, labor could inspire jagged divisions within the Court itself, and it could generate the kind of political backlash that would eventually produce the Norris-LaGuardia Act in 1932.

What in retrospect is most striking about the Taft Court's jurisprudence of race is that African Americans did not display this kind of political presence during the 1920s. The Court did not divide over questions of race. There were no dissenting voices to the Taft Court's policy of conciliation; there was literally no one on the Court prepared to speak on behalf of racial minorities.[270] And, until the unexpected battle over Parker abruptly materialized, there was no political backlash strong enough to require Northern political elites to take notice.

Eight years later, however, footnote 4 of *Carolene Products* completely reimagined the purpose of the Equal Protection Clause. Stone read the Clause as seeking to uproot the kind of "prejudice against discrete and insular minorities" that seriously curtails "the operation of those political processes ordinarily to be relied upon to protect minorities."[271] Underlying this proposed reformulation of equal protection doctrine lay an altered conception of African Americans. Stone had come to imagine Blacks as a group actually engaged in the "political processes" of the nation.[272] The great, forgotten controversy over Parker's nomination helped spark this momentous transformation.

The Taft Court

Notes

1. For a detailed study, see Stephen A. Siegel, *Justice Holmes, Buck v. Bell, and the History of Equal Protection*, 90 MINNESOTA LAW REVIEW 106, 139–43 (2005).
2. Silver v. Silver, 280 U.S. 117, 122–24 (1929). *Silver* was authored by Stone. On his return to Stone's draft opinion, Holmes wrote, "Yes indeed – I only think the 14th Am. so remote from the case that I wonder that you take such pains to fasten it down." (Stone papers).
3. *See, e.g.*, Chicago, R.I. & P. Ry. Co. v. Perry, 259 U.S. 548, 556 (1922) ("The contention that the Service Letter Law denies to plaintiff in error the equal protection of the laws is rested upon the fact that it is made to apply to public service corporations (and contractors working for them), to the exclusion of other corporations, individuals, and partnerships said to employ labor under similar circumstances. This is described as arbitrary classification. We are not advised of the precise reasons why the Legislature chose to put the policy of this statute into effect as to public service corporations, without going further; nor is it worth while to inquire. It may have been that the public had a greater interest in the personnel of the public service corporations, or that the Legislature deemed it expedient to begin with them as an experiment, or any one of a number of other reasons. It was peculiarly a matter for the Legislature to decide, and not the least substantial ground is present for believing they acted arbitrarily. We feel safe in relying upon the general presumption that they 'knew what they were about.'") (opinion by Pitney, J.; Taft, Van Devanter, and McReynolds dissenting); Arkansas Natural Gas Co. v. Arkansas Railroad Comm'n, 261 U.S. 379, 384 (1923) ("The reasons which influenced the classification are not disclosed on the face of the act, but the mere absence of such disclosure will not justify the court in assuming that appropriate reasons did not in fact exist. The presumption is that the action of the Legislature – which applies alike to all falling within the class – was with full knowledge of the conditions and that no arbitrary selection of persons for subjection to the prescribed rule was intended. The state Legislature is vested with a wide discretion in the matter and interference by this court may not be had merely because its exercise has produced inequality – every selection of subjects or persons for governmental regulation does that – but only where it has produced an inequality which is actually and palpably unreasonable and arbitrary.") (opinion by Sutherland, J.); Georgia Ry. & Power Co. v. Decatur, 262 U.S. 432, 439 (1923) ("[I]t is not shown that the classification in fact is unreasonable and arbitrary and, under the decisions of this court, we cannot say that it is obnoxious to the constitutional provision.") (opinion by Sutherland, J.); Stebbins v. Riley, 268 U.S. 137, 142–43 (1925) ("The guaranty of the Fourteenth Amendment of the equal protection of the laws is not a guaranty of equality of operation or application of state legislation upon all citizens of a state. ... It is not necessary that the basis of classification should be deducible from the nature of the thing classified. It is enough that the classification is reasonably founded in the 'purposes and policies of taxation.' It is not open to objection unless it precludes the assumption that the classification was made in the exercise of legislative judgment and discretion.") (opinion by Stone, J.); Roberts & Shaefer Co. v. Emmerson, 271 U.S. 50, 57 (1926) ("The inequalities complained of result from a classification which, being founded upon real differences, is not unreasonable, and the discrimination which results from it is not arbitrary or prohibited by the Fourteenth Amendment. It is

The Equal Protection Clause & Race

enough that the classification is reasonably founded upon or related to some permissible policy of taxation.") (opinion by Stone, J.).
4. *Brandeis-Frankfurter Conversations*, at 330 (July 6, 1924).
5. Felix Frankfurter to HFS (June 6, 1928) (Stone papers).
6. 262 U.S. 544 (1923).
7. *Id.* at 547-49.
8. *Id.* at 551.
9. In the Brandeis papers is a note from Sutherland saying "I am 'agin' you in this," and a note from McKenna saying "Under the other flag."
10. 172 U.S. 239 (1898).
11. *Blake* was very explicit on this point. *See Blake*, 172 U.S. at 261: "Without attempting to state what is the full import of the words, 'within its jurisdiction,' it is safe to say that a corporation not created by Tennessee, nor doing business there under conditions that subjected it to process issuing from the courts of Tennessee at the instance of suitors, is not, under the above clause of the fourteenth amendment, within the jurisdiction of that state. ... Nor do we think [the foreign corporation] came within the jurisdiction of Tennessee, within the meaning of the amendment, simply by presenting its claim in the state court, and thereby becoming a party to this cause. Under any other interpretation, the fourteenth amendment would be given a scope not contemplated by its framers or by the people, nor justified by its language."

In his opinion in *Kennedy Finance*, Van Devanter essentially evaded the force of *Blake* by contenting himself with an *ex cathedra* pronouncement: "It is enough to say that, when the plaintiff went into Wisconsin, as it did, for the obviously lawful purpose of repossessing itself, by a permissible action in her courts, of specific personal property unlawfully taken out of its possession elsewhere and fraudulently carried into that state, it was, in our opinion, within her jurisdiction for all the purposes of that undertaking. And we think there is no tenable ground for regarding it as any less entitled to the equal protection of the laws in that state than an individual would have been in the same circumstances; for ... 'a state has no more power to deny to corporations the equal protection of the law than it has to individual citizens.'" *Kentucky Finance*, 262 U.S. at 550.
12. *Kentucky Finance*, 262 U.S. at 553 (Brandeis, J., dissenting). As late as 1928 it could be observed in a treatise on constitutional law by a professor of political science at Johns Hopkins that although "corporations equally with natural persons are entitled to the protection" of the Equal Protection Clause, "as to foreign corporations, a State having the constitutional right to say whether a corporation not chartered by itself shall do business within its limits (interstate commerce excepted) the State may impose upon such corporations as conditions precedent to the enjoyment of the privilege, such special conditions as it may see fit." WESTEL W. WILLOUGHBY, PRINCIPLES OF THE CONSTITUTIONAL LAW OF THE UNITED STATES 350 (New York: Baker, Voorhis & Co. 1928).
13. A particularly saliant example of the Court using the Equal Protection Clause in this way is Power Manufacturing Co. v. Saunders, 274 U.S. 490 (1927), which is discussed in detail in Chapter 38, at 1195. *Saunders* was characterized as "the culmination of a series of cases extending the safeguard of the equal protection clause to foreign corporations." Note, 41 HARVARD LAW REVIEW 95, 95 (1927). *See* Hanover Fire Ins. Co. v. Carr, 272 U.S. 494 (1926); Air-Way Electric Appliance Corp. v. Day, 266 U.S. 71 (1924).

14. Thomas Reed Powell, *The Supreme Court and State Police Power 1922–1930 – VI*, 18 VIRGINIA LAW REVIEW 270, 301–2 (1930).
15. Quaker City Cab Co. v. Pennsylvania, 277 U.S. 389, 399–400 (1928). "The tax is imposed merely because the owner is a corporation. The discrimination is not justified by any difference in the source of the receipts or in the situation or character of the property employed. It follows that the section fails to meet the requirement that a classification, to be consistent with the equal protection clause, must be based on a real and substantial difference having reasonable relation to the subject of the legislation." *Id.* at 402 (citing *Power Manufacturing Co. v. Saunders*).
16. *Id.* at 402. In the words of one commentator: "Hitherto the general attitude of the courts has been that almost any tax imposed on a corporation but not on natural persons could be attributed to the advantages of the corporate organization. In contrast with that view, this decision represents a desirable tendency on the part of the Court, and one which will necessarily have an important bearing on the constitutionality of the numerous statutes in this country taxing the income of corporations." Note, 77 UNIVERSITY OF PENNSYLVANIA LAW REVIEW 120, 124 (1928).
17. Flint v. Stone Tracey Co., 220 U.S. 107, 155 (1911).
18. *Quaker City Cab*, 277 U.S. at 412 (Stone, J., dissenting).
19. *Id.* at 403 (Holmes, J., dissenting).
20. William H. Taft, *Recent Criticism of the Federal Judiciary*, in REPORT OF THE EIGHTEENTH ANNUAL MEETING OF THE AMERICAN BAR ASSOCIATION 246–47 (Philadelphia: Dando Printing & Publishing Co. 1895).
21. Holmes joined Brandeis's dissent. He wrote Brandeis, "I agree rejoicingly and dismiss the need of my shorter screed after this – unless to exhibit your thoroughness in sockdologizing." (Brandeis papers). In anticipation of his dissent, Brandeis had written Frankfurter inquiring about the work of Harvard Law Professor Edward H. Warren. Brandeis believed that Warren "had doubt whether on the whole business corporations had been a blessing or a damage to America – (as distinguished from unincorporated businesses)." LDB to Felix Frankfurter (March 29, 1928), in BRANDEIS-FRANKFURTER CORRESPONDENCE, at 329.
22. *Quaker City Cab*, 277 U.S. at 410 (Brandeis, J., dissenting). This paragraph was evidently too much for Stone, who wrote Brandeis asking him to drop it. "You have so many stronger reasons for your conclusions, fully expressed in the opinion, that the over-elaboration of this weaker one, to my mind, weakens the whole opinion. It will suggest to many minds that this is the real germ of your opposition." (Brandeis papers). But the passage was important to Brandeis, and he retained it. Stone declined to join Brandeis's dissent.
23. *See, e.g.*, Louis K. Liggett Co. v. Lee, 288 U.S. 517, 548–70 (1933) (Brandeis, J., dissenting).
24. LDB to Felix Frankfurter (October 23, 1922), in BRANDEIS-FRANKFURTER CORRESPONDENCE, at 123. In the 1920s, 80 percent of cases within federal diversity jurisdiction involved a corporation as a party. Felix Frankfurter, *Distribution of Judicial Power between the United States and State Court*, 13 CORNELL LAW QUARTERLY 499, 523 (1928).
25. Jordan v. Tashio, 278 U.S. 123, 130 (1928).
26. Holmes also appreciated the need for group power in the context of labor decisions, although for entirely different reasons than Brandeis. Lacking a normative theory of

The Equal Protection Clause & Race

democratic citizenship, Holmes was most concerned with issues of scale and organization in the context of a Darwinian struggle for power. He did not wish that struggle to be artificially distorted by judicial rulings. *See supra* Chapter 39, at 1243–44.

27. Louis D. Brandeis, *The Jewish Problem: How to Solve It*, AMERICAN ISRAELITE (June 24, 1915), at 1.
28. Louis D. Brandeis, *True Americanism*, in BUSINESS – A PROFESSION 366, 371 (Boston: Hale, Cushman & Flint 1933).
29. *Id.* at 372.
30. *Points Way to Lasting Peace*, BOSTON DAILY GLOBE (July 6, 1915), at 13.
31. *New Forms of Liberty*, CHRISTIAN SCIENCE MONITOR (July 12, 1915), at 16.
32. "The movements of the last century have proved that whole peoples have individuality no less marked than that of the single person; that the individuality of a people is irrepressible, and that the misnamed internationalism which seeks the obliteration of nationalities or peoples is unattainable. The new nationalism adopted by America proclaims that each race or people, like each individual, has the right and duty to develop, and that only through such differentiated development will high civilization be attained. Not until these principles of nationalism, like those of democracy, are generally accepted will liberty be fully attained and minorities be secure in their rights." Brandeis, *supra* note 28, at 373–74. The conflation of race and nationality was very common in the eighteenth and nineteenth centuries. MAE M. NGAI, IMPOSSIBLE SUBJECTS: ILLEGAL ALIENS AND THE MAKING OF MODERN AMERICA 23 (Princeton University Press 2004).
33. "The greatest criticism of Brandeis's jurisprudence of the 1920s, by twenty-first-century standards, is his 'remarkable indifference' to matters of race." MELVIN I. UROFSKY, LOUIS D. BRANDEIS: A LIFE 639–40 (New York: Pantheon Books 2009). Brandeis has been criticized for a "conspicuous evasion of public issues that dealt with inter-ethnic relations between African-Americans and Euro-Americans and his complicity in rendering judicial decisions that reinforced core principles of the segregation regime." Christopher A. Bracey, *Louis Brandeis and the Race Question*, 52 ALABAMA LAW REVIEW 859, 861 (2001).
34. THE NEW NEGRO: AN INTERPRETATION (Alain Locke, ed., New York: Albert & Charles Boni, Inc. 1925).
35. Alain Locke, *Foreword*, in THE NEW NEGRO, *supra* note 34. Locke compared the spiritual rebirth of "black folk" to a "Palestine full of a renascent Judaism."
36. Du Bois also used the term "race" in this way in his essay *The Conservation of Races*, in W.E.B. DU BOIS, WRITINGS 815–26 (New York: Library of America 1986).
37. Siegel, *supra* note 1, at 142–43.
38. E. Baskin Wright, *Constitutional Rights of the Negro*, in PROCEEDINGS OF THE ANNUAL SESSION OF THE SOUTHERN POLITICAL SCIENCE ASSOCIATION 6 (University of Chicago Press 1934). *See* T.R. POWELL, *The Supreme Court and State Police Power, 1922–1930 – IX*, 18 VIRGINIA LAW REVIEW 597, 634–35 (1932). For Stone's justification of this transformation of the Fourteenth Amendment, see HARLAN F. STONE, LAW AND ITS ADMINISTRATION 143 (New York: Columbia University Press 1915).
39. Nixon v. Herndon, 273 U.S. 536, 540 (1927).

40. O. Douglas Weeks, *The Texas Direct Primary System*, 13 SOUTHWESTERN SOCIAL SCIENCE QUARTERLY 95, 96–97 (1932).
41. 8 CONG. REC. 1079 (February 7, 1879). Windom was speaking in the context of advocating Black relocation within the Union. He wanted to encourage and promote "the partial migration of colored persons from those States and congressional districts where they are not allowed to freely and peacefully exercise and enjoy their constitutional rights as American citizens, into such States as may desire to receive them and will protect them in said rights." *Id*. at 1077. Summoning the full resources of free labor ideology, Windom argued that this migration would allow the newly freed African-American to "find a home where he could support himself and family more comfortably than is possible under existing circumstances; a home where the tenant would be transformed into the landlord; where his earnings could be devoted to the support and education of his children; where his manhood and his civil and political rights would be respected; where he would be taught to respect himself; a home where the new political and social conditions which would surround him would stimulate his ambition to excel, fire his zeal for improvement, and thereby develop his powers of usefulness to his country and his race; in short, he would exchange practical serfdom for manly independence, with all the advantages which such a change implies." *Id*. at 1079.
42. Darlene Clark Hine, *The Elusive Ballot: The Black Struggle against the Texas Democratic White Primacy, 1932–1945*, 81 SOUTHWESTERN HISTORICAL QUARTERLY 371, 372 (1978).
43. Note, 41 YALE LAW JOURNAL 1212, 1214–15 (1932); Hine, *supra* note 42, at 373; Thurgood Marshall, *The Rise and Collapse of the "White Democratic Primary"*, 26 JOURNAL OF NEGRO EDUCATION 249, 250 (1957).
44. Note, 2 UNIVERSITY OF CHICAGO LAW REVIEW 640, 641 (1935).
45. Hine, *supra* note 42, at 371.
46. *Id*. at 373. *See generally* WILL GUZMÁN, CIVIL RIGHTS IN THE TEXAS BORDERLANDS: DR. LAWRENCE A. NIXON AND BLACK ACTIVISM (Urbana: University of Illinois Press 2015).
47. *Nixon*, 273 U.S. at 540. The alleged violation of the Fifteenth Amendment was straightforward; by contrast the alleged violation of the Fourteenth Amendment was obscure. It was contained in Paragraph 13 of the Amended Petition, Transcript of Record, Nixon v. Herndon, No. 117, October Term 1926, at 6–7, and it stated:

> Plaintiff further says that [the statute] purports to be limited to primary elections for the nomination of officers by the Democratic party; that there are in the State of Texas two great political parties, the Democratic party and the Republican party; that by its terms, said act applies only to the Democratic party; that the effect of such act is to exclude all negroes from participation in the Democratic primaries, forcing them by implication to vote, if at all, only in a Republican primary; that said Act thereby discriminates as between the Democratic and Republican parties and attempts by a legislative enactment to determine the party with which a negro shall affiliate and deprives him of his rights as an American citizen to determine for himself his choice of parties; that such act is discriminatory, unjust, illegal and void and operates as an unwarranted, unjust and discriminatory interference with the free exercise of privileges of citizenship and suffrage enjoyed by the plaintiff, together with others of his race ... contrary to the provisions, letter and spirit of the Constitution.... And by such restriction upon his freedom of choice to determine for himself the political party with which he shall affiliate abridges his rights and privileges as a citizen of the United States guaranteed to him by the Fourteenth amendment of the Constitution.

The Equal Protection Clause & Race

48. Van Devanter was absent.
49. Giles v. Harris, 189 U.S. 475, 486 (1903); *See supra* Chapter 5, at 166.
50. 266 U.S. 32 (1924).
51. Brief for the State of Texas, Nixon v. Herndon, No. 117, October Term 1926, at 14.
52. *See* Robert Cushman, *Constitutional Law in 1926–1927*, 22 AMERICAN POLITICAL SCIENCE REVIEW 70, 91 (1928); James E. Pate, *The Texas White Primary Law*, 16 NATIONAL MUNICIPAL REVIEW 618 (1927); Note, 28 MICHIGAN LAW REVIEW 613 (1930); Note, 6 NEBRASKA LAW BULLETIN 312, 313 (1928); Note, *supra* note 44, at 642.
53. Newberry v. United States, 256 U.S. 232, 250 (1921). *Newberry* may indeed have inspired the 1923 Texas statute at issue in *Nixon*. *See* Weeks, *supra* note 40, at 114.
54. In 1924, a federal district court had rejected a challenge to the Texas statute on the ground that a primary election did not come "within the meaning of the Fourteenth and Fifteenth Amendments to the Constitution of the United States." Chandler v. Neff, 298 F. 515, 518 (W.D. Tex. 1924). In *Chandler*, the plaintiff had sought to enjoin the Texas statute. Citing *Giles v. Harris*, the court in *Chandler* rejected that challenge on the ground that "the power of a court of equity by way of injunction has never in England, nor in America, been extended to political affairs." *Id.* at 517.
55. "If we can assume that the decision would have been the same had the Fifteenth Amendment never been enacted," commented T.R. Powell, "then the Fifteenth Amendment seems to be superfluous." Powell, *supra* note 38, at 635.
56. *Ex parte* Virginia, 100 U.S. 339, 367 (1879) (Field, J., dissenting). The Fourteenth Amendment, said Field, "secures to all persons their civil rights upon the same terms; but it leaves political rights, or such as arise from the form of government and its administration, as they stood previous to its adoption. . . . Civil rights are absolute and personal. Political rights, on the other hand, are conditioned and dependent upon the discretion of the elective or appointment power, whether that be the people acting through the ballot, or one of the departments of their government." *Id.* at 367–68. In 1970, this same theory was reasserted by the second Justice Harlan in Oregon v. Mitchell, 400 U.S. 112, 154 (1970) (Harlan, J., dissenting) ("[T]he Fourteenth Amendment was never intended to restrict the authority of the States to allocate their political power as they see fit and therefore . . . it does not authorize Congress to set voter qualifications, in either state or federal elections."). For discussions of this issue at the time of *Nixon*, see Note, NEBRASKA LAW BULLETIN, *supra* note 52, at 313–14, and Note, 5 TEXAS LAW REVIEW 393, 393–94 (1927).
57. OWH to Harold Laski (March 17, 1927), in 2 HOLMES-LASKI CORRESPONDENCE, at 927.
58. *Nixon*, 273 U.S. at 540. Oddly, Holmes cited *Giles v. Alabama*, 189 U.S. 475 (1903), for the proposition that an action for damages would lie. In *Giles*, Holmes had decided that equitable relief was unavailable for the wrongful denial of the right to vote. After Holmes's opinion, the plaintiff in the case, Jackson Giles, sought to bring an action for damages to enforce his right to vote. The Alabama Supreme Court made short work of this action; its decision was upheld by the Supreme Court of the United States because it had been decided on an adequate and independent state ground. *See* Richard H. Pildes, *Democracy, Anti-Democracy, and the Canon*, 17 CONSTITUTIONAL COMMENTARY 295, 308 (2000).
59. In his return to Holmes's opinion, Taft wrote: "I concur though I suspect that some of the brethren who are sensitive as to the non-application of the 15th Amendment

THE TAFT COURT

under our decisions to a primary may ask for a little more elaborate statement of what our decision here is confined to. Perhaps not. Certainly I don't ask it. It suits me." (Holmes papers).

60. *Nixon* had throughout been conceived as a case whose outcome would depend on the question of whether a primary was an election for purposes of the Fifteenth Amendment. The Fourteenth Amendment claim in the original petition, see *supra* note 47, was brief and obscure, and seemed to refer to the Privileges and Immunities Clause. The State of Texas did not even discuss the alleged Fourteenth Amendment violation in its brief to the Court. Texas concentrated its argument on the point that a primary was not an election for purposes of the Fifteenth Amendment. Moorfield Storey authored Nixon's brief to the Court. Although he charged in passing that the Texas statute "denies [Nixon] the equal protection of the law guaranteed by the Fourteenth Amendment," Brief of Plaintiff-in-Error, Nixon v. Herndon, No. 117, October Term 1926, at 9, 21, he failed to offer any extended explanation of the allegation. There is a fuller discussion of the Fourteenth Amendment claim in Nixon's Reply Brief, which appears to have been written by Louis Marshall. Reply Brief for Plaintiff-in-Error, Nixon v. Herndon, No. 117, October Term 1926, at 27–34. The Reply Brief does not discuss the question of whether the Equal Protection Clause applies to political, as distinct from civil, rights. It instead asserts: "The vice of this legislation appears on its face. ... If this is not arbitrary classification by race and color; if it does not constitute a complete deprivation of the equal protection of the laws; if it is not an abridgment of privileges and immunities of a citizen of the United States, then it is impossible to conceive of any acts which come within those terms." *Id.* at 32–33. The ultimate language in Holmes's opinion appears to draw on this passage in Marshall's reply brief.

61. *Nixon*, 273 U.S. at 540–41. NAACP secretary James Weldon Johnson regarded *Nixon* "as one of the most far-reaching [decisions] since the Civil War." *Ruling Gratifies Negroes Here*, NEW YORK TIMES (March 8, 1927), at 6. By contrast, Arkansas Senator Thaddeus Caraway "expressed astonishment" at a decision "denying the right of a state to deprive Negroes of the vote." Quoted in GUZMÁN, *supra* note 46, at 78. The *Washington Post* remarked that "The mistake made by Texas was in enacting a law denying to colored citizens the right to vote. Undoubtedly the white men of Texas can organize as many private parties as they please, and may exclude negroes; or the negroes may organize and exclude the whites; but the State of Texas can not give these private actions the force of law." *The Negro's Right to Vote*, WASHINGTON POST (March 8, 1927), at 6. The *Post* believed that the significant political implication of *Nixon* concerned whether it implicitly overruled *Newberry* and empowered the federal government to regulate primaries: "The supremacy of the white man in some parts of the South can be maintained only by denying the vote to negroes. The nation has tacitly consented to the arrangement. If the Senate should extend its jurisdiction over primary campaigns, however, the question of the enforcement of the fourteenth and fifteenth amendment will force itself to the front."

62. What in retrospect we can say with some assurance is that there are two logical possibilities: Either Holmes conceived *Nixon* to involve the political right to vote, in which case he authored an opinion extending equal protection guaranties to political rights without briefing, argument, or dissent, or Holmes silently accepted Texas's argument that a primary was not an election and

implicitly categorized the right to vote in an officially regulated party primary as a civil rather than as a political right. Given McReynolds's concurrence in the outcome, given McReynolds's insistence that primaries were not to be regarded as elections, see *supra* text at note 53, and given McReynolds's opposition to political equality for Blacks, see *supra* Chapter 7, at note 85, the latter seems the most plausible interpretation.

63. LDB to Felix Frankfurter (March 9, 1927), in BRANDEIS-FRANKFURTER CORRESPONDENCE, at 278.
64. Note, *supra* note 43, at 1216.
65. Marshall, *supra* note 43, at 251.
66. Note, *supra* note 43, at 1216.
67. Hine, *supra* note 42, at 374; Note, *supra* note 43, at 1212. The executive committee of the Democratic Party subsequently excluded Blacks from voting. Lawrence Nixon again challenged the Texas white primary, and he was again victorious. See Nixon v. Condon, 286 U.S. 73 (1932); Note, 17 ST. LOUIS LAW REVIEW 155 (1932). On its third attempt, Texas managed to find a way to segregate the Democratic primary that the Court did not regard as involving state action, and Texas was awarded a victory in Grovey v. Townsend, 294 U.S. 45 (1935). It was not until Smith v. Allwright, 321 U.S. 649 (1944), that the Court was able at last to lay the white Democratic Texas primary constitutionally to rest. The story is told in DARLENE CLARK HINE, BLACK VICTORY: THE RISE AND FALL OF THE WHITE PRIMARY IN TEXAS (Columbia: University of Missouri Press 1979), and in Marshall, *supra* note 43.
68. See *supra* Chapter 5, at 163. In later years Holmes came vigorously to disapprove his early abolitionism. See *supra* Chapter 5, at note 6.
69. *Nixon*, 273 U.S. at 541 (emphasis added). It is difficult, if not impossible, to parse the exact logic of *Nixon*. One interpretation of the decision might begin with the premise that the Fifteenth Amendment did not apply to primary elections because they involved civil rather than political rights. See *supra* note 62. It would follow from this premise that the Fourteenth Amendment did apply to primary elections. This meant that the Equal Protection Clause prohibited states from regulating primaries with legislation containing arbitrary classifications. The only plausible purpose for Texas's application of a racial classification to its Democratic primary was to prevent Blacks from influencing the outcome of the general election. But because the Fifteenth Amendment did apply to general elections, any such purpose was unconstitutional. Even if the Fifteenth Amendment did not directly apply to primaries, therefore, it might nevertheless invalidate certain purposes for classifications applied to primaries. Classifications applied to primaries that embodied these purposes would thus be rendered arbitrary and hence unconstitutional under the Fourteenth Amendment.
70. "I have no respect for the passion for equality," Holmes wrote, "which seems to me merely idealizing envy." OWH to Harold Laski (May 12, 1927), in 2 HOLMES-LASKI CORRESPONDENCE, at 942. For a discussion of Holmes and race cases, see Thomas Halper, *Justice Holmes and the Question of Race*, 10 BRITISH JOURNAL OF AMERICAN LEGAL STUDIES 171 (2021). On the basis of a survey of Holmes's votes and decisions in cases dealing with race throughout his tenure on the Court, Halper concludes that "Holmes was genuinely indifferent to the plight of blacks." *Id.* at 195. Halper finds Holmes's record "inarguably appalling." *Id.* at 194.

71. In 1915, *Ruling Case Law* set forth this summary of the relationship between the Equal Protection Clause and racial classifications:

> While the true purpose of the fourteenth amendment was primarily to secure to the negro race equality of civil rights, it was not intended to abolish distinctions based on color, or to enforce social as distinguished from political equality, or a commingling of the two races on terms unsatisfactory to either, and therefore race and color have been recognized as a proper basis for classification for certain purposes, as in the case of laws requiring negroes to be provided with separate accommodations in the vehicles of common carriers and in the public schools, and various other segregation laws.

6 Ruling Case Law § 389 (1915).

72. 275 U.S. 78 (1927). For a description of the historical circumstances of the case, see G. Edward White, *The Lost Episode of Gong Lum v. Rice*, 18 GREEN BAG 2ND 191 (2015).

73. Rice v. Gong, 104 So. 105, 106 (Miss. 1925). The Chinese population in the area had originally been recruited after the Civil War to substitute for formerly slave labor, but Chinese immigrants refused to go into debt as sharecroppers, and they very quickly moved into mercantile positions as grocers to the Black population. R. Milton Winter, *Rosedale Presbyterians and the Mississippi Chinese: Changing Concepts of Equality in an Aristocratic Southern Town*, 78 JOURNAL OF PRESBYTERIAN HISTORY 169 (2000). Successful Chinese merchants were permitted to attend white schools in Rosedale, and as a result Chinese from throughout the region sought to establish residency. At that point "whites became alarmed and sought to exclude the Chinese." *Id.* at 170.

74. ROBERT SETO QUAN, LOTUS AMONG THE MAGNOLIAS: THE MISSISSIPPI CHINESE 46 (Jackson: University Press of Mississippi 1982).

75. *Rice*, 104 So. at 106–7.

76. *Id.* at 110. "Race amalgamation has been frowned on by Southern civilization always, and our people have always been of the opinion that it was better for all races to preserve their purity. However, the segregation laws have been so shaped as to show by their terms that it was the white race that was intended to be separated from the other races. ... The Legislature is not compelled to provide separate schools for each of the colored races, and, unless and until it does provide such schools and provide for segregation of the other races, such races are entitled to have the benefit of the colored public schools. ... If the plaintiff desires, she may attend the colored public schools of her district, or, if she does not so desire, she may go to a private school. ... But plaintiff is not entitled to attend a white public school." *Id.*

77. Sutherland was absent. In Stone's docket book, the case is marked "per cur," suggesting that at one point the Court perhaps thought to issue only a *per curiam* opinion. In the end, however, Taft assumed the duties of authorship.

78. *Gong Lum*, 275 U.S. at 85.

79. *Id.* at 84. It was common knowledge that the white and colored schools were not in fact equal. The white schools in Rosedale, where Martha Lum lived, were "vastly superior." Winter, *supra* note 73, at 170. After losing in the Supreme Court, the Lum family "moved to Elaine, Arkansas" where "Martha could attend white schools." White, *supra* note 72, at 204. During the course of the litigation "Mr. Lum stated ... [that] the school for Negro children was an inferior building, poorly equipped and

The Equal Protection Clause & Race

with an inadequate teaching staff." *Supreme Court Upholds Jim Crow Schools*, PHILADELPHIA TRIBUNE (November 24, 1927), at A1. *See Unfortunate Martha Lum*, HARTFORD COURANT (December 2, 1927), at 8 ("The essential point is ... [that] the facilities offered colored children in Mississippi are not the equal of those provided for white children."). Taft knew full well that separate did not actually mean equal. *See infra* note 80.

80. William Howard Taft, *The Negro Problem in America*, 50 SOUTHERN WORKMAN 10, 11, 13 (1921). Taft spoke eloquently of "the actual discrimination, especially in the Southern States, in the division of the school funds, the poor accommodations for colored people where there was segregation, and the failure to maintain the equality of convenience that the law required." William Howard Taft, *Booker T. Washington: Pathfinder of a Race*, 49 SOUTHERN WORKMAN 247, 254 (1920). Although Taft asserted that "no laws or public regulations should be permitted which deny equality of comfort and service to the Negroes in what all whites share equally," Taft, *The Negro Problem in America, supra*, at 13, he showed little inclination to pursue that issue in *Gong Lum*. Neither did he pursue it as president.
81. 163 U.S. 537 (1896).
82. 175 U.S. 528 (1899).
83. 59 Mass. 198 (1849).
84. *Gong Lum*, 275 U.S. at 86. "The question here," said Taft, "is whether a Chinese citizen of the United States is denied equal protection of the laws when he is classed among the colored races and furnished facilities for education equal to that offered to all, whether white, brown, yellow or black. Were this a new question, it would call for very full argument and consideration." *Id.* at 85–86. *See* Joseph S. Ransmeier, *The Fourteenth Amendment and the "Separate but Equal" Doctrine*, 50 MICHIGAN LAW REVIEW 203, 218–19 (1951).
85. *Gong Lum*, 275 U.S. at 85. "Most of the cases cited arose, it is true, over the establishment of separate schools as between white pupils and black pupils, but we can not think that the question is any different or that any different result can be reached, assuming the cases above cited to be rightly decided, where the issue is as between white pupils and the pupils of the yellow races. The decision is within the discretion of the state in regulating its public schools and does not conflict with the Fourteenth Amendment." *Id.* at 87.
86. White, *supra* note 72, at 203.
87. ADDRESS OF THE PRESIDENT OF THE UNITED STATES AT THE CELEBRATION OF THE SEMICENTENNIAL OF THE FOUNDING OF THE CITY OF BIRMINGHAM, ALABAMA 6 (Washington D.C. 1921).
88. *See, e.g.*, ISABEL WILKERSON, THE WARMTH OF OTHER SONS: THE EPIC STORY OF AMERICA'S GREAT MIGRATION (New York: Random House 2010); NICHOLAS LEMANN, THE PROMISED LAND: THE GREAT BLACK MIGRATION AND HOW IT CHANGED AMERICA (New York: Vintage Books 1992).
89. ADDRESS OF THE PRESIDENT, *supra* note 87, at 6. "The South may well recognize that North and West are likely to continue their drafts upon its colored population, and that if the South wishes to keep its fields producing and its industry still expanding it will have to compete for the services of the colored man. If it will realize its need for him and deal quite fairly with him, the South will be able to keep him in such numbers as your activities make desirable." *Id.* at 11. Harding stressed the impact of "restricted immigration" on reducing

the labor supply and so increasing the dependence of the South on black labor. *Id.* at 10.
90. *Id.* at 7. "Racial amalgamation there can not be. Partnership of the races in developing the highest aims of all humanity there must be if humanity, not only here but everywhere, is to achieve the ends which we have set for it." *Id.* at 8.
91. *Id.* at 9.
92. *Id.* Harding continued: "I would accept that a black man can not be a white man, and that he does not need and should not aspire to be as much like a white man as possible in order to accomplish the best that is possible for him. He should seek to be, and he should be encouraged to be, the best possible black man, and not the best possible imitation of a white man." Harding noted the effects of the World War on black expectations of equal citizenship:

> In another way the World War modified the elements of this problem. Thousands of black men, serving their country just as patriotically as did the white men, were transported overseas and experienced the life of countries where their color aroused less of antagonism than it does here. Many of them aspire to go to Europe to live.
>
> A high-grade colored soldier told me that the war brought his race the first real conception of citizenship – the first full realization that the flag was their flag, to fight for, to be protected by them, and also to protect them.... These things lead one to hope that we shall find an adjustment of the relations between the two races, in which both can enjoy full citizenship, the full measure of usefulness to the country and of opportunity for themselves and in which recognition and reward shall at last be distributed in proportion to individual deserts, regardless of race or color.

Id. at 7.
93. *Id.* at 10. It all comes "back at last to the question of education," Harding remarked. *Id.* With restrictions on immigration, the South would need to cultivate a capable work force, which would necessarily involve Blacks. It behooved the South, therefore, to provide the kind of education "that would fit every man not only to do his particular work as well as possible but to rise to a higher plane if he would deserve it. For that sort of education I have no fears, whether it be given to a black man or a white man." *Id.*
94. For a brilliant dissection of Harding's speech, see W.E.B. Du Bois, *President Harding and Social Equality*, 23 THE CRISIS 53 (1921).
95. ADDRESS OF THE PRESIDENT, *supra* note 87, at 7, 11.
96. The ideal of color-blindness in the political sphere was of course primarily signified by the Fifteenth Amendment.
97. 245 U.S. 60 (1918).
98. 273 U.S. 668 (1927).
99. It is noteworthy that Taft explained a decision like Bailey v. Alabama, 219 U.S. 219 (1911), which struck down an Alabama peonage statute under the Thirteenth Amendment, as enabling "the Negro to enjoy his economic right of free labor, and to enable him, in the competition between labor and capital, to take advantage of the increased demand for his services." Taft, *The Negro Problem in America*, *supra* note 80, at 13–14. We might also place the Taft Court decision in Yu Cong Eng v. Trinidad, 271 U.S. 500 (1926), in the category of protecting economic rights. At issue in *Yu Cong Eng* was the Chinese Booking Act passed by the Philippine legislature in 1926. The Act imposed severe criminal sanctions on

The Equal Protection Clause & Race

merchants who kept their books in any language other than English, Spanish, or a native Filipino dialect. At the time, some 12,000 Chinese merchants operated in the Philippines, a majority of whom could not understand any language other than Chinese. The law would effectively put these Chinese merchants out of business. The statute was challenged under the Due Process Clause and the Equal Protection Clause, both of which were by statute applicable to the Philippines. *Yu Cong Eng*, 271 U.S. at 524. At conference, Holmes and McReynolds voted to uphold the law, but the remaining seven justices voted to overturn it. Taft wrote a unanimous opinion for the Court striking down the statute under both the Due Process Clause and the Equal Protection Clause. His opinion stressed the former rather than the latter. Taft emphasized the law's draconian impact on "extensive and important business long established." *Id.* at 525. He noted that the law could achieve its purpose, which was to facilitate official inspection of merchant books for tax purposes, without prohibiting books kept in Chinese. The Philippine government could, for example, require additional books to be kept in Spanish or English. In support of his conclusion that the law as drafted was unconstitutional, Taft primarily cited due process precedents like Lawton v. Steele, 152 U.S. 133 (1894), Adams v. Tanner, 244 U.S. 590 (1917), Meyer v. Nebraska, 262 U.S. 390 (1923), and Pierce v. Society of Sisters, 268 U.S. 510 (1925). He also mentioned two cases that discussed the Equal Protection Clause – Holden v. Hardy, 169 U.S. 366 (1898), and Truax v. Raich, 239 U.S. 33 (1915) – although in neither instance did Taft cite any discussion in the cases that was specific to the Equal Protection Clause. *Yu Cong Eng* is thus probably best classified as a case in which the Court considered equal protection and due process as virtually interchangeable, as, in the words of *Holden*, "so connected that the authorities upon each are, to a greater or less extent, pertinent to the others." 169 U.S. at 382. It is true that in the last sentence of his opinion Taft casually refers to the fact that the law was obviously intended chiefly to affect the Chinese, "as distinguished from the rest of the community," *Yu Cong Eng*, 271 U.S. at 528, but he makes very little of this fact, not even bothering to cite Yick Wo v. Hopkins, 118 U.S. 356 (1886), or indeed any case at all. Taft's heart was plainly in what we would today characterize as the due process aspects of the case rather than in what we would classify as its equal protection dimensions. His concern was triggered by the law's massively negative impact on economic liberty.

100. GEORGE BROWN TINDALL, THE EMERGENCE OF THE NEW SOUTH 1913–1945, at 165 (Baton Rouge:Louisiana State University Press 1967).
101. William Howard Taft, *Inaugural Address*, 44 CONG. REC. 1, 4 (March 4, 1909). Taft added, however, that the Fifteenth Amendment "ought to be observed," and that he believed that "the tendency of southern legislation to-day is toward the enactment of electoral qualifications which shall square with that amendment." *Id.* Taft took no steps as president to enforce the Fifteenth Amendment, however, and by 1921 Taft was forced to concede that in eleven Southern states whites "organized and, by violence and lawless methods, and by statutes fair on their face but discriminating in operation and enforcement, have destroyed" the operation of the Fifteenth Amendment. "Ever since 1880 the so-called popular government in the South has rested on an illegal basis which is itself demoralizing to all concerned." Taft, *The Negro Problem in America*, *supra* note 80, at 10.

102. Taft, *The Negro Problem in America*, supra note 80, at 13. *See* William Howard Taft, *The Negro in Politics* (January 8, 1921), in VIVIAN, at 523. "In retrospect," said Taft, "we can see that it was a mistake to give the franchise to a mass of densely ignorant people, and that its extension ought to have been made to depend on education or property qualification. It was given with the high purpose of securing to the Negro the means of protecting himself in his newly conferred civil rights; as he used it in the South it was an injury to him and to all concerned and its evil effects continue until to-day." *Id.* Elsewhere Taft referred to the "fruitless and damaging effort to protect the Negro by giving him the suffrage and denying it to his former masters," which he believed "produced a saturnalia and a riot of ignorance and corruption in political power, on the one hand, and lawlessness and cruelty, on the other, making more painful reading in our history than even the internecine struggle of the war itself." Taft, *Booker T. Washington*, supra note 80, at 247.
103. *See* RICHARD R.W. BROOKS & CAROL M. ROSE, SAVING THE NEIGHBORHOOD: RACIALLY RESTRICTIVE COVENANTS, LAW, AND SOCIAL NORMS (Cambridge: Harvard University Press 2013).
104. ADDRESS OF THE PRESIDENT, *supra* note 87, at 6. *See* LOTHROP STODDARD, THE RISING TIDE OF COLOR AGAINST WHITE WORLD-SUPREMACY (New York: Blue Ribbon Books 1920); F.T. Lugard, *The Colour Problem*, 233 EDINBURGH REVIEW 267 (1921).
105. STODDARD, *supra* note 104, at 5. Drawing on "nineteenth-century French thinking on race," Stoddard believed that "the white race divides into three main sub-species – the Nordics, the Alpines, and the Mediterraneans. All three are good stocks, ranking in genetic worth well above the various colored races. However, there seems to be no question that the Nordic is far and away the most valuable type; standing, indeed, at the head of the whole human genus." IAN HANEY LÓPEZ, WHITE BY LAW: THE LEGAL CONSTRUCTION OF RACE 74 (New York: New York University Press 2006). As Madison Grant well expressed it, the Nordics constituted "'The Great Race.'" STODDARD, *supra* note 104, at 162.
106. STODDARD, *supra* note 104, at 166. Lugard, *supra* note 104, at 268:

> We may take it ... that Madison Grant has conclusively shewn that miscegenation between two sub-species of the same race tends to deterioration, and the loss of all that is best in each, while the union of opposite types, such as the Negro or Australoid with the Nordic, rapidly tends to the elimination of the latter, owing to the prepotency of the black race. This is indeed a very serious aspect of the colour problem. It is not a matter of race arrogance, but the exposition of a biological process, by which specialised types are bred out by the Mendelian law.

107. STODDARD, *supra* note 104, at 301.
108. "Civilization of itself means nothing. It is merely an effect, whose cause is the creative urge of superior germ-plasm. Civilization is the body; the race is the soul. Let the soul vanish, and the body moulders into inanimate dust from which it came." *Id.* at 300. So, for example, "unlovely *fin de siècle* phenomena, such as the decay of ideals, rampant materialism, political disruption, social unrest, and the 'decadence' of art and literature," *Id.* at 167, were all caused by incipient racial degeneracy. "Race," said Stoddard, quoting Grant, "is everything." *Id.* at 169.

109. *Id.* at 309.
110. Richard B. Sherman, *The "Teachings at Hampton Institute": Social Equality, Racial Integrity, and the Virginia Public Assemblage Act of 1926*, 95 VIRGINIA MAGAZINE OF HISTORY AND BIOGRAPHY 275, 277 (1987); Mae M. Ngai, *The Architecture of Race in American Immigration Law: A Reexamination of the Immigration Act of 1924*, 86 JOURNAL OF AMERICAN HISTORY 67 (1999); Kenneth M Ludmerer, *Genetics, Eugenics, and the Immigration Restriction Act of 1924*, 46 BULLETIN OF THE HISTORY OF MEDICINE 59 (1972).
111. STODDARD, *supra* note 104, at 259, 266. "Just as we isolate bacterial invasions, and starve out the bacteria by limiting the area and amount of their food-supply, so we can compel an inferior race to remain in its native habitat, where its own multiplication in a limited area will, as with all organisms, eventually limit its numbers and therefore its influence." *Id.* at 259–60. *See* Lugard, *supra* note 104, at 280 (stressing "the vital necessity of maintaining the purity of the white race-type by drastic immigration laws in those home-lands of the white races.").
112. Madison Grant, *Introduction*, in STODDARD, *supra* note 104, at xxxii.
113. STODDARD, *supra* note 104, at 305–06.
114. Thus Democratic Senator Harrison of Mississippi argued that "to encourage the negro, who, in some States, as in my own, exceeds the white population, to strive through every political avenue to be placed upon equality with the whites, is a blow to the white civilization of this country that will take years to combat. If the President's theory is carried to its ultimate conclusion, namely, that the black person, either man or woman, should have full economic and political rights with the white man and white woman, then that means that the black man can strive to become President of the United States, hold a Cabinet position and occupy the highest places of public trust in the nation.... I am against any such theory because I know it is impracticable, unjust and destructive of the best ideals of America. Place the negro upon political and economic equality with the white man or woman and the friction between the races will be aggravated." Quoted in *Praise and Assail Harding Negro Talk*, NEW YORK TIMES (October 28, 1921), at 4. Democratic Senator Heflin of Alabama proclaimed that "There is no escape from the conclusion that absolute political and economic equality between the white man and the negro means the wiping out of all color line in the partnership in business and in the election of negroes to office over white people. Social equality is next door to such a humiliating and disgraceful policy." *Id.* Republican Senator Willis from Ohio, by contrast, proclaimed that "The President's ringing statement in defense of political and economic equality of individual opportunity with recognition of absolute divergence in things social and racial is as courageous as it is true." *Id.*
115. 163 U.S. 537 (1896). *See* McCabe v. Atchison, T. & S.F. R. Co., 235 U.S. 151, 160 (1914) "[I]t is not an infraction of the 14th Amendment for a state to require separate, but equal accommodations for the two races.") (opinion by Hughes, J.).
116. BOOKER T. WASHINGTON, UP FROM SLAVERY: AN AUTOBIOGRAPHY 221–22 (Garden City: Doubleday & Co. 1901).
117. We now know, however, that in actuality Washington exercised a "politics of deception." He privately and discreetly "funded and organized legal challenges to Jim Crow, taking some cases all the way to the United States Supreme Court." Desmond Jagmohan, *Booker T. Washington and the Politics of Deception*, in

AFRICAN AMERICAN POLITICAL THOUGHT: A COLLECTED HISTORY 171 (Melvin L. Rogers & Jack Turner, eds., University of Chicago Press 2021). *See* AUGUST MEIER, NEGRO THOUGHT IN AMERICA 1880–1915, at 110–13 (Ann Arbor: University of Michigan Press 1966). For example, Washington secretly funded and supported the litigation in Giles v. Harris, 189 U.S. 475 (1903). Pildes, *supra* note 58, at 304–5.

118. *U.S. Duty to Help Hampton-Tuskegee Fund, Says Hoover*, WASHINGTON POST (April 19, 1925), at R10. Du Bois wrote that Washington "became during the administrations of Theodore Roosevelt and William Taft, from 1901 to 1912, the political referee in all Federal appointments or action taken with reference to the Negro and in many regarding the white South." W.E.B. Du Bois, *Dusk of Dawn*, in WRITINGS, *supra* note 36, at 606.

119. Taft, *Booker T. Washington*, *supra* note 80. *See Taft as Negro's Friend*, BALTIMORE SUN (March 17, 1908), at 2 ("Taft tonight praised Hampton Institute, Tuskegee and Booker T. Washington, and Booker Washington in turn praised Mr. Taft."). The next year, as president-elect, Taft shared a stage with Washington and remarked that "a race that can produce Booker Washington in a century ought to feel confident that it can do miracles in time." *Negro Is Needed, So Taft Asserts*, CHICAGO DAILY TRIBUNE (February 24, 1909), at 4. At the time, Taft characterized the race issue as a Southern problem. "We have 10,000,000 of negroes in the United States, and of that 10,000,000 I suppose 9,000,000 live in the Southern States." *Mr. Taft Pleads for Negro Schools*, NEW YORK TIMES (February 24, 1909), at 1. "The negro is absolutely essential to the development of the South. His labor the South needs, and the more you instruct that labor the more valuable he becomes to the South." *Id.* Taft believed that the race issue was "one of the greatest questions that has ever presented itself to the American people." *Id. See* JESSE TARBET, WHEN GOOD GOVERNMENT MEANT BIG GOVERNMENT: THE QUEST TO EXPAND FEDERAL POWER, 1913–1933, at 21 (New York: Columbia University Press 2022) ("Taft's nomination at the Republican National Convention and his victory in the November general election were also victories for Booker T. Washington. In his inaugural address, Taft devoted six paragraphs – about 20 percent of his speech – to a discussion of civil rights.").

120. *Taft Talks on Negro Problem*, COURIER-JOURNAL (August 27, 1910), at 1.

121. W.E.B. Du Bois, *The Battle of Washington*, 30 THE CRISIS 114, 115 (1925).

122. W.E.B. Du Bois, *The Souls of Black Folk*, in WRITINGS, *supra* note 36, at 398–99. On the clash between Du Bois and Washington, see DAVID LEVERING LEWIS, W.E.B. DU BOIS: BIOGRAPHY OF A RACE 1868–1919, at 238–342 (New York: Henry Holt & Co.1993). Robert R. Moton, who was for many years the commandant of cadets at Hampton and who later succeeded Washington as the head of Tuskegee, and who was also the only Black trustee at Hampton, thought it "self-evident that the Negro has practically no share in the making or the execution of the laws. He knows when he is segregated that underneath the segregation is the idea that he is inferior and unfit for association with decent people of every other race. . . . Separation, so far as I have been able to observe, has never meant equal treatment or equal accommodations on railroads or steamboats, in restaurants or on street cars, or anywhere else." Robert R. Moton, *The Negro and the South's Industrial Life*, 43 SOUTHERN

The Equal Protection Clause & Race

WORKMAN 411, 415–16 (1914). But the only solution that Moton could put forth – and this exemplified also Taft's and Washington's perspectives – was that the "Southern conscience ought to be aroused to the point of action where the white South will demand absolutely equal accommodations for both races in all places where there is local segregation." *Id.* at 416. As the second principal of Hampton, H.B. Frissell, who was much beloved by Taft, remarked, "Men like Mr. Carnegie and Mr. Taft are impressed with the great advantage which the South has over other parts of the country in having a homogenous body of laborers, all of them speaking the English language and most of them professing the Christian religion. They are also of a peaceable nature, which makes the strikes and labor uprisings of the North well nigh unknown in this part of the country. In order to render these laborers efficient it is only necessary that they become intelligent, and in order that they become law-abiding it is important that they have land and property of their own. ... The white man of the south has a responsibility for his brother in black. 'It is possible,' as Major Moton says, 'for the two to live together as brothers in Christ without being brothers-in-law.'" H. B. Frissell, *Rural Segregation*, 44 SOUTHERN WORKMAN 137–38 (1915). On Taft's admiration for Frissell, see William Howard Taft, *A Man of Poise*, 46 SOUTHERN WORKMAN 582 (1917).

123. Taft, *supra* note 101, at 5. Because Taft wished to encourage a growing "feeling ... among the intelligent, well-to-do, and influential element [of the South] in favor of the industrial education of the negro and the encouragement of the race to make themselves useful members of the community," he proposed to modify Roosevelt's practice of appointing Blacks to official federal positions in the South. "[I]t may well admit of doubt whether, in the case of any race, an appointment of one of their number to a local office in a community in which the race feeling is so widespread and acute as to interfere with the ease and facility with which the local government business can be done by the appointee is of sufficient benefit by way of encouragement to the race to outweigh the recurrence and increase of race feeling which such an appointment is likely to engender. There the Executive, in recognizing the negro race by appointments, must exercise a careful discretion not thereby to do it more harm than good." *Id.* In January 1921, Taft gave this same advice to incoming President Harding. "If he shall be able by his decision to secure Republican parties of strength in the various southern states, even if he disappoints Negro applicants for office in the South, he will greatly help the Negroes of the South, because we can be very sure that Republican white legislatures of the South will be quick to do justice to the negro in the division of school funds and that Republican executives will do all that is possible in the suppression of lynching." William Howard Taft, *The Negro in Politics*, *supra* note 102, at 524–25.

124. William Howard Taft, *Racial Prejudice* (June 2, 1919), in VIVIAN, at 220–21. For a very negative assessment of Taft's views on race, see DAVID W. SOUTHERN, THE PROGRESSIVE ERA AND RACE: REACTION AND REFORM, 1900–1917, at 121–22 (Wheeling: Harlan Davidson, Inc. 2005). Southern quotes a panel of Black ministers who declared, "At no time, since the Negro has been a citizen, has he been so thoroughly ignored as a part and parcel of this great government, as he has since William Howard Taft has been President of the United States." *Id.* at 122. Black Southern Republicans were particularly outraged at Taft's reluctance to

extend patronage to Blacks in the South. *See supra* note 123; Nikolas Bowie & Daphna Renan, *The Separation-of-Powers Counterrevolution*, 131 YALE LAW JOURNAL 2020, 2067 (2022).

125. *Taft Accepts Election*, BOSTON DAILY GLOBE (May 24, 1909), at 2.
126. James E. Gregg, *History and Educational Philosophy*, in DEPARTMENT OF INTERIOR, BUREAU OF EDUCATION, HAMPTON NORMAL AND AGRICULTURAL INSTITUTE: ITS EVOLUTION AND CONTRIBUTION TO EDUCATION AS A FEDERAL LAND-GRANT COLLEGE (Washington D.C.: Government Printing Office 1923), at 5 (Bulletin No. 27).
127. William Howard Taft, *The Influence of Hampton*, in HAMPTON NORMAL AND AGRICULTURAL INSTITUTE, *supra* note 126, at 3. In this respect, Taft was carrying on the tradition of Theodore Roosevelt. In his 1906 annual message to Congress, Roosevelt had remarked that "Of course the best type of education for the colored man, taken as a whole, is such education as is conferred in schools like Hampton and Tuskegee; where the boys and girls, the young men and young women, are trained industrially as well as in the ordinary public school branches. . . . Every graduate of these schools . . . who leads a life so useful and honorable as to win the good will and respect of those whites whose neighbor he or she is, thereby helps the whole colored race as it can be helped in no other way; for next to the negro himself, the man who can do most to help the negro is his white neighbor who lives near him." Theodore Roosevelt, *President's Annual Message*, 41 CONG. REC. 25 (December 4, 1906).
128. William Howard Taft, *The Influence of Hampton*, in HAMPTON NORMAL AND AGRICULTURAL INSTITUTE, *supra* note 126, at 4.
129. William Howard Taft, Address Delivered by Chief Justice William Howard Taft over the Radio on the Evening of March 23rd, 1925, and Broadcasted Through WJZ New York (Taft papers).
130. In 1925, Hampton boasted "an endowment of $8,500,000," which placed it "first among black schools and seventeenth among the 176 American colleges then possessing endowments valued at more than a million dollars." RAYMOND WOLTERS, THE NEW NEGRO ON CAMPUS: BLACK COLLEGE REBELLIONS OF THE 1920S, at 231 (Princeton University Press 1975).
131. *The Trustees' Meeting*, 43 SOUTHERN WORKMAN 366 (1914); *Taft Heads Hampton Board*, NEW YORK TIMES (April 25, 1914), at 24.
132. Howard V. Young, Jr., *William Howard Taft and Hampton Institute*, in STONY THE ROAD: CHAPTERS IN THE HISTORY OF HAMPTON INSTITUTE 146–47 (Charlottesville: University Press of Virginia 1977); *Tuskegee Institute Given Million Dollars*, THE CHICAGO DEFENDER (March 14, 1925), at 1; Sherman, *supra* note 110, at 287.
133. W.E.B. Du Bois, *Hampton*, 15 THE CRISIS 10, 10–11 (1917). In the end Hampton could not maintain the pure focus on vocational training that so entranced Taft. James E. Gregg, who became the third principal of Hampton in 1917 after the death of Frissell, see *New Head for Hampton*, NEW YORK TIMES (December 24, 1917), at 8, began to move Hampton slowly but surely in the direction of a legitimate college education. WOLTERS, *supra* note 130, at 232–34. By 1927, Du Bois was prepared to concede that Hampton has been "compelled to meet more modern educational standards . . . and to establish college courses." W.E. Burghardt Du Bois, *The Hampton Strike*, 125 THE NATION 471, 471 (1927). Hampton was thus "no longer

dealing with docile and half-grown elementary students, regimented to strict military discipline; she had to deal with older college men who were thinking for themselves." *Id.* Hampton had difficulty adjusting to this new reality. Its efforts to impose traditional student discipline on mature students who were more dedicated to the ideals of Du Bois than to those of Washington led to a student strike in fall 1927, which resulted in the Hampton administration in effect firing its entire student body. The story is told in WOLTERS, *supra* note 130, at 230–75. Taft was entirely supportive of the Hampton administration's harsh response. He wrote Gregg that "I have watched as well as I could through the newspapers the account of the strike of your students and the absurd extremes to which they went. I think rather than to yield to them it would be better to close up the Institute for some little time and let them think over the absurdities that they are now guilty of. Considering the advantages that they enjoy over and above their fellows in the matter of a free education, it is difficult to be patient with such an exhibition, and they ought to be taught a lesson that we shall not be bothered again. It is a disposition to ape the absurdities of other institutions – public schools – in some cities where the children are influenced by the wild ideas of their parents in the matter of democratic control of the school by the children. I have no doubt it has given you great concern, but I think you are pursuing the right course." WHT to James E. Gregg (October 16, 1927) (Taft papers).

134. Taft, *Racial Prejudice*, *supra* note 124, at 221–22.
135. *Id.* at 222. "The negroes are migrating to the North because of the demand for labor and the higher prices for labor there," Taft said, "and the South is beginning to realize the value of negro labor and the necessity for treating the negroes with more consideration than they have heretofore – a factor in the situation which makes for the good of the country." WHT to Mrs. Bellamy Storer (December 7, 1923) (Taft papers).
136. The story is well told in Richard B. Sherman, *"The Last Stand": The Fight for Racial Integrity in Virginia in the 1920s*, 54 JOURNAL OF SOUTHERN HISTORY 69, 74 (1988). *See also* J. Douglas Smith, *The Campaign for Racial Purity and the Erosion of Paternalism in Virginia, 1922–1930: "Nominally White, Biologically Mixed, and Legally Negro,"* 68 JOURNAL OF SOUTHERN HISTORY 65 (2002). The resulting eugenicist campaigns were in part responsible for the sterilization laws considered by the Court in Buck v. Bell, 273 U.S. 200, 208 (1927). *See* Sherman, *supra*, at 79–80.
137. John Powell, *Is White America to Become a Negroid Nation*, RICHMOND TIMES DISPATCH (July 22, 1923), at 52. Powell argued that "it would be no kindness to the Negro to fail to preserve the color line. For in the resulting amalgamation that civilization would be destroyed which is his only guarantee of decent and fair treatment." *Id.*
138. Sherman, *supra* note 136, at 78–79; Smith, *supra* note 136, at 65. The act was ultimately held unconstitutional in Loving v. Virginia, 388 U.S. 1 (1967).
139. *Dedication of Ogden Hall*, 48 SOUTHERN WORKMAN 258 (1919).
140. WOLTERS, *supra* note 130, at 231. Du Bois said of Hampton:

> Armstrong, the first Principal, was a kind-hearted philanthropist of fair education and sincere but narrow ideals. He gave his life to the work and made the shibboleth of "industrial" education popular. He himself believed in college training, music and mathematics; but he was trying to emphasize hard steady skilled work for recently freed slaves. Frissell [the second Principal] raised the

> shibboleth to a gospel which attacked college training and discovered a "new" education in the so-called "Hampton Idea." While Armstrong sought tolerance and silent acquiescence from the Southern whites, Frissell sought friendship and offered power. To secure this, he was forced to draw the color line more and more inside the school itself – separation by race in dining rooms, guests' houses, social assemblies, faculty activities – indeed, the thing became so intricate and baffling that it took more time and energy to avoid introducing Colonel Carter to George Jones, than to teach carpentry and farming.

> W.E.B. Du Bois, *Hampton Institute*, 36 THE CRISIS 277, 277 (1929).

141. WOLTERS, *supra* note 130, at 239.
142. James E. Gregg to WHT (September 3, 1925) (Taft papers).
143. The story is told in detail in Sherman, *supra* note 110.
144. *The Integrity of the Anglo-Saxon Race*, NEWPORT NEWS DAILY PRESS (March 15, 1925), at 4.
145. *Id.*
146. James E. Gregg to Walter Scott Copeland (March 17, 1925), in *Teachings at Hampton Institute*, NEWPORT NEWS DAILY PRESS (March 20, 1925), at 4.
147. *Teachings at Hampton Institute*, NEWPORT NEWS DAILY PRESS (March 20, 1925), at 4.
148. *Id.*
149. W.E.B. Du Bois, *Social Equality at Hampton*, 30 THE CRISIS 59–60 (1925). See W.E.B. Du Bois, *The Anglo-Saxon at Bay*, 30 THE CRISIS 10 (1925).
150. James E. Gregg to WHT (September 3, 1925) (Taft papers).
151. *Social Relations in Hampton Institute*, NEWPORT NEWS DAILY PRESS (May 26, 1925), at 4.
152. *The Charge against Hampton*, RICHMOND TIMES DISPATCH (July 14, 1925), at 6.
153. Taft advised Gregg not to "answer the questions at all because of the evident desire of the writer to get into a controversy that will not make for the good of our movement, and were written apparently for the purpose of stirring race prejudice." WHT to James E. Gregg (August 23, 1925) (Taft papers).
154. WHT to James E. Gregg (August 23, 1925) (Taft papers); James E. Gregg to WHT (September 3, 1925) (Taft papers).
155. About the question of social equality, Taft had himself written in 1921:

> The solution is not that the white race and the colored race shall mix socially or that we shall have a large element of mixed blood in our population. It is generally agreed that miscegenation does not make for the good of either race. There is room enough for both races to live well and pursue happiness in this country.... It is not to be expected that in half a century, or indeed in a century, they can catch up with the whites, who have behind them many centuries of civilization. It is not important to consider that. All that it is important to know is that, with the opportunities offered them, they have greatly improved their condition, that the average of intelligence and usefulness among them has been greatly enhanced, that they seek education, and that under the intelligent leadership of their own people they are making headway. It is a mere academic question whether they are as capable of sustaining as high a standard of intelligence and morality as the best of the whites. It is enough to know that they have plainly demonstrated that they can and do make good loyal American citizens, and that they grow better as they go on.

> Taft, *The Negro Problem in America*, *supra* note 80, at 11–12.

156. *Mixed Audiences – Again*, NEWPORT NEWS DAILY PRESS (November 12, 1925), at 4.

The Equal Protection Clause & Race

157. *Demand Law Compelling Separation of Races in Va.*, NEWPORT NEWS DAILY PRESS (November 28, 1925), at 1. Taft wrote Gregg: "Somebody has sent a clipping to me giving an account of a meeting held at Hampton, Virginia, on the 27th of November, at which a resolution was passed attacking the doctrine and teaching of social equality at Hampton, with its resultant tendency toward racial amalgamation. This is calculated to make a man, unless he is a Minister, use profanity. I don't know what the Legislature of Virginia could do, though the ingenuity of fools is sometimes very great. Does this grow out of anything except the wild imagination of a crank?" WHT to James E. Gregg (November 30, 1925) (Taft papers). At the meeting, Major J.B.L. Buck, a member of the Hampton faculty, "admitted that the white and colored people" of Hampton "ate together at the same table on terms of social equality." *The Plain Duty of Hampton Institute*, NEWPORT NEWS DAILY PRESS (November 29, 1925), at 4. "How then," Copeland wrote, "can the officers of the institution expect the white people of this community to feel otherwise than resentful? ... Hampton Institute in large part has lost the good will of the white community."
158. Sherman, *supra* note 110, at 288.
159. Taft, *Racial Prejudice*, *supra* note 124, at 221–22.
160. *The Plain Duty of Hampton Institute*, *supra* note 157.
161. "The leaders of the alumni association reported that a poll of prominent graduates and ex-students from all sections of the country indicated that any attempt to enforce segregation on the campus 'would destroy the great usefulness of the institution to Negro people, [and] would lose the friendship and confidence and goodwill ... which [it] has taken the school fifty years to win.'" WOLTERS, *supra* note 130, at 242.
162. *Negro Singers Quit Women's Concert*, NEW YORK TIMES (May 6, 1925), at 5.
163. *Race Musicians Walk Out at Music Festival*, NEW YORK AMSTERDAM NEWS (May 13, 1925), at 2.
164. *200 Negro Singers Refuse to Appear at Music Festival*, WASHINGTON POST (May 6, 1925), at 1.
165. Adjourned Meeting of the Board of Trustees (March 3, 1926) (Taft papers).
166. Sherman, *supra* note 110, at 290, 293.
167. *The Charge against Hampton*, RICHMOND TIMES DISPATCH (July 14, 1925), at 6.
168. WHT to S.C. Mitchell (March 10, 1926) (Taft papers). *See* James E. Gregg to WHT (March 10, 1926) (Taft papers).
169. Sherman, *supra* note 110, at 293.
170. WHT to B.B. Munford (March 15, 1926) (Taft papers). "I understand that there is a custom in Virginia," Taft said, "that in public assemblies the white people and the colored people sit in different parts of the assembly room .... In Hampton the custom has been regarded as not having application, for the reason that in the public assemblies there held, the students as the larger part of the audience sit in order by themselves, with a mixed faculty, and the remainder of the people present are comparatively few in number, and it would be quite inconvenient to make a division among them. ... It has been generally recognized ... that the presence of white visitors is only an incident in the life of the institution, brought about by the volition of visitors interested in its operation." *Id.*

171. *Id.*
172. James E. Gregg to WHT (March 26, 1926) (Taft papers).
173. WHT to Mrs. Frederick J. Manning (March 15, 1926) (Taft papers). Taft reported to his daughter that "There are a lot of cranks in Virginia who are getting excited on the subject of race intermingling. It is an outgrowth of the Klu [sic] Klux business and of the insanity of race prejudice which has led to the organization of an Anglo Saxon Society. A newspaper man came to Hampton to see a dancing exhibition, which I don't think ever to have been given at Hampton, and found that his wife would have to sit next to negroes." *Id.*
174. Clarence H. Kelsey to WHT (April 26, 1926) (Taft papers). Kelsey, Taft's intimate friend, see *supra* Chapter 26, at 840, was the vice president of the Hampton Board, and Taft's eventual successor as its president.
175. Quoted in Sherman, *supra* note 110, at 296.
176. Minutes of the 57th Annual Meeting of the Board of Trustees of the Hampton Normal and Agricultural Institute (April 22, 1926) (Taft papers).
177. Taft, *The Negro Problem in America*, *supra* note 80, at 12.
178. Du Bois, *supra* note 94, at 54–55.
179. Herbert J. Seligmann, The Negro Faces America 262–63 (New York: Harper & Brothers Publishers 1920).
180. Rice v. Gong, 104 So. 105, 110 (Miss. 1925).
181. Martha Lum's lawyers argued this explicitly to the Court:

> The white, or Caucasian, race ... thinks that in order to protect itself against the infusion of the blood of other races its children must be kept in schools from which other races are excluded. The classification is made for the exclusive benefit of the law-making race. ... If there is danger in the association, it is a danger from which one race is entitled to protection just the same as another. The white race may not legally expose the yellow race to a danger that the dominant race recognizes and, by the same laws, guards itself against. The white race creates for itself a privilege that it denies to other races; exposes the children of other races to risks and dangers to which it would not expose its own children. This is discrimination.

Gong Lum, 275 U.S. at 78–79. See Sora Y. Han, *The Politics of Race in Asian American Jurisprudence*, 11 Asian Pacific American Law Journal 1 (2006).
182. *Gong Lum*, 275 U.S. at 85.
183. HFS to WHT (November 11, 1927) (Stone papers).
184. Many who explicitly embraced the biological roots of race were nevertheless chary of frankly acknowledging the hierarchical structure implied by segregation. As the *Los Angeles Times* said in an editorial praising *Gong Lum*:

> That race segregation in cities is desirable and necessary has long been felt by the thinking men of all the races represented. Segregation plans are not predicated upon the assumption that any races are either superior or inferior, but upon their irreconcilable differences, making them as impracticable of mixture as oil and water. Most States already have laws prohibiting the intermarriage of different races. These laws are based upon recognized biological principles and experience and upon the natural pride which wishes to retain racial integrity.

Race Segregation, Los Angeles Times (November 23, 1927), at A4. *See* Robert Cushman, *Constitutional Law in 1927–1928*, 23 American Political Science Review 78, 96 (1929) ("These decisions do not rest upon any theory of

The Equal Protection Clause & Race

racial inferiority or superiority, but upon the ground that separate schools are necessary and desirable to maintain wholesome social relations between the races.").

185. "*Gong Lum* is an ugly, unfortunate case, arguably worse than *Plessy*. . . . [T]he Court placed its blessing on a scheme whose design cannot be defended as even formally race-neutral. White parents were able (indeed required) to send their children to one of the numerous white-only schools in Mississippi, while students of other races were designated 'colored' and lumped together into an undifferentiated mass at scattered, inferior schools. . . . [T]he system as a whole is inexplicable in terms other than the promotion of white supremacy. . . . [T]he Mississippi Constitution sought to protect a space for white racial purity; racial division was neither an unintended nor an instrumental consequence of the policy, but was in fact its goal." Jamal Greene, *The AntiCanon*, 125 HARVARD LAW REVIEW 379, 431–32 (2011).

186. Taft, *The Negro Problem in America*, *supra* note 80, at 13. "The continued development of the prudential virtues – industry and thrift – must be the basis of continually increasing the future of negroes as citizens of this country," Taft wrote when he was chief justice, "whereby they will obtain, by the necessity of the case, full recognition of their civil rights and the equal protection of the laws which the War Amendments of the Constitution were intended to secure." WHT to Cleveland G. Allen (December 24, 1923) (Taft papers).

187. Plessy v. Ferguson, 163 U.S. 537, 551 (1896).

188. Taft, *Racial Prejudice*, *supra* note 124, at 221.

189. Taft, *The Negro Problem in America*, *supra* note 80, at 13. *See supra* note 186.

190. While chief justice, Taft gave a radio address in which he acknowledged that Blacks "have their rights on paper, but those rights are not always preserved. They are formulated and declared and gradually improvement is being made in their maintenance." But, Taft said, "the negro could best help to maintain his own rights by proving to the community his usefulness as a citizen and his economic power and force and his growth in moral strength and restraint. It is the instilling of these truths in the negro race that is ultimately to secure the members of that race the full enjoyment of their constitutional rights." Taft, *supra* note 129.

191. TINDALL, *supra* note 100, at 160.

192. *New Supreme Justice*, CHATTANOOGA TIMES (November 25, 1922), at 4.

193. David Lawrence, *Sanford Owes Boost to Taft*, DETROIT NEWS (January 25, 1923), at 28.

194. On Holmes, see *supra* Chapter 5, at note 137.

195. As Taft once wrote: "It was part of my purpose, when President, to appoint men to the Federal Bench in the South who would convince the people of that section that the Court was not an alien court, but one in which justice could be found for the citizens of the South and the citizens of the North." WHT to William H. Barrett (October 12, 1922) (Taft papers).

196. Taft, *Racial Prejudice*, *supra* note 124, at 222.

197. *Plessy*, 163 U.S. at 551.

198. 261 U.S. 204 (1923). For good discussions of the case, see LÓPEZ, *supra* note 105, at 56–77; and Rogers M. Smith, *United States v. Bhagat Singh Thind*, in THE WILEY BLACKWELL ENCYCLOPEDIA OF RACE, ETHNICITY AND NATIONALISM (1st ed., Chichester: John Wiley & Sons, 2016).

199. Butler's docket book indicates that the decision was also unanimous in Conference.
200. *Thind*, 261 U.S. at 206–7. Thind seems actually to have been a member of the Sikh religion. Alexander Rocklin, *"A Hindu Is White although He Is Black": Hindu Alterity and the Performativity of Religion and Race between the United States and the Caribbean*, 58 COMPARATIVE STUDIES IN SOCIETY AND HISTORY 181 (2016).
201. Ozawa v. United States, 260 U.S. 178, 189 (1922). On Sutherland's attitudes towards ethnicity, see Victor Jew, *George Sutherland and American Ethnicity: A Pre History to "Thind" and "Ozawa,"* 41 CENTENNIAL REVIEW 553 (1997). In 1906, Roosevelt had vainly appealed for legislation "providing for the naturalization of Japanese who come here intending to become American citizens." Roosevelt, *supra* note 127, at 31.
202. Ozawa v. United States, Brief for Petitioner, at 71.
203. *Ozawa*, 260 U.S. at 182. The Ninth Circuit had certified questions in the case to the Supreme Court in 1917, but "political and diplomatic considerations kept the Supreme Court from answering these questions for five years." M. Browning Carrott, *Prejudice Goes to Court*, CALIFORNIA HISTORY (Summer 1983), at 126. At issue was Japan's ongoing assistance in World War I, as well as its participation in the subsequent Washington Naval Conference. *Id.* On the diplomatic context of *Ozawa*, see Robert C. Yamashita & Peter Park, *The Politics of Race: The Open Door, Ozawa and the Case of the Japanese in America*, 17 JOURNAL OF RADICAL POLITICAL ECONOMICS 135 (1985); Brant T. Lee, *A Racial Trust: The Japanese YWCA and the Alien Land Law*, 7 UCLA ASIAN PACIFIC LAW JOURNAL 1, 11 (2001); and *Japanese Naturalization*, NEW YORK TIMES (November 15, 1922), at 18. Wickersham stayed at Taft's home while he was arguing the case before the Supreme Court. WHT to Horace D. Taft (October 4, 1922) (Taft papers).
204. 1 Stat. 103 (March 26, 1790). Lower courts had reached inconsistent conclusions with respect to the naturalization of Japanese immigrants. The 1910 census listed "more than four hundred naturalized Japanese." Raymond Leslie Buell, *Some Legal Aspects of the Japanese Question*, 17 AMERICAN JOURNAL OF INTERNATIONAL LAW 29, 31 (1923). See Lee, *supra* note 203, at 9; Izumi Hirobe, *Naturalization Cases of Asian Immigrants from* In re Ah Yup *to* United States v. Ozawa *and* United States v. Thind, 2006 JOURNAL OF PACIFIC AND AMERICAN STUDIES 119, 122–23, available at https://repository.dl.itc.u-tokyo.ac.jp/records/37234#.YNQ4pzaA63I. In Yamashita v. Hinkle, 260 U.S. 199 (1922), for example, which was the companion case to *Ozawa*, the Japanese immigrant had been naturalized. At the end of the nineteenth century, no less an authority than John Wigmore had forcefully argued that Japanese were "white" for purposes of the 1790 statute.

> [I]n the scientific use of language and in the light of modern anthropology, the term "white" may properly be applied to the ethnical composition of the Japanese race. ... The connection of the Japanese with the typical "yellow" peoples is so slender, so lacking in vitality, so lost in the preponderance of the "white" element, that the fullest force should be given to the index of color. Having as good a claim to the color "white" as the southern European and the Semitic peoples, having to-day greater affinities with us in culture and progress

The Equal Protection Clause & Race

and facility of social amalgamation than they have with any Asiatic people, isolated as they are to-day from Asia in tendencies and sympathies and isolated as they have been in racial history, it would seem that a liberal interpretation should easily prevail, and that the statute should be construed in the direction indicated by American honor and sympathy.

John H. Wigmore, *American Naturalization and the Japanese*, 28 AMERICAN LAW REVIEW 818, 827 (1894). Despite Wigmore's protestation, the federal government began in 1906 to oppose the naturalization of Japanese aliens. Lee, *supra* note 203, at 10.

205. *Ozawa*, 260 U.S. at 195.
206. *See supra* Chapter 42, at 1415.
207. *Ozawa*, 260 U.S. at 197. "[T]o adopt the color test alone would result in a confused overlapping of races and a gradual merging of one into the other, without any practical line of separation." *Id.*
208. *Id.* The Taft Court was deadly serious about this holding. In May 1925, it held in Toyota v. United States, 268 U.S. 402 (1925), that a Japanese born in Japan could not be naturalized, even though he had from 1913 through 1923 served in the Coast Guard, and even though Congress in 1918 had enacted a statute authorizing "'any alien' serving in the forces of the United States 'during the time this country is engaged in the present war' to file his petition for naturalization without making the preliminary declaration of intention and without proof of five years," and even though Congress in 1919 had expanded this exception to "any person of foreign birth." *Toyota*, 268 U.S. at 409. The Court, in an 8–1 decision, held in an opinion by Butler that because "it has long been the national policy to maintain the distinction of color and race, radical change is not lightly to be deemed to have been intended." *Id.* at 412. The Court thus interpreted the 1918 and 1919 statutes implicitly to incorporate the 1790 racial limitations on naturalization. Taft, for the one and only time during his tenure as chief justice, cast a lone dissent without opinion. Oddly, both Butler's and Stone's docket books indicate that the case had been unanimous in conference.
209. *Ozawa*, 260 U.S. at 198. *Ozawa* received positive press coverage. Exemplary is the comment by the otherwise staid *Philadelphia Ledger*, noting that "anti-Japanese feeling ... is founded in great part in a dread of the competition of the brown and yellow man in trade and industry. It is, however, much deeper than that. It is an instinct toward racial self-defense and a determination that so far as possible America must be maintained as a 'white man's country.'" Quoted in *Japanese Barred from Citizenship*, 76 LITERARY DIGEST 14, 15 (December 2, 1922).
210. *Thind*, 261 U.S. at 210.
211. *Id.* at 209, 213. On Sutherland's attitude toward expertise, see Mark S. Weiner, *Naturalization and Naturalization Law: Some Empirical Observations*, 10 YALE JOURNAL OF LAW AND HUMANITIES 657, 664 (1998).
212. *Thind*, 261 U.S. at 210, 213. *See* Morrison v. California, 291 U.S. 82, 85–86 (1934). It is noteworthy that in this passage Sutherland includes the three "subspecies" of the white race that Madison Grant had identified in MADISON GRANT, THE PASSING OF THE GREAT RACE OR THE RACIAL BASIS OF EUROPEAN HISTORY 17–18 (New York: Charles Scribner's Sons 1916): the Nordic, the Alpine, and the Mediterranean. *See supra* note 105. It seems implausible that these three specific

subspecies of the white race were a matter of "common understanding" among "unscientific men."
213. Sutherland slides over the very complex history by which those of Slavic and Mediterranean descent became accepted as "white persons." MARY C. WATERS, ETHNIC OPTIONS: CHOOSING IDENTITIES IN AMERICA 2 (Berkeley: University of California Press 1990); MATTHEW FRYE JACOBSON, WHITENESS OF A DIFFERENT COLOR: EUROPEAN IMMIGRANTS AND THE ALCHEMY OF COLOR (Cambridge: Harvard University Press 1999); John Tehranian, *Performing Whiteness: Naturalization Litigation and the Construction of Racial Identity in America*, 109 YALE LAW JOURNAL 817, 826 (2000). In 1894, for example, Wigmore could affirm that "The national stocks of northern and of southern Europe differ so decidedly in general color that the latter can be termed 'white,' not in the ordinary sense, but only in contrast with the African negro." Wigmore, *supra* note 204, at 821.
214. *Thind*, 261 U.S. at 215.
215. *Thind* allocates "the power to identify racial difference" to "the racial instincts of the average American." Sherally Munshi, *"You Will See My Family Became So American": Toward a Minor Comparativism*, 63 AMERICAN JOURNAL OF COMPARATIVE LAW 655, 674 (2015).
216. Thind was later naturalized in 1936 in New York, where tensions between South Asians and local white populations was much less intense, which suggests the "importance of local racial dynamics" in the application of federal naturalization law. Vinay Harpalani, *To Be White, Black or Brown? South Asian Americans and the Race-Color Distinction*, 14 WASHINGTON UNIVERSITY GLOBAL STUDIES LAW REVIEW 609, 620 (2015).
217. *Plessy*, 163 U.S. at 551.
218. NGAI, *supra* note 32, at 40.
219. "Before *Thind*, roughly seventy Indians had been able to naturalize; after *Thind*, the Bureau of Naturalization began to strip even those Indians of their citizenship." Munshi, *supra* note 215, at 659.
220. *Hindus Barred From Eligibility for Citizenship*, SACRAMENTO BEE (February 20, 1923), at 2.
221. *Court Bars Hindus from Leaseholds on U.S. Lands*, SAN FRANCISCO CHRONICLE (February 20, 1923), at 1.
222. *Hindus Too Brunette to Vote Here*, 76 LITERARY DIGEST 13 (March 10, 1923).
223. Terrace v. Thompson, 263 U.S. 197 (1923); Porterfield v. Webb, 263 U.S. 225 (1923); Webb v. O'Brien, 263 U.S. 313 (1923); and Frick v. Webb, 263 U.S. 326 (1923). All four of these cases were argued on April 23–24, 1923. In 1925, the Court revisited the question of alien land laws in Cockrill v. California, 268 U.S. 258 (1925). *See* Carrott, *supra* note 203, at 134. *See also* Asakura v. Seattle, 265 U.S. 332 (1924) (holding that a Seattle ordinance forbidding Japanese aliens from becoming pawnbrokers was preempted by a 1911 treaty between the United States and Japan).
224. A week before circulating his draft opinions in *Terrace* and *Porterfield*, both of which were announced on November 12, 1923, Butler sent a note to Van Devanter: "In advance of circulation to the others, I am sending you Nos 28–29, two of the four Jap land cases; and I will appreciate your criticisms – as to substance, form, & everything – before officially circulating. Am at work on the other two & hope to

The Equal Protection Clause & Race

have them ready soon." PB to WVD (November 5, 1923) (Van Devanter papers). *O'Brien* and *Frick* came down a week later, on November 19, 1923.

225. For an historical analysis of Washington's alien land law, see Mark L. Lazarus II, *An Historical Analysis of Alien Land Law: Washington Territory & State 1853–1889*, 12 UNIVERSITY OF PUGET SOUND LAW REVIEW 197 (1989).
226. *Terrace*, 263 U.S. at 215–16.
227. *Id.* at 224 (McReynolds & Brandeis, J.J., dissenting). Butler noted in his docket book that at conference Van Devanter opined: "say cloud on title gives jurisdiction." Sutherland did not participate in the cases. Brandeis later wrote Frankfurter about the cropping contracts at issue in the cases:

> In connection with the Japanese Alien Land Cases, following matter arising incidentally should receive separate appropriate comment –
>
> The Jap. get ½ the crop – only;
>
> The owners get ½ for furnishing, practically, only the land (paying taxes thereon)
>
> I think throughout history you probably could not find such rack-renting as we have made common in America.
>
> The church took 1/10th. (I think even of its {*} lands)
>
> The Attica tenants thought 5 per cent to the landlord was high.

LDB to Felix Frankfurter (November 20, 1923), in BRANDEIS-FRANKFURTER CORRESPONDENCE, at 147–48.

228. *Terrace*, 263 U.S. at 218. "At common law, aliens, though not permitted to take land by operation of law, may take by the act of the parties; but they have no capacity to hold against the State, and the land so taken may be escheated to the State. In the absence of a treaty to the contrary, the State has power to deny to aliens the right to own land within its borders. The provision of the act which limits the privilege of ineligible aliens to acquire real property or any interest therein to that prescribed by treaty is not in conflict with the Fourteenth Amendment." Webb v. O'Brien, 263 U.S. 313, 321–22 (1923). This view of due process is in tension with *Truax*'s conception of Clause as guarantying minimum protections for property rights.
229. *Terrace*, 263 U.S. at 220.
230. Terrace v. Thompson, 274 F. 841. 849 (W.D. Wash. 1921).
231. *Terrace*, 263 U.S. at 220. Butler resolutely refused to interrogate the basis for the federal classification. "Congress is not trammeled, and it may grant or withhold the privilege of naturalization upon any grounds or without any reason, as it sees fit. But it is not to be supposed that its acts defining eligibility are arbitrary or unsupported by reasonable considerations of public policy. The State properly may assume that the considerations upon which Congress made such classification are substantial and reasonable." *Id.*
232. *Id.* at 221. "The allegiance of the farmers to the state directly affects its strength and safety." Webb v. O'Brien, 263 U.S. 313, 324 (1923). Some commentators accepted and expanded this argument: "The purpose of the discrimination is not to be taken as one of color. The discrimination is against those not eligible to become citizens. It is to the disqualification put upon them by Congress and not to the color *per se* that the State objects, and since there is no restriction upon the authority of Congress to legislate as to the eligibility of an alien to become a citizen, he is

remediless. The cases holding that discriminations against negroes are violations of the equal protection clause are not in point. The Fourteenth Amendment made them citizens; nothing has been done to make the Japanese and Malays citizens." Note, 10 VIRGINIA LAW REVIEW 384, 388–89 (1924).

Generalizations about the propensities of aliens formed the basis for the Court's unanimous conclusion in 1927 that the Equal Protection Clause did not invalidate a Cincinnati ordinance prohibiting aliens from running pool and billiard rooms. *See* Ohio *ex rel.* Clarke v. Deckebach, 274 U.S. 392 (1927) (opinion by Stone, J.). Cincinnati defended its ordinance on the ground "that billiard and pool rooms in the city of Cincinnati are meeting places of idle and vicious persons; that they are frequented by lawbreakers and other undesirable persons, and contribute to juvenile delinquency; that numerous crimes and offenses have been committed in them and consequently they require strict police surveillance; that noncitizens as a class are less familiar with the laws and customs of this country than native-born and naturalized citizens; that the maintenance of billiard and pool rooms by them is a menace to society and to the public welfare; and that the ordinance is a reasonable police regulation passed in the interest of and for the benefit of the public." *Id.* at 394. Stone reasoned that the question was whether "the ordinance, in the light of facts admitted or generally assumed, does not preclude the possibility of a rational basis for the legislative judgment and that we have no such knowledge of local conditions as would enable us to say that it is clearly wrong. Some latitude must be allowed for the legislative appraisement of local conditions and for the legislative choice of methods for controlling an apprehended evil. It was competent for the city to make such a choice, not shown to be irrational, by excluding from the conduct of a dubious business an entire class rather than its objectionable members selected by more empirical methods." *Id.* at 397.

233. 263 U.S. 225 (1923).
234. *Porterfield*, 263 U.S. at 233.
235. Thomas Reed Powell, *Alien Land Cases in United States Supreme Court*, 12 CALIFORNIA LAW REVIEW 259, 273 (1924). "Mr. Justice Butler," said Powell, "gives no hint that ineligible aliens are such mal-adroit cultivators of the soil that they are likely to turn it into waste places and in consequence to become charges on public charity," nor does the rationale of allegiance to the nation have "anything to do with the case when those whose un-allegiance or perhaps dis-allegiance is voluntary are left without restraint." *Id.* at 281.
236. Powell also compared the equal protection analysis in *Terrace* with what he called the "fantastic reasoning" of *Truax*:

> One discrimination which the ineligible alien did not see fit to complain of is that between agricultural land and other land. Some ingenious advocate might have urged that an ineligible alien suffered an unconstitutional injury under the equal-protection clause because he was restrained only in respect to agricultural land and not in respect to all land. Such an absurdity would hardly be worth mentioning but for the fact that a similar one has had the august sanction of the Supreme Court. In Truax v. Corrigan Chief Justice Taft lays down that employers are denied the equal protection of the laws by being foreclosed from enjoining picketing employes when they still may pursue that remedy against others.... Chief Justice Taft asserts that equal protection means equal protection against all similarly situated as well as for all similarly situated.... In logic this was no more absurd than it would have been

The Equal Protection Clause & Race

  to grant the ineligible alien relief under the equal-protection clause because he suffers only in respect to agricultural land rather than in respect to all land.

 Powell, *supra* note 235, at 277.

237. *Id.* at 277. As Powell said in a different context, "The opinions in these cases zealously avoided the genuine reasons motivating and possibly justifying such legislation and went on airy lines of loyalty which were made silly by the distinctions in one of the statutes which discriminated against aliens who could not become citizens, however much they desired it, in favor of those who chose not to avail themselves of the opportunities of naturalization open to them. . . . [W]e were asked to believe that the justification for excluding non-eligible aliens when non-declarant eligible aliens are not excluded is that an alien because of alienage is a menace on the land." Thomas Reed Powell, *The Work of the Supreme Court*, 40 POLITICAL SCIENCE QUARTERLY 71, 76 (1925).

238. Charles Wallace Collins, *Will the California Alien Land Law Stand the Test of the Fourteenth Amendment*, 23 YALE LAW JOURNAL 330, 331 (1914); Raymond Leslie Buell, *The Development of Anti-Japanese Agitation in the United States*, 38 POLITICAL SCIENCE QUARTERLY 57 (1923). As president, Taft had even been responsible for pressuring California to back off an early version of the statute at issue in *Porterfield* because the manifestly discriminatory framework of the legislation would have unsettled international negotiations with Japan. Buell, *supra*, at 60; Carrott, *supra* note 203, at 128; Lee, *supra* note 203, at 16–17; Note, *Brakes on Peaceful Penetration*, 37 HARVARD LAW REVIEW 372, 372 (1924).

239. *Taft Interposes in Japanese Case*, NEW YORK TIMES (April 24, 1923), at 13. Webb was California attorney general from 1902 until 1938, when he was replaced by Earl Warren. He was a state-wide leader in seeking anti-Japanese legislation. *Ulysses Webb, 82, California Ex-AG*, NEW YORK TIMES (August 1, 1947), at 17; *Ulysses S. Webb, Fought for Ban on Immigration*, NEW YORK HERALD TRIBUNE (August 1, 1947), at 18. In a prominent 1913 debate about alien land legislation, for example, Webb had famously proclaimed, "Better that we have no Oriental commerce than that 1,000,000 Japanese come to live in San Francisco. Rather let the lands of California be waste than that they be tilled by Orientals. God forbid that the morals of the white race be contaminated by the morals of the Orientals. Better that no Orientals ever cross the ocean than that we have Japanese children in our public schools." *Alien Land Bill Theme of Debate*, SAN FRANCISCO CHRONICLE (May 21, 1913), at 12. *See* MILTON R. KONVITZ, THE ALIEN AND THE ASIATIC IN AMERICAN LAW 159 (Ithaca: Cornell University Press 1946).

240. Webb, of course, immediately and forcefully grasped the implications of these cases. *Japanese Ruling Momentous, Says Attorney-General of California*, SAN FRANCISCO CHRONICLE (November 14, 1922), at 1. Webb had in fact filed an amicus brief in *Ozawa*, arguing:

> With a clashing of races, however, competing with each other for their very existence as in the agricultural development of the Western States, the racial type is of supreme moment. . . .
>
> To say that the white, the yellow and the brown races can not assimilate is but to express a truism which is recognized by everybody with any knowledge on the subject at all. . . .

> There are ... certain fundamental facts in the history of every nation which can not be ignored by far-seeing statesmen. In an agricultural country such as our Western States there can not continue to exist the American farm home life as America has known it if that life is to be placed in competition with the Oriental farmer. One or the other must survive and the inevitable result would be the survival of the Oriental farmer when his method of intensive agricultural development is opposed to that of the American farmer. The American family reared along the lines of American traditions with the father managing the farm, the mother presiding in the home and the children during their younger years attending school, can not compete with the Oriental farm life wherein children and mother join with the father in the actual farm labor, and in addition do not enjoy conditions of life which are demanded by the American standard of living. ...
>
> It is perfectly obvious that the average American man, woman or child if asked the question as to the race of the Japanese would without any hesitation answer that Japanese are yellow, brown, or possibly a mixture of those two races. Any one would be astounded on asking such a question to receive the answer that the Japanese are of the white race. They are popularly referred to over the world as the "little brown men" and such popular appellation bespeaks an understanding of our American people and of the civilized world that the Japanese are not of the white race.

Ozawa v. United States, Brief Filed by the Attorney General of the State of California as Amicus Curiae, at 120–25.
241. Compare Webb's rhetoric in *supra* note 239 with Copeland's rhetoric in *supra* text at note 145.
242. Taft, *supra* note 124, at 222.
243. *See supra* note 240.
244. *Sanford Succumbs to Sudden Attack,* WASHINGTON POST (March 9, 1930), at M1.
245. *Id.* On that very day Van Devanter wrote his good friend District Judge John C. Pollock:

> Today we were shocked by the sudden death of Mr. Justice Sanford. I have thought heretofore that he was not well and that his color was bad: but as he said he was well there was nothing which I could do. He died of uremic poisoning. In all probability his kidneys had not been functioning properly. He was a very kindly man, actuated by the best of motives, and found it difficult to think ill of any one. But he is gone and we shall soon find his place filled with another.

WVD to John C. Pollock (March 8, 1930) (Van Devanter papers).
246. Brandeis thought Parker "a laboring, conscientious judge ... but I hadn't the impression of striking qualities. The slight mention of P. by my brethren at the last conference, did not disclose or indicate that any one of them had been consulted." LDB to Felix Frankfurter (March 26, 1930), in BRANDEIS-FRANKFURTER CORRESPONDENCE, at 419. *See* LDB to Felix Frankfurter (April 1, 1930), in BRANDEIS-FRANKFURTER CORRESPONDENCE, at 419.
247. For a detailed account of the NAACP campaign against Parker, see KENNETH W. GOINGS, "THE NAACP COMES OF AGE": THE DEFEAT OF JUDGE JOHN J. PARKER (Bloomington: Indiana University Press 1990).
248. Quoted in Statement of Walter White, Secretary National Association for the Advancement of Colored People, in Hearing before the Subcommittee of the Senate Committee on the Judiciary (April 5, 1930), 71st Cong. 2nd SESS. 2, at 74.
249. *Id.* at 75.

The Equal Protection Clause & Race

250. Ironically, Parker had cited Harmon v. Tyler, 273 U.S. 668 (1927), to strike down a racially based Richmond zoning ordinance. Richmond v. Deans, 37 F.2d 712 (4th Cir. 1930). Parker explicitly rejected the argument that Village of Euclid v. Ambler Realty Co., 272 U.S. 365 (1926), had overturned Buchanan v. Warley, 245 U.S. 60 (1918). Parker's decision in *Deans* apparently led some Southern senators to question Parker's allegiance to white supremacy. Ron Hirsch Mendlesohn, *Senate Confirmation of Supreme Court Appointments: The Nomination and Rejection of John J. Parker*, 14 HOWARD LAW JOURNAL 105, 126 (1968).
251. R.V. Oulahan, *Senate and the Supreme Court: A New Test*, NEW YORK TIMES (May 11, 1930), at 53.
252. Walter White, *The Negro and the Supreme Court*, 162 HARPER'S MAGAZINE 238, 239 (1931).
253. *Id.* at 238.
254. A.H. Ulm, *Parker Rejection Shows Awakening of Negro Interest*, WASHINGTON POST (May 18, 1930), at M13.
255. PATRICIA SULLIVAN, LIFT EVERY VOICE: THE NAACP AND THE MAKING OF THE CIVIL RIGHTS MOVEMENT 140 (New York: The New Press 2009).
256. There is evidence that by the end of the decade Taft was well aware of the "organized negro vote in the north, a part of which the Democratic party is endeavoring to obtain." Henry M. Ward to WHT (April 7, 1928) (Taft papers). *See supra* Chapter 15, at notes 74 and 80.
257. Ulm, *supra* note 254. *See* Mark Sullivan, *Sullivan Sees Some Political Shadows*, HARTFORD COURANT (June 8, 1930), at E7 ("Several Northern Democratic Senators are now as responsive to the political potentiality of Negro voters as are the Republicans. During the last fifteen years great migrations of Southern Negroes have settled in such Northern cities as New York and Chicago. In these cities the Negro vote is as much appealed to by Democratic leaders as by Republican ones.").
258. *Hoover-Parker Victory Rests with Democrats*, CHRISTIAN SCIENCE MONITOR (April 17, 1930), at 6. *See President Is Firm in Backing Parker in Face of Attacks*, NEW YORK TIMES (April 13, 1930), at 1.
259. *See* Mendlesohn, *supra* note 250, at 138; Oulahan, *supra* note 251; *supra* Chapter 39, at 1247; *supra* Chapter 40, at note 143. Stone had evidently advised Hoover that Parker "might have serious trouble from the labor end & that he ... [ought] to look into the matter thoroughly before acting." LDB to Felix Frankfurter (April 15, 1930), in BRANDEIS-FRANKFURTER CORRESPONDENCE, at 421. Organized labor opposed Parker because in United Mine Workers of America v. Red Jacket Consolidated Coal & Coke Co., 18 F. 839 (4th Cir.), *cert denied sub nom.* Lewis v. Red Jacket Consol. Coal & Coke Co., 275 U.S. 536 (1927), Parker had followed *Hitchman* and enjoined the UMW from organizing mines in which workers had signed yellow-dog contracts. The protection of these contracts bespoke an individualistic understanding of the labor market, and, as William Green opined, "Appointments to the Supreme Court should be made with concern for the economic philosophy of the individuals as well as their legal attainments." Justices needed to understand "the realities of life and work." William Green, *Supreme Court*, 37 AMERICAN FEDERATIONIST 406 (1930). During the battle over Parker, labor insisted that courts recognize the reality that employees required unions in order to maintain the possibility of fair bargaining. The struggle over Parker demonstrated the revived political muscle of organized labor. The Parker nomination allowed labor to serve notice on a shocked Republican administration that

it would no longer tolerate using federal courts as instruments of employer domination based upon the premise of an individualistic labor market. The interests of employees as a group would have to be considered. Only two years after Parker's defeat, Congress would enact the Norris-LaGuardia Act, Pub. L. 72-65, 47 Stat. 70 (March 23, 1932), by a vote of 75–5 in the Senate and 363–13 in the House. The Norris-LaGuardia Act prohibited federal enforcement of the yellow-dog contracts that had aroused such opposition to Parker. *See Holds Validity of Injunction in Doubt*, BALTIMORE SUN (March 24, 1932), at 1. It also strictly limited federal court injunctions in the context of labor disputes, so that a notorious court order like that issued by Parker in *Red Jacket* would no longer be permitted. In reluctantly signing the measure, Hoover said nothing but released a letter from Attorney General William Mitchell saying that the constitutionality of the Act was so controversial that it was "not susceptible of final decision by the executive branch of government" and could "only be set at rest by judicial decision." Laurence M. Benedict, *Injunction Ban Signed*, LOS ANGELES TIMES (March 24, 1932), at 1. "There is little doubt from reading his letter but that the Attorney-General regards the law as clearly unconstitutional and believes that the courts will so rule whenever it is put to a legal test." *Id.* at 2.

260. *The People's Victory*, RALEIGH NEWS AND OBSERVER (April 24, 1930), at 4. The editorial was quoted disapprovingly on the floor of the Senate. 72 CONG. REC. 7949 (April 29, 1930).

261. Mendlesohn, *supra* note 250, at 137.

262. Parker would have his revenge twenty-five years later in the notorious case of Briggs v. Elliott, 132 F. Supp. 776 (E.D.S.C. 1955), when he was a member of a three-judge district court that decided *per curiam* that *Brown* did not hold that the Constitution requires "integration. It merely forbids discrimination. It does not forbid such segregation as occurs as the result of voluntary action." *Id.* at 777. *Briggs* was eventually overruled in Green v. County School Bd., 391 U.S. 430 (1968).

263. Brandeis wrote Frankfurter:

> 2. G.W. Anderson says: "Parker is a victim of the unpopularity of the Supreme Court." The Baltimore case was the last straw. And Taft's death removed the protection afforded by a widely loved personality. Thanks partly to the new C.J., his former allies are much chastened – in manner, at least.
> 3. Directly, Organized Labor has doubtless gained most by the encounter. It has, at least, reasserted itself; should be encouraged to activity & wider assertion in its demand; ought now to get rid of the yellow dog contract; and also otherwise make inroads on "Government by Injunction."
> 4. The Negro also has moved a step forward.
> 5. And, of course, the progressives of both parties.
> 6. Poor H.H. cuts a pitiable figure. It is truly pathetic. And he was hoist by the errors of his guardians....
> 7. Yes, Mitchell's figure is {a} sad one. And he, himself, must be very unhappy.

LDB to Felix Frankfurter (May 8, 1930), in BRANDEIS-FRANKFURTER CORRESPONDENCE, at 424–25.

264. SULLIVAN, *supra* note 255, at 141.

265. GOINGS, *supra* note 247, at 53. Mark Sullivan offered this contemporaneous analysis:

> Of the total of 40 votes cast or paired against Judge Parker, roughly 10 can be accounted for by the opposition to him expressed by leaders of negro organizations....

> In at least ten northern and border states ... negroes cast a sufficiently considerable proportion of the total vote to cause senators to take account of them. In such states the negroes express themselves, or more correctly, are expressed, by leaders who head organized groups of them. These leaders were energetic in opposition to Judge Parker. A senator from such a state undoubtedly had reason to feel that he might be putting his political life in the balance if he should vote to confirm Judge Parker.
>
> The number who voted against Judge Parker because organized labor opposed him perhaps was slightly smaller than the number who voted against him because of the opposition of negro leaders. Here again there are states in which organized labor composes a sufficiently large proportion of the electorate to be taken into account.

Mark Sullivan, *Senate's Desire to Control High Court Revealed as Judge Parker Is Rejected*, ATLANTA CONSTITUTION (May 8, 1930), at 8.

266. Carlisle Bargeron, *Parker Nomination Rejected by Senate in Close Vote, 41–39*, WASHINGTON POST (May 8, 1930), at 1.
267. William H. Hastie, *A Look at the NAACP*, 46 THE CRISIS 263, 263 (September 1939). Heywood Broun wrote that "The fight against the confirmation of Judge Parker for the Supreme Court was one of the most useful incidents which has ever occurred to give the American Negro a consciousness of his voting power. It might almost be said that inadvertently President Hoover did the race a great favor. Solidarity, or rather the lack of it, has been the trouble. Republicans have assumed that they could count on the Negro vote." Heywood Broun, *The Black Voter*, 37 THE CRISIS 369 (November 1930).
268. ADDRESS OF THE PRESIDENT, *supra* note 87, at 9–10.
269. It is no accident that the struggle over Parker was also an inflection point in Black voters abandoning the Republican Party and turning toward Northern Democrats.
270. Holmes made this point most mordantly when he sought to explain to his friend Lewis Einstein why he did not grant Sacco and Vanzetti relief in habeas corpus in 1927. Holmes observed that the only ground for granting a petition for habeas "was the alleged prejudice of the Judge. If justice was what the world is after, this case is not half so bad as those that are more or less familiar in the South. But this world cares more for red than for black." OWH to Lewis Einstein (August 14, 1927), in HOLMES-EINSTEIN CORRESPONDENCE, at 272. *See* OWH to Felix Frankfurter (September 9, 1927) (Holmes papers).
271. United States v. Carolene Products Co., 304 U.S. 144, 152 n.4 (1938).
272. This is certainly the image of minority groups advanced in John Hart Ely's subsequent and influential interpretation of the footnote as policing the pluralist bazaar. *See* JOHN HART ELY, DEMOCRACY AND DISTRUST: A THEORY OF JUDICIAL REVIEW 152–53 (Cambridge: Harvard University Press 1980).

EPILOGUE

Chief Justice Taft Exits the Scene

As the spring of 1929 and the inauguration of Herbert Hoover approached, members of the Taft Court were tired and not well. Van Devanter wrote his sister:

> Mr. Hoover probably will have the selection during his four years term of as many as five members of our Court. The Chief Justice's health is such that he will retire when he can, which will be in 1931. Mr. Justice Holmes will be 88 next month and cannot hope to be with us more than a year or two.[1] Mr. Justice Brandeis is 73 and not in vigorous health, although he probably is not contemplating retirement. Mr. Justice McReynolds will certainly retire when he can, which will be in 1932. He would retire now if he could. Mr. Justice Sutherland is not in good health and will certainly retire when he can which will be in 1932. I will be 70 in April and unless there is a great change for the better in Dollie's condition I shall retire during the year. I am making no public announcement but my mind is becoming pretty well fixed on retirement.[2]

American constitutional law would no doubt have taken a very different turn had Van Devanter's confident predictions proved accurate.

For Taft himself, a decade of overwork was beginning to tell. The slippages of age were becoming ever more apparent. Taft administered the constitutional oath of office to Hoover in March. The new president was required to swear to "preserve, protect and defend the Constitution of the United States." But Taft, attempting to administer the oath from memory, stumbled. Over nationally broadcast radio, he asked Hoover to "preserve, maintain, and defend" the Constitution.

A 13-year-old girl, who had listened to the ceremony over the radio, wrote Taft to say that "the 8th [Grade] History Class of the Walden Junior High would like to know if there was any particular reason" why the chief justice had asked Hoover

Epilogue: Chief Justice Taft Exits the Scene

to "maintain, protect and defend" the Constitution.[3] Taft wrote back a gracious letter that compounded the confusion.

> One cannot speak to the whole United States without having his words closely examined. ... [M]y memory is not always accurate, and one sometimes becomes a little uncertain, so that the variation from "protect" to "maintain" was a departure from the text but not the meaning. It certainly did not prevent the validity of the oath. When I was sworn in as President by Chief Justice Fuller, he made a similar slip, but in those days when there was no radio, it was observed only in the Senate Chamber where I took the oath. This shows how much more carefully one who is exercising a public duty must conduct himself. You are mistaken in your report of what I did say. What I said was "preserve, maintain and protect". What I should have said was "preserve, protect and defend", and you may attribute the variation to the defect of an old man's memory.[4]

The exchange of letters hit the front pages of the papers,[5] and Taft, who erred both in administering the oath and in recounting his administration of the oath, became thoroughly exasperated.[6] It did not auger well for the coming year.

Taft had long appreciated Hoover's executive capacities, although he found Hoover personally opaque and indecipherable.[7] In 1921, he had urged Hoover to enter Harding's Cabinet,[8] and he had early on supported Hoover's presidential aspirations, believing that he "would make an excellent President, although he has not had experience in a good many fields that he would be thrown into were he to come to the Presidency."[9] Taft professed to be "very much impressed by the greatness of the man and by his courage,"[10] and he dictated "a peon [sic] of joy" upon his election.[11]

Once Hoover took office, however, Taft began to have doubts. "I haven't made up my mind about Hoover," Taft wrote his son at the end of March. "Some of his appointments are very queer, and include what seem to me to be very undesirable persons from my knowledge of their past, but I hope I may prove to be wrong. I am very anxious that he should succeed."[12] Hoover was close to Stone, with whom Hoover had served in Coolidge's Cabinet, and, on taking office, Hoover pressed Stone to leave the Court and join the Cabinet as attorney general.[13] Only four days after Hoover's inauguration, Brandeis wrote Frankfurter that "I think the C.J. is not being called upon for advice by H. But Harlan has been; doubtless contributed to the Inaugural; & will be called upon for advice often hereafter."[14]

Taft felt displaced and hurt. He was especially offended by Hoover's insistent efforts to recruit Stone to chair the new National Commission on Law Observance and Enforcement while simultaneously having Stone remain on the Court. Hoover was "most anxious" to appoint Stone to chair the Commission.[15] Taft told his daughter that Hoover "sent for me to lunch with him" to discuss the matter.[16] Taft reported that Hoover wanted to put Stone

> on the Commission and still have him retain his place on the Court, and I told him I did not think it possible. I have suggested that if he needs the Court ... although we would hate to let them go, he could take members of the Court who could

retire. There are two of them at least he could take and who would make very good members. The best man in the United States for the place is Willis Van Devanter. ... Another man who is entitled to retire is Brandeis. I told the President that if he would take Van Devanter as Chairman and put Brandeis on with him, he would lay a basis for a Commission noteworthy in the history of the country and a Commission that would do something. I told him that Stone did not have the qualities and that Stone would not retire, but he did not seem convinced.[17]

In Taft's view, Hoover was "daft in respect to the qualities" of Stone, "because he has known him for a long time, and not being a lawyer has not had full opportunity to understand and gauge his qualities in action."[18] Taft thought that Hoover was "quite indisposed properly to weigh the limitations upon the Court's action."[19] "We are not disposed to give up an active member of the Court and retain him in the Court while he does work in another jurisdiction," Taft wrote his son. "We need all we have, because we can not very well render decisions in a number of cases, and those most important, without a full Court."[20] "Moreover, there was a good deal of grave doubt as to whether a member of our Court ought to be on the Commission and then have to pass on questions arising out of the proposals of the new Code or whatever may be developed."[21]

Taft grew increasingly frustrated with Hoover's importunities. He noted that Hoover "thinks that Stone is keen to get into the work. Stone tells me he is not and wishes to be let alone in the Court."[22] Eventually Taft was forced to call a meeting of the full Court to decide the question. The meeting was held on April 6, 1929, but before Taft could report its outcome to the president, Hoover again wrote Taft "to express my anxiety that you will be able to acquiesce in" the suggestion that Stone be permitted to chair the Commission without retiring from the Court:

> I realize the extra burden it imposes on the Court. ... I also realize the desire of the Court that its members should not, as in the past, head up commissions in public matters. On the other hand, it seems to me that this is so closely affiliated and so vital to the whole of the future of our judicial system that it would not comprise a precedent in your newly established custom.
>
> I have again this week, with the assistance of several of our best members of the Bar, traversed the personnel of the Bench and Bar of the whole country, and I have not received a single suggestion of a man who, in the view of these helpers, can adequately undertake the job with any hope of its successful consummation and the necessary support of its conclusions by the public, except Justice Stone. ...
>
> I now realize that I should not have launched and pledged my administration to this venture. Many of my advisers are strongly recommending that I should abandon the major purpose of this inquiry until some future successor can find himself in position to command the talent necessary to effectually carry it through.[23]

Taft grimly replied to Hoover: "[W]e had a meeting yesterday and confirmed the conclusion which by previous personal conferences with all the

Epilogue: Chief Justice Taft Exits the Scene

members of the Court, I had found to be its judgment. But in view of your letter, I shall ask the members to meet me in the morning ... so that I may submit the question to them again for further consideration."[24] As good as his word, Taft circulated a suggestion for a second meeting to the whole Court, attaching the president's letter.[25]

On April 8, Taft once again wrote to Hoover, saying that there has "been a misunderstanding between us, which a visit from Mr. Justice Stone this morning makes clear." Taft reported that the decision of the initial conference had been "taken upon a full understanding of your position in the matter," and that it was therefore "unnecessary ... to call a second meeting of the Court."[26] To his son Robert, Taft expressed exasperation and some suspicion of Stone's role:

> I have been going through ... a trial with Hoover, in which he has attempted to take from our Court, and still retain him on the Court, his favorite Stone. I opposed it and made some other suggestions which did not suit him, and he hammered at me through Stimson and through the Attorney General. But I submitted the question to the whole Court and they stood by me, every one, so that he had to come down. Stone presented the view that he would go but that he was not in favor of it. I am not quite sure what his attitude is in respect to that issue, because I think when he talked with Hoover, he took a little different view from that which he took when he talked with me. However, it is settled .... I rather think the best man they could get now would be George Wickersham, but I don't think that Hoover's friends like him. I think Hoover himself is disposed rather in that direction, but my impression is that Hoover is so much under the Progressive influence that it would be enough to be against George on account of his relation to me in the past, although I would think that George could put the thing through rather more promptly and effectively than any of them. Indeed I consider him a very much better man than Stone would be, because of George's experience.[27]

A decade later, Stone would write his sons that although Hoover was "very much enamored of the idea that I should head the Commission ... I was equally desirous of not serving in that capacity. ... I tried to convince him that such a service on my part was incompatible with my position as a member of the Supreme Court, both because it was too time-absorbing ... and because I felt that discussions of my action as chairman ... might readily impair my public standing as a member of the Court. I was not at all disposed to hazard such little reputation and public standing as I had by monkeying with the prohibition buzzsaw."[28] Eventually, Hoover accepted Taft's advice and chose as chair of the Commission George Wickersham, who had been Taft's attorney general and who at the time was the law partner of Taft's brother Henry.[29]

Taft's growing disenchantment with Hoover aligned with mounting divisions within the Taft Court itself. In declining Hoover's offer to join the Cabinet, Stone remarked to his former law clerk Milton Handler that "you know the battle of ideas that is going on in the Court and consequently know how difficult it would be for me to abandon the fight for anything else."[30] In the close confines of the Court, the struggle for ideas inevitably turned personal. "Stone is anxious to be Chief Justice to succeed me," Taft wrote his brother in January.³¹ Five months later Taft complained to his son:

> Hoover's attachment for Stone is very great. I had a notice from the Herald-Tribune this week that they had a report that I was going to retire in order that Stone might be appointed Chief Justice.... There has been a good deal of an effort to boost Stone by complimentary articles in places where it would seem as if they had come from the same source. ... I have no doubt that if I were to retire or to die, the President would appoint Stone as the head of the Court. I think in doing so he would make a great mistake, for the reason that Stone is not a leader and would have a great deal of difficulty in massing the Court. ... He definitely has ranged himself with Brandeis and with Holmes in a good many of our constitutional differences.³²

Tensions intensified over the summer. In mid-August, Van Devanter reported to Taft that he had just learned that "Mark Sullivan recently said in a confidential way that he was expecting Mr. Justice Stone to fully reorganize our Court in the course of four or five years. A friend in speaking to the President . . . commented on the possibility of his having several appointments to make to our Court and on the difficulty in getting the right kind of men for such positions. The President answered, 'Quite true, but if I can get Cardozo and some more like him I shall feel satisfied.' The friend is not an admirer of Cardozo but thinks that if he were selected as a successor to Holmes or Brandeis his selection would not be as objectionable as otherwise it might be."³³

Van Devanter confided to Butler that the anonymous friend was none other than William Mitchell, Butler's former law partner, whom Hoover had appointed attorney general on Van Devanter's personal recommendation.³⁴ Taft found Sullivan's comment "most interesting, but the fact that such purposes are revealed is not startling, for it is very easy to prophesy such a conclusion. All we can do is to hope that the old Scotch warning that 'The plans of mice and men "aft gang aglee"' may apply here. I agree that the substitution of Cardozo for others you mention would not be unsatisfactory on the whole, but it is a little hard to prophesy at a distance, and there may be others in the running."³⁵

The next month Butler wrote Taft to say that "My secretary heard [John T.] Suter, the Associated Press man, tell a group in the clerk's office that the President has told the newspaper men that he intends to make Stone Chief Justice. . . . It seems to me unbelievable that Hoover would do that. There is no vacancy and he has no right to assume that there will be one during the present term of Presidency. We all hope and believe that there would be no reason for making the announcement now even if it is the present purpose to promote Stone if & when there is opportunity."³⁶ "The President intends the best," Butler added, "but does not know. Those who have his ear ought to tell him the truth. It may not be too late to prevent bad mistakes."³⁷

Taft replied expressing confidence that the Court's conservative jurisprudence would not be disastrously reversed:

> What you say with reference to Stone's promotion to succeed me, I have no doubt has a good deal of truth in it, and it can hardly be called news. All that we

Epilogue: Chief Justice Taft Exits the Scene

can hope for is continued life of enough of the present membership of Court to prevent disastrous reversals of our present attitude. With Van and Mac and Sutherland and you and Sanford, there will be five to steady the boat, and while the appointment of Stone to be Chief Justice would give a great advantage for the minority, there would be a good deal of difficulty in working through reversals of present positions, even if I either had to retire or were gathered to my fathers, so that we must not give up at once.[38]

Speculation about Taft's replacement was rampant because Taft's health had taken a decided turn for the worse at the conclusion of the 1928 term.[39] As early as January 1929, Taft had expressed the wish "to go back to the old town [of Cincinnati], but if I did the city would be peopled with ghosts for me."[40] In May he wrote his elder half-brother Charles Phelps Taft,[41] to whom he was very close, saying that "I would like to come out to see your old town for two or three days just after the Court adjourns. . . . It will involve some risk on my part, but I have not been out to the old town for such a length of time that I feel as if I ought to go there just to register as a Cincinnatian for a little while."[42]

The long rail journey to and from Cincinnati landed Taft in the hospital. As he wrote Charles, "for some reason or other the trip by rail, to which I am not accustomed, created a cystitis, due to too great alkali secretion."[43] Although Taft longed "for the breezes of Murray Bay"[44] where his summer vacation home was located, he was instead forced "to go to the hospital for a little while, to rid myself of an inflammation in the bladder."[45] It was in Garfield Hospital on June 8 that the Supreme Court Building Commission met with Taft to finalize the submission of bills to Congress for the new Supreme Court building.[46] The hospitalization was widely reported in the press.[47] Eventually Taft left the hospital, but not before being spotted "pushed through Washington's Union Station . . . in a wheelchair, on his way to his summer home in Murray Bay . . . . Exhausted by a trip to Cincinnati and back, fearing recurrence of an old bladder ailment, Mr. Chief Justice had been hospitalized for five days."[48]

Taft's vacation in the summer of 1929 was plagued by persistent illness. On June 19, he wrote Van Devanter that "I have not settled down to normal condition and am still medicating . . . . My visit to Cincinnati was an error in that I forgot the limitation on my activities. I have to keep constantly before me that I can do so much and no more."[49] At the end of June, Taft found himself "in the embrace of a case of obstinate constipation" which was "exasperating" and "discouraging."[50] The upshot was that he experienced "trouble with both my digestion and my waterworks."[51]

To add insult to injury, he suffered yet a third ailment. He "was riding in a rough depot wagon over the links of the Golf Club and was bumped in such a way as to produce something like a local 'trauma', as the physicians say."[52] Taft was referring to a bad case of epididymitis, or "swollen testicles,"[53] which required him to use a wheel chair and then "a large and extensive suspensory bandage."[54] Taft decided to give up his annual birthday luncheon on September 15, with an attendance normally in excess of 100, "and postpone it until next year, hoping that I may live until then and really enjoy it."[55] "Altogether," Taft's personal secretary

Wendell W. Mischler reported to Taft's new law clerk, "he has had a very bad summer, and has been deprived of his vacation."[56]

In September, Brandeis wrote Frankfurter that "I fear the C.J. is less well than he was when the Term closed & that he is suffering still from his post term-Cincinnati excess."[57] The 1929 term was set to begin on October 7, and Taft was still feeling unwell.[58] On October 12, Brandeis reported that Taft "seemed pretty ragged at Conference."[59] Yet Taft, ever the optimist, remarked to his son that "everybody seems to be in good shape. Those who have been threatened with a little illness are happy, especially Justice Holmes. . . . I hope that we shall not be very much disturbed by differences of opinion."[60] And, in truth, on October 19 Brandeis revised his earlier assessment and noted to Frankfurter that "The C. J. seems much better at yesterday's & today's conferences."[61]

Ten days later the world spun off its axis. The bottom fell out of the stock market on Black Tuesday.[62] In the ensuing gloom, Taft wrote his brother "I am working along. I don't get as much work done as I would like to, but I am older and slower and less acute and more confused. However, as long as things continue as they are, and I am able to answer in my place, I must stay on the Court in order to prevent the Bolsheviki from getting control."[63]

Throughout the 1929 term Taft "gradually grew weaker."[64] By December he was openly confessing frustration at his failing capacities. He wrote his daughter that "I am frequently disappointed" in writing opinions, "because my mind moves slowly, and I have great difficulty in arranging my opinions as I would like to. I don't coordinate them as they ought to be coordinated on my first dictation of them, but that is incident I presume to my old age."[65] As Taft felt his intellectual powers wane, he mused about the survival of his own jurisprudential legacy. He wrote his brother, Horace:

> Of course we have a dissenting minority of three in the Court. I think we can hold our six to steady the Court. Brandeis is of course hopeless, as Holmes is, and as Stone is. Should Stone ever have the administration of the Chief Justiceship, he would find himself embarrassed in respect to a good many principles that we have declared as the result of a great many years of careful consideration. However, the only hope we have of keeping a consistent declaration of constitutional law is for us to live as long as we can, because should Hoover's administration continue, I do not doubt there will be an attempted revolution. Indeed I have understood from pretty reliable sources that Hoover has announced his purpose in this regard. I don't think that Hoover knows as much as he thinks he does, and that it is just as well for him to remember the warning in the Scripture about removing landmarks. The truth is that Hoover is a Progressive, just as Stone is, and just as Brandeis is, and just as Holmes is, but should the change take place, they will find themselves in a situation full of difficulties in determining how far they are going, especially when they have made the change and don't realize how far it will carry them.[66]

Horace was disturbed by Taft's evident depression. "Your letter sounds pessimistic, especially in regard to the court work," he wrote. "You and I have

Epilogue: Chief Justice Taft Exits the Scene

got to get used to the fact that we belong to the former generation and that things are sliding along. ... [I]t is a pressure like that of a glacier, which moves along irresistibly."[67] "You speak of my pessimism," Taft replied. "I suppose I must have had reference to the situation in the Court."

> My feeling with respect to the Court is that if a number of us die, Hoover would put in some rather extreme destroyers of the Constitution, but perhaps we are unduly exercised, because of the conservative members of the Court we have six, and two of the remainder are Brandeis and Holmes. Brandeis is seventy-three and Holmes is eighty-nine. He enters his ninetieth year next month. I have no doubt there is persistent hope, especially by the younger crowd of college professors, that in some way or other Holmes will be continued on the Court while the rest of us die off. The good luck of the Court in times past has been marked, and changes of a radical character have not been made all at once. More than that, when men are visited with the responsibility of change, they often find themselves rendered conservative by a fuller realization of the effect of the changes which when they haven't the responsibility they think they would make. I think the Court on the whole stands very well. Of course there are quite a number of extremists and we are likely to hear a good deal more from them than from the other side, and it is the dissenters who make the loudest noise. I think that Hoover is a new man and thinks that everything ought to be new. He will learn a good deal before he gets through. I think he is trying to do the best he can, and we can probably solve everything if we can only live, because delay makes for conservatism.
>
> So far as my personal health is concerned, it is not all that I would like to have it, and I have to go to the doctor a good deal with the view of avoiding bladder trouble. Dr. Hagner is very enthusiastic and quite optimistic, but the facts remain and I have got to give attention to his ministrations.[68]

In Taft's eyes Hoover intended a "revolution" executed by "extreme destroyers of the Constitution." But Taft believed he could outlast Hoover, for "delay makes for conservatism." Taft was certain he could use six votes to suppress "changes of a radical character." He imagined that the precedents he had worked to establish would remain sacred under the scriptural injunction "Remove not the ancient landmark, which thy fathers have set."[69] Yet it is clear that Taft nevertheless felt the ground moving beneath his feet.

Woven throughout his last letters is an oppressive sense of the fragility of mere court decisions in the face of the shifting tectonic attitudes of the public. The Court might be able to sustain the enforcement of the Volstead Act, but it could not by constitutional decision-making restore the sinking intellectual authority of *laissez-faire*. It could run up the flag of normative dualism, but it could not suppress the growing dominion of the federal government, nor could it forever deny the increasing importance of "the group system" in the marketplace. It could magnify the managerial effectiveness of the Court's own operations, but it could not reignite a dwindling faith in property as the keystone of civilization.

Taft's last letters are gloomy and pessimistic. His own sense of diminished personal capacity sharpened his apprehension of changing national attitudes. Even within his own precious Republican Party, the tide of opinion was running against him and toward a future that Taft feared would be embodied in the ruddy and robust figure of Stone. In Taft's eyes, Stone, like Holmes and Brandeis, had no respect for the Constitution, which "is the ark of our covenant and is the basis for the permanence of our Government."[70] Looking ahead, a weary Taft could foresee a long rearguard action to hold the line against a public opinion rapidly moving away from the conservative certitudes of the 1920s.

It was a struggle that Taft never lived to see. The ending for Taft came with merciful swiftness. On December 29, he received a telephone call from his son Robert notifying him that his beloved elder brother Charles "who has been ill now for six months, ... would not live through the day."[71] Taft immediately cancelled his many New Year engagements and made plans to travel to Ohio, taking with him a doctor to attend to his bladder so that "I can avoid what happened the last time I went to Cincinnati."[72] Charles died three days later, and the funeral was set for Thursday, January 2.

Stone wrote Taft a note of condolence. "We are sorry indeed to get the news of your brother's death. ... If you go to Cincinnati do take care of yourself and take a little rest before starting back."[73] Taft replied, "Thank you my dear colleague for your kind note of condolence. My brother Charley was very near to me all my life long and indeed he was the big brother to all of us and to my sister. I could not recount all that he did for us. The wrench that a separation like this makes in a life like ours is hard to bear. ... I hope to be with you next Saturday or next day."[74]

Taft was unstrung by Charles's funeral, as well as by the long rail trips to and from Cincinnati. Unable to sleep, he decided to take "a trip for a real rest of a month."[75] He fixed on Asheville, North Carolina. But after his return to Washington on January 3, his doctors would not let him leave, insisting that he instead be treated for four or five days in a hospital.[76]

Taft wrote Holmes on January 6:

> The strain through which I have been during the past summer and the illness of my brother and his death, has produced a nervousness resulting in insomnia that makes my doctors feel that I ought to separate from the work in the Court and avail myself of the practically seven weeks that intervene between now and the session beginning February 24th. I have consulted as many members of the Court as I could reach, after an urgent recommendation by my doctors that I delay any further work until I come back the 24th of February. ... Mrs. Taft will accompany me, and I shall hope that through you and the brethren it will not cause more inconvenience than the event makes necessary. I am hoping to be able to return again and try and pull my weight in the boat, and meantime ask you to bear with me as you are in the habit of doing as the "youngest" man in the Court.[77]

As he prepared to enter the hospital, Taft dictated the last letter he was ever to add to his long and memorable correspondence. Fittingly enough, it was to Van Devanter. "Nobody will be permitted to call me except you and Misch and Nellie.

Epilogue: Chief Justice Taft Exits the Scene

Those are the Doctor's orders. ... I am permitted to read enough to occupy my vacant mind, which I am sorry to say has been vacant too much of recent times. I expect to see you this afternoon at the hospital, and you have agreed to come. I sincerely hope that four or five or six days at the hospital will put me in a condition for the mountains of North Carolina. Love to Mrs. Van Devanter and yourself. You are a thing of joy forever!"[78]

Taft left for Ashville on January 14,[79] and thereafter his mind descended into a cloud of disorientation. Most likely he suffered a series of debilitating cerebral hemorrhages, for he lost concentration, memory, and focus.[80] Those around him soon came to the conclusion that "he may never resume his duties."[81] By January 27, Taft's wife could write their son Charles that "Your father is very well, but very cloudy – and he walks, old and very slow. ... As he gets stronger he is very anxious to go back to his Court – which is in session now. Helen went to Washington to see the Doctors, and Justices Van Devanter and Butler whom she talked to before – She wants to tell the doctors that they ought to come down and tell your father that he is not able to go on the Court again – and then he ought to resign – but the trouble is that he does not remember anything unless he does it immediately."[82]

Taft's descent into dementia was so rapid that, as Charles Evans Hughes put it, "the fear was entertained that unless he resigned at once he might lapse into a mental condition which would make it impossible for him to resign and in which he might continue for an indefinite period."[83] According to his son, Taft "was greatly worried that President Hoover would appoint Stone instead of Hughes as Chief Justice."[84] To prevent that eventuality, the Taft family turned to Van Devanter and Butler, who stepped forward tactfully to handle the transition.

On February 1, Van Devanter wrote Taft's son Robert:

> You doubtless know that your father has been rightly solicitous that in the event of his resignation he should be succeeded by some one well fitted by nature, education and experience to assume the duties of the Chief Justiceship. At different times he has indicated that he regarded either of two persons – former Justice Charles Evans Hughes and Attorney General Mitchell – as particularly qualified for the place, and he has indicated that another whose name need not be put down here was unhappily without needed qualifications.
>
> After you and other members of the family indicated a belief that your father should resign by way of better conserving his health and prolonging his life the matter of selecting a successor, in the event of resignation, was taken up very quietly and fully canvassed in authoritative quarters. The result has been that a possible successor whom you and others regarded as without needed qualifications has been entirely eliminated and it is now quite certain that one of the two whom your father and others have regarded as particularly qualified will be selected and also that he will accept.[85]

After a lifetime of influencing the selection of Supreme Court personnel, Taft managed for one last time to reach from virtually beyond the grave to affect the choice of yet another justice. We know that Van Devanter and Butler were charged by Attorney General William Mitchell to meet with Hughes in New York on January 28 to determine whether Hughes would accept Hoover's nomination.[86] Van Devanter would afterwards say to his sister that "there was a very narrow escape from the selection of one who would have been most unfortunate."[87]

Once the succession was settled, Van Devanter drafted a letter of resignation for Taft, which was submitted by Robert Taft and accepted by Hoover on February 3.[88] Later that same day, Hoover nominated Hughes to become the next chief justice.[89] Holmes wrote John Henry Wigmore: "I grieve over the enforced retirement of Taft, a most loveable man."[90]

His official life over, Taft made the long journey by train back from Asheville to Washington D.C. As he returned home, "several hundred persons were waiting in the rain on the lawn and sidewalks before the Chief Justice's house."[91] Taft's longtime secretary, Wendell Mischler, described the scene:

> He went to Asheville about three weeks ago for a complete rest there, but he did not improve at all. ... When the Chief Justice arrived here yesterday morning he was in a pitiable condition. I could never describe it to you. He was completely dazed and did not recognize anyone about him, but occasionally he would say "Darling" to Mrs. Taft. It took several very strong men to get him from his drawing room to the platform. He was perfectly helpless and could not walk a step. Then there was a hard time in getting him from the platform down to where there was a wheel chair for him. When he got to his automobile, these camera men, these flash light men, flashed the flash lights right in his face. They were just like so many vultures. They were not content with that but swarmed the lawn of the Chief Justice's house and waited for him there and repeated the same thing. It really was a disgrace, but there seemed no way to avoid it. ... He has been confused for such a long time. ... His going this way is really a tragedy. It is like some tall sturdy oak tottering. ... The physicians informed Mrs. Taft that it is only a question of a little time until he passes on.[92]

"By an unspeakable brutality," Holmes wrote Laski, "there was in one or more of the leading papers a photograph of him caught between the train and his house – with every spark of intelligence gone from his face. He has recurrences when he is more or less himself, but I imagine has no prospect of life, or reason to desire it. Hardening of the arteries and other troubles, I understand. We shall miss him much – but I shall welcome Hughes as an old friend."[93]

The transition from Taft to Hughes was expected to go smoothly and uneventfully. Even so astute an observer as Mark Sullivan predicted that Hughes would be quickly and unanimously confirmed. This was due to "the present and recent high public satisfaction with the Supreme Court."

> The times have been rather frequent when national policies or specific questions under consideration by the Supreme Court gave rise to acute public controversy. ... That there is no such controversy now is itself proof of the universal public contentment with the course of the court. In the 1928 Presidential

Epilogue: Chief Justice Taft Exits the Scene

campaign the Supreme Court never was mentioned even faintly as even the most minor kind of issue. The last occasion when dissatisfaction with any aspect of the court expressed itself in politics was in 1924. ... The movement came to nothing.[94]

The only cloud on the horizon, Sullivan noted scrupulously, was the "purely academic" issue of how to set rates for public utilities.[95]

Of course, this is not what happened. The "academic" question violently exploded, as senators from both parties unexpectedly and vehemently objected to the Taft Court's ratemaking decisions.[96] It was like a thunderstorm materializing out of thin air. Plainly the pressure had been quietly accumulating for some time. Perhaps the burst of anger was unleashed by the changed atmosphere of the stock market crash. But another possible explanation, and one favored by Brandeis, is that Taft, at the moment of his retirement, was "a widely loved personality" whose benevolence offered a kind of "protection" to the Court.[97] "Few public men have evoked such spontaneous and warm affection as has Taft," Frankfurter wrote Holmes. "He is a dear man – a true human."[98] The departure of Taft left the Court exposed to the unmediated consequences of its own decisions.

Taft was a unique chief justice in part because he had the preternatural capacity to charm even his worst enemies. "He now retires as Chief Justice," said the *New York World*, "with the personal good will of the entire nation."[99] Taft was widely respected for his candor and for his honest capacity for hard work.[100] Even Taft's nemesis, Senator Thaddeus H. Caraway of Arkansas,[101] remarked that Taft retired "without an enemy in the world. I love to see his smile. He had the happy ability of making friends of even his political enemies. Nobody in my lifetime is going to be as popular as Mr. Taft."[102] "What drew men to Mr. Taft and causes the nation's sympathy to envelop him now," opined the *Philadelphia Record*, "is not so much regard for his achievements as a sense of his humanness, his wholesomeness, his steady service to the nation through laborious years."[103]

After Taft's terrible and humiliating defeat in the election of 1912, said the *New Republic*, "no one would have ventured to predict that eighteen years later he would stand high in the affection of the American people. It was not so much that Taft had changed during these eighteen years, for he did not. It was partially that the United States reverted, after the war, to a frame of mind of which his own temperament was a better expression than before."[104] During the 1920s, Taft had been, as William Allen White put it, the "high priest of prosperity in the temple of legal stability."[105] Taft's commitment to the property rights he regarded as necessary for economic growth well accorded with the decade's priorities. But Taft's departure coincided both with the end of prosperity and with the sudden opening of new legal possibilities. It marked the genuine end of an era.

In his first years as chief justice, Taft had led the Court's turn to the right. With his eminent good sense, he had also moderated it. As his heart and health gave way, Taft became increasingly captive to the Van Devanter/Butler wing of the Court. After La Follette's decisive defeat in 1924, Taft allowed conservatives on the Court to overplay their hand. The result was an ever-growing if unexpressed anger at the Court's increasingly aggressive conservative agenda. There would eventually be the devil to pay for overreaching decisions like *West* or *Bedford Stone*. Taft would not personally experience the backlash,[106] but both Hughes and Parker would certainly feel its sting.

On February 10, the surviving members of the Taft Court sent Taft an unusual, eloquent, and heartfelt letter of regret, inimitably drafted by Acting Chief Justice Holmes:[107]

> We call you Chief still, for we can not quickly give up the title by which we have known you for all these later years and which you have made so dear to us. We can not let you leave us without trying to tell you how dear you have made it. You came to us from achievements in other fields and with the prestige of the illustrious place that you lately had held, and you showed in a new form your voluminous capacity for work and for getting work done, your humor that smoothed the rough places, your golden heart that has brought you love from every side, and, most of all, from your brethren whose tasks you have made happy and light. We grieve at your illness, but your spirit has given life an impulse that will aide whether you are with us or are away.[108]

It is unlikely that Taft ever read the letter, for by this time he had sunk into a peaceful oblivion. Van Devanter wrote a friend that "Taft's illness has been serious for about four weeks and has brought much sadness to me. He has arteriosclerosis and about four weeks ago it extended to the brain. Gradually his mind has given away.... Now he is very much beclouded, seldom recognizes any one and is practically unconscious of his surroundings. But happily he does not suffer and is not worried."[109]

Taft died quietly at home at 5:15 pm on Saturday, March 8, 1930. He was only 73 years old,[110] but he had, in Van Devanter's words, "strained the bow so much that it could not come back."[111] It is fair to say that Taft had worked harder than any chief justice in history. He literally worked himself to death. By remarkable coincidence, Sanford collapsed and died at noon on that very same day, which just happened also to be Holmes's eighty-ninth birthday.

The following Monday, four justices – Hughes, McReynolds, Butler, and Stone – were in Knoxville, Tennessee, to attend Sanford's funeral.[112] The four remaining justices – Holmes, Van Devanter, Brandeis, and Sutherland – convened a session of the Court, "but only for the purpose of immediately adjourning out of respect to their former chief magistrate."[113]

> The great patriarch of human liberty, Justice Oliver Wendell Holmes, of whose eighty-ninth birthday [on] Saturday death made such a mockery, headed the sorrow-laden quartet. There was the customary barking announcement of the court crier as they appeared in their black robes from across the corridor that separates the court from the justice's robing room, but that was the only resemblance to the usual openings of the court. Justice Holmes, bent more than usual, it seemed, walked past the chair in which Justice Sanford had been want to sit, now heavily draped, and took a seat in that occupied by Mr. Taft before he resigned.[114]

Epilogue: Chief Justice Taft Exits the Scene

The *New York Times* reported that "Only a few spectators and attorneys were in the room, and the sadness in the faces of the jurists was reflected in the gloom and silence in the chamber."[115] Holmes then stood up and spoke:

> On Saturday last, just as we were expecting him at a conference of the justices, we were informed that our brother, Justice Sanford, had become unconscious pending a slight operation. Five minutes later we received word that he was dead. . . .
>
> Afterward came news that the late Chief Justice had found relief from his hopeless illness in death.
>
> Such events must be accepted in silent awe.[116]

The Taft Court had well and truly ended. There was a moment of silent awe, and then all hell would break loose. But that is a story for another volume.

* * *

At the end of March, the usually placid and unemotional Van Devanter wrote a close friend, "I find myself missing [Taft] constantly."[117] But in this Van Devanter was increasingly alone. With Taft gone, conservatives on the Court were left without the cover of that immense goodwill which Taft effortlessly exuded. Within a decade the jurisprudence of the Taft Court, which had accurately reflected the ambivalences and uncertainties of the 1920s, would be utterly effaced. It would soon descend into an obscurity so deep that most law students cannot now name more than ten Taft Court decisions.

The achievements and personality of Taft himself would also be lost. Few now remember that Taft had forever altered the nature of the chief justiceship, the Supreme Court, or the federal judiciary. Few now recall his efforts at judicial reform or the construction of the contemporary Supreme Court Building. With the exception of *Myers* and possibly *Carroll*, few now can call to mind the judicial landmarks he thought he had established.

We tend to remember justices according to their words and thoughts. Holmes, who could express in living sentences a deep and austere account of the nature of law, will live in the American imagination, as will Brandeis, who could articulate an inspiring vision of the relationship between law and American democracy. But in this regard Taft was unfortunate. His actions were monumental, but his words and thoughts were ultimately prosaic. In his commitment to prosperity and the rule of law, he exemplified, but did not transcend, the best common sense of his era. Taft may have lived a most lucky life, but in historical time his fate has been cruel. He changed so much, but he himself has been lost to memory.

THE TAFT COURT

Notes

1. Fanny Holmes, Holmes's wife, would die on April 30, 1929. Taft offered this account to his son:

> Mrs. Justice Holmes died on Tuesday night. She had been dying for some days. She had suffered three falls since September and then had one that broke her hip. It occurred at night when she was alone with the Justice, and he not having anybody within call had to lift her on to the bed and could not get a doctor until the next morning. She then went through that dreadful treatment that they have to give in order to try to enable the limb to knit by putting it in a plaster cast, but it usually results fatally .... They say she was probably ninety. Mrs. Holmes has been a protector of Justice Holmes and has attended to everything connected with his living. He has a niece, a Mrs. Clark, who came to me on Sunday last and told me that Mrs. Holmes was dying, but that the doctor, who is my doctor, had not communicated to Justice Holmes what the impending result would be. Dr. Claytor was afraid that it might shock the Justice and that he would save him this. But Van Devanter and I sent for the doctor and told him that Holmes was a man who wanted to know the facts, and therefore that he ought to tell him. He did so, and Mrs. Holmes died on Tuesday night. I really had to take charge of the funeral with Mrs. Clark. I went down to see her and met the Judge, and he did everything that I suggested, so that we had Dr. Pierce and a harp for music. It was a beautiful day, and we went out to Arlington where by virtue of his war record Justice Holmes is entitled to lie with his wife. He has the most beautiful site in Arlington.... There is a great big beautiful tree on a large knoll, and I could not but feel envious that your mother and I did not have such a place.

WHT to Charles P. Taft 2nd (May 5, 1929) (Taft papers). Van Devanter wrote his sister that Fanny "was a bright woman, very plain and well informed, but without any religious belief. The Justice is like her in the last particular. They have no children. We were somewhat concerned about the funeral service, but the Justice has concluded to have one out of regard for the usual custom. The funeral service is to be at the house and is to be conducted by a Unitarian minister." WVD to Mrs. John W. Kelley (May 2, 1929) (Van Devanter papers).

Taft confided to his son Robert that Holmes "seemed very grateful to me for relieving him." WHT to Robert A. Taft (May 5, 1929) (Taft papers). Holmes "will feel lonely," Taft wrote his brother. "He will probably develop a good deal of activity for a time in Court work, but he is so old that he has no intimate friends, and Mrs. Holmes and he were people unto themselves, and it is in certain aspects quite pitiable." WHT to Horace D. Taft (May 1, 1929) (Taft papers). Taft nevertheless concluded that "It is a great mistake to suppose that he proposes to surrender because of her death. I went down to the house and ran into him the first day after her death. One of the first things he told me was that he did not propose to give up – that the matter would go right on. I suppose there are a good many who are counting on his retirement. If so, they miss their guess. He proposes to remain in the harness as long as the harness will hold him. He seems to have a great deal of reserve force. He wrote an opinion and sent it to me the day she died, and I don't know but I shall give him another one before the month ends." WHT to Robert A. Taft (May 5, 1929) (Taft papers).

Six days after Fanny's death, Holmes wrote Taft: "You must let me repeat once more – that your tender thoughtfulness and care in my trouble went to my heart and moved me deeply. They come from a beautiful nature. They can have come from nothing else. Affectionately yours." OWH to WHT (May 6, 1929) (Taft papers).

Epilogue: Chief Justice Taft Exits the Scene

Eleven days after Fanny's death, Brandeis wrote Frankfurter: "I saw O.W.H. a week ago today. He took the bait – telephoned me himself Wednesday asking me to come to see him & read me his piece – which is fine. Yesterday we had a Conference. I asked the C.J. to give him some opinions to write, one each week. Instead he gave OWH 3, with a promise on the donee's part not to write more than one a week. He is in fine form again, working as of old." LDB to Felix Frankfurter (May 11, 1929), in BRANDEIS-FRANKFURTER CORRESPONDENCE, at 372.

It is notable, however, that the next month Holmes wrote the Viscount Kentaro Kaneko: "I think I shall be ready to follow her when my turn comes. My work is done – even if I should live and write decisions for a year or two longer. I don't lose my interest in my work or in life, but I regard what may be left as a mere appendix. It doesn't matter whether it is longer or shorter, although I still enjoy it in a way – with half of me gone." OWH to Kentaro Kaneko (June 27, 1929) (Holmes papers).

2. WVD to Mrs. John W. Lacey (February 12, 1929) (Van Devanter papers). Dollie was Van Devanter's wife, who had been ill.
3. Helen Terwilliger to WHT (March 5, 1929) (Taft papers).
4. WHT to Helen Terwilliger (March 8, 1929) (Taft papers).
5. *Taft, Told of Mistake by New York Schoolgirl, Admits He Recited Oath Wrong to Hoover*, NEW YORK TIMES (March 14, 1929), at 1.
6. *See* WHT to Mrs. Frederick J. Manning (March 17, 1929) (Taft papers):

> I have been for eight or ten days subject to correspondence and editorial comment on a verbal mistake made by me, not only in my administration of the oath to the President, but in my correspondence in respect of it. The importance that even the Associated Press will give to such an incident, especially if a little girl appears in it, is a useful and significant comment on the difference between real importance in the news and that which makes for gossip in the newspapers. I was exasperated and impatient at it because there was no need of my writing the letter to the little girl. I made it personal, but she is probably not old enough, or at least her mother is not sensitive enough, to treat it as something not to be published. It has led to solemn newspaper articles, and I hope after a while will be transmitted to the pigeon hole, marked "Highly unimportant". But one can not tell.

The newspapers even sought to have Helen Terwilliger personally interview Taft. WHT to Robert A. Taft (March 17, 1929) (Taft papers). The best and most complete account of the events may be found in WVD to A.C. Campbell (March 18, 1929) (Van Devanter papers). Van Devanter noted that "the matter has got on the nerves of the Chief Justice and has been annoying him quite a little. The truth is that when he wrote the little girl he did so hastily because he was busy. There really was no manifestation of old age in either instance. He was embarrassed when he came to administer the oath and failed to read the paper which he had in his hand. And in writing the girl he did so too hastily, and therefore carelessly."

7. In 1925, Taft observed to his brother:

> I do not often see Hoover, and I find him not particularly suggestive and not interesting, unless you find a subject in which you are interested and in which he is, and then he can tell you a great deal more about it than you ever knew. He is a curious man. He has the reputation of being anxious to absorb credit in matters in which he takes part. I presume he has a good opinion of what he does in a particular enterprise where he shares it with others, but I don't know that he exaggerates his proper share. He is not communicative, and he has a capacity for

cutting off inquiry if he does not wish to be inquired of. But I think he is doing good work, and I think he has some clear ideas as to how he is going to do it. He and I are on very good terms because of his friendship for Bob. Bob's loyalty to him he knows, and he knows Bob's capacity, too. That always gave me a good idea of his judgment, which is natural.

WHT to Horace D. Taft (October 11, 1925) (Taft papers).
8. "I see that Hoover has been asked to enter the Cabinet. I think he was quite out of the notion of going into the Cabinet and he must have told some people that he would not enter such a Cabinet.... I telegraphed him yesterday morning urging him to accept. It will strengthen the Cabinet much. With him in it, the Cabinet will be a strong one." WHT to Helen Herron Taft (February 24, 1921) (Taft papers).
9. WHT to Mrs. Frederick J. Manning (April 1, 1928) (Taft papers).
10. WHT to Charles P. Taft 2nd (November 3, 1928) (Taft papers). Taft considered Hoover "one of our greatest men," "one of the strongest men I have known in public life." WHT to Horace D. Taft (October 31, 1928) (Taft papers).
11. WHT to C.S. Jobes (November 7, 1929) (Taft papers).
12. WHT to Charles P. Taft 2nd (March 31, 1929) (Taft papers). As early as January Taft had written his son Robert that "My experience with Hoover makes me think that he is a good deal of a dreamer in respect to matters of which he knows nothing, like the judicial machinery of our government. It is a great comfort to me to feel that neither you nor I ask any favors from him. I have tried to give him the benefit of the best information I have, but he is evently [sic] not at all impressed." WHT to Robert A. Taft (January 20, 1929) (Taft papers).
13. WVD to Mrs. John W. Lacey (February 12, 1929) (Van Devanter papers). Stone declined. "I would doubtless get lots of fun out of a Cabinet position," he said. "But I couldn't have the fun without abandoning responsibilities which I feel rest on me where I now am." HFS to Luther E. Smith (February 12, 1929) (Stone papers). According to Taft, Stone was "a little bit afraid to leave the Court and run the risk incident to his not getting back again." WHT to Horace D. Taft (January 31, 1929) (Taft papers). Stone did consent, however, to join Hoover's "Medicine Ball Cabinet." *Justice Stone Tests Medicine Ball Cabinet*, NEW YORK TIMES (April 12, 1929), at 21.
14. LDB to Felix Frankfurter (March 8, 1929), in BRANDEIS-FRANKFURTER CORRESPONDENCE, at 364.
15. WHT to Charles P. Taft 2nd (March 17, 1929) (Taft papers).
16. WHT to Mrs. Frederick J. Manning (March. 17, 1929) (Taft papers).
17. WHT to Robert A. Taft (March 17, 1929) (Taft papers).
18. *Id.*
19. WHT to Charles P. Taft 2nd (March 17, 1929) (Taft papers).
20. WHT to Charles P. Taft 2nd (March 31, 1929) (Taft papers).
21. WHT to Samuel H. Fisher (May 2, 1929) (Taft papers). It is quite striking to note the difference between this observation and Taft's early relative indifference to the possibility of conflicts of interests arising from his own law reform work. *See supra* Chapter 15, at 513.
22. WHT to Robert A. Taft (March 31, 1929) (Taft papers).
23. Herbert Hoover to WHT (April 7, 1929) (Taft papers).
24. WHT to Herbert Hoover (April 7, 1929) (Taft papers).
25. WHT to the Court (April 7, 1929) (Van Devanter papers).
26. WHT to Herbert Hoover (April 8, 1929) (Taft papers).

Epilogue: Chief Justice Taft Exits the Scene

27. WHT to Robert A. Taft (April 7, 1929) (Taft papers).
28. HFS to My Sons (November 3, 1939) (Stone papers).
29. *See A Commission with a Herculean Task*, 101 LITERARY DIGEST 5 (June 1, 1929).
30. HFS to Milton Handler (February 19, 1929) (Stone papers). *See* HFS to Sterling Carr (February 12, 1929) (Stone papers). A year later, Stone wrote frankly to Frankfurter, "I am bound to say that I feel a good deal of concern over some of our recent decisions." HFS to Felix Frankfurter (January 16, 1930) (Stone papers).
31. WHT to Horace D. Taft (January 31, 1929) (Taft papers).
32. WHT to Charles P. Taft 2nd (May 12, 1929) (Taft papers).
33. WVD to WHT (August 13, 1929) (Van Devanter papers).
34. WVD to PB (August 14, 1929) (Van Devanter papers); WVD to Mrs. John W. Lacey (February 12, 1929) (Van Devanter papers).
35. WHT to WVD (August 17, 1929) (Van Devanter papers).
36. PB to WHT (September 10, 1929) (Taft papers). Butler continued: "However there has been enough of publicity in reference to Stone's elevation – when taken in connection with the President's known desire to have him for Attorney General, Secretary of State and head of the Law Enforcement Commission, to indicate that there is an understanding between them and a purpose – even with indecent haste – to reorganize the Court for the accomplishment of some purpose."
37. *Id.* Butler reported the same news to Van Devanter, adding, "It is certain, I think, that the Chief Justice has not indicated a purpose to resign and the assumption that his death is imminent is not warranted; and, in any event would be in such bad taste that it ought not to be indulged. Even if it is the President's present purpose to promote Stone in case of a vacancy, there is no reason now to announce it. ... Already there has been enough of publicity in respect of Stone & the Chief Justiceship to warrant the giving of the President the truth and those who have his ear ought to tell him – the sooner & oftener the better. It may not be too late. Hoover wants to do the best, but he doesn't know or it may be impossible to get him to understand what a mistake it would be to carry out his present purpose. But every effort should be made. I have a letter from the Chief. He knows what Stone is at." PB to WVD (September 10, 1929) (Van Devanter papers). Van Devanter replied, "I note what you say about another matter of special interest to us and I agree with you that the time has come when it should be given real attention. In the last letter from the Chief he ... wrote rather pointedly about one subject in which we are interested and I think he is fairly alive to what is going on." WVD to PB (September 16, 1929) (Van Devanter papers). For an example of Van Devanter criticizing Stone's legal acumen, see WVD to PB (August 26, 1929) (Van Devanter papers).
38. WHT to PB (September 14, 1929) (Taft papers). A visitor to Taft at Murray Bay, Fred Starek, the former head of the War Finance Corporation, wrote Taft two weeks later to say that he had spent time "with Senator Root at Clinton. One of the things we discussed was the aspiration of a certain Associate Justice to which allusion was made in the conversation you and I had during our stroll down the village street. Needless to assure you, our talk was confidential. The Senator was deeply interested in the situation and is of the conviction that the gentleman in question is seriously lacking in the proper qualifications. I am sure he will co-operate earnestly in preventing a mistake in this connection. I shall go into detail when I see you." Fred Starek to WHT (September 25, 1929) (Taft papers).

THE TAFT COURT

39. At the end of the term, Taft decided that he would no longer hire as law clerks recently graduated law students, as did Brandeis, Stone, and Holmes. Instead he hired "a young man from the Clerk's office named Robertson. He is a good deal of an expert and has written a book on Supreme Court practice. My colleagues insisted that I ought to have him relieve me from a good deal of the executive work with which he is very familiar." WHT to Mrs. Frederick J. Manning (June 2, 1929) (Taft papers). *See* LDB to Felix Frankfurter (October 13, 1929), in BRANDEIS-FRANKFURTER CORRESPONDENCE, at 394–95 ("The C.J. has abandoned the practice of taking as law clerk a Yale graduate. Instead, he has taken as permanent Robertson, former Ass't Clerk. The man who wrote the book on L{ower}. C{ourt}. Jurisdiction. In view of the C.J.'s health, this is fortunate & should greatly facilitate his work, on certioraris, statements of jurisdiction & otherwise.").
40. WHT to Stephen H. Wilder (January 28, 1929) (Taft papers). In this letter Taft quotes – apparently from an imperfect memory – lines that James Russell Lowell had written on his sixty-eighth birthday:

> As life runs on, the roads grow strange
> With faces new, and near the end
> The Milestones into headstones change
> Neath every one a friend.

41. Charles was the editor of the *Cincinnati Times Star* and owned both the Philadelphia Phillies and the Chicago Cubs.
42. WHT to Charles P. Taft (May 5, 1929) (Taft papers). Taft worried to his younger brother Horace "whether I risk too much or not in planning to ... visit Cincinnati and Annie and Charley. ... I am hoping that it will not result in anything untoward. The doctor thinks it is all right." WHT to Horace D. Taft (May 27, 1929) (Taft papers). The next day he mused that "I am afraid I am facing a hot trip to Cincinnati, and I almost feel like giving it up." WHT to Horace D. Taft (May 28, 1929) (Taft papers).
43. WHT to Charles P. Taft (June 7, 1929) (Taft papers).
44. WHT to Theodore E. Burton (June 1, 1929) (Taft papers).
45. WHT to Charles P. Taft 2nd (June 7, 1929) (Taft papers).
46. *See supra* Chapter 17, at 562.
47. *See, e.g., Chief Justice Taft Goes to Hospital for Treatment*, NEW YORK TIMES (June 8, 1929), at 1; *Taft Is in Hospital; Illness Not Serious*, WASHINGTON POST (June 8, 1929), at 1; *Taft Victim of Illness*, LOS ANGELES TIMES (June 8, 1929), at 1. The *Washington Post* editorialized that "the public is anxious and somewhat alarmed over Mr. Taft's condition and will not feel reassured until he leaves the hospital. ... Every one in Washington is a personal friend and neighbor of Chief Justice Taft. His early recovery and continued robust health are prayed for by all." *Mr. Taft's Illness*, WASHINGTON POST (June 9, 1929), at S1.
48. *Chief Justice William Howard Taft*, 13 TIME MAGAZINE 54 (June 24, 1929).
49. WHT to WVD (June 19, 1929) (Van Devanter papers). *See* WHT to PB (July 3, 1929) (Taft papers); WHT to Clarence H. Kelsey (September 22, 1929) (Taft papers) ("I came through last year by the 3d of June in what I thought was excellent condition. I was unwise enough to go to Cincinnati to see my brother Charley, when it would have been very much better to come to Murray Bay and then settle down here.").
50. WHT to Horace D. Taft (June 25, 1929) (Taft papers). *See* WHT to WVD (July 4, 1929) (Van Devanter papers); WHT to OWH (July 4, 1929) (Holmes papers).

Epilogue: Chief Justice Taft Exits the Scene

51. WHT to Clarence H. Kelsey (July 16, 1929) (Taft papers). Taft believed that "I have really been sick ever since I left Cincinnati." WHT to Miss Maria Herron (July 3, 1929) (Taft papers).
52. WHT to George D. Seymour (August 20, 1929) (Taft papers). *See* WHT to OWH (August 26, 1929) (Taft papers).
53. WHT to Horace D. Taft (August 25, 1929) (Taft papers); WHT to Horace D. Taft (September 6, 1929) (Taft papers).
54. WHT to Francis R. Hagner (September 4, 1929) (Taft papers). Taft reported to a friend that "I have had three illnesses this summer, and ... while I enjoyed part of the summer, there is a good deal of it that I can not say I rejoice in.... If it were not that I have had such a glorious good luck in most of my life, I would feel impatient at the recurrence three times this summer of bad periods." WHT to George W. Burton (August 27, 1929) (Taft papers). *See* WHT to JCM (August 23, 1929) (Taft papers).
55. WHT to OWH (August 31, 1929) (Taft papers).
56. Wendell W. Mischler to Reynolds Robertson (September 6, 1929) (Taft papers). Van Devanter was especially concerned. "I am deeply interested in your getting back your vigor and I have an abiding confidence that you can accomplish it." WVD to WHT (July 29, 1929) (Van Devanter papers). Van Devanter's letter concludes, "with love to you and yours."
57. LDB to Felix Frankfurter (September 6, 1929), in BRANDEIS-FRANKFURTER CORRESPONDENCE, at 384.
58. Which of course did not prevent the press from reporting that Taft, "who started his vacation last spring in a wheel chair, seemed greatly improved by several months of rest." *Supreme Court Gets 259 Pleas as Fall Term Opens*, BALTIMORE SUN (October 8, 1929), at 2. *See Chief Justice Taft Returns to Capital Improved in Health*, BALTIMORE SUN (October 2, 1929), at 9.
59. *See* LDB to Felix Frankfurter (October 13, 1929), in BRANDEIS-FRANKFURTER CORRESPONDENCE, at 395.
60. WHT to Charles P. Taft 2nd (October 13, 1929) (Taft papers).
61. *See* LDB to Felix Frankfurter (October 19, 1929), in BRANDEIS-FRANKFURTER CORRESPONDENCE, at 396.
62. Taft wrote his son that "I was amused at your statement that now is the time to buy. There seem to be a good many of that view, so that you may find lots of people running the same way." WHT to Charles P. Taft 2nd (November 3, 1929) (Taft papers). Later that week, Taft again wrote his son: "I am afraid that we haven't gotten out of the panic, from what I hear. Stone, my colleague, has been over in New York, and he says that they tell him that there is a good deal of uncertainty and fear in Wall Street. It may be that we shall have to have some reductions in prices, so don't go too far in your purchases." WHT to Charles P. Taft 2nd (November 7, 1929) (Taft papers).
63. WHT to Horace D. Taft (November 14, 1929) (Taft papers). Contrast this passage with a nearly simultaneous description of the Court in an article in the *New York Times*:

> Dignified, aloof, alert, and at the same time a little weary, these nine robed men give forth a sense of power and wisdom.... Position, authority, tradition, a concept in the minds of men, have welded them into an abstraction made visible. They are justice incarnate. They know it, and so do the spectators. And the spectators like it. In a day when cathedrals are little more than examples of architecture, when Legislatures, State and national, hold little inspiration for

1513

any one who can read, the Supreme Court is a great comfort to the imagination. Here at least it is still possible to feel the majesty of the law.

Mildred Adams, *In the Supreme Court Law Is Majesty*, NEW YORK TIMES MAGAZINE (November 10, 1929), at 10.

64. *Taft Will Take Rest*, LOS ANGELES TIMES (January 7, 1930), at 1.
65. WHT to Mrs. Frederick J. Manning (December 16, 1929) (Taft papers).
66. WHT to Horace D. Taft (December 1, 1929) (Taft papers). At about this time Brandeis was writing Frankfurter: "No one on our Court thinks of retiring or dying, but Harlan wisely thinks it's time to ponder over possible men for the Court. We lost in Edwin B. Parker one of the best possibilities. Whom besides Cardozo, whom Harlan is keen for, would you suggest?" LDB to Felix Frankfurter (December 5, 1929), in BRANDEIS-FRANKFURTER CORRESPONDENCE, at 402. Brandeis's observations about possible retirements should be contrasted to Van Devanter's speculations, *supra* text at note 2. It might be that retirement came to seem less attractive as conservatives on the Court grew increasingly alarmed at Hoover. *See, e.g., supra* text at note 33.
67. Horace D. Taft to WHT (December 2, 1929) (Taft papers). Horace referenced a positive write-up of Holmes in the *New York Times – Justice Holmes, Champion of the Common Man*, NEW YORK TIMES BOOK REVIEW (December 1, 1929), at 4. "Holmes will be confirmed in his frivolous interpretation by such flattering comments as were made in the New York Times last Sunday in an article which you probably saw."

> Of course the old man enjoys popularity, as we all do, and his interpretation regardless of the limitations of the text of the constitution is popular. However, as you say, it is up to you to live as long as you can.
> As for Hoover, I think he is doing some remarkably good things, but I should suppose his ignorance of the constitutional law and the effect of certain interpretations would be as great as possible. To start by ignoring the language of the constitution and think that we can stop where we please is, to use Webster's phrase, as though a man should take the leap at Niagara and say that he would stop half way down. But cheer up. The worst is yet to come.

68. WHT to Horace D. Taft (December 8, 1929) (Taft papers). Horace replied, "As for the Court, you must try to be philosophical. Things seem to come around in the end." Horace D. Taft to WHT (December 12, 1929) (Taft papers).
69. Proverbs 22:28.
70. WHT to C.G. Taylor (November 23, 1927) (Taft papers).
71. WHT to PB (December 30, 1929) (Taft papers).
72. WHT to Charles P. Taft 2nd (December 30, 1929) (Taft papers).
73. HFS to WHT (January 1, 1930) (Taft papers).
74. WHT to HFS (n.d.) (Stone papers).
75. WHT to Charles D. Hilles (January 5, 1930) (Taft papers).
76. WHT to Horace D. Taft (January 6, 1930) (Taft papers). *See Illness Keeps Taft from Supreme Court; Chief Justice Will Recuperate in South*, NEW YORK TIMES (January 7, 1930), at 1 ("The Chief Justice complained of feeling ill upon his return to Washington Friday from Cincinnati [January 3], where he had gone to attend the funeral of his brother, and has suffered from extreme nervousness and insomnia. His condition caused worry to his associates, and he was counseled not to attempt to attend today's session of the court. Associate Justice Holmes, who is 88 years old, presided today, and will continue to do so until Mr. Taft returns.").

Epilogue: Chief Justice Taft Exits the Scene

77. WHT to OWH (January 6, 1930) (Taft papers). Brandeis reports that Holmes presided magnificently over the court during the interregnum between Taft's departure and Hughes's confirmation. "O.W.H. is indeed 'to the manor born,'" Brandeis wrote Frankfurter. "He is presiding with great firmness, alertness and joy. A marked rejuvenescence has been effected; and he is definitely without worry in those unaccustomed duties incident to his new office. It is several years since we have had so good a C.J." LDB to Felix Frankfurter (January 9, 1930), in BRANDEIS-FRANKFURTER CORRESPONDENCE, at 405. Two days later, Brandeis noted that "O.W.H. presided beautifully & calmly at today's conference. Stone says it was the best conference he has attended since coming onto the Court. I have begged H. not to write an opinion tomorrow & he half assented & I guess will refrain." LDB to Felix Frankfurter (January 11, 1930), *id.* at 406. Five days later Brandeis wrote that "We have very good days with O.W.H. presiding." LDB to Felix Frankfurter (January 16, 1930), *id.* at 406. The following week Brandeis commented that "O.W.H. continues to handle the C.J. duties well. But he said yesterday that he will be glad to have the C.J. resume sway." LDB to Felix Frankfurter (January 23, 1930), *id.* at 407.
78. WHT to WVD (January 7, 1930) (Taft papers). On this letter being the last written by Taft, see WVD to John C. Knox (March 11, 1930) (Van Devanter papers) ("His secretary tells me that I was the recipient of his last letter."). Mischler wrote Taft's brother Horace on January 11 that "The Chief Justice does not have a single letter brought to his attention, nor does he see anyone except Dr. Hagner and Justice Van Devanter." Wendell W. Mischler to Horace D. Taft (January 11, 1930) (Taft papers).
79. WVD to John C. Knox (January 14, 1930) (Van Devanter papers) ("Mr. Chief Justice leaves this evening for Asheville, North Carolina, for a well earned and needed rest."); *Chief Justice Taft on Way to Asheville*, NEW YORK TIMES (January 15, 1930), at 25 ("The Chief Justice walked to the train with an easy stride through the long concourse at the station. He did not seem to tire. He was in a cheerful mood."). On January 16, Van Devanter wrote a long, discreet letter to Horace. "I saw the Chief shortly before he started to the train. He was then looking better than at any time since his return from Cincinnati and he was in excellent spirits. ... The Chief has been carrying a heavy load recently and he was much affected by the illness of his brother, Charles P. ... I am very anxious that those about him shall not be misled by the improvement and give their consent to a premature return. Not improbably the chief will, when he begins to feel stronger, feel inclined to think of returning. He should be dissuaded from this. ... My belief is that with care, proper surroundings and an absence from real work and worry he may have several years of real happiness before him. But, after hearing all the doctors have to say, I tremble lest he may get back to work and suffer an impairment which would be impossible of repairment and difficult to bear." WVD to Horace D. Taft (January 16, 1930) (Van Devanter papers).
80. *See* Mrs. Frederick J. Manning to Robert A. Taft (January 25, 1930) (Taft papers). In this letter, Taft's daughter Helen refers to the matter of the resignation as not yet "settled."
81. WVD to Frank B. Kellogg (January 22, 1930) (Van Devanter papers). *See* WVD to Henry W. Taft (January 22, 1930) (Van Devanter papers).
82. Helen Herron Taft to Charles P. Taft 2nd (January 27, 1930) (Taft papers).
83. CHARLES EVANS HUGHES, THE AUTOBIOGRAPHICAL NOTES OF CHARLES EVANS HUGHES 291 (David J. Danelski & Joseph S. Tulchin, eds., Cambridge: Harvard University Press 1973).

84. Charles P. Taft, *My Father the Chief Justice*, 2 YEARBOOK OF SUPREME COURT HISTORICAL SOCIETY 5, 10 (1977). Hoover would argue to Hughes "that Taft would more readily resign if he knew that Hughes would succeed him." Merlo J. Pusey, *The Nomination of Charles Evans Hughes as Chief Justice*, 7 YEARBOOK OF SUPREME COURT HISTORICAL SOCIETY 95, 96 (1982).
85. WVD to Robert A. Taft (February 1, 1930) (Van Devanter papers). *See* WVD to Dennis T. Flynn (February 3, 1930) (Van Devanter papers).
86. Pusey, *supra* note 84, at 98; Elizabeth Hughes Gossett, *My Father the Chief Justice*, 1 YEARBOOK OF SUPREME COURT HISTORICAL SOCIETY 5, 12 (1976).
87. WVD to Mrs. John W. Lacey (March 6, 1930) (Van Devanter papers). From the little that can be discerned from his correspondence, Stone did not take the rejection well. When his former law clerk Milton Handler wrote to express sadness at Taft's resignation and disappointment at the president's nomination of Hughes instead of Stone, Stone could only bring himself ungraciously to reply: "It is well for us to remember though that one's capacity for useful work bears very little relation to high dignity that may be showered upon him. You know, being Chief Justice is a good deal like being the Dean of the Law School – he is obliged to do many things that the janitor will not. I do not think the post enlarges the occupant's capacity to do fine judicial work; it may diminish it. So I shall be contentedly sawing wood at the old stand, as usual." HFS to Milton Handler (February 5, 1930) (Stone papers). When Yale Law Professor and Librarian Frederick C. Hicks wrote Stone to say that he was "astonished and disappointed" in Hoover's nomination, Stone replied: "I am too familiar with the history of this country and the Court to have any illusions about appointments to high office. There are so many contending forces which control the matter that one who goes regularly about his business, without permitting himself or his friends to urge his claims, may well be passed by." HFS to Frederick C. Hicks (February 5, 1930) (Stone papers).
88. Hoover replied to Taft: "I was deeply pained at receiving your letter of resignation today. For some time I have been aware of the shock you received to your health and have been fearful lest this event should occur. In accepting your resignation I would like to add my personal appreciation of the long and distinguished service of a great American to his country." Herbert Hoover to WHT (February 3, 1930) (Department of Justice File Group #348).
89. On February 4, the normally restrained Hughes wrote Taft:

> I can not tell you how distressed I was at the news of your illness and that it seemed to be necessary for you to retire from the office that you have filled with such great distinction. The tributes that you so richly deserve and will so abundantly receive will demonstrate once more what a strong hold you have upon the affections of the people. Never has a Chief Justice had such a warm place in their hearts.

Charles Evans Hughes to WHT (February 4, 1930) (Taft papers).
90. OWH to John Henry Wigmore (February 5, 1930) (Holmes papers). That same day Holmes wrote Judge J.C. Hutcheson, Jr., "All quiet along the Potomac tonight – so far as I am concerned. As you know we have had a shock in the illness and resignation of the Chief Justice but our selfish anxiety is relieved by the appointment of his successor. So far as I am concerned one personal friend succeeds another. But I am very sorry at what seems the rather sudden turn

Epilogue: Chief Justice Taft Exits the Scene

taken by Taft's illness. He is just naturally loved by everyone – I shall be glad to be relieved from the worries and annoyances of being the presiding officer, as next month I shall be 89." OWH to J.C. Hutcheson, Jr. (February 5, 1930) (Holmes papers).
91. *Taft Is Very Ill; Carried from Train*, NEW YORK TIMES (February 5, 1930), at 2.
92. Wendell W. Mischler to Charles D. Hilles (February 5, 1930) (Taft papers); Wendell W. Mischler to Horace D. Taft (February 4, 1930) (Taft papers).
93. OWH to Harold Laski (February 14, 1930), in 2 HOLMES-LASKI CORRESPONDENCE, at 1224. On February 6, Mischler noted that Taft is "in a very weakened condition, and he hardly recognizes anyone. He just faintly recognized the President yesterday for a moment or two. It is a very tragic ending. ... The doctors say he can not last long." Wendell W. Mischler to John V. Farwell (February 6, 1930) (Taft papers).
94. Mark Sullivan, *Public Esteem for Court Called Aid to Hughes*, NEW YORK HERALD TRIBUNE (February 6, 1930), at 9.
95. *Id.* The *New York Times* agreed. "It is rather striking," it said, "that in contrast with the situation when Mr. Hughes served as an Associate Justice there are now no outstanding cases of national importance before the Supreme Court as he returns to it as its presiding officer. This is an unusual state of affairs. ... Thanks to the administrative ability of Chief Justice Taft, the congestion of the court's docket has been relieved and its business is in good shape." Richard V. Oulahan, *Supreme Court on the Eve of Changes*, NEW YORK TIMES (February 9, 1930), at 10.
96. *See supra* Chapter 27, at 891–94.
97. LDB to Felix Frankfurter (May 8, 1930), in BRANDEIS-FRANKFURTER CORRESPONDENCE, at 424.
98. Felix Frankfurter to OWH (March 3, 1930), in HOLMES-FRANKFURTER CORRESPONDENCE, at 249.
99. Quoted in *Press of Nation Praises Service of Taft as Chief Justice*, NEW YORK HERALD TRIBUNE (February 4, 1930), at 13.
100. "The man's outstanding characteristic," said the *Minneapolis Journal*, "is his amazing intellectual integrity. His refusal to compromise with his own conscience, his unwillingness to trim sail to fit prevailing political breezes, his scorn of popularity paid for with peace of mind." Quoted in *Press of Nation Praises Service of Taft as Chief Justice, supra* note 99, at 13.
101. *See, e.g., supra* Chapter 15, at 511.
102. Quoted in *Senators Pay Tribute to Taft, Favor Hughes*, NEW YORK HERALD TRIBUNE (February 4, 1930), at 13.
103. *Chief Justice Taft's Retirement*, PHILADELPHIA RECORD (February 4, 1930), at 6. The *Baltimore Sun*, which had throughout vigorously opposed Taft's jurisprudence and politics, editorialized:

> The resignation of William Howard Taft ... marks the close of a public career notable for its breadth and length of service. In its accomplishments it has been a spotty career, its triumphs lying largely in the field of skillful administration. Its transcendent quality, however, has been the lovable good humor with which it has been carried forward.
>
> No one has ever talked with Chief Justice Taft, even to leave thoroughly persuaded that his ideas are those of a century long past, without feeling that there is a lovable and kindly man.

Chief Justice Taft, BALTIMORE SUN (February 4, 1930), at 14.
104. 62 NEW REPUBLIC 112 (1930). As chief justice, the editorial continued, the nation was able "to appraise at their true value his good humor, utter honesty and indefatigable devotion to his tasks." *Id*.
105. WILLIAM ALLEN WHITE, A PURITAN IN BABYLON: THE STORY OF CALVIN COOLIDGE 351 (New York: MacMillan Co. 1938).
106. "It can be said of William Howard Taft," reported the *New Republic*, "that at the moment when he leaves the Supreme Court his reputation with the American people is undoubtedly higher than ever before.... [B]y his modesty, geniality and unflagging energy in his work, he has rehabilitated himself to an extent which no one would have ventured to predict eighteen years ago. If he has not been among the wisest and most profound members of the Court in interpreting legal principles to accord with changing conditions, neither has he been the rigidly inflexible." *The Week*, 61 NEW REPUBLIC 310 (1930).
107. OWH to Nina Gray (February 12, 1930) (Holmes papers) ("Last Saturday the judges thought a letter should be written to C. Justice Taft. I had to write it.").
108. JOURNAL OF THE SUPREME COURT OF THE UNITED STATES 169 (February 24, 1930).
109. WVD to Clarence D. Clark (March 1, 1930) (Van Devanter papers).
110. *Ex-President Taft Dies at Capital*, NEW YORK TIMES (March 9, 1930), at 1.
111. WVD to Dennis T. Flynn (February 3, 1930) (Van Devanter papers).
112. *Justice Sanford to Be Buried Today*, NEW YORK TIMES (March 10, 1930), at 5.
113. *Taft to be Laid to Rest Today in Arlington Cemetery*, WASHINGTON POST (March 11, 1930), at 2.
114. *Id*.
115. *"Silent Awe" Rules High Court Session*, NEW YORK TIMES (March 11, 1930), at 8.
116. *Id*.
117. WVD to Dennis T. Flynn (March 31, 1930) (Van Devanter papers).

Index

ABA. *See* American Bar Association (ABA)
Acheson, Dean
  Brandeis and, 212–13, 295–96, 329, 365
  Clarke and, 48–49
  on *Coronado I*, 1338
  Harding and, 681
  Holmes and, 192, 195
  McReynolds and, 273, 285, 290
  Van Devanter and, 231
Acquiescence. *See* "Norm of acquiescence"
Act of 1876, 402, 414
Act of December 23 1914, 490
Act of June 5, 1920, 996–97
Act of October 3, 1913, 460–61
Act of September 6, 1916, 600, 609
Act of September 14, 1922,
  generally, 454–55, 461, 462, 509
  Article III branch of government and, 451–53
  Conference of Senior Circuit Court Judges and, 451–53
  Judiciary Act of 1925 compared, 484–85
  new judgeships, creation of, 536–37
  new role of chief justice and, 452–53
  Norris and, 503–4
  prohibition and, 450, 982–84
  Taft and, 451–53, 463–64, 503–5, 544, 564
Adair v. United States (1908), 1230–31, 1245
Adams, John, 447
Adams, John Quincy, 168
Adamson Act, 774, 806, 1248–49, 1273–74, 1298–99
Addams, Jane, 1249–50, 1262, 1380, 1389
Addyston Pipe & Steel Co.; United States v. (1923), 1122
Adkins v. Children's Hospital of the District of Columbia (1923)
  appellate court decision, 777–78
  arbitrariness of statute and, 761, 762
  Borah on, 766, 789–91
  Brandeis in, 760, 764
  brief of appellees, 769–70
  Butler in, 756
  Coolidge and, 766
  Corwin on, 767
  dissenting opinions
    Holmes, 764–65, 775, 783
    Taft, 764, 765–66, 775, 783
  district court proceedings, 846–47
  Due Process Clause and, 755, 756, 772–73
  economic policy and, 834–35
  factual background, 755–56
  Fifth Amendment and, 755
  Frankfurter as counsel in, 756, 759, 760, 764, 773–74, 839
  freedom of contract and, 755, 756, 761, 762–63, 765, 778
  Gompers on, 777
  health regulation, statute as, 757, 759, 766, 772–73
  Holmes in
    generally, 772
    dissenting opinion, 764–65, 775, 783
    freedom of contract and, 765
    Lochner and, 765
    Sutherland compared, 765
    takings, minimum wage distinguished, 765
  hours of labor, minimum wage distinguished, 757
  judicial review and, 760
  justification for statute, 756
  La Follette on, 766, 789–91
  legal scholarship and, 766
  legislative intent, relevance of, 757, 765–66
  liberty and, 756–57
  Lochner and, 759, 765, 766
  McKenna in, 756
  McReynolds in, 756
  morality and, 762–63, 778, 834–35
  nexus between legislation and benefits of, 759–61
  Nineteenth Amendment and, 763–64
  property rights and, 757
  reaction to decision, 766, 767, 788, 789–91
  reaffirmance of decision, 766, 787–88
  reasonable relation standard and, 759
  Sanford in, 764
  Sutherland in
    generally, 391–92, 755, 756

1519

INDEX

Adkins v. Children's (cont.)
   arbitrariness of statute and, 761, 762
   authority of expertise and, 839
   economic policy and, 834–35
   freedom of contract and, 761, 762–63, 778
   Holmes compared, 765
   Lochner and, 759, 766
   morality and, 762–63, 778, 834–35
   nexus between legislation and benefits of, 759–61
   Nineteenth Amendment and, 763–64
   price controls, minimum wage distinguished, 759, 762–63
   Taft compared, 765–66
   voluntariness of employment contracts and, 763–64
   workers' compensation compared, 761–62, 763
   Taft in
     generally, 391–92, 760–61
     dissenting opinion, 764, 765–66, 775, 783
     legislative intent and, 765–66
     Sutherland compared, 765–66
   takings, minimum wage distinguished, 765
   Van Devanter in, 756, 764
   voluntariness of employment contracts and, 763–64
   workers' compensation compared, 761–62, 763
Administration of Court
   Brandeis and, 477
   chief justice, role of (*See* Taft, William Howard – in capacity of chief justice)
   Conference of Senior Circuit Court Judges (*See* Conference of Senior Circuit Court Judges)
   Holmes on, 477
   judicial reform, need for, 477
   Judiciary Act of 1925, (*See* Judiciary Act of 1925)
   McReynolds and, 477
   need for legislation, 477
   openness and, 477
   Taft as administrator (*See* Taft, William Howard – in capacity of chief justice)
   Van Devanter and, 230–31, 477
Administrative expertise
   administrative state and, 693, 694
   Brandeis and, 273, 736
   economic regulation and, 693, 719
   judicial deference to, 693, 694
   progressivism and, 690, 694–95
   World War I and, 707
Administrative state. *See also* Economic regulation
   administrative expertise and, 693, 694
   conservatism and, xxviii, 651, 922
   judicial deference and, 735–37, 739

   liberty and, 1068
   McReynolds on, 273
   Myers v. United States and, 416–17
   progressivism and, 690, 694–95, 923–24
   prohibition and, 922, 923–24
   Purity Extract and, 739, 825
   ratemaking (*See* Ratemaking)
   removal power and, 416–17
   Sutherland on, 41, 740–41, 800, 838, 839
   Taft and
     as president, 401, 403–4
     tension between efficiency and freedom, 393, 394
   World War I, impact of, 693, 707
Admiralty, 1176–77
Advisory opinions
   Taft and, 512, 514, 528
   Van Devanter and, 528
AFL. *See* American Federation of Labor (AFL)
African Americans
   civil rights and, 1460
   eugenics and, 1441, 1444, 1452
   Fifteenth Amendment and, 1434–37
   Great Migration, xxxiv, 1438, 1459, 1461, 1479
   Holmes and, 166, 1486
   lynchings
     Dyer Anti-Lynching Bill, 1418
     habeas corpus and, 1025, 1038–41
     Ku Klux Klan and, 1025
     lynchings by year and race 1882–1940, 1222
     NAACP and, 1036–37
     "Red Summer of 1919," 1221–22
     Taft on, 1036–37, 1222, 1226
   McReynolds and, 285
   "Negro Renaissance," 1434
   organized labor compared, 1461
   political power of, 1460–61
   political rights and, 1442, 1444–45, 1468–69
   primary elections and, 1434–37 (*See also Nixon v. Herndon* (1927))
   "Red Summer of 1919," 1221–22
   "separate but equal," 1442
   social equality (*See* Social equality)
   Taft and (*See* Race relations)
   voting rights and, 1434–37
   in World War I, 1221
Agency
   Coronado I and, 1311–12, 1347
   Norris-LaGuardia Act and, 1347–48
   Sayre on, 1311, 1348
Agriculture Department, 694
Aitchison, Clyde B., 175, 887
Alchon, Guy, 687
Alcorn, Robert H., 1045–46
Alien land laws, 1455–58, 1487–90. *See also Porterfield v. Webb* (1923); *Terrace v. Thompson* (1923)

INDEX

Allen, Charles Claflin, 1359–60, 1375–76
Allen, Henry Justin, 794, 806, 807, 808–9, 816
Allgeyer v. Louisiana (1897), 1193–94
Alpha Portland Cement Co. v. Massachusetts, 268 U.S. 203 (1925), 1188–89
Alphonso Taft Hall, 168
Alschuler, Samuel, 1325–26
Altgeld, John Peter, 1376–77, 1387
Aluminum Company of America, 149–50
Ambler Realty Company, 835–36, 837, 870
American Anti-Boycott Association, 1361
American Bankers' Association, 1236
American Bar Association (ABA)
  on Brandeis, 309
  Canons of Judicial Ethics, 513, 527, 626, 629, 638, 649
  Caraway bill and, 525
  Committee on Jurisprudence and Law Reform, 495–96, 532
  judicial reform and, 513
  Judicial Section, 451, 504–5, 1001
  Judiciary Act of 1925 and, 485, 495–96, 502–3
  on labor injunctions, 1375–76
  on prohibition, 1001
  Sutherland and, 39–40, 51, 740–41
  Taft and, 2, 451, 481, 503, 504–5, 507–8, 513
American Civic Association, 866
American Civil Liberties Union (ACLU), 1295
American Column and Lumber Co. v. United States (1921), 49–50, 696, 710, 711–12, 713–14, 715
American Federationist, 634–35
American Federation of Labor (AFL)
  on *American Steel Foundries*, 1253
  on *Bailey*, 1127
  on *Bedford Cut Stone*, 1333, 1334–35
  on Child Labor Amendment, 1219
  on compulsory arbitration, 1297–98, 1300
  Congressional overturning of Court decisions, proposed Amendment regarding, 1312
  cooperation and, 1313
  on *Coronado I*, 1309, 1311–12, 1337, 1352–53
  on "free labor," 1298
  on judicial review, 63, 614–17, 1340–41
  on labor injunctions, 1389, 1417
  on open shops, 1271–72
  on Parker, 1287
  on prohibition, 924–25, 940
  Railroad Labor Board and, 1257–58
  railroads and, 1257–58
  on Sherman Anti-Trust Act, 1333, 1334–35, 1349
  on Taft, 3
  on Taft Court, 1219, 1225
  on *Truax*, 1415, 1427–28
  on voluntarism, 1298, 1303
American Institute of Architects, 571, 866
"Americanism," public schools and, 832–33, 857–58
American Law Institute, 485, 673
American Liberty League, 103–4
American Linseed Oil; United States v. (1923), 696–97, 712, 713–14
American Medical Association, 991
American Missionary Association, 1443
"American plan," 1218–19, 1236, 1270–71
American Railway Union (ARU), 1229, 1322–23, 1375
American Society of Landscape Architects, 866
American Steel Foundries, 1240, 1242–43, 1244–45, 1246
American Steel Foundries v. Tri-City Central Trades Council (1921), 1239–48
  AFL on, 1253
  Borah on, 1233, 1247
  Clarke in, 1252–53
  Clayton Act and, 1241–42, 1283
  dissenting opinion (unpublished), 1283–84, 1286, 1290, 1294
  factual background, 1240
  Gompers on, 1253
  Hitchman distinguished, 1246–47
  Holmes in, 1277–78, 1283–84, 1286, 1290, 1292, 1294
  individualism and, 1245
  labor injunctions and, 1252
  Norris-LaGuardia Act and, 1245–46, 1247
  picketing and
    case by case determination, 1251
    direct versus indirect connection to benefits, 1246–47
    persuasion versus coercion, 1240, 1242–43, 1250–51, 1252, 1291–92
    purpose of, 1250
    purpose of picketing, 1242–43, 1246–47
  Pitney in, 1246, 1247, 1251–52, 1277–78
  reaction to decision, 1294
  rearguments in, 1239–40, 1278
  Taft in, 1239–40, 1242, 1244–48, 1250, 1278, 1292
  Truax compared, 1402, 1403
  in White Court, 1239–40
American Tobacco Co.; United States v. (1911), 276–77
American Tobacco Company, 261, 263, 277
Amicus briefs
  in *Euclid*, 837–38, 867–68, 873–74
  in *Myers v. United States*, 402
Anderson, Albert Barnes, 1325–26, 1329
Anderson, Henry, 108–9
Andrews, Lincoln, 949, 956
Angell, James R., 230
Anglo-Saxon Clubs, 1444, 1446, 1482

Index

Annen Realschule (Dresden), 296
Annual Conference on Weights and Measures, 733, 743, 745–46
Anti-Narcotic Act of 1914, 282, 1129–30, 1153–54
Anti-Saloon League
  generally, 917, 919–20, 960, 965, 1025
  Act of September 6, 1922 and, 464–65, 466–67
  on Brandeis, 977–78
  Eighteenth Amendment and, 964
  power of, 924, 925
  as single issue lobbying group, 924
  as "super-legislature," 748–49
  Taft and, 999, 1002
  Taft Court and, 966–67
  Volstead Act and, xxx, 924, 925
  Wayne Wheeler and, 464–65, 466–67, 924, 938–39, 965, 1002, 1022
Anti-Semitism
  Brandeis and, 36–37, 297, 309, 342–43, 349–50
  Holmes on, 217, 223
  of McReynolds, 36–37, 264–65, 290
  Taft on, 342–43
Anti-Slavery Society, 163
Antitrust law. *See also specific case*
  American Linseed Oil and, 696–97
  American Tobacco Co. and, 276–77
  Brandeis on, 696–98, 710, 713–14
  Butler on, 713–14
  Clarke on, 709–10
  Clayton Act (*See* Clayton Act of 1914)
  Commerce Department and, 696
  commodities exchanges and, 1156
  common law and, 1197–98
  Coronado I and, 1312 (*See also United Mine Workers of America v. Coronado Coal Co.* (1922) (*Coronado I*))
  federal common law and, 1197–98
  federalism and, 1132
  Holmes on, 190–92, 696–98, 713
  Hoover and, 697–98
  labor injunctions and, 1306
  labor market and, 1220, 1319
  Maple Flooring Manufacturers Ass'n and, 697
  McKenna on, 696–98, 713–14
  McReynolds on, 261–62, 276–77, 696–97, 713–14, 715
  monopolies
    Brandeis on, 337
    federal common law and, 1199–200
    Holmes on, 218
    McReynolds on, 276–77
    railroads as, 895
    Sherman Anti-Trust Act and, 1125
  normative dualism and, 1121–22
  open shops and, 1318–19

restraint of trade
  Coronado I and, 1313–14, 1315
  Sherman Anti-Trust Act and, 1358–59
  strikes and, 1313–14, 1315, 1317
  Sanford on, 713–14, 715
  Sayre on, 1370
  Sherman Anti-Trust Act (*See* Sherman Anti-Trust Act of 1890)
  shifts in jurisprudence, 696
  Stone on, 697, 714–15
  strikes and, 1307
  Sutherland on, 713–14
  Taft Court generally, 696, 700, 701, 709–11, 713–14, 1319 (*See also United Mine Workers of America v. Coronado Coal Co.* (1922) (*Coronado I*))
  Taft on, 713–14, 715, 1122, 1135, 1404–5, 1420
  trade associations and, 694–96, 697–98
  Van Devanter on, 710, 713–14
  World War I, impact of, 696
Appeals. *See* Judicial review
Appointments to Court
  Brandeis, 307–10, 343–44, 346–48, 349
  Butler, xxvi, 33, 61, 88, 102
  Clarke, 35
  by Coolidge, 33, 92, 122, 146–47
  Day, 59
  by Harding, 33, 58, 84, 92, 102, 612–14, 681–82, 949, 1239
  Holmes, 165–66
  Hughes
    as associate justice, 238
    nomination as chief justice, 879, 891–92, 1503–5
  Lamar, 238
  Lurton, 238
  McKenna, 117, 118
  by McKinley, 117, 118
  McReynolds, 263–64, 283
  nomination of Taft as chief justice, 4–5
    generally, xxvi, 20, 25, 949
    Daugherty and, 5
    Harding and, 4–5, 8, 529, 681–82, 949
  Pitney, 225, 238
  Republican Party and, 102–3
  Sanford, xxvi, 33, 85–86, 87–88, 90, 1452
  Stone, 33, 122, 125–26, 146–47
  Sutherland, xxvi, 33, 39
  by Taft, 225, 227–28, 238, 307
  by Theodore Roosevelt, 59, 91, 165–66
  Van Devanter, 225, 227–28, 238
  by Wilson, 35, 74, 263–64, 307–10
Arbitration
  generally, 793, 806
  AFL on, 1297–98, 1300
  Brandeis on, 798
  Charles Wolff Packing and, 814

INDEX

compulsory arbitration, 1255, 1275, 1297–98, 1300
  Harding on, 1275
  international arbitration, Taft and, 3
  public, intervention by, 1255
  Railroad Labor Board and, 1256–57
  Taft on, 816
  Thirteenth Amendment, 816
  Transportation Act and, 1300
  unions and, 1255
  "Voluntary Principle," 1255
  war versus, 17
Architect of the Capitol, 558, 559
Arizona Civil Code paragraph 1464, 1399–400, 1402, 1403, 1404, 1406, 1408, 1409–10, 1413, 1414, 1417, 1422. *See also Truax v. Corrigan* (1921)
Armstrong, Samuel Chapman, 1443
Arnold, Peri Ethan, 688
Arnold, Thurman, 1358
Article II judges, 416
Article II powers. *See* Executive power
Article III courts
  autonomy of, 564
  Caraway bill and, 511–13
  Circuit Courts of Appeal (*See* Circuit Courts of Appeal)
  comity and, 1210
  contempt, power to punish, 1382–84
  Court of Customs Appeals as, 514
  custom and public sentiment and, 1201
  district courts (*See* District courts)
  diversity jurisdiction (*See* Diversity jurisdiction)
  dockets
    bankruptcy cases in district courts, by fiscal year 1915–1930, 455
    civil cases in district courts in which United States is party, by fiscal year 1915–1930, 456
    criminal prosecutions in district courts, by fiscal year 1915–1930, 455
    district courts cases in which United States is not party, by fiscal year, 1915–1930, 456
    total number of district courts cases, by fiscal year 1915–1930, 454
  federal common law and, 1198
  federalism and, 1198, 1201
  federal question jurisdiction
    Norris on, 1214–15
    S. 3151 and, 516–18, 1214–15
  foreign corporations, access of, 1196–97, 1207
  judicial appointments (*See* Judicial appointments)
  judicial reform and, 451
  Judiciary Act of 1925 and, 485
  labor injunctions and, 1233, 1241, 1274, 1325, 1375, 1376, 1491–92
  management of, 452
  Norris and, 516, 518
  prohibition
    backlog of cases regarding, 949
    overwhelming judges, 949
    turning district courts into police courts, 949
  separation of powers and, 511–13, 564, 1382–84
  state courts compared, 510–11, 523–24
  system of corporate diversity jurisdiction, 1196, 1197
  Taft on, 451, 510–11, 523–24, 564, 1507
  Thomas Walsh and, 516
Article V, 971, 979–80, 1000–1, 1071
Ashurst, Henry F., 558, 584–85
Association Against the Prohibition Amendment (AAPA), 942–43, 970–71
"Associative state," 1260
Atkinson, Thomas E., 1056–57
Auerbach, Jerold S., 672–73
Auerbach, Joseph S., 989–91
Authority of expertise
  Adkins and, 839
  authority of finality versus
    Holmes on, 654–55
    Stone on, 655–56
  Brandeis and, 661–62
  Butler and, 659
  dissent and, 656–57, 664
  economic regulation and, 693, 719
  Euclid and, 839–40, 842–43
  Frankfurter and, 665
  functional account of law and, 129–30, 158–59
  Handler on, 671
  Holmes and, 654–55
  Hughes and, 655–56
  Jay Burns and, 736
  judicial deference to, 693, 694
  Learned Hand and, 656–57
  legal scholarship versus, 655–56, 657–59, 661
  Lochner and, 737
  Louis Pizitz Dry Goods and, 659
  Myers v. United States and, 657
  New Deal and, 665
  "norm of acquiescence" and, 664
  open debate and, 665
  punitive damages and, 659
  social policy and, 661–62
  Stone and, 655–56, 661–62
  Taft and, 657–59
  Taft Court generally, 654, 655–56
  tension with impartiality, 513
  Van Devanter and, 659

1523

INDEX

Authority of finality
  authority of expertise versus
    Holmes on, 654-55
    Stone on, 655-56
  dissent and, 629-30
  legal scholarship and, 661
  mandatory jurisdiction and, 654, 655, 665, 666
  "norm of acquiescence" and, 665
  supervisor of judiciary versus final appellate tribunal, Supreme Court as, 480, 484-85, 498, 603, 665-66
  Taft Court generally, 654-55
Automobiles
  Dormant Commerce Clause and, 1170, 1186, 1190-91
  searches
    generally, 1046, 1049
    Brandeis on, 390
    prohibition and, 1026-30 (See also *Carroll v. United States* (1925))
    Taft on, 390

Bache-Denman Company, 1304, 1316
Bacon, Henry, 556, 577, 578
Bailey v. Drexel Furniture Co. (1922), 1126-28
  AFL on, 1127
  Beck on, 1146
  Brandeis in, 1146
  Clarke in, 1146
  Congressional power and, 1126-28
  federalism and, 1103-4, 1132
  judicial review and, 1127
  La Follette on, 1127
  national market and, 1130-31
  normative dualism and, 1126-28
  reaction to, 1127
  Taft in, 1126-28, 1156
  Tenth Amendment and, 1126
Baker, Francis E., 1286, 1292-93, 1381-82, 1383-84
Baker, Newton D.
  on *Coronado I*, 1310
  Euclid and, 835-37, 838, 870-71, 872-73
  on labor injunctions, 1392-93
  on labor market, 1255
  minimum wage and, 776
  on workers' compensation, 776
Baker, Ray Stannard, 13, 1217
Balancing tests
  Dormant Commerce Clause and, 661-62, 1172-73
  intergovernmental tax immunity, 1115
  judicial authority and, xxxvii, 661-62
  social policy and, 129, 661-62
  Stone and, 129, 661-62, 1115, 1172-73
Baldwin, Roger, 1077-78
Baldwin, Simeon, 346-48

Ballinger, Richard A., 263, 302-4, 331, 333, 334-35, 403
Ballinger-Pinchot affair, 302-5, 308-9, 310-11, 331, 332-36, 350
Baltimore & Ohio R.R. Co. v. Goodman (1927), 206, 207
Baruch, Bernard M., 708
Bates, Ernest Sutherland, 281, 687
Beard, Charles A., 29
Beck, James M.
  on *Bailey*, 1146
  Judiciary Act of 1925 and, 483, 484, 495-96
  on labor market, 1279
  Myers v. United States and, 402, 420, 429, 440-47, 657
  on prohibition, 961, 980, 1006, 1013, 1024
  on Tenth Amendment, 986
Bedford Cut Stone Co. v. Journeymen Stone Cutters' Ass'n (1927), 787-88, 1324-35
  AFL on, 1333, 1334-35
  announcement of decision, 1330
  Brandeis in
    dissenting opinion, 1327, 1330-31, 1333, 1334, 1367
    reaction to decision and, 1333
  Circuit Court proceedings, 1325-26
  class considerations in, 1327
  Clayton Act and, 1330-32
  common law and, 1327, 1329-30
  concurring opinions, 1330
  dissenting opinion, 1327, 1330-31, 1333, 1334, 1367
  Duplex and
    Brandeis distinguishing, 1327, 1331
    Sutherland following, 1329, 1330
    Taft following, 1326, 1327-29, 1330
  equity and, 1326, 1327, 1334
  factual background, 1325
  Frankfurter on, 1332, 1369
  Green on, 1333, 1372-73, 1374
  Holmes in, 1326, 1330-31
  individualism and, 1334
  interstate commerce and, 1326, 1330, 1332
  involuntary servitude, charges of, 1331-32, 1333-34, 1368
  labor injunctions and, 1381
  Norris-LaGuardia Act, effect on, 1335
  reaction to decision, 1332-35, 1367, 1369-70, 1371
  Sanford in, 1326, 1327, 1330, 1365-66
  Sherman Anti-Trust Act and, 1325, 1326-28, 1329-32, 1365
  Stone in, 1326, 1327, 1328-29, 1330, 1365-66
  Sutherland in, 1326, 1327, 1328-30, 1332

INDEX

Taft in
  generally, 1362
  labor injunctions and, 1381
  lobbying of other justices, 1326, 1327, 1329–30
  reaction to decision and, 1334
  Sherman Anti-Trust Act and, 1365
  Thirteenth Amendment and, 1368
Benedict, Michael Les, 771
Bennett, Edward H., 557–58, 580
Bettman, Alfred, 836, 837–38, 840, 862–63, 865, 867–68, 869, 873, 876
Beveridge, Albert, 649, 1248–49
Bhagat Singh Thind; United States v. (1923), 1453–55
  alien land cases and, 1455
  biological construction of race, 1453, 1454
  Indians, racial classification of, 1453–55
  meaning of race in, 1453–55
  reaction to decision, 1455
  social construction of race, 1453–55
  Sutherland in, 1452, 1454, 1485–86
Bickel, Alexander M.
  generally, xxv, xxxviii
  on authority of Supreme Court, 652
  on Brandeis, 311
  on Dormant Commerce Clause, 1174, 1183–84
  on Holmes, 196–97
  on Taft Court, 652, 1174
  on Van Devanter, 238
Biddle, Francis, 301
Biological construction of race, 1453, 1454, 1482–83
Black, Forrest Revere, 992, 1030, 1058
Black, Hugo, 591
Black & White Taxicab & Transfer Co. v. Brown & Yellow Taxicab & Transfer Co. (1928), 173, 202, 1199–200, 1211–15
Blackstone, William, 534–35
Blakemore, Arthur W., 1049
Block v. Hirsh (1921), 723–24, 768, 793
Blodgett, Geoffrey, 577, 591
Bluefield Water Works & Improvement Co. v. Public Service Comm'n of West Virginia (1923), 884, 890
Board of General Appraisers, 402
Board of Trade v. Olsen (1923), 1129, 1152
Boards of trade
  Brandeis on, 1150
  Commerce Clause and, 1128, 1129
  federalism and, 1133–34
  interstate commerce and, 1128–29, 1133–34
  Taft on, 1150–52
Boiler Inspection Act, 1141–43
Bolshevik Revolution, 1218
Bonaparte, Charles J., 261
Bonbright, James C., 138, 906

Borah, William E.
  on *Adkins*, 766, 789–91
  on *American Steel Foundries*, 1233, 1247
  Daugherty and, 145
  Hughes and, 913–14
  judicial review, proposed legislation regarding, 616–17, 789–91
  League of Nations and, 18–19
  on *O'Fallon Railway*, 913–14
  Parker and, 1233
  on prohibition, 941–42, 950, 1001, 1021
  Taft and, 25–26, 766, 1247
  Van Devanter and, 234–35
Borchard, Edwin M., 324–25, 657–59, 674–75, 676, 788
Bourquin, George M., 681–82, 1153–54
Bowen, William A., 642
Bradley, Joseph P., 815
Brandegee, Frank B., 23, 524
Brandeis, Elizabeth, 764, 782–83, 869
Brandeis, Louis Dembitz
  generally, xxvii, 887
  ABA on, 309
  Acheson and, 212–13, 295–96, 329, 365
  in *Adkins*, 760, 764
  administration of Court and, 477
  administrative expertise and, 273, 736
  advice from, 322
  on alien land laws, 1487
  in *American Column and Lumber Co.*, 696
  on "Americanism," 859
  Anti-Saloon League on, 977–78
  anti-Semitism and, 36–37, 297, 309, 342–43, 349–50
  on anti-trust law, 696–98, 710, 713–14
  appointment of, 307–10, 343–44, 346–48, 349
  on arbitration, 798
  authority of expertise and, 661–62
  on automobile searches, 390
  in *Bailey*, 1146
  in *Baldridge*, 740
  Ballinger-Pinchot affair and, 302–5, 308–9, 310–11, 331, 332, 333–36
  in *Bedford Cut Stone*
    dissenting opinion, 1327, 1330–31, 1333, 1334, 1367
    reaction to decision and, 1333
  Bickel on, 311
  on "bigness," 337
  on boards of trade, 1150
  "Brandeis brief," 298–301, 329, 330
  Brewer and, 300
  Butler and, 61–62, 81, 617, 1068
  in *Carroll*, 390, 1030, 1069
  in *Casey*, 178–79, 221–23
  on *certiorari*, 224
  in *Charles Wolff Packing*, 798

1525

INDEX

Brandeis, Louis Dembitz (cont.)
  in *Chastleton*, 723, 730–31
  on child labor, 1107
  Clarke and, 35, 37, 46, 49–50
  on Clayton Act, 1242
  community and, 321
  conference cases
    number of votes recorded at conference that switched to join opinion by Brandeis, divided by number of Brandeis opinions in conference cases, 44
    percentage of Brandeis's dissenting votes in conference that Brandeis switched in order to join published Court opinion, 622
    percentage of Brandeis's published opinions that were unanimous in conference, 66
    percentage of Brandeis's unanimous published opinions that had dissenting or uncertain votes in conference, 66
    percentage of decisions in which Brandeis participated and switched vote in conference to join published Court opinion, 622
    percentage of decisions in which Brandeis participated and voted in conference with justice with whom most likely to vote, 233
    percentage of decisions in which Brandeis participated and voted with another justice in conference, 316
    percentage of decisions in which Brandeis participated and willing to switch conference vote to join Court opinion or join Court opinion despite registering uncertainty in conference, 43
  confirmation of, 309
  on Congressional power, 1149–50
  on Constitutional interpretation, 300–1, 312–13, 315, 389, 630
  Coolidge and, 361
  in *Coronado I* (See *United Mine Workers of America v. Coronado Coal Co.* (1922) (*Coronado I*))
  in *Coronado II*, 1316
  on corporations, 1432–33
  cultural pluralism and, 1433
  in *Davis*, 363–64
  Day, views on, 67–68
  on declaratory judgments, 324–25, 675
  on democratic participation, 318, 834
  Democratic Party and, 309, 326, 1059
  on democratic theory and judicial review, 313–14
  on despotism, 340
  in *Di Santo*, 644–45
  dissenting opinions
    law reviews cited in, 661
    "norm of acquiescence" and, 630, 631
    reluctance to dissent, 626, 628, 639, 640, 641
    views of, 617
  on diversity jurisdiction, 1197, 1208, 1214–15
  Dormant Commerce Clause and (See Dormant Commerce Clause)
  Due Process Clause and, 320, 1194–95, 1204–5
  early life of, 296–97
  on economic growth, 321
  on economic prosperity, xxix, 312, 315–16, 321, 1332, 1412
  on economic regulation, 129, 304–5
  Equal Protection Clause and, 1205, 1412, 1415, 1430–31, 1432–33, 1464
  on espionage, 1087–88
  in *Euclid*, 837
  on "experiments," 314–15, 1410–11
  expertise and, 273, 736
  facts, focus on, 300–2, 329, 645–46
  on federal common law, 817, 1201, 1212, 1216
  federalism and, 365, 366, 968–69, 1104
  First Amendment and, 315
  Fourteenth Amendment and, 298, 363–64, 1412
  Fourth Amendment and, 358, 1062
  Frankfurter and, 154, 195–96, 310–11, 350–51, 360–61, 444
  Franklin Roosevelt and, 295, 340
  on freedom of contract, 299–300, 313
  on freedom of speech, 127, 315
  FTC and, 271, 306–7, 825, 844–45
  in *Gambino*, 951
  Gold Clause cases and, 296
  Gompers and, 1305
  on grand jury requirement, 388–90
  Gray, as clerk for, 187, 297
  as "great Justice," 244, 373
  on group rights, 428–29, 1413, 1433, 1464–65
  Harlan and, 299–300
  on Harrison Narcotics Act, 1154
  in *Hill v. Wallace*, 1146–47
  in *Hitchman*, 1286
  Holmes and
    Brandeis views on Holmes, 173, 197, 205, 213–14, 215–16, 617, 1418
    comparison, 132, 212–13, 296, 298, 300, 301–2, 315–16, 320, 321, 323–24, 362–63
    Holmes views of Brandeis, 177–78, 217, 219
    opinions compared, 173, 218
    personal relationship with, 217, 297, 348
    professional relationship with, 219–21
    views on Holmes opinions, 173, 175–76
    voting alliance with, 176–80, 223–24, 315–16

INDEX

Hoover and, 708–9
on hours of labor, 298–301, 329, 339
"House of Truth" and, 168, 195–96
Hughes, views of, 223
ICC and, 317–20, 363, 365, 366, 367, 1137
on immigration, 859
on incorporation of unions, 1305
on individualism, 833–34, 1465
on innovation, 327–28
on intergovernmental tax immunity, 1119–20
on interstate commerce, 1128, 1183–84
on involuntary servitude, 1331–32
in *Jay Burns*, 734, 735–37, 744, 748
as Jew, 296–97, 309, 342–43, 349–50, 1433
judicial appointments and, 546
judicial authority and, 652
judicial deference and, 313, 315, 736, 737
on judicial reform, 461, 467–68
on judicial review, xxix, 313–14, 1412
judicial style of, 311, 315–16
Judiciary Act of 1925 and, 491–93, 499–500
Judiciary Committee hearings, 307, 309, 348, 349
on juries, 521–22
jurisprudence and, 296, 311, 315, 321, 345–46, 362–63
in *Katz*, 1030–31
on labor injunctions, 1380, 1411–12
labor market and, 1238, 1317
on labor violence, 1288, 1289–90
La Follette and, 305, 348
in *Lambert*, 988–89, 991
Landis on, 326
Laski and, 323–24, 358
on lawlessness, 1069–70
law reviews and, 659, 670
on law students, 325
as lawyer, 297–98
Learned Hand and, 89, 322
legacy of, 373, 1507
on legal education, 331
legal process school and, 315
legal scholarship and, 656–57
on leisure, 358–59
on liberty, 337
Lochner and, 298–300, 307
Lodge and, 344
on *mala prohibita* versus *mala in se*, 1086–87
in *Maul*, 1031
McKenna and, 120, 315–16
McReynolds and
 generally, 262
 Brandeis views on McReynolds, 265–66, 289, 292
 comparison, xxix, 267, 271, 273, 294, 295, 296, 315–16, 320–21, 834, 1068
 personal relationship with, 36–37, 265–66, 279–80, 287–88, 290

political support for, 262
in *Meyer v. Nebraska*, 828–29
on minimum wage, 765
on monopolies, 337
morality and, 295–96, 834
in *Moreland*, 388–90
in *Muller*, 298–300
in *Myers v. United States* (*See Myers v. United States* (1926))
on *The New Republic*, 330
Nixon and, 1436–37
"norm of acquiescence" and, 628
Norris and, 348
in *O'Fallon Railway*, 888, 889–90
on official lawlessness, 1072–74
in *Olmstead* (*See Olmstead v. United States* (1928))
opinions
 generally, 219
 under authorship of other justice, 361–62
 average number of days from argument to announcement of unanimous opinion, by justice, 1921–1928 terms, 86
 average number of pages in unanimous opinion by Brandeis, 1921–1928 terms, 174
 cost of printing, 351–52
 footnotes in, 218
 Holmes compared, 218
 independence of, 311, 315–16
 law reviews cited in, 659
 number of citations to law review articles in Brandeis Court opinions and dissents, 1921–1928 terms, 661
 number of citations to treatises and law review articles in Brandeis Court opinions, 1921–1928 terms, 662
 number of citations to treatises and law review articles in Brandeis dissents, 1921–1928 terms, 661
 number of opinions authored by Brandeis, 1921–1928 terms, 8
 number of opinions authored by Brandeis, 1921 term, 31, 32
 percentage of Court opinions authored by Brandeis, by term, 317
 persuasiveness of, 315–16
 reactions of other justices to, 352–55
 rhetorical structure of opinions, 645–46
 Taft, views of, 311–12, 348
 writing style of, 218, 311, 315–16, 645–46, 671
opposition to appointment of, 308–9
on pardons, 221–23
on Parker, 1490, 1492
in *Pennsylvania v. West Virginia*, 1160
as "people's lawyer," 297
performance on Court, 311, 315–16
in *Pierce*, 834

1527

Brandeis, Louis Dembitz (cont.)
Pitney and, 85, 97, 98
on price controls, 129
on privacy, 928, 1067–68, 1085–86
Progressive Party and, 306, 341
on prohibition (*See* prohibition)
promotion of democracy and
generally, 320, 321, 338–39, 1423
Holmes compared, xxix
ICC and, 317–20
Meyer v. Nebraska, 829
property rights and, 312–13
in *Truax*, 1410–11, 1412
trusts and, 305, 306
"property affected with a public interest" and, 819
on property rights, xxix, 311–13, 817
on prudent investment theory, 881–82
publications of, xxxvi
public good and, 297–98
public interest and, 298
race relations and, 1433–34, 1441, 1465
racial equality and, 1433–34
Railroad Labor Board and, 1302
railroads and, 317, 318–20, 363, 365, 367, 1139, 1140–43
on ratemaking, 881–82, 883–84, 888, 889–90, 902–3
reaction to appointment of, 307–8
on rehearings, 212
rhetorical structure of opinions, 645–46
in *Ribnik*, 820
Root and, 341–42, 346–48
Sacco and Vanzetti case and, 1040–41
Sanford, views on, 98
in *Saunders*, 1205
scientific management and, 317–20, 363–64, 365
on searches and seizures, 1056–57, 1075–76
on secondary boycotts, 1364–65
seniority of, 31
Sherman Anti-Trust Act and, 271
"social inventions" and, 298, 326–27, 366, 834
Socialist, viewed as, 308, 309
social values and, 314
on socioeconomic legislation, 296
in *Southwestern Bell Telephone*, 881–82, 883, 898, 900, 901–2
on *stare decisis*, 644–45
on statutes versus common law, 996
Stone and
Brandeis views on Stone, 128, 145–46, 152–53
comparison, 127, 132, 155, 157–58, 159, 324–25
professional relationship with, 33, 128, 157–58, 249–50

Stone views on Brandeis, 301
views on Stone opinions, 714–15
on strikes, 1248
Supreme Court Building and, 565, 569, 572–73, 592
Sutherland and
Brandeis views on Sutherland, 42, 56–57, 58
comparison, 315–16, 1068
opposition to appointment of, 309, 310–11
personal relationship with, 360
returns to Brandeis opinions, 352–55
Taft and
Ballinger-Pinchot affair and, 304–5, 308–9, 335–36
Brandeis views on Taft, xxxv, 6–7, 8, 27, 28, 29, 373–74, 1505
comparison, xxix, 8, 224, 311–12, 321, 388–90, 630–31
death of Taft and, 1506
health of Taft and, 380, 386, 1500
opposition to appointment of, 308–9, 343–44, 346–48
personal relationship with, 304–5, 310–11, 349–51, 892
as president, 304, 310–11
professional relationship with, 317, 351–52, 389–90
returns on Brandeis opinions, 352–55
Taft views on Brandeis, xxx, 89, 179–80, 1495–96, 1502
views on Brandeis opinions, 311–12, 348
views on Taft opinions, 8
on taxation, 323
in *Terrace*, 1455
in *Texas Transport & Terminal*, 1169, 1182
Theodore Roosevelt and, 305–6
Thomas Walsh and, 509
on tipping, 322
on Transportation Act, 317, 318, 1140–41
in *Truax (See Truax v. Corrigan* (1921))
on trusts, 304–5
on tyranny, 313, 418
in *Tyson*, 800
on unions, 338, 365, 1292, 1344–45
in *United States v. Lee*, 1062
Van Devanter and
Brandeis views on Van Devanter, 230, 231, 237, 243, 244, 247, 258, 617
comparison, 236, 237, 246
influence of, 231
personal relationship with, 254
professional relationship with, 247–48, 250, 251
on Volstead Act, 1030–31
voting on Court
number of percentage points by which Brandeis is more or less likely to join or author opinion for Court, prohibition

1528

INDEX

decisions versus nonprohibition decisions, 928
percentage of all decisions in which Brandeis participated and either joined or authored Court opinion, 1915–1920 terms versus 1921–1928 terms, 613
percentage of decisions in which Brandeis and Clarke participated and joined same opinion, by term, 38
percentage of decisions in which Brandeis participated and chose to be only dissenter, 1921–1928 terms, 269
percentage of decisions in which Brandeis participated and either joined or authored opinion of Court, 1916–1921 terms, 32
percentage of decisions in which Brandeis participated and either joined or authored opinion of Court, 1921–1928 terms, 10, 682
percentage of decisions in which Brandeis participated and either joined or authored opinion of Court, 1921 term, 32
percentage of decisions in which Brandeis participated and either joined or authored opinion of Court, by term, 1921–1928 terms, 614
percentage of decisions in which Brandeis participated and joined or authored opinion for Court, prohibition decisions versus nonprohibition decisions, 1921–1928 terms, 927
percentage of decisions in which Brandeis participated and joined same opinion of another justice, 1921–1928 terms, 316
voting alliances, 176–80, 223–24, 315–16
in *Weaver*, 738, 739–40
West and, 892
Wickersham and, 309
in *Williams*, 803
in *Willing v. Chicago Auditorium Ass'n*, 324–25
Wilson and, 195–96, 306–7, 340–41, 342–43, 350–52, 423–24, 977–78
on wiretapping, 358, 1085
in *Wisconsin Rate Case*, 1137
World War I and, 689
on yellow-dog contracts, 1233
Zionism and, 342–43, 349, 1433
"Brandeis brief," 298–301, 329, 330
Bread standardization. *See also Jay Burns Baking Co. v. Bryan* (1924)
generally, 732–33, 742–43
Annual Conference on Weights and Measures, 733, 743, 745–46
Butler and, 748
Due Process Clause and, 733, 734
Fifth Amendment and, 732–33
Fourteenth Amendment and, 733

freedom of contract and, 733, 734
Hoover and, 733, 743
judicial deference and, 733
price controls, 732–33
state legislation, 733–34
substantive due process and, 733, 734
White Court and, 733
in World War I, 733
Brennan, William J., 653
Brewer, David J.
Brandeis and, 300
on excessive legislation, 170
labor market and, 1289
on property rights, 198, 200
Breyer, Stephen, 485, 651
Bricklayers' Union, 1320–21
Briggs, John Ely, 1108–9, 1155
Brigham Young Academy, 51
Brigham Young University, 39
Brooks v. United States (1925), 1132–34, 1157–58
Broun, Heywood, 1213, 1493
Brown, Henry Billings, 239–40
Brown, L. Ames, 919, 932, 933
Brown & Yellow Taxicab Company, 1199
Brown v. Board of Education (1954), 651, 653
Bruce, William Cabell, Jr., 1004–5, 1006, 1155
Bruère, Robert W., 860–61
Bryan, William Jennings, 234–35, 255, 260–61, 882
Bryce, James, 692
Buchanan v. Warley (1918), 875, 876–77, 1440
Buck v. Bell (1927), 203–4
Buck v. Kuykendall, 267 U.S. 307 (1925), 1170, 1186
Buck, George S., 1004, 1007
Buckley, John, 1418
Buckner, Emory, 957–58
Budget
Coolidge and, 553
Taft and, 403–4, 423–24, 425–26, 447, 864
Budget and Accounting Act of 1920, 419–20
Budget and Accounting Act of 1921, 430
Building codes, zoning distinguished, 863
Building Commission, 553–55
Bullitt, Martin, 74
Bunn, Charles W., 496
Bureaucracy. *See* Administrative state
Bureau of Insular Affairs, 168
Bureau of Internal Revenue, 948, 954–55
Bureau of Mines, 694
Bureau of Prohibition, 1078
Bureau of Public Roads, 694
Burleson, Albert S., 263, 283–84, 411–12, 1268–69
Burlingham, Charles C., 72–74, 103–4, 111, 908
Burnham, Daniel H., 568

1529

Burns, William J, 125, 145, 151–52
Butler, Nicholas Murray, 105, 124, 674–75, 915, 980, 1072–74
Butler, Pierce
  in *Adkins*, 756
  on anti-trust law, 713–14
  appointment of, xxvi, 33, 61, 88, 102
  authoritarianism of, 63
  authority of expertise and, 659
  Brandeis and, 61–62, 81, 617, 1068
  bread standardization and, 748
  in *Carroll*, 1058
  as Catholic, 71
  in *Chastleton*, 723–24
  conference cases
    generally, xxxvii
    number of votes recorded at conference that switched to join opinion by Butler, divided by number of Butler opinions in conference cases, 44
    percentage of Butler's dissenting votes in conference that Butler switched in order to join published Court opinion, 622
    percentage of Butler's published opinions that were unanimous in conference, 66
    percentage of Butler's unanimous published opinions that had dissenting or uncertain votes in conference, 66
    percentage of decisions in which Butler participated and switched vote in conference to join published Court opinion, 622
    percentage of decisions in which Butler participated and voted in conference with justice with whom most likely to vote, 233
    percentage of decisions in which Butler participated and voted with another justice in conference, 65
    percentage of decisions in which Butler participated and willing to switch conference vote to join Court opinion or join Court opinion despite registering uncertainty in conference, 43
  confirmation of, 64, 881, 885
  on conscientious objectors, 151
  controversy regarding, 61–62, 63–64
  Cummins and, 903–4
  Daugherty and, 61, 102
  dissenting opinions
    generally, 82
    reluctance to dissent, 626, 638–39, 640
  Dormant Commerce Clause and, 1171, 1172, 1173–74, 1191
  Douglas, views of, 62, 75
  early life of, 62
  on economic prosperity, xxix
  on economic regulation, 65–66, 76
  in *Euclid*, 835, 839–40, 841
  on excessive legislation, 62–63, 76, 737
  as "failure," 244
  on federal common law, 1199–200, 1211
  Fourth Amendment and, 1047–49
  Gompers and, 903–4
  on government, 77
  Harding and, 61, 62, 63–64, 71
  in *Highland*, 720–23, 727, 728
  Holmes and, 62, 75, 83, 154, 172, 212
  Hughes and, 62, 75, 356, 1503–4
  on individualism, 76–77
  on intergovernmental tax immunity, 1112
  intolerance of, 63
  Jackson on, 63, 77, 82
  in *Jay Burns*, 734, 735–36, 737, 744, 751
  labor market and, 1317
  La Follette and, 78–79, 80
  law reviews and, 670
  legacy of, 373
  legal scholarship and, 659
  McReynolds and
    comparison, 267–68, 269, 270, 271, 274
    personal relationship with, 292
    voting alliance with, 266–67, 269
  Mitchell and, 63, 75–76, 82
  morality and, xxx
  in *Myers v. United States*, 404–6, 411
  National Oratorical Contest and, 378
  "norm of acquiescence" and, 626
  Norris and, 80, 903–4
  on official lawlessness, 1072–74
  in *Olmstead*, 1062, 1064–65, 1070, 1088–89
  opinions
    generally, 64–66
    average number of days from argument to announcement of unanimous opinion, by justice, 1922–1928 terms, 86
    average number of pages in unanimous opinion by Butler, 1922–1928 terms, 174
    draft opinions, 81
    footnotes in, 218
    number of citations to law review articles in Butler Court opinions and dissents, 1922–1928 terms, 661
    number of citations to treatises and law review articles in Butler Court opinions, 1922–1928 terms, 662
    number of citations to treatises and law review articles in Butler dissents, 1922–1928 terms, 661
    number of opinions authored by, 64–65
    number of opinions authored by Butler, 1922–1928 terms, 8
    percentage of Court opinions authored by Butler, by term, 65
    persuasiveness of, xxxvii, 64–65

INDEX

opposition to, 79–80
on pardons, 221–23
physical appearance of, 75–76
in *Porterfield*, 1456–57, 1486
on price controls, 720–23, 727, 728, 798–99
on prohibition
  generally, 926, 927–28
  in *Carroll*, 1058
  morality and, xxx
  normative dualism and, 974
  opposition to, 66–67
  rule of law and, 1003
on property rights, 62, 172, 356
railroads and, 76, 883–84, 890
on ratemaking, 881, 883, 884, 890, 902–3
recusal of, 885, 887–88, 903–4
reproduction theory of value and, 884
on rule of law, 77–78
Sanford compared, 91–92
Senate views on, 892
Stone and
  chief justice, consideration for, 1498–99, 1511
  comparison, 123–24
  personal relationship with, 144
  professional relationship with, 33, 81–82, 127
Supreme Court Building and, 552, 554, 555, 591
Sutherland compared, 58
Taft and
  death of Taft and, 1506
  health of Taft and, 1503
  intervention in nomination of, 536
  personal relationship with, 24, 71, 80
  professional relationship with, 61
  Taft views on Butler, 72–74, 117
  views on nomination of Taft, 5
  voting alliance with, 64, 394
on takings, 726–27
on taxing power, 1129–30
in *Terrace*, 1455–56, 1486, 1487
Thomas Walsh on, 903–4
on valuation of railroads, 897
Van Devanter and
  comparison, 64–65, 232–34, 256
  influence of, 231
  personal relationship with, 71, 231, 232–34, 254
  professional relationship with, 61, 232
  Van Devanter views on Butler, 72–74
  voting alliance with, 64
voting on Court
  number of percentage points by which Butler is more or less likely to join or author opinion for Court, prohibition decisions versus nonprohibition decisions, 928
  percentage of decisions in which Butler participated and chose to be only dissenter, 1922–1928 terms, 269
  percentage of decisions in which Butler participated and either joined or authored opinion of Court, 1922–1928 terms, 10, 682
  percentage of decisions in which Butler participated and joined or authored opinion for Court, prohibition decisions versus nonprohibition decisions, 1922–1928 terms, 927
  percentage of decisions in which Butler participated and joined same opinion of another justice, 1922–1928 terms, 64
  voting alliances, 64, 266–67, 269, 394
in *Weaver*, 738–39
Wickersham and, 72–74
Wilson and, 62
on workers' compensation, 77
World War I and, 699
Byrd, Harry F., 1447, 1448
Byrnes, James, 1221

Cadwallader, Wickersham & Taft (firm), 89
Caffey, Francis, 516
California Workmen's Compensation Act, 1176–77
Campbellites, 260, 269
Canons of Judicial Ethics (ABA), 513, 527, 626, 629, 638, 649
Caraway, Thaddeus H., 511–13, 526, 555, 1417, 1468, 1505
Cardozo, Benjamin
  on judicial supremacy, 169
  legal scholarship and, 656, 661
  on *Lochner*, 766
  McReynolds, personal relationship with, 36–37, 265, 287
  Taft, views of, 106, 1498
  on uncertainty, 667
Carolene Products Co.; United States v. (1938)
  Equal Protection Clause and, 1433, 1434, 1460, 1461
  privacy and, 1068
  segregation and, 1450
  Stone and, 127, 1068, 1450
Carroll v. United States (1925), 1026–30
  Brandeis in, 390, 1030, 1069
  Butler in, 1058
  common law and, 1029
  dissenting opinion, 1027, 1029–30, 1055–56
  Fifth Amendment and, 1029
  Fourth Amendment and, 1028, 1029
  Holmes in, 1030, 1058
  Lochner and, 1055
  McKenna in, 1049–52
  McReynolds in, 1027, 1029–30, 1055–56

INDEX

Carroll v. United States (1925) (cont.)
　novelty of automobile, 1027
　positive law and, 1027–29
　pragmatism in, 1055
　probable cause requirement, 1028–30
　Sutherland in, 1027, 1029
　switching of votes in, 1049–52
　Taft in, 390, 1027–29, 1049–52, 1054, 1055
　Van Devanter in, 1049–52
　Volstead Act and, 1027
Carrott, M. Browning, 1038, 1484
Carson, Hampton L., 642, 684–85
Carter, James Coolidge, xxxix, 169, 198–99, 1007
Casey v. United States (1928), 178–79, 221–23
Certiorari
　Brandeis on, 224
　conference cases
　　percentage of published conference cases that are unanimous as multiple of percentage of conference cases that are unanimous in conference, by jurisdiction by term, 1922–1928 terms, 625
　　percentage of unanimous conference cases, by jurisdiction, 624
　　percentage of unanimous conference cases, by jurisdiction by term, 1922–1928 terms, 625
　Evarts Act and, 477
　Frank Walsh on, 491–93
　Holmes on, 224
　Judiciary Act of 1925 and, 484, 600–3, 619, 626
　merits of case and, 493–94
　in *Olmstead*, 1063, 1083
　opinions and
　　generally, 608
　　average number of days from argument to announcement of full opinion, by jurisdiction by term, 1921–1928 terms, 607
　　average number of pages in full opinion, by jurisdiction by term, 1921–1928 terms, 607
　　percentage of full opinions that are unanimous, by jurisdiction by term, 1921–1928 terms, 608
　revised rule, 484, 497–98
　Supreme Court generally, 477, 484
　Taft and, 375, 380, 491–93
　unanimous opinions and, 619
　Van Devanter and, 493–94, 497–98
Chafee, Zechariah, Jr., 1030, 1044–45, 1071, 1072–74, 1095
Chain drug stores, 741, 754
Chamber of Commerce, 694, 1236

Charles Wolff Packing Co. v. Kansas Court of Industrial Relations (1923), 793–99
　arbitration and, 814
　Brandeis in, 798
　Fourteenth Amendment and, 796
　Frankfurter on, 811
　Frank Walsh on, 816
　Gompers on, 816
　managerial supervision by state and, 797–98
　McReynolds in, 798–99
　opinion below, 808
　"property affected with a public interest" and, 795–97
　reaction to decision, 810
　Taft in, 796–98, 812–13, 814–15
　unanimity in, 798–99
　Van Devanter in, 812, 813
Chastleton Corp. v. Sinclair (1924), 723–25
　Brandeis in, 723, 730–31
　Butler in, 723–24
　emergencies and, 723–25
　Holmes in, 723, 724, 728–29
　judicial notice and, 724–25
　McKenna in, 728–29
　McReynolds in, 728–29, 730
　Sanford in, 723–24
　Sutherland in, 723–24, 730
　Taft in, 724
　Van Devanter in, 723–24, 728–29, 730
Chicago Bar Association, 463–64, 504–5, 509, 530–31
Chief justice
　Conference of Senior Circuit Court Judges, role in, 452–53, 457–58
　expanded role of, 502
　Framers' conception of role, 506
　Holmes as acting chief justice, 1506, 1515
　Hughes
　　confirmation hearings, 892–94, 913–14, 915–16
　　nomination of, 879, 891–92, 1503–5
　judicial control and, 509–10
　judicial reform and, 504–5
　legislative process and, 502–4, 505, 511–13, 516–19
　Stone, consideration for, 1497–99, 1503, 1511, 1516
　Taft as (*See* Taft, William Howard – in capacity of chief justice)
　Van Devanter, campaign for chief justiceship, 21–23
Child labor
　Bailey, 1126–28 (*See also Bailey v. Drexel Furniture Co.* (1922))
　Brandeis on, 1107
　Coolidge on, 1147–48
　Dagenhart and, 969–70, 1103
　Day on, 1126

1532

INDEX

federalism and, 1103–4
Fourteenth Amendment and, 1131
Hammer v. Dagenhart and, 969–70, 1103
Harding on, 1147–48
interstate commerce and, 1126, 1130, 1179
National War Labor Board and, 1106–7
normative dualism and, 969–70, 1126, 1134
"property affected with a public interest" and, 1131
Republican Party and, 1147–48
state regulation of, 969–70, 1106–7, 1126, 1130, 1131
substantive due process and, 1158
Taft on, 1107, 1145–46, 1147–48
taxation and, 1126 (*See also Bailey v. Drexel Furniture Co.* (1922))
White Court and, 969–70, 1130
World War I and, 1103
Child Labor Amendment (proposed), 1104, 1147–48, 1219
Choate, Joseph H., 299, 341–42, 346–48
Cincinnati Law School, 1, 225, 449
Circuit Courts of Appeal
Conference of Senior Circuit Court Judges (*See* Conference of Senior Circuit Court Judges)
Evarts Act of 1891, 477–80
judicial appointments, 538–39
Learned Hand as circuit court judge, 542–43
Taft as circuit court judge (*See* Taft, William Howard – as circuit court judge)
Van Devanter as circuit court judge, 227
City-Beautiful Movement, 866
Civil service
Myers v. United States and, 407–8, 409, 411, 413
prohibition agents in, 956–57
removal power and, 407–8, 409, 411, 413, 429
Taft and, 433
Civil War
Holmes, impact on, 163–64, 168, 171, 172, 181–83, 184–85, 204
McReynolds on, 261
Clark, Charles E., 168, 768, 789
Clark, Tom C., 282
Clarke, Ida, 37–39
Clarke, John Hessin
Acheson and, 48–49
in *American Column and Lumber Co.*, 46, 49–50
in *American Steel Foundries*, 1252–53
on anti-trust law, 709–10
appointment of, 35
in *Bailey*, 1146
Brandeis and, 35, 37, 46, 49–50
on civil liberties, 46
on Clayton Act, 1242

in *Coronado I*, 1306, 1339
Day, views on, 67–68
dissenting opinions, 633
on diversity jurisdiction, 1208–9
Dormant Commerce Clause and, 1162
Frankfurter views on, 46
Harding and, 39
in *Hitchman*, 1233
Holmes and, 35, 46, 47, 206–7, 208
on juries, 521–22
on life on Court, 35–36, 47–48
McReynolds and, 36–37, 48, 265, 267
on minimum wage, 786–87
opinions
generally, 612
number of opinions authored by Clarke, 1921 term, 31, 32
on prohibition, 958–59, 993–94
as "radical," 35
replacement of, 33
retirement of, 36, 37–39, 49, 61, 599
Taft, views of, 35, 36–37, 46, 49
on Transportation Act, 1144
in *Truax*, 1401, 1402, 1409
on "unimportant" cases, 599, 600
in *United Zinc*, 46, 49–50
Van Devanter, personal relationship with, 47, 49, 231
voting on Court
percentage of all decisions in which Clarke participated and either joined or authored Court opinion, 1915–1920 terms versus 1921 term, 613
percentage of decisions in which Clarke and Brandeis participated and joined same opinion, by term, 38
percentage of decisions in which Clarke either authored or joined opinion of Court, 1921 term, 10
percentage of decisions in which Clarke participated and authored or joined opinion for Court, by term, 36
percentage of decisions in which Clarke participated and either authored or joined opinion for Court, 1916–1921 terms, 32
percentage of decisions in which Clarke participated and either authored or joined opinion for Court, 1921 term, 32
percentage of decisions in which Clarke participated and joined same opinion as another justice, 1916–1921 terms, 37
percentage of decisions in which Clarke participated and joined same opinion as another justice, 1921 term, 38
voting alliances, 37
Wilson and, 39, 49–50, 284, 599
on yellow-dog contracts, 1233

1533

INDEX

Clarkson, Grosvenor, 691
Class legislation. *See also* Race relations
  agricultural cooperatives and, 1405–6
  ambiguity regarding, 758
  common benefit contrasted, 758
  Connelly and, 1405–6
  Field and, 1404
  Fourteenth Amendment and, xxvi, 757, 1254, 1404–5
  Holmes and, 757
  individualism and, 1440
  Liberty Warehouse Co. and, 1405–6
  Lochner and, 758–59
  McReynolds and, 1406, 1421
  Natural Carbonic Gas Co. and, 236, 1024–25, 1403–4, 1406–8, 1409, 1456–57
  presumptive reasonableness of racial classifications, 1438
  reasonable relation standard and, 1404
  Stone and, 1421
  strict scrutiny and, 1421
  Sutherland and, 757, 1405–6
  Taft and, 757, 1404–6
  Truax and, 1404, 1406
  unions and, 1254
  Van Devanter on, 1404
Clay, Henry, 550
Clayton, Henry D., 452
Clayton Act of 1914,
  generally, 3, 306–7, 452
  American Steel Foundries and, 1241–42, 1283
  Bedford Cut Stone and, 1330–32
  Brandeis on, 1242
  Clarke on, 1242
  Coronado I and, 1348–49
  Duplex and, 1400–1
  Gompers on, 1241
  Holmes on, 1242, 1282
  interstate commerce, labor not deemed, 1280
  jury trial, right to, 1381, 1382–84
  labor injunctions and, 1241–42, 1282–83, 1378, 1399, 1400–1, 1403
  labor market and, 1280
  Michaelson and, 1381, 1382–84
  picketing and, 1250–51, 1290
  Pitney on, 1242
  purpose of, 824
  railroads and, 1394–95
  secondary boycotts and, 1361
  Taft on, 1241–42, 1281, 1404–5
  Truax and, 1415
  Wickersham on, 1241, 1280–81
Cleveland, F.A., 423–24
Cleveland, Grover, 72–74, 304, 1230, 1375, 1460
Coaldigger, Adam, 1022

Coal industry
  Dormant Commerce Clause and, 1163–64
  Highland, 720–23
  hours of labor in, 782
  as interstate commerce, 1135, 1178–79
  labor injunctions and, 1299
  price controls in, 720–23
  "property affected with a public interest" and, 1299
  Sherman Anti-Trust Act and, 1122
  strikes in, 1236, 1237–38, 1255–56, 1290, 1299
Cobb, Frederick Lyman, 931
Cohen, Morris, 196
Collective bargaining
  bargaining representatives, 1258
  Industrial Conference and, 1236–37, 1273, 1342–43
  National War Labor Board and, 1235
  Railroad Labor Board and, 1259–60
  Railway Labor Act and, 1260–61
  Taft on, 1237, 1273
  Transportation Act and, 1259–60
Collector v. Day (1870), 1111
Collier's, Ballinger-Pinchot affair and, 302–3, 304, 331, 332
Colorado v. United States (1926), 319–20
Columbia Law School, 122–23, 140–41, 147–48, 656
Comity, dual sovereignty and, 1210
Commerce Clause. *See also* Interstate commerce
  boards of trade and, 1128, 1129
  Congressional power and, 390, 1114, 1128, 1129, 1144, 1151, 1152
  Dormant Commerce Clause (*See* Dormant Commerce Clause)
  Taft and, 390, 1144
Commerce Department
  anti-trust law and, 696
  economic and statistical analysis and, xxvi
  Hoover in, 695–96, 697–98, 832, 1260
  standardization and, 695, 733
  World War I and, 696, 832
  zoning and, 865
Commission of Fine Arts, 551–52, 556, 568
Commission on Efficiency and Economy, 423–24
Commission on Industrial Relations, 14
Committee of Fifty, 934
Committee of Forty Eight, 1384
Common carriers, Dormant Commerce Clause and, 1173–74, 1185
Common law
  anti-trust law and, 1197–98
  authority of, 1198
  Bedford Cut Stone and, 1327, 1329–30
  Carroll and, 1029

1534

INDEX

Coronado I and, 1308, 1309
custom and public sentiment and, 200, 1198
dual sovereignty and, 1102
equity versus, 509
Fairmont Creamery and, 823
federal common law (*See* Federal common law)
Holmes on, 165, 173, 207
Hughes on, 823
Louis Pizitz Dry Goods and, 844
McReynolds on, 834
Meyer v. Nebraska and, 827–28, 834
Olmstead and, 1090–92
positive law versus, 823, 1309
reasonable relation standard and, 733, 734
secondary boycotts and, 1321–22
Sherman Anti-Trust Act, application under, 1319–20, 1381
statutes versus, 996–98, 1012–13
Stone on, 123–24, 141
Taft on, 199, 509
tyranny versus, 141, 823
The Common Law (Holmes, Jr.), 167, 297
Commons, John R., 789–91
Communications Act of 1934, 1066, 1084
Communitarian liberalism, 1069
Company unions, 1295–96
Competition. *See* Antitrust law
Compulsory school laws, 831, 856
Conference cases. *See also specific justice or case*
  defined, xxxvi
  dissent in
    percentage of dissenting votes in conference that justice switched in order to join published Court opinion, 622
    percentage of justice's unanimous published opinions that had dissenting or uncertain votes in conference, 66
  mandatory jurisdiction versus discretionary jurisdiction
    percentage of published conference cases that are unanimous as multiple of percentage of conference cases that are unanimous in conference, by jurisdiction by term, 1922–1928 terms, 625
    percentage of unanimous conference cases, by jurisdiction, 624
    percentage of unanimous conference cases, by jurisdiction by term, 1922–1928 terms, 625
  percentage of opinions in which justice participated and voted in conference with justice most likely to vote with, 233
  switching of votes in
    between conference and publication, 620–21
    number of votes recorded at conference that switched to join opinion of justice, divided by number of that justice's opinions in conference cases, 44
    percentage of decisions in which justice participated and switched vote in conference to join published Court opinion, 622
    percentage of decisions in which justice participated and was willing to switch conference vote to join Court opinion or to join Court opinion despite registering uncertainty in conference, 43
    percentage of dissenting votes in conference that justice switched in order to join published Court opinion, 622
  unanimous opinions
    generally, 620, 621–22, 637–38
    percentage of justice's published opinions that were unanimous in conference, 66
    percentage of published conference cases that are unanimous as multiple of percentage of conference cases that are unanimous in conference, by jurisdiction by term, 1922–1928 terms, 625
    percentage of published conference cases that are unanimous as multiple of percentage of conference cases that are unanimous in conference, by term, 624
    percentage of unanimous conference cases, by jurisdiction, 624
    percentage of unanimous conference cases, by jurisdiction by term, 1922–1928 terms, 625
    unanimous conference cases, 621
    unanimous conference cases, by term, 1922–1928 terms, 623
Conference for Progressive Political Action (CPPA), 1384, 1395–96, 1415
Conference of Representatives of National Trade Unions, 1400
Conference of Senior Circuit Court Judges
  Act of September 14, 1922 and, 451–53
  appropriations and, 469–70
  attorney general and, 453, 469
  chief justice, role of, 452–53, 457–58
  committees, 453
  creation, 451
  Graham and, 469
  increased manpower and, 454–55
  intangible factors associated with, 456–57
  managerial efficiency and, 452, 465
  meetings, 453

1535

Conference of Senior Circuit Court (cont.)
  new judgeships, creation of, 453, 462–63, 474–75
  opposition to, 452, 464–65
  powers of, 462
  recommendations of, 453, 466–69
  Sanborn and, 468, 469, 470–71
  success of, 454, 471
  United States Commissioners and, 514–16
  as voice of judiciary, 453–54
Conference on Unemployment, 698, 717–18
Conflicts of interest, appearance of, Taft and, 513
Congressional power. *See also specific Act*
  Bailey and, 1126–28
  Brandeis on, 1149–50
  Commerce Clause and, 390, 1114, 1128, 1129, 1144, 1151, 1152
  contempt, power to regulate, 1382–84
  Coronado I and, 1312
  Dayton-Goose Creek and, 390–91
  economic regulation and, 1122, 1125–26, 1128, 1129, 1132
  Eighteenth Amendment, enforcement power, 958–59
  executive power versus, 402–4, 407, 409, 411, 412–14, 415–16, 418
  expansion of, 690–91, 704, 728, 1121, 1501
  federal common law and, 1198
  federal grants to states and, 1122–23
  federalism and changes in, 1104
  form of power versus substance of power, 1128, 1129, 1130
  Fourteenth Amendment and, xxxii, 1215–16
  Frankfurter on, 1181
  Hill v. Wallace and, 1146–47
  intergovernmental tax immunity and, 1101
  interstate commerce, authority regarding, 1125–26
  judicial deference and, 1129
  McKenna and, 137
  morality and, 1133–34, 1157–58, 1159
  normative dualism and, xxxi, 970–71, 975, 1121–22, 1125–26, 1127, 1132–33, 1134
  Olsen and, 1129, 1152
  opposition to, 1131–32
  oversight of judicial review, 63, 614–17, 653, 789–91, 1312, 1396, 1415
  prohibition and
    enforcement power, 958–59, 1101
    judicial deference and, 928, 998–99
    McCulloch v. Maryland and, 973
    normative dualism (*See* Normative dualism)
    Purity Extract and, 973
    "property affected with a public interest" and, 720–21

railroads, authority over, 1101, 1123–24
Stafford and, 1313–14
stockyards and, 1125–26
"stream of commerce" and, 1166
Taft Court generally, xxxii, 1121–22
Taft on, 391–92
White Court and, 728
Wilson on, 1155
Wisconsin Rate Case and, 1313–14
World War I and, 690–91, 704, 1101
Connelly v. Union Sewer Pipe Co. (1902), 1405–6
Conner, Valerie Jean, 1269
Conscientious objectors
  Butler on, 151
  Holmes on, 151–52
  Stone on, 124, 144–45, 151
Conscription, 698–99
Conservatism
  administrative state and, xxviii, 651, 922
  Butler and, 63
  Carter and, 169, 1007
  Coolidge and, 717
  custom and public sentiment and, xxvii–xxviii, xxx–xxxi, xxxvii, 169
  freedom of contract and, 823
  Harding and, 717
  Holmes and
    as conservative, 204–5
    conservative suspicion of, 172–73, 179
  McKenna and, 118–20
  McReynolds and, 260
  natural law and, 170
  prohibition and
    administrative state and, 922
    ambivalence of, 922
    federalism and, 922
    liberty and, 924
  property rights and, 4, 311–12, 387–88
  Sanford and, 99
  Stone and, 143–44, 152
  Sutherland and, 41–42, 63
  Taft and, 8, 63, 1505–6
  Van Devanter and, 234–36
Conservative unions, 1248–49
Constitutional interpretation
  Brandeis on, 300–1, 312–13, 315, 389, 630
  custom and public sentiment and, 1200–1
  federal common law and, 1199
  Holmes on, 172–73, 202
  McReynolds on, 266–67
  organizations, status of, 1219–20
  Stone on, 124, 156
  Sutherland on, 39
  Taft on, 389, 398, 422–23, 630
  Thayer and, 359
  unions, status of, 1219–20

1536

INDEX

Contempt
  Article III courts, power of, 1382–84
  civil versus criminal contempt, 1395
  Congressional power to regulate, 1382–84
  jury trial, right to, 1381–84
  labor injunctions, for violations of, 1381–84 (*See also Michaelson v. United States* (1924))
  separation of powers and, 1382–84
Cook, Walter Wheeler, 140–41, 151, 155–56, 158–59
Cooks' and Waiters' Union, 1399
Cooley, Thomas M., xxvii, xxxviii, 39, 662, 844, 1254, 1378, 1393
Cooley v. Board of Wardens (1851), 1169–70
Coolidge, Calvin
  generally, 103–4, 683
  Adkins and, 766
  appointments to Court by, 33, 92, 122, 146–47
  Brandeis and, 361
  budget and, 553
  on Child Labor Amendment, 1147–48
  Daugherty and, 125
  on duty of states to enforce prohibition, 949–50
  on federal grants to states, 1122–23
  federalism and, 1104, 1107–8
  Gompers and, 1275
  Harding and, 717
  Holmes and, 168
  Hoover and, 698, 708
  inactivity of, 716
  judicial appointments and, 537–39, 545–46, 548
  Judiciary Act of 1925 and, 485, 501
  labor market and, 1224, 1275
  Lippmann on, 716
  "normalcy" and, 724
  on price controls, 777–78
  on prohibition, 958, 959–60, 1002, 1021
  reelection of, 120–21
  Stone and, 122, 125, 146–47, 153
  Supreme Court Building and, 555
  Taft and
    Caraway bill and, 512
    judicial appointments, lobbying for, 537–39, 543–44, 545–46, 548
    labor market and, 1253–54, 1385
    presidential campaign of Coolidge, 447
    retirement, 382–83
    rulemaking authority of Court and, 509
    Stone and, 132, 147
Copeland, Royal S., 517–18, 1061
Copeland, Walter Scott, 1444–47
Coppage v. Kansas (1915), 1231–33, 1245
Corley, Pamela C., 679

Coronado Coal Co. v. United Mine Workers of America (1925) *(Coronado II)*, 1315–17
  Brandeis in, 1316
  Holmes in, 1316
  intent standard, 1316–17
  interstate versus intrastate commerce, 1317
  McReynolds in, 1316
  normative dualism and, 1317
  Sherman Anti-Trust Act and, 1317
  Taft in, 1316–17, 1355
Corporations
  Brandeis on, 1432–33
  Equal Protection Clause and, 1431–33, 1463, 1464
  foreign corporations (*See* Foreign corporations)
  Stone on, 1433
  system of corporate diversity jurisdiction, 1196, 1197
  Taft on, 1432
Corruption. *See* Official lawlessness
Corwin, Edward S.
  on *Adkins*, 767
  on *Coronado I*, 1362
  on Dormant Commerce Clause, 1182
  on dual sovereignty, 1110
  on Dyer Anti-Lynching Bill, 1418
  on federalism, 1154–55
  on liberty, 853–54
  Myers v. United States and, 414, 434–36, 443, 444
  on removal power, 414, 434–36, 443, 444
  Taft and, 673
  on Taft Court, 682, 685
  on *Truax*, 1426
  World War I and, 718, 1106
Coursey, Joseph, 518–19
Court of Customs Appeals, 513–14
Cover, Robert C., xxv, xxxviii, 1025
Cozzolino, Robert, 700
Crane, Frederick E., 89
Cravath, Henderson and Gersdorff (firm), 261
Criminal law, prohibition and. *See* prohibition
The Crisis (NAACP publication), 1221, 1445
Croly, Herbert, 168, 1155–56, 1254–55, 1298–99
Cromwell, William Nelson, 151
Crowder, Enoch, 1233–34
Cubberley, Elwood P., 831, 856
Cudahy Packing Co. v. Hinkle, 278 U.S. 460 (1929), 1188–89
Cultural pluralism, 1433, 1434
Cummins, Albert Baird
  Butler and, 903–4
  Caraway bill and, 512, 524
  defendants' fees and, 519
  Judiciary Act of 1925 and, 482–84, 503

1537

INDEX

Cummins, Albert Baird (cont.)
   Myers v. United States and, 402
   United States Commissioners and, 515
Cummins Amendment of 1915, 633
Currie, David P., 986, 1403
Curtis, Charles, 550, 567
Cushman, Barry, 638, 745, 770, 787–88, 837–38, 1158, 1184
Cushman, Robert E., 434–38, 749, 750, 907, 1030, 1397
Custom and public sentiment
   Article III courts and, 1201
   Carter and, 169, 1007
   common law and, 200, 1198
   conservatism and, xxvii–xxviii, xxx–xxxi, xxxvii, 169
   Constitutional interpretation and, 1200–1
   federal common law and, 1198, 1199–200
   Fourteenth Amendment and, 824, 1102
   Holmes and, xxviii, 173, 202
   judicial supremacy based on, 169
   McReynolds on, 271–72, 312, 823
   in *Meyer v. Nebraska*, 828–29
   as narrative of Taft Court, xxvii–xxviii
   Olmstead and, 1068–69
   positive law versus, 995–96, 1071
   prohibition and, xxxvii, 923–24, 971, 994, 998, 1010–11
   race relations and, 1451, 1454, 1481
   reasonable relation standard and, 824
   segregation and, 1481
   Sutherland on, 998
   Taft Court generally, xxvii–xxviii, xxxii, 1102, 1198, 1199
   Taft on, xxix–xxx, 387, 824, 1134

Dahnke-Walker Milling Co. v. Bondurant (1921), 1167–68
Danelski, David, 69, 136, 138–39
Daniels, Josephus, 264, 279, 283–84
Darrow, Clarence, 1002, 1389
Darwinism, 169
Daugherty, Harry M.
   Borah and, 145
   Butler and, 61, 102
   Coolidge and, 125
   federalism and, 1103
   Frankfurter on, 145
   judicial appointments and, 536–37, 543
   judicial reform and, 449–51, 460, 462–63, 527
   Judiciary Act of 1925 and, 482–83
   labor market and, 1238, 1290–91
   Miller and, 104–5
   nomination of Taft and, 5
   on prohibition, 959–60
   Sanford and, 87–90, 109–10
   scandal involving, 125, 126
   Taft and, 25, 536–37, 540–41
   trade associations and, 696
Davis, John W.
   consideration for appointment to Court, 61, 72, 103–4
   Coronado I and, 1353
   Day and, 67–68
   dissenting opinions, views on, 634–35
   election of 1924 and, 737, 779
   on excessive legislation, 737, 750
   on freedom of contract, 779
   McReynolds and, 280
   Pitney and, 97–98
   on rent control, 729
   Sutherland and, 40–41, 51
   Van Devanter and, 229
   World War I and, 718–19
Davis v. Farmers' Co-op Equity Co. (1923), 363–64, 1183–84
Dawes, Charles Gates, 545, 584, 1037–38
Dawes Act, 847
Day, William L., 67
Day, William Rufus, 5
   appointment of, 59
   Brandeis, views of, 67–68
   on child labor, 1126
   Clarke, views of, 67–68
   in *Coronado I*, 1306, 1341–42
   Davis and, 67–68
   Dormant Commerce Clause and, 1161–62
   Harding and, 60–61
   health of, 60–61, 69
   Holmes and, 67–68, 206–7, 211
   on hours of labor, 328–29
   judicial deference and, 733
   Judiciary Act of 1925 and, 483–84, 491–93
   McKinley and, 59, 67
   number of opinions authored by Day, 1921 term, 31, 32
   in *Pennsylvania v. West Virginia*, 1161–62
   personal appearance of, 67
   personality of, 67
   Pitney compared, 85
   "property affected with a public interest" and, 793–94
   replacement of, 33, 61
   retirement of, 59, 67, 69, 70, 78–79
   Taft and, 59, 60–61, 67–68
   Theodore Roosevelt and, 67
   in *Truax*, 1418–19
   Van Devanter, views of, 67–68
   voting on Court
      percentage of all decisions in which Day either joined or authored opinion of Court, 1915–1920 terms versus 1921 term, 613
      percentage of decisions in which Day participated and either authored or

1538

INDEX

joined opinion for Court, 1916–1921 terms, 32
percentage of decisions in which Day participated and either joined or authored opinion of Court, 1921 term, 10, 32
percentage of decisions in which Day participated and joined same opinion as another justice, 1916–1921 terms, 60
percentage of decisions in which Day participated and joined same opinion as another justice, 1921 term, 60
on yellow-dog contracts, 1231
Dayton-Goose Creek Ry. Co. v. United States (1924), 390–91, 693–94, 899–900, 902, 912
Debs, Eugene, 1322–23, 1375, 1376–77
Debs; In re (1895), 1241, 1377, 1379
Decision of 1789, 434–36, 444
Declaratory judgments
  Borchard on, 324–25, 657–59
  Brandeis on, 324–25, 675
  Grannis and, 657–59
  Stone on, 673–74
  Willing v. Chicago Auditorium Ass'n, 324–25
Deference. *See* Judicial deference
Delano, Frederic A., 580–82
Dembitz, Lewis Naphtali, 296–97
Denison, Arthur Carter, 112, 538–39
Denison, Duncan, 515–16
Dett, Nathaniel, 1446–47
Dewey, John, 195–96, 331
Dickinson, Jacob M., 34, 261, 284, 341–42
Dietrich, Frank S., 473
Dignity, *Olmstead* and, 1068–69
Dill, Clarence, 893
Dillard, James Hardy, 1448–49
Dillon, John F., xxxix, 201, 359
Di Santo v. Pennsylvania (1927), 644–45, 1172, 1189–91
Disarmament Commission, 5, 23–24
Discretionary jurisdiction
  certiorari (*See* Certiorari)
  changing authority of Court, 481, 484, 600, 637
  conference cases
    percentage of published conference cases that are unanimous as multiple of percentage of conference cases that are unanimous in conference, by jurisdiction by term, 1922–1928 terms, 625
    percentage of unanimous conference cases, by jurisdiction, 624
    percentage of unanimous conference cases, by jurisdiction by term, 1922–1928 terms, 625
  dissenting opinions and, 619, 623
  expanding, 481, 484, 600, 637
  Judiciary Act of 1925 expanding, 484, 637
  mandatory jurisdiction versus discretionary jurisdiction
    1922–1928 terms, 626, 627–28, 665
    average number of days from argument to announcement of full opinion, by jurisdiction by term, 1921–1928 terms, 607
    average number of pages in full opinion, by jurisdiction by term, 1921–1928 terms, 607
    percentage of full opinions that are unanimous, by jurisdiction by term, 1921–1928 terms, 608
    percentage of published conference cases that are unanimous as multiple of percentage of conference cases that are unanimous in conference, by jurisdiction by term, 1922–1928 terms, 625
    percentage of unanimous conference cases, by jurisdiction, 624
    percentage of unanimous conference cases, by jurisdiction by term, 1922–1928 terms, 625
  unanimous opinions, 619, 623
  more dissention in conference, 623, 626, 627–28
  unanimous opinions
    1922–1928 terms, 626, 627–28, 665
    mandatory jurisdiction versus discretionary jurisdiction, 619, 623
    percentage of full opinions that are unanimous, by jurisdiction by term, 1921–1928 terms, 608
    percentage of published conference cases that are unanimous as multiple of percentage of conference cases that are unanimous in conference, by jurisdiction by term, 1922–1928 terms, 625
    percentage of unanimous conference cases, by jurisdiction, 624
    percentage of unanimous conference cases, by jurisdiction by term, 1922–1928 terms, 625
Dissent. *See also specific justice or case*
  authority of expertise and, 656–57, 664
  authority of finality and, 629–30
  benefits of, 669
  collective judgment of Court, individual expression versus, 652–53

INDEX

Dissent (cont.)
  in conference cases
    percentage of dissenting votes in conference that justice switched in order to join published Court opinion, 622
    percentage of justice's unanimous published opinions that had dissenting or uncertain votes in conference, 66
  criticism of, 629–30, 647
  Davis on, 634–35
  dissenting votes as percentage of full opinions, by term, 1916–1928 terms, 615
  Douglas on, 631, 648, 652–53
  Edward White on, 629
  external attacks on Court and, 614–17
  Frankfurter on, 647–48
  Hughes on, 631
  institutional solidarity of Taft Court versus, 626–27
  judicial authority versus, 649–50
  Judiciary Act of 1925, impact of, 631
  legal realism and, 621–22, 626
  legal scholarship, number of citations to
    in Court opinions and dissents, 1921–1928 terms, 664
    in Court opinions and dissents, 1997 and 2011 terms, 664
    in Court opinions and dissents, by justice, 1921–1928 terms, 661
    in dissents, 661
    in dissents, by justice, 1921–1928 terms, 661
  losing parties, importance to, 628, 629
  mandatory jurisdiction versus discretionary jurisdiction and, 619, 623
  "marketplace of ideas" and, 653
  minimization of, 610–12
  modification of opinions to avoid, 612
  "norm of acquiescence" and, xxxvii, 627–31
  opposition to, 610, 629–30, 647
  percentage of decisions in which justice participated and chose to be only dissenter, 1921–1928 terms, 269
  potential awkwardness of, 629
  principles of law versus particular parties and, 628–29
  publication of, 632
  purpose of, 629, 647–48
  race relations and, 1455
  Scalia on, 641–42, 664–65
  switching of votes, percentage of cases by justice, 622
  troublesome nature of, 649
District courts
  Conference of Senior Circuit Court Judges and, 462

dockets
  bankruptcy cases in district courts by fiscal year 1915–1930, 455
  civil cases in district courts in which United States is party, by fiscal year 1915–1930, 456
  criminal prosecutions in district courts, by fiscal year 1915–1930, 455
  district court cases in which United States is not party, by fiscal year 1915–1930, 456
  total number of district court cases, by fiscal year 1915–1930, 454
judicial appointments, 537
new judgeships, creation of, 453, 462–63, 474–75, 536–37
as "police courts," 515, 949
Taft, district judges and, 457, 458
Diversity jurisdiction
  Black & White Taxicab, 1199–200, 1211–15
  Brandeis on, 1197, 1208, 1214–15
  Clarke on, 1208–9
  Erie Railroad and, 1102, 1201, 1216
  federal common law and, 1197–98
  foreign corporations and, 1196–97
  Frankfurter on, 1208, 1213
  Holmes on, xxxii, 206
  importance to national market and, 1101–2
  labor market and, 1241
  Lee v. Chesapeake & Ohio Ry. Co. and, 1197
  Norris and, 516, 1214–15
  S. 3151 and, 516–18
  Stone on, 1213
  Swift v. Tyson and (*See Swift v. Tyson* (1842))
  system of corporate diversity jurisdiction, 1196, 1197
  Taft on, 1196–97, 1214–15
  Terral and, 1196
  Thomas Walsh on, 1196–97, 1214–15
  Van Devanter on, 1197, 1208–9
Docket books, xxxvi
"Domestic imperialism," 971, 982
Donovan, William J., 148, 712
Doran, James M., 950, 960
Dormant Commerce Clause
  generally, 1160
  Attleboro Steam & Electric Co. and, 1167–68
  automobiles and, 1170, 1186, 1190–91
  balancing tests and, 661–62, 1172–73
  Bickel on, 1174, 1183–84
  Brandeis and
    generally, 363–64, 1160, 1189
    direct versus indirect burden on interstate commerce, 1169, 1171, 1183–84
    electric utilities and, 1180–81
    foreign corporations and, 1182
    licenses and, 1189–90
    natural gas and, 1161–63

1540

INDEX

Butler and, 1171, 1172, 1173–74, 1191
Clarke and, 1162
coal industry and, 1163–64
common carriers and, 1173–74, 1185
Cooley and, 1169–70
Corwin on, 1182
Dahnke-Walker and, 1167–68
Day and, 1161–62
direct versus indirect burden on interstate commerce, 1169, 1170–74, 1183–84
Di Santo and, 1172
dual sovereignty and, xxxi, 1163, 1164, 1166–68, 1181–82
Due Process Clause compared, 1194
Duke and, 1173–74
economic policy imposed on basis of, 1171, 1173
electric utilities and, 1167–68, 1180–81
ferries and, 1186
foreign corporations and, 1168–69, 1182
grain and, 1174
Heisler and, 1163–64
Helsen and, 1171
Holmes and, 1160, 1161–62, 1171, 1188–89
ICC and, 1168
incompatibility with dual sovereignty, 1164, 1166, 1167–68
insurance and, 1193–94
"interests" and, 1165–66, 1167–68
intergovernmental tax immunity and, 1171–72, 1188–89
interstate versus intrastate commerce, 1125–26, 1163–67, 1168–70
Lemke and, 1174
licenses and, 1172
McKenna and, 1161, 1186–87
McReynolds and, 1160, 1161–62, 1168, 1186
Missouri ex rel. *Barrett v. Kansas Natural Gas* and, 1164
national market and, xxxii, 1101–2, 1168, 1174
natural gas and, 1160, 1161–63, 1164–66, 1187
Pennsylvania v. West Virginia and, 1160–63, 1167
physical movement of goods and, 1164–66, 1179–80
Pitney and, 1161–62
railroads and, 1186–87
ratemaking and, 1167, 1168
Real Silk Hosiery Mills and, 1168
sales taxes and, 1171–72
Sanford and, 1167
Shafer and, 1174
Stone and, 1171–73, 1188–89
"stream of commerce" and, 1166
Sutherland and, 1165, 1166, 1168–69, 1171

Taft and
 as justice, 1161–62, 1163, 1178
 as president, 1160–61
 recusal of, 1163, 1178
taxation and, 1185
Texas Transport & Terminal Co. and, 1169
transfer of title and, 1165–66
uniformity and, 1160–61, 1163, 1165, 1168
Van Devanter and, 1160–62, 1168
Webb-Kenyon Act and, 1160–61, 1177–78
West v. Kansas Natural Gas and, 1161
Double Jeopardy Clause
 dual sovereignty and, 1110
 Lanza and, 951–52, 1110
 prohibition and, 951–52, 964–65
Douglas, William O.
 Butler, views on, 62, 75
 dissenting opinions, views on, 631, 648, 652–53
 McReynolds, views on, 265
 Stone and, 123, 143–44, 597, 655
 Sutherland, views on, 42
 Van Devanter, views on, 254
Dowling, Noel T., 155, 1190
Dred Scott v. Sandford (1857), 766, 1070–71
Drinker, Henry S., Jr., 1362
Dual sovereignty
 comity and, 1210
 common law and, 1102
 Corwin on, 1110
 defined, xxxi, 951–52
 Dormant Commerce Clause and, xxxi, 1163, 1164, 1166–68, 1181–82
 Double Jeopardy Clause and, 1110
 federalism and, xxxi
 intergovernmental tax immunity and, xxxi, 1110–11, 1112
 interstate commerce and, xxxi, 1163, 1164, 1166–68, 1181–82
 Lanza and, 951–52
 normative dualism (*See* Normative dualism)
 prohibition and, 951–52
 "separate spheres" and, xxxi–xxxii, 970, 1121–22, 1128, 1163, 1166
 Stone on, xxxi–xxxii, 1114–15
 Sutherland on, 1116–17
 Van Devanter on, 257–58, 963
Du Bois, W.E.B.
 generally, 1221
 Hampton Institute and, 1443, 1445, 1479–80
 Harding and, 1449
 race relations and, 1465
 social equality and, 1442, 1449
 Taft and, 1442, 1451, 1476
 Theodore Roosevelt and, 1476
Due Process Clause
 Adkins and, 755, 756, 772–73
 Brandeis and, 320, 1194–95, 1204–5

1541

INDEX

Due Process Clause (cont.)
  bread standardization and, 733, 734
  class legislation prohibited under, 757
  Dormant Commerce Clause compared, 1194
  economic liberty and, 825–26, 1200–1
  economic regulation and, 733, 738, 802–3, 823, 824
  Equal Protection Clause compared, 1404, 1419–20, 1430–31, 1432
  Euclid and, 835
  Fairmont Creamery and, 823, 824, 825
  federal common law compared, 1200–1
  foreign corporations and, 1195
  fundamental rights and, 1408
  Holmes and, 208, 734, 739, 1194–95, 1202–4
  hours of labor and, 770
  insurance and
    contracts, 1193–94, 1202
    foreign insurance companies, 1194–95
    taxation, 1194, 1202–4
  Jackson on, 802–3
  judicial deference and, 733, 739, 740, 741
  liberty (*See* Liberty)
  McReynolds and, 830–31, 1194–95
  Meyer v. Nebraska and, 827–28, 830
  peonage and, 1472–73
  Pierce and, 830–31, 833–34
  progressivism and, 1379
  property rights (*See* Property rights)
  ratemaking and, 879–80
  reasonable relation standard and, 824
  return on property and, 879–80, 890–91 (*See also* Fair value test)
  Sanford and, 1194–95
  Stone and, 129, 617
  substantive due process (*See* Substantive due process)
  Taft and, 1402–3, 1408–9
  Taft Court generally, 685, 686–87
  taxation and
    generally, 752
    foreign corporations, 1195
    insurance companies, 1194, 1202–4
  Terrace and, 1455–56
  Truax and, 1402–3, 1408–9, 1411, 1415
  tyranny and, 824
  vagueness and, 845–46
  Van Devanter and, 257–58, 1204
  Weaver and, 738, 751
  West and, 890–91
Dunbar, William H., 1377–78, 1379, 1388
Duplex Printing Press Co. v. Deering (1921), 1242, 1324, 1361, 1367–68, 1378, 1400–1
Dyer Anti-Lynching Bill, 1418

Easley, Ralph, 1260
Eastman, Joseph, 887, 906

E.C. Knight Co.; United States v. (1895), 1121–22, 1125–26, 1338
Economic liberty, xxvi, 825–26, 1200–1, 1376–77, 1472–73
Economic planning, World War I and, 694, 705, 706
Economic prosperity
  Brandeis on, xxix, 312, 315–16, 321, 1332, 1412
  Butler on, xxix
  economic regulation and, xxix
  judicial review and, xxix, 292–93, 312
  judicial supremacy and, xxix, 292–93
  as narrative of Taft Court, xxviii–xxix, 879, 1200–1
  property rights and, xxix, 312, 387–88, 866, 879
  Sutherland on, xxix
  Taft on, xxviii–xxix, 321, 388
Economic regulation. *See also* Administrative state
  administrative expertise and, 693, 719
  Brandeis on, 129, 304–5
  Butler on, 65–66, 76
  Congressional power and, 1122, 1125–26, 1128, 1129, 1132
  Due Process Clause and, 733, 738, 802–3, 823, 824
  economic prosperity and, xxix
  Equal Protection Clause and, 1430
  Fourteenth Amendment and, 128, 298, 391–92, 757
  freedom of contract and, 722–23, 733, 734, 755, 759, 765–66
  Holmes on, 129, 1230
  Hoover on, 709, 715–16
  judicial power and, 1198
  McReynolds on, 291
  minimum wage (*See* Minimum wage)
  overbreadth and, 825
  price controls (*See* Price controls)
  ratemaking (*See* Ratemaking)
  "real and substantial relation" standard, xxvii
  Stone on, 128, 130–31
  Sutherland on, xxxix, 42, 129
  Taft and, 391–92, 723
  taxation, disguised as, 263, 1129–30, 1153
  White Court and, 825
Edge, Walter E., 1004–5
Education. *See* Schools
Efficiency Society, 932
Eighteenth Amendment. *See also* prohibition
  Anti-Saloon League and, 964
  authority under, 923–24, 928
  concurrent enforcement power, 968–69, 971–72
  Congressional enforcement power, 958–59
  Constitutionality of, 970

1542

INDEX

debate regarding, 922, 924
Double Jeopardy Clause and, 951–52, 964–65 (*See also Lanza; United States v.* (1922))
duty of states to enforce, 949–51
implementation of, 922
legislative history, 964
National Prohibition Cases and, 970, 972
ratification of, 917–18, 920, 925
repeal of, 928
Root on, 979–80, 1010
Section 1, 972
Section 2, 972
Sutherland and, 968, 971–72
Taft and, 926, 927–28, 973
Volstead Act (*See* Volstead Act)
World War I, impact of, 917, 921, 929–30
Einstein, Lewis, 175, 191–92, 210
Eisner, Marc Allen, 705, 706
Elections. *See* Primary elections
Eliot, Charles William, 678, 1217
Elliott, Richard N., 560, 561, 562–63, 582, 584, 588
Ellsworth, Oliver, 6
Ely, John Hart, 1493
Emerson, Ralph Waldo, 175, 210
Epstein, Lee, 637
Equal Protection Clause
  Brandeis and, 1205, 1412, 1415, 1430–31, 1432–33, 1464
  Carolene Products and, 1433, 1434, 1460, 1461
  civil rights versus political rights versus social equality, 1436, 1467, 1468, 1470
  class legislation and, 1419, 1430
  contemporary jurisprudence compared, 1433, 1434, 1437
  corporations and, 1431–33, 1463, 1464
  Due Process Clause compared, 1404, 1419–20, 1430–31, 1432
  economic regulation and, 1430
  federal government, applicability to, 1453
  foreign corporations and, 1195, 1431
  Frankfurter and, 1415, 1430–31
  fundamental rights and, 1407–8
  Gong Lum and, 1437
  Holmes and, 1205, 1403–4, 1419, 1431, 1432, 1464
  narrow tailoring, 1408, 1409–10, 1413
  Nixon and, 1469
  political rights and, 1444–45, 1467, 1468–69
  primary elections and, 1434–37 (*See also Nixon v. Herndon* (1927))
  race, failure to apply to, 1223
  race relations and, 1223, 1433, 1435, 1436, 1437–38, 1450, 1455–56
  reasonable relation standard and, 1406, 1431–32

segregation and, xxxiv–xxxv, 1436, 1437–38, 1450
"separate but equal," 1442, 1450–51
social equality and, 1446
Stone and, 1432, 1433, 1461, 1482
strict scrutiny and, 1408, 1413
Taft and, 1403–5, 1406–8, 1432, 1433, 1453
Taft Court generally, 1430, 1458
taxation and, 752
Terrace and, 1455–56
Truax and, 1403–4, 1406–8, 1409–10, 1412, 1415, 1430–31
Van Devanter and, 236, 1403–4, 1431
voting rights and, 1436
White supremacy and, 1442, 1450–51
women and, 780–81
Equity
  common law versus, 509
  labor injunctions and, 1377–78
  Michaelson and, 1382–84
  proposal to merge with law, 509
  Taft and, 509, 1380
Erdman Act, 1230
Erie Railroad Co. v. Tompkins (1938), 1102, 1201, 1216
Esch-Cummins Act, 1352
Eugenics, 203–4, 1441, 1444, 1452
Evarts Act of 1891, 477–80, 489–90
Evidence
  illegally obtained, 1063–64, 1079–80
  judicial notice, 363–64, 724–25, 735–36
  unconstitutionally obtained, 1062, 1063–64, 1065, 1083
Excessive legislation
  Brewer on, 170
  Butler on, 62–63, 76, 737
  Davis on, 737, 750
  progressivism and, 995
  prohibition and, 994–95
  Stone on, 123–24, 198–99
  "super-legislature," 748–49
  Sutherland on, 753
  Taft on, 56, 753, 1191
Exclusionary rule
  generally, 1044–45
  prohibition and, 1026, 1062
Executive power
  Congressional power versus, 402–4, 407, 409, 411, 412–14, 415–16, 418
  Harding on, 693, 705–6
  Jackson on, 418
  J.W. Hampton and, 401, 693
  Myers v. United States and, 407, 414–15, 416, 418, 426–27, 428, 431–32
  prohibition and, 1025–26
  removal power and, 407, 413–15, 416, 418, 426–27, 428, 431–32
  residual presidential power, 403

1543

INDEX

Executive power (cont.)
  "stewardship" theory of executive leadership, 402–3
  Taft Court generally, 693
  Taft on, 401, 402–4
  Theodore Roosevelt on, 402–3
  World War I, impact of, 692–93
Expertise
  administrative expertise (*See* Administrative expertise)
  authority of expertise (*See* Authority of expertise)
  legal scholarship (*See* Legal scholarship)

"Facial" versus "as applied" challenges in *Euclid*, 838–39, 871–72
Fact-finding
  generally, 844–45
  Brandeis and, 300–2, 329, 645–46
  in *Jay Burns*, 730, 735
  judicial notice and, 724–25, 735–36
Fairmont Creamery Co. v. Minnesota (1927)
  common law and, 823
  Due Process Clause and, 823, 824, 825
  judicial deference and, 823
  judicial intuition and, 823
  McReynolds in, 822–23, 825
  overbreadth in, 825
  reasonable relation standard and, 823
  Stone in, 845
  substantive due process and, 824
Fair value test
  generally, 138, 895
  cost of reproduction, 881, 882–83, 884, 885, 886, 887, 888–90, 897–98
  creation of, 880
  difficulty in applying, 880
  logical fallacy of, 880
  present value, 884, 890–91, 894
  prudent investment, return on, 881–82, 883–84, 885, 886–87
  Smyth v. Ames and, 880, 881, 882, 883, 884, 886, 895, 896, 899
Fallibilism, 360
Federal Bread Act (proposed), 734–35, 744–45
Federal Bureau of Investigation (FBI), 146, 151–52, 1089–90
Federal common law
  generally, xxxii
  anti-trust law and, 1197–98
  Article III courts and, 1198
  Black & White Taxicab and, 1199–200, 1211–15
  Brandeis on, 817, 1201, 1212, 1216
  Butler on, 1199–200, 1211
  Congress and, 1198
  Constitutional interpretation and, 1199
  Coronado I and, 1312

  custom and public sentiment and, 1198, 1199–200
  diversity jurisdiction and, 1197–98
  Due Process Clause compared, 1200–1
  economic liberty and, 1200–1
  Erie Railroad and, 1102, 1201, 1216
  Fourteenth Amendment and, xxxii, 1198–99
  Holmes on, 1199–200, 1201, 1211, 1212, 1214
  labor injunctions and, xxxiii, 1241
  McReynolds on, 1198–99
  national market and, 1197–98
  normative dualism and, 1201
  Stone on, 1212
  substantive due process and, 1200–1, 1215
  Swift v. Tyson and, 1197, 1209, 1211, 1212, 1213
  Taft Court generally, xxxii, 1197–200
  Taft on, 1198, 1210
Federal Council of Churches, 1270–71
Federal courts. *See* Article III courts
Federal Employers' Liability Act of 1908 (FELA), 257–58, 362–63, 521–22, 1132, 1156–57, 1295
Federal Estate Law of 1926, 752
Federal grants to states
  Congressional power and, 1122–23
  Coolidge on, 1122–23
  Massachusetts v. Mellon, 1123
  Tenth Amendment and, 1123
Federalism
  ambivalence of Taft Court, 1101, 1104
  anti-trust law and, 1132
  Article III courts and, 1198, 1201
  Bailey and, 1103–4, 1132
  boards of trade and, 1133–34
  Brandeis and, 365, 366, 968–69, 1104
  child labor and, 1103–4
  Congressional power (*See* Congressional power)
  Coolidge and, 1104, 1107–8
  Corwin on, 1154–55
  democratic authorship and, 970–71
  Double Jeopardy Clause
    dual sovereignty and, 1110
    Lanza and, 951–52, 1110
    prohibition and, 951–52, 964–65
  dual sovereignty (*See* Dual sovereignty)
  Fourteenth Amendment and, 1215–16
  Harding and, 1104
  ICC and, 1104
  intergovernmental tax immunity (*See* Intergovernmental tax immunity)
  liberty and, 1132
  McKenna and, 1163–64
  McReynolds and, 968, 975–76, 1153, 1154
  medical prescriptions and, 975–76
  normative dualism (*See* Normative dualism)

1544

INDEX

prohibition and, xxxi, 922–23, 969, 973, 1132
railroads and, 1104
states' rights and, 1104
"stream of commerce," 1145
Sutherland on, 968, 984–85, 991–92
Taft and, 1103–4, 1126–27
Taft Court generally, 1104, 1105
Transportation Act and, 1133–34
Wilson and, 1103, 1104
World War I, impact of, xxxi, 1103
Federal preemption
generally, 1198
McReynolds on, 273
Federal question jurisdiction
Norris on, 1214–15
S. 3151 and, 516–18, 1214–15
Federal Trade Commission (FTC)
Brandeis and, 271, 306–7, 825, 844–45
ICC compared, 825
judicial deference and, 824
McReynolds and, 271, 290–91
normative dualism and, 1132
reasonable relation standard and, 824–25
removal power and, 415–16
Taft and, 844–45
Fellow servant rule, 996–97
Fess, Simeon D., 558
Field, Stephen
class legislation and, 1404
Fourteenth Amendment and, 1467
"free labor" and, 1227
"Old Brick Capitol" and, 555
on property rights, 1227
Fifteenth Amendment. *See also* Voting rights
generally, 1220
African Americans and, 1434–37
Fourteenth Amendment, relation to, 1436
Holmes and, 166
Nixon and, 1435–36, 1468, 1469
primary elections and, 1467
prohibition compared, 1002
Taft and, 1440, 1446, 1451, 1473–74
Fifth Amendment
Adkins and, 755
Carroll and, 1029
Casey and, 178–79
Double Jeopardy Clause
dual sovereignty and, 1110
Lanza and, 951–52, 1110
prohibition and, 951–52, 964–65
Due Process Clause (*See* Due Process Clause)
grand jury requirement, 388–90
Highland and, 721
Lanza and, 951
Moreland and, 388–90
Olmstead and, 1063, 1083, 1084
presumptions and, 221–23

price controls and, 721
prohibition and, 951
Taft and, 311–12, 388–90
Taft Court generally, 686–87
takings
Adkins, minimum wage distinguished, 765
Butler on, 726–27
frustration of contract distinguished, 726–27
price controls distinguished, 726–27
prohibition viewed as, 1014
ratemaking viewed as, 879–81
Supreme Court Building, condemnation for, 555, 556–57
zoning viewed as, 837, 866, 872
First Amendment
Brandeis and, 315
Establishment Clause, 860
freedom of association, primary elections and, 1435–36
freedom of religion
Establishment Clause, 860
Free Exercise Clause, 833
Pierce, not relied on in, 833
freedom of speech
Brandeis on, 127, 315
Holmes on, 127, 320
Stone on, 127, 144
Free Exercise Clause, 833
Holmes and, 315
modern doctrine, 1423
overbreadth and, 825, 1422
vagueness and, 845–46
Fish, Peter G., 589, 1181
Fiss, Owen M., 1387
Flint v. Stone Tracy Co., 220 U.S. 107 (1911), 1113, 1188–89
Food Administration, 711–12, 717, 733–34, 742–43, 746–47, 810
Fordney-McCumber Tariff Act of 1922, 419
Foreign corporations
generally, 1206
access to federal courts, 1196–97, 1207
diversity jurisdiction and, 1196–97
Dormant Commerce Clause and, 1168–69, 1182
Due Process Clause and, 1195
Equal Protection Clause and, 1195, 1431
foreign insurance companies, Due Process Clause and, 1193–95
substantive due process and, 1193–95
taxation, Due Process Clause and, 1195
unconstitutional conditions and, 1206–7
venue and, 1195
Foreign languages in schools
prohibition on, 827–30 (*See also Meyer v. Nebraska* (1923))
World War I, impact of, 848–49

1545

Formalism, intergovernmental tax immunity and, 1111–12
Fourteenth Amendment
 Brandeis and, 298, 363–64, 1412
 bread standardization and, 733
 Charles Wolff Packing and, 796
 child labor and, 1131
 class legislation and, xxvi, 757, 1254, 1404–5
 Congressional power and, xxxii, 1215–16
 custom and public sentiment and, 824, 1102
 Due Process Clause (*See* Due Process Clause)
 economic regulation and, 128, 298, 391–92, 757
 Equal Protection Clause (*See* Equal Protection Clause)
 federal common law and, xxxii, 1198–99
 federalism and, 1215–16
 Field and, 1467
 Fifteenth Amendment, relation to, 1436
 Highland and, 721
 Holmes and, 170, 171, 202, 215–16, 749
 hours of labor and, 770
 Jay Burns and, 734
 judicial supremacy and, 169
 McReynolds and, 271–72, 291–92, 827–28, 834, 861
 Meyer v. Nebraska and, 827–28, 848
 Moore and, 1025
 Nixon and, 1466–67, 1468, 1469
 Pierce and, 830–31
 price controls and, 721
 primary elections and, 1467
 prohibition and, xxx, 1025–26
 ratemaking and, 903
 restrictive covenants and, 1418
 Stone and, 128, 129, 152
 strikes and, 1248
 Sutherland on, 42–43
 Taft and, 311–12, 388, 393, 1446, 1451
 Taft Court generally, 685, 686–87
 Thirteenth Amendment, relation to, 152
 Truax and, 1409, 1412, 1414, 1415
 Tumey and, 1025–26
 Van Devanter and, 257–58
 Weaver and, 739–40
 West and, 890–91, 894
 Williams and, 803
Fourth Amendment
 automobile searches
  generally, 1046, 1049
  Brandeis on, 390
  prohibition and, 1026–30 (*See also Carroll v. United States* (1925))
  Taft on, 390
 Brandeis and, 358, 1062
 Butler and, 1047–49

Carroll and, 1028, 1029
exclusionary rule
 generally, 1044–45
 prohibition and, 1026, 1062
Hester and, 1062, 1067
Holmes and, 1062
jurisprudence generally, 1053–54
liberal construction of, 1084
Maul and, 1031, 1059–60
prohibition and
 generally, 1026
 automobile searches, 1026–30 (*See also Carroll v. United States* (1925))
 exclusionary rule, 1062
 wiretapping (*See Olmstead v. United States* (1928))
Stone and, 1047–49
Sutherland and, 1047–49
Taft Court generally, 1047–49
Fowler, James A., 87–88, 90, 99, 101, 103, 109–10, 111
Fox, Austen G., 328, 964–65, 1464
Frankfurter, Felix
 Adkins, as counsel in, 756, 759, 760, 764, 773–74, 839
 authority of expertise and, 665
 on *Bedford Cut Stone*, 1332, 1369
 Brandeis and, 154, 195–96, 310–11, 350–51, 360–61, 444
 on *Charles Wolff Packing*, 811
 Clarke, views on, 46
 on Conference of Senior Circuit Court Judges, 453–54
 on Congressional power, 1181
 on *Coronado I*, 1308
 on Daugherty, 145
 dissenting opinions, views on, 647–48
 on diversity jurisdiction, 1208, 1213
 Equal Protection Clause and, 1415, 1430–31
 Holmes and, 168, 196, 367
 on hours of labor, 772–73
 "House of Truth" and, 168
 Hughes and, 915–16
 on intergovernmental tax immunity, 1120, 1149–51
 on *Jay Burns*, 749
 on judicial reform, 450, 451–52, 453–54, 461, 465, 470, 506
 on Judiciary Act of 1925, 481, 499, 609
 on labor injunctions, 1358, 1379, 1386, 1391
 labor market and, 776–77
 law reviews and, 670
 legal scholarship and, 670
 McReynolds, personal relationship with, 265
 on *Meyer v. Nebraska*, 829
 on *Michaelson*, 1397
 on minimum wage, 756, 767–68, 769
 "norm of acquiescence" and, 665

1546

INDEX

on *Pierce*, 860–61
on prohibition, 978
removal power and, 402
on socioeconomic legislation, 815
Stone, views on, 148, 151
Taft and, 6, 8, 19–20, 27, 106–7, 682–83, 1505
Theodore Roosevelt and, 305–6, 686
on *Truax*, 1427
Van Devanter, views on, 232, 253
on World War I, 687
Franklin, John Hope, 1221–22
Freedman's Bureau, 1443
Freedom of association, primary elections and, 1435–36
Freedom of contract
  generally, xxvii
  Adkins and, 755, 756, 761, 762–63, 765, 778
  "American plan" and, 1236
  Brandeis on, 299–300, 313
  bread standardization and, 733, 734
  conservatism and, 823
  Davis on, 779
  economic regulation and, 722–23, 733, 734, 755, 759, 765–66
  Highland and, 722–23
  Holmes on, 202, 765, 800
  Lochner and, 758, 772
  price controls and, xxvii
  as property right, 825–26
  reasonable relation standard and, 1406
  substantive due process and, 733, 734, 1193–94
  Sutherland on, 56, 199, 779
  tortious interference with contract and, 1233
  unions and, 1230
  voluntariness of employment contracts and, 763–64, 782, 1231–32
  yellow-dog contracts and, 1231–33
Freedom of religion
  Establishment Clause, 860
  Free Exercise Clause, 833
  Pierce, not relied on in, 833
Freedom of speech
  Brandeis on, 127, 315
  Holmes on, 127, 320
  Stone on, 127, 144
Free Exercise Clause, 833
"Free labor"
  generally, 826
  Adair and, 1230–31
  AFL on, 1298
  Coppage and, 1231–33
  Duplex and, 1324, 1361, 1367–68, 1378–79, 1400–1
  Field and, 1227
  historical development of, 1227
  Hitchman and (*See* Hitchman Coal & Coke Co. v. Mitchell (1917))

individualism and, 1228, 1229, 1230–31
railroads and, 1230–31
right to organize and, 1227–28
"scabs" and, 1228
The Slaughterhouse Cases and, 1262
Freund, Ernst, 749, 842, 875, 1004
Freund, Paul A., xli, 360, 361, 365, 592
Frey, John P., 1389–90
Friedman, Barry, 651
Friendly, Henry J., 310–11, 330
FTC. *See* Federal Trade Commission (FTC)
Fuller, Charles M., 745–46
Fuller, Melville Weston, 29, 135, 227, 240, 551
Full opinions. *See* Opinions
Functionalism in *Myers v. United States*, 409–10, 414–16
Fundamental rights
  Due Process Clause and, 1408
  Equal Protection Clause and, 1407–8
  Holmes on, 320
  individualism and, 53, 630, 1407–8
  McReynolds on, xxviii, 828
  Meyer v. Nebraska and, 828–29
  property rights as, 1408
  strict scrutiny and, 1408, 1413
  Sutherland on, 40–41, 53
  in Taft Court generally, xxviii, 828–29, 1407–8, 1413
  Truax and, 1407–8
Furuseth, Andrew, 40, 52, 1334–35
Future Trading Act, 1128–29

Galloway, Gail, xxxvi
Galloway, Russell, 687
Gambino v. United States (1927), 951
Garesche, Vital W., 537, 543–44
Gary, Elbert H., 339–40, 1236, 1272, 1275
George M. Bush & Sons Co. v. Maloy, 267 U.S. 317 (1925), 1186
Georgia Ry. & Power Co. v. Railroad Comm'n of Georgia (1923), 883–84
German Alliance Insurance Co. v. Kansas (1914), 792–93, 795–96, 799
German–American Mixed Claims Commission, 69
Gilbert, Cass, Sr.
  generally, 577, 586, 650
  on architecture, 590
  Commission of Fine Arts and, 568
  design of Supreme Court Building, 564–66
  managerial functionality and, 589
  plans for Supreme Court Building, 559–62, 577–79, 580–82, 587
  politics of, 577, 591–92
  selection as architect, 556–58
  Taft and, 556, 563–64, 586
Gillespie v. Oklahoma (1922), 1111
Gillman, Howard, 651

1547

INDEX

Gilmore, Grant, 1209
Glavis, Louis R., 302–3, 331, 332, 333
Godkin, E.L., 1263–64
Goff, Guy D., 111
Goldmark, Josephine, 299
Gompers, Samuel
  on *Adkins*, 777
  on *American Steel Foundries*, 1253
  Brandeis and, 1305
  Butler and, 903–4
  on *Charles Wolff Packing*, 816
  on Clayton Act, 1241
  Coolidge and, 1275
  on *Coronado I*, 1310, 1311, 1312–13
  on *Hitchman*, 1267–68
  on incorporation of unions, 1305
  on judicial review, 635
  Kansas Court of Industrial Relations and, 794
  on labor injunctions, 1239, 1290–91, 1314, 1379, 1386
  on *Michaelson*, 1385, 1386
  Sutherland and, 40, 54
  Taft and, 3, 14–16, 1239, 1273–74, 1277, 1282, 1393
  on Taft Court generally, 1307
  on tension in labor market, 1224
  on *Truax*, 1427
Gong Lum v. Rice (1927)
  Equal Protection Clause and, 1437
  labor injunctions compared, 1451
  Nixon compared, 1438
  prohibition compared, 1451
  racial classifications, 1438
  reaction to decision, 1433
  "separate but equal" and, 1450–51
  state court proceedings, 1437
  Stone in, 1450
  Taft in, 1437–38, 1450–51, 1471
  white supremacy and, 1483
"Good government" movement, 424–25
Good will as property right, 1408–9
Gordon, Sarah H., 1152–53
"Government by injunction," 1376, 1377, 1387, 1388
Graham, George S.
  Caraway bill and, 511, 524–25, 526
  Conference of Senior Circuit Court Judges and, 469
  Judiciary Act of 1925 and, 502
  United States Commissioners and, 515–16, 529–30
Grain Futures Act, 1128–29, 1151, 1197–98
Grand jury
  Brandeis on, 388–90
  Fifth Amendment, grand jury requirement, 388–90
  Holmes on, 388–89

Moreland and, 388–90
  Taft on, 388–90
Grand Trunk Pacific Railway, 450–51
Grant, Madison, 1441, 1444, 1450–51, 1452, 1485
Gray, Horace, 165–66, 187–88, 297
Gray, John Chipman, 165–66, 168, 187
Great Migration, xxxiv, 1438, 1459, 1461, 1479
Green, William
  on *Bedford Cut Stone*, 1333, 1372–73, 1374
  on cooperation, 1313
  on *Coronado I*, 1346–47
  on involuntary servitude, 1297–98
  Railroad Labor Board and, 1303
  on yellow-dog contracts, 1491–92
Greene, Jamal, 1483
Greene, Nathan, 1358, 1379, 1391
Gregg, James E., 1445–46, 1478–79
Gregory, Charles Noble, 1388
Gregory, Charles O., 1283–84, 1413
Grimes, Barbara N., 782
Griswold v. Connecticut (1965), 1069
Grubb, William I., 106
Gunther, Gerald, 829
Guthrie, William D., 854–55, 856, 859, 971–72

Habeas corpus, 1025, 1038–39, 1040–41, 1493
Hadley, Arthur Twining, 915, 943–44, 994, 1007–8
Haldane, Richard, 1342
Hale, Matthew, 792
Hale, Robert Lee, 140–41, 895, 912–13
Hamilton, Walter H., 874
Hamlin, Charles Sumner, 138, 264–65
Hamm, Richard F., 929–30, 955, 956
Hammer v. Dagenhart (1918)
  child labor and, 969–70, 1103
  interstate commerce and, 992, 1135, 1152, 1179, 1307, 1338
  labor market compared, 1307
  National Motor Vehicle Theft Act compared, 1157–58
  normative dualism in, 969–70, 1122, 1313–14
Hampton Institute
  generally, 1222, 1476–77
  Booker T. Washington and, 1443
  Du Bois and, 1443, 1445, 1479–80
  endowment of, 1478
  Ogden Hall controversy, 1443–49
  social equality and, 1444–45, 1446, 1448
  Taft and, xxxiv, 1443–49, 1478–79, 1481
  Virginia Public Assemblage Act of 1926 and, 1448–49
Hand, Augustus N., 7, 111, 528, 538–39, 547–48
Hand, Learned
  authority of expertise and, 656–57

1548

INDEX

Brandeis and, 89, 322
as circuit court judge, 542–43
consideration for appointment to Court, 89
Holmes and, 186–87
legal scholarship and, 656–57
on *Meyer v. Nebraska*, 829
"norm of acquiescence" and, 641
Taft and, 89, 457, 474, 542–43, 547–48
Theodore Roosevelt and, 305–6
on *Tyson*, 818
Handler, Milton C.
generally, 596
on authority of expertise, 671
consideration of Stone for chief justice and, 1497, 1516
on federal jurisdiction, 115
on Holmes, 208–9
Stone and, 127, 128, 153, 597
on *Truax*, 1421
Hankin, Charlotte A., 567
Hankin, Gregory, xl, 567
Hapgood, Norman, 17–18, 332, 635–36
Harding, Warren G.
Acheson and, 681
ambivalence of, 683, 698–99
appointments to Court by, 33, 58, 84, 92, 102, 612–14, 681–82, 949, 1239
on arbitration, 1275
Butler and, 61, 62, 63–64, 71
on Child Labor Amendment, 1147–48
Clarke and, 39
Coolidge and, 717
Coronado I and, 1312
criticism of, 63, 80
Daugherty and, 125
Day and, 60–61
Du Bois and, 1449
election as president, xxvi, 4, 692, 1238
on executive power, 693, 705–6
federalism and, 1104
"Harding Court," 92
Hoover and, 683, 688, 698, 716–17
inauguration of, 681
on individualism, 1440–41
intention to nominate Sutherland, 4–5
judicial appointments and, 536, 537
Kansas Court of Industrial Relations and, 794–95, 809
labor market and, 1224, 1238–39, 1253–54
on labor violence, 1238–39
on lawlessness, 1036
League of Nations and, 4
Lodge and, 683
Mellon and, 688
"normalcy" and, 681–83, 704
organized labor and, 1238–39
on prohibition, 922, 926, 948, 955

race relations and, 1438–39, 1442, 1446, 1449, 1452, 1460–61, 1471–72
replacement of Pitney and, 88–90, 100–1, 102
segregation and, 1452
on social equality, xxxiii, 1385, 1439, 1441–42, 1449
Sutherland and, 4–5, 21, 61, 740–41, 1238–39, 1276
Taft and
labor market and, 1238–39, 1253–54
lobbying for judicial appointments, 536, 537
nomination of Taft, 4–5, 8, 529, 681–82, 949
presidential campaign of Harding and, xxvi, 388
white supremacy and, 1441–42
Wilson and, 681, 705
"Harding Court," 92
Harlan, John Marshall
on hours of labor, 328–29
on involuntary servitude, 1368
opinions, 209
on ratemaking, 880
Harmon v. Tyler (1927), 1440
Harries, Meirion, 702, 704
Harries, Susie, 702, 704
Harriman, Edward A., 1109
Harris, William J., 505
Harrison, Benjamin, 1, 118, 698
Harrison Narcotics Act, 975–76, 1129–30, 1153–54
Hart, Henry M., Jr., 367–68, 1181
Harvey, George, 2, 1290
Hawley, Ellis W., 707, 709
Haynes, Roy A., 932, 933, 942
Health of Taft. *See* Taft, William Howard – health of
Heflin, James Thomas, 148, 584, 1475
Heisler v. Thomas Collier Co. (1922), 1163–64
Hellerstein, Jerome R., 1293
Helsen v. Kentucky (1929), 1171
Henderson, Gerard C., 706
Herrin Massacre (1922), 1345–46
Herron, M.C., 461
Hester v. United States (1924), 1062, 1067
Hicks, Frederick C., 1516
Highland v. Russell Car & Snowplow Co. (1929), 720–23
Hill v. Wallace (1922), 1146–47
Hilles, Charles D., 50, 100–1, 103, 104–5, 542, 715
Hillquit, Morris, 1228
Hiscock, Frank H., 30
Hitchman Coal & Coke Co. v. Mitchell (1917)
American Steel Foundries distinguished, 1246–47

1549

INDEX

Hitchman Coal & Coke Co. v. Mitchell (cont.)
  Brandeis in, 1286
  Clarke in, 1233
  Coronado I distinguished, 1365–66
  dissenting opinion, 1286
  Gompers on, 1267–68
  Holmes in, 1233
  labor injunctions and, 1378
  Pitney in, 1233, 1266
  property rights and, 1233
  yellow-dog contracts and, 1233
Hofstadter, Richard, 704, 921
Holden v. Hardy (1898), 40, 770, 1232, 1404
Hollinger, David A., 197
Holmes, Fanny, 1508–9
Holmes, Oliver Wendell, Jr.
  generally, xxvii
  as abolitionist, 163, 182, 184, 1437
  as academic, 164, 194
  Acheson and, 192, 195
  as acting chief justice, 1506, 1515
  in *Adkins* (*See Adkins v. Children's Hospital of the District of Columbia* (1923))
  on administration of Court, 477
  African Americans and, 166, 1486
  in *American Steel Foundries*, 1283–84, 1286, 1290, 1292, 1294
  on anti-Semitism, 217, 223
  on anti-trust law, 190–92, 696–98, 713
  appointment of, 165–66
  on authority of expertise versus authority of finality, 654–55
  in *Baldridge*, 740, 741
  in *Bedford Cut Stone*, 1326, 1330–31
  Bickel on, 196–97
  in *Black & White Taxicab*, 1200
  Brandeis and
    Brandeis views on Holmes, 173, 197, 205, 213–14, 215–16, 617, 1418
    comparison, 132, 212–13, 296, 298, 300, 301–2, 315–16, 320, 321, 323–24, 362–63
    Holmes views on Brandeis, 177–78, 217, 219
    opinions compared, 173, 218
    personal relationship with, 217, 297, 348
    professional relationship with, 219–21
    views on Holmes opinions, 173, 175–76
    voting alliance with, 176–80, 223–24, 315–16
  Butler and, 62, 75, 83, 154, 172, 212
  in *Carroll*, 1030, 1058
  on *certiorari*, 224
  charm of, 163
  in *Chastleton*, 723, 724, 728–29
  Civil War, impact of, 163–64, 168, 171, 172, 181–83, 184–85, 204
  Clarke and, 35, 46, 47, 206–7, 208
  class legislation and, 757
  on Clayton Act, 1242, 1282
  on common law, 165, 173, 207
  conference cases
    number of votes recorded at conference that switched to join opinion by Holmes, divided by number of Holmes opinions in conference cases, 44
    percentage of decisions in which Holmes participated and switched vote in conference to join published Court opinion, 622
    percentage of decisions in which Holmes participated and voted in conference with justice with whom most likely to vote, 233
    percentage of decisions in which Holmes participated and voted with another justice in conference, 179
    percentage of decisions in which Holmes participated and willing to switch conference vote to join Court opinion or to join Court opinion despite registering uncertainty in conference, 43
    percentage of Holmes's dissenting votes in conference that Holmes switched in order to join published Court opinion, 622
    percentage of Holmes's published opinions that were unanimous in conference, 66
    percentage of Holmes's unanimous published opinions that had dissenting or uncertain votes in conference, 66
  on conscientious objectors, 151–52
  conservative suspicion of, 172–73, 179
  on Constitutional interpretation, 172–73, 202
  Coolidge and, 168
  in *Coronado I*, 1306, 1341–42
  in *Coronado II*, 1316
  custom and public sentiment and, xxviii, 173, 202
  Darwinism and, 169
  Day and, 67–68, 206–7, 211
  dissenting opinions
    generally, 166–67, 190, 199, 211
    with Brandeis and Stone, 179–80
    "norm of acquiescence" and, 630
    reluctance to dissent, 626–27, 629, 630, 638–39, 642
    views of, 643
  on diversity jurisdiction, xxxii, 206
  Dormant Commerce Clause and, 1160, 1161–62, 1171, 1188–89
  Due Process Clause and, 208, 734, 739, 1194–95, 1202–4
  early life of, 163
  on economic regulation, 129, 1230

INDEX

Edward White and, 167, 192, 204, 211
energy of, 208
Equal Protection Clause and, 1205, 1403–4, 1419, 1431, 1432, 1464
eugenics and, 203–4, 1452
on "experiments," 171, 202, 203
fallibilism and, 360
on federal common law, 1199–200, 1201, 1211, 1212, 1214
Fifteenth Amendment and, 166
First Amendment and, 315
Fourteenth Amendment and, 170, 171, 202, 215–16, 749
Fourth Amendment and, 1062
Frankfurter and, 168, 196, 367
on freedom of contract, 202, 765, 800
on freedom of speech, 127, 320
on fundamental rights, 320
in *Gillespie*, 1111
on grand jury requirement, 388–89
as "great Justice," 244, 373
on group rights, 1464–65
on habeas corpus, 1038–39, 1040–41, 1493
Handler on, 208–9
at Harvard, 190–92
health of, 215–16, 1494, 1500
in *Hitchman*, 1233
on hours of labor, 203, 328–29
"House of Truth" and, 168, 195–96
Hughes and, 181, 186–87, 223, 656, 1504
as instrumentalist, 312
on intergovernmental tax immunity, 1111, 1112–13, 1114, 1119, 1149–51
in *Jay Burns*, 734
as judge, 164, 188–89
judicial aspirations of, 166, 167
judicial authority and, 650, 653
judicial deference and, 170, 178, 739–40
on judicial review, xxviii, xxix
judicial style of, 166, 173, 174–75, 192, 195–96
judicial supremacy, opposition to, 169–71
Judiciary Act of 1925 and, 485, 499–500
on juries, 173, 521–22
jurisprudence and, 168–70, 171–73, 179, 321, 345–46
labor market and, 1246, 1317
in *Lambert*, 988
Laski and, 182, 195–96, 217, 219–21, 485
law reviews and, 670
Learned Hand and, 186–87
legacy of, 373, 1507
on legal education, 1187
Legal Realism and, 165
legal scholarship and, 669
legislative supremacy and, 169–71, 201, 202
on *Lochner*, 765, 766
Lodge and, 165–66, 187–88

majoritarianism and, 201
McKenna and
  Holmes views on McKenna, 118–20, 137, 267–68
  personal relationship with, 118, 135–36
  professional relationship with, 120, 211
McReynolds and, 173, 260, 265–66, 269, 289
in *Meyer v. Nebraska*, 828–29, 852, 866
on minimum wage, 203
on monopolies, 218
in *Myers v. United States*, 404–5, 407, 414, 443
on natural law, 200–1
Nineteenth Amendment and, 780–81
in *Nixon*, 1435, 1436–37, 1467, 1468–69
"norm of acquiescence" and, 655
in *Olmstead*, 1062, 1068, 1069, 1070, 1079–80, 1089
openness of, 172
opinions
  average number of days from argument to announcement of unanimous opinion, by justice, 1921–1928 terms, 86
  average number of pages in unanimous opinion by Holmes, 1921–1928 terms, 174
  Brandeis compared, 173, 218
  Brandeis on, 173, 175–76
  brevity of, 174–75, 209, 210, 212
  dance metaphor, 218–19
  footnotes in, 218
  McReynolds compared, 173
  number of citations to law reviews in Holmes Court opinions and dissents, 1921–1928 terms, 661
  number of citations to treatises and law review articles in Holmes Court opinions, 1921–1928 terms, 662
  number of citations to treatises and law review articles in Holmes dissents, 1921–1928 terms, 661
  number of opinions authored by Holmes, 1921–1928 terms, 8
  number of opinions authored by Holmes, 1921 term, 31, 32
  obscurity of, 175, 212
  percentage of Court opinions authored by Holmes, by term, 173–74
  persuasiveness of, 173
  quickness of, 176
  song metaphor, 218–19
  speed of, 175–76, 189, 212, 213, 216
  Taft, views of, 175–76, 208–9
  Taft compared, 173
  Van Devanter compared, 173
  Van Devanter on, 176
  writing style of, 174–75, 176, 210–11, 213, 214, 218–19

1551

Holmes, Oliver Wendell, Jr. (cont.)
  on pardons, 221–23
  performance on Court, 166–67, 173, 174–75
  on picketing, 1243–44
  Pitney and, 97–98
  Pollock and, 177, 188, 191–92, 193–94, 195–96, 214, 219–21
  positive law and (*See* Positive law)
  presence of, 168
  on price controls, 129
  on prohibition
    generally, 926, 928, 1014–15
    in *Carroll*, 1058
    normative dualism and, 974
    positive law and, 928, 1000–1
    Volstead Act, recordkeeping requirements, 1030–31
  on property rights, 172, 205, 846, 1408
  publications by, xxxvi, 164, 167
  on public interest, 1255
  on ratemaking, 880–81, 896, 902–3, 912–13
  reaction to appointment of, 188
  as Republican, 180, 187–88
  reputation of, 168
  on responsibility, 189
  in *Ribnik*, 820
  Sanford and, 91–92
  in *Saunders*, 1205
  scholarship of, 153
  on secondary boycotts, 1321–22
  "self-denying judge" metaphor, 171–72
  Sherman Anti-Trust Act of 1890 and, 218, 362–63
  on sin, 205–6
  on skepticism, 184
  social custom and, xxviii
  on South, 184
  on *stare decisis*, 655
  on statutes versus common law, 996, 997, 1012–13
  Stone and
    comparison, 127, 128, 132, 155, 158–59
    Holmes views on Stone, 787–88
    influence on, 165
    professional relationship with, 33, 127, 128, 153
    Stone views on Holmes, 187
    views on Stone opinions, 714–15
  on strikes, 1248, 1263
  Supreme Court Building and, 569
  Sutherland and, 56–57, 172
  Taft and
    generally, 681–82
    as circuit court judge, 395
    comparison, 172, 180, 206–7, 312, 321
    death of Taft and, 1506–7
    farewell letter to, 1506
    health of Taft and, 1502
  Holmes views on Taft, 373–74, 395, 477, 486, 1143–44
  labor market and, 1244–46
  nomination of Taft and, 5, 23–24
  opinions compared, 173
  personal relationship with, 27–28, 194, 213–14, 1504, 1508–9
  Taft views on Holmes, xxx, 172–73, 179–80, 197–98, 205, 206, 208, 214, 223, 1502
  views on Holmes opinions, 175–76, 208–9
  views on Taft opinions, 8
Taney compared, 190
Theodore Roosevelt and, 165–66, 167, 187–88, 191–92
on threat of force, 1252
on trespass, 206–7
in *Truax*, 1401, 1402, 1409, 1413
in *Tyson*, 800
on unions, 1229, 1230
Unknown Soldier and, 689, 709–10
Van Devanter and
  comparison, 225, 229
  influence of, 231
  opinions compared, 173
  professional relationship with, 248–49
  Van Devanter views on Holmes, 173
  views on Holmes opinions, 176
on Volstead Act, 1030–31
voting on Court
  number of percentage points by which Holmes is more or less likely to join or author opinion for Court, prohibition decisions versus nonprohibition decisions, 928
  percentage of all decisions in which Holmes participated and either joined or authored Court opinion, 1915–1920 terms versus 1921–1928 terms, 613
  percentage of decisions in which Holmes participated and chose to be only dissenter, 1921–1928 terms, 269
  percentage of decisions in which Holmes participated and either joined or authored opinion of Court, 1916–1921 terms, 32
  percentage of decisions in which Holmes participated and either joined or authored opinion of Court, 1921–1928 terms, 10, 682
  percentage of decisions in which Holmes participated and either joined or authored opinion of Court, 1921 term, 32
  percentage of decisions in which Holmes participated and either joined or authored opinion of Court, by term, 1921–1928 terms, 614

INDEX

percentage of decisions in which Holmes participated and joined or authored opinion for Court, prohibition decisions versus nonprohibition decisions, 1921–1928 terms, 927
percentage of decisions in which Holmes participated and joined same opinion of another justice, 1921–1928 terms, 178
voting alliances, 176–80, 223–24, 315–16
on voting rights, 166
on war, 184–85
in *Weaver*, 738, 739–40
in *Williams*, 803
Wilson and, 194
on wiretapping, 173, 1084
on yellow-dog contracts, 1231, 1233
Holmes, Oliver Wendell, Sr., 163, 181, 182
Holsinger, Maurice Paul, 227, 236, 238
Hook, William Cather, 228
Hooper, Ben W., 1349
Hoover, Herbert
generally, 151–52
anti-trust law and, 697–98
Brandeis and, 708–9
bread standardization and, 733, 743
city planning and, 873
in Commerce Department, 695–96, 697–98, 832, 1260
Coolidge and, 698, 708
economic and statistical analysis and, xxvi
on economic regulation, 709, 715–16
Franklin Roosevelt and, 708–9
"good government" movement and, 424–25
Harding and, 683, 688, 698, 716–17
Hughes and, 879, 1503–4
on individualism, 1296
labor market and, xxxiv, 1238
on lawlessness, 1024, 1033–34
Norris and, 717–18
on *O'Fallon Railway*, 889
Parker, nomination of, 647–48, 1458, 1493
on price controls, 709
on prohibition, 925, 958, 1002, 1021–22
public works and, 562, 570
Railroad Labor Board and, 1260
Sherman Anti-Trust Act and, 697
standardization and, 695, 733
stock market crash and, 716
Stone and, 128, 145, 714–15, 1495–99, 1503, 1510
swearing in of, 1494–95, 1509
Taft and, 1494–99, 1501, 1509–10, 1516
trade associations and, 695–96, 697, 709
unemployment and, 717–18
on Volstead Act, 1024
Wickersham Commission and, 969, 1495–97
zoning and, 836, 865

Hoover, J. Edgar, 125, 1077–78
Horwitz, Morton J., 186–87, 1283
Hough, Charles M., 89–90, 106, 702, 1009
House, Edward M., 262, 263, 281, 283
"House of Truth," 168–69, 195–96
Howe, Mark DeWolfe, 29, 30
Howell, Clark, 546
Hoxie, Robert Franklin, 1228, 1372–73
Hughes, Charles Evans
generally, xxix, 517
appointment to Court
as associate justice, 238
nomination as chief justice, 879, 891–92, 1503–5
authority of expertise and, 655–56
Borah and, 913–14
Brandeis, views on, 223
Burton Wheeler and, 914
Butler and, 62, 75, 356, 1503–4
on common law, 823
confirmation hearings as chief justice, 892–94, 913–14, 915–16
on conscription, 698–99
Coronado I, as counsel in, 1306
on Court in Senate Chamber, 567
dissenting opinions, views on, 631
on "domestic imperialism," 982
Frankfurter and, 915–16
on group status of unions, 1261
Holmes and, 181, 186–87, 223, 656, 1504
Hoover and, 879, 1503–4
on hours of labor, 768–69
on interstate commerce, 1145
legal scholarship and, 655–56
Mitchell and, 1503–4
nomination as chief justice, 879, 891–92, 1503–5
on Railway Labor Act, 1260–61
as secretary of state, 1338
Stone and, 915–16
Supreme Court Building and, 564, 567
Taft and
comparison, 26
Conference of Senior Circuit Court Judges and, 474
death of Taft and, 1506
health of Taft and, 1503, 1516–17
Hughes views on Taft, 6, 395
Supreme Court Building and, 564
on trusts, 694–95
on unions, 1261
Van Devanter and, 230, 241–42, 244, 246, 1503–4
West, impact on confirmation hearings, 892–94
World War I and, 805
on yellow-dog contracts, 1231
Humphrey, William, 445

1553

INDEX

Humphrey's Executor v. United States (1935), 416
Hutchison, Hazel, 700

Immigration
  alien land laws, 1455–58, 1487–90
  "Americanization" and, 857–58
  Brandeis on, 859
  Chinese Americans, 1470
  eugenics and, 1441
  Indians, racial classification of, 1453–55
  Japanese, racial classification of, 1452–53, 1484–85
  Ozawa, 1452–53
  prohibition and, 925
  Stone on, 141
  Thind (See Bhagat Singh Thind; United States v. (1923))
  zoning and, 842, 843
Immigration Act of 1924, 858, 1441
Independent agencies
  Myers v. United States and, 416
  removal power and, 416
Indian land allotment
  generally, 847
  Stone and, 826–27
  taxation and, 826–27
  Theodore Roosevelt on, 847
  Van Devanter and, 227, 247–48
Indians, racial classification of, 1453–55
Individualism
  Adair and, 1245
  "American plan" and, 1236
  American Steel Foundries and, 1245
  Bedford Cut Stone and, 1334
  Brandeis on, 833–34, 1465
  Butler on, 76–77
  class legislation and, 827, 1440
  Coppage and, 1245
  Euclid and, 839–41
  "free labor" and, 1228, 1229, 1230–31
  fundamental rights and, 53, 630, 1407–8
  Harding on, 1440–41
  Hoover on, 1296
  incompatibility with regulation of labor market, 1228, 1230–31
  individual agency, property rights as necessary for, 825–26
  McReynolds on, 833–34
  Meyer v. Nebraska and, 827–28, 830
  Pierce and, 834
  Pitney on, 1234, 1236
  property rights and, 307, 312–13, 387–88, 826–27, 834, 838, 839–42
  race relations and, 1440–41
  Sutherland on, 767, 776, 826
  Taft on, 387–88, 870

unions and, 1254–55
yellow-dog contracts and, 1231
Industrial Association of San Francisco v. United States (1925), 1318–19, 1356–58, 1365
Industrial Conference, 1236–37, 1273, 1342–43
Injunctions. *See* Labor injunctions
Instrumentalism, intergovernmental tax immunity and, 1114–15
Insurance
  Dormant Commerce Clause and, 1193–94
  Due Process Clause and foreign insurance companies, 1193–95
  insurance contracts and, 1193–94, 1202
  taxation, 1194, 1202–4
  interstate commerce, not deemed, 1193–94, 1202
  "property affected with a public interest" and, 821
Intergovernmental tax immunity
  generally, xxxvii
  balancing tests, 1115
  Brandeis on, 1119–20
  Butler on, 1112
  Collector v. Day, 1111
  Congressional power and, 1101
  Dormant Commerce Clause and, 1171–72, 1188–89
  dual sovereignty and, xxxi, 1110–11, 1112
  formalism and, 1111–12
  Frankfurter on, 1120, 1149–51
  Gillespie, 1111
  historical background, 1111
  Holmes on, 1111, 1112–13, 1114, 1119, 1149–51
  instrumentalism and, 1114–15
  Long v. Rockwood, 1114
  Macallen Co., 1113–14, 1115
  McCulloch v. Maryland, 1111
  McReynolds on, 1114, 1118
  Metcalf, 1114–15
  Panhandle Oil Co., 1112
  patents, royalties from, 1114
  Sanford on, 1112
  Stone on, 129, 156, 1114–15, 1118, 1119
  Sutherland on, 1112, 1113, 1119–20
  Taft on, 1112
  Van Devanter on, 1112
Interstate commerce
  Bailey (See Bailey v. Drexel Furniture Co. (1922))
  Bedford Cut Stone and, 1326, 1330, 1332
  boards of trade and, 1128–29, 1133–34
  Brandeis on, 1128, 1183–84
  child labor and, 1126, 1130, 1179
  coal mining as, 1135, 1178–79
  Congressional power over, 1125–26

1554

INDEX

Dagenhart and, 992, 1135, 1152, 1179, 1307, 1338
Dayton-Goose Creek and, 390–91
direct versus indirect burden on, 1169, 1170–74, 1183–84
Dormant Commerce Clause (*See* Dormant Commerce Clause)
dual sovereignty and, xxxi, 1163, 1164, 1166–68, 1181–82
due process and, 1158
Hammer v. Dagenhart and, 992, 1135, 1152, 1179, 1307, 1338
Hill v. Wallace and, 1146–47
Hughes on, 1145
insurance not deemed, 1193–94, 1202
intrastate commerce versus
    Dormant Commerce Clause and, 1125–26, 1163–67, 1168–70
    strikes and, 1305, 1317–18
labor, 1280
labor injunctions and, 1306, 1378–79
McReynolds on, 1175
morality and, 1133
natural gas and, 1180
normative dualism and, 969–70, 1121–22, 1125–26, 1128, 1132–33, 1134
Olsen and, 1129
Stafford and, 1125–26
Stone on, 129
"stream of commerce," 1145
strikes and, 1305, 1317–18
substantive due process and, 1158
Sutherland on, 1177–78
Taft on, 1128, 1145, 1152
Transportation Act and, 1133–34
uniformity and, 1160–61, 1163, 1165, 1168
Webb-Kenyon Act, 1160–61, 1177–78
Wisconsin Rate Case and, 1167–68
Interstate Commerce Act of 1887, 633
Interstate Commerce Commission (ICC)
    Brandeis and, 317–20, 363, 365, 366, 367, 1137
    Colorado v. United States and, 319–20
    Dayton-Goose Creek and, 390–91, 693–94
    Dormant Commerce Clause and, 1168
    economic and statistical analysis and, xxvi
    federalism and, 1104
    FTC compared, 825
    judicial deference and, 825
    McReynolds and, 263, 281, 1137
    "property affected with a public interest" and, 825
    railroads and
        Congressional power and, 1123, 1124
        ratemaking, 693–94, 706, 884–90
    ratemaking and, 1136
    removal power and, 416
    Taft and, 366–67, 431, 1137

Taft Court generally, 693–94
Transportation Act and, 365, 366–67, 693, 706, 903
valuation of railroads, 884–90 (*See also St. Louis & O'Fallon Railway Co.* (1929))
Van Devanter and, 1137
Wisconsin Rate Case and, 1167–68
Intrastate commerce
    Dormant Commerce Clause and, 1125–26, 1163–67, 1168–70
    labor injunctions and, 1306
    strikes and, 1305, 1317–18
    Wisconsin Rate Case and, 1167–68
Involuntary servitude
    Bedford Cut Stone and, 1331–32, 1333–34, 1368
    Brandeis on, 1331–32
    Green on, 1297–98
    Harlan on, 1368
    Taft on, 816

Jackman v. Rosenbaum Co. (1922), 215–16
Jackson, Charles, 164
Jackson, Howell Edmunds, 261
Jackson, Robert
    on Butler, 63, 77, 82
    on Due Process Clause, 802–3
    on executive power, 418
    on judicial authority, 654
    labor market and, 1366–67
    on Stone, 146
James, Henry, 185–86, 212–13, 689
James, William, 185
James Everard's Breweries v. Day (1924), 973–74
    Lambert and, 974, 975
    normative dualism and, 973–74, 975, 976
    positive law and, 976
    Purity Extract and, 973
    Sanford in, 973, 974
    Tenth Amendment and, 973
Jantzen, Franz, 290, 577
Japanese, racial classification of, 1452–53, 1484–85
Jay, John, 569
Jay Burns Baking Co. v. Bryan (1924), 732–38
    authority of expertise and, 736
    Brandeis in, 734, 735–37, 744, 748
    Butler in, 734, 735–36, 737, 744, 751
    difficulty of complying with statute, 734–35
    fact-finding in, 730, 735
    Fourteenth Amendment and, 734
    Frankfurter on, 749
    Holmes in, 734
    judicial deference and, 735–36, 738, 741, 745
    judicial intuition and, 823

1555

Jay Burns Baking Co. v. Bryan (cont.)
   judicial notice and, 735–36
   Lochner compared, 736–37
   maximum weight and, 733–34, 735, 745–46, 747–48, 751
   McKenna in, 734
   overbreadth in, 735
   prohibition and, 939–40
   reasonable relation standard and, 735, 744
   substantive due process and, 734
   Sutherland in, 734
   Taft in, 734
   World War I and, 733
Jessel, George, 1200
Jews
   anti-Semitism
      Brandeis and, 297, 309, 342–43, 349–50
      Holmes on, 217, 223
      of McReynolds, 36–37, 264–65, 290
      Taft on, 342–43
   Brandeis as Jew, 296–97, 309, 342–43, 349–50, 1433
   private schools and, 833
   Zionism, 349, 1433
John P. King Mfg. Co. v. City Council of Augusta, 277 U.S. 100 (1928), 115, 224, 361–62
Johnson, Andrew, 404, 416–17
Johnson, Hiram, 7, 18–19, 25–26, 28
Johnson, James Weldon, 1221–22, 1468
Johnson-Reed Act, 858
Jones, Wesley L., 1004
Jones Act of 1920, 1282–83
Judges' Bill. *See* Judiciary Act of 1925
Judicial appointments. *See also specific person*
   Brandeis and, 546
   to Circuit Courts, 538–39
   Coolidge and, 537–39, 545–46, 548
   Daugherty and, 536–37, 543
   to district courts, 537
   Harding and, 536, 537
   political patronage and, 564
   Stone and, 537–38, 545
   Taft and
      as chief justice, 536–39, 540, 543–44, 545–47, 549
      as president, 61, 71, 1483
   Van Devanter and, 543, 547, 548–49
Judicial authority
   generally, 596
   authority of expertise versus authority of finality (*See also* Authority of expertise; Authority of finality)
      Holmes on, 654–55
      Stone on, 655–56
   balancing tests and, xxxvii, 661–62
   Brandeis and, 652
   Brown v. Board of Education and, 651, 653
   collective judgment of Court, individual expression versus, 652–53
   dissent and, 649–50
   Grannis and, 657–59
   Holmes and, 650, 653
   indeterminacy and, 650
   Jackson on, 654
   Judiciary Act of 1925, impact of, 485, 651, 665
   labor injunctions and, 1377–78
   law/politics distinction, 650, 666
   legal scholarship, Taft viewing as threat, 657–59
   New Deal and, 651
   "norm of acquiescence" and, 649
   Norris-LaGuardia Act and, 1220
   positive law and, 269, 270, 998–99, 1000–1
   public opinion and, 651–53
   supervisor of judiciary versus final appellate tribunal, 665–66
   Taft and, 393–94, 399–400, 649, 650, 653
   weakening of, 666
Judicial deference
   to administrative expertise, 693, 694
   administrative state and, 735–37, 739
   to authority of expertise, 693, 694
   Baldridge and, 741
   Brandeis and, 313, 315, 736, 737
   Congressional power and, 1129
   Day and, 733
   Due Process Clause and, 733, 739, 740, 741
   Euclid and, 839
   facts and, 736
   Fairmont Creamery and, 823
   FTC and, 824
   Holmes and, 170, 178, 739–40
   ICC and, 825
   Jay Burns and, 735–36, 738, 741, 745
   justification of, 359
   McReynolds and, 739, 831
   in *Porterfield*, 1456–57
   prohibition and, 928, 998–99
   Purity Extract and, 739
   Schlesinger and, 739
   Stone and, 127, 128, 131, 142
   substantive due process versus, 739
   Sutherland and, 741
   Taft and, xxix–xxx
   Weaver and, 739–40
   White Court and, 732, 739
Judicial ethics, 513, 527, 626, 629, 638, 649
Judicial legitimacy. *See* Judicial authority
Judicial notice, 363–64, 724–25, 735–36
Judicial recall
   La Follette on, 143
   Stone on, 124, 143
   Sutherland on, 41, 55
   Taft on, 55, 448–49, 459
   Theodore Roosevelt on, 41, 124, 143

INDEX

Judicial reform
  generally, 6, 14, 373, 397, 448
  ABA and, 513
  Brandeis on, 461, 467–68
  Conference of Senior Circuit Court Judges (*See* Conference of Senior Circuit Court Judges)
  costs, controlling, 449, 477, 490
  Daugherty and, 449–51, 460, 462–63, 527
  delay, eliminating, 449, 465
  Frankfurter on, 450, 451–52, 453–54, 461, 465, 470, 506
  Judiciary Act of 1925, (*See* Judiciary Act of 1925)
  Landis on, 445, 450, 451, 461, 465, 499, 506
  legislation for, 503–4, 505
  managerial efficiency and, 452, 465
  opposition to, 450, 452, 464–65
  prohibition, impact of, 450
  "proper executive principle," 450, 451
  proposals of Taft, 449–51, 460, 509
  Taft and
    as chief justice, 504–5
    as president, 397, 448
  unification of judiciary, 451–52, 464
  Volstead Act, impact of, 450
Judicial review
  Adkins and, 760
  AFL on, 63, 614–17, 1340–41
  Bailey and, 1127
  Borah, proposed legislation by, 616–17, 789–91
  Brandeis on, xxix, 313–14, 1412
  congressional oversight of, 63, 614–17, 653, 789–91, 1312, 1396, 1415
  criticism of, 63
  economic prosperity and, xxix, 292–93, 312
  Gompers on, 635
  Holmes on, xxviii, xxix
  La Follette, proposed Amendment by, 63, 614–17, 653, 789–91, 1312, 1396, 1415
  McReynolds on, 260
  Progressive Party and, 616–17
  Stone on, 131, 142
  Sutherland on, 41
  Theodore Roosevelt on, 124, 143
  Truax and, 1412
Judicial style of justices
  Brandeis, 311, 315–16
  Holmes, 166, 173, 174–75, 192, 195–96
  McKenna, 118–20
  McReynolds, 265, 267–68, 269, 272–73
  Pitney, 85
  Sanford, 87, 91–92, 114, 115
  Stone, 132–34
  Sutherland, 42–43
  Taft, 8–10, 27
  Van Devanter, 228–30, 232–34

Judicial supremacy
  generally, 200
  Cardozo on, 169
  custom and public sentiment, based on, 169
  democracy and, 198
  economic prosperity and, xxix, 292–93
  Fourteenth Amendment and, 169
  Holmes, opposition of, 169–71
  natural law and, 170, 200–1
  Stone on, 198–99
  text and, 200–1
Judiciary Act of, 1925
  generally, 6, 509
  ABA and, 485, 495–96, 502–3
  Act of September 14, 1922 compared, 484–85
  Beck and, 483, 484, 495–96
  Brandeis and, 491–93, 499–500
  certiorari and, 484, 600–3, 619, 626
  changes in jurisdiction under, 496
  Coolidge and, 485, 501
  Cummins and, 482–84, 503
  Daugherty and, 482–83
  Day and, 483–84, 491–93
  discretionary jurisdiction, expanding, 484, 637
  dissenting opinions, impact on, 631
  docket, effect on, 485
  evolution of Court under, 596
  final appellate tribunal versus supervisor of judiciary, Supreme Court as, 484–85, 498, 603, 665–66
  Frankfurter on, 481, 499, 609
  Graham and, 502
  Holmes and, 485, 499–500
  judicial authority of Court, impact on, 485, 651, 665
  Landis on, 609
  mandatory jurisdiction, reducing, 482–83
  McReynolds and, 491–93, 502
  "norm of acquiescence" and, xxxvii, 628, 631
  opinions, impact on, 599, 600–3
  origins of, 481–84
  Supreme Court Building and, 551, 564
  Sutherland and, 502
  Taft and, 373–74, 481, 484–85, 487, 496, 501, 504–5
  Thomas Walsh and, 491–93, 499
  unanimity, impact on, 619, 627–28
  Van Devanter and, 232, 482, 483–84, 485, 491–93, 494, 495, 500, 502, 503
  White Court and, 482
Judson, Frederick N., 1206–7, 1241
Juries
  Brandeis on, 521–22
  Clarke on, 521–22

1557

INDEX

Juries (cont.)
    Clayton Act, right to jury trial under, 1381, 1382–84
    contempt, right to jury trial, 1381–84 (*See also Michaelson v. United States* (1924))
    Holmes on, 173, 521–22
    labor injunctions as means of avoiding, 1377
    Sanford on, 521–22
    Stone on, 521–22
    Taft Court generally, 521–22
    Taft on, 509–10, 521, 522–23
    Van Devanter on, 521–22
Jurisdiction
    diversity jurisdiction (*See* Diversity jurisdiction)
    federal question jurisdiction
        Norris on, 1214–15
        S. 3151 and, 516–18, 1214–15
    Supreme Court
        discretionary jurisdiction, expanding, 481, 484, 600, 637 (*See also* Discretionary jurisdiction)
        mandatory jurisdiction, reducing, 480–81, 482–83, 600 (*See also* Mandatory jurisdiction)
        technical amendments to jurisdiction, 494
Justice Department
    Bureau of Prohibition, 1078
    Daugherty in (*See* Daugherty, Harry M.)
    McReynolds and, 261
    Sargent in, 221–23, 453, 457–58, 469, 538
    Stone in, 124, 125, 126, 146, 151–52, 1089–90
    Willebrandt in, 146, 934, 945, 955–56, 1063, 1072
J.W. Hampton, Jr. & Co. v. United States (1928), 401, 693

Kammen, Michael, 875
Kaneko, Kentaro, 1508–9
Karger, Gus, 15–16, 23, 460
Katz, Stanley N., xxxviii
Katz; United States v. (1926), 1030–31
Katz v. United States (1967), 1069
Keating-Owen Child Labor Act, 1126, 1132–33, 1145–46
Keller, Morton, 701
Kelley, Florence, 299, 789, 1127
Kellogg, Frank B., 71, 78–79, 1312
Kelsey, Clarence H., 840, 1482
Kennedy, David M., 704
Kennedy, Will P., 574, 589
Kentucky Finance Corp. v. Paramount Auto Exchange Corp. (1923), 1431
Keyes, Henry W., 552, 559–60, 582, 584
Killits, John M., 111
King, Will R., 421

Kirchwey, George W., 1021–22, 1034
Knappen, Loyal E., 112
Knights of Labor, 1322
Knutson, Anne Classen, 700
Koistinen, Paul A.C., 707
Ku Klux Klan
    "Americanism," public schools and, 833, 858–59
    lawlessness and, 1025
    lynchings and, 1025
    Pierce and, 833
    prohibition and, 925, 954–55, 1024–25, 1037–38, 1061
    Taft on, 1037–38
    Van Devanter on, 1037–38
    white supremacy and, 859
    Zimmerman and, 858, 1025
Kutler, Stanley I., xxxix
Kyvig, David E., 936, 1071, 1075

Labor injunctions
    generally, xxxvii–xxxviii, 1219, 1220, 1335
    ABA on, 1375–76
    AFL on, 1389, 1417
    American Steel Foundries and, 1252
    anti-trust law and, 1306
    Article III courts and, 1233, 1241, 1274, 1325, 1375, 1376, 1491–92
    Bedford Cut Stone and, 1381
    Brandeis on, 1380, 1411–12
    class hatred of, 1377–78
    Clayton Act and, 1241–42, 1282–83, 1378, 1399, 1400–2
    coal industry and, 1299
    contempt for violations, 1381–84 (*See also Michaelson v. United States* (1924))
    Coronado I, damages lessening need for injunctions, 1310
    criminal prosecution, as alternative to, 1377
    criticism of, 1376–78, 1379
    damages as alternative to, 1310
    Democratic Party and, 1377, 1387
    Duplex and (*See Duplex Printing Press Co. v. Deering* (1921))
    federal common law and, xxxiii, 1241
    Frankfurter on, 1358, 1379, 1386, 1391
    Gompers on, 1239, 1290–91, 1314, 1379, 1386
    Gong Lum compared, 1451
    "government by injunction," 1376, 1377, 1387, 1388
    historical background, 1375–76
    Hitchman and, 1378
    imprisonment for violations, 1379
    interstate commerce and, 1306, 1378–79
    intrastate commerce and, 1306
    Jane Addams and, 1380
    judicial authority and, 1377–78

INDEX

legitimacy of law, as undermining, 1378
Newton Baker on, 1392–93
Norris-LaGuardia Act and, xxxiv, 1335, 1465
Parker on, 1247
Pepper on, 1379, 1392
picketing and, 1240–41
Pitney on, 96, 1242
property rights and, 1233, 1411–12
secondary boycotts and, 1372
strikes and, 1237–38, 1249, 1326, 1332, 1375–76, 1379, 1380, 1381–82
Taft on
   generally, 1290–91
   American Steel Foundries, 1239–40, 1242, 1244–48, 1250, 1278, 1292
   Bedford Cut Stone, 1381
   as circuit court judge, 1335, 1379–80
   common law and, 1381
   equity and, 1380
   as "father of injunctions," 392, 395, 1239
   Michaelson, 1382
   as president, 14–15, 392, 395, 1380, 1393, 1402, 1404–5
   prohibition compared, 1380–81
   property rights and, 1402–3, 1408–9
   Truax (See Truax v. Corrigan (1921))
Thomas Walsh on, 1262
Truax (See Truax v. Corrigan (1921))
tyranny and, 1377, 1379
UMW and, 1314
yellow-dog contracts and, 1233, 1378–79
Labor market
   agency
      Coronado I and, 1311–12, 1347
      Norris-LaGuardia Act and, 1347–48
      Sayre on, 1311, 1348
   "American plan," 1218–19, 1236, 1270–71
   American Steel Foundries, 1239–48 *(See also American Steel Foundries v. Tri-City Central Trades Council* (1921))
   anti-trust law and, 1220, 1319
   arbitration *(See* Arbitration)
   bargaining representatives and, 1258
   Beck on, 1279
   Brandeis and, 1238, 1317
   Brewer and, 1289
   Butler and, 1317
   child labor *(See* Child labor)
   Clayton Act and, 1280
   contracts and
      breach of contract, 1266
      tortious interference with contract, 1233
      voluntariness of employment contracts, 1231–32
      yellow-dog contracts *(See* yellow-dog contracts)
   Coolidge and, 1224, 1275
   Coronado I, 1304–16 *(See also United Mine Workers of America v. Coronado Coal Co.* (1922) *(Coronado I))*
   Coronado II, 1315–17 *(See also Coronado Coal Co. v. United Mine Workers of America* (1925) *(Coronado II))*
   Dagenhart compared, 1307
   Daugherty and, 1238, 1290–91
   Democratic Party and, 1238
   direct versus indirect connection to benefits, 1246–47
   discrimination against employees based on union membership, 1230–31, 1234, 1267–68, 1301
   diversity jurisdiction and, 1241
   Frankfurter on, 776–77
   Harding and, 1224, 1238–39, 1253–54
   Hitchman (See Hitchman Coal & Coke Co. v. Mitchell (1917))
   Holmes and, 1246, 1317
   Hoover and, xxxiv, 1238
   individualism, incompatibility with regulation of, 1228, 1230–31
   individual versus group rights, xxxiii
   interstate commerce, 1280
   Jackson and, 1366–67
   labor injunctions *(See* Labor injunctions)
   juries, as means of avoiding, 1377
   Lochner and, 758–59
   managerial prerogatives and, 1233, 1236, 1258, 1260–61
   McKenna and, 1317
   McReynolds and, 1317
   Michaelson, 1381–86 *(See also Michaelson v. United States* (1924))
   minimum wage *(See* Minimum wage)
   National War Labor Board and, 1267
   Newton Baker on, 1255
   normative dualism and, 1317
   Parker and, 1355, 1491–92
   picketing *(See* Picketing)
   Pitney and, 1246, 1247, 1251–52, 1327–28
   Republican Party and, 1238
   right to organize, 1235, 1260–61, 1285
   Sanford and, 1317
   Sayre on, 1266, 1294
   secondary boycotts *(See* Secondary boycotts)
   Sherman Anti-Trust Act and
      generally, 1319–20
      Bedford Cut Stone, 1325, 1326–28, 1329–31
      Coronado I, 1305, 1306, 1309, 1311–12, 1314, 1315, 1322–23
      Coronado II, 1317
      Duplex, 1324

1559

Labor market (cont.)
  substantive due process and, 847
  Sutherland and, 1154–55, 1238–39, 1276, 1317
  Taft and, 1218, 1247, 1264, 1272, 1326
  tension in, 1217–19, 1224
  Theodore Roosevelt and, 1240–41
  union control of, Taft on, 1326
  unions (*See* Unions)
  Van Devanter and, 1317
  violence (*See* Labor violence)
  Wilson and, 1236–37, 1298–99
  World War I, impact of, xxxiii, 1233–34
  yellow-dog contracts (*See* Yellow-dog contracts)
Labor unions. *See* Unions
Labor violence
  generally, xxxii–xxxiii, 1217, 1248
  Brandeis on, 1288, 1289–90
  Coronado I and, 1304–5
  Harding on, 1238–39
  picketing and, 1240, 1248, 1252–53
  radicalism, charges of, 1248
  Stone on, 1295
  strikes and, 1249, 1250, 1399
  Taft on, 1248–50, 1288–89
Lacey, John W., 225
La Follette, Robert M.
  generally, 1314
  on *Adkins*, 766, 789–91
  on *Bailey*, 1127
  Brandeis and, 305, 348
  Butler and, 78–79, 80
  on *Coronado I*, 1309, 1310, 1344, 1350
  on judicial recall, 143
  judicial review, proposed Amendment regarding, 63, 614–17, 653, 789–91, 1312, 1396, 1415
  presidential campaign of, 616–17, 766, 851–52, 1384–86
  as progressive, 690
  Sutherland and, 40, 614–16
  Taft and, 25–26, 333–34, 614–16, 635–36, 851–52
  Transportation Act and, 903
  Treaty of Versailles and, 18–19
  on *West*, 892
La Guardia, Fiorello H., 464–65, 548–49, 724–25
Laissez faire
  decline of, 1501
  World War I, effect of, 690, 691, 702–3
Lamar, Joseph Rucker, 238, 307, 793, 804–5
Lambert, Samuel W., 974, 989–91
Lambert v. Yellowey (1926), 974–75
  Brandeis in, 988–89, 991
  Holmes in, 988
  James Everard's Breweries and, 974, 975

  normative dualism and, 974–75, 976
  positive law and, 976
  Sanford in, 988
  Stone in, 989
  Sutherland in, 974–75, 989
  Taft in, 988
  Tenth Amendment and, 975
  Van Devanter in, 988, 991
Landis, James M.
  on Brandeis, 326
  on judicial reform, 445, 450, 451, 461, 465, 499, 506
  on Judiciary Act of 1925, 609
  on *Michaelson*, 1386
Langdell, Christopher Columbus, 297
Lansing, Robert, 419–20
Lanza; United States v. (1922), 951–53
  Double Jeopardy Clause and, 951–52, 1110
  dual sovereignty and, 951–52
  Fifth Amendment and, 951
  prohibition, duty of states to enforce, 952–53
  reaction to decision, 965–66
  Tenth Amendment and, 952
Lasker, Bruno, 875–76
Laski, Harold
  Brandeis and, 323–24, 358
  Holmes and, 182, 195–96, 217, 219–21, 485
  "House of Truth" and, 168
Lauck, W. Jett, 715–16
Law and Its Administration (Stone), 123
Lawler, Oscar, 303–4, 334–35
Lawlessness
  Brandeis on, 1069–70
  crime wave, 1024, 1027, 1032, 1034
  Harding on, 1036
  Hoover on, 1024, 1033–34
  Ku Klux Klan and, 1025
  labor violence (*See* Labor violence)
  law enforcement and, 1061–62, 1069–70
  lynchings (*See* Lynchings)
  official lawlessness, 1062, 1069–70, 1072–74
  positive law and, 923–24, 926, 927–28
  prohibition and, 922, 925, 1024–25, 1061
  racial violence (*See* Racial violence)
  radical unions and, 1236
  "Red Summer of 1919," 1221–22
  strikes and, 1249
  Taft on, 1024, 1038
Lawrence, David, 108, 819–20, 1369
Law reviews
  Brandeis and, 659, 670
  Butler and, 670
  Frankfurter and, 670
  Holmes and, 670
  number of citations to (*See* Legal scholarship)
  Stone and, 659–61, 670

1560

Index

Taft and, 659, 671
treatises compared, 662
on *Truax*, 1414, 1419, 1422–23
Lawson, Steven F., 701
Leach, W. Barton, 216
League for Industrial Rights, 1361
League of Nations
  Borah and, 18–19
  Harding and, 4
  Taft and, 3–4, 18–19
  Theodore Roosevelt and, 3
  Wilson and, 3–4
League to Enforce Peace, 3
Lee; United States v. (1927), 1062
Lee v. Chesapeake & Ohio Ry. Co. (1923), 1197
Legal scholarship
  Adkins and, 766
  authority of expertise versus, 655–56, 657–59, 661
  authority of finality and, 661
  Brandeis and, 656–57
  Cardozo and, 656, 661
  Frankfurter and, 670
  Holmes and, 669
  law reviews
    Brandeis and, 659, 670
    Butler and, 670
    Frankfurter and, 670
    Holmes and, 670
    Stone and, 659–61, 670
    Taft and, 659, 671
    treatises compared, 662
    on *Truax*, 1414, 1419, 1422–23
  number of citations to
    in contemporary Court, 659, 664
    in Court opinions, by justice, 1921–1928 terms, 662
    in Court opinions, by term, 1921–1928 terms, 1997 term, 2011 term, 664
    in Court opinions and dissents, 1921–1928 terms, 664
    in Court opinions and dissents, 1997 and 2011 terms, 664
    in Court opinions and dissents, by justice, 1921–1928 terms, 661
    decline in, 678
    in dissents, 661
    in dissents, by justice, 1921–1928 terms, 661
    per Court opinion, 1921–1928 terms, 1997 term, and 2011 term, 659, 661, 662–64
    Taft Court generally, 662–64
  Stone and, 655, 656–59, 665, 677
  as supplementing Court's authority, 666
  Taft, hostility of, 659, 665, 670–71
  Taft Court, hostility of, 671

Taft Court and, 664
treatises
  function of, 678
  law reviews compared, 662
  Van Devanter and, 672
Lemke v. Farmers' Grain Co. (1922), 1174
Leuchtenberg, William E., 742, 920
Lever Act, 720–21, 722–23, 726
Lewis, John L., 1237, 1352–53
Lewis, Sinclair, 941–42
Lewis, William Draper, 1378, 1388
Liberty
  Adkins and, 756–57
  administrative state and, 1068
  Brandeis on, 337
  Corwin on, 853–54
  economic liberty, xxvi, 825–26, 1200–1, 1376–77, 1472–73
  Euclid and, 838, 842
  federalism and, 1132
  Lochner and, 772
  McReynolds on, 827–28
  Meyer v. Nebraska and, 827–28, 848
  Pierce and, 830–31, 855
  prohibition and, 924, 995, 1014
  substantive due process and, 828
  Sutherland on, 56, 199
  Taft on, 848
Liberty Warehouse Co. v. Burley Tobacco Growers' Co-Operative Marketing Ass'n (1928), 1405–6
Liberty Warehouse Co. v. Grannis (1927)
  declaratory judgments and, 657–59
  judicial authority and, 657–59
  Stone and, 657–59
  Taft and, 657–59
Lilienthal, David E., 1290–91, 1373, 1390–91
Lincoln, Abraham, 260–61, 416–17, 1241, 1338–39
Lincoln Memorial, 561–62, 1225, 1338–39
Lincoln Memorial Commission, 556
Linder v. United States (1925), 975–76
Lindsley v. Natural Carbonic Gas Co. (1911), 236, 1024–25, 1403–4, 1406–8, 1409, 1456–57
Link, Arthur, 306, 341
Lippmann, Walter
  on Coolidge, 716
  "House of Truth" and, 168
  on mastery, 690
  on *Meyer v. Nebraska*, 829
  progressivism and, 690, 700, 701, 716
  on prohibition, 920, 925, 942, 1004, 1005–6, 1023
  Taft and, 399–400
  on teaching of evolution, 853–54
  Wilson and, 692
  World War I and, 700, 1106

1561

INDEX

Little, Herbert, 589
Llewellyn, Karl, 105, 566, 593
Lloyd-La Follette Act, 429
Lochner v. New York (1905)
  Adkins and, 759, 765, 766
  authority of expertise and, 737
  Brandeis and, 298–300, 307
  Cardozo on, 766
  Carroll and, 1055
  class legislation and, 758–59
  freedom of contract and, 758, 772
  health regulation, statute as, 758, 771–72
  Holmes on, 765, 766
  hours of labor and, 758–59, 771
  impermissible motives and, 771–72
  Jay Burns compared, 736–37
  labor market and, 758–59
  liberty and, 772
  nexus between legislation and benefits of, 758
  reasonable relation standard and, 828
  Sutherland and, 759
  Taft and, 785–86
  Taft Court generally, 687, 759, 765, 766, 835, 998
Locke, Alain, 1434, 1465
Lockhart, William B., 1116
Lockwood Housing Commission, 1307, 1340
Locomotive Boiler Inspection Act, 366
Lodge, Henry Cabot, 165–66, 187–88, 344, 683, 692, 981
Lone Wolf v. Hitchcock (1903), 227
Long v. Rockwood (1928), 1114
Longworth, Nicholas, 558, 583
Louis K. Ligget v. Baldridge (1928), 740–41
Louis Pizitz Dry Goods Co. v. Yeldell (1927), 659, 844
Louisville & Nashville Railroad Company, 1199
Lowell, Abbot Lawrence, 333–34, 344, 984
Lowell, James Russell, 1512
Lowell Lectures, 297
Lubin, David M., 700
Lugard, F.D., 1441
Lum, Martha, 1437, 1450, 1482, 1486
Lurton, Horace Harmon, 59, 238, 263
Lynchings
  Dyer Anti-Lynching Bill, 1418
  habeas corpus and, 1025
  Ku Klux Klan and, 1025
  lynchings by year and race 1882–1940, 1222
  NAACP and, 1036–37
  "Red Summer of 1919," 1221–22
  Taft on, 1036–37, 1222, 1226
Lyons, Willie A., 756, 769

Macallen Co. v. Massachusetts (1929), 1113–14, 1115, 1119, 1188–89

Maguire, Sarah A., 770, 1420
Maher, James D., 476
Mandatory jurisdiction
  Act of December 23, 1914, 490
  Act of September 6, 1916, 600, 609
  authority of finality and, 654, 655, 665, 666
  conference cases
    percentage of published conference cases that are unanimous as multiple of percentage of conference cases that are unanimous in conference, by jurisdiction by term, 1922–1928 terms, 625
    percentage of unanimous conference cases, by jurisdiction, 624
    percentage of unanimous conference cases, by jurisdiction by term, 1922–1928 terms, 625
  dissenting opinions and, 619, 623
  Evarts Act of 1891, 477–80, 489–90
  final appellate tribunal, Supreme Court as, 596, 608, 665–66
  Judiciary Act of 1925 reducing, 482–83
  mandatory jurisdiction versus discretionary jurisdiction
    average number of days from argument to announcement of full opinion, by jurisdiction by term, 1921–1928 terms, 607
    average number of pages in full opinion, by jurisdiction by term, 1921–1928 terms, 607
    percentage of full opinions that are unanimous, by jurisdiction by term, 1921–1928 terms, 608
    percentage of published conference cases that are unanimous as multiple of percentage of conference cases that are unanimous in conference, by jurisdiction by term, 1922–1928 terms, 625
    percentage of unanimous conference cases, by jurisdiction, 624
    percentage of unanimous conference cases, by jurisdiction by term, 1922–1928 terms, 625
    unanimous opinions, 619, 623
  reducing, 480–81, 482–83, 600
  unanimous opinions
    mandatory jurisdiction versus discretionary jurisdiction, 619, 623
    percentage of full opinions that are unanimous, by jurisdiction by term, 1921–1928 terms, 608
    percentage of published conference cases that are unanimous as multiple of percentage of conference cases that are unanimous in conference, by

INDEX

jurisdiction by term, 1922–1928 terms, 625
percentage of unanimous conference cases, by jurisdiction, 624
percentage of unanimous conference cases, by jurisdiction by term, 1922–1928 terms, 625
Taft Court generally, 626, 627–28, 665
Mann, James R., 567–68, 691
Mann Act, 263
Manton, Martin T., 72–74
Maple Flooring Manufacturers Ass'n v. United States (1925), 697, 713–14, 715
Markets, McReynolds on, 273–74
Marshall, John, 7, 8, 29, 172–73, 1144
Marshall, Thurgood, 1436–37
Martineau, John Ellis, 464–65, 548–49
Mason, Alpheus Thomas, 331, 430, 1303
Massachusetts v. Mellon (1923), 1123
Maul v. United States (1927), 1031, 1059–60
McAdoo, William Gibbs, 262, 280–81, 942–43, 982–84
McBain, Howard Lee, 937, 952–53, 956, 1045–47
McCardle v. Indianapolis Water Co. (1926), 884, 885–86
McCarl, John Raymond, 430
McCormack, Alfred, 127, 249–50, 406, 426, 837–38
McCulloch v. Maryland (1819), 973, 1111, 1116
McGirr, Lisa, 919, 920, 933, 943, 1031
McGrain v. Daugherty (1927), 237
McKenna, Joseph
  in *Adkins*, 756
  on anti-trust law, 696–98, 713–14
  appointment of, 117, 118
  in *Block v. Hirsh*, 768
  Brandeis and, 120, 315–16
  in *Carroll*, 1049–52
  in *Chastleton*, 728–29
  Clerk of Court and, 476
  conference cases
    generally, xxxvii
    number of votes recorded at conference that switched to join opinion by McKenna, divided by number of McKenna opinions in conference cases, 44
    percentage of decisions in which McKenna participated and switched vote in conference to join published Court opinion, 622
    percentage of decisions in which McKenna participated and voted in conference with justice with whom most likely to vote, 233
    percentage of decisions in which McKenna participated and voted with another justice in conference, 119
    percentage of decisions in which McKenna participated and willing to switch conference vote to join Court opinion or to join Court opinion despite registering uncertainty in conference, 43
    percentage of McKenna's dissenting votes in conference that McKenna switched in order to join published Court opinion, 622
    percentage of McKenna's published opinions that were unanimous in conference, 66
    percentage of McKenna's unanimous published opinions that had dissenting or uncertain votes in conference, 66
  Congressional power and, 137
  death of, 140
  dissenting opinions, 138–39, 627
  Dormant Commerce Clause and, 1161, 1186–87
  early life of, 118
  federalism and, 1163–64
  in *German Alliance*, 792
  in *Heisler*, 1163–64
  Holmes and
    Holmes views on McKenna, 118–20, 137, 267–68
    personal relationship with, 118, 135–36
    professional relationship with, 120, 211
  incompetence, 117–18, 135, 138–39
  indecision of, 120
  in *Jay Burns*, 734
  judicial style of, 118–20
  labor market and, 1317
  McKinley and, 117, 118
  McReynolds and, 138, 272–73
  in *Michaelson*, 1382
  "norm of acquiescence" and, 617, 627
  opinions
    average number of days from argument to announcement of unanimous opinion, by justice, 1921–1924 terms, 86
    average number of pages in unanimous opinion by McKenna, 1921–1924 terms, 174
    number of citations to law reviews in McKenna Court opinions and dissents, 1921–1924 terms, 661
    number of citations to treatises and law review articles in McKenna Court opinions, 1921–1924 terms, 662

INDEX

McKenna, Joseph (cont.)
  number of citations to treatises and law review articles in McKenna dissents, 1921–1924 terms, 661
  number of opinions authored by McKenna, 1921 term, 31, 32
  percentage of Court's opinions authored by McKenna, by term, 121
  persuasiveness of, xxxvii, 120
  switching of votes, 120
  writing style of, 118, 135
  Pennsylvania v. West Virginia and, 1161
  performance on Court, 117–20, 135
  on price controls, 768
  on prohibition, 958–59, 977, 1049–52
  "property affected with a public interest" and, 804, 821
  on property rights, 312
  on ratemaking, 883–84
  on rent control, 118–20
  replacement of, 33, 617
  retirement of, 121–22, 125, 139, 402
  role on Court, 120
  on statutes versus common law, 996
  Taft and
    nomination of Taft and, 5, 23–24
    personal relationship with, 121–22, 135
    professional relationship with, 136
    Taft views on McKenna, 117, 118, 120, 137, 138
  temper of, 118
  on unions, 1230
  Van Devanter and, 117, 121–22, 227, 231, 232
  voting on Court
    percentage of all decisions in which McKenna participated and either joined or authored Court opinion, 1915–1920 terms versus 1921–1924 terms, 613
    percentage of decisions in which McKenna participated and chose to be only dissenter, 1921–1924 terms, 269
    percentage of decisions in which McKenna participated and either joined or authored opinion of Court, 1916–1921 terms, 32
    percentage of decisions in which McKenna participated and either joined or authored opinion of Court, 1921–1924 terms, 10
    percentage of decisions in which McKenna participated and either joined or authored opinion of Court, 1921 term, 32
    percentage of decisions in which McKenna participated and joined the opinion of another justice, 1921–1924 terms, 119
  in *West v. Kansas Natural Gas*, 1161
  wife, death of, 120–21, 139
  on workers' compensation, 1265–66
McKenney, Henry, 476
McKim, Charles F., 568
McKinley, William
  appointments to Court by, 117, 118
  on Court in Senate Chamber, 551
  Day and, 59, 67
  McKenna and, 117, 118
  Taft and, 1
McMillan Commission, 551, 554–55, 568
McNary-Haugen Act (proposed), 819–20
McReynolds, Ellen Reeves, 275
McReynolds, James Clark
  generally, xxvii
  1924 election and, 1418
  Acheson and, 273, 285, 290
  Act of 1916 and, 160, 482
  in *Adkins*, 756
  administration of Court and, 477
  on administrative state, 273
  admiralty and, 1176–77
  African Americans and, 285
  on age of justices, 34
  anti-Semitism of, 36–37, 264–65, 290
  on anti-trust law, 261–62, 276–77, 696–97, 713–14, 715
  appointment of, 263–64, 283
  as attorney general, 262–63, 272, 278, 282–83, 291
  Brandeis and
    generally, 262
    Brandeis views on McReynolds, 265–66, 289, 292
    comparison, xxix, 267, 271, 273, 294, 295, 296, 315–16, 320–21, 834, 1068
    personal relationship with, 36–37, 265–66, 279–80, 287–88, 290
    political support of, 262
  Butler and
    comparison, 267–68, 269, 270, 271, 274
    personal relationship with, 292
    voting alliance with, 266–67, 269
  as Campbellite, 260, 269
  Cardozo, personal relationship with, 36–37, 265, 287
  in *Carroll*, 1027, 1029–30, 1055–56
  in *Charles Wolff Packing*, 798–99
  in *Chastleton*, 728–29, 730
  on Civil War, 261
  Clarke and, 36–37, 48, 265, 267
  class legislation and, 1406, 1421
  on common law, 834
  community and, 321
  conference cases
    number of votes recorded at conference that switched to join opinion by

1564

INDEX

McReynolds, divided by number of McReynolds opinions in conference cases, 44
percentage of decisions in which McReynolds participated and switched vote in conference to join published Court opinion, 622
percentage of decisions in which McReynolds participated and voted in conference with justice with whom most likely to vote, 233
percentage of decisions in which McReynolds participated and voted with another justice in conference, 268
percentage of decisions in which McReynolds participated and willing to switch conference vote to join Court opinion or to join Court opinion despite registering uncertainty in conference, 43
percentage of McReynolds's dissenting votes in conference that McReynolds switched in order to join published Court opinion, 622
percentage of McReynolds's published opinions that were unanimous in conference, 66
percentage of McReynolds's unanimous published opinions that had dissenting or uncertain votes in conference, 66
confirmation of, 264
on confiscation, 291
on Constitutional interpretation, 266–67
on contractual interpretation, 270–71
controversy regarding, 263, 282
in *Coronado II*, 1316
criticism of, 263, 283
on custom and public sentiment, 271–72, 312, 823
Davis and, 280
Democratic Party and, 259–60, 262
dissenting opinions
  generally, 292–93
  reluctance to dissent, 627, 640, 641
Dormant Commerce Clause and, 1160, 1161–62, 1168, 1186
Douglas, views of, 265
Due Process Clause and, 830–31, 1194–95
early life of, 260–61
on economic regulation, 291
on entrepreneurship, 834
in *Euclid*, 835, 839–40
in *Fairmont Creamery*, 822–23, 825
on federal common law, 1198–99
federalism and, 968, 975–76, 1153, 1154
on federal preemption, 273
Fourteenth Amendment and, 271–72, 291–92, 827–28, 834, 861

Frankfurter, personal relationship with, 265
FTC and, 271, 290–91
on fundamental rights, xxviii, 828
in Gold Clause cases, 272, 292–93
gold standard and, 259
on habeas corpus, 1038–39
health of, 1494
Holmes and, 173, 260, 265–66, 269, 289
ICC and, 263, 281, 1137
on individualism, 833–34
on intergovernmental tax immunity, 1114, 1118
on interstate commerce, 1175
judicial deference and, 739, 831
on judicial review, 260
judicial style of, 265, 267–68, 269, 272–73
Judiciary Act of 1925 and, 491–93, 502
Justice Department and, 261
labor market and, 1317
on liberty, 827–28
on markets, 273–74
McKenna and, 138, 272–73
in *Meyer v. Nebraska*, 827–28, 830, 851, 870–71
in *Michaelson*, 1382
misanthropy of, 264–65
misogyny of, 285
on monopolies, 276–77
morality and, xxx, 269–74, 368, 834
in *Myers v. United States* (See *Myers v. United States* (1926))
Norris and, 263, 281
in *O'Fallon Railway*, 888, 908
in *Olmstead*, 1062, 1063–66
opinions
  average number of days from argument to announcement of unanimous opinion, by justice, 1921–1928 terms, 86
  average number of pages in unanimous opinion by McReynolds, 1921–1928 terms, 174
  erratic nature of, 286
  footnotes in, 218
  number of citations to law reviews in McReynolds Court opinions and dissents, 1921–1928 terms, 661
  number of citations to treatises and law review articles in McReynolds Court opinions, 1921–1928 terms, 662
  number of citations to treatises and law review articles in McReynolds dissents, 1921–1928 terms, 661
  number of opinions authored by McReynolds, 1921–1928 terms, 8
  number of opinions authored by McReynolds, 1921 term, 31, 32
  percentage of Court opinions authored by McReynolds, by term, 267

1565

McReynolds, James Clark (cont.)
    Taft, views of, 209
    writing style of, 265
  oratory and, 293
  overbreadth and, 825
  performance on Court, 265, 267–68, 269, 272–73
  personality of, 259–60, 264–65
  in *Pierce*, 830–31, 834
  Pitney, views on, 97–98
  in politics, 259–60, 275
  positive law versus, 269, 270
  pragmatism of, 261
  on prejudice, 854
  on price controls, 272, 291, 798–99
  primary elections and, 1435–36
  on private schools, 276
  on prohibition (*See* prohibition)
  promotion of republicanism and, 830
  "property affected with a public interest" and, 793–94
  on property rights, 320–21, 356
  racism of, 285
  railroads and, 393, 398
  on ratemaking, 881, 888
  reaction to appointment of, 284–85
  religion and, 260, 269
  Sanford and, 91, 100, 289
  on secondary boycotts, 1364–65
  Sherman Anti-Trustt Act of 1890 and, 261
  on social equality, 285
  as Southern Democrat, 264
  in *Southwestern Bell Telephone*, 883
  on statutes versus common law, 1012–13
  Stone and
    comparison, 267
    McReynolds views on Stone, 152–53
    personal relationship with, 126
    professional relationship with, 132–34, 160, 617–19
  Supreme Court Building and, 569, 572–73, 589
  Sutherland and
    comparison, 267, 270, 271, 273–74
    personal relationship with, 292
    voting alliance with, 266–67, 269
  Taft and
    comparison, 8, 267–68, 269, 270, 271, 274, 393
    death of Taft and, 1506
    health of Taft and, 382–83
    personal relationship with, 291
    Taft views on McReynolds, xxx, 265, 266–67, 286, 290
    views on McReynolds opinions, 209
    voting alliance with, 269
  on taxation, 282
  on taxing power, 1129–30
  temper of, 264, 279, 286
  in *Terrace*, 1455
  Tobacco Trust and, 262, 263, 277–78, 279
  on trusts, 271
  Van Devanter and
    comparison, 259–60, 267–68, 269, 270, 271, 274
    influence of, 231
    personal relationship with, 292
    Van Devanter views on McReynolds, 265
    voting alliance with, 266–67, 269
  voting on Court
    number of percentage points by which McReynolds is more or less likely to join or author opinion for Court, prohibition decisions versus nonprohibition decisions, 928
    percentage of all decisions in which McReynolds participated and either joined or authored Court opinion, 1915–1920 terms versus 1921–1928 terms, 613
    percentage of decisions in which McReynolds participated and either joined or authored opinion of Court, 1916–1921 terms, 32
    percentage of decisions in which McReynolds participated and chose to be only dissenter, 1921–1928 terms, 269
    percentage of decisions in which McReynolds participated and either joined or authored opinion of Court, 1921–1928 terms, 10, 682
    percentage of decisions in which McReynolds participated and either joined or authored opinion of Court, 1921 term, 32
    percentage of decisions in which McReynolds participated and either joined or authored opinion of Court, by term, 1921–1928 terms, 614
    percentage of decisions in which McReynolds participated and joined or authored opinion for Court, prohibition decisions versus nonprohibition decisions, 1921–1928 terms, 927
    percentage of decisions in which McReynolds participated and joined same opinion of another justice, 1921–1928 terms, 268
  voting alliances, 267–68, 269
  Wilson and, 262, 263–64, 266–67, 284
  on wiretapping, 1084
  on workers' compensation, 273–74, 1265–66
  World War I and, 263–64, 290
McReynolds, John Oliver, 260–61, 275–76

Index

Medical practice
  federalism and, 975–76
  narcotics, taxation and, 1129–30, 1133, 1153
  Nigro and, 1129–30, 1133
  prohibition and
    beer and malt beverages, 973–74 (*See also James Everard's Breweries v. Day* (1924))
    medical judgment and, 975
    wine and spirituous liquor, 974–75 (*See also Lambert v. Yellowey* (1926))
  Volstead Act and, 987–88
Mellen, Charles S., 263
Mellon, Andrew, 149–50, 557, 558, 572, 687–88, 1384
Mencken, H.L., 919, 938, 949
Merritt, Deborah Jones, 1116
Merz, Charles, 702–3, 919, 934–36, 940–41, 942–43, 955
Metcalf, Evan, 709, 717
Metcalf v. Mitchell (1926), 1114–15
Metzenbaum, James, 837, 840, 863
Meyer, Eugene, 941–42
Meyer v. Nebraska (1923), 827–30
  Brandeis in, 828–29
  common law and, 827–28, 834
  custom and public sentiment in, 828–29
  Due Process Clause and, 827–28, 830
  Fourteenth Amendment and, 827–28, 848
  Frankfurter on, 829
  fundamental rights and, 828–29
  Holmes in, 828–29, 852, 866
  individualism and, 827–28, 830
  Learned Hand on, 829
  liberty and, 827–28, 848
  Lippmann on, 829
  McReynolds in, 827–28, 830, 851, 870–71
  progressivism, divisions in regarding, 829, 852
  promotion of democracy and, 829, 830
  property rights and, 828
  Taft in, 828, 848, 849
Michaelson v. United States (1924), 1381–86
  1924 election and, 1384–86
  Clayton Act and, 1381, 1382–84
  equity and, 1382–84
  Frankfurter on, 1397
  Gompers on, 1385, 1386
  Landis on, 1386
  McKenna in, 1382
  McReynolds in, 1382
  reaction to decision, 1385–86
  separation of powers and, 1382–84
  Sutherland in, 1382–84
  Taft in, 1382
Michigan Public Utilities Comm'n v. Duke (1925), 1173–74
Miller, Nathan, 89, 103–5, 145

Milton, George F., Jr., 99, 113
Minimum wage
  Adamson Act, 1248–49
  Adkins (See *Adkins v. Children's Hospital of the District of Columbia* (1923))
  Brandeis on, 756
  Clarke on, 786–87
  Frankfurter on, 756, 767–68, 769
  Holmes on, 203
  hours of labor compared, 757
  Newton Baker and, 776
  price controls compared, 757, 759, 762–63
  purpose of legislation, 782
  railroads and, 793–94
  Stone on, 127–28, 159, 787–88
  Sutherland on, 391–92
  Taft on, 391–92
Minor, John B., 261, 262, 276
Mischler, Wendell W., xl–xli, 232, 588, 1499–500, 1504, 1517
Missouri ex rel. *Barrett v. Kansas Natural Gas* (1924), 1164
Missouri ex rel. *Burnes Nat'l Bank v. Duncan*, 265 U.S. 17 (1924), 1116–17
Mitchell, Wesley C., 706
Mitchell, William D.
  Butler and, 63, 75–76, 82
  defendant's fees and, 518–19
  Hughes and, 1503–4
  on Norris-LaGuardia Act, 1491–92
  on prohibition, 1078
  Stone and, 1498
  Supreme Court Building and, 555
  Van Devanter and, 241
Model Code of Judicial Conduct, 513
Model Zoning Enabling Act, 836
Montague, Gilbert H., 711–12
Moody, William Henry, 94–95, 227, 240
Moore, Charles, 559–60, 568, 576
Moore, John Bassett, 158, 885
Moore, Underhill, 140–41
Moore v. Dempsey (1923), 1025, 1039–41
Moreland; United States v. (1922), 388–90
Morrill, Justin Smith, 551
Morrison, Frank, 1297
Moses, George, 553, 569
Moton, Robert R., 1448, 1476–77
Muller v. Oregon (1908), 298–300, 736, 770
Munford, Mary Cooke Branch, 1447
Munn v. Illinois (1876), 732–33, 792, 795–96
Murchison, Kenneth M., 962, 965
Murphy, Walter F., 100, 107, 1072
Murphy v. Sardell (1925), 787–88
Mussolini, Benito, 591–92, 1297–98, 1333, 1371
Myers, Frank, 401–2, 419
Myers v. United States (1926)
  administrative state and, 416–17
  amicus briefs in, 402

1567

Myers v. United States (1926) (cont.)
  announcement of decision, 411, 433, 434
  Article II judges and, 416
  authority of expertise and, 657
  Beck and, 402, 420, 429, 440–47, 657
  Brandeis in
    generally, 404–5
    civil service and, 409
    dissenting opinion, 407, 408–10, 417–18, 428–29
    executive power and, 418
    separation of powers and, 418
    Stone, critique by, 409–10
  Butler in, 404–6, 411
  civil service and, 407–8, 409, 411, 413
  conference, vote in, 404–5
  Corwin and, 414, 434–36, 443, 444
  Cummins and, 402
  Decision of 1789 and, 444
  dissenting opinions
    Brandeis, 408–10, 417–18, 428–29
    Holmes, 407, 414, 443
    McReynolds, 407, 409–11, 412–13, 416, 430, 438–40
  executive officers applicable to, 408, 411, 413–16, 417
  executive power and, 407, 414–15, 416, 418, 426–27, 428, 431–32
  factual background, 401–2
  functionalism in, 409–10, 414–16
  Holmes in, 404–5, 407, 414, 443
  Humphrey's Executor and, 416
  independent agencies and, 416
  inferior officers, applicability to, 407–8, 409–10, 411, 412–13, 415–16
  McReynolds in
    generally, 404–5
    dissenting opinion, 407, 409–11, 412–13, 416, 430, 438–40
  office versus specific office holder, 414–15
  oral arguments in, 402
  originalism in, 412
  Pepper as counsel in, 402, 429, 443
  Perkins and, 407–8
  pragmatism in, 412, 436–38
  reaction to decision, 433, 436–38
  rehearing in, 402
  Sanford in, 404–5, 406, 411
  separation of powers and, 417–18
  Stone in
    generally, 402, 421, 426
    Brandeis, critique of, 409–10
    executive power and, 428, 431–32
    Taft, consultation with, 406–8, 411, 429, 430
  Sutherland in, 404–5, 406, 410–11, 426
  Taft in
    generally, 402
    administrative state and, 416–17
    Butler, consultation with, 405–6, 411
    civil service and, 407–8, 411, 413
    Decision of 1789 and, 444
    drafting of opinion, 405–8, 410–11, 427, 429
    executive power and, 405, 415, 426–27
    health of Taft, impact of, 410
    office versus specific office holder, 414–15
    pragmatism and, 412
    presidential experience, 402
    Sanford, consultation with, 406, 411
    Stone, consultation with, 406, 407, 411, 429, 430
    Sutherland, consultation with, 406, 410–11, 426
    Van Devanter, consultation with, 405, 406, 408, 410, 411, 432
    Vesting Clause and, 413–14
  Take Care Clause and, 440–47
  unitary executive and, 440–47
  unusual composition of decision, 411–12
  Van Devanter in, 404–5, 406, 408, 410, 411, 432
  Vesting Clause and, 413–14, 440–47
  writing style of opinion, 434

NAACP. *See* National Association for the Advancement of Colored People (NAACP)
Nagel, Charles, 227–28, 733
Narcotics, taxation and, 1129–30, 1133, 1153
Narrow tailoring, 1408, 1409–10, 1413
National Association for the Advancement of Colored People (NAACP)
  Booker T. Washington compared, 1460
  The Crisis, 1221, 1445
  Du Bois and (*See* Du Bois, W.E.B.)
  lynchings and, 1036–37
  Moore and, 1039–40
  Nixon and, 1435
  Parker nomination, opposition to, xxxiv–xxxv, 1223, 1458–59, 1460
  Taft and, 1036–37
National Bureau of Standards, 733
National Civic Federation, 1260, 1370
National Civil Service League, 956–57
National Commission on Law Observance and Enforcement. *See* Wickersham Commission
National Conference on City Planning, 837, 866
National Conference on Social Work, 924
National Conference on Valuation, 887, 906–7
National Consumer's League, 299, 756, 789
National Education Association, 857–58
National Grange, 1271–72

INDEX

National Labor Relations Act (NLRA), 1365
National Motor Vehicle Theft Act (NMVTA), 1132–33, 1157–58
National Oratorical Contest, 378, 383
National Prohibition Act. *See* Volstead Act
National Prohibition Cases (1920), 970, 972
National Recovery Administration, 340
National War Labor Board (NWLB)
  child labor and, 1106–7
  collective bargaining and, 1235
  discrimination against employees based on union membership and, 1234
  Frank Walsh in, 1234
  group rights and, 1257
  labor market generally, 1267
  post-war demise of, 1235–36
  Railroad Labor Board compared, 1256–57, 1258
  right to organize and, 1235
  success of, 1235
  Supreme Court precedents and, 1234
  Taft on, xxxiii, 765, 1106–7, 1234, 1235
  Wilson and, 2–3, 1234
  women and, 784–85
  yellow-dog contracts and, 1234, 1268
National Woman's Party (NWP), 555, 576, 779–80
Native Americans, Van Devanter and, 227, 247–48
Naturalization, 506
Naturalization Act of 1790, 1453
Natural law
  conservatism and, 170
  Holmes on, 200–1
  judicial supremacy and, 170, 200–1
  Sutherland and, 53–54
Nelson, Knute, 102, 241, 903–4
Nelson, William E., 199
Newberry v. United States (1921), 1467, 1468
New Deal, 565, 577, 651
New Freedom, 306, 692
New York City
  Commission on Building Districts and Restrictions, 863, 864
  Zoning Commission, 840
  zoning in, 836, 840, 862–63, 864
New York County Bar Association, 505
New York ex rel. *Bryant v. Zimmerman* (1928), 858, 1025, 1038–39
New York State Bar Association, 740–41
Niebuhr, Reinhold, 571
Nigro v. United States (1928), 1129–30, 1133
Nineteenth Amendment
  Adkins and, 763–64
  Holmes and, 780–81
  National Woman's Party and, 779–80
  Sutherland and, 52, 779–80
  Taft and, 780

Nixon, Lawrence A., 1435, 1469
Nixon, Richard, 1035–36
Nixon v. Herndon (1927), 1434–37
  Brandeis and, 1436–37
  Equal Protection Clause and, 1469
  Fifteenth Amendment and, 1435–36, 1468, 1469
  Fourteenth Amendment and, 1466–67, 1468, 1469
  Gong Lum compared, 1438
  Holmes in, 1435, 1436–37, 1467, 1468–69
  limitations of, 1437
  NAACP and, 1435
  political question doctrine and, 1436
  Privileges and Immunities Clause and, 1468
  Taft in, 1467
Normative dualism
  anti-trust law and, 1121–22
  Bailey and, 1126–28
  child labor and, 969–70, 1126, 1134
  Congressional power and, xxxi, 970–71, 975, 1121–22, 1125–26, 1127, 1132–33, 1134
  Coronado I and, 1313–14
  Coronado II and, 1317
  in *Dagenhart*, 969–70, 1122, 1313–14
  defined, xxxi, 969–70
  democratic authorship and, 970–71
  democratic legitimation and, 971
  federal common law and, 1201
  FTC and, 1132
  in *Hammer v. Dagenhart*, 969–70, 1122, 1313–14
  interstate commerce and, 969–70, 1121–22, 1125–26, 1128, 1132–33, 1134
  James Everard's Breweries and, 973–74, 975, 976
  labor market and, 1317
  Lambert and, 974–75, 976
  national market and, 1132
  positive law and, 971, 976
  prohibition and
    generally, 1122
    Brandeis on, 968–69, 974
    Butler on, 974
    criticism of prohibition based on, 970–71
    as "domestic imperialism," 971
    Holmes on, 974
    James Everard's Breweries, 973–74, 975, 976
    Lambert, 974–75, 976
    McReynolds on, 974
    Sanford on, 973, 974
    Sutherland on, 971–72, 974–75
    Taft on, 974, 987
    Van Devanter on, 972, 974
  Sherman Anti-Trust Act and, 1121–22
  Sutherland and, 971–72, 975, 1154–55

INDEX

Normative dualism (cont.)
  Truax and, 1409
"Norm of acquiescence"
  authority of expertise and, 664
  authority of finality and, 665
  Brandeis and, 628, 630, 631
  Butler and, 626
  dissenting opinions and, xxxvii, 627–31
  Frankfurter and, 665
  Holmes and, 630, 655
  judicial authority and, 649
  Judiciary Act of 1925 and, xxxvii, 628, 631
  Learned Hand and, 641
  McKenna and, 617, 627
  New Deal and, 651
  public opinion and, 634, 638
  stability of law and, 630, 631
  stare decisis and, 644–45, 648
  Taft and, 631
  Taft Court generally, xxxvii, 627–31
Norm of consensus, 627
Norris, George W.
  generally, 430
  Act of September 14, 1922 and, 503–4
  Brandeis and, 348
  Butler and, 80, 903–4
  diversity jurisdiction and, 516, 1214–15
  federal court jurisdiction and, 516, 518
  on federal question jurisdiction, 1214–15
  Hoover and, 717–18
  McReynolds and, 263, 281
  on *O'Fallon Railway*, 887
  S. 3151 and, 533, 534
  Taft and, 503–4
  on *West*, 892
Norris-LaGuardia Act of 1932,
  generally, 1220, 1263, 1281, 1461
  agency and, 1347–48
  American Steel Foundries and, 1245–46, 1247
  Bedford Cut Stone, effect of, 1335
  judicial authority and, 1220
  labor injunctions and, xxxiv, 1335, 1465
  Mitchell on, 1491–92
  right to organize under, 1285
  Taft Court, impact of, xxxiv
  Truax, effect of, 1465
  yellow-dog contracts and, 1247
North Dakota Nonpartisan League, 1191–92
Nourse, Victoria F., 770, 771–72, 1420
Nullification, prohibition and, 943–44, 1007–8
Nutter, George R., 113
NWLB. *See* National War Labor Board (NWLB)

O'Brien, David M., 638, 1202–4
Official lawlessness, 1062, 1069–70, 1072–74
Okrent, Daniel, 920, 938–39, 943
Old Brick Capitol, 555

Oliphant, Herman, 140–41, 158–59
Oliver Wendell Holmes Devise History of the Supreme Court of the United States, xxv
Olmstead, Roy, 1062–63, 1076–77
Olmstead v. United States (1928)
  announcement of decision, 1065
  Brandeis in
    generally, 657, 1064–65, 1070
    Carroll compared, 1069
    certiorari and, 1063, 1083
    custom and public sentiment and, 1068–69
    dignity and, 1068–69
    Griswold and, 1069
    illegally obtained evidence, 1063–64, 1079–80
    Katz and, 1069
    official lawlessness and, 1069–70
    privacy and, 1067–68, 1085–86
    promotion of democracy and, 1068
  Butler in, 1062, 1064–65, 1070, 1088–89
  certiorari in, 1063, 1083
  common law and, 1090–92
  custom and public sentiment and, 1068–69
  dignity and, 1068–69
  dissenting opinions, 1062, 1066, 1067–70
  evidence
    illegally obtained, 1063–64, 1079–80
    unconstitutionally obtained, 1062, 1063–64, 1065, 1083
  factual background, 1062–63
  Fifth Amendment and, 1063, 1083, 1084
  Holmes in, 1062, 1068, 1069, 1070, 1079–80, 1089
  McReynolds in, 1062, 1063–66
  official lawlessness and, 1062, 1069–70
  privacy and, 1067–68, 1085–86
  promotion of democracy and, 1068
  reaction to decision, 1070–71
  rule of law and, 1071
  Sanford in, 1062, 1063–65
  search or seizure, 1064, 1065–66, 1067
  Stone in, 1062, 1081–82
  Sutherland in, 1062, 1063–64, 1065–66, 1070, 1084
  switching of votes, 1078–79
  Taft in
    generally, 390, 1062, 1063–64, 1070, 1092–94
    certiorari and, 1083
    common law and, 1090–92
    official lawlessness and, 1070
    search or seizure, 1064, 1065–66, 1067
    trespass and appropriation, 1065–66, 1067, 1086
  trespass and appropriation, 1065–66, 1067, 1086
  Van Devanter in, 1062, 1063–65, 1092–94

Index

Olmsted, Frederick Law, Jr., 568, 873
Olney, Richard, 1230–31, 1375, 1387
Opinions. *See also specific justice or case*
  appellate docket
    appellate caseload of Supreme Court, by term, 1888–1930 terms, 478
    appellate caseload of Supreme Court, by term, 1910–1930 terms, 479
    percentage of decided cases on appellate docket disposed of by full Court opinion, by term, 1912–1929 terms, 601
  certiorari and, 600–3, 608
  conference cases (*See* conference cases)
  dissent (*See* Dissent)
  footnotes in, 218
  Judiciary Act of 1925, impact of, 599, 600–3
  legal scholarship, number of citations to
    in contemporary Court, 659
    in Court opinions, by justice, 1921–1928 terms, 662
    in Court opinions, by term, 1921–1928 terms, 1997 term, 2011 term, 664
    in Court opinions and dissents, 1921–1928 terms, 664
    in Court opinions and dissents, 1997 and 2011 terms, 664
    in Court opinions and dissents, by justice, 1921–1928 terms, 661
    decline in, 678
    in dissents, 661
    in dissents, by justice, 1921–1928 terms, 661
    per Court opinion, 1921–1928 terms, 1997 term, and 2011 term, 659, 661, 662–64
    Taft Court generally, 662–64
  length of opinions
    average number of pages in full opinion, by jurisdiction by term, 1921–1928 terms, 607
    average number of pages in full opinion: White, Taft, Rehnquist, and Roberts Courts, 605
    average number of pages in unanimous opinion, by author, 1921–1928 terms, 174
    average number of pages in unanimous opinion by Stone, 1924–1928 terms, 134
    average number of pages in unanimous opinion by Taft, by term, 379
    mandatory jurisdiction versus discretionary jurisdiction, 1921–1928 terms, 607
  mandatory jurisdiction versus discretionary jurisdiction
    generally, 600–3
  number of full opinions, by term, 1921–1928 terms, 602
  percentage of full opinions, by jurisdiction by term, 1921–1928 terms, 602
  percentage of full opinions that are unanimous, by jurisdiction by term, 1921–1928 terms, 608
  number of opinions
    number of full opinions, by term, 1912–2017 terms, 604
    number of full opinions, by term, 1921–1928 terms, 602, 605
    number of opinions authored, by justice, 8
    number of opinions authored, by justice, 1921 term, 31, 32
    reduction in, 603–5
  prohibition cases
    generally, 926, 945–47
    number of percentage points by which justice is more likely to join or author opinion of Court, prohibition decisions versus nonprohibition decisions, 928
    percentage of decisions in which justice participated and joined or authored opinion of Court, prohibition decisions versus nonprohibition decisions, 1921–1928 terms, 927
    percentage of full opinions that are unanimous, prohibition decisions versus nonprohibition decisions, 1921–1928 terms, 927
  switching of votes
    between conference and publication, 620–21
    dissenting votes, percentage of cases by justice, 622
    number of votes recorded at conference that switched to join opinion of justice, divided by number of that justice's opinions in conference cases, 44
    percentage of decisions in which justice participated and switched vote in conference to join published Court opinion, 622
    percentage of decisions in which justice participated and was willing to switch conference vote to join Court opinion or to join Court opinion despite registering uncertainty in conference, 43
    percentage of dissenting votes in conference that justice switched in order to join published Court opinion, 622
  time from argument to announcement
    average number of days from argument to announcement of full opinion, by jurisdiction by term, 1921–1928 terms, 607

1571

Opinions (cont.)
    average number of days from argument to announcement of unanimous opinion, 98–99
    average number of days from argument to announcement of unanimous opinion, by justice, 1921–1928 terms, 86
    average number of days from argument to announcement of unanimous opinion: White, Taft, Rehnquist, and Roberts Courts, 606
    unanimous opinions (*See* Unanimous opinions)
    voting alliances, 37, 42, 64, 87, 132, 176–80, 223–24, 266–68, 269, 315–16, 394
    writing style (*See* Writing style of opinions)
Originalism, 412, 646
Overbreadth
    economic regulation and, 825
    in *Fairmont Creamery*, 825
    First Amendment and, 825, 1422
    in *Jay Burns*, 735
    McReynolds and, 825
    price controls and, 845
    in *Purity Extract*, 825
    in *Tyson*, 825
    in *Weaver*, 738
Ownbey, James A., 125–26
Ozawa v. United States (1923), 1452–53

Packers and Stockyards Act of 1921, 390, 1125–26, 1197–98
Palfrey, John G., 193
Palmer, A. Mitchell, 124, 1237
Palmer raids, 124, 125, 295, 322
Pam, Max, 1278
Panhandle Oil Co. v. Mississippi ex rel. *Knox* (1928), 1112
Parker, Alton B., 341–42, 1337–38
Parker, John J.
    generally, 1460–61
    AFL on, 1287
    Borah and, 1233
    Brandeis on, 1490, 1492
    Hoover and, 647–48, 1458, 1493
    on interstate commerce, 1209
    on labor injunctions, 1247
    labor market and, 1355, 1491–92
    NAACP, opposition to nomination from, xxxiv–xxxv, 1223, 1458–59, 1460
    organized labor, opposition to nomination from, 1287
    race relations and, 1458–59, 1460
    rejection of nomination, 1460
    segregation and, 1492
    Senate debate on nomination, 647–48
Parrish, Frank M., 789
The Path of the Law (Holmes, Jr.), 164

Pearson, Drew, 154, 591
Peckham, Rufus, 209
Pegram, Thomas R., 934
Pendleton Act of 1883, 429
Pennsylvania Coal Co. v. Mahon (1922), 205, 215–16
Pennsylvania Railroad, 1257–59, 1260
Pennsylvania Railroad Co. v. United States Railroad Labor Board (1923), 1258–59, 1302
Pennsylvania Railroad System and Allied Lines Federation No. 90 v. Pennsylvania Railroad Co. (1925), 1259–60
Pennsylvania v. West Virginia (1923), 1160–63, 1167
Peonage, 1472–73
Pepper, George Wharton
    Ballinger-Pinchot affair and, 331
    on *Coronado I*, 1351
    on labor injunctions, 1379, 1392
    Myers v. United States, as counsel in, 402, 429, 443
    on prohibition, 1034–35
    Taft and, 105–6
Perkins, Frances, 768
Perkins, George W., 305–6, 339–40
Perkins; United States v. (1886), 407–8
Philips, Wendell, 41
Phillips, Nelson, 106
Picketing
    American Steel Foundries, 1239–48 (*See also American Steel Foundries v. Tri-City Central Trades Council* (1921))
    Clayton Act and, 1250–51, 1290
    direct versus indirect connection to benefits, 1246–47
    Holmes on, 1243–44
    intentional infliction of harm and, 1244, 1284–85
    labor injunctions and, 1240–41
    persuasion versus coercion, 1240, 1241, 1242–44, 1250–51, 1252
    purpose of, 1243–44, 1246–47, 1250
    Taft on, 1292
    Thomas Walsh on, 1294
    Truax
        persuasion versus coercion, 1402, 1403
        purpose of, 1399, 1402
    violence and, 1240, 1248, 1252–53
Pierce v. Society of Sisters (1925), 830–34
    Americanization and, 827, 832–33
    Brandeis in, 834
    Due Process Clause and, 830–31, 833–34
    Fourteenth Amendment and, 830–31
    Frankfurter on, 860–61
    freedom of religion not relied on, 833
    individualism and, 834
    Ku Klux Klan and, 833

INDEX

liberty and, 830–31, 855
McReynolds in, 830–31, 834
oral argument in, 859
parental control and, 855
public/private distinction, 830–31
reasonable relation standard and, 831
"standardization of children," fear of, 831–32
substantive due process and, 830–31, 833
Sutherland in, 873–74
Taft in, 831–32, 873–74
tyranny and, 831–32, 860–61
Pierson, Charles W., 984, 1004, 1105, 1155, 1177–78
Pinchot, Amos, 911
Pinchot, Gifford
Ballinger-Pinchot affair, 302, 303–4, 305–6, 333, 336, 340
as progressive, 690
prohibition and, 943–44
Theodore Roosevelt and, 305–6
Pitney, Florence, 84, 93–94, 95
Pitney, Mahlon
generally, 75
in *American Steel Foundries*, 1246, 1247, 1251–52, 1277–78
appointment of, 225, 238
Brandeis and, 85, 97, 98
on Clayton Act, 1242
in *Coppage*, 1231–33
in *Coronado I*, 1341–42
Davis and, 97–98
Day compared, 85
Dormant Commerce Clause and, 1161–62
in *Duplex*, 1242, 1324
early life of, 84
health of, 84, 93–96
in *Hitchman*, 1233, 1266
Holmes and, 97–98
on individualism, 1234, 1236
judicial style of, 85
on labor injunctions, 96, 1242
labor market and, 1327–28
McReynolds, views of, 97–98
opinions
average number of days from argument to announcement of unanimous opinion, by justice, 1921 term, 86
number of opinions authored by Pitney, 1921 term, 31, 32
performance on Court, 84–85
"property affected with a public interest" and, 793–94
retirement of, 84, 88, 94–95, 97
Sanford compared, 86–87, 99
on secondary boycotts, 1324
Taft and
labor market and, 1246, 1247, 1251–52
personal relationship with, 84, 97

replacement of Pitney and, 89–90, 100–1, 102
Taft views on Pitney, 94–95
talkativeness of, 97–98
in *Truax*, 1401, 1402, 1409–10, 1422
Van Devanter and, 93–95, 97, 228–29
voting on Court
percentage of all decisions in which Pitney participated and either joined or authored Court opinion, 1915–1920 terms versus 1921 term, 613
percentage of decisions in which Pitney participated and either authored or joined opinion of Court, 1916–1921 terms, 32
percentage of decisions in which Pitney participated and either authored or joined opinion of Court, 1921 term, 10
percentage of decisions in which Pitney participated and either joined or authored opinion of Court, 1921 term, 32
percentage of decisions in which Pitney participated and joined same opinion as another justice, 1916–1921 terms, 85
percentage of decisions in which Pitney participated and joined same opinion as another justice, 1921 term, 86
on workers' compensation, 85, 96–97, 1232–33
on yellow-dog contracts, 1231–33
Political question doctrine, 1436
Political rights
African Americans and, 1442, 1444–45, 1468–69
Equal Protection Clause and, 1444–45, 1467, 1468–69
segregation and, 1442
Pollock, Frederick
on federal common law, 1212
Holmes and, 177, 188, 191–92, 193–94, 195–96, 214, 219–21
on *Olmstead*, 1085
Pollock, John C., 21–23, 547, 673, 764
Porcellian Club, 181
Porterfield v. Webb (1923), 1456–57
Butler in, 1456–57, 1486
judicial deference in, 1456–57
Positive law
Carroll and, 1027–29
common law versus, 823, 1309
of Constitution, 1201
custom and public sentiment versus, 995–96, 1071
Holmes and
academic views of, 164, 169, 170, 171, 200–1, 202
Brandeis compared, 320, 321
judicial review and, xxviii

1573

INDEX

Positive law (cont.)
    labor market and, 1198, 1201
    prohibition and, xxviii, 998, 1000–1
    social custom and, xxviii
  James Everard's Breweries and, 976
  judicial authority and, 269, 270, 998–99, 1000–1
  Lambert and, 976
  McReynolds versus, 269, 270
  normative dualism and, 971, 976
  progressivism and, 995
  prohibition and
    generally, 918
    as challenge to, 923–24, 926, 927–28
    custom and public sentiment versus, 995–96
    Holmes and, 928, 1000–1
    Sanford and, 998–99
    Sutherland and, 995, 1010
    Taft and, 998–99, 1000–1
    Van Devanter and, 998–99
  rule of recognition and, 321, 1071
    Sanford and, 998–99
  statutes versus common law, 996–98, 1012–13
  Sutherland and, 995, 998
  Taft and, 998–99, 1000–1
  trademarks and, 1213–14
  Truax and, 1403
  Van Devanter and, 998–99
  Volstead Act and, 1451
Pound, Cuthbert W., 89, 104–5
Pound, Roscoe, 461, 670–71, 803, 996, 1010–11, 1012
Powell, H. Jefferson, 422
Powell, John, 1444, 1446, 1479
Powell, Thomas Reed
  on *Adkins*, 766, 768, 775, 778
  on alien land laws, 1488–89
  on *American Steel Foundries*, 1247
  on Butler, 72–74
  on *Coronado II*, 1355–56
  on Dormant Commerce Clause, 1189–90, 1191–92
  on Due Process Clause, 1201
  on federal common law, 202
  on *Hitchman*, 1266
  on intergovernmental tax immunity, 1117
  on *James Everard's Breweries*, 973–74
  on *Jay Burns*, 750
  on *Myers v. United States*, 445–46, 447
  on *Nixon*, 1467
  on *Pierce*, 855
  on Pitney, 96–97
  on *Porterfield*, 1457
  on price controls, 845
  on prohibition, 973–74

  on ratemaking, 895
  on *Terrace*, 1488–89
  Theodore Roosevelt and, 686
  on *Truax*, 1422–23, 1425–26
  on *Tyson*, 801
Power Manufacturing Co. v. Saunders (1927), 1195, 1205
Pragmatism
  in *Carroll*, 1055
  of McReynolds, 261
  in *Myers v. United States*, 412, 436–38
  in *Springer*, 436–38
  of Taft, xxx, 312, 390–91, 436–38
  of Van Devanter, 236–37
Precedent. *See* Stare decisis
Price controls
  Adkins, minimum wage distinguished, 757, 759, 762–63
  Brandeis on, 129
  bread, 732–33
  Butler on, 720–23, 727, 728, 798–99
  Charles Wolff Packing, 793–99 (*See also Charles Wolff Packing Co. v. Kansas Court of Industrial Relations* (1923))
  in coal industry, 720–23
  Coolidge on, 777–78
  employment agencies and, 801–2, 821
  Fifth Amendment and, 721
  Fourteenth Amendment and, 721
  freedom of contract and, xxvii, 722–23
  gasoline and, 802–3
  Highland, 720–23
  Holmes on, 129
  Hoover on, 709
  McKenna on, 768
  McReynolds on, 272, 291, 798–99
  minimum wage compared, 757, 759, 762–63
  other forms of police power distinguished, 792
  overbreadth and, 845
  "property affected with a public interest" and, 129–31, 157–59, 792, 793, 817
  ratemaking (*See* Ratemaking)
  Ribnik and, 801–2 (*See also Ribnik v. McBride* (1928))
  Stone on, 129–31, 157–59
  Sutherland on, 41, 129, 130–31, 798–99, 818
  takings distinguished, 726–27
  theaters and, 799–801, 818
  Tugwell on, 802
  Tyson, 799–801 (*See also Tyson & Brother v. Banton* (1927))
  Van Devanter on, 798–99
  Wilson and, 721, 722–23
Priest, Henry S., 980–81, 984, 1008
Primary elections
  African Americans and, 1434–37

1574

INDEX

Democratic Party and, 1434–37
Fifteenth Amendment and, 1467
Fourteenth Amendment and, 1467
freedom of association and, 1435–36
McReynolds and, 1435–36
Newberry and, 1467, 1468
Nixon (*See Nixon v. Herndon* (1927))
Pringle, Henry F., 1
Privacy
  Brandeis on, 928, 1067–68, 1085–86
  Carolene Products and, 1068
  Olmstead and, 1067–68, 1085–86
  prohibition and, 928
Private schools
  Catholics and, 833
  Jews and, 833
  McReynolds on, 276
  prohibition on, 830–34 (*See also Pierce v. Society of Sisters* (1925))
Privilege, Malice, and Intent (Holmes, Jr.), 1243–44, 1283, 1321–22
Privileges and Immunities Clause, 1468
Probable cause, *Carroll* and, 1028–30
Progressive Party
  Brandeis and, 306, 341
  judicial review and, 616–17
  on railroads, 901
  Taft and, 392–93, 398
  Theodore Roosevelt and, 2, 305–6
  Wilson and, 340
Progressivism
  administrative expertise and, 690, 694–95
  administrative state and, 690, 694–95, 923–24
  defined, 690
  Due Process Clause and, 1379
  economic liberty and, 1332
  excessive legislation and, 995
  La Follette and, 690
  Lippmann and, 690, 700, 701, 716
  Meyer v. Nebraska, divisions regarding, 829, 852
  Pinchot and, 690
  positive law and, 995
  prohibition and
    administrative state and, 923–24
    ambivalence of, 923–24
    federalism and, 923
    roots in, 921
    social reform and, 924
    World War I and, 917–18
  Sutherland and, 838
  Taft and, 89, 391–92, 448
  unions and, 1255
  World War I and, 690, 692
prohibition
  ABA on, 1001
  Act of September 14, 1922 and, 450, 982–84
  administrative state and, 922, 923–24
  AFL on, 924–25, 940
  Anti-Saloon League (*See* Anti-Saloon League)
  Beck on, 961, 980, 1006, 1013, 1024
  Borah on, 941–42, 950, 1001, 1021
  Brandeis on
    generally, xxxi, 926, 928
    normative dualism and, 968–69, 974
    takings and, 1014
    Volstead Act, recordkeeping requirements, 1030–31
  Bureau of Internal Revenue and, 948, 954–55
  Butler on
    generally, 926, 927–28
    in *Carroll*, 1058
    morality and, xxx
    normative dualism and, 974
    opposition to, 66–67
    rule of law and, 1003
  civil service, prohibition agents in, 956–57
  Clarke on, 958–59, 993–94
  concurrent enforcement power, 968–69, 971–72
  Congressional power and
    enforcement power, 958–59, 1101
    judicial deference and, 928, 998–99
    McCulloch v. Maryland and, 973
    normative dualism (*See* Normative dualism)
    Purity Extract and, 973
  constitutionality of, 970, 972
  Coolidge on, 958, 959–60, 1002, 1021
  criminal law and
    generally, xxx, 1024–25, 1031
    automobile searches, 1026–30 (*See also Carroll v. United States* (1925))
    executive power versus judicial power, 1025–26
    official lawlessness, 1062, 1069–70
    recordkeeping requirements, 1030–31
    warrantless searches, 951, 962–63, 1027, 1028, 1031
    wiretapping (*See Olmstead v. United States* (1928))
  cultural context of, xxx, 925, 926
  "culture war" regarding, 925
  custom and public sentiment and, xxxvii, 923–24, 971, 994, 998, 1010–11
  Daugherty on, 959–60
  debate regarding, 922, 924
  Democratic Party and, 925, 977
  district courts as "police courts," 949
  divisions in Court regarding, 926, 927–28
  "domestic imperialism," 971, 982
  Double Jeopardy Clause and, 951–52, 964–65 (*See also Lanza; United States v.* (1922))

1575

INDEX

prohibition (cont.)
  dual sovereignty and, 951–52 (*See also Lanza; United States v.* (1922))
  duty of states to enforce, 949–51, 952–53, 969
  Eighteenth Amendment (*See* Eighteenth Amendment)
  excessive legislation and, 994–95
  exclusionary rule and, 1026, 1062
  executive power and, 1025–26
  as expansion of federal authority, 918, 922, 948, 973, 1031
  federal courts, backlog of cases regarding in, 949
  federalism and, xxxi, 922–23, 969, 973, 1132
  Fifteenth Amendment compared, 1002
  Fifth Amendment and, 951
  Fourteenth Amendment and, xxx, 1025–26
  Fourth Amendment and
    generally, 1026
    automobile searches, 1026–30 (*See also Carroll v. United States* (1925))
    exclusionary rule, 1062
    wiretapping (*See Olmstead v. United States* (1928))
  Frankfurter on, 978
  Gong Lum compared, 1451
  Harding on, 922, 926, 948, 955
  Holmes on
    generally, 926, 928, 1014–15
    in *Carroll*, 1058
    normative dualism and, 974
    positive law and, 928, 1000–1
    Volstead Act, recordkeeping requirements, 1030–31
  Hoover on, 925, 958, 1002, 1021–22
  immigration and, 925
  inadequacy of federal enforcement, 948, 949
  Jay Burns and, 939–40
  judicial deference and, 928, 998–99
  judicial reform, impact on, 450
  Ku Klux Klan and, 925, 954–55, 1024–25, 1037–38, 1061
  lack of federal–state cooperation, 948–49, 955
  lack of legitimacy, 993–94, 1071
  Lanza and, 951–53 (*See also Lanza; United States v.* (1922))
  law enforcement and
    generally, 1031
    automobile searches, 1026–30 (*See also Carroll v. United States* (1925))
    executive power versus judicial power, 1025–26
    official lawlessness, 1062, 1069–70
    recordkeeping requirements, 1030–31
    warrantless searches, 951, 962–63, 1027, 1028, 1031
    wiretapping (*See Olmstead v. United States* (1928))
  lawlessness and, 922, 925, 1024–25, 1061
  lax enforcement by states, 948–49
  liberty and, 924, 995, 1014
  Lippmann on, 920, 925, 942, 1004, 1005–6, 1023
  Lodge on, 981
  McKenna on, 958–59, 977, 1049–52
  McReynolds on
    generally, 926, 927–28
    in *Carroll*, 1027, 1029–30, 1055–56
    morality and, xxx
    normative dualism and, 974
    rule of law and, 1003
  medical prescriptions and
    beer and malt beverages, 973–74 (*See also James Everard's Breweries v. Day* (1924))
    medical judgment and, 975
    wine and spirituous liquor, 974–75 (*See also Lambert v. Yellowey* (1926))
  Mitchell on, 1078
  morality and, xxx, 921–22
  National Prohibition Cases, 970, 972
  normative dualism and (*See* Normative dualism)
  nullification and, 943–44, 1007–8
  Olmstead (*See Olmstead v. United States* (1928))
  opinions
    generally, 926, 945–47
    number of percentage points by which justice is more likely to join or author opinion of Court, prohibition decisions versus nonprohibition decisions, 928
    percentage of decisions in which justice participated and joined or authored opinion of Court, prohibition decisions versus nonprohibition decisions, 1921–1928 terms, 927
    percentage of full opinions that are unanimous, prohibition decisions versus nonprohibition decisions, 1921–1928 terms, 927
  Pepper on, 1034–35
  positive law and (*See* Positive law)
  privacy and, 928
  progressivism and
    administrative state and, 923–24
    ambivalence of, 923–24
    federalism and, 923
    roots in, 921
    social reform and, 924
    World War I and, 917–18
  race relations and, 925
  reapportionment, and failure of, 925, 943
  religious roots of, 921

INDEX

repeal of, 928
Republican Party and, 945
Root on, 979–80, 1010
rule of law and (*See* Rule of law)
Sanford on
   generally, 926, 927–28
   federalism and, 973
   normative dualism and, 973, 974
   positive law and, 998–99
   rule of law and, xxx–xxxi, 1002–3
   Tenth Amendment and, 975
Saunders and, 1195, 1205
searches and seizures and
   generally, 1026
   automobile searches, 1026–30 (*See also Carroll v. United States* (1925))
   exclusionary rule, 1062
   under Volstead Act, 1057
   warrants, 951, 962–63
   wiretapping (*See Olmstead v. United States* (1928))
segregation compared, xxxiv, 1451
social custom and, xxviii
Southern Democrats and, 917–18, 936–37
state laws, 934–36
Stone on, 147–48, 974, 1010, 1030–31
Supremacy Clause and, 968, 977
Sutherland on
   generally, 926, 927–28
   in *Carroll*, 1027, 1029
   liberty and, 1014
   morality and, xxx
   normative dualism and, 971–72, 974–75
   positive law and, 995, 1010
   rule of law and, 1002–3
   Taft compared, 1023
Taft Court generally, 926
Taft on
   generally, 917, 918, 919, 921, 926, 927–28, 930, 941–42, 945
   in *Carroll*, 1027–29, 1049–52, 1054, 1055
   local option and, 1016
   normative dualism and, 974, 987
   opposition to, 999–1000, 1015–16
   rule of law and, xxx–xxxi, 1001, 1002–3, 1017–18, 1019, 1020
   Sutherland compared, 1023
   in *Tumey*, 1025–26
   Volstead Act, recordkeeping requirements, 1030–31
takings, viewed as, 1014
Tenth Amendment and, 952, 970, 973, 975
Tumey, 1025–26
tyranny and, 943–44, 982–84
United States Commissioners and, 514–16
Van Devanter on
   generally, 926, 927–28
   in *Carroll*, 1049–52

normative dualism and, 972, 974
rule of law and, xxx–xxxi, 1002–3
searches, 1031
Volstead Act, recordkeeping requirements, 1030–31
Volstead Act (*See* Volstead Act)
voting rights compared, 1002
Wayne Wheeler and, 464–65, 466–67, 924, 938–39, 965, 1002, 1022
Weaver and, 939–40
Wickersham Commission and, 940, 969, 1024, 1074–75
Wickersham on, 969, 978
Wilson on, 968
World War I, impact of, 917, 921, 929–30
Prohibition Reorganization Act of 1930, 466–67
"Property affected with a public interest"
Brandeis and, 819
Charles Wolff Packing, 795–97 (*See also Charles Wolff Packing Co. v. Kansas Court of Industrial Relations* (1923))
child labor and, 1131
coal industry and, 1299
Congressional power and, 720–21
Day and, 793–94
Edward White and, 793
employment agencies and, 801–2
Euclid and, 835, 879
gasoline and, 802–3
German Alliance and, 795–96
historical development of, 792–93
ICC and, 825
insurance and, 821
lack of jurisprudence regarding, 799
McKenna and, 804, 821
McReynolds and, 793–94
Munn and, 792, 795–96
Pitney and, 793–94
price controls and, 129–31, 157–59, 792, 793, 817
property connected with independent moral agency distinguished, 835, 879
railroads and, 793–94, 879, 1132
ratemaking and, 792, 879–80, 881, 882, 883–84, 891, 893–94
rent control and, 793
Ribnik and, 801–2
stockyards and, 1132
Stone on, 129–31, 157–59, 800–1, 802, 803
Taft and, 796–97
theaters and, 799–801, 818
Transportation Act and, 796
Tyson and, 799–801
utilities and, 879
Van Devanter and, 793–94
West and, 892–93, 1221
White Court and, 793–94

1577

"Property affected with a public interest" (cont.)
  Wickersham on, 810
  in *Williams*, 802–3
  World War I, impact of, 793
Property rights
  Adkins and, 757
  Baldridge and, 741
  Brandeis on, xxix, 311–13, 817
  Brewer on, 198, 200
  Butler on, 62, 172, 356
  conservatism and, 4, 311–12, 387–88
  economic prosperity and, xxix, 312, 387–88, 866, 879
  Euclid and, 840–41
  Field on, 1227
  freedom of contract as, 825–26
  as fundamental rights, 1408
  good will as, 1408–9
  Hitchman and, 1233
  Holmes on, 172, 205, 846, 1408
  individualism and, 307, 312–13, 387–88, 826–27, 834, 838, 839–42
  labor injunctions and, 1233, 1411–12
  McKenna on, 312
  McReynolds on, 320–21, 356
  Meyer v. Nebraska and, 828
  as necessary for individual agency, 825–26
  negative versus positive rights, 1403
  normative dimensions of, 827
  state duty to protect, 1402–3
  substantive due process and, 741, 828
  Sutherland on, 172, 312, 741
  Taft on, 4, 172, 311–12, 321, 356, 387–88, 392–94, 827, 847, 861
  Truax and, 1402–3, 1408–9
  Van Devanter on, 236
Proskauer, Joseph M., 647–48
Public sentiment. *See* Custom and public sentiment
Public Utilities Comm'n v. Attleboro Steam & Electric Co. (1927), 1167–68
Pullman Palace Car Company, 1322–23, 1375
Pullman strike (1894), 1229, 1230
Purcell, Edward A., Jr., 685, 1196, 1206–7, 1211, 1215
Purity Extract & Tonic Co. v. Lynch (1912), 739, 752, 825, 939–40, 973, 991

Quaker City Cab Co. v. Pennsylvania (1928), 1431–33

Race relations
  African Americans (*See* African Americans)
  alien land laws and, 1455–58, 1487–90 (*See also Porterfield v. Webb* (1923); *Terrace v. Thompson* (1923))
  biological construction of race, 1453, 1454, 1482–83
  Brandeis and, 1433–34, 1441, 1465
  Byrnes and, 1221
  Chinese Americans and, 1470
  class legislation (*See* Class legislation)
  The Crisis (NAACP publication), 1221, 1445
  custom and public sentiment and, 1451, 1454, 1481
  dissent and, 1455
  Du Bois and, 1465
  Equal Protection Clause and, 1223, 1433, 1435, 1436, 1437–38, 1450, 1455–56
  eugenics and, 1441, 1444, 1452
  Fifteenth Amendment (*See* Fifteenth Amendment)
  Great Migration, xxxiv, 1438, 1459, 1461, 1479
  Harding and, 1438–39, 1442, 1446, 1449, 1452, 1460–61, 1471–72
  Indians, racial classification of, 1453–55
  individualism and, 1440–41
  Japanese, racial classification of, 1452–53, 1484–85
  lynchings
    Dyer Anti-Lynching Bill, 1418
    habeas corpus and, 1025, 1038–41
    Ku Klux Klan and, 1025
    lynchings by year and race 1882–1940, 1222
    NAACP and, 1036–37
    "Red Summer of 1919," 1221–22
    Taft on, 1036–37, 1222, 1226
  McReynolds, racism of, 285
  national scope of issue, 1220–21
  Parker and, 1458–59, 1460
  primary elections
    African Americans and, 1434–37
    Democratic Party and, 1434–37
    Fifteenth Amendment and, 1467
    Fourteenth Amendment and, 1467
    freedom of association and, 1435–36
    McReynolds and, 1435–36
    Newberry and, 1467, 1468
    Nixon (*See Nixon v. Herndon* (1927))
  prohibition and, 925
  race riots, 1036–37
  racial classifications, 1438
  real estate, racial classifications and, 1440
  "Red Summer of 1919," 1221–22
  Republican Party and, 1222–23, 1438–39, 1441–42
  restrictive covenants and, 877, 1418
  "separate but equal" and, 1442, 1450–51
  social construction of race, 1453–55
  social instincts, 1451, 1452, 1453–55
  Taft and
    Booker T. Washington and, 1442–43

INDEX

Hampton Institute controversy, 1443–44, 1446, 1447–49, 1476–77
  as justice, 1483
  patience, advising, 1222–23, 1451
  as president, 1440, 1443, 1471, 1477–78
  Taft Court, ambivalence of, 1460–61
  Theodore Roosevelt and, 1478, 1484
  violence (*See* Racial violence)
  voting rights and, 1436 (*See also* Fifteenth Amendment; Primary elections)
  white supremacy (*See* White supremacy)
  Wickersham and, 1453
  Wilson and, 1221
  World War I, impact of, 1220–21
  zoning and, 842, 843, 875–76, 877, 1440
Racial violence
  generally, xxxii–xxxiii
  increase in, 1221–22
  lynchings
    Dyer Anti-Lynching Bill, 1418
    habeas corpus and, 1025, 1038–41
    Ku Klux Klan and, 1025
    lynchings by year and race 1882–1940, 1222
    NAACP and, 1036–37
    "Red Summer of 1919," 1221–22
    Taft on, 1036–37, 1222, 1226
  race riots, 1036–37
Radice v. New York, 264 U.S. 292 (1924), 780–81
Radin, Max, 1363
Railroad Labor Board (RLB)
  AFL and, 1257–58
  arbitration and, 1256–57
  Brandeis and, 1302
  collective bargaining and, 1259–60
  discrimination against employees based on union membership and, 1301
  Green and, 1303
  group rights and, 1257
  Hoover and, 1260
  managerial prerogatives and, 1258, 1260–61
  National War Labor Board compared, 1256–57, 1258
  Pennsylvania Railroad Co. v. United States Railroad Labor Board, 1258–59, 1302
  Pennsylvania Railroad System and Allied Lines Federation No. 90 v. Pennsylvania Railroad Co., 1259–60
  strikes and, 1288–89
  Supreme Court precedents and, 1257–58
  Taft and, 1258–59
  Transportation Act and, 796, 1256–58, 1259–60, 1302
Railroads
  Adair, 1230–31
  Adamson Act, 1248–49
  AFL and, 1257–58
  Brandeis and, 317, 318–20, 363, 365, 367, 1139, 1140–43
  Butler and, 76, 883–84, 890
  Clayton Act and, 1394–95
  Congressional authority over, 1123
  Congressional power and, 1101, 1123–24
  discrimination against employees based on union membership, 1230–31
  Dormant Commerce Clause and, 1186–87
  federalism and, 1104
  "free labor" and, 1230–31
  hours of labor and, 793–94
  ICC and
    Congressional power and, 1123, 1124
    ratemaking, 693–94, 706, 884–90
  McReynolds and, 393, 398
  minimum wage and, 793–94
  national market and, 1124
  O'Fallon Railway, 885–90 (*See also St. Louis & O'Fallon Railway Co.* (1929))
  Pennsylvania Railroad Co. v. United States Railroad Labor Board, 1258–59
  Pennsylvania Railroad System and Allied Lines Federation No. 90 v. Pennsylvania Railroad Co., 1259–60
  Progressive Party on, 901
  "property affected with a public interest" and, 793–94, 879, 1132
  Railroad Labor Board (*See* Railroad Labor Board (RLB))
  Railway Labor Act, 1260–61
  ratemaking and, 76, 390–91, 397, 706
  safety, 393–94, 398
  scientific management and, 317, 318–20, 363, 365
  Sherman Anti-Trust Act of 1890 and, 190–91
  strikes and, 1239, 1248–49
  Taft and, 390–91, 393–94, 397, 398, 1123–24, 1137–38
  Transportation Act and, 893, 1123, 1124, 1125
  unions and, 1384
  valuation of, 884–90, 897, 905 (*See also St. Louis & O'Fallon Railway Co.* (1929))
  Van Devanter and, 247–48, 1124, 1138–39
  World War I, during, 1124, 1143
Railroad Shopmen's strike (1922), 1313, 1381–82
Railway Labor Act (RLA), 1260–61
Rainey, Henry T., 885, 904
Ralston, Jackson Harvey, 616–17, 1417
Ransom, William L., 909
Ratemaking
  aggregate rates, 903

1579

Ratemaking (cont.)
  Bluefield and, 884, 890
  Brandeis on, 881–82, 883–84, 888, 889–90, 902–3
  Butler on, 881, 883, 884, 890, 902–3
  cost of reproduction, 881, 882–83, 884, 885, 886, 887, 888–90, 897–98
  Dormant Commerce Clause and, 1167, 1168
  Due Process Clause and, 879–80
  fair value test (*See* Fair value test)
  Fourteenth Amendment and, 903
  Georgia Ry. & Power Co. and, 883–84
  Harlan on, 880
  Holmes on, 880–81, 896, 902–3, 912–13
  ICC and, 1136
  land-value doctrine and, 906
  McCardle, 884, 885–86
  McKenna on, 883–84
  McReynolds on, 881, 888
  O'Fallon Railway (*See St. Louis & O'Fallon Railway Co.* (1929))
  "property affected with a public interest" and, 792, 879–80, 881, 882, 883–84, 891, 893–94
  prudent investment, return on, 881–82, 883–84, 885, 886–87
  railroads and, 76, 390–91, 397, 706
  Smyth v. Ames, 880, 881, 882, 883, 884, 886, 895, 896, 899
  Southwestern Bell Telephone, 881–83 (*See also Southwestern Bell Telephone Co. v. Public Service Comm'n of Missouri* (1923))
  Stone on, 884, 902–3, 905
  street cars and, 890–94 (*See also United Railways and Electric Co. v. West* (1930))
  substantive due process and, 879–80
  Sutherland on, 883, 902–3
  Taft Court generally, 879, 893
  Taft on, 880–81, 883, 888–89, 890, 897–98, 912
  takings, viewed as, 879–81
  utilities and, 881–84 (*See also Southwestern Bell Telephone Co. v. Public Service Comm'n of Missouri* (1923))
  Van Devanter on, 883
  West, 890–94 (*See also United Railways and Electric Co. v. West* (1930))
Rational basis review, 236, 256
Real Silk Hosiery Mills v. Portland (1925), 1168
Reapportionment
  failure of, 925, 943
  prohibition, effect of, 925, 943
Reasonable relation standard
  Adkins and, 759
  Baldridge and, 740–41, 754
  class legislation and, 1404
  common law and, 733, 734
  custom and public sentiment and, 824
  Due Process Clause and, 824
  Equal Protection Clause and, 1406, 1431–32
  Fairmont Creamery and, 823
  freedom of contract and, 1406
  FTC and, 824–25
  Jay Burns and, 735, 744
  judicial intuition and, 823, 824
  Lochner and, 828
  Pierce and, 831
  Schlesinger and, 739
  Terrace and, 1455–56
  Weaver and, 738–40
Reconstruction, 405, 427, 1225
"Red Summer of 1919," 1221–22
Reed, James A., 558, 560–61, 583, 587
Reed Amendment, 934–36
Rehnquist, William, xxx–xxxi, 508
Rehnquist Court, 605, 606, 927–28
Reich, Charles A., 846
Religion, 269, 355–56, 392
Removal power
  administrative state and, 416–17
  advice and consent of Senate and, 401–2
  Article II judges and, 416
  civil service and, 407–8, 409, 411, 413, 429
  Corwin on, 414, 434–36, 443, 444
  executive officers applicable to, 401, 402–3, 408, 411, 413–16, 417
  executive power and, 407, 413–15, 416, 418, 426–27, 428, 431–32
  Frankfurter and, 402
  Franklin Roosevelt and, 445
  FTC and, 416
  Humphrey's Executor, 416
  ICC and, 416
  independent agencies and, 416
  inferior officers, applicability to, 407–8, 409–10, 411, 412–13, 415–16
  Myers v. United States (*See Myers v. United States* (1926))
  office versus specific office holder, 414–15
  quasi-judicial and quasi-legislative offices and, 416
  separation of powers and, 417–18
  Taft and, 402, 404, 421–22, 436–38, 443
  Take Care Clause and, 440–47
  Vesting Clause and, 413–14, 440–47
  Wilson and, 419–20
Remus, George, 1080–81
Rent control
  Block v. Hirsh, 723–24
  Chastleton, 723–25 (*See also Chastleton Corp. v. Sinclair* (1924))
  Davis on, 729
  Edward White on, 728–29

INDEX

extension of, 731
McKenna on, 118–20
"property affected with a public interest" and, 793
White Court and, 723
World War I and, 723
Ribnik v. McBride (1928), 130–31, 801–2, 820, 821
Richberg, Donald R., 887, 903, 906–7, 909, 1385
Riesman, David, 565, 592
The Right to Privacy (Brandeis), 1067–68, 1087
Ritchie, Albert C., 950
RLB. *See* Railroad Labor Board (RLB)
Robb, Charles H., 774
Roberts, Owen, 98, 591
Roberts Court, 603–5, 606, 621–22
Rodgers, Daniel T., 703
Rogers, Henry Wade, 474–75, 1131–32
Roosevelt, Franklin D.
  generally, 1
  Brandeis and, 295, 340
  Court packing plan, 565–66
  election of, 925
  Hoover and, 708–9
  judicial authority and, 651
  removal power and, 445
  Taft and, 7
  Thomas Walsh and, 509
  Van Devanter and, 256–57
  Wickersham and, 978
Roosevelt, Theodore
  generally, 6, 7
  appointments to Court by, 59, 91, 165–66
  Ballinger-Pinchot affair and, 304
  Booker T. Washington and, 1449
  Brandeis and, 305–6
  Committee of Forty Eight and, 1384
  Day and, 67
  Du Bois and, 1476
  effect on Court decisionmaking, 19–20
  in election of 1912, 12–13, 305–6
  on executive power, 402–3
  Frankfurter and, 305–6, 686
  Holmes and, 165–66, 167, 187–88, 191–92
  on Indian land allotment, 847
  international arbitration and, 3
  on judicial review, 124, 143
  labor market and, 1240–41
  League of Nations and, 3
  Learned Hand and, 305–6
  McReynolds and, 261
  nationalism and, 1104–5
  Pinchot and, 305–6
  Progressive Party and, 2, 305–6
  race relations and, 1478, 1484
  Republican Party and, 4
  on residual presidential power, 403
  on secondary boycotts, 1360
  "stewardship" theory of executive leadership, 402–3
  Taft and
    executive power and, 402–3
    rift with, 1–2, 392–93
    views on Taft, 402–3
  Van Devanter and, 227, 234–35
Root, Elihu
  Brandeis and, 341–42, 346–48
  on Court in Senate Chamber, 550
  on Eighteenth Amendment, 979–80, 1010
  health of Taft and, 378, 384
  opposition to appointment of Brandeis, 341–42, 346–48
  on prohibition, 979–80, 1010
  Stimson and, 106–7
  Stone and, 1511
  Supreme Court Building and, 592
  Sutherland and, 39–40
  Taft and, 36–37, 72–74, 103–4, 388, 504
Rose, George B., 548–49, 810, 1205–6
Rose, John C., 108–9
Rose, U.M., 1263–64
Ross, Edward Alsworth, 932
Ross, William G., 636, 929–30, 1267
Rubin, W.B., 1147, 1279, 1293, 1349, 1417
Rule of law
  Butler on, 77–78
  Olmstead and, 1071
  prohibition and, 1001–3
  generally, xxx–xxxi
  McReynolds and, 1003
  Sanford and, 1002–3
  Sutherland and, 1002–3
  Taft and, 1001, 1002–3, 1017, 1018, 1019, 1020
  Van Devanter and, 1002–3
  Taft on, 1038
Rule of recognition, 321, 1071
Rules Enabling Act, 509
Rules of procedure, Taft proposal for, 509
Russian Revolution, 1218
Ryan, John A., 773, 789, 1354, 1390

Sabin, Pauline, 926, 944
Sacco and Vanzetti case, 672–73, 1040–41, 1493
St. Louis & O'Fallon Railway Co. (1929), 885–90
  Borah on, 913–14
  Brandeis in, 888, 889–90
  dissenting opinions, 888, 889–90, 908
  district court proceedings, 887
  fair value test, 886–87, 888–90
  Hoover on, 889
  ICC proceedings, 885–87
  McReynolds in, 888, 908

1581

St. Louis & O'Fallon Railway Co. (cont.)
  Norris on, 887
  reaction to decision, 889, 890, 908–9, 910–11
  Stone in, 908
  Taft in, 888–89, 890
Salinger, Benjamin I., 498
Sanborn, Walter H.
  Conference of Senior Circuit Court Judges and, 468, 469, 470–71
  on *Coronado I*, 1317, 1318, 1356
  S. 3151 and, 531
  on *Truax*, 1464
  Van Devanter and, 228, 484, 1205
Saner, R.E.L., 750–51, 1007, 1135–36
Sanford, Edward Terry
  in *Adkins*, 764
  on anti-trust law, 713–14, 715
  appointment of, xxvi, 33, 85–86, 87–88, 90, 1452
  in *Bedford Cut Stone*, 1326, 1327, 1330, 1365–66
  Brandeis, views of, 98
  Butler compared, 91–92
  character of, 114
  charm of, 113–14
  in *Chastleton*, 723–24
  conference cases and
    generally, xxxvii
    number of votes recorded at conference that switched to join opinion by Sanford, divided by number of Sanford opinions in conference cases, 44
    percentage of decisions in which Sanford participated and switched vote in conference to join published Court opinion, 622
    percentage of decisions in which Sanford participated and voted in conference with justice with whom most likely to vote, 233
    percentage of decisions in which Sanford participated and voted with another justice in conference, 88
    percentage of decisions in which Sanford participated and willing to switch conference vote to join Court opinion or to join Court opinion despite registering uncertainty in conference, 43
    percentage of Sanford's dissenting votes in conference that Sanford switched in order to join published Court opinion, 622
    percentage of Sanford's published opinions that were unanimous in conference, 66
    percentage of Sanford's unanimous published opinions that had dissenting or uncertain votes in conference, 66
  conscientiousness of, 99
  Daugherty and, 87–90, 109–10
  death of, 98, 1247, 1458, 1490, 1506–7
  dissenting opinions, 627, 640
  Dormant Commerce Clause and, 1167
  Due Process Clause and, 1194–95
  early life of, 86–87, 91, 113
  in *Euclid*, 837
  Fowler and, 87–88, 90, 99, 103, 109–10, 111
  Holmes and, 91–92
  on intergovernmental tax immunity, 1112
  in *James Everard's Breweries*, 973, 974
  as judge, 91
  judicial style of, 87, 91–92, 114, 115
  on juries, 521–22
  labor market and, 1317
  in *Lambert*, 988
  McReynolds and, 91, 100, 289
  in *Myers v. United States*, 404–5, 406, 411
  in *Olmstead*, 1062, 1063–65
  opinions
    average number of days from argument to announcement of unanimous opinion, by justice, 1922–1928 terms, 86
    average number of pages in unanimous opinion by Sanford, 1922–1928 terms, 174
    footnotes in, 218
    number of citations to law reviews in Sanford Court opinions and dissents, 1922–1928 terms, 661
    number of citations to treatises and law review articles in Sanford Court opinions, 1922–1928 terms, 662
    number of citations to treatises and law review articles in Sanford dissents, 1922–1928 terms, 661
    number of opinions authored by Sanford, 1922–1928 terms, 8
    percentage of Court opinions authored by Sanford, by term, 92
  persuasiveness of, xxxvii, 91–92
  writing style of, 91–92, 99
  performance on Court, 87, 91–92, 115
  personality of, 91
  Pitney compared, 86–87, 99
  in politics, 113
  positive law and, 998–99
  on prohibition (*See* prohibition)
  reaction to appointment of, 90–91
  in *Ribnik*, 820
  Stone, views of, 91, 98, 114–15
  Supreme Court Building and, 552, 554, 572–73
  Taft and
    intervention in nomination of, 536
    personal relationship with, 89, 112, 208

INDEX

Taft views on Sanford, 86–88, 99, 110, 117
Tenth Amendment and, 986
in *Tyson*, 800–1, 819
Van Devanter and, 231, 250–51, 1490
voting on Court
  number of percentage points by which Sanford is more or less likely to join or author opinion of Court, prohibition decisions versus nonprohibition decisions, 928
  percentage of decisions in which Sanford participated and chose to be only dissenter, 1922–1928 terms, 269
  percentage of decisions in which Sanford participated and either joined or authored opinion of Court, 1922–1928 terms, 10, 682
  percentage of decisions in which Sanford participated and joined or authored opinion of Court, prohibition decisions versus nonprohibition decisions, 1922–1928 terms, 927
  percentage of decisions in which Sanford participated and joined same opinion of another justice, 1922–1928 terms, 87
  voting alliances, 87
World War I and, 699
Sargent, John G., 221–23, 453, 457–58, 469, 538
Sayre, Francis Bowes
  on agency, 1311, 1348
  on anti-trust law, 1370
  on labor market, 1266, 1294
  on secondary boycotts, 1324–25
  on *Truax*, 1414, 1426
"Scabs," 1228
Scalia, Antonin
  dissenting opinions, views on, 641–42, 664–65
  originalism and, 412
Scheiber, Harry N., 1209–10
Schlesinger v. Wisconsin (1926), 739, 752, 986
Schmidinger v. Chicago (1913), 733, 735–36, 737, 738, 792
Schools
  "Americanism," public schools and, 832–33, 857–58
  Brown v. Board of Education, 651, 653
  compulsory school laws, 831, 856
  evolution, teaching of, 853–54
  foreign languages in
    prohibition on, 827–30 (*See also Meyer v. Nebraska* (1923))
    World War I, impact of, 848–49
  parental authority in, 850–51
  private schools
    Catholics and, 833

Jews and, 833
McReynolds on, 276
prohibition on, 830–34 (*See also Pierce v. Society of Sisters* (1925))
segregation in, 1437–38, 1486 (*See also Gong Lum v. Rice* (1927))
"standardization of children," fear of, 831–32
Schwimmer, Rozika, 151–52
Schwimmer; United States v. (1929), 151–52
Scientific management, 317–20, 363–64, 365
Scopes trial, 853–54
Seamen's Act of 1915, 40, 774, 1282–83
Searches and seizures
  automobile searches
    generally, 1046, 1049
    Brandeis on, 390
    prohibition and, 1026–30 (*See also Carroll v. United States* (1925))
    Taft on, 390
  Brandeis on, 1056–57, 1075–76
  exclusionary rule
    generally, 1044–45, 1062
    prohibition and, 1026
  prohibition and
    generally, 1026
    automobile searches, 1026–30 (*See also Carroll v. United States* (1925))
    exclusionary rule, 1062
    under Volstead Act, 1057
    warrants, 951, 962–63
    wiretapping (*See Olmstead v. United States* (1928))
  Taft on, 1056–57
  Van Devanter on, 1075–76
Secondary boycotts
  generally, 1227–28, 1359–60
  Bedford Cut Stone, 1324–35 (*See also Bedford Cut Stone Co. v. Journeymen Stone Cutters' Ass'n* (1927))
  Brandeis on, 1364–65
  Clayton Act and, 1361
  common law and, 1321–22
  compartmentalization and, 1323–24
  Duplex and, 1324
  Holmes on, 1321–22
  labor injunctions and, 1372
  McReynolds on, 1364–65
  opposition to, 1322, 1323, 1332–33, 1361, 1380
  Pitney on, 1324
  Sayre on, 1324–25
  Sherman Anti-Trust Act and, 1322–23, 1324
  strikes distinguished, 1359, 1360
  success of, 1322
  Taft on, 1320–24, 1361–62, 1363–64
  Theodore Roosevelt on, 1360
  tyranny and, 1322

1583

INDEX

Segal, Jeffrey A., 637
Segregation
   appeasement of Southern whites, xxxiv–xxxv
   Carolene Products and, 1450
   civil rights and, 1436, 1442
   custom and public sentiment and, 1481
   Democratic Party and, xxxiv, 1459, 1461
   Equal Protection Clause and, xxxiv–xxxv, 1436, 1437–38, 1450
   eugenics and, 1441, 1444, 1452
   Harding and, 1452
   institutionalization of, 1220
   Parker and, 1492
   political rights and, 1442
   popular instinct and, 1460
   prohibition compared, xxxiv, 1451
   Republican Party and, 1438–39, 1441–42
   in schools, 1437–38, 1486 (*See also Gong Lum v. Rice* (1927))
   "separate but equal," 1442, 1450–51
   social equality and (*See* Social equality)
   Southern Democrats and, 1459, 1461
   Southern strategy, 108, 1442, 1448–49
   Stone and, 127
   Taft and, 1451, 1452
   Taft Court deference to, xxxiv–xxxv, 1451–52
   white supremacy and, 1441–42, 1452, 1453
   zoning and, 842, 843, 875–76, 1440
"Self-denying judge" metaphor, 171–72
Seligmann, Herbert, 1449
Senate Chamber, Supreme Court in
   generally, 488, 550
   Hughes on inadequacy of, 567
   inadequacy of, 550–51
   McKinley on inadequacy of, 551
   Stone on inadequacy of, 552, 569
   Taft on inadequacy of, 550–51
Seo, Sarah, 1059
"Separate but equal," 1442, 1450–51
Separation of powers
   Article III courts and, 511–13, 564, 1382–84
   Caraway bill and, 511–13, 524–25, 526
   contempt and, 1382–84
   Michaelson and, 1382–84
   Myers v. United States and, 417–18
   removal power and, 417–18
   Springer and, 436–38
   Supreme Court Building and, 564
   Sutherland and, 436–38
Sessions, Clarence, 474–75
Seventh Amendment, 524
Severance, Cordenio, 810
Seymour, George D., 18
Shafer v. Farmers' Grain Co. (1925), 1174
Shaw, Lemuel, 1227, 1242

Shaw v. Gibson-Zahniser Oil Corp. (1928), 826–27
Shelton, Tom, 416–17, 525
Sheppard, Morris, 930
Sheppard-Towner Act, 1123
Sherman Anti-Trust Act of 1890,
   Addyston Pipe and, 1122
   AFL on, 1333, 1334–35, 1349
   American Column and, 696
   American Linseed Oil and, 696–97
   American Tobacco Co. and, 276–77
   Bedford Cut Stone and, 1325, 1326–28, 1329–32, 1365
   Brandeis and, 271
   coal industry and, 1122
   common law, application of, 1319–20, 1381
   Coronado I and, 1305, 1306, 1309, 1311–12, 1313–14, 1315 (*See also United Mine Workers of America v. Coronado Coal Co.* (1922) (*Coronado I*))
   Coronado II and, 1317
   E.C. Knight Co. and, 395, 1121–22
   Holmes and, 218, 362–63
   Hoover and, 697
   information sharing and, 696–97
   interpretation of, 1319–20
   labor market and
      generally, 1319–20
      Bedford Cut Stone, 1325, 1326–28, 1329–31
      Coronado I, 1305, 1306, 1309, 1311–12, 1314, 1315, 1322–23
      Coronado II, 1317
      Duplex, 1324
   Maple Flooring and, 697
   McReynolds and, 261
   monopolies and, 1125
   national market and, 1326
   normative dualism and, 1121–22
   railroads and, 190–91
   restraint of trade and, 1358–59
   secondary boycotts and, 1322–23, 1324
   shifts in jurisprudence, 696–98
   Stone and, 1356
   strikes and, 1122, 1359
   Swift & Co. and, 1122, 1125
   Taft and, 395, 1319–20, 1322–23, 1381, 1393
   trade associations and, 696–97
   unions and, 1314
Shields, John Knight, 88, 464, 634–35
Ship Mortgage Act, 270
Shipstead, Henrik, 78–79, 558, 583, 903–4, 1465
Shoddy, 738–40. *See also Weaver v. Palmer Brothers Co.* (1926)
Shoked, Nadav, 875, 876
Siegel, Stephen A., 686–87

INDEX

Simpson, A.W.B., 669
Simpson, George T., 869, 870
Simpson, Sidney Post, 1426, 1428
The Slaughterhouse Cases (1872), 1262
Smith, Adam, 763, 804, 1227
Smith, Al, 925, 950, 951, 961, 964–65
Smith, Ethel M., 779–80
Smith, F. Dumont, 812–13
Smith, Hayden, 405
Smith, Jesse, 151–52
Smith, Walter George, 358, 703, 847–48
Smith, Young B., 659
Smoot, Reed, 553–54, 572, 573, 574, 584
Smyth v. Ames (1898), 880, 881, 882, 883, 884, 886, 895, 896, 899
Snell, Bertrand H., 125, 525
Snyder, Brad, 194, 195–96, 198
Social equality
    Democratic Party and, 1461
    Du Bois and, 1442, 1449
    Equal Protection Clause and, 1446
    Hampton Institute and, 1444–45, 1446, 1448
    Harding on, 1385, 1439, 1441–42, 1449
    McReynolds on, 285
    Republican Party and, 1441–42
    Seligmann and, 1449
    Taft on, 1443–44, 1446, 1447, 1448, 1449, 1480, 1481
    Virginia Public Assemblage Act of 1926, 1448–49
Socioeconomic legislation, Stone on, 131
Soule, George, 704, 707, 815, 1395–96
Southern strategy, 108, 1442, 1448–49
Southwestern Bell Telephone Co. v. Public Service Comm'n of Missouri (1923), 881–83
    Brandeis in, 881–82, 883, 898, 900, 901–2
    dissenting opinion, 883, 901–2
    fair value test
        cost of reproduction, 882–83
        prudent investment, return on, 881–82, 883
    Holmes in, 901
    judicial conference in, 881–82
    McReynolds in, 883
    Taft in, 881–82
Spencer, Herbert, 51, 142
Springer v. Government of the Philippine Islands (1928), 436–38
Sprout v. City of South Bend, 277 U.S. 163 (1928), 361–62, 1169–70, 1185
Stafford v. Wallace (1922), 1116, 1125–26, 1143–44, 1150–51, 1152, 1313–14
Standardization
    generally, 709
    of bread (*See* Bread standardization)
    Commerce Department and, 695, 733
    Hoover and, 695, 733

"standardization of children," fear of, 831–32
World War I and, 733, 856
Stansbury, William R., 476
Stare decisis
    Brandeis on, 644–45
    Holmes on, 655
    "norm of acquiescence" and, 644–45, 648
Stayton, W.H., 934–36, 980–82
Steel Trust, 338
Steffans, Lincoln, 938–39
Steigerwalt, Amy, 679
Steuart, Justin, 938–39
Stevenson, Archibald E., 982, 984, 986
Stimson, Henry L., 6, 106–7, 168, 436–38
Stock market crash (1929), 562, 716, 1500, 1513
Stoddard, Lothrop, 1441, 1444, 1450–51, 1452, 1474–75
Stone, Harlan Fiske
    as academic, 122–23
    on anti-trust law, 697, 714–15
    appointment of, 33, 122, 125–26, 146–47
    as attorney general, 125, 126, 146, 147–48, 537–38, 1063, 1077–78, 1089–90
    authority of expertise and, 661–62
    on authority of expertise versus authority of finality, 655–56
    on autocracy, 719
    balancing tests and, 129, 661–62, 1115, 1172–73
    in *Bedford Cut Stone*, 787–88, 1326, 1327, 1328–29, 1330, 1365–66
    Brandeis and
        Brandeis views on Stone, 128, 145–46, 152–53
        comparison, 127, 132, 155, 157–58, 159, 324–25
        professional relationship with, 33, 128, 157–58, 249–50
        Stone views on Brandeis, 301
        views on Stone opinions, 714–15
    Burton Wheeler and, 126, 148, 149–50, 151–52
    Butler and
        chief justice, consideration for, 1498–99, 1511
        comparison, 123–24
        personal relationship with, 144
        professional relationship with, 33, 81–82, 127
    Carolene Products and, 127, 1068, 1450
    Carter and, 198–99
    chief justice, consideration for, 1497–99, 1503, 1511, 1516
    on civil liberties and civil rights, 124, 127
    class legislation and, 1421
    at Columbia, 122–23, 140–41, 147–48, 656

1585

INDEX

Stone, Harlan Fiske (cont.)
  on common law, 123–24, 141
  conference cases and
    number of votes recorded at conference that switched to join opinion by Stone, divided by number of Stone opinions in conference cases, 44
    percentage of decisions in which Stone participated and switched vote in conference to join published Court opinion, 622
    percentage of decisions in which Stone participated and voted in conference with justice with whom most likely to vote, 233
    percentage of decisions in which Stone participated and voted with another justice in conference, 133
    percentage of decisions in which Stone participated and willing to switch conference vote to join Court opinion or to join Court opinion despite registering uncertainty in conference, 43
    percentage of Stone's dissenting votes in conference that Stone switched in order to join published Court opinion, 622
    percentage of Stone's published opinions that were unanimous in conference, 66
    percentage of Stone's unanimous published opinions that had dissenting or uncertain votes in conference, 66
  confirmation of, 126
  on conscientious objectors, 124, 144–45, 151
  on Constitutional interpretation, 124, 156
  Coolidge and, 122, 125, 146–47, 153
  on corporations, 1433
  on Court in Senate Chamber, 552, 569
  on declaratory judgments, 673–74
  in *Di Santo*, 1172
  dissenting opinions
    with Brandeis and Holmes, 179–80
    reluctance to dissent, 626, 642
    views of, 647–48
  on diversity jurisdiction, 1213
  doctrine and, 129
  Dormant Commerce Clause and, 1171–73, 1188–89
  Douglas and, 123, 143–44, 597, 655
  on dual sovereignty, xxxi–xxxii, 1114–15
  Due Process Clause and, 129, 617
  early life of, 122
  on economic regulation, 128, 130–31
  Equal Protection Clause and, 1432, 1433, 1461, 1482
  in *Euclid*, 837–38
  evolving views of, 132, 155
  on excessive legislation, 123–24, 198–99
  in *Fairmont Creamery*, 845

  on federal common law, 1212
  Fourteenth Amendment and, 128, 129, 152
  Fourth Amendment and, 1047–49
  Frankfurter, views of, 148, 151
  Frank Walsh on, 151
  on freedom of speech, 127, 144
  functional nature of law and, 128–29, 155–56
  Grannis and, 657–59
  as "great Justice," 244
  Handler and, 127, 128, 153, 597
  Holmes and
    comparison, 127, 128, 132, 155, 158–59
    Holmes views on Stone, 787–88
    influence of, 165
    professional relationship with, 33, 127, 128, 153
    Stone views on Holmes, 187
    views on Stone opinions, 714–15
  Hoover and, 128, 145, 714–15, 1495–99, 1503, 1510
  Hughes and, 915–16
  on immigration, 141
  Indian land allotment and, 826–27
  on intergovernmental tax immunity, 129, 156, 1114–15, 1118, 1119
  on interstate commerce, 129
  judicial appointments and, 537–38, 545
  judicial deference and, 127, 128, 131, 142
  on judicial recall, 124, 143
  on judicial review, 131, 142
  judicial style of, 132–34
  on judicial supremacy, 198–99
  Judiciary Committee hearings, 126, 148, 149
  on juries, 521–22
  on labor violence, 1295
  in *Lambert*, 989
  law reviews and, 659–61, 670
  learning to be justice, 132–34
  legal scholarship and, 655, 656–59, 665, 677
  McReynolds and
    comparison, 267
    McReynolds views on Stone, 152–53
    personal relationship with, 126
    professional relationship with, 132–34, 160, 617–19
  in *Metcalf*, 1114–15
  on minimum wage, 127–28, 159, 787–88
  Mitchell and, 1498
  in *Myers v. United States* (*See Myers v. United States* (1926))
  in *O'Fallon Railway*, 908
  in *Olmstead*, 1062, 1081–82
  on open shops, 1357
  opinions
    average number of days from argument to announcement of unanimous opinion, by justice, 1924–1928 terms, 86

1586

INDEX

average number of pages in unanimous opinion by Stone, 1924–1928 terms, 134, 174
draft opinions, 81–82
footnotes in, 218
law reviews cited in, 659–61, 670
length of opinions, 132–34
number of citations to law reviews in Stone Court opinions and dissents, 1924–1928 terms, 661
number of citations to treatises and law review articles in Stone Court opinions, 1924–1928 terms, 662
number of citations to treatises and law review articles in Stone dissents, 1924–1928 terms, 661
number of opinions authored by Stone, 1924–1928 terms, 8
percentage of Court opinions authored by Stone, by term, 134
writing style of, 132–34, 676
performance on Court, 132–34
on price controls, 129–31, 157–59
professional fees and, 1114–15
on professionalism, 123
on prohibition, 147–48, 974, 1010, 1030–31
on "property affected with a public interest," 129–31, 157–59, 800–1, 802, 803
publications of, xxxvi
on ratemaking, 884, 902–3, 905
in *Ribnik*, 130–31, 802, 820, 821
Root and, 1511
Sanford, views on, 91, 98, 114–15
segregation and, 127
Sherman Anti-Trust Act and, 1356
social change and, 124, 142
on socioeconomic legislation, 127, 128–29, 131, 153–54, 155
on statutes versus common law, 997–98, 1012–13
substantive due process and, 847
Supreme Court Building and, 552, 554, 560, 569, 572–74, 578–79, 591
Sutherland and, 42–43, 50–51, 56–57, 58, 123–24
Taft and
 Caraway bill and, 512
 comparison, 123–24, 132, 158–59
 death of Taft and, 1506
 Grannis, 657–59
 judicial appointments and, 537–38
 personal relationship with, 1502
 professional relationship with, 128, 155
 Stone views on Taft, 7
 Taft views on Stone, 125, 132, 147, 179–80, 676, 1502
Tenth Amendment and, 989
Thirteenth Amendment and, 152

Thomas Walsh and, 149
trade associations and, 700
in *Tyson*, 129–30, 800–1
Van Devanter and
 chief justice, consideration for, 1498, 1511
 comparison, 132
 influence of, 231
 personal relationship with, 231
 professional relationship with, 33, 127, 155, 249–50, 636
 Stone views on Van Devanter, 230, 236
 Van Devanter views on Stone, 146–47
on Volstead Act, 925, 1030–31
voting on Court
 number of percentage points by which Stone is more or less likely to join or author opinion of Court, prohibition decisions versus nonprohibition decisions, 928
 percentage of decisions in which Stone participated and chose to be only dissenter, 1924–1928 terms, 269
 percentage of decisions in which Stone participated and either joined or authored opinion of Court, 1924–1928 terms, 10
 percentage of decisions in which Stone participated and either joined or authored opinion of Court, by term, 618
 percentage of decisions in which Stone participated and joined common opinion with another justice, by term, 133
 percentage of decisions in which Stone participated and joined or authored opinion of Court, prohibition decisions versus nonprohibition decisions, 1924–1928 terms, 927
 percentage of decisions in which Stone participated and joined same opinion of another justice, 1924–1928 terms, 132
 voting alliances, 132
in *Weaver*, 738, 740
Wickersham Commission, consideration for, 1495–97
in *Williams*, 803
on wiretapping, 1063, 1077–78
on workers' compensation, 124, 143
Stone, Kimbrough, 1318
Storey, Moorfield, 346–47
Storrs Lectures, 766
Story, Joseph, 662
"Stream of commerce," 1145, 1166
Strict scrutiny
 class legislation and, 1421
 Equal Protection Clause and, 1408, 1413
 fundamental rights and, 1408, 1413

1587

INDEX

Strikes
  Adamson Act and, 1248–49
  anti-trust law and, 1307
  Brandeis on, 1248
  in coal industry, 1236, 1237–38, 1255–56, 1290, 1299
  decreasing number of, 1313
  disruption to population, 1236
  Fourteenth Amendment and, 1248
  Holmes on, 1248, 1263
  improper purpose, 1248
  increasing number of, 1218, 1235–36, 1237–38, 1239, 1267
  interstate commerce and
    interstate versus intrastate commerce, 1305, 1317–18
    restraint of trade, 1313–14, 1315, 1317
  labor injunctions and, 1237–38, 1249, 1326, 1332, 1375–76, 1379, 1380, 1381–82
  picketing (*See* Picketing)
  Railroad Labor Board and, 1288–89
  railroads and, 1239, 1248–49
  secondary boycotts distinguished, 1359, 1360
  Sherman Anti-Trust Act and, 1122, 1359
  Taft on, 1248, 1256, 1274, 1277, 1300
  by UMW, 1237, 1255–56, 1345–46
  violence and, 1249, 1250, 1399
  Wilson on, 1274
Strong, Charles H., 1004–5
Substantive due process
  generally, 199, 770, 1216
  Adkins and (*See Adkins v. Children's Hospital of the District of Columbia* (1923))
  bread standardization and, 733, 734
  child labor and, 1158
  Euclid and, 835
  Fairmont Creamery and, 824
  federal common law and, 1200–1, 1215
  foreign corporations and, 1193–95
  foreign insurance companies and, 1193–95
  freedom of contract and, 733, 734, 1193–94
  interstate commerce and, 1158
  Jay Burns and, 734
  judicial deference versus, 739
  labor market and, 847
  ordinary business practices and, 824, 825
  Pierce and, 830–31, 833
  property rights and, 741
  property versus liberty, 828
  ratemaking and, 879–80
  Stone and, 847
  Taft Court generally, 740
  Weaver and, 738
Sullivan, Mark, 691–92, 708, 1491, 1492–93, 1498, 1504–5, 1517
Sumner, Charles, 550, 1215–16

Sumner, William Graham, 776–77, 826, 1322
Sumners, Hatton W., 583
"Super-legislature," 748–49
Supplemental Prohibition Act, 985, 987–88
Supreme Court. *See also specific justice or case*
  administration of (*See* Administration of Court)
  appellate caseload of Supreme Court, by term, 1888–1930 terms, 478
  appellate caseload of Supreme Court, by term, 1910–1930 terms, 479
  backlog of cases in, 477–81
    generally, 490, 500
    appellate caseload of Supreme Court, by term, 1888–1930 terms, 478
    appellate caseload of Supreme Court, by term, 1910–1930 terms, 479
  Building for (*See* Supreme Court Building)
  certiorari and (*See Certiorari*)
  chief justice (*See* Chief justice)
  Clerk of Court, 476
  Committee of Accounts, 477
  conference cases (*See* conference cases)
  decrease in number of opinions, 603–5
  discretionary jurisdiction, expanding (*See also* Discretionary jurisdiction)
    generally, 481, 484, 600, 637
    number of full opinions, by term, 1921–1928 terms, 602
    percentage of full opinions, by jurisdiction by term, 1921–1928 terms, 602
  dissent (*See* Dissent)
  expedited criminal cases in, 486–87
  as final appellate tribunal versus supervisor of system of federal law, 480, 484–85, 498, 603, 665–66
  judicial authority of (*See* Judicial authority)
  Judiciary Act of 1925 (*See* Judiciary Act of 1925)
  mandatory jurisdiction, reducing (*See also* Mandatory jurisdiction)
    generally, 480–81, 482–83, 600
    number of full opinions, by term, 1921–1928 terms, 602
    percentage of full opinions, by jurisdiction by term, 1921–1928 terms, 602
  opinions (*See* Opinions)
  percentage of decided cases on appellate docket disposed of by full Court opinion, by term, 1912–1929 terms, 601
  proposal for increasing number of justices, 495–96
  routine procedures, 595–96
  rulemaking authority, proposal for, 509
  in Senate Chamber
    generally, 488, 550
    Hughes on inadequacy of, 567
    inadequacy of, 550–51

INDEX

McKinley on inadequacy of, 551
Stone on inadequacy of, 552, 569
Taft on inadequacy of, 550–51
as supervisor of system of federal law versus final appellate tribunal, 480, 484–85, 498, 603, 665–66
technical amendments to jurisdiction, 494
voting fluidity in, 637
writ of error and, 600
Supreme Court Building
appropriations for, 554–55, 561, 562–63
Architect of the Capitol and, 558, 559
Bacon and, 556, 577, 578
Brandeis and, 565, 569, 572–73, 592
Building Commission and, 553–55
Butler and, 552, 554, 555, 591
classical design of, 564–65
Commission of Fine Arts and, 551–52, 553–54
condemnation for, 555, 556–57
Coolidge and, 555
costs of, 562
design of, 564–66
exclusively for Supreme Court, 564
funding of, 565
Gilbert and (*See* Gilbert, Cass, Sr.)
historical background, 550–51
Holmes and, 569
Hughes and, 564, 567
impatience of Taft regarding, 558
Judiciary Act of 1925 and, 551, 564
location of, 551–52, 557–58, 580–82
managerial functionality and, 564
McReynolds and, 569, 572–73, 589
Mitchell and, 555
model placed alongside Taft's casket, 563–64
press and, 589
representation of Taft in, 566
Roman design of, 565
Root and, 592
Sanford and, 552, 554, 572–73
selection of architect, 556
Senate Chamber compared, 564–65
separation of powers and, 564
Stone and, 552, 554, 560, 569, 572–74, 578–79, 591
Supreme Court Building Commission, 558, 559, 560–61, 562, 584, 587, 1499
Sutherland and, 569, 591
symbolism of, 565–66, 590
Taft campaigning for, 30, 374, 552–54, 570, 1507
Urgent Deficiency Bill and, 554–55, 561, 574–75
Van Devanter and, 552, 554–55, 556, 557, 559–60, 579–80, 583–85, 586, 587, 591

Suter, John T., 1498
Sutherland, Arthur E., 75, 204, 1089
Sutherland, George
ABA and, 39–40, 51, 740–41
in *Adkins* (*See Adkins v. Children's Hospital of the District of Columbia* (1923))
on administrative state, 41, 740–41, 800, 838, 839
on anti-trust law, 713–14
appointment of, xxvi, 33, 39
in *Baldridge*, 740–41
Ballinger-Pinchot affair and, 303, 310–11
in *Bedford Cut Stone*, 1326, 1327, 1328–30, 1332
Brandeis and
Brandeis views on Sutherland, 42, 56–57, 58
comparison, 315–16, 1068
opposition to appointment of, 309, 310–11
personal relationship with, 360
returns to Brandeis opinions, 352–55
Butler compared, 58
in *Carroll*, 1027, 1029
in *Chastleton*, 723–24, 730
class legislation and, 757, 1405–6
conceptualism of, 436–38
conference cases and
number of votes recorded at conference that switched to join opinion by Sutherland, divided by number of Sutherland opinions in conference cases, 44
percentage of decisions in which Sutherland participated and switched vote in conference to join published Court opinion, 622
percentage of decisions in which Sutherland participated and voted in conference with justice with whom most likely to vote, 233
percentage of decisions in which Sutherland participated and voted with another justice in conference, 43
percentage of decisions in which Sutherland participated and willing to switch conference vote to join Court opinion or to join Court opinion despite registering uncertainty in conference, 43
percentage of Sutherland's dissenting votes in conference that Sutherland switched in order to join published Court opinion, 622
percentage of Sutherland's published opinions that were unanimous in conference, 66
percentage of Sutherland's unanimous published opinions that had dissenting or uncertain votes in conference, 66

1589

Sutherland, George (cont.)
  on Constitutional interpretation, 39
  on custom and public sentiment, 998
  Davis and, 40–41, 51
  dissenting opinions, reluctance regarding, 626–27, 640
  Dormant Commerce Clause and, 1165, 1166, 1168–69, 1171
  Douglas, views of, 42
  on dual sovereignty, 1116–17
  early life of, 39
  on economic prosperity, xxix
  on economic regulation, xxxix, 42, 129
  Eighteenth Amendment and, 968, 971–72
  in *Euclid* (*See Village of Euclid v. Ambler Realty Co.* (1926))
  on excessive legislation, 753
  on federalism, 968, 984–85, 991–92
  in "Four Horsemen," 57–58
  Fourteenth Amendment and, 42–43
  Fourth Amendment and, 1047–49
  on freedom of contract, 56, 199, 779
  on fundamental rights, 40–41, 53
  Gompers and, 40, 54
  Harding and, 4–5, 21, 61, 740–41, 1238–39, 1276
  health of, 42–43, 57, 868, 1494
  Holmes and, 56–57, 172
  on hours of labor, 40, 41, 52, 54, 773
  on individualism, 767, 776, 826
  on initiative and referendum, 41, 55
  intention of Harding to nominate, 4–5
  on intergovernmental tax immunity, 1112, 1113, 1119–20
  on interstate commerce, 1177–78
  in *Jay Burns*, 734
  judicial deference and, 741
  on judicial recall, 41, 55
  on judicial review, 41
  judicial style of, 42–43
  Judiciary Act of 1925 and, 502
  labor market and, 1154–55, 1238–39, 1276, 1317
  La Follette and, 40, 614–16
  in *Lambert*, 974–75, 989
  on liberty, 56, 199
  Lochner and, 759
  McReynolds and
    comparison, 267, 270, 271, 273–74
    personal relationship with, 292
    voting alliance with, 266–67, 269
  on minimum wage, 391–92
  morality and, xxx, 762–63, 778, 834–35
  in *Myers v. United States*, 404–5, 406, 410–11, 426
  National Oratorical Contest and, 378
  natural law and, 53–54
  as "near great Justice," 244
  Nineteenth Amendment and, 52, 779–80
  normative dualism and, 971–72, 975, 1154–55
  in *Olmstead*, 1062, 1063–64, 1065–66, 1070, 1084
  on open shops, 1318–19, 1357
  opinions
    average number of days from argument to announcement of unanimous opinion, by justice, 1922–1928 terms, 86
    average number of pages in unanimous opinion by Sutherland, 1922–1928 terms, 174
    footnotes in, 218
    intellectual nature of, 44–45
    number of citations to law reviews in Sutherland Court opinions and dissents, 1922–1928 terms, 661
    number of citations to treatises and law review articles in Sutherland Court opinions, 1922–1928 terms, 662
    number of citations to treatises and law review articles in Sutherland dissents, 1922–1928 terms, 661
    number of opinions authored by Sutherland, 1922–1928 terms, 8
    number of opinions authored by Sutherland, by term, 44
    opinions of overturned, 44–45
    percentage of Court opinions authored by Sutherland, by term, 45
    persuasiveness of, 42
    writing style of, 44–45
  in *Ozawa*, 1452–53
  performance on Court, 42
  in *Pierce*, 873–74
  positive law and, 995, 998
  on price controls, 41, 129, 130–31, 798–99, 818
  progressivism and, 838
  on prohibition (*See* prohibition)
  on property rights, 172, 312, 741
  on ratemaking, 883, 902–3
  relations with other justices, 56–57
  in *Ribnik*, 801, 802, 820
  Root and, 39–40
  in Senate, 39–41, 51–52
  separation of powers and, 436–38
  social class and, 1439
  in *Springer*, 436–38
  on statutes versus common law, 996, 997, 998, 1012–13
  Stone and, 42–43, 50–51, 56–57, 58, 123–24
  Supreme Court Building and, 569, 591
  Taft and
    comparison, 58, 255
    death of Taft and, 1506
    personal relationship with, 1082

INDEX

political support for Taft, 56
professional relationship with, 41–42, 56
prohibition and, 1023
Taft views on Sutherland, 39, 50, 51, 117, 246
voting alliance with, 394
on taxing power, 1129–30
in *Thind*, 1452, 1454, 1485–86
on tyranny, 41, 55, 846
in *Tyson*, 800–1, 825
on "unimportant" cases, 609
Van Devanter and, 231, 236, 241–42, 246
on Volstead Act, 972, 998
voting on Court
  number of percentage points by which Sutherland more or less likely to join or author opinion of Court, prohibition decisions versus nonprohibition decisions, 928
  percentage of decisions in which Sutherland participated and chose to be only dissenter, 1922–1928 terms, 269
  percentage of decisions in which Sutherland participated and either authored or joined opinion of Court, 1922–1928 terms, 10
  percentage of decisions in which Sutherland participated and either joined or authored opinion of Court, 1922–1928 terms, 682
  percentage of decisions in which Sutherland participated and joined or authored opinion of Court, prohibition decisions versus nonprohibition decisions, 1922–1928 terms, 927
  percentage of decisions in which Sutherland participated and joined same opinion of another justice, 1922–1928 terms, 42
  percentage of decisions in which Sutherland participated and joined same opinion of another justice in conference, 43
  voting alliances, 42, 266–67, 269, 394
in *West*, 890–91, 892, 911–12
in *Williams*, 802–3
on wiretapping, 1066, 1084
on women's suffrage, 40, 52
on workers' compensation, 40–41, 52–53, 273–74, 775–76, 1421
World War I and, 720
zoning and, 868–69
Swan, Thomas W., 538–39, 548
Swift & Co. v. United States (1905), 1122, 1125
Swift v. Tyson (1842), 1197, 1209, 1211, 1212, 1213

Taft, Alfonso, 1
Taft, Charles P. 2nd, 1080–81
Taft, Charles Phelps, 1042, 1080–81, 1163, 1499, 1502, 1512, 1515
Taft, Helen Herron, 24, 1503
Taft, Henry W., 89, 106, 512, 517, 526, 532, 565, 1497
Taft, Horace D., 23–24, 788, 989–91, 1500–1, 1514
Taft, Robert A., 175–76, 194, 208, 1365, 1497, 1502, 1503, 1504
Taft, William Howard – generally. *See also specific topic*
  1924 election and, 1384–85
  ABA and, 2
  as administrator (*See* Taft, William Howard – in capacity of chief justice)
  AFL on, 3
  ambition of, 395
  Anti-Saloon League and, 999, 1002
  on anti-Semitism, 342–43
  Borah and, 25–26, 766, 1247
  Borchard and, 674–75
  on "bourbon employers," 1235, 1237
  Brandeis, Ballinger-Pinchot affair and, 304–5, 308–9, 335–36
  Cardozo, views on, 106, 1498
  as chief justice (*See* Taft, William Howard – in capacity of chief justice)
  as circuit court judge
    generally, 382–83
    Addyston Pipe, 1122
    appointment, 1
    Holmes on, 395
    Hughes, views of, 395
    influence of, 387
    on labor injunctions, 1335, 1379–80
    labor market and, 1229
    railroads and, 1137–38
    on secondary boycotts, 1322–23
    Sherman Anti-Trust Act and, 1319–20, 1322–23
    Thomas, 1322–23, 1326, 1329
    Toledo, 1379
  Coolidge and
    presidential campaign of Coolidge, 447
    retirement and, 382–83
    Stone and, 132, 147
  Corwin on, 673
  Daugherty and, 25, 536–37
  death of, 7, 27, 1506
  Du Bois and, 1442, 1451, 1476
  early life of, 1
  on economic prosperity, xxviii–xxix, 321, 388
  on election of judges, 399
  eugenics and, 1452
  on excessive legislation, 56, 753, 1191
  on factionalism, 1254, 1296–97
  farewell letter to, 1506

1591

INDEX

Taft, William Howard – generally (cont.)
Franklin Roosevelt and, 7
Frank Walsh and, 2–3, 15–16, 815, 1234, 1268
funeral of, 1506–7
Gilbert and, 563–64, 586
Gompers and, 3, 14–16, 1239, 1273–74, 1277, 1282, 1393
on Great Migration, 1479
Hampton Institute and, xxxiv, 1443–44, 1446, 1447–49, 1478–79, 1481
Harding, presidential campaign of, xxvi, 388
health of (*See* Taft, William Howard – health of)
Hoover and, 1494–99, 1501, 1509–10, 1516
Hough and, 89–90
on human nature, 388, 871
on individualism, 870
Industrial Conference and, 1273
on judicial recall, 459
on juries, 509–10, 521, 522–23
as justice (*See* Taft, William Howard – as justice)
on Ku Klux Klan, 1037–38
on labor violence, 1248–50, 1288–89
La Follette and, 25–26, 333–34, 614–16, 635–36, 851–52
on lawlessness, 1024, 1038
law reviews and, 659, 671
League of Nations and, 3–4, 18–19
Learned Hand and, 89, 457, 474, 542–43, 547–48
legal academia, tension with, 659, 665, 670–71
letters of, xxxvi, xl–xli
Lippmann and, 399–400
on lynchings, 1036–37, 1222, 1226
on makeup of Court, 31, 34
McKinley and, 1
NAACP and, 1036–37
on national capital markets, 355
National Oratorical Contest and, 378, 383
on National War Labor Board, xxxiii, 765, 1106–7, 1234, 1235
Nineteenth Amendment and, 780
Norris and, 503–4
organized labor on, 14–15
Pepper and, 105–6
personality of, 6–7, 1505
Philippines, as governor of, 1, 191–92
on political parties, 1254, 1296–97
as president (*See* Taft, William Howard – as president)
Progressive Party and, 398
on property rights, 4
public affection for, 1505
race relations and
generally, 1483

Booker T. Washington and, 1442–43
Hampton Institute controversy, 1443–44, 1446, 1447–49, 1476–77
patience, advising, 1222–23, 1451
on radicalism, 1272–73
on Reconstruction, 405, 427, 1225
rehabilitation of image, 1, 2–4, 13
religion and, 355–56, 392
Republican Party and, 4
Root and, 36–37, 72–74, 103–4, 388, 504
as secretary of war, 1, 847, 1229–30, 1240
segregation and, 1451, 1452
social class and, 1439
on social equality, 1443–44, 1446, 1447, 1448, 1449, 1480, 1481
on social reform, 356–57
as solicitor general, 1
Southern Democrats and, 341–42, 1459
Stimson and, 106–7
Theodore Roosevelt and
executive power and, 402–3
rift with, 1–2
views on Taft, 402–3
Thomas Walsh and, 510, 514, 520, 521, 530–31
von Moschzisker and, 89, 105–6
on War Labor Conference Board, 1234
Wickersham and, 531
Wilson and, 2, 17, 19, 307, 311, 341–42, 388, 422, 442–43
on wiretapping, 390
World War I and, 10–11, 699
Taft, William Howard – as circuit court judge
generally, 382–83
Addyston Pipe, 1122
appointment, 1
Holmes on, 395
Hughes, views of, 395
influence of, 387
on labor injunctions, 1335, 1379–80
labor market and, 1229
railroads and, 1137–38
on secondary boycotts, 1322–23
Sherman Anti-Trust Act and, 1319–20, 1322–23
Thomas, 1322–23, 1326, 1329
Toledo, 1379
Taft, William Howard – as justice
generally, 373
on accountability, 447
in *Adkins* (*See Adkins v. Children's Hospital of the District of Columbia* (1923))
in *American Steel Foundries*, 1239–40, 1242, 1244–48, 1250, 1278, 1292
on anti-trust law, 713–14, 715, 1122, 1135, 1404–5, 1420
on arbitration, 816
on Article III courts, 510–11, 523–24, 564

1592

Index

authority of expertise and, 657–59
on automobile searches, 390
in *Bailey*, 1126–28, 1156
in *Bedford Cut Stone* (*See Bedford Cut Stone Co. v. Journeymen Stone Cutters' Ass'n* (1927))
on boards of trade, 1150–51, 1152
Brandeis and
  Brandeis views on Taft, xxxv, 6–7, 8, 27, 28, 29, 373–74, 1505
  comparison, xxix, 8, 224, 311–12, 321, 388–90, 630–31
  death of Taft and, 1506
  health of Taft and, 380, 386, 1500
  opposition to appointment of, 308–9, 343–44, 346–48
  personal relationship with, 304–5, 310–11, 349–51, 892
  professional relationship with, 317, 351–52, 389–90
  returns on Brandeis opinions, 352–55
  Taft views on Brandeis, xxx, 89, 179–80, 1495–96, 1502
  views on Brandeis opinions, 311–12
  views on Taft opinions, 8
Butler and
  death of Taft and, 1506
  health of Taft and, 1503
  personal relationship with, 24, 71, 80
  professional relationship with, 61
  Taft views on Butler, 72–74, 117
  views on nomination of Taft, 5
  voting alliance with, 64, 394
Caraway bill and, 1417
in *Carroll*, 390, 1027–29, 1049–52, 1054, 1055
as centrist, 8–10
in *Charles Wolff Packing*, 796–98, 812–13, 814–15
in *Chastleton*, 724
on child labor, 1107, 1145–46
on Child Labor Amendment, 1147–48
Clarke, views on, 35, 36–37, 46, 49
class legislation and, 757, 1405–6
on Clayton Act, 1241–42, 1281, 1404–5
on collective bargaining, 1237, 1273
Commerce Clause and, 390, 1144
on common law, 199, 509
conference cases and
  generally, 6–7
  number of votes recorded at conference that switched to join opinion by Taft, divided by number of Taft opinions in conference cases, 44
  percentage of decisions in which Taft participated and switched vote in conference to join published Court opinion, 622

  percentage of decisions in which Taft participated and voted in conference with justice with whom most likely to vote, 233
  percentage of decisions in which Taft participated and voted with another justice in conference, 235
  percentage of decisions in which Taft participated and willing to switch conference vote to join Court opinion or to join Court opinion despite registering uncertainty in conference, 43
  percentage of Taft's dissenting votes in conference that Taft switched in order to join published Court opinion, 622
  percentage of Taft's published opinions that were unanimous in conference, 66
  percentage of Taft's unanimous published opinions that had dissenting or uncertain votes in conference, 66
on Constitutional interpretation, 389, 398, 422–23, 630
conventional views of, 387
Coolidge and, 1253–54, 1385
in *Coronado I* (*See United Mine Workers of America v. Coronado Coal Co.* (1922) (*Coronado I*))
in *Coronado II*, 1316–17, 1355
on corporations, 1432
on criminal law, 1035–36, 1380
criticisms of, 402–3
on custom and public sentiment, xxix–xxx, 387, 824, 1134
Day and, 59, 60–61, 67–68
in *Dayton-Goose Creek*, 390–91, 902, 912
on discrimination against corporations, 1432
dissenting opinions
  aversion to, 610
  minimization of, 610–12
  modification of opinions to avoid, 612
  "norm of acquiescence" and, 631
  reluctance to dissent, 638, 640
on diversity jurisdiction, 1196–97, 1214–15
Dormant Commerce Clause and, 1161–62, 1163, 1178
Due Process Clause and, 1402–3, 1408–9
economic regulation and, 391–92, 723
Edward White and, 681–82, 720
Eighteenth Amendment and, 927–28, 973
Equal Protection Clause and, 1403–5, 1406–8, 1432, 1433, 1453
equity and, 509, 1380
in *Euclid*, 837–38, 841, 843
on executive power, 401, 402–4
on federal common law, 1198, 1210
federalism and, 1103–4, 1126–27
Fifteenth Amendment and, 1446, 1451
Fifth Amendment and, 311–12, 388–90

1593

Taft, William Howard – as justice (cont.)
Fourteenth Amendment and, 311–12, 388, 393, 1446, 1451
Frankfurter and, 6, 8, 19–20, 27, 106–7, 682–83, 1505
FTC and, 844–45
in *Gong Lum*, 1437–38, 1450–51, 1471
on grand jury requirement, 388–90
Great Depression, impact of, 393–94
on group status of unions, 1253–54, 1256, 1261, 1269–70, 1308
on habeas corpus, 1040
Harding and, 1238–39, 1253–54
in *Hill v. Wallace*, 1146–47
Holmes and
generally, 681–82
comparison, 172, 180, 206–7, 312, 321
death of Taft and, 1506–7
farewell letter to, 1506
health of Taft and, 1502
Holmes views on Taft, 373–74, 395, 1143–44
labor market and, 1244–46
opinions compared, 173
personal relationship with, 27–28, 194, 213–14, 1504, 1508–9
Taft views on Holmes, xxx, 172–73, 179–80, 197–98, 205, 206, 208, 214, 223, 1502
views on Holmes opinions, 175–76, 208–9
views on Taft opinions, 8
Hughes and
comparison, 26
death of Taft and, 1506
health of Taft and, 1503, 1516–17
Hughes views on Taft, 6
ICC and, 366–67, 431, 1137
on individualism, 387–88
on integration of national market, 1195
on intergovernmental tax immunity, 1112
on interstate commerce, 1128, 1145, 1152
on involuntary servitude, 816
in *Jay Burns*, 734
judicial authority and, 393–94, 399–400, 649, 650, 653
judicial deference and, xxix–xxx
judicial style of, 8–10, 27
jurisprudence and, 312, 390, 394
on labor injunctions (*See* Labor injunctions)
labor market and, 1218, 1247, 1264, 1272, 1326
in *Lambert*, 988
on liberty, 848
Lochner and, 785–86
on makeup of Court, 46
McKenna and
nomination of Taft and, 5, 23–24
personal relationship with, 121–22, 135
professional relationship with, 136
Taft views on McKenna, 117, 118, 120, 137, 138
McReynolds and
comparison, 8, 267–68, 269, 270, 271, 274, 393
death of Taft and, 1506
personal relationship with, 291
Taft views on McReynolds, xxx, 265, 266–67, 286, 290
views on McReynolds opinions, 209
voting alliance with, 269
in *Meyer v. Nebraska*, 828, 848, 849
in *Michaelson*, 1382
on minimum wage, 391–92
in *Myers v. United States* (*See Myers v. United States* (1926))
on national market, 1195
as "near great Justice," 244
in *Nixon*, 1468
in *O'Fallon Railway*, 888–89, 890
on official lawlessness, 1072–74
in *Olmstead* (*See Olmstead v. United States* (1928))
in *Olsen*, 1129, 1152
on open shops, 1236, 1271, 1318–19, 1357–58
opinions
generally, 8
average number of days from argument to announcement of unanimous opinion, by justice, 1921–1928 terms, 86
average number of pages in unanimous opinion by Taft, 1921–1928 terms, 174
average number of pages in unanimous opinion by Taft, by term, 379
Brandeis, views of, 8
footnotes in, 218
health of Taft, effect of, 380, 386, 617–19
modification of opinions to avoid dissents, 612
number of citations to law reviews in Taft Court opinions and dissents, 1921–1928 terms, 661
number of citations to treatises and law review articles in Taft Court opinions, 1921–1928 terms, 662
number of citations to treatises and law review articles in Taft dissents, 1921–1928 terms, 661
number of opinions authored by Taft, 1921–1928 terms, 8
number of opinions authored by Taft, 1921 term, 31, 32
percentage of Court opinions authored by Taft, by term, 378
on opposition to Court, 614–16
organized labor on, 2–3

1594

INDEX

originalism and, 646
peonage and, 1472-73
on picketing, 1292
in *Pierce*, 831-32, 873-74
Pitney and
  labor market and, 1246, 1247, 1251-52
  personal relationship with, 84, 97
  replacement of Pitney and, 89-90, 100-1, 102
  Taft views on Pitney, 94-95
positive law and, 998-99, 1000-1
as pragmatist, xxx, 312, 390-91, 436-38
progressivism and, 89, 391-92, 448
on prohibition (*See* prohibition)
"property affected with a public interest" and, 796-97
on property rights, 172, 311-12, 321, 356, 387-88, 392-94, 827, 847, 861
Railroad Labor Board and, 1258-59
railroads and, 390-91, 393-94, 397, 398, 1123-24, 1137-38
on ratemaking, 880-81, 883, 888-89, 890, 897-98, 912
recusal of, 1163, 1178
removal power and, 404, 421-22, 436-38, 443
on rule of law, 1038
Sanford and
  personal relationship with, 112, 208
  Taft views on Sanford, 86-88, 99, 110, 117
on searches and seizures, 1056-57
on secondary boycotts, 1320-24, 1361-62, 1363-64
Sherman Anti-Trust Act and, 395, 1319-20, 1381, 1393
in *Southwestern Bell Telephone*, 881-82
in *Stafford*, 1125-26
on statutes versus common law, 996, 1012-13
Stone and
  comparison, 123-24, 132, 158-59
  death of Taft and, 1506
  Grannis, 657-59
  personal relationship with, 1502
  professional relationship with, 128, 155
  Stone views on Taft, 7
  Taft views on Stone, 125, 132, 147, 179-80, 676, 1502
on strikes, 1248, 1256, 1274, 1277, 1299
on supply and demand, 871
Sutherland and
  comparison, 58, 255
  death of Taft and, 1506
  personal relationship with, 1082
  political support of Sutherland, 56
  professional relationship with, 41-42, 56
  prohibition and, 1023
  Taft views on Sutherland, 39, 50, 51, 117, 246
  voting alliance with, 394
tariffs and, 191-92
on taxing power, 1129-30
tension between administrative efficiency and freedom, 393, 394
in *Terral*, 1196
Thirteenth Amendment and, 816
on Transportation Act, 1138
in *Truax* (*See Truax v. Corrigan* (1921))
in *Tumey*, 1025-26
in *Tyson*, 800
on unions, 1229-30, 1244-45, 1253-54, 1256, 1261, 1269-70, 1308
Van Devanter and
  appointment of, 227-28
  as closest confidante of, 231-33
  comparison, 232-34, 236-37, 254, 256
  death of Taft and, 1506
  health of Taft and, 1499, 1502-3, 1506, 1513, 1515
  personal relationship with, 225, 231-33, 251-52, 1507
  professional relationship with, 252, 253
  Taft views on Van Devanter, 99, 229-31, 242-43, 244, 245-46, 1495-96
  voting alliance with, 394
on Vesting Clause, 444
on Volstead Act, 1030-31
voting on Court
  number of decisions per term that Taft does not author or join majority opinion, 379
  number of percentage points by which Taft is more or less likely to join or author opinion of Court, prohibition decisions versus nonprohibition decisions, 928
  percentage of decisions in which Taft participated and chose to be only dissenter, 1921-1928 terms, 269
  percentage of decisions in which Taft participated and either authored or joined opinion of Court, 1916-1921 terms, 32
  percentage of decisions in which Taft participated and either joined or authored opinion of Court, 1921-1928 terms, 10, 682
  percentage of decisions in which Taft participated and either joined or authored opinion of Court, 1921 term, 32
  percentage of decisions in which Taft participated and joined or authored opinion of Court, prohibition decisions versus nonprohibition decisions, 1921-1928 terms, 927

1595

INDEX

Taft, William Howard – as justice (cont.)
  percentage of decisions in which Taft participated and joined same opinion of another justice, 1921–1928 terms, 235
  voting alliance, 64, 269, 394
  voting rights and, 1440, 1474
  Webb-Kenyon Act and, 1160–61, 1178
  in *Wisconsin Rate Case*, 1123–24
  on workers' compensation, 777
Taft, William Howard – as president
  generally, 1
  administrative state and, 401, 403–4
  alien land laws and, 1489
  anti-trust law, veto of bill prohibiting funds applied to unions, 1404–5
  appointments to Court by, 225, 227–28, 238, 307
  Ballinger-Pinchot affair and, 302–5, 308–9, 331, 333, 335–36, 350
  Booker T. Washington and, 1442–43, 1476
  Brandeis and, 304, 310–11
  budget and, 403–4, 423–24, 425–26, 447, 864
  civil service and, 433
  class legislation and, 1404–5
  on Congressional power, 391–92
  defeat in reelection bid, 1, 2, 13
  Dormant Commerce Clause and, 1160–61
  executive branch and, 26
  as "failure," 6, 15–16
  as "father of injunctions," 392, 395
  Fifteenth Amendment and, 1440, 1473–74
  Gilbert and, 556
  Hampton Institute and, 1443
  ineffectiveness of, 5–6
  international arbitration and, 3
  judicial appointments, 61, 71, 1483
  on judicial recall, 55
  judicial reform and, 397, 448
  on labor injunctions, 14–15, 392, 395, 1380, 1393, 1402, 1404–5
  legalistic conception of, 402–3
  mandatory jurisdiction, reducing, 480–81
  nomination for reelection, 26
  on pardons, 221–23
  pardons and, 248–49, 349–50
  political ineptitude of, 12
  Progressive Party and, 392–93
  race relations and, 1440, 1443, 1471, 1477–78
  removal power and, 402
  on secondary boycotts, 1322, 1323
  swearing in, 135, 1494–95
  Theodore Roosevelt, rift with, 392–93
  on war, 3
  Webb-Kenyon Act, veto of, 1160–61, 1178
Taft, William Howard – health of
  generally, 890

  blood pressure, 377, 381, 385
  Brandeis and, 380, 386, 1500
  Butler and, 1503
  certiorari, effect on, 380
  cognitive problems, 380, 385
  concerns of Taft regarding, 377, 378–79, 381–83, 384, 385–86, 1500–1, 1512, 1513
  decline in, 1494, 1499–501
  dementia, 1503
  epididymitis, 1499
  heart attack, xxxv, 380, 394, 410, 448, 539, 617–19
  heart palpitations, 377–79, 381–82, 384
  Holmes and, 1502
  hospitalization, 1499, 1502–3
  Hughes and, 1503, 1516–17
  McReynolds and, 382–83
  Myers v. United States, impact on, 410
  National Oratorical Contest and, 378, 383
  obesity, 377
  opinions, effect on, 380, 386, 617–19
  paroxysmal atrial fibrillation, 381–82, 384
  pessimism of, 1502
  retirement, 380, 382–83, 384
  Root and, 378, 384
  Van Devanter and, 382, 383–84, 1499, 1502–3, 1506, 1513, 1515
Taft, William Howard – in capacity of chief justice
  ABA and, 451, 481, 503, 504–5, 507–8, 513
  Act of September 14, 1922 and, 451–53, 463–64, 503–5, 544, 564
  administrative role of, 5–6, 26, 452–53, 457–58, 477
  advisory opinions and, 512, 514, 528
  Article III courts and, 451, 564, 1507
  bar, relationship with, 504–5, 507
  Butler, intervention in nomination of, 536
  Caraway bill and, 511–13, 524–25, 526
  certiorari and, 375, 491–93
  Clerk of Court and, 476
  confirmation of, 25–26
  conflicts of interest, avoiding appearance of, 513
  consensus, building, 610–12
  Coolidge and
    Caraway bill and, 512
    judicial appointments, lobbying for, 537–39, 543–44, 545–46, 548
    Judiciary Act of 1925, 485, 501
    rulemaking authority of Court and, 509
  on Court in Senate Chamber, 550–51
  criticism of, 5–6, 16, 504, 505, 507
  Daugherty and, 540–41
  on defendants' fees, 518–19
  discretionary jurisdiction, expanding, 481
  district judges and, 457, 458

INDEX

Edward White compared, 503–4
executive leadership and, xxxv, 457–58
expanded role of, 6, 373, 476, 502, 1507
expedited criminal cases and, 486–87
on federal court jurisdiction, 516–18
Harding and
  lobbying for judicial appointments, 536, 537
  nomination of, 4–5, 8, 529, 681–82, 949
Holmes, views of, 477, 486
impropriety, avoiding appearance of, 516
influence of, xxxv
judicial appointments and, 536–39, 540, 543–44, 545–47, 549
judicial control and, 509–10
on judicial recall, 448–49
judicial reform and, 504–5
Judiciary Act of 1925 and, 373–74, 481, 484–85, 487, 496, 501, 504–5
law and equity, proposal to merge, 509
law clerks and, 1512
leadership of, 7
legacy of, 7–8, 505, 1507
legislative process and, 502–4, 505, 511–13, 516–19
Lord Chancellor
  chief justice compared, 505, 507–8, 513, 518
  viewing role as, xxxv, 503, 504
mandatory jurisdiction, reducing, 480–81, 482–83
modification of opinions to avoid dissents, 612, 888–89, 1306–8
naturalization and, 506
nomination of, 4–5
  generally, xxvi, 20, 25, 949
  Daugherty and, 5
  Harding and, 4–5, 8, 529, 681–82, 949
on patent appeal legislation, 513–14
politics and, 504, 511–13, 516–19
prejudice, avoiding appearance of, 513, 516
on procedure, 508
Public Law No. 69–563 and, 518–19
resignation of, 7, 563–64, 891–92, 1504
on routines of Court, 595–96
rules of procedure, proposal of, 509
S. 3151 and, 516–18, 531, 532–33, 534
Sanford, intervention in nomination of, 536
on state courts versus federal courts, 510–11, 523–24
Supreme Court Building and (See Supreme Court Building)
swearing in of Hoover, 1494–95, 1509
United States Commissioners and, 514–16, 529, 530
workday of, 375–76, 385
Taft Court. See also specific justice
AFL on, 1219, 1225
ambivalence of, 11, 683, 696–97, 698–99, 1101, 1127, 1239, 1247–48, 1253–54, 1261
Anti-Saloon League and, 966–67
anti-trust law and, 696, 700, 701, 709–11, 713–14, 1319 (See also United Mine Workers of America v. Coronado Coal Co. (1922) (Coronado I))
authority of expertise and, 654, 655–56
authority of finality and, 654–55
Bickel on, 652, 1174
Congressional power and, xxxii, 1121–22
contemporary Court compared
  generally, 595–96, 603–5
  average number of days from argument to announcement of unanimous opinion: White, Taft, Rehnquist, and Roberts Courts, 606
  average number of pages in full opinion: White, Taft, Rehnquist, and Roberts Courts, 605
  number of citations to law review articles per Court opinion, 1921–1928 terms, 1997 term, 2011 term, 661
  number of citations to law reviews and treatises in Court opinions, by term, 1921–1928 terms, 1997 term, 2011 term, 664
  number of citations to law reviews and treatises in Court opinions and dissents, 1997 and 2011 terms, 664
  number of full opinions by term, 1912–2017 terms, 604
  percentage of full opinions that are unanimous, 1912–2017 terms, 611
  percentage of full opinions that are unanimous, White, Taft, and Roberts Courts, 603–8
Corwin on, 682, 685
criticisms of, 614–17, 1127, 1253, 1259–60, 1309, 1312–13, 1332–35, 1350–51, 1367, 1371, 1413–15, 1426, 1427–28
cultural context of
  generally, xxv
  divergent values of country, xxv–xxvi
  prohibition and, xxx, 926
  World War I, impact of, xxvi
custom and public sentiment and, xxvii–xxviii, xxxii, 1102, 1198, 1199
decrease in number of opinions, 603–5
democracy as narrative, xxix
dissent (See Dissent)
Due Process Clause and, 685, 686–87
economic prosperity as narrative, xxviii–xxix, 879, 1200–1
Equal Protection Clause and, 1430, 1458
executive power and, 693 (See also Myers v. United States (1926))

1597

INDEX

Taft Court (cont.)
  factionalism on, 617–19, 636
  federal common law and, xxxii, 1197–200
  federalism and, 1104, 1105
  Fourth Amendment and, 1047–49
  fundamental rights in, xxviii, 828–29, 1407–8, 1413
  Gompers on, 1307
  holding over of cases, 609
  holdover justices, 373 (*See also specific justice*)
  ICC and, 693–94
  ideological configuration of, 31
  ideological split in, 753
  institutional solidarity of, 626–27
  internal dynamics of, xxxvii
  judicial authority of (*See* Judicial authority)
  juries and, 521–22
  jurisprudence and, 596
  legacy of, 1507
  legal academia, hostility toward, 671
  legal scholarship and, 664
  Lochner and, 687, 759, 765, 766, 835, 998
  morality and, 835
  narratives
    blending of, xxix–xxx
    economic prosperity as, xxviii–xxix
    promotion of democracy as, xxix
    social custom as, xxviii
  "norm of acquiescence" in, xxxvii, 627–31
  Norris-LaGuardia Act, impact on, xxxiv
  opinions (*See also* Opinions)
    generally, 596
    writing style of, 603–8
  organized labor on, 63
  perception as reactionary, 681–83, 685, 686–87
  politics and, 504, 511–13, 516–19, 666
  prohibition and, 926
  promotion of democracy as narrative, xxix
  race relations, ambivalence regarding, 1460–61
  ratemaking and, 879, 893
  segregation, deference to, xxxiv–xxxv, 1451–52
  seniority on, 31
  social custom as narrative, xxviii
  substantive due process and, 740
  transformations in, xxxv
  "unimportant" cases in, 599–600
  white supremacy, deference to, 1452
  World War I, impact of, 10–11, 699, 1121, 1124, 1259–60
Taft-Hartley Act, 1365
Take Care Clause, 440–47
Taney, Roger B., 8, 29, 190
Tariff Commission, 693
Tariffs, 191–92, 693

Taxation
  Brandeis on, 323
  child labor and, 1126 (*See also Bailey v. Drexel Furniture Co.* (1922))
  Dormant Commerce Clause and, 1171–72, 1185
  Due Process Clause and
    generally, 752
    foreign corporations, 1195
    insurance companies, 1194, 1202–4
  economic regulation disguised as, 263, 1129–30, 1153
  Edward White on, 1126
  Equal Protection Clause and, 752
  Indian land allotment and, 826–30
  intergovernmental tax immunity (*See* Intergovernmental tax immunity)
  inter vivos gifts, 739, 752
  McReynolds on, 282
  narcotics and, 1129–30, 1153
Taxing power
  Butler on, 1129–30
  economic regulation disguised as taxation, 1129–30, 1153
  McReynolds on, 1129–30
  Sutherland on, 1129–30
  Taft on, 1129–30
Teapot Dome, 145
Tenth Amendment
  Bailey and, 1126
  Beck on, 986
  federal grants to states and, 1123
  James Everard's Breweries and, 973
  Lambert and, 975
  Lanza and, 952
  prohibition and, 952, 970, 973, 975
  Sanford and, 986
  Stone and, 989
Tenure of Office Act, 404, 410, 416–17
Terrace v. Thompson (1923), 1455–57
  Brandeis in, 1455
  Butler in, 1455–56, 1486, 1487
  district court proceedings, 1456
  Due Process Clause and, 1455–56
  Equal Protection Clause and, 1455–56
  McReynolds in, 1455
  reasonable relation standard and, 1456
  Van Devanter in, 1487
Terral v. Burke Constr. Co. (1922), 1196
Texas Transport & Terminal Co. v. New Orleans (1924), 1169
Thacher, Sherman, 1322
Thayer, James Bradley, 164, 186, 359
Thind, Bhagat Singh, 1453, 1484, 1486
"Third degree," 1074–75
Thirteenth Amendment
  Bedford Cut Stone and, 1368
  compulsory arbitration and, 816

INDEX

Coronado I and, 1331–32
Fourteenth Amendment, relation to, 152
peonage and, 1472–73
Taft and, 816
Thompson, Hope, 1373–74
Thompson, Walter, 930, 931, 981–82, 984, 1004
Three Needed Steps of Progress (Taft), 509
Tilton, Elizabeth, 925
Tindall, George Brown, 1473, 1483
Tobacco Trust, 262, 263, 277–78, 279
Toll, Seymour I., 842, 862, 864
Tortious interference with contract, 1233
Touster, Saul, 182–83
Trade associations, 694–96, 697, 700, 709
Trademarks, positive law and, 1213–14
Trading with the Enemy Act, 291
Transportation Act of 1920,
  arbitration and, 1300
  Brandeis on, 317, 318, 1140–41
  Clarke on, 1144
  collective bargaining and, 1259–60
  Democratic Party and, 1138
  federalism and, 1133–34
  ICC and, 365, 366–67, 693, 706, 903
  interstate commerce and, 1133–34
  La Follette and, 903
  "property affected with a public interest" and, 796
  Railroad Labor Board and, 796, 1256–58, 1259–60, 1302
  railroads and, 893, 1123, 1124, 1125
  Railway Labor Act and, 1260
  Taft on, 1138
  valuation of railroads and, 884–85, 886, 887–88, 889–90
  West and, 891
Treatises
  function of, 678
  law reviews compared, 662
  number of citations to (*See* Legal scholarship)
Treaty of Versailles (1919), 4
Truax, William, 1399, 1400
Truax v. Corrigan (1921)
  generally, 1386
  AFL on, 1415, 1427–28
  American Steel Foundries compared, 1402, 1403
  announcement of decision, 1402
  arguments in, 1401
  Brandeis in
    generally, 1401, 1402, 1413
    dissenting opinion, 1410–12
    Equal Protection Clause and, 1412
    "experiments" and, 1410–11
    judicial review and, 1412
    promotion of democracy and, 1410–11, 1412
  Clarke in, 1401, 1402, 1409
  class legislation and, 1404, 1406
  Clayton Act and, 1415
  Corwin on, 1426
  Day in, 1418–19
  dissenting opinions, 1409–12
  Due Process Clause and, 1402–3, 1408–9, 1411, 1415
  Edward White in, 1401
  Equal Protection Clause and, 1403–4, 1406–8, 1409–10, 1412, 1415, 1430–31
  factual background, 1399
  Fourteenth Amendment and, 1409, 1412, 1414, 1415
  Frankfurter on, 1427
  fundamental rights and, 1407–8
  Gompers on, 1427
  Handler on, 1421
  Holmes in, 1401, 1402, 1409, 1413
  influence of, 1415, 1428–29
  judicial review and, 1412
  law reviews on, 1414, 1419, 1422–23
  normative dualism and, 1409
  Norris-LaGuardia Act, effect on, 1465
  picketing
    persuasion versus coercion, 1402, 1403
    purpose of, 1399, 1402
  Pitney in, 1401, 1402, 1409–10, 1422
  positive law and, 1403
  positive versus negative rights in, 1403
  promotion of democracy and, 1410–11, 1412
  property rights and, 1402–3, 1408–9
  reaction to decision, 1413–15, 1419, 1426, 1427–28
  reargument in, 1401–2
  Sanborn on, 1464
  Sayre on, 1414, 1426
  state court proceedings, 1399–400, 1416–29
  Taft in
    generally, 392, 1413
    class legislation and, 1404, 1406
    Due Process Clause and, 1402–3, 1408–9
    Equal Protection Clause and, 1403–4, 1406–8
    fundamental rights and, 1407–8
    negative versus positive rights, 1403
    property rights and, 1402–3, 1408–9
    reaction to decision and, 1426, 1427
    state duty to protect property rights, 1402–3
  Van Devanter in, 1418–19
  in White Court, 1401
  writ of error, 1400
Truman, Harry, 6
Tucker, Henry St. George, 1103–4
Tugwell, Rexford G., 709, 793, 802, 819, 820
Tumey v. Ohio (1927), 1025–26
Tuskegee Institute, 1448, 1476–77

Twenty-first Amendment, 928, 1071
Tyson & Brother v. Banton (1927), 799–801
  Brandeis in, 800
  Holmes in, 800
  Learned Hand on, 818
  overbreadth in, 825
  "property affected with a public interest" and, 799–801
  reaction to decision, 801, 819–20
  Sanford in, 800–1, 819
  Stone in, 129–30, 800–1
  Sutherland in, 800–1, 825
  Taft in, 800

Ulm, A.H., 152, 501, 966–67, 1491
Unanimous opinions. *See also specific justice or case*
  generally, 610, 612, 617
  certiorari and, 619
  conference cases
    generally, 620, 621–22, 637–38
    percentage of justice's published opinions that were unanimous in conference, 66
    percentage of published conference cases that are unanimous as multiple of percentage of conference cases that are unanimous in conference, by jurisdiction by term, 1922–1928 terms, 625
    percentage of published conference cases that are unanimous as multiple of percentage of conference cases that are unanimous in conference, by term, 624
    percentage of unanimous conference cases, by jurisdiction, 624
    percentage of unanimous conference cases, by jurisdiction by term, 1922–1928 terms, 625
    unanimous conference cases, 621
    unanimous conference cases, by term, 1922–1928 terms, 623
  Judiciary Act of 1925, impact of, 619, 627–28
  mandatory jurisdiction versus discretionary jurisdiction
    generally, 619, 623
    percentage of full opinions that are unanimous, by jurisdiction by term, 1921–1928 terms, 608
    percentage of published conference cases that are unanimous as multiple of percentage of conference cases that are unanimous in conference, by jurisdiction by term, 1922–1928 terms, 625
    percentage of unanimous conference cases, by jurisdiction, 624
    percentage of unanimous conference cases, by jurisdiction by term, 1922–1928 terms, 625
    Taft Court generally, 626, 627–28, 665
  outward show of unanimity, 626
  percentage of full opinions that are unanimous
    1912–2017 terms, 611
    1921–1928 terms, 613
    by jurisdiction by term, 1921–1928 terms, 608
    prohibition decisions versus nonprohibition decisions, 1921–1928 terms, 927
    White, Taft, and Roberts Courts, 606
  persistence of unanimity, 619
  in Roberts Court, 621–22
  time from argument to announcement
    average number of days from argument to announcement of full opinion, by jurisdiction by term, 1921–1928 terms, 607
    average number of days from argument to announcement of unanimous opinion, 98–99
    average number of days from argument to announcement of unanimous opinion, by justice, 1921–1928 terms, 86
    average number of days from argument to announcement of unanimous opinion: White, Taft, Rehnquist, and Roberts Courts, 606
  in Vinson Court, 636–37
Unconstitutional conditions, 1206–7
Underwood, Oscar W., 856, 945
Unemployment, Hoover and, 717–18
Uniform Bills of Lading Act, 997–98
Uniform Procedure Bill, 528
Unincorporated associations, unions as, 1308–9
Unions. *See also specific union*
  agency
    Coronado I and, 1311–12, 1347
    Norris-LaGuardia Act and, 1347–48
    Sayre on, 1311, 1348
  arbitration and, 1255
  bargaining representatives, 1258
  Brandeis on, 338, 365, 1292, 1344–45
  class legislation and, 1254
  company unions, 1295–96
  conservative unions, 1248–49
  conspiracy, not deemed, 1227
  Constitutional interpretation and, 1219–20
  damages recoverable against, 1305, 1308–9, 1313, 1351
  decreasing membership in, 1219

INDEX

discrimination against employees based on union membership, 1230–31, 1234, 1267–68, 1301
freedom of contract and, 1230
group status of, 1228, 1253–55, 1256, 1261, 1269–70, 1308
Holmes on, 1229, 1230
Hughes on, 1261
incorporation of, 1305
increasing membership in, 1217–18, 1224
individualism versus, 1254–55
industrial unionism, 1269
lawfulness of, 1227
legal status of, 1219–20
McKenna on, 1230
progressivism and, 1255
public interest versus, 1255
radicalism, charges of, 1236, 1248
railroads and, 1384
right to organize, 1227–28, 1235, 1237, 1260–61, 1285
rise of restrictions on, 1227–28
secondary boycotts (*See* Secondary boycotts)
Sherman Anti-Trust Act and, 1314
Taft on, 1229–30, 1244–45, 1253–54, 1256, 1261, 1269–70, 1308
tortious interference with contract and, 1233
as unincorporated associations, 1308–9
voluntarism, 1231–32
World War I, impact of, 1217–18
yellow-dog contracts and (*See* Yellow-dog contracts)
Unitary executive, 440–47
United Leather Workers International Union, Local Lodge or Union No. 66 v. Herkert & Meisel Trunk Co. (1924), 1317–18, 1356
United Mine Workers of America (UMW)
 Coronado I, 1304–16 (*See United Mine Workers of America v. Coronado Coal Co.* (1922) (*Coronado I*))
 Coronado II, 1315–17 (*See also Coronado Coal Co. v. United Mine Workers of America* (1925) (*Coronado II*))
 District 21, 1305, 1308, 1311, 1313, 1315, 1316–17
 labor injunctions and, 1314
 organizing by, 1246
 strikes by, 1237, 1255–56, 1345–46
United Mine Workers of America v. Coronado Coal Co. (1922) (*Coronado I*), 1304–16
 Acheson and, 1338
 AFL on, 1309, 1311–12, 1337, 1352–53
 agency and, 1311–12, 1347
 announcement of decision, 1306
 anti-trust law and, 1312
Brandeis in
 generally, 1306, 1341–42, 1348
 damages recoverable against union and, 1309
 dissenting opinion (draft), 1306–8, 1336, 1341–42
Circuit Court proceedings, 1305
Clarke in, 1306, 1339
Clayton Act and, 1348–49
common law and, 1308, 1309
Congress and, 1312
damages recoverable against union, 1305, 1308–9
Davis and, 1353
Day in, 1306, 1341–42
 dissenting opinion (draft), 1306–8, 1336, 1341–42
district court proceedings, 1305
Edward White in, 1306
factual background, 1304–5
federal common law and, 1312
Frankfurter on, 1308
Gompers on, 1310, 1311, 1312–13
Green on, 1346–47
Harding and, 1312
Hitchman distinguished, 1365–66
Holmes in, 1306, 1341–42
Hughes as counsel in, 1306
importance of, 1304
interstate commerce versus intrastate commerce, 1305
judicial discretion in, 1314
"judicial legislation" in, 1309
labor injunctions, damages lessening need for, 1310
labor violence and, 1304–5
La Follette on, 1309, 1310, 1344, 1350
national union versus local union, 1305, 1311–12, 1347–48
Newton Baker on, 1310
normative dualism and, 1313–14
Pepper on, 1351
Pitney in, 1341–42
reaction to decision, 1309–11, 1312–13, 1350–51
restraint of trade and, 1313–14, 1315
Sanborn on, 1317, 1318, 1356
Sherman Anti-Trust Act and, 1305, 1306, 1309, 1311–12, 1313–14, 1315
Taft in
 generally, 1307, 1341–42
 agency and, 1347
 judicial discretion and, 1314
 labor injunctions and, 1314–15
 national union versus local union, 1311, 1347–48
 reaction to decision and, 1312–13, 1350–51

1601

INDEX

United Mine Workers (cont.)
    restraint of trade and, 1313–14, 1315
    switching of vote, 1306–8
    Thirteenth Amendment and, 1331–32
    UMW on, 1310–11, 1347
    Van Devanter in, 1306
    in White Court, 1306
United Railways and Electric Co. v. West (1930), 890–94
    Brandeis and, 892
    Due Process Clause and, 890–91
    Fourteenth Amendment and, 890–91, 894
    Hughes confirmation hearings, impact on, 892–94
    La Follette, Jr. on, 892
    Norris on, 892
    present value and, 890–91, 894
    property, incentive effects and, 891
    "property affected with a public interest" and, 891–93
    reaction to, 892–93, 894
    Sutherland in, 890–91, 892, 911–12
    Transportation Act and, 891
United States Commissioners, 514–16
United States Steel Corporation, 305–6, 339–40, 1236
United Zinc & Chemical Co. v. Britt (1922), 206–7
Upham, Fred, 100–1
Urban property, 839–42, 843
Utilities
    electric utilities, Dormant Commerce Clause and, 1167–68, 1180–81
    natural gas
        Dormant Commerce Clause and, 1160, 1161–63, 1164–66, 1187
        interstate commerce and, 1180
    "property affected with a public interest" and, 879
    ratemaking and, 881–84 (*See also Southwestern Bell Telephone Co. v. Public Service Comm'n of Missouri* (1923))

Vagueness
    Due Process Clause and, 845–46
    First Amendment and, 845–46
Valuation Act, 884–85
Van Devanter, Dollie, 242
Van Devanter, Willis
    generally, xxvii, 41–42
    Acheson and, 231
    in *Adkins*, 756, 764
    administration of Court and, 230–31, 477
    advisory opinions and, 528
    on anti-trust law, 710, 713–14
    appointment of, 225, 227–28, 238
    authority of expertise and, 659, 672
    Bickel on, 238
    Borah and, 234–35
    Brandeis and
        Brandeis views on Van Devanter, 230, 231, 237, 243, 244, 247, 258, 617
        comparison, 236, 237, 246
        influence on, 231
        personal relationship with, 254
        professional relationship with, 247–48, 250, 251
    Butler and
        comparison, 64–65, 232–34, 256
        influence on, 231
        personal relationship with, 71, 231, 232–34, 254
        professional relationship with, 61, 232
        Van Devanter views on Butler, 72–74
        voting alliance with, 64
    in *Carroll*, 1049–52
    certiorari and, 493–94, 497–98
    in *Charles Wolff Packing*, 812, 813
    in *Chastleton*, 723–24, 728–29, 730
    chief justiceship, campaign for, 21–23
    as circuit court judge, 227
    Clarke, personal relationship with, 47, 49, 231
    on class legislation, 1404
    conference cases and
        generally, xxxvii
        number of votes recorded at conference that switched to join opinion by Van Devanter, divided by number of Van Devanter's opinions in conference cases, 44
        percentage of decisions in which Van Devanter participated and switched his vote in conference to join published Court opinion, 622
        percentage of decisions in which Van Devanter participated and voted in conference with justice with whom most likely to vote, 233
        percentage of decisions in which Van Devanter participated and voted with another justice in conference, 234
        percentage of decisions in which Van Devanter participated and willing to switch conference vote to join Court opinion or to join Court opinion despite registering uncertainty in conference, 43
        percentage of Van Devanter's dissenting votes in conference that Van Devanter switched in order to join published Court opinion, 622
        percentage of Van Devanter's published opinions that were unanimous in conference, 66

INDEX

percentage of Van Devanter's unanimous published opinions that had dissenting or uncertain votes in conference, 66
confirmation of, 228
in *Coronado I*, 1306
Davis and, 229
Day, views on, 67–68
dissenting opinions, reluctance regarding, 626, 638–39, 640
on diversity jurisdiction, 1197, 1208–9
Dormant Commerce Clause and, 1160–62, 1168
Douglas, views of, 254
on dual sovereignty, 257–58, 963
Due Process Clause and, 257–58, 1204
early life of, 225–27
Edward White and, 21–23, 246
Equal Protection Clause and, 236, 1403–4, 1431
in *Euclid*, 835, 839–40
as "failure," 230, 373
Fourteenth Amendment and, 257–58
Francis Warren and, 225, 226–27, 228, 231, 238–41, 259
Frankfurter, views of, 232, 253
Franklin Roosevelt and, 256–57
free silver and, 259
Holmes and
    comparison, 225, 229
    influence on, 231
    opinions compared, 173
    professional relationship with, 248–49
    Van Devanter views on Holmes, 173
    views on Holmes opinions, 176
on hours of labor, 759
Hughes and, 230, 241–42, 244, 246, 1503–4
ICC and, 1137
ideology of, 234–36
influence of, 231
on intergovernmental tax immunity, 1112
judicial appointments and, 543, 547, 548–49
judicial style of, 228–30, 232–34
Judiciary Act of 1925 and, 232, 482, 483–84, 485, 491–93, 494, 495, 500, 502, 503
on juries, 521–22
on Ku Klux Klan, 1037–38
labor market and, 1317
in *Lambert*, 988, 991
in *Lee v. Chesapeake & Ohio Ry. Co.*, 1197
legal scholarship and, 672
McKenna and, 117, 121–22, 227, 231, 232
McReynolds and
    comparison, 259–60, 267–68, 269, 270, 271, 274
    influence on, 231
    personal relationship with, 292
    Van Devanter views on McReynolds, 265
    voting alliance with, 266–67, 269

Mitchell and, 241
in *Myers v. United States*, 404–5, 406, 408, 410, 411, 432
national market and, 1162, 1197
National Oratorical Contest and, 378
Native Americans and, 227, 247–48
in *Olmstead*, 1062, 1063–65, 1092–94
opinions
    average number of days from argument to announcement of unanimous opinion, by justice, 1921–1928 terms, 86
    average number of pages in unanimous opinion by Van Devanter, 1921–1928 terms, 174
    footnotes in, 218
    length of, 229
    number of citations to law reviews in Van Devanter Court opinions and dissents, 1921–1928 terms, 661
    number of citations to treatises and law review articles in Van Devanter Court opinions, 1921–1928 terms, 662
    number of citations to treatises and law review articles in Van Devanter dissents, 1921–1928 terms, 661
    number of opinions authored by, 228–29
    number of opinions authored by Van Devanter, 1921–1928 terms, 8
    percentage of Court opinions authored by Van Devanter, by term, 229, 230
    persuasiveness of, xxxvii, 231
    slowness of, 228–30, 240, 242–43, 245
    writing style of, 229, 242, 244, 245, 249–50
on pardons, 221–23
in *Pennsylvania v. West Virginia*, 1161
performance on Court, 228–30, 232–34
Pitney and, 93–95, 97, 228–29
positive law and, 998–99
pragmatism of, 236–37
on price controls, 798–99
on prohibition (*See* prohibition)
"property affected with a public interest" and, 793–94
on property rights, 236
public impression of, 244
railroads and, 247–48, 1124, 1138–39
on ratemaking, 883
rational basis review and, 236, 256
reassignment of cases, 229–30, 243
in Republican Party, 226–27
Sanborn and, 228, 484, 1205
Sanford and, 231, 250–51, 1490
in *Saunders*, 1205
on searches and seizures, 1075–76
Stone and
    chief justice, consideration for, 1498, 1511
    comparison, 132

1603

Van Devanter, Willis (cont.)
  influence on, 231
  personal relationship with, 231
  professional relationship with, 33, 127, 155, 249–50, 636
  Stone views on Van Devanter, 230, 236
  Van Devanter views on Stone, 146–47
  Supreme Court Building and, 552, 554–55, 556, 557, 559–60, 579–80, 583–85, 586, 587, 591
  Sutherland and, 231, 236, 241–42, 246
  Taft and
    appointment by, 227–28
    Caraway bill and, 512
    as closest confidante of, 231–33
    comparison, 232–34, 236–37, 254, 256
    death of Taft and, 1506
    health of Taft and, 382, 383–84, 1499, 1502–3, 1506, 1513, 1515
    personal relationship with, 225, 231–33, 251–52, 1507
    professional relationship with, 252, 253
    resignation of Taft and, 1503
    Taft views on Van Devanter, 99, 229–31, 242–43, 244, 245–46, 1495–96
    voting alliance with, 394
  in *Terrace*, 1487
  Theodore Roosevelt and, 227, 234–35
  in *Truax*, 1418–19
  on Volstead Act, 1030–31
  voting on Court
    number of percentage points by Which Van Devanter is more or less likely to join or author opinion for Court, prohibition decisions versus nonprohibition decisions, 928
    percentage of all decisions in which Van Devanter participated and either joined or authored Court opinion, 1915–1920 terms versus 1921–1928 terms, 613
    percentage of decisions in which Van Devanter participated and chose to be only dissenter, 1921–1928 terms, 269
    percentage of decisions in which Van Devanter participated and either authored or joined opinion of Court, 1916–1921 terms, 32
    percentage of decisions in which Van Devanter participated and either joined or authored Court opinion, by term, 1921–1928 terms, 614
    percentage of decisions in which Van Devanter participated and either joined or authored opinion of Court, 1921–1928 terms, 10, 682
    percentage of decisions in which Van Devanter participated and either joined or authored opinion of Court, 1921 term, 32
    percentage of decisions in which Van Devanter participated and joined or authored opinion of Court, prohibition decisions versus nonprohibition decisions, 1921–1928 terms, 927
    percentage of decisions in which Van Devanter participated and joined same opinion of another justice, 1921–1928 terms, 234
    voting alliances, 64, 233–34, 266–67, 269, 394
  on workers' compensation, 1265–66
  World War I and, 699
  in Wyoming, 225–27
Vanzetti, Bartolomeo. *See* Sacco and Vanzetti case
Veblen, Thorstein, 807
Venue, foreign corporations and, 1195
Vertrees, John J., 304, 331
Vesting Clause. *See also* Executive power
  Myers v. United States and, 413–14, 440–47
  removal power and, 413–14, 440–47
  Taft on, 444
Village of Euclid v. Ambler Realty Co. (1926), 835–43
  amicus briefs in, 837–38, 867–68, 873–74
  announcement of decision, 838
  authority of expertise and, 839–40, 842–43
  Brandeis in, 837
  brief of appellees, 870–71
  Butler in, 835, 839–40, 841
  district court proceedings, 836–37
  Due Process Clause and, 835
  "facial" versus "as applied" challenges, 838–39, 871–72
  factual background, 835–36
  individualism and, 839–41
  judicial deference and, 839
  liberty and, 838, 842
  McReynolds in, 835, 839–40
  Newton Baker and, 835–37, 838, 870–71, 872–73
  "property affected with a public interest" and, 835, 879
  property rights and, 840–41
  rehearing in, 838
  Sanford in, 837
  social value of home and, 877–78
  Stone in, 837–38
  substantive due process and, 835
  Sutherland in
    generally, 837
    on apartments, 842–43
    authority of expertise and, 839–40, 842–43
    Due Process Clause and, 835
    "facial" versus "as applied" challenges, 838–39, 871–72
    judicial deference and, 839

INDEX

liberty and, 838, 842
property rights and, 840–41
social value of home and, 877–78
switching of vote, 838, 843, 869
Taft in, 837–38, 841, 843
takings, zoning as, 837
urban property and, 839–42, 843
Van Devanter in, 835, 839–40
Villard, Oswald, 1427
Vines, Kenneth N., 636–37
Vinson, Fred M., 636–37
Vinson Court, 591
Virginia
  Massenberg Bill, 1446–47, 1448
  Public Assemblage Act of 1926, 1448–49
  Racial Integrity Act of 1924, 1444
Volstead, Andrew John, 102
Volstead Act
  generally, xxx, 5, 918
  Anti-Saloon League and, xxx, 924, 925
  Brandeis on, 1030–31
  Bureau of Internal Revenue and, 948, 954–55
  Carroll and, 1027
  duty of states to enforce, 950
  enactment of, 924–25
  fines under, 1053
  Holmes on, 1030–31
  Hoover on, 1024
  intoxicating beverages defined in, 939–40
  judicial reform, impact on, 450
  lack of legitimacy, 993–94
  medical prescriptions and, 987–88
  positive law and, 1451
  recordkeeping requirements, 1030–31
  searches and seizures under, 1057
  Stone on, 925, 1030–31
  Sutherland on, 972, 998
  Taft on, 1030–31
  Van Devanter on, 1030–31
  Wickersham on, 969, 979
  widespread contempt for, 1005–6
Voluntarism, 1298, 1303
von Moschzisker, Robert, 89, 105–6, 111
Voting fluidity, 637
Voting rights
  Equal Protection Clause and, 1436
  Fifteenth Amendment (*See* Fifteenth Amendment)
  Holmes on, 166
  primary elections
    African Americans and, 1434–37
    Democratic Party and, 1434–37
    Fifteenth Amendment and, 1467
    Fourteenth Amendment and, 1467
    freedom of association and, 1435–36
    McReynolds and, 1435–36
    Newberry and, 1467, 1468
    Nixon (*See Nixon v. Herndon* (1927))

prohibition compared, 1002
race relations and, 1436
Taft and, 1440, 1474
women's suffrage, Sutherland on, 40

Wadsworth, James W., Jr., 89
Wagner, Robert F., 647–48
Waite, Morrison R., 792
Waite Court, 637, 879–80
Walker, Robert Averill, 869
Walsh, Frank P.
  on *certiorari*, 491–93
  on *Charles Wolff Packing*, 816
  in National War Labor Board, 1234
  on Stone, 151
  Taft and, 2–3, 15–16, 815, 1234, 1268
Walsh, Thomas J.
  Brandeis and, 509
  on Butler, 903–4
  Court of Customs Appeals and, 514
  on diversity jurisdiction, 1196–97, 1214–15
  federal court jurisdiction and, 516
  Franklin Roosevelt and, 509
  Judiciary Act of 1925 and, 491–93, 499
  on labor injunctions, 1262
  on picketing, 1294
  rulemaking authority and, 509
  Stone and, 149
  Taft and, 510, 514, 520, 521, 530–31
Ward, Artemus, 679
Ward, Henry W., 532–33
War Industries Board (WIB), 694–95, 711–12
War Labor Conference Board, 1234
Warren, Charles B., 537–38, 545, 558, 634
Warren, Earl, 1489
Warren, Francis E., 225, 226–27, 228, 231, 238–41, 259
Warren, Sam, 297
War Service Committees, 694
War-Time Prohibition Act, 730–31, 929–30, 939–40
Washington, Booker T.
  Hampton Institute and, 1443
  NAACP compared, 1460
  "politics of deception," 1475–76
  Republican Party and, 1451
  "separate but equal" and, 1442
  Taft and, 1442–43, 1476
  Theodore Roosevelt and, 1449
Washington Naval Conference, 1484
Weaver v. Palmer Brothers Co. (1926), 738–40
  Brandeis in, 738, 740
  Butler in, 738–39
  Due Process Clause and, 738, 751
  Fourteenth Amendment and, 739, 740
  Holmes in, 738, 739–40
  judicial deference and, 739–40
  overbreadth in, 738

1605

Weaver v. Palmer Brothers Co. (cont.)
  prohibition and, 939–40
  reasonable relation standard and, 738–40
  Stone in, 738, 740
  substantive due process and, 738
Webb, Ulysses Sigel, 1457–58, 1489–90
Webb-Kenyon Act, 1160–61, 1177–78
Webster, Daniel, 550
Wendell, Barrett, 1010
Westenhaver, D.C., 837, 841–42, 866
Western Union Telegraph, 1234
West v. Kansas Natural Gas (1911), 1161
Weyl, Walter E., 692, 704
Wheeler, Burton
  Hughes and, 914
  Stone and, 126, 148, 149–50, 151–52
Wheeler, Everett P., 341–42, 1464
Wheeler, Wayne B., 464–65, 466–67, 924, 938–39, 965, 1002, 1022
White, Byron, 1422
White, Edward Douglass. *See also* White Court
  generally, 7
  in *Coronado I*, 1306
  on Court in Senate Chamber, 551
  death of, 5, 21–23, 1239–40
  dissenting opinions, views on, 629
  Holmes and, 167, 192, 204, 211
  on hours of labor, 328–29, 759
  legislative process and, 503–4
  McReynolds, views of, 21–23
  memorial for, 720
  "property affected with a public interest" and, 793
  on rent control, 728–29
  Taft and, 503–4, 681–82, 720
  on taxation, 1126
  in *Truax*, 1401
  Van Devanter and, 21–23, 246
  on workers' compensation, 1265–66
  writing style of opinions, 192
White, G. Edward, 57–58, 173, 770, 1438
White, Walter, 1458–59, 1460, 1491
White, William Allen, 6, 12, 19, 538–39, 692, 1505
White Court
  American Steel Foundries in, 1239–40
  bread standardization and, 733
  child labor and, 969–70, 1130
  Coronado I in, 1306
  economic regulation and, 825
  expansion of Congressional power and, 728
  judicial deference and, 732, 739
  Judiciary Act of 1925 and, 482
  opinions in
    average number of days from argument to announcement of unanimous opinion: White, Taft, Rehnquist, and Roberts Courts, 603–8
    average number of pages in full opinion: White, Taft, Rehnquist, and Roberts Courts, 603–8
    dissenting votes as percentage of full opinions, by term, 1916–1928 terms, 615
    percentage of all decisions in which justice participated and either joined or authored Court opinion, 1915–1920 terms versus 1921–1928 terms, 613
    percentage of full opinions that are unanimous: White, Taft, and Roberts Courts, 603–8
  prohibition and, 968
  "property affected with a public interest" and, 793–94
  rent control and, 723
  Truax in, 1401
  zoning and, 875
White supremacy
  Equal Protection Clause and, 1442, 1450–51
  Gong Lum and, 1483
  Harding and, 1441–42
  Ku Klux Klan and, 859
  Ozawa and, 1453
  Porterfield and, 1456–57
  racial violence (*See* Racial violence)
  segregation and, 1441–42, 1452, 1453
  "separate but equal" and, 1442, 1450–51
  social equality (*See* Social equality)
  Southern Democrats and, 1220, 1441
  Taft Court, deference of, 1452
  Terrace and, 1455–57
  Thind and, 1453–55
Whitman, Walt, 205
Whitten, Robert H., 842, 875–76
Wickersham, George W.
  Ballinger-Pinchot affair and, 302–3, 304, 332–34, 336
  Brandeis and, 309
  Butler and, 72–74
  on Clayton Act, 1241, 1280–81
  Franklin Roosevelt and, 978
  Kansas Court of Industrial Relations and, 808–9
  McReynolds and, 261–62, 277, 278, 279
  on prohibition, 969, 978
  on "property affected with a public interest," 810
  race relations and, 1453
  Taft and, 531
  Tobacco Trust and, 261–62, 277, 278, 279
  on Volstead Act, 969, 979
  Wickersham Commission and, 1497
Wickersham Commission
  generally, 530
  Hoover and, 969, 1495–97

1606

INDEX

prohibition and, 940, 969, 1024, 1074–75
Stone, consideration of for, 1495–97
Wiebe, Robert H., xxxviii, 30, 687, 841
Wigmore, John Henry, 196, 197, 654, 1044–45, 1484–85, 1504, 1516–17
Willebrandt, Mabel Walker, 146, 934, 945, 955–56, 1063, 1072
Williams, C. Dickerman, 349
Williams v. Standard Oil Co. (1929), 802–3
   Brandeis in, 803
   Fourteenth Amendment and, 803
   Holmes in, 803
   "property affected with a public interest" in, 802–3
   Stone in, 803
   Sutherland in, 802–3
Willing v. Chicago Auditorium Ass'n (1928), 324–25
Williston, Samuel, 113
Wilson, Edmund, 172, 918
Wilson, William, 1237
Wilson, Woodrow
   generally, 411–12
   1918 elections and, 692
   appointments to Court by, 35, 74, 263–64, 307–10
   Brandeis and, 195–96, 306–7, 340–41, 342–43, 350–52, 423–24, 977–78
   Butler and, 62
   Clarke and, 39, 49–50, 284, 599
   Commission on Industrial Relations and, 14
   on Congressional power, 1155
   election of, 2, 12–13
   federalism and, 1103, 1104
   Harding and, 681, 705
   Holmes and, 194
   Industrial Conference and, 1236–37
   labor market and, 1236–37, 1298–99
   on labor violence, 1217
   League of Nations and, 3–4
   Lippmann and, 692
   Lodge and, 692
   McReynolds and, 262, 263–64, 266–67, 284
   Myers v. United States and, 401–2
   National War Labor Board and, 2–3, 1234
   New Freedom, 306, 692
   price controls and, 721, 722–23
   Progressive Party and, 340
   on prohibition, 968
   race relations and, 1221
   removal power and, 419–20
   on strikes, 1274
   stroke of, 1238
   Taft and, 2, 17, 19, 307, 311, 341–42, 388, 422, 442–43
   War Labor Conference Board and, 1234
   World War I and, 690–91, 692
Windom, William, 1435, 1466

Wiretapping
   Brandeis on, 358, 1085
   Holmes on, 173, 1084
   McReynolds on, 1084
   prohibition and (*See Olmstead v. United States* (1928))
   Stone on, 1063, 1077–78
   Sutherland on, 1066, 1084
   Taft on, 390
Wisconsin Rate Case (1922), 366–67, 1123–24, 1136, 1137, 1138, 1167–68, 1313–14
Witte, Edwin E., 1265, 1266, 1288, 1293, 1295–96, 1332–33, 1351, 1369, 1370, 1390–92, 1424
Woll, Matthew, 15–16, 1272, 1374, 1391
Women
   Equal Protection Clause and, 780–81
   hours of labor and, 298–301, 329–30, 780–81
   McReynolds, misogyny of, 285
   National War Labor Board and, 784–85
   Nineteenth Amendment
      Adkins and, 763–64
      Holmes and, 780–81
      National Woman's Party and, 779–80
      Sutherland and, 52, 779–80
      Taft and, 780
   women's suffrage, Sutherland on, 40, 52
Women's Organization for National Prohibition, 926
Wood, Stephen B., 1107
Woodhouse, Barbara, 827
Woods, Arthur, 717
Woollcott, Alexander, 182
Workers' compensation
   Adkins, workers' compensation compared, 761–62, 763
   Butler on, 77
   Edward White on, 1265–66
   McKenna on, 1265–66
   McReynolds on, 273–74, 1265–66
   Newton Baker on, 776
   Pitney on, 85, 96–97, 1232–33
   Stone on, 124, 143
   Sutherland on, 40–41, 52–53, 273–74, 775–76, 1421
   Taft on, 777
   Van Devanter on, 1265–66
Workmen's Compensation Act, 449
World War I
   administrative expertise and, 707
   administrative state, impact on, 693, 707
   African Americans in, 1221
   "Americanization" and, 848–49
   anti-trust law, impact on, 696
   Brandeis and, 689
   bread standardization in, 733
   Butler and, 699

World War I (cont.)
  child labor and, 1103
  Commerce Department and, 696, 832
  Congressional power and, 690–91, 704, 1101
  conscription and, 698–99
  Constitutional limits on legislation during, 720
  Corwin and, 718, 1106
  cultural context of Taft Court, impact on, xxvi
  Davis and, 718–19
  economic cooperation and, 694–96, 708
  economic planning and, 694, 705, 706
  Eighteenth Amendment, impact on, 917, 921, 929–30
  executive power, impact on, 692–93
  federalism, impact on, xxxi, 1103
  foreign languages in schools, impact on, 848–49
  Frankfurter on, 687
  Hughes and, 805
  Jay Burns and, 733
  labor market, impact on, xxxiii, 1233–34
  laissez faire, effect on, 690, 691, 702–3
  Lippmann and, 700, 1106
  McReynolds and, 263–64, 290
  nationalism and, 692, 703
  New Deal, influence on, 690–91
  political culture, effect on, 691, 703
  progressivism and, 690, 692
  prohibition, impact on, 917, 921, 929–30
  "property affected with a public interest," impact on, 793
  race relations, impact on, 1220–21
  railroads during, 1124, 1143
  rent control and, 723
  Sanford and, 699
  standardization and, 733, 856
  Sutherland and, 720
  Taft and, 10–11, 699
  Taft Court, impact on, 10–11, 699, 1121, 1124, 1259–60
  trade associations and, 694–96, 697
  trusts and, 694–96
  unions, impact on, 1217–18
  Van Devanter and, 699
  Wilson and, 690–91, 692
Writing style of opinions
  Brandeis, 218, 311, 645–46, 671
  Edward White, 192
  Holmes, 174–75, 176, 210–11, 213, 214, 218–19
  McKenna, 118, 135
  McReynolds, 265
  Sanford, 91–92, 99
  Stone, 132–34, 676

Sutherland, 44–45
Taft Court generally, 603–8
Van Devanter, 229, 242, 244, 245, 249–50
Writ of error, 160, 224, 486–87, 496, 599, 600, 1400

Yellow-dog contracts
  generally, 1265
  at-will employment contracts, 1233, 1245–46, 1286
  Brandeis on, 1233
  Clarke on, 1233
  Day on, 1231
  freedom of contract and, 1231–33
  Green on, 1491–92
  Hitchman (*See Hitchman Coal & Coke Co. v. Mitchell* (1917))
  Holmes on, 1231, 1233
  Hughes on, 1231
  individualism and, 1231
  labor injunctions and, 1233, 1378–79
  National War Labor Board and, 1234, 1268
  Norris-LaGuardia Act and, 1247
  Pitney on, 1231–33
  tortious interference with contract and, 1233
  voluntariness of employment contracts and, 1231–32
Yntema, Hessel E., 677
Yost, Casper Salathiel, 516–17, 1345–46

Ziang Sung Wan v. United States, 266 U.S. 1 (1924), 1072–74
Zionism, 342–43, 349, 1433
Zoning
  building codes distinguished, 863
  Commerce Department and, 865
  Euclid, 835–43 (*See also Village of Euclid v. Ambler Realty Co.* (1926))
  historical development of, 836
  Hoover and, 836, 865
  immigration and, 842, 843
  Model Zoning Enabling Act, 836
  morality and, 840
  in New York City, 836, 840, 862–63, 864
  purposes of, 874–75
  race and, 842, 843, 875–76, 877, 1440
  security versus freedom, 841
  segregation and, 842, 843, 875–76, 1440
  social class and, 842, 877
  as social planning, 838
  split in jurisdictions regarding, 866
  status quo and, 841–42
  Sutherland and, 868–69
  takings, viewed as, 837, 866, 872
  White Court and, 875